The Birth of the Modern

The Birth of the Modern

WORLD SOCIETY 1815–1830

Paul Johnson

Weidenfeld and Nicolson
London

First published in Great Britain in 1991 by
George Weidenfeld & Nicolson Limited
91 Clapham High Street, London SW4 7TA

British Library Cataloguing in Publication Data
applied for

ISBN 0 297 81207 6

Printed in Great Britain by
The Guernsey Press Co. Ltd, Guernsey, Channel Islands.

*This work is dedicated
to my beloved wife Marigold
who restrains excesses,
corrects errors
and always encourages and inspires*

Contents

THREE The End of the Wilderness   165

FOUR World Policeman   286

FIVE Can the Center Hold?   356

SIX Honorable Gentlemen and Weaker Vessels   444

SEVEN Forces, Machines, Visions   541

EIGHT Masques of Anarchy   627

NINE Fresh Air and Drowsy Syrups

Preface

The title of this book requires some explanation. I present the fifteen years 1815–30 as those during which the matrix of the modern world was largely formed. Some may find this choice surprising. They might point instead to the decade of the 1780s as decisive, when the British economy was the first to achieve self-sustaining industrial growth, and the French Revolution began the process of sweeping away the ancien régime. It is true that modernity was conceived in the 1780s. But the actual birth, delayed by the long, destructive gestation period formed by the Napoleonic Wars, could begin in full measure only when peace came and the immense new resources in finance, management, science and technology which were now available could be put to constructive purposes. That is what I describe in my book.

The postwar years saw great and rapid changes in Britain and continental Europe, and still more fundamental ones elsewhere. The United States transformed itself from a struggling ex-colony into a formidable nation, growing fast in territory and population and embracing democratic politics. Russia, too, was expanding fast and at the same time was developing the fatal fissures in her society which were to engulf her in the immense tragedies of the 20th century. In China and Japan also the seeds of future catastrophes were being sown. Latin America came into independent and troubled existence, and the first stirring of modernity were felt in Turkey and Egypt, Southeast Asia, the Middle East and the Balkans. In India the British were moving deeper into the subcontinent and beginning to modernize it. They were breaking out of their coastal enclaves in South Africa and Australia and striking inland. All over the world, the last wildernesses, in the pampas and the steppes, in the Mississippi Valley and Canada, in the Himalayas and the Andes, were being penetrated or settled by the advanced societies, and their peoples were being subdued, in some cases annihilated. Never before or since had so much cheap land become available, and the hungry peoples of Europe were moving overseas in vast numbers to possess it.

These political, economic and demographic changes, all without precedent in their scale and future significance, were accompanied by powerful new currents in music and painting, literature and philosophy, some ennobling and refreshing, some sinister. The book attempts to show how deeply painters, musicians and writers were involved in the great events of these years. I have tried throughout not to compartmentalize politics and economics, science and engineering, the arts and literature, but to present them as they really were, closely enmeshed, reacting one upon another, parts of the seamless garment of a society exhilarated and sometimes bewildered by the rapid changes which were transforming it. The age abounded in great personalities; warriors; statesmen and tyrants; outstanding inventors and technologists; and writers, artists and musicians of the highest genius, women as well as men. I have brought them to the fore, but I have also sought to paint in the background, showing how ordinary men and women—and children—lived, suffered and died, ate and drank, worked, played and traveled, and I have something to say about animals, too, especially those noble creatures, the horse and the dog, and the exotic beasts that were now filling the new zoos.

The book deals with the whole world and has no one angle of vision. The United States, Russia, France and Germany necessarily occupy much space, as does the Spanish-speaking world and the major civilizations of Asia. A specially prominent place is accorded to Britain, for during these years Britain was the most influential of the powers, the only one operating simultaneously in all quarters of the globe. As the first nation to industrialize herself, she enjoyed a financial and technological paramountcy which for a time was unique. More critical decisions were taken in London than in any other capital, and they often affected not just power and money, but intellectual fashions and social trends. So what happened there is sometimes looked at minutely. But I also bring into close-up other key cities, some new, some old: Paris, Vienna, Saint Petersburg, New York, Washington, Canton, Buenos Aires, Mexico City, Cape Town, Sydney, Singapore, Montreal and Cairo.

While seeking to portray international society in its totality, I have striven hard not to fall into the trap which sometimes swallows social historians—that is, to leave out chronology and show a world which appears static. I hold strongly that chronology forms the bones of history on which all else is built. The world changed substantially in those fifteen years. In 1815 reaction seemed triumphant everywhere; by

1830 the *demos* was plainly on its way. Or again, in 1815 a poet, a scientist and a painter spoke the same language—I give many instances—but by 1830 it was increasingly difficult for them to understand each other; the sad bifurcation into two cultures was beginning. One impression the historian must always convey is this sense of the turning of the years, sometimes slow, sometimes fast, always relentless in its motion. While dealing with all aspects of society, I have also tried to show the world as dynamic, driven forward by a succession of major events—mass emigration, war, unprecedented economic expansion, followed by financial disaster, depression and anguished popular unrest. Hence, designing the structure of the book has been a formidable and fascinating challenge. Sometimes readers will have to bear with me while we retrace our steps a little before resuming the onward march: but we always get there in the end.

The first two chapters in particular involve an element of retrospective explanation, to set the scene. The narrative begins with the origin of that cornerstone of the modern, democratic world order, the Special Relationship between the United States and Britain. It demonstrates how this friendship between the two great English-speaking nations sprang, phoenix-like, from the ashes of the tragic and bitterly fought War of 1812. I describe how it culminated in the American victory of New Orleans, fought paradoxically after the historic Treaty of Ghent had already been signed. This, fortunately, as I show, left the belligerents exactly as they stood when the fighting started. Thereafter the strong and abiding community of interests between the two peoples did its healing work and the elements of a mighty, civilizing friendship began to come together. The narrative moves on to the Congress of Vienna, and here again we look back in order to show how the excesses of Bonaparte's imperial rule had roused the peoples of Europe against France. We see the Congress assembled to rebuild Europe in the aftermath of Bonaparte's first abdication (1814), its interruption by his return from Elba and final defeat at Waterloo (1815), and the way in which the peace settlement it devised, reinforced initially by the powerful currents of romanticism sweeping through the world, founded an international order which, in most respects, endured for a century. From this point the narrative begins to move forward again, and the book broadens out not only to take in society as a whole but to embrace all five continents as each, in turn, is harnessed to the accelerating chariot of progress.

Although this work thus tackles new problems in the presentation of history, it is not an attempt to prove a case. It is primarily an effort to bring back to life a remarkable epoch in world history, rich in grand

and bizarre events and in human characters. I want to make readers
enjoy exploring it as much as I do myself. To do so, I have tried to get
the men and women who lived in those days to tell the story in their
own words, using their letters and diaries, public and private documents, parliamentary exchanges and recorded conversations, songs,
poems and fictions. Those distant voices—happy and angry, shrill and
passionate, cynical, frivolous, humble and haughty in turn, evocative
always—constitute the vivifying principle of my book.

> Paul Johnson
> Over Stowey,
> Somerset

ONE

A Special Relationship

At dawn on Sunday, 8 January 1815, as the mist cleared, the British army attacked the heavily defended ditch and rampart guarding New Orleans. The town, which dated from 1718, was then the one big place on the far side of the Appalachian frontier, the key to the South and the Gulf of Mexico. The Louisiana Purchase of 1803, whereby Napoleon made over 828,000 square miles of French-claimed territory to the United States, thus increasing its national territory by 140 percent and making possible the creation of thirteen new states—all for the princely sum of $15 million, or four cents an acre—ensured its importance. Governor William Claiborne had said in the following year, in a letter to Thomas Jefferson: "There appears to me a moral certainty that in ten years it will rival Philadelphia or New York." He was proved right. Until the Ohio Valley could be firmly and cheaply linked to the East Coast, all the trade of the Mississippi had to go in and out through New Orleans.[1]

That, of course, was why the British wanted to take it. They wished to bring to a decisive end the War of 1812, which, since the abdication of Napoleon Bonaparte nine months before (6 April 1814) had released large naval and military resources from the European theater, was going their way. Their expedition had set forth on the night of 27–28 November 1814. It had 60 ships and 14,000 troops, most of them Peninsular veterans. Also on board were many officers' wives and a printing press—during the long wars against France the British had learned, for the first time, the art of propaganda.

But the troops were unwisely led. The force commander was Sir Edward Pakenham (1778–1815), a sprig of the Anglo-Irish nobility from Pakenham Castle, County Westmeath. The great Duke of Wellington had married his sister, Catherine, but that was the closest he got to military mastery. Money and connections had made him a major before he was 17 and a colonel at 21. There was no question of his courage.

Serving as major-general under his brother-in-law at Salamanca in 1812, he had been given his chance when Wellington told him to take his division straight at the French center, with the words "Now's your time, Ned!" He broke the French line and this, said Wellington in his dispatch, won the battle, though he admitted "Pakenham may not be the brightest genius."[2]

Pakenham arrived to take up his command only toward the end of December 1814, when the expedition had already landed, at Fisherman's Village on Lake Borne. The week before, the British navy had destroyed the U.S. gunboat squadron protecting the sea approaches to New Orleans. Had the divisional commander, Major General John Keane, dashed straight for the city he could have taken it, for the American commander, General Andrew Jackson, was frantically gathering men and putting up defenses. But Keane believed rumors that it was garrisoned by 20,000 men. When Pakenham at last arrived to take command, he found a plan in being for an attack on both sides of the Mississippi. He determined to carry it out as soon as possible. He was driven both by his own impatience and by a desire to maximize the British strategic position before the peace talks, which were already taking place, led to a ceasefire. But by this time Jackson had set up a formidable defensive line behind what was called Rodriguez's Canal, a ditch four feet deep and ten feet wide, which he deepened and reinforced with a mud rampart. Pakenham failed to make any dent in this position by artillery bombardment and so authorized a frontal assault on the fatal Sunday morning. All might yet have gone well for the British had the left arm of the two-pronged assault, up the almost undefended left bank of the river, been given time to take the ramp from behind. But the force landed in the wrong place and fell behind schedule. Pakenham, impatient as always, would not wait and fired the two Congreve rockets, which were the signal for attack.

A frontal assault against a strongly defended position not enfiladed from the rear was a textbook example of folly which would have made Wellington despair. In this case, it was made more murderous by the failure of the leading battalion to bring up the fascines to fill the ditch and the ladders to scale the ramparts. The result was a massacre of brave men. Jackson poured into the advancing redcoat lines a savage volume of grapeshot, canister, rifles and muskets. The attack wavered, and in goading on their men all three of the British general officers were shot down—Pakenham killed outright, Sir Samuel Gibbs, commanding the attack column, fatally wounded, General Keane taken off the field writhing in agony from a bullet in the groin. By the time the general commanding the reserve arrived to take over, the men were running.

Jackson, shrewd enough not to pursue and expose his men, had only 13 killed, 29 wounded and 19 missing. The British casualties were 2,037, of whom 291 were dead and another 484 missing without trace. It was all over by ten in the morning.[3]

Sadly watching this debacle was Captain Edward Codrington R. N., captain of the fleet under the command of Admiral Sir Alexander Cochrane, on board HMS *Tonnant*. Codrington was an uxorious man, devoted to his wife, Jane. They were a close couple, rather like Rear Admiral Croft and Sophia Croft in *Persuasion*, the novel so much concerned with the British navy which Jane Austen was to begin in six months' time. Captain Codrington wrote long, careful and frequent letters to Jane, and on Monday, the day after the battle, he gave her an account of it. Pakenham, he complained, should have used all the advantages of naval amphibious movement which Britain's supremacy at sea conferred and turned Jackson's position. He himself had told Pakenham, "[I] really thought this business should be done in the most regular, scientific manner, and not be a sacrifice of lives in an exhibition of bravery; and that I was sure that by forming a flotilla on the river with our boats, and landing a respectable force on the opposite bank during the night to take their batteries and turn them against them, we should oblige them to quit their present formidable position." All the other military men thought the assault should have been deferred, and then "we should have performed the most scientific and beautiful operation without loss of any moment as a prelude to our success, instead of throwing away the most valuable soldiers of our country by an attempt bordering on desperation." Even Pakenham had seemed to agree with him, but "rendered impatient" by the slowness of the turning movement, "which actually was succeeding very well," he gave the order to the assault: "It is certainly a fault in these Peninsula generals, their exposing themselves as they do. . . . Sir Edward Pakenham had even been reproved by Lord W[ellington] for exposing himself too much, and thus setting an example injurious to the welfare of the army." The fall of the three generals had turned a likely disaster into a certainty. "There never was," he summed up, "a more complete failure."[4]

Thus was lost and won one of the decisive battles of history. It was, as it happened, needless: by 11 January the first rumors reached the area that Britain and the United States had made peace—the treaty was actually signed at Ghent on Christmas Eve, 1814. On 25 January, the British fleet sailed out of Lake Borgne, with Pakenham's riddled body on board, pickled in a hogshead of rum. The expedition continued to fight until a formal order to cease fire was received, and on 11 February

Admiral Cochrane took Fort Bower, guarding Mobile, Alabama. But by the time he was ready to enter the town, a dispatch boat arrived with news of the peace, and in March he packed it in and set sail for Portsmouth. The failure to take New Orleans was thus a strategic reverse, which was to have momentous consequences.

Who was this man, Andrew Jackson, who had humiliated the most powerful amphibious power on Earth? As he played a formidable role in shaping the age which saw the birth of modernity, we must look at him closely. Jackson was born to fight, and especially to fight the British. He was of Black Protestant Ulster stock, at a time when the Presbyterian poor of Ulster hated British rule almost as much as did the Catholic Irish. His father, of Scots descent—farmers brought in to settle the Ulster border area as a fortified cordon—came from near Castlereagh, the town from which the British Foreign Secretary, the personification of the Anglo-Irish ascendancy, drew his courtesy title. He arrived in America in 1765, as part of a big Ulster migration; he and Jackson's elder brothers preserved many fragments of the Scots-Ulster dialect in their speech.[5] But he died before Jackson was born, on 15 March 1767, and the child's upbringing was entirely the work of his formidable mother. He was raised in the Waxhaw Settlement, South Carolina, a violent boy much given to swearing, a poor scholar who never learned to spell properly or mastered grammar. Some have seen his ignorance as an important clue to his character and performance. One of his early biographers, James Parton, wrote that his "ignorance of . . . everything which he who governs a country ought to know, was extreme. . . . His ignorance was a wall around him, high, impenetrable. He was imprisoned in his ignorance, and sometimes raged round his little, dim enclosure like a tiger in his den."[6] A powerful image, but perhaps misleading. Jackson, like Cecil Rhodes at the end of the century, lacked schooling, but, as with Rhodes, a powerful intelligence and an even stronger will gave a strange force to his writing and still more to his speech. Throughout his life, it helped to inspire dread in his opponents, racial and political.

As a boy, Jackson suffered from what was termed "slobbering," a source of his outbursts. It may have been a mild form of epilepsy, then a shameful complaint attributed to excessive masturbation. His interests were dogs and dogfighting, horses and horse racing, above all cockfighting. The first fragment of paper he preserved in his archive gives an Ulster recipe: "Memorandom: How to Feed a Cok before You Him Fight," which is dated "Orrange Town, in Orange Country, March the 22d 79." He was then twelve. It was his mother who gave a strongly masculine twist to his life and filled him with hatred of the British, whom she identified with the Anglican bigots who persecuted her church. A fragment of mother-and-son dialogue is preserved: "Stop that Andrew. Do not let me see you cry again. Girls were made to cry, not boys." "What are boys made for, mother?" "To fight."[7] He reported her dying advice to him as follows: "Avoid quarrels as long as you can without yielding to imposition. But sustain your manhood always. Never bring a suit in law for assault and battery or defamation. The law affords no remedy for such outrages that can satisfy the feeling of a true man . . . [But] if you ever have to vindicate your feelings or defend your honour [by dueling] do it calmly." Jackson added: "Her last words have been the law of my life."[8] This curious injunction from a mother, at a time when dueling was the scourge of society, especially in the South, and most women were beseechingly opposed to it, Jackson followed in one sense. But, in another, he rejected the plea to be ultramasculine. Throughout his life, his closest friends, all those whose advice he most valued and followed—often disastrously—were women. Like his great contemporary, Wellington, he was really happy only in the company of what were then called, quite mistakenly to judge by his and Wellington's experience, "the Weaker Vessels."

Jackson began his formal training as a fighting animal at the age of twelve, when he enlisted in the militia to fight the Revolutionary War against the British. His two elder brothers served too, one being killed at age sixteen; his mother nursed the wounded and died while the struggle still raged. Jackson was wounded and captured, then dealt a savage blow by the saber of a British officer, whose boots he refused to clean. "The sword reached my head," he later wrote to his official biographer, "& has left a mark there as durable as the skull, as well as on the fingers."[9] The mark of this assault was there, to stir his anti-British fury, to his dying day. His brother Robert was beaten by the same man. Jackson emerged from prison weakened by smallpox, and by the bouts of malaria which plagued him thereafter (he had one during the siege of New Orleans itself). He was an orphan at fifteen. Two years later he turned to a life in the law, which was in practice a blend of land grabbing, wheeler-dealing, office seeking and dueling, and perhaps could not have occurred in precisely this combination at any other time or place. The frontier, then in the process of rapid change and expansion, was rough, violent and litigious. Jackson became a pleader in court, attorney general for a local district, judge advocate in the militia. By age 27, he was already deep in land speculation, the easiest way for a man to become rich in the United States, but he was almost ruined by an associate's bankruptcy. The breakthrough came in

1796, when he helped to create the new state of Tennessee, serving first as one of its United States representatives, then as senator. He took office as a judge in the state's Superior Court and founded the first Masonic lodge in Nashville, where he settled in 1801, soon acquiring the fine estate at the Hermitage nearby. He was deep in local politics, but more important was his election in 1802 as major general of the Tennessee militia, the power base from which he carved his way to the top.

Jackson was known as a killer. His first duel, when he was twenty-one, was with Colonel Waightstill Avery. It arose from courtroom abuse, as did many duels in those days, especially in the South and in Ireland—the young Daniel O'Connell, eight years Jackson's junior, was equally vituperative and bellicose. On this first occasion, both men settled it by firing in the air, but in later duels Jackson usually shot to kill. A common cause of his fights was his marriage, in 1790, to Rachel Robards, an older woman, perhaps a substitute mother, whom Jackson loved passionately and fiercely defended until her death. This union proved invalid, and the Jacksons were jeered at; in 1794 they were forced to go through a second ceremony. Such legal muddles were common on the frontier and were later repeatedly used by Anthony Trollope as machinery for the plots of his novels. But at the time they were deadly serious.

In 1803, while he was a senior judge in Knoxville, Jackson had a fight with John Sevier, then governor of the state and its greatest hero. Rachel was the issue, for Sevier denied she was validly married to Jackson and accused him of "taking a trip to Natchez with another man's wife." "Great God!" responded the outraged Jackson, "do you dare to mention *her* sacred name?" Pistols were drawn—the men being aged 58 and 36, respectively—and shots were fired, but only a gawking passerby was grazed. Ten days later, however, there was another gun-fight between Jackson and various members of Sevier's family. In 1806 he fought a formal duel with Charles Dickinson, arising out of one of Jackson's frequent but earlier quarrels. He was wounded but contrived to hit Dickinson, who bled to death.[10] Seven years later Jackson, by then in his midforties, acted as second to a young man called Billy Carroll, and ran the duel in what was supposed to be the approved French fashion. But it ended with Carroll's opponent being shot in the bottom and the subsequent row—it was in the nature of dueling, with its absurd rules, often broken, that one duel provoked another—led Jackson to challenge Thomas Hart Benton, later a famous senator. This produced a violent melee in the streets of Nashville on 4 September 1813, fought with swordsticks, guns and even daggers. That was the odd thing about dueling: It was supposed to concern high honor and be confined to gentlemen, whose status it was designed to enhance. But it often ended in a sordid and undignified brawl, from which no one emerged with credit. Almost all Jackson's duels, in which he faithfully carried out his mother's injunction, struck a squalid note.[11]

The duels also left his body a wreck. Jackson was tall, a good six feet one, though he weighed only 145 pounds. This thin, erect body, crowned with a thatch of red hair and a thin, pain-lined face from which blue eyes blazed angrily, was soon chipped and scarred by the marks of a violent existence. Charles Dickinson's bullet broke two of Jackson's ribs and buried itself in his chest. It could never be extracted and, carrying bits of cloth with it, produced a lung abscess which caused him pain for decades and led to varieties of lung trouble and blood spitting. In the Benton duel he was hit in the shoulder and nearly had an arm amputated. The wound was staunched with elm poultices from an Indian recipe but the ball could not be prised out; it was embedded in his bone for twenty years and produced osteomyelitis. In 1825 Jackson, who was clearly accident-prone, stumbled in the dark going upstairs and ripped the wound open, causing massive bleeding from which he almost died and which recurred occasionally till the end of his life. On top of these fearful scars and bits of metal in his body, Jackson compounded his endemic malaria with dysentery, contracted on campaign, which plagued him repeatedly. For the first, and for his aching wounds, he took sugar of lead, both internally and externally; for the second, huge doses of calomel which rotted his teeth.[12]

Jackson met these misfortunes stoically and even with a species of heroism. He tried to anticipate the hemorrhages by opening up a vein. He would "lay bare his arm, bandage it, take his penknife from his pocket, call his servant to hold the bowl, and bleed himself freely." These atrocious auto-operations he carried on throughout his presidency, often in the middle of the night without a servant.[13] His acceptance of pain testified to his resolution, but left further scars on his psyche, which deepened his rages and bitterness. His unforgettably fierce but frail figure thus became an embodiment of angry will, working its purpose on his times.

That process began in earnest with the outbreak of the War of 1812. The origins of this needless, destructive and sometimes bloody and bitter war are obscure and debatable. Certainly, it could not have taken place had it not been for the mutual antagonism felt by many of the ruling men on both sides. Both Thomas Jefferson, Democratic-Republican president (1801–09) and his successor James Madison, Democratic-

Republican president (1809–17), survivors of the struggle for independence, were pro-French by cultural and political inclination and violently anti-British. On the British side, most of the Tory ministers saw American republicanism as a threatening ideology almost as dangerous as its French version, and found it difficult to recognize the United States as a "normal," legitimate country. .

In 1805 the great war against Bonaparte and his satellites had reached a kind of geopolitical stalemate. Admiral Nelson's dramatic victory at Trafalgar, in which the French and Spanish battle fleets had been virtually destroyed, gave Britain decisive supremacy at sea and ended any real prospect of a French invasion and conquest of Britain. A few weeks later, Bonaparte's equally decisive victory at Austerlitz destroyed the main Austrian and Russian armies; he followed this in 1806 by a relentless rout of the Prussian forces at Jena. Thereafter Britain was forced to carry on the struggle virtually single-handedly. Bonaparte was in control of the Continent. But Britain ruled the seas and oceans, including the Atlantic. To destroy British trade and industry, wherewith she financed her war effort and subsidized anti-French activity in Europe, Bonaparte set up what was known as the "Coastal System," banning ports throughout Europe to British commerce. In May 1806 Britain retaliated with the so-called Fox Blockade, whereby the Royal Navy closed the ports from Brest to the Elbe. After his victory at Jena, Bonaparte went a stage further, publishing the Berlin Decrees of 21 November 1806. They were based on a notional blockade and laid down that any ship coming direct from a British port, or having been in a British port after the decrees came into force, should not be permitted to use a Continental port; if such a ship made a false declaration, it was to be seized. All goods had to be accompanied by a "Certificate of Origin," and all goods of British origin or ownership were to be confiscated wherever found. This was what came to be known as the "Continental System."[14]

The British response was the first Order in Council of 7 January 1807, which prohibited trade "between port and port of countries under the dominion or usurped control of France and her allies." Bonaparte again hit back by extending his system to Turkey, Austria and Denmark, and, after defeating Russia at the Battle of Friedland, he forced her into the Treaty of Tilsit, July 1807, which extended it to the Tsar's dominions too. In November the British produced what was the central Order in Council, which in effect laid down that all trade with Napoleonic Europe had to pass through British ports.[15] The Americans (and other neutrals) complained that the only trade the Royal Navy would now allow them was precisely the kind Bonaparte had forbidden them, and he reinforced the point in his first Milan Decree, not only by laying down strict criteria for determining whether a neutral ship had touched at a British port, but by declaring that any ship which submitted to a search by the Royal Navy automatically forfeited the protection of its flag and was prizable. The Americans, harassed by both sides, passed the Non-Importation Act in April 1806, which banned most British imported goods, and embargoed all non-American shipping.[16]

It is important to grasp that all sides were divided. The mechanics and economics of international trade were little understood. Policies, shaped in ignorance, often produced the opposite effect of that intended. Bonaparte's Continental System led to trouble with all his allies and satellites and probably, in aggregate, weakened his war effort. The Orders in Council were difficult to understand and still more difficult to enforce. They probably did more damage to Britain than to anyone else, although they benefited the West Indian interest, since they prevented French and Spanish products from reaching the Caribbean. The Liverpool merchants and the Manchester manufacturers were hit, and they began to brief as their parliamentary counsel a young and sharp-witted Scots barrister, Henry Brougham, who will figure often in our story. Until he became a member of Parliament in 1810 he pleaded their case at the parliamentary bar; once elected, he campaigned ferociously against the Orders in Council and finally destroyed them in 1812—but not until after war had broken out.[17]

The Americans were also divided. The commercial interest in the New England states was pro-British and anti-French. These states were mostly Federalists, committed to trade and industry, as opposed to the predominantly agrarian Republicans of the South. They would happily have settled for cooperation with the British system or even war with France. The shipowners of Boston and Salem were not above asking for Royal Naval convoys, and from time to time the British encouraged their support by lifting the blockade of their ports and banning the impressment of their sailors. The British also treated American shipping in a cavalier manner when they chose. As early as 21 June 1807, the USS *Chesapeake*, a warship, was forced by Royal Naval units to surrender for refusing to allow herself to be searched for British naval deserters.[18] Bonaparte was equally haughty in his dealings with Americans, treating them as a subordinate nation under his protection. He broke his promises, and his warships, when they did succeed in penetrating the British blockade, behaved like pirates. Early in 1812 a marauding French squadron was burning American ships over a wide area of the Atlantic. As Senator Nathaniel Macon of North Carolina put it:

"The Devil himself could not tell which government, England or France, is the most wicked."[19]

Behind the New England sympathy with Britain was a much deeper resentment of the South and the constitutional system which gave its states, particularly Virginia, such a predominant role in American government. In the presidential election of 1812, New York, tired of the Virginia Dynasty, put up its favorite son De Witt Clinton to frustrate James Madison's bid for a second term. The issue was essentially the South and war or New England and peace. Clinton got the support of New York (29 electoral college votes), Massachusetts (22), Connecticut, New Jersey, New Hampshire, and other smaller states, making a total of 89 votes. Madison had Virginia (25) and Pennsylvania (25) and a group of southern and western states led by the Carolinas, Georgia and Kentucky, making a total of 128 votes. But the seven states which voted for Madison had a total of 980,000 slaves. These blacks had no voice in government whatever, but each 45,000 of them added an electoral vote to the state where they were held, giving the cause of the South and war a total of 21 electoral votes. Thus, the New England Federalists claimed that the freemen of the North were at the irresponsible mercy of the slaves of the South.[20]

The South and the burgeoning West favored war for imperial reasons. They thought it a heaven-sent opportunity to break into ill-defended Florida, held by Britain's new ally, Spain, and turn it into another state devoted to cotton, the South's fast-expanding staple product. They also thought of appropriating part, perhaps the whole, of Britain's colony Canada, likewise largely unprotected. The term *Manifest Destiny* had not yet been coined—it gained currency only in the 1840s—but it was implicit in the conviction of many American public men, who believed the United States had a "natural," indeed, a God-given, right to the whole of North America. The war might have been avoided even so. On 18 June 1812 Congress completed the constitutional formalities for declaring war on Britain. But two days later in Westminster, Brougham's motion for repealing the Orders in Council had elicited from Lord Castlereagh, on behalf of the government, a statement that they were suspended. An inexperienced American chargé d'affaires in London failed to get the news to President Madison with the speed it merited.

When war came, many in the South and West were elated. As Representative Felix Grundy of Tennessee put it, in a letter to Andrew Jackson, he was anxious "not only to add the Floridas to the south but the Canadas to the north of this empire;" these two areas would be "the Theatres of our offensive operations."[21] Even James Monroe, the Secretary of State and no fire-eater, was keen to grab Canadian territory, not necessarily on a permanent basis, but to strengthen America's hand in the peace process, which he hoped would begin soon.[22]

When the war began, it consisted of three primary forms of hostility: an American invasion of Canada; the naval war, on the Great Lakes and in the Atlantic; and the opportunities presented in the South to the American settler interest. Washington pinned its highest hopes on the first, but the attempt to conquer Canada was based upon two grave misapprehensions. The first was that Canada was a soft target. It was divided into two distinct colonies: to the East, Lower Canada, overwhelmingly French-speaking; and to the West and North, Upper Canada, thinly settled, mainly by people of British origin but with a growing American community. Washington believed that the French Canadians were an oppressed and occupied people, who identified with Britain's grand enemy, France, and would welcome the invading American forces as liberators. Nothing could have been more mistaken. The French Canadians were ultraconservative Roman Catholics, who had detested the atheistic French Revolution and regarded Bonaparte as a usurper and a madman. They wanted a Bourbon Restoration in France, which was also the aim of British war policy. The Quebec Act of 1775, much criticized in Britain at the time, had proved a wise act of liberal statesmanship. It gave the French community wide cultural, religious and political privileges, enabling them to maintain their Frenchness. They knew that as a state within the union, they could not hope for such a deal from the U.S. federal government. In fact they saw America as an ideologically committed state, wedded to Republicanism and militant Protestantism, both of which they detested. The war had actually strengthened their links to the British, and they viewed an American invasion with dread.

American prospects of success in Lower Canada were still further reduced by the fact that the New England states, to the immediate south, had no desire to march to Montreal. They did not exactly sit on their hands; they invested in British securities and did good business with the British forces. The British blockade did not extend to New England until near the end of the war, and by that stage two-thirds of the beef consumed by the British army was supplied from south of the border, chiefly from New York State and Vermont.[23]

The American invasion had a marginally better chance in Upper Canada, where there were only 4,500 regular British troops plus a militia of unknown quality. The recent infiltration of American settlers led Sir Isaac Brock, the Lieutenant Governor and Commander-in-Chief in Upper Canada, to take the view that the majority was disloyal. His only hope, he said, was to "speak loud and think big." But his fears were soon laid to rest when the ineptitude of the invasion became apparent, and local opinion lined up solidly behind the British authorities. Here we come to the second American miscalculation: Washington believed it could wage war and conduct an invasion over an immense stretch of territory on the cheap. Such an approach served the United States well over most of the activities of the state. It provided the cheapest government in the world, largely conducted on a self-help basis. The militia was a military form of self-help. It had worked well before, during the War of Independence. It would serve for the invasion of Canada. But an amateur, ill-trained soldier, who may fight hard and well in defense of his home, is less apt to do so for an invasion into unknown lands hundreds of miles away.

The forces Washington dispatched to annex Canada were a rabble, commanded by men who made poor "Ned" Pakenham look like a military genius. The state militias had no discipline. Every man selected his own ground to pitch his tent. No pickets were posted, no patrols sent forth at night. Neither militiamen nor Volunteers were anxious to cross the border. Many of the units flatly refused to fight at all outside U.S. territory, believing they were within their legal rights to do so. The Volunteers believed that if they crossed into Canada they automatically became liable to five years' service. Most of them were terrified of the Indians, and with reason, since the Indians massacred prisoners. Sending such troops into the wilderness, especially Indian areas, was asking for mutiny and wholesale desertion.[24]

The general officers did nothing to improve matters. The commander on the Niagara frontier in 1812 was Major General Stephen van Rensselaer of the New York militia. Scion of one of the oldest Dutch-American dynasties, he inherited a vast estate of nearly 150,000 acres, let to 900 tenant farmers, each with 150 acres under cultivation. Though Independence had ended the old baronies, this tract was known as the Van Rensselaer Manor and its owner was always termed "The Patroon," being "eighth in succession." Grandee he might be, but his troops refused to follow him, and his invasion collapsed ignominiously.[25] Further attempts were countermanded or ended in rout and disaster. Casualties, mainly from disease, exposure and Indian raids, were heavy. The generals blamed each other. General Alexander Smyth was accused by General Peter B. Porter, in the pages of the *Buffalo Gazette,* of arrant cowardice. They fought a duel on Grand Island, in which no one was hurt but which had an air of comic-opera buffoonery about it.[26] Later, Smyth was mobbed and his shortcomings posted on handbills. Some units fought each other with considerably more enthusiasm than they faced the British. In the camp at Black Rock there was a pitched battle between the Irish Greens from New York and Volunteers from the South, and both turned on the regulars brought in to end the riot. Others were jeered at by a contemptuous public. The U.S. Light Dragoons, raised in 1808, with the initials USLD on their caps, were branded Uncle Sam's Lazy Dogs.[27] By the end of 1813 the plan to conquer Canada had been, in effect, abandoned, and the British from Lower Canada had occupied a large part of Maine. Farther west, the border had shifted south; by the end of the war, the Americans were everywhere on the defensive and the Canadian settlers were optimistic about getting access to the Mississippi.

But on the Great Lakes the Americans fared better. After war broke out, Oliver Hazard Perry of Rhode Island built a serviceable fleet which inflicted a sharp defeat on Royal Navy vessels on Lake Erie. This led directly to one American land success in the theater, the Battle of the Thames won by Richard Mentor Johnson, and the killing of the much-hated Shawnee Indian chief Tecumseh. His dead body was found and skinned, the soldiers keeping long strips from his thighs to use as razor straps.[28] Such conduct was not unusual. The Canadians claimed that whenever they got the chance, the American invaders behaved savagely, burning Indian villages and settlers' homesteads, and even setting fire to small towns.

The naval victory on the Great Lakes spurred American efforts to challenge the British in the sphere where they claimed to be effortlessly supreme—the high seas. This was, increasingly, an area of high technology—the first such epoch in the history of warfare and an ominous portent for the future. Britain, now at the climax of the first phase of the Industrial Revolution, swarmed with highly qualified engineers and inventors. Americans still saw their country as essentially agrarian but there was no shortage of ingenious mechanics. Technological contacts between the two countries throughout this time, and indeed with France too, were frequent and close, despite the war. Most inventors were impelled by a mixture of patrotism and an overriding desire to get their fantasies off the drawing boards and into action, and thus often *in extremis* did business with whatever government, friend or foe, was prepared to put up cash.

The greatest military visionary of the age was the American Robert Fulton (1765–1815). He came from Little Britain (now renamed Fulton Township) in Pennsylvania, though ultimately his family was Irish, from Kilkenny. His father died when Fulton was tiny and he had a penurious childhood, redeemed by his amazing skill at drawing, combined with a strong mechanical aptitude—from the age of 13 he made his own pencils, paints and other art materials. In his teens he made his living as a painter of miniatures and may have worked under the then-leading portraitist in Philadelphia, Charles Willson Peale, who painted his portrait—it shows a brooding, tough-featured man, full of determination and rage.[29] Then he had a spell in London, studying with other American artists who were trying their fortunes there, such as Benjamin West and Gilbert Stuart. It was a characteristic of this age in which the modern world was born that many artists (and indeed poets) were fascinated by scientific advances and, conversely, that many of the best engineers, doctors and scientists were exquisite draughtsmen. Fulton's younger contemporary, Samuel Morse, who was to transform telegraphy, also began as a portrait painter. Fulton's obsession with propulsion, whether chemical or atmospheric, began as early as his passion for art. At thirteen he made a powerful skyrocket. At the same time he was working for the gunsmiths at Lancaster, his local county town, forging and designing guns; the next year he did an elaborate working drawing of a paddlewheel.[30] Throughout his life he produced superb blueprints of his projects, whether ships, canal schemes, or digging machines.

Fulton's Irish background may account for his bitter Anglophobia. He rationalized it by arguing that the Royal Navy was the chief obstacle to the freedom of the seas, to him the high road to human advancement. His ideology took him to France in 1798, where he stayed with an American couple who called him Toot, and offered to build General Bonaparte a submarine for use against the British. This was not the first time Americans had thought of undersea warfare as the means to destroy the hated British naval supremacy. As far back as 1776 the state of Maine had given £60 to the inventor David Bushnell to design a submarine, but it did not work when tried against British vessels. The French were interested in Fulton. He made the Ministry of Marine a diving machine in which he went down to a depth of 25 feet with three mechanics. Then he concentrated on underwater mines and torpedoes to be launched from a submarine provided with fresh air in a compression tank, called the *Nautilus,* the plans for which, dated 1798, can still be seen in the Archives Nationales, Paris. Like all Fulton's marine designs, it imitated the movements of a fish in water. The French offered him 400,000 francs if his machine succeeded in sinking a British frigate. The attempt took place in summer 1801 and was a failure, whereupon the French dropped Fulton, and his submarine was broken up.[31]

After the brief Peace of Amiens, the British, worried by Bonaparte's invasion plans, persuaded Fulton to come to London. The British painter and diarist Joseph Farington recorded a long description of how the submarine was supposed to work in his diary entry of 29 May 1803. The vessel could submerge, resurface and submerge again, was capable of remaining underwater for eight hours and could go down to 40 fathoms. It destroyed its targets with a gunpowder-filled "small machine which appears extremely like the back of a porcupine, having small pipes or quills standing out in every direction, any one of which being touched occasions a firepiece something like the lock of a gun to go off & the powder blows up." The submarine could proceed underwater at 3mph. Farington added: "This most dangerous and dreadful contrivance is said to be fully understood only by Fulton. He will shew the machine but there are certain mysteries about it which he has not yet communicated & says he *will not but in America.*"[32] Fulton's patriotic reservations, however, did not prevent him from drawing up an agreement, dated 20 July 1804—it is in his own handwriting and was kept by Castlereagh in his papers—in which he undertook to destroy by torpedo the French invasion fleet at Boulogne. The submarine was put on the back burner for the time being, but the torpedoes were made and tried out, under the code name Catamaran Expedition, on 2 October 1804. One of them worked, destroying a French pinnace and drowning its crew of 22. But the British Admiralty did not know this at the time, and the experiment was written off as a failure. There was another failure on 8 December. It was the politicians, not the Royal Navy, who were keen. As Admiral Sir John Jervis, Earl St. Vincent, said to Fulton: "Pitt was the greatest fool who ever existed, to encourage a mode of war which those who commanded the sea did not want and which, if successful, would deprive them of it." Once the news of Trafalgar reached England and ended the invasion scare, interest in Fulton's torpedo collapsed.[33]

Fulton returned to the United States and became involved in the first successful attempts to set up steamship services, which we will examine in due course. When the War of 1812 came, he reverted in the most determined fashion to his earlier plan to annihilate the Royal Navy by high technology. This time, having been able to buy some powerful steam engines made by the leading British firm of Boulton & Watt, he concentrated on enormous, steam-driven surface warships. The project, variously christened *Demologos* (1813) and *Fulton the First* (1814), was a twin-hulled catamaran with huge 16-foot paddles between the hulls. It was 156 feet long, 56 wide, and 20 deep and protected by a solid timber belt nearly five feet thick. With an engine powered by a cylinder four feet in diameter, giving an engine-stroke of five feet, it was, in fact, a large armored steam warship. The British were also working on a steam-powered naval vessel, HMS *Congo,* which they were building at Chatham, but it was a mere sloop. Fulton's battleship carried thirty 32-lb guns firing red-hot shot and was also equipped to fire 100-lb projectiles below the waterline. With its 120 horsepower developing a speed of up to 5mph and independent of the wind, it theoretically outclassed any vessel in the British fleet. Stories of this terrifying monster, which was launched on the East River on 29 June 1814, reached Britain and grew in the telling. The *Edinburgh Evening Courant* doubled the ship's size and credited her with 44 guns, including four giant 100-pounders. The newspaper added: "To annoy an enemy attempting to board it can discharge 100 gallons of boiling water a minute and, by mechanism, brandishing 300 cutlasses with the utmost regularity over her gunwales and works also an equal number of heavy iron pikes of great length, darting them from her sides with prodigious force."[34]

The British, with far greater technical resources at their disposal, were just as active and equally capable of devising means to conduct what they would later call, in an anti-German context, "frightfulness." They also had something approaching an overall plan for mastery of the world. In November 1810, a Scots military engineer, Captain Charles William Pasley (1780–1861), produced the first modern work of geopolitics, *An Essay on the Military Policy and Institutions of the British Empire.*

Pasley was a dauntingly intelligent Scot from Dumfriesshire, so clever that at eight he could translate the Greek Testament. At twelve he wrote a history of the "wars" between local gangs of boys, which he put into Latin in the style of Livy. An artilleryman in 1796, he transferred to the Engineers, which offered more opportunities for his ingenuity (he eventually became their colonel-commandant in 1853 and a full general in 1860). He saw active service in the Mediterranean, Italy, Spain, and the Low Countries, becoming a siege-and-explosives expert. He virtually invented the science of military engineering, so far as concerned the British, who had always been behind the French in this respect. But it was his *Essay,* his only political work, which attracted attention. He argued that Britain should drop its negative and defensive geopolitical posture of simply reacting to foreign threats. Instead it should devise a global strategy: "War we cannot avoid; and in war we cannot succeed merely by displaying the valour, unless we also assume the ardour and the ambition, of conquerors."[35] Pasley argued that Britain should annex Sicily and control the Mediterranean. She should consider a federal union with Sweden as a step to controlling the Baltic. The full resources of the Royal Navy and modern technology should be deployed to establish total control of the Atlantic. At the time he wrote, war with America looked increasingly possible: Pasley advocated conciliation (he was no warmonger, having seen too much of it) but if war came it should be vigorously prosecuted by raiding the American coasts.

As Pasley knew, not only ships but new devices, especially rockets, were available for such a project. In 1803 his colleague Colonel Henry Shrapnel (1761–1842) had invented the hollow case shot of shrapnel shell, an antipersonnel weapon used with devastating effect at Surinam the following year. It has proved one of the most successful, durable and devilish military devices of all time.[36] More important at this stage, however, were the chemical rockets developed by the offspring of a family of military inventors, William Congreve (1772–1828). His father ran the Royal Artillery laboratory at Woolwich, where young Congreve worked on explosive and propulsive devices: whereas Fulton was "Toot," he was "Squibb."

After the failure of the Peace of Amiens he was awarded £100 a month for his experiments. His first rockets were used at Boulogne in 1805, without much success, but later did some damage on the French coast and at Copenhagen in 1807, where he fired them wearing his laboratory gear of white hat and coat.[37] He created the Congreve Rocket in 1808. His essential invention was successfully to replace the paper and wood hitherto used by iron. This made the warhead far more damaging and permitted a stronger propellant, thus enormously increasing the range. He made five different types of missile, from a six-pounder to a 42-pounder, the last with a range of 3,000 yards, nearly two miles. He tried to construct rockets with warheads up to 400 pounds but could not find a sufficiently powerful propellant. This was something which the German chemical industry, already more inventive than Britain's, though smaller, would eventually supply.

It was Congreve's belief that rockets would eventually replace artillery, being much lighter and more mobile, and in this belief he has been largely justified. But he was a man before his time. The most successful battlefield weapon he produced was his 32-pounder, 3 feet, 6 inches long, with a 4-inch diameter, a 15-foot stick and a range of 2,750 yards. Congreves were used extensively in the Peninsula War, but field commanders complained they lacked firepower and accuracy. They could have a major psychological effect and were used with great success at the huge Battle of Leipzig in 1813. But their terror could rebound. Wellington disliked them because they frightened the horses. Since he had quite enough trouble already with his volatile cavalry, he tried to keep the Congreves off the field. At Waterloo he sought to break up the rocket unit, commanded by Major E. C. Whinyates R.A., and distribute its gunners among the conventional artillery. A staff officer told him: "But that, Your Grace, will break Major Whinyates's heart." "Damn his heart, Sir, let my orders be obeyed!"[38]

A further possible use of Congreves, however, was in the punitive bombardment of towns, especially those made largely of wood, which could be fired. Here was where the seaborne rocket capability fitted into Pasley's strategy. For this and other reasons, his book captured the imagination of the English. It quickly went through four editions. George Canning, who reviewed it anonymously for the *Quarterly Review*, called it one of the most important political works he had ever come across.[39]

Jane Austen, always fascinated by anything which raised the importance of the Royal Navy, in which two of her beloved brothers (both later admirals) served, pronounced it "delightfully written and highly entertaining"; it became one of her favorite books.[40] Most impressed of all, however, was the poet Robert Southey, who at one point in the 1790s had been, along with William Wordsworth, an ardent supporter of the French Revolution, but was now an equally fervid Tory and imperialist. Southey was about to become poet laureate when he read the book early in 1813. Pasley's scheme to raid the American coast attracted him strongly. If British peace terms were not accepted, Southey wrote to Sir Walter Scott, Britain should send a strong fleet to threaten American coastal cities with a missile attack of Congreves. "I would run down the coast, and treat the great towns with an exhibition of rockets . . . [until] they choose to put a stop to the illuminations by submission—or till Philadelphia, Baltimore, New York etc, were laid in Ashes."[41]

He expanded on the theme of British civilization imposed by military technology in a projected article for the *Quarterly:* "I am as ardent for making the world English as can be." But the piece was toned down so as not to offend foreign governments, and he got no support from his crony Wordsworth. Wordsworth deplored the notion of missile attacks and rejected Pasley's plan to use British industrial technology for conquest: "I wish to see," he wrote to Pasley, "Spain, Italy, France and Germany formed into independent nations; nor have I any desire to reduce the power of France further than may be necessary for that end. . . . My prayer, as a patriot, is that we may always have, somewhere or other, enemies capable of resisting us and keeping us at arm's length."[42] He persuaded Southey to see Pasley's policy not in terms of

conquest but of emancipation—Britain using her power and technology
to promote independent, constitutional governments all over the world,
a far more humane as well as practical idea, soon to be pursued with
great success by such Prime Ministers as Canning and Palmerston.[43]

But in the meantime Britain was at war and some of the "pigtails,"
as the brass hats were called in those days, were even more bloodthirsty
than Southey. Admiral Lord Cochrane (1775–1860), who had inherited
an impoverished Scots title and made a name for himself as one of the
most dashing and resourceful frigate captains, put forward to the Prince
Regent in March 1812 a comprehensive plan to bring the war to a rapid
conclusion by devoting immense resources to high-technology firepower: France was to be reduced by saturation bombardment of rockets, including poison-gas warheads. The government appointed a secret
committee to examine his proposals, which were shelved.[44]

A policy of "frightfulness" was nonetheless an option for the British
in pursuing the war against America. But the only instrument with
which it could in practice be pursued was the Royal Navy and, as
Cochrane had good cause to know, the navy was an imperfect instrument. The ships were sound, for the most part, albeit the hard-worked
frigates tended to be small and were undergunned by American standards. A much graver source of anxiety was the quality of the officers
and the loyalty of the men. In theory the "Senior Service" was run on
merit, but in reality everything which affected its commissioned officers
was determined by influence—"interest" as it was called. This was a
point Jane Austen illustrated again and again, especially in *Mansfield
Park* (1814), where the antihero Henry Crawford, in an unavailing
attempt to ingratiate himself with the heroine, Fanny Price, uses his
powerful connections in the Admiralty to get her beloved midshipman
brother William, who has no interest, "made lieutenant"—here, one
feels, Miss Austen was writing from the heart. When in 1814 the diarist
Farington was involved in a similar endeavor to get his nephew promoted from lieutenant to captain, assisted by his powerful friend the
Earl of Lonsdale, the earl was crisply told by John Wilson Croker,
M.P., throughout this period the political secretary to the Admiralty:
"Except in extraordinary instances where officers may have acquired
publick notice by some distinguished Service, Promotion is by Interest."[45]

The difficulty was even greater than Croker admitted. An officer
was far more likely to be promoted and given important commands if
he had the right political connections and displayed acceptable views
than if he did meritorious service. The army was Tory, the navy
Whig—or, rather, the best sea officers tended to be Whigs, since they

hated the way Tory ministers promoted their desk-bound colleagues. A case in point was James, Baron Gambier (1756–1833), son of a lieutenant governor of the Bahamas and nephew of an admiral. These connections in themselves might not have served him much, but he was attached to the Evangelical wing of the Tory party. William Wilberforce, M.P., and the best-selling Tory Evangelical novelist, Hannah More, were his dear friends. In 1793 Gambier held mass-catechisms on board his first major command, HMS *Defence,* a 74-gun battleship, which was known as a "praying ship," as opposed to a "fighting ship," in consequence. He distributed pious tracts throughout the fleet and was despised by his officers as a "blue light," keener on saving the souls of his men than on fighting the French. Gambier served twice as a Lord of the Admiralty, was raised to the peerage and ended his career as Admiral of the Fleet. But he hated the sea, and during his 63 years of naval service (he joined at the age of 11), he spent only 5½ years in sea commands and the rest as part of the entrenched Admiralty establishment.[46]

By contrast, Cochrane, a radical, regarded by the government and Admiralty alike as a troublemaker, was a first-class fighting commander who found it difficult to get any employment. His command of the famous frigate HMS *Imperieuse* was probably, in terms of enemy ships sunk or taken and damage done to enemy land forces, the most successful commission in the history of the Royal Navy. But, as he later put it in his *Autobiography,* "For these operations I never received the slightest acknowledgement from the Admiralty." Captain Frederick Marryat, later the famous nautical novelist, was, as a midshipman, an angry observer at the Battle of the Aix Roads, 11–14 April 1809, when the navy was instructed to take out the powerful French Rochfort squadron, sheltering in the roads. Gambier, during one of his brief spells at sea, was the fleet commander. Cochrane commanded the attack squadron. Along with Admiral Pelham, another famous frigate commander, Cochrane had an outstanding capacity for devising ingenious ways of killing the enemy—the two men were conflated in C. S. Forrester's fictional hero, Horatio Hornblower—and on this occasion he conceived and carried through a daring plan of entry involving fireships. He burned three French ships of the line, rendered three more unfit for further service, and disposed of two frigates as well. The rest of the French squadron were all aground the morning after the attack.

All that was needed, to reproduce another victory on the scale of Trafalgar, was for Gambier to take his battleships into the roads and blow the beached Frenchmen to bits or force them to lower their colors. But Gambier funked what he regarded as a hazardous venture and flatly

declined to go in. A much-relieved Bonaparte pronounced: "If Cochrane had been supported, he would have taken every one of our
ships."[47] There was much bitterness among the seagoing officers of the
fleet. Admiral Sir Elias Harvey, who had commanded the famous
"Fighting *Temeraire*" at Trafalgar and had hoped to be in charge of the
operation, told Gambier to his face: "I never saw a man so unfit for the
command of a fleet as Your Lordship," adding that he himself had been
disparaged "because I am no canting methodist, no hypocrite, no
psalm-singer and do not cheat old women out of their estates by hypocrisy and canting."[48] For this outburst Harvey was court-martialed and
dismissed the service.[49]

Cochrane was a witness to this scene and after Gambier refused to
support him inside the roads, the furious Scot openly accused his fleet
commander of cowardice in the face of the enemy and forced him to
demand a court-martial to clear his name. That turned into a political
farce, as Cochrane should have had the sense to know it would. An old
friend of Gambier was appointed to chair the court-martial, and he was
duly acquitted. Hannah More wrote in triumph to Lord Barham, First
Lord of the Admiralty: "terrible as Buonaparte is in every point of view,
I do not fear him so much as those domestic mischiefs—Burdett, Cochrane and Cobbett. I hope however that the mortification Cochrane etc
have lately experienced in their base and impotent endeavours to pull
down reputations which they found unassailable will keep them down
a little." The upshot was that Cochrane, the most effective ship commander of his day, was not given any further command by the Admiralty for forty years and had to seek his livelihood abroad, first in Chile,
then in Greece.

Against this background, it is hardly surprising that American naval
commanders, appointed and promoted entirely on their records,
achieved some notable successes in command both of regular warships
and of privateers. In 1814, in particular, privateers did immense damage
to British shipping in the western approaches to the British Isles. A
petition of the Liverpool merchants to the Admiralty described privateering as "a new method of warfare." In an address to the Crown, the
Glasgow merchants claimed: "In the short space of two years, above
800 vessels have been taken by that power whose maritime strength we
have hitherto held in contempt."[50] It is true that American losses were
also severe: Captain Marryat, on the frigate HMS *Spartan*, for instance,
sank or took scores of coastal vessels.[51] But what shook British official
confidence even more than the loss of mercantile craft was the failure
of regular warships to stand up to American units in single combat. The
new American "big" frigates, mounting 52 guns, were better designed

than were their British equivalents, as well as much larger; their guns were placed high over the waterline, a distinct advantage. They had twice as many officers as Royal Naval ships of similar tonnage, and most of them were better trained.[52] Captain Codrington, on station off the American coast, wrote to his wife on 10 July 1814, just after the USS *Peacock* captured HMS *Epervier:* "The system of favouritism and borough influence [in Parliament] prevails so much that many people are promoted and kept in commands that should be dismissed the service. And while such is the case, the few Americans, chosen for their merit, may be expected to follow up their successes, except where they meet with our best officers on equal terms."[53]

In the same letter Codrington put his finger on a further point of weakness. He pointed to the so-called crack ships, notable for their fresh paint, gleaming brasswork and dazzling decks, rather than their war records, and often commanded by well-born noodles with plenty of interest, as being responsible for the high and growing rate of desertions. Overdiscipline, he said, meant the sailors, "from being tyrannically treated, would rejoice in being captured by the Americans, from whom they would receive every encouragement." This, in fact, was happening increasingly. British sailors knew that if they contrived to desert or surrender, they would be welcome on U.S. naval vessels, where they could expect higher pay, better and shorter terms of service, finer food (though no daily allowance of rum) and more civilized treatment.

Even the good British captains were terrified of losing their skilled seamen. Farington noted in his diary that Captain Brooke of the *Shannon* frigate, who took the USS *Chesapeake* frigate off Boston, was so anxious to keep his crew that he burned prizes, "not regarding their value."[54] Captain Marryat, put in command of one of the new "big" frigates built by the Admiralty in response to the American 52-gun ships, found great difficulty in keeping her manned. HMS *Newcastle* was 1,556 tons, as big as a modern destroyer, mounting 58 guns and requiring a complement of 480. It was really a small ship-of-the-line (battleship). But it was hopelessly undercrewed, mainly by old men and boys; most of the trained seamen in the right age group had long ago deserted to Yankee ships, he complained. In Bantry Bay, before the ship left for the American station, some of the "waisters," as the worst elements in the crew, billeted admidships, were called, desperate to get ashore before the Atlantic crossing, rushed the gangway, knocked down the Marine sentry, stole a boat and, though fired upon, got safely ashore and escaped. In the year from February 1814 to February 1815, Marryat noted, over 100 out of a scratch crew of 350 deserted. Had the

Newcastle been involved with an enemy of equal size, Marryat lamented, it would have been a disaster.[55] American naval successes were thus due to daring Yankee officers commanding largely British crews. All the same, as Canning put it in the House of Commons, "It cannot be too deeply felt that the sacred spell of the invincibility of the British Navy has been broken by these unfortunate victories."[56]

It would be wrong, however, to suggest that the United States was actually winning the naval war. The U.S. Navy was not strong enough to fight a fleet action. The British retained effective command of the sea. When news of Bonaparte's abdication and the end of the European war reached New York early in June 1814, there was rejoicing in New England, marked by public dinners and thanksgiving services. But the return of the Bourbons to the French throne left America alone to face British wrath. Not that the British, as a people, were much interested in the war with America. They were obsessed by Bonaparte, and the skirmishing on the borders of Canada struck no chord. Neither wartime regulations nor the naval war prevented British citizens from visiting the United States. Francis Jeffrey, the famous editor of the *Edinburgh Review,* decided to go to New York to get married and spent more than three months in the United States (7 October 1813 to 22 January 1814), traveling to Washington and calling on President Madison. When the president asked him what the British thought of the war, Jeffrey was silent; pressed to reply, he finally said: "Half the people of England do not know there is a war with America, and those who did have forgotten it."[57] But the British cabinet and the military and naval authorities were keen to alter the strategic balance across the Atlantic now that peace with France had released large forces. The Royal Navy had 99 battleships and many hundreds of smaller warships, manned by 140,000 men. It was now possible to impose a close blockade of the U.S. Atlantic coast, and this was done, even off New England, to increase the pressure of the Federalist states on Washington to make peace. A naval striking force was also put together, and units of Peninsula veterans were shipped straight from France to the vast military depots Britain had built in Bermuda and Jamaica.

The object of these measures was to strengthen Britain's hand in the peace talks, which were now clearly coming. But they had a collateral purpose—punishment. There had been American atrocities in Canada almost from the start. They seem to have increased after President Madison appointed General John Armstrong (1758–1843) his secretary of war, with wide powers to direct the field armies. He had been aide-de-camp to Horatio Gates in the War of Independence and later a senator and diplomat; he had political ambitions and felt that a policy of ruthlessness might promote them. Monroe, then Secretary of State, hated him and saw him as a potential Bonaparte.[58] Armstrong sent an order to General William Harrison, the future president, to convert the British settlements on the Thames "into a desert," by conciliating the Indians and then turning them loose on the settlers. He also gave General McLure discretion to burn Newark. Madison commanded the Thames order to be revoked, and the burning of Newark was disavowed. One American colonel was court-martialed for a township burning. Terror was never official White House policy. Nonetheless, settlers had been murdered and their homes ruined. Sir George Prevost, the British commander in Canada, announced that it was his "imperious duty to retaliate on America the miseries" inflicted on Newark, and he proceeded to burn Buffalo, Lewiston and Manchester. Admiral Sir Alexander Cochrane, the naval force commander (he was the more conventional uncle of Lord Cochrane), wrote to Monroe, as secretary of state, informing him that in retaliation for the outrages in Upper Canada, his duty was "to destroy and lay waste such towns and districts upon the coast as may be found available"; he would refrain, he added, if the United States government made reparations to the Canadians.

In view of such warnings and the obvious threat from the amphibious British force, it is curious that the actual landing on the Chesapeake in August 1814 and the thrust to Washington took the U.S. authorities by surprise. The assault ships were commanded by Rear Admiral Sir George Cockburn, who succeeded in landing 5,000 troops under General Robert Ross and withdrawing them, largely unscathed, over a month later. In the capital, the cabinet and the army became inextricably confused, with politicians and generals rushing about, not quite knowing what they were doing. Madison himself, Monroe, Armstrong, the Secretary of the Navy William Jones and the Attorney General Richard Rush all made off to a hastily improvised defensive camp, "a scene of disorder and confusion which beggars description."[59] An eyewitness saw the president's wife, Dolley, "in her carriage flying full speed through Georgetown, accompanied by an officer carrying a drawn sword."[60] In fact, Mrs. Madison seems to have behaved with more sense than anyone else. She saved Gilbert Stuart's fine portrait of Washington, which hung on the dining-room wall of the President's house, "by breaking the frame, which was screwed to the wall, and having the canvas taken away."[61]

The British entered Washington, which was now undefended, on Wednesday 24 August. They fired a volley through the windows of the Capitol, went inside, and set it on fire. Next they went to the president's house, contemptuously known to Federalists as "the Palace"—it was unfinished and had no front porch or lawn—gathered all the furniture in the parlor and fired it with a live coal from a nearby tavern. They also torched the Treasury Building and the Navy Yard, which burned briskly until the fire was put out by a thunderstorm at midnight. Cockburn had a special dislike for the *National Intelligencer,* which had published scurrilous material about him, and he set fire to its offices, telling the troops: "Be sure that all the presses are destroyed so that the rascals cannot any longer abuse my name."

Ross pulled out his troops at 9 P.M. the following day, Thursday, by which time a cyclone and torrential rain had further confused the scattered American soldiers and cabinet ministers and compounded the miseries of thousands of refugees. The unpopularity of Madison, held responsible for a disastrous war, had been growing, and the sack of Washington was the last straw. There was a good deal of cowardice as well as incompetence. Codrington, reporting events to his wife Jane, wrote: "the enemy flew in all directions [and] scampered away as fast as possible." Madison, he added, "must be rather annoyed at finding himself obliged to fly with his whole force from the seat of government before 1200 English, the entire force actually engaged." Codrington claimed that the Americans had 8,000 troops defending the approaches to Washington, but "they ran away too fast for our hard-fagged people to make prisoners."[62] Madison himself was a fugitive. Dolley had to disguise herself: one tavern, crowded with homeless people, refused her admittance as they blamed her husband for everything. When she took refuge at Rokeby, the country house of Richard Love, the black cook refused to make coffee for her, saying "I done heerd Mr Madison and Mr Armstrong done sold the country to the British."[63] The middle states, like the South and West, had been strongly for war. Yet they made remarkably little effort to resist invasion. As one American historian put it: "In Maryland, Virginia and Pennsylvania there were then living not far from 1.5 million of whites. Yet this great population remained in its towns and cities and suffered 5,000 Englishmen to spend five weeks in its midst without once attempting to drive the invaders from its soil."[64]

The British, hardened and corrupted by 20 years of war fought all over the globe, were ruthless. Codrington related to his wife an incident that occurred on 31 August and concerned a grenadier of the Twenty-first Foot. "The poor fellow, fagged by a hard march, was stooping to fill his canteen at a well some distance from his comrades, when two Yankees leapt upon him, secured his musket, pinioned him and so forth. After going some little distance, he begged to have his arms untied that he might eat a mouthful of biscuit. This was granted, and as they were going on apparently in a very peaceable way, one of the two stepped forward to see if all was safe on the main road, while the other kept charge of the prisoner. They had not sat down five minutes when the *sentry* fell fast asleep. The soldier, watching his chance, got his knife out as quietly as possible and, contriving to cut the cord which secured his hands, he then seized his own musket from his enemy and knocked his brains out. But as he was desirous of making a complete job of it, he waited patiently for the return of the other, after examining his piece to see it was in good order for service, and the moment he came in sight shot him dead." What Jane Codrington thought of this incident is not recorded. Her husband was in no doubt: "You may think this, however soldier-like, a sort of legal butchery. But it is an act of well-performed duty nonetheless, and were it not so estimated, England would not be where it is."[65] Other naval officers disagreed. As the fleet ranged up and down the coast, bombarding Baltimore and sending parties ashore to fire smaller ports and towns, Captain Frederick Champier, another future naval novelist then serving on HMS *Menelaus* under Admiral Sir Peter Parker, wrote: "Let us hope that this disgracefully savage mode of warfare will never again be countenanced by civilised nations. It will be a blot on our escutcheon so long as the arms of England exist."[66]

At the time, however, these atrocities plainly increased America's war weariness. They also detonated a long-smoldering financial crisis. Even before the sack of Washington, the banks in Philadelphia and Baltimore had gone bankrupt. Immediately after it, the New York banks followed. The U.S. Treasury was in a mess, its longtime secretary, Albert Gallatin (1761–1849), having been dispatched to Europe in readiness for peace talks. Armstrong had been forced to resign when militia units simply refused to obey his orders, and Monroe had taken over the War Department in addition to the State Department—for an entire month, he later said, "I never went to bed." Federalist New England, its own banks sound, watched the disarray of the ruling Republicans and the ruin of the pro-war states with complacency. The Federalists held a convention at Hartford, Connecticut, in December 1814 to devise measures to bring the confused government and its war policy under stricter control, with the particular purpose of quashing a conscription bill, then before Congress, and limiting wartime interference with trade. Contrary to what many feared, there was no serious discussion of secession, but there was no predicting what would happen if the ruinous war continued.

Not all New Englanders endorsed its detachment. The strongly nationalistic diplomat John Quincy Adams (1767–1848), though a Bostonian himself, denounced the prevailing opinion in New England as substituting "faction for patriotism, a whining hypocrisy for political morals, dismemberment for union and prostitution to the enemy for state sovereignty."[67] The acid tone was characteristic—we shall be hearing a good deal more of it—but Adams's anger illustrated the deep divisions in what was still, after all, a new country.

But if the strain of the conflict was demoralizing the central states, a different situation was emerging on the third front, the South, almost entirely because of Andrew Jackson, the tall, thin angry man with the red hair and blazing blue eyes. Most people in the West and South wanted the war because they believed it would enable them to solve the "Indian problem." The new country had always been ambivalent about the Indians. An ordinance passed by the Continental Congress on 7 August 1786, which regulated Indian affairs, cut Indian country into two, at the Ohio River. North of the Ohio River and west of the Hudson River was the Northern District; the South was south of the Ohio and east of the Mississippi. Each district was under a superintendent, who felt some responsibility to his charges. To a limited extent the federal government had inherited the notions of the British colonial administration, to whom Indians were royal "subjects" with real as opposed to notional rights. But the United States was a settlers' country and Washington had to heed their views. In the South and the frontier states, the view was clear: the Indians must assimilate or move west.

It was a constitutionalist, rather than a racist, viewpoint. The United States was organized into states, counties, townships and parishes. The Indians were organized tribally. So organized, they lived by the pursuit of game. But the game was all gone or going. Tribal agriculture made inefficient use of the land. Tribal habits made Indians a constant security risk. They therefore had to detribalize themselves and fit into the American system. If they chose to do so, they could be provided with agricultural land (640 acres a family was a figure bandied about) and U.S. citizenship. This was, in fact, the option countless Indians chose. Many settled, took European-type names and, as it were, vanished into the growing mass of ordinary Americans. In any case there was no clear dividing line between redskins and whites. There were scores of thousands of half-breeds, some of whom identified with the whites and others who stuck to their tribes. But the bulk of the purebred Indians seem to have preferred tribal life, when they could choose. Very well, said the settlers, in that case you must move beyond the Mississippi, where there is still game and tribal life is possible.[68]

The War of 1812 made the settlers' viewpoint irresistible and gave them the physical opportunity to enforce it. The British did not hesitate to play the Indian card. Nor did the Spanish. Though not technically at war, the Spanish rightly feared American encroachment. As it happens, the Americans also used Indians when convenient, or indeed any other unintegrated group. Much of the Far South, especially near the coasts, was a lawless area, where no country's writ ran effectively. Groups of men—Indians, half-breeds, escaped slaves, mulattos—banded together, sometimes in sizable townships. Both sides in the war bid for their support when necessary. But the British pursued a systematic policy of organizing minorities against the United States. They liberated black slaves whenever they could and they armed the Indians. In the region of the Apalachicola River, then the boundary between west and east Florida, Major Edward Nicholls, with four officers and 108 Royal Marines, armed and to some extent trained over 4,000 Creeks and Seminoles, distributing 3,000 muskets, 1,000 carbines, 1,000 pistols, 500 rifles, and a million rounds of ammunition.[69] It had long been British policy to organize Indian resistance to American encroachment in the north.[70]

The Indians themselves were divided on whether to take advantage of the war—and the possibility of British arms supplies—to strike at American settlements. The most prominent of the war party, the Shawnee chief Tecumseh (1768–1813), had contrived, by his remarkable oratory and the predictions of his brother, "The Prophet," to organize a league of Indian tribes. He is reported to have told a gathering of Creeks, in October 1811: "Let the white race perish! They seize your land. They corrupt your women. They trample on the bones of your dead! Back whence they came, upon a trail of blood, they must be driven! Back—aye, back to the great water whose accursed waves brought them to our shores! Burn their dwellings—destroy their stock—slay their wives and children, that the very breed may perish! War now! War always! War on the living! War on the dead!"[71]

By the time war broke out, the militant Creek Indians, who carried bright red clubs, were known as the Red Sticks. Late in 1812 some of them went as far as Canada to massacre the demoralized American invaders. On their way back to the South, they murdered more Americans near the mouth of the Ohio, and this action, in turn, led to civil war among the Indians, for the Chickasaw, fearing reprisals, demanded that the Creeks punish the murderers. In the wild frontier territory north of the Spanish colonial capital of Pensacola, the American settlers, plus Indian "friendlies," attempted a massacre of the Red Sticks, led by half-breed Peter McQueen, who had his own prophets in the shape of High-Head Jim and Josiah Francis. The attempt failed, and the whites retreated into the stockade of another half-breed, Samuel Mims, who was pro-white, fifty miles north of Mobile on the Gulf. Rather grandly called Fort Mims, it was an acre surrounded by a log fence with slits for muskets and two gates. Inside were 150 militiamen—300 whites, half-breeds, and friendlies—and another 300 black slaves. Yet another half-breed, Dixon Bailey, was appointed commander. A slave who warned Bailey that the Red Sticks were coming was branded a liar and flogged, and on 30 August 1813 the gates were actually open when 1,000 Creeks attacked. Bailey was killed trying to shut the gates and all except 15 whites massacred. "The children were seized by the legs and killed by battering their heads against the stockading, the women were scalped and those who were pregnant were opened, while they were alive, and the embryo infants let out of the womb."[72] In all, the Creeks murdered 553 men, women and children and took away 250 scalps on poles.

At this point Jackson, as major general of militia in Tennessee, was ordered to take his men south to avenge the disaster. It was the opportunity for which he had been waiting. Like Henry Clay of Kentucky (1777–1852), Speaker of the House and leader of what were known as the War Hawks, and John Caldwell Calhoun of South Carolina (1782–1850), Jackson wanted every unassimilated Indian driven west of the Mississippi, and he wanted the states and the federal government to build roads as quickly as possible to bring in the settlers to secure the new frontier—just as his forebears had done in Ulster after the Battle of the Boyne. His arm was still in a sling from his latest duel, but he hurried his militiamen south, building roads as he went. With him was his partner in land speculation, General John Coffee, who commanded the cavalry, and a motley bunch of adventurers, which included David Crockett (1786–1836), also from Tennessee and a noted sharpshooter, and Samuel Houston (1793–1863), a Virginia-born frontiersman, then only nineteen.

The men who were to expand the United States in Texas and beyond were mostly blooded in this Creek War. And bloody it was. Two months after the massacre, on 3 November, Jackson's men surrounded the "hostile" village of Tallushatchee, and Jackson sent in Coffee with 1,000 men to destroy it. Coffee, Jackson reported to his wife Rachel, "executed this order in elegant stile [sic]." Crockett put it more truthfully: "We shot them like dogs."[73] Coffee killed every male in the village, 186 in all. Women were killed, too, though 84 women and children were taken prisoner. "We found as many as eight or ten dead bodies in a single cabin," wrote an eyewitness. Some of the cabins had taken fire, and half-consumed human bodies were seen among the smoking ruins. In other instances, dogs had torn and feasted on the bodies of their masters."[74] A 10-month-old Indian child was found clutched in his dead mother's arms. Jackson, always conscious of his own orphan status, and himself childless, promptly adopted the boy, named him Lyncoya, and had him conveyed to his house, the Hermitage. He wrote to Rachel that the child should be "well taken care of, he may have been given to me for some valuable purpose—in fact when I reflect that he, as to his relations, is so much like myself I feel an unusual sympathy for him."[75]

The week after the massacre, on 9 November, Jackson won what amounted to a pitched battle at Talladega, attacking a force of 1,000 Red Sticks who were besieging a "friendly" village, and killing 300 of them. At that point, under a different commander, the offensive would have petered out. The militia troops were obliged to provide only 90 days' service, rather like a medieval feudal army. The Volunteers undertook to serve for a year, but their term was running out. They had all had enough and wanted to go home. They said they would either march home, under Jackson, or mutiny and march home without him. This was the spirit that had ruined the Canadian campaign, and it threatened to ruin the multipronged campaign against the Creeks. An expedition by the Alabama Volunteers under General Ferdinand Claiborne had ended in disarray. The Georgia Militia, under General John Floyd, had lost 200 men in an attack on their badly posted camp and he had been forced by the malcontents to pull his troops out of the war.

Jackson was not going to allow his angry will to be bent by a military rabble. At various times he used the Volunteers to frighten the militiamen and his few regulars to frighten both. On 17 November he and Coffee and a few troops lined the road to stop mutinous militiamen from marching home. He said he would personally shoot any man who crossed the line. Back in camp he faced an entire brigade, his left arm still in a sling, his right clutching a musket which rested on the neck of his horse. It is likely the musket was not capable of being fired, but Jackson held the mob with his fierce glare until regulars with arms ready formed up behind him.[76] When the Volunteers, their term expired, decided to move off on 10 December, Jackson trained two small pieces of field artillery on them, loaded with grape, and when they failed to respond to his orders, he commanded the gunners, who were loyal militiamen, to light their matches. At that, the mutineers gave way. The men hated Jackson, but they feared him more. He wrote to Rachel that the Volunteers had become "mere whining, complaining Seditioners and mutineers, to keep whom from open acts of mutiny I have been compelled to point my cannon against, with a lighted match to destroy them. This was a grating moment of my life. I felt the pangs of an effectionate [sic] parent, compelled from duty to chastise the child."[77] It is unlikely that Jackson felt any such emotion; he always rationalized his acts in the language of a pre-Victorian melodrama. When a young militaman called John Woods, a mere boy of 18, refused an officer's order—while he was eating his breakfast—to return to his post, and grabbed a gun when arrested, Jackson had no hesitation in court-martialing him for mutiny and having him shot by firing squad, with the entire army watching. He stopped whiskey getting into camp. He made the men get up at 3:30 A.M., and his own staff half an hour before, to frustrate Indian dawn raids. Senior officers who objected to this kind of thing were sent home under arrest. The shooting of Woods had its effect. According to Jackson's aide-de-camp and later biographer, John Reid, "The opinion, so long indulged, that a Militiaman was for no offence to suffer death was from that moment abandoned and a strict obedience afterwards characterised the army."[78]

Under this iron rule, the army, paradoxically, attracted volunteers, and soon Jackson had a force of 5,000. He believed, like Wellington, in outnumbering the enemy, if possible, and he was thus able to attack the Creeks' main fortress, at Horseshoe Bend, which was defended by 1,000 men, with a column two or three times as large. But the place was very strong: a 100-acre wooded peninsula almost surrounded by water, with a 350-yard breastwork five to eight feet high with a double row of firing holes across its neck. It was, Jackson wrote, "well formed by Nature for defence & rendered more secure by Art." Indeed Jackson, who never underestimated the Indians, was impressed by their ingenuity— "the skill which they manifested in their best work was astonishing."[79] Jackson used various diversions, such as fireboats, and then stormed the rampart, proving in the act that scaling-ladders were not necessary. Ensign Sam Houston was the first man to get safely across the breastwork and into the compound. Both from the defense works themselves and from the experience of overwhelming them, Jackson learned much that was to be invaluable in the defense of New Orleans. What followed the breach of the wall was horrifying. The Indians would not surrender and were slain. The Americans kept a body count by cutting off the tips of the noses of the dead braves, giving a total of 557 dead in the fort and an estimated 300 drowned in the river. The dead included three leading "prophets" in full warpaint and feathers. The men cut strips of skin from the bodies to make harness for their horses. Jackson himself lost 47 whites and 23 friendlies.[80]

Thereafter it was a question of applying terror, by burning villages, confiscating food supplies and destroying crops. Jackson also built forts and roads. On 18 April 1814, Red Eagle, the nearest the Creeks had to a paramount chief, surrendered with other leaders. He is represented as saying to Jackson: "I am in your power. Do with me as you please. I am a soldier. I have done the white people all the harm I could. I have fought them and fought them bravely, and if I had an army I would still fight and contend to the last. But I have none. My people are all gone. I can now do no more than weep over the misfortunes of my nation."[81] Jackson spared Red Eagle because he was useful in persuading others to surrender and avoid a guerrilla war. Red Eagle was given a large farm in Alabama, where, like other successful Indian planters, he owned a multitude of black slaves; from time to time he visited Jackson at the Hermitage.[82]

But Jackson showed no mercy to the Indians as a whole, whether hostile or friendly. On 9 August 1814, at the fort called after him, he imposed on 35 frightened chiefs, most of whom had never lifted a finger against the Americans—hostile chiefs had fled to Spanish territory—a Carthaginian peace. Jackson was an impressive and at times terrifying orator, who left the huddled chiefs in no doubt what would be their fate if they failed to sign the document he thrust at them. They had, as it happened, documents of their own—letters of indemnity signed by the official U.S. superintendent for the southern region, Colonel Benjamin Hawkins, and by General Pinckney, Jackson's predecessor, which had been given to them in return for their support or neutrality. Jackson simply stated that the letters were invalid as they had not been authorized by Washington. Instead, his treaty of surrender imposed on the Creeks the surrender of 23 million acres, which was half their lands—three-fifths of the present state of Alabama and a fifth of modern Georgia. Jackson wrote gleefully to one of his business associates, John Overton: "I finished the convention with the Creeks . . . [which] cedes to the United States 20 million acres of the cream of the Creek Country, opening a communication from Georgia to Mobile."[83]

Jackson knew from long personal experience—he had been involved in land deals since 1795, and Rachel's father, John Donelson, a state surveyor, had got 20,000 acres of former Indian land near Chattanooga—the significance of this deal. In effect, it broke the Creeks as a self-conscious nation and made the surrender of the rest of their lands only a matter of time. The Treaty of Fort Jackson in fact was the tragic turning point in the destruction of the American Indians east of the Mississippi, the first of five similar seizures which over the next decade were totally to transform the South and Southwest. We will look at them later. For the present, we have to see Jackson as a man moving fast, who knew exactly what he was doing. He wrote urgently to Washington, begging the authorities and Congress to act quickly to settle and secure the frontier belt with fortified farms. He wanted a law to give "each able-bodied man who will settle upon this land a section at $2 an acre, payable in two years with interest—this measure would insure [sic] the security of this frontier and make citizens of the soldiers who effected its conquest."[84] This was an old Roman colonizing procedure, and in Tsarist Russia, military colonies were being set up in territories annexed from tribes at exactly the time Jackson wrote.

Settlement, however, was the long-term strategy. For the immediate future Jackson intended, whether he was authorized by Washington or not, to exploit the military advantage his victory over the Creeks gave him by destroying Spanish power. He was alarmed by the news of the British landings in the Washington area and rightly feared they would follow up their success by a move in the South. Before the end of August he had occupied Mobile, near the Florida border, and garrisoned Fort Bower on the key to the south of it. When British amphibious forces moved into the area in mid-September they found the fort strongly held and failed to take it. On 7 November, after careful preparations, Jackson occupied the main Spanish base of Pensacola. Spain and America were not at war, and Jackson had no authority for this act of aggression. He gave his reasons in a letter to Monroe, now doubling up as War Secretary, citing "The Hostility of the governor of Pensacola in permitting the place to assume the character of a British territory by resigning the command of a Fortress to them."[85] Washington, still recovering from the British incursion, was too shell-shocked to do anything about such insubordination, and by the time it recovered its poise, the Battle of New Orleans had been won and Jackson was a conquering hero, the only one the country had.

Jackson's moves frustrated the plan of the British fleet commander, Cochrane, to take Mobile and move inland to cut off New Orleans, freeing blacks and raising Indians as he went. Instead Cochrane decided on a direct assault on the city. Jackson moved there on 1 December, finding it virtually undefended. But by the time "Ned" Pakenham arrived to command the British assault force, Jackson's force and ruthlessness—he was already known to his men as "Old Hickory," and the Indians called him "Sharp Knife" and "Pointed Arrow"—had effected huge changes. He formed the local pirates, who hated Royal Navy ships, on which they were periodically hanged, into a defensive unit, operating out of Cat Island. He formed hundreds of free blacks into a battalion, with white officers but their own noncommissioned officers: all were paid a bounty of $124 and 160 acres of land taken from the

Indians. This unheard-of treatment of blacks brought an outraged protest from the Paymaster, who was told crisply: "Be pleased to keep to yourself your opinions on the policy of making payments of the troops with the necessary muster-rolls without inquiring whether the troops are white, black or tea."[86] Jackson brought as many troops into the defensive area as possible, though it was nothing like the 20,000 British intelligence reported, and began feverishly constructing his forward line. His tactics were not perfect. He failed to secure the left bank of the Mississippi, and this failure might have proved fatal had Pakenham been more patient. But his main defense, based upon his hard-won experience at Horseshoe Bend, was faultless. At a stroke, the man who had humiliated the conquerors of Washington became the most famous man in America.

By one of history's ironies, peace had already been concluded. This peace, the Treaty of Ghent, proved to be one of the most durable and decisive in world history and is worth examining in some detail. It was not without its lighter moments. While the British were still determined to pursue their war aims vigorously as long as the conflict continued, once France had surrendered in April 1814, they became increasingly anxious to settle the dispute with America, regarded as a mere hangover of a world war now at an end. The British press was making bellicose noises in late spring and summer 1814, but the grim fact was that 70 percent of Britain's entire government revenue was now devoted to servicing the debt contracted during the long struggle against Bonaparte, in which the British had not only paid for their own war effort but subsidized that of all their allies.[87]

Castlereagh first offered to treat at Gothenburg, but by the time Madison had accepted, the rendezvous was shifted to Ghent.[88] The first to arrive on 24 June 1814 was the American Peace Commissioner, John Quincy Adams, who came from Saint Petersburg, where he was U.S. minister, accompanied by his black valet Nelson (a favorite name among blacks, then as today, for the British admiral was celebrated for freeing slaves). Appointed to assist him was the Treasury Secretary, Albert Gallatin, representing the administration and Republican point of view, and the Federalist senator from Delaware, James Ashton Bayard. At the last minute Madison decided to add the aggressive westerner Henry Clay and the U.S. minister to Sweden, Jonathan Russell, to the American delegation. It would be difficult to conceive of a more ill-assorted team. Gallatin and Bayard, by definition, represented violently opposed interests. Clay was a thruster, whom Adams, a Harvard man and Boston Brahmin, regarded as very much less than a gentleman.

Russell was a quibbling nonentity. Adams felt he was the senior participant by virtue of his position and experience: The son of the second
president, he had spent a great deal of his life in embassies and was
fluent not only in languages but in international law. He was also highly
argumentative, thin-skinned, quick to take offense, and a superb hater.
He was a great compiler of enemies' lists, and toward the end of his life
drew up a paranoid table of thirteen men, including Jackson, Clay,
John C. Calhoun, William Crawford and Daniel Webster, who had
"conspired together [and] used up their faculties in base and dirty tricks
to thwart my progress in life."[89]

Adams held his fellow commissioners in low esteem. Bayard he
already hated and he came to dislike Clay intensely, though political
fortune was later to bring them into close and uneasy contact, as
President and Secretary of State. He found the hours of his colleagues,
who lodged at the same hotel, inconvenient. He himself got up at 5
A.M., in the dark, and worked busily by candlelight for hours, covering
endless sheets with his critical scribbles. He dined at one, the rest at
four, and then, he recorded in his diary, "They sit after dinner and
drink bad wine and smoke cigars which neither suits my habits nor my
health and absorbs time which I cannot spare." They also gambled,
which he deplored. On 8 September he recorded: "Just before rising [at
5 A.M.], I heard Mr Clay's company retiring from his chamber. I had
left him with Mr Russell, Mr Bentzon and Mr Todd at cards. They
parted as I was about to rise." The same thing happened a fortnight
later.[90] Clay not only liked to gamble but to gamble high; he got, Adams
reported sourly, "wearing and impatient" if Russell and Gallatin
wanted to play for low stakes. It also came to his shocked ears that Clay
had made a pass at a chambermaid. Clay, Adams said, was particularly
hostile to New England: he "rails at commerce and the people of
Massachusetts, and tells what wonders the people of Kentucky would
do if they should be attacked."[91]

There were, indeed, furious arguments within the American delegation reflecting the interests of different states. New England wanted
concessions from the British over Maine and Newfoundland fishing
rights, in return for giving Britain access to the Mississippi. Gallatin
urged that "if we should abandon any part of the territory it would give
a handle to the part there now pushing for a separation from the Union
and a New England confederacy, to say that the interests of the North-
East were sacrificed, and to pretend that by a separate confederacy they
could obtain what is refused to us." This statement brought an outburst
from Clay: "It was too much the practice of our government to sacrifice
the interests of its best friends for those of its bitterest enemies—that

there might be a party for separation at some future date on the Western states, too." At which point Adams accused him sharply of "speaking under the impulse of passion."[92] At one stage the bellicose Clay "was for a war three years longer. He had no doubt but three years more of war would make us a warlike people. . . . He was for playing *brag* with the British plenipotentiaries . . . the art of it was to beat your adversary by holding your hand, with a solemn and confident phiz, and outbragging him."[93]

At other times, however, Adams found Clay, along with the rest, insufficiently firm. There was much exchanging of notes between the delegations and, while "the tone of all the British notes is arrogant, overbearing and offensive, the tone of ours is neither so bold nor so spirited as I think it should be." Adams had accused his colleagues of pusillanimity from the start by being prepared to accept the British proposal that the talks should take place at the British lodgings in the Hotel Lion d'Or. This proposal was, he told Gallatin and Clay, "an offensive pretension to superiority. I referred my colleagues to Martens, Book vii, Chapter 55, Section 3, of his *Summary* [of diplomatic usage], where the course now taken by the British commissioners appears to be precisely that stated there to be the usage from ambassadors to Ministers of an inferior order." The others found Adams's pedantry and his habit of reading aloud to them from his copious notes and authorities tiresome. They also objected to his propensity to indulge in moralistic rhetoric, of a kind which Woodrow Wilson later epitomized, and in particular to his dragging God into their many arguments. Adams lamented: "The terms God, and Providence, and Heaven, Mr Clay thought were canting, and Russell laughed at them. I was obliged to give them up and with them what I thought the best argument we had." In this, as in other aspects of drafting, Adams usually found himself in a minority of one; no wonder.[94]

The question of a venue was soon settled by holding meetings alternately at each other's hotels, and in practice Adams found the British delegation more congenial companions than his colleagues. Despite their common religiosity, Admiral Gambier, the hymn-singing Evangelical who was the senior member of the British party, did not appeal to him. But he got on well with William Adams, who was what was termed a "civilian," that is, an expert on Roman law and international protocol: they spent many happy hours discussing genealogies and whether they could be remote cousins—a foretaste of that magical phenomenon, soon to emerge, the "special relationship."[95] Adams found bonds, too, with the third British delegate, Henry Goulburn (1784–1856), member of Parliament for the pocket borough of St. Germans, a wealthy man-about-town just touching thirty, later to be Chancellor of the Exchequer. Goulburn had blotted his copybook in the House of Commons, on his first election, by trying to take the oath in riding boots, a privilege reserved for County Members. But since then he had flourished, and was now Under-Secretary for War and Colonies and, along with Sir Robert Peel, Fred Robinson, John Wilson Croker, Lord Palmerston, and other rising stars, a member of Alfred's Club where the smarter ministerialists met to dine every Wednesday.[96] Adams, critical as always, found that the more he chatted with Goulburn, "the more the violence and bitterness of his passion against the United States disclosed itself," but he recognized Goulburn's superior Cambridge ton—the next best thing to Harvard—and found his social and intellectual fastidiousness a change from his colleagues.

It was with Goulburn, too, that Adams was able to get to the heart of the argument between the two countries. It was really around two issues, Canada and the Indians; they were interconnected. Britain feared the aggressive expansionism of the United States, of which the confiscation of Indian lands was the most obvious sign. This was taking place not only on a huge scale in the South, but in the north near Canada. America, having failed once to annex Canada, would, as its population and power increased, try again, and the continued presence of U.S. warships on the Great Lakes underlined this threat. Nor were these fears unfounded. Adams certainly wanted to absorb Canada and even, as he said, "strongly urged the expediency of avowing as the sentiment of our government that the cession of Canada would be for the interest of Great Britain as well as the United States." His colleagues regarded such a claim as ridiculous, since America had clearly been worsted on the Canadian frontier and the British were currently occupying over 100 miles of the coast of Maine. So Adams was turned down. In any case, Goulburn made it clear to Adams in private conversation that, for the British, Canada was the sticking point. The British wanted a joint British-American guarantee of the remaining Indian territory, so that British and U.S. frontiers in the north did not touch, the Indians constituting a *cordon sanitaire* in between. The British also wanted naval disarmament. Goulburn told Adams that "to save Canada" was Britain's "great object"; the United States had been determined to have it, and it had been preserved "by a miracle." So disarmament on the Great Lakes must come. America would never be in danger of invasion from Canada, which was "infinitely weaker." But "Canada must always be in the most imminent danger of invasion from the United States, unless she was guarded by some such stipulation as [the British] now demanded—that it could be nothing to the United States to agree not to arm upon the Lakes, since they had never actually done it before the present war. Why should they now object to disarming there, where they had never before had a gun floating?"[97]

To this argument, Adams countered that, leaving aside the question of warships on the Great Lakes for the moment, America could not accept any treaty that would require halting expansion at the expense of the Indians anywhere. It is curious that Adams, though reflecting the typical New England detestation of black slavery—it was one of the ruling passions of his life—had no feelings of compassion for the Indians. He gave Goulburn a robust defense of U.S. Indian policy at its most ruthless. The Indians would never settle. They would never be other than "wandering hunters." Settlement required land, and the only policy was to take it, compensate the Indians, and remove them farther "to remoter regions better suited to their purposes and mode of life." Taking a high moral line, which always came easily to him, he called such an attitude "liberality" and "an improvement upon the former practice of all European nations, including the British." As he saw it, "Between [such a policy] and taking the lands for nothing, or exterminating the Indians who had used them, there was no alternative. To condemn vast regions of territory to perpetual barrenness and solitude [in order] that a few hundred savages might find wild beasts to hunt upon it, was a species of game law that a nation descended from Britons would never endure. It was incompatible with the moral as well as the physical nature of things."[98] Adams told Goulburn that even if America signed a treaty limiting their right to push on, it would prove worthless—"It was opposing a feather to a torrent." The rapid increase in the American population placed it "beyond human power to check its progress by a bond of paper." In practice, Adams added, "the only real security for Canada" was Great Britain's ability to hurt the United States somewhere else."[99]

There were plainly huge gulfs between the two sides. The detailed haggling began when the British side put forward "heads of agreement" for a treaty, setting out their demands. The Americans pronounced it totally unacceptable and rejected it. It was withdrawn. Then the British, knowing well the divisions within the U.S. delegation, asked them to put forward *their* proposed heads of agreement. This request occurred on 31 October 1814. As the British expected, once the U.S. delegates began to draft the document, their unity fell apart over the conflict between New England and western interests. Meanwhile external events pressed. Originally, the British had been slow even to send their delegates to Ghent, believing that with every week which passed, the rapid transport of British reinforcements, released from France, across the Atlantic would strengthen their bargaining position, and the point was made by the burning of Washington. That, however, was followed by numerous U.S. sinkings of British ships, which discomposed the British team and encouraged Adams, Gallatin, and Clay to be more intransigent.

As the autumn dragged on, however, America's urgent need for a peace at almost any price became clearer. George W. Campbell, who had succeeded Gallatin at the U.S. Treasury, told Congress that if the war went on only until 1 January 1816, Congress would have to vote a further $50 million in taxation. When Congress showed no such disposition, he resigned. His successor, Alexander James Dallas, went further: he proposed not only a regular system of federal taxation, but a federal Bank of the United States, something many congressmen regarded with abhorrence. He formally certified that the U.S. Treasury was bankrupt and, unless it issued paper, was unable to pay its bills or salaries, including presumably those of the American delegation in Ghent. Meanwhile the banking crisis spread.

The administration's proposals to carry on the war more effectively likewise ran into Congressional obduracy. Monroe, as War Secretary, put forward a Militia Bill which sought to remedy the mutinous indiscipline of the American forces by rather more lawful methods than Jackson used. Christopher Gore, the Federalist senator from Massachusetts, denounced such a move as outrageous: "It is the first step on the odious ground of conscription, which never will and never ought to be submitted to by the people of this country while they retain any idea of civil freedom . . . and should be resisted by all who have any regard for public liberty or the rights of the states."[100] Since Congress would not act, the states in theory raised their own forces. But some refused to do so. Others, like New York, did so against strong public hostility. Public-spirited Americans, relishing legal argument, leapt into the debate: some argued that state armies were unconstitutional; others contended that federal conscription was, and more so. But the plain fact was that the U.S. Congress had failed to provide the country with either a currency or an army, at a time when part of its territory was under enemy occupation and much more was threatened. Against this background, it seemed to many that the federal government, with no troops or money, "sitting in the ashes of its former home," was on the brink of collapse, with the prospect of a New England breakaway. Peace was not merely desirable; it was a necessity.[101]

Oddly enough, in view of his previous patriotic hard line, it was Adams who first proposed, to his own colleagues, a way out of the impasse by a *status quo ante bellum* clause. Under this, each side would revert to its frontiers before the fighting started and, in effect, forgo any claims, as though the war had never taken place. The rest of the delegation thought the clause a nonstarter: the British would laugh and say "Aye, aye! Pretty fellows you, thinking of getting out of the war as well as you got into it."[102] In fact, the *status quo ante* formula was the simplest solution to a war which both sides now secretly admitted had been a mistake and urgently wanted to end. So it was accepted. Such matters as Newfoundland fisheries and navigation rights on the Mississippi were dropped. The actual issues of the war on both sides were ignored. All the treaty did was to provide for the cessation of hostilities immediately it was ratified; the release of prisoners; surrender of virtually all territory captured by either side; the pacification of the Indians; and the more accurate definitions of boundaries, to be handed over to three sets of commissioners. The last joint meeting was held on Christmas Eve, 24 December 1814, in the lodgings of the British delegation. It began at 4 P.M. and ended at 6:30, by which time six copies of the treaty had been signed and sealed. One of the U.S. clerks, Hughes, set off the same evening for Bordeaux to ship a copy with all speed to the U.S. government. The delegation's secretary, Henry Carroll, left two days later for London to take ship there, and he actually got to Washington first. Back in Ghent, there was a final, undignified row between Adams and Clay over who should keep the papers, Adams broadening the dispute into the charge that America would have got a better treaty if the rest of the team had followed his advice, and Clay shouting: "You *dare* not, you *cannot* you *SHALL* not insinuate that there has been a cabal of three members against you!"[103]

In fact, the administration and American public opinion generally regarded the treaty as excellent in the circumstances. The financial crisis and the impasse in Congress had continued. In mid-January Stephen Decatur, the best of the American naval commanders, had been obliged to lower his flag to the Royal Navy outside New York. This defeat was offset on 4 February when news of the battle of New Orleans reached Washington. But the British had withdrawn in good order and were engaged in further assaults on the coast. So when Carroll, later that month, entered New York harbor, clutching the treaty, in the sloop *Favourite,* he was received with profound relief. Most rejoiced at its terms, which might have been far worse. The Federalists pointed out that in view of the administration's war aims, it was a total defeat and humiliation. It was instantly approved by Congress, on 18 February 1815.[104] The British were also well content. Indeed, Castlereagh was relieved too; he was experiencing great difficulties at the peace congress in Vienna and was now anxious to concentrate the British fleet and mobile invasion force on the European side of the Atlantic.[105]

The Treaty of Ghent was one of the great acts of statesmanship in history. Those involved wrought more wisely than they knew. After the signing, Adams remarked to old Gambier: "I hope this will be the last treaty of peace between Great Britain and the United States."[106] It was. The very fact that both sides withdrew to their prewar positions, that neither could call the war a success or a defeat, that the terms could not be presented, either then or later, as a triumph or a robbery—all worked for permanency and helped to erase from the national memory of both sides a struggle which had been bitter enough at the time. Moreover, the absence of crowing or recrimination meant that the peace could serve as a plinth on which to erect the foundations of a friendly, commonsense relationship between the two great English-speaking peoples. Does that mean that Jackson's victory at New Orleans was of no consequence? Not at all. It was decisive in its way, for, though the treaty made no mention of the fact, it had in reality involved major strategic, indeed historic, concessions on both sides. Castlereagh, the wise man behind the mask of ice, was the first British foreign secretary who accepted the existence of the United States, not just in theory, but in practice as a legitimate national entity to be treated as a fellow player in the world game. This acceptance was marked by the element of unspoken trust which lay behind the treaty's provisions. For its part, the United States accepted the existence of Canada as a legitimate entity too, not an unresolved problem inherited from the War of Independence, to be absorbed in due course when America was strong enough. At the time it was a much greater concession than it looked, for neither the British nor the Americans yet seemed to have grasped that the road to expansion of both the United States and Canada lay not in depredations at each other's expense but in both pushing simultaneously and in friendly rivalry toward the Pacific Coast. In return, Britain, in effect, gave the Americans the go-ahead to expand as they wished anywhere south of the 49th parallel, at the expense of the Indians and the Spanish alike.

Hence, though Jackson's victory at New Orleans had no effect on the treaty itself, it determined the way it was interpreted and applied. The treaty was as important in what it did not say as in what it did. The Treaty of San Ildefonso (1800), by which Bonaparte secured the Louisiana Territory from Spain, said France could not dispose of it without first offering it back to its original owner. This Bonaparte omitted to do, so when he sold it to the United States in 1803, most nations, including Britain, did not recognize the purchase. In international law, as Britain saw it, America had no right to be anywhere on the Gulf of Mexico, including New Orleans and Mobile. Since the Treaty of Ghent said nothing about these territories, Britain would have been at liberty to hand them back to Spain had she been in possession of all or any of them at the time the treaty came into effect. As Monroe put it to Madison, if Jackson had lost the battle, that is exactly what Britain would have been tempted to do. The effect of Jackson's victory was to legitimize the entire Louisiana purchase in the eyes of the international community; henceforth we hear no more about its illegality. Equally, if Fort Bower had been taken before the war ended, instead of after, Britain could have occupied Mobile with the 6,000 men she had on the spot and might have been tempted to fortify and keep it as another Gibraltar, to checkmate any U.S. forward moves toward Britain's valuable colonies in the Caribbean.[107] The instructions given to Cochrane and Pakenham reserved the right to retain any conquests after the war, and the actual wording of the treaty would have made this provision lawful. As it was, Britain, in effect, renounced any such ambitions provided America left Canada alone. There were, of course, sound economic reasons for Britain to want friendly relations with the United States in the whole area. The financial significance of Britain's rich sugar colonies in the Caribbean was fast declining relative to the huge industrial expansion, based on finished cotton manufactures, which was taking place in Britain and for which the American South increasingly supplied the raw material. For America to expand in the South, putting more territory under cotton, was in the interests of both countries. But it was the New Orleans victory which clinched the switch of policy.

Equally, the victory meant that the slender provision the treaty made, on Britain's insistence, to protect the Indians, was nugatory. Under Article Nine, America agreed to end the war against the Indians, too, "and forthwith to restore to such tribes . . . all possessions . . . which they have enjoyed . . . in 1811 previous to such hostilities."[108] This clearly made the Fort Jackson Treaty invalid. Jackson himself argued that the 20-million-acre concession was a quite separate treaty between the Indians and Washington and had nothing to do with Ghent. Britain rejected this *force majeure* argument and, under pressure, Washington agreed. Jackson was told, "The President . . . is confident that you will . . . conciliate the Indians upon the principles of our agreement with Great Britain." But Madison had no grounds for such confidence: Jackson never obeyed orders he found uncongenial, unless absolutely forced. He simply instructed his men to keep the sullen, demoralized Indians moving west. Now that the British expeditionary forces had left for Europe, there was no power in the area to compel him. Washington did nothing, nor did the British. In fact, the American settler interest had now received carte blanche to pursue its destiny. That was the consequence of New Orleans.

In the meantime, and equally important in the light of history, the "special relationship," the foundations of which had been so grudgingly laid in those Ghent hotels, continued to prosper. In pursuance of the treaty, talks were held in Washington in 1817 to settle the Great Lakes and the Canadian border. On the American side was Richard Rush (1780–1859), from Pennsylvania, son of the great medical scientist Benjamin Rush who had signed the Declaration of Independence. When Monroe began his presidency in 1817, he appointed Adams his secretary of state in April, but Adams was en poste in Europe and did not arrive in Washington to take up the job until September, an indication of the difficulties of communication and travel at the time.

Meanwhile, Rush, a discreet Washington insider, did the work. It was just as well. Where Adams was quarrelsome, anti-British and ultra-expansionist—"the United States and North America are identical," as he put it—Rush was eirenic, a Princeton Anglophile and skeptical of overrapid expansion, which he thought would weaken still further the fragile state of the American economy. As he was to put it later, as Treasury Secretary, "The creation of capital is retarded, rather than accelerated, by the diffusion of a thin population over a great surface of soil." The current toast, at Fourth of July celebrations, was "to the United States Eagle, and may she extend her wings from the Atlantic to the Pacific, and fixing her talons on the Isthmus of Darien, stretch her beak to the Northern Pole."[109] But Rush, who had a healthy respect for British power, knew that such ambitions did not make sense with Britain an enemy; indeed, continued western expansion really hinged on having Britain as a friend. Rush's opposite number, the British minister in Washington, Sir Charles Bagot (1781–1843), thought along similar lines. He had come to Washington from the Paris embassy, and was to end his days as governor-general of Canada. Much of Bagot's life was spent smoothing relations between the two English-speaking powers. He was the brother of a peer of ancient lineage, was married to Wellington's niece, and his manners were impeccable. Even Adams, who liked no one, admired his "discretion"; he had, Adams wrote in his diary, "made himself universally acceptable. No English minister has ever been so popular"—adding, characteristically, "the mediocrity of his talents has been one of the principal causes of his success."[110]

Left to get on with it, these two professional fixers soon produced a draft treaty (1817), known as the Rush-Bagot Agreement, which was duly ratified at a convention the next year, Goulburn and his friend Fred Robinson signing it in London.[111] The treaty was approved by the U.S. Senate unanimously. It laid down the 49th parallel as the border between British Canada and the United States and strictly limited the number and size of armed ships on the Great Lakes. It could be described as the first and, in many ways, the most effective disarmament treaty in history. In practice it made it unnecessary for either side to defend a border both now accepted. This border was by no means undefended, as yet. The U.S. administration, fearing sneaky British attempts to impede settlement south of it by encouraging Indians to infiltrate, built an impressive series of forts to secure the advance west. The notion of "the only undefended frontier in the world" became reality only from the 1870s onwards. But it had its roots in 1817. Moreover, the deal led directly to joint Anglo-U.S. cooperation in facing up to other powers in the area, the first time the two countries had ever worked together on the world stage.

The area involved was the vast northwest of the North American continent, west of the Rockies, north of the 42nd parallel and south of 54 degrees. It was vaguely known as Oregon. Four powers had interests and claims there. The Spanish had pushed north from California from the 16th century onward. The British, too, had been on this coast in Drake's day and clearly had further claims if the 49th parallel settlement were pushed to its westernmost conclusion. In 1725 the Russians had hired the Danish navigator Vitus Bering to explore these waters, and his discovery of the Aleutian Islands in 1741 had led Russian fur traders to push into the region, leaping from island to island as they had earlier leapt from one river portage to another right across Siberia from the Urals to the Pacific. The Anglo-U.S. convention of 1818 extended only to the Rockies, leaving both nations in joint occupation of Oregon beyond. They therefore had a mutual interest in excluding the other two powers. Britain had already forced Spain to renounce some of her claims in 1790, following a high-handed Spanish arrest of British fur traders at Nootka Sound, near Vancouver Island. Moreover, Britain was the only power with a naval capability in the area, and if the Americans wanted to act against Spain at all, they had to do so in concert with the British, or at least with their acquiescence.

It was as well that during these years, British foreign policy was in the hands of Castlereagh. He was quite clear in his mind that the best way to protect Canada and other British interests in the hemisphere and the Northeast Pacific was to remain on friendly terms with the United States and to ignore any provocative behavior. Even so, Castlereagh's patience was sorely tested. In the South Jackson's determination to destroy organized Indian society east of the Mississippi and to replace it by white settlements—which we will look at in detail later—led him to act first and seek his government's approval afterwards, as did so many European imperialist generals in the nineteenth century. On 15 March 1818 Jackson's troops began an undeclared war against Spain by invading Florida, which the Spanish colonial authorities were incapable of defending. On 2 June Jackson even wrote to President Monroe, "I will ensure you Cuba in a few days," but Washington declined to send him the frigate that would have made it possible.[112]

Washington never explicitly authorized Jackson's acts of aggression. The only member of the cabinet who backed him wholeheartedly, on grounds of God-inspired manifest destiny, was Adams. Monroe gave him tacit support, in that he knew what Jackson's intentions were—the general had told him many times in writing he would move against the Spanish—and did not specifically forbid them. But later he denied collusion and said he was sick at the time. In a modern context, of course, Jackson's activities—which were plainly against the Constitution (which gave Congress the right to make peace and war) would have been exposed by liberal-minded journalists. In 1818, the general would have seized and expelled such reporters or possibly hanged them for treason. In any case there were no liberal-minded journals in the United States in 1818, at least on Indian questions; all were bellicose and expansionary. Moreover, Congress itself was happy to endorse the *fait accompli* by rejecting a motion of censure on Jackson for seizing Florida, on 8 February 1819, and the territory was formally conveyed from Spain to the United States two years later (17 July 1821).

The only power in a position to aid Spain was Britain, and Jackson offered a further provocation on 29 April 1818, with the judicial murder of two British subjects in Florida. Alexander Arbuthnot, a Scot aged 70, traded with the Indians from the Bahamas. He was, no doubt, a rogue of a kind, but he had certainly not incited the Indians against the whites—quite the contrary. His crime was that he loved them. So, too, did Robert Ambrister, a former Royal Marine lieutenant and, therefore, a peculiar object of detestation to Jackson. He, by contrast, had plainly urged the Indians to fight and offered to lead them. Jackson seized both men and put them on trial before a court of hard-faced American whites who equated friendly feelings toward "hostiles" with the butchering of settlers. The old Scot, who admitted selling gunpowder to Indians for hunting, was condemned to death. Ambrister, though clearly guilty as charged, the court liked better and, after sentencing him to be shot, altered the punishment to 50 lashes and a year's hard labor. Jackson ignored the revised sentence and shot the marine anyway, and he hanged Arbuthnot on the yardarm of the old man's ship.[113] This was just the kind of unlawful act against those who owed allegiance to the British Crown which Lord Palmerston was later to argue justified war, pleading the line *Civis Britannicus Sum*. But Palmerston was then only Secretary for War. Castlereagh, as Foreign Secretary, decided to bite the bullet. He wrote to the courtly Bagot in Washington that he had decided the two dead men "had been engaged in unauthorised practices of such a description as to have deprived them of any claim on their own government."[114]

Castlereagh also received much provocation from the prickly Adams in Washington. While actively negotiating a definite boundary line with Spain with Luis de Onis, the Spanish minister, Adams not only haughtily rejected Spanish demands that Jackson be disavowed and punished for his actions, but wrote a long, aggressive letter to George W. Erving, the U.S. minister in Madrid, setting out his views and telling him to transmit them, syllable by syllable, to the Madrid government. It is an exemplary essay, for neophyte diplomats, of attack being the best means of defense. The British were engaged in "a creeping and insidious war, both against Spain and the United States . . . to plunder Spain of her province and to spread massacre and devastation along the borders of the United States." Spain was to blame for not "controlling these wicked British activities." Old Thomas Jefferson, shown a copy, thought it "among the ablest compositions I have ever seen, both as to logic and style." It was, in fact, a detailed foreshadowing of the policy on Manifest Destiny.[115] Almost inevitably, a copy fell into Castlereagh's hands. Again, he chose to ignore the insult. He did not want war or threats of war. He valued the North American market too much and he recognized that the disintegration of the once-enormous Spanish empire in the Western hemisphere was to the advantage of Britain, as well as the United States. He had the perception, too, to grasp that much of Adams's slam-bang argument was rhetoric, born of a need to get the bile out of his system.

So Britain was content for the negotiations to proceed, and on 22 February 1819, a fortnight after Congress refused to disavow Jackson, Adams and Onis signed the treaty which bears their name, acknowledging the *fait accompli* in Florida. Far more important, the treaty agreed on a transcontinental line which, in effect, permitted the United States to pursue its destiny to the Pacific, though it left still under nominal Spanish control the territories of seven states, including California and

Texas, which the United States would subsequently seize from Spain's successor-state, Mexico. Adams called it "the most important day in my life"; the acknowledgment of a "definite line of boundary to the South Sea" formed "a great epocha in our history."[116]

The treaty was of significance for Britain, too, since it eliminated the Spanish factor from the efforts of the two English-speaking peoples to work out their claims in the Oregon territories, as they had contracted to do under the Rush-Bagot treaty. This was not easy. Plenty of people on the East Coast were anxious to stir up anti-British feeling. In Pennsylvania, for instance, the press was dominated by the *Aurora,* edited by William Duane, a malcontent Irishman who had been expelled from British India for sedition, and by the *Democratic Press,* edited by an English renegade, John Binns, who had been tried by a British court for high treason. Secretary of State Adams, who did not particularly like anti-British polemic issuing from any but his own lips and pen, noted in his diary that both men were "of considerable talents and profligate principles, always for sale to the highest bidder, and always insupportable burdens, by their insatiable rapacity, to the parties they support."[117]

But such spirits had ample ammunition to fire, especially since British and American traders occasionally came into conflict in the huge, wild, unmapped, and totally unsettled lands beyond the Rockies, particularly on and around the Columbia River, which flowed into the Pacific south of Vancouver Island. At the end of January 1821, Adams recorded a characteristic exchange, over American attempts to place a settlement on the river, with Bagot's successor, Stratford Canning (1786–1880). Canning was a less ecumenical type, cousin to the thrusting Tory politician George Canning, a grandee diplomat who was later to fit in well with Palmerstonian principles. He had raised an objection under the 1818 Convention. Adams: "Have you any claim to the mouth of the Columbia river?" Canning: "Why—do you not know that we *have* a claim?" Adams: "I do not know what you claim or do not claim. You claim India. You claim Africa. You claim—" Canning: "Perhaps a piece of the Moon?" Adams: "No, I have not heard that you claim exlusively any part of the Moon. But there is not a spot on this habitable globe that I could affirm you do *not* claim."[118]

Nevertheless, both powers cooperated to push out Russia, as hitherto they had excluded Spain and France. The Russians, who had no fleet in the region to face up to the Royal Navy, withdrew their claims and signed a treaty with America in April 1824, which fixed 54 degrees, 40 as the southernmost limit for her posts. A similar Russian agreement with Britain followed in February 1825.[119] It was as well that the

English-speaking powers acted against Russia when they did to halt its advance into the North American continent. As it was, the whole Pacific Coast (except Alaska) over more than 12 degrees of latitude was left to the Anglo-Saxon states, without any possibility of foreign intervention. In the minds of some American statesmen, Adams for instance, "the United States and North America are synonymous," and Britain had no place there—such sentiments underlay the formulation of the Monroe Doctrine as we shall see. But Britain was never to admit the doctrine in this sense. As George Canning, who succeeded Castlereagh as Foreign Secretary, told the amiable Richard Rush, now U.S. minister in London: "If we were to be repelled from the shores of America, it would not matter to us whether that repulsion was effected by the ukase of Russia excluding us from the sea, or by the new doctrine of [the United States] excluding us from the land. But we cannot yield obedience to either."[120] In fact, most Americans tacitly conceded that the British were not in the same category as the other European powers. Adams found this belief hard to swallow. The Anglo-U.S. frontier convention of October 1818 had to be renewed for another ten years, and as late as 14 February 1827, Adams, by now President, was minuting to himself: "I would leave the North-West boundary *in statu quo* rather than accept anything proposed by the British or concede anything to them. The prospects of our relations with Great Britain are dark."[121] But the prospects were not, in fact, dark. The logic of the Special Relationship was too powerful. The convention was renewed. Indeed the two powers jointly administered the huge Oregon territory, without much trouble, until 1848.

The development of mutual interests in the Western hemisphere, and on the two great oceans which protected it, was accompanied by a steady increase in personal contacts between British and Americans, at all levels of society. The year 1815 was a turning point in this respect, marking the beginning of the age of mass travel, even across the Atlantic and not just for the purpose of emigration. The British poured into New York and Boston and often wrote books about what they saw. A growing trickle of Americans came to Europe, especially to London. There were some stock British attitudes to Americans. Among the upper echelons of society feelings of hostility remained, especially among the older generation. King George III was always irritated at the thought that some of the painters he had patronized were of American origin, especially when they disagreed with him. He snarled at Sir William Beechey of the Royal Academy: "[Benjamin] West is an American, so is [John Singleton] Copley, and you are an Englishman, and if you were all at the Devil I would not inquire after you!" But when this remark was reported to the Prince of Wales, he thought it so funny he "laughed for ten minutes"—younger people had no bitterness about the War of Independence.[122] They did, however, point to a certain hypocrisy among Americans, on the lines of Dr Samuel Johnson's famous jibe: "Why is it we hear the loudest *yelps* for liberty among the drivers of Negroes?" This line was to be found among Whigs as well as Tories. The Irish poet Thomas Moore, much patronized by Whig grandees like the Marquess of Lansdowne and Lord Holland, even wrote an anti-American poem, "To Thomas Hume Esq., MD, from the City of Washington," sneering at the unfinished state of the United States capital,

> *where fancy sees*
> *Squares in morasses, obelisks in trees*

And

> *The Patriot, fresh from freedom's councils come*
> *Now pleased retires to lash his slaves at home.*[123]

On the other hand, the titled British upper class were already beginning to eye wealthy American ladies with a view to replenishing their fortunes, and the ladies were coming to London with matrimony in mind. The first grand Transatlantic liaison, forerunner of many which were to underpin the Special Relationship and produce such offspring of it as Sir Winston Churchill, occurred in 1825. Mrs. Harriet Arbuthnot, the Duke of Wellington's principal confidante, recorded in her diary, with some indignation, that the Duke's brother, the Marquess of Wellesley, who had governed both India and Ireland for the Crown, was proposing to marry the rich Marianne, widow of Robert Paterson and daughter of Richard Caton of Baltimore, who had actually signed the Declaration of Independence! Mrs. Paterson, she told the Duke, "had come to this country on a matrimonial speculation, and it was pretty well for the widow of an American shopkeeper to marry a marquess, the Lord Lieutenant of Ireland, and a Knight of the Garter." Stuff and nonsense, said the Duke, "The honours were all empty ones and the real facts were that Lord Wellesley was a man totally ruined. When he quitted Ireland, which he must soon do, he would not have a house to take her to or money to keep a carriage, that he had not a shilling in the world and moreover was of a most jealous disposition, a violent temper, and he had entirely worn out his constitution by the profligate habits of his life." He added that he himself had written to the lady and "stated all these objections."[124] Nonetheless, the marriage took place, and its success led both parties to conclude they had done a good deal, the first of many such.[125]

Among British progressives, who included so many opinion formers, writers and journalists, the ideological sentiment was overwhelmingly pro-American. Indeed, from the 1790s to the end of the 1860s, America was the favorite country of virtually all British intellectuals on the Left of the political spectrum, just as the Soviet Union was to be for Western intellectuals generally in the period 1918–45. Children of progressive parents were brought up to admire America. There is a revealing sentence in the *Autobiography* of John Stuart Mill, born in 1806. Describing how his father James Mill, a radical who worked at India House, made him, when he was eight, read through the volumes of the *Annual Register,* Mill wrote: "When I came to the American War, I took my part, like a child as I was (until set right by my father) on the wrong side, because it was called the English side."[126] Lord Byron had similar ideas planted in his mind by his progressive-minded mother.[127] Throughout his life, he applauded American Republicanism and looked on individual Americans with favor. "I like the Americans," he recorded in his diary on 7 December 1813. Nine years later he wrote to Moore, whose anti-Americanism, Byron argued, arose from some unfortunate business dealings, "I would rather . . . have a nod from an American than a snuff-box from an Emperor." Despite what he called "the coarseness and rudeness of its people," he praised the country as "a Model of force and freedom & moderation." He linked its political system with the best aspects of ancient Greece, especially Athens in its heyday. There is a long passage in his diary, written on 23 November 1813, in which he exalts the constitutional republic and its elected rulers as both the most moral and effective form of government, and the most glorious: "To be the first man—not the dictator—not the Sulla—but the Washington or the Aristides—the leader in talent and truth—is next to the Divinity!" He talked often of going to America, even buying land there and sharing its fortunes. He did neither, but until the end he saw the American pattern as the only hope for the future of humanity, noting in his diary: "There is nothing left for Mankind but a Republic—and I think that there are hopes of such . . . Oh Washington!"[128]

Liberals like Byron were so enamored of the general system of government in the United States that, like the political pilgrims to Russia in the 1930s, they were prepared to overlook or justify shortcomings which, in any other context, they would have deplored. Thus

Byron scarcely ever referred to the American slave states—the point on which all Tories pounced. John Stuart Mill, who emerged from his conditioning a reliable exponent of the progressive viewpoint, did not hesitate to defend, in an article in the radical weekly *Examiner,* Jackson's Indian removal policy, which had been criticized in *The Times.* "The conduct of the United States towards the Indian tribes has been throughout not only just, but noble," he wrote. "The Indians have occasionally been unjustly treated by several of the state governments who, like other people, are not the very best of judges in their own cause; but the Federal government has been the guardian and protector of the rights of the Indians on all occasions."[129] Another hard-line liberal, the Rev. Sydney Smith, writing in the *Edinburgh Review,* went so far as to justify the emerging caucus system as "nothing more than the natural, fair and unavoidable influence which talent, popularity and activity must always have."[130]

Smith, reviewing the spate of descriptions of America by travelers which appeared from 1815 onwards, listed in various articles the aspects of America which British progressives most admired. One was the cheapness of government: the President, Smith recorded with wonder, was paid only £5,000; the vice president, £1,000; and "their Mister Crokers [junior ministers] are eminently reasonable—somewhere about the price of an English doorkeeper or the bearer of a mace." There was, too, the assumption that America already had what Smith called "universal suffrage."[131] Smith also contrasted the mean and ungrateful British treatment of soldiers and sailors who served in the War of 1812 with American generosity: After the war, he told his British readers, "an [American] recruit honourably discharged from the service was allowed three months pay and 160 acres of land."[132] Nor did he fail to notice, being a liberal churchman, the spirit of religious freedom which pervaded the new republic. He noted: "The High Sheriff of New York last year was a Jew. It was with the utmost difficulty that a Bill was carried this year to allow the first Duke of England [Norfolk] to carry a gold stick before the King, because he was a Catholic!—and yet we think ourselves entitled to indulge in impertinent sneers at America." Smith thought it "hardly possible for any nation to show a greater superiority over another than the Americans in this particular [religious toleration] have done over this country." As for popular education, American efforts "put into the background everything that has been done in the Old World and confer deservedly upon the Americans the character of a wise, a reflecting and a virtuous people."[133]

Progressive-minded Britons who went to America for a time or permanently saw what they chose to see, for the most part. Thomas

Hulme, a radical entrepreneur from Lancashire, who employed 140 hands plus 40 apprentices at his bleaching mill near Bolton, toured the East Coast and parts of the new interior—Ohio, Pennsylvania, Indiana, and Kentucky—in summer 1817. He found Pittsburgh already a major coal-iron and manufacturing center, crowded with "skilful and industrious artisans and mechanics from all over the world," who were paid wages at twice the British level with much lower taxes. In Kentucky he met Mr. and Mrs. Johnstone: "They told us they had come to this spot last year, direct from Manchester, Old England, and had bought their little farm of 55 acres from a backwoodsman, who had cleared it and was glad to move further westward, for $3 an acre. They had a fine flock of little children, and pigs and poultry, and were cheerful and happy, being confident that their industry and economy would not be frustrated by visits for tithes and taxes." Like other progressives, Hulme wrote of the country's high moral and cultural tone: "I have had the pleasure to meet many gentlemen, very well-informed and possessing greater knowledge as to their own country, evincing public spirit in all their actions, and hospitality and kindness in all their demeanour. But if there be pensioners, male or female, or sinecure-place lords and ladies, I have yet to come across, thank God, no *respectable* people."[134]

Hulme's friend, the noisy Tory radical William Cobbett (1763–1835), fled to the United States in 1817 to escape prosecution for libel, and farmed for a year on Long Island, publishing an account of his experience on his return to Britain in 1819. Cobbett was no starry-eyed political pilgrim. He thought that British people would not like the way of life in the newly settled interior—"To boil their pot in the gipsy fashion, to have a mere board to eat on, to drink whiskey or pure water, to sit and sleep under a shed . . . to have a mill at 20 miles distance, an apothecary at a hundred and a doctor nowhere" was not acceptable. But life on the coast had never been better, for ordinary people, anywhere in history. He listed the food consumed in a year by a man and his family farming 154 acres: 14 fat hogs; 4 oxen, 46 sheep, suckling pigs and lambs; eggs from 70 hens, "good parcels of geese, ducks and turkeys but not to forget a garden of three-quarters of an acre and the butter of 10 cows, not one ounce of which is ever sold." Such plenty bred human kindness: "When one sees this sort of living, with the house *full of good beds,* ready for the guests as well as the family to sleep in, we cannot help perceiving that this is that *English Hospitality* of which we have *read* so much but which Boroughmongers' taxes and pawns have long since driven out of England."[135] Except for the blacks, "a disorderly, improvident set of beings," there was no poverty and no paupers, other than those deliberately exported from Europe. The last category could rapidly escape from indigence if they chose to work. "I have now been here *twenty months* and I have only been visited by *two beggars*"—one English, one Italian. Like almost every visitor, Cobbett wondered at the low taxes and absence of tithes: "American farmers cannot believe that Englishmen have to give a tenth of their crops to the parson. They treat it as a sort of *romance.*" He too noticed the high level of education: "There are very few really *ignorant* Americans of native growth. Every farmer is more or less of a *reader.*"[136] Finally, he noticed how naturally and peacefully the Americans were taking to the vote, without any of the fearful consequences predicted by opponents of reform in Britain. Virtually everyone, he pointed out, who exercised power in America was elected; there were no sinecures and no jobs without service. The electors decided all. And who were they? In Connecticut, "Whoever has a freehold worth a guinea-and-a-half a year, though he pays no tax and though he be not enrolled in the militia, has a vote. Whoever pays tax, though he be not enrolled in the militia and have no freehold, has a vote. Whoever enrols in the militia, though he have no freehold and pays not tax, has a vote. So that nothing but beggars, paupers and criminals can easily be excluded."[137] And the result was not anarchy, but good government.

Less politically committed visitors from Britain viewed the egalitarianism they found in America with mixed feelings. What they all noticed was the universal practice of shaking hands. In Britain handshaking was a sign of close friendship or kindly condescension. In Jane Austen's *Emma,* the humble Harriet Smith, on her first visit to the Woodhouses, was "delighted with the affability with which Miss Woodhouse had treated her all the evening, and actually shaken hands with her at last!"[138] But in America, the alternative, a mere bow, was regarded as anti-republican and pro-King. Captain Marryat, of the Royal Navy, who had been so worried about losing his badly crewed frigate during the war and who returned to America in more peaceful times to write a book about it, found he had to "go on shaking hands here, there and everywhere, and with everybody." The practice blurred social disinctions: it was "impossible to know who is who."[139] A British lady-visitor, Mrs. Basil Hall, also found the handshaking odd and everywhere missed the constant deference which the British took for granted. At the inns there was just, she wrote, "unbending, frigid heartlessness." Servants, when they existed at all, were insubordinate and not well trained. They simply could not provide the service the traveling British expected in hotels. There was no soap in the bedrooms, and a guest who asked for it was likely to receive a pert answer. This was what another British writer of a travel book called American "democratic rudeness."[140] Mrs. Hall, and many other visitors, likewise deplored the American habit of smoking cigars and chewing tobacco—a habit by no means confined to men—wherever they pleased, even in public buildings and churches. She found the floor of the Virginia House of Burgesses "actually flooded with their horrible spitting" and the floors of some churches black with "ejection after ejection, incessant from the twenty mouths" of the men in the choir.[141] The British visitor's habit of picking on uncouth American behavior was to reach a climax in the highly critical account written by Fanny Trollope, mother of Anthony. *Domestic Manners of the Americans*— the title was suggested by Mrs. Hall's husband—was published in 1832 and sold hugely, not only in London but in America, where it came out in a pirated edition with a hostile preface accusing her of not being a lady.[142]

But Mrs. Trollope, who had an unfortunate experience as a would-be entrepreneur in Cincinnati, admitted she did not like Americans. Most of the British who went there did, on the whole, and they grasped the point, which lay at the heart of the Special Relationship, that Americans were not "foreigners." They were part of the English-speaking family, poor relations in some ways, rich in others, but definitely bound by ties of blood, history, and custom, not least the Common Law tradition both Americans and English shared, but most of all by their tongues. There were some patriotic Americans who argued forcefully that the Americans should develop their own specific language, correcting English of its many imperfections, just as American statesmen had fundamentally improved the British constitution. As far back as 1790, the great American lexicographer and philologist Noah Webster (1758–1843), progenitor of the dictionary which is one of the permanent glories of American scholarship, argued: *"Now* is the time, and *this* is the country in which we may expect success in attempting changes favourable to language, science and government."[143] Three years later, his colleague William Thornton addressed the American people thus: "You have corrected the dangerous doctrines of European powers, correct now the languages you have imported, for the oppressed of various nations knock at your gates." If this were done, he argued "The *American Language* will thus be as distinct as the government, free from all the follies of unphilosophical fashion, and resting upon truth as its only regulator."[144] But there were three good reasons why the attempt to bring about a bifurcation of the tongues would never succeed. First, Thornton's practical proposal for reform involved a reformed system of spelling involving not only a phonetic mode, which people found ridiculous, but a series of signs he had invented, which was incomprehensible to everyone else.[145]

Similar drawbacks attended other schemes for rationalization, as indeed they have done ever since, from Basic English to Esperanto. Second, neither the Pilgrim Fathers of America, who wrote the language of John Donne and the King James Bible, nor those who wrote and signed the Declaration of Independence had expressed themselves on formal occasions in anything except the normal, correct English of their day. In 1802 a Scots immigrant coined the term *Americanism,* on the analogy of the "Scotticisms" which North Britons who came south were so anxious to leave behind. But it was almost impossible to find Americanisms in the public doctrines of the new Republic, and for a good reason. The statesmen of the 1770s and 1780s were students of Thomas Hobbes, and he had argued in *Leviathan,* with characteristic rigor, that a high, imposed discipline in language was necessary for social cohesion. Language was for human beings the chief organizaing principle and without it, "there had been amongst men, neither Commonwealth, nor Society, nor Contract, nor Peace, no more than amongst Lyons, Beares and Wolves."[146] Any social contract had to be written with terms of exact and universally understood meaning: "For one man calleth *Wisdome,* what another calleth *Feare;* and one *Cruelty* what another *Justice;* one *Prodigality* what another *Magnanimity* . . . such names can never be true ground of any ratiocination."[147] The Declaration of Independence and other constitutional acts were written in the light of this advice as though they were to be put on the Statute Book at Westminster, and clearly the common language of a state, particularly a new one, cannot be abruptly and artificially changed from that in which its constitution is written.

In any case, and this is the third reason, "the follies of unphilosophical fashion" are precisely the engines by which languages are created and grow, and they operate far more powerfully than the schemes of philologists ever could. They are continually adding depth, color and density, but above all richness and variety, to a living tongue. Moreover, as the American reformers tended to forget, such engines of fashion were operating on both sides of an Atlantic increasingly bridged by a constant stream of traffic. The United States was much less isolated from Britain in the years after 1815 than in, say, 1750. Travelers from Britain noted that the English spoken in various parts of the United States varied less fundamentally than did the regional dialects of Britain; there were, of course, bucolic turns of speech, but it was not difficult for an American to understand what was said to him wherever he went, for Americans—as visitors also noted—were constantly traveling. "Here," a Boston newspaper boasted in 1828, "the whole population is in motion whereas in old countries there are millions who have never been beyond the sound of the parish bell."[148] Travel worked as a constant unifying force against regional differences in speech. But equally, the growing Transatlantic contacts worked against further fundamental differences in pronunciation, vocabulary and grammar between American English and the parent tongue. In fact, there were in 1815 more American variants, in speech and structure, than there are now: the 19th century, for British and American English speakers, was one of convergence.

In both countries, neologisms were pouring out, perhaps at a faster rate than ever before. But in most cases they were rapidly adopted on both sides of the Atlantic, so for the first time a joint language was coming into being, adding to its vocabulary at twice the speed either could have done separately. It was, indeed, a great age for new words. The Germans produced *Zeitgeist* and *Weltanschauung,* and the French, *romantique* and *libérale,* the latter quickly adopted in England and given, by Byron, as the title to the newspaper he financed in 1820. But it was the Anglo-Saxons who were adding to their terms the fastest. Edmund Burke had produced *colonial, financial, expenditure, representation* [as in political] and *diplomacy.* Jeremy Bentham contributed *international.* Sir Walter Scott, characteristically, invented *stalwart, gruesome, free lance,* and *red-handed;* Byron, equally characteristically, *bored* and *blasé;* and Samuel Taylor Coleridge, *phenomenal, pessimism* and period terms, such as *Elizabethan;* from Thomas Macaulay, in the 1820s, came *constituency.*[149]

To these new terms of British origin, the Americans constantly added their own neologisms or adoptions from half a dozen tongues. *Cocktail* dates from 1806: in 1822 a *Kentucky Breakfast* was defined as "three cocktails and a chaw of terbacker." *Barroom* came in 1807; *mint julep,* in 1809; and a *long drink,* in 1828. There were borrowings from the Dutch, such as *boss,* and many more from the French, both Canadian and in Louisiana: *depot, rapids, prairie, shanty, chute, cache, crevasse.* From the Spanish another large crop, including *mustang* (1808), *ranch* (1808), *sombrero* (1823), *patio* (1827), *corral* (1829), and *lasso* (1831). The Americans used obsolete English words like *talented,* as well as pure neologisms like *obligate.* They adopted the German word *dumm,* which became *dumb,* meaning stupid. They were beginning to adopt Negro words and to coin a good many terms springing from their own political customs—not only *caucus* but *mass meeting,* for instance. There were settler's words like *lot* and *squatter.* There was also the beginning of a dangerous talent for euphemism: *help* as the democratic term for *servant.*

The journals of the great expedition carried out by Meriwether Lewis and William Clark in 1804–06, from Saint Louis across the Rockies to the Columbia River and the Pacific, published in 1814, introduced a wide range of terms never before heard in Britain: *portage, raccoon, groundhog, grizzly bear, backtrack, medicine man, huckleberry, war party, running time, overnight, overall, rattlesnake, bowery,* and *moose,* as well as adding new variant meanings to old English terms, such as *snag, stone, suit, bar, brand, bluff, fix, hump, knob, creek,* and *settlement.*[150] Above all, there was the fertile American capacity to coin phrases and amalgams: It was the Americans, not the English oddly enough, who invented *keep a stiff upper lip* (1815), plus *fly off the handle* (1825), *get religion* (1826), *knock-down* (1827), *stay on the fence* (1828), *in cahoots* (1829), *horse sense* (1832) and *barking up the wrong tree* (1833), plus a variety of less-datable expressions like *hold on, let on, take on, cave in, flunk out,* and *stave off.* As early as the 1820s Americans were trying to *get the hang of a thing* and insisting *there's no two ways about it.* At varying speeds most of these new words and expressions crossed the Atlantic, so it was soon apparent that the Americans were influencing the way the British spoke, as well as vice-versa.

What was not clear, for a time, was whether Americans could reciprocate the huge cultural influence of Europe, and especially Britain. Sydney Smith was, as we have seen, generous in praising many social and political aspects of American life, but in a brilliant and notorious passage in the *Edinburgh Review* in 1819, he argued that the Americans "during the thirty or forty years of their existence" had done "absolutely nothing for the Sciences, for the Arts, for Literature, or even for the statesman-like studies of Politics or Political Economy." Americans were fond of boasting, he noted, but where were "their Scotts, Rogers's, Campbells, Byrons, Moores or Crabbes—their Siddons, Kembles, Keans or O'Neills—their Wilkies, Lawrences, Chantrys?. . . . In the four quarters of the globe, who reads an American book? Or goes to an American play? Or looks at an American picture or statue?"[151] This was unfair, in part, especially over political philosophy. But it was, and indeed still is, inexplicably strange that after the brilliant start given by Jonathan Edwards, Benjamin Franklin, and Thomas Jefferson, American literature failed to add substantially to its laurels in the half century up to 1830.[152]

Shortly before Smith's strictures, the *Philadelphia Portfolio* published an essay by George Tucker, "On American Literature," drawing the contrast bewtwen the insignificant contribution Americans had made to English literature and the almost dominant position now occupied by Scottish and Irish writers. In the wake of Edmund Burke, Richard Sheridan, Jonathan Swift, Oliver Goldsmith, George Berkeley, and Thomas Moore from Ireland, and James Thomson, Robert Burns, David Hume, Adam Smith, Tobias Smollett, and James Boswell from Scotland, the two most influential novelists of the present period, Sir Walter Scott and Maria Edgeworth, were of Scottish and Irish descent. If two such small countries could have so disproportionate an influence, what was America doing? Tucker calculated that Britain, with a population of 18 million, produced every year between 500 and 1,000 new books; America, with 6 million, averaged 20. Four years after Smith's attack, it was in part echoed by Charles Jared Ingersoll in an address to the American Philosophical Society, "A Discourse concerning the Influence of America on the Mind." Ingersoll noted that both the *Edinburgh Review* and the *Quarterly* were now reprinted in America and sold the then-impressive number of 4,000 copies each. The *North American Review*, dating from 1815, was unknown across the Atlantic. Why? In the previous nine years, Ingersoll added, 200,000 copies of Scott's Waverley novels had been printed in America, while the novel form in American hands languished. The only explanation he could find was that there were few university graduates and hardly any professional authors in the United States.[153]

By this time, as it happened, the first professional American author had begun to make his mark on both sides of the Atlantic. Washington Irving (1783–1859) was 32 at the time of the Battle of Waterloo. His father came from the Orkneys, his mother from Falmouth, and his eldest brother was actually born in Scotland. His own American roots were not deep. In 1803, at age twenty, he made his first trip to Europe, and as soon as the War of 1812 was over, he returned to run a merchant house in Liverpool which he and his brother owned. Not until the business went bankrupt in 1818 did he turn to full-time authorship. He had little originality. His earliest writings, in which he "discovered" the Hudson, were based on an earlier generation of English writers who had discovered the Lakes. Later he based himself on Scott and Thomas Moore, catering deliberately to the English taste, which American readers were brought up to share. For his ideas he plundered German literature. There was nothing unusual in this. Many other writers did the same. Coleridge appropriated German philosophical notions. Others ransacked German folklore, for the Germans were considered unique in the fertility of their magic legends—what the young Alfred Tennyson, another neologist, was soon to christen fairy tales. A volume of German ghost stories, *Tales of the Dead,* was avidly scoured by

Byron and Shelley at the time when the latter's 18-year-old second wife, Mary, wrote her great scientific-gothic romance, *Frankenstein,* in June 1816. Setting out for Germany, Irving wrote: "I mean to get into the confidence of every old woman I meet with in Germany and get from her her budget of wonderful stories." But in practice he was heavily dependent on literary sources. His most famous character, Rip Van Winkle, and the *Legend of Sleepy Hollow,* came straight from Christophe Martin Wieland and Riesbeck's *Travels through Germany.*[154] He merely expanded the Winkle tale and gave it an American setting.[155]

Nevertheless, when Irving's first collection, his *Sketch Book,* came out in 1820, it was an immediate success. It got the stamp of approval from Byron and from the twin pillars of the literary establishment, Gifford of the *Quarterly* and Jeffrey of the *Edinburgh Review.* As his English publisher was John Murray, who also published *Waverley,* many people assumed the real author was Scott himself. Rush, the American Minister, passed on to Irving a long letter from Lady Lyttleton inquiring about the authorship, to which Irving replied, insisting he had written every word himself: "I speak fully on this point, not from any anxiety of authorship, but because the doubt which her ladyship has heard on the subject seems to have arisen from the old notion that it is impossible for *an American to write decent English."* [156] Irving was particularly gratified when the great actress Mrs. Siddons said to him at a party in her slow, deep, meaningless voice: "You have—made—me—weep."[157]

But, of course, one important reason for his success in England was what would later be called his "cultural cringe." He proposed to Murray, for example, that the poet Thomas Campbell be hired to lecture in New York to give "an impulse to American literature and a proper direction to the public taste." He genuflected to the right idols, paying a courtesy visit to Scott ("a sterling, golden-hearted old worthy"). He did his best to alleviate the outstanding grievance of the British literary and publishing industry—the absence of a copyright law in America and the systematic pirating of British books by American publishers. He was anxious, perhaps overanxious, to disassociate himself in English eyes from Republican, let alone radical, ideas: "There could be nothing more humiliating to me," he wrote to Murray, "than to be mistaken for that loose rabble of writers who are ready to decry everything orderly and established—my feelings go the contrary way."[158]

All these characteristics eventually led to the eclipse of his reputation and the fierce hostility felt toward him and his work by the first generation of American writers, led by Ralph Waldo Emerson, who repudiated English, indeed European, cultural colonialism. But they paid handsomely at the time. Because he was admired and read in England, he was admired and read in America. After the success of the *Sketch Book,* he told Murray he wanted 1,500 guineas for his next book. "This staggered Murray who, after a moment's hesitation, began 'If you had said a thousand guineas—' 'You shall *have* it for a thousand guineas,' said Irving, grandly."[159] For his life of Columbus, Murray gave him 3,000 guineas in 1828. He was immensely industrious and quick: He wrote a million words on Spain alone and over 3 million altogether. Moore recorded that in a mere ten days he "has written about 130 pages of the size of those in his *Sketch Book*—this is amazing rapidity."[160] In all, Irving seems to have earned from his writing over $200,000. When he started, Ingersoll had lamented in his address that 35 towns in America were named Waverly, and none after an American writer. By the time Irving was finished, not only little towns but big hotels and squares, steamboats, even cigars were named after him. "He is only fit to write a book and scarcely that," sneered Andrew Jackson, who objected to his being minister in Madrid. But that was an out-of-date view. At Irving's death, New York closed down; there were 150 carriages in his funeral procession and 1,000 waited outside the packed church.[161] He was the first American to achieve celebrity through literature. That was an important step in the growth of America's cultural self-confidence. It was also a critical stage in Britain's recognition of the United States not only as a legitimate entity but as a civilized one. And the fact that America's first internationally recognized professional writer wrote not merely in the English language, but in the English cultural idiom, was a subtle contribution to the Special Relationship.

In the years after 1815, the United States was not yet a great power, in the conventional sense. To be sure, it was acquiring a regular military establishment, with its trappings. From 1813, under the pressures of war, shakos were issued to U.S. infantrymen to replace the old-fashioned civilian top hats, made of beaver, which the men had worn hitherto. At the same time generals got the full treatment: a huge bicorne, with a solid gold eagle on the center of the cockade. The coat was plain blue, single breasted, but it had ten ball-buttons of gold and black herringbone embroidery across the chest and four chevrons on each forearm and one on each side of the collar—and the new coat was worn with high, cuffed boots.[162] But the regular army itself was tiny. Expanded to its wartime maximum of 46,858 in 1814—including Volunteers and militia it numbered 286,700—it had fallen to 16,743 by 1816 and to a mere 9,863 by 1822.[163]

But if the United States was not yet a great power, it was rapidly becoming, in many ways, a world power. As far back as 1784, the first American ship, rounding the Horn, had appeared in Chinese waters. The same year a U.S.-registered ship sailed up the Baltic and docked at Saint Petersburg. American whalers were now in both Arctic and Antarctic waters. Once the War of 1812 was over, American merchant ships reappeared in the Atlantic, in ever-growing numbers, enough of them by 1820 to be causing concern to the British Board of Trade.[164] They were numerous in the Caribbean, too, and in the Mediterranean—Byron was delighted to go aboard one of them in Genoa harbor. The U.S. Navy was also capable of global operations. One reason it was created in 1794 was to protect U.S. merchant ships from corsairs based on the Barbary Coast of north Africa, what is now Algeria, Libya and Tunisia. The reason for this was American pride: The United States government, unlike most European powers, refused to ransom captive seamen by giving the pirates money, powder, shot and weapons.[165]

America was thus already distinguishing itself by its refusal to follow time-honored European paths of compromise and its determination to take the high road of moral righteousness. Europeans might or might not approve—most did not—but the notion was striking and new. It was given its first formal expression in John Quincy Adams's opening address to Congress in 1825, when he signified that the modern world of idealism and ideology was being born, foreshadowing an enlightened superpower with a moral mission to change the planet for the better. "The spirit of improvement is abroad upon the earth," he said. "It stimulates the heart and sharpens the faculties not of our fellow-citizens alone, but of the nations of Europe and of their rulers. While dwelling with pleasing satisfaction upon the superior excellence of our political institutions, let us not be unmindful that liberty is power: that the nation blessed with the largest portion of liberty must, in proportion to its numbers, be the most powerful nation on earth, and that the tenure of power by man is, in the moral purpose of his Creator, upon condition that it shall be exercised to ends of beneficence, to improve the condition of himself and his fellow men." For America not to use its new and growing power was "treachery to the most sacred of trusts."

This assertive moral nationalism was noted by European statesmen, underpinned as it was by what struck them even more forcibly: the growth of the U.S. population. In 1815 it was 8,419,000. Fifteen years later, it has risen by more than half to 12,901,000, and the rate of increase was accelerating.[166] The land area of the new giant was expanding even more rapidly. Europe, used to judging power in terms of "souls" and hectares, rather than moral authority, registered the fact that America was progressing fast in all three. In its growing size, America was already being compared to Russia. The two nations were seen as having much in common: both strange and extra-European, almost alien; both, at the time, making loud moral noises; both, seemingly, portents of the future. These two big, hungry nations did not found colonies, as the older European states did; they simply swallowed territory and digested it. Alexander Herzen was to produce a classic definition of what they had in common and where they differed: "The United States sweeps everything from its path, like an avalanche. Every inch of land which the United States seizes is taken away from the natives forever. Russia surrounds adjoining territories like an expanding body of water, pulls them in and covers them with an everlasting, uniformly-coloured layer of autocratic ice."[167] There was, however, a further difference between the two, in the eyes of the statesman of the reestablished ancien régime in 1815. The United States was a vast ocean away. Russia was established, for the first time, in the heart of Europe, by virtue of her enormous, conquering army. This was one of many reasons why Castlereagh had been anxious to wind up the American war as fast as possible, so that Britain's resources and attention could be concentrated on the Old World.

TWO

The Congress Dances

The day General Jackson's men were slaughtering Sir Edward Paken-ham and his redcoats before New Orleans, poor "Ned's" brother-in-law, the Duke of Wellington, received orders from the British govern-ment to leave Paris, where he was Ambassador-plenipotentiary, and replace Castlereagh as chief British envoy in the Vienna peace talks, the celebrated "Congress." The prime minister, the Earl of Liverpool, him-self in the House of Lords, found he could not get the government's business done in the House of Commons without Castlereagh to man-age it. As Thomas Barnes, soon to be editor of *The Times,* put it, "his conciliatory tone, his graceful manners, his mildness, urbanity and invincible courtesy ensure him popularity and even fondness from the House."[1] So home Castlereagh had to go, and Wellington, the only British public servant whose prestige with European sovereigns was comparable, took over Congress. He rumbled across Europe by heavy coach, on roads slippery with ice. General Alava, who had traveled much with the Duke in Spain, said that when asked what time the party should set off in the morning, Wellington invariably answered: "Day-light"; and the dinner was always 'cold meat." "I began to have a horror," said Alava, "of those two words, 'daylight' and 'cold-meat.' "[2] The food, it is true, was game birds and pâté de foie gras, taken with claret, but there was a mere four hours' sleep at night in bad inns. Only the Duke undressed and, as was his invariable custom, fell asleep the moment he lay down. His two aides de camp, Lord William Lennox, son of the Duke of Richmond, and Colonel John Fremantle, had to doss down in their clothes in front of the stove.[3]

The Duke reached Vienna on 3 February and made his immediate entrance to the Congress, wearing a scarlet field marshal's uniform, with a velvet collar embroidered in gold wire, the stars of the Garter, Bath and Golden Fleece, and the solitary Peninsula medal, the one he prized most; white stock, white breeches. His entry caused a sensation, for he was the only professional general among the sovereigns and chancellors and one, moreover, known as *le vainqueur du vainqueur du monde*. He had not yet met Bonaparte in battle, but he had beaten all his best marshals and troops in Spain. He was now forty-five, two years younger than Jackson, three months older than Bonaparte—a lean, energetic man of five feet nine; brown from years in the Indian sun; hook nosed, but considered handsome by the ladies; his blue eyes less piercing than Jackson's, more of the lively kind; his brown hair short cropped. He had an abrupt manner of speech and a laugh, as the society poet Samuel Rogers said, like a man with whooping-cough.

Wellington came from an impoverished but noble Anglo-Irish Ascendancy family, who had gradually changed their name, Wesley, to the less plebeian Wellesley, in accord with their title as Earls of Mornington. Arthur Wellesley, born in Ireland in 1769, would not have it he was Irish: "Because a man is born in a stable, that does not make him a horse." After he had spent three undistinguished years at Eton, and a spell at the famous French riding academy in Angers, his mother the Countess, now a widow, put him to soldiering; he was, she said, "food for powder and nothing more."[4] In fact Arthur was a dreamy boy, loving music and skilled at playing the violin, though it is true that, at Eton, he thrashed the Rev. Sydney Smith's ugly brother, "Bobus" Smith.

He took to the army, albeit in the lowly form of a "Sepoy General" in India; men who had commanded native troops but had never beaten European armies were not highly regarded in military circles. In this sense, he had something in common with Jackson, who made his name beating redskins. Nevertheless, Wellesley's eight years in India were a thorough training in constant combat. He conquered Mysore, stormed Seringapatam, and fought the Second Mahratta War. This included the storming of Ahmednuggur, winning the ferocious battles of Assaye and Argaum, and culminated in the surrender of Gawilghur. He had lived for as long as three years in tents, commanded 50,000 men in the field and learned the key to success in war—"attention to detail." Asked to explain his later military success in Europe, he would say "All that is India."[5] After a spell as a member of Parliament and office as Chief Secretary to Ireland, he had moved to the Peninsula war-theater, eventually taking over as Commander-in-Chief after the death of Sir John Moore at Corunna. From April 1809 until the final Battle of Toulouse five years later, he had been engaged in continual fighting against the French invaders, fighting over 100 actions, winning eleven major battles and beating General Junot, Marshals Massena and Soult, and Bonaparte's brother Joseph. He rose swiftly up the peerage from viscount (1809), to earl

(1812), to marquess (1812) to duke (1814), becoming also in the process an English field marshal, the Portuguese Marshal-General and Generalissimo of the Spanish armies. Wellington had carried out many a strategic retreat, but he had never been worsted on the field.

He took a low view of the moral character of his armies. At various times he found his forces as a whole "infamous," "a rabble." The men were "the scum of the earth," a phrase he repeated many times. "None but the worst description of men enter the regular service." Or again: "People talk of their enlisting from their fine military feeling—all stuff—no such thing. Some of our men enlist from having got bastard children—some for minor offences—many more for drink." The noncommissioned officers were the only group to escape criticism, and even they got disgustingly drunk on the night of a victory. The officers were brave, but could not be got to pay "minute and constant attention to orders." The commissariat was "very bad indeed." The cavalry were useless: They charged head on, then "gallop back as fast as they gallop on the enemy"; they "never think of maneuvring," indeed cannot maneuver, "except on Wimbledon Common." The generals "make me tremble." The infantry, when properly trained, were all right, but even they had to be "ruled with a *rod of iron.*'"[6] On the other hand, no one grudged spending his armies more than did the Duke. He wept bitterly when his officers were killed and valued the lives of his soldiers more than did any other contemporary commander, attributing his compassion to the British constitution. As he put it later: "[Bonaparte] could do what he pleased; and no man ever lost more armies than he did. Now with me the loss of every man told. I could not risk so much. I knew that if I ever lost 500 men without the clearest necessity, I should be brought upon my knees to the bar of the House of Commons."[7] With all that, he was now the most successful warlord of his age. To the grandees of Vienna, he was the marshal who had never lost a battle.

As Wellington's star rose, Bonaparte's sank. By 1815 his moral capital was exhausted, except among the French professional army. A few intellectuals, scattered through Europe, still saw him as a force for progress and defended his iniquities. In England, William Hazlitt, a passionate, lifelong supporter, justified even Bonaparte's murder of the Duc d'Enghien. He defended Bonaparte in the way progressives were long to defend Stalin in the twentieth century. "The question with me is," wrote Hazlitt, "whether I and all mankind are born slaves or free . . . Secure this point and all is safe; lose it and all is lost . . . If Buonaparte was a conqueror, he conquered the grand conspiracy of kings against the abstract right of the human race to be free; and I, as a man, could not be indifferent which side to take. If he was ambitious, his greatness was not founded on the unconditional, avowed surrender of the rights of human nature. With him, the state of man rose too. If he was arbitrary and a tyrant, first France as a country was in a state of military blockade or garrison duty and not to be defended by mere paper bullets of the brain; secondly, but chiefly, he was not nor could be a tyrant by right divine. Tyranny in him was not sacred; it was not eternal; it was not instinctively bound in a league of amity with other tyrannies; it was not sanctioned by all the law of religion and morality."[8] Hazlitt worked for years to create a four-volume *Life of Napoleon* (1828)—an answer to Sir Walter Scott's highly critical nine-volume *Life* (1824)—which presented Bonaparte as the champion of humanity: "As long as he was a *thorn in the side of kings,* and kept them at bay, his cause stood out of the ruins and defeat of their pride and hopes of revenge. He stood, and he stood alone, between them and their natural prey. He kept off this last indignity and wrong offered to a whole people, and throughout them to the rest of the world, of being handed over, like a herd of cattle, to a particular family, and chained to the foot of a Legitimate throne. This was the chief point at issue—this was the great question, compared with which all others were tame and insignificant—whether mankind were, from the beginning to the end of time, born slaves or not? As long as he remained, his acts, his very existence, gave a proud and full answer to this question. As long as he interposed a barrier, a gauntlet, an arm of steel between us and them who alone could set up the plea of old, indefensible right over us, no increase in [his] power could be too great."[9]

As with Stalin's case, however, this ideological rhetoric bore little relation to the facts. Bonaparte was, or had been, a great law codifier, institutional reformer, road builder and, at times, state patron. As the young romantic French painter Eugène Delacroix put it—he was a natural son of the French plenipotentiary at Vienna, Talleyrand—"The life of Napoleon is the event of the century for all the arts."[10] In this sense, Bonaparte was in the 18th-century tradition of the Enlightened Despots. But in other respects his conduct looked forward to the horrifying totalitarian regimes of the 20th century. He was in no sense a democrat. To him, the people were a mob, *canaille,* to be dispersed, "by a whiff of grapeshot." His various constitutions gave less voting rights to the people than did the electoral system of the ancien régime, which produced the Estates General in 1789, and they were all based on the anti-democratic principle, "Confidence comes from below, authority from above."[11] Nor did Bonaparte, as Hazlitt foolishly supposed, stand for the principle of individual liberty. Indeed, he created the first modern police state, and exported it. Austria, Prussia, and Russia all learned from the methods of Joseph Fouché, Bonaparte's minister of police, from 1799 to 1814, and it is significant that when Jean-Baptiste Bernadotte, one of Bonaparte's marshals and trained in his system, became the effective ruler of Sweden from 1809, almost his first acts were to set up a secret police force and an espionage network, neither of which Sweden had ever possessed. As Bernadotte put it—he never learned more than a word or two of Swedish—"*Opposition—c'est conspiration!*"[12]

It is true that in some parts of Europe, notably Germany and northern Italy, Bonaparte, as conqueror, imposed some of the reforms introduced by the Revolution in France. But elsewhere reforms had been accomplished peacefully and in the local manner. Denmark, for instance, which was dragged into Bonaparte's wars and impoverished, had introduced prison and law reform, poor relief and, above all, land reform and the gradual abolition of labor services, as early as the 1780s; reforms of the tariff and a progressive abolition of the slave trade had followed in the 1790s; the country was in the process of securing for more than half the peasant-farmers the ownership of their land and of making education universal and compulsory—the involvement with Napoleonic France merely delayed the process.[13] In other parts of Europe, the Low Countries for instance, the invading French abolished ancient charters of rights and local elected bodies going back to the early Middle Ages. In Switzerland, with its traditions of cantonal self-government, Bonaparte began to chip off territory for France from 1798, and followed this with full-scale invasion the following year and the enforcement of a French-devised constitution which made the Swiss his puppets: it was his treatment of Swiss liberties which decisively turned the poet William Wordsworth against Bonaparte and all he stood for.

Everywhere Bonaparte moved there was plundering at bayonet point, not just of the peasants to feed his armies—the French never paid for any food or horses they took—but of churches, town halls, palaces and treasuries. The art collections of Germany, Italy, and Spain were looted for the Louvre and for the commandeered chateaux of Bonaparte's marshals, most of whom became millionaires to keep up the ducal and princely titles he bestowed upon them. (Bonaparte himself stashed away the then-colossal sum of £8 million.) If such things as Swiss bank accounts had existed, all would have had them. In fact, the French did the reverse in Switzerland, stripping the Bernese treasury of every coin it contained to finance their expedition to Egypt. When the French plenipotentiary, Brune, left Switzerland for Italy, the bottom of his carriage collapsed with the weight of the stolen gold he had stacked in its boot. Thus £10 million in cash disappeared, plus £8 million in good paper, mainly English bills. When the people resisted, they were shot. One French commander, General Schauenburg, slaughtered 500 men, women and children in the Nidwalden; whole villages were wiped out. Bonaparte's orders to his commanders were, You have the force, live off the land. When in 1808 Marshal Joachim Murat complained to Bonaparte about the difficulties of getting supplies in Spain, his master replied that he was tired of a general who, "at the head of 50,000 troops, asks for things instead of taking them." The letter, said Murat, "stunned me, like a tile falling on my head." The result was the brutal massacre of patriots, monks, priests, and shopkeepers outside Madrid, as immortalized in the terrifying painting, *The Third of May 1808* by Francisco de Goya (1746–1828).

Goya is an interesting case of the way in which civilized opinion swung against Bonaparte as the first decade of the century progressed. He came from Saragossa, the son of a master gilder, and progressed through the royal tapestry factory, as a designer, to painting royal and society portraits. He was enormously successful, though he painted girths, warts, wrinkles, and all; he used to quote Cervantes: "Where truth is, God is, truth being an aspect of divinity." A self-portrait shows him in bullfighter's kit, with candles in his hat and a fierce face. He had 19 children by his wife, sister of the painter Bayue, and more by a variety of mistresses, ranging from his high-born sitters to street girls. One of his mistresses gave him syphilis, and in 1792 he went stone deaf. Thereafter, fearsome creatures began to appear in his work. On one of his *Capriccios,* showing himself asleep at his drawing board, he inscribed, "The sleep of reason brings forth Monsters." In these times, when Bonaparte was seeking to impose the ideology of "enlightened" France on the rest of Europe by force, it was as though reason itself was bringing the monsters into being. Goya had long been interested in manifestation of violence combined with sex. In the 1790s he made many studies of bandits stripping naked women captives, then stabbing them to death. Even his arcadia paintings, cartoons for tapestries, have a streak of sex-war viciousness, as when he shows three militant women tossing a man in a blanket. He was fascinated by abnormality, too: giants, dwarfs, cripples, madmen, even cannibalism and demented animals—hence his horrifying studies of *Los Disparates (The Unequals).* The titles of many other canvases and prints tell their own tale: *The Courtyard of the Madhouse; The Road to Hell;* and *Madness Runs Amok,* the last showing the clothes of a madwoman gripped in the jaws of a horror-horse.[14]

These interests were not unusual in the Romantic Age, but Goya had them to an unusual degree. With the incursion of the French, the imposition of an alien regime, the revolt of the masses, and the long war which followed—the French armies passing up, down and across Spain like a red-hot rake—Goya's obsessions became politicized. He was, of course, a court painter, one whose living came from whatever ruler was currently in possession. His *Allegory of Madrid* began as a portrait of King Joseph Bonaparte, the French-imposed ruler, done in 1810; when Madrid was liberated in 1812, *Constitution* replaced Joseph's head; the head reappeared when the French retook the city a few months later, only to disappear finally in 1813, being replaced by Ferdinand VII's head in 1814.[15] But all the time, Goya's feelings were turning with increasing power and venom against the insensate folly of seeking to impose political ideas at the price of human flesh and blood. He came to identify himself with the Resistance and its dead. He said of his May pictures, done in 1814, that they were designed "to perpetuate with my brush" the "glorious revolt against the tyrant of Europe."

Goya was not unaware of war propaganda. The British artist R. K. Porter, a pupil of Benjamin West, had come to Spain with Sir John Moore's army and specialized in anti-French prints. His etchings, such as *Buonaparte Massacring 3800 men at Jaffa* and *Bonaparte Massacring 1500 persons at Toulon,* both from 1803, were circulated and copied widely in Spain and were used by Goya in planning his own massacre picture, an example of how a great artist elevates a crude but powerful idea into sublimity.[16] But when Goya came to do his Disasters of War series, he was no longer thinking in terms of propaganda as such. He was, rather, registering his detestation, as a human being, of what Bonaparte had done and was doing to Europe. There comes a point, his drawings insist, at which the original objectives of a war waged for ideals cease to be of the smallest consequence—are, in fact, quite forgotten—as the savagery and cruelty which war engenders, and which increase as it continues, consume everything, blind, heedless, insatiable. In the final stages of a war men kill and burn simply to eat, to survive. Thus war, especially ideological war, is the true sleep of reason, when the monsters appear. Goya's final comment emerged in 1819 when he moved to what he called "The House of the Deaf Man" in Madrid and painted on its walls his image of the naked, unseeing, mad, and gigantic Saturn—an allegory of the Bonapartist attempt to remake the world—gobbling his children.

This revulsion against Bonaparte's wars was something which English intellectuals like Hazlitt, Shelley and Byron did not feel because they had escaped the consequences. They had not seen, felt or suffered the horrors. Over 2 million people had died as a direct consequence of Bonaparte's campaigns, many more through poverty and disease and undernourishment. Countless villages had been burned in the paths of the advancing and retreating armies. Almost every capital in Europe had been occupied—some, like Vienna, Dresden, Berlin and Madrid, more than once. Moscow had been put to the torch. Copenhagen had been bombarded. That Goya's drawings did not exaggerate is confirmed by the account of George Sand, in her *Histoire de ma vie,* of her childhood journey in 1808 across stricken Spain, where her father was serving.[17] Sand lived off raw onions, sunflower seeds, green lemons, and soup made with candle-ends, shared with the soldiers. She remembered the noise of the wheels of the wagon in which she lay, crunching over the bones of a corpse in the road. She remembered clutching at the sleeve of a trooper, only to find his arm missing.

The wars set back the economic life of much of Europe for a generation. They made men behave like beasts, and worse. The battles were bigger and much more bloody. The armies of the old regimes were of long-service professional veterans, often lifers, obsessed with uniforms, pipe clay, polished brass, and their elaborate drill—the kings could not bear to lose them. Bonaparte cut off the pigtails, ended the powdered hair, supplied mass-produced uniforms and spent the lives of his young, conscripted recruits as though they were loose change. His insistence that they live off the land did not work in subsistence economies like Spain and Russia, where if the soldiers stole, the peasants starved. So in Spain, French stragglers were stripped and roasted alive, and in Russia the serfs buried them up to their necks in mud and ice for the wolves to feed on. Throughout Europe, the standards of human conduct declined as men and women, and their growing children, learned to live brutally.

Writers and artists who experienced the erosion of values during Bonaparte's tyranny abandoned their initial support for a man they once saw as a force for change. Benjamin Constant summed it up in his *De l'Esprit de la conquête* (1813): "Human beings are sacrificed to abstractions—a holocaust of individuals is offered up to 'the People' "—a truth the 20th century was to learn even more painfully.[18] In Germany the intellectuals initially supported French "liberation" because it ended the petty Courts where, paradoxically, German *Kultur* had been suppressed in favor of French *culture.* Some writers abased themselves before the Bonapartist life force. G. W. F. Hegel, from Stuttgart, ran a pro-French newspaper, the *Bamberger Zeitung,* mostly copied from the official French government organ, the Paris *Moniteur;*

he thought Bonaparte, whom he had seen ride through Jena in 1806, was the *Weltseele,* the personification of reason, and he applauded Bonaparte's troops even though they stole all his money. The editor-historian Ernst Ludwig Posselt, who ran the monthly *Europäische Annalen* and for a time the daily *Neueste Weltkund* of Tübingen, wrote of "the Emperor" as of a god and said that one of the highest slopes of the Alps should be cleared and "Napoleon" inscribed on it in giant golden letters so that the glint of them could be seen even in Germany. He argued that it was right for the Italians to hand over their works of art to the French because it was "their first step into the hallowed temple of liberty."[19] These Francophile publications were strictly controlled by the French authorities, who imposed total censorship of the press from start to finish and ended by suppressing even the most craven of the collaborationist sheets. They could not find the author of the critical pamphlet, *Germany in the Depths of Degradation* (1806), so they shot the publisher, Philipp Palm of Nuremberg. This was one of many such incidents, ignored by radical writers in England, like Hazlitt or Leigh Hunt, who risked no more than a year or two at most in comfortable prisons, but they gradually forced "enlightened" Germans into opposition.

Hence the years 1810–14 saw the intelligentsia, throughout the German states, swing decisively against Bonaparte. German romanticism, especially *Sturm und Drang* and its reverberations, was directed against the Napoleonic armies, administrators and propagandists, and the officially approved art forms of the French empire, which were classical-revival. Young German writers and artists joined the new volunteer units set up to help liberate German-speaking territory, as the empire began to founder. The painting by G. F. Kersting, *At the Advance Post,* shows three such intellectuals serving in his regiment in 1813. A year later, his friend Caspar David Friedrich painted the highly nationalistic *A Chasseur in the Forest,* showing a French soldier of occupation amid dark and threatening German trees, with a raven singing his death song.[20] The trouble with anti-Bonapartist feeling was that, in many parts of Europe where the leaning of the upper class toward French culture had long been resented, it broadened into hatred of France and the French as such. This was particularly true of Germany, where Francophobia, first among the intellectuals, then among the population as a whole, became a powerful and dangerous force for nearly 150 years.

The reaction against France was all the stronger because the German-speaking states had received the greatest humiliations at the hands of Bonaparte and had formed the background to his most arrogant displays. After the Battle of Jena in 1806, when Bonaparte crushed the Prussian army—once, under Frederick the Great, the finest in Europe—the north Germans watched in shame while large and well-provisioned garrisons surrendered to mere troops of French dragoons. The King, Frederick William III, showed himself a craven nonentity. Further south, the King of Saxony became a self-abasing French puppet, whose palace at Dresden Bonaparte treated as his hotel. Austria was no better. By 1809 it had been beaten by Bonaparte in four successive campaigns and was bankrupt, but nonetheless forced to pay an indemnity to the French and surrender territory. Its army was restricted to 150,000 men. The Habsburg monarch, Francis, could no longer call himself Holy Roman Emperor, since Bonaparte had abolished that ancient entity, which went back to Charlemagne. Francis himself was a feeble figure, who spent his time making toffee and endlessly stamping blank sheets of parchment with specimens from his huge collection of seals. When Bonaparte, who had discarded his wife Josephine for failing to give him an heir, demanded of Francis a further sacrifice in the shape of his eldest daughter, Marie-Louise, the head of the House of Habsburg, then the grandest ruling family in Europe, felt he had to assent. It is true that the Habsburgs had made their way in the world less by winning battles than by judicious marriages. But the shame was fearful. Marie-Louise, then 18, had been brought up to call Bonaparte "the Corsican Anti-Christ." It was as though the Britain of 1940, having surrendered to Hitler, had been forced to deliver Princess Elizabeth, elder daughter of King George VI, to the Führer as his bride. Marie-Louise, hitherto interested chiefly in whipped cream and her pet ducks, was happy to escape from her governesses and inquisitive priests to the glamor of the usurper's court at Fontainebleau. But the Courts of Germany felt the horror of an alliance which, in effect, sanctioned the murder of Marie Antoinette, another Habsburg princess and the bride's great-aunt, and legitimated a plebeian tyrant.

As it was, the military adventurers who followed in Bonaparte's wake, and their women, were already mingling with the ancient nobilities of Europe, which took their cue from above. Clemens Metternich (1773–1859), who had become Austrian Foreign Minister in autumn 1809 after the last Habsburg disaster at Wagram, was from one of the oldest families in Europe, which went back to the times of King Henry the Fowler and even Charlemagne. He was married to Eleonore von Kaunitz, diminutive granddaughter of the great Austrian chancellor—it was to her that Bonaparte, at a masked ball, had first broached the idea of marrying Marie-Louise. Metternich, an accomplished womanizer,

did not scruple to conduct an adulterous affair with Bonaparte's youngest and prettiest sister, Caroline, married to one of his marshals, Murat,
or to run this affair in tandem with another military wife, Laura
Junot, whose spouse was the Governor of Paris. When Mettenich
and Madame Junot were seen together at a Paris fortune-teller's,
Bonaparte's secret police were informed, and Caroline Murat, who
seems to have had access to their files, plotted revenge. On 13 January
1810, at yet another masked ball—they were the delight of the super-
rich in Bonapartist Europe—Caroline Murat told Junot that if he
broke into his wife's desk, he would find compromising letters. The
general did so, then threw a tantrum. First he said he would get Bonaparte to declare war on Austria again. Then he swore to challenge
Metternich to a duel. All he did in the end was to attack Laura with a
pair of scissors, leaving her (as she put it), "a blood-drenched wife, half
dead and cut to pieces by his own hands." He then confessed what he
had done to Madame Metternich, who responded dryly: "The role of
Othello ill becomes you."[21] The episode well conveys the atmosphere
of vulgar ostentation, vice and near-gangsterism which characterized
the meridian of Bonapartist Europe.

Worse was to come. In May 1812 Bonaparte moved his entire court
to Dresden, taking over the Saxon king's rococo palace and filling it
with wagon trains of French tapestries, wines, porcelain, china, glass
and furniture brought from Paris, along with hundreds of French cooks
and delicacies from all over the empire. His new empress, Marie-
Louise, was attended by duchesses with some of the oldest names in
France—Turenne, Montesquieu and Noailles—for the French noblesse
had, at this stage, capitulated to him too. At the first of a great series
of balls he gave, the kings of Europe and the Austrian emperor preceded
him into the room; then came his wife; finally, he was announced, quite
simply, not as king or emperor of this or that, but as L'Empereur![22]
There were two royalties not present at this abasement of European
legitimacy before their Corsican conqueror. The first was the English
Prince Regent, sitting behind his navy in London. The second was the
Tsar of Russia. Bonaparte had finally decided he had no alternative but
to deal with the Tsar as he had dealt with all the other Continental
sovereigns, and the gathering at Dresden was designed to launch his
"civilizing mission" to Russia. After a week of festivities he left for his
military headquarters on 28 May, to begin the invasion. The rulers
gathered at Dresden were obliged to contribute more than their approval. Bonaparte's Grande Armée was multinational, as were to be the
forces Hitler hurled at Russia in 1941: in addition to 200,000 French,
there were 147,000 German troops from the French-run Confederation

of the Rhine, plus 50,000 from the Prussian and Austrian forces, making nearly 200,000 Germans in all; there were 80,000 Italians and 60,000 Poles, and contributions from the Swiss, the Dutch, the southern Slavs, the Spanish and the Portuguese. Bonaparte's intention, after the conquest and dismemberment of Russia, was to have himself declared Emperor of Europe.[23]

Six months later, even Bonaparte's own war bulletin, the 29th issued on 3 December 1812, was obliged to admit that "an atrocious calamity" had overtaken the army. Two days later, Bonaparte himself abandoned it, plus his coach—which ended up in Byron's possession—and much else, and fled west by fast sledge, accompanied only by his personal staff chief, Armand de Caulaincourt, duc de Vicence. Bonaparte was no longer L'Empereur, but traveling as Caulaincourt's secretary, "Monsieur de Rayneval."[24] Thereafter, for Bonaparte, it was mostly downhill, though there were missed opportunities on the way. The last of any consequence came in June 1813, following two French victories and an armistice. By now Prussia and Russia were his sworn enemies and all his former satraps had deserted him except Saxony. Austria was neutral, since Metternich conceived it was in her interest to have a Habsburg-Bonapartist dynasty on the French throne and for France, accordingly, to keep many of her conquests. As Metternich put it to Caulaincourt, now Bonaparte's regular negotiator, "When it comes to anything which touches the soil of France, Napoleon and the Empress's father—as grandfather to the successor to the [French] throne—must think alike."[25] On 24 June Prussia, Russia and Austria drew up the Reichenbach Treaty, which offered Bonaparte the best peace he was likely to get. All he had to do was to dissolve his Grand Duchy of Warsaw, return various chunks of territory to Prussia and Austria, and give the Hanseatic towns, like Hamburg and Lübeck, back their liberties. The rest of his empire, including French frontiers up to the Rhine and the loot of Europe, he was to keep.

On 26 June 1813 Metternich put these terms to Bonaparte at an eight-and-a-half-hour interview, from noon to 8:30 P.M. It took place at at the Elsterwiese Castle outside Dresden, built by the puppet king for his mistress, the opera singer Camilla Marcolini—the little king was forced to hang about in his own waiting room and was finally told to go home. Both men were supreme egoists and they later gave conflicting accounts of their marathon talk. The essential point was that Bonaparte turned down the terms. Any concession, he said to Metternich, would be fatal: "My reign will not outlast the day when I have ceased to be strong and therefore to be feared." The conversation went round in circles, thirteen by Bonaparte's count. "I know how to die," he told

Metternich. "But I shall never cede one inch of territory. Your sovereigns, who were born on the throne, can allow themselves to be beaten twenty times and will always return to their capitals, But I cannot do that—I am a self-made soldier." Metternich: "I have seen your soldiers. They are not more than children." At this point Bonaparte threw his hat into a corner and shouted: "You know nothing of what goes on in the soldier's mind. I grew up on the field of battle. A man like me cares little for the lives of a million men." Metternich: "If only the words you have just spoken could be heard from one end of Europe to the other." Bonaparte: "I may lose my throne. But I shall bury the whole world in its ruins." Metternich: "Sire, you are a lost man."[26]

The three powers then proceeded to sign a mutual support convention which was to be the basis for the subsequent Holy Alliance, and in August, Austria too declared war on France. The armies met at Leipzig, the so-called Battle of the Nations, fought 16–19 October 1813, which ended in the destruction of Bonaparte's second Grande Armée of 700,000, by a force of 830,000 Russians, Austrians and Prussians. Not all these men were in the actual battle, where about 190,000 French and their allies faced 300,000. Bonaparte had no choice but to retreat to save his troops from total destruction, and he contrived to get back across the Rhine only 70,000 of them, of whom 30,000 quickly died of typhus. He raised fresh forces and maneuvered skilfully, but there could now be no doubt about the outcome. The British were advancing across the Pyrenees toward the Loire. The Prussians, Russians and Austrians all crossed the Rhine by February. Paris fell on 31 March. Until almost the end, Bonaparte refused to negotiate seriously or allow Caulaincourt to do so on his behalf—in this respect, too, Hitler was to be like him—but early in April, in negotiations with the Tsar, he suddenly capitulated and agreed to abdicate. In return, he got the island of Elba and a pension of 2 million francs. His empress was compensated by being made duchess of Parma. This agreement, called the Treaty of Fontainebleau, was entitled "A Treaty Between the Allied Powers and His Majesty the Emperor Napoleon."

Many had misgivings about this compromise, which left the man who had kept Europe in uproar for nearly twenty years free and even, in a small way, sovereign. Elba was preferred to other islands because Corsica and Sardinia were too big and he would not accept Corfu because it was too far away. His police chief Fouché, who had now deserted him and who knew his wiles, said he should be deported to the United States.

Metternich was particularly unhappy about the choice of Elba because it was so near Italy. Castlereagh thought it would be an easy matter for Bonaparte to jump from Elba onto the French coast, as happened. One suggestion was to intern him on Gibraltar, but this was attacked by Tory backbenchers: "We should be really sorry if any British possession were to be polluted by such a wretch. He would be a disgrace to Botany Bay."[27] The same argument applied to another place already being mentioned, the remote British station of Saint Helena in the south Atlantic. The British cabinet disliked an alternative Castlereagh put forward, to grant him asylum in the splendid British fort of Saint George on the Beauly Firth, designed by the Adam brothers, where Dr Samuel Johnson and James Boswell had dined with the garrison in 1783. Ministers thought that if Bonaparte found himself there, the Whig leaders would promptly serve them with a writ of habeas corpus forcing them either to bring him to trial or to free him. In the end, all agreed to Elba, fearing that the Tsar, a mercurial uncollegiate figure, might suddenly propose what Bonaparte now wanted— an abdication not in favor of the Bourbons but of his own son, the king of Rome. So all signed, but Metternich said: "There will be war again within two years."

Bonaparte did not take his degradation easily. His rage was said to be "supernatural," his "cries were those of a trapped lion." Since the Russian disaster, he had always worn a suicide pill round his neck, a practice followed by the Nazi leaders in 1945. In his case, it consisted of a tiny pouch of black taffeta containing a mixture of belladonna, hellebore and opium. He took it on 12 April but it did not work, producing merely spasms and nausea. His doctor offered no help. He had sworn the Hippocratic Oath and said, "I am no murderer."[28] So Bonaparte was hustled to the Mediterranean coast, with an escort of 60 lancers to protect him from the White Terror now raging in the countryside. Disguised in a blue servant's livery and with a tiny round hat on his head, he refused to cross to Elba on a French warship, as French naval officers hated him, and instead traveled on HMS *Undaunted*, reaching his new kingdom on 4 May 1814.

The brief Kingdom of Elba is one of the curiosities of history. Bonaparte attempted to keep a court there. He had a Grand Marshal of the Palace, a Military Governor, a Treasurer, four chamberlains, two secretaries, a doctor and chemist, a butler and chef and seven assistant chefs, two valets, two equerries, a Mameluke servant called Ali, two gentleman-ushers, eight footmen, a porter, a Director of the Gardens, a Director of Music and two women singers, a laundress and a washerwoman. He had 35 men working in the stables which housed 27 carriages and many of his favorite horses. But the court did not function as he wished. The local ladies and gentry were not up to the style of his receptions, or Drawing Rooms as they were then called, and he soon abandoned the farce. Instead, he played vingt-et-un and dominoes with his family, which included his mother and his sister Pauline Borghese. He bustled about his little kingdom, reorganizing it. But he was bored. He was also broke and his schemes to modernize Elba languished for lack of money. The court was expensive. He had brought with him nearly 4 million francs in cash, but this was soon spent and much of it appears to have been stolen. When he left France, he had relinquished his £8 million fortune, most of it in real estate or otherwise immovable, in return for a £100,000-a-year state annuity. But this was never paid, and when Castlereagh and Metternich reproached his Bourbon successor, Louis XVIII, the king merely raised the possibility of shifting Bonaparte to the Azores.[29] So Bonaparte could claim that the Treaty of Fontainebleau had never been honored. He was also frightened for his personal safety. He feared the Whites might assassinate him or that the Allies would suddenly sweep him off to a British station in the West Indies or Saint Helena. He had been allowed to keep 400 men of his Old Guard and a squadron of Polish cavalry; there was, too, the local militia. But Bonaparte was running out of cash to pay the regular troops, and fear of removal was one reason he determined to escape. The other more compelling motive, however, was the report that the restoration of the Bourbons was proving unpopular and that the people would welcome him back.

Needless to say, Louis XVIII (1755–1824) had not been greeted by most Frenchmen with any enthusiasm. He was old, enormously fat, lame and almost immobile, and had sat out the long war at Hartwell in Buckinghamshire. He was not wholly ungrateful. On his way back to Paris, he had said to the Prince Regent: "It is to the counsels of Your Royal Highness, to this glorious country, and to the steadfastness of its inhabitants that I attribute, after the Will of Providence, the reestablishment of my house upon the throne of its ancestors."[30] This statement, when published, aroused the wrath of Tsar Alexander, who attributed the downfall of Bonaparte chiefly to the "heroic sacrifices" of the Russian people—another phrase which was to recur in Hitler's time. No doubt Louis had heard the Tsar was not anxious to see the Bourbons back on their throne and had agreed to their return merely as a *pis aller* after other ideas, such as a regency by Marie-Louise or the enthronement of Bernadotte, proved even less acceptable. When, newly installed at Compiègne, Louis consented to receive the Tsar, he put him in bad rooms and gave him a chilly greeting. "One would think," Alexander complained, "that it was actually *he* who had put *me* on *my* throne." He was particularly disgusted when, at dinner, Louis insisted on following his own protocol and being served first—"*Moi avant!*" he called out decidedly. As a result, the Tsar refused to spend the night under his roof.[31]

One reason Louis insisted on being served first was that he was a very hungry, greedy man. His subjects called him *le Cochon*. Wellington related with relish that, dining with the king *en famille* with the princesses, he noticed a substantial dish of early strawberries brought in: "The King very deliberately turned [it] into his own plate, even to the last spoonful, and ate [it] with a large quantity of sugar and cream, without offering any to the ladies."[32] But greed, by the standards of the ancien régime, was a minor shortcoming. In general Louis was tolerant and unvengeful. There is no evidence that any substantial section of the French people wanted to replace him with a returned Bonaparte. In the army, however, it was a different matter. The marshals, rich and full of honors, had no particular desire to fight again and wanted to enjoy their gains—their enthusiasm for "the Emperor" had waned steadily since 1812. The career officers and the men thought otherwise: for them, Bonaparte meant service, action, promotion and loot.

Acting on this calculation, Bonaparte easily deceived his guardian, the British Commissioner Sir Neil Campbell, and using the brig HMS *Inconstant* which the Royal Navy had kindly provided him, landed on the Riviera, at Golfe Juan, on 1 March 1815. He took a peaceful Europe by surprise. Byron had got married a few days before the Battle of New Orleans and was already repenting at leisure—"I am," he reported to Thomas Moore on 2 March, in a "state of sameness and stagnation . . . playing dull games at cards—and yawning—and trying to read old *Annual Registers* and the daily papers."[33] Jane Austen was writing the final chapters of *Emma,* which she was to finish on 29 March.[34] Shelley had just deserted his wife and run off with William Godwin's daughter, Mary. J. M. W. Turner was painting his sun-filled arcadian canvas, *Crossing the Brook*. Gioacchino Rossini was writing *The Barber of Seville* and Ludwig van Beethoven his piano sonata Opus 101. Humphry Davy was working on the first miner's safety lamp. The news of Bonaparte's escape spread rapidly through Europe. Thanks to the highly efficient French telegraph system, the first to get the news was Louis XVIII on 4 March. The message also brought him the unwelcome intelligence that French troops and local authorities were putting up no resistance to the intruder. Soult, as commander in chief, stationed supposedly loyal regiments to bar Bonaparte's progress; they let him through or joined him. Marshal Ney said he would bring back Bonaparte "in an iron cage"; instead, he offered "the Emperor" his sword.

On Sunday 19 March old Louis decided to pack and flee.

Meanwhile the news had reached Vienna. The unfortunate Campbell had returned to Elba on 28 February, to find his charge gone and had immediately sent the news both to the Austrian consul at Genoa and to the British minister, Lord Burghersh, in Florence. Wellington always claimed that the letter forwarded by Burghersh reached him in Vienna first, and he broke the news to the rest of the Congress. Talleyrand said, "Mark my words, you will find him anywhere but in France—look to Italy." The Tsar burst out laughing.[35]

Metternich always claimed the letter from the Genoa consul reached him first, though he got the date muddled. It arrived on 7 March. He had been up working till 3 A.M. the night before. At seven his valet woke him with a message. Seeing it was only from the Genoa consulate, he put it on his night table and tried to go back to sleep. But he was restless and at 7:30 A.M. he opened the note. It said simply: "The Commodore of the British Elba squadron reports that Napoleon has left the island. That is all we know here."[36] By 8 A.M. Metternich was with the Austrian Emperor. Fifteen minutes later he saw the Tsar, and at 8:30 A.M. he was with the King of Prussia. At 10 A.M. all the plenipotentiaries met, and couriers were dispatched to mobilize the allied armies. As Metternich put it, "In this way war was decided on in less than an hour."[37]

Six days later the Congress declared Bonaparte an outlaw; he had, it stated, "placed himself beyond the protection of the law and rendered himself subject to public vengeance [vindicte publique]." Wellington signed this communiqué and was promptly attacked by the Whigs as having invited Bonaparte's assassination; he was, said Samuel Whitbread, MP, the Whig brewing millionaire, morally Bonaparte's murderer. But Wellington pointed out that vindicte meant "justice" not "vengeance" (it actually means "prosecution").[38] In fact, Wellington was too busy to worry about moral niceties since once it was confirmed that Bonaparte was back in Paris, without an arm being raised against him, it was clear war was inevitable. On 25 March the four principal allies each agreed to provide 150,000 men, the British to make up any shortfall in their contribution by financial subsidies. Soon a million men were set in motion to form a cordon sanitaire around France, from the English Channel to the Alps, and Wellington left for Brussels to take up command of the Anglo-Dutch forces, to the right of Marshal Blücher's Prussians.

Bonaparte found no trouble in establishing himself in Paris. He was accustomed to arriving there without an army and getting a new one.

Wellington used to assert that when Bonaparte arrived from Russia, having lost his first *Grande Armée,* he decided to give the Parisians something else to talk about. So he determined that "the woman dancers at the Opera House should dance *without their under-garments,* and actually sent an order to that effect—the women, however, positively refused!" concluded the Duke, with his whooping-cough laugh.[39] This time Bonaparte produced a liberal constitution, and progressive-sounding decrees issued from the presses as fast as he could dictate them. He took over the northern group of armies and moved them toward the Belgian frontier, planning to strike between the converging Anglo-Dutch and Prussian armies and beat each separately. The French troops rallied to him unanimously. This was as Wellington expected. When the Whig member of Parliament, Thomas Creevey, who was living in Brussels with his family to save money, asked the Duke "Do you calculate upon any desertion in Buonaparte's army?" Wellington answered: "Not upon a man, from the colonel to the private in a regiment, both inclusive. We may pick up a marshal or two, perhaps, but not worth a damn." The two men were in the Brussels Park, and at this point the Duke caught sight of a redcoat—an infantry private—gawping at the statuary. "There," he said to Creevey, "it all depends upon that article whether we do the business or not. Give me enough of it, and I am sure."[40]

In fact the Horse Guards in London, HQ of the British Army, was slow and reluctant to send him men. Instead of the 40,000 infantry and 15,000 cavalry he had asked for, he was sent only 30,000 of all arms, of which a mere 7,000 were veterans. He did not get the divisional generals and staff he named, and to command the cavalry he was sent the Earl of Uxbridge, with whom he had never worked. The Horse Guards, as usual, put personal interest before military efficiency. Wellington was anxious to conceal the weakness of his position and his own anxieties and that is why he encouraged the Duchess of Richmond to give her famous ball on 15 June. She said to him: "Duke, I do not wish to pry into your secrets . . . . I wish to give a ball and all I ask is, may I give my ball? If you say, 'Duchess, don't give your ball,' it is quite sufficient, I ask no reason." "Duchess, you may give your ball with the greatest safety, without fear of interruption."[41]

The Richmonds, as well as Creevey, were living in Brussels to save money—"on an Economic Plan," as they put it, like Sir Walter Elliot in *Persuasion*—the Duke having had an expensive spell as Lord Lieutenant in Dublin. With them were various daughters, almost grown up and needing husbands. The Duchess, bad tempered, mendacious and a gambler though she might be, was anxious they should attend balls.

Her eldest son, as we have seen, was with Wellington himself; three younger ones, from seven to fourteen, were under the care of a tutor, Spencer Madan, whose diaries illuminate these hectic weeks. They all lived in a large, ramshackle house the Richmonds had rented cheap in the poorer part of Brussels, "Laundry Street." Wellington called it the Wash House. The boys celebrated the approaching battle with a fraternal quarrel: "Lord Frederick despairing, I suppose, of convincing his brother by means of words, took up a heavy brass candlestick, perhaps with a view of throwing light on the subject, and gave his brother a blow of which he will carry the mark to the grave." Madan, an Oxford first, could teach little to what the duchess called her pickles and said that, without his close watch, "the house would be turned out of windows every evening, & there would be no end to their riots, *let alone* their pilfering the store-room, thrashing the maids, and sending out for red herrings and gin."[42]

The ball was held in the decked-out coachhouse of this place and was in the circumstances a success, supplying Byron with the most famous passage, perhaps, in his entire oeuvre, and Thackeray with a notable scene in *Vanity Fair*. Wellington kept his sangfroid because he was anxious at all costs to avoid a panic in Belgium which would block his reinforcement roads with refugees, but he was busy receiving messages and dispatching orders throughout the dancing and was off to the front, after two hours' sleep, at 5:30 A.M. the next morning. The Duchess's memory of the time was "I never took off my clothes for three days."

Waterloo, fought from 11:25 A.M. until nightfall, about 10 P.M., on 18 June, was a peculiarly savage and costly battle, a fitting climax to Bonaparte's long career of large-scale bloodshed. Because of Bonaparte's determination to destroy the army Wellington commanded by a frontal assault and because of the configuration of the ground, nearly 140,000 men and 30,000 horses, plus over 400 guns, were crammed into a lethal space of less than three square miles. Bonaparte had 71,947 men and 246 guns committed to the action, against Wellington's 67,661 men and 156 guns, and the majority of them were under fire, or actually in contact with their enemy, for several hours on that long, wet, misty and muddy day.[43]

Bonaparte lost the battle because he was not able to bring into action his additional 33,000 men under the Marquis de Grouchy, on his right, or prevent Blücher's Prussians, whom he had mauled two days before, from joining the battle toward evening. But the main reason was that he had underestimated the capacity of the British infantry to resist attack, though warned of their endurance on the morning of the battle by several of his marshals, who had suffered from it. Wellington had not been able to glimpse Bonaparte throughout the day—"No, I could not—the day was dark—there was a great deal of rain in the air"—but he had caught sight of Soult, writing an order, "most plainly." In fact, Bonaparte, when not on his white mare Désirée, commanded the French forces from a wooden tower his engineers had erected, though the combination of mist and cannon smoke did not allow him to see much.

Wellington was on his small but exceptionally strong chestnut, Copenhagen, which had carried him at three successful battles already. He had seen faster and handsomer horses than Copenhagen, he said, "but for bottom and endurance I never saw his fellow." The Duke mounted him at 6 A.M. on the day of Waterloo and did not finally dismount until 11 P.M., a matter of 17 hours, and including much movement across the arc of the allied forces. The Duke, as usual in battle, wore civilian clothes, cut military style, with a huge cocked hat, not worn broad on like Bonaparte, but pulled low over his face. He did not believe in making things easy for enemy snipers, trained to kill senior officers—unlike Nelson, at Trafalgar, who wore all his stars on the quarterdeck of the *Victory* and paid with his life. One of the Duke's veteran generals from the Peninsula, Sir Thomas Picton, also wore civilian trousers and coat, crowned by a top hat—he had hurried across from England and had not had time to change. A bullet passed through the hat (now in the Military Museum, Sandhurst) and killed him instantly, while he was leading the Gordon Highlanders in a charge. Wellington was in range of French artillery for eight hours, and a large grapeshot from one of the last rounds fired from the French lines—it was about 8 P.M.—passed over Copenhagen's neck and shattered the right knee of the cavalry commander, Uxbridge, who had to have his leg amputated. (The leg was put in a wooden coffin and buried beneath a willow in the garden of the cottage where the operation took place.)[44]

The battle was a case of attrition, not science. Bonaparte tried to break the Anglo-Dutch lines first with artillery, then infantry, then cavalry, then infantry and cavalry combined, finally with his Old Guard. The British cavalry proved brave but uncontrolled and therefore useless, as usual, but the infantry held firm, though an eyewitness saw Wellington "working his lips as if his mouth were dry with anxiety." Several of the French assaults were led by Marshal Ney personally; he knew his life would be forfeit if the battle was lost, for he had broken his oath to Louis XVIII. Ney had four horses shot under him, and when the last fell, he was seen through a gap in the smoke striking his sword in frustration against the barrel of an abandoned cannon. By

late afternoon Wellington was running out of aides de camp. Some
were scattered with orders about the battlefield. The Duchess of Richmond's son, Alexander, had been carried off the field with a shattered
leg, but unlike Uxbridge he died on the operating table. So the Duke
was driven to use as message carriers some stray civilians who, mysteri-
ously, had been swept into the battle: a young Swiss, a button salesman
from Birmingham, a commercial traveler from the City, mounted on a
pony.⁴⁵ By the early evening, it was clear Bonaparte's tactics had failed.
Wellington was not impressed by them: "Napoleon did not manoeuvre
at all. He just moved forward in the old style, in columns, and was
driven off in the old style."⁴⁶ By 8:30 P.M., with the Old Guard in
retreat, Wellington advancing, and the Prussians rolling up his right,
Bonaparte decided the game was up, got into his carriage, a *berline,* and
drove off the field. But the Prussians threatened to overtake him, and
he was forced to abandon his carriage, leap onto a horse, and ride south
with his escort of Red Lancers.

Waterloo, like New Orleans, was one of the decisive battles of
history. It finished off Bonaparte for good and introduced a period of
general European peace which lasted a century. No one doubted its
importance at the time, least of all Wellington. But he was appalled at
the cost. Battle-hardened as he was, the number of dead and savagely
wounded, including many personal friends and old comrades, left him
shaken. The battle he said had been "all pounding." He compared it to
two punch-drunk boxers slugging away at each other. It brought home
to him, perhaps as never before, the sheer horror and waste of war.
Creevey, who saw him the next day, just after he had finished his
dispatch, found him the reverse of exultant. He spoke with "the greatest gravity." "It has been a damned serious business. Blücher and I have
lost 30,000 men. It has been a damned nice thing—the nearest-run thing
you ever saw in your life." He "repeated so often its being *so nice a
thing—so nearly run a thing*" that Creevey asked if the French had
fought especially well. No, they had been as always. But he added—
without a trace of vanity, as Creevey testified—"By God I don't think
it would have done if I had not been there."⁴⁷

By this time the dispatch was winging its way to London in the
hands of the Hon. Henry Percy, almost the only one of Wellington's
aides de camp not to have been killed or wounded. Percy had been in
action all the previous day, but set off immediately, taking with him
two captured eagle standards. The sloop in which he crossed the Channel from Ostend was becalmed within sight of the English coast. But
Percy had rowed at Eton and, with some fellow passengers, seized oars
and got ashore in a gig. He reached London at ten in the evening, took

the dispatch to Earl Bathurst's house in Grosvenor Square, where the cabinet was dining, then went down to St. James's to present the eagles to the Prince of Wales. Then he collapsed. But he had been beaten to it. An agent of the London branch of the Rothschilds, waiting in Ghent, had picked up the news at breakfast on 19 June and got across the Channel using the fast fisher boats the Rothschilds hired from Folkestone. He reported to Nathan Rothschild at 2 New Court, St. Swithin's Lane in the City, then dashed to Lord Liverpool's house in Westminster: the Prime Minister got the news at two in the afternoon.[48]

When news of the horrifying casualties spread through London, some of the younger hospital surgeons immediately took coach for the Continent. They found an appalling scene at Waterloo. Many of the British wounded had been collected off the battlefield, but hundreds of them were still awaiting surgery. The field itself was still scattered with the stricken, lying amid the dead. Colonel Frederick Ponsonby had been cut up by French cavalry sabers and left for dead; he had been speared by a passing Polish lancer; given some brandy by a French officer; piled into a barricade of bodies by retreating French infantry; ridden over and tossed by Prussian cavalry; discovered by a British infantryman who stood guard over him throughout the night, while he felt the air pass in and out of his pierced lung; and finally taken off to a dressing-station at daybreak. He was known as "the Man Who Was Killed at Waterloo," and spotted twelve years later, as governor of Malta, by Captain Codrington's daughter, who found him "playing violent games of racquets with as much energy as the young soldiers around him."[49]

Ponsonby was lucky. Most of the wounded, especially the French, died on the field. Bonaparte's outstanding surgeon in chief, Baron Larrey, who had invented the "flying ambulance" for use on the battlefield and saved thousands of lives by training teams of surgeons to carry out quick amputations, was captured by Prussian cavalry, and his unit was scattered. Wellington's losses were not quite as high as he feared—just under 15,000 killed and wounded. The Prussians lost 7,000. French losses were 25,000, and of this last figure several thousands died of wounds before help of any kind reached them. But the arrival of the London surgeons was a help. The great Scottish surgeon and anatomist Charles Bell spent a week carrying out operations from dawn till dusk, until "his clothes were stiff with blood" and his arms "powerless with the exertions of using the knife." A superb draughtsman, he also did studies of Waterloo gunshot wounds, which were later made into oil paintings for the use of students. Some of his sketches were incorporated in his *Nervous System of the Human Body* (1830), the first textbook of modern neurology.[50]

Nor were the horses entirely forgotten. Sir Astley Cooper, then the outstanding London surgeon, attended the sale of the wounded Waterloo horses, considered fit only for the knacker's yard, bought twelve of the most serious cases, had them taken to his little estate in Hertfordshire, and began the systematic extraction of bullets and grapeshot. He saved the lives of all twelve and let them loose in his park. Then "one morning, to his great delight, he saw the noble animals form in line, charge, and then retreat, and afterwards gallop about, appearing greatly contented with the lot that had befallen them."[51]

The Napoleonic era now ended swiftly. The Allied armies entered Paris at the end of the first week of July, Wellington just in time to stop Blücher's Prussians from blowing up the Pont de Jena, which they saw as a symbol of their humiliation. He stationed British sentries on it. The Prussians were also demanding Alsace, Lorraine, Luxembourg, the Saar, plus a huge cash indemnity—all a foretaste of the Franco-Prussian War, 1870–71. They wanted Bonaparte shot. Bonaparte in the meantime had abdicated in a hopeless attempt to get his little son, the king of Rome, made ruler of France. Then, fearing for his life, he made for Rochefort on the coast, hoping to get a ship for the United States. But the port was blockaded by HMS *Bellerophon,* a famous Trafalgar veteran battleship, known in the navy as "Billy Ruffian." On 13 July Bonaparte decided his wisest course was to surrender to the British. He sent a message to the Prince Regent: "I come, like Themistocles, to throw myself upon the hospitality of the British people . . . . I place myself under the protection of their laws," and two days later went aboard the warship, wearing his green chasseur's uniform. He expected to be given comfortable asylum in England. But there was never any question of that. *Bellerophon* returned to British waters but Bonaparte was not allowed to land; instead, after some argument in the cabinet, the ship was ordered to proceed straight to Saint Helena with her prisoner, and Bonaparte never set foot on English soil even as a captive.[52]

Bonaparte was already part of history. The souvenir hunters had descended on Waterloo long before the last corpses had been cleared. In the circumstances, Wellington himself was lucky to get a dozen cuirassas; Sir Robert Peel bought "a good one" for two *Napoléons;* Croker paid one for a Cross of the Légion d'Honneur. The sheer devastation of the battlefield, adumbrating Flanders a century later, struck contemporaries. "The farm of Hougoumont," Croker recorded, "which was to the right of the action, was totally destroyed, the house and offices burnt and battered with shot, the trees around it (for it had an orchard and a little wood) cut to pieces."[53] Southey was appalled by what he found: "I had never before seen the real face of war so closely and, God knows, a deplorable sight it is!"[54] The exhibition industry was soon at work. Bonaparte's *berline*, in dark blue and gilt with red wheels, fell into the hands of the Prussians, and Blücher presented it to the Prince Regent. He quickly sold it for £2,500 to William Bullock, the show impresario, who had built the Egyptian Hall in Piccadilly, opposite Bond Street. Jane Austen had seen Bullock's thirty-five-foot boa-constrictor in 1811, "tho' my preference for Men and Women always inclines me to attend more to the company than the sight." Now he set up the carriage of the fallen dictator, complete with its bullet-proof panels, a camp bed; a traveling case of a hundred pieces, nearly all in solid gold; two "restorative bottles," one containing rum, the other old Malaga; two of its horses; and its young coachman, who had lost an arm in the battle. Londoners flocked to see it at the rate of 10,000 a day and it was gawped at by 800,000 in all, netting Bullock £35,000.[55]

In Saint Helena, Bonaparte, his small party guarded by the grim and suspicious Sir Hudson Lowe, was something, of a tourist attraction himself for passengers on ships which put in to provision there. One described him as "round and white, like a china pig." On 8 March 1817 the young William Makepeace Thackeray, then aged five, sent by his parents in India to school in England, landed briefly from the East Indiaman *Prince Regent*. His black servant, Lawrence Barlow, "took me a long walk over rocks and hills until we reached a garden where we saw a man walking." "That is he," said Barlow, "that is Bonaparte. He eats three sheep a day and all the little children he can lay his hands on."[56] The cost of guarding Bonaparte was enormous: over £400,000 a year, with 3,000 men employed on the island and aboard the covering squadron. It included the brig *Beaver*, commanded by Captain Marryat in 1821. Marryat said that Lowe believed there was a plot to rescue Bonaparte by submarine from Brazil. He was on shore when the ex-emperor died, on 5 May, and the next day attended his lying in state and was amazed at the unwrinkled ivory skin, youthful looks and feminine hands. A skilful artist, Marryat did a sketch of the face before the post-mortem took place, and another of the funeral.[57] The news attracted little interest in Europe. "Not an event," commented Talleyrand, "more a news-item."[58]

It was Charles-Maurice Talleyrand (1754–1838), once Bonaparte's Foreign Minister, who had been instrumental in securing the eclipse of his dynasty and, financed with £10,000 of British secret service funds, the restoration of the Bourbons.[59] After Waterloo, the Allied armies re-entered Paris in the last week of July 1815 and commenced a lengthy occupation. The return and defeat of Bonaparte had in some ways simplified matters and allowed the victorious powers to tie up all the loose ends of a European peace settlement. We must now look back a little and see how that settlement came about. It was important because it became one of the foundations of the modern world and was, in its own way, among the most successful and durable peace treaties in history.

In the aftermath of the Battle of Leipzig in autumn 1813, four great powers were hounding Bonaparte to destruction. Of these, Britain was the only one not interested in Continental acquisitions. What she wanted was a balance of power in Europe to guarantee a peaceful background to her expanding trade. The Royal Navy could look after the rest of the world. By balance, Britain meant two strong German powers, Prussia and Austria, both to deter France from further wars of conquest, and to counter Russia, whose forces were now in central Europe, and a France cut down to her prewar frontiers and in particular excluded from Belgium, which Britain wanted to be part of an enlarged Holland. During the long wars, Britain had made conquests all over the world. But she was prepared to hand most of them back to get the kind of European settlement which guaranteed a long peace. These notions were based upon the "scheme" drawn up by William Pitt, then Prime Minister, as long ago as 1804, but since updated by Castlereagh, now Foreign Secretary. In his "Memorandum to the Cabinet, 26 December 1813," Castlereagh suggested a general alliance of the victorious nations should be agreed on balance-of-power lines, subject to such safeguards as the guaranteed independence of Spain and Portugal and of Holland-plus-Belgium. Of her conquests, Britain was to keep the Cape of Good Hope (but pay Holland £2 million for it), Malta, Mauritius, Guadeloupe and two other West Indian islands, plus Heligoland (taken from the Danes). All the rest, including the whole of the Dutch East Indies, would be restored. This was a considerable concession, since the worth of the restored colonies was over £75 million annually (£31,048,000, French; £39,157,000, Dutch; £5,014,000, Danish).[60]

Two days after his memorandum had been approved by the cabinet, Castlereagh left for the Continent to represent British interests in the concluding stages of the fighting and at the subsequent peace congress. Accompanied by Fred Robinson, MP, and (as far as the Hague) by his wife, he traveled through the middle of one of the coldest winters ever recorded. The Thames was frozen over, and sheep were roasted whole on the ice. The Channel was enveloped for days on end in frozen fog. The Foreign Office party was not large—Joseph Planta, a senior official, and two clerks. There were four coaches in all, and the cost to the taxpayer was £10,546. Once Lady Castlereagh had been left behind, the men traveled without a pause, except to eat and change horses, sleeping in the carriage. "Robinson and I," Castlereagh wrote to his wife, "have hardly seen any other object other than the four glasses of the carriage covered with frost which no sun could dissolve, so that we were in fact imprisoned in an Ice House for days and nights, from which we were occasionally removed into a dirty room with a black stove, smelling of tobacco-smoke or something worse." Under his traveling cloak he wore a blue winter coat, red breeches and jockey boots, with a gold-banded fur cap on his head. We have a vignette of him, in the courtyard of a chateau, snatching a quick lunch: He propped his plate on the luggage-rumble of the carriage and stood on tiptoe to eat a sausage of partridge and sip a glass of champagne.[61]

Castlereagh was 44 when he set off to settle the fate of Europe. His father was born an Ulster squire and head of the local dissenting interest, not at all a grandee by the standards of the English ruling class. But, like the Habsburgs, he rose by judicious marriages: first to a daughter of the Marquess of Hertford, one of the richest men in England, then to a daughter of Marquess Camden, a Lord Chancellor. In due course he became a Marquess himself. Castlereagh's half brother and successor married a millionairess, the Vane-Tempest heiress, so that by the mid-1820s, in the space of half a century, the Vane-Tempest-Stewarts, Marquesses of Londonderry, had become one of the richest and loftiest families in the kingdom.

There were plenty of brains in the family and much artistic talent. Castlereagh was always cleverer than he liked to appear and, thanks to his stepgrandfather, Lord Camden, was well educated at St. John's, Cambridge. He was deeply musical and played the cello with distinction. In 1789, when he was only 20, his father paid out £60,000 to win him a contested seat in County Down against the great Downshire interest. This was in the old, corrupt Irish House of Commons. A decade later Castlereagh was instrumental in pushing through the Act of Union, whereby, as he put it, the British government, by distributing money and honors, "bought out the fee simple of corruption," abolished the Irish parliament and united the two kingdoms. He meant it for the best, believing union would be rapidly followed by Catholic Emancipation—which he favored all his life—the modernization of Ireland and the end of Irish poverty, among the worst in Europe. In fact, it merely opened another epoch of Irish misery and discontent.[62]

Castlereagh seems to us a mysterious figure because contemporaries give two conflicting accounts of him. To radical intellectuals, he was by far the most hated, because most formidable, figure in the Liverpool government. Shelley poured his vitriol on Castlereagh in "The Masque of Anarchy" and Byron repeatedly abused him in private letters and public verse, as, for instance, in the "epitaph" he sent Thomas Moore on 14 September 1820: "Posterity shall ne'er survey / A monument like this; / Here lie the bones of Castlereagh; / Stop, passer-by, and piss."[63] But neither Shelley nor Byron ever met him. Nor did his other abusers, such as Godwin, Hazlitt, Leigh Hunt and Charles Lamb. Outwardly, Castlereagh seemed reserved, even chilly, especially with strangers. But those who saw behind the mask found a delightful person. The Irish nationalist writer Sidney Owenson, later Lady Morgan, had been brought up to regard him as a monster. When she actually got to know him, staying at the Marquess of Abercorn's house, Stanmore Court, just outside London, she found him "one of those cheerful, lovable, give-and-take persons who are so invaluable in villa life. . . . His implacable placidity, his cloudless smile, his mildness of demeanour, his love of music, his untunable voice and passion for singing all the songs in the *Beggar's Opera,* and the unalterable good humour . . . rendered him most welcome in all the circle."[64] Mrs. Arbuthnot, on whom he called every day during the parliamentary season, found him kind, funny, sensitive, highly intelligent and one of the best companions in the world.[65]

Castlereagh was not without steel and could be very determined, even ruthless, when he felt he had to defend a principle. One such was loyalty and fair dealing between members of the same administration. He rightly saw George Canning as a contender with himself for the mantle of Pitt, and clearly both were jealous of each other. But in 1809, when Canning was Foreign Secretary and Castlereagh Secretary for War, what led to their duel was Castlereagh's well-founded belief that Canning was intriguing both to have him replaced and to torpedo the Walcheren Expedition the cabinet had backed and of which he was in charge. This went against all his notions not only of how a cabinet should be run but of honor itself. Hence his angry letter to Canning on 19 September: "You continued to sit in the same cabinet with me, and to leave me not only in the persuasion that I possessed your confidence and support as a colleague, but you allowed me . . . in breach of every principle both public and private, to proceed in the Execution of a new enterprise of the most arduous and important nature, with your apparent concurrence and ostensible approbation." The letter ended in a challenge, and the duel took place the next morning. The first shots both missed; in the second exchange, Canning was wounded "in the fleshy part of the thigh." The episode reflected badly on both men, and in Castlereagh's case hinted at the hysteria, under pressure, which was

to lead to his suicide in 1822. The Whig *Morning Chronicle* observed
two days later: "To suppose it possible, after the disgusting exhibition
they have made, to form out of their dispersed and disorderly ranks a
government that could stand, is the height of absurdity"—an illustration of the unreliability of newspaper prophecy, since the Tory administration carried on for another 21 years.[66] But it is significant that the
House of Commons, a good collective judge of character, did not hold
the challenge against Castlereagh, believing him to have been wronged,
and though Canning was easily the best speaker in the House and
Castlereagh often halting and almost incoherent, there was never any
question which of the two members of Parliament all parties preferred.
They respected Castlereagh for his courtesy, even to the most tiresome
Members, his fair dealings, his sincerity and, not least, for his truthful-
ness. The respect thus won was unquestionably the source of his immense parliamentary power during these times.

It also explains his diplomatic success. Even John Quincy Adams,
who discovered reasons for hating every Englishman he met, gave
grudging approval to Castlereagh. Caulaincourt, who had lengthy
negotiations with him 1813–14, found him "obliging, positive and
frank. He kept his word to me in everything." But most important of
all was the impression he made on Metternich. The first meeting of the
two men in January 1814 at the Three Kings Inn in Basel was a complete success, the foundation of a friendship which lasted until Castlereagh's death. As Metternich put it in a letter to his "serious" mistress, Wilhelmine, duchess of Sagan: "I cannot praise Castlereagh
enough. We get on as if we had passed our lives together." And later:
"Castlereagh behaves like an angel."[67] From their first conversation
together, the two men found they shared a similar view of Europe: a
region where peace was preserved by a careful balancing of interests,
and where no one power was ever in a position to act in an overbearing
way toward others.

This friendship was of great historical importance—the personal
element which made the success of the Congress possible. Their amity
was in itself odd. The two men were very different. Castlereagh could
be flirtatious with ladies, in an unpushy way, but at heart he was
strait-laced and a thorough Ulster Protestant. His devotion to Lady
Castlereagh, who soon joined him, was marked, and in Vienna, the
frivolous townsfolk—"Utterly frivolous!" as Beethoven put it—were
amazed to hear that, every Sunday morning, Castlereagh and his entire
family, staff, colleagues and servants, would gather in the drawing
room at 30 Minoritenplatz, his official residence, to sing hymns to a
harmonium.[68]

Metternich, by contrast, had no religious sense, other than a preference for Catholicism as the faith of the old order, and he was a lifelong
womanizer. Charles Nesselrode, the chief Russian negotiator, put it
romantically: he was "almost always in love"; Sir Edward Cooke, head
of the British Foreign Office, took a sterner view, pronouncing him
"intolerably loose and giddy with women." In this sense he was always
a security risk. Even more odd, his affairs were usually with the wives
of important personages, whose anger could do Austria incalculable
harm. As we have noted, while Austria was reeling and almost defenseless, Metternich had competitive affairs with the wives of two of Bonaparte's most powerful commanders, one of the women being the then-
Emperor's own adored youngest sister. The other, Laura Junot,
recorded in her memoirs that he loved "playing the Grand Gentleman
at his most elegant," dressing up happily in the magnificent red cloak
with black facings of a Knight of Malta. He adored parties, fine carriages, masked balls, assignations. She said that all his romances were
"dampened by sentimental tears"—he was a tall, handsome, blue-eyed
blond, curly haired, excessively vain German—and liked secret dashes
in hired cabs, rendezvous in ghostly grottoes and moonlight scampering
in and out of upper-storey windows. He was of the Gothic-minded
generation for whom Jane Austen wrote *Northanger Abbey* in 1798–99.
He had, it was said, a particular weakness "for Russian ladies with
soulful countenances."[69] One such was Katarina Bagration, daughter of
the great Russian general mortally wounded at the Battle of Smolensk.
Metternich had an illegitimate child by her. This affair was a source of
annoyance to Tsar Alexander I, who also loved Katarina, but did not
enjoy her favors until Metternich had lost interest; the irritation was all
the greater because by then Metternich had a new mistress, the clever
and bossy Duchess of Sagan, whom the Tsar had sought in vain. The
Tsar, who was also arrogant, and vindictive as well, hated being sexually upstaged by the mere servant of a fellow emperor.

"Confidential servant" is a better description. Francis II always
followed Metternich's advice. But the Habsburgs demanded subservience from even their most exalted ministers, and Metternich could
cringe and fawn appropriately before his master. By such methods he
became one of the longest-serving chief ministers in history, moving
into his official residence in Vienna, the Ballhausplatz, on 28 November
1809, and not leaving it until he was chased out by the mob in March
1848. Metternich was a conservative (like Castlereagh) rather than a
reactionary. He had in fact been taught by a radical tutor and attended
the free-thinking Strasbourg University. He supported the abolition of
the feudal dues paid by the peasants and favored streamlining the

absurdly centralized administrative machinery of the Habsburg state, which went back to the 16th century. But, like many other men of his age, his political thinking had been indelibly marked by witnessing revolutionary excess. Lord Liverpool had been present at the storming of the Bastille and had never forgotten it. Metternich had a similar experience the same year, as he recorded, characteristically, in his memoirs: "Surrounded by a number of uninteresting persons, who called themselves the people, I was present at the plundering of the Town Hall in Strasbourg by a drunken mob."[70] Later his own estates, and those of his wife, had been ravaged, confiscated, restored and ravaged again, and he had seen his country humiliated, ransacked, scorched and impoverished by revolutionary zealots and conquerors. He was not against constitutions, provided they were of organic growth and time honored, like Britain's, but he thought they were not for export. He wanted a quiet life, in which all, of whatever degree, from emperors to peasants, were secure in their own possessions and content with them, not seeking to aggrandize themselves at the expense of their neighbors. Kings should be satisfied with their frontiers, stick to their bargains, concentrate on keeping the show on the road. He thought nationalism a great evil and an unnecessary one. He was not even sure there was such a thing as a "nation." Language, race and sentiment did not, in his view, necessarily produce unity. Experience showed, he argued, that most men and women were more likely to be happy, in practice, under a hereditary sovereign who honored his obligations and their ancient rights than in a unitary monoglot state with a constitution drawn up on abstract principles and under a government claiming to be "the will of the people"—that is, an authoritarian dictatorship. But Metternich was not a theorist, even of monarchy. He was an empiricist, who accepted realities and was willing to compromise. What he wanted, above all, was a stable order that worked. And on that point he and Castlereagh, while differing on many detailed matters, saw eye to eye.

For dynastic reasons Metternich had been slow to abandon the Bonapartes. But the British would have none of it. "You can scarcely have an idea," Liverpool wrote to Castlereagh on 12 February 1814, "how *insane* people in this country are on the subject of any peace with Bonaparte"; and Stratford Canning added: "The Methodists and the women are particularly warlike."[71] But once the Bonaparte option had been ruled out and opinion had moved in favor of what the British had believed, all along, to be the obvious and simplest solution, the restoration of the Bourbons, the Castlereagh-Metternich axis was transformed into a tripartite union of reasonable men by the arrival on the scene of Talleyrand.

Talleyrand was fifteen years older than Castlereagh and twenty years older than Metternich, having been born in 1754 and seen much more of the world and its miseries than either. A streak of ineradicable bitterness ran through his entire life. Though the eldest son of well-to-do noble parents, he had been boarded out as a tiny child to a poor family in the Paris suburbs, where an accident lamed him permanently. His parents thereupon disinherited him in favor of his younger brother. Such a decision was by no means unusual in an age which still respected the notion of the Book of Leviticus that those destined for high service must be perfect in body—that was one reason why Byron was so ashamed of his twisted foot and took such pains to conceal it. There was also the practical consideration that the eldest son of a landed house must see military service. So Talleyrand was stripped and sent into the church, and though family influence got him benefices and a bishopric (of Autun), he hated the cloth and unfrocked himself at the earliest possible moment.[72] Under the Revolution and Empire he was in turn a member of the Estates General, a diplomat in London, an exile in the United States, a political conspirator under the Directoire, an adviser to Bonaparte first as Consul then as Emperor, becoming Foreign Minister, Vice-Grand elector, and Prince of Benevento. He amassed an immense fortune, and many useful contacts, by corruptly serving the interest of foreign governments. From 1807 he increasingly opposed Bonaparte's expansionary plans and transferred his allegiance to the Bourbons. When Bonaparte fell, it was part of Britain's bargain with Louis XVIII that Talleyrand, known as a man with whom sensible business could be done, should be in charge of French foreign policy.

Talleyrand had a curiously pretty face, and many women slept with him not just for his money. He was happier with them than with men, but not enthusiastic about either sex; and happiest of all with his chef, with whom he spent a full hour each day, planning meals down to the last sauce.[73] It must be said that, excommunicated but not released from his vows of celibacy, he married his low-born mistress, Mrs. Grand, though to do so was directly contrary to his interests. But in general he was mercenary, worldly, mendacious, treacherous and without scruples. In 1807 Bonaparte called him, in front of the entire court, *"merde en bas de soie"* ("silk-stockinged excrement"). Sainte-Beuve, in his brilliant essay on Talleyrand, wrote of the agonizing conflict he experienced between his admiration for his work and contempt for his character.[74] Most men hated or despised him. But they used him. As Metternich himself said: "Such men as M. de Talleyrand are like sharp-edged instruments with which it is dangerous to play. But for great evils drastic remedies are necessary and whoever has to treat them should not be afraid to use the instrument which cuts the best."[75]

Talleyrand was lazy; many of his official letters were not even dictated but written by a confidential clerk, then amended. But his mind indeed had a cutting edge. As Wellington said, at dinner he would not bother to talk most of the time, "and then suddenly he says something you remember all your life." What made him particularly valuable at the peace talks was his realistic view of France's requirements. He hated enthusiasm and its invariable consequence, excess. He said to his clerks: "*Surtout, messieurs, pas trop de zèle*" ("Above all, don't be too keen"). Bonaparte had brought himself and France to ruin because he had been too greedy for territory and power. Talleyrand fought brilliantly for France's essential interests, the frontiers and status with which she had begun the long struggle. But he asked for no more. He thus stood for the principle of moderation, alongside Castlereagh and Metternich, and upheld the aim, as they did, of a treaty which would prove durable and promote a long peace precisely because it left no grievances crying to heaven for vengeance.

There was a fourth significant figure at the talks, a loose cannon on the deck: Tsar Alexander I (1777–1825). He was 37 when the peace negotiations began and had been Autocrat of All the Russias since 1801, when his father, the mad Paul I, had been murdered, a crime of which Alexander may have had some knowledge and which certainly caused him uneasiness all his life. Alexander was notably clever, at a superficial level, and he suffered from that curse of the pre-Revolutionary age, a crypto-radical tutor. All his life he was devising schemes for reform, which he eventually abandoned or reversed, but which caused a great deal of trouble in the meantime. He feared he would go mad like his father. Others thought so too. Bonaparte said it would be difficult to find a sharper fellow: "But there is something missing. I have never been able to discover what it is"; he was "a decadent Byzantine" and, in reference to his favorite actor, "A Talma of the North." Talleyrand said darkly: "He is not for nothing the son of Paul I." The British ambassador in Saint Petersburg, Lord Walpole, reported: "The great oddness of the Emperor was suspected at a very early age, and medical men now here were brought over on that account."[76] But insanity was probably not his problem. Vicomte Chateaubriand was nearer the truth when he called him "a strong soul and a weak character—too strong to employ despotism, too weak to establish liberty." Metternich too saw him as essentially a lightweight: "Moving from one form of worship to another, from one religion to another, he stirred up everything, built nothing: everything about him was on the surface."[77]

However, in theory at least, in 1814–15 Alexander was the most powerful man on the Continent, with an enormous if ill-disciplined army which had fought its way right across Europe. In one mood he liked to present himself as a simple soldier: "I hate civilians. I am a soldier. I only like soldiers." He dressed in uniform: big epaulettes to conceal sloping shoulders; a vast green hat worn sideways like Wellington, with cock-feathers; a broad black belt; huge boots on his enormous feet, decked with solid gold spurs. But however he liked to think of himself, he was not the military type. After Austerlitz he had panicked. When Bonaparte invaded Russia he had stayed at his villa near Saint Petersburg during all the excitements of Borodino and the burning of Moscow, emerging only after the French were well and truly retreating. Nor was it true, as he claimed, that he was the inventor of the scorched-earth tactics which starved the Grande Armée: it was General Kutuzov who had won the war. In another mood Alexander was a man of the spirit. We will come to his religious manias in due course, but here it is appropriate to point out that he was also a man of the flesh, though perhaps he was more at home as a procurer or a voyeur than a seducer. Sir Thomas Lawrence, an assiduous collector of gossip during his lengthy portrait sittings of the great, said that the Tsar had helped Caulaincourt, when he was Bonaparte's ambassador in Saint Petersburg, to seduce the wife of a respectable married woman by posting her husband, a general, to Moscow.[78] And there was a curious episode in the Palais Palm, during the Congress, when the Tsar and a pretty Austrian countess had an argument about who could undress faster, a man or a woman. They went off to a bedroom to put it to the test, and she won. This episode scandalized the Papal Nuncio: "This is the kind of man by whom the world is governed—turning the palace of the emperors into a brothel."[79]

In essence, however, Alexander was a pseudo-intellectual. He corresponded with Thomas Jefferson about adapting American institutions, including the federal system, for Russian use. Nothing came of it. He toyed with various ideas produced by the French, but the only one which was realized was his creation, in 1802, of the MVD, an authoritarian instrument for internal control based on the Bonapartist Ministry of Police.[80] When the French front collapsed in 1814 he made a beeline for Paris, with all kinds of constantly changing ideas about who should occupy the vacant throne: Marie-Thérèse as regent, the King of Rome, the Duc d'Orleans (who finally got it in 1830), and Bernadotte. To propitiate and control him, Talleyrand invited him to put up, with his guard of gigantic Cossacks, at his house in the rue St Florentin. There, the Tsar lived on the first floor, while Talleyrand, as Vice-Grand Elector, summoned the senate, under his chairmanship, on the ground floor and in due course appointed Louis XVIII king, the Tsar meekly assenting. A clever, patient man did not find him hard to manage.

In the late spring of 1814, having settled Louis back on his throne, and as a preliminary fiesta to the peace conference arranged in Vienna, the potentates of Europe moved to London. Francis II refused to go: he did not wish to leave his seal collection and had no desire to be upstaged by the Tsar. But the rest went. It is odd to think of the Russian Autocrat being the hero of British progressive opinion, but so it was, his reputation as a reformer having preceded him. The Whigs, in particular, were anxious to fête him, and gave the nod to their section of the London mob. But some grandees in the old Whig tradition of antimonarchism did not like the junketings at all. From London, Lord Grenville wrote to his cousin, the Marquess of Buckingham, in his palace at Stowe: "We are full of very ridiculous preparations for very foolish exhibitions of ourselves to foreign sovereigns (if they do come here) in that character which least of all becomes us—that of courtly magnificence. Our kings never have, and I hope never will be able, to come near their neighbours in that respect."[81] Those remarks are a reminder that Britain was not a monarchy in the Continental sense, but more a constitutional oligarchy with a tolerated, titular sovereign.

The influx was preceded by the arrival, on 31 March, of the Tsar's sister, the Grand Duchess Katerina, a small, ugly, squat-nosed widow, full of mischief and malice. She had crossed the Channel in the *Jason* frigate, but in London she declined royal hospitality on the unspoken grounds that the Regent was a profligate man living apart from his wife. She had Princess Lieven, wife of the Russian ambassador, book her a floor of the new Pulteney Hotel in Piccadilly, at a cost of 210 guineas a week. She had an ill-timed meeting, on the stairs of that establishment, with the Prince Regent, who had called on her before she changed from her traveling clothes, and thereafter she was out to make trouble. She made a point of receiving all the leaders of the Opposition at the Pulteney, and the Lievens had great difficulty preventing her from infuriating the Regent by calling on his estranged wife, the Princess of Wales. A dinner the Regent gave for her at Carlton House turned into a disaster. She forced him to stop the band playing, on the grounds that "music makes me vomit," had an edgy conversation with him on the duties of spouses, then lapsed into obstinate silence. She then complained to her brother that the Regent was ill-bred, had tried to tell her dirty stories, and had "a brazen way of looking where eyes should not go"—all most improbable, since the one thing that could be said for the Regent was that he had admirable manners for formal occasions. Worst of all, she persuaded the Tsar to turn down the Regent's invitation to stay at St. James's Palace. Instead he joined her at the hotel.[82]

Alexander, King Frederick William and Metternich arrived in Dover at 6:30 P.M. on 6 June. The Whig Opposition were determined to exalt the Tsar at the expense of the Regent, who had not brought them into office when he at last had the power to do so. They had their mob ready when Alexander reached the Pulteney and appeared on its balcony at 2:30 P.M. on Tuesday. There were deafening huzzahs which could be heard in Carlton House, where the Regent was plucking up his courage to venture out and pay the call protocol demanded. At 4:30 P.M., he was obliged to send the humiliating message: "His Royal Highness has been threatened with annoyance in the streets if he shows himself. It is therefore impossible for him to come and see the Emperor." So the Tsar went to Carlton House instead and afterwards pronounced his host "a poor prince." Thereafter it was downhill all the way.

The festivities continued for nearly three weeks, punctuated by Congreve's spectacular fireworks displays in Green Park. The Prussian king and his family behaved well. He had been reluctantly dragged from Paris, where he spent his afternoons sliding down the "Russian Mountains" at the Montmartre fun fair. But he soon found consolations in London's Vauxhall and Ranelagh. He had only one detective, who followed him at a discreet distance, and the way the London crowd pestered him made him, Creevey reported, "sulky as a bear." But his sons made themselves liked, going on unaccompanied walkabouts.

The Tsar, on the other hand, engaged in a campaign of calculated rudeness to his host, keeping him waiting, dining with Opposition leaders like Earl Grey and the Duke of Devonshire, uniting with the Princess of Wales at a musical gala at the King's Theatre on Saturday 11 June, and constantly walking in Hyde Park, something he knew the Regent would not dare. He went to the British Museum, the Royal Exchange, St. Paul's Greenwich (where he had a fish breakfast at the Star and Garter), Westminster Abbey, Frogmore, Hampton Court, Ascot Races and a Quaker meeting—the usual tourist circuit. On 12 June the circus went to Oxford, the Tsar staying at Merton, the Prussian King at Corpus, the Regent and Blücher at Christ Church. There, after dinner in the Hall, a drunken Blücher addressed the company in incoherent German, "which was immediately and eloquently translated into English by the Prince Regent."[83] This was the Regent's one trick of the visit and was spoiled by the Tsar leaving early to drive through the night to join his Whig friends at Lady Jersey's ball, where he danced from 2:30 till 6 A.M. The bottom was reached on 18 June at a 700-place Guildhall banquet, costing £20,000, which was for men only. The Duchess Katerina nonetheless insisted on going and again had the music silenced; indeed, she even tried to stop the band playing "God Save the King." This exasperated Lord Liverpool, who could be quite fierce when roused; he complained to Princess Lieven: "When folks don't know how to behave they would do better to stay at home and your duchess has chosen against all usage to go to men's dinners."[84] The Tsar was also offhand. Creevey wrote happily to his wife: "All agree that Prinny [the Prince Regent] will die or go mad. He is worn out with fuss, fatigue and *rage*."[85] But by this time public opinion had begun to swing against the Russian couple. Even Lord Grey came to the conclusion that the Tsar was a "vain, silly fellow." The London crowds, exceptionally well behaved according to the diarist Farington, continued to love the Cossack general, Hetman Platov, who spoke only Russian but had sensational moustaches and baggy breeches, and old Blücher, with his huge pipes and soft peaked cap, but they no longer turned out for the Tsar.[86] His departure on 27 June passed almost unnoticed. It was during this visit that Castlereagh and Metternich came to the conclusion that Russia and its Tsar were not to be counted on as positive, constructive allies in the peace settlement. They would reconstruct the European order with the Tsar if possible, but without him if necessary.

In the early autumn of 1814 the powers gathered in Vienna for the Congress, which opened formally on 1 November. During the fortnight before there were feverish multilingual preparations to settle procedure, precedence and protocol. Previous large-scale peace settlements in Europe—Cateau-Cambresis in 1559, Westphalia in 1648, Utrecht in 1713—had been bilateral or trilateral deals, mainly endorsing frontiers determined by force. Vienna was the first modern peace conference: an attempt not only to settle all outstanding matters throughout Europe and to have decisions reached endorsed by all its states, but to draw up, as it were, a constitution for the entire European community as a means to underwrite international law and so preserve peace on a permanent basis. It was in fact a very ambitious venture, adumbrating the Treaty of Versailles and the creation of the League of Nations in 1918–19. Its procedures became the pattern for all international conferences, and many of its rulings on protocol stand to this day.

Vienna was in some ways an unsuitable place for such a meeting.

The endless wars and occupations had made it a pauper city, characterized by hunger marches and soup kitchens. A low-cost, supposedly nourishing broth, devised by the famous philanthropist and busybody Count Rumford and called after him "Rumford Soup," was dispensed to the many homeless people and refugees. The paper currency was worthless. Vienna was still a fortress-city, with a huge glacis cutting off the ancient inner town from the rest, and within the center rents were already the highest in Europe, higher even than London.[87] The conference pushed them up further, for the influx of delegates and lobbyists was vast. Royalties alone included the Tsar and his empress, four kings, one queen, two crown princes, three grand duchesses, and three princes of the blood. Then there were 215 heads of princely families.

These strutting potentates, in their gorgeous uniforms, came as Blücher put it, "like peasants to a fair." "All Europe," said Metternich complacently, "is in my antechamber." He relished his role. "The best Master of Ceremonies in the world," the Tsar contemptuously called him, "and the worst minister."[88] Kings and princes brought thousands of horses with them, but the 1,400 Francis II maintained in his palace stables were also kept busy. Some of the delegations were enormous. Castlereagh's was modestly kept down to Sir Edward Cooke, Planta and the young men from the Foreign Office. But the Tsar, besides his own large entourage, employed in effect four teams, headed respectively by Charles Nesselrode, who was the official Russian Foreign Minister, Karl vom Stein, who dealt with German affairs, Pozzo di Borgo, who handled France, and Adam Czartoryski, his adviser for Poland; in due course he added a fifth, John Capodistria from Corfu, whom he made joint Foreign Minister—and all these he played off against each other, seeking to be his own Foreign Minister in practice. Talleyrand also brought a large collection of experts, plus some of the best chefs in France, and he hired one of Joseph Haydn's pupils, Sigismond Neukomm, to play the piano softly—background music, hours at a time— while he worked at his desk at the Kaunitz Palace in the Johannesgasse. He had his pretty 21-year-old-niece, the Comtesse de Perigord (later Duchesse de Dino), as his hostess, since his own wife was not considered *sortable* (the other ladies would not receive her or attend her receptions). A high moral tone was set by the papal delegation, led by Cardinal Consalvi. There was some buffoonery from the Sultan of Turkey's team, with the ferocious Mavrojeni Pasha in charge. But the chief butt of the Congress was Pedro Labrador, from Madrid, a caricature Spaniard who specialized in frantic rages, haughty silences and maladroit demarches—"The most stupid man I ever came across," said Wellington, an experienced judge of difficult *hidalgos*. Rivaling him

was Admiral Sir Sidney Smith, the hero of the Siege of Acre, who was
the self-appointed representative of the anti-slave-trade lobby, but who
wearied the salons with his endless accounts of his victory and was
known as "Long Acre." Other lobbies included the Jewish elders, the
German publishing trade, who wanted an international copyright
agreement, the dispossessed German princes, the knights of Malta,
Swabia and the Wetterau—all wearing their special uniforms—and the
Association of Rhine Navigators.

Most of these bodies were dealt with by forming a series of special
committees, on House of Commons lines. To these were added, at
Castlereagh's suggestion, a Statistical Committee—to discover the
exact size of the populations being exchanged and partitioned—and a
Drafting Committee under the Congress Secretary, Friedrich von Gentz
(1764–1832), a Silesian pupil of Immanuel Kant, who had been Metternich's secretary since 1812. The last fortnight before the opening was
a frantic rush to settle how the Congress was to work. For the first time
the notion of Great Powers as opposed to Small Powers was formally
defined—a principle resurrected in the United Nations Security Council
130 years later. The idea was that the four victorious powers, Russia,
Prussia, Austria and Britain, would form this steering group. But on the
day before the Congress opened, 30 September, Talleyrand, by some
adroit maneuvering, insinuated France into the group, making it the Big
Five.[89] This made a sensible peace possible, for two reasons. First, it
undermined the idea that the Congress was a meeting of victors and
vanquished—the fatal distinction which made Versailles a failure in
1918—or of legitimate and "usurper" states. In fact, only Britain had
stuck to the principle of legitimacy throughout the two decades 1793–
1813. All the rest had done deals with Bonaparte at some time or other.

One of Talleyrand's aims was to rescue Saxony, Bonaparte's most
faithful ally, from dismemberment or extinction. When the Tsar protested that its king, the pathetic Frederick-Augustus, had committed
"treason to the common cause," Talleyrand replied icily, and with
telling effect, "Treason, Your Majesty, is a question of dates"—a reference to Tilsit and Erfurt, where Alexander had danced to Bonaparte's
tunes. Talleyrand had been present, privy to the secrets of both sides,
and knew exactly the extent of Alexander's own treason to the common
cause.

The second reason why France's elevation was helpful was that it
added a third, powerful party to the forces of moderation represented
by Castlereagh and Metternich. Castlereagh wanted, if possible, a
treaty without losers. Of course, there had to be some losses. Saxony

was an unavoidable loser and in the end saw two-fifths of its territory swallowed by Prussia. The other two losers were Poland and Italy.

Poland and France had been allies ever since Louis XV had married the daughter of the last truly Polish king, for whom France had provided, as a capital in exile, the city of Nancy, which he had superbly adorned. Metternich said he hated Paris because it "swarms with Polish Frenchmen and French Poles." Bonaparte had built up Poland as a military satellite of France, strategically placed between his three main opponents. The three now insisted on repartitioning her, but the actual frontiers were determined—as happened again in Eastern Europe in 1945—by the brutal fact of Russian occupation. The Tsar told Castlereagh, grimly, that he had 500,000 men there and that they "occupied every town and village."[90] Alexander played with the idea of creating his "own" Poland, as Bonaparte had created the Grand Duchy of Warsaw, and even wrote to the leading English political theorist, Jeremy Bentham, asking him to draw up a constitution for the new state. But this was just his pseudo-intellectual nonsense. His love for the Poles was not increased by the fact that, during the Congress, Czartoryski (the Tsar's adviser for Poland), with typical Polish imprudence, was having an affair with the Tsarina. The fact is, Alexander was determined to hang onto every inch of Poland he already occupied, with Prussia and Austria unwilling to let him drag off the carcass whole. Prussia was subservient to Russia throughout this period and settled for its Saxon gains. But Metternich fought hard for eastern Galicia, on Austria's behalf, provoking the Tsar into losing his temper. "You are the only man in Austria who would dare to oppose me in such rebellious terms." Metternich told Francis II that the Tsar was becoming "just like Bonaparte," and the Tsar complained to Francis about Metternich's language and suggested he should be dismissed. Francis merely remarked that it was best to "leave such matters to the Foreign Ministers"—negotiations, he implied, were not for sovereigns.[91] This was another step in the decline of Alexander's influence.

The fate of the third loser, Italy, was determined in practice by the same factor which operated in Poland—troops on the ground. Bonaparte had appealed strongly to the spirit of Italian nationalism, as the opening of the great novel by Stendhal (Marie-Henri Beyle, 1783–1842), *La Chartreuse de Parme*, published in 1839, eloquently testifies. The British had also favored constitutionalism, and in the early months of 1814, the British Minister on the spot, greatly exceeding his instructions, had actually called on the Italians to rise in defense of their liberties. He had promised the Genoese, for instance, the return of their ancient independence (26 April 1814). But Britain was not in a position to deliver Italian independence, unless the Italians themselves took it. A Milanese mob had tried to seize power on 20 April. But the Austrian army retook the city and spread all over Lombardy. The Habsburgs had ancient claims all over Italy but when a delegation of Italian nationalists came to see Francis II during the Congress he simply told them: "You belong to me by right of conquest." Metternich insisted Italy was not a nation but a collection of cities. Some belonged to Savoy, some to the Pope, some to Naples—and some to Austria. Indeed, he said, Austria was more than a city owner, since it had a right to Lombardy, an ancient kingdom "whose spirit was being rekindled." This was non-sense but during the summer there had been nothing to stop Francis II being proclaimed King of Lombardy (12 June) and formally annexing it, and in due course the Congress accepted the *fait accompli*.

The best the British could do was to build up the position of the House of Savoy by giving it, among other territories, Genoa. The British thus backed the eventual winner in the long struggle for a united, independent Italy, which culminated in the 1860s; but at the time it was realpolitik rather than justice. When the fate of Genoa was debated in the Commons, 13 February 1815, Samuel Whitbread, for the Opposition, launched a savage attack on Castlereagh, on high moral grounds, for giving the famous republic to a monarchy "equally imbecile as it is corrupt." He added that the Foreign Secretary should be "arraigned before the tribunal of the world"—the first mention in history of this imaginary body, usually called "the court of world opinion," and beloved of progressives from that day to this. Castlereagh, in reply, took the opportunity to restate the grand principle on which all his diplomacy was based: "The Congress of Vienna was not assembled for the discussion of moral principles but for great practical purposes, to establish effectual provisions for the general security."[92]

The strong position thus created for Austria in Italy was, in Castle-reagh's judgment, part of this "effectual provision" for a lasting peace. In the years 1805–12 Austria, which was no more than the Habsburg family firm, had almost disintegrated, leaving a gaping hole in the heart of east-central Europe. Castlereagh wanted a "big" Austria, which could field a powerful army, to keep the Russians not only out of central Europe but out of the Balkans, where Turkey was in danger of collapse. Hence the Austria which emerged from the Congress was almost double its previous size, annexing the Tyrol and Salzburg, Illyria in the Adriatic and nearly half Italy, since in addition to Lombardy and Venice, Francis, through his relations (including his daughter Marie-Thérèse) controlled various duchies. The Habsburgs now ruled more "souls" than any other family in Europe except the Romanoffs in Russia.

Prussia, as a fellow victor, was bound to be a gainer as well, and here again Castlereagh was content she should be. Holland was enlarged to take in Belgium, thus denying the French military access to the Flemish ports, those "daggers pointed at the heart of England." But to provide further security against French aggression, Castlereagh willingly brought Prussia to the Left Bank of the Rhine, for the first time. This was, as it turned out, a fateful step but it seemed to make good sense in 1814–15. With her gains in Saxony and the Rhineland, plus Westphalia and Swedish Pomerania, Prussia was now unquestionably the leading power in north Germany: a formidable barrier to France but, equally, a barrier to Russia, which had now pushed her "Oriental barbarism," as some saw it, to the western frontier of Poland.

These dispositions, producing a big Austria and a big Prussia, in effect dividing power in Germany almost equally between the Hohenzollerns and the Habsburgs, meant there was a fourth loser at the Congress, German nationalism. In the final stages of the struggle to overthrow Bonaparte, the German nationalist uprising had been as potent a factor as any other, and those who had participated in it naturally assumed its spirit would now be embodied in some kind of all-German federation. For Karl vom Stein (1757–1831), Bonaparte's bitterest German enemy, that meant a reconstitution of the Holy Roman Empire, which had been destroyed in 1806, in a modernized, constitutional form. His inspiration was the old Hohenstauffen Empire of the 10th to the 13th centuries but now endowed with formal guarantees of personal rights and public freedoms, a Diet representing all German landowners and their tenants as well as the cities, and an executive emperor who would collect taxes, run the administration, supervise central courts and command the army.[93] With the assistance of Tsar Alexander, to whom he had attached himself, he hoped to bring about this vision at Vienna.

But the forces arrayed against it were too great. Stein hated the petty German princes, seeing their sovereign pretensions as an enemy to German liberties and their collective weakness as an invitation to French invaders. But there were scores of them, all lobbying hard in Vienna. Moreover, there were big fish among the countless minnows. George III of England was also King of Hanover. The Danish king was Duke of Holstein. The Dutch king was Duke of Luxembourg. All these entities would, in effect, disappear in Stein's scheme or lose all their powers. Then again, who was to be emperor? Neither the emperor of

Austria nor the King of Prussia would allow the other to have the title, and both would unite to prevent it going to a third, who would inevitably eclipse their claims to speak for the Germans. Even Alexander soon lost interest in Stein's plan, seeing it to be impractical, and concentrated on his real object of hanging on to the maximum amount of Polish territory.

There was a feeling too among many sensible Germans that a united Germany would be too big for its own good—as indeed much of the 20th century was to prove. This attitude was well summed up by William von Humboldt (1767–1835), the Prussian diplomat and leading philologist, brother to the scientist Alexander von Humboldt. As adviser to the Prussian delegation, he argued strongly that Germany must be a confederation, not a unity. "One must never forget that the real purpose of the German confederation is . . . to ensure peace and to preserve the equilibrium of the Continent through natural gravity. It would be quite contrary to this purpose to introduce another collective state into the ranks of the European system, in addition to the bigger individual German ones. . . . No one could then prevent Germany, as Germany, from becoming another conquering state, a situation which no good German can want." He added that Germany "has derived great advantages in intellectual and scientific education from having no foreign policy"—if Germany acquired one, where would it lead her? Into the abyss? The truth, Humboldt hinted, was that Germany was too powerful to become united, a state like the others. It must be a European trustee: united for defense but not for expansion, devoting itself to science, education and progress.[94]

Metternich and the Prussian head of delegation, Prince Karl-August von Hardenberg (1750–1822), united behind this concept, and what indeed emerged was a loose, weak confederation of 34 sovereign princes and four free cities. They were all to work together "for the maintenance of the internal and external security of Germany, and the independence and inviolability of the Confederated States." There was indeed to be a federal diet, but one composed of officials nominated by the sovereigns. Constitutional rights, as such, were not mentioned; indeed, the Confederation was a perfect formula for conservative autocracy. Stein left the Congress in disgust once he knew he had lost the game, and before the Final Act was drawn up. The German nationalists despaired with him—as we shall see. Thus Germany emerged as two big states, balancing each other, with a weak *cordon sanitaire* of petty states between them. In fact the arrangement was bound, in the long run, to favor Prussia, which emerged not only as large but as largely German and was certain therefore to form the nucleus around which an eventual united Germany would cohere. Austria, on the other hand, now had a majority non-German population, her losses of German subjects compensated for by millions of Italians and Slavs. Her weakness, vis-à-vis pan-Germanism, was partly concealed by the fact that she was made president of the new Diet. But this was show. The reality was that frustrated German nationalists would now look to Berlin, not Vienna.

The "compensations" were carefully worked out down to the last "soul." It was Hardenberg, the Prussian, who insisted that all souls were equal; if Austria got so many Galician Poles, Prussia was entitled to an equivalent number of Rhineland Germans, since a Polish soul was worth, *sub specie aeternitatis*, as much as a German one. The Statistical Committee could work out the exact figures: thus were the tenets of medieval Christendom brought into the age of modern demography.

The real work was done by the Foreign Ministers during the morning sessions in Metternich's Ballhausplatz. The sovereigns met in the afternoon at the Hofburg Palace, most of them simply to confirm what their ministers had decided, Alexander, from time to time, to make trouble. But it was not all work. There was much praying: the Catholics crowding to the Karlskirche, south of the Vienna River, and Saint Stephen's Cathedral in the Inner City, to hear masses by Mozart and Salieri, the Protestants bawling out the metrical psalms in the embassy chapels. For the grandees, there was hunting, for stags, boar and hare, in the royal forests northwest across the Danube in Bohemia, and south east along the road to Hungary. There were gambling, tombolas, *tableaux vivants*, fake tournaments, balloon ascents, sleighing in the Wienerwald and parades in the Prater, where Francis II liked to stroll and talk in the Viennese dialect with the citizens—all this by day. At night there was more gambling, amateur theatricals, where plays by August von Kotzebue were staged, as in *Mansfield Park*, and professional performances in Vienna's two big "classical" theaters, the Leopoldstadt and the Burgtheater in the Inner City, the Theater an der Wien across the glacis, and others in the suburbs. The Wien specialized in spectacular scenery and effects—thunderstorms, cavalry charges, shipwrecks, battle scenes, and camels and even giraffes on stage, as well as horses and bears. There were balls and parties, coordinated by the hard-working Festivals Committee, under the enthusiastic supervision of Metternich himself. He darted about at night, from the big functions at the Ballhausplatz to the Palais Palm, where his current mistress, the Duchess of Sagan, and his former one, Madame Bagration, occupied confrontational wings, to his villa south of the glacis where he held private suppers.

Poor though it was, Vienna was well equipped for gaiety. There was, for instance, the Alollosaal, built in 1808. It had waterfalls, grottoes, a lake with swans, four "drawing rooms," which could accommodate 4,000 people; and above all, five ballrooms. Vienna was a dancer's paradise. Even the Castlereaghs took dancing lessons, though without much success. As with clothes and hairstyles, the kind of dance you practiced indicated your politics. The minuet stood for the ancien régime. In Washington they favored the cotillion, which was French and republican, at any rate not monarchical. Imperial Vienna had dropped the minuet—too old hat—but had produced its own extravaganza, new, exhilarating, daring, erotic and intensely athletic—the waltz. Vienna was a hive of buzzing composers who wrote for the ballroom—Muzio Clementi, the music boss of the city, and his pupils Cramer and Kalkbrenner; and Mozart's pupils Ebert and Hummel. Johann Nepomuk Hummel (1778–1837) had written the first waltz for piano, his Opus 27, in 1808; four years later, the new star from Silesia, Carl Maria von Weber (1786–1826) dashed off a brilliant series of six waltzes for Bonaparte's empress, Marie-Louise, and by the following year it was sufficiently established for Byron to write a satirical poem on the subject, The Waltz.[95] As he enviously noted, the intimate and close physical contact between the couple made it an entirely new kind of dance, a sexual break with the past. In Vienna there were dozens of waltz orchestras, led by the Michael Pamer band, which played at the largest of the Alollosaal's ballrooms, the Moonlight Hall—the feat there was to make a complete circuit, waltzing at top speed, eight times. This was something Metternich delighted in and was still young enough to do.

Then there was more substantial music, at the Opera House, where the new ballet Flore et Zephire was the star attraction, and in the dozens of churches and concert halls. There was an astonishing amount of new, high-quality music to be heard in Vienna in autumn and winter 1814. On 16 October, while the Congress was assembling, the choir of the Karlskirche gave the premiere of the first completed mass by Franz Schubert (1797–1828), a 17-year-old genius born in the northwest suburb of the city. The soprano solos were performed by a brilliant 14-year-old, Thérèse Grob. Schubert was in love with her and three days later, in a single afternoon, he wrote for her his first masterwork, Gretchen am Spinnrade, adapted from Johann Goethe's Faust.[96]

But the great man in Vienna was now Ludwig van Beethoven (1770–1827). He came from Bonn, was of Flemish descent, and had no time for the locals—"From the Emperor to the bootblack, all the Viennese are worthless"—but Vienna had a huge musical public as well as rich patrons.[97] Beethoven was the supreme musical innovator, one of the central pillars of the modern, and some of his music was repellent to conservatives. The final stages of the war had turned him into a popular, patriotic hero. To celebrate Wellington's decisive victory at Vitoria, he had written his Battle Symphony. It had received its first performance, in Vienna, in December 1813, with Salieri, Hummel, Spohr and other leading musicians taking part, playing the drums and directing the canonades. The same concert also saw the first performance of his magnificent Seventh Symphony. Two days before the Congress opened, on 28 October, the Opera House, by imperial command, gave a performance of *Fidelio* for the delegates and their wives, and on 29 November, with the conference in full swing, there was another Beethoven concert at the Hofburg, before both emperors and all the kings and princes. Indeed Beethoven had written a new work, *Chorus to the Allied Princes*, especially for the occasion, and a further topical item, his cantata *Der Glorreiche Augenblick*, "The Glorious Moment," had its first performance. To make up the bill there was the Battle Symphony and the Seventh Symphony again. Beethoven himself, "a short and stout figure," fairly deaf, conducted. Afterwards his great patron, the Russian Ambassador Count Andreas Razumovsky, and his pupil, the Archduke Rudolph, presented him to the sovereigns, who gave him purses of gold. Beethoven did not despise this overwhelming acclaim. "It is certain," he wrote, "that one writes most prettily when one writes for the public—and also rapidly." After the big concert he inserted a characteristic notice in the newspapers: "A Word to His Admirers. How often, in your chagrin that his depth was not sufficiently appreciated, have you said that Beethoven composes only for posterity! You have no doubt now been convinced of your error, even if only since the general enthusiasm aroused by his immortal opera *Fidelio!* The present finds kindred souls and sympathetic hearts for what is great and beautiful, without withholding its just privileges for the future!"[98] After the Christmas recess, Beethoven gave a further concert, this time a piano recital of his works, to celebrate the Tsarina's birthday on 25 January 1815, his last performance in public.

It is typical of the atmosphere of Vienna in winter 1814–15, indeed of Continental Europe in general at this time, that the secret police found it necessary to report extensively and repeatedly on attitudes toward Beethoven's new compositions and the musical taste of the Viennese public. It has been argued that there was a certain backhand merit in Stalin's attempts to censor and influence the works of Dmitri Shostakovich, Sergei Prokofiev, and Aram Khachaturian—at least it showed he took music seriously. The same could be said of Metter-nich's Vienna. "There are," one secret police report read, "two factions now forming, for and against Beethoven. In opposition to Razumovsky, Appolyi and Graft, who idolize Beethoven, there is a large majority of connoisseurs who do not want to hear anything composed by Herr van Beethoven."[99] The notion of a state political police, composed of plain-clothes officers operating in secret, was an importation from the totali-tarian system Bonaparte set up in France after his coup d'état of No-vember 1799. To have a secret police became, for the Habsburgs and for most European ruling houses who could afford one, the sign of a "modern" monarchy. Once the force was set up, it soon found enemies to observe. As early as 1803 Count Pergen, its head in Austria, warned Francis II of secret societies "dedicated to destroying the basic princi-ples of Christianity and monarchical government." He promptly re-ceived permission to monitor and act against all such types of conspira-tors, such as the Turnenbündler, the Illuminati, the Carbonari, the Burschenschaften and the Mazzinisti. Agents, often drawn from the impoverished upper classes, were known as *Vertraute höheren Standes*, and operated in cafés, restaurants, coffeehouses, private drawing rooms and banks. They rummaged, opened, bribed and steamed, to produce *Rapporte, Interzepte* and *Chiffons* (contents of wastepaper baskets). All prominent people were watched. Beethoven's conversation-books, which he used after he became totally deaf about this time, provide a curious record of the uneasy feeling the secret police generated: "An-other time—just now the spy Haenzl is here" (this in a café).[100]

The ubiquitousness of the Austrian police was well known. Since all mails were opened, Castlereagh used a team of King's Messengers to carry his dispatches home and his instructions back. They were dis-creet, resourceful men in black who suffered acute discomfort and often took grave risks to commute between the two capitals by the fastest route. All the indoor servants at the British delegation headquarters also had to be British—another taste of the modern world. But there were security lapses: not until three years later, in 1817, did the British discover that the Prussians had one of their ciphers. During the Con-gress, Baron Hager, who had succeeded Pergen as "president" of the Oberste Polizei and the Censur Hofstelle, worked night and day to have his reports ready for the Emperor each morning. Francis, who hated parties and left as early as he properly could, delighted in reading what had gone on. Much of the material was as trivial and inconsequential as a present-day gossip column: "In the evening [the king of Prussia] went out in civilian clothes with a round hat pulled down over his eyes; he had not returned at 10pm"; "Every morning a large block of ice is brought to the Emperor [of Russia], with which he washes his face and hands." The Habsburg family itself was included in the surveillance: the letters of both the Empress and her sister were opened, copied and resealed. But there is no evidence that Hager ever learned anything of importance by these methods. On the contrary, scraps of information were given undue significance precisely because they had been obtained in a furtive manner, and wrong inferences were drawn accordingly. Worse, the known existence of the system generated suspicion and impeded agreement.[101]

The real secret of the Congress did not remain one for long. On 3 January 1815 France, Britain and Austria drew up and signed an agreement to resist the Russo-Prussian hard line over Saxony and Poland. This "secret treaty" was a bit of a bluff to counter the bluffing of Alexander and Hardenberg. It became known—was, perhaps, deliberately leaked—and as a result the Eastern powers climbed down somewhat and an agreement was reached in February.[102] Six weeks later the escaped Bonaparte entered Paris and soon found a copy of the secret agreement in the Paris archives. He promptly sent it to Alexander. But the Tsar, who knew about it already in any case, was not to be taken in by so crude a ploy. He handed it back to Metternich with the words: "Let us kiss and let all be forgotten. Let us never mention this incident again but attend to more serious matters."

In fact the return of Bonaparte and his Hundred Days, far from disconcerting and dividing the Allies, served to unite them and speed up the work of the Congress. It meant, to Talleyrand's despair, that France got a poorer deal over her frontiers and lost most of the works of art Bonaparte had looted. In other ways it simplified matters. Murat, the King of Naples, who might otherwise have been left in possession of his kingdom, declared war against the Austrians on 30 March and called on the Italians to rise. He was defeated on 3 May by an Austrian army, which entered Naples three weeks later, thus ensuring that the kingdom was handed back to the Bourbons. The need to close ranks against Bonaparte also solved the "German problem" and agreement on the new *Diet* and much else was reached on 8 June. The next day, in the evening, all the decisions so far taken in Vienna were embodied in a draft final treaty, which was signed by all the Great Powers, plus Sweden, Spain and Portugal. The text, of 121 articles, then had to be copied out by hand for all the archives and for all the smaller powers to sign. This immense task, undertaken by Gentz's 26 secretaries, continued throughout the Waterloo campaign. It was finished only on the morning after the battle, while the wounded like Colonel Ponsonby were being carted to the dressing stations. On the evening of that day, from 9 p.m. till midnight, the minor powers and princes lined up to sign. It had been a weary nine months, with much pretentious theorizing. As Gentz put it: "I sensed as never before the futility of human endeavour, the failings of men who hold the fate of the world in their hands. . . . The fine-sounding nonsense of these gentlemen enveloped my mind in a fog of unreality."[103] But despite the "vaporizing," as Talleyrand called it, the agreement had a core of realism. In the end, all but the Pope and the Sultan of Turkey agreed to sign it. It proved durable. One of its main provisions, the incorporation of Belgium in the Netherlands, broke down in 1830. But the Franco-German settlements lasted till 1870. The European structure it created endured till 1914. It has shaped international meetings at every level up to the summit ever since.

The second overthrow of Bonaparte and the reoccupation of France meant that the scene of events now switched to Paris. Wellington, with his army, got there first and was soon installed in the Hotel de la Reynière, home of the banker Ouvrard. He was the man in charge and Britain was dominant during this phase of the peacemaking, which lasted 133 days and led to an Allied peace treaty with France on 20 November 1815. France lost some territory on the frontier, but Castlereagh vetoed the Prussian demand for Alsace-Lorraine. France also had to hand back some of her stolen art treasures to the Pope, the grand duke of Tuscany and the Dutch. She had to return to Venice its four bronze horses, which had been set up in the Place du Carrousel outside the Louvre Palace. When the workmen came to take them away there was a minor riot, in which British tourists joined in the hope of ripping off pieces as souvenirs. (This was an age in which Byron, of all people, carved his name—still to be seen—in the marble of the Temple at Sounion.) Further, an indemnity of 700 million francs was imposed and France had to accept (and pay for) an Allied occupying army for three years. The same day this new peace was sealed, representatives of the four great powers met again at Castlereagh's lodgings—Princess Pauline Borghese's superb house on the Rue St Honoré, which has been the British Embassy ever since—to sign a treaty of alliance. At Castlereagh's suggestion, Article VI provided for the four states to constitute a kind of security council which would meet from time to time to discuss "what would be most salutary for the repose and prosperity of nations and for the maintenance of the peace of Europe."[104] These conferences indeed took place: at Aachen, September–November 1818, which ended the occupation of France; at Troppau (modern Opava) in October–December 1820, which concerned itself with Italy; at Laibach (modern Ljubljana) the following January, and at Verona, September–December 1822, when Spain was the topic.

This "Congress System," admirable in principle, was unfortunately vitiated by an element of mysticism introduced by Tsar Alexander. And here we must pause to note that statesmen, however much they may think they are guided by the unalterable laws of realpolitik and national self-interest, are in fact as much influenced by cultural trends and fashions as everyone else. Castlereagh, Metternich, Talleyrand and Alexander lived in the same world as Beethoven and Byron, Turner and Victor Hugo, and felt the same intellectual breezes on their cheeks. During the long Revolutionary and Napoleonic wars, the civilized world had passed, by virtue of those strange but irresistible currents which determine cultural change, from the Age of Reason to the Age of Romanticism. During the years of fighting, misery and deprivation, the process was masked. In 1815, the transformation, almost complete, burst upon a society now at peace: that is one reason why I call this time the birth of the modern. It was not that men or women were less rational in 1815 than they had been in the 1780s; on the contrary, the world was every day being increasingly pushed, in practical matters, along the paths of scientific deduction and mechanical exactitude. Nor were they, in arrangements over marriage and money, for example, any more romantic; they were in fact the same mixture of hard-headedness and rashness they had always been. It was, rather, that they stressed different aspects of their behavior. In the 1780s it had been reason; now it was feeling.

In 1802 the Breton aristocrat François-René de Chateaubriand (1768–1848) had published a remarkable defense of the religious impulse, *Le Génie du christianisme,* which proved one of the most influential books of the new century. It originally included his autobiographical story *René,* published separately in 1805, which introduced to the world the brooding, melancholic, self-obsessed young man who was to be the emblem of the romantic movement, to inspire Byron and, through Byron's poetry, countless others. But *Le Génie* was more than that. It explained why, as the French themselves had discovered during the atheistic 1790s, religion was a necessary part of human life—and always would be so—why reason and the cold intellect were not enough, and why Blaise Pascal had been right to insist that "the Heart has its reasons which Reason knoweth not." There was a particular passage which struck home. Chateaubriand noted the extraordinary impact on the human senses of the sound of church bells heard from afar across the countryside, especially after a period when they had been long silent—the voice, as it were, of the deity speaking, and touching the hearts of ordinary men and women in a way no other sound could. The passage was apt, for at the time the book appeared Bonaparte was making the Republic's peace with the church, and the bells, long unlawful, could be heard again. In effect Chateaubriand was drawing attention to what had always been true but had never before been so clearly perceived: the centrality of the irrational.

By 1815 the cultural tide which the Breton Viscount was the first to take was sweeping all before it. Settling down on 8 August to begin *Persuasion*, Jane Austen, by training and inclination a model of sense rather than sensibility, nonetheless found herself creating a romantic heroine, Anne Elliot, whose intense feelings were her own. The following month, Tsar Alexander, who had read Chateaubriand's book with enthusiasm and had now drunk deep of the new romantic springs in Paris, drafted the text of a piece of romantic politics which became known as the Holy Alliance. He asked his fellow sovereigns—as persons, as "souls"—to sign a declaration that henceforth they would conduct their relations with each other "upon the sublime truths which the Holy Religion of Our Saviour teaches . . . the precepts of Justice, Christian Charity and Peace." These precepts "must have an immediate influence on the Councils of Princes and guide all their steps" so that all governments would henceforth behave as "members of one and the same Christian Nation."[105]

The proposal that kings should behave like Christians aroused, as might have been expected, much opposition. The Pope was outraged by this attempt of a Russian Orthodox schismatic to invade his spiritual province. The Sultan would take no guidance from an infidel. Wellington and Castlereagh laughed at what the latter called "this piece of sublime mysticism and nonsense" and promptly advised the Regent that he must on no account sign it as it was contrary to Britain's Protestant constitution. But Alexander was not deterred by such criticism, which he attributed to "the genius of evil." His mood was exalted. The intellectual atmosphere of Paris was exactly to his taste. There, the pseudoscientific theories of Franz Mesmer (1734–1815), who had experimented with the curative powers of magnets and the vivifying force of electricity, had finally taken over society, and in the salons people were "mesmerizing" each other by what they called "animal magnetism." A year later, by the shores of Lake Geneva, Mary Shelley was to write her tale of a man-monster brought back to life by huge electrical shocks, but in the meantime the Parisians were curing their migraines and *crises de foie* by using the pile-batteries recently introduced there by the Italian physicist Alessandro Volta (1745–1827) and "electrifying" each other. Every kind of occult gnosticism flourished at what the Parisians now called séances.[106]

Alexander had been moving in this direction for some time, especially since the French invasion of 1812 had caused a religious revival in Russia. He gave a ready ear to prophets and a readier one to prophetesses. Prince Golitsyn, whom Alexander had made Procurator of the Holy Synod, in effect Minister for Religious Affairs, got Bible mania in consequence and teamed up with the Grand Master of the Imperial Court, Koshelev—another religious dabbler—to promote the teachings of various fashionable religious figures, such as Saint-Martin, Lavater and Swedenborg. The two men founded the Russian Bible Society and induced Alexander to join and finance it. Some 189 "chapters" were set up throughout the Russian empire, and the Tsar forced the reluctant Metropolitans of Moscow and Kiev, plus other religious dignitaries, to serve on its committee—only the Jesuit Superior refused and was expelled accordingly. Bible reading among the Russian *muzhiks* produced ecstasies and sects: the Dukhobors who took it as their only guide in life, the Moloknants who would drink nothing but milk (like most English Methodists), and the Skoptsy or eunuchs, organized by a religious entrepreneur, Kondrati Selivanov, who induced high-society people to attend his gatherings. They also flocked to hear the Bavarian illuminist Jung-Stilling and the predictions of Madame Guyon, founder of Théologie Astrale. Alexander took an interest in all these activities and in the mystic freemasonry then fashionable, to which his two ministers had introduced him. He was particularly impressed by one of Selivanov's followers, Katerina Tatarinova, head of an ecstatic dancing community whose Bible readings induced rites similar to those of the whirling Dervishes. Katerina spun like a top in a white transparent chemise, then screamed out her prophecies to the goggling Tsar. By now an avid Bible reader, he asked her to explain the esoteric meanings of various passages.[107]

One which struck him, as he read Revelations while awaiting the outcome of the Hundred Days, was the verse: "And there appeared a great wonder in Heaven: a woman clothed with the sun." Lo and behold! the "woman" turned up at his headquarters at Heilbronn on 4 June 1815. She was Julie von Wietgenhof, a Latvian from Riga, who had married a diplomat called Baron Krudener. Madame Krudener had become a born-again Christian when a handsome, would-be seducer, who had bowed to her in the street, dropped dead instantly. She preached and prophesied, giving a fairly unsophisticated message: "Be filled with divine creations! Let the Life of Christ permeate your spiritual body!"[108] She had mystic views about the Russians, whom she regarded as "the sacred race" and "a simple folk who have not drunk the cup of iniquity," and she referred to Alexander as "the elect of God" and "a living preface to the sacred history which is to regenerate the world." It is not surprising that he had heard of her, and when she talked her way into his hotel—"Everything requires a certain amount of charlatanism," as she put it—he greeted her with pious joy and they spent several hours together, she ranting, he praying and weeping. She followed him to Paris and put up at the Hotel Monchenu, next door to his quarters in the Elysée Palace. He had a hole knocked in the wall which separated them, and they held nightly prayer-séances. The relationship was entirely chaste, since Madame Krudener was by now a portly, middle-aged woman with gray hair parted in the middle, pale skin and hollow eyes. Her influence reached a climax on 10 September 1815, when she was the Egeria at an impressive "Holy Review" of the Russian armies, held on the Plain of Vertus on the Upper Marne, in front of eight altars. Some 150 squadrons of cavalry, 600 guns and 100 battalions of infantry thundered past while the Tsar saluted her, in Sainte-Beuve's phrase, as "the Ambassadress of Heaven." In the evening the Tsar wrote to her: "This day has been the most beautiful in my life. My heart was filled with love for my enemies. I prayed with fervour that France might be saved."[109] It was at this point that he conceived the idea of the Holy Alliance.

The difficulty about an alliance based upon the personal oaths of princes is that it presupposes some ability on their part to make it succeed. It would be difficult to conceive of a less talented group of men than those who occupied the thrones of Europe in the years after Waterloo. Compared to, say, Frederick the Great and Catherine the Great, even Joseph II and George III, they were all nonenties, with the exception of Alexander, and he was a dilettante, a *flâneur*. The Regent had never done anything in his life, except collect things. He came to believe that he had taken part in the big cavalry charge at Waterloo, and his descriptions of it, listened to in embarassed silence by the court and ending with the appeal: "Wasn't it so, Duke?" always evoked Wellington's chilly response: "As Your Royal Highness has so often observed." Louis XVIII meant well, but was by now totally inactive, too stout to walk at all. Wellington said that when he presented Louis with the Garter and tied the ribbon round his calf, "it was like putting your hands round the waist of a young man." It might have been a different matter if Bernadotte had been brought in to run France but, in a diminished Sweden, he was very much at the periphery. The head of the House of Orange was industrious but small-minded. The House of Savoy was incorrigibly provincial, the Bourbons of Naples irredeemably stupid. Ferdinand VII of Spain was not the monster his enemies depicted—as we shall see—but he was that thoroughly ineffective type, the impoverished despot, and a remarkably large proportion of his time was spent raising tiny loans with which to pay his palace servants.[110] Francis II was more lazy than anything else, and the King of Prussia just tagged along behind the Tsar.

It was during this period that effective power, even in the monarchical despotisms, began to shift for good into the hands of the ministers. And men like Metternich were clearly going to play safe. He took the original text of the Tsar's manifesto, which Francis II was reluctant to sign as it stood—he felt, rightly, that politics and religion rarely mix well—and made significant alterations. He turned it into a political document condemning revolutions wherever they might occur, and reasserted the principles, which all Christian sovereigns were bound to uphold, of legitimacy, order and established law. The Holy Alliance thus became, in practice, not an idealistic, let alone a romantic, instrument of social improvement, but a bond by which the signatories agreed to combine to resist popular pressure for constitutions. As such, it was unacceptable to Britain, even to the more conservative Tories. Mrs. Arbuthnot, speaking for Castlereagh and Wellington, dismissed the Holy Alliance in her diary as "all sorts of wild schemes of establishing a general police all over Europe and sending the troops of one country to keep order in another; and any Englishman of good sense and conduct would have been able to show them the folly of such schemes."[111]

This aspect of the postwar system did not work, though it was tried in Spain and Italy, as we shall see. By the end of the 1820s it had broken down and been tacitly abandoned. While it lasted it was the golden age of the political police, who provided its underpinning. As Beethoven, who was shrewd about such things, pointed out, all this was the fault of the Revolution. "Before the French Revolution," his Conversation Book recorded, "there was great freedom of thought and political action. The Revolution made both the government and the nobility suspicious of the common people, and this has led by degrees to the present policy of repression." Police supervision was irritating as well as ridiculous. Joseph Blochlinger, the headmaster of the school attended by Beethoven's beloved nephew Karl, wrote in the Conversation Book, during the Laibach meeting: "The Congress is working on a law that will lay down how high birds may fly and how fast hares may run." August Kanne, editor of the *Allgemeine Musikalische Zeitung,* wrote in the Book that the police system produced economic crisis because it was designed to keep in the manner to which they were accustomed 38

courts, which meant "something like a million princes and princesses—
no wonder Germany is poor." But as Beethoven said, the actual effect
of the postwar repression on people's lives, even on the lives of writers
and artists, was minimal: "All over Germany things are exactly as they
were before the so-called democratic disturbances . . . The real scholar
and independent thinker was no more persecuted then than he is
now."[112]

There is another point, which students of the period have not
perhaps sufficiently stressed. The neologism *Zeitgeist* was much bandied about in the years after 1815. But what exactly was the "spirit of
the age"? Was it, as some contemporaries and many later historians
have supposed, a burning desire for reform? Did the writings of Byron
and still more Shelley thus incarnate it? If that was indeed the *Zeitgeist*,
why did it prove, in practice, so feeble a spirit? Granted the general
inefficiency of the various political police forces—for which the evidence is abundant—and granted the ramshackle nature of the repressive regimes, why did the forces which sought to overthrow them prove
so ineffective? Why were the German students and the Italian *carbonari*
and the Spanish liberals so easily dealt with? "We are many, they are
few," claimed Shelley. If so, why did the few find it so easy to hold the
many down? It may be, in fact—and close inspection of the evidence
seems to point this way—that the "many" failed because they were, in
fact, the "few." Behind the ostensible *Zeitgeist* pressing for change,
there was a hidden but more powerful *Zeitgeist* anxious for stability.
After two decades of wars and cruelty and privation, most people,
whatever their class, wanted to return to the civilized values and the
absence of violence which they, or their parents or grandparents, could
vaguely remember. In this sense "repression" was a welcome phenomenon for most people, for those whom a later age would call "the silent
majority," and one achievement of the years 1815–1830 was that they
saw, by and large, a return to stability and the civil settlement of
disputes, thus laying the foundations of a century which was to witness
enormous improvements in the human condition brought about primarily by the absence of war and civil disturbance.

There was another factor. Many people felt that the changes taking
place, naturally, spontaneously and in ways no government could possibly prevent, as the result of the industrial, scientific and cultural revolutions sweeping through the advanced countries of the world in the years
after 1815, were as much as society could conveniently digest. Even in
the political sphere, changes were constant. Switzerland, the Netherlands and Poland got new constitutions. Baden and Bavaria enacted
constitutional laws for the first time. Sweden recognized the constitu-

tion of Norway, its possession, and Russia recognized that of Finland. Even Cardinal Consalvi, the papal secretary of state, enacted reforms in the papal territories. The constitution Louis XVIII brought with him was more liberal than any of Bonaparte's. But more important than such formal provisions were the changes within those areas of society the political process could not penetrate—attitudes, assumptions, passions, values, prejudices, and leading ideas. While Congress danced, the tunes were changing. And to examine how and in what direction, we must begin by looking more closely at that proud, deaf, enraged man with the Conversation Books.

Beethoven was a key figure in the birth of the modern because he first established and popularized the notion of the artist as universal genius, as a moral figure in his own right—indeed, as a kind of intermediary between God and Man. His friend Bettina von Arnim said he "treated God as an equal." He seems to have felt that, by virtue of his creative powers, he had some kind of direct contact with the Deity, and that he, as a great artist, was an anointed one, like the prophets in the Bible. He was the first to assert that the artist was the arbiter of public morals, that he spoke for "suffering humanity." In 1821 Shelley, in his *Defence of Poetry*, called the poet "the unacknowledged legislator of the world," but Beethoven was already making the claim twenty years before and, what is more, on behalf of the musician, then a lowly species. Poets had been honored since the days of Homer, but even at the end of the 18th century, musicians were low- or middle-ranking servants in the households of the great or minor cathedral functionaries. In 1781 Mozart had been placed below the valets in the Archbishop of Salzburg's household. Antonio Salieri, the court Kapellmeister in Vienna and arbiter of its music from 1788 for nearly forty years, never pushed himself socially; he belonged to the old world and set foot outside the city only four times in half a century. Salvatore Cherubini, ten years Beethoven's senior and the musical boss of Paris, called his younger colleague Hector Berlioz "a savage" because he entered the Conservatoire through the door reserved for the gentry. Such men might be proud of their art, but they knew their place.

Beethoven would have none of such subservience. There was an important episode at Teplitz in 1812 when Beethoven was with Germany's great poet, Johann Wolfgang von Goethe (1749–1832). Goethe was more than 20 years Beethoven's senior, world famous and a man of consequence—ennobled, a privy councillor and in effect Chief Minister to the Duke of Saxe-Weimar. He was a pioneer of romanticism but he still belonged to the old world. Beethoven lectured him on the true

status of the artist. He said that Goethe should not hesitate to be rude
to the great, as Beethoven was to his pupil the Archduke Rudolf. He
added: "I told them that they might be able to hang a decoration round
a man's neck but that this did not make them any better than the next
man. They could make a privy councillor or a minister but they could
not make a Goethe or a Beethoven. Therefore they must be taught to
respect what they cannot make and are far from being themselves—it
does them good." At this point—the two men were walking in the
public gardens—the Empress of Austria and various dukes approached
with all their attendants. Beethoven turned to Goethe: "Now keep your
arm linked in mine, they must make way for us, not us for them."
Goethe was flustered and embarrassed; he withdrew his arm, took off
his hat in respect and stepped aside. Beethoven, his arms crossed,
walked straight through the crowd of dukes, "only moving his hat a
little." The dukes parted to make room for him "and all of them
greeted him kindly." At the end of the path Beethoven waited for
Goethe, who had been bowing deeply. "I have waited for you," he said,
"because I honour and revere you as you deserve. But you have done
too much honour to those there."[113]

Beethoven got away with this high line because public attitudes
toward music were already changing. The traditional aesthetic view of
music was low: music appealed only to the senses. Indeed the kind of
romantic music Beethoven was producing had its roots in what the 18th
century called sentimentality, contrasting with the rationalism of serious life; its soft, quivering tone was thought to embody *Seelenlaut*, the
"sound of the soul," which Jean-Jacques Rousseau said was the source
of all music.[114] Immanuel Kant, summing up 18th-century aesthetic
theory, admitted that music could "move the mind in a variety of ways,
and very intensely." Its impact lasted only for a moment, since "it
speaks by means of mere sensations without concepts and so does not,
like poetry, leave anything over for reflexions."[115] But from about 1800
music was seen as increasingly significant because it heightened self-
awareness, now regarded as desirable. As Hegel put it, music "made the
listener more clearly aware of the workings of the inner self." He
added: "The special characteristic relating the abstract inner-conscious-
ness most closely to music is *emotion,* the self-extending subjectivity of
the ego."[116] Emotion, then, created forms of knowledge as serious as
reason, and music, as a key to it, became more serious, too. Besides,
music was increasingly used to enhance serious meaning.

Poetry, including most notably Goethe's own, was being turned into
songs, cantatas, operas and even symphonies. It was characteristic of
this new approach that Beethoven crowned his greatest symphony, the

Ninth in D Minor, with a setting of Schiller's *Ode to Joy*. Old rational-
ists like Goethe might not like this—when Schubert sent him a collection of his settings and asked permission to dedicate it to him, he never
even got a reply. But the public was enthusiastic. Music was soon seen
as the interpreter, the enhancer, of poetry. A man like Thomas Moore
quickly achieved a worldwide reputation as a great lyric poet precisely
because he *sang* his poems in the drawing rooms of the great. Indeed
music came to be revered, increasingly, as a key to all the arts. Thomas
Cole, the first major American landscape artist, tried to create what he
called a "color piano." Germaine de Staël, emerging around 1810 as a
major arbiter of aesthetic fashion, popularized a German phrase which
was going around, that "music is frozen architecture." There was
discussion, about this time, of a super-art which would combine all
the arts—a notion which finally took shape in Wagner's "music-dra-
mas"—and in which music would be the central, cohering force.[117]
Soon some would argue that music was the queen of the arts, since, as
Henriette, sister of the philosopher Feuerbach, put it, it enabled "spirit
to speak directly to spirit."[118]

But great cultural revolutions come about not just through innumerable invisible forces working in the background, but by the actions
of giant figures in the foreground. Beethoven changed the content of
music. 18th-century opera was largely about sexual intrigue—among
Mozart's operas, Beethoven characteristically approved only of *The
Magic Flute* (1791). His own *Fidelio* (1804–05) shifts the ground fundamentally to the brotherhood of man and the glory of fidelity. His Fifth
Symphony in C-minor, composed in 1807—its first London performance, in the Argyll Rooms, took place on 15 April 1815, during the
Hundred Days—operates at the highest level of human intellect and
emotion. He changed the forms, too, dramatically, to handle the increased *gravitas* of the content, thus provoking fury as well as frantic
applause. When the Ninth Symphony was first performed in Vienna on
7 May 1824, and some in the audience burst into cheers for the fifth
time, the Police Commissioner stood and shouted "Silence!" Hector
Berlioz tells us that when the Baillot players gave the first Paris performance of the C-Sharp Minor Quartet (Opus 131), 200 people attended,
of whom 90 percent had left halfway through: "Shortly the chaos
seemed to unwind and just when the public's patience gave out, mine
revived and I fell under the spell of the composer's genius . . . Here is
music then which repels almost all those who hear it and which, among
a few, produces extraordinary sensations."[119]

Beethoven himself reinforced the controversy his work aroused by
the high claims he made. If Bettina von Arnim is to be believed, his

music-conversation was spattered with key words: *boundless, eternal, infinite, pure sensation, passion, power, ecstasy, excitement, the spirit, the senses, enthusiasm,* and *incomprehensible.* He said: "Music is a greater revelation than the whole of wisdom and philosophy." "I know well that God is nearer to me in my art than to others, I consort with him without fear, I have always recognised and understood him." Or again, using the electrical metaphor artists were so attached to around 1815: "Music is the electric soil in which [the seed of] the spirit lives, thinks, invents. Philosophy is a striking of music's electrical spirit. . . . All that is electrical stimulates the mind to musical, flowing, surging creation. I am electrical by nature." And the divine theme again: "Music is founded on the exalted symbols of the moral sense: all true [musical] invention is moral progress. . . . The divine . . . lends to the imagination its highest effectiveness. So art always represents the divine, and the relationship of men toward art is religion: What we obtain from art comes from God, is divine inspiration."[120]

It is important to grasp that Beethoven was not consciously trying to turn music into a secular religion. He was neither agnostic nor atheist, deist nor Unitarian, but a Roman Catholic. It is significant, however, that he was a warm admirer of Father Johan Michael Sailer, a leader in the religious revival which accompanied the nationalist upsurge in Germany after the Battle of Jena in 1806. He later became Bishop of Ratisbon, the great cathedral city where the emperors were crowned and whose choir was (and is) world-famous. Sailer was the first prominent churchman to understand what romanticism was about and adapt it to the religious purpose. He studied Chateaubriand's great book and derived from it the notion that a man who is conscious of his human dignity can accept as real and true only those elements in the traditional body of faith that he has made his own, by his intellect or by his inner feelings.

Strictly speaking, this subjective approach to faith, in orthodox Catholic eyes, is a heresy known as Fideism. But it was becoming the most powerful element in the rebirth of religion now taking place all over Europe, and it was to receive endorsement at the highest intellectual level in the philosophy of religion which John Henry Newman began to work out toward the end of the 1820s. Indeed Sailer's view that the church was an organic development, just as romantics believed poetry grew from nature, was to be a key element in Newman's faith. Beethoven seems to have seen Sailer as the only kind of cleric who could keep him within the church, and three of his devotional works were found among the composer's books at his death. Equally Sailer loved Beethoven's music, as a means whereby men came to God. But it cannot be denied also that, for some—and for an increasing number as the decades went by—the new kind of transcendent music Beethoven wrote, and the new importance he gave to music in the intellectual and moral cosmos, did constitute a secular substitute for religion: There was a new faith, and Beethoven was its prophet. It was no accident that, about this time, new concert halls were being given temple-type facades, thus exalting the moral and cultural status of the symphony and chamber music (as opposed to the opera). New theaters were Greek, churches themselves Gothic, museums, Egyptian—but the concert hall was the setting for the new high priest, the composer.[121]

Superficially, Beethoven was an unlikely man to bring about this revolution. He was born in 1770, his father a run-of-the-mill court musician, his mother a chambermaid who died of tuberculosis when he was 16. He was trotted out as an infant prodigy at age six, began full-time work as a performer at age ten and had no non-musical schooling thereafter. He could not even multiply, adding up endlessly instead—one reason he got into such a mess over money. He read a lot—Homer, Schiller, Shakespeare, Goethe—but was well described by the German historian Albert Leitzman as "the last of the hermit autodidacts of genius." He often talked pseudo-intellectual nonsense. His health was wretched, and its progressive ravages can be traced in over 50 portraits.[122] In the 19th century it was widely believed that Beethoven was the victim of venereal disease or alcoholism or both. In fact his troubles were not of his making. By age 21 he was already suffering from chronic colic and diarrhea, accompanied by intermittent fevers and septic abscesses.

His deafness first appeared when he was 27. It is now diagnosed as otosclerosis, the cartilage rim of the opening of the inner ear turning into bone, thus immobilizing the ossicle whose base fits in the opening and transmits the sound waves—quite common and usually hereditary. There are periods of quiescence but the disease is progressive. By the end of his twenties Beethoven was hearing incessant noises, ringing and whistling, and suffering from ear- and headaches, especially in winter. Noises caused him intense distress; he stuffed his ears with cotton wool, and during the bombardment of Vienna in 1809, he covered his head with cushions. By 1805, at age 34, he could not hear the wind instruments in the *tutti*. By 1812 visitors had to shout. Five years later, he could no longer hear music at all and was effectively stone deaf. For his multiple ailments, he tried various treatments, including the notorious Brown's Treatment of Opposites, credited with killing more people than all Bonaparte's wars. But most doctors would not handle him; he was too difficult. He refused to stick to a strict diet banning wines, spirits, coffee and spices, and this may have made matters worse. His death, at age 57, seems to have been caused by the complications of jaundice, contracted seven years before. The autopsy revealed his liver to be in an appalling state. Modern diagnosis, however, suggests that he may have suffered from the specific form of immunopathic disease called systemic lupus erythematosus, which begins in early adulthood and becomes chronic (with intermissions), the symptoms including emotional instability, rashes and redness of face, rheumatism and liver disease.

Beethoven, in short, was an increasingly sick man all his adult life and his maladies determined his behavior. He gave vent to the rages of the chronic sufferer from stomach pains and the frustrations of the deaf composer. But by a supreme moral irony, his appalling conduct actually sanctified his status as an artistic genius and intermediary between the divine and the human. And that was a sign of the times. In an earlier age, society would have found Beethoven merely repulsive. He showed a lifelong determination to dominate his family, invoking the law if he saw fit. At 18 he had taken charge, having his father declared incompetent as an alcoholic. He tried to prevent the marriages of both his brothers, in each case declaring their wives immoral. When his brother Karl died in 1815 of tuberculosis, Beethoven insisted on an autopsy, accusing the widow of poison. He then pursued her in the courts for five years, accusing her of theft and prostitution and unfitness to bring up his nephew, Karl. He got legal custody of the boy in 1816, and Karl became a pathetic prisoner of the composer's obsessive love, as his pleas in the Conversation Books reveal: "Will you let me out a little today? I need recreation." "I only want to go to my room." "I am not going out. I only want to be alone a little." "Will you let me go to my room?" The perhaps foreseeable result was that Karl tried to kill himself with a pistol in 1826, later telling the magistrates: "I have become worse because my uncle insisted on making me better."[123]

Beethoven's overbearing selfishness was compounded by his failure to marry and the loneliness it bred—"Oh God," he wrote in anguish, "may I find her at last, the woman who may strengthen me in virtue, who is permitted to be mine."[124] But no one was willing to be Beethoven's wife. Few would even be his servants. One witness described him hurling a dish of food at his housekeeper. An early biographer, Anthon Schindler, recounted an episode in August 1820: "As soon as we entered we were told that, in the morning, both of Beethoven's maidservants had run away—at some time after midnight there had been a scene which disturbed everyone in the house because, tired of waiting for their master, both had fallen asleep and his dinner had been spoilt. In the drawing room, behind a locked door, we heard the Master singing, howling and stamping over the fugue for the *Credo* [Mass in D]. After listening to this almost gruesome sound for some time, we were just about to leave when the door opened and Beethoven stood before us, a wild look on his face, almost terrifying. . . . 'A fine household!' he said. 'They've all run away and I have had nothing to eat since yesterday noon!' "[125]

Beethoven seems to have quarreled with everyone sooner or later. He was frequently abusive. His sister-in-law was "Fatlump," her daughter "Little Bastard." His faithful Bohemian music-copyist, Wolanek, after consistent ill-treatment, wrote a letter of reproach. Beethoven drew lines across it from corner to corner, then wrote over it in letters two inches high: "*Dummer, Eingebildeter, Eselhafter Kerl*"—"stupid, conceited, asinine fellow"—then added: "Compliments from such a worthless fellow—better to pull his asinine ears." He added more abuse on the other side of the page. Wolanek had been "pilfering my money." Indeed, Beethoven accused virtually everyone with whom he had business dealings of dishonesty. The truth was rather different. Whether deliberately or through forgetfulness and muddle, he cheated most of his publishers. Letters he wrote in 1822 show him claiming to be at work on three different masses and promising them to at least five publishers, though he completed only the Mass in D (Opus 123), and that he sold to a sixth. Two of the original five were later accused of "playing a trick" or "playing a Jewish trick on me."[126]

Sometimes his abuse exploded into violence; he is described as hurling a plate of stew at a waiter, hitting Prince Lichnowsky with a chair, and striking members of his family. From about 1816 on, often servantless and neglected, he was seen out walking in old clothes, his hat on the back of his head, singing or rather roaring—he composed on his walks—striding down the fashionable Helenethal, forcing even the emperor and the empress to stand aside, or in the country lanes, waving his arms, making a "barking" noise and frightening the cattle, with dogs snapping at his heels and boys throwing stones at him. In 1819 he was spotted composing at a window, having forgotten to put on his trousers; the next year he was mistaken for a tramp, arrested and put in the cells, and had to be rescued by friends.[127]

Such behavior, far from rendering Beethoven disreputable in the eyes of the musical world—or at any rate, its more advanced echelons—made him more fascinating. These were the eccentricities of genius—the follies, agonies and hallmarks of a man's titanic struggles with the forces of creation, his divine madness. There was also a strong element of pity. A 17-year-old soprano, Wilhelmine Schroder, described his last appearance as a conductor, 3 November 1822, trying to direct the musicians and singers in his *Fidelio,* "with a bewildered face and unearthly, inspired eyes, waving his baton back and forth with violent gestures. . . . If he thought it should be *piano* he crouched down almost under the conductor's desk, and if he wanted *forte* he jumped up with the strangest gesture, uttering uncanny sounds"; then suddenly breaking down, he shouted "Out, quick!," ran home, flung himself on a sofa and covered his face with his hands.[128]

Many visitors described Beethoven's increasingly painful efforts to play. Louis Spohr noted: "the pianoforte was badly out of tune, which Beethoven minded little, since he did not hear it; and secondly there was scarcely anything left of the virtuosity of the artist which had formerly been so greatly admired. In *forte* passages the poor deaf man pounded the keys until the strings jangled, and in *piano* he played so softly that whole groups of tones were omitted, so that the music became unintelligible."[129] In 1818 the great London firm of Broadwood sent him their latest model, described in the invoice as a "Six-octave Grand Pianoforte No. 7362, tin and deal case," which was shipped to Vienna via Trieste. But it did not yet have an iron frame and could not stand up to Beethoven's increasingly violent efforts to hear it. Soon, according to one visitor, Johann Andreas Stumpff, it was "in a most miserable state. When I opened it, what a sight confronted me! The upper registers were mute and the broken strings were in a tangle, like a thorn-bush whipped by a storm."[130] Other visitors—and there was a constant procession— told similar tales, in a mixture of wonder, sorrow and admiration.

Despite his miseries, Beethoven often laughed, sometimes joked, was kind—for instance to the child Franz Liszt, though as a rule he hated infant prodigies—and was always impressive composing. This was accompanied by "excessive washing" and, wrote Gerhard von Breuning, when Beethoven had been sitting at table for a long time writing music, "he would hurry to the washbasin and pour jugs of cold water over his heated head"—vast quantities of water would thus pour onto the floor, then down through the boards onto the neighbors below, causing an uproar.

Beethoven much admired Weber's *Der Freischütz* and so was glad to see the composer, but Weber's description, given in his life by his son Max, was full of compassion: Beethoven's room was "dreary, almost sordid," "in the greatest disorder: music, money, clothes lay on the floor, linen in a heap on the unclean bed, the open grand piano was covered in thick dust, and broken coffee cups lay on the table." Beethoven's hair was "dense, grey, standing straight up, quite white in places, the forehead and skull extraordinarily wide and rounded, high as a temple, the nose square like a lion, the mouth nobly formed and soft, the chin broad with those marvellous dimples, formed by two jaw-bones capable of cracking the hardest nuts." In the midst of "a broad, pock-marked face" and beneath "the bushy, sullenly-contracted eye-brows," Weber noticed small, shining eyes "fixed benevolently" on him. But when he asked if Beethoven ever considered going on tour, the old man made a hopeless gesture of trying to play the piano and shouted "Too late!"[131]

Thus, in countless anecdotes and eyewitness accounts was built up the composite picture of the archetype martyr to art, the new kind of secular saint who was taking over from the old Christian calendars as a focus of public veneration. Rousseau had started the cult of the divine genius in the 1770s and 1780s, but he had appealed to a comparatively narrow circle of aristocratic admirers. Beethoven, too, had begun his career in the world of patronage. But he had broken out of it decisively into the much wider universe of a European, indeed a world, mass market of music consumers, fed by commercial publishers, public con-cert halls and impresarios, in a combination capable of rewarding performers and composers far more handsomely than even the most munificent princely sponsor. Beethoven, as much by his personality and genius-image as by his astonishing works, played a major role in creat-ing this new commercial market, but was perhaps too old and ill, in the post-1815 period, to exploit it fully.

That was the work of the younger generation, notably of Gioac-chino Rossini (1792–1868), four years younger than Byron, the other international figure who, next to Beethoven, symbolized uncontrolla-ble, outrageous genius. Rossini was the only child of a radical-minded, quarrelsome town trumpeter and of a flirtatious mother—her sister was the local harlot—which made for an unpromising background in Pesaro, part of the papal states. Rossini later told a biographer: "With-out the French invasion of Italy I would probably have been an apothe-cary or an oil merchant."[132] As it was, under the aegis of the French, his father got a teaching job in the Academy at Bologna, then (as Stendhal said) the musical capital of Italy, and the young Rossini, who had begun composing at age 11, soon followed him there to get a thorough musical training. By age 13 he had already acquired a rich mistress and could write out an entire score from memory. Five years later, Venice, the most enterprising Italian city in presenting new music, gave him his chance by putting on his first opera, *La Cambial di Matrimonio* (1810). Then, early in 1812, came a huge success in Milan with his earliest masterpiece, *La Pietra del Paragone*. It ran for 53 performances and secured for its composer not only a handsome financial reward, but exemption from military service—an important point since, of the 90,000 Italian conscripts Bonaparte swept up later that spring for his Russian campaign, hardly any came back.[133]

When the wars ended, the whole of Europe opened up for the young Italian genius. His main base was the San Carlo theater in Naples, run by one of the new-style international impresarios, Domenico Barbaia, who had made himself a millionaire in gambling concessions—he specialized in roulette, then an ultra fashionable novelty. Thanks to the Naples gambling concession, Barbaia subsidized the San Carlo, providing it with what Berlioz called the best orchestra in Italy, and giving his new composer-star a generous contract: In return for composing one opera a year, Rossini was allowed to travel and perform where he liked.[134] In Rome in 1815, Rossini's contract for what became *The Barber of Seville* was in the old style: He was paid in coin, plus a "hazel-coloured jacket with gold buttons." Thereafter it was all cash, in a musical world which was now richly rewarded; the postwar saying went, "For a cavatina, a city; for a rondo, a province." Rossini increased his growing wealth by pinching Barbaia's mistress, Isabella Cobran, then the highest-paid soprano in Italy, and making her his first wife. Of the 18 operas he composed between 1815 and 1823, ten were written for her.

In these years Rossini commuted between the four biggest opera houses—Naples, Rome, Milan and Venice—but did not despise the smaller ones either, quickly becoming the most traveled man in the history of music. He was soon a cult figure, perhaps the best known, certainly the most revered, in the whole country. His arias, wrote one English traveler, W. R. Rose, were sung by workmen, "with as much passion as the most *tolerolo* tunes are bawled about in England," and in May 1819 Byron gave a vignette of him in Venice: "There has been a splendid opera lately at San Benedetto—by Rossini—who came in person to play the harpsichord—the people followed him about—crowned him—cut off his hair "for memory"—he was shouted for and sonnetted and feasted—and immortalised much more than either of the emperors."[135] A fortnight later, in Pesaro, he felt grand enough to refuse to bow to the British Prince Regent's estranged and disreputable wife, Caroline of Brunswick, and as a result her lover, Bartolomeo Bergami, organized a riot at the theater and forced him out of town. No matter: Rossini simply crossed the place off his list and never set foot there again; the Pesarese felt it their loss.[136] At Milan's La Scala, for the opening of his brilliant *La Gaza Ladra* (1817) and *Semiramide* (1824), he could command the services of the world's greatest stage designer, Alessandro Sanquirico, who produced stupendous sets. Then, in 1822,

Barbaia took the entire San Carlo company, plus a new opera by Rossini, *Zelmira*, to Vienna, where he had taken over the Kärntnertortheater.

It was the first time an international musical venture had been mounted on this scale, testifying to improved traveling conditions, and it led to a prolonged bout of Rossini-fever in Europe. Thereafter Schopenhauer, Heine and Hegel were all, for a time, entranced by a cult of the south, the last solemnly intoning: "Italian music is made for Italian throats as assuredly as Strasburg *pâté de foie gras* is made for the throats of gourmets."[137] On this visit Rossini was received by Beethoven, who told him, "Write more *Barbers*" and "stick to *buffa*"—all he thought Italians were fit for. Coming from a German, this was rude and perhaps intended to be. In the artistic hierarchy, *opera buffa*, where chorus and sets were small and costumes did not have to be historically accurate, came below *opera seria* and *opera semiseria* and only just above the spoken theater, music hall and circus.[138] In fact Rossini, while boasting he could set a laundry list to music, was a profoundly serious artist, much given to melancholia and depression, and of his 34 operas only 13 were *buffa;* the majority were *semiseria* (3) or *seria* (18). He made possible Verdi just as surely as Beethoven himself made possible not just Weber but Wagner.

All the same, Rossini reveled in the new millionaire's world of international musical show business to which Barbaia introduced him, with its contract battles, rows and litigation. He was a ruthless showman. He thought nothing of transferring arias from one opera to another. He scribbled, almost overnight, highly paid concert pieces, oratorios, even operas for the solemn monarchical junketings of postwar Europe—the Congress of Verona, the marriage of the Duc de Berri, the coronation of Charles X. He gave the public what he thought it wanted, altering the story line without the slightest hesitation. Byron described one of Rossini's Shakespearean ventures: "They have been crucifying *Othello* into an opera—all the real scenes with Iago cut out—and the greatest nonsense instead—the handkerchief turned into a *billet doux*—and the first singer would not *black* his face—for some exquisite reasons assigned in the preface—scenery, dresses and music very good." Rossini's opera ended with Othello and Desdemona in each other's arms.[139]

From his triumph in Vienna, he swept on to Paris in November 1823, his fees increasing with each season. The French artistic world gave him a grand dinner in the new leading restaurant, Le Veau Qui Tette, attended by 150 people, including the singer Pasta, the painter Horace Vernet and the composers Auber and Herold; the event was so much talked about that it prompted a satirical play by Augustin-Eugène Scribe. The next month Rossini was in London, settled in sumptuous rooms in the new Regent Street (Number 90), a perfect venue for a visiting theatrical celebrity. His operas were performed at the King's Theatre, Haymarket, but he sang and played all over the place. Rendering *Largo al Factotum* before George IV in Brighton, he seemed to one observer "more like a sturdy, beef-eating Englishman than a sensitive, fiery-spirited native of the soft climate of Italy." Thomas Moore found his piano playing "miraculous"; Leigh Hunt labeled him "the smart schoolboy" compared to Mozart, "the true man of sentiment," but admitted that anyone who did not enjoy Rossini's music must "lack animal spirits."[140] The money earned, even by Rossini's standards—he had been astonished by the poverty of Beethoven's apartment—was prodigious. His wife was paid £1,500 for the season, Pasta £1,400; he himself got 50 guineas for a single drawing-room appearance, which included writing his name in the family's songbook, and he charged 100 guineas for an hour's music lesson (the usual professional fee was 1 guinea); he may well have cleared £30,000 on this trip.

Indeed, if Italy and Austria were the leading producers of music, it was the big cities of the Anglo-Saxon world, with their expanding, increasingly wealthy middle class, which were the leading consumers. As early as 1815 the Handel and Haydn Society of Boston sought to commission work from Beethoven. Four years later the Beethoven Society was formed in Portland, Maine, and the same year New York saw its first performance of Rossini's *Barber of Seville* (Mozart's *Figaro* had to wait till 1824). But it was London, already by far the world's biggest city, which provided the richest market. Britain could boast no composer of note—John Braham's "When the Bosom Heaves the Sigh" and "The Death of Nelson" (1811), and Sir Henry Bishop's "Home Sweet Home" (1823) were characteristic products—but it had the best paying audiences. The London Philharmonia Society, started in 1813, soon became a power in the musical world and Beethoven repeatedly testified to its generosity and high standards. Its orchestra was not enormous: a maximum of 50 players, compared to 55–60 in some Continental orchestras, and up to 75 in opera houses.[141] But it was backed by the London music-publishing industry, which in the years after 1815 rapidly became the largest in the world, reinforced by the great firm of George Thomson in Edinburgh.[142] And behind this vast output, in turn, was that increasingly ubiquitous article of furniture and culture, the pianoforte.

*   *   *

In the years after 1815 no article was more symbolic of middle-class values and wealth than was the pianoforte. It was the sign not merely of respectability but of culture. In Jane Austen's *Emma*, published in January 1816, the "large and populous village" of Highbury (based on Leatherhead in Surrey) contained no less than five "instruments," as they were called, and these are merely the ones we hear of in the narrative. It was the same all over provincial England. A James Gilray print (1809) portrays "Farmer Giles and his Wife showing off their daughter Bella on her return from school"—she plays a square piano by Longman & Broderip. The rise of the piano had been rapid and its reverberations felt throughout the world of music. Beethoven's early sonatas had been written as much for the harpsichord as for the primitive pianos then available. But it was the piano which made the player's technique "brilliant"—a vogue word of the time. Mozart had been happy to keep his hands close to the keys. But in the new age of musical genius, a touch of theater became obligatory. Clementi was the first to start raising and flourishing his hands while playing; Dussek, another leading player-composer, took the next step by putting himself sideways, his right profile to the audience, the lid of his grand piano open; Moscheles, who took over as the top pianist in the 1820s, specialized in the whole range of virtuoso techniques and exhibitionism the audiences now demanded.

As the technology advanced—Stein of Augsburg introduced escapement, Pierre Erard of Paris devised the critical "repetitious action," while Broadwood improved the tonal volume and sonority and invented the sustaining pedal—Beethoven set the pace. He forced the manufacturers to provide more sophisticated and powerful instruments by writing music which would have been unplayable a decade before.[143] His first two piano concertos were written for a five-octave piano. The Waldstein sonata required six octaves. This is what the piano sent to him by Broadwood provided, but when he came to write Opus 106 in B (1818), he found it inadequate. This sonata, afterwards known as the Hammerklavier, requires 6½ octaves and the piano must stand up to over 20,000 notes. It thus needed greater reliability and a stronger frame, as well as a wider range. The firm of Conrad Graf supplied such a piano—Beethoven's last, which had four strings for each note, but even this Beethoven wrecked. However, Broadwood, which had been experimenting with iron tension bars as early as 1808, produced a model in 1821 which had various metal parts, and Erhard quickly followed. The Americans, who had been making their own pianos, based on Broadwood, since the late 1770s, were not far behind. In 1825 Alpheus Babcock cast the first one-piece iron piano frame.

It was the growing sensationalism of the playing these powerful instruments made possible which turned the piano into the new household altar of the middle class. Everyone wanted to be a Moscheles. The composers and publishers responded with more modest targets. In 1817 Clementi, who made pianos in both London and the Continent, published simultaneously in Leipzig, Paris and London Volume One of his *Gradus ad Parnassum,* piano-playing exercises which became standard fare for an entire generation. George Thomson of Edinburgh had innumerable orchestral works by Haydn, Beethoven, Johann Hummel and Weber transcribed for piano. He also published hundreds of settings of Irish, Scottish and Welsh folk songs—much to the taste of post-1815 young romantics—to join the musical versions of Moore's *Irish Melodies,* printed in Dublin from 1807 to 1834. In addition, there were études (the fashionable new name for "exercise"), *valses brillantes,* polonaises—Frédéric Chopin's first, childish effort was published in 1817—and endless sonatas written by Cramer, Steibelt, Dussek and Clementi, joined from the mid-1820s by the young Felix Mendelssohn.

To satisfy the insatiable demand of the middle class to play these works, John Bernard Logier started to teach groups of 20 in two-hour sessions and invented an instrument of pedagogic torture, the Chiroplast, Patent Number 1446, made in Soho Square and launched in Chiroplast Hall in Dublin. By 1819 Logier had eight of his piano-teaching academies scattered throughout Britain and Ireland. Meanwhile Broadwood was increasing production. Between 1782 and 1802, the firm had made 7,000 square (or upright) pianos and 1,000 grand pianos. The piano, with its many identical parts, was well adapted to mass production and the division of labor and, indeed, to the use of steam power. By the second decade of the 19th century Broadwood was employing 600 workers and producing 1,700 instruments a year. There were perhaps 40 or 50 other makers in London alone. John Julius Angerstein (1735–1823), the Russian-born millionaire financier, used to say that the best index of the growth and prosperity of London was the number of music shops: When he first came to the city, there were only two; by 1816 they were at every street corner in the better parts.[144] Mass production had brought down the price too. In 1780 the Broadwood square piano cost £21, plus half a guinea for packaging and delivery. By 1815 a much bigger, better and stronger model cost only £18.3s, carriage-paid. That was the price Frank Churchill, in *Emma,* would have paid for the "instrument" he had surreptitiously delivered for the benefit of Miss Jane Fairfax.[145] In the United States, however, pianos cost much more, between $200 and $600 which, at a time when a skilled carpenter in a big city made $400 a year, ruled them out for all but the wealthy. In Vienna there were in the 1820s 65 piano makers, mostly small scale, but few middle-class families could yet afford to buy a piano. In France they were a rarity outside Paris. Berlioz, born near Lyons, the son of a prosperous doctor, complained that there was no piano in the house or even in the entire neighborhood until 1818.[146] It was in England that the piano first emerged as the proof that the middle class was taking over the cultural leadership from the old nobility.

Aristocratic influence was strongest in Germany simply because there were 38 courts and each had at least one opera house, usually two—one reason for the large number of opera houses in Germany today. But even in Germany there were signs of a middle-class takeover. One portent was the first international music festival, organized by Spohr in 1810 at Frankhausen in Thuringia. Another was the appointment in 1823 of Carl Heinrich Breidenstein, at Bonn University, to the first lectureship in music, a position soon raised to a professorship. A musical press emerged: Vienna's *Allgemeine Musikalische Zeitung* dates from 1817. The equivalent in Berlin followed in 1823. In London the *Quarterly Musical Magazine* appeared, and *The Times* appointed its first regular "musical reporter," the wealthy manufacturer Thomas Alsager: it was in his house that the first London performance of Beethoven's Mass in D was given in 1832. The conductor on that occasion was Moscheles, the piano virtuoso, a sign that the professional conductor, who finally killed off the old controlling voice in music, the *Kappelmeister* of the nobility, was slow to emerge. Before the conductor took over, there was no one to defend the integrity of the music. Bonaparte, for instance, ordered C.-S. Catel's *Les Bayadères* to be performed with all instruments muted and all the marks ignored.[147] The conductor, when finally put in charge, could rule out such interference and ensure a new work was properly rehearsed. But that was still rare in the 1820s and it was one reason why Beethoven's revolutionary new works did not always come off. When his Ninth (Choral) Symphony got its first Leipzig performance in March 1826, only the individual parts were available; the conductor had never seen the score.[148]

More important, however, was the fact that music was increasingly written for the commercial (that is middle-class) market. Beethoven retained a few patrons until the end, but by 1815 he was writing primarily for publishers. Franz Schubert, 27 years his junior, wrote for the market from the start of his earning career. He was in fact the first to compose essentially for the middle-class drawing room and concert hall. Indeed he was middle class himself. Almost all his predecessors came from an upper-servant background of court or chapel players. His father was a schoolmaster and he got a good general education, as well as a good professional one as a boarder at the Imperial Chapel School. He was small, just over 5 feet 1 inch (Beethoven, at 5 feet 6 inches, was the same height as Bonaparte), an important handicap because it got him out of military service during the final, costly stages of the French wars. Unfortunately it also, combined with his ugliness and nearsightedness, made him unattractive to women and drove him to the use of prostitutes, which made him syphillitic and ended his life in 1828 when he was 32. Schubert was extraordinarily prolific: He wrote his first song at age 14, and during the next fifteen years composed over 600 more, plus ten symphonies, six masses, operas and cantatas and a quantity of instrumental chamber music. He worked with great fluency: A note on the score of the first movement of his B-flat string quartet (D 112) says it took him 4½ hours. Five of his loveliest Goethe songs (D 255–59) were composed in a single day, 19 August 1815. In that one year he composed 189 works, including four operas, though he also had to teach on most mornings.

Schubert is often cited as a tragic failure, crushed by a harsh commercial world. It is true that his larger works were usually rejected by publishers, and Acts Two and Three of one of his operas seem to have been used by a servant to light fires. His Eighth Symphony (The Unfinished), on which he worked in autumn 1822, was not performed until 1865. But it seems likely that Schubert did not finish it because he associated it with the episode in which he contracted syphilis.[149] His failure to earn a larger income by selling his works, and thus his dependence on teaching, was due to his lack of organization, business acumen and push, rather than commercial indifference—nothing that a good agent could not have put right.

Even as it was, his appeal to the new middle-class market was strong. From May 1816, when he was twenty, his piano works and, above all, his songs were performed in a house in Vienna's Erdberggasse at weekly musical evenings which became known as Schubertiads. The spread of his fame was greatly accelerated by his alliance with a fine baritone, called Johan Michael Vogl, whose voice had a huge range, taking in the full tenor register, and who sang Schubert's songs with superb aplomb and perfect enunciation so that the force of the poetry—especially Goethe's and Schiller's—came through. By the mid-1820s, Schubert was becoming well known even outside Vienna—the Leipzig *Allgemeine Musikalische Zeitung* compared him to Beethoven (1826). There was a ready market throughout Europe and in the American East Coast for the quality of art songs he produced, and commercial success must have followed. But from 1823, when the disease took hold, he had intermittent, increasingly frequent, periods of poor health. Syphilis, unlike gonorrhea, did not usually yield to mercury treatment—the two maladies were not even distinguished until 1832—and Schubert, in despair, turned to drink, which made matters worse. He was, if anything, a victim of the bohemian life which one part of his nature seemed to crave.

That was the verdict of his friends, who blamed the influence of Byronic notions, so potent in the years after 1815 and transmitted in this case by Schubert's crony, Franz von Schober. To Schubert's early biographer, Ferdinand Luib, one friend wrote: "By Schubert's seducer I mean Franz von Schober . . . there reigned in this whole family a deep moral depravity, so it is not to be wondered that Franz von Schober went the same way. But he in addition devised a philosophical system for his own reassurance . . . to his adherents he alone was all, not only prophet but God himself, and apart from his oracles he was willing to tolerate no other religion, no morals, no restraint."[150] Here was the other side of the coin showing the artist-genius as intermediary with the deity, as demigod—or demiurge; here was a world in which art flourished, but God had been expelled and chaos reigned. Schubert, in the other side of his nature, rejected bohemia and its lack of restraint and discipline. On June 16, 1816, he took the occasion of the 50th anniversary of Salieri's appointment in Vienna—he, as it were, standing for old-fashioned musical decorum—to denounce in his diary "the eccentricity which is common among most German musicians" and—with Beethoven clearly in mind—"that eccentricity which confuses the tragic and the comic, the sacred and profane, pleasant and unpleasant, heroic strains and mere howling, which engenders in people feelings not of love but of madness."[151]

Schubert was later to revise these views, notably on Beethoven himself, but coming from a gifted young artist just turned twenty, they reflect the great chasm which was opening, not merely between artistic bohemia and conventional life, but between the increasing pace of artistic innovation and the corresponding desire among the majority—including many artists themselves—to apply the brakes. Was it the role of artists to sustain, enrich and ennoble society, or to overthrow it and replace it with another, better one? For the first time, among artists of all kinds and everywhere, we find these questions discussed in letters and diaries. But it was mixed up in many cases with the question of their own place in society. By 1820 the middle-class artist was a fact. In music perhaps Schubert was the first but close behind him were Hector Berlioz (1803–69), Felix Mendelssohn (1809–47) and Frédéric Chopin

(1810–49), to list only three. Such young men, well educated—intellectuals, in fact, rather than craftsmen—were the reverse of servile. They were highly articulate, with a tendency to intellectualize their work. They struck a new note of arrogance. Berlioz referred to "the imperious and irresistible nature of my vocation," as though artistic self-dedication had replaced religious duty. William Blake (1757–1827) wrote of those who rejected his work: "Theirs is the loss, not mine, and the contempt of posterity." August Wilhelm von Schlegel (1767–1845) asserted that artists were to the rest of mankind what man was to the rest of creation.[152]

The new feeling might be called consecrated egoism: The artist believed he had an overriding duty to follow his particular genius on behalf of humanity. Granted this belief, where did the artist fit in the social structure? Agonizing over this question, the painter Benjamin Robert Haydon (1786–1846), one of the sharpest and most self-revealing diarists of his time, covered pages with uneasy musings. A generation before, he would have seen it his duty to society to paint its portraits. Now, "My whole soul and body raises the gorge at Portraits! . . . When I painted Poetry, night and day, my mind and soul were occupied. Now, as soon as the Sitter is gone, I turn from his resemblance with disgust!" (16 February 1825). Two days later: "God grant me no more sitters till I am starving!" Portrait painting was servile work, not fit for a true artist, endowed with divine imagination. Haydon expected to be treated with dignity. He recorded with disgust that George Canning, then Foreign Secretary (and himself the son of an actress), was less "civil" to him than was the nobility: "At dinner I received, as a Young Painter of Genius [this was in 1808] more attention . . . from Lord Dartmouth & Lady Harrington, than from Canning. Indeed Canning stood with his back to the Fire, as we were rising to go to the Ladies, with evident wide-legged aristocratic indifference—I stood by him—not a word passed—not a word of notice, though he had heard me widely aluded to during the Evening, & paid particular attention to by Lord Dartmouth, who praised my first painting . . . Now as Canning was a parvenue himself, this was not quite genuine."[153] But Haydon noticed, with irritation, that an aristocrat expected to be listened to by artists even when discoursing on their own territory. At an exhibition, "A Man of Rank came up to me and said, 'Do you know, Mr Haydon, I think Titian's grounds were so-and-so.' As long as I listened he appeared pleased, but this was putting a poker into a powder-barrel. I exploded and poured forth all I had obtained from experience and reading. He looked grave—hummed—talked of the weather & took off his hat with a 'Good Morning!' "

Haydon despised painters who aped their betters, sneering at the highly successful sculptor Francis Chantrey (1781–1841), son of a carpenter: "When he set up his carriage it was not to be borne—it was all: 'John, tell Richard to desire Betty to order Mrs Chantrey's maid to tell Mrs Chantrey to send down my snuff-box.' But he had nothing but contempt for artistic squalor either: 'When my table is laid it is fit for Lord Egremont [his patron] to sit at, whereas the greater part of Artists, with a squalling child, a Pot de Chambre, a gridiron and a press-bed, look like artists & these people like these things.' "[154] Haydon thought the artist should be a member of the respectable middle rank, belonging to society and separated from it only by the invisible curtain of his own high-minded artistic integrity. If he despised the sitter, he saw the continuing need for the Patron. In the United States, however, such an oppressive figure was no longer acceptable: "Patronage—degrading word" said William Dunlap, addressing New York art students at the end of the 1820s. "Every artist who has the feeling of a man, or more especially of a Republican Man, will spurn the offer of patronage as debasing to himself, his art and his country."[155]

If artists, as a new, self-contained, disengaged element in society— outsiders and judges, rather than participants—no longer willingly submitted to the aristocratic patron, neither did they accept the yoke of their new paymasters, the middle classes, without resistance and anger. Indeed it is a significant fact of history that artists preceded the political radicals in their attacks on the bourgeoisie. In 1815 proponents of reform still identified themselves with the middle class against the dominant landowning element. But the artists were already becoming suspicious. German intellectuals, adapting a term of abuse used by university students against townsmen, coined the word *Philister,* which reached Britain as *philistine* in the years after 1815. Byron, not without a strong tincture of this new intellectual snobbery, as well as its old social variety, used another neologism, *tourist,* in contemptuous denunciation of the gaping English who came to stare at him on Lake Geneva or in Venice. Yet another term of abuse came into vogue at this time, to describe the unenlightened many as opposed to the artistic, literary elect: *vulgarité,* invented by Germaine de Staël (1766–1817).

De Staël was the only daughter of Jacques Necker, the great financier who tried to save the French monarchy from its follies on the eve of the Revolution, and she inherited his fortune. From the early 1790s until her death—sometimes in France, sometimes in exile—she was a catalyst of liberal political and literary ideas, thanks to her massive determination and energy. She occupies a central if hard-to-define place in the birth of romanticism. F. R. Rontiex, who wrote the first history of the movement in the 1820s, perhaps came closest by calling her *"notre gran' maman a tous"*: as we would say, perhaps, the den mother of the romantics.[156] Her own literary output was considerable. Her patronage was important. She was married to a penniless Swedish diplomat, from whom she carefully protected her money and her famous estate at Coppet on Lake Geneva. According to Wilberforce, she set her cap at William Pitt, Europe's most famous bachelor, and she tried to pursue Bonaparte into his bathroom.[157] In the wake of Bonaparte's armies, she traveled through Germany, and it was there that she first discovered, like Coleridge before her, the riches of German idealist philosophy and identified herself with the principles of liberty and burgeoning nationalism. The result was her most influential book *De l'Allemagne* (1810), which was seized and destroyed by Bonaparte's censors. She herself was exiled to Coppet.

There followed a period of exiled wandering during which De Staël became the best-known woman in Europe. She was of course a Swiss, not a Frenchwoman, and, in a sense, the first European—itself a portent—whose own preferences lay with the Germans and the English. She could not be dismissed as a bluestocking because she played a notable part in organizing resistance to Bonaparte in northern Europe. Accusations that she got her best ideas from men—notably August Wilhelm Schlegel—were patently silly (the same charges, as we shall see, were brought against George Sand).[158] Men thought she talked too much, women that she dressed too young; neither took her on in conversational combat if they could help it. In Russia in 1811–12, she was described to Alexander Pushkin by a woman eyewitness as "a hefty woman of fifty"; her clothes were "inappropriate . . . her speeches were too long and her sleeves too short." In Stockholm, 1813, she appeared at the theater "declaiming, with her hands, feet and lungs, to the great amusement of the entire pit, who stared at her wide-eyed and open-mouthed, though continuing to eat apples." Another Swedish eyewitness reported her "stout, very thick-set . . . kept her head thrown back and never seemed to stop looking at the ceiling with her lively and mobile eyes . . . mouth always half-open even when not talking, which happened rarely."[159]

From Sweden she moved to London in winter 1813–14, when the publisher John Murray finally brought out her book on Germany, paying her £1,500 for it. When she appeared at Lord Lansdowne's, a vast, eager society crowd climbed on tables and chairs to get a glimpse of her. Among those she met was Byron: The two fascinated each other. She praised his poetry and tried to reconcile him to his wife. He dotted references to her throughout his letters and scraps of reminiscence: "as frightful as a precipice"; "she writes octavos and talks folios"; "her works are my delight and so is she herself—for half an hour." He noted, at Samuel Rogers's house, that she declined to leave the table with the other ladies, in fact "she always lingers so long after dinner that we wish her in—the drawing room."[160] On her London visit she was usually squired by Sir James Mackintosh, a leading progressive intellectual sometimes misleadingly known as "the Whig Cicero," a confirmed muddler, fuddled with opium. He volunteered to take her to dinner at the country house of Lord Liverpool, the Prime Minister. This was Coombe House, sometimes known as Coombe Wood, set in 670 acres at the end of Richmond Park on the south side of the Putney Road, a mile or so from Richmond on Thames. It was notoriously difficult to find, as many a cabinet minister discovered. Mackintosh took her first by mistake to Addiscombe, then got lost; it was dark by the time they found the right direction and they then had to get out of their carriage and walk along a muddy track through a wood, arriving two hours late. De Staël held forth in the hall: *"Coombe par ci, Coombe par la—nous avons été par tous les Coombes d'Angleterre!"*—the unmistakeable voice carries across nearly two centuries.[161]

One of those waiting for her was the Admiralty Secretary Croker, who portrayed her with "an ugly mouth and one or two prominent teeth" but "eyes full, dark and expressive," "singularly unfeminine and if in conversation one forgot she was ugly one also forgot she was a woman." But able, secure men valued her. Byron found her "the cleverest, though not the most agreeable woman" he had ever met. Wellington, who liked strong-minded women with brains, found her agreeable too—"the most agreeable woman he had ever known" he told a stony-faced Mrs. Arbuthnot—but criticized the way she "lost her head" when discussing politics. He told her: "I detest political arguments and don't want any with you." She replied: *"Et moi, discuter sur la politique, c'est vivre!"*[162] She did not see the line where politics ended and other matters—like literature or art—began. For her, politics was or included the arts. In such an age, how could an artist not be involved, committed?

Yes, but committed to what? De Staël answered—liberty. But there again, in the years after 1815, liberty meant different things to different people. Bonaparte claimed that, in conquering Europe, he was liberating it from ancient structures and ideas. Hazlitt and others agreed with him, and when this venture finally ended at Waterloo, Hazlitt went on a depressed, self-destructive bout of drinking which nearly killed him. But for most Europeans—Russians, Germans, Dutch and Spanish especially—the destruction of Bonaparte's armies amounted to "patriotic wars of liberation," restoring national dignity and independence. The France to which De Staël returned in 1814–15 was a divided and confused country, numbed by the huge loss of manpower, glad of peace at almost any price. Louis XVIII was trundled back to power, twice, in the wake of the Allied armies true enough, but it is not accurate to say he had no popular backing. Conservative Catholicism had proved notably adept at raising mobs, especially in Paris, in the 16th and 17th centuries, and by the second decade of the 19th century, a religious revival, which Chateaubriand had adumbrated, was well under way. It found secular, militant expression in 1810, when the first right-wing resistance order was founded, precursor of many others from that day to this. The order was run by Ferdinand de Bertier from the traditional aristocratic quarter of the Faubourg St. Germain in Paris and called itself Les Chevaliers de la Foi. Medieval in sentiment, it employed the new cell techniques of freemasonry to enforce secrecy and conceal the identities of its higher officers. The secretary of the Paris Banner was Louis de Gobineau, father of the future racial theorist and author of the ominous *Essai sur l'inegalité des races humaines* (1854). De Gobineau *père* organized the market porters into formidable anti-Republican street gangs, and the Paris example spread to the provinces, especially in the northeast and the west, forming the "right-wing France" which became a permanent part of French voting patterns. On 14 March 1814, with Bonaparte's armies crumbling, the knights, led by Gobineau, organized a highly successful coup in Bordeaux on behalf of the Bourbons. Without it, they might never have recovered their throne; indeed, Louis XVIII always referred to it as "the Miracle of Bordeaux." In Paris royalists seized the presses and Chateaubriand plastered the wall with posters advertising his personal manifesto, full of the new romantic phraseology, *On the Necessity of Rallying to Our Legitimate Princes.*[163]

These royalist cadres were unable to prevent the return of Bonaparte in March 1815—they were forced into hiding—but once they reemerged after Waterloo, they took a fierce revenge. They were called *miquelets* or *verdets*, the more ruthless ones *nervis*. As the anti-Nazi Resistance was to do in 1944, they seized power by taking over the town halls, then settling down to massacre Imperialists and Republicans, plus any Protestants or Liberals they could lay their hands on. The killings began in Marseilles on 25 June. They spread to Avignon, where Marshal Brune was lynched and his body tossed into the Rhône, and Toulouse, where General Ramel was murdered; at Nîmes 100 Jacobins and Imperialists were slaughtered. But any further killing was prevented by the armies of occupation, which at one time numbered

1,200,000. Once a provisional government was established, the legal "white terror" which followed was on a relatively small scale, some 3,746 cases passing through the civil and 237 through military courts, most of them ending in light sentences or acquittals. The principal blood sacrifice was Marshal Ney, executed on 7 December 1815, chiefly because his supporters boasted the authorities would not dare.[164] Purges of government employees were heavy, involving about one-third (estimates vary from 50,000 to 80,000). None of this satisfied the ultra-royalists, swept to power by elections on 14 and 22 August 1815 to form what was called a *Chambre Introuvable*. They put their faith in the Comte d'Artois, the king's brother, later Charles X.

Louis XVIII himself was a conciliator. He was an absolute stickler for precedent in matters of protocol: Scarcely able to walk, he fell down on parade in 1816 while inspecting troops but angrily rejected the assistance of a young officer and waited, flat on his back, until the "proper person," the Captain of the Guard, was summoned to help him up. But in politics he wanted peace. The constitutional charter of 1814, a liberal document by Bourbon standards, was to some extent his work. In 1817 he put through an electoral law which introduced direct voting for the first time since 1789, albeit on a restricted franchise, with a 300-franc tax requirement. This was equivalent to $60 or £12 and was high by American or even by British qualification levels. In practice, it restricted the electorate to 10,000 landowners or members of the haute bourgeoisie. On the other hand, the voting was free. Under both the Republic and the Empire, fraud, intimidation and violence by the authorities made a mockery of all the electoral arrangements, and Bonaparte's parliaments in particular were rubber-stamp bodies. Under the Bourbon restoration, every Chambre elected proved itself independent and unruly, despite changes introduced in 1820 and 1824 designed to make deputies more docile.[165]

Louis's administration meant well. The head of it, the Duc de Richelieu, amnestied many convicted Imperialists. The king's favorite was the young minister of Police, Élie Décazes, a mere 25, who fed the King with salacious gossip collected by his agents and in return received cloying notes from his childless master: "My Élie, I love you, I bless you with all my soul, I hold you close to my heart. Come and receive the tenderest embraces of your friend, your father, your Louis."[166] But Décazes was no cipher, and he kept an eye on the ultras, as well as the Imperialists, leading to a showdown in the cabinet with the ultra interior minister, the Comte de Vaublanc. Décazes: "You are nothing more than the Minister of the Comte d'Artois and you would like to secure more power than the king's own ministers." Vaublanc: "If I were more powerful than you I would use my authority to have you indicted for treason because you are, Monsieur Décazes, a traitor to King and Country!" The King struck Vaublanc's name off the ministerial list.

If Louis and most of his ministers meant well, the difficulty was that none of them knew how to run a constitutional system. The ancien régime had been an absolute monarchy. The republic had been been ruled by a revolutionary elite punctuated by terror, chaos and *complots*. The Empire had been as close to a modern totalitarian dictatorship as the means of the day permitted. Louis knew he had to rule by some form of consent but a letter he wrote to Décazes 20 January 1819 shows he still saw himself as a quasi-divine source of authority: "It is my will which should do everything. Responsible ministers tell the king: 'Here is our opinion.' The king replies: 'This is what I want done.' If the ministers, after thinking it over, believe they would not be risking too much to follow this view, they will follow it. If not they will say they cannot. Then the king will submit if he thinks he cannot do without his ministers. If the contrary, he will find new ones."[167] This was the kind of system George III of England had tried to enforce as a young king in 1760 and it had proved unworkable then. By 1815–20, the world had moved on; people were wealthier, better educated, much more insistent on their rights. And if Louis did not understand constitutional monarchy, nor did his ministers grasp the nature of cabinet government. One minister, Count Louis Molé, gave a revealing account. Décazes always arrived up to 45 minutes late. After waiting a bit, the Duc de Richelieu would start. Décazes then arrived, sat down without apology, handed Richelieu his police reports, and started to write his letters. Richelieu read the reports. Various ministers spoke. No one listened. "The minister whose turn it was to report spoke to deaf ears until, wanting to have some decision, he begged, in a discouraged tone, the Prime Minister and the Favourite to give him some attention. When I saw it was always going to be this way, I did the same as the others and only listened when something interested me. Most of the time I walked about the room. Gouvion slept. Richelieu and Décazes read or wrote. Pasquier warmed himself by the fire."[168]

On the other hand, ministers could have learned how to do it, and some of them were already learning by 1820. The suffrage could have been steadily broadened, as was happening in the United States throughout this time, and would happen in Britain from 1832 onwards. The constitutional Charter of 1814 was in some ways a contradictory document. Article Five upheld freedom of religion, but Article Six made Roman Catholicism the state religion. Article Eight stated "All Frenchmen have the right to publish and have printed their opinions" but added the qualification "provided they comply with the laws intended to prohibit abuses of that liberty."[169] In practice, however, freedom of speech and publication prevailed and the political education of the French proceeded more rapidly than ever before in the country's history. As Alphonse de Lamartine (1790–1869), the new lyric poet whose *Méditations poetiques* brought him instant fame in 1820, insisted: "The constitutional government . . . by the very novelty of a regime of freedom in a country which had undergone ten years of enforced silence, accelerated more than at any other time in our history that expression of ideas and that steady and lively murmur in Parisian society."[170]

In short, from 1815 France moved abruptly from a closed society where individualism was suppressed and writers conformed, ceased to publish or went into exile, into a free market in opinions. The change came just in time, for during the previous dozen years, France had completely lost the intellectual leadership of the world which she had held in the second half of the 18th century. The world which reopened to French talent in 1815 was a new, more complex and much more invigorating one than the one that had closed at the end of the 1790s. To begin with, it was far more international. Where once educated men and women, throughout Europe and in North America, turned chiefly to the Greek and Latin classics, they now explored a growing range of modern literature outside their own countries. In 1808, for instance, in a famous series of lectures, "Dramatic Art and Literature," delivered in Vienna, Schlegel had introduced the great Spanish playwrights, such as Calderón, to the more enlightened subjects of the Habsburgs. All over Europe Shakespeare was being translated, acted, set to music, turned into operas, illustrated, put on canvas, carved in stone. There was a Continental craze for Celtic ballads. Though Macpherson's "translations" of Ossian had been exposed by Dr. Samuel Johnson as far back as the 1770s, by 1815 versions circulated in all the main European languages, sold in prodigious quantities and were plundered by poets and artists for subject matter. By 1815 too, Byron's *Childe Harold* was translated and read everywhere, and in his wake followed Sir Walter Scott's ballads and romances.

But the biggest factor of all was the international discovery of German literature: the forest tales of the *Nibelungenlied* and other sagas, the idealist philosophy of Kant and his followers, the lyrics and dramas of Goethe, and above all Schiller's verse plays. Schiller had died in 1805, but his European impact was cumulative. As Scott put it, "I am, like the rest of the world, taken in by the bombast of Schiller."[171] Washington Irving thought the high point of poetic excitement was

reached in Schiller's *Wallenstein,* as he read it in Coleridge's translation
of 1800. Coleridge himself, overwhelmed by Schiller, thought him better than John Milton—a view shared, among others, by Thomas Campbell, Robert Southey and Hazlitt.[172] Schiller's work was also one of the
climaxes of De Staël's book on Germany, now at last available in
France, and from 1815 French readers—and still more her writers—
devoured German poetry. For the first time since the 16th century,
French culture became highly receptive to foreign influences.

There were exceptions to this growing cosmopolitanism. In much of
Germany, the younger generation, brought up during the rising against
Bonaparte, was strongly nationalistic. A symbol of their feelings was
the Berlin War of Liberation Monument (1818–21), by Karl-Friedrich
Schinkel, a novelty in itself because it was made of cast-iron with
Gothic trimmings. Schinkel was the ringleader in the campaign to
restore and complete Cologne Cathedral, the focal point of Germano-
Gothic enthusiasm, which cast its enormous shadow over the Rhine,
now another symbol of pan-German aspirations. Postwar German nationalism tended to be xenophobic, or at least francophobic. The students organized themselves into *Burschenschaften,* sworn associations
which flaunted their Christianity, rejected alike Anglo-Saxon constitutionalism and France's cult of Reason, rejected indeed the entire modern world and wanted to go back to the Middle Ages, to the Hohen-
staufen Empire, whose black, red and gold colors they brandished.
They formed the world's first youth movement, wore their hair long,
grew beards—for them a symbol of their Teutonic race—and at their
first mass rally in the Wartburg in 1817 they reintroduced medieval
book burning, throwing into the flames not only the works of philosophers they did not like but the *Code Napoléon.* Their leader, Friedrich
Ludwig Jahn, taught them slogans such as, "If you let your daughter
learn French, you might just as well train her to become a whore."[173]
The German courts, especially Berlin and above all Vienna, found
this new and ugly nationalism inconvenient, indeed dangerous, and by
a curious irony turned against the romantic current which had swept
the French from their possessions. Wedded to divine-right monarchy
they might be in politics, Lutheran and Roman Catholic in religion, but
in practice they found it more congenial—and safer—to prefer rationalism to the deep emotions now being stirred, to stick to the classical
rather than risk the romantic, and favor frivolity over high seriousness.
While their police inspectors tried to stop audiences applauding Beethoven symphonies too lustily, their favorite dramatist was August von
Kotzebue (1761–1819), whose rather risqué comedy *Lovers' Vows,* in

Mrs. Inchbald's translation, was the controversial choice of the young people for their amateur production in Jane Austen's *Mansfield Park*.[174] Kotzebue subjected the *Burschenschaft* movement to some well-merited ridicule, and they resented it bitterly. Jahn taught his student followers physical fitness and encouraged them to wear uniforms and to carry, in their belts, a huntsman's dagger to emphasize that they were earnest— pure forest folk rather than money-grubbing town dwellers. In 1819 one of the keenest of them, Karl Ludwig Sand, used his dagger to stab Kotzebue to death. In the ensuing uproar, Sand was hanged and became an instant martyr, and Metternich rushed through his cowed Diet the Karlsbad Decrees (1820), which dissolved the student movement and set up an inter-German agency to investigate subversion.

In France there was a much more open battle between classicism-reason, on the one hand, and romanticism-unreason on the other. Again the authorities, in their desire for order, found themselves taking up an illogical position. The years 1815–20 were the first in which "isms" began to be generally discussed and to play a leading role in politics and culture. No wonder old fogeys like Louis XVIII were puzzled. Even the experts were confused. In 1824, to settle the matter once and for all, two leading French scholars, Dupuis and Cotonet, tried for a year to define *romanticism* and gave up in despair.[175] By the mid-1820s, about 150 definitions had been produced, none generally acceptable. De Staël herself had epitomized the classical-romantic clash as "writing which imitates that of the ancients and, on the other, that which springs from a medieval outlook . . . one having its origins in paganism, the other in the spirit of religion."[176] A lithograph produced in the 1820s and entitled *The Great Battle between the Romantic and the Classic at the Door of the Museum*, shows a naked antique figure armed with a javelin and a Doric column fighting a man in 16th-century dress with a rapier and a gothic spire.[177]

Such visual definitions were probably the most useful. In any case, it was quite clear where Bonaparte had stood: He favored, patronized, and backed the classical. This was partly a reflection of the Revolutionary-Republican origins of the regime, rooted in the classical revival of the 1780s–90s in matters of taste, and Roman republicanism and Athenian democracy in matters of politics. But it was also linked to the grandiose concepts of Napoleonic Imperialism. In his personal taste, Bonaparte might have a weakness for the stories of Ossian, "the Northern Homer," as he liked to call him: for his palace at Malmaison, he commissioned one of his favorite painters, François Gérard (1770– 1837) to create a fantasy concept, "Ossian," and for his bedroom in the Quirinale, the palace he occupied when he was in Rome, he got Jean-

Auguste-Dominique Ingres (1781–1867) to paint a ceiling decoration entitled *The Dream of Ossian*.[178] But both these painters belonged strictly to the classical school, and all the sumptuary apparatus of the Empire—furniture, tapestries, insignia, Eagles, medals, uniforms, public buildings, even sabers, helmets and breastplates—were of classical form or inspiration.

Bonaparte, who paid as much attention to artistic propaganda as he did to secret policing, spent much effort and money to popularize images from the great empires of antiquity. The ruins of Herculaneum and Pompeii had been uncovered as long ago as 1738–48, but it was only in 1812 that François Mazoi, under the patronage of Bonaparte's sister, Caroline Murat, began to publish his magnificent folio edition of the sites.[179] Earlier Bonaparte had backed Vivant Denon, who was with him on his famous invasion of Egypt in 1798, in publishing his two superbly illustrated volumes on the great empire of ancient Egypt (1802).[180] It was Denon again, by now Bonaparte's Minister for the Arts, in effect, who acted as adviser to the state porcelain factory at Sèvres when, in 1810–12, it produced its *Service Egyptienne,* with its stunning centerpiece based on the temple at Luxor, which Bonaparte presented to Tsar Alexander. A duplicate of this dessert service, perhaps the grandest artifact of the age—and a symbol of a system of state patronage of the arts which was now yielding to commercial capitalism—was ordered for Bonaparte's ex-wife, Josephine, as a divorce present. But it was never taken up and Louis XVIII generously bestowed it on Wellington.[181] Bonaparte, then, was a classicist-Imperialist in his artistic policy, and the iconlike portrait he got Ingres to paint of him in 1806, the year of his crowning victory over the Prussians at Jena, shows him as such. It is entitled *Napoleon on His Throne,* was intended to overawe his already subservient legislators in the Chambre des Députés, and shows Bonaparte full front, as Jupiter, Caesar Augustus and Charlemagne all rolled into one. It is perhaps the most ridiculous portrait ever painted by a great master but there can be no doubting its intentions—it is an emphatic statement of classicism as the official art of France.[182]

In 1815, then, all that had to go. It mattered not that Louis XVIII, being a member of the older generation, was himself a classicist. The winds of change were blowing, and the old order could not resist them. Besides, was there not blood as well as treason on the hands of the outgoing artistic establishment? Just as Ney was needed as a blood sacrifice from the ranks of Bonaparte's marshals, so the arts Bonaparte patronized had to yield a victim, too. The choice fell on the painter

Jacques-Louis David (1748–1825), and a very appropriate one it was. David was a revolutionary, a friend of Robespierre, who had embraced him after his great speech on 8 Thermidor saying, "If you drink the hemlock I shall drink it with you." He was lucky to keep his head, for he had not only been the leading iconographer of the Terror but had belonged to the Committee of National Safety and signed death warrants.[183] Under the Empire he had become the most famous, highly paid and powerful painter in the world.

Bonaparte revived the title of First Painter, invented for Charles LeBrun by Louis XIV, and bestowed it on David, who responded with cringing servility and unparalleled professional skill. A snatch of conversation survives of the two discussing the special gallery to be built for the series David painted for the coronation. *Bonaparte:* "What should it be named?" *David:* "The Gallery of the Coronation." *Bonaparte:* "No—the Gallery of David. There is a Rubens Gallery and this will be called the David Gallery." *David:* "The difference here is great, for while Rubens was a greater painter than Marie [de Médicis] was queen, Napoleon is a greater emperor than David is a painter." Typical of his attempts to ingratiate was his brilliant but outrageous "Napoleon in his Study," which shows the emperor hard at work, the hands of the clock pointing to 4:13, a candle indicating it is night, the *Code Napoléon* on the desk with a sword on a chair. No wonder Bonaparte liked it: "You have understood me, *mon cher David,* in the night I am occupied with the happiness of my subjects and during the day I work for their glory!"[184] All things considered, the restored Bourbons treated David generously, but he instantly succumbed to Bonaparte's flattery when, at the beginning of the Hundred Days, the emperor visited his atelier: "Very good, Monsieur David, continue to illustrate France!" He not only accepted high office under the Usurper but signed the fatal *Acte additionelle.* The Law of 12 January 1816, which spared many Bonapartists from the pains and penalties of treason, was only passed after an angry debate, the ultra-royalist Count de la Bourdonnaye insisting: "To stop their criminal conspiracies we must use irons, executions and torture—death and only death can frighten their accomplices and put an end to their plots!" But even this lenient law could not save David, who was sentenced to exile and ended his days in Brussels.

It was, however, characteristic of the inconsistencies of the divine-right monarchs that the Bourbons retained the services of another leading painter, Baron [Anton Jean] Gros (1771–1835), who had likewise flattered Bonaparte but played his legal cards more skillfully. Indeed David himself, thrown out of France, was instantly offered the post of Minister for the Arts, at a higher salary, by the King of Prussia (he had the grace to decline it).[185] Nonetheless the fall of David was a tremendous blow to the classicists and was felt as such. Who was now their champion? The obvious candidate, in terms of style, was Antonio Canova (1757–1822). This brilliant scion of a family of stonemasons, from Possogno in the Dolomitic foothills of the Alps, had ended Baroque sculpture, almost at a stroke, in 1783–87, and introduced neoclassicism, with his stupendous tomb of Pope Clement XIV in Rome. For the next quarter-century he was probably, in most people's eyes, the world's greatest living artist, even if David had been more honored in France. Canova had been Bonaparte's favorite sculptor and had served Bonaparte's family well, producing, among other choice works, a moving seated figure of Madame Mère (Bonaparte's mother) and an astoundingly erotic half-naked figure of Pauline Borghese, Bonaparte's sister, on her bed.[186]

But then Canova was everyone's favorite sculptor. He held no ideological brief. He had designed and carved another epoch-making tomb in the Augustinekirche, Vienna, which houses the Habsburg dead, for Maria Christina, daughter of the great Maria-Theresa and sister of the executed Marie-Antoinette.[187] That he was a "classicist" there could be no doubt. He had seen the Pantheon marbles, brought to London by Lord Elgin—"They are flesh, true flesh" was his comment—and, in consequence, produced his carnal-ethereal *The Three Graces,* the most widely admired, and copied, piece of sculpture in the entire 19th century.[188] But his allegiance, such as it was, lay with legitimacy and Catholicism: in 1813–15 he had sculpted a colossal statue of *Religion,* intended to mark the triumph of Rome over atheism and republicanism, which by a strange irony ended its days in the distinctly Protestant setting of the parish church of Belton. In 1815 as papal commissioner he had succeeded, with the help of Castlereagh and Wellington, in getting the French authorities to disgorge the antique and Renaissance masterpieces Bonaparte had looted from the Vatican—plus many other Italian art treasures.[189] Moreover, in the new, post-1815 world, Canova was growing old and losing his nerve. Commissioned to sculpt Washington for the state house in Raleigh, North Carolina, he had tried to show the President delivering his final address to Congress in bare knees wearing a Roman toga, and the result was a disaster.[190] Even more preposterous was his colossal statute of the ferocious Ferdinand Bourbon of Naples, one of the ugliest men of his time, whom he presented in female dress as Minerva.[191]

Canova's obvious successor was Bertel Thorvaldsen (1770–1844), whom the old man had promoted, and who had followed the master to the extent of producing his own *The Three Graces.* Thorvaldsen was astonishingly gifted, one of a group of northerners (he was half-Icelandic, half-Danish) who were now bringing Scandinavia to the forefront of European art. But he would not leave Rome, he was lazy (albeit productive), often drunk, and patrons found it hard to gouge their commissions out of his studio—Byron's repeated efforts to get his hands on the bust Thorvaldsen had done of him can be traced in the volumes of his correspondence. Moreover, he worked mainly for the Danish royal family—who sent armed frigates to pick up the results—and the strange Ludwig, Crown Prince of Bavaria.[192]

Not surprisingly, then, the years after 1815 found the once all-powerful French classicists on the defensive. Their last remaining redoubt was the Académie Française, under its embattled Perpetual Secretary, Louis-Simon Auger. Auger accused the romantics, in a fierce speech delivered on 24 April 1824, of subverting the laws of French literature, dividing the national genius, and various other cultural crimes. The poet Emile Deschamps, whose translations had played a notable part in bringing English, German and Spanish authors to French readers, and whose journal La Muse Française was the flag bearer of the romantic movement in Paris, replied that all the finest European writers now repudiated classicism. He listed Byron, Chateaubriand, De Staël, Schiller, Joseph De Maistre, Goethe, Thomas Moore, Scott, Lammenais, and the Italian poet and dramatist Vincenzo Minti. Indeed during the 1820s the romantics carried all before them, and Auger, in despair, committed suicide in 1829.[193] The romantics were bound to win, if only because of their ages. When Auger delivered his attack, every one of the "Forty Immortals" for whom he spoke had been born before 1790, most of them before 1770. The romantics came from the decade 1795–1805. The historian F.-A. Mignet had been born in 1796, the poet Alfred de Vigny in 1797, the historian Jules Michelet in 1798, the novelist Honoré de Balzac in 1799, the novelist Prosper Mérimée and the historian Edgar Quinet in 1803, George Sand in 1804. The year 1802 had been a particularly fertile one in letters, seeing the births of the orator J.-B.-H. Lacordaire, the novelists Alexandre Dumas and Victor Hugo. These young people were "the generation of Empire"—they had, as Alfred de Musset put it, been "conceived between battles, attended school to the rolling of drums."[194]

But they were violently anti-Bonapartist. Taking their cue in this and other respects from Chateaubriand, they repudiated both the Republic and the Empire, and they embraced the ancient monarchy, with its links to the medieval past they found so stimulating. Unlike the younger English romantics, such as Byron, Shelley, Keats, Leigh Hunt and Hazlitt, they had no admiration for Bonaparte—they had actually experienced what it was like to live in his police state. If anything, they were reactionaries, in the true sense: They wanted to delve back into the past.

In this respect, Victor Hugo, by far the most important, was also the most typical. He had personal reasons for repudiating the recent past, too. He and his two brothers were children of a one-parent family. His father, Sigismund Hugo, was a professional soldier who had flourished mightily under Bonaparte, becoming a general and a count. As a boy Hugo had traveled in his father's wake, across the Alps into Italy, all over Spain and (like the infant George Sand) had seen the dark side of Imperial glory, the rotting corpses, burned villages, starving peasants—images which became part of his dark, tragic, Gothic imagination. The general had met and married Hugo's mother, Sophie Trebuchet, while suppressing the Vendée rising, an event which was to provide the background to Balzac's magnificent novel, Les Chouans. But Sophie was by birth and conviction a royalist and soon regretted her choice. The couple fought, then separated (1812) in a welter of lawsuits—she demanding restitution of conjugal rights, he suing for divorce—in which the boys became pawns. This kind of marriage breakdown, envenomed in the courts, which we tend to regard as a 20th-century phenomenon, was in fact becoming common in the second decade of the 19th, as we shall see. The boys sided with their mother, a resolute lady who brought them up, as the phrase then went, "by hand." As Hugo put it, "I learned, from a strong-minded mother, that one can be the master of events."[195]

In one respect, though, the young Hugo, a precocious child who seems to have read a prodigious amount of Greek, Latin and modern literature in his early teens, repudiated his mother. She was a Voltairean skeptic who had not even bothered to get him baptized: When he wanted to marry he had to get his friend Father Lamennais to fake the necessary certificates.[196] He became a fervent Catholic, as most clever, imaginative young men did. He was later to write: "Nothing is more powerful than an idea whose time has come." He knew this from experience. He was overwhelmed by Le Génie du Christianisme when he read it, aged 14, and wrote in his diary: "I must be Chateaubriand or nothing!" The date was 10 July 1816, and the idea whose time had come was Catholic royalism.

By the age of 17 Hugo was already editing and publishing his own magazine, Le Conservateur Littéraire (modeled on Chateaubriand's Le Conservateur), in which over a period of 16 months he wrote 112 articles and 22 poems. His poems, overwhelmingly on royalist themes, were not only widely published but won prizes in competition with established figures like Lamartine. He won the Golden Lily for his ode on the reinstatement of the statue of Henri IV on the Pont Neuf. It was one of the most fortunate times in history for able young men. Instead of being called to slaughter on Bonaparte's battlefields, they were fêted and rewarded by a state anxious to reestablish France's role as the leading literary nation. Old Louis XVIII read Hugo's poems and made constructive criticisms. The king's brother D'Artois also admired him. In 1822, when he was barely twenty, he was granted a pension of 1,200 francs a year from the king's Privy Purse, plus a further 2,000 francs from the Interior Ministry. This enabled him to get married, something he was anxious to do, for his strong sexual urges conflicted with his dedicated chastity.

Much later in life Hugo was to claim he had slept with over 2,000 women in his youth. But there is not a word of truth in it. All the evidence, especially from women, testifies to extreme prudishness. He was described as "a young man with a high forehead and the formidable gift of virginity."[197] He had been in love with Adèle Foucher from the age of 16. She later wrote: "A pin the less in my tucker made him angry. The slightest hint of license in my talk shocked him, and it is not hard to realise how mild such 'license' must have been in a family so strict that my mother refused to admit that anyone could even hint at a lover in connection with a married woman—she did not believe such a thing was possible!"[198] His own letters confirm he was an outstanding prig at this time. Of Adèle's young friend Julie Duvidal, who had started to teach drawing, he said: "It is quite enough to ruin that young woman's reputation that she has turned herself into an artist. A woman has only to belong to the public in one way, for that public to believe she belongs to it entirely. . . . Is it fitting that a woman should lower herself to the level of painters, where she will find herself cheek by jowl with actresses and dancers?" In another letter he rebuked Adèle herself for lifting her dress and so revealing her ankles, when crossing a muddy street: "I could wish, my dear Adèle, that you were less fearful of dirtying your skirts when walking in the street. . . . I cannot describe to you the agonies I went through yesterday in the Rue des Saints-Pères at seeing the woman whom I respect making herself the target for impudent glances."[199]

Clearly even the young Hugo thought a great deal about sex, so his pension and marriage came just in time. In old age he stated that he and Adèle copulated nine times on their bridal night.[200] That seems an altogether more plausible claim. The young couple were much sought after in royalist literary circles. At the head was Chateaubriand himself, at 27 rue Saint Domenique. There was, Adèle wrote, "something regal in his posture, in the inflections of his way, in his manner of assigning those introduced to him what he considered to be their due place in the hierarchy of fame." He had an icy way of indicating when he was bored. On one visit "the Viscount left his bed and had himself sponged down and massaged, stark naked, in the presence of his surprised disciple . . . one was in the presence of a genius, not a man."[201] The younger romantics felt more at ease at the gatherings held by the critic Charles Nodier of *La Quotidienne*, in the library of the Arsenal, where D'Artois had appointed him director. There all the contributors to the *La Muse française*—royalists, medievalists, Catholics—met weekly for two hours of solid conversation, from eight till ten in the evening, after which they had some old-fashioned dancing for which Nodier's beautiful daughter Marie played the piano.

Hugo had now begun to write fiction as well as verse and would soon turn to theater also. The themes were Gothic, violent, often supernatural, dealing with death and especially with madness—a worrying subject, close to Hugo's heart, since on the day of his marriage, his brother Eugène had gone raving mad, apparently from jealousy, and chopped up all the furniture with a saber. His first big story, *Han d'Islande* (1823), a tale full of horrors, evoked from Alfred de Vigny the comment: "You have laid in France the foundations of a Walter Scott." Much of this story was read aloud at Nodier's salon, as were Hugo's poems. There was a good deal of stylized swooning from the ladies and melancholic posturing from the young men. An eyewitness described one occasion when, after Hugo had read one of his Gothic odes, a man approached him, overcome with emotion, lifted his hand, raised his eyes to heaven, and then—after a silence—intoned: *"Cathedrale! Ogive! Pyramide!"*[202]

If the romantics reveled in drama, not to say melodrama, that was natural. It was a theatrical age. Chateaubriand himself had some of the characteristics of a great actor. Long before Byron, he perfected the open-necked, disheveled, "windswept" look—that is how Anne-Louis Girodet portrayed him in a famous painting, circulated in print by the hundred thousand, the perfect image of romantic histrionics. Writers and artists liked a touch of stagey madness. Their favorite character was Hamlet. He symbolized, as Hugo put it, "the permanent condition of man . . . the discomfort of a soul in a life unsuited to it." He added: "His strange reality is our own reality, after all." Chateaubriand saw the play as an epitome of romanticism. It had everything: a mad hero, or better still a hero feigning madness, a mad heroine, skulls, graves, a ghost—"the challenge of the sentinels, the screeching of the night-bird and the roaring of the sea"—and, not least, actors as artists, with

Hamlet himself the archetype actor-artist.[203] The great actor François-Joseph Talma (1763–1826) specialized in playing a romantic Hamlet in the great new Théâtre Française he had helped to found in the rue de Richelieu. Paris was the theatrical city par excellence: Not only did it boast splendid and enterprising theaters, it was a drama in itself.

Superficially, Paris was becoming a classical city. On the Left Bank, Jean-Francis Chalgrin (1739–1811) had completed the vast West Front of Saint Sulpice, with its twin towers, in the last years of the *ancien régime;* a little farther east, the great dome of the Panthéon, by Jacques Germain Soufflot (1713–80) had been finished in the early 1790s. The Empire had powerfully reinforced this classical impress. Charles Pércier (1764–1838) and Pierre Fontaine (1762–1853) refashioned in classical style the north side of the Louvre Palace and set up the Arc du Carrousel (1806), based on the great Arch of Septimius Severus in Rome. Meanwhile Chalgrin had designed the enormous and splendidly situated Arc de Triomphe, started in 1806 and under construction throughout the years of the Bourbon restoration, while Bernard Poyet was putting a 12-columned portico, based strictly on Roman architectural principles, on the front of the Chambre des Députés, where the new "free" parliament sat. Above all, across the bridge on the Right Bank was arising the masterpiece of Pierre-Alexandre Vignon (1763–1828), the dramatic church of the Madeleine, a colossal replica of an octostyle peripteral Roman temple, spectacular by virtue of its island site and grand flight of steps leading to its podium raised 23 feet above ground level.

These striking new buildings caught the eye of the British tourists who poured over from the summer of 1815 onwards—there were 30,000 of them a year by the early 1820s—but their overriding impression, contrasting Paris with London, was how *old* it was. The essayist Charles Lamb (1775–1834), who came over in 1822, thought Paris made London look "new and raw" it was "so delightfully old-fashioned."[204] The city seemed Gothic, medieval, still surrounded by its toll wall with 32 access points guarded by troops. British visitors found the air astonishingly clean and clear, the Seine limpid and transparent compared to the murky Thames. There was some streetlighting from oil lamps, hanging from cords and swaying in the wind, but no boulevards as yet, the medieval street plan virtually intact. This was romantic but there were inconveniences. No pavements at all were laid until the late 1820s. The British artist William Callow noted: "The streets . . . were laid with cobblestones with gutters running down the centre and without any side-pavements, there was no sanitation and whenever there was a storm the streets were flooded."[205]

This dark, ancient, odiferous city was full of exotica and excitement. It was growing fast, leaping from half a million at the turn of the century to 622,000 in 1811 and 714,000 in 1817.[206] Many of the newcomers were foreigners. In the years after 1815, Paris rapidly became the most cosmopolitan city in the world, as immigrants flooded in from all over Europe, so that by the end of the Restoration they made up 55 percent of the registered electors. Some of the best salons were kept by foreigners: In the summer of 1821 the well connected were entertained by the Ladies Holland, Blessington and Oxford from England, Lady Morgan from Ireland, the Countess Apponyi from Austria, the Princess Bagration from Russia. Lower down the scale a man could enjoy, it was said, the favors of girls of every race and color on earth at one of 163 licensed brothels, which housed 2,653 registered prostitutes (there were over 15,000 unregistered ones).[207] Women were highly visible in Paris. They ran many businesses. They drove post chaises or *coucous*. They were reputed to be promiscuous, and it was a fact that every third child born in Paris was illegitimate. They were certainly lightly-clad: a famous Rowlandson cartoon has a visiting John Bull goggling at Paris ladies with their low-cut dresses and exposed ankles and calves.

But the excitement lay above all in the Paris shows. Paris specialized in everything that was visually stimulating, and it was during these years that the effort to satisfy the ever-more-demanding curiosity of the vulgar began to make increasing use of modern technology—a process which was to carry society into the photographic, the cinematic and finally the television age. Most of the ideas came, initially, from Paris, but were rapidly carried to London, much bigger and richer, for large-scale commercial exploitation. The notion of a devastating visual coup for a mass audience was the work of the great stage designer Giovanni Servandoni (1695–1766), a Florentine by origin and an architect, as well as a man of the theater—it was he who first conceived the great West Front of Saint Sulpice. His Paris sets were stupendous and overwhelmed the English actor David Garrick when he saw them.

Among Servandoni's pupils was a young man from Strasbourg, Philippe Jacques de Loutherbourg (1740–1812), who was impressed by a show he saw at the Versailles palace in 1770, in which automata, driven by clockwork, performed in an ingenious mixture of light and shadow. He put together a new combination—magic lantern devices (which were old), clockwork, transparencies, jointed cutouts worked with strings or sticks—and took it to London the next year, where it caught on immediately. A decade later, the first modern lighting system, the Argand Lamp, which replaced the old wick with an incandescent cylinder, so enabling light to be concentrated and project images onto a screen, gave him the idea for what he called the eidophusikon. He presented it at his home in Lisle Street, off Leicester Square, where he built a miniature theater with a stage 10 feet wide, 6 feet high and 8 feet deep, in many ways like a giant television screen. Here he displayed sequences of dawn, noon, sunset, moonlight, fog, cataracts—based on America's Niagara Falls, already famous—and a Satan-dominated "fiery lake." He had a concealed battery of Argand lights, with yellow, blue, green, purple, and red glass slides to produce every possible color combination. Revolving cylinders filled with stones and shells of different sizes and thin copper sheets produced weather sound effects, while program music was provided by Dr. Charles Burney on a harpsichord, a foretaste of the early movies. In the Pandaemonium scene, this *son-et-lumière* effect produced real terror, the five-shilling middle-class customers fighting to get out of the 150-seat theater.[208] The painter Thomas Gainsborough was so impressed that "for a time he talked of nothing else—he thought of nothing else—and passed his evenings at that exhibition in long succession"; indeed, he made a show-box of his own, now in the Victoria and Albert Museum in London.[209]

In 1785 Loutherbourg transferred his techniques, on the largest possible scale, to Covent Garden Theatre, for a presentation he designed of Captain Cook's voyages, *Omai or a Trip Round the World*. The new *Daily Universal Register,* which became *The Times* in 1788, enthused: "The scenery is infinitely beyond any designs of paintings the stage has ever displayed. To the rational mind what can be more entertaining than to contemplate prospects of countries in their actual colourings and tints—to bring into living action the customs and manners of distant nations—to see exact representations of their buildings, marine vessels, arms, manufactures, sacrifices and dresses?" It was a spectacle, the paper added, "the most magnificent that modern times has produced."[210]

This digression into the late 18th century has been necessary because these innovative stage devices set up a chain reaction which was not merely to give birth to new schools of painting, but to revolutionize the visual expectations of ordinary men and women and to transform the way in which civilized societies saw the wider world. In 1800 Paris produced the Phantasmagoria, brought to London in the winter of 1801–02 by the French showman Paul de Philipstal. It was the invention of a Belgian physics professor, Etienne Robert, and illustrates the way in which technologists were beginning to interest themselves in show business. An advanced version of the magic lantern, with adjustable lenses and mounted on a moving carriage, projected from behind a semitransparent screen ghostly images of Voltaire, Rousseau, the murdered Marat and other celebrities, who appeared to emit frightening smoke clouds, in a semidarkened theater, and—above all—advanced upon the audience until, amid thunder and lightning flashes, they vanished at the point of contact.[211] One of Philipstal's London slide painters, Henry Langdon Childe (1781–1874), conceived in 1807 the brilliant idea of using two lanterns, focused on the same area of screen, each equipped with a comblike shutter, which allowed the operator to "dissolve" one picture into the next, so that the enthralled viewer was no longer conscious of the mechanical contrivance behind the images. This was the point at which the magic lantern ceased to be just a toy and became a key instrument of scientific education.[212]

The process was accelerated when Thomas Drummond of the Royal Engineers produced in 1826 a steady, powerful beam for lighthouses by applying a mixture of oxygen and hydrogen to small balls of lime. This "Drummond Light," as Drummond was the first to admit, was the invention of Goldsworthy Gurney (1793–1875), one of a small group of scientists associated with Sir Humphry Davy and Michael Faraday at the Royal Institution. We shall be hearing more about him. Once the new light appeared on the seacoasts, its possibilities were immediately grasped by those in show business. Rechristened Limelight, it was soon transforming the stage and, replacing the Argand lamp, it enabled lanterns to project and pinpoint a hugely powerful beam and so to illustrate lectures attended by 2,000 people or more.[213]

All these devices were essentially aimed at increasing verisimilitude. For though the public wanted Gothic terror and romantic emotions, it also wanted—perhaps more than anything else—realism. The details had to be right. However ingenious the projection, there were angry complaints the moment coaches were seen to be moving backwards or ships to be carrying inappropriate rigging. On this point, as always, Jane Austen caught the spirit of the age when she had Admiral Croft, in *Persuasion,* complaining to Anne Eliot of the sea painting he is examining in a Bath shop window: " 'What a thing is here, by way of a boat. Do look at it. Did you ever see the like? What queer fellows your fine painters must be, to think that any body would venture their lives in such a shapeless old cockleshell as that. And yet, here are two gentlemen stuck up in it mightily at their ease, and looking about them at the rocks and mountains, as if they were not to be upset the next moment, as they certainly must be. I wonder where that boat was built' (laughing heartily). 'I would not venture over a horsepond in it.' "[214] Showmen, and increasingly the artists who worked for them, knew they faced a highly critical audience who insisted on accuracy. The poet John Keats (1795–1821), just coming to the fore in the postwar age, spoke for all when he declared in his "Ode on a Grecian Urn," "Beauty is truth, truth beauty." The audience admired the new scientific shows and found them beautiful, only in so far as they felt them to be true. Huge ingenuity of mind was brought to bear to satisfy this demand. In Paris, there was Uranorama, Noerama, Goerama, Cosmorama. But the most enduring system used to bring visual truth to captive audiences was Panorama.

The idea of reproducing the most gigantic effects of the external world on two-dimensional surfaces was not new—the first multisheet woodcut giving a bird's-eye view of an entire city, Venice, was produced in 1500.[215] But it was only in the Edinburgh of the mid-1780s, then an extraordinary forcing ground for talent and ingenuity of every kind, that Robert Barker, a portrait painter, walking on Calton Hill, thought of drawing the entire 360-degree prospect on a series of frames, so that the viewer could stand in the middle and admire it all, just as if he were on the hill itself. But the effectiveness of the illusion depended on the sheer size of the depiction, as well as on the detail, and the size, in turn, demanded a purpose-built circular exhibition hall. In 1794 Barker, who had moved to London to exploit his idea, erected a vast circular shed on the east side of Leicester Square, where the Odeon Cinema now stands—the first move toward making the Square the center of London's popular entertainment industry. The shed housed a 1,479-square-foot canvas of London, which Barker and his 16-year-old son had painted from the top of the Albion Sugar Mill. The panorama was on two levels, London above, the Fleet at Spithead below, and the suspension of the circular images 30 feet away from the viewers helped the illusion. The idea was commercially so successful that it was soon adopted in Paris, Berlin and Saint Petersburg. Almost every landscape artist in need of steady employment had a shot at panoramas, including Thomas Girtin, whose Eidometropolis (1802), a circular view of London 108 feet long by 18 feet high, done from the top of the British Plate Glass Manufactuary, now survives—alas!—only in a few sketches.[216]

It was only with the end of the wars, however, and the prospect of international showmanship, that panoramas became big business and attracted the best brains on both sides of the Channel. The first to make a fortune was the leading Paris scene designer, Louis-Jacques Daguerre, who specialized in trompe l'oeil effects. His sunlit scenery for the Paris Opéra's Aladdin in February 1822 is a legend in French theater history. Five months later he opened his Diorama, as he called it, in a specially built 350-seat theater at 4 rue Sanson, and its success was such that he rapidly engaged a pupil of the architect John Nash, Augustus Charles Pugin, to build an improved version, at a cost of £10,000, in London's new Regents Park area. This amphitheater, seating 200, pivoted through a 73-degree arc, from one "picture" to another. Each picture was seen through a 2,800-square-foot window, made of calico, painted half translucent, half opaque, the opaque lit by frontal light, the trans-lucent from behind, which created the illusion that the picture itself exuded brilliant light. The intensity, placing and color of the light were varied by an elaborate system of pulleys, cords, slides and shutters. The huge pictures, painted by Daguerre himself and his colleague Jean Bouton, came from Paris, though they portrayed British subjects— Canterbury and Holyrood for instance—as well as Chartres and the Cloisters of Saint Wandrille. The drawback of the system was that it operated entirely by natural light and so could not function in the evening, and fog, increasingly common in London as the quantities of coal it consumed mounted, was a disaster. All the same, the Diorama grossed £3–4,000 a year for Daguerre.[217]

The most sensational London panorama, however, operating at the frontiers of the available technology, was in the Regents Park Colos-seum. This was the idea of a land surveyor, called Thomas Horner (1785–1844), probably the finest draughtsman of estate maps who has ever lived. In 1820 he began to work on a vast panorama of London as seen from the Bull's-Eye Chamber of the lantern above St Paul's dome. The next year the cathedral architect, S. R. Cockerell, erected wooden scaffolding above to repair the ball and cross, and Horner got permis-sion to superimpose a cabin above it from which to make his drawings, using his special optical telescope. This invention by the painter Corne-lius Varley (1811) not only magnified the object, but projected it onto a flat surface, allowing the draftsman to trace its outlines.[218] To get to his cabin studio each day, Horner had to climb 616 stairs and four long external ladders, and taking advantage of the long summer days, he set to work at 3 A.M. each morning, before the household fires began to belch obscuring smoke. In high winds and storms, the work was ex-tremely dangerous, and Horner was often deathly cold, fortifying him-self with large quantities of port, in the belief (as he put it) that "spirits at this level lose more than half their strength."[219] He nonetheless produced over 2,000 drawings, and with the help of the painter-engineer Edmund Parris—who had invented elaborate machinery in restoring Thornhill's paintings inside the dome below—he succeeded in reproducing them in paint, enlarged 16 times, to make an inward curving, 134-foot-diameter canvas covering 24,000 square feet. Nothing on this scale and difficulty, involving daunting problems of aerial and linear perspective, had ever been attempted before—or since, for that matter.[220]

To house this immense work, the young architect Decimus Burton (1800–81), then aged only 23, designed an immense 16-sided polygon of stucco-covered brick crowned by a 115-foot-high dome, 30 feet wider than St Paul's itself. The canvas was mounted within, the interior of the dome itself being painted as sky. The panorama, which showed London in detail to a distance of 20 miles, could be viewed from two different levels, with comfortable seats to sit in and binoculars to examine the details. To get up there you either mounted a spiral staircase within a huge central pillar or went up in what was called the "Ascending Room," London's first hydraulic lift. On ground level were further spectacles, including a Swiss Cottage, with a panorama of the Alps, and an "African Glen."[221]

Every effort was made to increase realism at these shows. In the Diorama, to intensify the effects of light on the screen, the audience sat in darkness, an innovation since houselights in theaters were not put out until near the end of the 19th century. You were shown to your seats by lamp-carrying attendants, like usherettes in a modern movie theater. The Saint Paul's panorama was enhanced by real masonry and ironwork on the platforms. The multiplication of panoramas, of Paris, Rome, Venice, Florence, Athens, Saint Petersburg and many other sights, served for the middle classes as a substitute for the Grand Tour, in the days before Thomas Cook created the all-in package. As *Blackwood's Magazine* put it, "Panoramas are among the happiest contrivances for saving time and money in an age of contrivance. What cost a couple of hundred pounds and half a year half-a-century ago now costs a shilling and a quarter of an hour."[222] But even the experts and the much-traveled elite loved these shows. The Duke of Wellington was a frequent visitor to the Diorama. J. G. Wilkinson, the classical scholar and author of *The Topography of Thebes,* took Thomas Moore to see the panorama of Thebes. In 1827 Moore went with Mary Shelley to see the Geneva panorama in Leicester Square, and she pointed out to him Byron's Villa Diodati and the place where she had written *Frankenstein.*[223] Wordsworth himself was a gratified fan of panoramas, as he describes in *The Prelude.*[224] No wonder: it was the writings of Byron, Scott and Wordsworth that incited customers to go to these travel shows in the first place, and what they saw sent them back to the romantic poets and novelists.

It is hard for us, in the last years of the 20th century, our senses numbed by the endless succession of sensational images of the world we receive through photographs, movies and television, as well as global travel, to grasp the impact of these new technologies on the vision of early 19th-century men and women. The connection between visual astonishment and the emotions—indeed between sight and spirit—had been perceived even in antiquity, giving rise to the notion of sublimity. Longinus defined it as a lifting up of the soul to ecstasy so that it took part in the splendors of divinity. Sheer size was clearly a major element in this process. The American writer James Fenimore Cooper—whom we shall examine in more detail later—saw himself as a novelist of the sublime because of the vastness of the lakes and forests described in his narratives. Richard Payne Knight (1750–1824), the leading aesthetic theorist of the early 19th century, thought that, by contemplating largeness the human mind was "grasping at infinity" and so "expands and exalts itself." Later, John Ruskin was to produce the most comprehensive definition: "Anything which elevates the mind is sublime, and elevation of mind is produced by the contemplation of greatness of any kind, whether of matter, space, power, beauty or virtue."[225] But that was, perhaps, to expand the term too far; ordinary people were more likely to be awed, and so sublimated, by scale than by anything else.

By the early decades of the 19th century, to achieve the sublime was one of the cardinal aims of all the arts. Hence one of the most characteristic features of the age was the cult of the gigantic. Wordsworth's vast spiritual and aesthetic autobiography in verse was so large it never was, or could be, realized. Beethoven's symphonies and masses grew longer and longer, and in the 1820s the young French romantic Hector Berlioz began to operate on an even bigger scale. But naturally it was in painting that the trend was most obvious. Loutherbourg was a pioneer. In the 1780s and 1790s he created huge atmospheric scenes, with titles like *Dawn over London, Storm at Sea, Hannibal Crossing the Alps, Woodcutters Defending Themselves Against Wolves, The Navy Relieving Gibraltar,* and featuring suns, moons, fog, smoke and snow in profusion, both for his light shows and for ordinary exhibition in his house. These were eight feet wide and six feet high, sometimes even bigger. Such canvases cannot be dismissed as peepshow material. They were major works of art, as a visit to the Tate Gallery in London will confirm. Indeed it is impossible to imagine Turner without this mentor, and his impact on many of the younger generation of painters was tremendous.[226]

Loutherbourg achieved his best effects in the legitimate theater—like his master, he was the best scene painter of his generation—and it was to the stage that some of the most ambitious younger painters turned. As London itself grew in size—by the end of the wars it was six miles across—the demand for more, and better, theatrical entertainment grew too. Under the old system, going back to Charles II's day, the two theaters-royal, Covent Garden and Drury Lane, had a legal monopoly to perform the drama (that is, the spoken word) by royal patent. But nine so-called minor houses were licensed by Justices of the Peace to put on variety, melodrama, sub-operatic pieces, musical dumb shows and animal acts. By 1815 the distinctions were becoming confused and more and more theaters opened, so that there were over 30 before the old patent system was finally scrapped in 1843. The ever-growing public demanded bigger and better theaters and, above all, more elaborate staging. Hitherto the craft of scene painting had been in the hands of a small number of monopolistic, trade-union-minded families—the Frenches, the Orans, the Greenwoods, the Whitemores, and especially the Phillipses at Covent Garden. They worked in meticulous detail which was counterproductive: the higher the quality of the work, the poorer the effect in the stalls.

Work on the theory of optics pointed to broad, stylized effects, and at the turn of the century a young man from Astley's theater, John Grieve (1770–1845), showed the Covent Garden management how to achieve them. He set up the spectacle of *Timour the Tartar*, painting in a day, at a fourth of the cost, what had taken the old Phillips gang a month. The actor Joseph Cowell recorded: "In the same room [Grieve] was splashing into existence a cottage or a cavern with a pound brush in each hand [while] Phillips would sit for hours with a rest-stick and a camel's hair pencil, shaping the head of a nail."[227] Grieve's approach enabled the theater to put on new productions in record time, and soon its rival, Drury Lane, was employing two brilliant young artists, David Roberts (1796–1864) and Clarkson Stanfield (1794–1867), to do the same. These were humble lads from poor families. Stanfield came from Sunderland, the son of an Irish Roman Catholic provincial prompter, and tried his luck at sea before taking up his father's profession. Roberts was the son of an Edinburgh shoemaker and graduated from housepainting, which paid him 18 shillings a week, to scenery, for which he got 30 shillings. By the end of the 1820s Drury Lane was paying him £10 for a six-hour day.[228] These men painted literally hundreds of superb sets, all of which have disappeared, and as Roberts put it in his memoirs "Stanfield and myself . . . completed the overthrow of the race of legitimate scene-painters."[229]

This scenic revolution, 1815–17, came to a climax when gas lighting reached the London theaters two years after Waterloo. Gas in the form of piped firedamp had been used to light offices in northern England since the early 18th century and it was the big mill owners, and some Birmingham manufacturers, who began to use it on a large scale in the first decade of the 19th. In 1812 a German immigrant, F. A. Windsor, set up the Gas, Light & Coke Company in London, and by 1814 the whole parish of Saint Margaret's, Westminster, was lit by gas. As early as December 1816 London had 26 miles of gas mains, and the following spring the network reached the theater district. By comparison Paris lagged behind, though the arcades of the Palais Royale were lit by gas in 1819; Baltimore was the first in America, lighting some streets by 1816; Berlin got its first gas lighting in 1826, installed by a British company.

Gas was important for many reasons. It was much more powerful than oil lighting. Envoy John Quincy Adams found the new gaslights in the City, near the Mansion House, in December 1816 "remarkably brilliant," shedding a light "almost too dazzling for my eyes."[230] It was thus strongly favored by the police and the London justices. As the Lambeth Stipendiary put it, "Without presuming to play on words, I regard gas as essential to an enlightened police," and there was a rush to put mains in the so-called criminal quarters.[231] Gas was also cheap: a third to a quarter of the cost of oil. Not least, it was much safer. Tumbled oil lamps were the cause of most fires, especially in London, and though gas was smelly and theoretically liable to explode, it was not a source of house fires. Hence insurance premiums dropped once gas was installed, and this was a key point for the theaters, nearly all of which had been burned down at one time or another. Grieve, Roberts and Stanfield took immediate advantage of gas lighting by introducing a new glaze which lent great depth to their powerfully top-lit scenery. Theatergoers from 1817 onwards were dazzled by the realism of the sets and the colossal size which rapid production techniques made possible.

Painters were among the most impressed. Some already had an itch for gigantism. As far back as 1789–91 the Anglo-American artist John Singleton Copley (1738–1815) had produced his astounding *Defeat of the Floating Batteries,* which was 25 feet long by 18 feet high. The Swiss immigrant Henri Fuseli, or Füsli (1741–1825), produced a series of paintings illustrating Milton, just before the turn of the century, which measured 13 feet by 12 feet. He was influential, being professor of painting at the Royal Academy schools. To crown all, the President of the Academy, Benjamin West, another Anglo-American (1738–1820), celebrated the end of the wars (1814) by a *Christ Rejected by Caiphas,* which was no less than 38 feet long, provoking a snarl from Hazlitt that he was "only good by the acre." In Waterloo year the newly founded British Institution, one of whose functions was to promote contemporary native art, offered £1,000 for a canvas "expressing in an allegorical spirit the Triumph of Wellington." It had to be at least 21 feet by 16 feet. James Ward, a master of the grandiose—his vast *Goredale Scar* is one of the treasures of the Tate Gallery—won the prize with a 35 × 22 foot monster.

The postwar theater powerfully reinforced this trend, persuading many of the younger artists that fee-paying exhibitions of prodigious works were the way to fortune. Some, like Benjamin Robert Haydon, and West himself, put their giants on show in their own houses. Others used public rooms, especially the Egyptian Hall in Piccadilly. To it came Le Thière's *Judgment of Brutus* (26' × 10') in 1816 and the following year, the Chevalier Wicar's *Son of the Widow of Naim* (30' × 21').[232] Indeed, the cult was spreading in Europe. In 1821–22 the Bavarian painter Josef Anton Koch produced his spectacular *The Schmadribach Waterfall*, now in the Munich Pinakothek. Three years later a Waterloo picture by the Fleming Pieneman was so big that, when brought to London, it had to be shown in a vast temporary shed in Hyde Park. The young Frenchman Théodore Géricault (1791–1824), who spend a gooa deal of time in London and was much influenced by James Ward, dismissed his own masterpiece, *The Raft of the Medusa*—big enough in all conscience—as "a mere easel picture." "Real paintings," he added, "must be done with buckets of colour on walls a hundred feet long."[233]

Where would it all end? Within twenty years, it was overwhelmingly apparent that in cultivating the gigantic, painting had taken a wrong turning; the quest for truth was to be pursued in quite a different direction, and the signs of it were already apparent, as we shall see. But at the time it is not surprising that the attractions of immensity should have turned young painters' heads. William Etty (1787–1849), later to establish himself as England's greatest painter of the nude, usually on a small scale, did some huge pictures during these years. So did an ambitious young emigrant from Ireland, Francis Danby (1793–1861), whose sensational light effects and subject matter, as in his *Sunset at Sea after a Storm*—bought by Sir Thomas Lawrence—and his *The Upas or Poison Tree in the Island of Java* (1819), had more than a touch of show business.[234]

But the master of the gigantic was undoubtedly Danby's contemporary and bitter rival, John Martin (1789–1854), who for a time made himself the most popular artist in Britain, perhaps in the world. Martin was born hideously poor, in a one-room farm building in Northumberland, the son of an unemployed tanner who produced 13 children, of whom only five survived infancy. Like many another artist, he got his start working for a coach builder, painting coats of arms on the doors, but in 1815, by some miracle, he surfaced as drawing master to the

Prince of Wales's only child, Princess Charlotte.[235] From this point, he began to paint huge canvases on biblical subjects. He held one-man shows at the Egyptian Hall, but also took his exhibits around the country, to raise popular interest in mezzotint versions, which sold by the tens of thousands. Most of his monsters vanished into the maw of a Lancashire collector, Charles Scarisbrick of Southport, and after his death were destroyed or met many indignities as Martin's reputation collapsed. So complete was his eclipse, indeed, that his three great Judgment paintings—now in the Tate—were sold for £7 the lot in 1935.[236] But in the 1820s the public loved them. The greatest success was *Belshazzar's Feast* (1820), the idea for which he got from a conversation with the American painter Washington Allston, who had had an unsuccessful shot at the subject himself.[237] The *Feast* was shown at the British Institution in 1821 and not only won the first prize but proved so attractive to the public that the exhibition had to be extended three weeks. It was then bought by the publisher William Collins—just beating the duke of Buckingham, who bid 800 guineas—and shown to thousands more at his premises, 343 the Strand.

Most Royal Academicians were jealous of Martin's success, which they attributed to his unseemly huckstering, and they refused to elect him to the academy. And, as Charles Lamb shrewdly pointed out, Martin hovered uneasily between the sublime and the ridiculous: The backgrounds were "stupendous," but the figures were too distinct, instead of being shrouded in mysterious obscurity.[238] Haydon, no enemy to size, nonetheless ridiculed Martin's reported remark of his *Fall of Babylon* (1819): "I meant that Tower" (pointing) "to be Seven Miles high!" "The association," wrote Haydon in his *Diary,* "is preposterous . . . when he makes a great Creator 15 inches high, paints a sun the size of a bank token, draws a line for the sea and places one leg of God in it and the other above & says, 'There, that horizon is twenty miles long and therefore God's leg must be sixteen *relatively,* if that horizon is twenty'—the artist deserves as much pity as the poorest maniac in Bedlam."[239] The last sneer was cruel, for it was known that a streak of madness ran in Martin's family; indeed, his brother Jonathan in 1829 expressed his own form of giganticism by trying to burn down Britain's biggest cathedral, York Minster, and spent the rest of his life in Bedlam.

Martin himself was by no means insane. Even his wildest visions were anchored in reality, though it was often the reality of the distant past or the unrealized future. He was fascinated by science and engineering. Inspired by Gideon Mantell, the geologist, he was the first man to paint the antediluvian world in *The Country of the Iguanodon.* He not only painted on the largest scale, he wanted to transform the real world by huge public works. He translated his vision of the biblical Euphrates into actual plans for embanking the London Thames on the most sumptuous scale. He put forward detailed proposals, in pamphlets, for revolutionizing London's water supply and sewage system, surrounding it with greenbelts, equipping it with a magnificent transport network, and clearing slums for exotic public gardens—all these ideas, and others, echoing images from his giant canvases. Nor were these mere pipe dreams. He actually sat on the board of the Metropolitan Sewage Manure Company. Virtually all the large sums he earned from his art vanished in efforts to turn London into a modern Babylon, in bank crashes and in other hazards which afflicted entreprenurial Georgians.[240]

The whole of Martin's work was inspired by the same consciousness which underlay the cult of gigantism in its many manifestations—a consciousness that man, the educated, civilized man of Europe and North America, was suddenly, in these years, breaking out of his inhibiting enclave and taking possession of the entire world. He was, to use an image of Shelley's, Prometheus unbound, taller than any of his forbears, stronger, more intelligent, better equipped by science and engineering, prepared at last to enter into his global inheritance. The modern age was beckoning him into the wilderness, to conquer it.

No one expressed this notion more powerfully than a young man much influenced by Martin's work, the American landscape painter Thomas Cole (1801–48). Cole came from Lancashire, where he had trained as a woodblock engraver, emigrating with his family in 1818. His father tried to run a wallpaper manufactory in Ohio, and Cole did the designs. His sisters set up a girls' academy, and they and Cole read hugely in Wordsworth, Byron, Coleridge, and Keats—they were all true romantics, worshipping Nature. But how best to serve the deity? Then Cole read Washington Irving's dictum (1820): "He . . . who would study nature in its wildness and variety must plunge into the forest, must explore the glen, must stem the torrent and scale the precipice."[241] Cole took this advice: "Every morning, before it was light, he was on his way to the banks of the beautiful Monongahela, with his paper and pencils. He made small but accurate sketches of single objects—a tree, a leafless bough. Every twig was studied and as the season advanced he studied the foliage, clothed the naked trees and by degrees attempted extensive scenes."[242] Inspired by the scale and intensity of Martin's work, which he knew only in mezzotint at this stage, he made a long, solitary trip up the Hudson river in 1825 and painted the Catskills in autumn. The result was his *Falls of the Kaaterskill* (1826), the most influential canvas ever produced in North America, which caused a sensation in the New York art world, led to the creation of the Hudson River School, and acted as a beacon for Cole's pupil Frederick Edwin Church, perhaps the greatest American landscape artist. For the first time, the majestic scenery of the American outback had been systematically studied on the ground and put on canvas.[243] This brilliant painting was indeed well timed. It epitomized the spirit which underlay the Promethean search for the sublime and the immense—an awareness that the last age of the wilderness was at hand, that modern man was, at that very moment, in the process of conquering and taming it forever.

THREE

The End of the Wilderness

On 5 September 1812, two days before the Battle of Borodino, the artist and diarist Joseph Farington paid a visit to Trimlingham Telegraph House in Norfolk. There he found a retired naval officer, Lieutenant Enfield, and his wife, who together ran the station round the clock, for which they were paid the modest sum of 6 shillings a day, plus accommodation, free coal and candles. The house, with its huge semaphore beams swaying above in the wind, was very isolated. Enfield complained he "only saw a newspaper once a week." But the station was a vital link in a new system of communication which was beginning to annihilate distance and, quite suddenly, was accelerating the process whereby the advanced West was conquering the world and stamping it ineradicably with its own version of civilization. Enfield explained that he could make, or receive, a message from the Admiralty in London in 6 to 7 minutes. The record, he added, was a message-and-answer between London and the Portsmouth base, which had taken only 4 minutes 30 seconds.[1]

For this the Royal Navy had to thank its French enemies. The French had long been ingenious about communications. They ran a high-grade state academy, the Ponts et Chaussées, specifically to train engineers whose job was to maintain and improve France's military-based road system. In 1790 one of its graduates, Claude Chappe, who came from a family of distinguished scientists, had devised the semaphore system. Appointed Ingénieur-Télégraph in 1793, he set up the Paris–Lille line, the first leg in what became a 3,000-mile system. The British soon adopted this idea, first on the London–Deal route, which transmitted messages to the Fleet on the Downs, using a moving shutter device which got the time down to one minute; other routes followed. By 1815 the Americans had a short-range system working in Boston. Semaphore worked by code but it was not until the 1830s that the Massachusetts portrait painter, Samuel Morse, devised an efficient one.

In the meantime, semaphore could only handle very short messages efficiently, was confined to land and the daylight hours, and was baffled completely by mist or fog. It was heavy on manpower, too, since the stations at best could not be more than 10 miles apart. War ministries liked it because special lines could be set up to enable the politicians to control generals on campaign—thus in 1822, for the French invasion of Spain, Paris had itself linked by semaphore to Bayonne. But it was one of those good ideas not susceptible to fundamental improvement. In April 1829, the system was nearly 40 years old but when news of the election of Pius VIII reached Toulon from Rome, at 4 A.M., it still took till noon to get to Paris.

Perhaps most important, semaphore was not open to the public: There was no money in it for the entrepreneur. The future lay with the electric telegraph. Not long after Waterloo, Goldsworthy Gurney, whom we have already come across, was observing from Somerset House Terrace an experiment to use wire as a lightning conductor on ships' masts and announced: "Here is an element which may, and I foresee will, be made the means of intelligible communication."[2] He grasped that the key lay in combining the new Voltaic battery with the magnet, and work on this principle was conducted in London in 1816. But Gurney was diverted by the promise of mobile steam power, so it was a diplomat, F. Schilling von Candstadt (1787–1837), working at the Russian legation in Munich, who first transmitted electrical impulses through wire; but his device was no more than a toy. Here again, it was the opening of a commercial opportunity, the first long-distance passenger rail lines, which led the new Great Western Railway to lay down a working electric telegraph line—and that was not until 1838.

For all practical purposes, therefore, the public in the post-Waterloo era continued to depend on the post, which itself was limited by the speed of horses and boats driven by wind power, and thus dependent on the weather. Charles Lamb groaned that when he wrote to his friend Thomas Manning (1772–1840) the Orientalist and the first Westerner to set foot in Lhasa, capital of Tibet, it took six months for his letter to reach Canton.[3] But people wrote a vast number of letters all the same. Even in France, regarded as backward in this respect, the number of letters leaving Paris each day had risen to 36,000 by 1826, plus 60,000 newspapers and magazines and 10,000 other pieces of printed matter.[4] In London, outgoing mail had long passed the daily 100,000 mark. Correspondents, especially women, cultivated tiny handwriting and "crossed" their letters, that is, turned them upside down or sideways and wrote in the spaces, to save paper, weight, and so postage. The accent was always on economy. Ink was usually homemade from powdered galls, camphor and water (most cookery books contained a recipe for it). A steel pen still cost a shilling, so people made do with quills, which needed constant sharpening with a penknife, a service which kind cousin Edmund performed for little Fanny Price in Jane Austen's *Mansfield Park*.[5] Those in "public offices," that is, government departments or monopolies, were expected to provide steel pens for acquaintances. Charles Lamb, a £600-a-year accounts clerk in East India House in Leadenhall Street, smuggled out no less than 200 steel pens for the use of his old schoolfellow, Samuel Taylor Coleridge, a notorious consumer of writing materials. He also abstracted sheets of Slade's Original Hand-Made Blotting Paper, just coming in during the postwar years, though not envelopes, which he thought newfangled and objectionable.[6] Letters were not yet stamped: the recipient paid. Sir Walter Scott grumbled that his fan mail cost him £150 a year. Since incoming mail at East India House was automatically paid for on arrival at the registry, Lamb got all his letters free by telling correspondents to address their letters to him at the office; he even had Coleridge's mail sent there, but in such cases writers were told to spell his name "Lambe," so he did not open Coleridge's letters.[7]

Cheating to get free postage was a national passion. Members of Parliament got their letters "franked," which meant that the letters cost the recipients nothing and all who were remotely connected with a member of Parliament expected him to oblige them with a frank. But the member of Parliament had to write the address in his own hand. Why was the public so anxious to defraud the Post Office? In Britain at least there was less criticism of the actual service than there is today. In *Emma*, Jane Austen, an enthusiastic user, paid it a famous tribute, having Jane Fairfax sing its praises to the chorus of John Knightley: " 'The Post Office is a wonderful establishment!' said she. 'The regularity and dispatch of it! If one thinks of all that it has to do, and all that it does so well, it is really astonishing! It is certainly very well regulated. So seldom that any negligence or blunder appears! So seldom that a letter, among the thousands that are constantly passing about the kingdom, is even carried wrong—and not one in a million, I suppose, actually lost! And when one considers the variety of hands, and of bad hands too, that are to be deciphered, it increases the wonder.' " Knightley's answer was that "The public pays and must be served well."[8]

In fact the excellent service was run by comparatively few people: 1,129 in Britain and 347 in Ireland operated the 61 mail coaches, pulled by 4,000-plus horses, and the 54 packet boats; the Post Office staff of all ranks came to 4,000.[9] It had been set up originally as an exclusive service for government, and a high proportion of its work was still

Crown business—the Admiralty, for instance, received about 4,000 letters a day from all over the world, and its rule was that each must be answered the day of reception. That made 24,000 pieces of mail a week from one government department.[10] Carriage of private mail had started as a privilege long before it became a right and the cost was high: local post, in London, was only one penny but in the British Isles as a whole it varied from 4d to 1s8d; in France, Germany, Italy and the United States it was much higher. But in relation to real wages the cost was coming down, and the speed of delivery was certainly improving. At the beginning of the century, for instance, a letter posted in London on a Monday afternoon in time to catch the outgoing night mail at 5 P.M., reached Matlock, in Derbyshire, at 7 P.M. the following evening, and you could get it then if you sent to the local Post Office. But your outgoing mail would not leave until 6 A.M. the next morning.[11] By 1821, however, mails were averaging 11mph or even more, round the clock, and a letter posted in Manchester at 4 P.M. would be in London next morning by 10A.M.[12] In this respect Britain was indeed the first "modern" country; the figures from France, where a Paris–Marseilles letter might still take a week or even a fortnight, and from Germany were poor by comparison. It was no better in the United States: In 1828 Martin Van Buren noted that a letter from the White House took five days to reach him in New York.[13]

The delays increased dramatically if a sea crossing was involved. The diarist Farington noted with pleasure and surprise, as far back as 1798, that a letter from County Mayo in the west of Ireland took only 65 hours to reach him in London. Yes, but that was because the Royal Mails handled the stage across the Irish Sea in one of their packets. The internal mail systems now run by Britain, the United States, Canada and most European countries did not pretend, as yet, to handle letters and packets crossing international waters. That was a private affair. To send a letter from the United States to Britain, you addressed it by domestic U.S. Mail to a shipping house on the coast, enclosing money to cover ocean travel and inland postage in Europe. The captain of the transatlantic ship was the real carrier, and passengers sometimes undercut him by agreeing to take letters at 25 to 50 cents apiece. But the total cost of a letter from the New World was never less than a day's wages, or two days' wages in the other direction. Time taken was rarely less than two months, even if the letter was an important official dispatch carried by fast frigate. In 1817 the new president, James Monroe, wrote to John Quincy Adams in London, summoning him to be Secretary of State, on 6 March; it reached Adams only on 16 April, the fastest of four identical letters sent by different routes.[14]

All the same, from the end of the wars the number of letters carried doubled every five years. So did the travelers. The itch to move long distances was now irresistible, though all were well aware of the risks and horrors. In his first two years of office as Irish Secretary, Sir Robert Peel had to cross the Irish Sea no less than nine times, usually in the stormy season; he complained mightily of the "horrible Welsh roads" and the absence of a pier at Dunleary, the port for Dublin (work began on one in 1817), but most of all of the crossing itself. It took seven hours if he was lucky, often 14, once (in August 1815) no less than 33 hours: "Two nights and a day," he moaned to J. W. Croker, "Wretched beyond description . . . Men all sick and the women and children thought they were going to the bottom."[15]

From the safety of the age of rail, romantic writers like Charles Dickens dwelt nostalgically on public coaches but as even such a traditionalist as Robert Surtees (1803–64) admitted, the very "latest and best of the old stage-coaches were dreadful, slow and uncomfortable . . . Who hasn't a lively recollection of the musty old horrors?"[16] Tales circulated of outside passengers freezing to death. J. M. W. Turner (1775–1851) painted a watercolor of a beleaguered diligence caught in a snowdrift on Mont Tarrar, with travelers huddled round a fire waiting to be rescued. This picture was based on personal experience, for he braved long-distance Continental travel in 1802, 1817, 1819, 1820, 1821, 1825, 1826, 1828 and 1829; on the last occasion he wrote from Italy: "The snow began to fall at Foligno . . . the coach from its weight slid about in all directions. . . . I soon got wet through and through till at Sarre-Valli the diligence slid into a ditch and required six oxen, sent three miles back for, to drag it out; this cost four hours, so we were 10 hours beyond our time at Macerata, consequently half-starved and frozen, we at last got to Bologna. . . . But there our troubles began instead of diminishing. . . . crossed Mont Cenis in a sledge—bivouacked in the snow with fires lighted for three hours on Mont Tarrar while the diligence was righted and dug out . . . the same night we were again turned out to walk up to our knees in a new-fallen drift."[17]

The sheer slowness of much coach travel was daunting. Farington, trying to get to Harlech over the Chair, "a very mountainous road," had to hire four horses for his post chaise, but found it still took him "3 hours and 40 minutes in going 10 miles." Richard Wharton, MP, Chairman of Ways and Means, told him that he left Lowther Castle at 3 P.M. on 26 October 1808 to go to Old Park, his house 50 miles away, and did not get there till 3 A.M., nearly dying in the process.[18] There were other hazards. Large parts of Italy were bandit ridden, one reason

why Byron always carried two loaded pistols when traveling there.
Harriet Campbell, a 14-year-old English girl who kept a remarkable
diary of a journey to Florence in 1817, wrote of the route across the
Appenines: "The whole of this road is considered very dangerous and
as we certainly expected to be attacked I was in a comfortable state of
fear the whole day."[19] She related that bandits not only killed and
stripped travelers, but burned bodies and coach alike, making off on the
horses. In Britain by 1815 the age of the highwayman was over but
robbers swarmed on the coach routes and often clambered onto vehicles without the drivers being aware of it. In her diary Mrs. Arbuthnot,
wife of the Joint Secretary to the Treasury, related a typical incident on
28 October 1820: On the road to Woodford, "about three miles from
London, some thieves cut Mr Arbuthnot's dressing-box from the top of
the carriage and got off with it."[20] In France, goods wagons had to be
closely guarded for the same reason, partly because they traveled so
slowly. An official enquiry in 1811 revealed that it took 18–22 days for
goods from Paris to reach Nantes, 8–10 to Rennes, 10–22 to Orleans
and 36–40 to Lyons. Even as late as the 1840s the "ordinary" speed of
French carts was only 25–33 kilometers a day.[21]

No figures are available for the total number of road accidents but
they were probably more numerous, per person per hour spent traveling, than today. Horses were often nervous creatures who bolted at the
least unexpected noise. A wealthy widow, Mrs. Mary Wagner of Brighton, who kept a diary from 1814–29, related a typical incident. While
she was paying a call in London, the coachman got out to ring a
doorbell which had a loud peal. The horses "went off"; a "mob of
labourers" tried to stop them, "which terrified the horses so much"
they began to gallop. Happily the reins got entangled round a lamppost,
which "brought the horse down" and she and her daughter were able
to get out, otherwise the carriage would have been "dashed." "Those
who saw us," she concluded, "say they never saw such an escape."[22]
Fatal carriage accidents were common. When the Princess of Wales's
barouche overturned near Leatherhead, her lady-in-waiting, Miss Chol-
mondeley, was "killed instantly." The coachman had taken a corner
"too close." Farington's friend Mrs. Thelwall Salusbury died when
broken glass from her overturned carriage severed an artery in her neck.
This time, the coachman was prudent and sober and the cause was "the
darkness of the night and a narrow lane." Ayscough Boucherett, member of Parliament for Grimsby, died when the pole of his curricle broke
on a steep hill. The royal surveyor and architect James Wyatt was killed
when his chaise overturned near Marlborough, "his head striking the
roof of the carriage with great force." Here again, a bad road was to

blame.[23] Few roads indeed would permit carriages to proceed at top speed without risk. Thomas Telford, surveying the traditional main road to Holyhead (and Ireland) over its Welsh section, declared the entire stretch constituted an "extreme danger." Over an 85-day period in 1810 he discovered the mail coach was 1 to 5 hours late 71 times out of 85 in the Holyhead direction and 75 out of 85 going to London, while shackles and springs were broken and the vehicle frequently overturned.[24]

The situation was far worse in America, even in the eastern states. American stages had soft tops, mere leather curtains buttoning onto the wooden panels of the bottom half; not only did they fail to keep out wind, rain and snow, they offered much less protection when accidents occurred.[25] The roads were highly dangerous. Henry Addington, who kept a diary in New York State, 1822–25, noted that "bad patches," whose "ferocity" was "fearful," often stretched for four or five miles. The worst were "corduroy roads" of mere logs placed across swamps, producing "an uninterrupted series of plunges from one hole to another." No wonder he often passed "the wreck of a coach or waggon by the side of the road."[26] On a long journey anywhere in the United States, a traveler had to expect his coach to be overturned at least once, usually twice; in 1829 a man traveling from New York to Cincinnati and back reported the coach had been overturned nine times.[27]

Granted the evils of the roads, coachmen should have proceeded slowly. In fact, travelers were so frustrated by the length of journeys that they commanded, begged, and bribed drivers to go well beyond the speed of safety, flogging often weak and overtaxed horses up inclines and forcing them to gallop frantically on the level stretches. In any case, those in the transport industry looked on horses strictly from the financial viewpoint. They called a 1 in 22½ gradient "an easy trotting slope," though a loaded coach weighed two tons. Gradients were often 1 in 9, for instance on the busy London–Bath road at Kingsdown Hill, or even higher.[28] Horses were expendable and were expended ruthlessly. Those who pulled fast coaches lasted only, on average, three years. A big London coachmaster like William Waterhouse, operating from the Swan-with-Two-Necks, a famous coaching inn in Lad Lane, owned 400 horses, working 50–100 miles outside London and expected them to last no more than four years. John Eames, another coachmaster, who owned the White Horse, Fetter Lane, and the Angel, Saint Clements, kept 300 horses. William Horne of the Golden Cross, Charing Cross, running 40 coaches pulled by 400 horses, renewed his stock every four years. Hack horses were plentiful and cheap, bought and sold at horse fairs, where up to 50,000 beasts were on offer, in a country where the horse population probably numbered over 5 million. There was an equally high ratio of horses to human beings in the United States, 1 in 4 by 1820, and 15,000 full-time teamsters by the 1830s. Men like Waterhouse, Eames and Horne, who knew how to manage and exploit horseflesh, made fortunes. Greatest of the coachmasters, William Chaplin (1787–1859), began life as a coachman, then progressed to owning coaches and horses—60 coaches and 1,200 horses—and switched to rail just in time, ending up as Chairman of the London & South-Western; he died worth £500,000.[29]

The horse trade itself was the most consistently dishonest industry in Britain, as Surtees delighted to remind his readers. Indeed one reason why garages tend to cheat customers today over repairs is that they had their origin in horse mongering, thus preserving an unbroken tradition of fraud. Uninstructed purchasers often paid handsome sums for vicious or overnervous animals that were not fit to ride. The result was countless accidents involving ridden horses, especially in towns. It is hard to think of any active man, from the Duke of Wellington himself to the President of the Royal Academy, Sir Thomas Lawrence, who was not thrown at some time. Deaths from horse falls were often lingering. A typical case was that of the 4th Earl of Buckinghamshire, father-in-law of "Prosperity" Robinson, MP, later Prime Minister as Viscount Goderich. The Earl fell off in St. James's Park, tried to struggle on with his job as President of the Board of Control, but died (according to Robinson) "after the greatest affliction in which I have ever seen a man."[30] Another politician who was to die from a horse fall was Sir Robert Peel, who suffered three days of "exquisite agony." The son of Samuel Wilberforce, MP, Bishop "Soapy Sam" Wilberforce of Winchester, was likewise killed by his horse, though in his case death was "instantaneous." Robinson's Cabinet colleague William Huskisson, MP (1770–1830) was thrown by horses more than once and was also badly injured when his carriage was smashed up in Hampshire in 1817 as a result of a broken axle-tree (a frequent occurrence); he survived, as we shall see, to be the first person killed by a train, 15 September 1830. Clearly he was accident-prone.[31]

Deaths from urban horse falls seem to have increased after 1815, as the streets became more crowded, horsemen jostling with carts and carriages. In France, where passenger travel was now doubling each year, 300 coaches were leaving Paris every day by 1824, while 2,100 fiacres or cabriolets carried people within the walls. Regular omnibuses came to the city in 1826, thus carrying out a scheme first suggested by Blaise Pascal in the 17th century. By 1829 the main company had 100 vehicles carrying 30,000 daily.[32] At this point, Shillibeers Omnibuses appeared in London. They thundered alongside the coaches which, in addition to the royal mails, ran on the 600 services which operated from London. There were 883 routes based in provincial towns. Bristol had 80 by 1828, of which over 50 ran daily; there were 13 Bristol–London services, some daily, some putting on two or even three coaches for each departure. The Bristol coaches careered into Bath all day from 7 A.M. to 8 P.M.—no wonder the country-loving Anne Elliot, in Jane Austen's *Persuasion,* found it so disagreable.[33] The noise of iron-shot wheels banging over unevenly cobbled main streets was absolutely deafening, much louder than most traffic noise today, though it did sharply diminish at dark. Fallen or even dead horses were a familiar sight and the stench of horse manure was the most characteristic odor of an early 19th century city, with scores of waifs scrambling to gather the detritus into bags to earn a penny or two.

The roads would have been easier if more people had been prepared to travel by public transport. But then as now, it had many drawbacks—inconvenient schedules, stops for meals at bad, extortionate inns, pestering peddlers in the coach yard, inexplicable delays. If you got on a mail coach (which went faster than the private services) in West or Central London, you found it wasted a whole hour picking up mail at St-Martins-le-Grand before setting off for its destination. There were elaborate rules about who had the right to sit inside: As a boy of 14 traveling in France in 1820, John Stuart Mill, already self-righteous, not to say priggish, asserted his privilege to an inside seat by virtue of "seniority in the coach," forcing a woman to sit outside.[34] Above a certain class, women would not travel coach unless they had an escort or chaperone. It was an American characteristic, which shocked visitors and new immigrants, that females frequently traveled long distances alone. In Europe, elaborate arrangements had to be made—see the case of Fanny Price's journeys in *Mansfield Park*—to ensure that ladies got "protection." If they did go alone, they often dressed as young men (and dressed their daughters as boys) both to avoid unwelcome attention and to spare their clothes.

For all these reasons, those who could conceivably afford to "keep their carriage"—which meant a coachman, groom, stables and coach house as well as the cost of the vehicle itself and purchase (or hire) of horses—did so. It was the surest, most coveted and eagerly worked-for and saved-for mark of gentility. Thus the number of privately owned vehicles was constantly increasing. By 1824, on the Norfolk and Bristol Turnpike, Massachusetts, chaise drivers outnumbered horsemen by four to one.[35] In Britain not only the number but the variety of carriages leapt briskly after 1815; indeed there were as many types and makes as there are cars today. By 1829 the Bath Trust, which ran the local toll roads, had notices saying it charged 4d for "every horse or other beast drawing any coach, barouche, sociable, berline, chariot, landau, chaise, phaeton, curricle, gig, caravan, cart upon springs, hearse, litter or other light carriage, except stage-coaches."[36]

A coach was a generic term for a four-wheel vehicle with at least two seats capable of holding six people inside (at a pinch). A barouche held four inside and two on top, plus a coachman, of course, and a groom if there was one. A landau was like a standard coach but with the body open. A demilandau or landaulet opened only from the front, the hood folding down at the back. A barouche-landau was a grand vehicle—the reason Mrs. Elton in *Emma* boasted about her sister's—hung high on C-springs, with a double folding hood which enabled it to be completely closed in rain. A sociable was low hung, with two seats facing each other, the gentleman sitting in front with his back to the driver, the lady facing, covered by its half-hood. A berline was old-fashioned by 1815 and characterized by an extra back seat covered by a hood. A chariot was a half-enclosed three-seater and a postchariot carried two, though often with a rumble for two servants behind. A chaise, also holding three, was the commonest family carriage, the post chaise being a faster version carrying two. Phaetons and gigs were two-wheelers, beloved of young men, though the smarter ones had curricles. They are described in William Felton's *Treatise on Carriages,* a contemporary handbook, as "being generally used by persons of eminence [and] on that account preferred as a more genteel kind of carriage."[37] The Bath Trust list of vehicles is by no means exhaustive. Other types I have noted in letters and diaries of the day include the cabriolet, stanhope, brougham (this only came in about 1830), dioropha, amamphton, clarence, britzka, pilentum and whiskey.[38] There were many more personal vehicles, such as Lady Morgan's Dublin carriage, colored bright green, with enormous wheels, and described as a "dangerous contraption," especially when driven down back streets by her nearsighted husband wearing his dark-green glasses.[39]

With all this clutter on the roads and streets, parking first became a problem after 1815, especially on the sides of roads, and the earliest parking regulations date from 1820; prototype "carriage parks" appeared a year or two later. Road surveyors were the first category of officials empowered to take proceedings against vehicle owners who parked unlawfully.[40] In the 1820s traffic jams also became common, and not only in big cities. As the immigrants poured into the United States and those on the coast moved west with all their belongings, the main roads across Kentucky, for example, jammed tight several times a week, with wagons loaded with goods and people nose to tail for stretches of many miles.[41] But it was the London jams which became notorious in the postwar years. Here is Mrs. Arbuthnot on her first such experience, 29 May 1820, after a Convent Garden performance of *Virginius* by John Sheridan Knowles, staring Charles Kemble, Daniel Terry and W. C. Macready: "We left the place at 11 o'clock and in Piccadilly we got into a crowd of carriages caused by a party at Lady Charleville's and were kept there, unable to move either way, for above two hours; at the end of which time, when we *were* able to move, I was so tired I went home. I never saw such a quantity of carriages and never was so bored and provoked."[42] Boston, Philadelphia and New York developed their own variety of jams, often lasting for hours, when large flocks of hogs, sheep and cattle were driven into town, mingling with heavy goods wagons driven by eight horses.

Premechanical travel was unquestionably expensive, however you did it. By stagecoach, travel from Boston to New York in 1820 cost $10 to $11, two days' wages; New York to the then-frontier in western Ohio was $80, two months' wages. In Britain it was comparatively more expensive in terms of wages: 4d to 5d a mile inside the coach, 2d to 3d outside, and a coachman, guard and porters all expected to be tipped. So working men could not afford to take a stagecoach and went by wagon or walked. On the Continent, stage travel could be even dearer because of the multiplicity of barriers and tolls, which mounted up and were paid at the end of each stage by passengers on a pro rata basis. From Ostend, Farington paid 28s.6d for a stage of 15 miles, "perhaps the dearest travelling in Europe."[43] Getting through a shut town gate after dusk at Brussels, for instance, cost you a fine of 1s.9d. Such extras existed in the United States and Britain, too, but only for private toll roads and bridges. Thus, to cross a bridge on the Upper Thames, you had to pay 1s for a chaise, 2d for a horse. To get from Maidstone to Sevenoaks direct, a distance of seven miles, you had to pay at five turnpikes; to avoid them meant traveling 15 miles, an extra hour-and-a-half, perhaps two. But to choose your route meant taking your own carriage, and that meant hiring posthorses en route. (Your own horses had to be rested, which doubled your traveling time.) Big posting inns not only kept about 60 horses for the stages but a further 50–60 for private hire, singly, in pairs or in two pairs. There were always two postboys, ready booted and spurred, for the shout "Horses on," which they could manage in perhaps two minutes. A pair cost up to 1s.6d a mile, plus 3d a mile for the postboy who traveled with them; the four required for a heavy carriage, plus two boys, would thus tot up to 3s.6d a mile, up to five times the inside coach fare. If you hired the chaise as well, the cost doubled so you paid ten times the coach.[44] Nonetheless, angry men who had missed the stage, impatient men who would not wait for it, browbeaten men whose wives would not tolerate the close proximity of sweaty or rain-sodden bodies, and social-climbing men who would not travel by public conveyance on principle, all paid up.

The rich, then as now, spent a fortune on travel. At Doncaster Races in 1827, Thomas Creevey noted that the Duke of Devonshire arrived in a coach and six with 12 outriders; Earl Fitzwilliam brought two coaches and six with 16 outriders.[45] Lord and Lady Holland always traveled with two carriages, the second containing their personal servants and, among other things, bed linen, Lady Holland refusing to sleep in any but her own, like the fashionable Mrs. Churchill in *Emma*. But other big spenders were, increasingly, the ultra-busy, highly successful professional men who constituted, from 1815, the first generation of inveterate travelers in history, rather like the Concorde commuters of today. The architect Wyatt told Farington "that his professional journeys are now so many that he computes he travels 4,000 miles in a year"—and, of course, it killed him in the end. Twenty years later, in 1821, his colleague John Nash calculated he "travelled in the Three Kingdoms 11,000 miles in the year" and spent £1,500 annually hiring chaises. Dr. Sinclair, a busy physician, claimed he rode 9,000 miles a year, an astonishing total.[46] J. L. McAdam, the road builder, clocked up an average of 2,000 miles a year over three decades. His rival, Thomas Telford, did much more, "living like a soldier always on active service." "You know I am tossed about like a Tennis Ball," he remarked. "The other day I was in London and since then I have been in Liverpool and in a few days I expect to be in Bristol." This was impressive talk in 1815. His assistant, the grim-visaged John ("the Tartar") Mitchell, Inspector of Highland Roads, rivaled Dr. Sinclair with his yearly average of 8,800 miles on horseback.[47] But perhaps the most-traveled celebrity of these years was Rossini, the first truly international musical star, who not only roamed between Paris, Vienna and London, but commuted between Milan, Venice, Rome, Naples and other Italian opera houses, along atrocious roads, often in coaches pulled by mules, which he called *bestie buggierone.*[48]

Such men bellowed forth their complaints about everything that was wrong with the way they were forced to travel and were seconded by scores of thousands of lesser folk. For the first time in history, and especially in Britain, transport became a prime subject of public and even political debate. But what was to be done? One obvious solution was to make better roads. That meant, to begin with, better mapping. Here the French, inventors of the *théodolite,* were the traditional leaders in triangulating their entire country. London had been done in 1787 but the Ordnance survey, set up in 1791 to triangulate Britain, did not finish the work until 1852; the United States did not even begin until the 1830s.

Better maps meant more rational routes for roads, and the Enlightened Despots of the Continent, not having parliamentary pressure groups to consider, had been efficient at replacing traditional tracks with "scientific" highways. They had also, for military reasons, conquered natural barriers. Catherine the Great had begun the great Siberian highway. Joseph II of Austria had put a modern road through the Arlberg Pass. Bonaparte, the last and greatest of them, had not only completed 14 highways radiating from Paris along which to hustle his troops but had opened the spectacular Simplon Alpine route in 1805 and the Mont Cenis pass in 1810. The same year 17,000 vehicles used it to travel from Savoy to Italy. French roads, made to the specifications of the 18th-century engineer P. M. J. Tresaguet, were reckoned the best: a bottom layer of big stones hammered into contours which determined the surface camber, a further layer making a total foundation of about seven inches, then a surface of three inches "to be of pieces broken to about the size of a small walnut."[49] He claimed such roads ought to last at least ten years. Some did. Others were badly made. All were expensive and thus depended on the will of central government, which tended to be weak unless driven by warlike necessity.

The man who discovered how to make good roads cheaply—one of the magic keys to modernity—was a complete amateur. John Loudon McAdam (1756–1836) was the son of a minor Ayrshire laird. He made a comfortable fortune as a merchant (and loyalist) in the United States and returned to set himself up as a country gentleman, moving to Bristol in 1798. That was how he got himself involved in roads, for the better ones, the turnpikes, which constituted 17 per cent (19,275 miles) of the whole by the end of the wars, were run by trusts on which the local gentry, from a 20-mile radius, sat. The radius had to be limited by the need to get "the attendance of gentlemen at meetings, who will not ride further from home than they can attend in an evening"; the Bath Trust met monthly, "the Saturday nearest the full moon" (a necessity for travel on unlit country roads, so dinner parties, for example, were planned to coincide with strong moonlight). As a trustee, McAdam became fascinated and appalled not so much by the cost of building roads but by the vast expense of maintaining them and the poor results, no matter how much was spent. From about 1800 he turned himself into an unpaid road inspector, traveling 30,000 miles and scrutinizing every main road in Britain, questioning turnpike officials and trustees everywhere. He came to the conclusion that most roadwork in Britain was actually counterproductive, and he caused a sensation when he gave evidence before a Parliamentary Select Committee in 1811.

Like Tresaguet, McAdam believed the stones used for roads were too big. He told the committee members: "Every piece of stone put into a road which exceeds an inch in any of its dimensions is mischievous." You could not get a smooth surface without small stones, and smoothness was the key to a good, durable road. "Any person," he said, "who will take the trouble to follow a carriage on the road will see that the wheel does not *pass over* the materials of which the road is formed, but they are constantly at almost every step encountering the pressure of the wheel and the carriage must be lifted up by the force of the [horses] so as to surmount it; the effect on the road is either to leave a hole, if the stone is displaced, or that the wheel makes a hole by falling from the height to which it was forced by the obstacle." The result was constant discomfort and often danger, as on 30 November 1811, when a Bath coach "hit a heap of unbroken stones in the middle of the road and upset, killing the coachman and injuring several passengers."[50]

From thousands of hours of careful observation, McAdam worked out that the point of contact between the wheel and the road was no more than an inch longitudinally; any stones larger than that would lie loose until wheels either pushed them out of the way or crashed down heavily after bumping on them, in either case making a hole which rapidly became a rut. Earth and sand, supposedly used as a binder, merely created dust and added to the expense. From time to time, repair men came along, using the same bad materials and producing the same result at huge cost. The only advantage was that roads were thereby raised to a high level and contained masses of material which could be put to good use by the right method. This was to make sure the "native soil" was dry by proper drainage at the sides. Then, dispensing with foundations, "a road made of small, broken stone, without mixture of earth, will be smooth, hard and durable." If the stones were small enough—they had to pass through a two-inch brass ring and might not measure more than six ounces on a portable scale carried by the surveyor—the weight of the traffic itself consolidated the surface instead of destroying it.[51]

When McAdam gave evidence in 1811 he asserted that only two stretches of road in the entire country, near Bridgwater and Kendal, conformed to his principles. But the entire main road system could, he calculated, be McAdamized to a width of 15 feet for a cost of only £968 a mile. He felt so strongly that in 1816, though sixty years old, he agreed to be surveyor to the Bristol Trust, the largest in the country, running 149 miles of roads. He made such a success of this job that he acted as a consultant to major trusts throughout Britain and his system became standard in the 1820s. He stressed he was not an engineer; he did not plan road routes. He was merely a surveyor, but he insisted that this was a very necessary profession which ought to be raised in the public esteem to the level of apothecaries and solicitors—an example of how, in these years, specialized expertise was taking over. The service he provided included the whole science of road management: construction, directions for selecting and training staff and laborers, contracting for materials and services, and financial control and accounting.[52]

McAdam was a hard man. He thought most trusts amateurish and incompetent, often content to auction off their tolls to "farmers," such as Louis Levy, who farmed up to half a million of tolls within 60–80 miles of London.[53] Thanks to his admirer Thomas Pelham, Earl of Chichester, Postmaster General, and, as such, the largest turnpike user in Britain, McAdam forced trusts to amalgamate and accept professional direction by surveyors who were properly trained and certified honest. When such could not be found he moved in his sons and nephews, of which there was a plentiful supply. He was ruthless in getting the cheapest possible labor. He would not employ men by the day, as he believed them naturally idle; everything was piecework. That was the system in Bristol itself, where he had 280 men on piecework. Any fall in agricultural wages or a general depression helped him to contain costs. Whenever he could he employed paupers, old men and women, children and workless farmhands, who got 10d a ton for breaking stones to the standard size. "The heavy work is done by the men," wrote his son James, "the light work with small hammers by the women and children, so that whole families are employed."[54] The work was drudgery. On the other hand, argued McAdam, it was regular and sure; without it such families would have been destitute or starved. By 1820 McAdam and his system, first in Bristol and the West Country, then in Devon and Cornwall, then all over England, were producing hard, smooth surfaces over which carriages could travel as fast as horses could pull them, and at a cost which was continually falling. During the years 1820–37, England got the best road system since the fall of the Roman Empire.

McAdam was not without his professional critics, who suspected the quality of his roads. Among them was Thomas Telford (1757–1834), perhaps the most remarkable man of all, in an age of great men.

He was the son of a shepherd of Eskdale, a remote Scots valley north of Carlisle. His father died the year he was born, and he was brought up in great poverty by his widowed mother, who counted herself lucky to get him apprenticed to a stonemason in nearby Langholm. There the Duke of Buccleuch was building a New Town, and Telford's stonemason's mark can still be seen on the bridge and doorways.[55] He loved to work with his hands, in iron as well as in stone, and his singular virtue was the capacity to combine superb craftsmanship, by himself and others, with a passion for the latest technology and massive powers of organization. He thus rose to build bridges, roads, canals, harbors, embankments and other public works on a scale not seen since Roman times, to create the first Institute of Civil Engineering and lay down its superlative standards, and, at the same time, to remain an artist-craftsman, even a visionary.

From Langholm Telford moved to Edinburgh, where he developed a passion for reading and writing poetry and for architecture, serving Robert Adam and Sir William Chambers, who brought him to London to work on Somerset House. There he met William Pulteney, reputedly the richest commoner in Britain. Pulteney was also a member of Parliament for Shrewsbury, and he took Telford there, to restore the castle and to be Surveyor of Public Works for the county. Telford was thus fortunate to breathe the exhilarating air of two of the most dynamic cities in Europe—Edinburgh, an unsurpassed center of art and learning, and Shrewsbury, then the new focal point of advanced technology. Its school, under Samuel Butler, had recovered the prestige it enjoyed in the 16th century in Sir Philip Sidney's day, and the place was also notable for Charles Bage's multi-story iron-frame building, the first in history, and the vast coal and iron workings of William Hazeldine. Telford was adept at spotting talent and quickly gathered one of the finest teams of craftsmen ever assembled, including John Straphen, his master mason. He built the local jail and various churches, including St. Mary Magdalene, Bridgenorth, a brilliant design using giant Tuscan columns and Doric pilasters, which reveals that Telford was in touch with the latest classical developments in France.[56] He also studied the technical treatises of J. R. Perronet, then the leading international authority on bridge building, and incorporated Perronet's ideas in the 40 bridges he built in the district, though he also made the fullest use of the local cast-iron techniques.[57]

Telford's adventurous combination of traditional and advanced technology is brilliantly illustrated by the Ellesmere Canal, which included the great Chirk and Portcysullte aqueducts, "some of the most impressive monuments to canal engineering ever to have been built."[58]

Chirk consisted of ten 40-foot spans taking the canal 70 feet over the surface of the Ceiriog river valley. To save the huge weight of a masonry floor, Telford built the water-channel bottom of cast-iron plates, which also acted as a continuous tie to hold together its masonry walls. Portcysullte is even more astounding—you have to stand underneath it to grasp the majesty of its 1,007-foot stretch, 127 feet above the Dee. It could not have been built at all by conventional means. The piers are hollow with cross walls to save weight. The huge economy of materials is compensated by superb-quality masonry. The trough was again of iron. The 100-foot-high earth-bank approaches were the greatest raised at that time. All these works have survived, in their original form, for nearly 200 years. The mortar contained bullock's blood for extra strength in the thin layers. The joints between the metal plates—still perfect—were rendered with Welsh flannel soaked in syrup and boiled for hours. Only two inches of iron stood between the barges and the floor 127 feet below. Nothing like it had been seen since the age of Marcus Aurelius.[59]

It was primarily Telford's success as a canal builder which determined the British government to put him to work on what they regarded as the most important project in the kingdom, transforming the London–Holyhead road, the key section in the route to Dublin. Its importance had increased immeasurably since the Act of Union (1801) quadrupled, and more, the traffic. Once the wars were over the Holyhead Road Commission (1815), with Telford's long and critical report on the existing road before it, set in motion the various acts which led to the spending of £750,000 of public money, an unprecedented sum then.[60] Telford's direct route, avoiding the delays of the north and south Wales variations—which went back to medieval, indeed Roman days—was designed to the highest-speed specification: "that horses," as he put it, "may easily and rapidly trot over the whole road, ascending or descending, with a loaded coach," in safety and at average speeds of eight miles an hour. The width had to average 40 feet and must never be narrower than 30 feet, with an 18-foot minimum of graveled surface in the center and top gradients of only 1 in 30, apart from some special sections. This involved huge works on a scale never yet seen outside the Alps—the Chirk embankment, the Glyn Diffwys Pass, and the road through Nant Ffancon, for example. Telford, having settled the entire route, began work on the most dangerous sections first, in the hope of cutting accidents and saving lives. He was sometimes too late—just before work started on the Glyn Diffwys pass in autumn 1816, the mail overturned on an acute bend in the old road, hurling people and luggage into the abyss 100 feet below.

The work was pushed with great speed and determination, inspired by the new British pride born of the Waterloo victory, symbolized by the magnificent bridge over the Conway at Bettws, with roses, leeks, thistles, and shamrocks in its spandrels. There was a new and entirely modern spirit of organization combined with an almost medieval attention to the beauty of detail. Huge depots were set up for materials. Overhanging trees were felled and hedges replaced by stone walls. For the first time, retaining walls contained possible landslides. The milestones were magnificently carved from fine, hard limestone, at a cost of 55d each, and they, plus most of the rest of the road furniture, are still there, like the road itself. The tollhouses, four-room bungalows of great simplicity and elegance, were deliberately built by Telford to the highest standard, so that he could attract respectable people to run the tolls honestly and so greatly increase the revenue. Throughout, the road expresses enviable drama and panache. Telford, in the autobiography he wrote at the end of his life, put it truthfully: "This road, established through a rugged and mountainous district, partly along the slopes of rocky precipices and across inlets of the sea, where the mail and other coaches are now enabled to travel at the rate of nine or ten miles an hour, was indeed an arduous undertaking which occupied fifteen years of incessant exertion."[62] It became, at a stroke, the world's fastest all-weather road.

As a fitting climax, it included the latest technical marvel, the Menai Bridge (opened 30 January 1826), which took the route across the straits into Anglesey. The Admiralty insisted that it be high enough to allow the tallest warships to pass underneath. So arches 52 feet 6 inches wide were chained to towers 153 feet high to give a total suspended span of 579 feet and clearance of 100 feet. No one had ever built a suspension bridge of this size before. Each of the 16 chains, composed of links 98 inches long, took 2 hours 20 minutes to raise into position, a terrifying operation which Telford supervised himself. He used a special hydraulic press designed by the great machine-tool inventor, Joseph Bramah, to determine the strength and size of the cables, and then tested them to a 100 percent safety margin on a machine he himself had made in Shrewsbury. To protect them from erosion he put them, still hot, into a bath of linseed oil, then dried them on stoves. For accurate drilling, he and Bramah created a revolutionary new jig. As a result the bridge, despite heavy traffic and often appalling weather, survived without major repairs until 1939, and it is still in use.[63]

Telford's great road played a major part in opening up north and central Wales to modernity and so was part of a process by which the remaining wildernesses of Europe were being subdued. His impact on the Scottish Highlands was still more decisive. Telford had been working for the British Fisheries Society and the Scottish Canals and Highroads Commissioners since the early years of the century, and most of the projects he set on foot were finished by the early 1820s. The trouble with the Highlands was that they had no proper infrastructure of roads and ports. This was one reason why the clansmen, when "cleared" from the overcrowded glens to make way for sheep, cattle and deer—as we shall shortly see—had not much alternative but to cross the Atlantic. Some roads had been built after the Fifteen and the Forty-Five rebellions, but mainly for military purposes, to link forts. Unlike the Continental despotisms, British governments were conducted on laissez-faire principles as a rule. They were not in business to create transport systems—that was for the local authorities or private enterprise. They forked out £750,000 for the new road to Wales because it was part of the strategy to bind Ireland to the Union. They also put up money in Scotland, but only on condition local interests provided matching sums. In practice, however, the lairds proved only too willing to drag their country into the 19th century. They rightly recognized that their large but often threadbare estates would increase markedly in value once the area was opened up to commerce and sport. This willingness to spend must be remembered when they are criticized, often with reason, for putting profit before people in the glens. But equally, implementing Telford's great schemes involved the government in an unprecedented way in Scotland's civil affairs. The Tory governments of the day were often slow and fumbling, but they were not doctrinaire and sometimes showed themselves remarkably willing to take risks and respond to public needs. Thus a combination of governmental intervention and farsighted generosity by the landed interest created the modern Highlands.[64]

But it was Telford who made all possible. No other man has, single-handedly, changed so completely the face of an entire region. The poet laureate Robert Southey (1774–1842) had an unrivaled opportunity to judge the extent of the transformation when he toured the installations with Telford himself in 1819—the year of Peterloo, when Keats was writing "Hyperion" and Shelley, "Prometheus Unbound"—and set down an illuminating account of it.[65] Southey was fair-minded, awarding praise and blame as deserved. Edinburgh had "a rage for splendid building, [but] you might smoke bacon by hanging it out of the window." Soon after they crossed the border into Perthshire, the only county which refused to do a deal with Telford to improve its roads, the horses stumbled: "We're in *Perthshire*, Sir," the driver remarked sourly. But Telford nonetheless had already built 920 miles of roads and rebuilt 280 miles of the old military ones, over which the chaise rattled along. Southey cursed the Duke of Montrose for "disfiguring . . . the most beautiful spot in the whole islands of Great Britain" by selling his woods on Loch Katrine "for the paltry sum of £200"—the Timber company made £3,000 profit.[66] He praised the Earl of Breadalbane for moving his clansmen off the uplands and into the valley, "a wonderful improvement . . . both for the country and for them." He commended Dundee, where Telford had built "a huge floating dock and the finest graving dock I ever saw. The town expends £70,000 on these improvements." There were "marks of well-directed industry everywhere. Flax, potatoes, clover, oats and barley, all carefully cultivated and flourishing."[67]

Everywhere Southey applauded Telford's bridges. There were 1,117 of them, ranging from simple arches over streams to monsters, often in glens where no bridge had existed before.[68] By comparison, the few earlier bridges, mostly by General Wade, looked "very insecure." There was a superb Telford seven-arch bridge at Dubkelt, paid for by the Duke of Atholl, the government chipping in £5,000. Southey was particularly struck by Telford's many iron bridges, especially the 150-foot span of Craigellachie, near Elgin: "A noble work it is . . . beautifully light, in a situation where the utility of lightness is instantly perceived." Of Bonar Bridge he wrote: "As I went along the road by the side of the water I could see no bridge; at last I came in sight of something like a spider's web in the air—if this be it, thought I, it will never do! But presently I came upon it, and Oh! it is the finest thing that ever was made by God or man!"[69]

No place Southey saw seemed to be without Telford's mark on it. At Bervie, "a mere £2,000" spent on a Telford pier was "securing commercial success" to a small port. Much machinery had been put in: "The stones are lifted by a crane, with strong iron cramps or pinchers; and an iron railroad is in use, which is carried from pier to pier, wherever it is wanted." At Aberdeen, for a cost of £3,000, Telford had provided a kirk heated by steam from under the aisles, "plates of perforated iron being laid along the middle of them." He saw a big ship enter the new, "very fine" harbor, also by Telford. It had cost £100,000, but the improvements had already raised the harbor dues to over £8,000 a year. True, he saw a beggar in the street, but he was "reading his Bible." At Banff Telford's £15,000 pier produced "a busy scene—handcarts going to and fro on the railroads, cranes at work charging and discharging huge stones." At Cullen, where £4,000 had been spent, Southey had "a proud feeling" to see "the first talents in the world

employed by the British government in works of such unostentatious
but great, immediate, palpable and permanent utility." He saw the
fishing fleet come in—a thing "impossible before." In fact "This whole
line of coast is in a state of rapid improvement, private enterprise and
public spirit keeping pace with national encouragement, and it with
them." At Fraserburg £14,000 had been spent; at Peterhead, £20,000:
"Wherever a pier is wanted, if the people or the proprietor of the place
will raise half the sum required, Government gives the other . . . public
liberality thus directed inducing individuals to . . . expend with a good
will much larger sums than could have been drawn from them by
taxation."[70]

The "improvements" were just reaching the wild West Coast when
Southey got there, his chaise and horses being the first carriage ever to
reach Strome Ferry by the new 100-mile stretch of Telford road. And
Southey was overwhelmed by the huge scale of the work on the Caledonian Canal, which Telford was driving through the Great Glen from
coast to coast. The locks were "large enough to admit a 32-gun frigate,
the largest that has ever been made." Immense difficulties had been
overcome, the bottom "being a mud so soft that it was pierced with an
iron rod to a depth of sixty feet." Telford solved the problem by the
huge compressive weight of earth and stones left 12 months to settle,
then a pit sunk in it "and the sea therein founded and built." Southey
saw at work the dredging machine, "an engine of tremendous power"
which "brings up 800 tons a day." Beyond Ochy he passed through the
famous "deep cutting," a scene of frenzied activity like a vast anthill,
rest periods marked by a horn sounding. Then at Loch Lochy there was
the "staircase lock," a multiple of eight locks in succession over a
stretch of 500 yards, giving an upward lift of 64 feet—"the greatest
work of its kind which has been ever undertaken in ancient or modern
times." To Southey all this tremendous activity brought to vivid life the
cult of the gigantic one saw in the art galleries. Here was "the greatest
piece of masonry in the world," with "the powers of nature brought to
act upon a great scale in subservience to the purpose of man: one river
created, another (and that a huge mountain stream) shouldered out of
its place, and art and order assuming a character of sublimity."[71] As for
Telford himself, "a man more heartily to be liked, more worthy to be
esteemed and admired, I have never fallen in with."

Telford's achievements were so great, and so durable—more than
75 percent of his enormous output is still in use, 150–200 years later—
that the historian has to face the paradox that had society paid more
regard to his foresight, it would have been far greater still. From 1795
to 1835, Telford, McAdam and their followers built the finest road

system in Britain the world had ever seen. The result was a steady and at times dramatic increase in traveling speeds, as well as in comfort and safety. Telford's road to Holyhead, for instance, reduced the time from London from 41 to 28 hours. Rich men and military dispatch riders, with no expense spared and who did not mind ruining horses, had clocked up sensational times in the first decade of the century. As early as 1799 the millionaire William Beckford was getting from Fonthill to London, a distance of over 90 miles, in as little as 7 hours. In 1809 Lord Lonsdale, another millionaire, was averaging 9–10 miles an hour in his highly sprung carriage drawn by six horses. He also had contrived to ride 150 miles in a single day, on post horses, taking 15 hours, a remarkable exploit; he had ridden, indeed, 100 miles on the same horse.[72]

The effect of road improvements was to make such times easily attainable by coach and thus within the reach of the middle class, an excellent example of technology turning luxuries into commonplace necessities. The price was coming down too. By the end of the 1820s the average speed of the commercial coach from London to Manchester was as high as 12mph. Palmer's Coaches took only 16 hours on the London–Bath route, though it is true these were "specials," the ordinary coach, with six inside, 14 outside, taking 34 hours. Prices were lower than on the official mails and the seats more comfortable. But their coachmen sometimes dawdled to suit their own convenience. The mails, on the other hand, allowed only 30 minutes for major stops and ran strictly to time. Except in the worst weather, you could rely on their punctuality, an increasingly important point as everyone acquired watches and more and more businesses ran by the clock. The mails were generous with luggage, too, whereas the coaches weighed it carefully and anything over the 14-pound free allowance was charged at a penny a pound. Mails had harder seats, but you could sometimes get a whole side (to seat three) to yourself and stretch out—in that case travelers like Farington would travel more stages without stopping for the night. On 23 August 1836 the Exeter Mail contrived to get from London in a mere 16½ hours, cutting the already fast time by 3½ hours.[73]

Such speeds were impressive by comparison with the past but they represented the end of a line of development—the horse could go no faster. Telford had been aware of the need for a new system of road propulsion since he first began to create modern roads in the early years of the century. While it was the bump and crash of the wheel which destroyed badly made roads, once you had a well-made "scientific" road surface of the kind he and McAdam provided, the attrition came largely from the horses's hooves, by a factor of three to one.[74] In short, the horse had to be eliminated in favor of the power-driven wheel. Then you could have modern roads everywhere providing surfaces for speeds which were without limit. Telford always thought on the grandest possible scale. The sheer size of the earth-moving, rock-blasting, cutting- and embankment-making of his Holyhead road and his canals in Wales and Scotland was equal to anything which was to come in the early rail age, 1830–50. Edmund Burke, in his famous essay on the sublime (1757), the most influential tract on aesthetics ever published in the Anglo-Saxon world—it affected thinking on art as much as Adam Smith's *Wealth of Nations* (1776) revolutionized business theory—lists the qualities of the sublime as Astonishment, Terror, Obscurity, Power, Privation (Vacuity, Darkness, Solitude and Silence), Vastness, Infinity, Succession and Uniformity, Magnificence, Light, Colour, Magnitude in Building and Difficulty.[75] The great industrial concerns and their attendant cities which were arising in England in the early decades of the 19th century fulfilled many of these conditions of sublimity, but when it came to Magnitude in Building and, above all, Difficulty, Telford was the supreme engineer-architect of the sublime. His works inspired awe because ordinary people could not imagine how they got there without a miracle. He set the tone for other architects. Typical was the giant Highgate Archway which John Nash built (1812–13) at the northwest entrance to London to carry the traffic of Hornsey Lane over the A1. This not only adumbrated the future rail viaducts but was a distant intimation of modern large-scale road intersections.[76]

Telford would have loved to build a high-speed national road system solely for long-distance traffic—a motorway network, in short, 150 years before such came into being. While building his Holyhead road he realized that such highways ought to bypass towns completely, running straight from one terminus to another, serviced by special inns en route. On this point he was overcome by local trading interests, especially shopkeepers, who insisted the road ran in the traditional manner through their towns, thus in the end wrecking them as civilized places and works of art.[77] Telford ran into even more frustrating opposition in his efforts to promote a powered road vehicle. The solution, of course, was the internal combustion engine, which eventually emerged to do the job. A gas-engine patent had in fact been lodged in 1794, and as early as 1824 such engines were made and used for pumping.[78] But this line of development was not pursued because it had to compete with a rival source of power already in process of spectacular evolution—steam.

*   *   *

Steam power was essentially an 18th-century invention pioneered in France but developed in Britain, chiefly in the mining industry. In the year of the American Declaration of Independence and *The Wealth of Nations*, 1776, James Watt set in motion the first modern steam-pumping engine. One which his firm, Bolton & Watt, installed the next year, 1777, continued to function until the first decade of the 20th century. Bolton & Watt engines, and others built on similar principles, were soon put to a huge variety of uses—one, for instance, powered the monster Telford used on his Caledonian Canal. The problem was to make them mobile. A ship, as we shall shortly see, was quickly perceived as a natural steam engine platform. But on land? Here again, a genius of the lowliest origins, like Telford, carried through the revolution. George Stephenson (1781–1848) came from the great northeast coalfield. He and the outstanding painter of the sublime, John Martin, were born in neighboring villages and were equally poor. Like Telford, Stephenson came from a family of shepherds, though his father worked as an engine man at the pits.

The Industrial Revolution, which first developed its irresistible momentum in the 1780s when Stephenson was a little boy, is often presented as a time of horror for working men. In fact it was the age, above all, in history of matchless opportunities for penniless men with powerful brains and imaginations, and it is astonishing how quickly they came to the fore. Capitalists, often swell landowners like Lord Wharncliffe, Lord Ravensworth and the Earl of Strathmore, who constituted the Grand Allies, owners of the West Moor Mine where Stephenson got his start, were anxious to recognize, promote and reward talent. Pits opened and shut quickly, the men were used to change and mobility, and the abler among them thought constantly in terms of innovation. Stephenson had no education. At eighteen he could not read or write. But by then, he had been a herdsman and a welder, had driven a gin horse, and had served as an assistant fireman, fireman, then engineer—mending shoes and clocks in his spare time; the year before he had been put in charge of a giant new pumping engine at a major pit, consulting with the man who made it, a brilliant designer called Robert Hawthorne. By eighteen he was in love with steam machinery as the young Keats and Shelley were in love with poetry. He found these hissing, pounding, difficult and massive objects creatures of romance, as indeed they were, and are.

Stephenson got his supreme chance in 1811 when the new pumping engine at the ultradeep High Pit failed and he was called in to transform it and make it work efficiently. His success led the Grand Allies to put him in charge of all machinery at their pits on a retainer of £100 a year, and he worked in addition as a civil engineer for other firms. He learned to read and write, attended night school, and used the excellent education he provided for his son Robert, born in 1803, to advance his own. Robert had to ride 10 miles a day on a donkey to attend classes in Newcastle and teach his father in the evenings when he got back—they read volumes of science and technology together.[79] The father, often with the son observing and helping, designed and built 34 different stationary engines at this time, including a giant 200 horsepower pump which drew water from 50 fathoms at 2,000 gallons a minute. When the Grand Allies decided to use steam to power their coal-wagon trains they commissioned Stephenson to design the engine.[80]

Stephenson's early locomotives were tricky. Only one driver in three could manage them and no one except George Chicken could be trusted to run one safely at night. But Stephenson was an indefatigable man who worked on problems until he solved them, and he gradually devised an efficient control system. Like Telford he thought big, too, and systematically increased the power of his creations. Then again, he was surrounded by inventive men, one of whom went on to found the Belgian rail system, another to design the York & North Midland, a third to create the Midland Railway.

Like Telford again, Stephenson had a natural eye for simplicity and elegance of design, and his engines were beautiful in their way. Indeed these men of the Northeast, capitalists and inventors alike, were keen to adorn as well as serve their society. When they set up their routes, to and fro and within the coalfields, they hired Ignatius Bonomi, son of the great Joseph, to design their bridges, of which Skerne Bridge, Darlington, remains an outstanding example. They were humanists in their way, and the power-god they brought into existence had almost a human face. As the head of one of the greatest engine firms, Colonel Kitson Clark, put it, "There is nothing so serviceable or so valuable to mankind as the steam locomotive. A machine easy to make, easy to run, easy to repair, never weary from its birth in mint condition to the days that saw it worn, dirty and old; wasteful as nature and inefficient as man, very human in characteristics, far from ideally economic in action but, like our race, ever in a stage of development, master in emergencies, its possibilities of improvement inexhaustible."[81]

It was this adaptable creature that Telford wanted to put on his ideal road system. He was not opposed to rails or tramways in their place. Wooden rails had been used in German mining since the early 16th century, and in Britain since the 1580s; in the Lowther pits near Whitehaven they had been replaced by iron rails since 1738. By 1815 hundreds of miles of iron track had been laid in the industrial districts for bulk carriage, and for ten years there had even been a 4-foot-gauge railway carrying passengers from Croydon to Wandsworth. All these routes were horse drawn. Telford was as anxious as anyone to put the locomotive to work. But he felt strongly that those running on rails should be confined to bulk goods and should essentially serve as feeders and outlets to the canal system, a slow but cheap and efficient method of heavy transport which now radiated all over the country. He opposed the idea of a steam-powered rail network for general traffic, including passengers. On 19 April 1821, a fateful date in transport history, a group of Northeast businessmen, led by Edward Pease, got a Bill through parliament to construct a steam rail route from Darlington, in the remote Aukland coalfield—hitherto underdeveloped because of the carrying distance—to Stockton-on-Tees. Stephenson was hired as chief engineer and Pease boasted: "If the railway be established and it is a success, as it is to convey not only goods but passengers, we shall have the whole of Yorkshire and next the whole of the United Kingdom following the railways."[82]

By 1824, when the line was almost complete and Telford had the opportunity to study its proposed timetables, he realized there was a fundamental objection to the whole notion of a transport system based on fixed rails: Only the company which owned the track could, in practice, operate the vehicles on it. This offended the basic principle of British monopoly legislation which, for instance, forbade a canal-owning company to operate barges on its own waters. But such a law could not, for safety reasons, apply to rails, which would never be open to the general public. Railways, then, were by unalterable definition inefficient and uneconomic because they required an expensive, special track for their exclusive use. To get competition, you had to run rival tracks—as indeed was to happen—which would be even more wasteful. If one company went bankrupt, what would happen to its track? And if railways prospered, what would happen to the modern road system Telford was building? It would decay—yet more waste.

Telford wanted transport companies to run fleets of carriages on his new roads.[83] That meant getting the weight down. He found a willing ally in young Goldsworthy Gurney, who from 1823 began to design lightweight engines, reduced from four tons to 30 hundredweight by using a new "steam-jet" or blast system to produce power. Ironically, this propulsion system was quickly incorporated by Stephenson into his track engines, especially the *Rocket*. Unfortunately, neither Gurney nor Telford had a powerful lobby to back their schemes. The army showed some interest, and in July 1829, at the request of the Quartermaster-

General, Gurney made a return journey from London to Bath in his steam engine on the common road at an average speed of 15mph. This inspired Sir Charles Dance to set up a regular service between Gloucester and Cheltenham, a distance of nine miles, which operated for three months in 1831, taking as little as 45 minutes on the journey.[84]

But by then it was too late. The mining and industrial companies were heavily committed to the fixed track system. In 1821 a Morpeth engineer called John Birkinshaw had perfected a fast and cheap production method of making wrought-iron "I" section rails in convenient 15-foot lengths, which meant that the track itself could be laid quickly. The Stockton–Darlington railway was a commercial success and was followed by heavy investment in the far more ambitious Liverpool–Manchester Railway, in which George Stephenson was also involved. He now had his own engine-production company, the best of its kind in the world. He did not believe that road engines could ever safely develop the power and speed which rails made so easy. On 25 August 1830, three weeks before the new Liverpool–Manchester Railway opened, he took out his Northumbrian on a test run, with the pretty actress Fanny Kemble beside him on the footplate. She had just had a sensational success in *Romeo and Juliet,* which was now playing in Liverpool, and she was treading on air. She wrote to a friend that she was "horribly in love" with George Stephenson, finding his "mode of explaining his ideas" to be "peculiar and very original, striking and forcible." His accent might be "north country" but his language was without "the slightest touch of vulgarity or coarseness." As for the engine, she found it "a snorting little animal which I felt rather inclined to pat." It "set out at the utmost speed, 35 miles an hour, swifter than a bird flies. You cannot conceive what that sensation of cutting the air was; the motion as smooth as possible too. I could either have read or written; and as it was I stood up and with my bonnet off drank the air before me . . . When I closed my eyes this sensation of flying was quite delightful and strange beyond description. Yet strange as it was, I had a perfect sense of security and not the slightest fear."[85]

There indeed was the case for rail, and neither Telford nor Gurney really got the chance to put the rival one for road. By the end of the 1820s, the rail lobby was well capitalized and powerful in Parliament. The rail men did not want steam carriages on roads at any price. Moreover, for the time being, they had a powerful ally in the horse-and-coach lobby. They recognized the threat of rail and were making desperate efforts to raise the speeds of coaches to meet it. But the threat of steam coaches on the roads was far more immediate, especially if the coaches went at averages of 15mph or even—God forbid!—20mph. The

toll interests stood to gain enormously, in the long run, by the development of mechanical traffic on the roads, for if steam succeeded there,
other and less objectionable forms of propulsion would follow; the
internal combustion engine might have come in twenty years or even
ten, instead of 60. But for the moment the toll owners were entirely in
the hands of the coach-mail-horse lobby. This combination, plus the
rail interest, was irresistible in Parliament, which passed prohibitive
tolls specifically designed to discriminate against steam vehicles on the
roads and wreck the notion commercially. In 1831 Gurney persuaded
a Select Committee to agree that the steam carriage was "one of the
most important improvements in the means of internal communications ever introduced" and that the blocking legislation should be
"repealed immediately." But by this time the Commons was totally
embroiled in the Reform-Bill crisis and nothing was done.[86] The death
of Telford in 1834 settled the matter. First England, then the world,
invested in hundreds of thousands of miles of fixed track and the
motorway age was delayed for over a century. The stages and mails, so
determined to keep the steam carriage off their roads, had been mortally wounded by rail before the end of the 1840s. Tolls fell in value, and
road technology, given such a tremendous impetus by Telford and
McAdam, stagnated.

Wind power at sea put up a much fiercer resistance to steam power
because its technology was more flexible than horsepower. But the race
for greater speed and reliability was if anything even more relentless
because the sea was such a hostile element and delays so objectionable
to travelers. Indeed sometimes they could not set off at all. When the
Duchess of Richmond, heading for Brussels, went on the Dover–
Boulogne Channel crossing in 1814, with her three boys, their tutor
Spencer Maidan, her daughter, and various servants—a total of 17, plus
a barouche and a barouche-landau—they were forced to wait an entire
week at Dover for a favorable wind, staying at Wright's Hotel, one of
the most expensive in the world. Maidan reported that the Duke of
Orleans and his suite had been charged £100 there just for breakfast.
The duchess's party finally got off on a sloop-of-war and Maidan, "by
Captain Denman's order," was sent "a glass of madeira and a biscuit
every half-hour and some cold fowl and ham when I chose it," and thus
"escaped sea-sickness altogether."[87] In autumn 1821 Leigh Hunt set off
for Italy at the invitation of Byron and Shelley to edit a new paper, the
Liberator, beyond the reach of the English law of criminal libel. He got
on board in London, accompanied by his wife, six children, and a goat,
on 15 November. The winter of 1821–22 was one of the worst ever

recorded, and by 22 December the ship had got no further than Dart-mouth. The Hunts were so exhausted they went ashore, thus forfeiting their passage money, and endless delays and fears of storms meant they did not get off again until 13 May 1822, reaching Leghorn (Livorno) in July.[88] There were similar tales of horror from all over the world. When Stamford Raffles, the creator of Singapore, and his wife Sophie traveled from the British base at Bencoolen in Sumatra to Calcutta in 1817, they had to put up with a "miserable" boat "which has no better accommo-dation than one small cabinet with only a porthole to admit air, where centipedes and scorpions roved about without interruption." They lost a mast in the Bay of Bengal monsoon, Sophie added, and the Hoogly River pilot "got so drunk" he stuck them on a sandbank where they remained for four days until rescued.[89]

At its best, however, sail at least had the advantage of cheapness. It cost far less to travel from Edinburgh to London by boat than by coach. At Gravesend there were 700 watermen and fishermen and you could bargain with them to take you down into East Kent or up into Essex or Suffolk for a few shillings. There were risks of course, especially on the Thames, where big barges often ran down and sank small passenger boats—that was how the art dealer Van Der Gucht was drowned, leaving a wife and eleven children.[90] But if you avoided grasping racket ports like Dover, nipping up the coast by small boat was a smart way to travel before the rails came. The amount of inshore boat traffic, as a study of the paintings of Turner, who loved to paint it, reveals, was enormous. On a September day in Cromer, Farington found himself surveying a vast panorama of small vessels—luggers, colliers, yawls and so on—going about their daily business; he counted 97 sail in sight at one time.[91] Moreover, these ships were often highly efficient, one reason why so many of them survived till 1914. It was a long time before rail could transport Newcastle coal ("sea coal" as it was called) to London cheaper than the sail colliers. The Geordie ships were regarded as the best training possible for seamen because crews were made to work hard and efficiently, though many of their skippers were illiterate, could not read charts and felt their way by lead lines. They had no shoes or socks, wore trousers made of pilot cloth and known as "fearnoughts" and sleeved vests, and then asserted their dignity by tall chimney-pot hats, though they went aboard by swarming up the cable chain. "Geordie Fashion" was what sailors meant by a hard life from the captain, as opposed to "Blackwall Fashion" or the nautical term "full and plenty" (a full crew, enough food).

The colliers looked clumsy but these two-masted vessels, square rigged on both the fore and main masts, were, in their own way, miracles of advanced sail technology: their brig-rig, as it was called, enabled them to stop and start quickly and go forward and backward. Brigantines, cutters with square yards and stunsails, ketch-rigged and cutter-rigged yachts, luggers and yawls, or ingenious combinations of them, led to many postwar improvements in wind power which prolonged the age of sail by decades. Smart young men with more money than sense often got maritime architects to design them ultrafast little cruisers with which to astonish their friends, rather as today they sport Ferraris or Jaguars. That was how Shelley killed himself. From envy of Byron's much bigger yacht *Bolivar,* he acquired the very fast *Don Juan,* only 24 feet long, but with twin mainmasts and schooner rigging, and bullied his architect into raising its speed still further by a rerig and false prow and stern—the result "sailed like a witch" but was equally lethal and duly took its owner to the bottom in June 1822.[92] But speed could be safe. The most impressive invention of all was the big, fast clipper, an American peacetime development of the two-masted Yankee schooner designed in Baltimore for privateering during the War of 1812. China-trade tea clippers of 1,000 tons or more and immigrant clippers twice their size began to appear around 1820. These superb creations, the modern frontier of a technology which had been evolving for 6,000 years, are the only sailing ships known to have logged more than 400 sea miles in a day, then the fastest travel on Earth.

It was no accident that the best new designs came from America. The post-1815 spread of maritime traffic on the lakes and rivers of North America was one of the biggest single growth points in a civilized world which was growing fast almost everywhere. Canadian and United States timber prices were the lowest on record and the East Coast shipbuilding industry expanded at such a rate that by 1840, when 90 percent of the world's shipping was still made of wood, American and Canadian yards were producing half of it. Not until iron took over did British yards reestablish themselves as the world's biggest producers (by 1892–94, the United Kingdom was launching 81.6 percent of all ships built).[93]

Needless to say, even in 1815 iron was clearly coming for sea transport, as it was coming on land. This development was a godsend to a small country like Britain, whose noble woods and few forests had been savagely reduced by the needs of the Napoleonic Wars, but which was rich in iron ore and coking coal to smelt it. Wooden ships had many advantages, not least the fact that they could be repaired in yards anywhere in the world or just beached on a friendly, tree-lined shore. They were strong, too. It is worth remembering that HMS *Victory,* a 100-gun ship of 2,162 tons, laid down at Chatham in 1759 (though not completed till 1778), carried the flag of 14 admirals, including Nelson, was involved in eight major actions in 34 years, was not paid off till 1835 and still survives.⁹⁴ But ships made of wood developed weaknesses if built beyond a certain length; in 1811 theoretical studies by Thomas Laing demonstrated that the safe maximum length was about 300 feet. By contrast, the length of bars of iron for transverse frames was almost limitless, and iron ships could dispense with a keel and be built to virtually any size.⁹⁵ And, if steam-power was coming for ships, it seemed anomalous, as well as a fire risk, to put an iron engine in a wooden hull.

Steam was certainly coming on water. The French had built a steamboat and tried it on the Seine as far back as 1775, but the power proved too weak; five years later, the Marquis Jouffroy d'Abbans went up the Saone near Lyons in a 182-ton paddle wheeler he called the *Pyroscaphe*. There were some American experiments in 1787, but Robert Fulton, who started to build steamboats when he returned to America in 1806, has the best claim to be the father of commercial steam navigation. His first patented boat, which had its trials on the East River on 9 August 1807, was described as "an ungainly craft looking precisely like a backwoods sawmill mounted on a scow and set on fire.'" But it went 150 miles to Albany in only 32 hours, and back downriver in 30. Fulton was able to write in triumph: "The power of propelling boats by steam is now fully proved," adding, in the light of the Louisiana Purchase, "It will give a cheap and quick conveyance to the merchants on the Mississippi, Missouri and other great rivers which are now laying open their treasures to the enterprise of our countrymen."⁹⁶

Fulton was the first to grasp that shallow-draft steam-driven craft were ideally suited to river work. In military hands, as we shall see, these craft were a prime instrument which enabled the West to penetrate the great rivers of Asia and Africa and subdue their peoples. Fulton's main aim however was to cut the cost of goods and passenger travel. His *Steam Boat* started its commercial service a month after its trials and within weeks was carrying 90 passengers. Each boat he built was better than its predecessor, and in 1812 he introduced a reliable thrice-weekly service, the whole trip costing $7 each way or $1 for each 20-mile stage, well below the rival cost of coach travel. Wartime meant he had difficulty getting Boulton & Watt engines from England, which required export licenses from the British government, but once peace came, this and other services, including a New York–Jersey City steam ferry, exploded. By then Fulton was dead, of a neglected cold which became pneumonia. The day of his funeral, the legislature went into mourning and the New York shops shut—they respected inventors in those days. Fulton's first peacetime (and posthumous) vessel, the *Chancellor Livingstone* (1816), the earliest to use coal, looked almost beautiful, and it certainly offered comfort—a galley, bar, berths, and a dining saloon. (The corridor system was used on this boat and became the model for the first American railroad carriages. By contrast, early British rail carriages were modeled on stagecoaches and had separate doors and compartments—a distinction between the two systems which prevailed until the mid-20th century.) By 1823 the Hudson Steamboat Company was a huge success, owning five boats valued at £132,000, grossing £30,000 annually and returning 8 percent on its capital.[97]

Fulton got the service going by virtue of a monopoly privilege in the New York area. Colonel John C. Stevens of Hoboken, barred from New York for this reason, built a steamboat called the *Phoenix* and started to run her commercially from Trenton to the Delaware estuary in 1809, the first commercial service at sea. The beginnings of competition led to a mass of lawsuits over privilege and over copyrights—the United States was already in the process of becoming a lawyers' paradise. But nothing could stop the steam conquest of America's tremendous rivers. In 1811 at Pittsburgh, an eastern financial syndicate launched a monster of 371 tons, the *New Orleans,* to go downriver. Shortly after General Jackson's victory made the South safe again, the *Enterprise* made the first trip *upriver,* against powerful currents, managing New Orleans–Louisville, with stops, in only 25 days. That trip was the breakthrough. Four years later there were 31 steamboats on the Mississippi and Ohio, jumping to 75 in 1825 and to nearly 400 by 1830. They were owned in small groups or even individually and the fierce competition they generated forced down freight prices and fares. In pre-steam days it had cost $5 to carry 100 pounds up to Louisville. It had dropped to $2 by 1830, and soon fell to 25 cents.[98] Cost-effectiveness was achieved by the high-pressure engine, reducing the draft and enabling designers to pile on decks above the waterline and so increase carrying space. The weird shape thus created by techno-economic factors soon assumed a beauty all of its own—the early Industrial Revolution constantly bred new and graceful forms as well as pollution and ugliness. The shallow draft meant that all rivers could be used high up their courses: Within fifteen years steamboats had reached Nashville, Knoxville, Pittsburgh and the Alleghenies on the upper Ohio, and there were hundreds of river ports, kept open by elaborate dredgers, by canals and by locks over falls and rapids.[99]

The British effort in steamships was initially dictated by the desire to maneuver warships independently of wind and weather so they could, whenever desired, "break the line," a tactic first used by Admiral Rodney in 1780 at Martinique. At the Carron Ironworks near Stirling, the great armaments factory which invented the fast-action Carronade gun, they experimented with double- and triple-hulled craft, driven by paddles worked by manpower. But the men became tired too easily. Then a young engineer, William Symington, made two steam engines which were put into a small pleasure boat and tried on Dalswinton Loch near Dumfries on 17 October 1788. On board were a local laird, Sir William Monteith, three of his servants who acted as crew, Patrick Miller, the rich banker who owned the works, Symington, the future inventor Alexander Naysmith, the tutor to the Miller household and, most improbably, the poet Robert Burns.[100] Watching from the shore was a young, sharp-eyed Borderer, Henry Brougham.

The craft developed a speed of 4–5mph, but this historic episode did not produce a fleet of steam warships, the Admiralty preferring its strongly built sailing ships which could take a tremendous pounding and deliver hundred-ton broadsides all day. Even at the end of the Napoleonic Wars, warships driven by steam were still only at the building stage, and they were soon canceled. The first European steam warship of any size, the *Rising Star* (1817–18), was a product of private enterprise. It was fully rigged too and was commissioned by the rebel and adventurer Lord Cochrane to liberate Chile; it inaugurated the steam era in the Pacific. Steam was seen as more useful for short distances, because early engines demanded so much wood or coal. In 1812 the *Comet,* built in Glasgow and operating on the Clyde, became the first commercially successful steamship in Europe. These Clydeside steamers were soon operating up the west coast of Scotland as far as Inveraray, and one of them, the *Eagle,* was brought to London to work as a Thames pleasure cruiser in 1819. It left Hungerford Market stairs at 9 A.M. and went as far as Gravesend, stopping en route and returning by 4:30 P.M.—31 miles each way for the modest fare of 1s, 1.6d on Sundays; it had a tiny kitchen for refreshments and it provided playing cards, table games and even an orchestra.[101]

The British, on the other hand, were quicker than the Americans to use iron to supplement steam. Their iron boats went back to 1787, when John Wilkinson launched a 70-foot barge of bolted cast iron on the Severn, and from the end of the wars onwards enormous iron barges dominated the Clyde coal trade. In 1820 the British got an iron boat across the Channel and two years later the first true iron steamship, assembled on the Thames from parts prefabricated in Staffordshire, steamed down-Channel and up the Seine. Getting across the Channel by the fastest and easiest method was already an obsession among imaginative engineers on both sides of it. There was much talk of a Channel Tunnel. The 26-mile stretch of water had, in fact, been crossed by air in 1785, when the French inventor François Blanchard, accompanied by John Jeffries, an Anglo-American, went from Dover to the Forest of Guines in a balloon, equipped with a parachute the Frenchman had likewise devised. Aeronautics was now a flourishing science, at least in theory. During the big invasion scare of 1805, a print presented Bonaparte's forces arriving by balloon and tunnel, the British retaliating with giant man-carrying kites.[102]

The year before this print appeared, a Yorkshire landowner, George Cayley (1773–1857), wrote an essay on the mechanical principles of flight, and in 1809, for the first time, he correctly set down the theory of heavier-than-air motion.[103] Cayley got his passionate interest in science and mechanics, and his considerable theoretical understanding over a wide area, from the Nonconformist tutors of the Dissenting Academy tradition—Oxford and Cambridge made virtually no contribution to science or technology during this period. His range of inventive imagination was astonishing. His idea for a hot-air engine powering an aeroplane, engraved on a silver disk, can be seen in Kensington Science Museum, and his papers, which came to light in 1927, included designs for a helicopter with four-bladed rotors. Cayley inherited a baronetcy and a large estate, but in the intervals of running it, he established the first agricultural allotments, helped to found the British Association for the Advancement of Science and the Regent Street Polytechnic, improved the acoustics at Covent Garden, invented a tension wheel for aircraft carriages, forerunner of the bicycle wheel, served as a member of Parliament, and lobbied the government to provide funds for scientific research and development. He also worked on airships, a mechanical hand, caterpillar tractors, buffers for trains, rail safety and the internal combustion engine.[104]

The last point was of critical importance, since Cayley understood very well what was required for powered flight: "The whole problem is confined within these limits, viz. to make a surface support a given weight by the application of power to the air"—which meant not only lightweight materials but a lightweight engine. He knew that an internal combustion engine was far more likely to meet this criterion than steam and in his key 1809 paper he described such a power source, "igniting inflammable powders in closed vessels . . . by inflammation of spirits of tar." He believed "the engine itself need not exceed 50 lbs in weight."[105] The difficulty was that fuel for a "closed combustion" engine exceeded in cost steam-engine fuel by a factor of eight.

Even more serious was that Cayley lacked the mechanical skill to make his own engines. He had a workshop at his Yorkshire house, Brompton Hall, presided over by an engineer called Vick, but he lacked a close practical associate of the caliber of Stephenson or Naysmith. He made endless observations of birds to discover the ratios of size, weight, strength, speed, and wing beats, and he carried out aerodynamic experiments with airflows around streamlined solids to determine the best designs to achieve lift. He discovered that much more power was needed for take-off than in regular flight, so that aircraft engines must be capable of "doing more than their constant work," and that wings would require a hollow structure. He wrote that he remained "well convinced that Aerial Navigation will form a more prominent feature in the progress of civilisation during the succeeding century." But like Charles Babbage, the inventor of the computer, as we shall see, he was frustrated by the nonavailability of lightweight materials and cheap functional parts.[106] The best he could do was to sponsor and invest in the Adelaide Gallery, off the Strand. The object of the gallery was to get the public interested in the scientific future by exhibiting such new devices as a steam-driven machine gun, said (falsely) to have impressed the Duke of Wellington so much that he had declared, "If I had had the steam-gun at Waterloo it would have been over in half an hour instead of lasting all day."[107]

The public was interested in these possible developments, but on a strict basis of *cui bono.* And people wanted science for different purposes. Shelley, the most scientific minded of all the romantic poets, more so even than Coleridge, believed that scientific invention had the social purpose of redeeming the mess that man, and still more God—or rather the belief in God, since He Himself did not exist—had made of the world.[108] Shelley, like Cayley, saw the world and progress, as it were, from a birdman's-eye view. He planned to explore Africa by balloon on a mission of social progress, insisting: "The shadow of the first balloon, which a vertical sun would project precisely underneath it, as it floated silently over that unhappy country, would virtually emancipate every slave, and would annihilate slavery for ever."[109] His *Witch of Atlas,* with energy supplied by electricity and magnetism, is the earliest great poem of space travel.[110]

Not many, however, shared Shelley's enthusiasm for scientific travel as the way to the stars, both metaphorically and literally, or even Sir George Cayley's more modest aim to escape from the restraints and friction of the Earth's surface. They were adventurous enough, they wanted to travel far, and frequently—it was the first age of mass long-distance travel—but their objects were speed, comfort, safety and economy. In the years after the war, substantial and accelerated progress was being achieved on all four counts. The wars had brought vital advances in seamanship which were rapidly applied when peace came. The accumulation of records of deep-sea soundings meant that the number of positions correctly fixed in latitude and longitude, only 109 in the early 18th century, had risen to over 6,000 by 1817.[111] In the 1820s, Francis Beauford, hydrographer to the Admiralty, began the accurate series of charts covering the entire globe and known as Admiralty Pilots. In the same decade the British perfected the chronometer. The compass, still unreliable in 1820 (the Admiralty reported that half the navy's compasses were worthless), was rapidly improved. There was a revolution in shore guidance. As late as 1807 the key Eddystone Lighthouse in the Channel was lit merely by 24 candles. In 1819 Augustin Fresnel designed a modern lighthouse lens and burner for the French Ministry of Marine and devised a system of identifying flashes. In the mid-1820s both the British and the French authorities embarked on major lighthouse programs, much assisted by the invention, in 1824, of Portland cement, by a Wakefield bricklayer, Joseph Aspdin, who heated a mixture of chalk and clay at temperatures high enough to sinter it, that is, make it coalesce without melting. The British reorganized Trinity House, which ran the coastlines and, at the same time, founded the Royal National Institute for the Preservation of Life from Shipwreck (1824), which provided lifeboats, and started work on Lloyd's Register of British and Foreign Shipping (1834), which supplied the data and the impetus for scientific safety measures. The Americans, hitherto backward, began to take safety at sea seriously from 1820, raising the number of lighthouses on their coasts from 55 to 256 and adding 30 lightboats and over 1,000 buoys.[112]

Travel on water remained hazardous. Even a great East Indiaman, regarded as the safest vessel afloat, might go down, as happened to one commanded by Wordsworth's brother Jim. And steam, a boon in so many ways, created brand-new perils, especially on the rivers it queened. Up to the 1840s, nearly one-third of the Mississippi steamboats were lost in accidents. Burst boilers were so common—150 were recorded up to 1850, with 1,400 killed; the real total was much higher—that Charles Dickens, for instance, was strongly advised to sleep at the back of the boat. In February 1830 the *Helen McGregor* was leaving Memphis, Tennessee, when the head of her starboard boiler cracked, and the explosion killed 50 souls, flayed alive or suffocated inhaling the steam.[113] All the same, the number of those lost at sea, as a proportion of those traveling, began to fall steadily after 1815.

Greater speed, greater comfort, and cheaper prices went hand in hand. From the end of the wars, the establishment of official packets, to Dublin, to Calais and soon across the Atlantic, set new standards for sea travel, as the mails had done on land, especially when they were equipped with steam engines. Croker, returning from Dublin where he had been for George IV's official visit, reported to Peel on 29 August 1821: "Sailed in the steam-packet, the wind quite against us, very strong. . . . We had a rolling and disagreeable passage of 10 hours and 50 minutes." That was bad enough, but, he added, "The sailing packet, which had sailed 24 hours before us, we passed at sea, and she cannot arrive for 12 hours after us. If she has any passengers on board, they must have passed a miserable time. I sat in my carriage on deck."[114]

During the 1820s, steamers were no longer content to dominate the rivers and the narrow seas, but roamed farther and farther afield. The first company specifically founded to run seagoing steamships, the General Steam Navigation Company, began to operate paddle wheelers from London in 1824, initially to Kent coast towns like Margate and Ramsgate. The next year the *Enterprise,* 470 tons, 120 horsepower, became the first steamer to reach Calcutta, taking 103 days plus 10 days refueling, a very impressive performance. In 1829 a Bombay-built steamer, the *Hugh Linday,* 411 tons, 160 horsepower, made the trip to Suez with mails, and the next year the London–India short route was completed when a mail steamship traveled from Falmouth to the eastern Mediterranean. Both the Peninsular & Orient and the Pacific Steam Navigation Company date their origins from 1829. Steam cut the cost of sea travel first by half, then by three-quarters. It was coming down even without steam. Steam came late to transatlantic travel because of the difficulty of carrying enough fuel across so huge a stretch of water, but the rapid development of packet services from 1815 cut times and cost and promoted reliability. By 1829 there were packets sailing from London to New York twice a month, Liverpool to New York and Le Havre to New York three times a month each, Liverpool to Boston once a month, and frequent sailings from Hamburg to New York, too.[115] Once transatlantic packets, which carried mail, cabin passengers and light freight—prototypes of the regular service—began to function, fares became highly competitive and fell steadily. This in turn affected the immigrant boats. By 1816 the cheapest fare from Europe to New York had dropped to £10, and by 1830 it had halved again. By then the fare from Ireland to Quebec was usually as little as £2.10, and on occasions it fell to 15 shillings.[116]

*   *   *

I have described at length these huge advances in every aspect of the transport systems available to the peoples of the advanced nations because they were behind a process of unique importance in bringing the modern age into being—mass migration across continents. Huge numbers of men, women and children began to move from the Old World into the new settlements on the edge of the wilderness, or even directly into the wilderness itself.

In sheer numbers, it was the greatest population movement in history to date, and it began to change the actual face of the planet with growing rapidity. The process whereby Europeans colonized and settled large parts of the globe was not accidental. It began and ended primarily for demographic reasons. Europe was the first continent in which death rates began to fall substantially faster than birthrates. As a result its population rose much faster than in Africa and Asia, from about 150 million in 1750 to over 400 million in 1900. In 1750 Europe had one-fifth of the world's population; by 1900 it had risen to a quarter, despite a huge net outflow of emigrants.[117] After 1900 the rate of European population growth began to slow down and by the 1930s had been overtaken by the other continents; decolonization followed soon after, and even a net migration into Europe. In the 19th century however Europe was moving into its expanding cities and out into the world. Britain was the leader in both. This reflected the population growth rates. The population of all European states was rising, but some much faster than others. France's was the slowest. It had traditionally been the largest European state in terms of people, though Russia had overtaken it in the 18th century and Austria in 1814–15. In 1800 France had 28.3m people. By 1870 this had risen to 37.7m. The Germans, less than 20m in 1800, had passed France by 1870 to reach 41.1m. The Italians had jumped from 17.2m in 1800 to over 26m and the Spanish from 10.5m to 16.2. The British population had risen fastest, from 10.5m in 1800 to over 26m in 1870, a near-threefold increase.[118]

Hence, the British were the greatest urbanizers as well as the most numerous colonists. In the half-century 1800–50, England led the table for the annual percentage rate of urbanization with 0.36 percent. Then came Scotland and Belgium, the United States (with 0.16) and Saxony. France was only 0.10, Russia and Austria very low indeed with 0.04 and 0.03 respectively.[119] By 1815 Britain was well on the way to becoming the first urbanized society. At the opening of the century, 20 percent of its population lived in cities and towns of more than 10,000 people. By 1851, the year of the Great Exhibition, it had risen to 38 percent, and if you included towns of over 5,000, more than half the population was now urbanized.[120] In the years 1815–1830, this process of urbanization was proceeding briskly and obviously in Britain. People were both exhilarated and alarmed. An 1829 print by George Cruikshank, *London going Out of Town—or—the March of Bricks and Mortar,* shows hostile armies of chimneypots forming up to cross the river dividing countryside from town, while a continuous arc of bricks constitutes an invasion bridge: trees, animals and haystacks flee in terror, while behind the chimney-pot men massed ranks of back-to-back houses and dense clouds of coal smoke are preparing to follow.[121]

An expanding population thus drifted into the big towns, whose own birthrates were rising much faster than death rates—a combination which was to push the total of those living in London to nearly 2.5m by mid-century. But many of those leaving the overcrowded countryside knew they had little hope of making a living in the cities and preferred to risk emigration. If we include Ireland, the population of the United Kingdom in 1801 was a little under 15m. By 1821 it had jumped to over 21 million, and ten years later it was about 32 million, of which Ireland made up nearly 8m. The increase would have been even bigger without emigration. In the years 1815–40 alone, over a million left the British Isles—499,899 to British North America, 457,765 to the United States, 58,449 to Australia and New Zealand, and a little under 10,000 to South Africa.[122]

The millions flowing out from Britain and Ireland were joined by hundreds of thousands more from north and central Europe. The exodus was essentially a postwar phenomenon. It began when the first peace came in 1814: 7,000 Irish moved to Newfoundland (plus 3,000 the next year), only to find that the peace had hit the fishing industry there, and the British government had to provide assistance.[123] The big outflow started in 1815. Events leading up to Waterloo delayed it until the late summer, when the season for transatlantic travel normally ended. This year, however, immigrant ships, braving gales and ice, continued to reach North Atlantic ports throughout the autumn and winter. The volume increased the following year, particularly toward the end of it, since 1816 was "the year without a summer" in Europe. There was torrential rain and even sleet and snow during the summer months, wrecked harvests, and distress and starvation in the countryside, while the postwar industrial recession was hitting the towns. In central Europe the roads were crowded with ragged wanderers. Peasant prophets arose. Tsar Alexander I, anxious to increase his stock of "souls" to populate recent and anticipated conquests in Eastern Europe, the Caucasus and Asia, sent out propagandists who stressed the riches awaiting those who settled in his dominions. One such envoy was his friend Madame Krudener, whom we have already met. She traveled through Europe with her revivalist team of 40, preaching the claims of the Third Rome, as Moscow was called. In Summer 1817 Alexander's agents persuaded 700 Mennonites, regarded as "good" immigrants, to march 700 miles from Württemberg to found a colony in south Russia. But most central European emigrants, like the British and Irish, went to North America. A regular emigrant boat service was started down the Rhine, from Basel, Cologne and other centers, to the Dutch ports. Boats were built solely to get them down the big Continental rivers, and this was how steam was first used on inland waterways in central Europe.

The American journalist Hezekiah Niles (1777–1839), who ran *Niles's Weekly Register* from 1811 onward, in many ways America's best journal of record at this time, reckoned that 50,000 reached the United States in 1816, though this figure was later revised downward. His more careful calculations for 1817, based on shipping lists, suggest that 30,000 immigrants arrived during the season up to early September. (The U.S. federal government did not yet produce statistics.) Of these half came to New York and Philadelphia, though some went straight over the Appalachians into the Ohio Valley. Britain provided 20,000 of the arrivals, Germany and central Europe 8,000, and France 2,000.[124] At this stage there was no regulation at all. The British, who wanted to direct their emigrants to Canada rather than the United States, tried to limit British ships to one passenger to every two tons of registry against a ratio for foreign ships (chiefly American) of one in five. But fierce protests from Washington led them to give American ships equality of treatment from the beginning of the 1816 season. Apart from this, no authority on either side of the Atlantic bothered about who was going where or how.

In a sense, it was an astonishing moment of freedom in the world's history. An Englishman, without passport or papers, health certificate or any other documentation—without luggage for that matter—could plunk down £10 at a shipping counter in Liverpool and go aboard. He got nothing but water on board and had to provide his own food. He might go down to the bottom but, if lucky, in due course he went ashore in New York, no one asking him who he was or where he was going. He then vanished into the entrails of the new society. Many could not afford £10. They went on subsidized ships to Canada where, if they were Irish, they got cheap rides or lifts on coastal boats which got them to Massachusetts or New York. There was no control and no resentment at any of these arrivals. In 1818 the Scottish immigrant James Flint wrote: "I have never heard of another feeling than good wishes to them."[125] In five years, over 100,000 had come to the United States from Europe.

The age of innocence ended in the winter of 1818–19, when the effects of America's first bank crisis began to be felt. We will deal later with its political significance, which was considerable. Its effects on immigration were immediate. Unemployment rose. New arrivals were the first to be laid off or to meet blunt refusals when they tried for jobs. The Philadelphia cotton mills employed 2,325 in 1816; by autumn 1819 the number had dropped to 149.[126] John Quincy Adams, always quick to strike a doleful note, recorded in his diary on 24 April 1819: "In the midst of peace, and of partial prosperity, we are approaching to a crisis which will shake the Union to its centre."[127] The news of trouble arrived in Europe too late to affect the 1819 sailings, so tens of thousands continued to arrive throughout the spring and summer. Some cities, like New York, made frenzied attempts to stop them coming. For the first time domestic opinion swung brutally against immigrants. One observer, Emanuel Howitt, wrote that the Yankees now [1819] regarded the immigrant "with the most sovereign contempt . . . a wretch, driven out of his wretched country, and seeking a subsistence in this glorious land."[128] It would never be "glad confident morning again."[129] In March 1819 Congress introduced its first regulation, a two-persons-for-five-ton rule for incoming ships, effective from September—the beginning of control. In response to German colony founders, who demanded special treatment, Adams, as Secretary of State, laid down federal policy, such as it was, in a rescript published in *Niles' Weekly Register*. The American Republic, he said, invited nobody to come. "It would keep out nobody. Arrivals would suffer no disadvantages as aliens. But they could expect no advantages either. Native-born and foreign-born faced equal opportunities. What happened to them depended entirely on their individual ability and exertions, and on good fortune."[130]

The American crisis of 1819 gave others their chance to grab immigrants. Brazil was keen. In summer 1819 Portuguese agents persuaded 2,200 German-speaking immigrants from Freiburg to set up the colony of New Freiburg near Rio. Two years later, only 800 were still alive. Despite this failure, another batch of up to 5,000 Germans from Hamburg and Bremen left for Brazil in 1822.[131] The Tsar seized the opportunity too, needing colonists especially for his new conquests in the Caucasus. He was particularly keen on fundamentalist religious sects, rightly believing they made good farmers in rough territory. Before the American crisis, these movements were badly organized. Thus, of 14 columns of wagons, carrying 1,500 families, which left Ulm in Germany in summer 1817, only a third reached Tiflis, capital of Georgia in Transcaucasia—2,000 men, women and children died on the Lower Danube. But this disaster did not serve as a deterrent, especially when America turned sour. At this stage at least, the "pull of the East" was much stronger for the Germans, and the Tsar reinforced it by legislation in 1820–24 which offered them free or cheap land, a moratorium on taxes, and exemption from military service—the last an important point in Russia, where it could be a long and heavy burden, especially for alien groups such as Jews. For every German emigrant to America, 25 went to Russia, chiefly Russian Poland, making a total of 250,000 in the decade, transforming large areas of countryside and dozens of small towns, where they set up industries behind high Russian tariff walls— and stored up intractable problems for the future.[132]

The pause in migration to America did not last long. A critical change took place in Ireland in 1821–22. Hitherto emigrants had come almost entirely from the North, from Protestant families who were a bit better off and could afford the fare. But when the potato crop failed in 1821, part of an ominous series of failures which was to culminate in the catastrophe of the mid-1840s, the British government tried to organize mass emigration from the south the following spring to avert famine. In counties like Mayo, Clare, Kerry and Cork, where emigration was not yet the pattern, alarm spread. People thought the grim-looking ships were transports, taking them to bondage in Australia. Once the truth was known, the idea of going to America, at virtually no cost, caught on in the poorest parts of Ireland. These Catholic Irish, most of them violently hostile to British rule, had no wish to go to British Canada—which is where the Colonial Office was dispatching them—and thought all North America militantly Protestant. But when the first wave of 1822–23 wrote home showing how easy it was to slip from Canada to the United States and pointing out that Catholics enjoyed equal rights there, the rush to get out was on. In 1825 no less than 50,000 southern Irish applied for a mere 2,000 assisted places on a Colonial Office scheme, a foretaste of the mass exodus which was to transport a third of the Irish population to America.[133]

This movement of Irish was part of an accelerating buildup of immigrants from all over Europe in the early 1820s, when 6,000 to 10,000 a year entered the United States. In 1826 the figure rose 50 percent to 15,000; two years later it doubled again to 30,000. In 1832 it passed the 50,000 mark and thereafter fell below it only twice. The 1820s was thus the key decade in the Europeanization of huge areas of the world. In terms of numbers the main target was North America, but the phenomenon was global. Mass immigration had at last taken off.

The process had been slow to get going. In the year 1800, after more than 200 years of colonization of southern South America, there were still only 500,000 whites there. In the Americas as a whole there were no more than 5m whites, plus 1m blacks. There were 10,000 whites in Australia; none at all, as yet, in New Zealand. But the diaspora which began in the 1820s meant that, by the second half of the 20th century Europe had taken over much of the world's temperate zones. North of Mexico, 80 percent were of European descent. In Argentina the figure was 90–99 percent, in Uruguay, 90 percent, in Australia, over 90 percent, in Brazil, 85–95 percent. In the southern temperate zone as a whole, 75 percent of inhabitants were entirely of European ancestry.[134]

What caused the rush? As we have seen, it was the availability of increasingly speedy, cheap and safe transport which provided the physical means to relieve the population pressure. But there were many other factors. The European winters of 1825–26 and 1826–27 were very long and horrifyingly cold; the winter of 1829–30 was one of the coldest ever recorded and had all kinds of consequences, including political ones, as we shall see. These climatic disasters produced serious food shortages, especially in Ireland and Germany. The theories of Thomas Malthus, that growing overpopulation would be corrected by natural disasters including famine, filtered down to the masses, often in hideously distorted forms. Men wanted to get their families out of Europe to escape from what they feared was impending starvation.

Then there was the tax burden. At the end of the wars, Europe was a painfully overtaxed continent. Almost everything was taxed, often heavily. Sydney Smith fulminated in the *Edinburgh Review* against "Pitt's system," which slapped duties on "every article which enters into the mouth, or covers the back, or is placed under the foot—taxes upon everything which is pleasant to see, hear, feel, smell or taste—taxes upon warmth, light and locomotion—taxes upon everything on earth, and the waters under the earth—or everything that comes from abroad, or is grown at home—taxes on the raw material—taxes on every fresh value that is added to it by the industry of man—taxes on the sauce which pampers man's appetite, and the drug that restores him to health—on the ermine which decorates the judge and the rope that hangs the criminal—on the poor man's salt and the rich man's spice—on the brass nails of the coffin and the ribands of the bride—at bed or board, couchant or levant, we must pay—the schoolboy whips his taxed top—the beardless youth manages his taxed horse, with a taxed bridle, on a taxed road—and the dying Englishman, pouring his medicine which has paid 7 percent, into a spoon that has paid 15 per cent, flings himself back on his chintz bed, which has paid 22 per cent—and expires in the arms of an apothecary who has paid a license of £100 for the privilege of putting him to death. His whole property is then immediately taxed from 2 to 10 per cent—beside the probate, large fees are demanded for burying him in the chancel—his virtues are handed down to posterity on taxed marble—and he is then gathered to his fathers, to be taxed no more."[135]

On the Continent, there were tens of thousands of customs barriers, imposing duties on almost anything which crossed them. The British were spared internal customs, but they groaned under the income tax. The income tax was the most unpopular tax since ship money in the 17th century. The radicals saw it not merely as a monstrous burden, but as an "inquisitorial" intrusion into the privacy of a man's financial affairs. In his great campaign against the tax in 1815–16, Henry Brougham produced evidence that income-tax returns had been sold as wastepaper and used to wrap up cheeses, so a customer might eat his cheese and devour the financial secrets of a fellow citizen simultaneously. His success in getting the Commons to abolish the tax on 18 March 1816 by a majority of 238 to 201 dumbfounded the government and was one of the most popular political victories of the decade.[136] But if the government was not allowed to tax you in one way, it would tax you in another. The real problem was the cost of government itself. The radicals wanted to reduce it drastically. It would be a different matter when they got control of it themselves and began to devise utopian schemes for spending public money. At this stage they saw governmental expenses as arising chiefly from excessive armies and navies, and pensions and sinecures for the well born and well connected. All these must go.

In the United States, however, they had never existed. There the army was one-fiftieth the size of Prussia's. America's *per capita* expense of government was 10 percent of Britain's. There were no tithes, because there were no established clergy. No poor rates, because virtually no poor. An American farm which kept eight horses paid only $12 annually in tax. To Europeans such figures seemed incredible Not only were American wage rates high, but you kept what you received. There wer other advantages. No conscription. No political police. No censorship. No legalized class distinctions. All classes wore the same clothes. Employers and their hands ate at the same table. No one called anyone "master." Europeans learned these things from personal letters from relations or neighbors who had already taken the plunge—letters which circulated round the village or were read aloud to rapt gatherings round the fireside. These most potent of all emigration agents were reinforced

by the American president's annual messages to Congress, which served
as liberal manifestos—especially when Andrew Jackson began to produce them at the end of the 1820s—and were often published *in extenso*
in European newspapers. As the *Dublin Morning Post* put it on 11
January 1830: "We read this document as if it related purely to our
concerns."[137] In Germany there was pressure from the authorities on
newspapers not to publish the president's message, which was regarded
as subversive—as indeed in a sense it was, for it made a point of
stressing American social and political virtues, in contrast to European
vices.

Perhaps the most potent of all American virtues, in European eyes,
had nothing directly to do with good government. It was the price of
land. In the early decades of the 19th century, good land—land that was
accessible and secure, ready to be cleared and worked by an industrious
family with a small capital—was cheaper than at any time in history,
before or since. It was a unique moment, which could never conceivably
occur again. The last great primitive hunting grounds of the world,
thinly populated, if at all, and enormous in extent, were suddenly open,
by virtue of the transport revolution, to farming settlement. In Russia,
another 120 million acres were being seized from the indigenous pastoral and hunting tribes—in the Transvolga and the Crimea, on both
sides of the Caucasus, in southern Siberia and south-central Asia—and
handed over to landlords and soldiers, free peasants and liberated serfs.
Many of the new owners got their estates or plots for nothing as part
of a deliberate state policy of turning over traditional tribal grazing to
intensive farming and settlement. From the end of the wars, and continuing throughout the 19th century, up to 18 million people—including
immigrants from central Europe as well as Russians moving south and
east—benefited from this process.[138] Much the same thing was happening in Argentina, where the policy was to sell, rent or if necessary grant
free land cleared of Indians in large, pastoral parcels to settle the
frontier. In the 1820s there was a Law of Emphytensis under which
settlers got land titles in return for annual rent to the state, initially
small and soon rendered derisory by inflation. Land went out thus in
enormous parcels of up to 675 square kilometers. The average parcel
was 150–300 square kilometers, but the Anchovena family got 864 s.k.
The army, which drove the Indians off in the first place, received free
grants—generals, 186 square kilometers, colonels, 155 square kilometers, and the rank-and-file, who got 10 square kilometers. One civilian
contractor, who supplied the weapons which made Indian clearance
possible, got a free grant of 3,100 square kilometers, probably the

largest single land transfer ever recorded. Much land was immediately sold on the open market, where the price was rock bottom but slowly rising—from 0.11 gold pesos a square kilometer in 1800 to 0.30 in 1826. By midcentury the price had jumped to 2.00 gold pesos, a rise of 2,000 percent in 50 years. The free market in land meant that small settlers of very modest means could benefit, though it is true the big winners were powerful or rich individuals and British, French, German, and Creole land companies. In the 1820s, 6.5 million acres were carved up among 122 families and partnerships, and ten people got over 130,000 acres each.[139]

In Australia during the 1820s the land-purchase rule laid down by the governor, Lieutenant-General Ralph Darling, was that "respectable" people could receive grants of one square mile (640 acres) for every £500 they were prepared to invest, up to a maximum of 2,560 acres, or four square miles—that meant an acre of land cost considerably less than £1. Those wanting more could buy up to 9,900 acres, but then they had to bid for it by competitive tender.[140] Thus, as in Argentina, many large estates were established, and there were complaints that the system favored the rich. But some early colonial experts argued from the start that healthy agricultural colonies could not flourish without substantial landowners to take risks and to set an example of scientific farming. In any case, there was certainly land enough in Australia, at low prices, for as many free settlers as wished to farm there.

In Cape Colony, which was finally assigned to Britain by the settlement of 1814–15, land was acquired by conquest, rather than by settlement and had to be defended. In 1811–12 British troops had driven the Xhosa across the Fish River, freeing the Zuurveld for European occupation, and in 1820 up to 10,000 British settlers went out to farm it. But few remained on the small farms allocated them. Most returned to the Cape itself. The Boers, or Afrikaaners, most of them descended from Dutch settlers of the second half of the 17th century—about 25,000 by 1815—found by experience that, outside the Cape area, farms had to be large to be viable and that the necessary land could be acquired only by invading black hunting areas. In the quarter century 1800–1824, about 130,000 square kilometers were thus taken over, the bushmen hunting bands being exterminated or driven north. By 1800 settlers had reached the Orange River, which in effect became the official frontier in the next few years, and by 1825 large-scale settlement had pushed across the Orange, into land depopulated by the ravages of Zulu imperialism. By 1829 some Boers were farming as far as the Harts River. With every year that passed, tens of thousands, sometimes hundreds of thousands of acres were falling into European hands. It had to be paid for in sweat and blood rather than in cash.[141]

Europeans, therefore, were moving into the former hunting grounds of the world's primitive peoples in five continents. But it was in the United States, in addition to its political advantages, that the lure of cheap land was most potent. The American government was inefficient in many ways but it was extraordinarily effective at getting settlers—not necessarily immigrants, many being New Englanders moving west—onto newly available land. The basis of the system was the Modifying Act of 1796, which priced land at $2 an acre but allowed a year's credit for half the total paid. A further act of 1800 provided for federal land to be sold at new offices in Cincinnati, Chillicothe, Marietta and Steubenville, Ohio—that is, on the frontier. The minimum purchase was lowered from 640 acres, or a square mile, to 320 acres, and the buyer paid only 25 percent down, the rest over four years. So a man could get a big farm—indeed, an enormous one by European standards—for only about $160 cash (£30–£40). Four years later, Congress halved the minimum again. This put a viable family farm well within the reach of millions of prudent, saving European peasants and skilled workmen. During the 1820s, minimum prices for federal land were often below $2 an acre, and the government land sales were frequently on a prodigious scale. During the first 11 years of the 1800 Act, 3,374,843 acres were sold to individual farmers in what was then the Northwest alone, plus a further 250,000 in Ohio. The postwar period accelerated the land transfers. From 1815 half a million acres of Illinois passed into the hands of small and medium-scale farmers every year. It was the same story in the South. In western Georgia the state granted plots of 200-plus acres free to holders of lottery tickets with lucky numbers. In Alabama, government land sales suddenly jumped to 600,000 acres in 1816 and three years later had risen to 2,280,000 acres a year.[142] In the fifteen years 1815–30, more people acquired freehold land in the United States, at rock-bottom prices, than at any other time in the history of the world.

And what land! In parts of Indiana, Illinois and Michigan—the "Lake Plains"—a vast glacier known to geologists as the Wisconsin Drift had in prehistoric times smoothed off the rocks and hills and laid down a deep layer of rich soil containing all the elements needed for intensive agriculture. For settlers steeped in the Old Testament, it was Canaan, "God's Country." It yielded a third more than the rest of the country—"Egypt" to them. There were countless individual success stories, though few were without a daunting element of hardship and risk. Thus, the Ten Brook family moved to what became Parke County, Indiana, in autumn 1822. The soil was rich, but virgin. There were 27 of them altogether—three interrelated families, three single men, two teamsters, 13 horses, 21 cows, two yoke oxen, and four dogs. Their first priority was to build a strong cabin. Then, working throughout late autumn and winter, they had cleared 15 acres by the spring and fashioned 200 fence rails. They had 100 bushels of corn for winter feed and spring planting. They began ploughing and planting on 12 June 1823, and put two more acres to potatoes and turnips. The spring brought seven new calves, and that first summer they made 40 twelve-pound cheeses, sold in the market at a dollar each. The harvest was good, too; they not only ground their own corn but made 350 pounds of sugar and 10 gallons of molasses from the same soil they cleared for corn. The sheer fertility of the soil made all the labor worthwhile, and their leader, Andrew Ten Brook, recounted later: "After the first year, I never saw any scarcity of provisions. The only complaint was that there was nobody to whom the supplies could be sold."[143]

A similar story came from Greene County, Illinois, where Daniel Brush and a small group of Vermonters settled in spring 1820. "A prairie of the richest soil," Brush wrote, "stretched out about four miles in length and one mile wide . . . complete with pure springs of cold water in abundance." Once a cabin, 16 feet by 24 feet, had been built, they began the backbreaking task of ploughing up the prairie. This done, Brush wrote, "No weeds or grass sprang up on such ground the first year and the corn needed no attention with plough or hoe. If got in early, good crops were yielded, of corn and fodder." He added: "Provisions in abundance was the rule . . . no one needed to go supperless or hungry to bed." Some of these postwar settlements became celebrated for their rapid rise to prosperity. One such settlement was Sangamon County in Illinois. Another was Boon's Lick, which became Howard County in 1816, a belt 60 miles wide on both sides of the Missouri River. It boasted superb land, pure water, plenty of timber as required, and fine scenery. By 1819, the *Missouri Intelligence*, produced in the little town of Franklin, offered a spring toast: "Boon's Lick—two years since, a wilderness. Now—*rich in corn and cattle!*" It was widely reputed to be the best land in all the West.[144]

These families were among the lucky ones. The process of land purchase and settlement in the United States was varied and frequently modified, and there were many anomalies and iniquities. In much of the South there was a method known as indiscriminate location. You bought a warrant for a stated acreage. You then picked acres to this amount from unsold public lands. The land chosen was then surveyed by the public surveyor and a certificate was issued. The claim was advertised and if no counterclaim was asserted during the prescribed period, a formal grant of the freehold was made by patent. In New England, a prior survey was made and the land was divided into compact townships, subdivisions and tracts sold at auction. This system was generally adopted in the West when the expanding states began to hand over title to western lands to the federal government. Townships six miles square and lots of one square mile were offered in advance of settlement. But there were countless exceptions for historical and other reasons.[145] The tendency was for the land price to come down, and during the 1820s it was often as low as $1.25 an acre.

To a modern mind, it is surprising that this price was regarded by many as too high and there were loud demands for cheaper or even free land. Many settlers were termed *squatters*, though the term did not have its present-day meaning—it signified simply that they got there first. They usually paid good money, but made the purchase after the survey and before the land was "sectionalized" for the market. Their title might thus be challenged by nonresident purchasers. By the end of 1828, two-thirds of the population of Illinois were squatters, and Thomas Benton, Senator 1821–51, made himself their champion. He argued against a minimum price for western lands, proposing instead price grading by quality, and he pushed through legislation to protect squatters' titles to land they had improved. Investors who bought land for speculative purposes, not intending to work it themselves, were hated, especially on the frontier. A Methodist preacher recorded that at Elkhorn Creek, Wisconsin, "if a speculator should bid on a settler's farm, he was knocked down and dragged out of the [land] office, and if the striker was prosecuted and fined, the settlers paid the expense by common consent among themselves. But before the fine could be assessed, the case must come before a jury, which of course must be selected from among the settlers. And it was understood that no jury would find a verdict of guilty against a settler in such a case because it was considered self-defence. [So] no speculator dare bid on a settler's land, and as no settler would bid on his neighbour, each man had his land at Congress price, $1.25 an acre."[146]

Speculators might be unpopular, but they were also indispensable in many cases. They built towns like Dayton, Manchester, Portsmouth, Columbus and Williamsburg, and they organized pressure on Congress to put through roads. But much of the speculation was on credit, and speculators went bust if they could not resell land quickly enough and at the right price. That is how foreign groups like the one organized by Sir William Pulteney, MP, acquired huge tracts. Pulteney's agent spent over $1 million building infrastructures—stores, mills, taverns, even a theater. A group of bankers from Amsterdam formed the Holland Land Company, acquired 4 million acres in northwest New York and western Pennsylvania, put in roads and other services, and eventually (1817) made a profit by selling land in 360-acre plots at $5 an acre (and 10 years' credit).[147] But as a rule settlers preferred cheap land to the provision of an infrastructure, which they could create for themselves. Moses Cleveland, agent of the Connecticut Land Company, contrived to sell good land at a dollar an acre, with five years' credit, and to found the village named after him, which became, in time, a mighty city. It was from Cleveland that William Henry Harrison (1773–1841) played a critical role in creating the new state of Ohio, then moved on to govern Indiana and finally to become America's ninth president.[148]

Land speculation, state building and politics were closely connected. When a popular public figure like General Jackson bid for a town lot, no one bid against him; he acquired his estate and became a reasonably wealthy man through land sales, though by the end of the war he had ceased to take much interest in money. His aide, General Coffee, formed the Cypress Land Company, bought land at Muscle Shoals and laid out the town of Florence, Alabama, where speculators and squatters bid up the government minimum to $78 an acre.[149] Coffee, and others in the Jackson camp, made fortunes this way. The New York politician Martin Van Buren (1782–1862), who became Jackson's Secretary of State, also became rich through land deals; he got large parcels of land in Otsego County for a tithe of their true value—one 600-acre holding, for instance, he bought for $60.90—and he bought land cheap when settlers' lands were sold up at sheriffs' auctions for nonpayment of taxes.[150] Land dealing was the foundation of many historic American fortunes at this time.

The truth is that the Americans, having laid down ground rules by Congressional statute, in effect allowed a free market in land in the instinctive belief that this was the best and quickest way to get the country settled. This instinct proved correct. Though there was some skulduggery and political corruption and a few fortunes made the easy way, the settlers themselves would not tolerate any blatant manipulation of the rules and responded to it with force, usually successfully. On the whole rough justice was done. It was not in the general interest for land to be too cheap, or so argued Edward Gibbon Wakefield (1796–1862), a land agent who became the chief theorist of settlement in the second quarter of the century. His theory rested on the assumption that without a "sufficient price," men became landowners too soon, and no labor was available for estates which set the technological pace and, in each district, provided examples of efficient farming for family farms to follow.[151] Certainly, the American evidence seems to suggest that, on balance, areas where speculators were active and land prices were somewhat higher tended to be more efficiently settled than others. The Americans assumed that human nature being what it is, a market in land would develop and speculators emerge and, therefore, provided a legislative framework for both.

By contrast, the British in Canada tried to eliminate the market and speculation altogether—on the highest principles of public service—and ended up with a bureaucratic mess, endless delays, and speculation still emerging in the form of corruption. One open-minded British expert, H. G. Ward, who had witnessed both systems, made a devastating retrospective comparison of them to the House of Commons in 1839. In Canada, he complained, the British government "had conferred grants of land on half a hundred different principles, mostly wrong, and through personal edicts of the Secretary of State instead of under statute." Fearing speculators, it had actually played straight into their hands. By contrast, the American system attracted multitudes, who quickly settled and set up local authorities that soon acted as a restraining force on antisocial operators. The system worked because it was simple and uniform and corresponded to market forces. "There is one uniform price fixed of $1.25 an acre [minimum]. No credit is given [by the federal government]. There is a perfect liberty of choice and appropriation at this price. Immense surveys are carried on, to an extent which strangers have no conception of. Over 140 million acres have been mapped and planned at a cost of $2,164,000. There is a General Land Office in Washington with 40 subordinate district offices, each having a Registrar and Receiver. . . . Maps, plans and information of every kind are accessible to the humblest persons. . . . A man if he pleases may invest a million dollars in land. If he miscalculates it is his own fault. The public is, under every circumstance, the gainer."[152]

The proof that the system worked was in the historic fact—the rapid and successful settlement of the Mississippi Valley. This was one of the decisive events of history. In the years 1815–30, America became dynamic, emerging from the eastern seaboard bounded by the Appalachian chain and descending into the great network of river valleys beyond. By 1830 it was well on the way to achieving its manifest destiny of reaching to the Pacific and becoming a great constitutional power in the world. The Mississippi occupation, involving an area of over 1,250,000 square miles, the size of Western Europe, marked the critical point at which the United States ceased to be a small, struggling ex-colony and turned itself into a major nation.[153] The speed with which representative governments were set up was an important part of the dynamism. In addition to Kentucky and Tennessee, the first Trans-Appalachian territories to be settled, through the Cumberland Gap in the mountains, Ohio became a state in 1803, Louisiana in 1812, Indiana in 1816, Mississippi in 1817, Illinois in 1818, Alabama in 1819, and Missouri in 1821, with Michigan and Arkansas soon to follow.

Washington contributed by road making. The National Road, a broad, hardened thoroughfare across the Appalachians, was open in 1818 as far as Wheeling (West Virginia), from where settlers could travel along the Ohio River; by the early 1830s, the road had reached Columbus, Ohio. Farther south, roads were built by state and federal governments in collaboration or by thrusting military men like Jackson, who in 1820, as commander of the Western Army, opened the road he had strung between Florence, Alabama, and New Orleans, the best route into the lower Mississippi area. There were also the Great Valley Road, the Upper Federal Road, and the Fall Line Road. These roads were rough by the McAdam-Telford standards of Britain, but far superior to anything available in Latin America or Australia.

In any case, across the mountains, there were plenty of rivers, all facing in the direction of settlement: south, west, and, above all, southwest. Even before the steamer came, there were hundreds, then thousands, of flatboats and keelboats to float settlers and their goods down the rivers. By the end of the 1820s, 3,000 flatboats were floating down the Ohio each year.[154] In 1825 the opening of the great Erie Canal to traffic, linking the Atlantic via the Hudson River to the Great Lakes, made easy access possible to the Lake Plains. From that point on, steamboats were ubiquitous in the Mississippi Valley, not only bringing in settlers but transporting growing quantities of their produce to the East, to feed and clothe its exploding urban population—only 7 percent of the nation in 1810, over a third by midcentury.

The tidal wave of migrants included not only farmers but traders and entrepreneurs. One who left a record was Elijah Iles, merchant, who moved to the Sangamon River country in 1823, to the site of a place called Springfield—then only a stake in the ground. He marked out an 18-foot-square site for a store, went to Saint Louis to buy a 25-ton stock of goods, chartered a boat, shipped his stock to the mouth of the Sangamon, and then had his boat and goods towed upriver by five men with a 300-foot tow rope. Leaving his goods on the riverside— "As no one lived near, I had no fear of thieves"—he walked 50 miles to Springfield, hired wagons and teams, and got his stuff to the new "town," where his store was the first to open. It was the only one in a wide district later divided into 14 counties—"Many had to come more

than 80 miles to trade." Springfield grew up around him. They built a
jail for $85.75, marked out roads and electoral districts, "precinks" as
they called them, and levied a tax on "horses, neat cattle, wheeled
carriages, stock in trade and distillery." By 1822 the town had its own
roads, juries, an orphanage, a constable, and a clerk. The key figure in
such developments was the county clerk, who often doubled as school-
teacher and was paid half in cash, half in kind.[155]

Indianapolis was another growth point. It was laid out only in 1821.
The next year it had one two-storey house. By the following year it still
had only 90 families, but it had already acquired a newspaper, an
important engine of urban dynamics. The population topped the 1,000
mark in 1827, and 21 months later a visitor wrote, "The place begins
to look like a town—about 1,000 acres cut smooth, ten stores, six
taverns, a court-house which cost $15,000, and many fine houses."[156]
The pattern was this: First came traders, doubling up as bankers when
required, then proper banks, with lawyers at roughly the same time.
The lawyers lived by riding with the local judge on a horseback circuit,
by which they became well known and sat in the legislature the moment
it was set up—so the grip of the attorneys was firm from the start.
Justice was fierce and usually physical, especially for thieves and, above
all, for horse thieves. The pillory, ears cut off and publicly nailed up,
and branding on the cheek were becoming rare by 1815, but whipping
continued to be a universal punishment. The tone of settler justice was
well set in Madison County, Tennessee, in 1821 when a local thief,
"Squire" Dawson, was sentenced "to be taken from this place to the
common whipping post, there to receive twenty lashes well laid on his
bare back, and that he be rendered infamous, and that he then be
imprisoned one hour, and that he make his peace with the state by the
payment of one cent."[157] Imprisonment was costly, fining pointless
when he had no money—but there was no shortage of bare back.

Churches were probably, in practice, more important than courts in
keeping down crime and settling disputes. The Baptists, the Methodists,
and the Presbyterians were well geared to frontier evangelism; the
preacher rode round his parish until the church was built, and the
church's opening was a mark in the advancement of a settlement, akin
to acquiring a newspaper and a bank.

The churches brought with them Bible classes and Sunday
schools—they were engines of literacy. But in the towns, however new
and small, schools, public and private, rose like mushrooms. Three
years after Jane Austen described Mrs. Goddard's "real, honest, old-
fashioned Boarding-school" in *Emma,* an advertisement in the *Blakeley
Sun,* 2 February 1819, announced a remarkably similar-sounding estab-

lishment opened by Miss Campbell in Mobile, Alabama, whose "principal advantages" were to be "providing Young Ladies with a liberal and solid education—in drawing the attention to such pursuits as are lasting and useful as well as elegant and ornamental—in substituting the more important acquirements of the mind in lieu of the frivolous pursuits which engage the time and talents of the majority of the rising generation."[158]

Solid or frivolous, the rising generation—the average age in the United States in 1815–30 was sixteen—was populating the vast area stretching north from New Orleans to the Great Lakes. A few figures tell the tale more eloquently than do words.[159]

STATE	POPULATION		
	1810	1820	1830
Ohio	230,760	581,434	937,903
Indiana	24,520	147,178	343,031
Illinois	12,282	55,211	157,445
Missouri	19,783	66,586	140,455
Alabama	9,046	127,901	209,527
Mississippi	31,306	75,449	130,621
Louisiana	76,556	153,407	215,739
Tennessee	261,727	422,823	681,904

These newcomers, for the most part, worked hard—they had no alternative—but for those who came from Europe especially, there was an all-pervading sense that they had indeed come to a promised land. William Forbes, a Scots immigrant from Peterhead, who settled and farmed in Allagan County in the new Michigan Territory, wrote in wonder of the ways crops sprang up with "a rapidity that staggers the belief of those accustomed to the slow growth of a colder climate." He marveled too at the genial summers: "Morning and evening delicious sitting out of doors in the shady side of the house or trees at breakfast or supper, eating melons in [the middle of] the day, not a cloud, pure blue sky, light and heat. Cattle breaking away to get into the deep shadow of trees or into the river to cool themselves—drinking water by the gallon which distils from you in large drops in a few minutes—dress shirt and trousers and straw hat. This never lasts three or four days until it is succeeded by a thundershower falling in torrents for one hour, then all is fair and cool and fresh again."[160]

*   *   *

This idyllic picture, however, conceals a hideous paradox. Forbes came from one of the poorest parts of Europe, where, despite Telford's miracle working and the efforts of government and enlightened lairds alike, there were too many people for the land to support. Scots from the Highlands and the uplands of southern Scotland and their near-kin, the Scots Ulstermen of the Irish North, were being driven off their ancestral acres by a combination of destitution and "clearances" by reforming landlords. In the Highlands and Islands in particular the depths of degradation caused by overpopulation were abysmal. Around the turn of the century, the Church of Scotland missionary to the islands, John Buchanan, described the scallags of Harris, whose wages were a mere £2 a year, plus four pairs of shoes, if male, and one-sixth of this, plus two pairs of shoes, if female. He defined a *scallag* as "a poor being who for mere subsistence becomes a predial slave to another, whether a sub-tenant, a tacksman or a laird. [He] builds his own hut, with sods and boughs of trees . . . five days a week he works for his master, the sixth he is allowed to himself for the cultivation of some scrap of land on the edge of some moss or moor on which he raises a little kail or coleworts, barley and potatoes. These articles, boiled together in one mash, and often without salt, are his only food, except in those seasons and days when he can catch some fish. . . . The only bread he tastes is a cake made of the flour of barley."[161]

There is no evidence that the plight of the scallags had improved by 1815; in some ways, they were better off than sub-tenants, who had to pay rent. Evidence offered to the Parliamentary Select Committee on Emigration, 1826–27, revealed that on North and South Uist, a third of the population was landless and utterly dependent on the charity of the local laird, Macdonald of Clanranald. In 1817 he had had to fork out £4,500—a devastating sum for a Highland laird—to buy them meal, plus a further £1,100 the following year. On Tiree, half the families were destitute, subsisting on the bounty of the other half. The lairds were resorting to desperate measures. Maclean of Coll would not allow the sons of crofters to marry without his consent; if they nonetheless did so, he drove them off his island. On the mainland, one crofter wrote to Archibald Campbell, MP (1827): "It has been utterly impossible for us to pay this year any rent to our landlords, consequently the little property we now possess becomes theirs and we cannot expect that they will let us houses for another year. We have no other prospect but that we shall be turned to the street, without a blanket to cover either ourselves or children, or implements to work at our trades."[162] By the end of the wars evictions were increasing and deliberate, systematic clearances of penniless tenants, to make way for sheep, cattle or deer forests, were becoming common.

The worst, or at any rate the best-known, instances were the clearances in Sutherland in 1807–21, in the far north of Scotland, where perhaps as many as 10,000 people were cleared by the Countess of Sutherland and her husband Lord Stafford, and their factor and tenant, Patrick Sellar. Sellar's methods in Strathnaver in 1814, when he used armed men, savage dogs and fire to clear the crofters from their huts, which were then burnt to the ground, became a legend of infamy, and he himself was tried for arson, but acquitted. Even Southey, touring with Telford, and no enemy to "improvement," deplored forcible clearing. He admitted the need for action: "I have never, not even in Galicia, seen any human habitations so bad as the Highland *black-houses*." Those who lived in them were "quiet, thoughtful, contented, religious people, susceptible of improvement and willing to be improved" and he thought slow changes would have worked. But to enforce "a sudden and total change of habits" was unconscionable, and "to expel them by process of law from their black-houses, and if they demur in obeying the enactment to oust them by setting fire to these combustible tenements—this surely is as little defensible on the score of policy as of morals."[163]

The Sutherlands, to do them justice, tried to provide work for those who were driven from the glens, besides building roads and bridges. They invested £14,000 in building a fishing port, harbor and curing station. Southey noted that the Marquess of Stafford was spending the entire revenue from his wife's estates, £5–6,000, plus a similar sum from his own property, trying to provide the dispossessed with a secure livelihood. But these well-meaning schemes, in Sutherland and elsewhere, rarely worked, so the emigrant ships beckoned. Between the end of the Seven Years War, 1763, and the end of the Napoleonic Wars, 1815, about 52,000 Scots left for North America—a rate of about 10,000 a year—despite much opposition from the government, many lairds and the anti-emigrant lobby, which got the Passenger Act (1803) passed to make emigration too expensive. After 1815, however, opposition ceased, the government began to provide assisted places on emigrant ships, and a growing number of lairds put positive pressure on the poor to leave. By 1830 the annual rate of Scots emigrants passed the 6,000 mark, the great majority of them Highland and Island paupers.[164]

But what were these dispossessed clansmen, the progeny of hunters and warriors, pastoralists and herdsmen, driven from their glens and islands, actually doing when they crossed the Atlantic? They were serving as economic foot soldiers in a surge of European settlement which was subjecting the Indians of North America to a similar process of eviction and exile. Therein lay the tragic irony. The Scots were not alone. In various parts of Europe where the social organization was closest to tribalism—in parts of Scandinavia, in Brittany and Galicia, and in the Swiss, Bavarian and Austrian Alps, not least in north and west Ireland, where over 20,000 left for North America in 1830—men and women from one failed form of primitivism were leaving to pass the death sentence on another. But it was the paradox of enforced Scots emigration which was the most poignant.

The paradox is underlined by the work of two great popular artists of the time, Edwin Landseer and James Fenimore Cooper. One of the concerns of the Romantic movement was the pathos of the savage in a modernizing world, the decline of traditional ways of living. Sir Walter Scott was the first to conjure up, for millions of readers, the poetry and nobility of Scottish clan life, just at a time when it was vanishing forever. But it was Edwin Landseer (1803–73) who gave it visual reality. This child prodigy, son of a leading engraver and perhaps the most naturally gifted painter England has ever produced, was drawing cows and sheep in the fields between Marylebone and Hampstead at the age of six. When only twelve he won the Society of Arts silver medal for a drawing of a hunter and by eighteen he had already earned over £1,000 by selling such superb animal studies as *Fighting Dogs Getting Wind* (1818) and *The Seizure of a Boar* (1821) to aristocratic collectors. He was 21 and already celebrated when he first went to Scotland, to stay with the Duke of Atholl at Blair Atholl and paint *The Death of the Stag in Glen Tilt*, a magnificent evocation of Highland primitivism. He also stayed with Scott, to paint him and his dogs—"the most magnificent things I ever saw," wrote Scott, "leaping and grinning on the canvas"— and to plan his ambitious historical celebration of bloodsport, *The Hunting of Chevy Chase* (1826–27). Thereafter he stayed in the Highlands every autumn, usually living in huts of birch and turf, sleeping on beds made of heather. The Earl of Tankerville described him in Glenfeshie in the Cairngorms, "a little, strongly-built man . . . busily employed in gralloching his deer. This he did with great quickness and dexterity. [He] let the head hang over, to display the horns, and then, squatting down on a stone opposite, took out of his pocket what I thought would be his pipe or whiskey-flask—but it was a sketchbook!"[165] Landseer added a further dimension of savage liberty by making his hostess, the Duchess of Bedford, his mistress, a liaison tolerated by the Duke, a much older man. A fellow guest described their life in the glen: "Here we have been now above a week, living on venison, grouse, hares, partridge, blackcock, ptarmigan, plovers, salmon, char, pike, trouts, beef, mutton, pork etc., all killed by ourselves and nearly on the spot—at any rate all (even red deer and ptarmigan) within a mile of the house. The ladies have only the dress of the country shape and material. . . . The gentlemen wear the kilts, and in short everything is picturesque in the extreme."[166]

More than any other artist, Landseer promoted the cult of the Highlands, but he did not romanticize the life there. His *Duke of Atholl in the Glen Till* painting is the epitome of the relentless hunter, huge, with tremendous stamina, brave but passionate and hungry for blood in his pursuit. Landseer made no concessions in his dauntingly accurate presentations of mauled, fur-torn, bleeding, dying animals. And he was as interested in the stalkers and keepers—and their children—as in the grand lairds. By the end of the decade of the 1820s, he had produced some remarkable genre paintings, showing the life of the glens in all its unrelenting poverty—*An Illicit Whisky Still in the Highlands, The Poacher's Bothy, An Interior of a Highlander's House* (it belonged, in fact, to a gillie). The violent and lawless side of existence in the mountains is shown with breathtaking realism and a stoical fatalism—the people are hunters and are themselves hunted—which leaves no room for sentiment or humbug. Landseer never "pitied the plumage but forgot the dying bird"; he painted both exactly as he saw them. The tragedy of Landseer's work is that it came, in a sense, too late. When Highland life was still vibrant, as it was up to 1745, even in some ways until 1800, there was no one to paint it. By the time of Landseer's coming in the 1820s, it was rapidly becoming a replica, to be enjoyed in increasingly artificial conditions by the rich and those who attended to their sport. The genius of Landseer is that he made the replica seem so real.

That, in one sense, applies to James Fenimore Cooper (1789–1851), the first American writer to make the North American continent a reality to European readers. By the time his fiction presented it, in the 1820s, the wilderness-America he knew as a boy was fast disappearing. Born in the year of the French Revolution, the twelfth child (out of thirteen) of a congressman-judge, Cooper grew up on a 40,000-acre tract of land in upper New York State. In the 1780s and 1790s his father acted as agent for both settlers and investors in land, including Madame de Staël and her father, and at one time owned 750,000 acres and controlled still more. Judge Cooper wrote in his *Guide to the Wilderness,* published in 1810, "In 1785 I visited the rough and hill country of Otsego, where there existed not an inhabitant nor any trace of a road. I was alone, 300 miles from home, without bread, meat or food of any kind. Fire and fishing tackle were my only means of subsistence. I caught trout in the brook and roasted them on the ashes. My horse fed on the grass that grew by the edge of the waters. I laid me down to sleep in my watchcoat, nothing but the melancholy wilderness around me. In this way I explored the country, formed my plans of future settlement, and meditated on the spot where a place of trade or a village should afterwards be established."[167] But this was a posthumous publication, since the year before the judge had fallen victim to the violence of frontier politics and was shot to death as he left a meeting in Albany. His son James was then twenty. He had gone to Yale at thirteen, been expelled, served at sea and later, as a married man, struggled hard to keep the inheritance from his father together. He turned to novel writing as a means. His first effort was a failure, his second sold well, his third, *The Pioneers* (1823), introduced what became known as the Leatherstocking tales, centered on his frontiersman-hero, Natty Bumppo, and made him world-famous.

The five Leatherstocking novels, called after Natty's deerskin leggings, and, above all, *The Last of the Mohicans* (1826) introduced the first substantial character in American fiction. Natty is indeed a recurrent American ideal type, putting honor and character above money and position, not so very different from the Ernest Hemingway hero who would emerge almost exactly a century later. More important however was the background of the American woods, where civilization came to an abrupt end and the wilderness began. Cooper skillfully employed his father's experiences and made the frontier reality of a generation before seem fresh and contemporary, rather as Dickens was to project his 1820s childhood into the 1840s. His presentation of Indian life in the recesses of New York State—already finished by the time he wrote of it—came as a delightful shock to East Coast Americans and a revelation to Europeans.

In some ways, Cooper was strongly opposed to immigration, or at least its consequences for the wilderness. He stressed again and again that Natty, the true frontier scout, shoots the abundant wildlife merely to live, whereas the invading white multitude slaughters it. What struck the more acute observers of the retreating wilderness was the sudden revelation of the almost immeasurable fertility of animal life in its pristine condition, especially the colossal flights of birds which took place at certain times. There is a fine April scene in *The Pioneers*, when the ice on the lake breaks up and countless thousands of migrating pigeons appear: "Here is a flock that the eye cannot see the end of. There is food enough in it to keep the army of Xerxes for a month, and feather enough to make beds for the whole country." To the strongly expressed disapproval of Leatherstocking, the honorable hunter, the entire village goes out to massacre the birds, filling even its signal-cannon with duck-shot, and justifying the holocaust by claiming the creatures eat the seed.[168]

Cooper saw such outrages against nature as symbolic of American loss of virtue, just as he saw the disappearance of Indian life, with its innocence and nobility, as well as its cruelty and savagery, as—in the long run—a defeat for the civilization which is responsible for it. But his mixed emotions and subtleties were largely lost on his European readers, on whom his tales acted as a lure and a magnet. Before Cooper, ignorance of the realities of American life was profound. It was not uncommon, in the years after 1815, for intending immigrants in England to write to the Colonial Office asking for grants to go to "the Virginia Plantations." Many, on arrival, were astonished to find there was no king. The Germans, on the other hand, knew there were no royal families in America—*Kein Koenig dort*—and that was precisely its attraction to a burdened people in a country where there were thousands of princes. But they knew little else until Cooper's novels arrived and were read aloud at village clubs which specialized in books about America.[169] Cooper acted as the great recruiting-sergeant for the Hamburg and Bremen emigrant ships. *The Pioneers* was published in Britain and France the same year it appeared in America, and within 12 months it had found two rival German publishers, who, of course, paid no attention to copyright. Cooper was seen as a remarkable realist, especially in Germany, and no less than 30 publishers eventually put out German versions of the Leatherstocking tales, especially *Der letzte Mohikaner*. In France, where he was described as *"le Walter Scott des sauvages,"* 18 different publishers competed.[170] But the popularity of Cooper was Europe-wide, eventually worldwide. Russian translations followed in abundance, and his works soon appeared in Spanish, Italian and Portuguese, and eventually in such tongues as Egyptian, Turkish and Persian. By the end of the 1820s, children all over Europe and even the Middle East were playing at Indians and learning to walk "Indian file."[171]

Here, then, we have the tragic paradox of these years—the dispossessed exiles of a broken clan system hurrying to occupy the conquered lands of New World tribesmen and the books which sang the elegy of the American Indian encouraging their readers to hasten his destruction. The years 1815–30 were decisive in the downfall of Indian power and property in the United States. The Indians' one hope of survival lay in the limited protection accorded by British authority in the north and

Spanish in the south. In the south General Jackson killed all hope by extinguishing Spanish rule in Florida and transforming it into an American territory. In the north, the American government accepted, from the treaty of Ghent onwards, that it could not have Canada. But it was determined, on its side of the border, to break the remains of the British-Indian alliance by expelling Canadian trappers from Indian villages—they had a community of economic interests against the farmer-settlers—and by bringing the Indians firmly under Washington's control. So a great fort-building program was begun in the Northwest, akin to the system of barracks which the British were putting up all over India. Each fort could house 100 or more soldiers and consisted of a strong timber or stone palisade with a blockhouse at each corner. Older forts were updated and strengthened—Forts Wayne and Harrison (1816) Forts Shelby in Detroit, Gratiot and Mackinac on Lake Michigan, Dearborn and Clark (1817)—new forts were added, Forts Edward in west Illinois, Armstrong on Rock Island, Crawford at Prairie du Chien, Howard on the Ox River (1816) and Forts Snelling on the Upper Mississippi, Saginaw in Michigan and Brady at Sault Sainte Marie (1819–22). By the mid-1820s, British influence in the entire region was dead, and the settler-authorities could do what they liked.

In the south, Jackson made possible the removal of all organized Indian life west of the Rockies by the destruction of Spanish power in 1817–18. Even earlier he had begun to sign dispossession treaties with the Cherokees (1816, 1817) and the Chickasaws (1816). The usual method was to bribe the chiefs into signing away their tribal lands. Jackson was sent $60,000 worth of bribe goods by Washington for this purpose. To do him justice, he did not like this method. He wanted the Indians to be turned into American-style farmers. "It is high time," he wrote to John Calhoun, the war secretary, in 1819, "that the Legislature should interpose its authority and enact laws for the regulation and control of the Indian tribes." They should be pushed into "settled agriculture" and provided with its "instruments"—all this would be "more humane and just than by corrupting their Chiefs to acquire their Country."[172] He protested that what he was doing was "not from choice but from instructions" and he required written authority to hand out goods and money.

Nonetheless, Jackson did was he was bid, using his fearsome presence to frighten the chiefs into signing quickly and without argument. The first three treaties gave the Choctaws and Cherokees a total of $64,000 annually, part for 10, and part for 20 years, plus about $20,000 in immediate cash and merchandise. In return, the tribes surrendered hundreds of square miles of land, allowing Jackson to link Washington directly to New Orleans, build a military road, and so prepare the attack on the Spanish.[173] Once the Spanish were out of the way, the removal policy went ahead without pity or respite. In essence it went back to the presidency of Thomas Jefferson, who said bluntly that if the Indians failed to assimilate and adopt white ways, "we shall be obliged to drive them, with the beasts of the forests, into the Stony Mountains [Rockies]."[174] For the 1817 Cherokee Treaty, the Indians were told that they could stay only if they abolished their tribal law system and accepted American state and local governments—in that case, they got 640 acres each. Otherwise they had to hand over 2 million acres in Tennessee, Georgia, and Alabama, receiving, in return, a similar territory west of the Mississippi, though even there Washington retained the right to build roads and set up military posts. When 67 chiefs signed a joint document rejecting the proposal, Jackson had each of them brought to his tent separately, beginning with the most malleable, and urged them to "look around and recollect what happened to our brothers the Creeks." The signatures were duly withdrawn, and all the chiefs then put their marks on the new treaty of 8 July 1817. Over the next two years, 6,000 Indians were thus removed, each receiving a rifle and ammunition, a blanket and a brass kettle or beaver trap. In 1818 Jackson stripped the Chickasaws of their remaining land in Kentucky and Tennessee. The treaty was carried out by bribing the mixed-blood leaders even before the talks began—Levi and George Colbert got $8,500 each, their brother James $1,666 and two other influential half-Indians $666 each.[175] The treaties all contained prefaces, providing the philosophical justification for what they contained. This one asserted that the land had already been paid for by the white men long ago, when England granted it to the states of Virginia and North Carolina. Then America had conquered England, a fact confirmed by the treaty of 1783. The United States had kept the white men away from it so that its president their father, could allow his red children to hunt game on it, but "the game is now gone and his white children now claim it from him"; he "cannot keep it from them any longer." The Indians got $300,000 compensation, spread over 15 years—Jackson's fellow commissioner, Isaac Shelby, protesting that it was far too much.[176]

The reasoning in this particular preamble is so lame that one wonders why the American plenipotentiaries bothered to include it. But in a way it accurately reflects Jackson's philosophy. He saw the Indians as irresponsible. They did not know what was good for them and a paternalistic government, which did, had to decide for them. Removal was rather like the Highland clearances in this respect, since it contained an element of altruism. But it was also a system of apartheid, based on the premise that Indians, if organized in their form of society, could not live with the whites and had to be kept apart. They could indeed accept U.S. citizenship—the 1817 treaty was the first to hold this out—but only as individuals. If they wished to retain their collective identity, as a "nation," then they had to go.[177] Exactly as with apartheid, removal was defended precisely because it gave the Indians the chance to "preserve their own ways and traditions."

Indeed, as with apartheid, the destruction of the Indians was enveloped in a thick covering of religiosity. Jackson was particularly good at moral outrage. While expelling the Spanish, he regarded their Indian allies as monsters of depravity. He wrote in triumph to his wife in April 1818: "I had Francis the Prophet and Homallee Mecko hung on the 8th. They will foment war no more." After he executed the two Britons, Arbuthnot and Ambrister, he wrote to Calhoun, his political boss: "The proceedings of the court martial in this case, with the volume of testimony justifying their condemnation, presents scenes of wickedness, corruption and barbarity at which the heart sickens."[178] But when he found that the Georgian militia had dared to burn a village of his Indian allies, he wrote in fury to the Governor, William Rabun, expressing his consternation "that there could exist within the United States a cowardly monster in human shape that could violate the sanctity of a flag, when borne by any person, but more particularly when in the hands of a superannuated Indian chief worn down by age. Such base cowardice and murderous conduct as this transaction affords has not its parallel in history and should meet with its merited punishment." The "monster" was Captain Obediah Wright whom Jackson had put in chains, expecting the Georgians to hang him. Captain Wright was, of course, acquitted by a Georgian jury, and Governor Rabun replied to Jackson by accusing him of seeking to impose a "military despotism" on "the liberties of the people of Georgia." Nonetheless, Jackson succeeded in gouging out $8,000 compensation for "his" Indians.[179]

Behind the moralizing and the religiosity, however, was humbug, and it is hard to decide whether there was more of it in the North or in the South. The process of removal speeded up when the Monroe administration endorsed it in 1825. In the North, the chief scourge of the Indians was General Lewis Cass (1782–1866), a hero of the War of 1812 and governor of Michigan Territory 1813–31. In August 1825 Cass called a conference of 1,000 leaders of all the Northwest tribes at Prairie du Chien and told them to agree on their tribal boundaries. Once this was done, he pounced on each tribe separately. In 1826 he forced the Potawatomi to hand over a vast tract in Indiana. The Miami handed over their last lands in Indiana for $55,000 and an annuity of $25,000.

In the years 1826–30 the Indians were forced to surrender not only their original lands, but their new reservations, as the settlers poured into the area and the land market warmed up. In spring 1827 one chief, Red Bird, led some Winnebagos in a rising, but this action simply provoked the building of a new fort. A more serious Indian war broke out in 1829, when a white mob drove Indians from their fields at Sauk Town, producing massacres and counter-massacres. The war was eventually put down by overwhelming American force, including the use of steam gunboats. As a result the Indians were pushed right across the Mississippi or left in small pockets, and the remaining 190,879,937 acres of Indian land passed into white hands, at a cost of a little over $70 million in gifts and annuities.[180]

Cass was not a thug. He later went on to hold high diplomatic and political office and he set down his views in an essay, "The Policy and Practice of the United States and Great Britain in their Treatment of Indians," published in the *North American Review*, 1827.[181] What, he said, he could not understand was why the Indians, after 200 years of contact with the white man, had not "improved." It was a "moral phenomenon"—it had to be—since "a principle of progressive improvement seems almost inherent in human nature." But "the desire to ameliorate their condition" did not seem to exist in "the constitution of our savages. Like the bear and deer and buffalo of his own forests, an Indian lives as his father lived, and dies as his father died. He never attempts to imitate the arts of his civilised neighbours. His life passes away in a succession of listless indolence, and of vigorous exertion to provide for his animal wants or to gratify his baleful passions . . . he is perhaps destined to disappear with the forests."[182]

Cass was making generalizations for which he had no evidence. The Indians varied greatly in their adaptability. In the years after 1815 there were probably about 500,000 in all, and the Creeks, Cherokees, Choctaws, Chickasaws and Seminoles, who bore the brunt of white aggression in these years, had long been known as the Five Civilized Tribes. If the Indians varied in their degree of culture, so did the whites. It was ironic that the territory that was keenest to assert the superiority of "civilized" white values was Arkansas, the most socially backward territory in the United States. Arkansas's whites tended to be solitaries—isolated hunters, trappers and primitive farmers—clannish, self-sufficient in their way, and extremely violent. Its 14,000 inhabitants got a territorial government in 1819, but both the courts and the legislature were ruled by duels as much as by debate or law. In 1819 the brigadier general commanding the militia was killed in a duel, and five years later the same thing happened to a superior court judge, his opponent being his colleague on the bench and the cause a squalid game of cards. One observer described the Wylie clan as "the same as the Indians." The Wylies were illiterate, "wonderfully ignorant" and "as full of superstitions as their feeble minds were capable of, believing in Witches, Ghosts, Hobgoblins, Evil Eyes. . . . They did not farm, had no fences round their shanty habitations and appeared to have lived a roving, rambling life ever since the Battle of Bunker Hill when they fled to this wilderness." The Flanagan Clan "respected no law, human or divine, but were slaves to their own selfish lusts and brutish habits."[183] Yet Arkansas, setting the pattern for poor whites throughout the expanding Europeanized world, was harder on Indians than any other territory or state. Like the harsh English Statutes of Kilkenny in medieval Ireland, Arkansan laws tried to end contact between whites and Indians for fear that the former might go native. It was unlawful to sell Indians liquor or horses. Testimony from anyone with a quarter or more Indian blood was inadmissible in the courts. The legislature denounced the local Cherokees as a "restless, dissatisfied, insolent and malicious tribe, engaged in constant intrigues."[184]

The Indians, for their part, were often contemptuous of Arkansas white "civilization." The head of a Cherokee delegation, Nutararuh, was quoted in the *Arkansas Gazette,* published in Little Rock (April 23, 1828), as claiming that in Arkansas Indians were more advanced than whites when it came to farming, building, clothes, morality and even reading and writing. "But if civilisation consists of pitched battles, to murder one another, or in shooting our neighbours and brothers in streets and places of public resort, then we are in a woeful state of barbarism." In fact, many of the Indians were making great advances. John Quincy Adams, an ultra-critical observer who strongly backed the removal policy, had to admit, as Secretary of State, that a delegation of Cherokees who came to see President Monroe in January 1824 were "most civilized." "These men," he recorded in his diary, "were dressed entirely according to our manner. Two of them spoke English with good pronunciation and one with grammatical accuracy."[185] Three months later, during a cabinet discussion on what Monroe called "the absolute necessity" that "the Indians should move west of the Mississippi," Secretary of War Calhoun asserted that "the great difficulty" arose not from their savagery but precisely "from the progress of the Cherokees in civilisation." He said there were 15,000 in Georgia and increasing just as fast as the whites. They were "all cultivators, with a representative government, judicial courts, Lancaster schools and permanent property." Their "principal chiefs," he added, "write their own State Papers and reason as logically as most white diplomatists."[186]

What Calhoun said was true—some Indians were doing exactly what the whites claimed they wanted them to do, assimilating and adopting white forms of social and political organization. But—and this was what was objectionable—they were doing so as a homogenous Indian unit. A Cherokee national council went back as far as 1792 and from 1808 there was a written legal code. In 1817 a republic was formed. An upper house or senate was chosen from the council, 13 members elected for two-year terms, while the rest of the council made up the lower house. Three years later, the territory was divided into eight congressional districts, each mapped and provided with police, courts, powers to collect debts and authority to raise taxes and pay salaries. In 1826 a Cherokee spokesman described the whole system in a public lecture in Philadelphia, and the following year a national convention drew up a written constitution. It was patterned on America's, giving the vote to "all free male citizens" over 18, except those of African descent. The first elections were held in summer 1828, though a Supreme Court had already been functioning for five years. The republic had its own paper, the *Cherokee Phoenix,* edited by Elias Boudinot. Its first issue appeared on 28 February 1828. The republic's capital, New Echota, was quite an elaborate place, with log houses, a fine Supreme Court building, and a few two-story brick homes, including one owned by Joseph ("Rich Joe") Van, which is still to be found near what is now Chatsworth, Georgia.[187]

The destruction of this ordered community is a particularly poignant tragedy within the larger tragedy of Indian removal. The contemporary evidence suggests that the community went a long way to diminish the evils which whites generally associated with Indians. Its courts were severe on horse thefts. There was even a plan to enforce prohibition and the *Phoenix* campaigned strenuously against alcohol. The authorities urged all Indians to work and provided the means. There were 2,000 spinning wheels, 700 looms, 31 grist mills, eight cotton gins, 18 schools—using both English and a newly developed written version of the Cherokee tongue. The 15,000 members of this settled community owned 20,000 cattle and 1,500 black slaves, like any other "civilized" Georgians. But its existence, and still more its constitution, violated both state and federal law, and in 1827 Georgia petitioned the federal government to remove the Indians forthwith. The discovery of gold brought in a rush of white prospectors and provided a further economic motive. The election of General Jackson at the end of 1828 sealed the community's fate. In his inaugural address he insisted that the integrity of the state of Georgia came before Indian interests. Congress decreed that, after 1 January 1830, all state laws applied to Indians, though it simultaneously denied them the right to testify in any case involving a white. Five months later, it passed a Removal Bill authorizing the president to drive any eastern tribe across the Mississippi, if necessary by force. The Indians appealed to the Supreme Court (*Cherokee Nation v The State of Georgia*), but it ruled that the tribe did not constitute a nation within the meaning of the constitution and so could not bring suit. The end came over the next few years, brought about by a combination of force, harassment—stopping of annuities, cancellation of debts—and bribery. The Treaty of New Echota, signed in December 1835 by a greedy minority led by Chief Major Ridge, ceded the last lands in return for $5.6 million, the republic broke up, and the final Cherokee stragglers were herded across the Mississippi by U.S. cavalry three years later.[188]

The sight of Indian families heading west with their meager possessions was a harsh symbol of the dawning age of mass European settlement. In winter 1831, in Memphis, Tennessee, Comte Alexis de Tocqueville, in America to study the penal system on behalf of the French government, watched a band of Choctaws being marshaled across the Mississippi. "The Indians had their families with them," he wrote, "and they brought in their train the wounded and the sick, with children newly-born and old men on the point of death." He added: "Three or four thousand soldiers drive before them the wandering race of the aborigines. These are followed by the [white] pioneers who pierce the woods, scare off the beasts of prey, explore the course of the inland streams and make ready the triumphal march of civilisation across the desert." He noted that the Indians were deprived of their rights "with singular felicity, tranquilly, legally, philanthropically, without shedding blood and without violating a single great principle of morality in the eyes of the world." It was, he concluded, impossible to exterminate with "more respect for the laws of humanity."[189]

De Tocqueville was not quite correct in suggesting that the expulsion of the Indians was viewed by all whites as moral and proper. In fact in Georgia and elsewhere in the world, some white clergy were already deeply concerned by what they saw as the sinful injustice of it all. In Georgia a number of missionaries actually encouraged the Indians to resist. On 15 September 1831, eleven of them were convicted of violating state law and sentenced to four years' hard labor each. Of these, nine got their freedom by submitting and taking the oath of allegiance to Georgia. Two appealed to the Supreme Court and had their convictions overturned; but Georgia, encouraged by President Jackson, defied the court's ruling.[190]

*   *   *

In Latin America clerical restraints on the dispossession of Indians and the occupation of their land were largely removed by the expulsion from Spain in 1767 of the Jesuits, the most powerful and active of the missionary orders, who made the protection of Indians from white predators and the preservation of their culture prime concerns. The Jesuits were hated by settler interests and attacks on them in Latin America began long before the formal expulsion order. In Argentina, which with its wide pampas and Indian hunting tribes most closely resembled North America, the Jesuits were hurriedly rounded up and sent back to Europe. Their mission stations were devastated and never fully re-established even after the restoration of their order. Missionaries raised lone voices on behalf of the Indians but they lacked the organization and financial power the Jesuits had once deployed. It was after 1815 and the withdrawal of Spanish power that the systematic assault on Indian life began in earnest. The pampas Indians had originally hunted on foot the indigenous deer, alpaca, rhea, otters and other creatures. From the 17th century, European animal imports—horses, cattle, sheep, goats, pigs, dogs—ran wild and multiplied at an astonishing rate. This situation tended to occur wherever in the world the European settled, but it was particularly marked in the Americas. It has been well observed that "in the late 18th and early 19th century the advancing European frontier . . . was preceded into Indian territory by an advance-guard of semi-wild herds of hogs and cattle, tended, every now and then, by semi-wild herdsmen, white and black."[191] Feral herds of European animal imports were most numerous in Argentina, where wild horses, above all, increased until they were counted in millions. With horses, the Indians not only flourished but traded with the settlers in reins, bridges, saddles, lassos, bolas and other hunting gear. They also, however, began to raid settlements, especially during periods of drought, as in 1820, 1824 and 1828–30.

The result was a repetition of what was occurring in the United States. Punitive expeditions were sent out and forts were built. By the early 19th century, the Indians had been cleared as far as the Salado River, 100 miles from Buenos Aires. Then the line of forts was gradually pushed farther. As the land thus secured was carved into big ranches, the head station of each *estancia* became a fort, with a moat, cannon, and look-out towers. Its cowboys were armed and trained as Indian fighters.[192] In addition to the forts, cavalry expeditions, known as *entradas,* were sent out to ravage Indian territory. Dashing young commanders made their reputations as hammers of the Indians, rather like Jackson and Cass in the United States. In the 1820s General Estanislao Lopez conducted various campaigns against the Indians in the north, when not persecuting his own countrymen. Since he decapitated his white opponents and exposed their heads in iron caps, the mind reels at what he did to the Indians, though it is known he rounded up young males for sale as ranch slaves. Another prominent 1820s Indian fighter was General Juan Mañuel de Rosas (1793–1877), who, like Jackson, went on to become his country's national leader and earn a reputation as "the Caligula of the Rio Plata."[193]

The years 1815–30 were decisive in Argentina's history. In 1815 less than 9 percent of its white population was foreign born. Then came the rush: Italians from Genoa, Spaniards from Galicia and the Basque country, French, Scots, Irish, Welsh and English. By 1822 Buenos Aires was already a big city of 55,416 inhabitants, with an annual growth rate of 2.6 percent. To support this growing immigrant population, the pampas had to be exploited quickly—by 1829 hides and salted meat had already risen to 65 percent of the total exports.[194] For every poor immigrant who came in from the Celtic fringes, the mountains and slums of Europe, a plains Indian had to suffer. General Rosas pushed the frontier up to the Colorado River and set up a new fort at Bahia Blanca. He signed treaties on the lines of those negotiated by Jackson, under which some Indians got regular rations of sugar and tobacco, as well as cattle and horses. But in essence the policy was expulsion or extermination, and the fighting was savage. The young Charles Darwin (1809–82), visiting Argentina in 1831 to collect material for what was later to become *The Cruise of the Beagle,* observed that the slaughter of young Indian males "is a dark picture, but how much more shocking is the unquestionable fact that all the women who appear above 20 years old are massacred in cold blood! When I exclaimed that this appeared rather inhuman, [the gaucho] . . . answered, 'Why, what can be done? They breed so!' " It was his experience in these parts which led Darwin sadly to conclude: "When civilised nations come into contact with barbarians, the struggle is short, except where a deadly climate gives its aid to the native race."[195]

Climate provided some protection in the Brazilian interior, in parts of the Andean states, and in Central America, but little or none in Argentina, the United States, or Canada, except in the far north. There, the indigenous population of Indians and Eskimos owed its partial preservation to the ineptitude and uncertainties of British policy and to disagreements among the settlers themselves. For a variety of reasons Canada did not duplicate the dynamism which characterized American society in the years 1815–30. The war had left the Canadians violently anti-American: they saw Americans as wanton aggressors motivated by rapacity, and in 1815 all new land grants to American citizens were prohibited. As a result of this general hostility to American immigrants, Canada did not share in the huge shift to the west. The Saint Lawrence River was the traditional and natural highway to the west, but its appeal was sharply reduced when the great Erie Canal opened in 1825. Canada needed canals and locks, too, to eliminate rapids and porterage, but the majority French speakers of Lower Canada opposed spending public money on projects which benefited the majority English speakers of Upper Canada. The race-and-language divide poisoned every aspect of life. In some ways Canada was like what South Africa was to become, with the French analogous to the Boer Afrikaaners, much older in settlement, highly conservative, lacking an entrepreneurial tradition, and bitterly resenting the newer English-speaking arrivals who possessed it.

The British government was not much interested in Canada and did all the wrong things. From 1815 the United States moved toward protectionism to build up its local industries; the British moved toward free trade for their own economic reasons; the Canadians were caught in between. New York port, open all the year round, prospered mightily; Montreal and Quebec, shut for six months and lacking a canal policy, stagnated. In 1822 the British brought forward proposals for union, which would, in time, have welded Canada into one English-speaking nation. But the proposals were dropped in the face of opposition from both communities, for different reasons. Under the Quebec Act (1791), the French speakers of Lower Canada were allowed to retain their basic institutions, which were static and reactionary. The Act was intended to be conciliatory but it failed in its long-term object, for the French saw the English, who were prepared to take risks and invest, grabbing control of everything. They found themselves becoming tenants or laborers on the old seignories, now owned by the English, or lumberjacks in the new English timber firms. Every English effort to charter firms, found townships or exploit Canada's enormous landed resources brought furious French protests.[196] Race and language divisions were deepened by religious ones.

In a way Canada was like Ireland, a Catholic majority ruled by a Protestant regime. The Church of England in Canada was aggressive, negative, greedy and conservative. Far from protecting Indians, it was much more interested in thwarting Methodists and Catholics, and it was at the heart of the so-called Family Compact that ran Upper Canada. Its strident spokesman was John Strachan (1778–1867), an Aberdonian immigrant who became a member of the local executive council in 1815 and Archdeacon (later, first bishop) of Toronto in 1827.

He vigorously upheld the Anglican monopoly of marriage services and the law which forbade the Methodist and Baptist churches to own property. He regarded Methodists as subversive pro-Americans. In a sense this was true since in the United States Nonconformity was the characteristic religion and a chief engine of rapid settlement and U.S. economic dynamism. As President of the Board of Education Strachan's aim was to keep all schools and colleges under Anglican control and impose religious tests on teachers. The Catholics retaliated by stopping students from attending college at all. Canadian education stagnated under this oppressive combination of Protestant sectarian fury and Catholic obscurantism.[197]

The net result was the birth of a virulent form of French cultural nationalism, led by Louis-Joseph Papineau (1786–1871), speaker of the Lower Canada assembly from 1815. He was an old-style landowner with a passionate belief in the virtues of the quasi-feudal seigneurial system, which he saw as a quintessential French institution tied to French civil law and upholding the cultural integrity of French Canada. His political philosophy was a mixture of Locke and Blackstone, Montesquieu and Voltaire, but his spirit was more akin to Chateaubriand's romanticism. His vision was of happy, hard-toiling peasants serving benevolent lords in a weird and unworkable combination of paternalism and utopian democracy.[198] The British Colonial Office regarded Canada as primarily a military posting and sent out grandee generals, usually Peninsular veterans, to govern it. These men had no idea of how to handle a man like Papineau, who eventually took Lower Canada into a destructive rebellion. Typical of them was the amiable duke of Richmond, whose wife gave the famous pre-Waterloo ball. The duke was a famous real-tennis player and reputed to be the best wicket keeper in England. But he quickly fell foul of the local parliament, taking refuge in the outback where the salmon fishing and game shooting were unparalleled. There his big dog Blücher made friends with a tame fox, which promptly bit the Duke; he died mad, suffering from the classic symptoms of hydrophobia (1819).[199] His successor, the 9th Earl of Dalhousie (1770–1838), another Peninsular hero, got into a row with parliament which resembled a comic version of Charles I's dealings with the Commons in the 1630s, and refused to recognize Papineau as speaker on the grounds that he had been personally insulting.

The French speakers were not the only troublemakers. Canada seems to have swarmed with do-it-yourself lawyers, including a pest named Robert Gourley, born in Fife in 1778, who came to Canada at the age of forty after a long career as a vexatious litigant in Britain.

Gourley instantly teamed up with local malcontents and began a campaign for Canadian independence. The authorities twice tried him for sedition but juries acquitted him; they next tried to deport him, under the 1804 Aliens Act, directed against subversive Yankees and Irishmen, but this action resulted in him hovering noisily on both sides of the Niagara Falls, which constituted the frontier. When they finally got him back to Britain, he published a hostile, sometimes valuable, work, *A Statistical View of Upper Canada*, engaged in yet more lawsuits, physically assaulted the Lord Chancellor, Lord Eldon, and struck his own counsel, Henry Brougham, with "a small whip," saying, "You have betrayed me, Sir, I will make you attend to your duty!"[200]

Even if the British had taken Canada more seriously the task would have proved difficult, with men like Gourley and Papineau selectively looking across the frontier to the example of the United States, where democracy was developing rapidly and unpredictably during these years. Part of the problem was the inheritance of old chartered companies, whose privileged business, fur trading, was antipathetic to settlement. In 1670 Charles II had given the Hudson's Bay Company exclusive rights over all western Canada, but in practice during the 18th century the rights had been exercised by the North West Fur Company. In 1810 the Hudson's Bay Company fell into the hands of an eccentric Galloway peer, Thomas Douglas, 5th Earl of Selkirk (1771–1820). He convinced himself that Canadian settlement was the only answer to the problems created by the overpopulation and clearances of the Scottish Highlands and reversed the company's traditional policy of hostility to farming. Forty-five million acres of the Red River Valley, comprising much of what is now Manitoba and Minnesota, were made over to him personally, and he sent in the warlike Captain Miles MacDonnell at the head of 100 Highlanders, each of whom was promised a farm after three years' service. From Fort Douglas, which he built, MacDonnell proclaimed himself Governor and Chief Magistrate. The North West Fur Company likewise recruited armed men, mainly mixed-blood Indians, and between 1814 and 1818 the two companies fought a minor war, with sieges, pitched battles and daring raids, in some of which the Earl took an active part. Selkirk won the sympathy of Sir Walter Scott who wrote: "I never knew in all my life a man of more generous and disinterested disposition." But the Compact families who ran Upper Canada and regarded the North West Fur Company as "their" firm, sided against Selkirk. He was fined £2,000 and retired hurt to England, where he complained vociferously of shortcomings in Canadian justice and administration.[201]

Such episodes, to say nothing of the noisy complaints of Gourley, were not good advertisements for Canada as a land of opportunity, particuarly in face of the competition from nearby America. As I noted, most of the Irish who were encouraged to go to Canada went on to Boston. The Scots tended at first to congregate in Nova Scotia, whose population rose by 40,000 in the decade beginning in 1815, New Brunswick increasing by 5,000 to 6,000 people a year. In the same period the population of Upper Canada doubled to 150,000, and there were some successful large-scale settlements. Colonel Thomas Talbot enticed 30,000 to his domain on the shores of Lake Erie. The Canada Land Company, with 1 million acres on Lake Huron, had settled 2,500 and disposed of 450,000 acres by 1834. But even by the end of the 1840s Upper Canada still had less than half a million people and everything was on a small scale compared to the striking progress made in the United States.[202]

Unlike North America and Argentina, most of Africa was effectively protected by a "deadly climate," or, rather, by yellow and blackwater fever; "bloody flux"; "breakbone fever"; and, not least, countless parasites. João de Barros, one of the early Portuguese explorers of the Guinea Coast, noted the anger of God who, having created a potentially bottomless source of wealth in tropical Africa, "has placed a striking angel with a flaming sword of deadly fever who prevents us from penetrating into the interior to reach the springs of this garden."[203] Nothing had changed in this respect by the early 19th century. On home stations the annual death rate among British regular soldiers was 15 per 1,000. In the tropical West Indies, during the years 1817–36, it varied, depending on the island, between 85 and 130 per 1,000. In West Africa it was 500. If a unit was dispatched to the coast, half of it would be dead within a year. But in South Africa it was a different matter. Cape Colony, as it became, has one of the healthiest climates and most fruitful ecologies on Earth.[204] But it was a long time before the British appreciated its value. The Royal Navy liked it simply because it was a more convenient place for reprovisioning than Saint Helena.

In Cape Colony, the Cape Squadron rendezvoused and the big China tea ships, "great towering castles," struck south "in search of the westerly winds which were to sweep them half round the globe," then catch the monsoon to Canton. "Each ship," wrote Captain Basil Hall, commanding their Atlantic naval escort, "sent a boat to us with letters for England, to be forwarded from the Cape. This was probably their last chance for writing home . . . their friends would hear nothing [more] of them till they presented themselves 18 months afterwards."[205]

The British government grumbled at the annual cost of the station, £100,000—more if there was any trouble with the natives. It disliked the local white population of Afrikaaners and more recent Boer settlers from Holland, who were as insubordinate as the Irish. But efforts to encourage British settlers and so to alter the demography in Britain's favor did not succeed, and the colony had a low grading. Even by 1830 the official establishment was less than 1,800, plus one frigate and half a dozen sloops and brigs, mostly used on anti-slave trade patrols.

All the same, the pattern of modern southern Africa was set in these years. Developments among blacks in the interior were just as formative as were the movements of whites on the periphery. Large-scale slave trading by highly organized Arab bands led a growing number of native kings to go to war in pursuit of slaves. The influence of Arab predation was felt as far south as the Cape, where the generic term for blacks was kaffir, the Arab-Islamic expression for "unbeliever" (spelled as giaour in North Africa). Speakers of the Bantu tongues—the word was a Zulu term for "the people"—had been moving into the healthier climate of southern Africa from the early modern period, probably even longer than the Dutch had been settled in the Cape. By about 1800 they were in contact with Boer settlements along the line of the Fish River.[206] In the first two decades of the 19th century a kind of political revolution took place in black society, leading to much bigger and better organized states, run by warrior chieftains who operated a system of military clientage, rather like the bastard-feudalism of the 14th–15th centuries in Western Europe. The Zulu, Swazi, and Sotho kingdoms, which still keep their identity, emerged at this time. The most successful of the warrior-kings was a fearsome man called Dingiswayo. His army was formed from military peer groups in what has been called "the age-regiment system," based on circumcision, initiation ceremonies and constant training.

When Dingiswayo was killed in battle, probably in 1817, his role was taken by one of his protégés, Chaka, whom he had put on the Zulu throne. In an age of remarkable men, Chaka stands high, though he does not exactly excite admiration. He was a military organizer of the stature of Frederick the Great or Bonaparte. He invented, or at least perfected, a battle strategy in which his impis or regiments formed themselves into a "chest," with "horns" on either side, encircling an attacking enemy. He rejected the hurling of assegais and replaced it with the tactic of locking shields and using short stabbing-spears. These methods were instilled by endless drilling and mock battles, one of which was witnessed by the Anglo-Irish trader, Henry Francis Fynn, in 1824.[207] From 1818 Chaka campaigned every year, conquering tribes, taking young men for his impis, building up an empire. Most of his soldiers were household troops and he replaced the traditional tribal council of elders with an assembly of formation-leaders known as *indunas*. His state was essentially militaristic, its structure underpinned by the fortress-towns he built, rather like King Solomon's chariot-cities. Each regiment had attached to it herds of royal cattle of a particular color, to supply uniform hides for their shields. As the herds expanded with wars and conquest, each impi had a direct interest in success. Commanders who grew arrogant and were tempted to form breakaway kingdoms were hunted down by Chaka's death squads.

Chaka himself was terrified of being overthrown by his heir. So he never married, and any woman found pregnant by him was executed instantly. He seems to have associated celibacy with virility. His warriors were expected to be chaste, and fornication was a capital offense. The young women, called his wards, were likewise organized in age-regiments and harshly drilled too, though they performed elaborate dances, rather than fought. They were given as wives to male age-regiments when they completed their years of active service. Chaka was thus able to engage in a scale of warfare, involving tens of thousands of professional soldiers, never seen in black Africa before.[208] But, like other tyrannies, his was "tempered by assassination." The first attempt was in 1824, when Fynn was there to dress his wound and cure him. Four years later, the tyrant was unhinged by the death of his mother and prohibited sexual intercourse entirely as a sign of mourning. At this point, various of his brothers conspired with other generals to stab him to death, like Julius Caesar.

By this time, however, the consequences of Chaka's imperialism—and he was not the only conqueror: Moshoeshoe created a similar Sotho confederation on the High Veld during the 1820s—were being felt throughout southern Africa. It might be thought that the existence of these fierce military states would have acted as a deterrent to Boer settlers who wished to push into the interior. Quite the contrary. The effect of the new black military system and the endless wars it waged was to concentrate the African population in areas the tyrants controlled directly and to denude large areas of what is now Natal, the Orange Free State and the Transvaal. Reports of these changes reached the Cape and persuaded those Boers who wished to move that land was there for the taking. And many did wish to move. They found British rule oppressive from the start. They were acclimatized Africans, who followed the laws of their continent—laws which applied equally to animal and human species, to blacks, whites, and coloreds. The racial mix of Cape Colony was already extremely complicated and becoming more so. There were, for instance, large numbers of mixed-race off-spring of Boers and slaves imported from Asia, mainly of Malay stock, who later formed the large, distinct community known as Cape Coloreds. There were Bastards or Bastaards, mixed-race Euro-Hottentots, another distinct people, who tended to retreat to the frontiers of settlement; their more settled elements, which became known as Griqua, possessed horses and firearms and a regular government of chiefs ruling from towns. There were freed slaves of various races, and many more still unfree. A calculation of 1820 showed that in the colony there were 42,975 "free burghers," 1,932 free blacks, 31,779 slaves belonging to burghers, and 26,974 Hottentots and Bastards.[209] To the Boers, with 180 years' experience living on the continent, each community struggled to survive or went under, exactly like animals and the black tribes of the interior, by force, courage and cunning. The Boers were committed to the process which young Charles Darwin would soon characterize as natural selection and Herbert Spencer, also a schoolboy at this time, would call "the survival of the fittest."[210]

The new British rulers, however, were committed to a different process, the rule of law. In their case this was an uneasy combination of the English Common Law, including the Mansfield Judgment of 1772, which declared slavery unlawful in England, and statute law, including the Act abolishing the slave trade of 1807, plus various altruistic notions derived from the Bill of Rights, Habeas Corpus, Locke, Blackstone and the New Testament. Britain's global efforts to suppress the slave trade and to limit slavery as an institution will be examined in the next chapter, but it is important to note here that an official hostility to slavery in any form envenomed, from the start, relations between British rulers and Boer subjects, even though slavery itself was not made unlawful throughout British territories until 1834. Successive governors sought to encourage emancipation and took active steps to punish the ill-treatment of slaves or any other indentured or compulsory laborers. Once British rule was established, such groups benefited automatically from the parliamentary statute of 1797, which abolished the torture of suspects and criminals. In 1813 the number of strokes that could lawfully be inflicted on a slave was limited to 39, the first of a number of liberal ordinances.[211] Britain had from the start also taken a close interest in the treatment of the settled natives, framing a Hottentot Code in 1809, which gave them a legal status. As far as the blacks were concerned, the code was a two-edged instrument. It introduced, for the first time, pass laws, which were to plague black Africa for a century and a half. Various designated groups of blacks could not change their district without a pass from a local magistrate. Hottentots had to have a fixed address, a farm or mission-station, or they could be arrested for vagrancy. A further ordinance of 1812 gave a farmer the right to ten years' service from any children up to the age of eight who were brought up on his farm, and one of 1819 gave him the service of farm orphans up to the age of 18.

This code, however, made master-servant relations in southern Africa subject to law for the first time, and therein lay the source of the Boer's antagonism. Blacks might not be able to bring charges against their oppressive masters themselves, but white missionaries could do it for them. Many of the first charges were dismissed as frivolous, but eight convictions for assault on blacks were secured and the indignation aroused among the Boer community was extreme—for the first time a formal legal process had intruded into a paternalistic, self-regulating society. Moreover, the news of convictions encouraged blacks to report atrocities. In 1811–12 Governor St. John Craddock ordered a special judicial investigation to inquire into and try any such offenses, which passed into Boer folklore as the Black Circuit. Two farmers were convicted of murdering blacks. A more serious incident arose out of a complaint against a farmer, Freek Buzuidenhout, in April 1813, by a black called Booy for nonpayment of wages. The farmer ignored repeated court summonses, and on 10 October 1815 four white officials and soldiers and a dozen native troops arrived to arrest him. He resisted and was killed by a *pandour* or black soldier. At his funeral, vengeance was sworn and dozens of Boers took to arms, trying to enlist the support of neighboring Xhosa tribesmen, who were also smarting from the heavy arm of British justice. On 18 November government troops surrounded 60 rebels at Slachtenek, killing Freek's brother Hans and forcing the rest to surrender. Five of the ringleaders were convicted and hanged—the executions being a particularly gruesome event, since the gallows collapsed when the men were swung up and they all had to be rehanged.[212]

The Slachtenek rebellion was the direct antecedent of the Great Trek of the 1830s and the formation of Boer republics outside British control—thus, in due course, leading to the Boer War and the modern tragedy of apartheid. The culture shock administered to the Boers by British notions of justice was never overcome. The big Boer farmers did not mind reasonable regulations to stop brutality to black laborers, since they could afford to treat their hands decently, rather as, in England, large-scale well-capitalized factory owners like Sir Robert Peel's father welcomed factory legislation which cut down unfair competition. Most of the Slachtenek rebels were landless men, poor whites, with nothing to distinguish them from the blacks but their color and faith. Many of them had already been in trouble with the law. Their complaints, which emerged in evidence at their trials, were pretty elementary: "Hottentots were preferred to the burghers"; "The black nation was protected and not the Christians"; government was *gelykstelling,* leveling; it "favored" blacks.[213] They were the exact equivalent of the Wylies and Callaghans of Arkansas. But the diary of an educated Boer woman, Anna Steenkamp, which has survived, reveals that more thoughtful people also regarded the intrusion of the British legal process as brutal, insensitive, and destructive of the true relationship which ought to govern black-white and master-servant relations—an offense not only to natural justice but to the laws of God. They hated and rejected the emerging British-run society in which they were suddenly made to feel moral outcasts—a feeling which still determines Afrikaaners' feelings toward the outside world.[214]

The offense to the Boers' religious feelings was envenomed by the fact that British policy was increasingly shaped, both in London and locally, by pressure from the missionary lobby. It was in the years after 1815 that liberal, London-led Christian churches first began to play a leading role in the politics of southern Africa, adding another formidable piece to the modern chessboard of race. The Evangelical Anglicans and the English and Scots Nonconformists had enjoyed an unprecedented triumph—the first outstanding, single-issue victory by a lobby—when they got the slave trade outlawed in 1807. That out of the way, Britain's permanent annexation of the Cape from 1809 presented them with a fresh opportunity to promote the rights of nonwhites. They fell on it with relish. Indeed it is probably true to say that the London Missionary Society, the operating agency, was more interested in southern Africa than the British government.

After the occupation of the Cape, the first impact of the London Missionary Society on London opinion was the arrival in 1810 of the Hottentot Venus, a black drover's daughter, who had been brought to Europe by a Boer named Hendrik Cezar for exhibition in Piccadilly. The Cape governor, Lord Caledon, gave permission for this exercise, in the belief it would provide useful publicity for the new colony. In fact it provoked a scandal. The lady, Sartje, was chiefly distinguished by her enormous bottom, and as her arrival coincided with an attempt to replace the Percival administration with what was termed a Broad Bottom ministry, the cartoonists went to town. The lady was put on show within reach of the mob and pinched and poked with canes and parasols. "This inhuman baiting," wrote one eyewitness, the famous actor Charles Matthews, "the poor creature bore with sullen indifference, except upon some great provocation, when she seemed inclined to resent brutality, which even a Hottentot can understand."[215] Under Evangelical pressure, the Attorney General intervened, bringing witnesses to complain that Sartje was "enclosed in a cage on a platform raised about three feet above the floor . . . The Hottentot was produced like a wild beast, and ordered to move backwards and forwards, and come in and out of her cage, more like a bear on a chain than a human being." But it was found on enquiry that she did not object to this routine, which raised profits, of which she got half herself. After a provincial tour, she went to Paris where she was painted in the nude and examined by the founder of comparative anatomy, Baron Georges Cuvier (1769–1832), but succumbed to a combination of alcoholism and smallpox.

The advent of the Hottentot Venus opened a lively debate on race. Cuvier got permission to dissect her, especially her genitalia, on which he wrote an elaborate report in the *Mémoires du museum d'histoire naturelle,* 1817. At this time, "scientific" race theory, which dominated the second half of the 19th century, with baleful results in the 20th, had not been developed. The question was, as it were, open, and discussion, unlike today, was uncensored and uninhibited. Travelers circa 1815 tended to write more sympathetic accounts of blacks than would those a generation or two later.[216] Most people accepted the view, put forward by Montesquieu in *De l'Esprit des lois* (Paris 1748), that a temperate climate accounted for a higher level of achievement among northerners. One standard work, Edward Long's *History of Jamaica* (1774), argued that Negroes were a separate species, halfway between humans and the higher apes. Another, Charles White's *An Account of the Regular Gradations in Man* (1799), asserted, to the contrary, that there was an ascending hierarchy of races. The debate between the polygenists and the monogenists, as they were known, was taken a stage further by the leading early 19th-century ethnologist, J. C. Pritchard, in his *Natural History of Mankind,* who distinguished a hierarchy of Negro types. "Tribes having what is termed the Negro character in the most striking degree," he wrote, "are the least civilised. The Pepels, Nisagos, Ibos, who are in the greatest degree remarkable for deformed countenances, projecting jaws, flat foreheads and for other Negro peculiarities, are the most savage and morally degraded of the natives." But others, he noted, had "nearly European countenances" and were correspondingly "civilised" (a word, be it noted, of recent coinage, which came into general circulation only about 1815).[217]

A third view, favored by the German idealists, was of upward progress, though it was not clear whether improvement occurred in successive races or within them over time. The Christian Evangelical position was emphatically the second. In the 1797 edition of the *Encyclopedia Britannica,* a work they influenced, the entry on Negro asserted that any apparent inferiority was due to the effects of slavery. It was a constant theme of missionary literature, 1815–30, that backward races were the victims of their environment—a writer of 1816 made the point forcibly by showing the Bulom of Sierra Leone offering sacrifices to a cannon ball—and that knowledge of Christianity could raise them, sooner rather than later, to the level of whites. The constitution of the Aborigines Protection Society laid down that "the complete Civilisation and the real Happiness of Man can never be secured by anything less than the diffusion of Christian principles."[218]

Hence the Evangelical missionaries who went out to Cape Colony had a clear ideological standpoint which ran counter to the Boers' empirical assumption of a permanent master-servant relationship between whites and blacks. The first outspoken leader of the London Missionary Society there, a Dutchman, Johannes van der Kemp, organizer of the litigation which produced the Black Circuit, asserted the ultimate absolute equality of the races. He deliberately married the daughter of a slave woman from Madagascar to underline the point that missionaries must throw in their lot with the black people.[219] His sudden death in the middle of his campaign to get elementary justice for blacks left the society without a leader until Dr. John Philip (1775–1851) arrived at the Cape in 1819.

Philip, the son of a weaver-turned-schoolmaster from Kirkaldy (Adam Smith's town) in Fife was one of scores of exceptionably able, heroically determined, self-educated lowland Scots who were leaders in transforming the world at this time. His remarkable life is imperfectly recorded because his sons and grandsons were lazy about writing it and the mass of papers he had accumulated, together with a draft-biography by W. H. Macmillan, were destroyed in a fire at the University of Witwatersrand in 1931.[220] Philip went into textiles and at 21 was running a power mill in Dundee. He then joined the Evangelical Union, which was the Scottish form of Congregationalism, took a degree at the famous Hoxton Theological College and got an American doctorate (he was enrolled at both Columbia and Princeton).

In Cape Colony he filled the specially created post of superintendent of missions, creating a network of 26 of them, plus substations, which covered the entire country and constituted almost an alternative system of government, often better informed than the real one. Philip himself covered the ground by making six-month tours by ox cart, 12 in all, and his notes on these odysseys constitute a valuable archive on the early history of the colony. The missionaries were accused of cutting off the blacks from their roots—mission-educated children spoke English, rather than their native languages—and Philip was constantly criticized for ignoring Afrikaaner opinion (though he seems to have spoken the language). But his knowledge of the blacks was unrivaled and he was the first European on the entire continent who put the blacks' interests first and presented their views forcefully to the authorities. He founded the tradition of white Christian churchmen in Africa giving their moral sanction to the black quest for rights. It was from his house that Robert Moffat set out to found his mission station in Bechuanaland in 1820 and that David Livingstone began his first northward journey in 1841.

Philip was a superb administrator and a formidable politician with powerful contacts. His son-in-law, for instance, was the editor of the only Cape daily paper, the *Commercial Advertiser*. It was useless, Philip argued, simply to get a conviction on a particularly atrocious case of ill-usage; the object must be general reform. His efforts, working through the Evangelical network in London, led to the appointment of a Commission of Inquiry (1822), whose terms of reference were expanded to include not only slaves in the Cape, but "free persons of colour" (that is, all black laborers). When the commissioners arrived in the Cape, Philip presented much of the evidence they received, went on long journeys to collect more, and in 1826 himself sailed to London to lobby the Colonial Office. He was behind the resulting Fiftieth Ordinance, "For Improving the Conditions of the Hottentots and Other Free Persons of Colour," and saw to it that it was endorsed by an Order in Council to prevent bureaucratic evasion. Philip felt the ordinance did not go far enough, in that it was discriminatory, and he would not rest until the civil and criminal law was made color blind by the Master and Servant Law (1842), which treated blacks like any other citizens.[221] Blacks did not get the vote but coloreds did, and the law marked the acceptance of what was known as "Cape policy," which remained the standard until the Afrikaaner Nationalists won power in 1948 and began to implement apartheid.[222]

With his one-track mind, powerful voice and tireless self-righteousness, Philip made few friends in the Cape Colony. He was much disliked by the Colony's officials, whom he bitterly denounced in print for backsliding. One of them successfully sued him for libel. The Boers hated him. As one account put it, he became "one of the most hated figures in any national history" and "Dr Philip" was, for generations of South African whites, "the most comprehensive term of abuse possible.[223] The tragedy is that much of this odium was incurred in vain. Philip's object was the creation and recognition of a series of indepen-

dent African states. But settlers continued to push into black lands, and
when blacks retaliated by stealing cattle, the Boers formed what became
known as "commandos" to inflict collective punishment on any black
villages within reach. Philip warned: "I consider it highly impolitic to
drive the Caffres [sic] to desperation . . . if you deprive a pastoral people
of their herds you instantly convert them into banditti [and they] attempt to live by plunder." He presented a good deal of evidence to show
that punitive raids—of exactly the kind carried out against Indians
throughout the Americas—were not the answer. Some people in positions of authority agreed with him. In 1822 General Bourke, the Acting
Governor, ordered that military patrols should not enter black territory
unless stolen cattle were actually in sight. But when black raids increased, the order was countermanded and patrols authorized to follow
spoor. This was followed by reprisals carried out by commandos. One
missionary reported that these activities, whether by troops or commandos, were self-defeating, since it was usually impossible to identify
which *kraals* (villages) were responsible for the theft, and the whites'
revenge was undiscriminating: "In most cases the guilty escape with
impunity, while the innocent are deprived of their means of support and
reduced to want and misery"—thus being forced into banditry themselves. Moreover, the military, who in the end had to take the decisions
about security, always saw frontiers as lines to be secured. Experiments
with a neutral buffer zone to keep black- and white-held territory apart
did not work: it quickly filled with Boer farmers, who drove the blacks
out, and the raiding recommenced. Then the military started to think
about a new frontier, yet farther north—and so the area of white
domination was constantly expanded, a process punctuated by more
violent outbreaks known as "Kaffir Wars."[224]

Philip's activities, however, were sufficiently effective in braking the
speed of white advance and bringing to book farmers who abused their
black laborers to provoke the Boers into the act of breakaway desperation known as the Great Trek. Philip was fighting for a moral cause.
The Boers retaliated with what, for them, was a moral gesture—they
were just as ready to respond with the outraged rhetoric of religiosity
as was General Jackson in his campaigns to remove the Indians. "We
complain," wrote the Trek leader, Piet Retief, in his manifesto, "of the
unjustified odium . . . cast upon us by interested and dishonest persons
under the cloak of religion, whose testimony is believed in England, to
the exclusion of all evidence in our favour; and we can see, as the result
of this prejudice, nothing but the total ruin of the country. We are
resolved, wherever we go, that we will uphold the just principles of
liberty; but whilst we will take care that no one shall be held in a state

of slavery, it is our determination to maintain such regulations as may suppress crime and preserve proper relations between master and servant."[225]

Hence, the Boers set off to carve out independent republics for themselves, in a spirit of indignant rectitude not unlike the Pilgrim Fathers in the United States. One spirit of self-righteousness, that of Philip and the London Missionary Society, had provoked and strengthened another, that of Afrikaaner Christian fundamentalism, while yet a third, the pained and punctilious irenicism of the Colonial Office, anxious to do the right thing by all parties, satisfying none, irritating all, presided over and sought to contain the deepening conflict. Thus, the modern South African problem came into existence. In origin it was broadly the same as that created by the whites in the temperate zones of North and South America, but with one crucial difference. In the temperate Americas, the Indians were virtually annihilated, and so their white supplanters took all and their 20th century progeny were able to enjoy their inheritance with an easy conscience. In southern Africa, the restraints imposed by the Colonial Office mentality were sufficient to allow the black peoples not only to survive but to multiply, and thus to prolong the moral doubts surrounding European settlement into the 20th century, when in due course they became overwhelming.

However, even in the years 1815–30, the moral issues raised by population movements were, and were seen to be, complex and not easily resolved. In the Americas, the Indians, had they possessed the power, would not merely have "removed" the white settlers but exterminated them, as some of their chiefs frankly admitted. Black African leaders were no different, as the Kaffir and Zulu Wars were to show. In all these conflicts developing across the globe, no race had a monopoly of virtue or evil. The truth is, during the early 19th century, the revolution in transport and the growth in population made huge movements of people not only possible but inevitable, and the historian should avoid making neat sums in moral arithmetic about the rights and wrongs of it all. In any case, it is important to remember that a high percentage of those who shifted from one continent to another in these years did so against their will. We will examine slavery in the next chapter but it should be pointed out here that perhaps half the intruders who replaced Indians in such areas as Brazil, Venezuela, and the southern United States were African blacks.

Nor were blacks the only involuntary migrants. The rapid growth in population brought with it a huge increase in crime throughout Europe, which bewildered the authorities in all countries. They raised their hands in helpless horror, much as they do now, while criminals filled to bursting expensive new prisons as fast as they could be built. Governments executed as many as public opinion would stomach. They buried alive serious but noncapital offenders and recidivists in offshore island fortresses, if they possessed any. If they were lucky enough to have colonies, convicts were dumped in them, society squaring its conscience by the belief they would "redeem" themselves, an ancient Christian concept which received secular reinforcement at the end of the 18th century from Rousseau's doctrine of the New Man.

Penal colonies varied from horrifying to chaotic. But the earlier alternatives were usually worse. Spain abolished the unspeakable punishment-galleys in 1748, sending convicts instead to *presidios* in North Africa, Puerto Rico, and Cuba. France also abandoned the galley system, and in the 1790s republican governments dumped 5,000 convicts in Guyana. Russia had been exiling criminals to beyond the Urals since the 16th century, and in 1763 abolished capital punishment for most offenses, substituting banishment with hard labor to Siberia. Under Alexander I the new penal system was implemented on a large scale. It was called "sending east," a sinister euphemism resurrected by the Nazis in the early 1940s for their Jewish "final solution." In the early 1820s, the first of what was to total over 900,000 enforced immigrants (187,000 criminals, 513,000 political exiles and 216,000 accompanying family or servants) began to trundle out to Siberia in heavily guarded wagon trains.[226]

In various parts of the world, Britain as the largest colonial power presided over involuntary movements of ever greater magnitude, though the degree of compulsion and servitude varied widely. About 3 million bonded workers were transported from India and the Pacific Islands, beginning in the 1820s. British-ruled India and Ceylon (as it was then called) also dispatched convicts, 11,000 to the Andaman Islands, up to 6,000 to Sumatra, and 16,500 to what is now Malaysia. Indian rogues, chiefly dacoits, thugs (members of Thugee sects) and murderers serving life sentences, were also sent from 1815 to Mauritius, where Darwin found 800 of them making roads. Indian convicts built the harbor and city of Singapore, which began to arise at this time. Lady Raffles, wife of the founder of Singapore, testified in 1818 that "it rarely happens that any of those transported have any desire to leave the country . . . they form connections and find so many inducements to remain that to be sent away is considered by most a severe punishment."[227] From 1812 convicts, employed chiefly as quarrymen and stonecutters, built the magnificent naval base in Bermuda, now one of the architectural treasures of the New World. They were paid 3*d* a day, a penny to spend, two to keep for their release. About 1,400 were guarded by the 400 marines of the garrison. The prisoners got three-quarters of a pound of fresh beef four times a week, plus pork three times a week, and their daily allocation included 1¼ pounds of soft bread and a gill of rum.[228] Gibraltar's public buildings were the product of the same system.

Traditionally, however, most British transports, as they were termed, went to the Americas, chiefly Virginia and Maryland, where they worked in a harsh form of indentured labor. Before the War of Independence, about 50,000 were sent and there was no inherent reason why the system should not have continued after it. Britain did not mind processing other country's convicts, rather as now it specializes in handling foreign nuclear waste. It cheerfully shipped Hanoverian rogues to its empire, and proposals to accept German convicts for transport to the Antipodes were discussed in the 1820s and 1830s. But in practice sending British transports to free America did not work, so they were put instead in hulks at Chatham, Portland, Plymouth and other naval stations, where they served as cheap dockyard labor, building breakwaters, dredging harbors and stripping rust from chains and anchors. These fearsome hulks, which Charles Dickens knew about in Kent as a boy, form the background to the magnificent opening chapter of his *Great Expectations* (1861). Hulk-prisons, indeed, rotted away and cried to Heaven for vengeance all round the coasts of France, Spain, Italy and northern Europe. From the late 1780s, however, British governments, conscious that they were living in an age of enlightenment and improvement, preferred the Australian alternative.[229]

Captain James Cook, accompanied by the botanist Joseph Banks, had explored the eastern coast of Australia, and taken possession of it for King George III in 1770. The decision to use it for a penal colony was made in August 1786, and the First Fleet of 11 ships carrying 1,000 convicts, at a cost of £84,000, arrived in 1788. This was the beginning not only of the most successful penal experiment in human history, but of a great modern nation. By the 1880s, less than 100 years later, Australia had the fastest-growing economy and enjoyed the highest per capita income in the world. Nonetheless, the birth and early development of Australia was, and among historians still is, surrounded by controversy. About 160,000 convicts were dispatched there over eight decades, and the last transport, Samuel Speed, sent to Western Australia in 1864 for arson, survived until 1938. But almost from the start voices were raised against the system. As early as 1837 a parliamentary select committee recommended it be ended, though it continued in some form until 1867.

Transportation necessarily involved and inevitably produced many horrors. They were mitigated by strong, intelligent leadership, and woefully increased by incompetence. The First Fleet was well managed by an outstanding officer, Captain Arthur Phillip, who became governor of the new colony. But no one was in any doubt that it was a fairly desperate undertaking. An English local paper reported: "Each of the transport ships going to Botany Bay has two guns loaded with grapeshot pointed down the hatchway where the convicts are to be, and which will be fired on them should any riot or mutiny happen." A witness to the embarkation said that the Portsmouth shops were all closed and the streets were lined with troops as a convoy of 30 wagons loaded with convicts passed through to the harbor.[230] The voyage lasted up to eight months and could be appalling. On the badly managed Second Fleet, 267 died aboard and and three vessels alone landed 486 sick convicts of whom 124 died almost immediately. The dead were thrown naked into Sydney harbor. An army officer aboard, Captain Hill, pointed out that the masters of the transport ships, unlike slave captains, had no financial interest in landing their human cargo in healthy condition: "The slave traffic is merciful compared to what I have seen in this fleet." Evidence given to Parliament in 1812 showed that those transported included boys and girls of 12 and men and women over 80. Men and women were crowded into the same ships, and the Reverend John West, who later organized the Australasian Anti-Transportation League, testified: "Both male and female prisoners were commonly forwarded together. The officers and soldiers selected companions for the voyage, and a sentence of transportation commonly included prostitution."[231]

By 1815 complaints had brought dramatic improvements. Transport ships were obliged to carry surgeons, who got a bonus, depending on the number who safely landed. Separate ships were assigned for women and later for juveniles. There were elaborate provisions for inspection. Indeed the years 1815–30, which saw the making of Australia, might be termed the golden age of transportation. But golden is a relative term. A new country cannot be built from the human detritus of an old society without many shameful episodes. One historian summed up the attitudes of the "immigrants" thus: "mateship, fatalism, contempt for do-gooders and God-botherers, harsh humour, opportunism, survivors' disdain for introspection, and an attitude to authority in which private resentment mingled with ostensible recognition were the meagre baggage of values the convicts brought with them to

Australia."[232] But there is fierce disagreement whether the convicts, as a whole, constituted a criminal class or were closer to a cross section of British and Irish society.[233] Peter Cunningham, surgeon-superintendent on the transport *Recovery* (1819), said that it was routine to put under the heading "occupation" on the indents the term "labourer" in order to disguise the real one, "thief." On the other hand, an analysis of 19,711 convicts transported to New South Wales in the years 1817–40, a third of the total sent to New South Wales and a quarter of all arrivals, shows that most were first offenders who were guilty of petty theft. A majority had been employed as free laborers in the normal way and often committed work-related crimes, such as stealing tools. Most crimes were unpremeditated and lacked the kind of planning one associates with a criminal class.[234]

The women may have been of a lower moral order than the men. This was the contemporary view. Opinion was unanimous that all the female transports were whores. But a statistical investigation of 2,210 women who were transported to New South Wales from 1825 to 1840 shows that the true figure was between 20 and 30 percent.[235] Many women were debauched on board. During an official investigation (1820) into prostitution on board the *Janus,* carrying 104 women, two Catholic chaplains, the Revs. Philip Connolly and Joseph Therry, who tried to stop prostitution on board, testified that the captain, who usually had two or three women in his cabin, was to blame. They said that when the ship stopped at Rio, they complained to the British commodore there, and as a result bolts and bars were put up to prevent unauthorized entrance to the women's quarters. But as soon as the ship set sail, the sailors removed them. Women convicts were also corrupted on arrival, especially if they were sent to the female factory at Parramatta. Commissioner J. T. Bigge reported: "In their passage from Sydney, great irregularities take place. The women frequently arrive at Parramatta in a state of intoxication after being plundered of such property as they had brought from the ship with them . . . the night of their arrival at Parramatta, those who were not deploring their state of abandonment were *traversing the streets.*"[236] Two years later John Nicol, a sailor on the *Lady Juliana* carrying 245 females, reported that they included "Mrs Barnsley, a noted sharper and shoplifter, who openly boasted that for a century her family had been swindlers and highwaymen . . . Mrs Davis, swindler and fence, and Mary Williams, receiver of stolen goods" and Nelly Kerwin, who he described as "a female of daring habits"—she specialized in impersonating sailors' wives to draw their pay. Immediately they got ashore Mrs Barnsley sported a crucifix, persuaded the locals she was a Catholic being transported for her religious convictions, and collected "presents"; later she ran a brothel for which she also served as midwife."[237]

Nicol added, however, that most of the women were "harmless, unfortunate creatures, victims of the basest seduction." He said that, once at sea, "every man on board took a wife," himself included. "The girl with whom I lived was Sarah Whitelam . . . of modest and reserved turn, as kind and true a creature as ever lived"; she bore him a son. Indeed, many women arrived pregnant. Once in the Parramatta factory, they found themselves in an informal marriage market. Both convicts and free settlers went there to select wives. An eyewitness testified: "The women are turned out, and they all stand up as you would place so many soldiers, or so many cattle in fact at a fair . . . The [free] man goes up and looks at the women; and if he sees a lady that takes his fancy he makes a motion to her, and she steps on one side. Some of them will not, but stand still, and have no wish to be married; but this is very rare . . . I have known of convicts going, and having the pick of one or two hundred women without finding one to please them—the lowest fellows you can fancy have said, It wouldn't do, they could not get one to suit. But if he finds one to please him, they get married." There were other reports of women being sold as wives for a gallon of rum or a five-pound note.[238] Such unions were often unofficial. One shocked witness asserted that "almost the whole of the Australian population was living in a state of unblushing concubinage." Court cases give fitful gleams of illumination into the lives of the women. On 13 June 1813, a woman convict who had served her term was followed to her Sydney lodgings in Pitt Street by two drunken officers of the 73rd. Her landlord, Holness, another ex-convict, said to them "Oh, oh, if it's F——— you want, I can give you enough if you do not be off." He died in the subsequent fight and the two officers were fined a shilling and given six months in jail for "felonious killing."[239]

Sarah Whitelam, Nicol's girl, had been sentenced to seven years for stealing a lady's dress. That was a typical sentence. Most women were transported for theft, usually from their employer. All but 5 percent had occupations, and the vast majority (77 percent) were in domestic service as kitchen maids, cooks, housemaids, laundresses, nursemaids, seam- stresses, and dairymaids. A third stole clothes, a fifth money, a few cloth, yarn and jewelry. Violence among women convicts was very rare.[240] Some, clearly, were incurable thieves. Nicol reported that a woman on board, caught stealing from the hold, was given 12 strokes with a cat-o'-nine-tails. In the early 19th century, society habitually used the whip to impose order on those who had no property to confiscate, women and children included. But, hardened as its upholders were to the infliction of physical punishment, there was a point at which they lacked the stomach to go on. In 1814 Jeffery Hart Bent kept a diary of the voyage while going out to be a judge on the new New South Wales Supreme Court. He described a woman convict, sentenced to the pillory, who simply banged her head on the deck and held her breath till black in the face—the captain, advised by the surgeon, had no alternative but to remit the punishment.[241]

Bent complained that he could not bear to hear the screams of convicts being flogged. The lash was in constant use, rising to a total of 332,810 in 1835.[242] But beatings were not a regular feature of convict life; two-thirds received only one or none at all. The real horrors arose over the treatment of the few thousand who were regarded as incorrigible. In the early days, justice was swift. A convict from the First Fleet, James Barrett, aged 17, was hungry and stole some food. On 8 February 1788 he was charged, convicted, sentenced and hanged within an hour. A generation later the Rev. Samuel Marsden J.P.—clergy were often magistrates—flogged one of his convict servants who then "went bush" and committed another offense before being recaptured. Marsden sentenced him to be hanged and administered the last rites on the scaffold. If not hanged, recidivists were sent to Norfolk Island, three miles by five miles, 600 miles from Sydney, and one of the world's worst penal settlements in the years 1815–30. There, Father Bernard Ullathorne (1806–89) a Catholic chaplain and later a famous Archbishop of Birmingham, witnessed a mass hanging of 31 men after a convict revolt, which took place in front of 2,000 sullen inmates herded behind stockades manned by armed soldiers.[243] Some of the cruelties, inflicted more out of desperation than sadism, almost defy belief. There was the case of Charles Answerson, born in a workhouse, an orphan, sent to sea at nine, who received a head wound at Navarino and became violent thereafter when angry or drunk, and was transported at age 18. For repeated offenses, even on Norfolk, he was put on nearby Goat Island for two years, with trumpet irons on his legs and riveted to a rock by a 26-foot chain. He slept in a hollowed rock, his only shelter being a wooden lid with holes in it locked into position at night, and he was fed from a dish pushed toward him by a pole. Fellow convicts were forbidden to speak to him, on pain of 100 lashes. He was then aged 24, but looked twice his age. But this pathetic inmate, regarded as a wild beast, was befriended and rehabilitated by a humane superintendent, Captain Alexander Maconochie RN, and was eventually put in charge of the signal station.[244]

Indeed, most convicts were able to redeem themselves. While still serving their sentence, they were obliged to work, either for the government or for private masters 5½ days a week, an average of 56 hours. Prison laborers in Russia did 76–84 hours and in Spain, 62–88 hours; slaves averaged 70–75 hours. Indeed, 56 hours compared well with free labor in England, where agricultural workers did 57 hours a week; miners, 42–48; royal dockyard workers 63, tailors 72, cotton-workers 72–90, metalworkers, 78–84; and factory children 72–84.[245] Outside the special punishment settlements, their food, clothing and accommodations were perhaps the best enjoyed by prisoners anywhere in the world. On the King's birthday, 4 June 1819, to celebrate completion of the superb new barracks he had built for them, Governor Lachlan Macquarie (1761–1824) dined with the 600 convicts it accommodated off a fine meal of beef and plum pudding and drank toasts with them in punch. The convicts gave him three cheers.[246]

Three cheers was the characteristic symbol of convicts' approval, and it is significant that even the 1,000 transports of the First Fleet gave three cheers as their ships left England—they preferred Botany Bay to English hulks or prisons. Certainly by 1815, after the reform of the shipping procedures, the terrors of transportation had been much reduced. At a hearing of the Police Committee three years later, Superintendent Cotton, in charge of Newgate Prison in London, testified disapprovingly: "The generality of those who are transported consider it as a party of pleasure, as going out to see the world; they evince no penitence, no contrition but seem to rejoice in the thing, many of them to court it." He complained that some called out to his warders, after sentence, "The first fine Sunday we shall have a glorious kangaroo-hunt at the Bay."[247] This was a gross exaggeration. But Edward Gibbon Wakefield, from a three-year observation of Newgate prisoners, said he could not recall a case of a convict really fearing transportation—most thought they had a better chance that way. By 1835, Governor William Cope of Newgate concluded that "19 out of 20 were glad to go."[248]

The truth was, it was in the interests of masters using assigned convict laborers to treat the men well. James Macarthur, a large-scale farmer in New South Wales, admitted as much to a Select Committee, adding, "The principle on which we have conducted our establishment is, where a man behaves well, to make him forget if possible that he is a convict." Convicts got a ticket-of-leave (probation) after serving four years of a seven-year sentence, or after six years of a 14-year sentence. Thereafter they were free men in a country where land was cheap and plentiful, labor was scarce, wage rates were high and mortality rates were low. Australia was exceptionally healthy for Europeans. The death rate for troops, even including the return voyage, averaged only 16.8 per 1,000 per annum. Child mortality was only one-eigth of that in Britain. Until 1831 convicts got free medical treatment in the colony's hospitals, where the standard of care was probably higher than at home.

But if Australia benefited the convicts, they in turn benefited the colony. Indeed, they made it during its formative years. Though free settlers began to come out in small numbers as early as the Second Fleet, even by 1820 there were only 943 of them plus 333 women and 665 children (most of them wives or children convicts). Even in 1840 over 70 percent of all labor was convict. For a new colony, settlement by unfree laborers with real incentives to behave and get on was the ideal formula. By 1815, when the system was properly organized, all transports had to be passed fit for the four-month voyage and were thus above the average British health standards. Females had to be under age 45, males 15–50 years.

The demographic profile was far more efficient for colony-building purposes than that of free immigrants. Among both males and females, there was a high degree of preconviction mobility, an advantage for settlers. The overwhelming majority were male, and over 80 percent were in the 16–25 age group. Free immigrants tended to be both older and younger—30 percent of them were under age 16—and less than half (47 percent) formed the optimum 16–35 age group. With the constant flow of fresh batches of convicts, much of the burden of schooling, trade-training and care of the elderly was avoided for the first two generations. Indeed, in the formative years up to 1830, over 65 percent of the total population were working males. This was a huge economic advantage. The convicts seem to have had roughly the same proportion of skilled and semiskilled workers as the rest of the population, but it is a curious fact that, of English convicts, 75 percent could read or write (or do both), against 58 percent for the general population. Among women convicts, too, there was above-average literacy. This significant proportion of well-read literates early formed an Australian labor aristocracy. In 1826 Sir Robert Peel recommended that such men be sent to outstations as pioneers. But the competition for their services was too great. The men were able to take full advantage of the incentive system. Masters who were known to get the best out of convicts and to provide them with opportunities were assigned the most skilled convicts by the government. William Cox, the "squire" of Richmond, who earned favor with the government for this reason, but also as a hard-working Justice of the Peace and builder of the first road across the Blue Mountains in 1815, aroused a lot of jealousy because he secured a carpenter, two sawyers, a painter and glazier, two blacksmiths, a butcher, a tanner, a tailor, a harness maker and three cobblers. His estate at Clarendon even had a textile shop that processed wool into clothes.[250]

Such a work force provided the human means to make the colony a success. But it was the leadership of Macquarie, during the key dozen years after 1810, which ensured that the means was effectively joined to ends. Macquarie was yet another of those energetic, able, obstinate and self-righteous Scots—he was an islander, the son of a Mull laird—who made such a mark at this time. Like Philip in Cape Colony, he lacked flexibility and the ability to see any viewpoint but his own. So he made countless enemies who dragged him down. But he has the strongest claim to be called the creator of Australia. He saw its boundless opportunities and appointed official explorers, including G. W. Evans, the cartographic expert. It was Macquarie who encouraged Cox to drive the highway across the Blue Mountains, finished the same month that Jackson won the Battle of New Orleans. Four months later, just before Waterloo, he went across it to found the first interior town of Bathurst, seeing this magnificent country as what he called "a chance for sober industrious men with small families from the middling class of free people to receive from 50 to 100 acres of land." By this time, indeed, land in the immediate Sydney area was running out, and it was Macquarie's stress on exploration which led to the discovery of the Liverpool Plains to the north of Sydney in 1818 and, the following year, to the breakout toward rich lands in the southwest. By 1820 Australia had spread outside its original enclave, just as the United States was spreading across the Appalachians and well into the Mississipi Valley.[251]

Macquarie had been enjoined by Castlereagh, in his original instructions, "to enforce a due observance of religion and good order, and to take particular care that all possible attention be paid to the due celebration of public worship." He carried out these orders with zest. Almost his first act was to shut public houses during Divine Service; reduce their number; raise the duty on spirits, end Sunday trading and, most insistently, forbid by proclamation "the scandalous and pernicious custom so generally and shamefully employed throughout the territory of persons of different sexes cohabiting and living together unsanctioned by the legalities of matrimony." He made Sunday church attendance for convicts compulsory and set up Sunday schools for the colony's children. It was his aim to transform Sydney from a moral slum into a grand, righteous city, and he set on foot an enormous public works program: state buildings, barracks, fortification, schools, hospitals, roads, squares, and bridges. These buildings were erected of fine, hard stone by skilled convict laborers and were designed by an architect

of solid genius, Francis Howard Greenway. Born in 1777, he had practiced in Bristol and Bath, but in 1812 had been charged with forging a
building contract. His death sentence was commuted to 14 years' transportation, and two years after his arrival in Sydney, Macquarie made
him Civil Architect (30 March 1816) at 3 shillings a day, using him as
extensively as the prince employed Nash. Greenway not only built early
19th-century Sydney, but advised Macquarie on the design of the townships—each with a church, schoolhouse, jail, and guardhouse—which
he placed in the midst of his new settlements. Their names ring with the
England of those times, Pitt Town, Castlereagh, Liverpool, Wilberforce, Windsor, and Richmond. Thus the visual grace of Regency Bath
and Bristol was seen in New South Wales, too.[252]

Macquarie's patronage of Greenway was not to the taste of Sydney's free elite, who had come out to New South Wales to invest their
money profitably and to lord it over a convict multitude. They objected
to the expense too, and soon their complaints echoed through Sydney
and winged their way to Lord Bathurst at the Colonial Office. The rage
of the free righteous against the convict wicked rose in a crescendo
when the Governor, determined to honor and encourage freed convicts
who had made good, invited four of them to dine at Government
House—D'Arcy Wentworth, the head surgeon, his assistant William
Redfern, Andrew Thompson, a large-scale farmer, and Simeon Lord, a
leading merchant. These "emancipists," as they were termed, had hitherto been excluded from Sydney's polite society. The Governor compounded his affront to the *bien-pensants* by making Thompson a magistrate. The Chief Chaplain and instant hanger, the Rev. Samuel
Marsden, put himself at the head of the opposition and declined to
serve on a turnpike commission with two of these ex-convict bigwigs.
Worse, when Thompson died, he said he would not attend the funeral
of a man who had "once been an evil-liver." Macquarie, a veteran of
America, India, Egypt and Spain, and former commander of the 73rd,
was furious at what he regarded as insubordination. He said that were
Marsden's appointment not a civil one, he would have him court-
martialed.

Opposition based on (as he saw it) humbug and moral snobbery
merely strengthened Macquarie's resolve to do right by the emancipists.
"I am Happy," he wrote to Bathurst, 'in feeling a Spirit of Charity in
Me, which shall ever Make Me despise such Unjust and Illiberal Sentiments."[253] That was not the kind of letter to reassure the Colonial
Secretary that he had a sensible man in charge of a far-distant settlement. And indeed the dispute was petty in many ways. The Governor
rowed with the Forty-sixth Regiment, the other battalion quartered in

Sydney, and "Ensign Bullivant drew on the wall of the Guard Room a full caricature of Macquarie in a position of ignominy with indecent scurrilous labels under it." Its officers refused invitations to Government House. Macquarie, for his part, made public his objections to the contents of Marsden's sermons. On 4 January 1817 the governor's secretary, J. T. Campbell, published a letter in the *Sydney Gazette,* under the pseudonym Philo Free, denouncing Marsden as "the Christian Mahommed," who, under the cloak of religion supplied the South Seas natives with Bibles and booze "to his own pecuniary profit and personal glory." Marsden sued for libel and got £200 damages.[254]

Matters came to a head in December 1817 when the Governor, feeling he did not have the full support of Bathurst, sent in his resignation and summoned the Chaplain General to his presence, feeling now free to say what he thought. In front of "a number of people," he told Marsden: "Viewing you *now,* Sir, as the *Head of a seditious low Cabal,* and consequently unworthy of mixing in Private Society, or intercourse with me, I beg to inform you that I never wish to see you *except on Public duty;* and I cannot help deeply lamenting that any Man of your *Sacred Profession* should be *so much lost* to every good feeling of Justice, generosity and gratitude, as to manifest such deep-rooted malice, rancour, hostility and vindictive opposition towards one who has never injured you . . . [shouting] I command you, Sir, that you never set foot in Government House except on public duty!" Marsden: "Your Excellency may rest assured that I will be very particular in not violating Your Excellency's commands in *that* respect."[255]

Bathurst's response to all this was to send out a former Chief Justice of Trinidad, J. T. Bigge, as Commissioner to make an inquiry. He arrived in Sydney in September 1819 and quickly discovered the real issues behind what seemed a series of personal quarrels. Macquarie wanted to run New South Wales primarily as a place where convicts were rehabilitated. While anxious to explore the vast country, he was perhaps influenced by the demographic profile of the transports, which was overwhelmingly urban, into an overconcentration on building up towns. Marsden, on the other hand, saw the colony as a place where free settlers with sufficient capital—he was well-to-do himself and farmed 4,500 acres—could exploit both cheap convict labor and the limitless natural resources of the country to create a rustic paradise based on sheep. One particular point at issue concerned the constitutional rights of freed convicts. Should they, as Governor Macquarie held, eventually vote, alongside free settlers, for a legislative assembly, and in the meantime serve on juries? Or was it, as Marsden maintained, wrong to risk the property of free men at the hands of jurors who had once been felons? The issues were important and the debate curiously modern.

On the whole, Bigge accepted Marsden's case, and a heartbroken Macquarie read his report as a rejection of his entire administration.[256] It might have been expected that the more liberal-minded English would have taken Macquarie's side. Not at all. Both Marsden, who submitted written evidence, and Bigge himself were much more efficacious in presenting their case than the angular and excitable governor— who was, after all, a mere soldier by education. It was an early example of the growing importance of good public relations in an age when the press was growing in power every year. Sydney Smith, writing in the key Whig journal, the *Edinburgh Review,* accepted Bigge's measured arguments uncritically and held up Macquarie to ridicule as a preposterous fellow, whose building schemes moreover were outrageously expensive. "Ornamental architecture in Botany Bay!" sneered Smith. "How it could enter into the head of any human being to adorn public buildings at the Bay, or to aim at any other architectural purpose but the exclusion of wind and rain, we are at a loss to conceive." The Governor was clearly "wrong-headed" and "very deficient" in "good sense"; whereas, Smith added, it was clear that Mr Marsden was "one of the best and most enlightened men in the settlement" as well as "a gentleman of great feeling."[257] Thus rejected by his natural supporters, Macquarie (whose resignation had been accepted even before Bigge reported) died a disappointed man.[258]

As it happened, both Macquarie and Marsden were justifed by Australia's subsequent development. Australia became the greatest sheep-raising country on earth, but also the most urbanized, with over 80 percent of its population living in five big cities. As for ornamental architecture in Botany Bay, the Sydney Opera House of the 1970s was to outrun its estimates more comprehensively than any other public building of the 20th century. Nor did Macquarie's retirement end the rococo rows in which the colony already specialized. His successor, Sir Thomas Brisbane, a military protégé of Wellington's, soon acquired a multitude of critics in Sydney, a town which delighted in public abuse, press scurrility, sending complaining petitions home, and vexatious litigation—as well as varieties of religious mania in which Brisbane, an imprudent man, enthusiastically joined. He was peremptorily recalled in 1825: "It has been expedient to relieve your Excellency and appoint a successor." His successor, yet another Peninsular veteran, Ralph Darling, likewise ran into trouble by backing the Australian Agricultural Company, which planned to exploit state lands with convict labor by investing £1 million, and was denounced by envious rivals as an outrageous monopoly. Both sides wrote pamphlets against each other and drank belligerent toasts at big public dinners held at such hostelries as Mrs. Hill's Hyde Park Tavern, and the issues of principle were invariably envenomed by mutual accusations of seducing maidservants, drunkenness, secret sales of intoxicating liquor, and illegal floggings, the small change of life in Botany Bay.[259] When Darling too was recalled, the Sydney Monitor headlined: "He's Off! Reign of Terror Ended!"

But Australia marched inexorably on. Queensland was settled in 1824, Western Australia five years later, and South Australia in the 1830s. It proved impossible to halt Macquarie's policy of integrating former convicts into the colony's life at every level; they were doing too well and in the long run money talks louder than records. Of the men Macquarie had at his table, both Wentworth and Lord founded dynasties. Lord had been convicted in Manchester in 1790 for stealing muslin and calico worth tenpence. In Sydney he worked as a servant, then at a bakery, whose owner, Mrs. Bligh, set him up as an auctioneer. By 1806 he was trading successfully in coal, timber, grain, South Sea products, sealskins and sheepskins. He built a woolen mill to manufacture cloth and produced a range of items never before manufactured in Australia. His appointment as a justice was furiously resented in Westminster, no less than in Sydney. Henry Bennet, MP, son of a Whig earl and a parliamentary and penal reformer who should have known better, complained in the Commons: "As soon as [Lord] came down from the seat of justice he got into a cart and sold blankets, one of the most indecent acts that could possibly be exhibited."[260] Bigge had him removed from the bench accordingly, but Bennet's remarks were beginning to seem archaic even at the time, and Lord went on to become a plutocrat, to built a three-story mansion in Macquarie Square, "the best house in Australia," and to rear an enormous and prosperous family, whose names are commemorated in streets all round the Bay.[261]

Even richer was Samuel Terry, born in 1776 and transported in 1801 for stealing geese. From a stonemason's gang at Parramatta, he graduated to selling spirits from a small shop in exchange for worn convicts' clothes. He gave rise to the general complaint that convicts did not prosper as farmers, even when given land—it was "too much like hard work"—but, if they had enterprise, they sold the land and set up as spirits dealers. In fact Terry, having run a successful public house, exchanged it for land grants and by 1820 had 19,000 acres. Three years later, he was known as "the Richest Outlaw in Australia" or "the Botany Bay Rothschild," and he died worth over £1 million.[262] Another landowning family was the Wentworths, established by the surgeon

D'Arcy Wentworth, of Portadown, Ulster. Wentworth was not strictly speaking a transport, but had twice been convicted for highway robbery and discharged in 1789 only on condition that he go out to Australia as superintendent of convicts in Botany Bay. He became rich through land grants in Parramatta, financed from the hospital's rum contract and Pacific trading. He had a son by a female transport, Catherine Crowley, who called himself W. C. Wentworth. He was educated in England; saw himself as a Byronic hero, took part in the first drive across the Blue Mountains, became very rich, practised at the Bar, founded a new paper, *The Australian,* and sought the hand in marriage of the daughter of John Macarthur, the leading free-settler landowner.[263]

Macarthur, one of the first military free-settlers, who had a wool station of 9,600 acres at Camden, indignantly forbade the union, which led to a historic feud with reverberations for decades. He built himself an English-style stone manor house at Camden and his aim was to create a New South Wales aristocracy of pure "free" blood. He signified his moral earnestness by laying down a vineyard to discourage the burning Botany Bay taste for spirits, thus founding a mighty industry. In fact, said the emancipist rumor factory, Macarthur nonetheless secretly distilled spirits and bribed governors Brisbane and Darling with casks of brandy; it also asserted that his original trade was as a stay maker and that his wife had stuffed mattresses. Even Macarthur, moreover, was forced to conciliate the convict lobby, asserting that only two transports had ever been punished on his estates and that none had ever petitioned to be withdrawn from his service. This may well have been true. Macarthur was an excellent sheep farmer who believed in large-scale wool production to make English machine manufacture of woolen products independent of raw material from Saxony, Austria and Spain. His object was rapidly achieved but only because he recognized that a growing number of successful sheep farmers and managers were former convicts. Even in 1821, the emancipists were able to claim that they numbered 7,506 adults, worth £1,123,600, against of the free settlers' net worth of merely £597,464. The wealth of convicts continued to expand rapidly in the 1820s, and by the end of the decade, it was increasingly difficult to distinguish between the two interests, both of which were manifestly contributing to and sharing abundantly in the success of the whole experiment.

The losers, of course, as in the United States, Canada and Argentina, were the aborigines. In New South Wales the climate provided them with no protection, whereas for the British, it was more benign than their own environment at home. Even in Queensland, which was tropical, settlement in the 1820s came late enough for settlers to take effective steps to protect their lives, stock and crops.[264] At no point during the early settlement did any British official act on the assumption that aborigines had any proprietary rights; it was simply assumed that the Crown owned all by virtue of Cook's act of possession. The natives were never designated with tribal names. Nor was it known if they had any. In fact it proved difficult to make any intellectual contact with this stone-age people. The first governor, Phillip, was well disposed but baffled. He estimated there were 1,500 aborigines living in the neighborhood of Botany Bay when the First Fleet arrived, and he issued orders that no one was to molest them or attempt to take away their hunting weapons. But he was disobeyed, often by his own officers.

Moreover, he was frustrated by the secretiveness of the aborigines and their apparent lack of curiosity about the new arrivals. Eventually he seized two by force, planning to educate them and then free them so they could tell their kindred of European advantages. But one died of smallpox and the other escaped. Two more were taken and named Colnee and Bennelong. Colnee contrived to vanish into the bush, even wearing leg irons. Bennelong seemingly liked his captors, and Phillip, when he retired, took him back to England, where he met George III and was lionized. But on his return to Sydney, he was quickly killed, in a tribal fight or city brawl—tales vary. This cautionary story was not encouraging. Nor were later efforts to make contact. The explorer Evans, traveling 100 miles west of Bathurst, came across an aborigine who was so terrified that he climbed up a tree, crying piteously, "so much so that he could have been heard a mile away," he reported to Macquarie; the more Evans spoke to the aborigine, the more he cried.[265]

Macquarie, anxious as always to befriend the unfortunate, made considerable efforts, as he put it, "to bring these poor unenlightened people into an important degree of civilisation, and to instil into their minds, as they gradually opened to reason and reflection, a sense of the duties they owed to their fellow kindred and society." Unfortunately, as he had to admit, they had "no sense of duty." A farm he set up on the north side of Sydney Harbor did not flourish. He started a school under a William Shelley, but most of the parents quickly took their children away.[266] On 28 December 1816 he invited all the chiefs to meet him in the marketplace at Parramatta. Some 179 took part in the feast, the chiefs on chairs, the rest on the ground, consuming bream, roast beef and a cask of grog. Macquarie produced 15 children who had stayed at the school and put them through their paces. One chief, delighted, exclaimed: "Governor—that will make good settlers—that's

my picaninny!" At another meeting, 1 January 1818, Macquarie told
the chiefs that he was pleased "by the very decent and orderly appearance of the tribes." A third meeting at the end of 1818 brought together
chiefs from distant areas, reflecting the growing confidence of even the
wilder tribes in the good intentions of the British, or so Macquarie
reported. The aborigines had even learned to give the governor three
cheers. The *Sydney Herald* reported on 17 April 1819 that a 14-year-old
girl had won first prize in a mixed school, refuting those who claimed
that the natives were incapable of mental improvement. True, some
aborigines had retreated to the wilds, but this was not surprising since
the whites would give them no employment above that of kitchen boy.
It was now proved, the paper concluded, that aborigines were fit for
decent jobs.[267]

But this proved a false dawn. Most contacts were disastrous, especially when aborigines got access to liquor. Whites often made them
drink to get them to fight, what the *Sydney Gazette* called "that most
shameful, cruel and barbarous custom of encouraging black people to
murder or mangle one another for the sport of learned, polite and
refined Europeans."[268] Thus the men provided blood sports for whites,
and the women worked in white kitchens. Whalers and sealers along
the coast, often absconders or emancipists, used the women as concubines, sometimes paying them, and to peg out skins. The male aborigines hit back by spearing cattle. Then the settlers demanded troops. At
the end of 1821, the Rev. Ralph Mansfield was told by a native who had
learned some English: "Black men die fast since white men came. Old
black men nigh all gone. Soon no black men, all white men."[269]

Some whites, and by no means all of them of low education, simply
would not accept that aborigines had basic human rights at all. When
Nathaniel Lowe of the Fortieth was charged with murdering an aborigine, his counsel, Dr Robert Wardell, argued that the very trial was
irregular since because aborigines were not allies, subjects or enemies
of the king of England, they did not have the legal status of human
beings, and killing them was not murder. Wardell quoted a German
anthropologist to the effect that the aborigines were cannibals, and
Christians had a moral right to exterminate such grievous sinners.
Lowe was acquitted without being called to give evidence.

Australian juries throughout the 1820s and into the 1830s refused to
convict whites of capital crimes against nonwhites, just as in the United
States and South Africa. At Myall Creek in northern New South Wales
in 1838, a group of convict hands from the Dangers' station herded 28
aborigines, men, women, and children, whom they accused of stealing,
into a hut, where they roped them together and slaughtered them. The

governor, Sir George Gibbs, had 11 convicts arrested and tried; all were acquitted. The *Sydney Monitor,* which upheld aboriginal rights, denounced the verdict as a conspiracy between convict and landlord interests: "The verdict of acquittal was *highly popular!* It was only with exertion that the Chief Justice could prevent the audience *from cheering!* Such was their delight! The aristocracy of the colony, for once, joined heart and hand with the prison population in expression of joy at the acquittal of these men. We tremble to remain in a country where such feelings and principles prevail. . . . For the verdict of Thursday shows that only let a man or a family be sufficiently *unpopular* with the aristocracy and the prison population of the colony *conjoined* (in this case) and their murder will pass unheeded. Money, lucre, profit—these are thy Gods, O Australia!"[270] Such protests led directly to the re-trial, the following month, of seven of the accused; they were found guilty and hanged, not without furious complaints from the *Sydney Herald.*

In Tasmania (originally Van Diemen's Land), where the first whites had landed in September 1803, the misunderstanding between the races was total. The island, especially its almost impenetrable west coast— still wild today—was regarded as a dumping ground for convicts not wanted in New South Wales. The convicts occasionally escaped from the fearsome convict settlement and "went bush," where they died or (in some cases) became cannibals. The natives were quite different from mainland aborigines, with wooly hair, flat noses, full lips, large ears, and expressive faces. In May 1804 a group of whites—liberated convicts, up-country settlers, and sealers—opened fire without warning on a native hunting party, who had no weapons other than pointed sticks and clubs. This became the pattern for what the authorities described as "the murders and abominable cruelties practised upon the natives by the white people." Part of the trouble was that it was hard to find decent men to serve in responsible positions in Tasmania. The Anglican chaplain, the Rev. Robert Knopwood, and the Catholic priest, Father Philip Connolly, were reported to get drunk together "and roar through Hobart arm-in-arm." One Lieutenant Governor, Colonel Thomas Davey, though admirable at putting up official buildings—the island abounds in delightful 19th-century architecture of all periods—was accused of a catalogue of crimes: he "dressed in short sleeves"; fornicated with convict females, "called people by their Christian names" or "even nicknames," and became intoxicated, often in the company of male convicts, "by day and night," in the Bird in Hand in Argyll Street. Despite such complaints, it took two years to get rid of "Mad Tom," as he was known.[271]

In 1820 a Russian naval officer, Captain Bellinghausen, visited Hobart in command of a ship called the *Discovery*. He reported that, by this stage, the natives of Van Diemen's Land lived in a state of perpetual warfare with the whites. Hating the English because of the behavior of the first settlers, they destroyed sheep, not for food but for revenge. He described a native chief, Boongaree, who visited his ship and told him: "This is my land." But he added that the chief and his wife were inveterate cadgers, who shouted and swore when refused gifts. Bellinghausen said he had reached the conclusion that contact between the races had been an unrelieved disaster. The natives had acquired all the vices of the Europeans, especially smoking and drinking—their desire for drink was so great that, though they hated work, they would toil all day for it—and had made no educational progress at all. They now owned nothing. All that was left to them was their memory of former independence and a smoldering desire for vengeance.[272]

By 1823, when Mad Tom was finally succeeded by Colonel George Arthur, the aborigine population of Tasmania, estimated at 5,000 when the white man first landed, had shrunk to 500. Arthur's first proclamation was to order settlers to stop "maliciously and wantonly firing at, injuring and destroying the defenceless aboriginals." Unlike his predecessor, he was severe and would not issue a license to sell liquor to anyone living with a woman not his wife. The *Hobart Town Gazette* described him as "a Gideonite of tyranny." Perhaps for this reason he failed to stamp out atrocities against the natives. Indeed in those times Tasmania, with its mysterious animals—Devils and Tigers, still plentiful then—its cannibal convicts in the bush, and its fearsome punishment colony at Macquarie Harbor, was not easily controlled by anyone. A convict called Charles Routley, with an iron hook instead of a hand, escaped from the harbor, murdered six men, sewed the body of one of them in a bullock's skin, roasted it and ate it and, when finally run down, waved his iron hook in the dock and cursed God and man (though he repented on the scaffold).[273] Runaway convicts were the worst enemies of the aborigines, who did not distinguish between these predators and peaceful settlers.

Arthur found by bitter experience that Tasmanian natives were less stoical than their apathetic distant relations on the mainland and could react to injustice with ferocity, especially if they got hold of firearms. They had learned a war cry, used when attacking farms: "Fire, you white bastards!" In November 1826 they murdered seven whites on the Macquarie river. Arthur issued a proclamation: "The series of outrages which have of late been perpetrated by the Aborigines of the colony, and the wanton barbarity in which they have indulged by the commis-

sion of murder in return for kindnesses in numerous instances shown
to them by the settlers and their servants, have occasioned the greatest
pain to the Lieutenant-Governor and called for his most anxious consideration of the means to be applied for preventing the repetition of
these treacherous and sanguinary acts." This uneasy language indicated
that Arthur was moving toward a policy of extermination, or at least
"removal." If, he continued, there appeared a "determination" by a
native tribe to attack, "any person" might arm himself and "joining
himself to the military, drive them by force to a safe distance, treating
them as an open enemy."[274]

This was ineffectual, and two years later, as attacks on whites
continued, the colony's chief legal officer openly threatened: "Let them
be removed, or they will be exterminated." In spring 1829 Arthur set up
a reserve on Bruny Island, appointing a guardian, G. A. Robinson, who
learned the aborigines' language.[275] Four months later he ordered a
roundup, with the object not of killing the aborigines but of corralling
them and "reducing them to civility." About 3,000 men, armed with
muskets and sounding bugles, began the drive on 7 October. After six
weeks they admitted failure; two aborigines had been shot, two captured. The reserve failed, too: All who were sent there died of apathy.
Thereafter the remaining natives were hunted down individually. The
Hobart Museum preserves the skeleton of Truganini, the last of them.
She was a woman, born about 1803; her uncle was shot by soldiers, her
sister was kidnapped by escaped convicts for sex, and her mother was
killed by sealers. The aborigines had been in Tasmania for 30,000 years
and were exterminated in two generations.[276]

The New Zealand Maoris had even less protection from the climate
than did the Australian natives. New Zealand proved to be the healthiest station in the entire empire, with military death rates of 5.3 per 1,000
per annum, less than a third of those in Australia (or at home). The
Maoris were saved by a combination of factors: their intelligence and
militancy; the fact that New Zealand was never a convict settlement;
and the leading role played by missionaries from the start. New Zealand was first used as a whaling station. The Industrial Revolution
enormously increased the demand for lubricants, and whereas steam
engines could use palm oil, which was cheaper, the oil of the sperm
whale was discovered to be ideal for the new machinery in cotton
factories, raising machine revolutions from 500 to 20,000 an hour.[277]
But whalers who put into New Zealand inlets were liable to be attacked
and their crews cannibalized. The Maoris had, for instance, killed and
eaten the captain and crew of the *Boyd* in Whangaroa Bay in 1810.

Cannibalism was so detested in the South Seas at this time, especially because it was believed to be a contagious evil which could spread to whites, that there was always a danger of punitive expeditions being launched against those who practiced it. Fearing this, Chief Chaplain Marsden decided to evangelize the New Zealanders and led an expedition which landed there on 28 November 1814. The brig *Active* carried 35 on board; they included Marsden, his three missionaries (Kendall, Hall, and King), their wives and children, eight Maori helpers, two Tahitians, mechanics, and one runaway convict. Negotiations were begun to buy land from the natives on behalf of the Church Missionary Society of London. On Christmas Day Marsden began a service with the Old Hundreth and preached on the text from St Luke, "Behold I bring you tidings of great joy." Then the Union Jack was raised, which was, Marsden reported, "a pleasing sight signalling the dawn of civilisation, liberty and religion in this dark and benighted land."[278]

This was in some ways another false dawn. Marsden himself was disconcerted to be offered by the Maoris several decorative heads. These were heavily tattooed, cooked, stuffed with flax, and apparently much prized in Sydney. They were entered on customs manifests as "Baked Heads from New Zealand" and then exported to Europe. They were by no means cheap, being priced, according to the amount and quality of the tattooing, from one to two guineas. Marsden decided to stamp out the trade. But when the Maoris, at his behest, refused to sell any more, the traders massacred them to get their heads. It was reported that Captain Stewart, of the brig *Elizabeth,* took part in a deal involving the slaughter of 500 Maoris. It was said that the native sellers even paraded living victims before buyers. Part of the problem was that the Maoris wanted to sell the heads because they were anxious to buy weapons, especially axes and muskets, in return.[279] They were extremely warlike. In 1815 they would give two hogs for a small axe, 150 baskets of potatoes and eight pigs for a musket. The greatest Maori chief, Hongi Hika, head of the Hgapuhi, even went to England in 1820 on an arms-purchase mission. He sought not only the latest muskets but a double-barreled gun, which in his eyes conveyed the highest prestige. George IV won his heart by presenting him with a suit of chain armor. On his return, he embarked on a war of conquest, wearing his chain mail and firing five muskets. He received a ball in his chest (1827), but lived another year with the hole, which he could make whistle. Many thousands were killed in these tribal wars, and the casualties would have been even higher if all the warriors had secured the guns they craved. In 1830–31 Australia exported over 8,000 guns and 70,000 pounds of gunpowder to New Zealand, almost all of it to Maoris.[280]

The Maoris lacked the strength to prevent the Europeans from moving in and transforming their country into the world's largest sheep park. But they were fierce enough, and the influence of the missionaries was pervasive enough, to prevent genocide.

In general, however, the spread of the Europeans into the "empty" portions of the globe was fatal to their indigenous peoples, who were annihilated or reduced to museum-specimen remnants of their former hordes. This was particularly true of many of the peoples and tribes of central Asia. So far we have looked at colonization mainly from Western Europe, beginning in the late 15th century and reaching a new pitch of intensity in the years after 1815. But the thrust of the Russians eastward had been at work even longer, and that, too, now began to accelerate. The Russians themselves had only moved east into what is now considered their heartlands around Moscow in the 10th century. They came from eastern Germany, Poland and Byelorussia and were an early instance of the *Drang nach Osten* usually considered a peculiarly German susceptibility but which in fact predates the evolution of a specific German people. The Russians are not usually seen as colonizers in the West. In fact, they were perhaps the most extensive and thorough colonizers in history, especially since the mid-16th century. The famous Russian historian V. O. Kliuchevski, writing in 1937, argued that colonization is the fundamental fact of Russian history, to which all its other features are related.[281]

To the east the Russians faced two frontiers: the forest frontier and the steppe frontier. The forest frontier was inhabited only by primitive groups, some still in the stone age when the Russians arrived, like the Australian aborigines or the Amazonian tribes. Although the Russians crossed the Ural Mountains in force only in the 1580s, they were already a majority in Siberia by about 1700.[282] Up to the end of the 17th century the fur trade was one of the main sources of revenue of the Russian state and its largest export; the advance into Siberia was driven by the exhaustion in European Russia of fur-bearing animals. Russia had no need of a transport revolution because a vast system of rivers made penetration possible. Once they crossed the Urals, the Russians colonized by river transport in much the same way that the Americans used the Ohio and Mississippi–Missouri rivers when they crossed the Appalachians two centuries later. At every portage link between the rivers, the Russians built fortified monasteries or *ostrogs* (forts), of which Moscow itself was a very early example. They leapt from one river system to the next, building ostrogs as they went: from the Volga to the Ob, the Yenisei, the Lena, the Amur. When they reached the Pacific and reconnoitered the Kuriles and the Aleutians, they stuck to the same principle: The sea was simply a broader river, and the key islands guarding the passages and dominating island chains were natural sites for ostrogs to be fortified. The Russian fur trappers would have gone right across North America had not the Western Europeans got there first and (as we have seen) had not the Royal Navy been available to prevent them.[283]

For the Russians, the fur trade and conquest were identical. The government was the chief fur trader and exacted fur tribute from conquered natives. It authorized private traders but had an option on their best furs and taxed the rest at 10 percent. The state church reinforced government power. The fur trade was enormously lucrative, acting as a sharp incentive both to the state and to private colonizers. One black fox pelt would buy a plot of over 50 acres, pay for the erection of a cabin and stock of up to 5 horses, 20 cattle, 20 sheep, and fowls. In time the portage system was replaced by canals. The earliest, 1703–09, was the Upper Volga Waterway, which linked its higher reaches to the Baltic. But the explosion of river transport, as in the West, came in the early 19th century. By then the waterway was carrying 5,000 boats a year, and it was soon joined by the Narvsky System (1808), another route to the Gulf of Finland, the Tikhvin Waterway (1811), linking the Mologa, a Volga tributary, to the Siaz, which flows into Lake Ladoga, and the Northern Dvina system, built 1824–28. By 1830 the Volga, which has a basin of 1,080 rivers, streams and lakes, was effectively canalized, linking the river systems of Eastern Europe to Russian Asia. As a result, the European population of Siberia began to increase rapidly. In 1724 it was counted at a mere 400,000. By 1858 it was 2.3 million, mostly Russian settlers, harbingers of an even greater migration of 5 million, nearly all of them peasants, which by 1911 had transformed the demography of this vast portion of the Earth's surface and made it 85 percent Russian.[284]

The second frontier, the steppes, was much tougher going for Russian imperialism. In the Ukrainian steppes, the Russians had to deal with the Turks; farther east there were nomadic tribes with strong traditions of warlike independence. The conquest of Central Asia took over 300 years. There was an important connection between the two frontiers, for it was the government's profits from furs which financed its drive to the southeast. The key phase of the conquest, which began in 1725, bore many strong resemblances to the ousting of the Indians in North America, though it had additional, and disagreeable, Russian overtones. The great imperialist, the Russian Clive or Jackson, was State Councillor Ivan Kirillovich Kirillov, who significantly began his career in the Tsar's secret police. Kirillov established Orenburg as the forward garrison-town at the junction of the Or and Ural rivers, a move well described as "one of the most outstanding events in Russian history."[285] Kirillov justified his forward operations as defensive, punitive raids against native "bandits"—a term the Russians were still using in their operations in Afghanistan 250 years later, in the 1980s. He described his methods to the Senate in 1735 as beginning with a network of forts, "and thus, surrounding the bandits on all sides, seize their wives, children and property and livestock and completely destroy their homes and punish the main instigators as an example to the others . . . in order that their roots will be completely torn out." Men captured in "rebellion" were executed; those who surrendered voluntarily were deported; minor offenders were sent to regiments in the Baltic region as conscripts or as slave laborers to the Ural mines.

The ruthlessness and cruelty were notable, even by the standards of the day. Tribesmen's heads were cut off and stuck on posts for display. One Bashkir prisoner, who starved himself to death in protest at the atrocities, had his dead body beheaded and his head displayed all the same. In summer 1740 the commander in Sakmarsk, General-Prince Vasily Urusov, calculated that he had executed 432 Bashkirs, given 301 a knouting and mutilation (ears or noses, or both, cut off), and sent 1,862 to Russia as serfs, army or navy conscripts, or slave laborers. The rules seem to have been these: The worst rebels were executed; those over thirty went to the mines; and the young men under 30 had their noses cut off and were flogged and then, together with wives and children, were moved to distant villages. Urusov was advised by a native "expert," "When in doubt, exterminate." The total number of Bashkirs was about 100,000, and of these, 28,511 were listed as killed or executed; were made conscripts, serfs, or slave laborers; or were "distributed." Thus, in a single decade, the Bashkir race was effectively reduced by nearly a third.[286]

This phase has been described in a little detail because it indicates that Russian genocide of the nomadic hunter and pastoral peoples began earlier than that in the Americas, southern Africa, and Australasia and was (Argentina excepted) considerably more deliberate and systematic. Moreover, this pattern, established in the 1730s, continued decade after decade, into the 19th century and beyond. The Russians had a variety of motives. They wanted to become middlemen, like the Portuguese, Dutch and British, in the world trade in exotic eastern products. They wanted to raise revenue from tribute to pay for the defense of their existing possessions, in effect to finance increasingly aggressive wars of conquest—a familiar imperialist logic. They were looking for deposits of base and precious metals, the state owning or controlling the metallurgical industry. Finally, and most of all, they wanted land.

Why did the Russians want more land, when they had so much already? The answer lies in geography, climate and method. The Russians were originally pastoralists, but slowly became agriculturalists as they created the Russian state radiating from Moscow. The Finns and the Turks, the indigenous natives, treated farming as supplementary, rather like the Indians in North America, relying chiefly on hunting, fishing, and breeding suitable livestock. They had good reasons for doing so. In the forest zone, the earth is *podzol*, short of natural plant food, so the farmer has to get at the subsoil, which means deep, difficult ploughing. The cold in winter grows worse as you move east. Thus there is a short farming season: only four months, mid-May to mid-September in much of Russia; the rest of the year the soil is hard as iron and covered in snow. So many Russian farmers had only 50 percent or even less of the farming time enjoyed in West and Central Europe. In the Baltic area rain is plentiful, but there the soil is poorest. In much of central European Russia the heaviest rain comes in July and August: "A small shift in the timetable of rain distribution can mean drought in the spring or early summer, followed by disastrous downpours during the harvest."[287] Farmers also have to keep their livestock inside for two extra months, so the animals miss the early spring grazing and are thin when finally put out. The stock is poor, the meat poor, dairy products poor, manure poor, draft animals poor. In short, the Russians, who had only the basic medieval plough, the *sokha,* which scratches the surface, until well into the 19th century, should not have concentrated on European-style farming at all. But they did. Hence, as one historian put it, "Their heavy reliance on farming under adverse natural conditions is perhaps the single most basic cause of the problems underlying Russian history."[288]

Over the centuries, mainly because of the distribution of rainfall, Russia has had one bad harvest out of three. And yields were always low. Typical medieval yields in Europe were three or fourfold rising to six or sevenfold by the end of the 17th century. By about 1830 British yields were 1 to 10. Until the second half of the 19th century, Russia was not able to improve on medieval yields. In bad years she only got a twofold yield or less; only in the best years was the yield as high as 1 in 5. In Scandinavia they got much better yields; so did German Junkers who ran Baltic estates within the Russian Empire. Hence, climate alone was not to blame.

In most of Russia, the urban population was tiny, there were few markets and a general absence of economic incentive to improve and invest. Writing in 1801, a German agricultural expert asserted there was no other European country where "agriculture is practised so negligently." A contemporary expert on Russia agreed the Russian peasants had a unique talent for "ravaging the land."[289] As their own land became exhausted, the Russian peasants pushed for more. They practiced, in effect, extensive, as opposed to intensive, agriculture. The peasant therefore backed and benefited from Russia's endless conquests, and their conscript sons provided the cannon fodder. Hunger for land increased as birthrates rose and death rates fell in the late 18th and early 19th centuries, pushing the population from less than 18 million in 1750 to 68 million a century later. The drive was always to get more pastureland under the plough, to rape "virgin land"—the phrase is significant, and the policy was still in force under Nikita Khrushchev as late as the 1960s.

Land hunger then was the energizing force of Russian imperialism. It explains the intensity and tenacity with which its conquests were colonized and made permanent. And because the peasants, by universal consent the "heart and soul" of Russia, were behind the colonization drive and the church sanctified it, Russians of every degree and inclination were imperialists. Even among the intellectuals—a significant addition to Russian society in the years after 1815, as we shall see—it is hard to find any opposition, at least until the closing decades of the century. Leo Tolstoy supported the imperialists; indeed, as a young man he was one. Alexander Herzen likened Russia's conquest of central Asia to America's "manifest destiny" drive to the Pacific; it was a sign of Russian youthfulness and vitality. It was in fact the hard unanimity of Russian opinion which made possible the dispossession and, in many cases, the destruction of ancient races—the Ostyaks and Cheremises, the Udmurts, Chuvashes, and Tatars; the Kalmuks; the Karakalpaks and Turkomen; the Little, Middle, and Great Horde; the Uzbeks; the Jungars, and many others. Where peoples survived, as subjects of the Tsar, their young men were often militarized and made into agents of the drive east and south. Thus, the mounted Cossacks became a powerful arm of the Russian army and learned to subdue others, as they had once been crushed themselves. Outside the mountain areas, 90 per cent of the Russian army of conquest was on horseback.

The French invasion of Russia in 1812, and still more their expulsion, served to give Russia a unity it had never before possessed, and this in turn intensified the territorial drive once it was resumed in 1815. Russia, like Austria and Prussia, was the great gainer from Bonaparte's long wars—the Holy Alliance, as it were, was a grace after meat. In

1809 Russia had got the Grand Duchy of Finland; in 1812 Bessarabia; in 1815 the Grand Duchy of Warsaw. Alexander I formally annexed Georgia outright, with its mountains, plains, and coasts, in 1801, but it was only in 1815 that he began to impose absolute control on its independent peoples. It was part of a general policy of exploiting territories already regarded as Russian. The Russification and organized development of Siberia, for instance, began under M. M. Speransky, governor general in 1819–22. But in Siberia there were no "hostiles"; its forest-hunters with their stone-age weapons had long ago been exterminated. Georgia was a different matter. There were Christians in this region, both Orthodox and Armenian, who looked to Holy Mother Russia for protection, lacking anything better. There were also Muslims, who looked to Turkey or Persia. Russia's conquests of Islamic peoples were always her hardest; indeed, they remain incomplete, and resistance endures to haunt Russia's rulers today. Russia's great ally, however, then as now, was the Sunni-Shia conflict. The predominantly Sunni Turks and the Shia Persians could hardly ever be got to cooperate against Russian aggression. Even when they did so their armies had to be camped well apart, since if their rival calls to prayer could be overheard, religious riot invariably followed.[290]

In 1816, in pursuit of his policy of "thorough" in Georgia, Alexander appointed General Yermoloff commander in chief in the region. This successful general was often described as "Russia's Wellington." He had been Barclay de Tolly's chief of staff during the French invasion and afterwards commanded the Russian guard in the drive to Paris. But he had not a scrap of the Iron Duke's humanity. Jackson at his ruthless worst was a mere echo of Yermoloff at his mildest. He was a giant, a terrifying figure who slept wrapped in his cloak, even in a Saint Petersburg state bedroom, his sword at his side. His locks were ragged, his ways simple, his manners rude. He was a comprehensive hater. He hated all non-Russians. Arriving at Alexander's antechamber, he asked a crowd of glittering generals: "May I enquire, gentlemen, if any of you speak Russian?" He had a particular hatred of the British, because of their success in India, and of Germans, because of their success in Russia. Asked what favor he aspired to, he replied: "To be made a German—then I shall be able to get everything I want." He was cruel— "at least as cruel as the natives themselves," his colleague General Erchert reported—but his cruelty was calculated. "I desire that the terror of my name," he said, "should guard our frontiers more potently than chains or fortresses . . . out of pure humanity I am inexorably severe. One execution saves hundreds of Russians from destruction and thousands of Mussulmans from treason."[291]

This assertion was wishful thinking. Unlike a General Rosas in the Argentine, who was equally cruel but who possessed the means to make his cruelty effective, Yermoloff created problems rather than solved them. He served in the Caucasus for a decade and seems to have learned nothing there. His approach was simple. The entire region, in his view, was already legally part of the Russian empire, whether actually conquered or not. All its inhabitants were therefore Russian subjects, and their submission must be total. Anything less was rebellion; and the punishment for rebellion was death, though there might occasionally be room for a certain politic magnanimity. His attitude indeed was closer to that of a Roman legionary commander of the 2nd century AD than to that of an educated man born at the end of the Enlightenment. But then his regiments were like the Roman legions, being based in the Caucasus generation after generation. Most of the men served 25 years consecutively. Yermoloff's strategy was Roman too—massive, fixed defenses and heavy firepower. He built gigantic, cavernous fortresses and made devastating use of artillery (the natives had none). This strategy still held good when Tolstoy, who served there, wrote his story, "The Woodcutting Expedition," set in the 1850s.

But the fact that the Russian campaign to subdue the region was still going on in the 1850s is the best testimony of the failure of Yermoloff's methods. Pushkin might write smugly, "Bow down thy snowy head, O Caucasus/ Submit: Yermoloff comes," but the snowy head did not submit. The General's conduct was so ferocious that the natives were always in revolt. His "victories" were successive "punishments" of "rebellions" which were themselves the product of earlier "victories." There were serious setbacks too. In 1818 one of his commanders, Colonel Pestel, later a leading Decembrist, made a rash attack on Bashli, lost 12 officers and over 500 men (Russian troops below the rank of sergeant had no official identity—they were merely "souls"—so casualty figures are approximate). His entire force was nearly annihilated and had to be rescued. With this in mind, and to punish the Chechens for stealing horses, Yermoloff launched a punishment raid in September 1819. He chose the large village of Dadi-Yourt on the banks of the Terek. On the 15th of the month, without warning, he surrounded it with six companies of the Kabarda Regiment, 700 Cossacks and six pieces of artillery. The Chechens were then ordered to leave immediately and retire beyond the Soundja. When, as expected, they refused, the attack began at dawn. Each house was taken separately, after a battering by artillery, in fierce hand-to-hand fighting, usually at bayonet point. As a rule, when the front drew near, the Chechens got their wives and children out of the way. But on this occasion, there was no time. So they slaughtered their own womenfolk, like the Jews at Masada. They even killed their children, to prevent them being sent to the Tsar's mines or conscripted in his hated armies. But some women took part in the fighting, attacking the Russians with knives. Others deliberately incinerated themelves in the flames of their burning homes. In the end the Russian infantry could not do the job, and the Cossacks had to be dismounted and sent in. The fighting lasted many hours, and at the end of it only 14 native men, all wounded, were left alive. There were 140 women and child prisoners, many of them wounded, too. About 300 were dead. The village was blown up and left a blackened ruin.[292]

This horrific reprisal, far from ending Chechen resistance, provoked a *jihad*, or holy war. Indeed, it did more than that. It gave rise to a new and intense form of Muslim fundamentalism known as Muridism. In Islamic theology, a Murid is "one who desires" [to find the way] as opposed to a Murshid, "one who shows." Murids are thus men studying the Muslim faith, often monks of a kind, and their particular devotions and beliefs are a form of mysticism, common in Persia, known as Sufism. In the Caucasus this mystic fundamentalism took an exceptionally militant form, and Muridism, as it developed in the 1820s, may be classified as the earliest organizational response of Islam to European colonialism, which was to appear in many guises in the 19th and 20th centuries, and is with us yet. Yermoloff's reaction to the beginnings of Muridism was to intensify his punishment raids, and the conflict deepened. He came to see the natives not as military opponents, but as personal enemies. Tales of atrocities shocked even hard hearts in Saint Petersburg. In 1826 the new Tsar, Nicholas I, himself one of the harshest of the Romanovs, wrote to Yermoloff ordering him to court-martial one general Vlasoff for "gross cruelty and injustice" to the Chechens. The following year he sacked his commander in chief. But by then it was too late. The conflict developed into a war of independence under the great resistance leader Shamil, who held out until the end of the 1850s. It left scars which still ache and threaten to burst open today.

Historians who study these sweeping European incursions into the last hunting preserves, pastures, and fastnesses of the primitive peoples tend to concentrate on such violent episodes and to blame the cruelty and folly of governors and generals. But the truth is that the principal damage inflicted on native stocks was not the result of deliberation or even unthinking savagery by the whites. As the Europeans spread into the wilderness, they brought with them their own cattle and crops, their animals and vermin, their insects and diseases. It was not just the human invader but their accompanying pathogens and microorganisms, animals, and weeds that, in deadly combination, destroyed the indigenous peoples. As Darwin put it, "Wherever the European has trod, death seems to pursue the aboriginal."[292] The nonhuman settlers flourished, in most cases, as mightily as did their transporters. Horses, cattle, sheep, goats, dogs, and pigs—often gone wild—multiplied ravenously and competed with the natives and with their animals for available food supplies. Sheep were fatal to the original inhabitants of the Highland glens, and no less engulfing in Australia and New Zealand. The multiplication of horses and cattle on the Argentine pampas was another case of animals destroying men. European rats and rabbits were even more unwelcome intruders. In North America the settlers introduced Kentucky Bluegrass and white clover, dandelion and nettles, couch grass, Shepherd's Purse, and sow thistle. Some of these plants were as imperialist as their masters. Sorrowing Indians called the ever-spreading plantain "Englishman's foot." In Argentina, European wild plants took over until, today, they constitute 75 percent of the whole on the pampas, now covered by Old World grasses and clovers. Darwin, in Uruguay in 1832, noted the ecological damage inflicted by the European wild artichoke. It is calculated that in North America, Australia, and New Zealand, the proportion of weeds of European origin varies from 60 to 90 percent.[294] Insects too played their part. According to Thomas Jefferson, even the honeybee was seen as a threat. The Indians, he wrote, called it "the English fly" and "look on [bees] with an evil eye as an omen of the white man's approach."[295]

But it was European diseases which had the most direct impact. By the early 19th century, as a result of generations of worldwide commerce, Europeans had built up greater immunities than any other race. Most of the major killer diseases were frequently epidemic or endemic in Europe. Smallpox, one of the most effective of all human destroyers, which covers immense distances with great speed, appeared in the New World in winter 1518–19, and over the decades and centuries killed many more Indians than guns did. In Argentina, in the early 19th century, it was far more destructive than General Rosas. By 1815 the British, at least, were beginning to master it by mass vaccination. But across the Atlantic it continued to take a fearful toll of the native peoples. There was an Indian legend of the Smallpox Rider: "I am one with the White People . . . Sometimes I travel ahead of them, and sometimes behind. But I am always their companion and you will find me in their camps and their houses. . . . I bring Death.''[296] The only New World disease the Europeans brought back with them was venereal syphilis, which developed into a major killer and was, in turn, reexported by them. Syphilis was one of a package of diseases the Russians brought to Siberia, along with typhus, measles, scarlet fever and, of course, smallpox. These scourges, especially the last, killed more than half the Tungus, the Yakuts, the Ostyaks, the Samoyeds and the Yukaghirs. Smallpox was a big destroyer in southern Africa and in Australia, where it made its appearance among the aborigines the year after the First Fleet entered Botany Bay and eventually killed a third of them. Sailors, among whom syphilis and tuberculosis were so common as to be almost classifiable as occupational diseases, distributed them throughout the great southern oceans.[297] Syphilis was particularly destructive to peoples, such as the Siberian forest dwellers and the Maoris, who practiced sexual hospitality to friendly strangers.

But if the European taming and transformation of the wilderness destroyed lives, it also preserved them on an increasing scale, throughout the 19th and 20th centuries, by providing the food surpluses which fed the world's rapidly growing population. It was in the decade after Waterloo that the solid foundations were laid for these gigantic surpluses—in Canada and the United States, in Argentina and Uruguay, in Australia and New Zealand. By the 1980s these six countries alone accounted for 30 percent of all the world's food exports and more than three-fifths of the wheat exports. The kind of high-investment, high-techology extensive farming—in which production is measured per farmer, rather than per acre—implanted by European settlers in areas almost designed by nature to receive it, saved the human race from the demographic catastrophe which the Rev. Thomas Malthus was gloomily predicting at this time. All these consequences must be carefully weighed together in history's scales of justice.

All the same, there is a clutch at the heart as we read descriptions of the wild, unspoiled vastnesses in these years, the last of their existence. Mrs. Anna Jameson (1794–1860) left this little portrait of Ontario: "The seemingly interminable line of trees before you, the boundless wilderness around, the mysterious depths amid the multitudinous foliage, where foot of man hath never penetrated, which partial gleams of the noontide sun, now seen, now lost, lit up with a changeful, magical beauty; the wondrous splendour and novelty of the flowers; the silence, unbroken but by the low cry of a bird, or hum of an insect or the splash and croak of some huge bullfrog; and the solitude in which we proceeded, no human being, no human dwelling, in sight.''[298]

Two thousand miles to the southwest, at almost exactly the same time, the young Richard Henry Dana (1815–82) was seeing the empty bay of San Francisco: "All around was the stillness of nature. There were no settlements on these bays and rivers, and the few ranches and missions were remote and widely separated. . . . On the whole coast of California, there was not a lighthouse, a beacon or a buoy. . . . Birds of prey and passage swooped and dived about us, wild beasts ranged through the oak groves, and as we slowly floated out of the harbour with the tide, herds of deer came to the water's edge."[299] Inland, at this time, wandering through the great forests of the Californian slopes of the Rockies, was a solitary, daring young Scot from Scone, David Douglas (1798–1834), a superb gardener and botanist, collecting specimens on behalf of the Hudson's Bay Company. Accompanied only by a little dog and wearing a complete suit—jacket, waistcoat, and trousers—of bright red Stuart tartan, he sent back to the Old World 50 trees and shrubs and over 100 plants never seen there before, including the splendid spruce which still bears his name. In 1823, 1824–27, 1829–32, and 1832–34, he crossed and recrossed the Rockies in Canada and the United States, often seeing not a single human being for months at a time.[300]

But the hoofbeats of progress were already sounding. In the years after 1815 American skin traders and whalers, looking for the fine oil in increasing demand as New England industrialized, were active off the California coast. Hardy men were looking for overland routes too. In 1826 Jedediah Strong Smith, "the Knight of the Buckskin," made his way on behalf of the Rocky Mountain Fur Company to Salt Lake City, along the Virgin River to Colorado, then to the San Gabriel Mission on the Pacific. In 1827–28 he made his way back to the Salt Lake, having thus discovered two viable routes. Also across the Rockies in 1828 went the Kentuckians Sylvester Pattie and his son James Ohio Pattie who pacified the locals by producing the anti-smallpox vaccine and immunizing 22,000 of them. Farther north, the Oregon Trail was being opened up.[301] These were heady years for American expansionists, whose number was growing fast. Thomas Hart Benton, Senator for Missouri, was urging settlement west of the Rockies as early as 1818. Seven years later he saw the United States as a great power in the Pacific, completing Columbus's unfinished work and finding the western route to India. Pointing to the West, he intoned: "There is the East, there lies the road to India." Europe, he argued, was on its way down. America should turn her back on it, exploit its geopolitical advantages by dominating the oceans, grab the commerce of Asia and become the fulcrum of the world.[302] Americans, both in government and in the media, were already developing the characteristic rhetoric of common-man-democracy-plus-technology which was to sanctify and legitimate their ascent to superpower status. There was, argued the *Southern Quarterly Review* in November 1828, "neither justice, nor wisdom, nor humanity" in "arresting the progress of order and science" by trying to halt westward expansion. Americans had a moral duty to proceed, and in any case there were plenty of "unproductive and barren wastes" which could be "reserved for the roaming barbarian." "Science," thundered Jackson in one of his messages to Congress, "is steadily penetrating the recesses of nature and disclosing her secrets, while the ingenuity of free minds is subjecting the elements to the power of man and making each new conquest auxiliary to his comfort."[303]

The Europeans and their overseas progeny were not yet everywhere. Though the whites had broken out of their Cape enclave at the southern tip, the penetration of most of Africa was only just beginning. Australia, still overawed by what its greatest historian has called "the tyranny of distance," had not yet been crossed, though in 1828–30, Governor Darling's outstanding military secretary, Captain Charles Stuart, discovered and named the Murray River by an overland route, reaching the ocean at the spot where Adelaide now stands.[304] But seamen, driven by the lust for seals and whale oil—and, to be fair, by the desire for knowlege—were reaching out to both poles. Captain Bellinghausen, whom we came across in Tasmania, circumnavigated Antarctica in one voyage in 1820–21, naming the Peter I and Alexander Islands. Two years earlier, the British sealer William Smith visited the South Shetland Islands, as he called them, and in 1820 the Anglo-American team of Edward Brandsfield and Nathaniel Palmer sighted the northern tip of the Antarctic Peninsula itself. In 1823 James Weddell entered what became known as the Weddell Sea, and the outline of the basic map of the region was completed in 1830 by another Englishman, John Biscoe, in the course of a further circumnavigation. Meanwhile, at the London Admiralty, John Barrow (1764–1848), its permanent secretary, was promoting Arctic voyages by Captain John Ross (1818), William Parry (1819–20, 1821–23, 1824–25, and 1827) and Captain John Franklin (1819–22, 1825–27). On 6 June 1824, Mrs. Arbuthnot and the Duke of Wellington paid a visit to Deptford to see the *Griper*, which was being fitted out by Captain George Lyon (1795–1832) for an Arctic expedition. Captain Lyon had been with Parry on his second voyage. They found him "in high spirits," and Mrs. Arbuthnot's sharp eyes noted the way in which new technology was now coming to the aid of exploration. The *Griper* was small but "very comfortable, with means for conveying hot air all round her." All were issued with insulated Arctic clothing. "There is a new way by means of glueing two pieces of cloth together with liquid indiarubber of making them completely air- and watertight. . . . Captain Lyon's fur bag for sleeping in was covered with this linen, his stockings were two glued together." She also inspected the first inflatable pillow: "In general [it] lay flat and could be packed in the smallest compass but furnished with a cork at the corner by blowing through which for a short time the pillow became distended with air and formed a most comfortable rest for the head." But she objected to the "nauseous smell" of all this rubber magic.[305]

The spread of human activity into all quarters of the globe, still more the astonishing increase in the speed at which travel was possible, led to a growing consciousness that the world was a finite and vulnerable place, which needed to be protected. In the years after Waterloo, poets, artists, and sportsmen, from different motives, came together to protest at the threat presented by "progress." It was most obvious in the spread of cities and the visible monstrosities they bred. In Glasgow, Charles Tennant's Saint Rollox soda works, the biggest chemical factory in the world, swallowed up 100 acres of the surrounding countryside and by pouring sulphuric acid on salt, produced immense clouds of hydrochloric acid gas, one of the first recorded instances of modern large-scale industrial pollution. The resulting uproar from outraged citizens and landowners led Tennant to build a chimney 455 feet high to disperse the poisonous smoke high in the atmosphere. But this ugly artifact aroused almost as many objections, being higher than any cathedral and visible for fifty miles. Sir Walter Scott thought it "intolerable." In the London area, the sportsmen grumbled that their territory was being engulfed year by year. In the early 1820s, Grantley Berkeley, master of the Old Berkeley staghounds, described how hounds "ran our stag up to Number One, Montagu Street, Russell Square . . . the deer having backed up the steps and set his haunches against the street door."[306] By the end of the decade all that was finished. Indeed, even Croydon, "the Melton of the South," which at the time of Waterloo housed the Surrey, Lord Derby's Staghounds, two packs of foxhounds and two of harriers, was under threat, and Surtees's cockney MFH, John Jorrocks, Master of Fox Hounds, was an anachronism before he reached print—though as a fictional character he is eternal. The hunting fields near Pinner, once celebrated, were being swallowed up by market gardens, which formed the advancing outer escarpment of urbanization, Lord Alvanley complaining: "Melon and asparagus beds devilish heavy, up to our hocks in glass all day."[307]

Poets and artists raised their voices against urban sprawl. On 23

October 1825 the historical painter Benjamin Robert Haydon walked to Hampstead from central London and complained, "Since I was in this road last, streets, in fact towns, have risen and the beautiful fields at the beginning were disfigured by cartwheels, stinking of bricks and whitened by lime!—these wounds on solitude, purity and nature are horrid."[308] From his house overlooking Derwentwater, the Poet Laureate Robert Southey fumed against the "terrible evil" of giant cities. The Luddite riots of 1811 had confirmed his fears that industrialization, because of its brutal nature, was certain to generate murderous mobs. He wrote that even in Keswick they were afraid of unemployed laborers descending from Carlisle, Whitehaven, and Cockermouth, what he called the "ugly fellows." He asked to be sent two pistols and a watchman's rattle, because Coleridge's deserted wife Sara, who shared the house, wanted to give the alarm "when the ugly fellows come."[309] Southey advocated positive, coercive steps to reduce the cities and re-create village life. But how? The letters of William and Dorothy Wordsworth and Dorothy's diaries are full of despairing complaints at the invasion of Lakeland valleys by city dwellers, and the erection of "hideous" villas by rich men which destroyed cherished views. From Paris, Eugène Delacroix raged against the English whom he held responsible for the ravages of factories, the explosion of cities, and the (to him) suicidal rush to go faster. "I hate," he wrote "those English steamboats whose shapes are so shabby. [I feel] great indignation against those races that know nothing except speed. May they go to the devil at top speed in their machines and 'improvements,' which are turning man himself into a machine."[310] The greatest protest of all came from Rossini, Europe's most successful musician, who in the mid-1820s virtually abandoned his career, saying he could not continue as the "modern world" took over. Music, he wrote, "this art which has its sole basis in 'idealism' and 'sentiment' cannot separate itself from the times in which we live, and idealism and sentiment have nowadays been exclusively turned over to 'steam', 'jobbery' and 'the barricades.'"[311]

Modernism, industrialization, urbanization were already generating a formidable protest literature which went back to Rousseau and incorporated Restif de la Bretonne and Louis-Sebastien Mercier in France, Thomas Jefferson in the United States, and William Blake and the Lake poets in England.[312] Sensitive people wanted, somehow, to retreat to nature, which meant, as they saw it, retreating into the past, into their childhoods, into history. It was the great unifying theme of Wordsworth's lifework. It was, too, behind much of the quest for the Gothic. Rural picnics, a feature of the times—they play a prominent part in *Emma* and in Dorothy Wordsworth's *Journals*—were a Gothic fancy. People, if they could afford it, made their gardens look "wild" and "ancient" by putting in bits of Gothic apparatus. John Byng recorded in his diary coming across a Lincolnshire parson's garden "almost cover'd with cloisters, seats etc. all made of roots of trees and moss, to correspond with a hermitage in the centre."[313] In the years after 1815, "rustic" garden furniture made its appearance, along with rock gardens and painted wooden or plaster gnomes (imported from ultra-romantic Germany). Some proud owners of Gothic grottoes (not entirely new: Wallenstein had one in the 1620s) even hired poor old men to sit in them as hermits to impress visitors. The poet Thomas Moore, visiting the aesthete Thomas Bowles, noted in his diary on 1 September 1818: "His parsonage house at Bremhill is beautifully situated, but he has a good deal frittered away its beauty with grottos, hermitages and Shenstonian inscriptions—when company is coming, he cries 'Here, John, run with the crucifix and missal to the Hermitage and set the fountain going'—his sheep-bells are tuned in thirds and fifths."[314]

The cult of gardens, which was spreading rapidly down the social scale in the years after 1815, was one way of protesting against the modern world, holding it at bay. At the top, the Duke of Marlborough created at White Knights in Hampshire a 36-acre flower garden which many believed to be the finest in the world. Captain Gronow said that the Duke, though heavily in debt, "would give Lee & Kennedy £500 for a curious plant or shrub." Mrs. Arbuthnot, who visited it 14 January 1821, found it tended by 23 gardeners: "It is said," she noted, "that the gardens have cost the Duke £40–50,000 and that he owes Lee & Kennedy £10,000 for plants."[315] As men invaded the wilderness, at least they brought back exotic specimens to gladden European eyes clouded by urban horrors. The spruce Douglas found in the Californian Rockies soon flourished in English gardens, thanks to Lee & Kennedy. So did the Sitka. The first wisteria arrived from China in 1818 and was planted at Chiswick. Two years later bedding-out was introduced for what were known as Italian Gardens. In the wake of the wisteria came lupins and petunias, dahlias and calceolarias, and countless other novelties from five continents. The Royal Horticultural Society went back to 1804, but it was only with the peace that it began to exercise a palpable influence not only on gentry gardens but on the middle class. By 1826 one leading nurseryman—a new trade in itself—was listing in his catalog over 1,400 species and varieties.[316] Even before 1815 the wives of parsons, doctors, lawyers and mere tradesmen kept fine gardens in and around country towns and villages. After it, however, and especially as the 1820s progressed, a new phenomenon appeared—the London and especially the suburban garden.

Indeed it found a crusading advocate. John Claudius Loudon (1783–1843), the son of a farmer from Cambuslang in Scotland, served an apprenticeship as a nurseryman and landscape gardener and then set up in business as a rustic propagandist. He designed and built two semidetached houses in Porchester Terrace, Bayswater, a part of London hitherto known as "Kensington Gravel Pits." The area was just being urbanized, though you could still watch the haymakers in nearby fields, and Holland House, down the road, was a major estate. John and his wife Jane Well Loudon lived in one of the houses—a prototype of the suburban villas which spread all around Victorian London—and his three sisters lived next door. Together they wrote, illustrated and published books which often sold tens of thousands of copies—*The Suburban Gardener and Villa Companion, Gardening for Ladies,* and *The Lady's Companion to the Flower Garden.*

Jane Loudon taught ladies of leisure how to garden in the same way that Mrs. Beaton taught them to cook, but Loudon himself was both a scientist and an inventor: He selected and popularized the shrubs and flowers which would flourish in suburbia, and he produced such devices as a flexible wrought-iron sash bar which made curvilinear glazing possible and so revolutionized conservatories and hothouses. He was the first writer to insist that it was not merely proper but positively moral for ladies and gentlemen to dig and plant their own gardens—as he and his wife and sisters did themselves. He advised on architecture, furnishing and equipment and showed how houses could open into gardens to form a satisfying environment for suburban life. But above all, he presented the garden as a defense against the moral degeneration which Southey and others insisted cities must bring. Loudon preached against such despair and gave people hope that beauty and nature could still hold their own in an industrialized society. He helped to lay foundations for the optimism which was to characterize the Victorian era and, in his own way, was one of the most influential minds of the century.[317]

Nor was Loudon the only mind working on the defenses which needed to be erected against the destructive thrust of the modern world which was growing with startling speed under men's eyes. In North America and Australasia a few thoughtful men were already noting the speed at which entire species of animals, unknown in Europe, were being hunted out of existence or exterminated as mere vermin. Darwin was later to bring this problem to the forefront of science. But it was in southern Africa that the first active steps were taken to arrest the forces of annihilation. Already in 1798 the last blaanbok or bluebuck was slaughtered.[318] Present-day place-names in the Cape indicate other species which disappeared from the region early in the 19th century—Elandsberg, Rhenoster, Kop, Quaggafontein, Spruit, Wildebeespan, Hartbeeskuil. The Boers cleared most of the Cape of game with their *roer*, a large powder musket firing homemade balls, long before the coming of the breech-loading rifle. They used professional black hunters, *Khoikhoi,* who were issued with a carefully counted number of rounds and had to bring back the same number of, for example, buffalo in order to be paid. The effect on game-numbers was devastating. The post-Napoleonic age had an insatiable taste for ostrich feathers. The best plumes cost sixpence or even a shilling, and since a good bird might have 45 fine ones, it could easily be worth £3 to £4 to the hunter. By the 1820s there were still ostrich on the Boer frontier, but they were dwindling fast. In 1820–22 Thomas Pringle, who led a group of Scots settlers to Glen Lyndon on the Baavares River, reported that game was now scarce—zebra, elephant, hartebeest, antelopes, and quagga were seldom seen. The wildlife of Cape Colony was being sacrificed to the export trade. In 1815 only £59 worth of ivory was exported from the Cape. By 1825 it had risen to £16,586. In the five years from 1820, the value of exotic hides rose from £2,324 to £23,544. Export of horns had leapt from nothing to £6,621 by 1829.[319]

The earlier Dutch government had dabbled in conservation and control but without much success. By the early 1820s it was clear that the virtually unrestricted destruction of game, which in North America had cleared it from a 100-mile belt running down the Atlantic coast, could not be allowed to continue in Cape Colony. On 12 July 1822, the governor, Lord Charles Somerset, introduced regulations which are of considerable importance historically because they constitute the first modern conservation plan, which became the prototype for others throughout the world. He said he was laying down closed seasons because the "rapidly increasing population" of the colony made it "daily more necessary to guard against the total destruction of game." He divided wild animals into three categories: royal game, which were protected—this included threatened species, such as elephant and hippos, for which a special license to shoot was required from the governor himself; shootable game, which could be killed by those in possession of a license, but only in season; and, finally, vermin, for which no license was needed. This last category included, surprisingly enough, leopard, which were still plentiful and highly destructive of livestock; if you produced a skin, the government would pay you a reward. Governor Somerset's regulations were a complex and impressive legislative framework, which later allowed threatened or nonthreatened species to be added to or taken off the prohibited lists.[320] The pity is that such rules were not quickly adopted in other territories being Europeanized at this time. Indeed, even in other British colonies, where enlightened authority was strong enough to overrule settler or native opinion, action came only slowly; India, for instance, was not to begin protecting its elephant stocks until 1873.[321]

At least a start had been made. But, at this birth of the modern world, roamed by predatory men armed with increasingly effective means of killing and traveling at speeds which accelerated each year, most assaults on nature went unheeded, and crimes against humanity remained unpunished. The world was becoming one, the wilderness was being drawn into a single world commercial system, but there was as yet no acknowledged law. Who was to play the world policeman?

FOUR

World Policeman

At 2:30 on a blazing hot afternoon, 27 August 1816, the British 100-gun battleship HMS *Queen Charlotte* led an Anglo-Dutch fleet commanded by Admiral Edward Pellew, Lord Exmouth, into the outer harbor at Algiers and anchored 100 yards from the mole head. Almost immediately guns from the heavily defended town opened fire on the ships. This was the provocation for which Exmouth had been waiting and he gave orders to begin the bombardment. The episode is worth looking at in some detail. It was the first instance in which the West deliberately used its increasingly superior technology to subdue a nonwhite power in the cause of civilization and humanity. But it also raised important questions about the principles and values of the West and the consistency with which they were applied.

Algiers, with a population of 50,000, was the most notorious of the Barbary Coast towns which preyed on Christian shipping in the Mediterranean. Tunis, near the site of ancient Carthage, was another pirate town, and so was Tripoli in Libya. Many other harbors were frequented by Muslim pirates along the North African coast, but these three were the most dangerous predators and the focus of Western attention. Officially they were provinces of the Ottoman Turkish Empire, and their beys or pashas were appointed by and responsible to the Sultan in Constantinople. They recruited their troops from his dominions in Anatolia and sometimes came to his assistance when he was in trouble. But for all practical purposes they were independent.[1] Their principal trades were kidnapping, hostage taking, slavery and ransom. In the early 19th century slavery was almost ubiquitous in the world—in some parts of the West, as we shall see, it was growing fast—but the Barbary Coast, stretching 1,500 miles from the Straits of Gibraltar to the Gulf of Sirte in Libya, was unique in being the only area where white men and women were subjected to it in large numbers. The Barbary pirates, using what would now be called a fundamentalist

interpretation of Islam as their pretext, regularly kidnapped Christian
livestock from Italy, Malta, Sicily, Sardinia and Corsica and from the
ships of all nations sailing the Mediterranean. In the 17th century their
corsairs had cruised in the waters of Northern Europe as well and at
one time Algiers had held as many as 25,000 white Christians as slaves.
Over three centuries, Western nations, alone or in combination, had
launched 17 expeditions against the coast. None had achieved a permanent solution to the problem. Algiers, Tunis and Tripoli were all
strongly fortified, and their defenses were constantly updated to the
limits of Turkish military technology. On the whole the West preferred
to negotiate, keeping consuls for this purpose and using intermediaries
from the large local Jewish communities. Wealthy captives could usually obtain ransom without difficulty. The rest were treated with varying degrees of barbarity. Few were actually behind bars, being allowed
to roam the town, prevented from escaping by chains weighing 50
pounds. Torture was used to obtain conversions to Islam: "turning
Turk," as Western sailors called it. Crucifixion, the bastinado, impale-
ment and castration were routine. Well-connected women prisoners
were ransomed quickly and were not usually molested. But rape was
also common and there were tales of Christian women being mutilated
and murdered. Most women who could not raise a ransom were, if
pretty, married off to locals, or put into harems as concubines. To make
them fat and thus increase their salability, they were forced to eat large
quantities of bread dipped in syrup.[2]

The West's supine attitude toward the horrors of Barbary piracy
had long aroused fury in some quarters. Officers of the British navy
were particularly incensed since seamen were frequently victims of the
trade. They could not understand why the huge resources of the world's
most powerful fleet were not deployed to root out this evil affront to the
international law of the sea, once and for all. They could not understand why liberal parliamentarians, who campaigned ceaselessly to
outlaw the slave trade by parliamentary statute, took no interest in
Christian slavery. Admiral Nelson wrote in 1799: "My blood boils that
I cannot chastise these pirates. They could not show themselves in the
Mediterranean did not our country permit. Never let us talk about the
cruelty of the African slave-trade while we permit such a horrid war."[3]
But William Wilberforce, MP, and the other Evangelical liberals, who
finally got the slave trade made unlawful in 1807, flatly refused to help.
They were concerned with the enslavement of blacks by whites and did
not give the predicament of white slaves a high priority on their agenda,
an early example of double standards. For want of a better champion
the victims had to make do with Admiral Sir Sidney Smith (1764–1840),

who in 1814 formed the Knights Liberator of the Slaves in Africa and, as we have seen, lobbied frantically at the Congress of Vienna. He knew more about the subject than anyone else alive but was a notorious bore and egoist whose calls public men dreaded. As a colleague put it, he was "kind-tempered and generous and as agreeable as a man can be supposed to be who is always talking of himself."[4] He helped to publicize the problem by a book he put out at the end of the war but he could not persuade Liverpool and Castlereagh to act.

More effective in this respect were the exploits of the Americans, who put the British government on its mettle. The activities of the corsairs, who did not scruple to kidnap Yankee sailors, led to the new republic's first experiment in geopolitics. It was principally on their account that Congress decided to establish a navy in 1794, and America consistently refused to ransom captives in the European way by handing over money, powder, shot, and arms to the Muslims. As President Jefferson put it, "Millions for defense, not one cent for tribute." From 1803 Washington, in effect, made war against the beys. In one episode in 1805 American marines marched across the desert from Egypt into Tripolitania, forcing Tripoli to make peace and surrender all American slaves, and giving rise to the famous line in the U.S. Marine Corps anthem "From the Halls of Montezuma to the Shores of Tripoli." Immediately after the Treaty of Ghent was signed, when the cruising season of 1815 opened, Washington sent out a squadron under Stephen Decatur to punish the Barbary towns for violations of previous agreements. He forced the Bey of Tunis to pay $46,000 in compensation, and in Tripoli he also exacted a fine and secured the release of some Danish and Neapolitan slaves. His squadron was relieved by five of the new "big" frigates under Commodore William Bainbridge who, in June 1815, achieved a remarkable moral victory over the Bey of Algiers, who was given exactly three hours to comply with an American ultimatum to hand over all U.S. captives plus a cash compensation; the Bey capitulated on time. There is some doubt about the permanent effectiveness of this American intervention, since all the pirate rulers repudiated their treaties once American ships were below the horizon. But news of it created a sensation in Britain and led to irresistible pressure on the government to order a similar display of British naval power.

Exmouth, put in charge of the operation, was of Cornish origin, the son of a Dover packet captain. He had joined the navy at 13, the same year as Nelson (1770), and made a name for himself as the most successful frigate captain of the 1790s. He was a tall, immensely powerful man, famous for the speed with which he could climb a mast, a strong swimmer who had rescued men overboard on several occasions, an officer who always led from the front. But he was also a cerebral commander, who kept right in the forefront of weapons technology, planned his operations with immense care and insisted on a thorough training for them.[5] Exmouth's original instructions were not to use force but to negotiate treaties, under which the beys would renounce slavery for all time. He actually ransomed, in the old fashion, a total of 1,530 Christian slaves, of a variety of nationalities, for 489,750 Austrian dollars. But news of this deal was badly received by the British public. Further negotiations came to nothing; the beys renounced all previous agreements, both with the Americans and the British, and on 23 May soldiers of the Bey of Algiers massacred over 100 Sicilian fishermen who enjoyed theoretical British protection. It was at this point that Exmouth received orders to enter Algiers harbor and destroy it if his force was fired on.

Exmouth had earlier detached the frigate *Banterer,* under Captain Charles Warde, an expert cartographer, to make a detailed survey of the Algiers defenses. Warde made excellent inshore charts, located all the Algerine batteries and identified the exact location and caliber of nearly 600 cannon, including a monster 20 feet long, then the largest in service in the world. Nelson had been so impressed by the Algiers defenses that he calculated it would take 10 ships of the line to silence them. Exmouth believed he could do it with five, plus five frigates, provided they were specially equipped for the operation, though in the event his force was reinforced by a Dutch squadron of five frigates. Exmouth took with him 11 artillery experts from Woolwich Arsenal who were working on new gunsights and a recently developed high-velocity gun designed by Congreve and made at the great cannon foundry at Carron in Scotland. He also had a detachment of 91 Royal Engineers, expert sappers and miners, and a squadron of the Royal Horse Artillery with Congreve rockets. At Gibraltar his artillery specialists made tests to discover the best ways of destroying guns protected by masonry. He fitted his ships with extra equipment to allow them to anchor fore and aft and to maneuver easily to sight and resight their guns. He reinforced their decks and sides to withstand heavy shot. Boat platforms and rafts were constructed to mount additional mortars and rockets, and floating mines were loaded with gunpowder. All inflammable material which could be dispensed with was taken off the ships to guard against red-hot shot. Wherever possible rope cables were replaced by steel links. On the battleships, 12-pounder carronades, each loaded with 300 musket balls, were mounted in the crosstrees. Finally the fleet exercised vigorously throughout the voyage and off the coast to improve its fire drill and accuracy.

Exmouth opened fire at 2:45 P.M. and his first broadside wreaked appalling destruction among the Algerine gun-crews, the *Charlotte* alone killing over 400 gunners. This set the pattern. The Admiral was particularly lucky with his 24-pound short-barreled carronades, which were specially designed for use against fixed batteries at short range. The raft-mounted armaments, under the command of midshipmen seeing their first action, served their turn. The rockets set fire to the Algerine fleet, huddled in the inner harbor, and later to most of the fort and town. The pirates were by no means easily cowed. They launched a sortie of 40 small boats crammed with men and cannon, but Exmouth coolly brought his broadsides to bear and blew 35 of them out of the water; the rest fled. The pirates had one minor success: the *Impregnable,* badly handled by her captain, was hit by an Algerine mortar shell which inflicted nearly 150 casualties. Indeed all their guns continued to fire until silenced. One of Exmouth's lieutenants, J. F. Johnstone, lost his arm, and the admiral had him taken to his own cabin and tended him personally (he was to die within sight of Plymouth). He himself had two musket balls through his clothes, another smashed his telescope and a fourth broke the spectacles in his pocket. A spent shot hit him in the leg, drawing blood, and a deck splinter struck him on the jaw. The mutual battering lasted over eight hours and was probably the most intense ever to have taken place to that date. At 11 P.M., all Algerine guns having ceased to fire and the town in flames, Exmouth called it a day and withdrew his ships.[6]

Detailed reports which the admiral obliged all commanders to submit showed that the new carronades and gunsights had performed well. Over 100 tons of powder had been used to fire 38,667 round shot weighing approximately 500 tons from the ships; the bomb rafts had fired 960 10- and 13-inch shells and several hundred rockets. This barrage had sunk virtually the entire Algerine navy—5 frigates, 4 large corvettes, 32 gun- and mortar boats and many smaller craft. It had killed 5,000 to 8,000 soldiers and civilians and damaged or destroyed virtually every building in the town. The British and Dutch lost no ships, but had 141 killed and 742 wounded. The fleet had sustained more damage than was easily observable from the shore and, fearing a return and landing, the Bey gave in. He released all the slaves he had, 1,642 (18 of them British, most Neapolitans and Sicilians), formally forswore holding Christians as slaves forever, and restored to liberty the British consul, who had been under house arrest. He also surrendered 382,500 Austrian dollars, in sacks of 1,000, which went to pay for the cost of the expedition, calculated at £1 million.[7]

This devastating "punishment," as it was termed, by no means ended the depredations of Moslem pirates and kidnappers, which continued until the French finally invaded and occupied Algeria at the end of the decade. But at the time it seemed pretty conclusive. The West had given an impressive exhibition of its new firepower. The Orient had bowed its bloodied head. In October Exmouth returned to London in triumph, to a viscountcy, the freedom of the City of London, a gilt sword decorated in diamonds and a piece of plate valued at 1,400 guineas. Bells were rung all over Christendom. He got the Order of Saint Maurice and Lazarus from the Sardinians, of Saint Willem from the Dutch, of Charles III from the Spanish, and of Saint Ferdinand from the Neapolitans. The Pope sent him a cameo.[8] From the Tsar, who was taking time off from organizing the Holy Alliance, came a handwritten letter of congratulations and thanks for his services to Christian souls.

Ironically enough, most of these sovereigns presided over nations which engaged in the slave trade themselves. The Tsar's own country ran the largest system of forced labour on earth, under the name of serfdom. It had many aspects, not the least interesting of which was the Russian capacity—to become such a feature of the modern world—to present crimes against humanity in the guise of utopianism. Six years before Admiral Exmouth blew up Algiers, Alexander himself had paid a visit to an estate called Gruzino, 75 miles east of Saint Petersburg. It was owned by an artillery general called Alexis Alexandrovich Arakcheev, victor of the campaign against Sweden which had given Finland to Russia. Arakcheev had been born in 1769, the same year as Bonaparte and Wellington, into a family of minor nobles. His mother was known as "The Dutchwoman" because of her passion for well-scrubbed floors, a trait her son inherited. His regard for tidiness was reinforced when he was taken into the military household of Alexander's mad father, the Tsar Paul. Russia was traditionally a slovenly as well as a grotesquely inefficient country, and its reformist rulers have tended to pounce on the visible, external signs of its shortcomings, the messy clutter in which it conducts all its affairs, in the hope that, by clearing up this, all the rest will follow. Paul, though mad, was in the reformist tradition, and at his estate at Gatchina, also outside Saint Petersburg, he had placed all his serfs under military discipline, assembled from them a small private army run on the ferocious lines of Frederick the Great's guards regiments, and turned the whole place into a smart-looking barracks. Arakcheev was formed by this tradition and transplanted it to Gruzino, but in a far more methodical and intensive manner.[9]

Indeed, Arakcheev's Gruzino has a strong claim to be considered the first modern experiment in social engineering, an attempt to create the New Man who, Rousseau had argued, could be born in the right conditions. The estate was 35 square kilometers and contained 2,000 "souls." The general destroyed all the old wooden buildings and put up new model villages of brick and stone. He drained the muddy roads and paved them. He dug a lake, with an island in it, on which was a temple. He built belvederes and towers, each of which was equipped with a clock. For all this he employed a professional architect, Minut, a ferocious taskmaster, of whom the peasants said: "He simply ate people." The clocks dictated their work-, meal- and bedtimes, something unheard of in Russia. Woods and thickets, in which idle peasants could skulk, were rooted out. Pig keeping was banned, outhouses pulled down, private plots forbidden. Drinking bouts were severely punished; indeed the general tried to stamp out liquor altogether, a constant aim of Russian reformers then and now.

The idea was to get all the peasants to work, ten hours every day of the year except Sundays. Orders, dictated by the General personally, were issued regularly, numbered and dated, as in the army. A typical one dealt with broken windows (another army obsession under the heading "Barrack-room Damage"). Another reflected the growing totalitarian flavor of the experiment: "Brief rules for the peasant-mothers of the District of Gruzino: (1) Every mother must feed her baby at least three times a day." In theory Gruzino had some of the characteristics of a miniature welfare state. There was a hospital and a school. The general got regular health reports. Vaccination against smallpox was compulsory. But the inhabitants had even less control over their lives than ordinary serfs. In an effort to raise the birthrate, lists were compiled of nubile unmarried females and widows capable of childbearing, and pressure was put on them to find partners. But the General had to approve such unions. A note from him on one damsel reads: "I agree [to her marriage]. But if she does not know her prayers by Lent, I shall have her soundly whipped."[10]

Therein lay the catch of Arakcheev's utopia. He found himself unwilling to abandon the most characteristic and incorrigible aspect of Russian backwardness—the universal reliance on savage physical punishment. Sir Robert Porter, who traveled in Russia at this time and published a book about it, described some of the terrible punishments he witnessed. A coachman, who had murdered his master, was sentenced to be knouted to death. Porter saw him struck over 200 blows, during more than an hour, before being pronounced lifeless. Then the man's nostrils were torn out by pincers. At this point he got up. If he had lived, he would have been sent to Siberia for life; in fact, he died of his wounds the next day.[11] Colonel Gribbe, who served under Arak-cheev, wrote: "Nearly the whole of Russia groaned under blows. People were flogged in the army, in schools, in towns and market-places, in the stables, in their homes."[12] Children and pregnant women were beaten to death and runaway serfs torn to pieces by dogs. Women as well as men administered these ferocious penalties. Princess Kozlovskaya whipped the breasts and sex organs of her women serfs. Countess Saltykob kept one of hers in a cage for three years. Arakcheev was quite capable of such atrocities, but on the whole he strove to make his punishment system as systematic and orderly as everything else. A first offense was punished by a "stable whipping"; for the second, men of the Preobrazhensky Regiment were used, wielding thick rods known as "Arakcheev Sticks." All floggings were recorded in an estate Punish-ment Ledger, and the General inspected backs to see that chastisements had been thorough. Each peasant also carried, at all times, a personal punishment book, in which his or her offenses were listed along with the sentence. There was a walled jail, known as "The Edicule," and in church women offenders were made to wear iron collars and to pray to be forgiven for their sins in front of the congregation.

Whether Tsar Alexander, on his visit, was made aware of these aspects of Gruzino is not clear. Probably not: Russian authorities have always been skilled in showing visitors only what is intended to be seen. Arakcheev's own parson, Father Feodor Malinovsky, wrote a guide-book to the place, comparing it to the Hanging Gardens of Babylon. At all events the Tsar was overwhelmed by what he saw. He, like his father, had a craze for order. Now he had seen that it could be imposed, even on sprawling, slothful, filthy Russia. "The order which prevails here is unique," he wrote enthusiastically to his sister, the Grand Duch-ess Katerina. "The streets of the villages here have *precisely that kind of cleanliness* which I have been trying so hard to see established in the cities." He said he wanted her husband to visit it, too, and note in particular four features: "1. The order which prevails everywhere. 2. The neatness. 3. The construction of roads and plantations. 4. A kind of symmetry and elegance which pervades the place."[13]

Gruzino did not merely impress Alexander; it launched him on a large-scale utopia of his own. He had long been worried about the institution of serfdom. He accepted the argument that it was wrong. Indeed he thought it monstrous. But he could not actually bring himself to do anything about it. Now here was an opportunity. Serfdom was linked to army recruitment. As we have seen, Russia was under a perpetual compulsion to acquire more land. Hence she needed an enormous army, for conquest and occupation. By the beginning of our period it had reached nearly a million men, the great majority of whom had been serfs. Under the system of recruiting decrees, landowners and state peasant communities—state peasants having marginally higher rights than privately owned serfs but still being unfree laborers of the state—had to surrender to the army a fixed number of recruits. The compulsory service lasted 25 years, in effect an entire working life. For a man to be selected was a life sentence. You might even call it a death sentence, since, once discharged, he was unemployable and without property and had to beg. Alexander now saw a way to solve this problem. He decided to found a whole series of military colonies all over Russia, modeled on Gruzino. They would constitute islands of neatness and order—an archipelago, in fact—amid the great Russian sea of squalor. Using Arakcheev's methods, he would gradually reform the entire Russian countryside, taking soldiers from the barracks and transforming them into skilled soldier-peasants. If the system was set up on a sufficiently large scale, the colonies would provide all the soldiers Russia needed, so conscription could be abolished. At the same time the colonies would produce everything the soldiers needed, so the peacetime army would be self-supporting. The Tsar explained his ideas to Arakcheev, put him in charge of the scheme, and told him to get to work immediately.

By a savage irony of a kind common in Russia, the place Arakcheev and the Tsar selected for the first, one-battalion experiment, in Mogilev Province between Minsk and Smolensk, was peculiarly unsuitable. It was a piece of crown land which had been leased for three years, at a price of 11,000 rubles, by a group of free peasants who had managed to club together to form a voluntary cooperative. It was precisely the kind of spontaneous experiment in progressive agriculture which the Tsar, if he had had any sense, should have encouraged. Instead he destroyed it. Without any warning, on 9 November 1810, at the onset of winter, the place was surrounded by a unit of the Eletsky Musketeers. The peasants, who were busy building their new homes, were rounded up and ordered to move south to the Novorossisky region. Their lease was annulled. Most of them never saw their new "home," but perished on the way from cold and hunger. Nothing could illustrate better the absence of the rule of law in Russia and the ruthless frivolity of the Tsar's utopian whim.[14]

The French invasion and the Russian advance to Paris interrupted the scheme, but it was resumed with added fervor and on a huge scale in 1816. While Exmouth was liberating Christians from slavery in Algiers, the Tsar and Arakcheev were subjecting "souls" to a new form of it in Holy Mother Russia. The second colony was sited on the Volkhov river in the Novgorod District, near Gruzino, so Arakcheev could inspect it regularly. This time the peasants were not removed but found themselves simply incorporated in the experiment, without warning or choice. The land was bought from the owners by compulsory purchase at a low price. Merchants were kicked out. The territory was then closed to outsiders, taken out of the administrative framework completely, and Arakcheev was given sole responsibility for everything which took place within it, being answerable himself only to the Tsar. Over the next five years 90 battalions were thus settled in Novgorod Province, 12 in Mogilev, 36 in the Ukraine, and 240 squadrons of cavalry in three settlements in the south. The archipelago included 750,000 men, women and children, completely cut off from the rest of the country—towns, roads, ministries, taxes, police, courts, everything. No one from outside could get in, except as an officially approved visitor. Even more sinister, once you were inside the archipelago, you could not leave it. This applied to officers as well as men. The system had its own 24-volume law code, and in theory anyone accused of an offense was tried by a "jury" of his peers. In practice, all was determined by Arakcheev and his subordinates.

Gribbe, an officer in the main Novgorod colony, left a description of Arakcheev. He wore an ordinary gray trench coat, was of "medium height, round-shouldered, with thick dark hair *en brosse,* a low forehead, small, terribly cold, colorless eyes, inelegant nose shaped like a shoe, long chin, tightly compressed lips, no one ever having seen him smile or laugh . . . voice very nasal."[15] He was scarcely educated and the 11,000 books in the library he accumulated were taken down from the shelves only for their regular dustings. But he was skillful at making "digests" or summaries of "problems," together with potted "solutions," and these Alexander loved. The Tsar, as his reign progressed, developed the habit of making Arakcheev an intermediary between himself and his ministers and giving him special assignments. Hence, in the five years after the war ended, Arakcheev accumulated more personal power than anyone else in the vast country except the Autocrat himself. It was this which enabled him to get the military colonies going and to expand them so rapidly. The final aim of Alexander and Arakcheev was an archipelago which included a million soldiers and four-fifths of the crown peasants, a total of 5 million men, that is, between a quarter and a third of Russia's entire male population. The target was never achieved, though the number of people within the system, including women, passed the million mark.

This huge exercise in social engineering had two egregious characteristics: fraudulence and cruelty. In theory, after receiving initial large-scale state subsidies, the system was self-supporting and even profitable. By 1826 Arakcheev boasted it had a "capital" of 32 million rubles. In the north it owned quarries, mills, and three steamships, and its construction gangs numbered 30,000 men. But these were slave laborers, and the investment funds themselves were raised by heavy taxation within the colonies, supplemented by heavy fines for "offenses," the sale of liquor licenses, and other privileges. Moreover, state funds were poured into the system in a variety of concealed ways and it is likely that the entire scheme was run at an immense loss, not unlike the state farm collectives and industries set up in Russia a century later. The accounts were elaborate essays in deception and self-deception and there is evidence of widespread corruption among the system's officials, high and low. Almost everyone connected with it had something to hide. In 1823, one of its top bureaucrats, General Maevsky, described the atmosphere at its central office in Liteinaya Street, Saint Petersburg, as "like that of a secret underground temple in Egypt. On people's faces you could read only fear."[16]

Probably the best aspect of the experiment was education. Arakcheev had been converted to the Bell-Lancaster method, which was used extensively, and large numbers of children were taught to read and write in well-built schoolhouses. Every settlement had a library, at any rate in theory. The schools, hospitals, fire stations, billiard rooms, reading rooms, chapels, and even restaurants (for officers only) were what impressed international visitors who were taken on conducted tours. They also noticed that each peasant house had a proper latrine, and they were handed figures showing huge increases in crop yields. These kind of propaganda-visits, to become so familiar in the 20th century, were then new, and visitors had not yet learned to be skeptical. Some wrote enthusiastic accounts. A typical dupe was Marshal Auguste Marmont, who had administered Dalmatia under Bonaparte and whose testimony was therefore regarded as expert. To pass through the gates of a military colony, he wrote, was to enter "a terrestial paradise." He added: "In no other country can one find an appearance of material well-being superior to that of the peasants of the colonies, although 20 years ago their poverty was extreme."[17]

In reality, though, teaching the peasants to read merely raised their awareness that something was fundamentally wrong with the whole idea. There were five categories of "settlers." The first, "cantonists," were children aged 7 to 18. They wore uniforms, had military training, were under military discipline, and were subject to the army, not to their parents. At the other end of the age scale were "veterans," who were excused from all work and got free food, clothing, and accommodation. In between were "active soldiers," "reservists," or "settled soldiers" (peasants). But in practice, these categories were meaningless since the authorities simply used man- or woman power as convenient. No one had any rights at all. Again, in theory, each family was supposed to have land of its own, 16 acres in the north, 40 in the south, and be provided with sets of tools. But these supposed property-owning peasants could not dispose of their land or even determine how to farm it. The land could be taken from them for a variety of offenses, including "lack of merit"—in practice at the whim of the regimental bureaucrats who ran the colonies.

As the peasants saw it, they had less liberty than privately owned serfs, since Arakcheev determined how they should arrange the furniture in their houses and plan their gardens—especially if their particular colony was on the official visitors' circuit—and, indeed, how they should spend the little free time left to them. They knew, if the visitors did not, that the benefits of the system were largely on paper. As Maevsky put it: "From the outside all seemed in order; closer examination revealed chaos. Cleanliness and order were the colony's first concern. But imagine a house in which the people and the food are freezing. Imagine a cow which is maintained like a rifle, but whose fodder is twelve versts away in a field. Imagine that the woods had been burned down and that new roofing or building material had to be bought in Porkhovo . . . then you begin to have an idea of state economics."[18] Maevsky said that in theory the colonies were endowed with all modern luxuries, from baths to maternity homes, but "thrift and cleanliness" destroyed the purpose of everything. Hospital floors were polished like parquets, and patients did not dare tread on them for fear of making them dirty and being punished—they entered and left through the windows. A great many of the facilities were never used, but were kept "for inspection."

The peasants, unlike the visitors, knew that the system was universally corrupt. Bread, produce, tools, textbooks, hospital equipment—anything salable, in fact—was embezzled. Sick lists were faked. The figures bandied about were largely imaginary. Most of the key officials were artillery officers, cronies or subordinates of Arakcheev, ill-educated, unimaginative, knowing nothing of farming but aware simply that their boss demanded order and cleanliness. So that is what they provided, and they pocketed anything that was going.

Alexander's utopia was thus built on lies and fraud—and a growing element of violence. As the concealed losses mounted and it became more difficult to hide them, fines increased, rules were tightened, production quotas were raised, and punishments made more severe. The peasants felt themselves hemmed in by ever-growing restraints on their lives. By one of those mysterious swings in fashion, the early decades of the 19th century were a time of marked prejudice against beards, at any rate in what were regarded as advanced societies. In England and France, beards were rare among the educated classes, though young men began to sport moustaches in the decade 1815–25. In the United States, where beards were to become all the rage in the 1860s, a man who grew one in the 1820s courted ostracism or violence. When Joseph Palmer of Fitchburg, Massachussetts, entered church wearing a beard in 1830 he was not only denied communion but later assaulted by a group of parishioners who tried to shave him forcibly.[19] The fashion changed in the 1850s, and by 1874 only two out of 658 British members of Parliament were beardless; but during the years after Waterloo, however, beards were identified with radicalism in the West. It was characteristic of Arakcheev that, aware of these "civilized" trends and hating unshaven men in any case as an insult to military discipline, he should order all male peasants in the colonies to cut off their beards. All objected furiously. Some, especially in the south, belonged to cults, such as the Old Believers, who regarded shaving as sinful and resistance to it the road to martyrdom. At one colony, over 200 men chose to be beaten to death rather than conform to Arakcheev's edict.[20]

Such incidents caused little stir, being lost in the immensities of Russian space. But from 1819 the mutinies began. The first occurred in June, at a new colony in the Ukraine, where Russian notions were hated anyway. The peasants went on strike and Arakcheev hurried down to suppress it. He sentenced 275 men to death, then commuted the sentences to *spitzruten*. This was a Prussian army penalty in which offenders were forced to pass a dozen times through files of 1,000 men, each armed with a stick—soldiers called it "going through Green Street." Afterwards, "you could only tell by their heads that these were men and not slaughtered meat."[21] The Tsar wrote Arakcheev a sympathetic letter. He urged severity—"The colonies will be set up come what may, even if I have to cover the road from St Petersburg to Novgorod with corpses"—but lamented the suffering which inflicting such punishments must cause "to your sensitive soul."[21]

There were other mutinies, notably in October 1820, among the Tsar's own Semyonovsky Regiment. Alexander attributed them to "secret societies," but the truth was that the military colonies were unpopular among regular soldiers as well as among peasants. Barclay de Tolly, a leading hero of the war against Bonaparte, said that the colonies were a system for turning good soldiers into bad peasants and good peasants into bad soldiers. There was much grim satisfaction among generals who were not involved in the system when the unrest struck at Arakcheev's own hearth in autumn 1825. Despite his puritanical ways, the General led an irregular life. In 1806 he had formally married Anastasia, the 18-year-old daughter of a respectable landowner. But by then he had already acquired a mistress, in the shape of a serf-woman called Nastasia Milkina. He had bought her through an advertisement, common enough in Russia, where a strong man would be put up for sale at 500 rubles, a child fetching as little as 10 kopeks. Then he had fallen in love with her, given her her freedom, made her his housekeeper and finally put her in charge of the whole estate. Descriptions of her vary. One says she had jet-back hair and eyes; the peasants thought her a gypsy, who could "do magic." The English investigator Lieutenant John Sherwood, who later unraveled the Decembrist Conspiracy, called her "a drunken, fat, pock-marked, uneducated, evil and loose woman."[22] She gave Arakcheev a son, Shumsky, who had red hair (usually regarded as a bad sign in the 19th century), was put into the Horse Guards but became an alcoholic, an embarrassment to the General in his anti-alcohol campaign. His mother would have made a better soldier; she "had the figure of a grenadier," and she was certainly brutal enough even for the General's taste.

On Thursday 10 September, after Arakcheev had left Gruzino to inspect the Novgorod colonies, Nastasia was murdered by her servants. It was one of the great and fascinating crimes of the age. The woman had committed atrocities against so many people on the estate that, as with the victim in an old-fashioned detective story, everyone had a motive for killing her. Arakcheev's own detailed account, written for the Tsar's eyes only, surfaced and was published in 1900. There were three young maids in the house, Praskovya, Tatanya and Feodosya, and Praskovya's young brother, Vassili Antonov, worked in the kitchen. Three days before, Nastasia Milkina had had Praskovya scourged twice and put the two other maids in the house jail. On the Thursday morning, Nastasia woke at five, summoned Praskovya, but fell asleep again. The girl then decided to revenge herself and summoned her brother from the kitchen. He arrived with a knife. At that point the dog woke up, waking Nastasia in turn, and a terrible struggle took place. Nastasia lost two fingers trying to grab the knife and was stabbed in the head repeatedly, until it hung from her shoulders only by its skin. When Arakcheev returned in the evening and found the gory mess, he almost went out of his mind. He refused to eat or shave, wore the woman's bloodstained handkerchief round his neck, and wrote to the Tsar: "For 22 years she slept on the ground in front of my bedroom, but for the last five years I asked her to use a camp bed. . . . In all the 27 years I could never persuade her to sit in my presence. As soon as I entered the room she would stand up, and to my request that she should sit down she would reply: 'Little Father, I want everyone to see I am your true servant and nothing else.' " At her graveside, the frantic General shouted out to the assembled estate people: "Kill me, you villains! You have taken my only friend from me. Now I have lost everything!" But he exacted a fearful revenge all the same. A total of 24 servants were sentenced to the knout—Antonov, to 175 blows; Praskovya, to 125; and the two other girls, to 70 each. Gribbe left an account of the executions which took place in a field at Gruzino, in front of thousands of people. Fires had been lit because of the intense cold and the knout men were well primed with vodka from a giant black bottle. Both Praskovya and her brother died under the knout. The sentences were illegal because all were under eighteen.[23]

The military colonies never recovered from this psychological blow to Arakcheev's self-esteem. He himself lost most of his state authority when his protector Alexander died later the same year; the final blow to the system came in 1830–31, when the cholera epidemic which was slowly harrowing the world hit Russia and was attributed by suspicious peasants in the colonies to the new health measures and hospitals. In the northern colonies, the peasants rose, murdered the officers and set fire to the hospitals and other public buildings. The new Tsar, Nicholas I, who had never liked the system anyway, introduced changes which destroyed it. Thus the first modern experiment in social engineering ended. Its significance was the ease with which it could be introduced on a scale to determine the lives of a million people, on the mere whim of a solitary autocrat who consulted no one and sought the approval of nothing. It pointed to fundamental weaknesses in Russian law and attitudes which were ominous for the future, when social engineering could be conducted on a much larger scale.

The chief, and fatal, weakness was the absence of rights. Arakcheev could have his teenage servants beaten to death and their families had no means of redress, though his act was against the law. The law meant nothing because it was not enforced except when convenient to authority. Why was this absence of the rule of law tolerated? Because everyone's rights were subsumed in the overriding rights of le pouvoir. In the early 19th century the systems of slavery in the Americas and of serfdom in Russia were often compared because both were growing rapidly. In west and central Europe, serfdom had declined rapidly from the 15th century onwards, and was extinct in any recognizable form by

1800. But in Russia it had actually expanded in the 16th and 17th centuries. Indeed the Code of 1649, confirming the practice of half a century, abolished the time limitation on the forcible return of runaway peasants, thus consolidating the institution in a form which endured until it was abolished in 1861.

As the peasant population increased, so did the number of serfs. They were divided into private serfs and state peasants, but the distinction was really false. All peasants belonged to the land where they lived, they were *glebae adscripti*, attached to the soil, a category going back to the late Roman Empire. They had to live and work where the official cadaster of residence said they belonged. But they were not *kholopy* or chattel slaves, whose owner could dispose of them at will. They were *krepostnye*, who had duties, including the duty of paying taxes to the state. So the state disliked slaves, whom it could not tax, and helped to stamp them out, while promoting serfdom, which brought in revenue. In practice however it farmed out the serfs to their landlords, who made themselves responsible for their taxes. This practice increased the landlords' power over the serfs and was convenient to the state, which collected its taxes more easily. In 1805 Michael Speransky, a man of some importance in Russia during Alexander I's early, reforming period, laid it down that Russia had only two estates—"slaves of the sovereign and slaves of the landlords." But, he added, the first category was "free" only by comparison with the second. One historian, N. Khlebnikov, trying to unravel the system in 1869, when it had been ended by law, defined private serfdom as follows: "The peasant was enserfed neither to the land nor to the person [of the landlord]: he was enserfed, if I may say so, to the state; he was made a state worker through the intermediacy of the landlord."[24]

It is at this point that the difference between unfree labor in Russia and in the Americas becomes of overwhelming importance. In the United States, for instance, the slave was an unfree being living in the midst of citizens with full rights, rather like in ancient Athens. In Russia, by contrast, the serfs simply formed one category of people in a servile system which allowed no one whatever to dispose freely of his time or his belongings. Neither freehold land nor personal rights, in the Western sense, had any meaning in Russia. It was what Thomas Hobbes called a "Patrimonial Monarchy" or Max Weber "a Patrimonial Regime," in which the autocrat, or the state he personally embodied, disposed of all resources, human or material. Such concepts as individual rights or liberties, the rule of law, or limitations on the exercise of authority simply did not exist. Peasant serfdom was therefore merely the most visible and widespread form of bondage. As a rule, both landlords and merchants, let alone minorities like the Jews, had to reside exactly where the state decided.

This monarchical-state power was exercised through the institution of the *tiaglo,* the Russian equivalent of the French *taille,* which means "to pull." Everyone had to yield the state either services or money, or both, at a certain place, where it was due; the *tiaglo* pulled you toward it. If you moved to evade it, you were manhunted, whether you were a city dweller or a peasant. Not only was it your duty to pay; it was also your duty to denounce those who did not pay. Denunciation was, in practice, the only way a peasant could effectively act against a landlord. Failure to denounce, whether for nonpayment or any other crime against the state, such as conspiracy, was itself ranked as "treason," and the entire family was implicated in the traitor's guilt. In practice however all did denounce because neighbors had to make good the losses suffered by the state when one of them absconded. Thus shopkeepers, merchants and dealers watched each other carefully. It was easier for a peasant to run off behind "the Rocks" (the Urals) than for a tradesman to evade paying taxes and stay in business. The state might not care much what one subject did to another, but where its own needs were concerned, it was zealous and made no distinction between thought and deed. Opposition to authority, an opposition cast of mind, was only one degree less punishable than an overt act of treason. It was such assumptions which were to make it so easy for Russia to pass from a patrimonial monarchy to a totalitarian dictatorship.

The serfs were merely the least free members of a servile society in which no one except the Tsar himself was truly free. The frontiers were always sealed. To go abroad, you had to obtain, by petition to the Tsar, a *proezzhaia gramota*. If a merchant traveled without one, his property was confiscated and his relatives were liable to be tortured to find out why he did it and sent to Siberia. Experience showed that Russians who went into the West and could make their living there, or managed to get their property out, rarely wished to return. Foreigners, too, required an entry visa and were not generally welcome. If they looked at things too closely, they were treated as spies—one reason why there are so few drawings of Russia in this period. Russians were forbidden to make unauthorized contact with foreign visitors. Only in 1703 did foreign or domestic news cease to be a state secret in Russia, and thereafter both remained in meager supply. Accurate news was called *kuranty* (from the Dutch *krant,* newspaper) and was supplied to the Tsar himself and to top officials on a "need-to-know" basis. Others were kept in the dark and expected to like it, though news did circulate by word of mouth and in letters and manuscripts.

It is of the nature of oppressive societies to induce a feeling of hopelessness among those who live in them. Even Tsar Alexander himself felt overwhelmed by Russia's weaknesses and wrongs. He, the only free man, was a prisoner of its problems. A would-be radical at the beginning of his reign, he lacked the courage and integrity to set about a fundamental restructuring, started schemes of reform here and there, raised dust and devils, then became increasingly conservative in the face of the incipient anarchy his dabblings threatened to produce. "Educated" Russia sighed and relapsed into apathy or, as we shall see, indulged itself in conspiracies scarcely less frivolous than the Tsar's utopian ventures. The nobility, served and indulged by a groveling multitude, felt ultimately powerless and chained to the lazy and incompetent human ants they appeared to own. Everyone, when they thought at all, was conscious of a huge weight of moral iniquity pressing down, and despaired of shedding the burden.

The feeling that slavery incarcerated its supposed beneficiaries as well as its victims was just as strong in those parts of the United States where it was ubiquitous and growing. Slavery had been abolished in Rhode Island in 1774, the year before the first antislavery society was founded in Philadelphia. Vermont made it unlawful in 1777, Pennsylvania in 1780, and in 1787 an ordinance forbade it in the then Northwest Territory, which extended from what is now Ohio to Wisconsin. But it is notable that the American Constitution of the same year, while at no point explicitly conferring the right to own slaves, seems implicitly to concede it. Article I speaks of "the whole number of free persons" and then of "three-fifths of all other persons" (that is, nonfree or slaves). It was this article which gave slave-owning states the right to consider their slaves as voting fodder (on a three-to-five basis with free men), while denying them the right actually to vote. But more significant still was Article IV, Section 2, paragraph 3: "No person held to service or labor in one State, under the laws thereof, escaping into another, shall, in consequence of any law or regulation therein, be discharged from such service of labor, but shall be delivered up on claim of the party to whom such service or labor be due." This passage not merely by implication conceded the lawfulness of slavery but bound the federal government to uphold it by preventing these mysterious persons, nowhere referred to as slaves, from "escaping."[25]

The deviousness of the Constitution on this issue reflected the pangs of conscience of the Virginia elite. Three years later the first census (1790) revealed that there were nearly 700,000 slaves in the United States, 20 percent of the total population and over 40 percent in the southern states. The Constitution prevented Congress from abolishing the slave trade (as distinct from slavery) until 1808. In fact all the states had ended the legal importation of foreign slaves by 1803, and Congress was able to exercise the power to ban the trade completely in 1807. But large-scale smuggling and high birthrates continued to swell the total slave population, and the value of the slaves themselves rose steadily.[26]

Well-meaning men found themselves entangled in the toils of the system. Thomas Jefferson was a typical example. We have to accept his word that he hated slavery. At age 44, he wrote to his brother-in-law in 1787 saying that, once his debts had been cleared, "I shall try some plan of making [his slaves'] situation happier, determined to content myself with a small portion of their liberty [crossed out] labor."[27] He argued that slavery corrupted the entire society where it flourished: "The whole commerce between master and slave is a perpetual exercise of . . . the most unremitting despotism, on the one part, and degrading submission on the other. . . . The man must be a prodigy who can retain his manners and morals undepraved by such circumstances." He foresaw endless servile insurrections: "We have the wolf by the ears, and we can neither hold him nor safely let him go." The insurrections would get worse until the whites were forced "after dreadful scenes and sufferings to release them in their own way." Unless the blacks were freed "by the generous energy of our own minds," emancipation would come "by bloody process." "I tremble," he added, "for my country when I reflect that God is just; that his justice cannot sleep for ever."

But Jefferson did not get out of debt and did not free his slaves. On the contrary, he acquired more. In 1802 he was unwilling or unable to deny an accusation in the *Richmond Recorder* that he kept a slave concubine, Sally Hemings, and had a son Tom and other children by her. (Sally was, in fact, a quadroon; two of her children passed into white society.) His letters show that he conformed to slave-owning practices in numerous ways. Thus, of a runaway slave, James Hubbard, he wrote: "I had him severely flogged in the presence of his old companions." He sought what he termed "young and able negro men" and "a breeding woman" for purchase. He noted the increased value of his human property: "The value of our lands and slaves, taken conjunctly, doubles in about twenty years. This arises from the multiplication of our slaves, from the extension of culture and the increased demands for lands." By 1822 he had no less than 267 slaves.[28]

Jefferson's fellow Virginian and successor as president, James Madison, also owned slaves all his life, though he was even more critical of the institution. He tried to make a rule not to sell slaves in the open market. He appointed one, his former valet at Princeton, Sawney, to be a farm overseer, and told another of his overseers, a white, to treat slaves "with all the humanity and kindness consistent with their necessary subordination and work."[29] In 1819, two years after he ceased to be president, he gave his views to the Philadelphia abolitionist, Robert J. Evans. The slaves ought to be freed, gradually, in an equitable manner "consistent with the existing and durable prejudices of the nation." But he thought the whites would have insuperable objections to a thorough incorporation, so the free blacks would have to be removed. Universal manumission would be financed by raising $600 million, from the sale of 300 million acres, one-third of the disposable public land, at $2 an acre. The freed slaves would then be resettled in Africa by transforming the American Colonisation Society, organized in 1816 with Madison as a life-member, into a federal agency superintended by a senior member of the government."[30]

A decade and a half later, Madison again gave his views, by now far more despondent, to the English economist Harriet Martineau. "With regard to slavery he owned himself almost to be in despair," and admitted "all the evils with which it has ever been charged." He was frightened by the rapid increase in Virginia's slave population—a third of his own slaves, he told her, were less than five years old. Those, he said, who saw slaves going cheerfully off to church, gaily dressed, and claimed they were happy, were simply deluding themselves—it was not true. The institution of slavery degraded the minds of the whites and ruined families of blacks and white alike. It even instilled cruelty to animals. He thought Congress had the power to forbid the internal slave trade, but for a final solution he still put his faith in African colonization. He insisted to Miss Martineau that white women were also slaves in the sense that they were kept in a state of fear and could not trust their own black servants. He complained bitterly of the "helplessness" of a country "cursed with a servile population." He wanted all men of good will to speak out against slavery so that "we may destroy it, and save ourselves from reproaches and our posterity the imbecility ever-attendant on a country filled with slaves."[31] But Madison, like Jefferson, could not emancipate himself. In 1834, aged 83, he sold 16 able-bodied slaves to a kinsman for $6,000, they giving "their glad consent" because of "their horror of going to Liberia"—so much for the African solution. Despite his many promises to free his slaves, the will he drew up the next year did not set them free; to do so would have impoverished his widow. Thus another well-meaning man went to his grave with a guilty conscience.[32]

*   *   *

Opponents of slavery in the north had little sympathy for these southern dilemmas. John Quincy Adams, who spoke for many of them, set down in his diary with relish some revealing views his cabinet-colleague, John Calhoun of South Carolina, confided to him in March 1820. Calhoun said that in Carolina "domestic labour was confined to the blacks and such was the prejudice that if he, who was the most popular man in the district, were to keep a white servant in his house, his character and reputation would be irretrievably ruined. . . . It did not apply to all kinds of labor, not for example to farming. Manufacturing and mechanical labor was not degrading. It was only manual labor—the proper work of slaves. No white person could descend to that. And it was the best guarantee of equality among the whites." On which Adams commented savagely: "In the abstract [southerners] say that slavery is an evil. But when probed to the quick on it they show at the bottom of their souls pride and vainglory in their condition of masterdom."[33]

It was not, as Adams knew very well, simply a matter of racial prejudice. There was anti-black prejudice throughout the North, too. De Tocqueville noticed it.[34] What puzzled him was that it was just as strong in areas where blacks were few. As Adams discovered when he was in Russia, the people of a country where men and women serfs were regularly beaten to death were still shocked by American racial prejudice. He noted (5 August 1812): "After dinner I had a visit from Claud Gabriel, the black man in the Emperor's service, who went to America last summer for his wife and children, and who is now come back with them. He complains of having been very ill-treated in America, and that he was obliged to lay aside his superb dress and sabre, which he had been ordered to wear, but which occasioned people to insult and even beat him."[35] A few years later, from Pennsylvania, came the first suggestions that blacks had a peculiar propensity to crime, the Governor publicly expressing his fear of a rising black crime rate, noting particularly robberies, assaults and burglaries. Both Ohio and Indiana had a legal requirement that on entering the state, blacks must post a $500 bond as a security for good behavior. In the North, legal and constitutional discrimination against blacks was almost universal. In 1821 New York State's constitutional convention virtually adopted universal manhood suffrage: Anyone who possessed a freehold, paid taxes, had served in the state militia, or even merely worked on the highways could vote—but only if he was "white"; the same convention actually increased the property qualification for blacks from $100 to $250. In 1838 Pennsylvania likewise adopted universal manhood suffrage, but again on a "whites-only" basis. Anti-black color bars were routine among trade unions, especially craft ones.[36]

Northerners like Adams, however, brushed aside the problem of discrimination and concentrated relentlessly on the institution of slavery itself. It was his view that it made southerners, who had a sense of masterdom which northern people did not feel, look down on their fellow Americans. "It is among the evils of slavery," he noted, "that it taints the very sources of moral principle. It establishes false estimates of virtue and vice." Hence, "if the Union must be dissolved, slavery is precisely the question on which it ought to break!" It was during these years that a feeling of bitterness and mutual moral incomprehension began to develop between those enveloped in the institution and those who were not. Madison, while admitting its evils, blamed the fanaticism of the northern abolitionists for the increasing tendency of southerners to produce elaborate defenses of slavery. This raised the debate to an ideological level, and people dug in on both sides, whereas it ought to have been simply about devising practical means to get rid of the curse. But people like Adams, on the other hand, saw the issue increasingly in apocalyptic terms. He dismissed the African colonization schemes Madison and other southern moderates favored as contemptible efforts to pass the responsibility to the federal government; they were, he snarled, "ravenous as panthers" to get congressional appropriations for their ill-conceived schemes. For him slavery was a huge moral issue, the greatest of the day. In another of his talks with Calhoun, the latter admitted that if the Union dissolved over the issue, "the South would be from necessity compelled to form an alliance offensive and defensive with Great Britain. I said that would be returning to the colonial state. He said yes, pretty much, but it would be forced upon them." To Adams, grinding his teeth in fury, it was only to be expected that the evil defenders of a wicked institution should ally themselves with the grand repository of international immorality, the British monarchy. To him, if the union could be preserved only at the price of retaining slavery, then it were better it should end, especially since in the breakup slavery itself would perish: "If slavery be the destined sword in the hands of the destroying angel which is to sever the ties of this union, the same sword will cut asunder the bonds of slavery itself. A dissolution of the Union for the cause of slavery would be followed by a servile war in the slave-holding states, combined with a war between the two severed portions of the Union . . . its results must be the extirpation of slavery from this whole continent and, calamitous and devastating as this course of events must be . . . , so glorious would be its final issue that, as God shall judge me, I dare not say it is not to be desired!"[37]

In the United States, as in Russia, there were misapprehensions on both sides of the argument about the nature and consequences of unfree labor. Madison, for instance, "spoke often and anxiously of slave property as the worst possible for profit." He used to say that Richard Rush's 10-acre farm near Philadelphia brought in more money than his own 2,000-acre one worked by slaves. But this was self-deceiving nonsense. The horrible truth, which decent men found it difficult to admit, was that modern technology and the advance of science did not necessarily work hand in hand with justice and human progress. In Russia, it is true, serfdom was seen as a relic of the past, something the rest of Europe had got rid of in its upward path, which Russia was bound in time to follow. There were strong economic arguments against it, which grew stronger with every decade of the 19th century and were reflected first in a relative, then in an absolute decline in the number of serfs. In 1795 there were 9,787,997 serfs, or 53.9 percent of the population. By 1833 the number of serfs had risen to 11,447,203, but they were now only 44.9 percent of the population. Twenty years later more than half the peasants were free and the number of serfs was falling fast. Emancipation, when it came in the 1860s, was the coup de grace for an institution in terminal decline.[38]

But while technology was undermining serfdom in Russia, it was strengthening slavery in the United States. The result was again reflected in the demography. The American slave society was the only one in the West to develop a high growth rate by increased births, as opposed to an artificial increase by the acquisition of more slaves from Africa. The lawful import of slaves ended in 1808. Smuggled slaves never reached a total of more than 15,000 in any one year, and were probably canceled out by manumissions. Yet the total slave population rose from 1,119,354 in 1810 to 3,963,760 in 1860. This impressive 2 percent annual growth rate was achieved almost entirely by high birthrates of 50-plus per 1,000 and low death rates of under 30 per 1,000. This rapid population growth was due primarily to good material conditions.[39]

Why were conditions good? Because growing cotton by unfree labor was a boom industry. Indeed in the years after 1815, cotton was probably the most valuable agricultural staple in the world, and slaves, though at the end of the profits-continuum, inevitably shared in its prosperity. The reduction in the price of cotton and the increase in its availability from 1780–1850 was one of the best things that ever happened to the world. Sensible people had long dressed in cotton if they could afford it. As Samuel Johnson observed, clothes made from vegetables, like cotton (and linen), could be made truly clean and cool, whereas clothes made from animal materials, like wool and silk, retained an element of grease whatever you did to them. The trouble with cotton was its expense. Up to the point where the cotton industry industrialized itself, to produce a pound of cotton thread took 12 to 14 man-days, against six for silk, 2 to 5 for linen, and one to two for wool. With fine cotton muslin, the most sought after, the value-added multiple from raw material to finished product was as high as 900.[40] No other article of apparel was so expensive, apart from the best furs. However, it was precisely this labor intensivity of the trade, and the rising demand for its products as western society became wealthier and more fastidious, that acted as a spur to invention and investment. This was the reason cotton figured right at the center of the first phase of the Industrial Revolution.

It was in the 1770s that Richard Arkwright's spinning machine and James Hargreaves's jenny were introduced in England. The consequence was dramatic. In 1765 500,000 pounds of cotton had been spun in England, all of it by hand. By 1784 the total had risen to 12 million, all of it by machine. The next year the new Boulton & Watt steam engines were first used to power the spinning machinery at a factory in Papplewich, Nottinghamshire. That, effectively, was the Big Bang of the Industrial Revolution—and it was during the 1780s that Britain became the first country in history to achieve self-sustaining economic growth.

More than any other product, cotton was susceptible to cost reductions produced by labor-saving machinery and steam power. By 1812 the cost of cotton yarn was one-tenth of what it had been even in the 1770s. Moreover, the big British cotton factories showed themselves continually ravenous for new technical improvements, so that in the years after 1815 the industry went through a second phase of innovation. The new mill which the engineers William Fairbairn (1789–1874) and John Kennedy (1769–1855) built in Manchester in 1818 introduced a revolution in high-velocity gearing that replaced the ponderous masses of cast iron held in position by huge wooden beams, using energy on a prodigious scale, with slender wrought-iron rods in light frames or suspended by hooks, all-metal machines whose revs were ten times their predecessors. The new-style cotton works coming on-stream in Britain in the early 1820s cut costs still more dramatically. Indeed by the early 1860s, the price of cotton cloth, in terms of gold bullion, was less than 1 percent of its price even in 1784, when it was already made by machine.[41] There is no instance in world history of the price of a product in potentially universal demand coming down so fast. As a result British-made cotton came within the means not just of the exploding populations of the advanced West, but of the rest of the world. By the beginning of 1830, finished cotton made up more than half of Britain's exports.

But Britain grew virtually no cotton herself. Where was the raw material to supply this colossal new industry to come from? Traditionally, raw cotton came to Europe from the Middle East, especially Egypt, and India; later, it came from Brazil and the West Indies, too. The more southerly states of America did not supply cotton. In so far as the South had a plantation economy, they produced mainly tobacco. The South first started to grow cotton for export only in the early 1780s, when the Industrial Revolution had already begun. When the first bale arrived from the United States at Liverpool in 1784, it was refused entry. Under the Navigation Acts, imports could be landed only from British ships or ships of their country of origin—the ship which landed the bale was American and the customs officers did not believe that cotton was grown in the United States.[42] American exports of cotton to Britain were still on a small scale until the early 1800s, when the effects of introducing the cotton gin suddenly brought the price of cotton crashing down.

The cotton gin was the invention of Eli Whitney (1765–1825). He was a case, common at this time, of a natural mechanical genius, for he was born on a poor farm and discovered his talent by working on agricultural tools, then paid his way through Yale as a mechanic. In Savannah, Georgia, he became fascinated by the intractable problem of separating the cotton lint from the seeds—the factor which made raw cotton costly to process. Watching a cat claw a chicken and end up with clawfuls of mere feathers, he got the idea for a solid wooden cylinder with headless nails and a grid to keep out the seeds, while the lint was pulled through by spikes, a revolving brush cleaning them. The supreme virtue of this simple but brilliant idea was that the machine was so cheap to make and easy to operate—a slave on a plantation, using a gin, could produce 50 pounds of cotton a day instead of one. Whitney's invention was instantly pirated, though he patented it in 1794, and it brought him no more than $100,000 in all. But by 1800–10 his gins had transformed production and made the United States the chief supplier of cotton to the British manufacturing industry's rapidly rising demand.[43] In 1810 Britain was consuming 79 million pounds of raw cotton, of which 48 percent came from the United States. Twenty years later imports were 248 million, 70 percent from the United States. By

1860 the total was over a billion pounds of which 92 percent came from
Southern plantations. During the same period, the cost fell from 45
cents a pound to as low as 28 cents (Liverpool landing prices).[44]

This huge growth in the cotton industry, rising at 7 percent compound annually, soon made cotton America's largest export trade and
perhaps the biggest single source of the country's growing wealth. It
also created "the South" as a special phenomenon, a culture, a cast of
mind. And this in turn was to a great extent the consequence of General
Jackson's destruction of Indian and Spanish power in the lower Mississippi Valley. The Old South—Virginia, the Carolinas, Georgia—was
not suited to growing cotton; it was if anything tobacco country. The
new states General Jackson's ruthlessness made possible, especially
Alabama, Mississippi, and Louisiana, now constituted the Deep
South, where cotton was king, and slavery on a vast and growing
scale underpinned it. The population of these states multiplied more
than threefold in the 20 years from 1810 to 1830. This growth in
population was the result of an internal migration from within the
United States, for the most part, settlers moving from New England,
where land was now scarce, or the Old South, where, in some cases, the
land was becoming exhausted. The rush began after the Treaty of
Ghent made normal relations with Britain possible and so spurred the
cotton export trade. "The *Alabama Fever*," wrote James Graham, a
North Carolina tobacco planter, to a friend on 9 November 1817,
"rages here with great violence, and has *carried off* vast numbers of our
Citizens . . . if it continues to spread as it has done it will almost
depopulate the country."[45]

This migration moved the plantation system from Virginia, the
Carolinas, and coastal Georgia inland to west Georgia and west Tennessee and to the Deep South. But Old South and New South were still
linked—by chains of slavery. Before the cotton boom, the price of
slaves in the United States had been falling: In the quarter century
1775–1800, it slid by 50 percent. Now it began to rise. In the half
century 1800–50, it rose, in real terms, from about $50 to $800–$1,000.
For every 100 acres under cotton in the New South, you needed at least
10 or perhaps as many as 20 slaves. The Old South was unsuited to
cotton but its plantations could, and did, breed slaves in growing
numbers. Slave breeding now became the chief source of revenue for
many of the old tobacco plantations, the ban on imported "new" slaves
from 1808 merely increasing the value of the homebred variety.[46]

In the New South the sudden arrival of paddle steamers in the years
after 1815 accelerated the growth of the plantation economy and raised

its profits. Thanks to slavery, a cotton plantation could be laid out and in full production in two years. It was possible to harvest a crop even in one year, and "a man who stood in a wilderness fewer than 12 months ago now stood at a dock watching his crop load out for the English factory towns." The frontiersman thus became part of a commercial economy and "cotton made it possible for a man to hang a crystal chandelier in his frontier log cabin."[47] A case in the records illustrates how quickly money could be made from plantation cotton. Early in 1823 a man in western Georgia planted cleared land with cotton, sold it in May with the crop established, cleared land in Alabama that autumn, planted and sold the farm, and then repeated the process in Mississippi; he ended up with 1,000 acres freehold, which had cost him $1,250 and two years' work.[48] But of course, this rapidity would have been impossible without slavery. Madison was out of date and out of touch when he laid down that slaves did not make money for farmers. Had he been right the system could have been ended in the second quarter of the century. In fact slaves made fortunes for those who owned and skillfully exploited them. There were thousands of small planters as well as big ones. A few plantations were worked by the white families which owned them. But over 90 percent had slaves, and from the early 1820s a new kind of large-scale specialist cotton plantation, using hundreds of slaves, began to dominate the trade.

These large plantations were supplied increasingly by slave-rearing plantations which were also highly commercial. With monogamous marriages, only 10–15 percent of slave women produced a child each year. Deliberate slave breeding involved the provision of sires for all nubile females, so that 25–40 percent of the female slaves produced a child each year.[49] The notion that Southern slavery was an old-fashioned institution, a hangover from the past like serfdom in Russia, was wrong. It was born of the Industrial Revolution, high technology and the commercial spirit catering for mass markets of hundreds of millions of consumers. It was very much part of the new modern world. That was why it proved so difficult to eradicate. The value of the slaves themselves formed up to 35 percent of the entire capital of the South. By midcentury their value was over $2 billion in gold; that was why compensation was ruled out, because it would have amounted to at least ten times the entire federal budget.

Hence it was the early 19th century world cotton boom which created "the South" as we understand it, a geographic entity united by its defense of slavery. In 1815 and for a few years thereafter, few people in the southern states had the moral hardihood to defend slavery, at least in public. They tended to support an "African solution," agreeing with the humanitarians on this point. President Monroe supported legislation in 1819 to permit the creation of Liberia (though he was not willing to allow the United States actually to purchase territory in Africa for this purpose). Monroe's support is why in 1824 the capital of the new colony was named Monrovia. But very few slaves wanted to go there, even to obtain their freedom. From that day to this, in fact, hardly any black Americans, slave or free, have shown any desire to return to Africa. But from 1819 onwards, as the financial potential of plantation cotton became obvious, the political stakes rose too, and opposition to slavery in the South declined sharply, partly because many Quakers and Methodists emigrated north and west to get away from it.

From this point some Southerners began openly to defend slavery as an institution, and with increasing bravado and brilliance. In February 1820 Adams noted bitterly in his diary that in Congress "all the most eloquent orators" were "on the slavish side." There might be "a great mass of cool judgment and plain sense on the side of freedom and humanity," but "the ardent spirits and passions are on the side of oppression."[50] This was the point at which north and south began to bifurcate decisively and indeed at which the term *the South* came into general parlance. The southern apologists were still, in their hearts, ashamed of slavery. That is why they used a euphemism. To them, it was not slavery—a word they never spoke, if possible—but "the peculiar institution." The use of euphemisms was to become an outstanding characteristic of the modern world which was being born, and nowhere was it employed more assiduously than in the South's defense of unfree labor.

Indeed, it is a curious thing that although the maintenance of slavery required an immense structure of law, the term *slavery* itself hardly ever appears in the constitutional documents of the slave states. Slavery was dealt with legally at the municipal level, and it is in the regulations of townships and counties that you have to look for the term. There was no general, authoritative survey of these bylaws and the courts made heavy weather of sorting out the legal implications of an institution they hesitated even to name. But when they did grit their teeth and name it, the implications were odious. In 1828 the Kentucky Court of Appeals ruled in *Jarman v. Patterson*: "However deeply it may be regretted, and whether it be politic or impolitic, a slave by our code is not treated as a person but as a *negotium*, a thing, as he stood in the civil code of the Roman Empire."[51] Thus, black marriage contracts, for instance, however validly made, were held in law to be "dormant" when a signatory had slave status, coming to life only if he or she was manumitted. Therefore, it was lawful to separate husbands and wives, or both, or either from their children, at a sale of slaves. In *Cannon v. Jenkins* in June 1830, the judge admitted "It would be harsh to sever the ties which bind even slaves together." But, he added, "it must be done, if the executor discovers that the interests of the estate require it."[52]

It was widely believed in the North that owners sometimes deliberately put a slave to death without legal punishment. This belief was not entirely true: All slave states hanged whites, from time to time, for the wanton murder of slaves. But it was true that the slave was held to be abandoned by natural and common law. Justice Ruffin, of the Supreme Court of North Carolina, in the case of *The State v. Mann* (December 1829), spoke of "the harsh but necessary discipline of the slave," though he added that its exercise was "a curse of slavery to both the bond and the free portions of our community." If the administration of "discipline" was held by the courts to be "necessary," then it was only a short step to the situation in some southern states where cases of killing by "undue correction" were dealt with merely by a full statement of the facts and a confession of fault. Thus in *State of South Carolina v. Raines* (May 1826), Raines was able to clear himself of what seems, on the facts, the atrocious murder of a subordinate slave.[53]

Perhaps the most revealing judgment was given by the chief justice of the Supreme Court, John Marshall (1755–1835), in *Boyce v. Anderson,* in which the owners of four slaves drowned by the steamboat *Washington* sued for negligence. "A slave," ruled Marshall, "has volition and has feelings which cannot be entirely disregarded. . . . He cannot be stowed away as common [cargo]. . . . He resembles a passenger."[54] The use of the words *entirely* and *resembles* are particularly significant because they reflect the perhaps unworthy but nonetheless genuine dilemmas of the legal mind confronted by the awesome clash of moral principle and commercial interest which slavery presented. In law, a Russian serf had much more protection than an American slave. But the law was completely disregarded if an owner had power, and the cruelties Russians regularly inflicted on their serfs would not have been tolerated in the Deep South, either by the law or by society. Moreover, the writhings and hesitations of the courts suggested that, sooner or later, they would reach solutions and that they would veer toward humanity rather than property.

In this sense the hypocrisy of the South, as an implicit admission of guilt, was a healthy sign. In any case, the South believed that the north was equally hypocritical. Once the cotton boom started, southern planters lived up to the hilt of their incomes and borrowed largely to acquire and expand their plantations. America already had a reputation as a nation of big spenders—it was a characteristic which struck de Tocqueville forcibly—and southern planters were the first of them. They borrowed money from the factors on the coast, who did not grow cotton themselves but traded in it for shipping east and acted as bankers to the growers. These factors, in turn, were indebted to New York agents and banks, which is where most of the heavy interest charges eventually went. So the North made money out of the South's shame— or so Southerners argued. But if the North already disposed of most of the money power, the balance of political power still rested with the South and, indeed, continued to do so until the end of the 1850s. From 1789–1860 southerners dominated the federal government. Eight out of 15 presidents were southern slave owners and three more were so-called doughfaces, northerners with southern principles. Four of the southerners served two terms, but none of the northerners did so. The South also dominated the Supreme Court and the Senate up to 1850, if not the House of Representatives, though even in the House a gentleman's agreement not to agitate the slavery issue usually held good.[55]

The Southern grip on the political system explains why the great Missouri Debate of 8 December 1819 to 26 February 1821, which produced the historic "Missouri Compromise," was really a victory for slavery. The original constitution of the United States was a hidden compromise on the issue in that it allowed the states equality in the Senate and permitted the South to count three-fifths of its slaves in the allocation of seats in the House. This balance was maintained in practice by admitting a free state every time a new slave state was created. Hence in 1819, for the second session of the fifteenth Congress, there were 22 states, 11 in each camp. But by this time, the population was growing far more rapidly in the North than in the South. Missouri, which had been a territory since 1812, practiced slavery, and its constitution reflected the fact. If it was admitted to the Union as a slave state, Congress would, in effect, be permitting the extension of slavery beyond the Mississippi. On the other hand, the northerners wanted to admit Maine as a free state. What they proposed was to admit both states while imposing such constitutional restrictions on Missouri as to turn it from a slave to a free state. Southerners believed that if the North won the battle over Missouri, its next step would be to introduce progressive emancipation throughout the South.

When the debates began, with Henry Clay stating the South's case and James Tallmadge and John W. Taylor of New York on the other side, Representative Thomas Cobb of Georgia asserted: "You have kindled a fire which all the waters of the ocean cannot put out, which seas of blood only can extinguish."[56] President Monroe wrote to Jefferson on 19 February 1820: "I have never known a question so menacing to the tranquility and even the continuance of the Union as the present one." He kept out of the debate, but was planning to use his veto on any bill which made Missouri a state under restrictions, on the grounds that such a measure "if not in direct violation of the Constitution, is repugnant to its principles."[57] The compromise proposal eventually submitted by Clay as a bill accepted Missouri as a slave state and Maine as a free state, but made slavery unlawful in the Louisiana Territory north of latitude 36"30".

This compromise set a precedent for Congress to exclude slavery. But it also recognized that Congress had no right to impose upon a state seeking admission conditions which did not apply to existing states. Hence the way was opened for Arkansas and Florida to be admitted as slave states. As part of the compromise, Missouri undertook to pass a public act declaring that its constitution—which instructed its legislators to enact laws excluding Negroes and mulattoes from exercising rights—did not contravene the federal Constitution. It duly did so, in a defiant text which declared itself unnecessary, not binding and *ultra vires* on the part of Congress. Monroe nonetheless accepted the text as sufficient and admitted Missouri by proclamation on 10 August 1821. Four years later Missouri passed legislation "concerning [free] negroes and mulattoes" excluding them from the state unless they could prove they were citizens of another state by showing their naturalization papers, an impossibility by definition, since they had not been naturalized.[58]

The Missouri Compromise, then, was broadly in the interests of the South, reflecting its predominant political power. The passionate controversy certainly served to bring into existence the South as a self-conscious political entity. The compromise itself served to postpone any threatened breakup of the union for the best part of three decades, during which time the whole of America flourished. But the agreement, by drawing an actual geographic line between slavery and freedom, seemed to lay down the frontier of a future conflict. Jefferson called it "a fire-bell . . . the knell of the union"; and Adams, from the opposite standpoint, described it as "a mere preamble—a title page to a great, tragic volume." By postponing the showdown, however, it did something of great historical importance. If the Union had broken up in the early 1820s, the North would not have possessed the physical power to coerce the South, especially a South allied to Britain. The outcome would have been two Americas, and the history of the entire North American continent—and so the world—would have been quite different. Forty years later, however, the preponderance of the North was sufficient to keep the United States in one piece. So the compromise did not toll the knell of the Union; in the long run, it tolled the knell of slavery.

Meanwhile, the number of slaves rose, and antagonism between the races festered. Lynching was an American institution—it went back to the 1780s, to the last phase of the Revolutionary War, when Colonel Charles Lynch used "lynch law" against British Loyalists in Virginia Piedmont. It was used increasingly against blacks, but in the early decades of the 19th century, it usually expressed itself in 39 lashes (in accordance with the Old Testament); hanging came later.[59] Slave risings were not unknown. The earliest took place in 1712 in New York City, and in 1741 rumors there that another was planned produced a preemptive white rampage against blacks, the first recorded race riot in American history.[60] There was always excited talk of risings, among whites and blacks alike. In 1822, a free black, Denmark Vesey, a well-to-do Charleston carpenter, tried to organize a revolt, inspired apparently both by the Missouri debates and by the Book of Exodus. The rising was planned for 16 June, but word got out and the Richmond authorities struck at dawn, arresting 131 blacks; Vesey himself was caught a week later. During the summer he and 36 others were hanged, 43 others were transported, and 48 were whipped.[61] Most of Vesey's associates were skilled craftsmen, such as blacksmiths; they also tended to be strongly religious. Nine years later, another Virginian black, Nat Turner, also a religious radical inspired by Exodus, led a group of 60 slaves on a murderous foray, killing between 50 and 60 whites, before being hunted down and hanged.[62]

The Turner affair, though often described as "the greatest slave rising in American history," was, in fact, on a small, local scale. Granted the scale of slavery in the South, organized rebellions were rare. But individual slaves constantly ran away, and the South's efforts to get the North to enforce the old 1793 Fugitive Slave Law or to enact a more efficient one continued to envenom relations between the two sections of the nation. Slave rising were much more extensive and successful in the Caribbean area, where pockets and colonies of runaway slaves were common in the years after 1815. In the Deep South blacks who successfully evaded immediate pursuit often found refuge in these enclaves. Although slavery was highly profitable and well organized in the United States, there were in fact many more slaves in Central and South America. About 75 percent of the millions who were forcibly transported across the Atlantic went there.[63] Moreover, outside the Anglo-Saxon zone, and especially under Portuguese rule, cross-race unions and even marriages were common, producing multitudes of mulattoes (half-white, half-black), quadroons (products of white–half-black unions), and *sambos* or *zambos* (product of black–half-black unions).

Brazil, in particular, was an early example of a multiracial society. Indeed, it has been argued that in the early 19th century it had more bonds with Angola, Dahomey, and the Guinea Coast than with the "mother country," Portugal.[64] Brazil had an enormous number of slaves, continued to import them as long as it could, and (despite many promises) did not make slavery unlawful until the late 19th century. The slaves were often cruelly treated and lived an average of no more than 15 years in servitude. If they ran off and were recaptured, they were sent to the galleys for ten years, and horrible physical punishments were inflicted on them. Brazil's slaves came from many different parts of Africa, and it was government policy not to allow a large grouping from any one tribe of Africans to become numerically dominant in Brazil as a whole, to prevent uprisings. Bantu from Angola were preferred, being tall, submissive, adaptable, and easily converted to Christianity. Blacks from Dahomey were less tractable, especially if they were Muslims. The Hausas proved the most restless: they were behind all the big risings in 1806, 1813, 1814, 1822 and 1835.[65] These were put down with ferocity. But some Latin American revolts succeeded, especially during the wars of liberation, and manumission was much commoner in Latin America than in North America. Slaves and freed blacks lived in the same communities, the distinction between them being much less absolute than farther north: Latin American law, indeed, tended to treat slaves as persons, not as objects. But one must not exaggerate the compassion that these owners displayed. There were none of the guilt feelings of a Jefferson or a Madison. A rare surviving letter written by the mother of Simón Bolívar, the "Liberator," shows her discussing the purchase and sale of slaves and mules in the same paragraph. She will not buy a black woman—past childbearing age. A slave has escaped; she hopes he will be caught. She writes: "It makes one grieve to pay 300 pesos for slaves which you cannot use for more than eight years"—a short life span even by the usual Latin American standards. She calls them throughout "pieces."[66]

Only in the Caribbean were slaves actually in the majority in some islands. Most were there because of the huge and rising European demand for sugar. The consumption of sugar had risen steadily in the 18th century, when the first nonalcoholic drinks, coffee, cocoa and tea, became widely available (few people in towns and cities drank plain water because it had to be boiled first). The first commercial beet sugar had been produced in 1801 in Germany, and during the wars its consumption in Continental Europe had been boosted by the British naval blockade. After 1815 the Prussian government, which had no sugar colonies, subsidized the beet industry. But even as late as 1830, most European sugar was still coming from the tropics, especially the Caribbean.[67] These sugar islands, where blacks greatly outnumbered whites, were made for revolts. In the early 1790s, revolutionary French governments encouraged them, in the name of the Rights of Man, and Britain, which had over 600,000 slaves in her West Indian colonies, took a repressive line. Later in the wars, and especially after Britain outlawed the slave trade in 1807, these roles were reversed.

The French sugar colony of Saint Domingue (later Haiti) was the western third of the island of San Domingo, Spain having the rest. There were 500,000 slaves; 50,000 whites, mainly French; and at least 30,000 freedmen, or *affranchis*. The French abolished slavery there in 1793. The British occupied the colony and reintroduced slavery, then handed it back at the Peace of Amiens in 1802, by which time the French were in favor of slavery again. The result was a revolt, and a successful one, for the *affranchis,* who normally sided with the French and property, joined the slaves.

Haiti's first constitution (1805) was racial. All Haitians of whatever shade were to be known as *noirs;* no white could own property. When the original ruler, Jean-Jacques Dessalines, died in 1806, the territory split into two, the north under a black, Henri Christophe, the south and west under mulattoes led by Alexandre Petion. In 1815 the restored Bourbon government in France, under pressure from dispossessed planters, sent missions to both halves. Franco de Medina, appointed to negotiate with the north, was captured and his secret instructions were opened. They showed that France planned to restore colonialism and white supremacy. A few of the mulatto and black elites would be given equality with whites; very fair-skinned Negroes would be issued with *lettres des blancs,* and mulattoes would be put below whites—"It is of the first importance to preserve for the whites some superiority over the coloured class of the first rank"; then, in order, would come "shades between mulattoes and blacks," free blacks, and unfree plantation blacks to be returned "to the situation in which it stood before 1789." Troublemakers would be "transported to the Island of Ratau." Interrogated, Medina said this meant they would be executed—"It is an invention of the Minister [of Marine, Baron P. V. de] Malouet, not to wound the philanthropic feelings of His Majesty."[68] These terms were published in a work printed in Exeter in 1823, entitled *An Essay on the Causes of the Revolution and Civil Wars of Hayti,* by Baron Pompée

Valentin de Vastey, a prolific writer on race and colonialism who, though a mulatto, identified with the blacks. At a Te Deum to celebrate the unmasking of the French plot, De Vastey preached a violent sermon during which Medina was made to stand on a bench in disgrace and was nearly lynched afterwards. After some wriggling, the French government decided to recognize Haiti's independence, consider it a *colonie commerciale,* and negotate an exclusive trade treaty. De Vastey argued against this decision, too. His works show he was fully alive to the dangers of neocolonialism, and he laid it down flatly that Haiti should refuse to grant "an *exclusive* commerce to any nation whatsoever."[69]

Vastey might be regarded as the first black supremacist—the first writer, at any rate, to try to rewrite cultural history with an aim to remove what he saw as a white bias. He argued that Africa was "the cradle of the sciences and the arts" and that Egypt, Carthage and Ethiopia had been civilized when the Gauls were savages. He saw the independence of Haiti as a prelude to a general revolution in Asia and Africa, in which "five hundred million men, black, yellow and brown, spread over the surface of the globe, are reclaiming the rights and privileges which they have received from the author of nature."[70] In fact Haiti remained isolated. It sent help to the insurgents against Spanish rule in South America but this was not reciprocated since the new rulers feared the contagion of revolt among their own black slaves. So Haiti was not invited to the first Pan-American Congress at Panama in 1825. Nor was the United States friendly. On behalf of the South, Senator Thomas Hart Benson of Missouri argued that recognition by the United States would be to reward a slave insurrection. America, he said, "should not permit black Ambassadors and consuls to . . . give their fellow-blacks in the United States proof in hand of the honors that await them for a like successful effort on their part."[71] This anti-black argument prevailed and Haiti did not get American recognition until 1862, after the outbreak of the Civil War.

Britain, though friendly, did not accord Haiti recognition until 1825, by which time Haiti had come to an agreement on compensating French planters for their assets. Yet the Haitian leaders rightly recognized Britain as their best friend among the white powers. Henri Christophe was in regular correspondence with British antislavery campaigners, and he refused to incite revolts in British colonies. Baron de Vastey wrote: "England is the principal power in Europe that took a lively interest in our fate. It is England who first of all proposed the abolition of the slave trade and endeavoured to ameliorate the conditions of slaves. It is England who, by an order in council, considered us independent and sent directly and legally her ships to Hayti. We should then be, of all things, the most ungrateful and injust were we ever deficient in gratitude to the people and government of England." He went so far as to argue that much of Africa, despite its civilized heritage, was barbarous and that it was the mission of "noble and generous England" to civilize it by an enlightened colonial policy, since it could be "civilised only by conquest."[72]

It is not hard to see why a black advocate like De Vastey was an Anglophile. Though the French Revolutionary government had been the first to condemn slavery root and branch and to proclaim universal rights irrespective of race, the British had actually done a great deal more in practical terms to promote these objectives. That was only just: British appetites and interests had been important in building up international slavery as a huge commercial force. The British per capita consumption of sugar was the highest in the world. Even in the 1790s Britain had imported 70,000 tons of sugar a year. Of incomes derived from overseas, including Ireland, William Pitt told the House of Commons in 1798, about 80 percent came from the West Indies. By the time Jane Austen came to write *Mansfield Park* and *Emma,* in both of which the West Indies and slavery crop up, the English were consuming about 171 pounds of sugar a head each year.[73] The richest men in Britain, richer even than the Indian nabobs, were those with successful West Indian estates, such as William Beckford (1760–1844), whose income was reported in 1797 to be £155,000, plus £75,000 in duties paid to the government.[74] The great port of Liverpool, and the fortunes of men like W. E. Gladstone's father, John Gladstone, MP, were built largely on slavery. The total number of slaves carried across the Atlantic from Africa is a matter of dispute. At one time, the number was thought to have been as high as 15 million or even 20 million. Now a figure of 11.5 million is thought more likely, of whom 9.5 million were landed safely.[75] During the 1790s and the early years of the 19th century, the proportion of this trade carried in British ships had been rising fast, as the Royal Navy cleared the seas; indeed, between 1793 and 1807 it more than doubled.

But if the British carried heavy responsibilities, they were also prime movers in abolition. Thomas Clarkson (1760–1846), the most learned and indefatigable of the humanitarians, gives in his history of the abolitionist movement a long list of writers who argued against slavery, from Aphra Behn and Daniel Defoe, through Alexander Pope, William Shenstone, Richard Savage, James Thomson and Thomas Day.[76] Samuel Johnson in particular had attacked slavery on every occasion. He described Jamaica as "a place of great wealth, a den of tyrants and a

dungeon of slaves." At Oxford he toasted "success to the next revolt of
the Negroes in the West Indies."⁷⁷ On 22 June 1772, an important date
in world history, Lord Chief Justice Mansfield effectively ended the
legal status of slavery in England by ruling that it was "so odious that
nothing can be suffered to support it but positive law . . . Whatever
inconvenience, therefore, may follow from this decision, I cannot say
that this case is allowed or approved by the law of England; and
therefore the black must be discharged." The *Somerset* judgment covered Ireland, and six years later the Scottish judges took a similar line,
so by 1778 slavery ceased throughout the British Isles, and 14,000
human beings, worth £500,000, got their freedom.⁷⁸

Britain became not only the first slave-free area in the world, but a
base for the first international campaign with a humanitarian purpose.
Although the Quakers had already set up regular committees to organize antislavery agitation, it was Clarkson's decision in 1785 to devote
his life to the cause which produced what was, in effect, the prototype
modern pressure group. He traveled 35,000 miles to gather information,
interviewing witnesses, measuring slave quarters, examining mortality
rolls, and collecting actual specimens of leg shackles, thumbscrews,
instruments for opening the mouths of recalcitrant slaves, and other
gruesome artifacts of the trade. In 1791 he launched the movement
nationally with a network of Correspondence Committees, which,
among other things, distributed copies of William Cowper's *The
Negro's Complaint* and a beautiful cameo of a slave begging help, made
by Wedgwood. William Wilberforce had become a convert in 1787 and
the next year his friend William Pitt passed the first Act to regulate
conditions in the trade. The French Revolution paradoxically delayed
abolition because it allowed slave-trading interests to associate abolitionists with Jacobinism. But Clarkson and Wilberforce kept up the
fight throughout the 1790s and beyond and gradually forced the trade
to base its case solely on military and economic necessity, thus conced-
ing all the moral arguments against it. This in turn allowed the government to proceed with various ameliorating acts to humanize it.⁷⁹

Many of the campaigners, like Wilberforce himself, lived in Clap-
ham; the house next door to his, owned by Henry Thornton (1760–
1815), MP, a wealthy bachelor, was used for meetings of the "Clapham
Sect." Thornton's brother John, James Stephen (1758–1832), and Wil-
liam Smith (1756–1835) were also members of Parliament. Charles
Grant (1746–1823) was on the Court of Directors of the East India
Company; John Shore, Lord Teignmouth (1751–1834), was Governor-
General of Bengal; and Zachary Macaulay (1768–1838) was to become
Governor of the West African freed slave settlement in Sierra Leone.

The original members of the Clapham Sect were of the generation which reached maturity during the American War of Independence and were imbued with a strong sense that many things were fundamentally wrong with Britain and required reform. Ending the slave trade was only one of them, but it was the issue which most engaged their strong religious fervor, which was Evangelical—what we would now call fundamentalist. Not all lived in Clapham. Clarkson operated from central London and the Rev. Charles Simeon (1759–1836), from Cambridge, where he was a fellow of King's College and perpetual curate of Trinity Church, training generations of well-born young men in their duties as high-minded reformers. The Clapham focus, however, gave a family air to the sect. Many members of the sect intermarried, and their children carried on the work—Charles Grant, Jr., for instance, became a reforming Colonial Secretary and James Stephen, Jr., became head of the Colonial Office staff. Thomas Babington Macaulay (1800–59), MP, a leading reformer on a wide variety of fronts, was the product of a Clapham Sect union.[80]

The size, comparative wealth and social importance, and not least the members' nearness to the central machinery of the government of the British Empire, explains why the sect was able to exert a growing measure of influence. Its first big encouragement came in 1802 when Denmark made the slave trade unlawful. Two years later, the moderates among the slave trade became downright abolitionists. In 1807 an abolition Bill was passed, first through the Lords, then the Commons, and got the King's assent on 25 March 1807. James Stephen, who had 11 years' experience at the West Indies bar, insisted that this initial victory formed merely a platform on which the real reforming process—to end not merely the trade but the institution of slavery itself throughout British dominions and then the world—could begin. He recognized that in such a cause, publicity was vital. Nothing effective would be done, he claimed, "to check colonial crimes until we blazon them to the English public and arm ourselves with popular indignation."[81] An Enforcement Bill of 1811 for the first time made participation in the slave trade a transportable offense, but Stephen insisted this did not go far enough. He wanted compulsory registration machinery so that the right of property to individual slaves could be tested in the courts. In short, he was now shifting the thrust of the reform from ships to colonies. In 1815 he published, anonymously, the *Report of a Committee of the African Institute on the Reasons for Establishing a Registry of Slaves*. The case was accepted by the government, and by 1819 all British colonies had established registers.

The story of the way in which Britain moved against the slave trade and slavery itself is immensely complicated, but instructive in showing how fundamental improvements in the human condition are brought about. The opposition to reform was formidable. The West India Committee, looking after the interests of 1,800 planters, 1,200 of whom lived in Britain, bought up boroughs to protect its parliamentary position. It was said to be able to control the votes of 60–70 boroughs, including those of 56 members of Parliament who had a direct financial interest in slavery.[82] But the Felony Act of 1811, which threatened slavers with Botany Bay, began to knock the stuffing out of the interest. In *Mansfield Park,* Jane Austen shows Sir Thomas Bertram forced to dash out to the West Indies and spend a good deal of time there restructuring his estates to cope with the new legislation. Moreover, mass opinion was being roused, thanks to the efforts of Clarkson and Stephen to draw the gruesome facts of slavery to the attention of a hitherto largely indifferent public. By the time Jane Austen came to write *Emma,* it was plausible to show the officious Mrs. Elton deploring slavery just to be in the swim. As far back as 1797, William and Dorothy Wordsworth and their friend Samuel Taylor Coleridge had sweetened their tea or coffee with honey rather than use sugar, branded in their eyes with the shame of slavery. By 1815, such boycotting had become common and was used for a variety of political purposes. In autumn 1819, for instance, the radical *Black Dwarf* urged readers to "hit the government's pocket" by refusing to buy goods with heavy duties, and it showed them how to use hay tea instead of real tea and to mix roasted peas with mustard to make a substitute brew for coffee.[83] Cobbett had a different recipe for *ersatz* coffee in his *Examiner*—roasted wheat.

Avoiding sugar as a protest against slavery was by far the most popular of these boycotts. In 1828 the antislaver William Nais published a pamphlet devoted to the subject. "If we purchase the commodity," he argued, "we participate in the crime. The laws of our country may hold the sugar-cane to our lips, steeped in the blood of our fellow-creatures; but they cannot compel us to accept the loathsome potion." He calculated that a typical family, using 5 pounds of sugar a week, and a similar proportion of rum, which boycotted both for 21 months, would "prevent the slavery or murder of ONE fellow-creature; eight such families in 19½ years will prevent the slavery or murder of ONE HUNDRED!" If one in ten joined the boycott, he concluded, slavery in the West Indies would be abolished. He urged readers to use sugar from nonslave sources, such as the East Indies.[84] There is no evidence that the boycott ever reached such proportions. But it did enable ordinary people to believe they were taking part in the campaign. W. E. Forster, the Victorian statesman who first introduced compulsory schooling, remembered well the care his mother, Anna, took to avoid West Indian sugar.[85]

The success of the antislavery lobby lay in its ability to operate simultaneously at a number of levels. The facts were assiduously collected and documented by experts like Clarkson, Stephen, and Zachary Macaulay, who had been a horrified 16-year-old bookkeeper on a Jamaican plantation and returned after five years to edit the *Anti-Slavery Reporter* and to marry the sister of Wilberforce's friend, Thomas Babington. Unlike his more famous son, he was "a stern, silent man with a quick step and keen grey eyes" or, as a friend put it, "the silent father of the greatest talker the world has ever known." Like his son, however, he had a fabulous memory; he soaked up facts and blue books and docketed them all in his mind. Wilberforce used to say: "Let us look it up in Macaulay."[86] Stephen, who married Wilberforce's sister, was their most accomplished writer, who wrote the master handbook of the campaign, *Slavery Delineated*.[87] Wilberforce himself was the top parliamentary front man. He had two important virtues. First, he was funny. Stephen's son, Sir James, said that "no prejudice, dullness or ill-humour" could resist "his contagious mirth," as "irresistible as the first laughter of childhood."[88] In the Commons humor was a priceless asset, since debates on reform, as Thomas Creevey put it, were "uncommon dull." The second reason for Wilberforce's popularity in Parliament was that the members knew he possessed extraordinary powers of sarcasm and vituperation but was too good-natured to use them except in rare and provoking circumstances. At the same time, Wilberforce was both snobbish and deferential and always treated authority with respect. He had none of the self-righteous incivility of the zealot and always preferred conciliation and diplomacy to hectoring. Thus, he often persuaded ministers to go farther along the path of reform than they had originally intended. It is a striking tribute to the regard in which politicians held him that, when he finally got a second reading for his anti-slave trade Bill, the whole house of Commons, including many who had voted against him, cheered the little man, who sat "bent in his seat, his head in his hands the tears streaming down his face."[89]

Reinforcing Wilberforce was the less likable but far more formidable Henry Brougham. He framed and pushed through, and then saw to the enforcement of, the 1811 Felony Act. A ship's surgeon turned factor was sentenced to seven years transportation and his black assistant, a mere pawn, three years' hard labor. Two Britons operating the trade on the West African coast, caught in a Royal Navy raid, each got 14 years transportation.[90] These were among the few prosecutions needed, the

Act being so comprehensive and severe and inspiring such terror. It applied to any British subject anywhere in the world who bought or sold slaves or carried them with a view toward selling them, and it applied to foreign nationals in British territory. As far as the British Empire was concerned, it killed the trade dead and must be accounted one of the most effective pieces of legislation in history.

But, like Stephen, Brougham went from abolition of trading to registration of slaves and then to abolition in toto, a campaign he introduced in the Commons on 15 May 1823. Brougham argued with great force that slavery made it impossible in practice to give slaves the protection of the law. The whole system ought to go but in the meantime the government had a duty to take steps to end the worst cruelties on the estates. As a result of this debate, the Colonial Secretary, Lord Bathurst, sent a dispatch (28 May) to West Indian governors ordering two specific reforms—an absolute ban on the flogging of women and a regulation which forbade the drivers to carry or use whips in the fields. These reforms were more significant than Bathurst realized: the women slaves were much more difficult to manage than were the males, and the whip was a symbol of authority. Bathurst's dispatch also insisted that husbands and wives should not be separated and that religious instruction should be provided.[91] The understanding, between him and the antislavery lobby, was that the new regulations would be given a three-year trial.

On the former Dutch colony of Demerara, now British, where the treatment of slaves was traditionally harsh, the dispatch was received on 7 July. There were 78,000 slaves on the island and only one clergyman, John Smith, a Congregationalist, to look after them. The planters withheld the dispatch from publication. The slaves got to hear of its existence and believed that it ordered their emancipation, or at least the end of flogging (which was true, in part). As a result, on 18 August they rose on 50 estates, under the leadership of Jack Gladstone, from the Gladstone plantation. Only one white man was killed, but some planters were placed in the stocks. There followed a savage three-day repression. About 200 slaves were killed, 47 were executed, and others were sentenced to as many as 1,000 lashes. Since some of the ringleaders had belonged to Smith's congregation, he was put before a military court and sentenced to death. This sentence had to be confirmed from London, but in the meantime, Smith died in his damp dungeon on 6 February 1824.

The Smith case caused an uproar in Britain and did more than any other episode to inflame mass public opinion against slavery. As Brougham was able to show, Smith's trial broke all the elementary rules of English jurisprudence—hearsay evidence was admitted, additional evidence by the prosecution was put in after the defense had concluded, and there were many other irregularities. As Lord Dudley and Ward, himself owner of a Jamaican plantation, told the peers with West Indian properties, they "could not afford to disregard the cry of indignation which had come from every corner of the kingdom." Smith's diaries, which were made public, were heartbreaking, and Brougham made much of his martyrdom in a 10-day debate in the Commons in which he delivered one of his most scorching speeches.[92] From this point on, people with West Indian incomes liked to keep quiet about them, and Brougham rightly noted that the time had now come for the national movement to extract pledges from parliamentary candidates to vote against slavery. This took time to organize, but it led directly to abolition throughout the Empire in 1834.

It is not surprising that it took a quarter of a century to change the legal framework which made slavery possible in British territory. It was one of the oldest and deep rooted human institutions. Slavery was also more profitable than ever before. A single voyage from east to west across the Atlantic, carrying 800 slaves, netted a profit of £60,000 in the hardest currency, gold. Whatever the abolitionists said in their pamphlets, slave-plantations, especially the big, well-run ones where conditions were best, made big profits, and the West Indian interest, which was close to the heart of British politics, was terrified that if Britain ended slavery, her competitors would benefit. It was therefore important all along for Britain, which was always first in the antislavery cause, to ensure that other nations followed close behind, both in trading and employing slaves.

It is at this point that we must consider the role of the Royal Navy as the world's policeman. After the destruction of French and Spanish naval power at Trafalgar in 1805, the Royal Navy controlled the oceans and high seas and was able to impose a close blockade on Europe. It was well equipped and trained to stop and search vessels for contraband, so the Act of 1807 merely added another item, the detection of slaving, to its duties. Wartime conditions allowed it to act in a highhanded manner, if necessary boarding ships which appeared suspicious and taking them into harbor. The prospect of prize money sharpened the professional zeal of its captains. With the peace all this changed. In theory by 1814–15 most European nations had abolished the slave trade. In practice, only Britain was keen to suppress it. The first peace treaty with France (1814) gave her five years to abolish trading in slaves and handed back all her old slave depots on the African coast. This

agreement outraged the British public, and the antislavery lobby organized 806 mass petitions signed by no less than 750,000 people. As a
result Castlereagh had to make mutual policing agreements with major
powers a prime object of his peace policy. As he wrote to the British
ambassador in Madrid: "The nation is bent upon this object. I believe
that there is hardly a village which has not met and petitioned upon it.
Both houses of parliament are pledged to press it and the ministers must
make it the basis of their policy."[93] Castlereagh was lucky in the case
of France because Bonaparte, to curry popular favor during the Hundred Days, had abolished the slave trade, and abolition was written into
the second treaty (1815). At Vienna Castlereagh secured a general
statement from the powers condemning the trade, and he was able to
buy out Spain and Portugal, which agreed to limit the trade to south of
the equator in return for British waivers on loans and £300,000 in cash.
In return for a further £400,000, Spain signed a formal treaty in 1817
which provided for the abolition of slave trading even south of the
equator in 1820, mutual rights of search and mixed courts of British and
Spanish judges to try slavers—an excellent early example of international cooperation to put down transfrontier crime. A treaty with the
Netherlands, 4 May 1818, also provided mutual rights of search, and
Portugal agreed to similar terms.[94]

But it was one thing to sign treaties with European governments,
and quite another to make them meaningful in distant parts, especially
when former colonies became independent. Britain had a great deal of
trouble with Brazil, the prime market for slaves south of the Caribbean,
despite treaties with both Portugal and Brazil itself. Article Ten of the
treaty Britain signed with Brazil in 1810 specifically provided for the
gradual abolition of the slave trade. But this was evaded. So were
repeated agreements with both Portugal and Brazil to restrict the trade
to the southern hemisphere. Despite patrols by enforcement cruisers of
the Royal Navy, Bahia alone received 40,000 slaves in the years 1813–
17. In the three-year period 1815–17, Rio got 18,480 slaves from Angola
alone, and Pernambuco 15,342.[95] Another loophole was opened by the
attitude of the United States. Although America, as we have seen, had
herself abolished the slave trade, emotional wartime memories prevented the U.S. government from agreeing to mutual rights of search,
which allowed Royal Naval patrols to stop and board American ships.
This meant in practice that the American law was not enforced, for the
United States did not then possess the naval resources to mount regular
cordons. Since the Royal Navy was ordered to be punctilious in dealing
with American ships, any slaver could trade with impunity under the
United States flag.[96] From 1825, in theory, an American could be

hanged by the government for slaving, but none was until Lincoln became president. British diplomacy had more success, initially, with liberated Spanish colonies. In July 1821 Simón Bolívar's Gran Colombia passed what were known as "free womb laws," which freed children of slaves, if not their parents. But the serfdom of children, under the guise of "apprenticeship," was reimposed when the confederation broke up into Venezuela, Colombia and Ecuador. Chile, under strong British influence at the time, was the most libertarian, ending slavery and banning the trade in 1823. But in most other Latin American countries, slavery continued well into the 1840s, and some countries returned to trading—Colombia sold 800 slaves to Peru as late as 1845. Mexico ended slavery in the 1830s, but peonage in many severe forms continued. Uruguay followed Chile in ending slavery in 1842. Then came Colombia and Bolivia in 1851, Ecuador in 1852, Argentina in 1853, and Venezuela and Peru in 1854—the last two still having 58,000 slaves between them in that year.[97]

British policy was concerned not merely with bringing pressure on receiver-countries to end slavery but with suppressing the trade itself on the high seas and preventing African societies from gathering and exporting human beings. At the Colonial Office in 1816, there was a tiny establishment of 14: the Secretary of State, Earl Bathurst, his Under Secretary, Henry Goulburn, MP, the Permanent Secretary, a librarian, a translator and nine clerks. According to Goulburn, "several" of the clerks were employed on slavery-law enforcement duties all the time.[98] The enforcement of the antislavery law seems to have had priority over any other policy objective. As Castlereagh put it in a letter to the Opposition Whig Lord Holland: "The task is a most difficult one; and the more because the object is really felt by every Englishman and is urged by our newspapers and other publications with all the earnestness, not to say violence, with which we are accustomed to urge such objects, without consideration to the prejudices and feelings of others."[99]

Castlereagh and Bathurst, two converts who eventually became zealous, if never enthusiastic, suppressors of the trade, realized that Britain had to avoid antagonizing other powers whose cooperation was essential if slavery was ever to be ended. But it was hard not to be angered by the cynicism of governments which claimed to be civilized. From 1819, a senior naval officer was ordered to report annually on the state of the trade. Commodore Sir R. G. Collier, presenting the second report (16 September 1820), noted: "England, certainly, the whole world must acknowledge, has most faithfully abandoned the trade. America may be considered next in good intentions." He reported that the United States had sent naval units to Africa and other parts and "is engaged in its suppression with great sincerity." Spain was bad: "If Spain be sincere, she can show it only by compelling her colonies to observe her engagements." Holland was also bad—"in her colonies also the trade is encouraged"—and Portugal was no better. "But France, it is with deepest regret I mention it, has countenanced and encouraged the slave trade, almost beyond estimation of belief." In fact, "France is engrossing nearly the whole of the slave trade," so that in the last 12 months "60,000 Africans have been forced from their country, principally under the colours of France," and taken chiefly to Martinique, Guadaloupe, and Cuba. The Commodore feared that unless the Royal Navy had "the full powers of a belligerent" the laws against the trade "will become a mockery."[100]

But there was never any question of the navy getting such powers in peacetime. It had to do the best with the limited search rights it had under various treaties, which often gave the slaver the benefit of the doubt. On a small naval craft, copies of the treaties took up a large amount of space in the captain's cabin and had to be instantly available.[101] Off West Africa, the navy had operated an antislave squadron since 1808. An Admiralty Court to prosecute slavers had been set up in Freetown, which was the capital of the largest of a series of settlements established for freed slaves since the Mansfield judgment. Freetown had originally been run by the Sierra Leone Company (1791), under such governors as John Clarkson, brother of Thomas, and Zachary Macaulay, but by 1808 it was penniless and the Colonial Office had to take over. By 1815, with new batches of freed slaves continually arriving, its population had risen to about 10,000.[102] Freetown also had what was called a Court of Mixed Commission, to deal with foreign slavers. Two judges, one British, one from the country of the ship's registration, heard the case; if they disagreed, an arbitrator was appointed. If the ship was found to be slaving, the human cargo was freed, other cargo impounded, and the captain and crew returned under arrest to their country of origin.[103] In 1816 the British set up a new resettlement colony for freed slaves north of Sierra Leone, on the island of Saint Mary in the Gambia River, called Bathurst.

South of Sierra Leone was the American settlement of Liberia. As we have already noted, Liberia's primary purpose was to settle American freed blacks, of whom there were at least 250,000 by 1815. They were second-class citizens in the United States. As Henry Clay put it: "The laws it is true proclaim them free but prejudice more powerful than laws denies them the privilege of free men." However, only 17,000

American blacks were willing to go to Liberia in the first quarter century of its existence, the rest preferring to remain U.S. citizens, albeit inferior ones. The colony itself was a private venture, but the American government agreed to pay for the settlement of additional ex-slaves freed by its naval activities off the African coast. In 40 years, however, the U.S. Navy brought in only 5,722 ex-slaves, known as "Congoes."[104]

These early West African colonies had to be defended by cannon and stockades from the local native rulers, who rightly saw them as a threat to their profits from the slave trade. The whole of West Africa was geared to domestic slavery and to the slave trade. Many of the coastal towns were former fishing villages, which had become depots for the trade. But slavery had always been part of black African society. It was the usual method of recruiting labor for wealthy farms, for ironworks and gold mines. Slaves were also used to transport goods in long-distance trade and as a form of negotiable currency in transactions. Skilled laborers, such as blacksmiths, were usually slaves. For the chiefs, the transatlantic export trade was a bonus on top of these other aspects of their traditional slave system, but it was a valuable one and they were most reluctant to give it up.[105] The years after 1815 saw a growing British effort to explore and map the interior of Africa, as well as the coast. The Colonial Office, in supporting such ventures with cash and equipment, reminded explorers that ending the slave trade was the primary object. "You will endeavour by every means in your power," Bathurst ordered Hugh Clapperton, who was setting out on the Sokoto Expedition on 30 July 1825, "to impress on [the ruler's] mind the very great advantages he will derive by putting a total stop to the sale of slaves . . . [which] will cause him to be ranked among the benefactors of mankind."[106] This argument was unlikely to impress unless it was backed by more practical inducements.

It would have been a different matter if the colonies of freed slaves had obviously flourished. There were, it is true, one or two success stories. In Bathurst, a black who had bought his freedom in America set up as a merchant and branched out into government contracting and shipowning, dying rich in 1842.[107] In Monrovia, a newspaper, the *Liberia Herald,* was launched by James Russwurn, one of the first blacks to graduate from an American university. A more important case was Charles Heddle, son of a Senegalese mother, who began to grow and trade in groundnuts, palm oil, kernels and benniseed, operating from both Freetown and Gambia, but he retired to a château in France when he had made his pile. It took a long time, and much effort and cash from the British and later the French government, before exports in such tropical products became a viable alternative, in the eyes of African rulers, to the slave trade. Hence, as long as Brazil was prepared to pay good prices for slaves, the trade continued.

To reinforce its high seas patrols, the British government was driven to what became known as "gunboat diplomacy." The first mention of it came in a letter from Bathurst to one of the West Coast governors, Charles Turner, 19 December 1825. When native chiefs prove recalcitrant in cooperating with antislavery measures, he wrote, "A Gun Boat, or vessel of a similar description containing 40 or 50 men, who should be chosen from those most inured to the climate, would . . . serve as a rallying-point for such of the Neighbouring Tribes as may be disposed to cooperate heartily in suppressing the Slave Trade; and would materially relieve the Cruizers employed on this coast."[108] The first steamboat arrived on the coast in 1827; steam was important because it enabled authority to push right up the rivers, where sail was baffled. Local vessels were also taken into service to blockade parts of the coast, though such cordons had to be arranged with the consent of the tribes in the area. Indeed, the "rules of guidance" for naval officers and others holding commission to suppress the trade show the strict limits within which the British men on the spot had to act.[109]

On the West Coast, at least, some of the most inveterate and cunning slave operators were detribalized blacks, mulattoes, often freedmen or sons of former slaves, who had returned from Brazil to make their fortunes. One such black, Petro Kogio, based at Anecho, "raided for slaves and bought Manchester cottons," operating under a respectable front of palm oil. Another palm-oil dealer was George Lawson, a Fanti from Accra and former steward on a slaver, who "saluted all flags and provided false information for naval officers," dealt widely in slaves, and founded the rich Lawson dynasty. Another liberated slave, Francisco Felix Da Souze, acted as a slave broker for inland kings: "His riches and hospitality became the legend of the coast and he charmed even missionary opponents with manners which were easy and graceful and exhibited the finished gentleman."[110] The coast abounded with such rogues. An eyewitness described how the trade operated in the 1820s: "As soon as a vessel arrives at her place of destination, the crew discharge her light cargo, with the manacles intended for the slaves, and land the captain at the same time. The vessel then cruises along the coast to take on country cloth, ivory, a little gold dust etc., and if a British man-of-war be near, the crew having nothing on board to excite suspicion, in most cases contrive to get their vessel searched whilst trading with the natives. . . . They return to the place where the cargo has been loaded and communicate with the captain on shore [who tells them] the exact time he will be in readiness to embark. The vessel then cruises a second time up and down the coast till the appointed day when she proceeds to take in her living cargo."[111] The profits for the wily were huge. A slave bought for £15 or £20 in Lagos would fetch £50 to £80 in Brazil, and sometimes as much as £120. The vessels were often fast clippers, usually built in New England and even flying the American flag, though more usually French and Portuguese. They could outpace most Royal Naval ships.

The failure to stamp out the slave trade with the speed the antislavery lobby demanded brought constant accusations from the lobby that British naval officers, and colonial governors, were halfhearted. Naval and Colonial Office papers show this accusation to be untrue. Naval officers with direct experience of the trade grew to hate it and often risked their careers by exceeding their authority in suppressing it. Most colonial officials were punctilious and often zealous in carrying out Parliament's wishes. Governor Robert Farquar of Mauritius, though criticized by the lobby, "hated the slave trade with a passion which became, in a few years, almost an obsession."[112]

One problem the British faced was the sheer extent of the trade. The Atlantic passage got the most attention, but there was an enormous volume of slaving throughout the Indian Ocean, most of it in the hands of Arabs. The Arab slave network stretched as far as the West African coast, where the Arabs worked closely with black Muslim chiefs, but whereas the French and Portuguese dominated the Atlantic long-distance trade, the trade in the Indian Ocean and adjoining seas was largely in Arab hands. The center of the trade was Zanzibar Island, where it was estimated in 1835 that two-thirds of the population were slaves. With the exception of the Masai and the Somalis, all the tribal groups of East Africa were milked by Arab slavers. The hinterland, wrote one British naval captain, was like a vast hunting preserve, which the Arabs worked in the slaving season each year "as you might work a [grouse] moor after the 12 August."[113] Arab dhows could make the 2,400-mile trip from Zanzibar to Arabia in 17–18 days. On arrival, boys up to age 10 fetched a maximum of $15, teenagers up to $30. Females cost more and might go for $40, if pretty. They were often used for sex, then returned to the slaver at a reduced price. The Habashi, or Abyssinian, females were the most highly prized, fetching up to $150, and Abyssinian males were also in demand as servants in princely households. Most of them were Christians, and their liberation became a particular object for naval officers and missionaries alike. The slaves were taken up the Persian Gulf and landed at Bushire for transfer to the

Persian interior, or at Basra for Mesopotamia and southwest Turkey. But Arab slavers also operated right down the coast to Mozambique and transferred their haul to European-owned slavers for transatlantic shipment.

It was a huge coast for the Royal Navy to cover and the first thing the service had to do was map it. By 1830 a tremendous effort, led by Captain Philip Morgan, Lieutenant J. M. Guy, and Captain George Brucks, had succeeded in producing reliable coastal charts stretching as far as the Persian Gulf. Twenty years later the entire coastline of the Indian Ocean had been accurately mapped.[114] The charts were desperately needed because naval antislavery missions usually involved penetrating river estuaries and sending parties upriver in small boats, gigs, pinnaces, cutters, and the like. The losses from disease on this coast, particularly around and south of the equator (as in West Africa) were horrifying. Captain William Owen, commanding a warship assigned to the coast from 1821 to 1826, lost more than half his crew in less than two years, and of the 44 officers who served under him, only 13 returned to England. There was not much in it for those serving in the navy, other than the occasional satisfaction of putting villainous traders behind bars. They did a discreet amount of "liberation," especially of the jewelry with which Arab traders liked to adorn pretty slaves to raise their price. But until 1833, when the government sensibly introduced official prize- and bounty money, all they got were occasional cash presents from antislavery societies.[115]

At all times naval commanders had to avoid offending local rulers or falling foul of the law, not least in India (Bombay was particularly difficult). Hence, their rejoicings at "a fair cop." Englishmen who were caught could expect to be savagely punished, even in a marginal case. Commander J. C. Hawlings of the East India Company's sloop-of-war *Clive* was sent to East Africa to recruit black volunteers for the East India Navy. At Lindi, he got 34 in return for a cash payment of $2,000. The "volunteers" turned out to be slaves; he was charged with piracy in the Bombay Supreme Court and got seven years' transportation to Botany Bay.[116] Gradually, during the years 1815–30, Admiralty courts were set up throughout the region and registers were compiled. But often the most effective way in practice to stop smuggling of what were called "new Blacks" to slaving centers was simply to bribe the chiefs, as Castlereagh had bribed the European governments. On 23 October 1817, Ramada, the Hova chief on Madagascar, signed a treaty prohibiting the sale or transfer of slaves, in return for which Britain agreed to pay him an annual indemnity of $1,000 gold and $1,000 silver, plus 100 barrels of gunpowder, 100 muskets, "one full-dress coat," and "other dress stuff" for his troops. Three years later the treaty was renewed, with a further British promise of training craftsmen and musicians in England to "form a band for the regiment of guards of His Majesty the King of Madagascar."[117]

The British naval personnel did not always like these dubious deals with local potentates. There was a strong Evangelical tradition in the navy, and many officers were deeply religious. These officers were as fierce as missionaries in deploring the wickedness of natives. They liked, for instance, the Seychelles because of its excellent climate and vegetation; but they deplored the practice of incest there—"too common to take notice of," as one officer reported; a native official there, he added, was "the son of his grandmother by his own brother."[118] Another ship's master, ordered by the Admiralty to send in notes on places he visited, reported of Muscat in the Gulf: "Inhabitants of Muscat. As to manners, they have none. As to their customs, they are very beastly." He reported to his commanding officer: "There, Sir, I have obeyed orders and you will find all I could write about these black fellows, and all they deserve."

In fact, Muscat was the capital of Oman, whose sultan, Seyyid bin Sultan Ali Bu Saidi, was assiduously cultivated by the British as a valuable ally in the anti-slave trade effort and in much else. Richard Burton was later to call him "as shrewd, liberal and enlightened a prince as Arabia ever produced."[119] Born in 1791, the sultan began to establish his rule at age fifteen and made it a point always to cooperate with Britain, and especially with the Royal Navy, in return for support against his many enemies. Though Muscat had been a traditional slaving center, he agreed to abandon the trade, despite the loss of revenues, in return for British support in building up a navy. He learned to sail ships and slowly acquired a fleet not only of modern merchantmen, but of sloops, corvettes, and frigates, augmented, in 1826, by the 74-gun *Liverpool*, a ship of the line built for him in Bombay. He thus built up "a more efficient naval force than all the native princes combined, from the Cape of Good Hope to Japan," and by its means established a maritime empire from Aden to the head of the Persian Gulf. The British looked benevolently on his growing power, since they could ensure it was exercised in their interest, as well as that of humanity. So they not only supplied him with arms but made him a Member of the Royal Geographical Society and sent him a service of silver-gilt plate (unfortunately put in the wrong box, so that the Sultan, eagerly opening his present, found only a large tombstone intended for the grave of a British sailor who had died in the Gulf).[120]

The arrangement with Oman was just one aspect of a growing

British penetration of Arabia and its environs, made permanent by the establishment of "residences" in Basra and Baghdad. From 1812 the senior British resident in Turkish Arabia was renamed Political Agent. This marked the foundation of a British presence in the area which was to last until the 1960s. And the Arabian presence was itself only one segment of an enveloping cloak of empire and influence which Britain was flinging across all the oceans, including the Indian one. The foundation of this power was the Royal Navy and, indeed, it was the needs of the navy, in harbors, docks and arsenals, which increasingly dictated the points at which this growing empire, fundamentally a maritime one, touched land. Equally it was the strength and activity of the navy which held the Empire together and which made its influence felt well beyond its nominal possessions.

In the years 1815–30, this navy, in absolute terms, was much weaker than during the Napoleonic Wars, but in relative terms, its strength was unparalleled. At the time of the Peace of Amiens (1802–03), the then-prime minister, Dr. Addington, told the Commons that Britain, with 202 ships of the line, had a superiority of 60 over the French, Dutch, and Spanish ships combined. After Trafalgar in 1805, the superiority was even greater: Britain had 250 ships of the line, the whole of the rest of Europe only 239. By 1812 Britain still had 250, as against about 100 French ships, plus 42 ships belonging to Denmark, Russia, and Sweden. These were theoretical strengths. Only a portion of the fleet was actually in commission—manned, fitted and supplied—at any one time. It is also worth noting that by no means all British ships were built in Britain. In the years 1793–1815 the Royal Navy captured from France alone 113 ships of the line and 205 frigates, of which 83 ships of the line and 162 frigates passed into British service. When the wars finally ended, France had to surrender 31 battleships, and all other European navies laid up or scrapped many units.[121] This enabled Britain to make huge cuts. At the time of Waterloo, the navy, already much reduced, had 99 battleships in commission and a total of 140,000 seamen on the pay lists. Two years later, only 13 battleships were commissioned, and 19,000 men. There were 60 admirals, 850 captains, and over 4,000 lieutenants on the active list, the great majority of them unemployed.[122] Indeed, you might say that Jane Austen's *Persuasion*, published the same year, is a tale of what happened to English society when unemployed naval heroes, like Admiral Croft and Captain Wentworth, "came ashore." Both these officers were rich because they had been in the right place at the right time and collected fortunes in prize money. Under the Cruisers Act (1708), renewed at the beginning of each war,

Crown rights to the value of captured vessels were divided into eighths: three-eighths went to the captain of the ship which took the prize, one-eighth to the commander in chief of the fleet or squadron, one-eighth to the officers, one-eighth to the warrant officers, and two-eighths to the crew. Thus, when the Spanish treasure ship *Hermione* was captured by the frigates *Active* and *Favourite* in 1762, and "condemned in prize" for £519,705, each of the captains received £65,000 and even the ratings (enlisted men) got £485 each. In 1793 the *San Iago*, carrying £25 million in specie, made £50,000 for the Admiral, Hood, and £30,000 each for the captains of the squadron. Again, in 1799, two frigate captains got £40,000 each when they forced two Spanish ships to surrender off Finisterre. Lord Exmouth, the victor of Algiers who began life penniless, made himself a rich man by his prizes as a frigate commander and bought a handsome estate in Devon. But these were exceptions. Most naval actions brought no prizes. No one present at Trafalgar, the greatest battle of all, got a penny. As the Royal Navy cleared the seas, the chances of prize money fell, and with the peace, it virtually ceased. Five out of six officers were idle on half-pay, and ratings, apart from gunner-specialists on seven-year contracts, were hired and discharged for specific service, as in the mercantile marine.[123] In the first years of peace, the navy was not an attractive career for ambitious men.

During the 1820s, as the Empire spread itself, the active navy expanded marginally. In 1827, for example, there were 17 capital ships in commission. The remaining 78 were laid up and dismantled, their guns lying by the thousands in neat rows at naval depots. But these 17 were formidable ships, each carrying 74 to 100-plus smooth-bore big guns. The biggest ship weighed about 4,500 tons and carried up to 1,000 officers and men. Such ships were built entirely of oak and a three-decker consumed 900 acres of 3,500 full-grown trees. They were driven by 50,000 square feet of canvas—11 square sails on 3 masts, plus 3 jibs, 4 staysails, 10 stunsails, and a spanker, with 2 sets of each aboard—and were fitted with 80 tons of spars, 900 blocks, and 34 miles of rope, some of it 6 inches thick. Windpower could not drive them, even with that enormous spread of sail, at much over 10 knots, but they could ride any weather and stay at sea for years, if necessary. They were the most frightening things on earth, looking enormous close-to, and each broadside weighed 1,928 pounds, carrying huge destructive power. As deterrents, they were well worth their £120,000 cost to a far-flung empire. By the mid-1820s, however, they were comparatively rare, most battleships being two-deckers, costing only £70,000, between 2,900 and 3,800 tons, firing a broadside of just over 1,000 pounds and sailing rather faster. In addition Britain had 124 frigates of 700 to 1,700 tons, carrying 28 to 50 guns and 180 to 460 men, plus 110 sloops of 16–20 guns, and a number of cutters and schooners. There were at least 45 frigates and 70 sloops in commission at any one time.[124]

The 1820s navy, which had cost £14.5 million to build and required £6,126,000 annually to maintain, had a total of 349 ships "in condition for service," mounting 15,710 guns. On paper it looked formidable. But only half the ships were commissioned and of these a third or more were on home service. Britain's global responsibilities were discharged by 9 two-deckers, 33 frigates, and 60 sloops, distributed between eight foreign stations—North America, South America, the West Indies, the East Indies, the Mediterranean, West Africa, the Cape and Lisbon. The capital ships were nearly always in the Atlantic, though sometimes in the Mediterranean. Far-flung stations rarely saw them. The real work was done by the frigates and sloops.

The slender resources of Britain's active naval power, covering millions of square miles of ocean, were adequate simply because there was no real rivalry. In 1815 France had retained, by way of overseas possessions, only two West Indian islands, Senegal in West Africa, and three posts on the Coromandel Coast of India (Pondicherry, Chandernagore and Karikal); it took her in effect 15 years, until 1830, before she was ready to expand colonially again. Holland had been reinstated by Britain as a colonial power in Southeast Asia primarily because Castlereagh needed her as a "strong" power in Europe, but, as we shall see, steps were taken to neutralize her Asian pretensions. The Spaniards still held the Philippines, but they lacked the cash for anything except to hang on grimly—indeed, these islands were themselves subsidized from Spanish Mexico. The Portuguese, in addition to Macao off the South China Coast, had three stations in India, including Goa, but Goa was dependent on British protection. They also had Mozambique in East Africa, but it was bankrupt. The one formidable and expanding colonial power was Russia, and it was British policy to keep her bottled up in the Black Sea—hence the necessity to ensure that Turkey remained formidable in that area.[125]

For all practical purposes, the South Atlantic, the South and Central Pacific, and the South Seas generally were controlled solely by Britain. From 1815 and for many decades, the Indian Ocean was a British lake. There, the power of the Royal Navy was reinforced by the East India Company, which had its own army and navy. The French strategist Baron Charles Dupin, in an address to the Institut de France, enviously remarked: "From the banks of the Indus to the frontiers of China, from the mouths of the Ganges to the mountains of Tibet—all acknowledge the sway of a mercantile company, shut up in the narrow streets of the City of London."[126] The big East Indiamen, insured for £250,000 or more, weighed up to 1,200 tons. They operated a monopoly of the Britain–India trade until 1813 and were preponderant in it until the 1840s, and they retained the monopoly of the China trade until 1833. In 1801 the Company had 122 of them, not counting India-built ships, averaging 870 tons; the larger ones mounted 30 to 40 guns, could deal with raiders of all sizes, and even see off a ship of the line. Traveling in groups, as they usually did, they were immune to the attacks of all but a major naval power.[127] But in the last resort, the security of the sea-lanes carrying this immensely valuable traffic depended on the Royal Navy.

The navy, in turn, depended on bases, which became increasingly important as coal-fired steamboats began to join the fleet in the 1820s. Ships using wind power could be provisioned at sea, careen themselves on any deserted tidal beach, and at a pinch could stay out of harbor for years. But steam warships, though vital to the Navy's increasing security role because of their ability to follow slavers, pirates, and other antisocial elements upriver, needed coaling stations. And, in general, the smaller the force available, the more need for secure, well-equipped bases, which could keep the maximum units on patrol. The Treasury's parsimony decreed that only two squadrons of frigates and sloops were available to police the 17 million square miles of the Indian Ocean. But the same desire to protect the taxpayer made it hard for the navy to build up the network of bases it needed. Right at the end of the Napoleonic Wars, it was able to move from the inadequate harbor at Cape Town to Simonstown, 23 miles to the south, a superb natural harbor which became, and remained until the 1960s, one of the world's great naval bases. Simonstown was the headquarters of the Cape Squadron. The British could also use the good harbors, such as Delagoa Bay, on the coast of Mozambique. They had an arrangement with the ruling Hovas in Madagascar, an island from which the navy had ousted the French in 1811, to supply them with arms and, from 1818, with missionaries, who built 50 schools, in return for base facilities.[128] Farther along the ocean route to India, they now had the former French colony Ile de France, renamed Mauritius, which became a minor base. In India itself, the harbors were poor, with Bombay, the main port of entry on the west, being particularly unsatisfactory. In 1815 the navy surveyed the magnificent natural base at Trincomalee in Ceylon and drew up plans to make it the center of the main fleet at the head of the ocean. But again, pressure from the Treasury was felt, and even as late as 1830, the new base was not fully equipped and many units continued to use Bombay.

The navy's quest for bases was intermeshed not only with Treasury policy but with Colonial Office thinking. That brings us to one of the least known but, in some ways, most influential men of the era, Henry, 3rd Earl Bathurst (1762–1834), who was Secretary of State for War and Colonies for 15 years, 1812–27, the whole span of the Liverpool ministry. The Colonial Office was a department created in the 1790s by hiving off a small section (two clerks) of the Home Office and gluing it onto the War Office. It was Bathurst who created it as an institution in its own right. This was an odd thing for a man of his temperament to do, for he was by nature conservative, reticent and, above all, silent: so conservative, indeed, that after the passing of the Reform Bill, he refused to have anything further to do with politics or even to hear the political news; so reticent that he never went out in society unless forced; and so silent that, though a member of Parliament for the family borough of Cirencester, Gloucestershire, from 1783 until he succeeded to his father's peerage in 1794, and for most of that time a junior minister, he spoke so seldom that he had left no impression at all on the parliamentary records.[129] But he was not exactly a diehard. He voted for the abolition of the slave trade as early as 1786 and always acquiesced in change when fairly convinced it was needed, then enforced the new measures with energy. He was a politician of the old school (his father had been Lord Chancellor), and by the 1820s he had amassed a combined income from offices, real and nominal, of over £10,000 a year—nor was he backward in securing more for his kin. But he was scrupulously honest and insisted on honesty in others; even Mrs. Arbuthnot, who disliked him intensely, admitted that "there cannot be a more disinterested man."[130]

Above all, Bathurst was experienced and assiduous. He had been at the Treasury, the Exchequer, and the Board of Control (India) and had been President of the Board of Trade and, for a short while, Foreign Secretary, before taking over War and Colonies. He knew more about how the central machinery worked than any other member of the Liverpool government. He was a minister of the old school, too: That is, he ran the office and made all the political decisions himself. To some extent, as was proper, he shared responsibilities with his parliamentary under-secretaries, in succession Goulburn and Wilmot Horton, both because they were unusually able and because they had to answer for the office in the Commons. But nothing of consequence was ever delegated to civil servants. The clerks were there to copy letters, not to write them; the Permanent under-Secretary was there to ensure that the clerks did their business.

It is impossible to understand the old system of government in Britain, especially its virtues, without grasping the fact that the good, and successful, ministers did the actual work. William Pitt was very much a prime minister in this tradition; he could stand up in the Commons and answer in detail, and without notice, questions about every aspect of his government, as William Cecil had done more than 200 years before. Pitt's protégés, Castlereagh and Canning, were like-wise omnicompetent ministers, and the tradition was carried on by Peel and Palmerston, with whom it finally died in 1865. At Bathurst's de-partment, the civil servants finally took over under Sir James Stephen, Permanent Under-Secretary from 1836 to 1848, and even before that, in 1833, Henry Taylor, senior clerk in the West Indian Department, had boasted: "I have been employed, not in the business of a clerk, but in that of a statesman. . . . I have been accustomed to relieve [ministers] from the trouble of taking decisions, of giving directions, of releasing despatches and writing them . . . the more important the question has been, the more have I found my judgment to be leant upon."[131] But in Bathurst's time, he and his Number Two were still everywhere in charge, despite the continuous increase in business.

Bathurst and his Colonial Office worked from 14 Downing Street, which he ran like a gentleman's London house. The building was not perfect—the cellar regularly flooded in heavy rain—but it was conve-nient, and as its work increased, the office spread into two nearby properties. The clerks were not bound to arrive before 11 A.M., but if they came earlier, Bathurst gave them breakfast (this was also the practice at East India House, where Charles Lamb worked—indeed, there the senior officials got breakfast whatever time they arrived). They had to remain till 4 P.M. "or until the business of the office be over." Under Bathurst, the 4 P.M. knocking-off time became academic. In 1806 the Colonial Office had received 1,653 letters (totaling 8,054 pages) and dispatched 902 (922 pages). After four years of his adminis-tration, the figures had risen to 4,487 (22,269 pages) received and 3,161 (2,957 pages) sent. Eight years later, in 1824, incoming letters had jumped again to 7,491 (35,836 pages) and outgoing letters to 4,957, though the last, totaling 5,257 pages, showed that Bathurst was still keeping his instructions short.[132] With 36 territories, many expanding fast, to oversee, he was in the midst of this constant inflow of queries and outflow of orders. "For a sedulous discharge of the peculiar duties of his office," Wilmot Horton wrote of him, "no public man who has ever filled that situation was more remarkable."[133] He liked replies to incoming dispatches to go out, if possible, by return mail, as at the Admiralty. There was an 8 P.M. mail coach for Falmouth, the last port at which outgoing dispatches could be taken aboard ship, and when ships were leaving for the West or East Indies, there was a frantic rush to get replies ready for the post. Taylor, chief clerk from 1825, said they sometimes worked till 2 A.M. They were particularly busy when Parliament sat, for the number of printed papers laid before the Commons rose from 14 folio pages in 1806 to 2,200 in 1825.

It was one of the characteristics of the post war world to demand systematic statistics, particularly on slavery and emigration which the Colonial Office began to supply from 1821; these statistics were in what was called Blue Books, from the color of the volumes sent out to governors to fill in.[134] Much of the work was wrapped up in elaborate security. Letters were marked in an upward gradient of Private, Confidential and Secret, Private and Confidential, the last category supposedly seen only by the two "politics," though the Registrar probably also knew their contents. Taylor recorded that in March 1824 he was "working in [14] Downing Street night after night till one or two in the morning, in the preparation of a paper which was immediately printed on the Foreign Office private press and laid before the Cabinet. . . . A clerk was sent to see the types broken up and to receive the printer's declaration that he had delivered all the impression taken off and kept no copy. The impressions delivered I was directed to keep under lock and key and give to no one."[135]

Bathurst made his staff work hard, but—unlike Palmerston, another fierce taskmaster—without rendering himself unpopular, probably because he had an excellent sense of humor and, while hating to make speeches, loved to tell stories. Charles Greville, once his private secretary, said his conversation consisted entirely of anecdotes.[136] Bathurst was also respected for working exceptionally hard himself, writing rapidly in an exquisite hand, his drafts requiring scarcely any corrections, and was known as a skilled compromiser and good Cabinet man, adept at getting his colleagues to endorse his decisions. He built up a library of reference works and newspaper clippings, put in a mapmaking machine, installed a full-time cartographer and got the office to make effective use of one of the earliest copying machines, which went back to 1799. The machine used dampened sheets of very thin paper, which were read holding them up to the light because the writing was reversed. Under Bathurst, it was now in action "daily," producing, according to Horton, "an extreme saving of time and labour."[137] It was one of Bathurst's strengths that he was throroughly familiar with the office's archives and could not be bamboozled by appeals to precedent;

long before his 15 years came to a close he knew more about the Empire than any one else alive.

Bathurst had no colonial policy, at any rate in theory. What he did, in characteristic English fashion, was to evolve a code of practice based on pragmatic decisions. In effect he authorized British representatives to do what was right, when something demonstrably needed doing and there was no one else to do it. To a limited extent, then, he was responsible for Britain becoming an unofficial world policeman. But the role was curbed, at all times, by Treasury restraints. Not only was the Treasury mean in itself, the whole thrust of reformers and radicals was in favor of economy. Edmund Burke had begun the campaign as a means of curbing the power of the Crown. The campaign succeeded, backed as it was by all the "rational" intelligentsia, led by Adam Smith and Jeremy Bentham, and it certainly made the government more efficient and less corrupt. But it made cutting governmental expenditures a moral as well as a political objective, an end in itself. We are accustomed, in the late 20th century, to a political spectrum in which the Left favors public spending and the Right seeks to reduce it. In the early 19th century the postures were reversed. The radicals were outraged by the size of governmental departments, the salaries paid to bureaucrats, and the fact that 60 percent of governmental revenues went for servicing the national debt (which they wanted eliminated by a capital levy). It was the radical Brougham, as we have seen, who buried income tax. From 1820, a sharp and parsimonious member of Parliament from Aberdeen, Joseph "Economy" Hume (1777–1855), who had made a fortune as a surgeon in India, began to go systematically through governmental accounts, querying even the most beggarly items, and encouraging colleagues and Commons committees to use their muscle to cut "waste" and "jobs" of all kinds.

Hence, Bathurst had to fight hard to retain the means for the Colonial Office to do what he believed was indispensable. There was nothing left for adventures. And in any case he was far from being an imperialist. The source of many of his office jokes was the activities of the Permanent Under-Secretary at the Admiralty (formally known as the Second Secretary, the political, or First Secretary being the redoubtable John Wilson Croker, MP). Sir John Barrow (1764–1848), who held this key post, with one brief interruption, from 1804 to 1845, was an imperialist of the same type as Captain Pasley—that is, he believed that law and civilization were usually coterminous with British authority and that to extend the third was to promote the first two. Bathurst liked to pretend that Barrow was a fire-eater. He once wrote on a paper in which Barrow proposed a forward move: "If coveting Islands or Foreign Settlements is a breach of the Tenth Commandment, he is the greatest violator of the Decalogue in the Kingdom."[138] To which Barrow might reply that, while Bathurst had never stuck his nose beyond Dover Beach, apart from the gentlemanly "grand tour," he himself had been all over the world and had seen its horrors and knew from experience how beneficent the presence of a British frigate could be, or even a British crown colony.

Barrow had been born in a cottage in Ulverston, at the southern tip of the Lake District—he called himself a "North Lancashireman." By prodigious efforts, he had made himself a first-class mathematician and geographer, and throughout his life he was an enthusiast for scientific exploration. He was behind the huge naval effort which, in one generation, charted the world's coasts and oceans, and he effectively founded the Royal Geographical Society. He had been the first Englishman to go up in a balloon, had hunted whales off Greenland, had gone to China with Lord Macartney's famous embassy, had traveled thousands of miles, mostly on foot, in Cape Colony and beyond (marrying a Boer girl); and had become an expert on the movements of icebergs.[139] He knew the workings of the navy and the colonial system from on-the-spot observation, and if he was inclined to be too security conscious—always proposing another forward base to "protect" an existing base—he was also painfully aware of the opportunities that Britain was missing, through misplaced economy, to exploit her naval preponderance in the interests of humanity. He was an indignant foe of slavers, pirates and other human jackals.

Barrow's strength, in his tussles with Bathurst, was that there was no lack of adventurous men on the spot who were prepared, in the tradition of Robert Clive, to put the Union Jack where it was needed. Deep anger had been caused, among British experts on the East, by Castlereagh's decision in 1814 to restore to the Dutch all their East Indies possessions. Castlereagh wanted a strong and wealthy Holland to contain France from the north, and he wanted to demonstrate that Britain approached peacemaking and the future security of Europe in a spirit of generosity, seeking not (like Prussia, Russia, and Austria) to grab territory and "souls," but to make the world safe for trade.[140] To those who knew the Indies, Castlereagh's decision made no sense, since the Dutch were then monopolists who hated free trade with all their hearts. The humanitarians among them were particularly indignant because of the bad Dutch record.

Among the younger men, the one most determined to remedy what he saw as Castlereagh's fatal error was Thomas Stamford Raffles

(1781–1826). This thin, sickly looking, intensely earnest and obsessive polymath was, literally, a child of the Empire, having been born aboard the West Indiaman of which his father was captain. At age 14 he was put into the East India House, in Leadenhall Street, as a clerk, where he quickly showed the zeal and enthusiasm his colleague Charles Lamb, six years his senior, so clearly lacked. In 1805, aged 24, he was sent east as assistant to the Chief Secretary in Penang Island, the British outpost off the northwest coast of Malaya, at the princely salary of £15,000 a year. Two years later he was promoted to the number two post and, when Britain took over the Dutch possessions, he was put in charge of Java, which he ruled from August 1811 to March 1816.

Raffles was essentially an autodidact, who mastered geography, anthropology, botany and zoology largely on his own. He possessed, Sir Joseph Banks, President of the Royal Society, wrote of him, "a larger stock of useful talent than any other individual of my acquaintance." He had a particular gift for teaching himself oriental languages. He was much helped by John Leyden, another phenomenal Scot, the son of a Highland shepherd, who had taken an honors degree in Hebrew at Edinburgh University at age 10, then went on to master medicine and to make himself the first international authority on the languages of the Far East. Leyden was a tiresome pedagogue who talked incessantly in what the Governor-General of India, Lord Minto (1751–1814), termed "a shrill, piercing and at the same time grating voice," but he enabled Raffles to master Malay and related tongues, and it was Raffles's ability to talk fluently in the local languages which made the young man such an effective negotiator.[141]

A further point in Raffles's favor, and the key to understanding him, was his deep sympathy with the peoples of the region. Raffles hated cruelty, especially to the defenseless, whether they were native villagers or animals. He opposed slavery with a passion that rivaled Wilberforce's, and made himself enemies in high Leadenhall Street places by manumitting the East India Company's slaves on the smallest pretext. He was delighted when Minto, visiting Malacca, insisted on blocking up the local prison, a hole in the rock, destroying all the instruments of torture found there, and freeing all the slaves and indentured laborers. He wanted the Dutch swept out of the Indies for good, writing to Minto (10 June 1811) that "solely attentive to their own commercial interests [the Dutch] have in their intercourse with these regions invariably adhered to a more cold-blooded, illiberal and ungenerous policy than has ever been exhibited towards any country, unless we except the conduct of the European nations towards the slave-coasts of Africa." In the Island of Banda, for instance, the "original inhabitants" had been "entirely extirpated" for the crime of resisting Dutch usurpations. The natives of Guah and Soping had "displayed great courage and magnanimity of character," but had been "hunted down with a perseverence worthy of a better cause." What he wanted was for the various sultans to invest the governor-general with the ancient Malay title of *Bitara* or Lord Protector, which would confer on him "a general right of superintendence" but "might be so limited by treaty as to remove any occasion of suspicion from the native power."[142]

The idea of a protectorate was supported by local native rulers and by the more enlightened Dutch colonists, but it was, of course, ended by Castlereagh's Euro-centered diplomacy. In 1816 Raffles returned to England frustrated, for the moment, accompanied by an enormous quantity of native art, manuscripts, carvings, stuffed animals, insect collections, plants, and textiles, altogether weighing over 30 tons. He promptly wrote and published a two-volume *History of Java,* had himself elected a fellow of the Royal Society, was knighted and made influential friends at court, in the Whig and Tory establishments, and in intellectual and social circles. When he returned to the East in 1817 as Governor of Bencoolen in Sumatra, where the British had been established since the 17th century, he had lined up a powerful selection of supporters in London, with whom he remained in correspondence. Back in the East, he found the British economic position had deteriorated. The Dutch, far from showing any gratitude to Britain for her generosity, were busy driving British traders from the areas they controlled and moving to occupy any remaining islands which Britain might use as an entrepôt. Raffles had already warned the government that the Dutch would do so. He advocated "our taking immediate possession of a port in the Eastern Archipelago, the best adapted for communicating with the native princes, for a general knowledge of what is going on at sea and on shore throughout the archipelago, for the resort of the independent trade and trade with our allies, for the protection of our commerce and all our interest, and more especially for an entrepôt for our merchandise."[143]

Raffles now pressed the new Governor-General, Lord Hastings (1754–1826), for a quick decision, since the Dutch were taking up all the options still left to Britain. Hastings was not a man of the Enlightenment like Minto, but a grandee rather, who conducted himself like a monarch, paid his court chamberlain £3,000 a year, and drove in his carriage with grooms running beside each horse, six mace-bearers preceding it. What chiefly impressed him about Raffles, whom he thought "too clever by half," was that he was in regular correspondence with the Duchess of Somerset. But at least Hastings was prepared to take responsibility. Getting an answer from London might take well over a year. He accordingly decided to act himself, issuing instructions based on a draft Raffles had prepared, which, in effect, allowed him to select and buy a suitable site. The orders were dated 28 November 1818 and Raffles sailed from Calcutta 10 days later, lamenting "I much fear the Dutch have left us hardly an inch of ground to stand upon. My attention is principally directed to Johore and you must not be surprised if my next letter to you is dated from the site of the ancient city of Singapore."[144]

Singapura was Sanskrit for "the Lion City" and was the only town on an island the size of the Isle of Wight, a quarter mile from the mainland of Johore (now Malaysia). It was a crumbling walled city, untouched since the 14th century. As Raffles said, "It is a child of my own. But for my Malay studies, I would hardly have known that such a place existed: not only the European but the Indian world was ignorant of it."[145] He arrived there in the late afternoon of 28 January 1819, and immediately began both negotiations with the local authorities and the construction of a fort, equipped with 12 guns and manned by a mere company of sepoys. Nine days later there was an elaborate installation ceremony at which a formal treaty was signed: the local sultan or *tunku* was to be given 5,000 dollars annually in return for giving the East India Company the right to build and maintain a settlement. In return for British protection, the tunku undertook not to give political rights to any other European nation. But the port was to be free. Raffles laid down all the specifications for the harbor installations—Martello tower, palisades, entrenchments, and batteries of 10-pounder guns inside a stronger, permanent fort, together with accommodation for 30 British gunners, plus native troops.

The coup was arranged quickly—Raffles himself was in Singapore less than two weeks—and if the Dutch governor-general of Java, Baron van der Capellan, had shown some nerve and attacked the settlement straight away, it is unlikely that the British base would have survived. The nearest British force of any size was in Penang, and its Commander, Colonel Bannerman, was jealous of Raffles's flashy career and refused to send the reinforcement of 200 men requested. We now know that if the post had fallen, the Court of Governors of the East India Company would have forbidden Hastings to retake it. But Capellan hesitated, and when news of the treaty reached Calcutta, the press—now growing in influence in India as, indeed, throughout the Europeanized world—reacted enthusiastically. The *Calcutta Journal*, reflecting commercial opinion, declared that the founding of Singapore was the most welcome event in the whole history of the China trade, and it congratulated Hastings on his dash and foresight. That was enough for the Governor-General. Having received Raffles's own account on 16 March, he wrote to him: "The selection of Singapore is considered highly judicious and your proceedings in establishing a factory there do honour to your approved skill and ability." He rebuked Bannerman for his lack of cooperation, and the extra 200 men were dispatched forthwith.[146]

When Raffles returned to Singapore at the end of May, he found that "already a population of about 5,000 souls has collected under our flag. . . . The harbour is filled with shipping from all quarters." The newcomers were mainly Chinese, moving in from many surrounding islands—the beginnings of an enormous Chinese diaspora which, in the 20th century, was to constitute some of the most successful mercantile and industrial communities on earth. Raffles laid out the new town, with sites for merchant houses and quarters for Chinese, Malays, and Indians; he built a circular road for European carriages and a bridge over the river. He wrote home that he was now going to devote himself to "the advancement of a colony" which he thought would become "one of the most important and at the same time one of the least expensive and troublesome, which we possess. Our object is not territory, but trade; a great commercial emporium and a *fulcrum,* whence we may extend our influence politically as circumstances may hereafter require. But taking immediate possession we put a *negative* to the Dutch claim of exclusion, and at the same time revive the drooping confidence of our allies and friends. Our free port in these seas must eventually destroy the spell of Dutch monopoly; and what *Malta* is in the West, that may Singapore become in the East."[147]

The foundation of this great port, one of the most remarkable commercial transactions in history, was blessed by success right from the start. In the first two-and-a-half years, 2,839 ships entered and cleared, 383 of them European, and the population jumped to 10,000; the next year all records were broken, the depot's trade now exceeding that of Penang and Malacca put together. It was a striking advertisement for free trade, a portent for the future, and Raffles was able to leave finally for England in June 1823, his mission and lifework accomplished. Like many European pioneers in the East, he sacrificed much for the sake of his work. His first wife, Olivia, one of the great beauties of the age, for whom Thomas Moore wrote many love poems, succumbed to the panoply of oriental killer diseases; so did four of the five children he had by her and her successor, Sophie.[148] The East India Company showed little practical appreciation of his services, not only refusing him a pension or gratuity but claiming that he owed it £22,000 for exceeding authorized expenditures. Raffles died of apoplexy on 12 April 1826, three months after receiving this demand. Shortly before, he had bought a 112-acre estate at Hendon near Wilby. The local vicar, who had money invested in West Indian slave plantations and hated Raffles for his strong emancipationist views, refused to allow a memorial tablet to be put up in the church.

But Raffles, in common with others who pushed British interests in the East, was not primarily interested in the acquisition of wealth. His chief wish was to spread the rule of law, with all races subject equally to it, and trade flourishing freely in consequence. By setting up Singapore, he wrote to Wilberforce, "the foundation has at least been laid on which a better state of society can be founded." Through it, "our commerce will extend to every part [of Southeast Asia], and British principles will be known and felt throughout."[149] He admired the native races of Asia, especially those which had not been crushed by the horrors of the caste system, and he sensed the coming Asian revolution. One of his first projects in Singapore was to found a college for the sons of native rulers, to introduce them to the notions of European jurisprudence and science and the art of constitutional government. He planned to provide schools for the whole population.

Raffles was likewise among the enlightened elite of his time in believing that empire was not just about the creation of wealth or even justice, but about the acquisition of knowledge. As governor of Bencoolen, he investigated a primitive race on the Sumatran coast called the Battas, from which the Malays had sprung. His friend, the anthropologist William Marsden, who wrote the first history of the island, called them cannibals.[150] Raffles visited them with his second wife Sophie, and found that the charge was true. The Battas, he reported, ate their victims—criminals and prisoners of war—alive: They tied them up, cut a slice off, then dipped it in salt and a sauce of lime and chillies. Their code made such feasting obligatory. "Should we never be heard of more," he wrote to the Duchess of Somerset, "you may conclude that we have been eaten." But, he added, "the Battas are not a bad people . . . they write and read, and think as much or more than those brought up in our National Schools."

It was one of Raffles's rules that there should never be any necessity for British troops or sepoys to fire on the aboriginals, provided officials knew the local languages. He was equally interested in the flora and fauna. He described to the Duchess his tame orang-utang: "Not much above two feet high, he wears a beautiful surtout of fine white woollen, and in his disposition and habits [is] the kindest and most correct creature imaginable; his face is jet black and his features most expres-

sive . . . always walks erect and would I am sure become a favourite in
Park Lane." At Bencoolen he had a menagerie and a magnificent garden, which he tended himself, specializing in exotic flowers. These
included a giant bloom, which he said 'measured across from the
extremity of the petal rather more than a yard, the nectarium was nine
inches wide and as deep; estimated to contain a gallon and a half of
water and the whole flower to weight fifteen pounds"—it was later
named the *Rafflesia Arnoldi*. When Raffles left for home in 1823, his
devoted Malay servant, Abdullah, who wrote a little book about him,
described the packing up of his collections: "There were thousands of
specimens of animals whose carcasses had been taken out but stuffed
like life. There were also two or three trunks of birds in thousands and
of various species, and all stuffed. There were several hundred bottles
of different sizes filled with snakes, scorpions and worms, and topped
up with gin to prevent corruption. . . . two boxes filled with different
corals and shells, mussels and bivalves of all kinds. On all these articles
he placed a value greater than gold, and he was constantly coming in
to see that nothing was hurt or broken."[151] By one of the strokes of
misfortune that embittered Rattles's last years the entire collection was
destroyed in a fire at sea. But in his brief retirement, Raffles contrived
to found, and become the first president of, the London Zoological
Society, and if he had lived, he would have succeeded Joseph Banks as
President of the Royal Society, too.

Raffles's interest in zoology, botany, and anthropology was characteristic of a determined and growing effort by the East India Company
and many of its leading servants to create an empire of knowledge, as
well as of commerce, in the Orient. One of the world's greatest botanical gardens was founded at Sibpur, on the river outside Calcutta, and
its superintendent, Dr. William Roxburgh, established a tradition of
research there which continues to this day. Another leading botanical
research garden was established at Samalkot, in the Madras Presidency—this one specializing in tobacco, pepper, and cardamoms—by
Roxburgh and his successor, Dr. Benjamin Heyne. At Saharanpur in
Uttar Pradesh, the speciality was Himalayan plants and medicinal
herbs, its brilliant superintendent, John Forbes Royle, retiring in 1831
to become Professor of Materia Medica and Therapeutics at the new
University of London. The East India Company set up various menag-
eries, specializing in birds, mammals and reptiles, and all these institutions carried out regular and elaborate expeditions to collect specimens
and acquire information, gradually spreading their activities to the
great mountain ranges of the north, and to the jungles of northern

Assam, Ceylon and Southeast Asia. The purpose was not merely scientific—one object was the establishment of the great Assam tea-growing industry—but the research effort established for the world the basic knowledge of the natural history of south Asia. It also produced some of the most sumptuously illustrated volumes ever compiled, such as Roxburgh's *Plants of the Coasts of Coromandel,* Royle's *Natural History of the Himalayan Mountains,* and Patrick Russell's *Fishes of Coromandel.* Vast quantities of specimens were sent home to find their way eventually to Kew, the Royal School of Mines, the British Museum, and institutions throughout the West.[152] The efforts of the East India Company were not unique. Most British colonial stations in the period 1815–30 joined in the growing knowledge hunt, appointing experts, if funds were available, setting up gardens and museums and dispatching specimens to England. The Royal Navy was an important part of this endeavor. Not only did it develop, thanks to Barrow, its own exploration, cartographic and scientific program, but it made itself available to transport the fruits of others' work. Barrow issued official Admiralty instructions for the correct packing and storage on ship of plants, coins, books, maps, prints, and statuary.[153]

All the same, the Royal Navy's primary duty was to secure the sea-lanes. That goal was in the forefront of Raffles's mind when he set up the port at Singapore. In the important paper he wrote in 1819, "British Commercial Policy in the East Indies," he adumbrated much later attitudes by arguing that Britain's role in the East was not primarily as a ruler but as an educator, drawing out the latent qualities and energies of the local states. He thought that British and Asian interests were not merely compatible but mutually reinforcing. India's textile industry, he pointed out, was being destroyed by imported English mass manufactures, but farther east, it was possible to "ensure a market for the manufactures of India, and thus promote its industry and prosperity." He thought acquiring more territory for the Crown "comparatively unimportant" and even perhaps "objectionable." He stressed that "trade and not territory is our object." In his view, Britain's interests were best promoted by "improving the energies and resources of [the native] states, upholding their independence and strengthening their power and importance." What he called "our interference" should be intended "not to depress but to raise those states, and by the establishment of a free and unrestricted commercial intercourse to draw forth their resources while we improve our own."[154] Raffles's vision was of a community of independent Asian states under enlightened, educated and constitutional rulers.

None of this vision was possible until international maritime law was established. It was a source of regret to Britain that other civilized powers were so reluctant to assist in the police effort needed to put down not merely slaving but high-seas and inshore piracy, endemic throughout the Indian Ocean area but especially in the Persian Gulf and on either side of the Singapore Straits. By 1815–20, for instance, the United States mercantile marine was carrying more than half the important Sumatran pepper trade, but it was rare for the United States Navy to keep a frigate (or at most two) in the region. The British authorities were pleased when Andrew Jackson, as president, retaliated against a pirate attack on a U.S. ship off the northwest coast of Sumatra by sending the frigate *Potomac* to bombard the marauders' lair, Batu.

But this was unusual. Normally the Royal Navy had to act alone or with such local allies as it could secure. And the tasks were formidable. In the Persian Gulf, pirate sheikhs were protected by the Wahabis— forebears of the present rulers of Saudi Arabia—whom the British were not anxious to antagonize, at least till the Napoleonic Wars were over. In 1815 the Gulf pirates took a small East India Company ship and massacred its crew; they nearly captured the ruler of Oman's 49-gun frigate, with Saidi himself aboard. Twelve months later, the company's 14-gun sloop *Aurora* had to fight desperately to defend her convoy from swarms of pirate dhows, and the same year the pirate sheikh of Ras-el-Khyma took three valuable cargo ships from Surat, flying the British flag, and slaughtered between 50 and 60 of their passengers.[155] The Indian government was unable to mount a retaliation strike immediately, since it had its hands full with campaigns against the Mahratta and Pindari confederacies. But it had one stroke of luck: Mehemet Ali, the "enlightened despot" of Egypt—whom we will examine in due course—was a mortal enemy of the Wahabis. In 1818 he contrived to capture both their capital and their emir, Abdullah ibn Saud, thus reducing the size of the military problem the company faced. In 1819, then, the company, plus its Omani ally, launched a joint amphibious force against the main pirate base at Ras-el-Khyma on the Straits of Hormuz. They killed 300 pirates, wounded 700, took the town after a week's siege, and eventually compelled the sheikh to surrender with 1,000 of his men. This was not the end of the matter—indeed, piracy tended to break out whenever British naval forces left the area—but it led to the signature of a general treaty with all the Arabian Coast and Persian Gulf tribes in January 1820. Since Britain had by then learnt that when dealing with Arabs, covenants without swords were useless, British enforcement bases were set up at Kishm Island on the far side of the Hormuz Strait and Bassador on the southern tip. These bases provided a diplomatic-naval framework for security which slowly became a reality as steam warships and long-range guns came into service.[156]

In Middle Eastern waters, therefore, the British were essentially trying to back the peaceful traders and farmers against the pirate tribes, within a system of general law. Once the right treaties were signed and the alliances were in place, it was only a matter of time before advancing naval technology did the job. But at the eastern end of the Indian Ocean and in the western Pacific, geography, in the shape of scores of thousands of islands and shallow channels, made piracy almost ineradicable. It was impossible even to map the entire area, especially the seas between the archipelagos of the Celebes and the Philippines, where even in the late 20th century nautical charts still mark portions "Dangerous Area (unsurveyed)." The impact of Western progress in some ways aggravated the problem. The peoples of the region were by no means unsophisticated, especially in the use of weapons, but they were still largely organized in traditional hunting and raiding societies, where piracy (as the West called it) was not only acceptable, but was regarded as more manly than farming. Such societies, as in the Scottish Highlands, had now disappeared in Europe, and they were being rapidly eliminated or pushed inland in the Americas, southern Africa, and Australasia.

In Southeast Asia, however, the increase in commerce of every kind which Western intrusion was bringing and which, in turn, raised the volume of native trade, made piracy far more lucrative in the second and third decades of the 19th century than it had been a generation earlier. Particularly succulent targets were the growing fleets of Chinese-owned craft carrying luxuries, such as edible birds' nests, to the Chinese mainland for the delight of wealthy merchants and mandarins grown rich on the tea and opium traffic. Such stolen cargoes were easily sold in scores of ports. The ships themselves were burned or, if fast, pressed into pirate service. Those aboard were casually slaughtered or, if rich, ransomed. Occasionally pilgrims to Mecca were spared. There were pirate gangs in every harbor, often openly displaying their trade—some, indeed, even lurked, though furtively, in the new port of Singapore. The chief threat, however, came not from the skull-and-crossbones type of buccaneer, but from entire villages or even sizeable princedoms organized for predation. George Windsor Earl, an 1820s expert on piracy, put it thus: "A petty chief of one of the Malay states, who has either been ruined by gambling or is desirous of improving his fortune, collects as many restless spirits as he can muster and sails for one of the most retired islands in the neighbourhood of Singapore. Here he erects a village as a depot for slaves and plunder, and then lies in wait with his armed *praus* for the native traders to pass. If successful, his forces increase and the village becomes a small town. Eventually his fleet becomes sufficiently numerous for sub-division into several squadrons."[157]

The worst area was the western coast of Malaya, sheltered from the monsoon. But there at least the praus were small and did not attack large vessels. The Lanuns and Balanini from the Philippines were far more efficient and ambitious. They conducted annual campaigns, during the pirate season, equipping fleets of up to 200 praus, each of 50–100 tons, sweeping the seas, dividing into squadrons of 20 or so if convenient, and passing right up the Malay coast and into Siam. Old naval hands thought them far more formidable than anything to be encountered in the Caribbean. Indeed, the Spanish authorities had been fighting them for 300 years, and with far less success than they managed on the Spanish Main. By 1820 Spain had no teeth at all. The obvious power to put them down, by attacking and burning their bases, as had been done in Algiers and the Strait of Hormuz, was the East India Company. But with economy all the rage in Westminster, the company was undergrowing pressure from the government, on which it depended for its monopoly privileges, to raise profits and reduce expenses. The easiest method of cutting its outgoings was to refuse all requests for punitive expeditions. The company had no territorial ambitions. All it wanted was to carry on its trade peacefully, at a minimum cost, and the cheapest way to do so was by local deals with rulers, if necessary with pirate-sultans. The company, for instance, had a policy of noninterference in Siam, despite the fact that the authorities there had only nominal control over much of the coast, from which pirates operated with impunity.[158]

Against this background, the Royal Navy did its best with limited resources. Experienced naval officers did not regard the Malay private praus, let alone the Philippine ones, as easy targets. They had lateen sails, but were driven mainly by skilled oarsmen and were deadly in a calm. In addition to a formidable array of spears, kris and muskets, they mounted swivel guns at bow, stern and quarters and could overpower the smaller Western naval craft, such as brigs, especially if they ran aground while searching the ill-charted islands. The praus often held surprising numbers of fierce men, who hid behind bulwarks until a gong sounded for boarding. During the 1820s the Royal Navy got all commercial vessels voyaging in the region to fit antiboarding nets. Naval officers, normally so keen on boarding at cutlass point, were wary of praus, whose crews often hid in the hold and speared the boarding party upwards through the bamboo decks. What the navy preferred to do was to sink the praus by gunfire, no easy matter. The alternative was to mount search-and-destroy operations on the pirate coasts and islands. The ideal craft for these operations were the new flat-bottom steam warships, mounting big guns. But neither the company nor the navy was yet ready to supply them for Southeast Asia, so such missions often had to be conducted in rowing boats, launched from warships and commanded by young lieutenants or midshipmen, in peril of their lives. For most of the 1820s, a brig and a schooner, sometimes backed by a sloop from the East Indies Squadron, constituted the only patrol on the Singapore Straits. Things improved in 1830 when Rear Admiral Sir Edward Owen arrived to take charge and began a systematic study of the patterns and economics of piracy, as a prelude to devising countermeasures. Some naval experts thought piracy could never be wiped out in these waters, just as today's police are skeptical about eliminating burglary in New York and London or eradicating the Mafia in Italy. Owen was not so pessimistic, but he concluded that naval forces, however strong, could not succeed alone: the structure and way of life of local societies had to be changed.[159] The only way to do that, as the next generation discovered, was by direct rule—colonialism, in short—just the solution Raffles believed was unnecessary.

Therein lay the dilemma, from which there seemed no escape as the 19th century progressed. As trade expanded, as Western ideas spread, increasing portions of the earth's surface required international policing, usually by Britain as the only constable available; and a policeman tended to change, almost imperceptibly, into a ruler. Many in London felt strongly that Britain could afford neither the resources nor the national will to take on these added responsibilities, particularly in view of her heavy duties as a guarantor of the European peace. In Europe, Britain pursued a judicious middle path: opposed, on the one hand, to revolutionary solutions promoted by violence, and deprecating, on the other, unreformed absolutism, not the least when dressed up in mystic religious garb. The British watchword was constitutionalism. But Britain, whether she liked it or not, was herself going through a demographic and industrial revolution of unprecedented magnitude, which was setting up strains within her society which at times seemed unendurable. In the years after Waterloo, these strains reached a climax, and the question then arose: Would the new world policeman lose control in his own hearth and home? Could the center hold?

FIVE

Can the Center Hold?

On 13 December 1817, the poet William Wordsworth wrote from London to his patron, literary admirer and mighty Lakeland neighbor, William Lowther, second Earl of Lonsdale: "This morning I heard of a piece of absurdity which Your Lordship will permit me to mention." A young friend from Troutbeck, studying law in one of the Inns of Court, had passed on a rumor to him that "certain persons had agreed to oppose your Lordship's interest for the County of Westminster at the ensuing election." Ridiculous though it might seem, Wordsworth continued, that anyone should seek to challenge the almighty Lowthers in the Lake District, where they controlled seven of the 10 seats in Cumberland and Westmorland, he had to report that £2,000 had been collected for this purpose and none other than the infamous radical lawyer, Henry Brougham, had been asked to undertake the contest. A week later Wordsworth wrote to the earl again. The news was only too true: At the general election, due the following June–July, the Earl's eldest son, William, Viscount Lowther, and his younger son, Colonel Henry Lowther, who held the two county seats for Westmorland—hitherto unopposed—would face the redoubtable Brougham, who had promised to lead a crusade to overthrow the "tyranny of the Lowthers." Wordsworth added: "Your Lordship has only to point the way in which you wish me to exert myself."[1]

The following Sunday Wordsworth was involved in a bit of awkwardness, at one of the most memorable dinner parties in the history of English literature. He and his family were linked to the Lonsdales in many ways, but none more decisively than through Wordsworth's governmental job, as Collector of Stamps for Westmorland, which the Earl had obtained for him in March 1813. The Collector got 4 percent on the stamps he sold and, in theory, the job was worth £400 a year. But Wordsworth had to pay his retired predecessor a £100 pension from the profits and, in practice, he made no more than £200 himself. Moreover, the job was by no means a sinecure, as most people supposed. It involved appointing and supervising the local stamp sellers, the equivalent of village postmasters today, and standing security for them if they defaulted; corresponding with the Commissioner of Stamp Duties in London, John Kingston; keeping the hugely valuable stock of stamps safely—a duty the nervous Wordsworth took seriously; compiling elaborate accounts; and inspecting all the stamp sellers once a quarter. This last obligation, which Wordsworth conflated to an annual tour on horseback, was the reason his best friends—Thomas Clarkson, the antislavery campaigner, Charles Lamb, the lawyer-diarist Henry Crabb Robinson—were delighted with the appointment. They thought Wordsworth led too isolated an existence at his house, Rydal Mount, in Grasmere, and that the work would get him about, meeting people, jogging along through some of the finest scenery in the world, and so inspire him to write more poetry.[2]

But the job was undoubtedly a government appointment, obtained through patronage and influence, and as such anathema to radical intellectuals, who (then as now) included most writers. Wordsworth, and his friend and Lakeland neighbor Robert Southey, now the Poet Laureate, were already objects of suspicion to them. Having once been enthusiastic supporters of the French Revolution—Wordsworth had been in Paris at the time, later recording "Bliss was it in that dawn to be alive/But to be young was very heaven,"[3]—both men had later broken with republicanism over its excesses and aggression, Wordsworth being particularly outraged by the destruction of Swiss liberty, and had moved into the conservative camp. To suspicious radical minds, Wordsworth's office, like Southey's laureateship, seemed like sordid rewards for services rendered to a reactionary Tory government and establishment. Leigh Hunt, who with his brother John ran the radical weekly *Examiner,* asserted flatly in 1815: "Mr. Southey and even Mr. Wordsworth have both accepted office under government of such a nature as absolutely ties up their independence." Wordsworth, whom he acknowledged was or had been a great poet, was now "marked as government property." William Hazlitt, another former admirer, attacked Wordsworth repeatedly, especially in a notorious review of *The Excursion* in Hunt's paper, and made a general sneer at poets: "They do not like to be shut out when laurels are to be given away at court—or places under government are to be disposed of—in romantic situations in the country. They are happy to be reconciled on the first opportunity to prince and people, and to exchange their principles for a pension."[4] Wordsworth's acceptance of the collectorship was also attacked by his fellow poet John Keats, who had never even met him, and by his London acquaintance, the history painter Benjamin Robert Haydon.

Haydon had the desire to bring Wordsworth and Keats together, and the meeting was accomplished on this famous Sunday, 28 December, at a dinner the artist gave in his "painting room"—the word studio was then thought French and affected—at his house in St. John's Wood, then a bohemian suburb of London. On the morning of this "immortal dinner," as Haydon recorded in his diary, the Stamp Commissioner, Kingston, called on him and asked for an introduction to Wordsworth, whom—he said—he had often corresponded with on official business and deeply admired, but had never met. Haydon told him to come along after dinner that day. The meal itself, which took place against the background of Haydon's gigantic *Christ's Entry into Jerusalem,* on which he was then feverishly working, was a distinct success. In addition to Wordsworth and Keats, there was Thomas Monkhouse (1783–1825), a cousin of Wordsworth's wife Mary, a rich merchant and giver of literary parties himself, and Charles Lamb. Later they were joined by the famous traveler Joseph Ritchie and the engraver John Landseer (father of Edwin Landseer, the painter). According to Haydon's account, "We had a glorious set-to—on Homer, Shakespeare, Milton and Virgil. Lamb got exceedingly merry ["tipsey" according to Keats's version, in a letter to his brothers] and exquisitely witty, and his fun in the midst of Wordsworth's solemn intonations of oratory was like the sarcasm and wit of the Fool in the intervals of Lear's passion." They had an argument about Voltaire, and drank to him, and about Isaac Newton, and drank to "Newton's health and confusion to mathematics"; and "it was delightful to see the good humor of Wordsworth in giving in to all our frolics without affectation and laughing as heartily as the rest of us."[5]

"When we retired to tea," continued Haydon, "we found the [Stamp Commissioner]. In introducing him to Wordsworth, I forgot to say who he was." After a while, Kingston, a senior bureaucrat who was perhaps unused to literary gatherings, suddenly demanded of Wordsworth: "Don't you think, Sir, Milton was a great genius?" Keats and Wordsworth looked at each other. Lamb, who had been dozing by the fire, focused on Kingston and asked: "Pray, Sir, did you say Milton was a great genius?" "No, Sir," said the man testily, "I asked Mr. Wordsworth if he were not." "Oh," said Lamb, "then you are a silly fellow." "Charles, my dear Charles," said Wordsworth. There was a pause. Then Kingston started again: "Don't you think, Sir, Newton a great genius?" There was some laughter. Keats, giggling, buried his nose in a book. Lamb, seizing a candle, went over to Kingston and held it to his head and said, "Sir, will you allow me to look at your phrenological development?" Kingston ignored this question and moved closer to Wordsworth. "I have the honour of some correspondence with you, Mr. Wordsworth." "With me, Sir?' said Wordsworth, "not that I remember." "Don't you, Sir?" said Kingston, "I am *the Commissioner of Stamps."* There was, said Haydon, "a dead silence," broken by Lamb's repeated "Do let me have another look at that gentleman's organs." At that point, Haydon recorded, "Keats and I hurried Lamb into the painting-room, shut the door, and gave way to inextinguishable laughter." Kingston was huffy and, at first, "irreconcilable," and Wordsworth had to humor him as best he could. But he was persuaded to stay to supper, during which, at intervals, could be heard Lamb's voice from the next room: "Who is that fellow? Allow me to see his organs once more."[6]

Haydon called the occasion "a night worthy of the Elizabethan age," made memorable not so much by the low comedy of the Kingston episode as by Wordsworth's "fine intonation" as he recited Milton and Virgil and by Keats's "eager inspired look" in response. Later Keats used to tell a garbled version of the story, much to Wordsworth's disadvantage, which contradicts his own letter written at the time. He said that, for his first meeting with Wordsworth, he called at the poet's house and was kept waiting a long time. When Wordsworth finally entered, "he was in full flower, knee breeches, silk stockings etc., and in a great hurry as he was going to dine with one of the Commissioners of Stamps." Keats related this encounter "with something of anger."[7] For the reason behind his anger, we have to look at an episode that took place later in the year. Though Keats disapproved of Wordsworth's stamp job, he had not yet understood the nature of his links with the Lowthers and his plans to fight on their side in the forthcoming election, although it soon became a talking point in literary London. Two months after the Haydon dinner, Hazlitt, with the election in mind, made a "contemptuous" attack on Wordsworth during a public lecture on Robert Burns, and in his essay *On Respectable People,* written at this time, he added: "The only way for a poet nowadays to emerge from the obscurity of poverty and genius is to prostitute his pen, turn pimp to a borough-mongering lord, canvass for him at elections, and by this means aspire to some importance, and be admitted on the same respectable footing with him as his valet, his steward or his practising attorney."[8] All this passed Keats by, and on 27 June, walking through the Lake District as a prelude to a tour of Scotland, he planned to call on Wordsworth and inquired about him from a waiter at the Bowness Hotel on Lake Windermere. By this time, the General Election was in full fury. The waiter "said he knew [Wordsworth], and that he had been here a few days ago, canvassing for the Lowthers. What think you of that," Keats added—he was writing to his brother Thomas—"Wordsworth versus Brougham!! Sad—sad—sad—and yet the family has been his friend always. What can we say?" He hoped to get Wordsworth's defense of himself in person, and next day, after "a Monstrous Breakfast"—he was a hungry young man of 22—called at Rydal Mount, but found the poet away, electioneering. So "I wrote a note for him and stuck it up over what I knew must be [Dorothy] Wordsworth's portrait." He could not resist some sarcasm about "Lord Wordsworth" who "instead of being in retirement" had "himself and his house full in the thick of fashionable visitors quite convenient to be pointed at all the summer long." Three weeks later, still disgusted by Wordsworth's flouting of the radical orthodoxy, he wrote a set of vulgar verses, much concerned with buttocks and arses, mocking Wordsworth, Southey, the Lowthers and, for good measure, the Chancellor of the Exchequer, Nicholas Vansittart.[9]

We will come to the election itself shortly, but first it is necessary to pause and examine why it is that John Keats, not a man much interested in politics, rather one who simply reflected the prevailing notions of his friends, should feel so depressed by Wordsworth's allegiance and why the latter should have committed himself so wholeheartedly to upholding the government. Why did these poets of different generations—Wordsworth was now 48—but of similar sensibilities, who were both, in their different but complementary ways, bringing about in English literature a Copernican-type revolution comparable to the philosophical revolution Immanel Kant and his followers had already achieved in Germany, find themselves on opposite and hostile sides of the great political divide which then severed Britain and indeed the whole of Europe? The answer to this question takes us to the heart of the politico-economic debate which raged in the years after Waterloo.

The first point to be grasped is that the romantic movement produced heightened sensibilities, felt (even if unconsciously) at every level of society. One chief way in which this new sensitivity expressed itself was in increasing awareness of poverty and concern for the poor. Men and women could see wealth increasing on all sides, while science and technology seemed to make all things possible for humanity. For the first time in history, resignation before the suffering and degradation inherent in the human condition was no longer necessary. Why, then, was there still so much poverty, and what ought society to do to relieve it? All decent, intelligent people, whatever their political sympathies, asked themselves these questions. The three poets often seen as "reactionaries" in the post-Waterloo years, Southey, Coleridge and Wordsworth, felt as much compassion for the poor as did anyone, as their writings abundantly testify. Wordsworth, in particular, knew a good deal about the poor, at least in his part of the world. He returned to the subject again and again, differentiating carefully between various kinds of poverty, for instance, in "The Old Cumberland Beggar," and insisting, particularly in his superb poem "Michael," that a poor man could have as wide and intense a range of feelings as one of soft nurture and education, and be capable of high nobility. For Wordsworth, poor people were never statistics, but they remained individual human beings, and his sister Dorothy's diaries and letters are dotted with detailed references to the poor people she encountered, her conversations with them and her efforts to relieve their want.

Foreign visitors to Britain were struck by the contrast between riches and destitution, particularly in London, visibly the wealthiest city in the world. On 8 November 1816 John Quincy Adams, then the American Minister in London, found, while walking through Brentford, an exhausted man in the street who told him he had not eaten for two days. "The number of these wretched objects I meet in my daily walks is distressing," he recorded. "Not a day passes but we have beggars come to the house, each with a different, hideous tale of misery. The extremes of opulence and want are more remarkable and more constantly obvious in this country than in any other that I ever saw."[10] Four years later, another foreigner, Théodore Géricault (1791–1824), left a remarkable visual record of poverty in London—wretched human beings, tired workmen, ruined horses, begging dogs, suffering and squalor. His drawings, watercolors, and lithographs of pain and poverty in the midst of a gigantic, opulent modern metropolis, done in 1820–21, constituted, in fact, a new form of the sublime.[11] But the reactions of people like Adams and Géricault were impressionistic and lacked a long-term basis for comparison. Adams recorded the worst moment of the postwar recession, Géricault the beginning of the economic upswing which produced the unprecedented general prosperity of the first half of the 1820s; their reactions convey no sense of movement, for better or worse.

For careful English observers, however, there was no doubt that, despite the swings of economic misfortune, of which the years 1816–19 were the most severe, the general condition of the country was slowly improving. The population might be growing fast—that was obvious—but at least the vast majority were fed. On the Continent, periodic famines persisted up to the 1830s. In England, Scotland and Wales they were already a thing of the past by 1815. The most difficult and dangerous period had been the 1790s, when the growth in population had not yet been met by the increasing productivity of British agriculture, and war conditions cut off supplementary supplies from Eastern and Central Europe as well as from France. In December 1795, for instance, the House of Commons passed an unprecedented motion calling for the adoption of a voluntary system of bread and grain rationing, owing to a one-third failure of the wheat crop.[12] There were times, up to the turn of the century, when many poor people in limited areas of the country actually came close to starvation.

But the chance that popular distress might lead to an overthrow of the system by force was much reduced by the reactions of the British possessing classes to events in France, which served as both a warning and an incentive. A large number of the British political elite had actually visited Paris during the years 1789–93 and had themselves witnessed firsthand some of the most formidable episodes of the Revolution. A typical example was Lord Liverpool, who had watched the mob storm the almost undefended Bastille and then massacre the garrison. He was left with a lifelong impression, which remained in his mind throughout his fifteen years as Prime Minister, 1812–27, of the fragility of lawful authority which hesitates in the face of violence and of the barbarism which seizes an aroused populace once it realizes that the powers that be have lost the will to govern. During the perilous decade of the 1790s, William Pitt, though in most respects a liberal who believed in steady reforms, did not hesitate to acquire emergency powers to suppress insurrection, even to the point of suspending *habeas corpus* (1794), and in so doing he had overwhelming support in parliament. He also provided the physical force to back up the law by making it possible for those who opposed revolutionary violence to enlist in the Volunteers and militia, and—in a country that traditionally rejected the notion of a standing army—he built barracks in which regular troops could be housed within range of expanding industrial towns like Nottingham, Sheffield, Birmingham, and Manchester. This too seems to have been done with the support of local opinion.[13]

If the possessing classes were willing to take measures to defend the existing order—a posture they maintained right up to the resignation of the Wellington ministry in 1830—they also showed restraint and forbearance, by and large, in the face of the sporadic violence which distress provoked. Indeed, without this restraint, the history of Britain during this period would have been different and much more savage. Parliament suspended *habeas corpus* twice and was willing to pass repressive legislation quickly when convinced there was a genuine threat to order. But at no point did it show itself a reactionary body committed to a general policy of ruling by military and police force. A similar attitude prevailed in the decisions taken at Quarter Sessions, which in practice were more important in the lives of most people than sittings of Parliament.[14] Justices of the Peace were most reluctant to use force, especially in times of distress when crowds of angry people were brought together by want, not by sedition. The bench of Justices of the Peace invited deputations, rather than read the Riot Act.[15] JPs often faced large mobs unarmed and unaccompanied even by constables. In extreme cases, they used the threat of force, rather than force itself, and this threat was usually successful, for the mob feared the military, especially the cavalry and above all the regular cavalry.

Commanding officers, and still more their junior squadron and troop commanders, were equally reluctant to give the order to fire, partly because they felt they had no quarrel with the mob, partly because they feared prosecution for murder before hostile juries. Voluntary bodies were not reliable when food was the issue; during the famine of 1801, some urban Volunteers resigned or even deserted. For all these reasons force was little used.[16] Indeed, as in Ulster today, soldiers, both regulars and volunteers, often had to face abuse and occasional stones for hours without retaliation of any kind. Few were provoked, even after the Riot Act had been read, and judges were disinclined to be severe in times of shortage—at no point was the land covered in gibbets.

Indeed, some of those who felt that the free working of the market was the only long-term solution to mass poverty criticized the possessing classes for their feeble response to mob violence. The Rev. Thomas Malthus denounced "the extreme ignorance and folly of many of the higher classes . . . particularly the clergy." He said that by denouncing "middlemen" as the cause of shortages they actually encouraged riots—"half the gentlemen and clergy of the country," he wrote, were thus liable to be prosecuted "for sedition."[17] Both the country gentry and the urban middle class—whose social conscience became an important phenomenon from the 1790s onwards—took elaborate steps to interfere in the workings of the market, much to the fury of experts like Malthus. Cooperative mills and mill clubs were set up to bring down the price of grain. Justices of the Peace were enthusiastic in prosecuting cases of fraud. To remedy commercial abuses, the Birmingham middle class subscribed to set up the Flour & Bread Company (1796), and a similar venture in Manchester, designed to break "monopolies," attracted £6,000 in start-up capital. The Birmingham company initially sold only to subscribers—Matthew Boulton bought 400 of its shares for the workers in his engine business—but it proved so successful that it was soon opened to all. Such ventures, in one form or another, were launched in all big centers of population.[18] There was also direct charity on an enormous scale, especially during the lean winter months, a feature of British life during the Napoleonic Wars which is impossible to quantify and can only be illustrated. "Such a Christmas," recorded an Oldham weaver in December 1802, "for Roast Beef pies and Ale etc as was never witnessed by the oldest person living for Such was the power of All Families by the Goodness of all Sorts of Trade that one family vied with Another which could Give the Greatest treat to its neighbour and nothing but mirth Glee and Harmony was seen during this Great Festivity."[19] This relative absence of class war during the food shortages of 1794 to 1801 helps explain why Britain was able to survive the last famines without much violence and why the war against Republican France was backed by the nation—indeed, its resumption in 1803 was surprisingly popular.

The last serious food shortages occurred in 1801. Thereafter actual food riots were rare. The war years 1803–14 were generally prosperous, with real wages rising. Popular disturbances were not unusual, but sprang from a variety of causes. In 1809, for instance, theatergoers at Drury Lane in London rioted against a sudden increase in the price of seats and continued to do so until the "Old Price" was restored. In 1810 there were riots among prisoners at Dartmoor and Porchester Castle, overcrowding and bad food being blamed, and disturbances among the Plymouth dockyard workers. In 1811 there were riots in Liverpool and Peterborough, and at Hertford students at the East India College rose up against their masters. The next year, rioters sacked the News Room at the Manchester Exchange, and in Nottingham there was a riot to celebrate the assassination of Spencer Percival, the Prime Minister, in the lobby of the House of Commons. These last riots, and many others, were termed "Luddite," called after "Ned" Ludd, supposedly a Leicestershire youth who broke some labor-saving machinery in 1799. Increasingly, the pattern of rioting, in so far as there was one, changed from protest against food shortages or high food prices to protest against unemployment, short time, wage cuts and, above all, the machinery held to be responsible for all these evils.

In winter 1811–12 there were many such disturbances in the manufacturing districts of Lancashire, Yorkshire and the Midlands. Again in 1814 there were riots among Bilston colliers, Tynside keelmen, Suffolk farm laborers, London shipwrights and Lancashire handloom weavers, some against machinery, though in every case local factors, often unique, were determinant.[20] The year 1812 was particularly bad since there was a recession in trade and its effects were widely felt. This, if anything, was the unifying factor. Some of the authorities tended to be alarmist. In June 1812 a Deputy Lieutenant of the West Riding asserted that the area was going "the direct Road to an open Insurrection" and "except for the very spots which were occupied by Soldiers, the Country was virtually in the possession of the lawless . . . the disaffected outnumbering by many Degrees the peaceable Inhabitants."[21] But this view was not widely shared. Lieutenant-General Thomas Maitland (1760–1824), member of Parliament for Haddington Burghs at the time, who favored stern measures against "seditious persons" in Yorkshire, was nonetheless adamant there was "no real bottom" to Luddism. "At present," he maintained, "the whole of these Revolutionary Movements are limited to the lowest orders of the people generally, to the places where they show themselves; and that no concert exists nor no plan is laid, further than is manifested in the open acts of violence that are daily committed."[22]

The violence seemed serious only in limited areas and for short periods. Elsewhere in the country, people were almost unaware of it apart from what they read in newspapers. Throughout this period the authorities had more armed clashes with smugglers, on the East and South Coasts and in the Bristol Channel, than with factory or agricultural workers. Many conscientious letter writers and diarists of the period do not mention economic disturbances. It is illuminating that Jane Austen, always keen to achieve verisimilitude, whose *Emma* describes the year 1814 and is set in Leatherhead, only a day's ride from central London, shows the easily alarmed Mr. Woodhouse frightened not by rioters—they do not impinge on his life at all—but by a group of gypsies, or "campers," who try to rob Emma's "little friend," Harriet Smith. This was "a very extraordinary thing"; according to Emma, "nothing of the sort had ever occurred before to any young ladies in the place" and "all the youth and servants in the place were soon in the happiness of frightful news."[23] It is also worth pointing out, to put the disturbances in perspective, that they did not make much impact on the crime figures. When alarmed, authority could react harshly to machine breaking. In 1813 it went so far as to hang 13 Luddites at York Assizes. But if we take, say, the years 1812–16 as a whole, acts of political-economic violence were only a tiny fraction of felony indictments, the overwhelming majority of which were for theft (in the towns) and poaching (in the countryside).

Unrest, moreover, lacked the coordination of a common program and clearly identified leaders. In the early 1790s there was vague agreement among militant extremists that the government should be over-thrown by force, as had happened in France. In the late 1820s there was vague agreement on "parliamentary reform." In between, discontent was not focused on a definite aim. Even the demonology varied. Some-times it featured Castlereagh, sometimes the Home Secretary, Lord Sidmouth, and his spies, Oliver, Castle and Edwards, sometimes mod-ern machinery, sometimes the Corn Laws; and sometimes high taxa-tion, but as often as not, the chief villain was the Prince Regent, whose name and habits were familiar to all and who was universally criticized for laziness, extravagance, unfaithfulness and a total lack of public spirit. But dislike of the Regent did not constitute a political program.

An acknowledged, national leader, such as Daniel O'Connell was to become in Ireland in the 1820s, might have been able to impose an agreed agenda of reform. But there was no such person in Britain. Some radicals harked back to the French-style Jacobinism of the early and mid-1790s and were known as "Jacks" or "Old Jacks." Some, like the muscular Christian radical Thomas Evans, called themselves "Spen-ceans," followers of the London bookseller Thomas Spence (1750–1814), a millenarian who favored nationalization of land, a single tax, self-supporting communities run on socialist principles, and other ideals beloved of radical dreamers, then and for long after. Some Spen-ceans were mild and bookish; others, like Arthur Thistlewood (1770–1820) and the two James Watsons, father and son, plotted bloody insurrection relentlessly. There were quasi-constitutionalists, like Henry ("Orator") Hunt (1773– 1835), who usually tried to stick within the law and eventually became a member of Parliament himself. There were loners like William Cobbett, who called himself a Tory. There was the rich Sir Francis Burdett (1770–1844), who sat in Parliament from 1796 onwards and strove for radical reforms from within the system, and Francis Place (1771–1854), the breeches maker, who adum-brated the program later adopted by the Chartists but who likewise eschewed violence. There was Major John Cartwright (1740–1824), brother of the famous inventor, Edmund, a former magistrate and militia officer, who in 1812 tried to steer agitation into constitutional channels and give it middle-class leadership by forming Hampden Clubs, which originally had a landed-property qualification of £300 a year. In January–February 1813, Cartwright held 35 public meetings throughout the north, west, and Midlands in 30 days—an indication of the growing speed of travel—but he was already in his mid-seventies, too old for the job.[24]

One or two of these men had something approaching a national reputation—Cobbett for his writings, for instance, and Hunt as a pub-

lic speaker. Others were obscure. Their most striking common characteristic was their loathing of each other. Burdett and Place hated Cobbett and Hunt, Hunt hated Cobbett, both of them hated Thistlewood,
and among the Spenceans, there were violent personal animosities between Evans, Thistlewood and Watson and between all of them and
Hunt. If such popular leaders could be induced to enter the same room
together, the outcome, as likely as not, would be fisticuffs. When a
public dinner of radicals was held in 1827 in honor of Burdett and John
Hobhouse, Byron's friend—they were the two members of Parliament
for Westminster—Hunt and Cobbett both appeared with their followers and caused a rumpus. Cobbett objected when Burdett's health was
toasted and insulted Hobhouse, a small man, by calling him "Burdett's
Sancho Panza," whereupon Hobhouse seized a stick and attempted to
administer a thrashing. Cobbett jumped on a table to harangue, was
knocked off it "with the loss of part of my waistcoat," and finally
hustled out of the room by outraged Burdettites.[25] It was impossible to
construct a platform of speakers at a mass meeting which represented
the radical movement as a whole.

The differences and animosities were fully reflected in the radical
press, which included Henry White's *Independent Whig*, T. J. Wooler's
Black Dwarf, the Hunt brothers' (Leigh and John) *Examiner*, Cobbett's
Political Register, and the many scurrilous sheets with names like *The
Cap of Liberty* and *Medusa*. Such publications abused each other as
often as they did the government. The government and its friends
studied them nervously, from time to time, and occasionally prosecuted, though doing so had become much more difficult since Charles
James Fox's 1792 amendment to the law of libel, which allowed the jury
(as opposed to the judge) to decide whether the words complained of
were libelous. Juries, especially those in the London area, were usually
unpredictable, notably in cases involving freedom of the press. In the
years 1808–21 the authorities embarked on 101 prosecutions for seditious libel, and as often as not failed to get a conviction. Even when they
did, the modern reader is led to wonder whether it was worthwhile.

Nobody actually liked going to prison, whatever the conditions,
and when Cobbett was threatened with a prosecution for seditious libel
in 1810, he tried to plea-bargain with the attorney general, offering to
give up the *Political Register*, then selling a handsome 6,000 copies a
week. The government refused, and he got a two-year sentence. But
once in Newgate, Cobbett not only lived in comfort in the former
governor's residence, for which he paid 12 guineas a week—"Not much
worse than living two years in London in lodgings," sneered "Orator"
Hunt—but edited his paper there, publishing it twice a week instead of

once a week and raising its circulation, thus recouping his prison fees and making a handsome profit. A portrait by J. R. Smith shows him in Newgate, sitting at his editorial desk in a comfortable armchair, behind him a fine painting of Hampden hanging in a gilt frame against velvet drapery. A visiting Frenchman, Louis Simond, gave an amazed description of seeing Cobbett in prison, holding forth, writing against the government, seeing friends, and receiving political deputations.[26] Cobbett himself claimed that during his incarceration he had been visited by individuals and deputations from 197 different cities and towns all over Britain and Ireland.[27]

The treatment in jail of Leigh Hunt (1784–1859) was still more extraordinary. Hunt came from a family of Philadelphia loyalists who had been expelled when the United States became independent. His father, Isaac, was a chronic insolvent and Hunt's earliest memory was of a room in the King's Bench Prison for Criminals and Debtors. In due course Hunt became a notorious cadger himself—he figures as Harold Skimpole in *Bleak House,* Dickens claiming, "It is an absolute reproduction of the real man"—and his wife, Mary Ann, whom he married when she was 14, developed a remarkable skill for writing begging letters.[28] Hunt was an infant prodigy, a "Blue Coat," or product of Christ's Hospital, from whence came many writers and journalists at this time, among them Charles Lamb, Samuel Taylor Coleridge and the great *Times* editor, Thomas Barnes (if a London journalist was not a Blue Coat, he was probably a Scot). At the age of only 16 he published his first volume of poems, *Juvenilia,* which was a huge success and, as he put it, "made [me] fit for nothing but an author."

The one solid member of the family was his elder brother John, a printer, and it was John who started the *Examiner* in 1808. It was a weekly, published on Sunday, of 16 pages and only two columns a page, which made it more legible than most dailies (though the type was poor). Its circulation gradually rose to 7,000—3,000–5,000 was the usual break-even range—and, as Jeremy Bentham testified, was the most highly regarded weekly among "political men." It was not particularly radical, but had many brushes with the law. In January 1811, thanks to their counsel, Brougham, the Hunt brothers were acquitted of seditious libel for publishing an article critizing the army's punishment of 1,000 lashes as excessive and implying that Bonaparte's soldiers were treated more humanely. A year later, on 22 March 1812, Leigh Hunt wrote, possibly with the assistance of Charles Lamb, a ferocious attack on the Prince Regent. Prosecution inevitably followed, and both brothers were convicted of a "foul, atrocious and malignant libel"; they were sentenced (3 February 1813) to a £500 fine and two years' imprisonment.

Leigh Hunt served his sentence in the Surrey County Gaol, in the Borough. (John Hunt was imprisoned separately.) Wealthy prisoners could usually make themselves comfortable, but Hunt was already £500 in debt when sentenced, and it is not clear who paid for his "extras." At all events, he was allotted two fine rooms in the prison infirmary, which the staff painter and carpenter decorated to his taste. The barred windows were disguised by venetian blinds. The walls were papered with rose trellising and the ceiling was "colored with clouds and sky." Hunt was allowed to install his family and servant and his own possessions, including a large library and a piano. On top of the bookshelves was a bust of Homer—"there was no other such room," wrote Lamb, "except in a fairy-tale." Outside there were a green fence, a plot of grass, flower beds and specially planted trees, including an apple tree whose fruit supplied Hunt's favorite tarts. In his library Hunt conducted his extensive journalistic practice and received visitors. Barnes, then Hunt's assistant, wrote: "It became fashionable in progressive circles to be seen in his prison" (and to send hampers of delicacies). Brougham popped in. Hazlitt stayed to talk. Haydon was allowed to bring along his 12-foot *Judgment of Solomon* to show Hunt. Thomas Moore called and (like others) wrote a poem about the prisoner. Byron paid a visit and christened Hunt "the wit in the dungeon." When Jeremy Bentham came, he found Hunt playing a game called battledore. Throughout the sentence, Hunt continued to edit the *Examiner,* frequently going for the government—and it is worth pointing out that he need never have gone to prison at all if he and his brother had undertaken to forgo, in future, personal attacks on the Regent.[29]

To the modern mind, there sometimes seems to be an element of playacting in the political contest between the government and the radicals during these years. This is probably an illusion. The struggle was serious, because all had before them the indelible memories of events in Paris, from which such torrents of blood had flowed. But its intensity varied enormously. Many towns and districts, including entire counties, never experienced any disturbances. Others were quiet year after year, then were shocked by a sudden flash of violence. Occasionally, there was a general sense of crisis. The distress at the end of the long wars, 1815–16, was particularly widespread, compounded of a collapse in agricultural prices, heavy unemployment and the discharge of scores of thousands of soldiers and sailors. The wars were over, but the bills were still being paid, in the shape of servicing a huge national debt. The uproar led by Brougham in Parliament over the income tax reflected a general view that the burden of taxation was unbearable and must come down.

Landowners and farmers felt particularly harassed. There were new duties on hops and barley, in addition to taxes on farm horses, sheep-dogs and leather, county and highway rates and a crushing poor rate. The agricultural interest had made handsome wartime profits, but most of them had been reinvested in buying new land, draining, fencing, hedging and rebuilding; in addition, loans and mortgages had been taken out. Then, with alarming speed, peace brought a fall in the price of wheat from 134s a quarter in August 1812 to 52s6d in January 1816. The rural economy was shaken from top to bottom—farmers and landowners in the first place, then a knock-on effect hitting town and village tradesmen. A petition to the Commons dated April 1816 de-scribes one Cambridgeshire parish in which every inhabitant was now classified as a pauper except one—and this unfortunate gentleman was himself becoming impoverished because he had to pay the entire rates. There were suicides. Tenants-at-will simply walked out. Land went out of cultivation. On the Isle of Ely, 18 farms were reported abandoned. In Norfolk land worth £1.5 million was on the market; no buyers. According to John Grey of Dilston, Northumberland, in a letter to the *Times,* small landowners who were entirely dependent on income from agriculture had become "mere agents between the tenants whose rents they receive and the tax-gatherers and mortgagees to whom they are transferred."[30] To make matters worse, the weather in 1816 was horri-bly wet—much of the harvest was ungathered in October. Wealthy noblemen did what they could. Lord Bridgewater of Ashridge took 800 men into his employ, having a rule never to refuse work to men who wanted it.[31] The Duke of Portland reduced his tenants' rent on a sliding scale with the price of corn.

Such potentates had income from coal mines and city property. For most landowners and virtually all farmers, the only remedy was protec-tion—the system known as the Corn Laws. Parliament, where the landed interest was not only paramount but all-pervasive, responded. Corn laws in one form or another had existed from the Middle Ages. The Act of 1815 banned corn imports altogether until the home price reached 80 shillings a quarter. Its effects were widely felt in Europe. In Prussia, for instance, the collapse of the export trade in corn produced an agrarian crisis; within a decade, 154 knights' estates were under sequestration.[32] At home, the elements of a mighty internal quarrel, which was to last 30 years, quickly emerged. The farmers did not think they were being greedy. For the half century up to 1815, their interest had made the fewest demands for help from the state, though they thought themselves highly taxed. During the war, they had in effect operated a system of free trade. Now they made demands for a tariff of between 84 and 105 shillings. What they got, 80 shillings, was just enough to keep land in cultivation and no more than the manufacturers got through customs duties.[33] But mill owners and their hands saw ruin ahead: How could foreigners afford to buy our cottons and woollens if we refused their grain? And city dwellers generally rose up against a "tax on bread." The London streets were already crowded with combustible material, notably unemployed ex-servicemen, and the result was the most extensive riots the capital experienced in the whole period, directed not just against public buildings but politicians, too.

As such, the riots cast an illuminating light on the relationship between governors and governed in early 19th-century England. Could a Danton and a Robespierre have been found among the mob and those who led it? And, if found, would they have risen to take charge of any successful insurrection? These are not easy questions to answer. During the Westminster election, which pitted the radical Horne Tooke (1736–1812) against Charles James Fox (Whig) and Sir A. Gardner (Tory), the diarist Farington recorded a snatch of conversation between Gardner and one of Tooke's backers, John Thelwall, then regarded as a dangerous revolutionary. Gardner, looking Thelwall over: "Your countenance is not so alarming and threatening as to cause apprehension." Thelwall: "No, I am not so like a Tyger as *you* are." Tooke himself, Farington reported, was always ostensibly good-humored when talking to members of the ruling establishment, but once, while talking to John Hoppner RA, he said savagely of Pitt and Dundas: "If I had one on each side I should soon have a knife in their guts."[34]

The only successful political assassination of the period, of Spencer Percival on 12 May 1812, was actually carried out by a deranged broker with a personal grievance, John Bellingham. But eyewitness accounts testify that the news of the killing was greeted with joy in some quarters, perhaps whipped up by the radical press—the *Examiner* carried a vicious attack on Percival only two days before he was killed. In Newcastle-under-Lyme, the Manchester reformer Archibald Prentice said he saw a man running down the street shouting: "Percival is shot—hurrah!" According to Cobbett's *Register,* the London mob called out to Bellingham on his way to the scaffold "God bless you!" and tried to rescue him (but then they often cheered convicted murderers). Coleridge said he knew a pub where, for years afterwards, it was the custom to drink Bellingham's health, and Shelley, who could be bloodthirsty at times, began in 1814 a long poem inspired by the event, to be called *The Assassins*, though he never finished it.[35]

The authorities reacted to Percival's murder with savage speed, trying, convicting, and hanging the assassin in short order (though it is only fair to note that Bellingham refused to repent, confess, or apologize to Percival's family, saying he had dispensed justice with God's approval). But sometimes the response to personal violence directed against ministers was surprisingly casual. Almost exactly six years after Percival was killed, an aggrieved army lieutenant, David Davies—he had cut off his penis in a fit, then unsuccessfully applied for a pension—called at the War Office and shot the Secretary of State, Lord Palmerston, as he was going up the stairs. The ball bruised and burned the Minister, passing through his clothes and lodging in the wall. "Pam" went into his office and worked, and when the famous surgeon, Astley Cooper, who had been summoned, arrived, Pam refused to be examined, saying he was "too busy." He saw the family doctor in the evening who advised him to be "kept low and eat no meat."

Palmerston, as a prominent minister, was involved in the anti-Corn Law riots, which broke out on 6 March 1815, five days after Bonaparte landed in France from Elba. The Bill was then going through Parliament (it became law on 23 March) and the mob first attempted to storm Parliament and bring the proceedings to a violent end. There had been some warning, so the entire metropolitan police force, such as it was, plus 50 extra constables, were on duty. They prevented the mob storming the chamber, but not from assaulting members of Parliament as they tried to make their way in. John Wilson Croker was dragged from his carriage, struck repeatedly, and forced to promise he would vote against the Bill. Croker at least was a Minister and a hard-line conservative. But their next victim was a harmless Irish baronet, Sir Frederick Flood, member for County Wexford, whose speeches evoked laughter or an exodus. According to Flood's account, he was not only torn out of his coach but flung around "just like a mackerel from Billingsgate market." He added: "I thought they meant to quarter me." Sir Robert Peel later loved to tell the tale that, when pressed by the mob for his name, Flood said: "I will not equivocate with ye. My name is Waters."[36]

After complaints from members of Parliament, Charles Abbot, the Speaker, had some footsoldiers and cavalry deployed, whereupon the mob declared it would go and attack the private houses of various people connected with the Bill, naming Lord Eldon, the Chancellor, Ellenborough, the Lord Chief Justice, Fred Robinson, MP and the Earl of Darnley. Eldon managed to get some soldiers. Ellenborough hurried back, addressed the mob, made popular noises and persuaded it to disperse. Various ministers took precautions. Palmerston, then living in Stanhope Street, told his servants to barricade his doors and windows. His instructions were to do nothing until "the first discharge of stones." Then they were to reply with "a volley of small shot" to "pepper the faces of the mob without any danger of killing them," as an "earnest of what a further perserverence in the attack might produce."[37]

Palmerston was lucky that his orders were not put to the test, as the experience of Robinson proved. Hearing that all Darnley's windows had been broken and admitting that a controversial member of Parliament "had to expect" such treatment—an interesting comment on the age—Robinson moved himself and his ultranervous wife to his father-in-law's, leaving the servants to protect his own house in Old Burlington Street, Mayfair. The mob duly arrived, broke all the windows, smashed the iron railings in front, battered down the door, destroyed the furniture, and (said Robinson in sworn testimony later) "threatened to murder the servants if they did not say where I was to be found." Soldiers then arrived, and the mob left. The next day the mob returned, broke in again, and chased three male servants—the butler, coachman and a footman, upstairs—at which point the servants equipped themselves with pistols and "swan shot." For a time cavalry prevented further violence, but when the troopers left in the evening, the mob returned yet again and attacked. Some soldiers within the house used blanks, but swan shot was also fired. A midshipman, Edward Vyse, was killed, and a widow, Jane Watson, mortally wounded. Burdett, who had himself been cheered by the mob, rose in the Commons three days later to remark: "No man knows whether he is safe in going along the streets if people are to be placed in ambuscade and allowed to fire through doors and windows." Robinson, replying, burst into tears, and thereafter was known as "the Blubberer." A Middlesex jury brought a charge of willful murder against the butler, James Ripley, and three soldiers. All were eventually acquitted, but only after having been in peril of the gallows for some weeks.[38]

Apart from Robinson, all the political victims seemed to have displayed remarkable sangfroid. Captain Gronow, shortly to fight at Waterloo, saw the mob break all the windows in St James's Square, throw stones and mud at the Life Guards with cries of "Down with the Piccadilly Butchers!" and by drawing his sword prevented the Bishop of London's doors being broken down. He then wandered into King Street, where he found Lord Castlereagh, "a particularly handsome man," dressed "in a blue coat buttoned up to the chin, a blue spenser, kerseymere breeches, long gaiters, shoes covered by galoshes and a white neckcloth." The Foreign Secretary was "quietly looking on while his windows were being broken by these ruffians." He warned Gronow that, in future, he should be more discreet than to interfere with rioters, adding "the mob is not so dangerous as you think." He seemed "perfectly calm and unconcerned."[39] Croker, nursing his bruises, dismissed the whole business in a letter to Canning: "Our riots, which are a good deal exaggerated in the public papers, are subsiding and never were, I think, at all serious. But you know how timid all constituted authority is on such occasions."[40]

In December the following year, which marked the climax of the postwar disturbances, the authorities were obliged to take the matter a little more seriously. Though economic conditions, despite the bad harvest, were already improving by the winter of 1816, a meeting at Spa Fields on 2 December, at which "Orator" Hunt was to speak, attracted a large crowd, including a number of Spenceans. Two weeks before, one of them had proposed the old Jacobin toast, "May the last of the Kings be strangled with the guts of the last priest." On the day itself, the Watsons, who had been acquiring Dutch courage—young Watson was actually drunk—detached a section of the crowd, before Hunt had even arrived, and led them on a march on the City, breaking into gunsmiths' shops on the way, to seize firearms. Their aim was to storm the Tower, in imitation of the taking of the Bastille, and use the heavy weapons stored there to carry through a coup d'état. But the plan was easily frustrated by a charge of the City police, led by the Lord Mayor. Young Watson went into hiding and later escaped to America disguised as a Quaker. His father was tried for treason. As Farington recorded, most people, including Lord Grey, leader of the parliamentary reformers, believed him guilty. But, despite the efforts of Ellenborough, three members of the jury would not convict him at any price, so he was acquitted.[41] All the same, the Spa Fields riot seems to have antagonized public opinion. Efforts to hold more big meetings the following February and March ended in failure, and the focus of discontent shifted away from London and toward the north.

It is hard to believe that an insurrection could ever have overthrown the system by force. The odds were stacked too heavily against it. The ruling class was rooted in the countryside and there they were solidly backed by the farmers, most of whom had votes. There was occasional trouble in rural areas—serious trouble at the end of the 1820s, as we shall see—mainly because agricultural wages responded too slowly to fluctuations in food prices. When the price of wheat collapsed, farmers cut wages. Wheat was back at 116s a quarter by June 1816, but wages were still low; there was, accordingly, trouble in Essex, Suffolk, Norfolk, Cambridgeshire, and Huntingdonshire that summer and an actual armed revolt on the Isle of Ely. But these were more a rural form of strike action than a rising with a political program, and if they became anything more ambitious, they were easily dealt with by the local volunteers, cavalry officered by the gentry, whose troopers were the sons of farmers and rural shopkeepers.

Farmers might vote Whig or Tory, according to local allegiance or friendship, the wishes of their landlords, family tradition, habit or even personal conviction, but it was rare to find one who did not back authority as such. Cobbett accused the farmers of cowardice but they had a clearer view of their interests than he did.[42] Over the past century they had improved their position immeasurably. Enclosures of common land had put them almost on a level with the gentry in terms of buying goods, rather than simply growing and making them. By Continental standards, though not by American ones, British farms were enormous—not least in Scotland, where the farms of East Lothian were reported to be the best managed in the world. It is true that there were still 250,000 farms of less than 100 acres, but the average was climbing steadily to reach 111 acres, in England and Wales, by 1851, when the first figures became available. Half the farmland of England was in holdings of 200 acres or over, nearly one-sixth in 500-plus units. The smaller farms were nearly always rented, though 10 percent of the total was owned by a cultivating freeholder. What surprised Continental visitors were the good relations between tenant farmers and landowners. There might have been antagonism because the Law of Fixtures and the laws governing distraint and distress were, theoretically, hard on tenants. In practice, however, the bonds of the hunting field, where farmers and gentry mixed and swore as equals, and the unwillingness of landowners to be hard on men whose votes they had to solicit periodically, ensured harmony.

Then again, the bigger farmers were beginning to identify with the possessing class. It was rare for them to make fortune like the rising manufacturers, but they were hardheaded, money-minded men—a point well made by Jane Austen in *Emma,* whose heroine's appraisal of young Farmer Martin as a commercially minded man reflected the current opinion of the gentry. The bigger tenant farmers enjoyed sporting rights if their leases were for life and their rents £150 a year or more. That is why George Knightly, the squire in *Emma,* calls Martin "a gentleman-farmer," much to Emma's annoyance. A man farming 400–500 acres now built a house for himself of 200 square feet, with two reception rooms, two kitchens, an office, and at least four bedrooms.

His parlor had a sofa, a bookcase and engravings on the walls; he gave dinners; his wife and daughters bought their clothes in the market town; and his son, if educated, often served as an officer in the militia or yeomanry.[43]

Cobbett deplored this social advance. "The English farmer has of late years," he snorted, "become a totally different character. A fox-hunting horse; polished boots; a spanking trot to market; a 'get out of my way or by G——d I'll ride over you' to every poor devil on the road; wine at his dinner; a servant (and sometimes in *livery*) to wait at his table; a painted lady for a wife; sons aping the young squires and lords; and a house crammed up with sofas, pianos and all sorts of fooleries."[44] But the best landlords, like Coke of Norfolk, who owned 60,000 prime acres and never had a farm unlet even in the worst days of 1815–16, rejoiced at this social improvement—it was what he had spent his life trying to bring about: "I am proud to have such a tenantry, and heartily wish that, instead of drinking their port they could afford to drink their claret and champagne every day."[45]

But as the farmers rose socially, a gap widened between them and their laborers. Everyone noticed it. One witness at a parliamentary inquiry (1830) stated: "When I was a boy I used to visit a large farm-house where the farmer sat in a room with a door opening to the Servants' Hall and everything was carried from one table to the other. Now they will rarely permit a man to live in their houses, and it is in consequence a total bargain and sale for money, and all idea of affection is destroyed."[46] Cobbett, as usual, put it more crudely: "Why do not farmers now *feed* and *lodge* their workpeople as they did formerly? Because they cannot keep them *upon so little* as they give them in wages."[47] But this was only part of the explanation. Young men preferred to live in lodgings, if possible, valuing their freedom. And middle-class families no longer wanted to live, as it were, over the shop, with employees on the same premises. Exactly the same process was occurring in the towns, where apprentices, clerks, shop assistants and mechanics were moving out of their employers' attics and into boarding houses, and the employers themselves, as often as not, were leaving their premises for houses in more salubrious parts of town—led at the top by the Rothschilds, who gave up living at New Court in the City and bought houses in Piccadilly and Park Lane. This was all part of the immense longing for domestic privacy that characterized society at every level in these years.

Whatever the reason, however, it increased the social and political bifurcation of farmers and their hands. The difference of interest was underlined by the method of paying poor relief in the south and Midlands. In the 1790s Berkshire magistrates had invented a dole system under which parish rates met the difference between actual wages and what was considered a living wage. This system was widely adopted because its advantages to farmers were obvious. But it drew no distinction between the industrious and the idle, and it was an early example of what we have come to call the "poverty trap." A man with savings or a bit of property would not be employed by farmers because he was not eligible for dole. It meant that farmers could avoid paying living wages at the price of paying higher rates, and it made them seem grasping and exploitative and, in self-defense, zealous upholders of authority. In France, nearly 5 million farms were under 26 acres and only 140,000 over 100 acres. In the various German states, 50-acre-plus farms made up only 6 percent of the total.[48] In both countries, therefore, millions of farmers could and did identify themselves with the poor. In Britain only a tiny minority had this feeling. Farmers might express sympathy with distressed laborers who were rioting for a better living—some unquestionably did—but in face of efforts to overthrow the system, they closed ranks behind it. George Eliot, a girl at the time, whose father ran a large farm and engaged in most aspects of agricultural economics, has left us a striking picture of how he saw the world: "To my father's mind the noisy teachers of revolutionary doctrine were, to speak mildly, a variable mixture of the fool and the scoundrel; the welfare of the nation lay in a strong government which could maintain order; and I was accustomed to hear him utter the word 'Government' in a tone which charged it with awe, and made it part of my effective religion, in contrast with the word 'Rebel,' which seemed to carry the stamp of evil in its syllables, lit by the fact that Satan was the first rebel."[49]

Alongside the farmers were the clergy, especially the diocesan bishops and parish incumbents of the established Anglican church. As clerical diaries show—a typical one is that kept by the Rev. William Holland, rector of Over Stowey, Somerset—parsons and farmers bickered over the payment of tithes.[50] But their economic and social interests were broadly similar. The bishops not only sat in the House of Lords *ex officio,* but their incomes and manner of life were similar to those of the landed nobility. At the top was a man like William Howley (1766-1848), Bishop of London (1813-28), then Archbishop of Canterbury for twenty years. Howley was the last of the prince-archbishops and the last to make a personal fortune out of ecclesiastical revenues. He coincided with the beginning of "income rationalization" in the church, and on his death the Ecclesiastical Commissions reduced the stipend of his see to a mere £15,000 a year—thus beginning the process whereby, in our time, bishops have become comparatively poor men and have changed their politics accordingly. Howley, however, had a career and attitudes that embodied traditions going back to the Middle Ages. He was educated at William of Wykeham's great 14th-century foundation, Winchester College—where he "knocked down [Sydney Smith] with a chessboard for checkmating him," said to be the only violent action in his entire life.[51] He then proceeded to the other Wykehamist institution, New College, Oxford. Next, in the customary manner, he tutored the son of a leading landowner, the Marquess of Abercorn, who secured him preferment. In due course he became a grand pluralist, accumulating the rectory of Bradford Peverell, the vicarages of Bishop's Sutton and Andover, a canonry of Christ Church, and the Oxford Regius Professorship of Divinity—the whole topped by London, again obtained for him by Abercorn. In the Lords he supported George IV against his wife Caroline on the grounds that "a King can do no wrong either morally or physically," and that got him Canterbury. There, with the disdain of a true pluralist, he had himself enthroned by proxy, which evoked the comment from an envious and half-admiring Sydney Smith: "A proxy sent down in the Canterbury fly, to take the Creator to witness that the Archbishop, detained in Town by business or pleasure, will never violate that foundation of piety over which he presides—all this seems to me an act of the most extraordinary indolence in history."[52]

As the last old-style primate, Howley wore solid-gold shoe buckles and drove everywhere in a coach and four. When he dined out, no one left the room until he rose to go. At Lambeth Palace, he gave regular banquets to which guests (if of a suitable social position) invited themselves, and at these, wrote an eyewitness, "the domestics of the prelacy stood, with swords and bag-wigs, round the pig, the turkey and the venison." When, after chapel in the evening, he crossed Lambeth courtyard to "Mrs Howley's Lodging" (so called because, at the palace, no woman was then allowed to enter the official parts, even to dust the furniture), he was preceded by men bearing flambeaux. W. E. Gladstone later used to quote him as saying that "the revival of religion in England sprang from the horrors of the French Terror"; be that as it may, he showed a Castlereagh-like *insouciance* when rioting mobs identified him with the possessing classes. During a Reform Bill riot in 1831, his coach was pelted in the streets of Canterbury, and his chaplain complained that he had been hit in the face by a dead cat. Howley: "You should thank Almighty God that it was not a live one." When he died, he left the then-immense fortune of £120,000, entirely acquired through church preferment.[53]

There was nothing new about men like Howley backing authority, however. What was new was the growing affluence of the parish clergy, often for the same reasons which were making farmers well-to-do. This statement needs qualification. There were about 4,000 livings worth less than £150 a year, regarded as the clerical breadline. Some Perpetual Curacies (which were freeholds) might be worth only £75—Anthony Trollope's Rev. Josiah Crawley, Perpetual Curate of Hogglestock in *The Last Chronicle of Barset* (1867), was based on bitter truth. But one expert, Morgan Cove, worked it out that, if all clerical revenues, from prelates down, were pooled, the result would be an average income of only £167 for each ordained cleric. Lord Eldon's brother, Sir William Scott, MP, who acted as parliamentary law spokesman for the church, defended the inequalities of the system: "As the revenues are at present distributed, the clergy as a profession find an easy and independent access to every level of society. . . . Alter the mode of distribution and you run the risk of producing a body of clergy resembling only the lower orders of society [and] . . . and infected by a popular fondness for some other species of a gross, factious and a fanatical religion."[54] Sydney Smith defended the inequalities on the grounds that the existence of "the prizes of the church" was the only way to tempt men of great ability and superior education to enter it; if you leveled incomes, all you would get would be clergy "little less coarse and ignorant than agricultural labourers [and] the clergymen of the parish would soon be seen in the squire's kitchen, [this] in a country where poverty is infamous."[55]

As it was, there were quite enough prizes, just at the parish level, to secure a regular intake of first-class Oxford and Cambridge graduates. The enclosures added greatly not only to the wealth of farmers but to the incomes of rectors and vicars. An enclosure needed an Act of Parliament and no such Act could be promoted without the agreement of the holder of the tithes, that is, the parish clergymen or the individual or institution who appointed him. This was usually obtained by the landlord commuting the tithe, by agreement with the holder, with a gift of land. Thus, the glebe was expanded at a time when the value of almost every kind of freehold land was rising, as a result of improved agricultural productivity and urban spread.

Churches were raising their leases and generally improving their assets. The parishes of Manchester, Bury, and Rochdale, for instance, got Acts passed allowing them to let out their glebes in building lots on 99-year leases. At the same time, tithes were being extended to newly cultivated lands or ones hitherto exempt. It was in the southern counties and the Midlands up into Lincolnshire and Yorkshire that enclosures were most common, and the glebe was often doubled and trebled in these areas.[56] At Combe Florey, Sidney Smith regarded the glebe as small: in fact, it had a cosy farm of 60 acres, plus several acres of woodland and a huge formal and kitchen garden surrounding a handsome and spacious house.[57] In a generation or so, and especially in the years 1815–30, a large number of parish clergy rose to gentry status, often building the vast late-Georgian rectories which, in the last years of the 20th century, are eagerly sought by the very rich. They took up hunting and other field sports, gave their daughters seasons in London; and, above all sat on the Bench. It was as Justices of the Peace that the parish clergy most closely identified themselves with the possessing classes and the maintenance of order, and clerical justices were often the most resolute (or severe) in putting down disorder. *The Times* quoted a clerical Justice of the Peace, chairman of the bench in Manchester, addressing an accused rioter after the St Peter's Fields disturbance in 1819: "I believe you are a downright blackguard reformer. Some of you reformers ought to be hanged and some of you are sure to be hanged—the rope is already round your necks."[58] This was the Rev. W. R. Hay, who had represented the civil authority on the occasion, read the Riot Act, and ordered the soldiers to intervene. His critics said he was presented with the valuable benefice of Rochdale in consequence.[59]

From 1809 onward the government sought to reinforce clerical allegiance by financial generosity. That year Spencer Percival provided the first of 11 annual parliamentary grants of £100,000 "for the augmentation of poor livings," part of a process which, combined with the rise in returns from glebeland, was to raise average stipends to £286 by the mid-1830s. Then in 1818 came the Church Building Commission, provided initially with £1 million of public money, which was charged to design and build parish churches in new or greatly expanded industrial towns and cities, and which, in conjunction with the voluntary-funded Church Building Society, raised the number of new Anglican churches put up in the first three decades of the century to over 500, at an average cost of £6,000. Altogether, the government put £6 million into this effort. Critics said that many of the new churches in Manchester for instance, were seldom full, and that only a third of the places in "parliamentary churches" were free of pew-rents.[60] But this criticism was to miss the point. Attending an Anglican parish church, especially in the big towns, was a sign of respectability and status, and middle-class people expected to pay pew-rents. Indeed, they would not frequent all-free churches, the first of which dated only from 1795–98 (Christ Church, Bath, built by Archdeacon Charles Daubeny).

One reason why the government was willing to fund money for church buildings was its fear of the competition from other Christian sects—Nonconformist and Roman Catholic for instance—which, it felt, might be less attached to the existing order, particularly since they were still subject to many legal disabilities. The weakness of the Anglican system was that it was designed to promote decorum, rather than religious enthusiasm, and its incumbents were selected and trained accordingly. J. A. Froude later described the clergy of the 1820s: "They were gentlemen of superior culture, manners and character. [The average incumbent] was a man of private fortune, the younger brother of the landlord perhaps and holding the family living; as it might be the landlord himself, the advowson or right to appoint the clergyman being part of the estate. His professional duties were services on Sundays, funerals and weddings on weekdays, and visits when needed among sick people. In other respects he lived like his neighbors, distinguished from them only by a black coat and white neckcloth, and greater watchfulness over his words and actions. He farmed his own glebe, kept horses, shot and hunted moderately and mixed in general society. He was generally a magistrate, he attended public meetings, and his education enabled him to take a leading part in county business."[61]

That was all very well, but the parson could not electrify his congregation and produce that emotional alternative to political passion which, since the French Revolution, was felt to be needed and which other churches—the Roman Catholic, with its theatrical glitter and appeal to the senses, and the Nonconformist with its thunder and terror—so abundantly provided. It was against this background of emotional starvation that the Evangelical movement found an increasingly important place in Anglicanism. Wilberforce and his lay and clerical friends might be devoted to ending the slave trade, and even slavery itself, but in domestic politics they were wholly committed to preserving and even reinforcing the existing order, employing in this cause all the resources of salvation and damnation. They also, and to an increasing extent, began to bring into the battle the brains and imaginations of women. During the years 1815–30, the most powerful single force in the Anglican defense of social order was the writings of Hannah More (1745–1833).

Hannah More was, essentially, an 18th-century bluestocking, the fourth of five sisters who became successful and prosperous schoolteachers (all left substantial fortunes). She moved in the literary circle of Johnson and Garrick, but in 1787 underwent a religious conversion at the hands of the ferociously gloomy Calvinist divine John Newton, Cowper's friend, whose pessimistic style of preaching and hymn writing had a peculiarly mesmeric effect on women. She was already a skillful writer, but henceforth, Newton said, she must "wield a consecrated pen." In 1788 she produced her first work of social piety, *Thoughts on the Importance of the Manners of the Great to General Society,* which hammered home the message of her lifework—the need for the privileged to set a good example and for the poor to follow it. She wrote with fervor, simplicity, and considerable power. Seven large editions were sold out in five months. In 1792, alarmed like other Evangelicals by the bloodthirsty atheism of the French Revolution, she added a political dimension to her work, and at the same time gave it an attractive quasi-theatrical form, by publishing *Village Politics by Will Chip.* This was not merely a huge popular success; it was further promoted by government, which bought up tens of thousands of copies and sent them for distribution among the supposedly disaffected in Scotland and Ireland.

Hannah More's literary genius lay in directness and brevity, and her books—some were little more than tracts or pamphlets—were accordingly cheap. All over the English-speaking world, well-to-do, right-thinking folk had them reprinted at their own expense and distributed them free to servants, employees, farm laborers and any one else at their mercy. In every British village, the poor could expect to receive, at the appropriate season, food, old clothes, sometimes a little money, but always a slim printed work by Hannah More. From the mid-1790s she produced three pieces of writing a month: a short story, a ballad, and a meditation for Sunday reading. They were called the Cheap Repository Tracts, cost a penny each, and were afterwards bound into volumes. Cobbett admired them greatly and distributed them in the United States; in fact, they had a profound effect on his own popular style and public persona. More than this, they became the pattern for all 19th-century popular religious literature and, indeed, for much political propaganda.

Hannah More was the first person to sell over a million copies of a work, and in the first year of publication alone, more than 2 million got into print. In 1809 a more substantial book, *Coelebs in Search of a Wife,* appeared, epitomizing in story form her social message of piety, good works, duty, and obedience to duly constituted authority, but also wittily mocking the vanity and folly of society as it was. It was an instant and continuous success: 11 enormous editions were sold in England in nine months and 30 more in the United States. It was still being reprinted two decades later. In a way it constituted the foundation document of 19th-century morality. Since many of her pamphlets were given away and the poor did not have to pay for them, the vast circulations they achieved may exaggerate their true impact. How many were thrown away unread? We do not know. But the fact that she had so many imitators, lay as well as religious, suggests she got her message across. Moreover, *Coelebs* cost 12 shillings and within a year had cleared its production expenses of £5,000 and made her a profit of £2,000, as much as Sir Walter Scott got for one of his best-sellers costing 2 guineas.[62] Even the tracts were collected in bound volumes and sold in prodigious numbers. In one way or another, her writings made their entry into more homes, high and low, than Maria Edgeworth, Walter Scott, Mrs. Radcliffe and Lord Byron—her chief rivals in popularity—all put together. It is striking that her collected works were published in 8 volumes in 1801, 19 in 1818, 11 in 1830 and 6 in 1834—until then no other author had had 4 complete editions published in his or her lifetime. The record held until Dickens broke it toward the end of his life.[63]

Hannah More was not alone. One of her imitators, the Rev. Leigh Richmond (1772-1827), sold 4 million copies of *The Dairyman's Daughter* (1809) in 19 languages.[64] And there were others. The Hannah More phenomenon, in fact, indicates that Anglican Evangelicanism, intelligently presented and well backed by social leaders, could and did make more effective use of the cheap printing processes now available than the secular radicals. They beat the Nonconformists at their own game, too, at least until about 1830. Not that most of the sects were disturbers of established order. This was a view put about by many Anglican parsons, but reflected more their fear of competition than a genuine political threat. It is true that Unitarianism tended to be radical: indeed for many, this system of belief, not strictly Christian, was merely the gradual road to outright atheism. It attracted "progressive" thinkers who, unlike William Godwin, were unwilling to admit they believed in no God at all. This was Hazlitt's early background: his eyes to modernity were opened when he first heard Coleridge preach a Unitarian sermon—that of course was in Coleridge's radical days when he almost became a full-time Unitarian minister.[65]

Radical extremists, especially in the London area, sometimes doubled as Dissenting ministers, or at least presented themselves as such. An Act of 1812, designed to give relief to Nonconformity, virtually repealed the old repressive Conventicle and Five-Mile Acts. It also gave relief to the Unitarians since it abolished obsolete penalties for those who denied the Trinity. But its chief effect was to allow almost anyone to open a a "place of worship" even in city centers. A radical agitator who ran into trouble with authority in his secular persona could take out a license as a Dissenting minister, call himself a Prophet and rechristen his meeting place a chapel. They were often in scruffy stables and the like—one, run by the Prophet Stiggins and the sinister "Shepherd," is described in *Pickwick Papers,* though Stiggins's object was more to extract money from foolish middle-aged women than to overturn the government.

Thomas Evans, leader of the Spenceans, was a licensed minister with a chapel in Archer Street. His favorite terms of political abuse, directed at Tories and Whigs alike, were pagan atheist and Jesuitical, and his radical program was set out in a pamphlet called *Christian Policy* (1816). How sincere Evans was in his religious beliefs it is impossible to say, but it is obvious that another radical prophet, the former sailor Robert Wedderburn, who ran a chapel in Hopkins Street, was a fraud. Wedderburn's mother had been a black slave and, like his assistant, the printer Thomas "Black" Davidson, he was a lascar, the British nautical term for a mulatto, who had come to radicalism via the religiosity of the antislavery movement. Wedderburn was publicly a licensed minister but privately "captain" of the Sixth Section, the most militant of all the London radical groups. He and Davidson urged the congregation to drill and arm themselves, and they held military parades after chapel service. They were an early instance of the belief that clerical status offered some protection to law-breaking radicals in their battle with authority and in addition attracted some respectable people otherwise deterred by revolutionary notions. Such clerico-progressives were to become commonplace in the 20th century, but in the years after 1815 they were new.[66]

These two groups apart, however, it is hard to think of any religious sect which was predominantly anti-authority. The Church of Scotland, though driven by ferocious internal disputes on dogma, was united in backing employers against strikers, and police, courts and judiciary against rebels. Congregationalists or Independents were likewise conservative, the 1812 Act having removed their last grievances. The Methodist clergy usually backed the mill owners in Lancashire and Yorkshire and the Midlands industrialists in rows with their workers, though it is a myth they were always pro-government. The Welsh Methodists tended to be radical. When their parliamentary champion, Sir Francis Burdett, fell foul of the Commons, the Member of Parliament who moved his committal to the Tower, Sir Robert Salusbury, not only had his London house attacked by the mob but had the bank which he owned in Monmouth subjected to a run organized by local Methodist ministers. Methodists in southeast Wales, led by their preachers, clerical and lay, were said to be "Democrats to a man."[67] Some Methodists in Staffordshire and Cornwall were radical too. In general, however, Wesleyan teaching on social matters followed the same directions as Evangelicalism, urging industry, thrift, punctuality, deference to superiors and respect for all lawful authority. The Roman Catholics, at least in England, were much the same. Their clergy campaigned hard for relief from legal disabilities, which they finally got in 1829; that apart, however, priests were strongly pro-order, in line with the ideology of the Papal States, which next to Naples was the most reactionary kingdom in Italy. Irish Catholic immigrants, already numerous in Glasgow, Liverpool and Manchester, were another matter, easy mob-fodder. But such activities produced an equal and opposite reaction among the Protestant working class, slowly becoming a powerful conservative force in all three of these big cities, and soon in Birmingham too.

In general, it must be emphasized that radical violence was usually counterproductive, in rural and urban areas alike. Not only the middle class, already huge and growing rapidly, but the church-and-chapel-going elements of the working class, who saw themselves as "respectable," closed ranks when the stones flew and responded strongly to government appeals for order. The Bank of England, with 900 clerks, one of the largest employers in the capital, had its own corps of volunteers. Lord's ground in St. John's Wood, already the home of English cricket, was willingly handed over for militia drilling. Londoners with carriages freely provided them for the rapid transit of troops (though the government possessed power to commandeer them).[68] The pages of Farington's diary are crowded with instances of how the middle classes, from a combination of patriotism and fear of the mob, organized themselves to support government, artists, for instance, clubbing together to form their own corps or raising money for the war effort.[69] This feature of the war years persisted right into the 1820s, when the radical threat died away. At times there was genuine fear of the mob. When the mob threatened the house of Sir Robert Salusbury's aunt, Mrs. Salusbury, in Russell Street, where he normally stayed in London, he tried to sleep at a hotel but none would accept him for fear of having their windows smashed. Smashed windows, indeed, tended to induce bourgeois pusillanimity at times.

Normally city dwellers expressed their approval of a public event by putting candles in their windows at night—"illuminating" as it was called. They might also refuse to do so. "Illuminating" was the earliest form of public opinion poll. In times of social unrest, however, mobs would sometimes order householders to illuminate, to celebrate the acquittal of a radical hero by a Middlesex jury, for example, on pain of having their windows broken if they failed to comply. Such orders were often cravenly carried out, but they were bitterly resented. People disliked being put in fear by social inferiors they despised. Farington records the case of a lady, quietly playing cards in her house in Charlotte Street, who had a heart attack when she heard the sounds of a rampaging mob and "died of fright."[70] Such incidents were much resented. Throughout these times respectable people considered the government too weak rather than too strong. In a discussion with Farington at the time of the Burdett rioting, Turner's friend William Calcott RA argued that people should gang up together to defend their houses against stone throwers: "He spoke of the weakness and impolicy of the present administration and of the imprudent lengths they had gone."[71] The postwar suspension of *habeas corpus* was generally popular and any decisive move by government to keep the streets orderly and the mob cowed was usually greeted with approval.

There is also some doubt about the seriousness of the mob, especially in London. Contemporary reflections and eyewitness accounts suggest that many of those who composed it were in quest of excitement and booty (especially drink) rather than fundamental political change. They cheered the footguards and hissed the cavalry, as though attending some kind of theatrical performance. When Lord Eldon arrived for the victory thanksgiving service at St Paul's in 1814, the mob hissed him, believing him to be Ellenborough, who presided at the Cochrane Trial; when Eldon returned from the service he was stopped by members of the mob at Charing Cross who offered their apologies for the mistaken identification.[72] In any case, what constituted a mob? A thousand people? Two thousand? So far as one can judge from the accounts, it was rare for more than a few hundred people to engage in serious violence. Nor was it difficult to organize a mob for any purpose in a population in which the average age was 16 and vast numbers of people of all ages were underemployed and hung about the streets. At the time the Watsons were trying to get a London mob to march on the Tower, the Gloucester by-election of September 1816 saw Bransby Cooper, brother of Astley Cooper the famous surgeon, stand as a ministerialist and try to overthrow the Whig hegemony. The Whigs controlled more votes, and Cooper failed narrowly, 849 to 730, but he rejoiced that "the mob is ministerialist . . . the populace is fully with us." In this case the money was on the side of the opposition, the Whigs spending £25,000 to get their man in, but the people backed the government.[73] In late Georgian England, in any given political contest, there was liable to be a mob, potential or actual, at hand. But those who had

CAN THE CENTER HOLD?

been mobbed might raise one of their own. People brought up in these times were used to it. Hence, Mr. Pickwick's remark: "It's always best on these occasions to do what the mob do." "But suppose there are two mobs?" suggested Mr. Snodgrass. "Shout with the largest," said Mr. Pickwick.[74]

Nothing much separated the mob, whether friendly or otherwise, from the powerful. The amount of protection afforded the mighty of the earth was astonishingly little. Throughout the civilized world, government was an intimate matter. Whether he was going through an unpopular phase or a popular one, the Duke of Wellington went riding through the London streets every day, attended only by an unarmed groom. Ordinary people gave him letters about grievances and talked to him; he answered them politely, if abruptly. He thought little of popular cheers. Indeed he positively disapproved of troops cheering their generals, "as coming close to an expression of opinion."[75] He ignored booing, or even a stone or two. When a mob shouted at him outside Parliament, "No hero! We want no hero!" he seemed "very much amused by it," as his friend Mrs. Arbuthnot noted in her diary on 8 September 1820. Six weeks later "as we passed through Bedford a great crowd collected round the inn and loudly cheered [him]." He thought that amusing, too.[76] What he could not bear was people staring at him, especially at mealtimes. At his country house in Hampshire, Strathfield Saye, he had the following hand carved on a wooden notice board: "Those desirous of seeing the Interior of the House are requested to ring at the door of entrance and to express their desire. It is wished that the practice of stopping on the paved walk to look in at the windows should be discontinued."[77]

But rulers had to get used to being stared at close to, and addressed. The King of Spain, Ferdinand VII, supposedly a tyrant, traveled through the country in an ordinary coach, without an escort of any kind. He made good speed on the atrocious roads, changing horses every seven miles and averaging 12-14 miles an hour.[78] But while the horses were being changed, he always talked to whatever gawpers and urchins were around. The Austrian Emperor, a booby in some ways, was always friendly; he walked in the Vienna public gardens almost every day, talking to people. The King of Prussia perambulated Berlin; he had an aide de camp follow a discreet few paces behind, but no detective.[79] George III, in his walks, did have a detective, one McManus, and sometimes a Bow Street runner as well.[80] But he was very forthcoming to whoever crossed his path, the only problem being that he insisted on doing all the talking.

It was the same across the Atlantic. President Monroe liked to ride

THE BIRTH OF THE MODERN

in the countryside around Washington, dressed in a dark coat, light knee-length pantaloons, white top boots, and a dark beaver hat. Attended by a single black groom, he would "chat with folks." The same groom was in attendance at his second inauguration, 5 March 1821, which Monroe went to "in a plain carriage," admittedly drawn by four horses, but with no escort whatever. Monroe was regarded as a bit "formal" because he complained that foreign ministers dropped into the White House in the afternoon without invitation and expected to get tea and that likewise they thought he should call on them informally.[81] His successor, Adams, though stuffier than Monroe in some ways, was even more accessible and informal in others. In Washington's summer humidity, he wore only a black silk ribbon around his neck, instead of a cravat; this was reported by a Philadelphia newspaper, which added that he wore no waistcoat either and even went to church barefoot.[82] The last item seems hard to credit but it is certain that, during his presidency, Adams went swimming stark naked in the Potomac whenever he could, attended by his black servant Antoine in a canoe. These swims usually took place before breakfast and apparently lasted between one and two hours. The Potomac was by no means a tame river and on 13 June 1825 the President was nearly drowned when the canoe was capsized by a fierce breeze in midstream; he lost his coat, waistcoat and one shoe.[83]

It may be that American presidents were expected to be more available than European heads of state and heads of government. In winter, when it was too cold to swim, Adams insisted on a daily four-mile walk but took it early, before many people were about, to avoid buttonholing. But he seems to have spent several hours every day receiving members of the public, who arrived without notice or invitation. Many had dreadful tales of woe. "The succession of visitors," he recorded, "from my breakfasting to my dining hour, with their variety of objects and purposes, is infinitely distressing." He noted, 22 November 1826, a visit from a Mrs. Weeden: "She said she had rent to pay and if she could not obtain money to pay it this day, her landlord threatened to distrain upon her furniture." He had, he added, "many" such visitors. On 19 June 1828 he recorded a visit from the wife of a convict called Willis Anderson, sentenced to 10 years for mail robbery: "The importunities of women are double trials. I had refused this woman three times, and she had now nothing new to allege. I now desired her not to come to me again." The truth is that early 19th-century society, though much more brutal than ours in many ways, was more humanitarian in others. Many cases which would now be dealt with cursorily at a low bureaucratic level were then dealt with by the president face to face. Two weeks after trying to get rid of Mrs. Anderson, Adams had to receive a Mr. Arnold, who said he had been traveling and found himself in Washington without money; he would be "much obliged" to the President for a loan to see him back home to Massachusetts, "which I declined."[84]

If the president was not protected from visitors even in the White House, it is not surprising that American statesmen were even more vulnerable on the road. Traveling to Washington in 1829 to take up his post as Secretary of State, Martin Van Buren stopped at the City Hotel in New York and found the barroom crammed with people waiting to see him (mainly to ask for jobs). He held a meeting of them, said he was tired from travel and that they must write their business on cards. Then he went to bed but was immediately woken up by the angry Senator from New Hampshire, Levi Woodbury, who complained he had not been offered a post in the cabinet. When Van Buren finally got to Mrs. Miller's boardinghouse in Washington, after a horrible six-hour ride from Baltimore, another crowd of people were swarming all over the building, and he had to listen to them for an hour, escaping only by telling them—which was true—that he had to see the president.[85] The newly elected President Jackson, likewise proceeding to Washington, enjoyed no privacy, especially on the river steamer. Frances Trollope saw him at Cincinnati and recorded "the brutal familiarity" to which he was exposed at every place the boat stopped: "there was not a hulking boy from a keelboat who was not introduced." She noted particularly an exchange between the President-elect and "a greasy fellow." "General Jackson, I guess. Why, they told me you was dead." "No. Providence has hitherto preserved my life." "And is your wife alive too?" The General shook his head; she had only just died and he was inconsolable. "Aye, I thought it was one or t'other of ye."[86]

British ministers did not quite have to put up with this sort of thing. Deference was still a force, though everyone noticed it was much less all-pervasive in 1815 and after than in the 1790s, especially in the industrial north. In Manchester, for instance, it was now common for working men to decline to doff their caps when gentry passed in their carriages. When passersby addressed Wellington, they usually did so politely, however. He replied in kind. He would see them, too, at Apsley House, or Number 1 London, as it was known, provided they were respectably dressed. Most impressive perhaps, he would always answer their letters, invariably in his own hand, though usually in the third person. The historian is astonished by the number of letters early 19th-century statesmen wrote to members of the public who had complaints, requests and information to convey. But Wellington, though one of the busiest, was especially punctilious. In the years 1815–30 he must have written thousands of holograph notes, brief for the most part, in answer to correspondents unknown to him. He kept this up even while Prime Minister. To give only one example, on 12 October 1830, when his government was already in terminal difficulties, he received a complaint from the painter Haydon that the new government in France was going to embark on a policy of giving employment to historical painters—why could not Britain do the same? Haydon apparently sent his letter to the Duke at 9 A.M. By 2 P.M. he had the duke's reply, in his own hand, explaining exactly why it could not be done.[87]

Government was thus an intimate business, close to the governed, small in scale, conducted from buildings which were essentially private houses. When Palmerston took over the War Office in 1809 he was amazed at its vast size—no less than 23 messengers, for instance, plus those in the "Foreign Department," which handled mercenary troops, chiefly Germans, in British pay. The explanation was the growing amount of paperwork. In 1797 the War Office had issued only 14,253 letters and warrants a year; by 1820 the figure was 112,239, one reason being, Palmerston complained, the spread of literacy among the lower orders, so more of them made claims. Once the war ended, he set about vigorously (he claimed he often worked from 7 A.M. to midnight) reducing paperwork, costs, and the number of clerks. By 1821 he had got the entire staff down to 136 and proposed to reduce it still further to 122. At the same time he increased efficiency by forcing the clerks to register everything systematically. If they could not put their hands instantly on any letter he wanted, they were in trouble. "If any paper is lost after the 28th Instant," he noted in August 1816, "I shall mark my displeasure in an effectual manner on the clerk at the head of the subdivision." Any "carelessness and inattention" in the writing of official letters meant he sent them back for recopying. "I *insist* upon obedience to my repeated orders," he snarled in May 1817. "Let them take care I have no further occasion to take notice of any neglect."[88]

Palmerston poked into everything and was liable to burst into the clerks' rooms without warning, hoping to find them roasting their backsides against the fire instead of at their desks. It was a grievance with him that the clerks' hours had shrunk to 11 A.M. to 4 P.M. and that they got Saturday off during the parliamentary recess, though in theory they were supposed to work as many hours as the Secretary of State required, six days a week throughout the year, getting only Good Friday and Christmas Day off. He had the satisfaction of virtually doubling the amount of real work they performed. In return they hated him. One clerk had his revenge by habitually supplying the opposition

Morning Chronicle with snippets damaging to his boss, and Mrs. Arbuthnot wrote that when he left office in May 1828, the clerks as a whole were only just prevented from illuminating the building (when he left the Foreign Office in 1841 they actually did so).[89]

Sir Robert Peel performed the same kind of efficiency-promoting exercise when he was at the Irish Office. Moving to the Home Office in 1821, however, he found a very limited staff: 14 senior officials and clerks, a précis writer, a librarian, plus a few porters, cleaners and messengers. The Home Office's meager human resources, indeed, ruled out any practical possibility of running Britain as a police state, despite what critics of the system claimed. Peel, anxious as he was to save every penny, thought the setup inadequate to discharge its statutory tasks and housed in such a way as to be positively unhealthy.[90] But of course the Home Office did not run or even invigilate the country in the way an Interior Ministry did in Continental Europe. In so far as anything at all was done, the instrument was the Justices of the Peace at Quarter Sessions, whose main work was not judicial at all but administrative and legislative. They made new local laws by pretending to interpret the old. They set a county rate and approved parish rates, and they saw to it that parishes produced funds and/or labor or both to mend bridges. These sessions, or assizes, brought out most of the leading figures in the county, lay and clerical (about half the Justices were parsons by 1815) four times a year. The justices were such men as the large and silent Mr. Musgrove in *Persuasion*. Mrs. Musgrove commiserated with Admiral Croft's wife on her husband's absences at sea, adding *"I know what it is, for Mr Musgrove always attends the assizes, and I am so glad when they are over and he is safe back again."*[91] Since the justices combined executive, legislative and judiciary functions all in one, they could when they met take any action they saw fit to deal with local emergencies.

Edward III had devised the system in the 14th century as an instrument of central government, but by 1815 justices of the peace were, rather, symbols of self-government and decentralization. They had little to do with London. They were chosen by the lord lieutenant, who was, by custom, the largest or the next-largest landowner in the county. Party politics were rarely the determining factor in any of these appointments. At any one time, a majority of the justices were Tories, since most of the gentry, and a big majority of the clergy, were Tory. Equally, a majority of the lords lieutenant were Whigs, since more than two-thirds of the biggest landowners were Whig. It was very rare, indeed, for the government, acting through the Crown, to deprive a lord lieutenant of office, though it did happen—the earl of Carlisle was ousted from the East Riding in 1780, and another Howard, the duke of

Norfolk, from the West Riding in 1798. It was almost equally rare for a justice of the peace to be sacked. There was a good deal of self-imposed restraint on all sides to keep party politics out of local government, thereby making it possible for the elites of local communities to deal, as a whole and on a friendly basis, with authority in London. This system was a weighty source of stability for England during these difficult years, and it led the great French historian Elie Halévy to describe the Quarter Sessions as, with one exception, "the most original and most characteristic of all British institutions."[92]

The exception was the cabinet, which was a nebulous concept. Foreigners conceded that it must work, since Britain's position in the world was preeminent. They accordingly sought to imitate it, usually unsuccessfully. As we have noted, it did not function well in Restoration France. It existed in the United States, but at the end of the 1820s President Jackson began to sidestep it. The British made it work partly because it suited their inclination to have no formal rules. It was chaired by a man often known as the prime minister (also as "the first minister" and sometimes just "the minister"), though the post had no official existence. The formal title was First Lord of the Treasury. Constitutionally, a number of grandees, such as the archbishop of Canterbury, the lord chamberlain, the master of the horse, and the groom of the stole, were cabinet ministers, though they were not involved in politics. They attended only to hear the approval of the royal speech at the beginning of each session of Parliament, or to decide periodically whether capital convictions in London should be carried out, an occasion known as "the Hanging Cabinet."[93]

The real cabinet consisted of the effective heads of departments. Occasionally, a senior figure who had been dismissed from office sought to go on attending.[94] More often, a doubtfully attached minister failed to turn up or came rarely. Lord Ellenborough, in his diary, complained in 1828 that Charles Grant (1778–1866) "never comes to a cabinet yet he sits on the Treasury bench." He would "reappear at a cabinet dinner" without warning.[95] Sometimes a minister would skip a meeting because he did not approve of what was likely to be decided or because he feared a row. Meetings usually took place over dinner in the London house of one of the wealthier ministers. Ellenborough recorded on 2 July 1828, "Cabinet dinner at Lord Bathurst's. The Chancellor not there. I expect he thought we should have an angry discussion and chose to be absent and so clear of it. . . . We had a great deal of useless talk, a large portion of which originated in Lord Bathurst's being rather drunk." Drunkenness, indeed, was a cabinet hazard, Sidmouth (home secretary until Peel took over) being a particular offender. As Lord Melville wrote to Charles Bragge-Bathurst, on 26 January 1825: "Lord Sidmouth, as you know, has left us. We were therefore quite orderly and abstemious."[96] Ellenborough noted a remark of Lord Lyndhurst (1772–1863): "The Chancellor said to me, 'We should have no cabinets after dinner. We all drink too much wine and are not civil to each other.' "[97] As a rule, however, the problem of cabinet management did not lie in drink but in pride. Ministers tended to be difficult and assertive either because, as House of Lords grandees, the proud owners of rentals over £100,000 and many scores of thousands of acres, they felt themselves to be above the ordinary rules of politics, or indeed of nature; or because as House of Commons stars with personal followings, they were out for the offices of senior colleagues or indeed the prime minister's own, and maneuvered accordingly.

Men like William Pitt, and later Peel and Palmerston, outstanding ministers and House of Commons performers, were able to rule the cabinet as prime ministers by virtue of their talents and status. Indeed, all three, in their day, were autocrats. For a man like Lord Liverpool, it was not so easy. He was not particularly rich. He had no personal following. He was no orator. He had endless difficulties with George IV, on the one hand, and, on the other hand, had to keep in harness a team of able, ambitious, and often rival colleagues, like Castlereagh, Canning, Peel, Huskisson and Wellington. The strain, over 15 years, was considerable, and sometimes it told. He would threaten to resign or complain piteously of his woes. Wellington, while admitting he was "a superior man," complained he was also "a sensitive plant."

As long as Castlereagh was alive, the Commons was in loyal and safe hands; but after his death Liverpool was always nervous about Canning, now the dominant figure. Colleagues thought he deferred to Canning too much and, as Wellington put it, "Canning's empire over Lord Liverpool was more that of fear than love."[98] The duke was often asked to "have a word" with Canning, on Liverpool's behalf; indeed, the prime minister often used a second colleague to deal with a third. Even so, his nerve occasionally cracked, and there were various accounts of him losing his temper. Charles Arbuthnot related that "when annoyed at something that had happened [in cabinet]," Liverpool would "break a chair to pieces by dashing it against the ground." Once, during a cabinet dinner at Castlereagh's house, Liverpool was told that Lord George Cavendish had decided to vote against the government, which was not surprising, since he was a Whig. "Lord Liverpool began beating himself with his arms, in the most violent manner, and exclaiming in a sort of scream, 'Damn the Cavendishes! Damn the Cavendishes!' till at last he burst out of the room, continuing these gestures and exclamations through the hall to his carriage, to the great astonishment of the servants."[99] It is not related what happened in the cabinet meeting the prime minister left so dramatically. However, with all his nerves and tempers, Liverpool contrived to take the cabinet and the nation through fifteen difficult and potentially catastrophic years, from very rough to comparatively smooth waters, and it is a measure of his skill that, once he departed in 1826, the old system began to fall apart and, within four years, was doomed.

One reason why Liverpool succeeded in keeping the rickety old coach on the road was that he was much tougher than he seemed, especially over the disposal of patronage. Patronage, in the form of jobs, sinecures, titles, honors, and pensions, was the capital government needed to stay in business. A government survived by its prudent conduct of the nation's affairs. But it also survived by the judicious skill with which the prime minister doled out Crown patronage to the families and connections of members of Parliament and the nobility who owned or influenced their seats. This was the eighteenth-century system, built up by Sir Robert Walpole, which Liverpool inherited. But he was facing two difficulties. The first was the greed of the monarch, first as prince regent, then from 1820 as King George IV, who wanted to distribute choice jobs and titles to his own cronies (and their relations), who were usually not in politics and could do nothing to get the government's business through the Commons. Liverpool showed great resolve and obstinacy in rejecting George IV's importunities, flatly refusing, for instance, to put through the necessary paperwork that would have given a Windsor canonry to Charles Sumner, tutor to the children of Lady Conyngham, the king's mistress. George hated him accordingly. Liverpool also sharply turned down a royal request for a privy councilorship for the king's factotum, Sir William Knighton, provoking a cry of rage from George that was expressed in a letter to Wellington. Despite Knighton's great services to the nation, complained the king—one can picture the duke's ironic smile as he read these words—"the return is Lord Liverpool's *usual* absurd, weak and disgusting conduct. Depend upon it that Lord Liverpool, if he lives till doomsday, will never be corrected or made fit for the high office to which I raised him, and I should consider it a mercy to be spared the irritations to which I am constantly exposed."[100]

This letter cut no ice with the duke, for he was well aware of the second problem facing Liverpool: the growing shortage of governmental patronage of any kind. When he himself became prime minister five years later, he was to complain bitterly that there was virtually none left. British radicals insisted that the government's patronage, and its opposition to parliamentary reform, were organically connected. Yet it is a curious fact that, in the United States, as we shall see, both the extension of the right to vote and the growth of the spoils system were proceeding simultaneously, one feeding the other.

But while Tammany Hall and its system were being built up in New York, Walpole's system was being gradually dismantled in Britain. The process had begun with Edmund Burke's famous speech on "economical reform" in 1780 and had been proceeding ever since, silently and stealthily, almost unknown to the public.[101] There were two big commissions of inquiry, followed by a complicated mass of statutes, winding up or transforming offices and sinecures many of which had been in existence since medieval times. These statutes included 22 George III Chapter 75 (dealing with plantations and colonies), 22 George III Chapter 81 and 23 George III Chapter 82 (Exchequer), 24 George III Chapter 38 (Tax Office), 25 George III Chapter 31 (Royal Navy), 25 George III Chapter 52 (Audit of Public Accounts), 27 George III Chapter 13 and 29 George III Chapter 64 (Customs and Excise), 38 George III Chapter 89 (Salt Board), 38 George III Chapter 86 (Customs sinecures), 39 George III Chapter 83 (Auditors of Land Revenues), 43 George III Chapter 16 (Royal Navy), 45 George III Chapter 47 (War Office), and 46 George III Chapter 141, which dealt with the so-called subordinate treasuryships. In addition, there were many special acts dealing with the problem and a mass of temporary legislation suspending obnoxious practices from year to year. In 1810 George Holland, MP, on behalf of the Treasury, summed up the results of 40 years of "economical reform" in a remarkable speech, which was printed as a pamphlet.[102] He said that more needed to be done, and would be done; the process was continuous.

I list this legislation in detail because it indicates how complex was the process of turning a medieval country into a modern one by piecemeal reform, rather than by violent revolution. But it was happening— Britain was being transformed from a country ruled by corruption into one where the central government was fundamentally honest—and it was because ministers knew it was happening that they had a confident belief that the British constitution was basically sound, that the system could be reformed from within, and that they ought to resist cries for radical change. It is important to grasp this point because it explains why Liverpool and his colleagues saw themselves not as reactionaries but as progressive reformers, albeit cautious ones.

Some sinecures were abolished outright. Others ended when the existing holder died, a very British way of doing things. One of the most outrageous "jobs" had been the four tellerships of the Exchequer, whose fees, especially in wartime, amounted to about £25,000 a year each. The Act of 1784 reduced them to fixed salaries of £4,000, but existing holders continued to enjoy the fees. One of them, the marquess of Buckingham, did not die till 1813. The last, Lord Camden, was still alive in 1819, but made a deal with Liverpool and voluntarily surrendered his rights under 59 George III cap. 43.[103] Needless to say, Lord Liverpool, like other senior operators of the political system, had "places." So did his dependents—his valet, for instance, drew a salary as a War Office messenger, without doing the work. But Palmerston was putting a stop to such jobs, and that sinecure, too, lapsed with the person. In 1796, to give another example, the deputy secretary at the War Office, Matthew Lewis (father of the novelist "Monk" Lewis), combined this role with that of chief clerk, drawing the salaries of both, plus a multitude of fees amounting to a total to £18,000 a year.[104] But all that kind of thing had gone, or was going—as old men died and their office "freeholds" were abolished—by the years 1815–20.

There was, moreover, much more effective supervision of those who held the jobs. Obviously, in the case of Liverpool's valet there was an agreement to exempt him from doing the work, as in many modern trade union practices, such as the "ghost dockers" of the Dock Labour Board, finally abolished in 1989. But most so-called sinecures involved appointing a deputy, who actually did the work, and who was paid a portion of the official fee, the holder pocketing the rest. As we have seen, as a receiver of stamps, Wordsworth did not really have a sinecure. For a comparatively meager net income, which never amounted to more than about £500 a year, he had to do a lot of traveling and inspecting, and he had to ensure that the subordinates he appointed were responsible people. That was why he was not always willing to accept Lowther's nominations for these humble posts. He was terrified that the great mass of stamped paper he kept in his house in a vast iron chest might be stolen or that one of the sub-collectors would run off to America, owing him for the stamps. In either case, he would be held responsible. The default of a deputy was by no means a remote contingency. It happened in the case of a fellow poet, Thomas Moore, who through the influence of his grandee Whig friends, such as Lord Lansdowne, had been given an Admiralty sinecure in Bermuda. This sinecure involved collecting and ultimately transmitting large sums to the authorities, and Moore was careless in the man he appointed. In 1818 the deputy disappeared, leaving a deficit of over £6,000, for which Moore was legally responsible. The consequences, which dogged the poet for five years, can be followed in his diaries.[105] The government was willing to let officeholders have deputies, but was relentless in holding the principal to task if money went missing. In 1819 Moore was forced to flee to Paris to avoid arrest for debt and he was not able to return to London until Spring 1822 when, after a lot of maneuvering by his well-placed friends, the remaining debt was reduced to one thousand pounds, which Lansdowne paid (Moore repaid him in due course). Without the ability to draw on such influence, Moore might have been ruined and spent the rest of his life in exile. Indeed, he might even have gone to jail; that is what happened to Theodore Hook (1788–1841), the novelist and editor of *John Bull,* who was likewise let down by subordinates, even though he was on the spot at the time, and who was in prison from 1823 to 1825 for shortages in his accounts as treasurer of Mauritius.

Men far more sagacious than Hook and Moore were sometimes caught. Joseph Farington, RA, *éminence grise* of the Academy and a man universally respected for his prudence, was receiver of crown rents for Oxfordshire and Berkshire (the latter including the honor of Windsor). The profits of the job were not much over £300 a year, though he might be lucky if a big long-term lease fell due. In 1798 he had appointed as his deputy—that is, the man who actually did the work of collecting and transmitting the rents—a man named William Henry White. White appeared highly respectable and was actually recommended by the Treasury. He worked as deputy to a number of sinecurists. But he seems to have been speculating with the money that passed through his hands and was caught by the postwar financial collapse that began in the autumn of 1815. On 11 December, Farington got the horrible news that White had disappeared with debts of at least £42,000; it was unlikely that his property would pay even 2 shillings on the pound. Farington discovered that the deficiency, as far as he himself was concerned, was £2,663.13.6, "such has been the conduct of this villain in return for the confidence I had placed in him." As with Moore, what happened next can be followed in harrowing detail in Farington's diary.[106]

Another unfortunate sinecurist, one Baseley, was faced by White's fraud with a deficiency of £33,000, and that is the last we hear of him—he clearly went to jail as a hopeless bankrupt or fled to France. Farington survived, thanks to a timely loan of £980 from his brother Bob and by endless visits to the Treasury and other governmental departments accompanied by assiduous lobbying of his political friends. He thereby managed to get the matter settled quickly without interest piling up (in Hook's case the affair dragged on from 1817 to 1823). But this involved the intervention of three senior members of the government—the prime minister; the chancellor of the Exchequer; Nicholas Vansittart, the postmaster general; and Charles Long, as well as William Huskisson, then chairman of the Commissioners of Land Revenue, all over a matter of (by then) less than £2,000. Nothing gives clearer insight into the smallness and intimacy of government in those days than reading about this affair, blow by blow, in Farington's entries. Or, indeed, into the perils of receiving patronage.

Yet patronage, rapidly dwindling though it might be, remained for the time being the oil that kept the machinery of government working. The prime minister and his leader of the House of Commons, first Castlereagh, then Canning, had to keep his parliamentary majorities up to get the money supply and legislation through. He did so through the whips, and it is significant that the official title of the chief whip, even to this day, is the patronage secretary. In the last resort, everything depended on the House of Commons and how it felt. It was a curious, irrational, unpredictable, and always formidable assembly. Though the most powerful body in the world, and just at the beginning of its worldwide influence, it met in grievous discomfort. The chamber was only 50 feet long by 33 wide and could seat fewer than 350 of its 658 members, even when they were squashed together. In 1791 an "air machine" had been put in to "draw off the bad air" after dinner, much needed in view of the quantity of wine the members drank.[107] Richard Wharton (1764–1828), the member for Durham and, as chairman of ways and means, one of the most hard-working men in the Commons, complained it was an unhealthy life for those who took their duties seriously and spent long hours there, especially in winter, when the windows had to be shut (the "machine" did not work well). But he pointed out that in 1808, for instance, only one member out of the 658 died, and he was Admiral Rainier, aged over 80. Wharton attributed this to the fact that the keen members who attended late sittings did not keep carriages waiting but walked home.[108] "Home" might be some distance—not until 1812 did a ruined baronet, Sir James Colleton, who had recently emerged from the King's Bench Prison, conceive the useful idea, in conjunction with Lady Colleton, of running a boardinghouse for members of Parliament in Jermyn Street, charging them £400 a year each.[109] Since 1790, however, there had been a House of Commons caterers, Bellamy's, which supplied, among other things, the pork pies Pitt remembered on his deathbed, and the oranges that orators sucked from time to time during a long speech (Brougham kept his top hat full of them, sliced in two, when going full blast).[110]

There were many of these long orations. In the Walcheren Debate, March 1810, the first four speeches took a total of fourteen hours.

Richard Brinsley Sheridan's speech against Warren Hastings in February 1787 lasted over five hours. Sheridan was outdone by Brougham's speech on law reform, 7 February 1828, which went on for six hours and three minutes precisely. Brougham is said to have "held the House" on this occasion.[111] Charles Bell, the famous surgeon, recorded that Brougham "delivers himself in a measured, slow, continuous flow of words . . . sawing first with one hand, then with the other, and generally holding out two fists straight before him."[112] But members of Parliament were not, as a rule, impressed by oratorical pyrotechnics. Brougham's brilliant speech attacking the Prince Regent on 20 March 1816 misfired. Thomas Creevey received a detailed description from the member for Essex, Charles ("Squire") Western (1767–1844), calling it "a speech which, for power of speaking, surpassed anything you ever heard, and by which he has damned himself past redemption. . . . Where the devil a fellow could get such lungs and such a flow of jaw surpasses my imagination. I was sitting in the gallery and he made my head spin in such a style I thought I should tumble over. When I recovered, I began to think—this will never do—impossible—I will go down and see what other lads think of it. I soon found that everybody was struck in the same way, and even more." Sir Samuel Romilly summed it up: "very injudicious."[113]

Brougham might have a forensic hit with a speech. He might have a flop too, and on these occasions the Commons made its views unmistakable. The radical Samuel Bamford, on his first visit to the Commons gallery, witnessed Brougham in trouble: "At times he is heard in the pauses of that wild hubbub, but again he is borne down by the yell which awakes on all sides around him. Some talked aloud. Some whinnied in mock laughter, coming like that of the damned from bitter hearts. Some called 'order, order,' some 'question, question'; some beat time with the heels of their boots; some snorted into their napkins; and one old gentleman in a side-gallery coughed himself from a mock-cough into a real one and could not stop until he was black in the face."[114]

The typical backbencher's attitude to oratory is summed up in various sayings of James Fergusson (1735–1820), the member for Aberdeenshire. When Fergusson first set off for Parliament, his mother had told him: "Never expose yourself, James, to be tried for a rape, for your broad shoulders will cause a jury to think it probable that you made the attempt, and your face will make it manifest that it must have been against the will." This big, ugly, shrewd man stayed in Bellamy's when Pitt was speaking. " 'What,' said they. 'Won't you go to hear Mr Pitt?' 'No,' he replied, 'why should I? Do you think Mr Pitt would go to hear me?' "[115] At the end of his life, Fergusson "was wont to say that he had heard very many fine speeches in his time on *baith* sides of the question, and on coming down to the House he had *vary* often changed his opinion, but *naver* his vote."[116]

The oratory, effective or not, was provided by a tiny proportion of the House. In the Parliament of 1790, for instance, a mere 19 speakers, led by Pitt and Fox, made 5,100 out of over 9,000 speeches, or more than 57 percent. More than half the members never spoke, and of the talking members, perhaps a quarter spoke only once. As far as I can discover, of the members who were returned for the borough of Preston in Lancashire during the forty years, 1790–1830, two in each Parliament, none ever spoke at all. Many were there, as Burke once put it, chiefly to "maintain the consequence of their families." The member for Dundalk, P. C. Bruce, admitted he was there simply for his "amusement and gratification" (it cost him £12,000 over five years).[117] The members who sat from 1790 to 1820, 2,143 in all, formed a remarkably good cross section of Britain's ruling class in its broadest definition. The average age of members on first entering the Commons was 33, and of the House as a whole, 44.[118] Many were very long-serving, especially the County members, who were nearly always noncareerists, there by virtue of their local family status. In many cases, their fathers and grandfathers had sat in the House: One-third of all members were sons of members, past or present.[119] Occasionally, minors were elected, quite unlawfully, but they were rarely unseated on these grounds; they did not attempt to speak or vote until they passed their twenty-first birthday. Of the 2,143 members, 148 sat for 25–30 years, another 119 for 30–35 years, 72 for 35 to 40 years, and another 72 for 40 years or more. Those who sat for more than 40 years included Palmerston (an Irish peer), who sat for 57 years (his father having sat for 40) and Sir John Aubrey, who sat for 58 years, in seven different constituencies.

The Commons was representative in other ways. There were 25 bastards and 50 who acknowledged having bastards themselves; 23 were divorced. Sir John Saint Aubyn had 15 children by the mistress he eventually married. Over 100 had 12 or more children and 6 had 17 or more; Sir Edward Knatchbull, Bt., had 20, his heir 15. About 10 percent got into trouble; at least 200 were ruined financially and 35 died abroad in consequence. Indeed, freedom from arrest for debt was one reason men sought to enter the Commons, though their privilege lapsed the moment Parliament was dissolved—and seven former members during this period died in debtors' prison. In 1818 Robert Christie Burton, MP, was actually in jail for debt but applied to the Speaker for relief, and the Commons directed he be freed; when Parliament was dissolved, he fled abroad. About 15 members were in the House primarily to escape arrest for debt, but many others took advantage of it.[120] During a thirty-year period (1790–1820), only one member was actually taken into custody for being roaring drunk in the House, but many were alcoholics or drug addicts. On May 25, 1811, we are told, every single Irish member present was intoxicated during the debate on Catholic Relief. Only five members were expelled for fraud, though many more deserved it. At least 35 members verged on insanity or were definitely insane—they included the Earl of Bective, "a chattering, capering, spindle-shanked gaby," whose adultery with Lady George Thomas Beresford caused her husband to commit *her* to an asylum. The varieties of madness found, ranging from egomania and senile dementia to persecution mania, were pretty typical, my researches show, of society as a whole, though members of Parliament were more likely to try to shoot each other than was the average citizen. At least 19 committed suicide, 6 while mad.[121]

Members of Parliament came from 240 different schools. By 1790 Eton had overtaken Westminster as the leading supplier of members, with about 400 as against 239; Harrow, with 177, overtook Westminster in 1826. Charterhouse provided 35 and Rugby 27, and Edinburgh High School had at least 20—no other school totaled more than 10. By 1818 over 60 percent of the members had been to a university, Oxford leading with a total of 531 in this period, against 414 from Cambridge. Thanks to the efforts of its dean, Cyril Jackson, Christ Church provided more members, 285, than all the other Oxford colleges combined; Trinity, Cambridge, had the next highest (151), followed by Saint John's, Cambridge. Over 500 members were entered for an Inn, and 225 called to the Bar. The religious spread was wider than might be thought, though obviously it involved fraud over oath taking. The most interesting nonconformist group was the Unitarians, though there was also a convert to Greek Orthodoxy, two Irvingites, and a Plymouth Brother.[122]

If we leave aside peers, most of the richest men in the country got into the Commons.[123] What was striking, especially in the years after 1815, was the growing number of self-made men. Over 100 rich members who sat in the House during the period had made their own fortunes, not just from obvious trades like brewing and distilling, but from, for instance, pharmacy, corn dealing, estate jobbing and portrait painting (Nathaniel Dance). Some had humble origins—Robert Macbeth was an ex-waiter, William Roscoe had been a wandering scholar-poet, James Mackintosh and Francis Horner were intellectuals, William Taylor was an opera manager, and Joseph Richardson was a playwright.[124]

However, when all was said and done, the hard core of the Commons was composed of ministerialists and those belonging to or dependent upon the nobility. The Celtic fringe provided much of the corrupt element. The Scots members were mostly managed and rewarded by the machine built up by Henry Dundas, Lord Melville, a machine which continued to function after his death. The Welsh were not formally managed, but were generally subservient to power in the hope of tidbits. Amazingly enough, they were also silent, as a rule. Of 74 Welsh members in the period, 46 never spoke at all and another 10 spoke only once or twice. Sir Thomas Mostyn "barked and hallooed but never spoke in the House." The most corrupt were the 100 Irish members, managed by Dublin Castle. They included Denis Browne, known as "the Great Leviathan of Mayo," whose family had a monopoly of governmental patronage in the county. Another was G. H. Rochford of Westmeath, who voted for ministers in return for jobs and pensions for his sons. He complained in 1812 that their "emoluments," as he put it, had fallen from £1,100 a year to £600; hence, government was "considerably in arrears of favours."[125]

To maintain a majority, the government had not merely to satisfy these Irish, Scots, and Welsh members, adding in English placemen; it had also to content the big fish of the House of Lords. Each Parliament included, on average, 170 sons of peers. Certain rich and highly "political" families were overrepresented. During the period, the Ponsonbys, the Townshends (both branches), and the Butes, Stuarts and Stuart Wortleys each produced 9 members; the Spencers and Fanes, eight each; the Cavendishes, Bouveries, and Somersets, seven each; and a good many, including the Clives, Smiths (Carrington), Cocks, Fitzroys, Manners, Wellesleys and Leveson Gowers, six each. Two branches of the Dundas family produced 123 between them, but that was Scotland, of course. Early in April 1827, a few weeks after Liverpool was knocked out of office by a stroke, Croker sent Canning, who was shortly to become prime minister, two memos showing the power of the aristocracy in the Commons and, therefore, the need to conciliate at least some of its bigger members.[126] He showed that 33 peers between them returned 116 members, proving "how impossible it is to do anything satisfactory towards a government of this country without the help of the aristocracy." His conclusion, and a very important one it is, was that "the *old Tory* and the *steady Whig* aristocracies have at least 150 Members in the House of Commons, not by influence or connection but by direct nomination, and that no Government which did not divide them could stand for any length of time." Croker further noted that of the 100-plus members returned by the 33 peers, only 18 held office (they included Canning and himself), the inference being that the grandees were content with influence and honors, rather than with exercising direct power.

The electoral system, of which the landed aristocracy was so salient a component, was very complex and probably more representative of national opinion than modern democrats are prepared to allow, albeit that in England, for instance, the electorate numbered only 190,000 (counties) and 123,000 (boroughs), a total of 313,000.[127] Moreover, at any one general election, only a minority of seats were contested—in 1818, for instance, of 190,000 county electors, only about 36,000 got the chance to vote. In the counties a man had to have a freehold worth at least 40 shillings a year to vote, but since a freehold was interpreted loosely to include leaseholders for life, annuitants, mortgage holders, placeholders, and church benefices, the county electorate included many poor men. So did the boroughs, since they embraced household, freeman, scot-and-lot corporation, burgage and freeholder franchises, computed in innumerable different ways. Individual electorates varied from about 5,000 voters downward. The larger the electorate, the more likely the seat would be contested, at any rate when party feelings ran high; on the other hand, such seats were very expensive to fight.

In Middlesex for instance, there were about 6,000 voters. Two elections there were reckoned to have cost Sir Francis Burdett £56,000, "and he has probably paid £3–4,000 more to persons procured on his account."[128] Yorkshire was even bigger: About 20,000 were eligible to vote, and when Wilberforce won the seat in 1807 against all the might of the Whigs, he racked up a total of 11,806 votes, the highest anywhere until Brougham fought and won the same seat in 1830. But the cost was ruinous. Earl Fitzwilliam, the richest man in Yorkshire, whose son, Lord Milton, came in second in the poll, said he would spend up to £150,000, which meant forfeiting up to £5,000 a year of his income. In fact, he forked out about £100,000, and the third and losing candidate, Henry Lascelles, son of the earl of Harewood, spent slightly less. Wilberforce's backers, all over the country, raised £112,000 by subscription, of which £28,000 was actually spent (the remaining £84,000 was returned). These huge sums, in terms of purchasing power, were comparable to expenditures on a modern American presidential election.

Yorkshire and Middlesex were unusual, of course; when contested, they tended to produce a result that genuinely reflected national opinion—in Fox's words, "Yorkshire and Middlesex between them make all England." But there were other big constituencies: Westminster, for example, had about 12,000 voters out of a total population of 158,210;

Burdett stood there, too, raising his total election expenditure to over
£100,000.[129] Contested electioneering could, indeed, be ruinous. The
Northamptonshire election of 1806, for instance, knocked out the marquess of Northampton and Lord Halifax, who had property there; it
was a decade before either recovered. Sir John Hadley D'Oyly, Bt.
(1754–1818), who had made a fortune in India, was undermined by an
Ipswich election that cost him £20,000 and eventually had to go back
to moguling.[130] In 1816 at a by-election, Edmund Pollexfen Bastard had
to spend £25,000 defending the family's Devon seat, where the electorate was 8,000 against the Fortescue interest—he won, but the cost
knocked *him* out financially, and two years later he had to raise a
subscription to fight the general election.[131]

All big constituencies cost money when contested, but the level of
corruption varied enormously. There were 1,600 voters in Hull, "and
it is a regular custom to pay a great majority of that number 3 guineas
a man," though the money changed hands only after the polls to avoid
infringing the anti-corruption acts. At Stafford, another corrupt place,
each election cost Sheridan about £8,000.[132] The trouble was that
spending a great deal did not guarantee actually sitting in the House,
since large numbers of elected members were unseated on bribery
petitions. Thus, in 1806, Coke and Wyndham spent £70,000 getting the
latter elected for Norfolk. On behalf of their opponent, Colonel Wode-
house, two society ladies, Mrs. Berney and Mrs. Atkins, rode through
Norwich in a barouche bearing his colors. Coke-Wyndham supporters
hired and dressed up two prostitutes in imitiation and paraded them.
This affront was decisive in getting Wyndham unseated on petition.[133]
At Barnstaple, still another corrupt place, in 1818, Sir Mannasseh
Lopez, Bt. was found to have raised the customary payments to electors
from £3 to £5 and was not only unseated but tried for bribery. Acquitted in Devon, he was found guilty of similar charges in Grampound,
where his agent had paid £35 each to 40 electors, though he later sold
this "interest" to somebody else. For this incidents, he was convicted,
fined £10,000, and sentenced to two years' imprisonment.[134] (He nonetheless died worth £800,000, then a colossal fortune.)

The Lopez case was exceptional, however, and bribery, at any rate
in a direct sense, was much less common than critics of the system
proclaimed. Colonel Mark Wood, who returned from India worth
£200,000, bought an estate that included the parliamentary borough of
Gatton for £90,000. But he found that the seven tenants, all voters,
could not be bribed, though offered up to £500 each.[135] Many accusations directed against particular boroughs were false. Reading, with a
population of 9,421 and about 600 electors, was said to cost £4,000 in

"treats," "and this without any man receiving a farthing by way of a bribe." But Francis Annesley (1734–1812), who represented it for 32 years, being elected five times, told Farington that it never cost him more than £200.[136] Annesley, however, was a popular local man, who treated the people of Reading with consideration and worked for their interests.

Palmerston, who hated forking out money for any purpose, left his safe seat at Newport because it cost him about £7,000 every few years and got himself returned for Cambridge (which carried much more prestige) at a by-election in 1811. Between then and 1826, it cost him virtually nothing, since he was returned unopposed at three general elections (1812, 1818, and 1820). In 1826 he found himself branded as a "Catholic" and opposed by two of his governmental colleagues— Copley, the attorney General, and Goulburn, standing as "Protestants." Liverpool declared himself neutral, provoking Palmerston's complaint: "L. has acted as he always does to a friend in personal questions—shabbily, timidly and ill." The incident soured Palmerston's relations with the Tory establishment and had important consequences, as we shall see. All the same, the contest only cost him £700, to reimburse the traveling expenses of his nonresident voters, not then regarded as bribery.[137]

The truth is that, once a man was established in a seat and provided he sought to represent all the people of the place on a nonpartisan basis, the likelihood of his being challenged was small. A sensible, fair-minded man could thus earn himself a seat for life. This applied particularly in county seats, but occurred also in a large number of English boroughs with middling electorates. Of course, if a member took a step, in or out of Parliament, which affronted a sizable section of his constituents, then he could expect to be opposed next time. The great merit of the system, then, was that in many constituencies it encouraged members of Parliament to rise above the party level and work in the general interest. This was called "preserving the peace of the country."

As a result, under the unreformed system, there were always more walkovers than contests. In the thirty years 1790–1820, thirteen counties did not have a single contested election and nine counties had only one. Yorkshire's Wilberforce election of 1807 was very expensive, but it was the only time the county went to the poll in nearly 80 years (1742–1820). In Staffordshire it was said that "this county has been without a contest for so many years that the voters hardly know what it means." It was not uncommon for a properly qualified freeholder to pass an adult lifetime without having the chance to exercise his vote. But few minded, provided the sitting member was acceptable. Most "respectable" people regarded the social harmony of the locality as more important than political point scoring; there was an instinctive hostility toward whoever provoked a contest, whether it was the sitting member by his partisanship or an intruder by his ambition. Hence the tremors set up throughout Westmorland—reflected in Wordsworth's initial incredulity—when it was learned that Henry Brougham, of all people, was to take the opportunity of the 1818 general election to force a fight for the county.

In Westmorland there had been no contested election for 44 years. Nor was it surprising. When Croker sent Canning his list of peers who returned members of Parliament, at the head of it stood the Earl of Lonsdale (1787–1872), with no less than nine. This political empire had been built up by his predecessor, Sir James Lowther, first Earl of Lonsdale (1736–1802). The Lowthers were a ramifying family connection who had lived in the Lake District for over 700 years, but James, by inheritance, united the properties of three branches and eventually owned over 100,000 acres, the towns of Whitehaven and Cockermouth, and coal mines that brought him over £25,000 a year.[138] He became one of the richest men in Britain, and a miser to boot. But his passion was politics. In 1754 the Lowthers ousted the Tuftons as the most active political dynasty in the Lakes, when the Tuftons agreed to share with them the representation of Appleby, in consequence of which no contest was held there for nearly eighty years, 1754–1832. That left eight seats in the two counties of Westmorland and Cumberland. As a young man, James Lowther ousted the Wyndhams from the two Cockermouth seats; in 1768 he forced the Duke of Portland's interest to share the two Cumberland seats and at the same time secured possession of the two Westmorland ones (one for a Lowther, one for a "friendly").[139] Finally, in 1790 he reached a compromise with the Howards to share the Carlisle seats. He also bought his way into two seats in the south of England.

Lowther's success was due to his obsessive attention to detail, his extensive knowledge of the immensely complex electoral law (especially Land Tax Assessment, which governed the right to vote), his ability to create "mushroom" freeholds—five hundred of his miners thus got the vote—and his willingness to spend a lot of money acquiring vote-holding territory. He waged a ferocious battle, for instance, to buy the Forest of Inglewood, which carried 300 freehold votes, from the duke of Portland, spending £150,000 and almost ruining the duke in the process.[140] By the turn of the century, he had ousted or tamed all his competitors in the Lakes, controlling seven out of its ten seats, and made himself the dark prince of borough mongers. He was also universally and passionately hated.

It is unclear what Lowther's object was in building up and maintaining this empire. He got himself an earldom—but that was probably his due anyway by virtue of his vast possessions. He did some good things: He was responsible for bringing the young William Pitt into Parliament in 1781. He had no general political philosophy, but he had strong views on matters of detail and insisted that "his" members of Parliament, including his brother Robert, voted in line with his wishes. Probably his main motive was the simple desire to exercise despotic power. This desire was what James Boswell discovered when, foolishly supposing that Lowther might bring him into the Commons, he agreed to accept the dogsbody job of Recorder of Carlisle. This legal official had to put a formal stamp on the Earl's dirty electioneering work in the borough. The final volume of Boswell's diaries contains a detailed and harrowing description of what it was like to be one of the Earl's dependents.[141] Boswell pronounced him "a monster," "mad," "a brute." Horace Walpole said it was difficult to decide whether the Earl was more unpleasant in private or in public. Alexander Carlisle recorded that he was "more detested than any man alive, as a shameless political sharper, a domestic bashaw, and an intolerable tyrant over his tenants and dependents"; he was "truly a madman, though too rich to be confined."[142] He seems to have been an opium addict: Farington said that Lord Mulcaster told him Lowther was too stingy to employ doctors and "would be his own physician—took laudanum not by drops but in quantities measured by the finger." Thus, he was "never disciplined" and "always irregular." He "threw all his letters and papers into a room together, then heaped them in baskets." Often he flatly refused to pay what he owed, simply challenging his creditors to take him to court, where they would be confronted with a battery of attorneys. At the same time, he hoarded money. At his death £16,000 was found in guineas, which he had carefully sorted into three huge bags, labeled "Indifferent," "Very Perfect," and "Super Excellent."[143]

It is not surprising, then, that Lowther was known as "the Bad Earl" or "Wicked Jimmy." Among the many locals he defrauded was Wordsworth's father, John Wordsworth. The family had come from Yorkshire several generations earlier, had acquired land near Penrith, married into the local minor gentry (Wordsworth's maternal grandmother was a Crackenthorpe of Newbiggin Hall) and taken up positions of trust. Wordsworth's paternal uncle, Richard, for example, was collector of customs at Whitehaven, so his own stamp job was very much in the family tradition. So was electioneering for the Lowthers. His father

John was an attorney; Bailiff and Recorder of Cockermouth; coroner at Millom; and, above all, chief law agent to the Bad Earl. Among his many duties was looking after the Earl's interests at election time, which involved confidential disbursements. The Earl, however, declined to refund him or even to pay his routine fees, exploiting the loyalty of the Wordsworth family. By the time John Wordsworth died in 1783, the money the earl owed him amounted to over £5,000, an enormous sum for a man of his class. Applications on behalf of his five children, who were left badly off, were totally unavailing, and the debt was still unpaid in 1802 when the Earl finally went to his maker.

The new head of the Lowthers, William (the earldom was revived in his favor in 1806), later labeled "William the Good," was painfully aware of his predecessor's evil record, having himself suffered much at his hands. He at once set about making whatever reparation was in his power to injured people. He repaid the Wordsworth debt with interest, making £8,500 in all, and this sum was divided up among the five, William and his sister Dorothy getting £1,800 each.[144] But he did more. He was a literary man, chairman of the local book club, and greatly admired Wordsworth's poetry. In 1806 Wordsworth was anxious to purchase a small farm of eighteen acres at Broad How in Patterdale; it had a magnificent view over Ullswater, and he wished to build a house there. He made an offer of £800 for it, but the rector of Patterdale was also in the running, so, being greedy, the woman who owned it raised the price to £1,000. Wordsworth did not have the extra £200, since he had lent most of his inheritance to his brother John. His friend Thomas Wilkinson told the Earl, without Wordsworth's knowledge or permission, and the money was produced. Wordsworth was greatly embarrassed, but the position was quickly regularized, the £200 being set against a mortgage, and the debt was paid back to the Earl within three years (though Wordsworth never built the house he planned). The Earl seems to have behaved with great delicacy, as well as generosity, in the matter, and it was the beginning of a long friendship.[145] Lonsdale was anxious that Wordsworth should be able to devote himself to his poetry, and was disturbed, according to a story told by Samuel Rogers in his memoirs, to hear that Wordsworth and his family "deny themselves animal food several times a week," being "in such straitened circumstances." Hence, the stamp job. At the same time, Wordsworth, who had had a number of unsatisfactory homes, including Dove Cottage in Grasmere, delightful (Dorothy remained devoted to it) but tiny, found a permanent resting place in Rydal Mount (1813), two miles away on the Ambleside road, which he rented from the widowed Lady Fleming. The house had superb views, was surrounded by a magnificent

wild garden of the kind Dorothy loved, and was a "gentleman's house."
It remained Wordsworth's home until his death 38 years later in 1850.

It is important to understand this background for two reasons. First
it explains Wordsworth's attachment to the Good Earl, and his anxiety
to battle on his behalf at the 1818 election. The Earl's two sons, Viscount Lowther and Colonel James Lowther, held the two Westmorland
seats, and either could have been ousted by Brougham's incursion. A
careful study of the vast number of letters that passed between the poet
and the Earl from December 1817 to the end of the election in July 1818,
and indeed their subsequent correspondence, shows that at every stage
Wordsworth was even keener on victory than was the head of the house
of Lowther. Far from being a hired hand earning his place, he was an
enthusiastic champion of what he saw as a worthy cause.[146]

This brings us to the second point. Many of Wordsworth's fellow poets
and writers criticized his identification with the Lowther interest because they did not understand or care about the localism that lay at the
center of his art. Wordsworth was, and felt himself to be, a creature of
the fells and their valleys, almost a part of the soil, linked to its people
by countless relationships stretching back generations and by memories
from earliest childhood, an intimate network of connections now reinforced by his job, which took him on horseback all over the territory.

Other writers, by contrast, had cut themselves off from their roots
and had become cosmopolitan wanderers, owing allegiance more to
their caste as intellectuals than to any particular place. Even those who
shared Wordsworth's increasingly conservative views were dislocated.
Southey no longer went back to his native Bristol, but had settled in
Keswick like any other villa owner or "income" as the Cumbrians
called them. Coleridge had finally turned his back on Ottery Saint
Mary, even though he still had traces of a Devon accent, and was as
happy (or unhappy) in London as anywhere. As for the critics, they had
turned themselves into men from nowhere. Thomas Love Peacock was
no longer interested in Dorset, where he was born. Hazlitt had no
feelings for Wiltshire or Leigh Hunt for Surrey. Keats was a Hampstead
cockney who longed for the south and got there, alas, too late. The
most localized was Charles Lamb, as passionately devoted to his native
London and its environs as Wordsworth was to his fells—that helps to
explain the great sympathy each felt for the other.

Byron had renounced his English and Scottish allegiance; was selling his ancestral estates in Nottinghamshire; and by 1818, had left for
good, to lead the life of a voluntary exile on the Continent. Shelley had
long since forgotten Sussex and was now also a wanderer. On April 20,

1818, by which time the election campaign was entering its paroxysm, he was sightseeing in Milan and writing to Peacock: "The number of English who pass through this town is very great. They ought to be in their country in the present crisis. Their conduct is wholly inexcusable."[147] The comment is characteristic not only of Shelley's double standards and his fond belief that rules which must be enforced strictly on others never applied to him, but to his alienation from Britain, his feeling that he could influence it only by his writings. Both Byron and Shelley thought their country *in extremis*. Neither felt they had a duty to be there, playing a part in the drama, though it is true that Byron talked occasionally of "taking a troop of horse," like a Roundhead squire, if civil war should break out. Both derived their entire incomes from Britain—about £7,000 a year in Byron's case and under £1,000 a year in Shelley's—from inherited family money invested in consols, land, mortgages, and the like, though Byron was now supplementing his *rentier* resources with large sums earned by his writings. Their moral position, in relation to the "condition of England" question, was thus equivocal.

But if Byron and Shelley lived from books and resided abroad—it did not matter much where—Wordsworth was not a bookish man. Wordsworth's library was pitifully small; he read the mountains and lakes and his fellow Westmorlanders and Cumbrians. He was absurdly self-centered, vain, narrow in many ways, a little grasping in others, but he was from first to last a local patriot. He nailed his colors to the mast of freedom and independence.[148] He saw the yeoman-farmers of the dales—called, significantly enough, "statesmen"—as essentially free even if they observed a proper respect for grand local families like the Lowthers and deferred to these families' views on national issues. His feeling for the dalesmen made him identify with the Swiss: that was why Bonaparte's enslavement of the Swiss finally turned Wordsworth against revolutionary republicanism and the agressive, conquering spirit that went with it.

In a long letter to his old friend James Losh, surveying his whole political pilgrimage, he admitted he had changed his views: "I should think that I had lived to little purpose if my notions on the subject of government had undergone no modification—my youth must, in that case, have been without enthusiasm, and my manhood endued with small capacity of profiting by reflection."[149] But he claimed that he had stuck to his libertarian principles and had turned against France only when its rulers "abandoned the struggle for liberty, gave themselves up to tyranny and endeavoured to enslave the world." This was why he learned to oppose the Whigs and radicals, too, because they "pandered" to "the tyrant Bonaparte." But they also "pandered" to the mob, and that was a further reason for resisting them. To Wordsworth, tyranny could be exercised not only by individuals like Bonaparte, but by the hydra-headed collective of masses of ignorant, maddened people.

He had the born countryman's fear of huge cities—"For upwards of 30 years the lower orders have been accumulating in pestilential masses of ignorant population," he wrote.[150] He thought this process, which he saw as contrary to nature, had produced sinister changes in the national character, breeding a spirit of aimless rebellion. That was why he had supported the suspension of habeas corpus the previous year, in 1817. "The ties which kept the different classes of society in a vital and harmonious dependence on each other," he wrote, "have within these thirty years either been greatly impaired or wholly dissolved. . . . Farmers used formerly to be attached to their landlords and labourers to their farmers who employed them. All that kind of thing has vanished, in like manner the connection between the trading and landed interests of county towns undergoes no modification whatever from personal feeling, whereas within my memory it was almost wholly governed by it. A country squire, or substantial yeoman, used formerly to resort to the same shops his father had frequented before him . . . a connection which was attended with substantial amity and interchanges of hospitality from generation to generation."[151]

What Wordsworth feared, in this dawn of the modern age, was the growing process of rationalization and depersonalization of economic life brought about by capitalist enterprise. He felt himself to be defending a rural arcadia. He was trying to protect not just the beauty of the dales from the "villa mongers," who almost without exception had made their money in the towns, but the purity of spirit of the innocent dalesfolk from mercenary urban corruption. He did not see the capitalist and the mob as opponents; on the contrary, they worked in conjunction to destroy rural values. It was of the nature of the Whigs and radicals, with their city money made in manufacturing, to whip up the mob against the landed interest. He referred repeatedly to "the democratic activity of the wealthy, commercial and manufacturing districts," which were "natural hotbeds for Jacobinism." These districts would invade the Lakes and take over. And who was there to resist them, except families like the Lowthers? He knew that some decent Cumbrians thought the landed interest had too much political power, but "I would ask a well-intentioned native of Westmorland or Cumberland who had fallen into this mistake if he could point to any arrangement by which Jacobinism can be frustrated except by the existence of large estates continued from generation to generation in particular families."[152]

That was the essence of Wordsworth's case, set out in two major political articles written at the beginning of the campaign, and in innumerable letters in the years 1815 to 1821. To him, the "invasion" of Westmorland by Brougham personified the entire, gigantic struggle between rural good and urban evil—Brougham was the modern world in arms—huge and hideous, glib, unscrupulous, ungodly, and out for anything he could get. True, he had a theoretical local connection, being distantly descended from the Cumbrian squirearchy, but his father had married the daughter of an Edinburgh boardinghouse keeper and lived there. Brougham had been born in Edinburgh, educated there, learned his law and his radicalism there, was a founder-member of the infamous *Edinburgh Review,* and had come south, breathing fire and Jacobinism, to impose its leveling principles on the English countryside.[153]

Wordsworth believed Brougham was an atheist and that profound religious issues were involved in the election. He was struck by the coincidence that the same month that Brougham's candidacy became known, the publisher William Hone (1780–1842) was aquitted of various charges of printing blasphemous parodies of the Litany and the Athanasian Creed; as Dorothy Wordsworth put it, "The acquittal of Home is enough to make one out of love with English juries."[154] In a letter to Lonsdale on 18 January 1818, Wordsworth swore he would fight all out, being "assured that this attempt is no common affair of county politics but proceeds from dispositions and principles which, if not checked and discountenanced, would produce infinite mischief not to Westmorland only, but to the whole kingdom."[155]

In fact, Brougham's intervention was not as sinister as Wordsworth thought. The initiative came from a London Committee for the Emancipation of the County, inspired by the local Whig gentry who accused the Lowthers of being too "greedy." It did, indeed, look bad, as the Earl admitted, that both the county seats were held by his sons. But this situation had come about by accident, and Lonsdale said he would be glad for one to retire if a suitable replacement could be found. In any case, as he repeatedly claimed throughout his long life, unlike his predecessor, he had never told anyone how to vote. But his chief adversary, the Earl of Thanet, was determined on a fight, and since he put up £4,000 of the £6,000 initially subscribed, he was given the choice of champion. He picked Brougham. "Wickedshifts," as Brougham was known, was at first reluctant because he already had a safe seat in Lord

Darlington's pocket borough of Winchelsea. But it seemed a good chance to get his revenge on Lonsdale, who had turned down his rather brazen request for a Westmorland seat in 1806.[156] Once committed, however, Brougham regretted it. He discovered that his chief backer, Thanet, was an incorrigible gambler who spent most of his time in Continental casinos. There was infighting between his London committee and the local one. Worse, the Whigs, who thought him a counterjumper, were treacherous, and some of them (the Cavendishes) secretly backed the Lowthers. The experience, he wrote, showed him "the futility of all party connection"; party was "a dupery of sixty or seventy people who don't reflect, for the benefit of two or three sly characters who go about earwigging the powerful ones for their own purposes."[157]

Wordsworth was finally convinced that Brougham was nothing but a vulgar adventurer when Lonsdale sent him (on 18 January 1818) a copy of Brougham's letter begging him for the Westmorland seat in 1806. This letter proved that the great radical had himself tried to make use of a "system" he now denounced as "iniquitous." Wordsworth repeatedly asked Lonsdale's permission to publish this extremely damaging letter, but the Earl thought it would be ungentlemanly. Wordsworth's long and numerous letters, chiefly to the Earl, giving a blow-by-blow account of the campaign, provide perhaps the best description we have of how an early 19th-century election was fought in a country district. They are supplemented by more vivid flashes in Dorothy's letters, often to Mrs. Clarkson, wife of the antislavery campaigner, who was on the other side.

Election toasts were drunk "in a bottle of Cowslip Wine." It was vital to win the friendship of the local attorneys, for after a gap of 44 years, there was no record of freeholders for electoral purposes. Both sides had to employ lawyers to prevent the other cheating, the Land Tax Assessment being the only authority. But many of the attorneys disliked each other, and "if you employed one you made enemies of the others." You were in trouble if the local lawyers were not on your side, since many voters asked their advice, or were given it anyway. Wordsworth told the Earl he regretted that all the key lawyers were not given a retainer right at the start; he had had to conciliate one of them, Isaac Wilson, who was "picqued at being overlooked."

Many such aspects were "a matter of great delicacy." In Langdale, where they ought to get 19 out of 20 votes, "eight or 10 hang back, complaining that the licence was taken away from the only Public House in the dale." He was furious that John Curwen, the Whig member for Carlisle, while passing through Ambleside, "finding there was a crowd in the Kitchen of the Inn, took his tea there and commenced agitator among them." Or again: "It is shocking that the whole of Longsleddale should be against us, through the influence of a single village orator." Wordsworth knew all the local personalities on both sides—many had been at school with him in Hawkshead. He describes sticky dinner parties at which both "blues" (Whigs) and "yellows" (Tories) were present and the issue of the moment tactfully avoided, adding "My son is a complete yellow, having got the jaundice, poor lad. . . . The daffodils are anxiously looked for that the *young* ladies in Rydale may adorn their bonnets with them."

The election was the making of the earl's two sons. Lord Lowther had never been in a political fight before; now he entered into the battle with relish. Even young Colonel Lowther, described by Dorothy as "painfully shy," began to blossom. On 11 February, the two sons made what was called "a grand entry" into Kendal, the county town, as a prelude to a canvass, and all hell broke loose. By some muddle the Whig-Radical mob had got drunk on liquor supplied by the Lowthers and attacked the Tory procession. By a miracle, wrote Wordsworth, "no lives were lost," though one of his old schoolfellows, the Rev. John Fleming, was "suffering considerably—a Stone, the size of a Man's Hand, struck him on the back and caused a spilling of bood." The Tory committee, a bunch of craven fellows, according to Wordsworth, were all for abandoning the canvass and surrending to the mob. But Lord Lowther was undaunted, insisted on calling on every elector in the town to solicit his vote, and got through it all triumphantly. Indeed, Wordsworth reported, "the outrages committed at Kendal" would "surely be of great use to our cause." He told the Earl of a conversation he had overheard in Ambleside between a chimney-boy an an apothecary's apprentice. Boy: "What have you to do with elections here?" Apprentice: "We *were* all Blues, but we're turning. My master promised his vote to Brougham, but he'll give it to the Lowthers. He says he doesn't like such blackguard work."[158]

Wordsworth had been warned that as a government employee, his participation in the election might be illegal, and Brougham's brother, James, was determined to bring an action against him. So when Brougham made his "grand entry" into Kendal on 23 March, Wordsworth lay low, leaving the reporting to Dorothy, who was determined to hear "Wickedshifts" speak, "as I never before heard a parliament man." The speech took place in "a heavy shower of snow and hail," but the "multitude of heads, fearless of the storm, one condensed line in motion wedging in the Horsemen and the Carriages, which all slowly streamed on together, was grand." But, Dorothy added, "you could hardly single out a gentleman—blackguards by the score—and multitudes of young lads."

Brougham spoke from the center window of their Whig friend Wakefield's house, wearing "a dark coat, yellow waistcoat and a very large blue silk hankerchief tied round his neck. . . . I could have fancied him one of the French Demagogues of the Tribunal of Terror at certain times when he gathered a particular fierceness into his face." She thought him "very like a Frenchman" with "nothing of the Westmorland countenance." Dorothy was thrilled and terrified that much of Brougham's speech was devoted to attacking her brother. Wordsworth had published two major articles on the campaign, which were circulating as handbills.[159] Now Brougham retaliated by describing him, without actually mentioning his name, as "one of these vassal underhand anonymous writers . . . the first who had descended to personalities in the content, a Man who held a Sinecure in this County and who had no other property besides, or very little . . . I do not speak of his poetry but of his laboured compositions in prose . . . far harder work for his readers than the *duties* of his Place furnished him with."[160]

As he spoke, said Dorothy, "he looked ready to lead a gang of Robespierrists to pull down Lowther Castle and tear up the very trees that adorn it." She was particularly frightened by his use of the word "independence." "Oh, that is a mischievous word! It is the motto of the servants, of the Girls working at Trades, comb-makers, straw-hat makers etc, and, really, walking Kendal streets in the evening of one of these bustling days of Easter Week, the numbers of disgusting females shouting Brougham and Independence was so great you might have supposed the whole of the female population turned out. I could not have believed it possible that so many impudent women and girls were to be found in Kendal."

Wordsworth, too, reporting to Lonsdale, expressed his concern at "the *ferment of dissatisfaction* in the County." He found "such a hostility among the lower ranks, including servants, daylabourers, handicraftsmen, small shopkeepers, to whom must be added many who from education and situation in life ought to know better, that if it went by counting heads Mr. B would sweep all before him." Brougham had been going round addressing mobs of people: "There are instances in which Mr. B had harangued to hundreds, and not above three or four freeholders there. In Patterdale there was only one. Yet his words were not thrown away. If the Father were not there, two or three of his sons were, the Mother also probably—these catch the infection and, uniting their forces, become too strong for the old man."[161]

Wordsworth particularly noticed that the young were turning radical, and he thought this was due, in great part, to the fact that the local press, the *Kendal Chronicle* and the *Carlisle Patriot* favored the Whigs. A plan of his to take over the *Kendal Chronicle* failed, and he finally persuaded Lonsdale to set up a new weekly, the *Westmorland Gazette,* to fight not only this election but all subsequent ones, for Wordsworth rightly foresaw that the unchallenged reign of the Lowthers was over. The first issue of the new paper appeared on 24 May, edited by a professional journalist Wordsworth brought from London. But the editor proved unsatisfactory. It was then that Wordsworth turned, almost in despair, to his difficult friend Thomas de Quincey (1785–1859).

De Quincey was a fine classical scholar, the son of a merchant who died worth £1,600 a year, but he had reduced himself to poverty by a combination of generosity, opium taking (which he had started at Oxford) and improvidence. He was a passionate admirer of Words-worth's poetry. In 1807 he had contrived to get a letter of introduction to the poet at Dove Cottage, but had been too shy to deliver it. When he finally did so, Wordsworth had been furious at the delay in getting the letter. Like Liverpool, Wordsworth took his anger out on the chairs. Instead of smashing them—he couldn't afford to—he "moved them around angrily." But he soon fell for De Quincey's relentless flattery and Dorothy was delighted with him: She was only five feet tall herself, but De Quincey, she wrote, was so "diminutive" that she had the unusual experience of looking down on him. De Quincey became im-mensely attached to the Wordsworth children, especially the luckless little Catherine, and when she died, he was heartbroken. He tutored the poet's son John, and his fine library, which he carried about with him, proved a further attraction. When he finally decided to settle in the Lakes, the Wordsworths made Dove Cottage, which they no longer used, available to him.

There was, however, a gradual falling-out. The Wordsworths no-ticed, as they had already sadly seen in the case of their former intimate, Coleridge, that De Quincey was an addict. As Wordsworth's sister-in-law, Sara Hutchinson, put it, "He doses himself with opium and drinks like a fish." Worse, in Dorothy's eyes, he cut down her precious wild plants at the cottage to get more light in at the windows.

Finally, De Quincey did the unthinkable: He seduced a local girl, Peggy Simpson, the daughter of a "statesman," who presented him with a son. The Wordsworth were particularly sensitive on the point of "incomes" laying their hands on innocent village girls. There had been a celebrated case in 1802 when the maiden known as the Beauty of

Buttermere had been deceived by a plausible scoundrel—Coleridge had written eloquently on the subject. Only a year later Hazlitt had assaulted another local girl, and Wordsworth and Coleridge had been obliged to save him from a mob of angry vigilantes and smuggle him out of the district. Now De Quincey had committed the same unforgivable sin. In his case, it is true, he was prepared to marry the girl and did so (1817). But this marriage made matters worse, if anything. The Wordsworths disapproved of cross-class marriages, at any rate in their own backyard. Besides, Dorothy thought Peggy stupid. When De Quincey had lent Peggy Oliver Goldsmith's *Vicar of Wakefield*, she had been disappointed to learn from him that the characters were not real people. Peggy, wrote Dorothy, was a "dully, heavy girl . . . reckoned a Dunce at Grasmere School." Dorothy and Wordsworth's wife Mary refused to call on the bride.[162]

Hearing that Wordsworth was starting a paper, De Quincey wrote to him for a role in opposing "the infamous levelling doctrines of Mr Brougham." He admitted there were doubts about "my competence . . . in punctuality, I mean, and power of steady perseverance," but added he was much "altered since I last had the happiness to associate with you." Wordsworth at first turned him down, but when the London journalist failed, he recommended De Quincey to Lonsdale, despite his reservations "on the score of punctuality" as "a most able man, one of my particular friends."[163] So De Quincey got the job, being paid £9 for the first three issues, thereafter a guinea a week. De Quincey proved a more enthusiastic Tory partisan than anyone else, accusing Brougham of being a spy on the Continent, calling him a "mobocrat," infuriating the editor of the *Kendal Chronicle* by claiming that editors "in general" were "low-bred mercenary adventurers—without manners—without previous education—and apparently without moral principles," and generally hotting up the contest. Lonsdale had to send urgent messages through Wordsworth begging De Quincey to tone the paper down.

De Quincey's leading articles were also criticized on another score, as being "too metaphysicising." Indeed, under his editorship the columns of the paper were crammed with articles on Kant, Herder, Herschel, and other luminaries not normally drawn to the attention of Westmorland folk, as well as six poems by Wordsworth and much other poetry. But De Quincey was also fascinated by violent crime—a taste that eventually (1828–29) produced his famous essays "On Murder Considered as One of the Fine Arts," so that he balanced German idealism with some lurid court cases, especially rape, described in great detail and never omitting the appearance of the girls—"a beautiful little girl of fifteen," "a very pretty, interesting English girl of 19," and so on.[164] In the eighteen months he edited the paper, De Quincey established the *Gazette* on a firm foundation; it still flourishes today.

How much he influenced the result of the election, however, is doubtful, since his first issue appeared only during the actual polling, 30 June–3 July. Wordsworth had feared intimidation even in the Dales, but special constables were enrolled; troops were available; and Lowther supporters, including colliers from their West Coast mines, were brought in to counteract the Blues mob. Most voters preferred to stick with the Lowthers against the "outcome," and the two brothers won comfortably, polling 1,211 and 1,157 against Brougham's 889. There was a riot in Kendal the day after the result was declared, and troops were called in. But by this time Wordsworth was already engaged, as the Blues were, in creating new freeholds, in preparation for the next time.

During the campaign, Wordsworth had become intimate with the Lowthers. Lord Lowther had spent three days at Rydal Mount and Wordsworth himself had stayed at Lowther Castle. His election letters to the Earl were now spiced with the kind of nonpolitical gossip both loved—"one of the young ladies at Calgarth has eloped with the butler."[165] So it continued for many years. The great political empire the Bad Earl had created did not survive for long—the Good Earl was not sufficiently interested in politics to keep it up—but the Lowther brothers continued to represent Westmorland long after Brougham had vanished into the Lords. Indeed, young Colonel Lowther may have been, as Dorothy Wordsworth described him, "like a rustic from one of our mountain vales," but he hung onto the seat for 55 years, triumphantly surviving two Reform Bills, and ended his life as Father of the House of Commons (1867).[166]

Nor was the government disappointed with the 1818 general election as a whole, though it was impossible to compute the result accurately until Parliament assembled in the autumn and the members began to vote. The chief issues had been parliamentary reform, restrictions on civil liberty, the Catholic question, taxation, and retrenchment (the two last being the most important). Considering all the government's postwar difficulties and the fact that no less than 120 constituencies went to the polls, the most in nearly thirty years, ministers were happy to lose no more than 11 seats. They admitted they had done badly in London—"The great source of all evil is this metropolis," Lord Liverpool wrote—but Lord Granville pointed out that in the turnover of members of Parliament, the government had exchanged "a great many absent and idle supporters for those of a more zealous and active nature," and this was reflected in higher majorities for the government, as we shall see, during the key year 1819. On 18 May 1819, in a letter to Lord Morley, Canning exulted in the government's strength: On a motion of censure by the Whig leader Tierney, three days before, the figures had been 357 to 178, a two-to-one majority for the government; the Speaker said that no less than 540 members were present and "there was never so great a *positive* number in a majority as 357 and never before was so immense a proportion of the whole House of Commons accounted for in a division."[167] So much for the consequences of the general election of 1818.

We must not regard it as surprising that writers like Wordsworth and De Quincey were so heavily involved in electioneering. In this birth of the modern age, literature and politics were intimately connected. A large proportion of the poetry written at this time alluded to political events and beliefs. Many poets—Wordsworth, at times, Shelley always—believed the prime object of their poems was to influence public attitudes. Only three years after the election, Shelley was to write his *Defence of Poetry,* in which he argued that poets, by virtue of their "intellectual beauty" or imagination, were "the unacknowledged legislators of mankind." Nor was it incongruous to find Brougham pitted against Wordsworth. On the contrary, it was entirely appropriate that the supreme defender of the natural order, as Wordsworth was becoming, should be locked in irreconcilable combat with such an outstanding champion of rational progress.

Brougham had one foot in politics, the other in literature, as did so many other men of this time. He came from Scotland, which next to France itself had been the chief forcing house of the European Enlightenment, and from Edinburgh, where this great intellectual movement was coming to a grand climax in the years after 1815.

In the first three decades of the 19th century, probably more clever and gifted men were gathered in Edinburgh than any other comparable city in the world. They had a Renaissance sense of universalism, ignoring the frontiers which separated poetry and fiction, science and engineering, art and architecture, and academic and public life, seeing understanding and achievement in all these spheres as a *continuum*. The unifying factor was a passionate belief in self-improvement by study and practice, in the need for education for all. The most influential teacher of the Scottish Englightenment, Thomas Reid (1710–96) had taught that human fulfilment was to be achieved, if at all, through knowledge, and this maxim was bred into the bones of the Scots intelligentsia.[168]

Typical of these men was the great Scots painter Alexander Naysmith (1758–1840), father of James, the inventor of the steam hammer.

Naysmith began humbly as a trainee housepainter, attended night
classes at the Trustees Academy and then worked in the studio of the
portraitist Alan Ramsay, of whom Samuel Johnson rightly observed:
"You will not find a man in whose conversation there is more instruction, more information and more elegance than in Ramsay's."[169] Naysmith was not only a landscape painter but a practical landscape "im-
prover." Half-architect, half-engineer, he was fascinated by the way in
which civilized man embellished the natural landscape with his artifacts. James Naysmith said it was his father who made him a scientific
engineer.[170] Alexander Naysmith's drawings contain ideas for bow-
and-string and other bridges, how to roof wide spaces, axial arrangements for propellers, engines, compression rivets and so on, as well as
for a multitude of buildings and their arrangements. There was more
than a touch of Leonardo da Vinci in the variety of his interests. In the
early years of the century, he had effectively founded Highland landscape painting with his four magical canvases *East and West of Loch
Tarbert,* commissioned for engraving by Campbells of Stonefield.[171]
But even more important was his practical work in the expansion of
Edinburgh New Town to the north and east, which after 1815 took in
the Calton hill area. This work gave Naysmith a matchless opportunity
to give concrete expression to his theories of how natural beauties could
be enhanced by man-made improvements.

Edinburgh as a city thus came to be a striking visual expression of
the epistemology of the humanist intellectuals who dominated its thinking, their theory of knowledge taking shape in granite and sandstone,
rocks, grass, and vistas.[172] In 1824–25 Naysmith painted four vast urban
landscapes of the Edinburgh he had helped to bring into existence. They
are some of the best panoramas ever done of a complete city as an
organism. They capture the dynamism of economic change; epitomize
Edinburgh at the height of the Scottish Enlightenment; and provide, as
it were, a powerful visual comment on the modern age now being
born.[173]

Brougham, an invading monster of disorder to Wordsworth, liked
to appear rather differently against his Edinburgh background, as an
apostle of calm rationality, writing on every aspect of science as well as
law, literature and public policy, and carrying the torch of Scotland's
enlightenment to illuminate the dusty recesses of Westminster. In fact,
as Wordsworth would have been keen to know, there was a strong
hooligan element in the Edinburgh intellectuals, a loonish boisterous-
ness of the kind that always made James Boswell ashamed of his fellow
countrymen. Brougham later boasted in his *Memoirs* that their constant practice "after an evening at the Apollo or at Johnny's," was to

"parade the streets of the New Town" and "wrench the brass knockers off the doors" or "tear out the brass handles of the bells"; he said that at his father's house, a closet was "literally filled" with their "prodigious" spoils. Saying farewell to the brilliant Francis Horner when he left for the English Bar in 1803, they "staggered from Fortune's Hotel" and "twisted off the enormous brazen serpent" which hung over Manderson's chemist shop.[174] Sixteen years later, richer and in many cases famous, they were still ready for horseplay. The painter William Calcott, RA, dining with their leader, Jeffrey, at his "country House" two miles from the center of Edinburgh, was amazed at his host's casual attire—"He wore a Jacket and Trowsers and half-boots and had a silk hankerchief around his neck"—and the fierce conversational competitiveness of his distinguished Scots guests. They drank deeply of champagne and "after sitting some time after dinner, an eminent pleader at the Scots Bar put his wineglass in his waistcoat pocket and saying, 'We have sat long enough' threw up the window and leapt through it to the grass plot and, being followed by the rest, they drank champagne and played at leap-frog."[175]

Francis (later Lord) Jeffrey (1773–1850) was the man who, together with Horner, had created (1802) the "Great Gun" of the Enlightenment and progress, the *Edinburgh Review,* which among other things was the platform from which Brougham launched himself. The idea for the paper came from the Englishman Sydney Smith, who edited the first issue; thereafter Jeffrey got control. Smith, the son of an Eastcheap merchant, who embraced the church only when his father died without leaving him any money, refused to have Brougham on the editorial committee, saying he was "violent and unreasonable" and guilty of "indiscretion and rashness." But Brougham contributed seven articles to the opening issue nonetheless, forced his way onto the committee from the third issue, and then, wrote Jeffrey, "did more work for us than anybody."[176]

Initially, the *Review* was more ecumenical than Whiggish, including in its circle Sir Walter Scott; John Murray, the publisher; Thomas Campbell; and the future Lord Cockburn. The committee met for supper every Friday. On one such occasion Brougham persuaded the entire distinguished group, plus Thomas Thomson, the clerk of Edinburgh Sessions, all of them drunk on a "strong punch" made of rum, sugar, lemons, marmalade, and calf's-foot jelly, to steal the Galen's Head hung over Gardiner's the apothecary. They were nearly caught by the Watch and had to run for their lives.[177] In 1808 the break with Scott and his fellow Tories came when Jeffrey not only savaged *Marmion* but, together with Brougham, wrote an ultra-radical article calling for a "salutary, just and necessary revolution" in Spain. They claimed that it would have "the full approval of the English people" and added the significant sentence: "And who then shall ever more presume to tell us that the people have nothing to do with the laws but to obey them, with the taxes but to pay them and with the blunders of their rulers but to suffer from them?" This statement was taken to be a call for fundamental change in Britain, too. The Earl of Buchan put the issue on his front doorstep and kicked it savagely into the street. Scott, more constructively, went into immediate cabal with Murray to start a rival, which became the *Quarterly*.[178]

Even from the start, however, the *Edinburgh* had always been an attacking journal, seeking to raise the temperature. A typical assault was directed in the 22nd issue (January 1808) by Brougham, writing anonymously, of course, on Byron's *Hours of Idleness*. Byron, after thoughts of "rage, resistance and redress," said he drank three bottles of claret, wrote 20 lines, and "felt considerably better"; on 16 March he published a remodeled version of an early poem as *British Bards and Scotch Reviewers*.[179] The *Edinburgh* also savaged the Lake poets—Wordsworth, Coleridge, and Southey—Jeffrey beginning his scourging of the third edition of *Lyrical Ballads* (1802) with the words, "This will never do." Indeed, the attacks on the Lake school became fiercer as those poets' political views moved toward the Tories, political and literary factors being almost inextricably intermingled.

In return, the Lake poets hated the magazine and its contributors. Three years before the Westmorland election, Wordsworth told Farington that he refused even to read the *Edinburgh*, "for however much he may despise such matters he would not have it buzz in his thoughts" or have the opinions of the dreadful Jeffrey "floating in his memory."[180] A thirst for revenge at Brougham's literary criticism undoubtedly gave edge to the participation by Wordsworth and his admirer De Quincey in the 1818 campaign.

Others hit back in print. Cobbett responded to an assault on him in the *Edinburgh* in 1807 by a campaign of vituperation which lasted many years. Its editors and contributors were "Northern leeches"; "hunters after the public money"; cowards; selfish, with "profligate principles"; "parasites and place-hunters"; "arrogant and stupid"; "shameless Scotch hirelings"; "toad-eaters"; and Scotch bloodhounds who "fatten on the cowardice and credulity of the nation," exhibiting "the most profound ignorance that ever disgraced the human mind." Jeffrey was "Old Mother Mange" or "Old Shufflebreeches," his colleagues "hireling hacks"; "prime pieces of Scotch humbug"; "conceited, pert, arrogant, impudent and insolent coxcombs"; and a good deal else.[181]

Southey also retaliated, joining the group of contributors, which included Canning and Scott, whom the *Quarterly*'s first editor, William Gifford (1756–1826) assembled to "dust the Whigs' jackets." Southey knew the *Edinburgh* to be mendacious. Jeffrey had printed an article stating that each of Southey's poems sold less well than its predecessor. This statement was the reverse of the truth: *Kahama* sold more copies than any of the earlier works, and *Roderick* (1814) did even better, clearing all Southey's debts to his publisher, Longman.[182] The poet laureate believed in hitting back; like Wordsworth, he was terrified of the mob and believed the *Edinburgh* to be an "intellectual mob." He was all for suppressing seditious newspapers, since he thought they were the direct causes of violence, and in his article on "Social Unrest" in the December 1812 issue of the *Quarterly*, he called for those who are convicted of seditious libel to be transported (Gifford cut this statement as being too extreme).[183]

But Southey was not vituperative, and the malicious abuse was left chiefly to Croker. Croker dealt with the press all his life, especially during the long years he spent in government. The *Quarterly* was a prime vehicle for his anonymous articles, done "in the most profound secrecy." Croker attacked enemies of the government, Whigs and Radicals alike, on principle, and innovative poets just for the hell of it. His 1818 *Quarterly* review of Keats's *Endymion* was generally supposed, in radical literary circles, to have hastened the poet's death (not so: Keats's tuberculosis followed the usual, tragic course) and provoked Byron's quatrain: "Who killed John Keats? / 'I' says the *Quarterly* / So cruel and Tartarly / Twas one of my feats."

Croker, to do him justice, had many good deeds to his credit; it was he, for instance, who got Theodore Hook out of jail. But not for nothing did one obituarist describe him as "a man who would go a hundred miles through sleet and snow, in a December night, to search a parish register, for the sake of showing that a man was illegitimate, or a woman older than she said she was."[184] Sometimes he would lead the entire pack of *Reviews* (monthly and quarterly magazines) in a campaign against a vulnerable target, especially a radical woman, for though the *Reviews* scratched out each others' eyes, they also ganged up to pick on an outsider. Thus, in 1821, when Sidney Owenson, Lady Morgan, published her two-volume *Italy*, the wolves were out. They hated Lady Morgan as a woman writer; as an ardent Irish nationalist; and, quite possible, as a revolutionary, and they were further incensed by the news that the publisher Colburn had paid her the immense sum of £2,000 for the book. Byron hailed the book as "fearless and excellent" in the *Quarterly*, but Croker began the attack by calling for a Royal Commission to inquire into her age, not doubting it would pronounce her "a female Methuselah"; more seriously, he demanded that the Irish law officers begin an investigation to see if the knighthoods bestowed on her husband and brother-in-law, being before the Union, were illegal.

The *Edinburgh* dismissed her as "an ambulator scribbler of bad novels," adding for good measure an attack by Hazlitt on her book on *Salvator Rosa*, in which he asserted that women had no business involving themselves in art history and criticism. *Blackwoods*, another Edinburgh review, described her as "the ci-devant Miladi," a "petticoated ultra-radical author" who had produced "a monstrous literary abortion." The Anglican *British Review* assailed her in verse: "She spewed out of her filthy maw / A flood of poison, horrible and black / Her vomit full of books and papers. . . ." Then, contradicting itself, it accused her husband of writing it, pronouncing him guilty of "intellectual hermaphroditism." When Lady Morgan rebuked her critics in the second edition, the *Edinburgh* returned to the attack. She was "an Irish she-wolf" a "blustering virago," a "wholesale blunderer and reviler"; she wrote while "maudlin from an extra tumbler of negus in the forenoon," and, noting that her father was an actor, the *Edinburgh* ordered her to return to "the stroller's barn where she was bred."[185]

This kind of scurrility, usually with political overtones, was spurred by the knowledge that writing was not only increasingly influential with the masses, but was big business. The *Quarterly* supported the Bell system and the *Edinburgh* the Lancaster systems but both favored rapid progress toward universal education; Southey and Wordsworth agreed that it was the only way to draw the fangs of the mob. "The nation that builds on manufactures sleeps on gunpowder," Southey wrote, and only literacy could damp down the explosives.[186] But as literacy spread and the population grew, thousands more readers joined the market for books every year. Lady Morgan's publisher Henry Colburn (c1785–1855) was merely the outstanding example of the new-style entrepreneurial publishers who were prepared to borrow heavily, pay well, cut prices and market their novels and even nonfiction by the thousands, possibly the tens of thousands. For this end, Colburn lined up Harrison Ainsworth and Captain Marryat, Bulwer Lytton and the young Benjamin Disraeli, and he reinforced his list of novels by launching or taking over literary boosters, such as the *New Monthly Magazine* (1814), the *Literary Gazette* (1817) and the *Athenaeum* (1827). In

1818 he brought out *Evelyn's Diary* and seven years later the newly deciphered *Pepys Diary,* and he concentrated on cheap, standard editions of novels suitable for circulating libraries.

Circulating libraries were a Scots innovation, going back to 1728 but much expanded and reinforced in the 1790s by Dissenters who were anxious to break the Anglican monopoly of higher education. The new or growing industrial towns prided themselves on their subscription libraries, some of which were huge and luxurious. Thus, Liverpool had the Athenaeum, opened in 1799, whose splendid building, which cost £4,400, housed 6,000 books and a coffee room, for 450 subscribers at 2 guineas a year each. Its rival, the Union News Room, was equally lavish.[187] The new bathing resorts, proliferating all along the south and east coasts, and the inland spas, likewise increasing, specialized in subscription libraries which dealt mainly in novels, for which the Colburns provided the fodder. The head of Jane Austen's family might be a clergyman, but all the Austens were "great Novel-readers & not ashamed of being so."[188] The novel was becoming not merely respectable but acknowledged as a major literary art form. As Jane Austen herself put it in *Northanger Abbey,* in the novel "the greatest powers of the mind are displayed."

The change in attitude was due, in large part, to the work of Walter Scott (1771–1832), who defined the novel as "a fictitious narrative accommodated to the ordinary train of events." Scott practiced this narrative first in verse with *The Lay of the Last Minstrel* (1805), *Marmion* (1808) and *The Lady of the Lake* (1810), then from 1814 with his *Waverley* series in prose. These works were important in all sorts of ways, not least because they gave further impetus to the growth of historical consciousness that was a striking feature of the age and an important sign of modernity. Scott was the first prominent author to go to considerable lengths to get details of a period correct and thus to give his fiction what appeared, to contemporaries, to be an astonishing air of realism. In this respect, all his successors, such as Alessandro Manzoni, Victor Hugo, Prosper Mérimée, Alfred de Vigny, and James Fenimore Cooper, were indebted to him. Even historians were profoundly influenced by his sense of period. Thomas Babington Macaulay, for instance, possessed a sophisticated historical outlook of a kind Edward Gibbon, with all his great merits, did not possess. The difference between Macauley and Gibbon, as his biographer G. M. Trevelyan put it, was due "almost wholly to the Waverley novels."[189]

But perhaps Scott's chief importance lay in the way his popularity permanently expanded the market available for serious poetry and prose fiction, not only in Britain but throughout the civilized world. His works were as eagerly read in Europe and North America as at home. *The Lady of the Lake,* in its first year of publication, sold out its 2 guinea de luxe quarto edition print of 2,050 copies, plus 20,000 copies of the cheaper octavo, and by the end of the wars over 100,000 copies of the three major verse-novels were in print. By 1818, according to Scott's biographer J. G. Lockhart, he was regularly making £10,000 a year from his novels.[190] Scott's success opened the way for many more serious novelists, including Jane Austen, and it is appropriate that Scott, always generous to fellow writers, was the first major figure to hail her genius in a survey of her work he published in the *Quarterly* in March 1816. He recognized that she dealt in a new kind of realism, "copying from nature as she really exists in the common walks of life, and presenting to the reader, instead of the splendid scenes of an imaginary world, a correct and striking representation of that which is daily taking place around him."[191] It was this quality that made Austen the favorite novelist, first of the Prince Regent, then of the young Disraeli, who read *Pride and Prejudice* "at least 16 times."

It was, above all, the market for novels that made it possible to run the mass book sales which the wholesalers Cadell & Davies held at this time. Cadell told Farington in December 1817, "with tears in his eyes," of the huge success his recent three-day sale had enjoyed, attended by 120 booksellers, all of whom he treated to a sumptuous dinner. At one of these sales in 1819, the publisher Murray sold £16,000 of books in a single day; Cadell himself died, a sheriff of London, worth over £150,000.[192] Of course, authors starved in garrets and languished in the Marshalsea (though in all the cases I have studied, such as William Godwin, Leigh Hunt, De Quincey, and Hazlitt, personal mismanagement was responsible). But it was now not merely possible but common for fortunes to be made through the printed word, by writers, publishers, printers and booksellers.

The feeling that vast sums were to be made out of literature was a potent factor in the personal antagonisms among writers during these years. But there were other causes. One was the sheer importance that people attached to literary sentiment, especially in poetry. A hard-bitten professional painter like J. M. W. Turner was passionately attached to reading and thinking about poetry, without which it is impossible to understand his more imaginative work. His colleague, Martin Archer Shee, RA (1769–1850), later to be president of the Royal Academy, another highly businesslike artist, was also a poetry fanatic. As Farington recorded: "Shee told me that so much does Poetry occupy his mind that, at every leisure moment, in the streets or in his [painting] room, his mind turns to that subject: it is his refuge when he wishes to get rid of any unpleasant feelings."[193] In *Persuasion,* Jane Austen cleverly presents a young Royal Navy captain, James Benwick, as successful and efficient as his fellow commanders—and no doubt as bloodthirsty—whose devotion to poetry transcends his life.

Another factor was the growing tendency of writers and artists to congregate in circles for mutual support and instruction. Wordsworth and Coleridge formed the first of these circles in West Somerset in 1797, when Coleridge was living in Nether Stowey and Wordsworth in nearby Holford, and together they assembled *Lyrical Ballads* and launched English romantic poetry. Later they, plus Southey—and, from time to time, Hazlitt, De Quincey, and others—formed the Lake District circle. Other coteries gathered around Keats in Hampstead and Lamb in Highgate. There was the Pisan Circle, created by Byron and Shelley, and the Nazarenes, formed by the Germans while in Rome. In Paris, after 1815, young painters like Delacroix and Géricault congregated in Horace Vernet's studio; later another group formed in the Forest of Fontainebleau. For writers like Victor Hugo and De Vigny, there were rival *Cénâcles.* These intense groupings, hothouses for gossip, rumor, and malice, were fertile in producing rows, both between the groups and within them.

Some of these quarrels were entirely personal. Hazlitt antagonized many just by his aggressive way of arguing. Charles Lamb's brother John, described as "jovial and burly" and essentially peaceable, was once provoked into knocking Hazlitt down over some dispute about the colors of Holbein and Van Dyck; Hazlitt said he did not mind the blow—"nothing but an *idea* hurts me."[194] Therein lay the main source of discord: the war of ideas. Ideas were combustible, both in morals and politics, the two often being connected. One fissure which ran right across the literary scene, tending to divide writers into two huge camps, was the acceptance or rejection of absolute morality. Traditionalists like Jane Austen and the mentor she most admired, the poet George Crabbe (1754–1832)—"she would sometimes say, in jest, that if she ever married at all, she could fancy being Mrs Crabbe, looking on the author quite as an abstract idea"—believed strongly in natural or absolute morals, which could not be changed by man.[195] In the view of Austen and Crabbe, the demands of absolute morality come before the needs, real or supposed, of society; this is why, for instance, in her most serious novel, *Mansfield Park,* Jane Austen has Fanny reject the marriage proposal of Henry Crawford, even though it is strongly supported by her benefactors, the Bertrams. On the other side of the divide was the utilitarian or relative morality first preached by Jean-Jacques Rousseau in the 1770s and 1780s, then thunderingly expanded in William Godwin's *Enquiry Concerning Political Justice* (1793), which presented moral systems as changeable to suit the convenience and promote the happiness of human beings. Among writers it was one of the most influential books for a generation, forming the mind of Shelley and, for a time at least, impressing Wordsworth, who found it liberating. Wordsworth's *Guilt and Sorrow* (1795) expresses the characteristic Godwinian idea, so typical of moral relativism, that it is society, not individual wickedness, which creates the criminal.[196]

Later, however, Wordsworth came to reject Godwinism almost totally and range himself wholly with the absolutists. The division between the camps took on a more direct political character as the aggressive behavior of Bonapartist France showed where relative morality led. This division reached a climax with the Battle of Waterloo, which Wordsworth and Southey saw as a wicked and unnecessary slaughter for which the monstrous ambitions of one man and his deluded supporters were entirely responsible, while Hazlitt, Byron and Shelley saw it as a catastrophe for progress, opening a new dark age of monarchical reaction. On 27–28 April 1816 Godwin, returning from Scotland, stayed with Wordsworth at Rydal Mount, where they had a fearful quarrel about Waterloo, Godwin (according to Crabb Robinson) quitting Wordswith "with very bitter and hostile feelings."[197] Southey, on the other hand, brought out a patriotic poem, in his capacity as poet laureate, called *The Poet's Pilgrimage to Waterloo*—he had visited the battlefield—presenting the event as a struggle between good and evil. Southey was particularly incensed because the victory bonfire that the citizens of Keswick had built on the top of Skiddaw had been prematurely ignited by the "subversive rabble." So he and his friends had to carry up the fuel to build a new one, the celebration finally being held on 21 August 1815, when Wordsworth spoiled the feast by accidentally kicking over the kettle of water needed for the punch.[198]

The trouble with Southey was that he got everything from books and newspapers and rarely moved outside his library. His son Cuthbert said that, in Keswick, "I do not think there were twenty persons in the lower class he knew by sight."[199] Southey believed the Skiddaw sabotage, and much else, was the work of a circle of atheists centered in Keswick who read Thomas Paine's *The Rights of Man* and plotted armed revolt. This was the fear behind the aggressive article Southey wrote for the *Quarterly* in 1816 calling for censorship of subversive writing. Even in its published form, as toned down by Gifford, it caused more anger among the radical writers than anything else that appeared at this time. It brought from Hazlitt three savage articles in the *Examiner,* one of which contains perhaps the longest sentence in the English language—certainly the longest abusive one—about Southey's repellent "marriage" to "that detestable old hag," Legitimacy.[200] Byron wrote that Southey was entitled to change his mind about politics, but not to "bring to the stake" those who "now think as he thought." Southey, said Byron, was "a dirty, lying rascal."[201]

The political dispute was envenomed by reports, usually false, of what one side had said about the other. The radical poets blamed any review in the *Quarterly* criticizing their work on Southey. Thus, Shelley believed Southey had called him "the *blackest of villains*" and had written a dismissive review of his *Revolt of Islam.* When he wrote accusingly to Southey, the latter replied he had had nothing to do with the review: "I have never in any of my writings mentioned your name or alluded to you even in the remotist hint, either as a man or an author." In fact, Southey thought that Shelley had "talents of a high order." However, he added—warming to the task—he felt that Shelley's writings were "so monstrous of their kind and so pernicious in their tendency" that he would feel "the deepest compassion" for their author, had not such opinions "brought immediate misery on others, and guilt which is all but irremediable on yourself." This was a reference, of course, to the suicide of Shelley's deserted first wife, Harriet, and much else. It brought a defensive scream from Shelley, protesting that Southey's charge arose "merely because I regulated my domestic arrangements without deferring to the notions of the vulgar. . . . I am innocent of ill, either done or intended; the consequences you allude to flowed in no respect from me." This defense, in return, brought a relentless reply. Southey said he had no great hopes that Shelley would repent, but there might be a chance: "for though you may go on with an unawakened mind, a seared conscience and a hardened heart, there will be seasons of misgiving, when that most sacred faculty you have laboured to destroy makes itself felt." When he got the news of Shelley's drowning, Southey wrote: "I knew that miserable man and am well acquainted with his dreadful history . . . the most tragic which I have known in real life." He thought that Shelley's "natural feelings to have been kind and generous. But he adopted the Devil's own philosophy that nothing ought to stand in the way of his own gratification."

In contrast, Southey thought that Byron was "wicked by disposition"—the head of the "Satanic school."[202] News of what Southey both said and wrote about him—true and false—reached Byron in Italy. Byron was particularly angered by a report (which proved to be untrue) that Southey, referring to the time when Byron and Shelley had spent part of the summer of 1816 on the Lake of Geneva with Mary Godwin and her half-sister Claire Clairmont, had accused the two poets of constituting "a league of incest." For a time Byron seriously thought of returning to England to force Southey into a duel, though in the end nothing came of it.[203]

But if the divided writers never actually came to blows, much of their work in the post-Waterloo years can be fully understood only in terms of the grand political quarrel. The *Excursion,* which Wordsworth published in 1814 after Bonaparte's first abdication, celebrates the defeat of the France created by scoffers and moralists like Voltaire and Rousseau; its failed Revolutionary, the Solitary, is based on the radical Wordsworth had known in the 1790s, John Thelwall, and its heroes are all men who have renounced utopianism and sought salvation through individual moral virtue. England's triumph, the poem continues, will be meaningless unless Englishmen seek piety and Godly duty; the strength of England lies in its simple, innocent villages, clustered round their churches. Shelley read the poem when he returned to England in September 1814, and his response, *Alastor,* written after Waterloo in September 1815, tells of the tragedy which befalls the poet who follows Wordsworth's advice. Byron's response, to Wordsworth and to many other attitudes he disagreed with, was *Don Juan.* Mary Shelley's *Frankenstein,* written under the influence of both radical poets, can also be seen as a criticism of Wordsworth: in the novel, the pursuit of solitary, individual idealism, as opposed to the collective humanitarianism advocated by Shelley, leads to positive evil.[204] Thomas Love Peacock replied to the Lake poets in *Melincourt,* which can be read as an attack on both Southey and Wordsworth, in *Nightmare Abbey* and in *Maid Marion.* Keats, perhaps despite himself, was involved in this literary shadow-boxing. Classified by both sides as a radical, he found himself, in consequence, praised in the *Examiner* and attacked in the *Quarterly* and, after his death, saluted as a hero in Shelley's *Adonais,* in which Southey appears as a supernumerary villain.

The warfare moved to a climax in the years 1818–19, envenomed, needless to say, by Wordsworth's well-publicized efforts to hold Westmorland for the Lowthers. Wordsworth's two electioneering addresses were assailed with peculiar ferocity by Peacock, who accused him of laying down the doctrine that only the rich were fit for Parliament and that members of Parliament should be appointed by the House of Lords, a perverse interpretation of Wordsworth's complex and by-no-means implausible case. Wordsworth was not the only traditionalist poet involved in the campaign. In Wiltshire George Crabbe, vicar of Trowbridge, made no secret of his support for the protectionist candidate, John Benett (1773–1852) who, as it happened, was an old-fashioned Whig. The local mob, including many of his own parishioners, "hissed and hooted" him, and he "rated them soundly." On the day he set out to vote in Devizes, "a riotous, tumultuous and most appalling mob besieged his house," threatening to destroy his chaise and tear him to pieces if he set off. "In the face of this furious assemblage, he came out calmly, told them they might kill him if they chose but, whilst he lived, nothing should prevent him giving a vote at the election, according to his promise and principles, and set off, undisturbed and unhurt to vote for Mr. Benett." Crabbe, unlike Wordsworth, was unlucky with his candidate.[205]

How far Wordsworth was responsible for the success of the two Lowthers against Brougham is arguable. Analysis of unpublished Lowther papers, especially Lord Lowther's reports to his father, strengthens Wordsworth's view that the deferential vote was in rapid decline, that few squires could deliver more than a handful of electors, and that everything really depended on an efficient organization, a thorough canvas, and the activity of professional party managers at the grass roots. Money mattered, too, of course: In 1820 Brougham came close to winning one of the Westmorland seats primarily because his organization spent £15,000 as opposed to a mere £7,000 in 1818. But the most important thing was the machine: Modern electioneering had already dawned.[206] In so far as he played a part in setting up and manning the machine, Wordsworth was instrumental in the Lowther triumph. At all events, he was held responsible by the radical poets and writers, whose anger against him rose to a crescendo in the 18 months that followed. It was this tradition of the radicals' abuse of Wordsworth which Robert Browning imbibed as a boy and regurgitated in his brilliant but unjust poem, *The Lost Leader*.

Wordsworth worked hard to defend his side in the 1818 election because he felt, in the closing months of 1817, that events were moving toward a climax. Southey (and Shelley for different reasons) thought the same. In March 1817, Southey was tentatively offered the editorship of the *Times:* he was to write a daily leader, take part in the management, and be paid £2,000 a year plus a share of the profits.[207] Southey was unwilling to take it on—he could not bear the thought of living in London—so Thomas Barnes, who turned out to be a reformer, got the job instead. But Southey continued to sound the alarm from his book-lined study high above Derwentwater. He saw society impaled on the horns of a fearful dilemma as a result of industrialization, which he hated. "We are far," he wrote, "from that state in which anything resembling equality would be possible; but we are arrived at that state in which the extremes of inequality are becoming intolerable. They are too dangerous, as well as too monstrous, to be borne much longer."[208] But short of turning back the clock to a preindustrial age, what could the government do? Well, argued Southey, it could at least take a firm line with subversives, deploying the legislative and physical weapons to maintain order and protect its supporters from mob violence. As it was, ministers were feeble: "Are they so stupid," he asked, "as not to know that their throats as well as their places are at stake?" He himself, he added, was doing all he could to help them, but his efforts were more likely to bring attacks of revenge on himself than a salutary stiffening of government policy.[209]

Southey's fear of an armed insurrection increased in 1817, 1818 and in the early months of 1819. He believed that agitation was well organized, using benefit societies and parish clubs as structures and the methods of the Wesleyans and Quakers as examples. Thus, funds were accumulated which could sustain strikes and even buy arms. He was terrified of an army mutiny, particularly since radical members of Parliament like Sir Francis Burdett were widely known to favor the abolition of flogging in the army. Fortunately, the mob, egged on by the radicals, always insulted the soldier: if they had endeavored instead to conciliate them, "the existing government would not be worth a week's purchase, nor any throat which could be supposed to be worth cutting safe for a month longer."[210] He was particularly distressed that the subversive press was capturing the imaginations of young people. The line dividing literary men, as he knew, was chiefly one of generations (he said to Shelley: "The real difference between you and me is that I am twenty years older"). Believing that delay favored the radicals, he wanted to bring matters to a head and smash them: "the longer revolutionary principles are allowed to be disseminated, the greater will be the danger—for in the end they will make it a struggle between youth and age and the weakest will go to the wall."[211]

Shelley, writing from Italy, was likewise anxious for a showdown. He illustrated Southey's belief that industrialization, by poisoning the traditional social order, injected people—elites as well as masses—with a spirit of destruction presented as "liberty," of course, but in reality leading to chaos and death. Shelley did not mind being ranked on the side of Satan. He smacked his lips over words like *atheism, anarchy,* and *assassin,* which were among his favorites. He was particularly attached to the term *demogorgon,* which was supposed to be the name of the infernal powers that the ancients regarded as unspeakable: Just to pronounce it produced colossal evil. The spell was first broken by the Christian writer Lactantius in the fourth century AD. Shelley learned of the name from Milton's *Paradise Lost* ("the dreaded name of Demogorgon"), and he liked to talk, as did other educated radicals, of "Demogorgon dethroning Jupiter," that is, the mob overthrowing the Liverpool government by force.[212]

For Shelley, as for other radical poets, 1819 was the key year. It produced Keats's majestic unfinished poem *Hyperion*, describing a revolution in which the Titans are overthrown by the collective gods of Olympus. The poem was among Shelley's favorites and was found, open in his pocket, on his dead body; it is likely he was reading it almost up to the moment his yacht was overwhelmed by the storm. Also in 1819 Shelley produced *Prometheus Unbound*, in which the humanist hero revolts against Jupiter and religion on behalf of mankind. There was, in 1818–19, a counterpoint between the British radical press, aimed at the literate masses, and anti-establishment poets, seeking to conjure up the radical elite. A paper like the *Black Dwarf*, for instance, praised the mass meeting as the supreme weapon because it forged the people into a single-minded unit and, even more important, banished their fear of authority: "The spark of patriotism runs with electric swiftness from pulse to pulse until the whole mass vibrates in unison. Then, despots, tremble, for the hour of retribution is at hand!"[213] Shelley, likewise, invited the British masses to rise in his *Masque of Anarchy:* "Rise like lions after slumber / In unvanquishable number / Shake your chains to earth like dew / Which in sleep had fall'n on you / You are many—they are few."

Was Shelley's arithmetic correct? Were the revolutionaries many and the defenders of order few? The critical question, Could the center hold? was put to the test in the second half of 1819. The timing was accidental, in some ways perverse. The London riots at the end of 1816 had come, as might have been expected, in the very trough of the postwar recession. Since then, economic conditions had greatly improved. The 1818 harvest was below average, but trade was reviving strongly; when Liverpool went on a tour of the south in September 1819, he concluded that "the agricultural counties are in a state of progressive prosperity." In the disturbed districts "nothing can be worse or more alarming," but the country as a whole was more prosperous than at any time since the war, perhaps since he entered public life 30 years before.[214] If there was discontent, it was certainly not reflected in Parliament. On 1 July Burdett had tabled a motion calling for political reform, but it attracted only 58 votes, a record low figure.[215] Parliament dispersed two weeks later in a good-tempered mood.

The danger lay not in economic facts, but in the growing sophistication of the extraparliamentary radicals. This time the threat did not come from London. Arthur Thistlewood and James Watson were still active and occasionally preached violence—earlier in the year, Thistle-wood had challenged the home secretary, Lord Sidmouth, to a duel and had been committed briefly to jail—but they found it impossible to raise a mob. Northern and Midlands radicals openly sneered at the timidity of London workers. One such radical was the ferocious "Mrs. Wilson" from Manchester, who came to London to collect money for the purchase of arms. Mrs. Wilson founded a female union and at-tended meetings at the White House tavern with a loaded pistol wrapped in her hankie, and threatened to use it when crossed. She called the Londoners cowards, but made the error of conducting an open affair with her fellow Northerner John Hill, who had fled after trying to shoot Joseph Nadin, Manchester's terrifying deputy consta-ble; Mrs. Hill promptly went to the police.[216]

In the manufacturing districts, where there were still pockets of distress, workers were more militant and their leaders were more enter-prising. From June onwards they organized a series of mass meetings, of a menacing but orderly nature, which engaged in mock elections. In July there was a spectacular one in Birmingham, which elected the radical agitator Sir Charles Wolseley as the people's "legislative attor-ney." Wolseley, like Liverpool, had been present at the fall of the Bastille, but had been more appreciative; indeed, he sometimes talked as though he had led the assault. The government regarded him as a menace, charged him with sedition and got a conviction. He was sen-tenced to 18 months' imprisonment, but the constable who arrested him was shot outside the court.[217] The meetings continued. There was talk of a national convention, elected by universal male adult suffrage. The next big gathering was to take place in August at St. Peter's Fields in Manchester and was expected to attract textile workers from a radius of twenty miles, some from towns still hit by the recession. It was to be addressed by "Orator" Hunt. Hunt was popular among the masses, who sometimes wore medallions of him round their necks and laid down flower "portraits" of him in village streets. He was not liked by those who knew him. Leigh Hunt shuddered exquisitely when they were confused. He detested the Orator's "vulgarity" and wrote, in the *Examiner:* "He never utters a sentence worth hearing." An important eyewitness, Samuel Bamford, described him as "gentlemanly in his manner and attire," over six feet tall, "extremely well-formed . . . his leg and foot were about the firmest and neatest I ever saw." His intention was to avoid any unlawful incitement, but once on the plat-form, he "worked himself furious. . . . His voice was bellowing; his face

swollen and flushed; his gripped hand beat as if it were to pulverise."²¹⁸
In any event, he nearly always said something which could be construed
as breaking the law by incitement to riot.

Hence, news of the Manchester meeting, fixed eventually for Monday 16 August, set alarm bells ringing, especially in Sidmouth's head.
Sidmouth had been warning his colleagues all year of coming trouble
in the north, from which he received constant and alarming reports. He
pointed to the events of 1817, when there had been the "Ardwick
Conspiracy" near Manchester in March, the "Pentridge Rising" in
Derbyshire in June, and an armed march of Nottingham workers led by
a man named Jeremy Brandreth. These were isolated events, far away,
but if they had occurred in the Home Counties, Parliament would have
been terrified. Indeed, a ploy called "the March of the Blanketeers" was
precisely designed to carry the agitation to London, just as the Marseilles men had stormed Paris in 1792. In the north, sporadic violence
and attacks on mills had continued throughout 1818 and into the first
half of 1819. The atmosphere was tense, with magistrates, police, and
mill masters fierce and aggressive toward "reformers"; their hostility
was reflected in the mood of the regiments of local yeomen. The general
feeling in the north, among ordinary respectable citizens, as well as
officials, was that the civil power was too weak. J. Norris, the able and
active stipendary magistrate in Manchester, forwarded to Sidmouth
numerous documents to this effect. In reply the Home secretary told
justices of the peace that no doubt the opportunity would arise "for
their energy to display itself" and they could count on "the cordial
support of the government."²¹⁹

But how exactly should magisterial energy display itself? The law
was unclear, and both sides knew it was unclear. There was an im-
memorial right under the Common Law for people to assemble in
public and petition the Crown. There was also the 1714 Riot Act—
aimed at Jacobites, not would-be Jacobins—which said that if any
persons to the number of 12 or more were unlawfully, riotously, and
tumultuously assembled together to the disturbance of the public peace
and did not disperse within one hour of being commanded to do so by
a justice of the peace, in the form set out in the act, they should be guilty
of a felony. Moreover, the justices might arrest the rioters and were free
from liability if any of them were killed or injured.²²⁰ That was all very
well. But what if the right of assembly was exercised by a vast number
of people, who came together not riotously and tumultuously but in an
orderly, disciplined and drilled manner? That was the new radical
strategy, and it was much more frightening to the law-abiding than

were the old, scruffy, haphazard riots of the past. In the view of the Lord Chancellor, Eldon, excessive numbers themselves broke the law. As he put it to the House of Lords, "numbers constituted force, and force terror, and terror illegality."[221] To him, the mere fact of bringing, say, 100,000 people into the center of a great town or city, to demand political changes Parliament had just refused to make by a huge majority, constituted a breach of the king's peace.

That was the view to which the Lancashire magistrates also inclined. They pointed, moreover, to the militaristic nature of these gatherings. Eleven days before the meeting, Norris informed Sidmouth that large quantities of flags and caps of liberty were being distributed in preparation, adding: "The drilling parties increase *very extensively* and unless some mode be devised for putting this system down, it promises to become a most formidable engine of rebellion." Sidmouth agreed. The day before the meeting, taking a few days' anxious rest in Broadstairs, he wrote to Admiral Exmouth: "The laws are not strong enough for the times [and] they must be made so."[222] The truth is, there was no precise law forbidding people to organize and even arm themselves in a military manner, provided they did not actually threaten or practice violence. A valuable insight into what mass militarism involved is provided by the memoirs of Bamford, who was an active participant. Bamford published them many years afterwards, in 1844, when his views had changed, but their essential veracity has not been successfully challenged.

Bamford came from Middleton, a small weaving town five miles to the north of Manchester. In 1816 Joseph Nadin, the Manchester police chief, had arrested and charged him with high treason. He was conveyed to London by two ultrapolite King's Messengers and made no less than five appearances before the Privy Council, a striking example of the intimate manner in which government was still conducted. There he found Sidmouth, a "tall, square and bony figure . . . with thin and rather grey hair: his forehead was broad and prominent and from their cavernous orbits looked mild and intelligent eyes."[223] Also present was the attorney general, Sir Samuel Shepherd, who "made frequent use of an ear-trumpet," and "a good-looking person in a plum-coloured coat, with a gold ring on the small finger of his left hand, on which he sometimes leaned his head as he eyed me over"—this was Castlereagh. Sidmouth was courtesy itself, behaving to Bamford rather like a university proctor toward an unruly undergraduate. A fellow conspirator, "Doctor" Joseph Healey, had the council constantly in fits of laughter. Bamford's brief spell in Coldbathfields Prison also casts a curious light on class warfare (if that is the right term) as practiced in early nineteenth-century Britain.

Bamford shared a room with three beds, ten yards by three. "At the head of the room a good fire was burning and we found a stock of coal and wood to recruit it at our pleasure. There was also a number of chairs, a table, candles and other requisites." The next day food, a kettle, and knives and forks arrived, and he found himself "wishing that all at home, and all others who deserved it, might have as good a breakfast as ourselves. At noon we dined on a quarter of pork, with potatoes and other vegetables; to dilute which each man was allowed a pot of porter, and pipes and tobacco were added. Our supper was tea and cold meat and thus, so far as diet was concerned, we lived more like gentlemen than prisoners." He added that they were able to pass on their surplus food to women prisoners in the next yard.[224]

Bamford returned to political activism after his release and led a well-drilled contingent to the Manchester meeting. He describes the preparatory drilling parties in great detail. The object, according to him, was to "disarm the bitterness of our political opponents by a display of cleanliness, sobriety and decorum" and to end taunts about "our ragged, dirty appearance." But Bamford's district was largely nonmilitant. Others were different. And even in his area there was an undertone of force. The "units" were drilled by former noncommissioned officers, discharged from the regular army, and the military appearance was increased by the practice of giving thunderous hand claps on the order "Fire!" Bamford saw few firearms but many had formidable sticks. The drilling took place on a large scale and involved huge numbers. Whether or not the object was to inspire terror, that was certainly the effect, as is suggested by a report of drilling and hand clapping (dated August 9) sent by two Rochdale Justices of the Peace, John Beswick and John Crossley.[225]

The actual events of 16 August were described by numerous eyewitnesses, the best known being John Tyas, who reported it for the *Times*, was arrested and was highly critical of the authorities.[226] He and his newspaper, which was anti-violence but pro-Reform, played a major part in creating the image of "Peterloo" and the "massacre."[227] Bamford, who has a full description of the day, as seen by himself and, separately, by his wife, said he was surprised that the authorities allowed such a vast number of people into Manchester in the first place. In his unit, he insisted that "no sticks, nor weapons of any description" might be "carried in the ranks." He claimed that if an insurrection had been intended, protesters would not have brought their wives and (in some cases) children. But many of the wives were arrayed in women's regiments; there were, for instance, the 156 members of the Oldham

Female Reform Club and a somewhat smaller group from Royton. Bamford described the various bodies converging on Manchester. Each one hundred men had a leader "distinguished by a sprig of laurel in his hat." There was also a senior rank of officer, described as "a principal conductor," attended by a bugler to give his orders: "At the sound of a bugle, not less than 3,000 men formed a hollow square."[228] Tyas confirmed this description: "The Reformers from Rochdale and Middleton marched to the sound of the bugle, and in very regular time, closing and expanding their ranks, and marching in ordinary and double-quick time, according as it pleased the fancy of their leader to direct them." These groups may not have been armed. But others were. Another eyewitness, Robert Mutrie, a special constable on duty, who sent an account ot his brother in Scotland, said that the "poor deluded people" converged on the fields "in regular military order with monstrous clubs over their shoulders." As they marched through the streets, he noted, they rattled their sticks against the railings and houses. Some, he added, had pistols.[229]

Against this background, Norris and his fellow magistrates behaved with some irresolution, first permitting about 80,000 people to assemble, then ordering the arrest of "Orator" Hunt. They had built up a substantial force of special constables, six troops of the fifteenth Hussars and the local yeomanry, mostly sons of local manufacturers and publicans but including a wine merchant, a cheesemonger, a butcher and even a dancing master. What followed when the Justices of the Peace decided to intervene and arrest those on the platform was what always happens, even today, when armed men who are not trained and equipped for riot control attempt to enter a vast crowd. The yeomanry simply rode into the assembly and began to hit out with the flat of their swords. According to Mutrie, they identified a group of 100 special constables as an armed mob and bowled them over; he himself was struck on the head with a saber. The crowd panicked and ran, many being trampled underfoot. Eleven died, including a constable and a cavalryman; there were over 100 injured, some of them women. There was fighting over a large area. Mutrie related that "after we had been exposed to the pelting of stones for an hour or two," the cavalry commander "got into the most furious passion and swore to Mr Norris that if he did not immediately read the Riot Act he would order his men to their quarters." The act was then read, the infantry formed a hollow square in New Cross, and parties of cavalry charged in all directions to clear the streets. Mutrie says he was on duty all day and "I got very little sleep all that week as being in the very heart of the disturbances." Reformers, he added, "continue to meet in the nighttime for drilling exercises." Not for a week was calm restored in Manchester and its neighborhood.

Peterloo has gone down in national folklore as an unwarranted abuse of official authority. In the short term it worked very much in the interests of the government. That may explain why one or two radical historians argue that Sidmouth planned it all.[230] The consequences were felt at two levels. Among the radicals, at any rate the extraparliamentary ones—Brougham publicly deplored mass meetings of the Manchester type—there was an initial resolve to answer blood with blood. In several northern towns, pikes were made from wooden staves with a groove at the top into which a knife (carried secretly in the pocket) was inserted. These blades, costing from 1 shilling to 3 shillings, were marketed in Manchester by Naaman Carter, who sold them on installment and touted them round smaller towns and villages. Bamford was one customer, and his utterances then—"May the Tree of Liberty be planted in Hell, and may the Bloody Butchers of Manchester be the Fruit of It!"—belie his later account. He said that militants were sharpening scythes, old hatchets, screwdrivers, rusty swords and big nails: "anything which could be made to cut or stab was pronounced fit for service."[231] But reports of these doings merely spurred the law-abiding to form associations of loyalists. And, one by one, those involved in leading the Manchester business were pulled in. Orator Hunt, Bamford, and others were arrested on 26 August.

Released on bail, Hunt made a triumphant entry into London in September, organized by the "Committee of Two Hundred," but was eventually tried, convicted, and sentenced to two years in prison. For once, the government found no difficulty in getting juries to convict, having shrewdly reduced the charges from high treason to misdemeanor. The radical press talked violence. *Medusa* wrote of "the necessity of constantly wearing arms," the *Cap of Liberty* urged that "Reform cannot be obtained without bloodshed." But in London no one stirred. Even in the north, the level of violence in the last three months of 1819 was the lowest in the year. Those radicals who were still at liberty divided sharply into violent and nonviolent wings. Watson was imprisoned for nonpayment of a bill incurred during Hunt's reception. Hunt hinted that Thistlewood was a government spy. Cobbett, returning from America in November, got a rousing reception in Liverpool but made no reference to Peterloo and talked about currency reform. In short, the military ardor so marked between June and August vanished in the flash of those clumsily wielded sabers, and the dead bodies left on St. Peter's field probably saved many more lives.

At the governmental level it took some time to formulate policy, partly because ministers were scattered for the holidays. It is amazing how reluctant they were to come back. Liverpool, himself spending as much time as possible in rural comfort at Kingston, in the house Madame de Staël had discovered so hard to find, had difficulty, throughout September and October, gathering a cabinet of more than six or seven.[232] Sidmouth's instant reaction was to endorse the conduct of the Manchester Justices of the Peace, get the Prince Regent to send a letter of approval that also praised the "forbearance" of the military, and reiterate his pleas to Liverpool for new anti-subversive legislation. Wellington was delighted and assured Sidmouth jovially that "the radicals will impeach you for this, by God they will!" Even Canning, the government's most liberal member—in some ways—approved: "To let down the magistrates would be to invite their resignations and to lose all gratuitous services in the counties liable to disturbance for ever." To be sure, the muddling of Norris and Co. was "provoking," but then the law was inadequate. "What is wanted," Canning told Liverpool, "is not a sudden & temporary measure . . . applicable to pressing but passing emergency, but a well-considered addition to the means which the present laws afford for repressing Evils . . . of deep root and thriving malignity."[233]

Liverpool hesitated over new legislation, partly because the law officers had not pondered the problem—and were notoriously slow anyway—partly because he was not sure what "the country gentlemen" (MPs for the counties) would think. The year before they had given him fearful trouble over providing more money for the royal princes. He had summoned them to a meeting at his Westminster residence, Fife House, to read them the parliamentary equivalent of the Riot Act, only to get a bloody nose instead and be told "some home truths."[234] Granted their attachment to "liberties," he hesitated to ask for more restrictions or even to get Parliament back early to test their mood. But the Whigs played into his hands. They, as it turned out, were much more divided than were the government's supporters, a majority backing what the Manchester justices had done, though not necessarily how they did it. But some called for an inquiry into the "massacre" and held meetings to this effect. In October the line of this faction was endorsed by Earl Fitzwilliam, a leading Whig grandee and the richest landowner in Yorkshire. Fitzwilliam was also Lord Lieutenant of the West Riding. His behavior caused outrage, being seen as an insult to the Regent and an affront to the whole principle of order in the north, where it was most needed. Liverpool stopped hesitating, seized eagerly on Fitzwilliam's tactical error, and sacked him on 23 October 1819. Parliament was hastily summoned for 23 November and the law officers were hounded back from the grouse moors and told to get to work immediately on bills to restrict public meetings of a minatory nature and subversive newspapers. Liverpool calculated that since some of the Whigs had irresponsibly identified themselves with the forces of anarchy, there would now be no difficulty getting the country gentlemen to back tough measures. He was right. The first of the Six Acts got its Second Reading on 2 December and all were passed into law by large majorities by Christmas. Many Whigs voted with the ministers, and they endorsed a provision to add 10,000 men temporarily to the army.[235]

The Six Acts are often cited, even today, as an archetypal repressive law code by those who clearly do not know what they contained. The first act prohibited unauthorized meetings to train men in the use of arms. The second authorized Justices of the Peace in areas legally defined as disturbed to search for arms, even in private houses, and to seize arms carried by individuals if they had reason to believe the intention was to break the peace. These provisions are still on the statute book. The third act made it hard for those accused of sedition to postpone trial; Castlereagh accepted an amendment by Brougham to rule out delays by the Crown as well, and this amendment too passed into the law as it exists today. The fourth act provided a stricter definition of seditious meetings and made it difficult to call one of more than 50 people; and it ruled out the use of arms, flags and military formations. Here, again, Castlereagh willingly conceded a Whig amendment that exempted indoor meetings. This act eventually disappeared, but part of it was revived in the 1936 Public Order Act to deal with fascism, and that, too, is still English law. The two truly repressive acts dealt with the press, authorizing the seizure of the whole of an issue containing an item of blasphemy or sedition, making the second offense transportable—that was what Southey wanted—and subjecting pamphlets that commented on the news to newspaper duty if they cost less than sixpence. The whole operation was extremely skillful, since it did not involve suspending habeas corpus—always an emotional stumbling block for Parliament—and was put through quickly and overwhelmingly, often with the cooperation of the Whigs.[236] It was also highly effective, ruling out any possibility of a return to the military-style mass meetings of the summer.

Finally, in February 1820, Liverpool and his colleagues enjoyed an uncovenanted stroke of luck which, in the public's eyes at least, vindicated their tough approach to subversion—Arthur Thistlewood achieved his revolutionary apotheosis. This illegitimate son of a Lincolnshire farmer was five feet ten, dark and sallow, with arched eye-brows and a military appearance—he had served in both the regulars and the militia. He seems to have plotted violence against authority for over twenty years, though there were brief periods when he supported constitutional reform. He had been arraigned for treason three times and had served twelve months—he complained he had been forced to sleep "two or three in a bed" in Horsham Gaol—for challenging Sidmouth to a duel. By mid-Autumn 1819 he had despaired of raising the London rabble. They were, *pace* Shelley, few not many now. Instead he determined on assassination.

Terrorism was in the European air. A month after Peterloo, radical German students had murdered the pro-Imperialist playwright Kotzebue, whose work figures so largely in *Mansfield Park*. In France plans were maturing to kill the ultimate heir to the throne, the much-hated Duc de Berri. Thistlewood's original scheme was to destroy the entire Parliament, rather like Guy Fawkes. But he decided he lacked the resources for such a large-scale operation. Instead, he determined to murder the cabinet, plus, if possible, the Prince Regent; seize Coutts or Childes' bank to get cash; raid the Tower for arms, and set up a provisional government in the Mansion House. But by this time, December 1819, he was being closely watched by a spy, George Edwards, whom the Home Office had planted in his entourage. Edwards was brought into Thistlewood's "Secret Committee of Thirteen," then into his inner executive of five, and finally was made his sole confidant. The successful murder of the Duc de Berri on 13 February was an inspiration to Thistlewood's circle, and Thistlewood was delighted when Edwards drew his attention to an item in the *New Times* announcing a cabinet dinner at Lord Harrowby's for 23 February. Thistlewood promptly hired a loft over a stable in Cato Street and assembled about 25 of his followers there on February 23. The plan was to force their way into Harrowby's house and then for James Ings, a butcher designated as secretary to the "Provisional Government," to enter the dining room, saying: "My Lords, I have got as good men here as the Manchester yeomanry—enter, Citizens, and do your duty." The heads of Castlereagh and Sidmouth were to be cut off, put on pikes and carried through the streets.

The gang had firearms, bombs, and hand grenades and were busy priming them when the police, tipped off by Edwards, entered the loft at 8:30 in the evening. Thistlewood contrived to kill Police Constable Smithers with a sword and got away, but was found the next day.[237] Of the gang, Thistlethwood, Ings, and three others were capitally convicted and hanged on May 1, an event recorded from life by Géricault in a brilliant pen-and-wash drawing, *Public Hanging in London*.[238] (In this drawing, Thistlewood has an intense stare as he resists the spiritual counsel of the Rev. Mr. Cotton, and a woman faints in the background.) Five of the rest were transported. The details of the assassination plan were gruesome in the extreme and sent a thrill of horror through the nation; for a moment or two, the plan almost made ministers popular and wiped out rapidly fading memories of Peterloo.

But the nation quickly turned to other and much more intriguing matters. For, while Thistlewood was plotting to exterminate the cabinet, old King George III, hopelessly mad for more than a decade and almost forgotten, finally breathed his last on 29 January 15 at 8:30 in the evening. His death made the Prince Regent king and, equally significant socially, it made his estranged wife queen. She had long been living in Italy, supposedly with her majordomo, Bergami. It was hoped she would continue to disport herself there, and ministers had vaguely talked of providing £50,000 a year to make her exile attractive. But shortly before Thistlewood went to the gallows, she announced her intention of coming to London to reclaim her rights, and on 5 June she actually arrived in Dover. Thus began the Queen Caroline Crisis, which transfixed the entire nation for a year, and from which the nation emerged transformed beyond recognition.

SIX

Honorable Gentlemen and Weaker Vessels

The one constant political fact about Britain in the fifteen years after Waterloo was the unpopularity of the sovereign, first as Prince Regent, then as George IV. It was the first thing foreigners visiting London noticed. John Quincy Adams, watching the Regent arrive to open Parliament on 28 January 1817, heard "a mixture of low but very audible hissing, of faint groaning, and still fainter attempts to raise a shout." The Household Cavalry stood ready to drive back the mob, the Life Guards with drawn sabers. He heard their squadron commander say repeatedly, "in a tone of extreme earnestness, 'Keep them back! Keep them back!' " "There were among the crowd," added Adams, "great numbers of very wretched and ill-looking persons. One said: 'He's gone into a strong hysteric.' Another said: 'Throw mud at him!' "[1]

Dislike of the Regent was not confined to the lower orders. The Regent was not, to be sure, the only member of the royal family to be hated. George III, a much-loved monarch, had had 15 children, eight sons and seven daughters. The daughters were virtually unknown to the public, but all the surviving sons were disapproved of, though in varying degrees. The Duke of Cumberland was a scoundrel, widely suspected of having murdered his valet. The Duke of York had been involved in a disgraceful business, through his mistress, of selling army commissions when he was commander in chief. The Duke of Clarence had lived off the earnings of *his* mistress, the successful comedy actress Mrs. Jordan, by whom he had 10 children, then cast her off to marry a German princess. The Duke of Kent's life followed a similar pattern, and when he finally brought his bride to England, he had to borrow £5,000 from Earl Fitzwilliam and Lord Dundas. Parliament was constantly being asked to vote money to rescue George III's sons from bankruptcy and to keep them in idle profligacy. As Liverpool frequently complained, no other kind of business was so difficult to get through the

House of Commons. Nor was this surprising. Wellington calculated that the brothers between them "at one time or another" had "personally insulted every gentleman in the kingdom."

But George IV, no doubt because as heir apparent he had been more indulged and flattered than his brothers, was by common consent the worst of the lot. His instinct was always to desert and betray. He had abandoned his old friends, the Whigs, when his father's madness made him Regent and kept the Tories in office, but he proved the greatest single burden the Tories had to bear. As the diaries of Mrs. Arbuthnot and much other contemporary material show, he was a serious and permanent obstacle to any kind of good government because his habit was always to plot against the men in charge. Not the least of Liverpool's merits was his ability to out maneuver this difficult and treacherous prince. Personal relations with him were always slippery because, like most royal persons—the same is true today—he wanted it both ways; he practised familiarity when it suited the mood of the hour, but insisted on ceremony the moment he felt his dignity infringed. One second he was humbly beseeching Liverpool to give jobs to his hangers-on, the next he was telling the prime minister: "Leave the room, Sir!" It was thought shocking he should call Lord Dundas "Tom"—no one else did. He even dared to call Wellington "Arthur"—much to the duke's annoyance—though a minute later, not liking the advice he received, he snapped; "Hold your tongue, Sir!" Often cringing or cowardly, he could be savagely insulting to senior ministers: "My Lord," he said silkily to Lord Chancellor Eldon, "I know your conscience always interferes except where your interest is concerned."[2]

Men disliked him particularly because he was an inveterate liar. Indeed, he was a fantasist who could convince himself that certain imaginary things had happened. He would threaten all kinds of things one minute, for effect, then forget what he had said and do the opposite. He would abruptly change his mood from resentful fury, vowing revenge, saying he would dismiss his ministers on the spot, to bland politeness or even affability, with no explanation at all. In the end, as Mrs. Arbuthnot put it, "The King is such a blockhead nobody minds what he says."[3] Some of his inventions were trivial and pointless. Lady Cowper said that at Brighton, the King talked of her mother Lady Melbourne (Byron's confidante), who died 6 April 1818, "and said he used, during her last illness, to walk across [Brighton] parade to her house every day . . . and that at last she died in his arms." Lady Cowper added that her mother died in London, not Brighton, and that the King "so far from calling to see her and having her die in his arms had never even sent to inquire after her."[4]

Men also hated him because he was lazy, unpunctual, and inconsiderate. The punctilious John Quincy Adams was enraged, when calling at Carlton House to say farewell officially to the Regent, at the appointed time of 2:30 P.M., that he was not admitted until 4 P.M. When he complained, the assistant master of ceremonies, Chester, just laughed; he said the Regent "led a singular kind of life . . . he had not risen when we came, and was scarcely ever out of his bed till three in the afternoon."[5] Adams was comparatively lucky. At Berkeley Castle, the Regent kept a large dinner party (and the food) waiting for two hours because he disliked "country habits" and would not dine before 8 P.M.[6] Rossi, the sculptor, attending the Prince to work on a small portrait head he had commissioned, was kept in attendance five hours, and then dismissed without being seen. The next day he had to wait three more hours, while the Prince tried on 40 pairs of boots and saw two tailors.[7] His idle selfishness—the *déformation professionelle* of heir-apparent royalty—was, at times, hard to credit. Sleeping badly himself, he would ring for a footman constantly during the night to demand the time, though his own watch hung at the head of his four-poster. He was not loath to wake up ministers either. His lady friends would frequently intercede on behalf of convicted felons, knowing he was softhearted about hanging anyway, and persuade him to exercise his royal prerogative of mercy. When Sir Robert Peel, as Home Secretary, stayed with him at Brighton Pavilion, he was accustomed to being roused in the small hours by a tear-stained monarch who said he could not sleep for worry and forced Peel to go over with him the current list of condemned men.[8]

One collateral reason why men disliked George IV was that he was very much a ladies' man, always surrounded by petticoats. It was characteristic of him that he was the first man to take over the new institution of lunch, hitherto regarded as a meal eaten exclusively by women—*Pride and Prejudice* shows the two eldest Bennet girls being thus entertained in an inn by their younger sisters[9]—and give luncheon-parties at Windsor. On 3 June 1820, for example, Farington noted that Lawrence, Samuel Rogers and his daughter were among those taking *lunch* (he underscored the word disapproving) at the castle.[10] Over women, George waxed sentimental, at least at a superficial level, and the opportunity to hug, kiss, and pay compliments even, on occasions, led him to put up with personal inconvenience. John Wilson Croker, who accompanied him on his state visit to Dublin, recorded that at the official "Drawing Room" at Dublin Castle, "no less than 1,000 Irish ladies were presented" and the king "kissed them all." Then the officials told him he could go, so he got undressed and went to bed. At that point, said Croker, "300 more ladies" were discovered, who had not been kissed, "and with great good nature [the King] put on his fine coat, came back to the Presence Chamber, and went through the ceremony of kissing 300 ladies more."[11]

The fact that George preferred female company did not mean that ladies liked him; quite the contrary. Outside his own family, all the women with whom he was intimately connected came to regret it. Perhaps his greatest love, Mrs. Fitzherbert, whom he actually married, albeit unlawfully, came to regard him with a mixture of distaste and weariness. In January 1795 she told Nathaniel Dance, RA, that her connection with the prince had actually *cost* her £8,000, "and if he would pay that sum and trouble her no more she would be contented." She said she had "lived the life of a Galley Slave for four years past."[12]

His marriage the same year to Princess Caroline of Brunswick was a complete disaster from the start. It must be remembered, to do him justice, that the bride was not his choice but his parents'—George III and Queen Charlotte made a pitiful mess of the marital arrangements for every one of their children—and that he found her unpleasing from the start. However, in an age when a majority of marriages, and virtually all royal ones, were arranged, he might have put more effort into making it succeed. However, he was then under the influence of a new mistress, Lady Jersey. Lady Jersey may have had a hand in the selection of Caroline—"all well-informed persons," wrote Lord Holland, "agree that the preference of the Princess of Brunswick was the choice of Lady Jersey and Lady Harcourt"[13]—anticipating the marriage would not work, and she certainly encouraged him to destroy it.

According to a diary Caroline kept when she was first married, which later disappeared but was peddled around and read in 1821, the Prince was drunk the night of the marriage. "When he came into her room," Mrs. Arbuthnot recorded, "he was obliged to leave it again; and he remained away all night and did not return till the morning; that he then obliged her to remain in bed with him and that that is the *only time* they were together as husband and wife"—and the point at which their only child Charlotte, who died in 1817, was conceived.[14] The couple cohabited barely a fortnight, and soon there was hatred on both sides. Caroline had been brought up without much refinement and was laughed at in any event, but the Prince and Lady Jersey were seen slipping brandy into her wine to get her drunk and behave yet more foolishly.[15] In 1796 the Prince and Caroline parted for good, though not in any legal sense.

Drink was one reason women disliked the Prince. He did not become an alcoholic until toward the end of his life, but as early as the

1790s he was accustomed to spend from six till midnight at the dinner table, beginning with "ten Bumber toasts" (there were six bumper glasses to the bottle).[16] As the years went by, he switched from wine to spirits. Mrs. Arbuthnot reported in February 1822: "The Duke of Wellington was at Brighton ten days ago and told me that the quantity of cherry brandy [the King] drank was not to be believed, and that he did not believe he could eat anything without that sort of stimulus."[17] Respectable women objected that, after drinking, his conversation was liable to become obscene and, as the Tsar's sister noted, he was too fond of peering down their cleavages. Mrs. Arbuthnot voiced a common complaint when she blamed him for society's low moral tone. It would be a "good thing," she wrote, "if the ladies will *pull up* a little and set their faces against the barefaced liaisons which are becoming the fashion. . . . It is all the King's fault. He has let down the royal dignity, has received at his court the Duchess of St Albans and Mrs Manners-Sutton, both *des femmes entretenues* [kept women] & now one is almost laughed at if one objects to receiving any woman, however atrocious her conduct."[18]

Ladies also, and increasingly, objected to his physical appearance. As a young man he had been unusually good-looking, "an Adonis," but by early summer 1817 he had grown so fat that he could not longer endure the discomfort of stays and "let loose his stomach." When he attended the opening of Waterloo Bridge on the second anniversary of the battle—an event recorded in a striking painting by John Constable, RA—Lord Folkestone reported that his stomach "reached his knees." Another observer of this occasion, Cobbett, described him as "an uncommonly large mass" weighing "perhaps a quarter of a ton."[19]

George IV was not without gifts. He played the cello "quite tolerably," according to the composer Joseph Haydn. He had a good bass singing voice and often sang in company with "gaity and spirit." As late as 12 January 1822, he was reported to have sung, from memory, "Glorious Apollo, Mighty Conqueror," "Lord Mornington's Waterfall" (which was encored), *"Non Nobis, Domine,"* "and several other glees and catches." Above all, he was an outstanding mimic, especially of actors and politicians—he could do Blücher and Talleyrand; fat Louis XVIII (in French); and his own ministers, notably the Duke of Wellington, Liverpool, Peel (with accent) and the tearful Robinson. He was, said the cosmopolitan boulevardier, Séguier, "the most remarkable Mimick I ever heard in my life."[20]

But as he grew older, his gifts were discounted by tipsiness and by the excessive tedium of his ceaseless chatter. All the royal family were "most unquiet men and women," according to the society portrait painter John Edridge, who added: "The Duke of York talks till he sweats." George III was just as bad as his children, and once he went mad, his talk became continuous, whether or not anyone was listening. George IV had this propensity to a high degree, and ministers and the court alike were forced to listen to his incessant anecdotage, having heard it all before and knowing well that most of it was untrue. This, in the last resort, was why even his favorites, who grew rich by him, found their intimacy with him insufferable. His factotum, Sir William Knighton, called him "the great Beast" and said he was sick of his "indecent conversation"; the king, for his part, Mrs. Arbuthnot reported, "began talking about Knighton, abused him and showed evidently that he feared and hated him, as a madman hates his keeper."

Lady Conyngham, his last and nastiest mistress, did not attempt to conceal her irritation and contempt. At Windsor, in October 1823, she told Wellington frankly "that the whole thing bored her to death and that she would go away and have done with it." This remark provoked an explosion from the Duke, who said to her: "If you had asked my advice in the beginning as to whether you should get into the scrape or not, I would have urged and advised you by all means to keep out of it. But now that you are established here, that it has been entirely your own seeking, that you have driven out everybody that used to be here, for God's Almighty' sake, don't make a fresh scandal by leaving him!"[21]

But there was one group of women for whom George could do no wrong: his unmarried sisters living at Windsor Castle, in what they termed "the Nunnery." He was the only one who cared and did his best for these pathetic creatures. George III had neither found them husbands nor allowed them to marry men of their choice. When he finally went irrecoverably insane, the Queen became even more selfish. By 1812 the eldest daughter had contrived to get herself married to the King of Württemberg and the younger daughter was dead. But that left four old maids still at Windsor. The Queen would not even permit them to go to London. She expected them to live with her, "attending my distress," as she put it, sacrificing their lives, or what was left of them, to her comfort. She had grown enormously fat, "as though," someone put it, "she was bearing all her 15 children at once." Her face was red and swollen with erysipelas, and she was extremely irritable. Their eldest brother was their only family confidant and support, and their letters to him illuminate their gruesome existence. A letter to George from Princess Augusta, then aged 44, in December 1812, described a "dreadful scene" in which the Queen accused her and her three sisters, Elizabeth, 42; Mary, 36; and Sophia, 35, of "lack of delicacy and affection." The sisters bore this criticism in a "perfectly respectful" manner but "the Queen was too violent to allow it." When she said she would "never forgive them," Elizabeth placed her hand on the family Bible and intoned "May *God* forgive you, for saying so!" At this remark the Queen countered: "I should not be surprised if you gave me a box on the ear," which produced in Elizabeth "a hysteric fit" (this last is the Queen's own account).[22] George tried to make peace, on this and other occasions, but the pleading letters continued. Sophia wanted to marry one of her father's equerries, Major General Thomas Garth, a tiny man, disfigured by a large birthmark and 33 years her senior. She pleaded for the union, which, of course, was not allowed, then excused herself for trading on her brother's good nature. How sick of his sister, she wrote, George must be: "*Poor old wretches* as we are, *four old cats*, a *dead weight* upon you, *old lumber* to the country, like *old clothes*. I wonder you do not vote for putting us in a *sack* and *drowning* us in the *Thames*."[23]

Augusta also wanted to marry an equerry, an Irishman, Lieutenant General Sir Brent Spencer. They had, she told her brother, loved each other for seven years, adding: "I now beseech you, my dearest, to consider *our situation*. If it is in your power to *make us happy, I know you will*. Of course it will be necessary to keep it a secret and it must be a *private marriage*." No such union took place. There were rumors of an illicit marriage between Sophia and Garth, and even of a son, Thomas. But both sisters lived on, officially as old maids, into the 1840s. Mary, in 1816, managed to marry her cousin, the Duke of Gloucester, more as an escape than from any liking. He was, wrote Baron Stockmar, "large and stout, with weak, helpless legs . . . prominent, meaningless eyes . . . a very unpleasant face with an animal expression." Two years later Elizabeth was finally allowed to marry the Prince of Hesse-Homburg, who had proposed to Augusta 14 years before but had been vetoed by the family. He was now 49, "reputed to wash at the most infrequent intervals and smelled of garlic and tobacco."[24] He was also fat, and bending down to pick up the Queen's fan, his trousers split with a tremendous crack. To the public, he was "Prince Humbug." But the Princess got to like him and called him "Bluff."[25]

Fond as he was of his sisters, George despaired of their problems. He hated his parents and went as little as possible to Windsor, which they had turned into a museum of the past, smelling of ancient drains and musty with absurd rituals. It was, for instance, forbidden for the pages to wake up the royal family by knocking on their bedroom doors. Instead they touched a piece of wood that made a rattling sound; it was known as "the Scratches." It was a complaint of the Regent's that, after the King went mad, there was no proper person to manage the finances at Windsor. The Queen and the Princesses foolishly trusted the accounts to an ingratiating writing master, Bolton, who proved to be a rogue and ran off with £40,000; they were poor in consequence.[26] The Regent washed his hands of the castle, though oddly enough when he became King himself and grew old, he spent more and more time there.

London and Brighton were his preferred playgrounds, and he transformed both. His impact on Brighton was less surprising, for when he first went there in the 1780s, it was still a small town. London was a different matter: a vast and ancient city, peculiarly resistant to systematic improvement, whose conservatism had defied the efforts of the gifted Charles II and his brilliant master architect Christopher Wren even when the accident of the Great Fire gave them a matchless opportunity to rebuild on the grand scale. George, as Regent and King, was much more successful, and it is odd that such an indolent, purposeless, weak-minded and inconstant flibbertygibbet should have had more impact on the physical appearance of London than any other ruler in English history. Indeed, he may fairly be said to have created the first modern metropolis. It is true that he could draw on the services of a large and able group of architects. There were more good (and a few outstanding) architects working in England in the years after 1815 than at any other time, before or since. The official Board of Works had three of the highest class, John Nash (1752–1835), John Soane (1753–1837) and Robert Smirke (1781–1867), all men of exceptional drive, organizing power, and impressive output. But there were many others in private practice and available for royal commands: Samuel Pepys Cockerell and his son Charles Robert, Benjamin Dean Wyatt and Jeffrey Wyatt (or Wyattville), George Dance and Thomas Cundy, George Gwilt, William Atkinson, William Wilkins and William Chadwell Mylne, together with younger men like Joseph Kay, Decimus Burton and Anthony Salvin. These were only some of the more prominent names.[27]

As with all the grandest architectural schemes, George IV's plan to transform and beautify London was not exactly carried through as he intended, and he was particularly unlucky with the palaces he built or altered. But his project for linking the traditional royal estates and buildings around Westminster and St. James's Park by a series of great terraces and avenues to the splendid collection of villas he was creating around his new *rus in urbe*, the Regent's Park, was broadly speaking carried through despite all the difficulties. At the same time, the state was, with his encouragement, paying for the erection of a vast series of new buildings: dozens of churches, the Customs House, Law Courts and Post Office, the Treasury and Privy Council offices, the British Museum and the National Gallery (built in 1834–38 but planned in George's day, when the concept of Trafalgar Square replaced the clutter of the old royal mews west of Charing Cross), and the Bank of England. Famous theaters, like Covent Garden, Drury Lane and the Haymarket, were rebuilt on a grander scale. Immense new clubs, like the Athenaeum and the United Services opposite it, came into magnificent existence.

All these operations were related to an overall plan in which John Nash, making the best possible use of the Crown Lands for determining the sitings and relationships, was the central figure. Nash was a superb diplomat, coaxing, suggesting, coordinating, pleading, piloting, and bargaining, and always with the authority and support of the Regent-king at his command. Some people laughed at him, especially when they saw him entertaining in marine profusion at his East Cowes Castle in the Isle of Wight, surrounded by nouveau riche London financiers and northern manufacturers. Mrs. Arbuthnot found him "a very clever, odd, amusing man, with a face like a monkey," dismissing his wife as "a vulgar bore" (she was the daughter of a rich coal merchant).[28] But by the end of the 1820s, he had no need of a monument: it was there already in a transformed London. *Metropolitan Improvements*, a book published in 1827 by James Elmes with drawings by T. H. Shepherd, records page by page the vast changes made by the sovereign and his factotum over two decades. Its subtitle, significantly, was *London in the 19th Century*.

The key stroke in the creation of modern London was to drive John Nash's new Regent Street through the old slums of Soho. Doing so effectively divided the West End from the squalor and poverty to the east of it, and allowed the creation of modern Mayfair and the great new upper- and middle-class housing estates which soon came into existence to the west of it: Belgravia, Knightsbridge and, eventually, Kensington. To the north of Hyde Park, Bayswater was then known as Kensington Gravel Pits and dotted with the little villas and cottages of artists; soon that, too, would be built over by immense middle-class terraces. By 1825 Regent Street had been built, and Nash was busy clearing the ground for Trafalgar Square.

By a fortunate chance, we have a detailed record of all these demolitions and rebuildings in the work of George Scharf (1788–1860), a Bavarian artist from Munich, the birthplace of lithography, who joined the British army as a baggage master, fought at Waterloo and came to London in 1816. Scharf was an unlucky man, a commercial failure who underpriced his work and hated asking to be paid, thus dying poor; and his masterpieces, two gigantic five-feet-long watercolors recording the building of New London Bridge (1830) were both destroyed in the 1940 Blitz. But every day, whatever the weather, he began sketching London and its life from 5 A.M., working for ten hours, and many of these quasi-photographic drawings have survived.

Scharf was particularly good at showing the old London juxtaposed with the emerging new. At the bottom of the new Regent Street, in the Quadrant, was the elegant Westminster Dairy, a brand-new milk shop supplying St. James and Mayfair, which he drew in 1825. Its supplies, however, came from the northern and western suburbs, so its milk was not as fresh or pure as that sold by the Cow Keeper, which Scharf also drew, in Golden Lane in the City (a desperately wicked area), since the cows which supplied it were in a stable behind the shop, being exercised in the yard and fed turnips, hay, and grain (45 quarters a week for 25 cows, each of whom provided nine quarts of milk a day).[29] Scharf also drew the milkmaids, who took the milk from the London cow stables, starting at 3 or 4 A.M. each morning and doing twice-daily rounds of the street, calling out "Milk below!" or *Mio-mieau,* meaning half-water—hence the noise cats were supposed to make. They were good singers, strong girls from Wales (later Ireland) and had to be, for their yoke weighed up to 130 pounds, and they were paid nine shillings a week, plus breakfast.

The streets, in the years up to 1830, were still full of people selling things—brushes, clothes horses, tables, chairs, footstools, fruit in season, hot gingerbread and potatoes from portable charcoal stoves, prints pinned inside an itinerant's umbrella. Scharf drew these things; the men who ground and mended knives and repaired furniture; and the countless street musicians, "vile yellow Italians," as the young, noise-hating Thomas Carlyle called them; ingenious one-man bands; a blind man who played the violin while working machinery to play a cello with his foot; a cripple who operated his band from a dogcart; and a man, carrying his baby on his back, playing his instruments and wearing as headgear a giant model ship.

Scharf's pencil also reported on the coming of mass advertising to London, especially since the huge "improvement" schemes led to a rash of giant hoardings for display ads. He showed the parades of unemployed men, hired sometimes in dozens, sometimes fifty at a time, to march in file through the streets, holding aloft placards advertising goods, rather like Roman standard-bearers. He recorded the first appearance, in 1828, of "sandwich-men," a new device which Charles Dickens called "a piece of human flesh between two slices of pasteboard," designed to draw attention to the battle scenes enacted at the Egyptian Hall, Piccadilly. Placard men were sometimes dressed in outlandish clothes, were preceded by a horse and cart containing a German band, or carried floats displaying giant waterproof boots or hats.

Robert Warren, who invented what he called "Japan Liquid Blacking," was a major advertiser. (Blacking was then big business and highly competitive because men cared desperately about the shine of their boots—Beau Brummell said he mixed his blacking "with the best champagne" to get the right sheen.) Warren was a pioneer of the display ad in newspapers, using woodcuts of highly polished boots, but he also mounted processions of grotesque blacking bottles, with men inside them. His rivals, operating from Hungerford Stairs, where Dickens briefly and shamefully worked sticking on labels, ran processions of 20-foot-high shining boots.

Scharf drew the giant caddies which stalked through the streets advertising tea, and inside one of which Dickens was later to conduct an interview for *Household Words;* walking coffee mills, hatboxes, iron stoves, and other advertising monstrosities. He also recorded mobile street shows, of which there were thousands—a stuffed alligator, live cannibals, a fat lady; an armless boy; and kaleidoscopes, patented by Sir David Brewester in 1817, of which 200,000 were sold in London and Paris in three months. He drew the Fantocini Marionette Theatres, very tall, since they were operated from above, not, like Punch and Judy, from below, preceded by a man with a pipe and drum, paid 4s a day, and run by a Scotsman named Grey who reckoned to make an average of 18s6d in half an hour. Then there were clockwork figures from Germany; walking tableaux of mechanical soldiers worked by turning a handle; and, not least, countless peepshows, the big ones pulled by a donkey, the smaller ones mounted on a man's back.

Scharf recorded the rapid changes of these years. Ladies still had to scamper under the dripping overhead pipes which linked the oil carts to the lamp shops, trying to avoid getting their dresses spoiled. But the lamp shops were going fast as the gas mains spread rapidly through London. Scharf's drawings show them being installed, narrow pipes set at right angles to the mains taking the gas to individual houses. He also showed experiments in paving: the growth of traffic noise led to a 150-yard stretch of Oxford Street being surfaced in 12 different materials, wood finally being chosen and used to cover all the thoroughfares. He also showed Covent Garden, rebuilt and transformed from a vast cluster of open stalls into a modern fruit-and-vegetable market; the Piazza Hotel, from whose coffee room in 1809 Richard Brinsley Sheridan watched his Drury Lane Theatre burn down, remarking, "Cannot a man take a glass of wine by his own fireside?" and the new Opera House, equipped with its own gas-works, which blew up in 1828, killing three people.

Scharf showed the first shopping arcade in Exeter Change, and the Change's famous elephant, Chunee, which in 1826 went on musk and had to be shot; the new Regent Park Zoo, built from 1826, with Jack, its Indian elephant, Toby, its Russian black bear, and the shop that sold cake, fruit, and nuts by the bear-pit and provided long sticks with which to feed the bears. "Their character," wrote one observer, "may be studied by exciting their jealousy and ferocity, which the bystanders abundantly do by giving them cakes at the end of a long pole."[30] He drew the British Museum, with people signing the visitors' book; the attendants in Windsor Livery—blue coats with scarlet collars and cuffs—the three stuffed giraffes which guarded the top of the main staircase; and Smirke's new building, now the main entrance, going up in 1827. Scharf liked novelties, such as the Gallery of Practical Science, which opened in one of Nash's pepper-pot buildings on the Strand and contained model paddleboats on a 100-foot canal, and the world's first machine gun, steam operated and firing bullets at 20 a second; or the Regent Street Polytechnic, which had a life-size diving bell with six men inside it. But he also liked the old, especially the fast-disappearing 17th- and 18th-century shop fronts, some adorned with superb painted carv-ings of the goods sold or the owner's names and initials in elaborate wrought iron. Behind one, a Queen Anne building at 96 St. Martin's Lane, was central London's last great vine, stretching 100 feet around the back garden and from which, in the 1820s, was regularly made a pipe of wine (100 gallons).

Scharf drew the old livery stables, of which there were 450 in London in 1827, soon badly hit by the arrival of the first regular omnibuses in 1829, and the big coaching inns, clustered by the dozen at the city's main entrances. Each coaching inn contained a smithy, a vet's shop, a coachmaker's and a wheelwright's. Scharf drew them on the very eve of the railway age. He also drew their ill-fated immediate rival, Goldsworthy Gurney's steam carriage. Fond as he was of the old shops, Scharf, like many other visitors to London, was amazed by the new ones rising in Regent Street and Oxford Street. The coming of plate glass made a vast difference. Some shops now had panes of 24 × 36 inches or even 30 × 40 inches. One Regent Street fur shop had a center pane in each main window half an inch thick, 9 feet by 5 feet and costing 50 guineas each.[31] Grand shops like these began to display spacious, elegantly designed interiors, with plush armchairs. The assis-tants, both male and female, were now chosen for their handsome, well-groomed appearance, like the footmen and housemaids in the private residences of Mayfair and St. James.[32] Indeed, shops were made to look as much as possible like fashionable drawing rooms.

London drawing rooms themselves were becoming bigger and more luxurious. They were losing their 18th-century formality and empty spaces, their squareness and regularity and acquiring what Jane Austen called "the proper air of confusion" by being decked out with "a grand piano forte and harp, flower-stands and little tables placed in every direction. Such an overthrow," she added ironically, "of all order and neatness."[33] The new Athenaeum Club was founded by John Wilson Croker (who also gave Nash invaluable assistance in getting his schemes through Parliament) because, he explained, "the University Club, the Travellers, the United Services and other such clubs had superseded and destroyed the old coffee-houses, and I considered that literary men and artists required a place of rendez-vous also." It was the masterpiece of the young Decimus Burton, who gave it the finest drawing room in the quarter, occupying the entire first-floor front.[34]

These years saw not only the transformation of London's exterior, at any rate in the West End, but the rise of a new art, interior decoration, a term coined by its founder, the wealthy connoisseur Thomas Hope (1770–1831), who believed that the furniture and fittings, colors and decorative patterns of each room should be planned in the tiniest detail. When Sir Walter Scott, intending to turn Abbotsford, the neo-Gothic mansion built on the profits of his verse-novels and *Waverley,* into a museum of Scots-baronial romance, inquired of a London architect-friend, "Pray is there not a tolerable book on upholstery—I mean plans for tables, chairs, commodes and such like?" he was told that, apart from a French book on Bonaparte's palaces, the only one was Hope's *Household Furniture and Interior Decoration,* published in 1807.[35] Hope was the dominent force, not only in theory but in practice, since his London house, filled with treasures and exquisitely decorated, and his beautiful home in Surrey, Deepdene, were much admired and imitated. Deepdene was the house from which John Claudius Loudon, who visited it in 1829, drew many ideas for his own writings on suburban villas.[36] But Hope was not alone. Another influential amateur was Charles Long, MP (1760–1838), Liverpool's paymaster general, who advised George IV on collecting, was a trustee of the British Museum and the new National Gallery, and had a finger in every important artistic pie. Long used Humphrey Repton, and the library–drawing room which he and Repton designed for his house at Bromley Hill, Kent, was regarded by many as the "perfect Room."[37]

Such houses, whether in London or the country, now all had attached conservatories, to accommodate the new passion for specimen plants of every kind, especially exotics—the hothouse was about to explode into a phase of giganticism culminating in Chatsworth, itself the prototype for the immense Crystal Palace. The Deepdene conservatory was, for admirers like Loudon, the centerpiece of the entire house. At his London home, Carlton House, the regent built himself an astounding gothic conservatory that seems to have been modeled on the Henry VII late-Perpendicular chapel in Westminster Abbey, with elaborate fan-vaults. He used this conservatory for banquets, the long center table being decorated with a fountain and a stream with mossy banks, and with goldfish swimming in it.[38]

During these years, English decorative innovations, like the conservatory, were adopted all over the world. This fact, in itself, was a novelty. In the 16th and 17th centuries, notions of visual elegance had come from Italy and in the 18th, from France. But the last authentic French style adopted by the international market and accepted as the desired norm by aristocrats and aesthetes everywhere had been Louis Seize. This style had been followed in quick succession by Directoire, Consulat, and Empire, but all had been discredited by association with Bonaparte, his *arriviste* court and, not least, by his total defeat. Its motifs had then been swept into oblivion by the restored Bourbons, leaving a vacuum in civilized taste. In the years after Waterloo, when British prestige was at its highest for a decade or more, the vacuum was filled, to a great extent, by English Regency, the first and perhaps the last time in history that the English have determined an international decorative style.[39] Indeed, the only competitor was the Biedermeier fashions of Metternich's Vienna, a city that was a by-word for fusty provincialism, except in music—the term was much later and derogatory—and that was imitated only in east-central Europe. For art and architecture, the cosmopolitan minded, even if they were French, tended to look to London. That, it must be said, was, in great part, the Regent's doing.

In clothes fashions, honors were evenly divided between London and Paris. It was during these years that the great axiom of modern sumptuary law was laid down: for fashions, men looked to Savile Row, women to the Rue de Rivoli. The French Revolution had brought about dramatic changes in women's dress, introducing a simplicity that the French believed they had taken from English rustic custom. Women's dress was supposed to be puritanical, but with its skimpy, clinging textiles and low neckline it rapidly developed not only a high exposure of female flesh but underlined the curves of what was still nominally covered. The English notion of "gay Paree" dates from the brief Peace of Amiens, 1802–03, when English visitors flocked to the French capital and brought back shocked-intrigued tales of how little the Parisian ladies wore. From that moment, French fashions dominated the lives of middle- and upper-class Englishwomen, who pored over Parisian magazines smuggled in at some danger, along with the brandy and scent. Once Waterloo was over, the grand Whig ladies actually bought their clothes in Paris. They also adopted another French innovation, the corset, originally known as a divorce, because it was the first undergarment to separate the breasts, pushing them up to form a fleshy shelf.

What women would not do, for a long time, was wear drawers or knickers, which the new style really demanded, partly because, until now, drawers were worn only by men, prostitutes and high-kicking opera dancers, especially in Paris (hence Wellington's anecdote about Bonaparte's return from Moscow). Instead, women wore "invisible petticoats," like strait waistcoats but drawn down over the legs, forcing the wearer to take short steps.[40] But gradually, as the 1820s progressed, the disadvantages of ladies not wearing drawers became apparent— Thomas Rowlandson specialized in depicting one of them—and by 1830 the basic components of modern women's underclothes were in place. Equally if not more important for most women was the growing cheapness of easily washable cottons. The reformer Francis Place (by trade a tailor), in his manuscript notes on "Manners and Morals," now in the British Museum, welcomed the dramatic improvement in the appearance of working-class women in the 1820s, made possible by "cleanly cotton gowns made pretty high round the neck."[41]

For men, modernity came with the adoption of trousers, perhaps the greatest of all watersheds in the history of men's fashion. Indeed, it might be said that of all the enduring achievements of the French Revolution, the most important was the replacement of *culottes*, or breeches, by the baggy trousers worn by peasants and working men, the *sans-culottes*. The adoption by the new French ruling class, in the 1790s, of trousers as a sign of solidarity with the masses was greeted with horror elsewhere. Several countries tried to ban them. But the term *trousers* that was generally adopted was, significantly, English, dating back to the late sixteenth century, and once the Savile Row tailors began to produce the garment, they quickly took it up-market, making it tight fitting and attractive to wear. One of the key innovations of George "Beau" Brummell (1778–1840) was to introduce a strap at the bottom of each leg, which went under the shoe or boot and stretched the trousers still tighter. These fashionable versions were made of light-colored nankeen, a close-woven cotton, or of fine doeskin leather for riding. The result was that they showed off the male leg to even greater advantage than breeches and satin stockings, which did justice only to the calf. Older men in authority, whose spindle shanks did not benefit from advertisement, denounced them as obscene and Pope Pius VII condemned them outright in a bitter rearguard action which lasted until his death in 1823.[42]

We come now to an important historical point, a change which in some ways permanently altered the relationship between the sexes. Until the second decade of the 19th century, both sexes had dressed for display, wearing the richest fabrics and the brightest colors their means afforded. Both used quantities of powder, if they had the money, and rouge, face cream and other cosmetics, if they moved in fashionable society. Jane Austen, in Persuasion, has Sir Walter Elliot, being a former "beau," not only use "Gowland" himself (it was a lotion made by the cosmetician Mrs. Gowland around 1815) but recommend it to young ladies, including his daughter.[43] Sir Walter particularly criticized the appearance of naval officers, who were exposed to all types of weather, and censured them for not doing more to improve their complexions.

But naval men were often just as anxious as anyone else in society to make the best of themselves. Admiral Codrington's daughter left a description of how, as a little girl, she was allowed to sit on a stool in her father's dressing room while he completed his toilet. She would sit "reading to him Miss Edgeworth's charming little stories," the Admiral correcting her punctuation pauses as she did so, while watching "the successive processes of the dress of those days." First came shaving. Then, elaborate powdering: "There was the white powdering cloth spread out on the carpet, the powder puff which seemed to me to be a fairy's work, the matter-of-fact powder knife which cleared off the fairy's work from forehead and temples"; finally, there was "the critical operation of putting on the neckcloth. This was a square yard of very finest jacconot, very carefully folded, begun behind, crossed in front, crossed again behind, finally met in front, the numerous little folds being confined by the neat little bow into which the ends were tied under the chin. This surmounted the very full and broad shirt-front of very finest cambric."[44]

As part of their uninhibited masculine display, men sought to draw attention to the best points of their bodies, just as women did, and were admired accordingly. This was the last period in history in which men could closely scrutinize the physical beauty of their own sex without being thought homosexual and women could comment on the male form without raising eyebrows. When Jane Austen's Sir Walter took up his station in Bond Street, Bath, to observe the world, he thought it just as natural to note the beauty of male faces and figures (or rather the lack of it) as of the female ones. Every woman's eye, he added, was always on his friend Colonel Wallis because of his "fine military figure, though sandy-haired." It was not unusual for society men, artists, and others to gather to see a particularly fine specimen of masculine beauty. Farington recorded attending a breakfast given by the well-known doctor, Anthony Carlisle, at which "Gregson the Pugilist" was displayed in the front drawing room, stripped naked, to be admired "on account of the fineness of his *form*." The gentlemen wandered round him for half an hour while he "struck poses": "all admired the beauty of his proportion," though Benjamin West, the president of the Royal Academy, drew their attention to "something of heaviness about the thighs." Later Gregson was exhibited at Lord Elgin's, so he could be compared with the males among the Parthenon marbles. Farington also went with West and Sir Thomas Lawrence, RA, to see the naked form of a "handsome black man," a sailor of just under six feet, "like the Farnese Hercules," and "the finest figure they had ever seen."[45]

Women, as well as men, admired the following points: slender waists; strong or broad chests, clustery hair, and, above all, well-made calves. Until about 1825 it was considered quite proper for a lady to comment on a gentleman's legs, which were carefully observed and compared. Men did the same. Old Horace Walpole, Lord Orford, told Farington that he could always recognize "a Cavendish leg": of Lord Walpole's son, whose mother was a Cavendish, he "insisted that if through a window he only saw the legs of Mr. Walpole in motion he should say he was a Cavendish."[46] When Thomas De Quincey published his reminiscenses of Wordsworth, one of the passages that gave most offense to the poet, his wife and sister concerned legs: "[Wordsworth's] legs were pointedly condemned by all the female connoisseurs in legs that ever I heard lecture upon that topic; not that they were bad in any way which would force itself upon your notice—there was no absolute deformity about them; and undoubtedly they had been serviceable legs beyond the average standard of human requisition; for I calculate, upon good data, that with these identical legs Wordsworth must have traversed a distance of 175,000 to 180,000 English miles—a mode of exertion which, to him, stood in the stead of wine, spirits and all other stimulants whatsoever to the human spirits; to which he has been indebted to a life of unclouded happiness, and we for much of what is most excellent in his writings. But, useful as they have proved themselves, the Wordsworthian legs were certainly not ornamental; and it was really a pity, as I agreed with a lady in thinking, that he had not another pair for evening dress parties, when no boots lend their friendly aid to mask our imperfections from the eyes of female rigorists . . . . A sculptor would certainly have disapproved of their contour."[47]

There, however, spoke the fading voice of the early 19th century. For, though gentlemen continued to wear breeches and silk stockings on formal evening occasions for some decades, trousers were worn for all other events by 1820, and the empire of the trouser continued to expand until it embraced virtually the whole world and has retained its power to this date—the most enduring masculine garment in history. By the mid-1820s, tight trousers of the Brummell type were out and have remained out, so male calves gradually lost their appeal. This was part of a wider change in which, for the first time, men handed over to women the leading role in sartorial display. It is true that, for some time to come, a number of men, particularly when they were young, wore bright clothes to attract attention. When Martin Van Buren went electioneering in 1828, he wore a beige swallow-tailed coat with matching velvet collar, an orange cravat with lace tips, white duck trousers, a pearl-gray waistcoat, silk stockings and yellow kid gloves, and he topped the whole with a large, broad-brimmed beaver hat covered in longish fur.[48] The young Benjamin Disraeli cut a similar figure in the 1820s and even later. Though forced by the new custom to abandon breeches and hose, which he favored, he insisted that his trousers be of green velvet. The French, too, stuck to bright colors and exotic textiles, even into the reign of Louis Philippe, the first French king to appear in trousers at court.

But that was because the French were behind in male fashions. The movement toward simplicity and severity came from London and was increasingly dictated by the tailors themselves. Originally, like trousers, it had had a political impulse. The Whig grandees, like their Puritan predecessors 150 years before, dropped wigs and adornment as a democratic gesture. At the famous Westminster election of November 1795, the Duke of Bedford and Charles James Fox were spotted wearing little round hats which, when doffed, revealed short natural hair underneath: "[The duke's] hair cropped and without powder—Fox also cropped and without powder, his hair grisly grey."[49] This Whig-Radical tradition continued. In 1816 Lord Milton, heir to Earl Fitzwilliam, wore nothing but black, with lank hair and buckles in his shoes; he looked "like a Methodist."[50] Brougham was the same. He was said, in Scotland, to wear tartan trews, but in London Harriet Martineau recalled "not a morsel of his dress being anything but black, from the ridge of his stock to the toes of his polished shoes. Not an inch of white was there to relieve the combined gloom of his dress and complexion."[51]

But, as with trousers, what began as a political fad soon became an enduring fashion.

Here, again, Beau Brummell was the key figure, not merely civilizing trousers, but inventing the black-and-white clad male. He taught that the aim should be simplicity and clothes which followed the natural lines of the body, though he was not averse to a little discreet padding or even a corset, which he called a "belt." Above all, a man should avoid "a mountebank appearance" by eschewing flashy colors and fabrics. Brummell favored black or dark gray outer garments, elegance flowing from the cut and the fit, with spotlessly white linen below. Thus, he invented the concept of evening dress as we know it. His stress was always on elementary points, obvious now but by no means taken for granted in the early 19th century, such as cleanliness. A gentleman should bathe once a day and change his linen at least once; he should wash, not oil, his hair, and keep it neatly cut; shave daily and closely; and avoid unguents, perfumes, and other greasy things. Not least, he should take regular exercise and keep his figure trim, for that was what, in the end, made clothes look elegant.[52]

This new kind of English decorum was successfully put to the test at the Congress of Vienna, where Lord Castlereagh, usually in black and white and adorned only by the blue Garter ribbon, stood out from the braided and bedizened peacocks who surrounded him. By the 1820s Paris fashionables like Eugène Delacroix, not the son of Talleyrand for nothing, were already having their clothes made in London.[53] Brummell had sanctioned a little light makeup for men—pale brown "and a touch of rouge." His successor as arbiter of London male fashion, Count d'Orsay, did not. By 1830 makeup had been virtually abandoned. By this date, indeed, the modern sartorial chasm between the sexes, with the men moving toward monochrome sobriety and uniformity, was beginning to open, at any rate in English society. In appearance, at least, men were becoming more obviously masculine; the line that marked them off from women was being more firmly drawn than ever before.

Yet, paradoxically, there was one exception to this trend. In the early 19th century gentlemen ceased to wear swords and took to carrying umbrellas instead. Thereby hangs a tale. One of the infallible signs of modernity was the decline of dueling. Yet it did not vanish as quickly as sensible men expected. Indeed, its survival, even—it might be said— its rebirth, was evidence that in certain respects the French Revolution and its aftermath brought not progress but retrogression. Christian societies had always, officially at least, condemned dueling. All the churches opposed it vehemently, in practice as well as in theory; it was one of the few sins that clergymen did not commit (except, occasionally, in Ireland). Law codes did not distinguish between a duelist who killed his opponent and a willful murderer, though what the courts did was a different matter. In the 18th century hostile state and clerical opinion was reinforced by the intelligentsia and, increasingly, by the spirit of the Enlightenment. Dueling was attacked by Jonathan Swift and Richard Steele, Daniel Defoe and Henry Fielding, Tobias Smollett and Samuel Richardson, in Carlo Goldoni's plays, the writings of Baron Montesquieu, in Denis Diderot's *Le Neveu de Rameau*, and Jean-Jacques Rousseau's *La Nouvelle Héloïse*, in the comedies of Richard Brinsley Sheridan and Oliver Goldsmith, and in Jeremy Bentham's *Morals and Legislation*. Anyone who troubled to think seriously about dueling condemned it. One of the few exceptions was Samuel Johnson, who was prepared to put the social (not the moral) argument for dueling and did so on a famous occasion at General Oglethorpe's in 1772, but even he "fairly owned that he could not explain the rationality of dueling."[54]

All the evidence suggests that dueling was in rapid decline in the 1780s. Hence, the sensation when in 1789 Captain Lennox of the Coldstream Guards, heir to the Richmond dukedom, shouted out a challenge to the King's second son on the parade ground (he said the Prince had insulted him). The affair took place on Wimbledon Common on 26 August, the Prince deliberately firing into the air. Lennox's shot grazed the Prince's hair, and Lord Rawdon, the royal second, later claimed that, by delaying the order to fire, he had unsteadied Lennox's aim and so saved the Prince's life. Be that as it may, the affair caused outrage. The officers of Lennox's regiment passed a resolution stating he had "behaved with courage . . . but not with judgment," and he was forced to resign his commission and join a line regiment. Indeed, Lennox was obliged to fight another duel, being challenged by an Irish barrister, Theophilus Swift, "for firing at the King's son" (Swift was seriously wounded, but recovered).[55]

While these events were taking place, however, dueling on a large scale was being reborn in Paris. Once the class war began in earnest, Royalists began challenging Republican deputies, such as Mirabeau, and pro-Republican army officers and noncommissioned officers began to take up the challenges on their behalf. The Jacobins opposed dueling, but between Thermidor in 1794 and Bonaparte's coup in 1799, it revived with great fury, and Bonaparte himself did nothing to stop it. He claimed it was "wasteful," but he also said he had been "out" himself once. His code did not forbid it. Indeed his habit of setting his generals against one another, to prevent them combining against him, actually encouraged dueling, as did still more the general spirit of militarism and violence that his campaigns bred all over Europe. In most of the armies, especially his own, it spread downwards through the ranks, and in many countries middle-class civilians now felt entitled to challenge their social superiors, as well as each other.[56] Waterloo and the peace did not end the habit, for Bonapartist veterans took to challenging officers from the armies of occupation, especially the British, as well as their Bourbon opponents. Captain Gronow, in his *Reminiscences,* related many such episodes, some of them horrifying. He claimed that in every case the French were the aggressors, but he also told of the exploits of a British engineer colonel who killed three French officers in duels in 1815–16, one of whom he had provoked into a challenge by beating him on the head with a *baguette,* or long French loaf of bread, in a restaurant.[57]

The Bonapartist revival of dueling spread to societies where it had been little known before, especially the United States. Dueling was introduced by French émigrés in the 1790s and reinforced by Republicans fleeing from the White Terror in 1814–15. It spread north from New Orleans and took a strong hold in "backwoods" states like West Virginia, Kentucky and Tennessee. Soldiers (of all ranks) were the worst offenders, but editors, poets, politicians, even doctors, were almost as bad. Jackson, as we have seen, set the worst possible example. Some of his duels came to nothing, but when he killed Charles Dickinson in 1806, it was on his second shot (the first had been a half cock), his opponent having been placed by force back on his mark.[58] It is curious, looking back on it, that more was not made of Jackson's violent past when he ran for president in 1824 and 1828, though the "Coffin Handbill" distributed by his opponents did him some harm. The answer is that, though every state forbade dueling by statute (in North Carolina it carried a death sentence), too many legislators and judges fought duels for the law to be held in anything but contempt. Governor James Hamilton of South Carolina was involved in no less than fourteen duels, wounding his opponent on every occasion. Some of the most famous names in American political history fought each other. On 10 July 1804, Aaron Burr killed Alexander Hamilton at Weehawken, New Jersey, on the same spot where Hamilton's son Philip had been killed three years before. Henry Clay exchanged shots with Humphrey Marshall on 19 January 1809; Thomas Hart Benton killed Charles Lukas on 27 September 1817; James Barron killed the great naval hero Stephen Decatur three years later; two Georgia congressmen, William Cumming and George McDuffie, fought on the banks of the Potomac in 1822; and McDuffie challenged two other congressmen, one of whom responded; four years later, again on the Potomac, Henry Clay fought another political duel, this time with John Randolph of Roanoke. Courtroom insults led to duels between attorneys and between attorneys and judges and, in Arkansas, between superior court judges, one of whom was killed by a colleague.

President Monroe set his face against dueling, at any rate in the White House. Sir Charles Vaughan, the British minister, dining there officially, noticed that whenever he made a remark, the French minister bit his thumb. "Do you bite your thumb at me, Sir?" he asked angrily. "I do, Sir!" Both diplomats left the table instantly and rushed into the hall. They already had their swords crossed before Monroe knocked them up with his own and ordered their carriages.[59] But his disapproval did not stop him giving the Treasury secretaryship to William Crawford, who had fought various duels, in one of which he killed Peter Van Allen, the solicitor general of the Western Circuit.[60] The leading American treatise on dueling, The Code of Honour (1838), was written by John Lyde Wilson of South Carolina, a state where all participants in a duel faced a penalty of a year in prison and a fine of $2,000. But American duels rarely went by the rule book. Often the notion of dueling was just a socially tolerated excuse for physical violence, including murder. When Henry Clay, John Quincy Adams's secretary of state, was seeking someone to challenge as a result of accusations that he got his post through a "corrupt bargain"—we will go into this later—he was told to be "on your guard" against the Jacksonians, as "a thousand desperadoes would think it a most honourable service . . . to shoot you."[61] But Clay at least was a fighting man. Jackson's Treasury Secretary, Samuel Ingham, was not. He declined a challenge from his cabinet colleague John Eaton over the "Mrs. Eaton Affair"—that, too, we will examine in due course—and as a result, Eaton arranged to have him waylaid in the streets and beaten up. Ingham's appeals to the president were rejected; he was forced to arm himself and hire bodyguards, finally "fleeing from Washington on the 4 o'clock stage," a retreat which the President scornfully described as "infamous," "ridiculous," and "cowardly."[62] Some so-called American duels were multiple affairs, fought with a variety of weapons, including rifles, and the violence of the Frontier from the 1820s onwards was directly related to coarse "affairs of honour."

In Europe there was more attention to the niceties, especially in Germany where, during the long Napoleonic Wars, dueling become more common than anywhere else in the world. It was the rule there that a physical blow could be avenged only by a duel fought to the death. Anthony Carlisle, the famous surgeon, used to tell with relish the tale of a Mr. Richardson, a boxer who punched a Baron Hompesch on the nose, knocked him down, and was forced to duel with pistols. Richardson received a ball that passed through the liver and lungs and grazed his heart. To prevent "inflammation," Carlisle engaged in "vast evacuations," taking no less than 236 ounces of blood from Richardson's arm (over two weeks), "besides three quarts from his side."[63] The patient lived. In Prussia duels were not even criminal, if fought according to the code among officers and gentlemen. They were particularly popular among students throughout German-speaking Europe. The diarist Henry Crabb Robinson noted in 1815 that in Jena alone there were 147 duels during the summer, among a student population of 350.[64] But the duels were fought with sabers, as a rule, and were rarely fatal, the object being to inflict and receive honorable scars. Saber duels could, of course, end in a killing. Madame de Staël's son, Albert, who was in the Swedish army, fought one in a Baltic resort with a Russian officer, who severed his head with one stroke.[65] In the Russian army, saber dueling was fought under strict rules, which forbade head wounds. Nadezhda Durova, who enlisted in the Russian cavalry as a man, acted as a second in such duels—she was careful not to get involved as a principal—and described them in her memoirs as "ridiculous," since "the two adversaries bowed down almost to the ground."[66]

In Russia as in Germany, the higher the rank, the more likely pistols would be used. Pistols would have been the weapons in the threatened duel, over a woman, between Tsar Alexander and Klemens Metternich. They were also the weapon that killed Aleksandr Pushkin, Russia's national poet, in 1837. In Russia, the Third Section, or secret police, kept close control over dueling, and there were rumors that they could, had they wished, have prevented this one. But Pushkin was the kind of hothead through whom dueling flourished. While in internal exile in Bessarabia, he involved himself in many childish duels. He fought two with army officers in 1822, the first spoiled by a blizzard, the second rendered abortive by bad shooting. There were other frustrated duels in his life, and he deserves little sympathy for the 1837 affair, from which no one emerged with credit except Tsar Nicholas I, who gave Pushkin's widow a pension and looked after his children.[67]

The more one examines the details of actual duels, the more sordid and dishonorable the institution appears. Crabb Robinson had nothing but contempt for what he saw at Jena, which he ascribed to "the ineradicable German love of brawling." Byron was equally dismissive of Italian dueling, "indistinguishable from dogfighting." He witnessed a collision between a husband and a *cavaliere servente* at the Benedetto Theater in Venice in December 1816. It was, he said, a *"maledetto scopalotto,* much swearing and scuffling ensued and both parties rolled skirmishing out into the passage—but showed no science—all rowly-powly—the vulgarest roundabout hitting you ever saw."[68] At the killing level, there was little distinction between dueling, family feuds of the Montague-Capulet kind and assassination; in the Papal States, where dueling was strictly forbidden and even punished, there were more murders than anywhere else in Italy, perhaps for that reason. As late as the decade 1879–89 no fewer than 2,759 duels were officially recorded, most of them with saber or rapier, but producing 50 deaths nonetheless.[69]

In Britain, essentially a civil society, the reemergence of dueling in the early nineteenth century was unquestionably due to the militarism encouraged by the long wars. It has been argued that dueling was also a rearguard action fought by the gentry class to distinguish itself from those below it. Hunting, steeplechasing, racing and gambling were risky activities associated with the aristocracy, made honorable by the courage or recklessness they required; dueling was the supreme example of this denial of the materialism of the middle class, or so the argument runs.[70] But in its last, lurid phrase, dueling was as much the habit of middle-class army officers, lawyers, and even journalists as the high-born. It was particularly common in India, a largely military society, among British officers who lacked the social pull and money to serve in a smart regiment at home. Scotland and Ireland (though not Wales, where it was almost unknown) saw many duels, right up to 1830 and beyond, perhaps because they retained traditions of clan warfare and private justice. But, here again, the middle-class element was as blood-thirsty as was the nobility. Edinburgh lawyers enjoyed the risky sport of threatening, and occasionally even fighting, duels, over courtroom exchanges or printed sallies. Boswell's heir, Sir Alexander Boswell, was killed by James Stuart of Dunearn at Auchtertool in 1822, for writing anonymous squibs, just as his father used to do. The case was important because Stuart, having fled abroad, returned to face trial and, despite having killed Boswell with a second shot, was acquitted to the general satisfaction. Lord Cockburn wrote in his memoirs, "No Scotch trial in my time excited such interest."[71]

Ireland was worse. It swarmed with half-pay officers, like Captain Macnamara, who had "killed three or four men" and who practiced the pistol regularly; on board ship he kept his hand in by "having fowls that are to be killed placed before him on Hen Coops & he shoots off their Heads with Pistol balls."[72] As in America, the worst possible example was given by parliamentarians and lawyers. It was an Irish characteristic, too, that duelists often killed not merely their enemies but their friends and relations. Richard Martin of Connemara, member of Parliament for Galway, 1810–12 and 1818–27, and often known as "the King of Connemara," killed his cousin in a duel and fought so often he was known as "Hairtrigger Rick." Oddly enough, he was also strongly opposed to capital punishment, deplored any kind of ill-treatment of dumb beasts, and helped to found the Society for the Prevention of Cruelty to Animals, ending his life with a new nickname, "Humanity Martin."[73] Irish elections produced rich crops of duels. At the Wexford County election in 1807, the Tory candidate, William Alcock, challenged and shot dead the Whig, William Colclough, "for trespass in canvassing the freeholders of an elderly widow," regarded as a social crime in those parts. The fight was watched by hundred of people, including various justices of the peace, but the then Chief Secretary, the future Duke of Wellington, reported to London that "as it was reckoned fair in Ireland, it created no sensation."[74] A judge and jury were unanimous against conviction.

Daniel O'Connell (1775–1847), "the Liberator," was another noted Irish duelist, a habit he acquired as a notoriously abusive barrister, keeping "his eye in" while riding on circuit by shooting at the dogs which snapped at his horse's heels. In his heart O'Connell never really approved of dueling, which was condemned fiercely by the Irish Catholic Church and no less so by his wife. But it was the fashion at the Irish Bar, where Lord Norbury was said to have "shot himself up to the Bench." The ridiculous thing was that O'Connell was just as likely to get into a broil with a friend or one of his numerous relations as with a political (or legal) opponent. Stendhal, on a visit to Ireland, noted that "people who are breakfasting cheerfully with one another may meet two hours later on the field of battle."[75] In 1801 O'Connell was in trouble for caning a cousin in open court. Twelve years later, also in court, he called opposing counsel, one of his drinking cronies, a liar; had a volume of statutes hurled at his head; and was kicked on the shins. Both episodes nearly led to duels to the death. In 1815, having described the Dublin corporation as "beggarly," he was challenged by one of its members, a grocer, whom he fatally wounded. Since this was a straight Catholic-Protestant affray, he had no trouble getting absolution from the Catholic archbishop of Dublin, Murray, who intoned when he heard the result of the duel, "Heaven be praised! Ireland is safe!"[76] Later that year, O'Connell muddled himself into a duel with Sir Robert Peel, no less. The chief secretary despised dueling even more than did O'Connell and, in the event, outsmarted him by hastening to

Calais for the encounter (thus establishing his own valor) while ensuring that O'Connell was arrested on the way and bound over to keep the
peace.[77] Thereafter the Liberator got his son Morgan to deputize for
him, as when he was challenged by the society smarty, Lord Alvanley,
whom he termed "a bloated buffoon." But Morgan was not always
prepared to oblige. When the young Benjamin Disraeli, standing at the
Taunton by-election in 1835, described O'Connell as "an incendiary
and a traitor" and the Liberator replied by asserting that Disraeli was
a "lineal descendant" of "the impenitent thief on the Cross," Disraeli
issued a challenge, but neither father nor son would meet him. The
affair dissolved in embarrassment for O'Connell and successful self-
advertisement for Disraeli, who noted complacently in his diary: "Row
with O'Connell in which I greatly distinguish myself."[78]

The fact that as late as 1835—and in peacable England, too—an
aspiring politician could believe his prospects would be helped by an
abortive duel shows the peculiar tenacity of the institution even in an
unreceptive area. In England dueling was not so much an aristocratic
institution in the early 19th century as one patronized by ex-public
schoolboys, who learned to fight with their fists in the most ferocious
fashion in the schoolyard. At Charterhouse, William Makepeace
Thackeray got his nose broken and flattened in one such fight and
recorded that in his time a formal battle between two boys went to 102
rounds.[79] At Harrow, Lord Palmerston—who, oddly enough, in a lifetime of illicit love affairs and political abuse, never fought a duel—had
a furious fistfight with another future prime minister, Lord Aberdeen.
At Eton, W. E. Gladstone recalled, "Hardly a day passed without one,
two, three or even four more-or-less mortal combats." His biographer
recorded: "The Windsor and Slough coaches used to stop under the
wall of the playing fields to watch these desperate affrays, and once at
least in these times a boy was killed" (Lord Ashley, son of the Earl of
Shaftesbury).[80] Boys were taught—by other boys, not the masters—that
insults should not go unredressed but be avenged by fists, though
according to certain rules; in adult life fists easily became firearms.

But outside the army (and, to a limited extent, the navy), duels were
more talked about than fought. Here, as always, Jane Austen got it
right: Mrs. Bennet is terrified, in *Pride and Prejudice,* that Mr. Bennet
will "fight Wickham" for debauching his youngest daughter, but Mr.
Bennet himself shows no such desire. In 1840, when the cavalry fire-
brand Lord Cardigan was tried in the House of Lords for fighting a duel
with Lieutenant Tuckett, his counsel, Sir W. Follett, QC, asked
Croker's advice about the historical background. Croker listed all the
duels involving members of Parliament, both in the Lords and in the

Commons, over the past 100 years. The total came to 13, not counting abortive ones. The duels were fought by six prime ministers, Bath, Pulteney, Shelburn, Pitt the Younger, Canning, and Wellington, plus Fox (not technically a prime minister), Castlereagh (who was almost a prime minister), and Peel (who was challenged twice but who never fought). Some of these duels sprang directly from political actions or words spoken in Parliament or cabinet maneuvering. The most serious duel was between Castlereagh and Canning in 1809, arising from Canning's intrigues behind the other's back to become number two in the government. Wilberforce, like all Evangelicals, deplored dueling, saying it lowered Britain's prestige throughout Europe. But in many of the duels, for example the Duke of Wellington's with the Marquess of Winchelsea in 1829 over Catholic emancipation, one or both of the parties fired wide (the Duke was then aged sixty and hated the institution). Three of the thirteen duels were fatal, and in each the victor was brought to trial; in half a dozen there were wounds, none serious. The list was not a particularly long one, though Croker admitted that it might not be exhaustive, since "duels are seldom matters of record, at least in such volumes as have indexes."[81]

Literary duels were about as common as political ones, though, here again, there was usually more hot air than powder. Lord Byron, whose immediate forebear, the fifth, or "Wicked Lord Byron," had killed his cousin Mr. Chaworth in what was more "a confused scuffle" than a duel in 1765 and had been convicted of manslaughter, was, to some extent, obsessed by dueling. Perhaps to compensate for his lame foot, which ruled out swordplay, he made himself an expert shot, took his pistols everywhere, and practiced wherever possible—on board ship, on the Venice Lido, in the Ravenna pine woods—though he aimed at bottles, not chicken heads. Thomas Moore recorded in his diary that Wedderburn Webster told him "that one day he travelled from Newstead [Abbey] to town with Lord Byron in his *vis-à-vis* [carriage]; the latter kept his pistols besides him and continued silent for hours with the most ferocious expression possible on his countenance." When asked what was the trouble, "Byron only answered that he had always had a sort of presentiment that his own life would be attacked some time or other and that this was the reason of his always going armed."[82] When young, Byron had nearly fought Wellington's aide de camp in Malta—"a rude fellow, who grinned at something, I never rightly knew what"—but accepted the officer's explanation and apology. He almost had a duel with Thomas Moore in 1818. But I find it inconceivable that the two poets could actually have fought at all, let alone tried to kill each other.[83]

Threatened duels figure largely in Byron's letters, but he is at his most posturing and unconvincing on the subject. Byron threatened "that dirty, lying rascal Southey" over the "League of Incest" accusation, saying he would prove him a liar "in ink—or in his blood, if I did not believe him to be too much of a poet to risk it." Moore noted on 4 March 1822: "[Byron] has called out Southey, as I expected he would, and he has done right—no man should suffer such a letter as Southey's, signed with his name, to pass without this sort of notice . . . Lord B. ought not to have brought it on himself, but having done so, there was but this left for him. Neither will any harm result from it as Southey I am sure, will not meet him."[84] There is something infantile about one poet thus commending another for challenging a third, knowing that nothing is going to happen. But Byron went on muttering threats, at any rate on paper, right to the end. In Greece, three weeks before his death, when one of his officers wanted to fight two others, he wrote to his banker-friend Douglas Kinnaird that he had put all three under arrest "and if there is any more challenging I will call all out and wafer one half of them."[85]

Unfortunately, the posturing among writers did, occasionally, come to blows. Captain Marryat had to fight a duel with an author who had taken mortal offense at a review. But that exchange was bloodless. The most serious case occurred in 1821. John Scott (1783–21) was an Aberdonian, who had known Byron at the High School before he went to Harrow. He came to London, established himself as a journalist, married the daughter of Paul Colnaghi, the art dealer—they were both friends of John Keats, Robert Benjamin Haydon, and their circle—and in January 1820 was made editor of a new monthly, the *London Magazine,* started by the publishing firm of Baldwin, Craddock & Joy. The paper was immensely successful almost from the start, Scott proving himself an editor of genius and, in particular, launching Charles Lamb's *Essays of Elia* and William Hazlitt's *Table Talk.* But by the end of the year, he had fallen foul of the most ferocious of the Scottish Tory journals, *Blackwood's Magazine.* Scott criticized the journal and the man whom he supposed to be its editor, J. G. Lockhart, in his paper. Lockhart, a typically belligerent Edinburgh barrister, notorious for the abuse he published in *Blackwood's,* went to London to demand satisfaction, enlisting the London barrister Jonathan Christie as his second. Scott refused to meet him, Lockhart "posted" him as a coward and went back north. Christie, left to deal with the affair, somehow got entangled in a challenge to Scott himself, and this time a duel was fought, at Chalk Farm, the London favorite for such affrays. Scott was mortally wounded, Christie and Scott's second, Hazlitt's friend P. G. Patmore, both fleeing to the Continent. All agreed it was a bad business. Sir Walter Scott, who had hitherto been ambivalent about dueling, as were a number of Romantics, strongly advised Lockhart, his son-in-law and later his biographer, to give up partisan writing for *Blackwood's*. But the damage was done. The *London Magazine* never found a worthy replacement for John Scott, and as a result, Lamb gave up writing *Elia*. Hazlitt's work suffered, too; it also made him nervous for the rest of his life. In May 1826, Haydon saw the poets Moore and Rogers admiring the paintings in Lord Stafford's art gallery. He added: "Hazlitt was there, and as he saw Moore he came up and whispered to me, 'I hope he won't challenge me.' On seeing anybody he has attacked, his predominant feeling is personal fear."[86]

But by 1826 the likelihood of a writer being shot for penning a bad review was small. With Peel, who by this stage saw dueling as a barbarous relic of the past, at the Home Office, magistrates were increasingly alert to stop duels before they took place. Police officers, like the famous Nagle of Manchester, did not hesitate to pull in excitable gentlemen, even if they were army officers, and courts, which had once merely fined duelers who were convicted of manslaughter £10, began to impose prison sentences. Croker's note marked the 1820s as the period when dueling went into rapid decline as memories of the great wars faded. By the time he wrote it, he calculated that no more than half a dozen members of the House of Lords had fought one and perhaps as many had acted as seconds. So British society began to treat the duel as a joke in bad taste, the umbrella became a more useful instrument to carry around London, and the rest of the civilized world slowly followed its example in this matter, as it already did with other masculine fashions.

The decline of dueling was a matter of great satisfaction for women, who had never encouraged or even approved of it, at any rate in England. Dueling women were not entirely unknown. A woman born in 1795 who called herself James Miranda Stuart Barry, studied medicine at Edinburgh disguised as a man, then served abroad as an army surgeon. She was court-martialed for vexatiously challenging fellow officers who mocked her high voice and lack of inches.[87] But the only celebrated all-woman duel which took place, perhaps inspired by the painting of two women fighting with swords, done by the sinister José de Ribera around 1636 and now in the Prado, was fought between Princess Metternich and Countess Kielmansegg, both women emerging slightly wounded.[88]

Women were more assiduous in invading that other theater of masculinity, gambling. More money was made and lost gambling in the half century 1780–1830 than perhaps at any other time in history. Casinos were opening up all over Europe, to attract the plungers who had hitherto gambled in private clubs, like Brooks's. From 1815, English high rollers like Lord Thanet and Lord Alvanley regularly visited the cross-Channel casinos and the German gambling-spas, where a much wider variety of games, including the newly fashionable roulette, were held than in London clubs. Roulette was the basis of the fortune of Domenico Barbaia, the millionaire owner of the San Carlo opera house and Rossini's great patron.

Some casinos now admitted ladies, who quickly demonstrated that they could become at least as addicted as men. Farington recorded in his diary an account of a Miss Pelham as "an extraordinary instance of suffering from the passion of gaming." Miss Pelham had lost her fortune of £70,000 yet "carries every guinea she can borrow to the gaming table, where she will weep and lose. When she has lost what money she has about her, she will solicit a loan of a few guineas from any person near her, even from a stranger." He also found himself lending £25, through an intermediary, to the Duchess of Devonshire, another gambler, who promised to repay it "next week." Thus, he noted, "in my humble situation I was enabled to aid and assist a Great Duchess from my little purse." When the Duchess and her sister, Lady Bessborough, wanted cash to gamble, they "would go to a tradesman's shop and order £100 worth of goods on condition of the tradesman advancing them £50 [in cash] which was also made a debt." At her death, her accumulated debts were said to top £200,000, and the Duke, whose own income was about £130,000 a year, agreed to pay them, though not the interest.[89] Another gambling lady was the Duchess of Richmond, who was rumored to have ruined her husband by losing £30,000 to Marshal Blücher in Paris, after the Battle of Waterloo; certainly, he did not take her with him when he went out to govern Canada.[90] But it was not unprecedented for society ladies to gamble. More shocking was the spread of gambling to the middle classes, even to clerical circles. Farington was intrigued to hear that the Bishop of Down, in puritan Ulster, had felt obliged to insure his life, with the Amicable, for £6,000: his wife had a "passion for cards" and "lost money."[91]

George IV's great matrimonial struggle with his wife, in which each, at least for a time, gave as good as they got, served for millions, and not just in Britain, to illuminate, illustrate, and in a curious way ennoble the battle of the sexes that was taking place in countless humbler households. It was an unequal battle, of course. Women were far weaker than men in law than they were in physical strength. Not many men agreed with Samuel Parr, "the Whig Doctor Johnson," who believed that women did not have souls. But the majority united in denying women rights. The law in Britain, and to a great extent in the United States, gave women few legal rights as single persons, and still fewer as wives. The leading legal authority, William Blackstone, laid down in his *Commentaries on the Laws of England:* "By marriage, the husband and wife are one person in law, that is the very being or existence of the woman is suspended during the marriage, or at least is incorporated and consolidated into that of the husband, under whose wing, protection and cover, she performs everything."[92]

The wife's position was not quite as bad as Blackstone's statement sounds. Common Law provided wives with the right of dower, roughly one-third of their estate. And the *jus mariti* really extended only to movable or personal property that the wife owned on marriage or subsequently acquired. The husband could do what he liked with it, and if he got into debt, his creditors could seize it. The *jus mariti* extended to the wife's earnings. A little episode in Mrs. Gaskell's life tells it all. Her husband William was a perfectly decent Unitarian minister, who loved and encouraged her. When she sold her first story, *Mary Barton,* she was astounded to receive a check for the, to her, magnificent sum of £100; she adds, "and William composedly buttoned it up in his pocket." However, if the wife owned real property, all the husband had was the *jus administrationis:* He could keep its rents and profits, but could not sell it. Moreover, if he owned land, he was restricted in selling it by her right of dower. The husband was liable for his wife's debts and torts and had a legal obligation to support her, though she, in turn, must "serve" and "provide him with *consortium.*" He might be liable for criminal acts committed by her, especially if he were present, because the presumption was that he coerced her into committing them. In fact the woman's status on marriage changed absolutely, and she became in some ways like a soldier, an infant, a slave, an alien or a bankrupt in that the description "married women" affected everyone's dealings with her in law.[93] A married woman could not make contracts, except as a husband's agent in small matters, could not sue or be sued unless the husband was joined with her; could not make a will, dispose of her property, appoint a guardian for her children or even recover damages.

However, as we shall see in this and other matters, the notional position in law did not correspond to the reality by the early 19th century. The system of male dominance was beginning to break down and women entered into favorable marriage contracts which made nonsense of Blackstone's dicta; they ran businesses and acted as administrators and executrixes of estates. This was already true of England by 1815 and was rapidly becoming still more true of the United States, where there was an amazing variety of legal rulings, some reflecting Spanish and French traditions as well as English (and Scottish) ones. In the more primitive parts of the country, the law favored the man. A court decision at Ocala, Florida, on 12 May 1814, resolving a dispute over property between an elderly nonwhite and his wife, read: "Be it known throughout Christendom that the husband is the head of the wife and whatever is hers is his, and come weal and woe, peace and war, the right of all property is vested in the husband."[94] In the North and West, however, the woman's position in law was improving rapidly, even though the first important Married Women's Property Acts, in New York and Pennsylvania, did not come until 1848. By then 17 states had passed statutes giving women a legal capacity.[95]

In France, the Revolution initially brought some relief to women. In September 1792 a law was passed providing for divorce by mutual consent, and for the rest of the 1790s about one in three French marriages ended in divorce. But the Directory reversed much of the progressive legislation passed in 1791–94 and Bonaparte himself was hostile to women's claims. "Women in these days require restraint," he laid down. "They go where they like, they do what they like. It is not French to give women the upper hand. They have too much of it already." His Napoleonic civil code retained divorce by consent only if both sets of parents also agreed, and the procedure, under Articles 133–34, was made difficult. There was differentiation on "marital offences": a man could sue for divorce on grounds of simply adultery, the wife only if the husband's concubine was brought into the home (Arts. 229, 230); an adulterous wife could be imprisoned from three months to two years, being released if the husband agreed to take her back, while an adulterous husband was simply fined (308, 309); divorce on grounds of cruelty was retained, however. Articles 376–77 gave back to the father the right, on simple request, to have rebellious children correctively imprisoned, and Articles 213–14 restored the legal duty of "wifely obedience." Unless the wife was a registered trader, her right to handle money was severely restricted by Articles 215, 217, 268 and 776. A wife who murdered her husband could offer no legal defense; a husband who murdered his wife was entitled to several pleas. On political activity, there was no permanent progress. Women's clubs had flourished from the summer of 1789, but they were outlawed as early as 1793. The Committee of Public Safety ruled that women could not take part in government, enjoy political rights or meet in clubs. This antiwoman line was reinforced under Bonaparte, and when the Bourbons returned the whole thrust of their governments was to restore the patriarchal society of the 18th century.[96] In the rest of Europe the pattern was broadly similar: a brief period of reform, followed by a partial or total reimposition of the status quo ante.

The French Revolution, then, had little permanent effect on the status of women. It had, it is true, opened a general debate on the topic. Mary Wollstonecraft's *Vindication of the Rights of Women* (1792) was one result. But much of the discussion was hostile to women. Between the mid-1780s and his death in 1806, Restif de la Bretonne, for instance, poured forth a torrent of books dealing with women, which rationalized and reinforced all the ancient prejudices and were widely read, as they were believed to be licentious. A typical sentence in *Le Thésmographe* reads: "By property, every man has something which is exclusively his, of which he is lord and master: his wife, his children, a piece of land, house, furnishings, money." He argued, "Women do not have the principle of life. It is annexed to the male and is his glorious prerogative. He is the one who gives it, to be developed in women." The role of women was to please men, since "The first sex is made for work and business, to acquire experience and enlightenment. To please is not its essence."[97]

It is surprising how many of the romantic writers, whether radical or conservative—or first one then the other—held antifeminine views. In particular, they detested the idea of highly educated women. "The longer I live," Coleridge wrote, "the more do I loathe in stomach and deprecate in judgment *all* blue-stockingism." Byron took particular exception to his wife's interest in mathematics—"the princess of parallelograms" as he scornfully called her—and he and his friend John Cam Hobhouse, another antifeminist, were described by Moore as quoting with relish the lines from *Don Juan:* "But oh! ye lords of ladies intellectual/Come, tell us truly, have they not hen-pecked you all?"[98] Shelley, it is true, held strong theoretical views about the equality of women, but the actual blow-by-blow history of his relations with them—his mother, his sisters, both his wives, his female followers like Elizabeth Hitchener, and his female servants—show him always in the role of exploiter. That was a role also filled, in different ways, by Wordsworth, with his "harem" of wife, sister, and sister-in-law; by Chateaubriand; by Victor Hugo; and by Stendhal, the last always treating women, indispensable though he found them, with a certain amused contempt. Contemptuous, too, was the note of John Keats's couplet (1817) on

Woman: "God! she is like a milk-white lamb that bleats/For man's protection."

Henri Fuseli, the Swiss immigrant who became a key figure in English romantic art and head of the Academy School, seems to have had a lifelong fear and hatred of (as well as dependence on) women. One of his earliest drawings, *The Henpecked Husband,* done when he was in his teens, shows a prostrate man with a beautiful wife putting her foot on his neck and is inscribed: "You fool, your mare rides you, you are saddled with the dowry." There is another, much later, drawing by Fuseli, *Symplegma: a Man with Three Women,* in which three women are subjecting a man to various sexual indignities; indeed, it is arguable that they are actually killing him. Among his works not meant for publication are many drawings of courtesans who are sexually injuring and mutilating young boys. Fuseli, indeed, coined the word. *Paidoleteria,* murderess of children. Such drawings, and his many portraits of his wife, reflect hostile feelings to women. In his works he often put his wife's features on destructive and cruel women, such as Medusa, and he repeatedly shows her as domineering, cold and obsessed with herself.[99]

The long Napoleonic Wars held back any progress for women, with their stress on militarism and their tendency to silence the few, like William Godwin, who were prepared to put their case. With the peace, however, heterodox voices began to be heard again. On 15 August 1823, the liberal *Morning Chronicle* published a long, well-argued letter signed "A Lover of Justice," in which the complaint was made that a Queen's Square magistrate, dealing with a complaint by a woman servant, had simply accepted the denial of her employer and had banned reporters from his court because they reproduced the woman's story.[100] The case was of some interest because the servant was employed by Lady Caroline Lamb and the employer was her husband William, later Lord Melbourne and prime minister. The "Lover of Justice" was none other than John Stuart Mill (1806–73), then aged 17, and this was his first attempt to expose the consistent denial of equal justice to women in the courts. It was during the 1820s that Mill started his campaign against wife beating and, in particular, the almost total failure of the courts to bring those who indulged in it to justice. It was the beginning of a long odyssey, culminating in his powerful and influential book, *The Subjection of Women* (1869), but Mill was already arguing in the 1820s that freedom was a necessary constituent of happiness and applied as much to women as to men.

Mill was not the only one. Two years after his first letter on women's rights appeared, William Thompson published a powerful profeminist tract with the descriptive title *An Appeal of One Half of the Human Race, Women, Against the Pretensions of the Other Half, Men, to Retain them in Political, and Thence in Civil and Domestic Slavery.* He insisted that the home was not, as was claimed, "the abode of calm bliss," but "the eternal prison-house of the wife. . . . The house is *his* house, with everything in it; and of all the fixtures the most abjectly *his* is his breeding-machine, the wife."[101] The same year, the feminist cause in London was joined by the fiery figure of Flora Tristan, the illegitimate daughter of a French émigré, who had learned lithography with the French engraver André Chazal—it was a trade in which many women were found—married him, then spent much of her life trying to escape from him. Her experience personalized the struggle, for not only did she fight a long legal battle for a formal separation, but suffered and survived a determined attempt by Chazal to murder her. She saw herself as a follower of Mary Wollstonecraft, but also as part of a movement, in both France and Britain, in which women were becoming active in organized political protest.[102]

In the 1820s, Frenchwomen in particular showed a good deal of spirit. During the years of poor harvest from 1826 onwards bands of angry women, often accompanied by children—one-parent families we would call them—roamed parts of France, especially in the north, attacking food merchants and forcing them to reduce prices.[103]

Women were also making progress in France at a more intellectual level, sometimes in odd ways, thanks to the teachings of Claude-Henri Saint-Simon, the eccentric social philosopher, and his followers. Saint-Simon had been primarily concerned with bringing industrialists into the business of government and had not directly advocated rights for women. But his insistence that "spiritual powers" would replace "brute force" in the world was a pointer toward a bigger role for women in running society. After his death in 1825, Barthelémy Prosper Enfantin, his successor, tackled the issue directly. He argued that it was precisely the absence of a feminine element in the power structure that had led to the destruction of the French Revolution through "politics, terror, war and violence." He set up communal living centers, *maisons au famille,* and cooperative workshops where tailors and seamstresses worked side by side. In 1828–29 he reorganized the movement on a religious basis, with a strong element of mysticism and a Catholic-style hierarchy. He produced the idea of a *couple-pape* leadership, the he-pope standing for "reflection," the she-pope for "sentiment." This idea would give women more power than might be supposed since the

Saint-Simoniens thought feeling a more important bond in society than reason.

At one time Le Père Enfantin, as he was known, had about 300 full-time women followers in Paris, and another 100 in Lyons, with branches in the United States and Egypt. When he lectured on sexual equality he sometimes attracted over 1,000 people. He began to advocate free love as one form of women's emancipation, and, as might have been expected, his movement degenerated into messiahism and sex orgies. In 1832 he and his lieutenant Michel Chevalier were jailed for "corruption of public morals." But some of his women acolytes formed a separate movement of female Saint-Simoniens, called themselves "New Women," and asserted the right to take complete control of their sexual lives. One of them, Pauline Roland, publicly declared "I want to become a mother with the paternity unknown" and eventually had four children by different fathers, none of whom she married. Some of the attitudes and activities of these women adumbrated the feminism of the late 20th century—they ran a paper called the *Tribune des femmes*, to which only women were allowed to contribute—but at the time, they had no lasting impact; indeed, their extravagances served to discredit French feminism until the end of the century.[104]

Part of the difficulty in making steady progress toward giving women an equal place in society arose from the inability of male intellectuals to separate their reason from their feelings and appetites. Even Godwin, the first male feminist, broke his rules by marrying, of all people, Mary Wollstonecraft, and then had to watch helplessly as she died, like so many unemancipated women, after giving birth to her child, the future Mary Shelley. The only feminist from this epoch who remained consistent was Mill who, from first to last, set his sights on practical objectives, such as trying to ensure that husbands who brutalized their wives were prosecuted. Mill's correspondence with Auguste Comte, the most considerable of Saint-Simon's onetime disciples, makes instructive reading. Comte originally held violently hostile views on women, no doubt, in part, because of his unfortunate first marriage to a Palais Royal prostitute, Caroline Massin. He told Mill that in the whole of the animal creation, the exceptions to the principle of male superiority were found only in the lowest reaches, among the invertebrates; that women were incapable of abstract thought; that they had done nothing in poetry, music, or painting; and that they should not only be denied power but forbidden to enter public offices. But he changed his mind completely in 1845 when he met Clothilde de Vaux— her husband had deserted her a decade before—and then began to create his quasi-religious *système de philosophie positive*, in which women play an important part. He laid down that women were the incarnation of physical, intellectual, and moral beauty and were the guardians of art. Madame de Vaux became the Patron Saint of Humanity, and even his maidservant, Sophie Bliot, was elevated to the role of Significant Proletarian. The striking thing is that Comte was taken seriously both in his antifeminine and his profeminine phases, in the latter attracting such formidable disciples as George Eliot, probably the most influential woman writer of the century.[105]

Progressive male thinkers, then, tended to be inconsistent, volatile, and, in any event, ineffectual, and women had to look after themselves. Women were more successful than one might suppose. Indeed, once one begins to study early 19th century society in detail and examines individual case histories, it becomes impossible to sustain the notion of a paternalistic society in which women were uniformly downtrodden. The great French portrait painter, Elisabeth-Louise Vigée Le Brun (1755–1842), whose work anticipated the relaxed feminine fashions of the Revolution and who was the real inventor of the "Empire" dress— rather as Byron's sartorial interpretation of Rousseau created the poet-bohemian look for men—always insisted that women were most suited to exercising indirect power through their intelligence, wit, and intuition. A feminist in her own way, particularly successful with mother-and-daughter studies known as *materines*, she argued that women were more favored by a secure, traditionalist society which they could manipulate than by one based on abstract principles which was bound to end in violence and militarism. Of the 1780s she wrote: "The women reigned then [in France]. The Revolution dethroned them"; they returned to power in the wake of the Bourbons.[106]

In a civil society like Britain's, women had more political influence, both direct and indirect, than might be supposed. As individuals, women could not, by law, vote in parliamentary elections, but as property owners, they participated in local elections and even returned members to Parliament. Of the two members for Ripon, for instance, the heiress Mrs. Allanson and her sister Mrs. Lawrence nominated one each. When Mrs. Allanson died in 1808, she left her share to her niece Miss Lawrence, who eventually nominated both members, until her death in 1845.[107]

As wives, too, women were players in the political game, not always to the public benefit. The formidable George Canning was enabled to go into politics by his marriage to Joan Scott, who brought him her half-share of the £200,000 made by her father, General Scott, at the gambling tables. Canning was made to earn it. Thomas Moore reported that, dining with the Cannings in Paris in 1821, he was intrigued to see that Mrs. Canning would not allow her husband and his friends to linger over their wine—the traditional time when men discussed politics out of femine earshot—but demanded he join her in the drawing room. Canning, he wrote, "rather sheepishly submitted—*her* looks all the while showing what a scene might have ensured had he resisted. This corroborates what I have heard of her temper."[108]

Canning's successor as prime minister, Fred Robinson, Viscount Goderich, was still more under the influence of his wife, Lady Sarah, a hypochondriac, who took to the sofa, from time to time, convinced she could not walk and was on the point of death and whose fears and alarms, tears and tantrums, kept her equally lachrymose husband in a constant tizzy. The diarist Emily Eden recorded: "She thinks and talks of nothing but her health," and her demands on her husband's attention and energies was a principal reason why his government was so short-lived. Charles Greville, the secretary to the Privy Council, recorded that "in the midst of all the squabbles which preceded the breaking-up of [Goderich's] Administration, he went whining to the King and said 'Your Majesty don't know what vexation I have at home, with my wife's ill-health, etc.' The King, telling the story, said: 'God damn the fellow, what did he bother me about his wife for: I didn't want to hear all the stories about her health.' " Lady Goderich, Greville added, "was a principal cause of all his follies, she never left him any repose, sent for him 20 times a day, even in the midst of his cabinets, and he was weak and silly enough to give way to her fancies, for she had persuaded him she would die if she was thwarted."[109]

Goderich's successor, in turn, the Duke of Wellington, was perhaps more influenced by a woman than was any other British prime minister—not indeed his wife, from whom he was estranged, but by Mrs. Arbuthnot (wife of a junior minister), who had earlier been a close confidante of Castlereagh. Rumors that she was the Duke's mistress are quite baseless, but her journals show that he discussed politics with her more intimately than with any of his colleagues. She often stood up to Wellington in his most formidable moods—perhaps the only person to do so—and occasionally he would rush out of her house in a rage, unable to bear being contradicted or, worse, outargued. Her dislike of Peel, never at ease with any woman except his beautiful and adored wife—hence Wellington's remark, "Peel has no manners"—was gradually transmitted to the Duke himself, and, as we shall see, it was the breach between the two men which destroyed the government late in 1830, so opening the way to the Reform Bill. Mrs. Arbuthnot is almost a textbook case of how important women could be in the politics of the old system.[110] The women were of even more significance on the Whig

side, for they were more zealous and attached to the party than were
their husbands, and it was the efforts of Lady Holland, Lady Melbourne, and Lady Cowper, as hostesses, confidantes, and even lovers,
which kept clever young men like Lord Palmerston from throwing in
their lot wholly with the governing Tories.[111] Without its womenfolk,
the Whig Party might well have disappeared between 1810 and 1830.

Individual case histories repeatedly demonstrate that women were
not in practice the downtrodden second-class citizens which their legal
disabilities might suggest. There are innumerable stories of spirited
women in France, not least Victor Hugo's Breton mother, Sophie
Trebuchet, whose royalist views did not accord at all with the Republican careerism of Hugo's father, one of Bonaparte's generals. For much
of the time, she refused to live with him, having her own royalist lover;
her three sons sided with her, and she was, in effect, head of a one-
parent family—a tough lady, used to traveling all over Europe on her
own, suing in the courts, dealing with governments and badgering
banks.[112] Farington was astonished, when traveling through France, to
see how often women were in charge of local businesses. Women ran
the inns, even when married; "the Husband appeared quite a Cypher
in what related to Guests."[113] One benefit the Revolution did confer on
women was to increase the amount of schooling available to them. As
a result, the female literacy rate began to rise steeply in France during
the early decades of the 19th century, especially from 1815 on, when
places in elementary schools expanded faster than did the population;
by 1830 the literacy rate for women was 60 percent, by 1848, 80 percent.[114]

Literacy was a great liberator for women; but having jobs, making
themselves financially independent, was, then as now, an even bigger
factor in raising their self-confidence. The Kendal girls whom Dorothy
Wordsworth found so "impudent" in 1818, holding political views and
calling out pro-Brougham slogans, were earning weekly wages, often
good ones. It was the same at the other end of the country, in Essex,
where the *Chelmsford Gazette* reported on 12 September 1823 that the
local silk works was paying such high rates that girls employed there
had been "mistaken for persons of distinction." Two young women
entered the parish church of Saffron Walden, "dressed most elegantly
in silks of their own production, to which were added fashionable
bonnets, plumed with nodding feathers. The clergymen politely directed the strangers to be shown to a pew suitable to their appearance,
and at the conclusion of the service enquired of the clerk whether he
knew these elegantly-dressed young ladies, when behold it was discovered that they were two girls from the Walden silk manufactory."[115]

Women were beginning to go on local expeditions alone, though not everywhere. Jane Austen's Emma Woodhouse did not like to go out by herself, even to her friend's house on the other side of the village [Leatherhead]: "She had ventured once alone to Randalls, but it was not pleasant and that is why she was so glad to have Harriet Smith available.[116] But in Scotland, Farington noted, "The principal convenience to women in Edinburgh is that they may pass from street to street singly, as at Bath, and do not require a Companion while paying their visits and holding such intercourse."[117] Visiting Paris with Fuseli, he was impressed by the fact that "respectable women" could be seen in restaurants "without causing remark."[118]

Women were not only moving about more freely, but were entering a widening range of paid occupations. Much of the high-quality work in art reproduction was performed by wives and daughters of engravers, though they did not necessarily get any credit for it. Women were also becoming involved in publishing. The Juvenile Library, for instance, which produced excellent books for children, such as the Lambs' *Tales from Shakespeare,* was run almost entirely by Godwin's second wife, Mary Jane Clairmont. Women had been doing increasingly well on the stage, of course, since the mid-seventeenth century. The problem there was not so much earning money, as keeping it. A typical case was Dorothy Bland, born in 1761 of an Irish father and Welsh mother, both on the stage, unmarried. At 20 she was working in Richard Daly's Dublin company and was soon "ruined" by her employer. Pregnant, she fled to England and was soon calling herself "Mrs. Jordan" (there never was a Mr. Jordan). She bore a Mr. Ford, son of a court physician and co-owner of Drury Lane, three children; he introduced her to the Duke of Clarence, by whom she had ten more. She became a great star, specializing in roles which allowed her to show off her superb legs in tight-fitting hose and breeches—"a privileged being sent to teach mankind what he wants, joyousness," as Lamb described her. Hazlitt added: "She rioted in her fine animal spirits and gave more pleasure than any other actress."[119] She earned prodigious sums, much of which, as we have noted, went to her royal lover. By the time he cast her off and married, in 1811, her earning power had gone, the financial provision made for her proved inadequate, her many children—some of whom did well for themselves—proved callous, and she died almost destitute at Saint Cloud in 1816.[120]

Even larger sums were made after Waterloo by such operatic *prime donne* as Pasta, Colbran, and the superb Spanish mezzo-soprano Maria Malibran (1808–36). Rossini called Malibran the "only" interpreter of his music and encapsulated her in the most comprehensive compliment ever paid by a great composer to an interpreter: "Ah, that marvellous creature! She surpassed all her imitators by her truly disconcerting musical genius, and all the women I have known by the superiority of her intelligence, the variety of her knowledge and her sparkling temperament. . . . She sang in Spanish (her native tongue), Italian, French, German, and after eight days of study she sang *Fidelio* in English in London. She sketched, painted, embroidered, sometimes made her own costumes; above all, she wrote. Her letters are masterpieces of subtle intelligence, verve, of good humour, and they display unparalleled originality of expression."[121] Alas, when she was 28, she and her talents were wiped out in a commonplace early 19th-century manner: blood poisoning following a miscarriage.

Women were also active behind the operatic scene. At least two operas were composed by Mrs. John Serres, the London songwriter, and the libretti of both Schubert's best operas, *Rosamunde* and *Euryanthe,* were written by a woman, Helmin von Chezy. Neither woman got much credit, or cash, for her work.[122] By the 1820s women were appearing as soloists in concerts. Clara Schumann's mother, Marianne Wieck, seems to have played piano concertos in public as early as 1819. Clara was born the same year. Both her mother and her father, who ran a musical library and piano business, were superb piano teachers. But they divorced, and Clara was brought up by a dumb nursemaid and could not pronounce a single word before she was five. She seems to have understood music before speech, and by age seven was playing the Hummel G-major concerto, opus 73; four days before her eighth birthday, she gave her first public performance, of Mozart's E-flat concerto, and by 1830, as a solo performer, she could fill the Leipzig Gewandhaus.[123] Perhaps it is not surprising then that she matured to become the first woman to influence the course of European music, first through her husband Robert, then through her pupil and protégé Johannes Brahms.

Women were also beginning to earn their living in growing numbers as writers, especially in London and Paris. Indeed, I suspect that if a full count could be made, perhaps as many as a third of the writers in London were women. In Charles Lamb's circle alone, there was the historian Lucy Aikin; the poetesses Joanna Baillie, Anna Barbaud, Sarah Flower, and Matilda Bentham; the novelists Fanny Holcroft, Elizabeth Inchbald (who also wrote plays), Anne Manning, Elizabeth Benger; authors of children's books like Isabella Jane Towers and Maria Hack; Mary Cowden Clark, who compiled the first *Complete Concordance of Shakespeare;* Elizabeth Fenwick, who wrote texbooks; the biographer Isabella Blackford; and better-known names like Mary

Russell Mitford, author of *Our Village;* Hannah Moore, Fanny Burney; her stepsister Sarah Burney; and Mary Shelley.[124] The last named, Godwin's daughter, had her first story published in 1809, when she was ten, and her half sister, Jane (later Claire) Clairmont, complained that in their family "if you cannot write an epic poem or novel, that by its originality knocks all other novels on the head, you are a despicable creature, not worth acknowledging."[125]

Women in early 19th-century literary families were often superlatively educated. Coleridge's daughter Sara, though virtually abandoned by her father, was kept up to the mark by her mother and her Uncle Southey. In 1812, Coleridge, paying a now-rare visit to Keswick, was impressed by his 9-year-old girl, who "reads French tolerably and Italian fluently, and I was astonished at her acquaintance with her native language. The word 'hostile' occurring in what she read to me, I asked her what 'hostile' meant. She answered at once, 'Why, inimical: only inimical is more often used for things and measures and not, as hostile is, for persons and nations.' "[126] It was to this remarkable and loyal daughter that Coleridge owes his immense reputation today: she sacrificed most of her life to compiling various books, including his *Biographia Literaria, Table Talk, Collected Poems, Literary Remains, Constitution of Church and State,* and *Lectures on Shakespeare,* from the primeval chaos of his unpublished papers, thus rescuing him from oblivion and, as it were, inventing Coleridge, the master of philosophy and prose.[127]

The education of Elizabeth Barrett Browning (1806–61) was even more intensive, as is revealed by various autobiographical essays, giving a history of her intellectual development, which she wrote in her teens. "At four I first mounted Pegasus [began writing poetry]" and before she was six was given a ten-shilling note by her father for "verses on virtue." "At seven I began to think of forming my taste." Between ages seven and eight she read the history of England, Rome, and Greece "and began poetry in earnest"—Scott, Pope's *Iliad,* Shakespeare. "At eleven I wished to be considered an authoress—novels were thrown aside, poetry and essays were my studies." From this year she read Latin and Greek with her tutor, Daniel McSwiney, and began work on her first major poem, *The Battle of Marathon,* which her father had privately printed in 1820, when she was 14.[128] A year later one of her poems appeared in the *New Monthly Magazine,* and by 1826, when she was 19, she had written enough poetry to fill her first volume, *An Essay on Mind and Other Poems.* She had been writing Greek verse for many years, and the volume attracted the attention of the classical scholar and aesthetician Uvedale Price (1747–1829), author of the famous *Essay on the Picturesque,* which formed the taste of an entire generation. Thus began a correspondence between the elderly scholar and the frail young poetess—she was described as having "curls like the pendant ears of a water-spaniel and poor little hands, so thin that when she welcomed you she gave you something like the foot of a young bird"[129]—which ranged over the whole field of classical literature but especially the accenting, metrication, and pronunciation of Greek and Latin poetry. Some of the letters written to her by the fierce old Welshman, a formidable, bald man with a big hooked nose and piercing eyes, were (including Greek quotations) 6,000 words long, and her answers, commenting on the manuscripts he sent her, reached 4,000 words or more.[130]

The early decades of the 19th century were crowded with such clever women, some of whom managed to establish themselves in a difficult world. From Ireland came Maria Edgeworth (1767–1849), whose novel *Castle Rackrent* (1800) was the first of a series of historical-regional novels dealing with the Irish "problem" from the standpoint of an enlightened Ascendancy family. Like Elizabeth Barrett, she was culturally force fed by an adoring father, of whose 22 children (by four wives) she was the favorite. Richard Lovell Edgeworth owned a large estate in County Longford. His life and his daughter's were deeply entangled; not only did they collaborate on her earlier books, but he involved her in the running of his property. When he died in 1817, and his heir, her brother Lovell, revealed himself to be an incompetent drunk, Maria took over completely. Writing educational textbooks and didactic novels, running a farm, managing often insolvent tenants, setting up a model school, organizing famine relief, persuading Protestants and Catholics to attend the same Bible classes, "explaining" Ireland to a host of important contacts on frequent visits to London—the diminutive Maria, who renounced marriage for the sake of her father and duty, revealed administrative abilities of a high order, as well as steely willpower.[131] Whereas Elizabeth Barrett, if born a hundred years later, must have ended up an academic, Maria Edgeworth would surely have gone into politics.

But what of Sidney Owenson, better known as Lady Morgan? Her sensational novel, *The Wild Irish Girl,* appeared five years after *Castle Rackrent* and answered its high-minded Protestant reformism with tirades of romantic Irish nationalism. Lady Morgan claimed she was born in a small boat on Christmas Day 1776, on a rough crossing to Dublin. Her father was a handsome, drunken, twice-bankrupt actor-manager, a cofounder with Wolfe Tone of the Irish nationalist theater; her mother was an infatuated English Wesleyan. The girl learned Latin from a hedge-schoolmaster, French at a Huguenot-run school in Clontarf and then was "finished" at Mrs. Anderson's School for Young Gentlewomen in Dublin. She acquired a remarkable, unassorted mass of information, much of which she incongruously inserted into her novels. Her wild Irish girl speaks Latin and Greek, as well as Gaelic, and the text is disconcertingly pedantic—the author had a spell as a governess—punctuated with words like *exility, supererogatory,* and *eleemosynary.* However, the book went into seven big editions in two years and brought celebrity on both sides of the Irish Sea. It, and its successors, also earned the author considerable sums, and by 1812, when she was 38, she had saved over £5,000. This enabled her to marry a Dublin doctor, Charles Morgan. Morgan was an idle man who was soon living off her earnings, but the arrangement suited her. Her marriage contract stipulated that she was to keep both her savings and any future earnings, and she was well content to pay the household bills in return for the freedom he granted her to range over France and Italy, as well as London, and publish what she pleased. Moreover, through Morgan, she acquired a title. A prominent doctor, suitably subservient to Dublin Castle, did not find it difficult to acquire a knighthood. Sidney's sister, Olivia, likewise netted a doctor-husband with a "K"—the Irish capital was contemptuously referred to as "the City of Dreadful Knights."

As a titled novelist-celebrity, the wild Irish girl, as some called her, ran a salon and was by far the most famous woman in Ireland, albeit with a host of outspoken enemies, as we have seen. She had a slight physical deformity. A friendly eyewitness described her at a viceregal reception: "Hardly more than four feet high, with a spine not quite straight, slightly uneven shoulders and eyes, Lady Morgan glided about in a close-cropped wig, bound by a fillet or solid band of gold, her large face all animation and a witty word for everybody."[132] And, unlike most women in her position, she was also a superb cook and not ashamed to admit it. In the 1820s she herself cooked a famous dinner she gave for the visiting violinist, Niccolò Paganini, and her diary records an occasional, very Irish, entry such as: "Poor old Mrs Casey broke down from nervousness (or whiskey) in the kitchen and I had to dress half the dinner myself, which everyone allowed was supreme, particularly my *matellote d'anguille* and my *dinde farci à la daube!*" Paganini, too, enjoyed his dinner, saying *"Bravissimo! Eccellentissimo!"*[133]

Many able and energetic women enjoyed the kind of freedom Lady

Morgan earned for herself. Rich widows who were sensible enough not
to remarry formed a special category. The most notable of them was
Mrs. Walker of Liverpool, the most powerful hostess in London, with
the possible exception of one or two Whig ladies. Mrs. Walker was the
daughter of one successful America-trade merchant, and married another. Even in her husband's day, she had entertained lavishly in London, taking their plate, worth £20,000, to the capital for the season, in
a specially built wagon. When her husband died, she began her "great
routs" at £5,000–£6,000 a time, as the goggling Farington noted:
"Grapes only have cost £500—on some occasions the fruit £700." He
added: "The Plans of her entertainments are formed by herself, she has
a talent and taste for it." Once she was fully established, even the
Regent could not get invitation cards for his cronies, unless she liked
them.[134]

Some women took charge of their lives with a firm hand. Lady
Charlotte Bertie (1812–95) eldest daughter of the 9th Earl of Lindsey,
recorded: "I have given myself almost a man's education from the age
of 12 when I first began to follow my own devices." She ran her eye over
two attractive men before dismissing them as inadequate and then
picked as her husband the South Wales ironmaster John Guest, member
of Parliament for Merthyr Tydfil. Her diaries illuminate how far a
strong-minded woman could go, and when she had to defer to her lord
and master. "Knowing that most wives are but looked upon as nurses
and housekeepers, very justly too," she wrote, "I have striven hard to
place myself upon a higher level—and dear [Guest], who knows how
sensitive I am on this point and who really does think that some women
are rational beings, has always aided and encouraged me."[135] Despite
producing 10 healthy children and having one miscarriage, being pregnant 90 months in all, she got to understand thoroughly her husband's
business and as his health failed, ran the ironworks herself. She was in
and out of the workshops, constantly going underground in the firm's
coal mines, seeing to orders, keeping the books. "It is now more congenial to me," she recorded, "to calculate the advantage of half-per-cent
commission on a cargo of iron than to go to the finest ball in the
world." She proved herself a formidable boss, facing down striking
colliers when her competitors opted for appeasement.[136]

Women who actually wanted to enter a man's profession, like the
army surgeon Miranda ("James") Barry, had, of course, to cross-dress.
This happened, I suspect, far more often than was realized, especially
since respectable women often wore men's dress, and dressed their girls
as boys, for long-distance travel. Simón Bolívar's last mistress, Manuela

Saenz, always wore men's dress when riding and clothed her two attendant Negresses, Natan and Jonatas, likewise; she carried a pistol and sword, too.[137]

Sometimes cross-dressing had lesbian implications, not always perceived even by sharp-eyed contemporaries. Thomas Malone, the Shakespearean scholar, recounted: "The singularities of Mrs Damer are remarkable—She wears a Man's Hat, and Shoes, and a Jacket also like a man—thus she walks about the fields with a hooking-stick. . . . The ecstacies on meeting, & tender leave on separating, between Mrs Damer and Miss Berry, is whimsical. On Miss Berry going lately to Cheltenham, the servants described the separation between her and Mrs Damer as if it had been the parting before death."[138] More often, women wore men's garments from necessity.

The number of women who enlisted as merchant seamen, naval ratings and soldiers was probably quite large (about 20 women are believed to have taken part in the Battle of Trafalgar, on the English side, though they were mostly wives and mistresses, concealed below decks). But we know of them only rarely. The case of the Cavalry Maiden, Nadezhda Durova, came to light because her uncle petitioned the Emperor Alexander I for her release and the war minister, then the notorious Arakcheev, was given her curriculum vitae. This and other documents remained in the official archives. Other details were supplied by Durova herself, when Pushkin published her memoirs in his magazine.[139] Pinning down her career and motives is complicated because she sometimes lied. She was born in 1783, daughter of a minor official. As a girl she hated needlework and deliberately ruined it. She often strayed, so that her mother threatened to tie her down with a rope. Her father wished she had been a son. Her mother told her gruesome tales of the fearful lot of women in Russia. She was plain and had a bad bout of smallpox which left her face pitted. She loved riding, had a horse she called Alcides and used to ride him when she was supposed to be asleep. "I was prepared at the dead of night to go into a graveyard, a forest, a deserted house, a cave or a dungeon." This courage and love of horses led her to enlist, dressed as man, in a Polish cavalry regiment. She claimed this took place when she was sixteen. But Russian military records show she was 23, and the fact is that she married at 18, had a son, and (it seems likely) ran away and enlisted to escape a family row over an affair with a Cossack captain. She served with distinction and was promoted to sergeant. After her identity was discovered, a personal order from the emperor allowed her to continue in the army, though he shifted her to a Russian hussar regiment and made her an officer. As an officer, she fought at the fearful Battle of Friedland, and at Borodino in

1812, where a cannonball bruised her leg and her gloveless hand nearly froze in the cold, clutching her saber. She retired in 1816 to look after her father, having served almost 10 years. She was in no sense a lesbian or a transvestite, but rather an adventurous woman who simply could not bear the disadvantages and limitations of being a member of the "weaker sex."

The most notorious cross-dresser and self-emancipationist of the age, Aurore Dupin, or George Sand (1804–76), also adopted male clothes for practical rather than sexual reasons. Her father, Maurice Dupin, was aide de camp to Bonaparte's dashing cavalry commander, Joachim Murat, and grandson, through his mother, of the famous Marechal Maurice de Saxe, son of the king of Poland; George Sand was second cousin, albeit by illegitimate descent, of both Louis XVIII and Charles X. Her childhood was unsettling because her father married an innkeeper's daughter and died when Sand was four. The child was battled over by her vulgar but religious mother and her snobbish but Voltairean grandmother, on whose Nohant estate she was brought up, eventually inheriting it. Her grandmother thought she was too fond of her mother—she told the child it was "unchaste" to sleep in her mother's bed—and when Sand was 13 informed her that her mother was an immoral woman who had given birth to an illegitimate child (Sand's elder sister Sophie), who was not fit to live with them. Sand later wrote that this revelation gave her "a huge internal wound, a searing emptiness in place of my heart . . . I no longer loved myself. If my mother was contemptible, then so was the fruit of her womb."[140] The same year, the girl was packed off to the Couvent des Anglaises, near the Panthéon in Paris, one of the best schools in France, run by English nuns under their superior, Madame Canning. The good girls were called *les sages;* the bad ones *les diables;* the easily led ones in between were *les bêtes.* Sand was first rebellious, the worst of the devils; then puzzled and mixed up, the most stupid of the beasts. Finally, she entered an acute religious phase at 15, became the most pious of the wise virgins and seriously considered becoming a nun. The moment her grandmother heard of this plan, she took her away, back to Nohant.

It was at this point that Sand began her cross-dressing. Her half brother Hippolyte, a Hussar corporal and accomplished horseman, broke for her a mare called Colette and taught her to ride astride, with a man's cap to keep her hair in place. The cross-dressing was encouraged by her science tutor and first beau, Stéphane de Grandsagne. He taught her to fire pistols and wear a complete man's outfit while riding. This was not as odd as it might seem. Few Frenchwomen then rode at all. It was one of Théodore Géricault's delights, when he came to

London at this time, to watch the tall English ladies riding their magnificent horses in Hyde Park—he drew many studies of them, which he called *Amazones*. If Sand dressed as a man while riding with Stéphane, it attracted no attention. He got the idea from a local nobleman, Count Omer de Villaines, who liked to go riding and hunting with his daughter and dressed her up in male blouse, cap, and trousers, "without being bothered," as Sand put it, "by the clothes which render women powerless at an age when they have the greatest need of developing their strength."[141] Thereafter Sand always dressed in men's clothes for her outdoor activities—riding, walking, sketching, scientific collecting.

By a curious coincidence, when her grandmother died and left her Nohant, Sand, now aged 17, went to stay at Plessis-Picard, where a retired cavalry officer, James du Plessis, lived with his wife and five daughters. To enable his daughters to ride and to compensate for the fact that he had no son, he dressed the four eldest as boys in red cavalry trousers with silver-button jackets. There, Sand went riding with her fellow amazons and there she met another retired army officer, Casimir Dudevant.[142] They married in September 1822 and went to live at Nohant, Sand eventually giving birth to a son, Maurice, and a daughter, Solange. Unlike her mother and grandmother (and all the other females in her family, so far as our information goes), Sand was a virgin when she married and she remained faithful for three years. But her husband was not interested in books or art or nature or ideas, and he was violent. In 1825 she spilled sand in his coffee and he slapped her face, hard, in front of many people. That was the beginning of her self-liberation, completed the same year when they went to the Pyrenees, her first experience of grand-scale romantic scenery, and she met a lover. The marriage then slowly disintegrated, and she drifted to Paris and the literary life, her husband remaining on the estate but making her a small allowance from its income.

George Sand's life and ideas repay study because they are so rich in the inconsistencies that mark the reactions of even the cleverest people to the dawn of modern ideas and habits. In Paris, Sand continued to dress as a man because it was cheap. Honoré de Balzac said about this time that it was impossible "to be a woman in Paris," that is, to dress smartly, on less than 25,000 francs a year. Sand had only 5,000 for all her living expenses. When she first got to Paris, she recounted, "my delicate shoes cracked open in two days, my pattens sent me spinning, and I always forgot to lift my dress. I was muddy, tired and runny-nosed, and I watched my shoes and my clothes—not forgetting my little velvet hats, which the drainpipes watered—go to rack and ruin with alarming speed."[143] She also discovered that dressed as a man, she could get into the theater pit, where women were not admitted, for half the price of a gallery seat. For her writing she adopted the name of J. Sand, later changed to G. Sand, then Georges, finally George Sand, for a complicated variety of equally practical reasons.[144] All the same, there is something odd about her change of name. Her grandparents had changed theirs during the Revolution, and Sand seems to have become confused about her identity. Her husband and one of her lovers, Frédéric Chopin, called her Aurore. Reviewers called her Monsieur Sand. Her daughter Solange and another lover, Alfred de Musset, called her George. Her contracts referred to her as Madame Dudevant. After the death of her husband, she liked to be called, as she was entitled, Madame la Baronne, though her last lover called her Madame Sand. She sometimes, in her *Journal Intime* of the 1830s, referred to herself in the masculine, and in private letters she was inclined to use the third person—"George," "poor boy." Addressing groups of women, she referred to "your sex," not "ours."

The confusion is not surprising, for in her own day Sand was unique, *sui generis*. Her romantic novels like *Indiana* (1832) *Valentine* (1832), and *Lelia* (1833) sold prodigiously, and some of her literary peers hailed her as a major figure. Chateaubriand (it is said) read the three-voume *Lelia* at a sitting, and wrote to her, "You will live, Madame, and be the Byron of France." But her singularity made her notorious. Some men saw her as a threat to their predominance, others as a portent of sexual chaos. Thomas Carlyle called her a high priestess of "a strange new religion, named of Universal Love, with Sacraments mainly of Divorce, with Balzac, Sue & Company for Evangelists, and Madame Sand for Virgin . . . a new, astonishing Phallus-Worship."[145] To Baudelaire she was "a latrine." (This kind of abuse continued; later in the century Nietzsche called her "a writing cow"; in our own time, V. S. Pritchett used the expression "a thinking bosom.") In fact, Sand was neither doctrinaire nor promiscuous in sexual matters, though she was often inconsistent. Her views on women strike one today as sensible and moderate; she might be called a skeptical feminist. She was certainly interested in the subject: Her library included nearly 150 collections of letters, memoirs and novels by women. She wrote, in her diary: "[Women] are mistreated, reproached for their stupidity imposed on them, scorned as ignorant, their wisdom mocked. In love they are treated like courtesans, in conjugal friendship like servants. They are not loved, they are used, they are exploited."[146] On the other hand, she was highly critical of some propositions put forward by advanced feminists of the 1820s and 1830s, as she made clear in her *Lettres à*

Marcie, written for the paper run by the liberal-Catholic evangelist, the Abbé Lamennais. She was much too shy to be a strident propagandist for her sex, too retiring even to keep a salon. She talked little, and her voice was often inaudible.

There is no basis for the accusation, made by Alfred-Victor de Vigny from jealousy, that she had a lesbian relationship with the actress Marie Dorval. Sand befriended Dorval, who had had a wretched life, and after Dorval's death looked after and educated her children.[147] But she was generous to many, especially to women who were bruised by a harsh, male world; these women included Aline Chazel, daughter of the feminist Flora Tristan, but Sand thought Tristan's own feminism "infantile." Sand inherited from her mother, who was immensely gifted with her hands—she could tune a piano perfectly, for instance—a passion for needlework, and defended it with equal ardor. Indeed she approved of all kinds of housework: "Housework dulls the mind only for those who spurn such tasks and do not know how to look for what can be found in everything—skilful work, well-performed."[148]

Sand was certainly not oversexed, as many supposed. She regarded her own sexuality as a burden. She took the subject seriously, however, and was continually disillusioned and saddened by what she experienced and saw. She thought the sex drive was as strong in women as in men, but that most men were incapable of equal and lasting relationships, while most women were likewise incapable of brief encounters. Women needed long-term husbands or lovers. Hence, women tended to be chained by their sexuality, instead of liberated. Their best defense was to make themselves financially independent, as she had. She was not so foolish as to suppose herself to be less vulnerable than any other woman. With her background—no father, brought up by two women who hated each other, a conventionally brutal and unfaithful husband—what she wanted was affection. She had three long-term lovers, and 12 in all, none entirely satisfactory. Her considered view of sex—rather modern and sophisticated, certainly not libertine—was that it was a messy business, tragic only if you worried about it too much. But she could not help herself. When she split with Alfred de Musset, her diary records that she prayed frantically to God to bring him back to her, promising, "I shall be devout and my knees shall wear out the stone paving of the church."

Sand's skeptical feminism was characteristic of many of the ablest women who came to intellectual maturity in the 1820s. Harriet Martineau (1803–76) had a more settled background than did Sand, having been brought up in an affectionate Unitarian family in East Anglia. But her father's textile firm went bankrupt, and she had to earn her own living. Moreover, the onset of otosclerosis when she was twenty left her increasingly deaf, with no sense of smell and defective taste. Thereafter, she used an ear trumpet, equipped with an ivory cup and earpiece joined by a flexible tube, which she threw across to people so they could talk to her. This severe handicap produced occasional bouts of hysteria and sometimes, like so many clever women of her time, she took to her sofa for weeks.[149] But as a rule she was exceptionally hardworking, vigorous and productive.

The prime influence during her adolescence was the great Unitarian preacher Lant Carpenter, who argued that the spread of literacy and the ability of women to get themselves published now offered them unprecedented opportunities to improve the morals of society. He instanced Maria Edgeworth, Hannah More and Mrs Barboud, and prophesied that if a really outstanding woman writer emerged, "in the scale of utility she will probably stand unrivalled among her contemporaries."[150] Martineau accepted his challenge; "I believe myself possessed of no uncommon talents, and of not an atom of genius. . . . My aim is to become a forceful and elegant writer on religious and moral subjects, so as to be useful to refined as well as unenlightened minds."[151] She achieved this aim by publishing highly successful moral tales about economics, rather as Hannah More had done on social behavior. *The Rioters* (on machine breaking) and *The Turnout* (on wages) were mid-1820s' best-sellers, and Martineau went on to become by far the most influential woman who has ever professed "the dismal science."[152]

The first articles Martineau published, when she was nineteen, in the Unitarian *Monthly Repository,* concerned the place of women in society. She rejected as rubbish the traditional argument that women's interests were protected by their menfolk. This idea, she insisted, was manifestly untrue in many cases. Some women had no husband or father; others required legal protection from them. "I declare that whatever obedience I yield to the laws of the society in which I live is a matter between, not the community and myself, but my judgment and my will. Any punishment inflicted on me for the breach of the laws, I should regard as so much gratuitous injury; for to those laws I have never, actually or virtually, assented. I know that there are many in England who agree with me in this. The plea of acquiescence [in male "protection"] is invalidated by us."[153]

Martineau's theme, which ran consistently throughout her life, was that women had to get themselves properly educated and then become visible, active, ubiquitous and constructive across the whole range of public activities. One of her most fundamental criticisms of American society revolved around the political nonexistence of women there, which she insisted contradicted its democratic principles. But she hated feminist theory, scorned "rights" campaigns, and deplored any kind of feminist activity that deepened the already tragic divisions between men and women. Her theme was, let us get real women into actual, important jobs, and forget about abstractions. But it is significant that she considered marriage an important job—at any rate for some (she remained unmarried). She set her face like flint against unmarried couples. When the radical activist W. J. Fox, editor of the *Repository*, where she worked, ended his unhappy marriage and set up house with another woman, Martineau broke with him, and she made public her disapproval both of the irregular (though highly proper) union of John Stuart Mill and Mrs. Harriet Taylor, and of George Eliot's "marriage" to G. S. Lewes.

In this respect Harriet Martineau was typical even of highly educated and ambitious women. Most books written by women on women insisted that a strict view of marriage worked in women's long-term interests, even at some sacrifice. Sarah Ellis's *Wives of England*, which Lady Charlotte Guest read attentively—it was a present from her husband—argued that "in the case of a highly gifted woman, even when there is an equal or superior degree of talent than that of her husband, nothing can be more injudicious or more fatal to her happiness than an exhibition even of the least disposition to presume upon such gifts." The *Saturday Review* put it more bleakly: "Married life is woman's profession. . . . By not getting a husband or losing him, she may find she is without resources. All that can be said of her is, she has failed in business and no social reformer can prevent such failures."[154]

Jane Austen, as usual the most balanced commentator (by implication as a rule, not directly) accepted marriage as woman's profession, regretted her failure to marry, and rejoiced at the compensation afforded by her own growing success as a writer (cut short by her death in 1817 just as her fame was spreading), but insisted marriage was a partnership. The marriage of Elizabeth and Darcy in *Pride and Prejudice* is to be a partnership of like-minded people; it is the same with Fanny and Edmund in *Mansfield Park*, Fanny being the junior who subtly transforms herself into the senior partner. Emma and Mr. Knightley are also to be partners, despite the disparity in their ages—he marries her not because she is subordinate but because she is "open." All these people are, or become, "sensible." Anne Elliot, in *Persuasion*, is sensible, too, except in one respect, and she remedies that; her marriage with Wentworth is to be a partnership, on the lines of Admiral and Mrs. Croft, who are presented for our admiration.[155] But Jane

Austen's novels also demonstrate, mirroring the many actual examples glanced at in her letters, that people often fail to be "sensible" and that, as a result, marriages cease to be partnerships and end as tyrannies, chasms, fictions, or plain disasters.

If one casts a net into the sea of marriage in the years 1815–30, one comes up with such an amazing variety of specimens as almost to defy any generalization. One is aware that long-term changes are taking place, but they are difficult to pin down or quantify. From 1750 onwards, in Western societies, there was a shift toward more, and earlier, marriages, and so more fertile ones. The traditional pattern of late marriages, multiple remarriages, and substantial celibacy—all because of property factors—changed. This change raised the birthrate, and, since infantile mortality was falling too, helps to explain the demographic revolution which was taking place, especially in England. There, Lord Hardwicke's Marriage Act of 1753, designed to end irregular forms of marriage, made lawful marriages easier. There was also a huge rise in premarital pregnancy and bastardy. Illegitimacy rates in south Lancashire and north Wales, for instance, may have been as high as 30 percent in the early 19th century. For one reason or another, young people were finding it easier to have sex together. The parish clergy did their best to push young people into marriage. In the 1820s one Hampshire vicar, the Rev. John Monkhouse, would enter a pregnant bride in the parish register as "whore" and a common-law wife as "kept mistress."[156] From the same period, surviving diaries of two Somerset rectors, William Holland and John Skinner, show them negotiating marriages to avoid the birth of bastards. Skinner recorded a pathetic conversation between an angry Mrs. Brimble and her pregnant daughter: "If thou doesn't ha him, I will put a whittle in thy throat." "I'll ha he, but he doesn't want ha I."[157]

Bastardy was not confined to the poor—far from it. Of the 2,143 members of the House of Commons in 1790–1820, 25 were acknowledged to be illegitimate, and at least 50 others had illegitimate children. Sir St. John Aubyn, MP, had 15 children by two mistresses before finally marrying the second. Farington recorded that Aubyn bitterly regretted, at the end of his life, having no legitimate children, and attributed his vicious life to his clergyman-tutor, who wrote books on religious subjects but was "so depraved as actually to lead his pupil into scenes of vice with women."[158] Lord Chedworth had a mixed brood: three sons, two of them illegitimate, and two daughters, one illegitimate.[159] Of course, bastards might marry well, even if they had no money. Thomas Gainsborough was delighted to marry an illegitimate daughter of the

Duke of Beaufort. Of William IV's 10 children by Mrs. Jordan one daughter married Lord Erroll, the premier Scottish Earl; another, Lord Falkland, a third, Lord de L'Isle and Dudley—all good matches—but another daughter was obliged to marry the illegitimate son of Lord Holland, and a son had to make do with the illegitimate daughter of Lord Egremont.[160] Many prominent figures were bastards: John-Julius Angerstein, for instance, the great financier who helped to create the National Gallery. But at least he knew who his father was. Another of Farington's merchant-friends, John Wilson, did not know who his father was, but suspected it was "probably Captain Coulbourne of the Royal Navy or Sergeant Kempe of Lewes."[161] Many prominent figures had bastards: Metternich (by a daughter of General Bagration, the Russian commander in chief); Wordsworth; Byron; Shelley, and Lady Harriet Cavendish, daughter of the Duke of Devonshire. Sidney Smith's sister-in-law gave birth to a bastard on board ship going to India, and when Smith went through his 84-year-old father's papers in 1826 he discovered provision had been made for a son his father "had begotten of a respectable housemaid when he was well over seventy."[162]

In France the number of people born out of wedlock was enormous—some believed up to 50 percent of the population of Paris were bastards. But the illegitimacy rate was falling. It was higher in industrial areas, especially towns, where migrants from rural areas were numerous. The figure was 18–25 percent in some northern towns, against a national average of 7.5 percent, and much lower in rural Brittany and the Basque country. The lower rate in Brittany and the Basque country may have been because the Napoleonic Code, by abolishing the old *recherche de paternité,* sharply reduced the rights of unmarried mothers. The local *bureaux de bienfaisance* and similar charities would not help unmarried mothers, who tended to be forced into prostitution. But if the illegitimacy rate was falling, so was the French birthrate as a whole. Indeed, about this time France became the first major country in history where, as a matter of choice, large numbers of people began to reduce the size of their families. The birthrate per 1,000 fell from an estimated 35–40 at the turn of the century to 32.9 in 1816–20, 31.4 in 1821–5, and only 30.5 in 1826–30. By the early 1820s, families of five or more children still made up 14.2 percent of the total, but the proportion was falling fast. By the end of the 1820s, the declining birthrate was a matter of concern to France, which traditionally had possessed a huge demographic advantage over its neighbors—especially since in England and Germany, its chief enemies, population was rising fast.[163]

In an odd way, George Sand's family illustrates all three of these trends: the ubiquity but also the decline in illegitimacy and the falling birthrate. On her father's side, her grandfather and great-grandfather were both illegitimate. So was her paternal grandmother (who brought her up), who at age 15 had been married off to the Count of Horn, bastard son of Louis XV; on her wedding night a valet was sent to caution her against intercourse with her husband because he had venereal disease. Before Sand was born, her father had an illegitimate son and her mother, an illegitimate daughter, and it offended her feminist sense of justice that her grandmother would allow her half brother, being male, to live with them, but not her half sister. She herself was only just legitimate, since her parents married a bare month before she was born. Her husband, too, was illegitimate. Sand was probably the first woman of her family in three generations to conceive her first child in wedlock, though her second was almost certainly conceived, though not born, outside it. In her circle, to produce two children was now the maximum.

The forms and legal validity of marriages varied. In many parts of England, "bundling" (sleeping together) took place between young people who might, or might not, be formally engaged. In parts of Dorset, Devon and Cornwall, girls had to prove themselves fertile before a marriage was agreed to. Farington noted in Polperro: "The men & women marry at a very early age, & generally signs of connection make it necessary for the credit of the female. But when this sign does appear the men are very faithful; and [when] a marriage has been solemnised there is no after reproach."[164] In Yorkshire, women kept a thumb free when hands were joined in marriage, as a sign of refusal to be dominated. The clergy did not like this practice, nor the big, semi-pagan public weddings, involving the entire village and much drunkenness, dancing, rice throwing, roping, chaining, mock battles, and such obscene customs as "the race for the garter." Parsons, squires and mill masters united to put down such expensive orgies, urging families to save their money to set up house. David Wilkie's brilliant *Penny Wedding,* a picture of the year at the 1819 Royal Academy exhibition, was a sign of the way things were going. Parsons and civil authorities alike were also keen to stop couples marrying in parishes where they were not known by falsely swearing to residence. "Common Law marriages," that is unions neither solemnized in church after the calling of banns, nor registered with the state by license, were very common in the century 1750–1850. They were known as "jumping over the besom," "besom weddings," "living tally," and other terms, varying with the county. Shoemakers and cobblers, a traditional antinomian group, called their common-law wives "tacks" ('If thee tak, I tak thee"). Other groups among whom non-church marriages were common were miners, sailors, canal workers, costermongers, sweeps and dustmen. Chapel ceremonies were conducted long before Nonconformist marriages became lawful in 1837. At the Laurence Street Chapel, Birmingham, Charles Bradley defiantly conducted his own marriage: "Before this congregation, I, Charles Bradley junior, give you, Emma Harris, this ring to wear as a memorial of our marriage, and this written pledge stamped with the impression of a United Rights of Man and Woman, declaring I will be your faithful husband from this time forward." It is likely that in the early decades of the 19th century, one in seven couples in England was not lawfully married or was "living tally."[165]

Elopements were common. They occurred both when parents would not consent or when partners could not stand their spouses. Of Angerstein's four half sisters, some legitimate, some not, Mrs. Hanker eloped to India with Colonel Straubenzee and Mrs. Ibbetson eloped to Portugal. The colonies offered wide opportunities for such escapades, especially South Africa, where there seems to have been no enforcement of the marriage laws in the period 1815–30, and Australia, where the number of couples getting lawfully married actually declined at this time.[166] By accident or design, many couples were bigamous. As long as neither partner caused a row, the authorities rarely took note, and if they did, the couple could slip across a frontier, to Dublin, Edinburgh, or France. This happened to the husband of one of the Regent's mistresses, Mrs. Crouch; he fled to Boulogne.[167] The nearness of Scotland, with radically different marriage laws from England, was a constant temptation to high and low alike. So-called Gretna Green marriages, just across the Scottish border, were cheap, quick and private. Only a small proportion of those eloping to Gretna Green were rich runaways, like Lady Sarah Fane, heiress to Child the banker, who married the 5th Earl of Jersey there, defying both sets of parents. When Farington, who took a detailed interest in such things, visited Gretna Green, he found that three men, none ordained, were conducting marriage ceremonies, the chief being Joseph Paisley, "a large fat old Man of 70 Years of age . . . a tobbaconist & never had an education or any Clerical function . . . drunk & improvident." He said that the business was managed by the drivers of the carriages who brought the couples. They judged from the couples' appearance how much they should advise Paisley to charge, the terms varying from 50 to as low as 5 guineas. That settled, the ceremony was performed immediately by reading the Church of England service before two hired witnesses; couples and witnesses then signed the register, and all was over. The average number of weddings thus performed each year was "40 to 50," though a total of 72 had been recorded.[168]

The older generation was overbearing in dictating or vetoing marriages among the young if the young lacked resolution. Anne Elliot, in *Persuasion,* who loses seven years of happiness with Captain Wentworth by bowing to the prejudices of her older mentor, Lady Mason, will have struck a chord in many female hearts; the novel went down well on the Continent, too, where it was translated into French and German. But at least Anne got a second chance, and took it. Victor Hugo's friend, Alfred de Vigny, fell in love with Delphine Gay, the beᵔutiful girl who played the piano at one of the *Cénacles* they frequented. His mother, the Comtesse Léon de Vigny, wanted him to make a rich marriage and turned the girl down. The poet weakly consented. Then, in 1825, he plucked up courage and defied his family by marrying Lydia Bunbury—it was fashionable for French intellectuals to marry English girls in the 1820s. De Vigny found their long legs and fair complexions irresistible, "straight out of *Ossian,*" as he put it. But Lydia proved difficult, a sofa-invalid, a snob, more keen on titles than on poetry.[169] Franz Schubert was still more unlucky. His failure to take the risk of running off with the teenage soprano Thérèse Grob— her mother forced her to marry a master-baker instead—led to lasting regret ("I still love her") and seems to have driven him away from marriage and into the arms of prostitutes, with fatal results.[170]

Robert Schumann was more determined. At the age of 20 he went to live with Friedrich Wieck as a piano pupil and soon fell for his brilliant daughter Clara. As a pianist he was a late starter and made disastrous use of a mechanical finger strengthener. (These devices were popular at the time: George Sand was forced to use one to help her handwriting.) The machine lamed the weaker finger of Schumann's right hand, and after months of ineffectual treatment, such as brandy-and-water bathing, herb poultices, and immersing it in the blood of a freshly killed ox, he was forced to give up any idea of a career as a pianist and concentrate on composing. For this reason, and perhaps because he knew Schumann had already contracted syphilis, Wieck hotly opposed Robert's marriage to Clara, and it took place only after a ferocious court battle.[171]

The case of the painter John Constable was more like Captain Wentworth's. As the son of a yeoman-miller, he came from a lower social grade than the girl he loved, Maria Bicknell, whose family were lawyers and clergymen. Moreover, by this time, 1811, he was already 33 and had sold few paintings. Maria refused to elope with him: "People cannot live now on four hundreds a year, it is a bad subject, so adieu to it." Constable was miserable, and used to wait outside her house in the cold, in the hope of an occasional glimpse of her. By 1816 he was forty and had been hanging around her for seven years. But he was beginning to dispose of his work for reasonable sums, and his staunchest patron, Archdeacon Fisher, offered to marry them if Constable could persuade Maria to elope. The painter hesitated, hoping to overcome the views of his main opponent, Maria's grandfather, the Rev. Durand Rhudde, "for the very idea of sneaking into the family is shocking [to me]." But doing so proved impossible and they were finally married in 1816, in defiance of the family, Fisher performing the ceremony at St. Martins-in-the-Fields (a friendly Anglican clergyman was an alternative to Gretna Green). Constable's bittersweet conclusion was, "We have been great fools not to have married long ago."[172]

Runaway marriages, often involving crossing the class barriers, were prompted by love, ambition, and cupidity in almost equal proportions. When the young barrister Daniel O'Connell, who came from the old Irish-Catholic gentry of Kerry, fell in love with his distant cousin Mary, from a lowlier branch of the clan—she had no money either—the head of the clan, "Hunting Cap" O'Connell, vetoed the marriage; the couple eloped, and the future Liberator was deprived of half his inheritance in consequence.[173] On the other hand, Edward Gibbon Wakefield (1796–1862), the ambitious son of a land-agent, seems to have been prompted by simple greed when he talked an heiress into a Gretna Green marriage. He was duly convicted of enticement and served three years in Newgate—it was there that he undertook the studies that made him the outstanding theorist of colonization. Ambition may also have prompted young George Repton, son of the landscape gardener, to elope (1817) with the daughter of Lord Eldon, the Lord Chancellor. Repton's was not strictly speaking a cross-class marriage, since Eldon himself was the son of a Newcastle coal merchant. But his official position made him, in rank, second only to the sovereign, and, more to the point, both he and his brother, Sir John Scott, had become immensely rich through the law. The daughter was forty and, rather like George III's girls, sick of being penned at home where her chief duty was to read to her father. The case attracted much attention and may have been in Dickens's mind when he later devised the elopement of Alfred Jingle and Miss Wardle. Repton had met the daughter while working in the office of John Nash and living in his house on the Isle of Wight, and Nash was furious at what he considered a breach of trust. The Eldons swore they would never speak to their daughter again, and when she asked for her clothes they simply sent her court dress in a parcel, without a note or acknowledgment of her letter. But

Eldon soon relented. He missed his daughter, "having a wife of such a disposition as to deprive him of domestic comfort: when he has a dinner to give he does it at a tavern."[174]

This marriage succeeded very well, and to judge by the cases I have come across, cross-class unions were as likely to succeed, or fail, as were any other kind. Lord Berkeley, head of one of the oldest and grandest families in the country, married a butcher's daughter; this marriage worked well enough, but there was trouble after his death. Lord Egremont, the great art patron, took a farmer's daughter as his mistress, she calling herself "Mrs Wyndham," the family name. But soon after he married her, he started to be unfaithful, and they separated. Lord Erskine also married his mistress, by whom he had had several children. Wanting to legitimate them, he took the woman to Scotland for a quick union. His legitimate son by an earlier marriage tried to prevent it, but Erskine evaded him "by wearing a woman's dress." The newly married couple settled in Hampstead where, in 1820, Erskine was said to be "under the domination of the woman." The great banker Thomas Coutts (1735–1822), founder of the firm, had better fortune. He, too, married his mistress, Mrs. Mellon. Mrs. Arbuthnot commented disapprovingly in her diary: "She lived with Mr Coutts many years before his first wife died, was an actress, and now, because he has left her his whole fortune, she gives balls and breakfasts and is invited by every body." In fact, Coutts treated her like his daughters, settling £2,000 a year on her, plus £100,000 cash. She made his last years happy: even when he was eighty, she used to ride with him in his carriage to his bank every day at 9 A.M.[175]

Another successful cross-class marriage took place in defiance of the Duke of Richmond. The Duke was wary on this point because of the experience of his aunt, the Duchess of Leinster. The Duchess had engaged a young Scottish tutor, a Mr. Ogilvie, to teach her sons. When she was widowed, six years later, she married him, saying he was such a good disciplinarian. The family loyally supported her decision, but Dublin society complained he was uncouth. Hence, when the Duke's daughter, Lady Sarah, fell in love with a widower of 38, General Sir Peregrine Maitland, who had commanded a brigade at Waterloo and was known as the handsomest officer in the army, her father refused his consent. Maitland, he said, did not have an income to uphold her status, she had no money of her own, and he had none to give her. So he did not invite Maitland to the victory ball he gave in Paris. When the general did not come to the ball and Lady Sarah discovered he had not been invited, she immediately changed out of her ball gown, put on traveling clothes and went straight to the general's lodgings; they were

married on 9 October 1815. In due course Wellington, who liked Maitland and, still more, Lady Sarah, pulled his rank and brought about a
reconciliation with Richmond. The marriage proved blissful and was
often quoted as proving that elopements need not lead to disaster.[176]
This was exactly the kind of story which Anthony Trollope, a schoolboy at the time, found intriguing and which he used to such effect in his
novels.

A more sinister tale, adumbrating Mr. Murdstone in *David Copperfield,* is painfully related by Farington in his diary. Though a working
painter himself, he came from an ancient Lancashire gentry family,
some branches of which were wealthy. His cousin, John Hammond,
had, unwisely in Farington's opinion and as events proved, left his wife
his fortune abolutely. The widow, in her forties and with two adolescent daughters, promptly fell in love with a much younger man, John
Smith, from an uncertain background—his father claimed to be a solicitor—who was plainly after her money. Despite Farington's considerable efforts to prevent the match, or to secure the inheritance of the
widow and her daughters, it took place. There was much contempt for
Mrs. Hammond, who "was going to marry a young man who had not
a sixpence," and relations and friends threatened to break off all contact. Successive diary entries tell the sad tale: Mr. Smith persuading the
new Mrs. Smith to settle all her money on him; the sacking of Grey, old
Mr. Hammond's faithful manservant; an expensive trip to Paris, where
one of the unhappy daughters died from a neglected illness; Mr. Smith's
moves to get the other daughter's inheritance settled on him; and the
girl's evident fear of her stepfather. An attorney Farington employed
reported: "He thought Mrs Smith now felt herself under authority—&
that she was not well used." Farington's death in 1821, and the end of
his diary, conceals from us the final outcome.[177]

Another pathetic little saga concerns the Irish artist Francis Danby
(1793–1861), who, with a more settled home life, might have become
one of the greatest painters of the era. The son of a Wexford squireen
(minor landowner), whose wealth had been destroyed in the 1798 rebellion, Danby came to England to make his fortune as a painter. In 1814
he settled in Bristol among the gifted group of amateurs and professionals who formed around Edward Bird, RA, and Edward Rippingille and
that included the notable American painter Washington Allston (1779–
1843). That summer Danby went around Somerset painting portraits of
well-to-do farmers. He related: "I took a great fancy to one of their
servants, a little, red-faced, bare-footed wench. My Irish brogue, I
suppose, was against me, and I could not succeed however in any way
but by promising to marry her." So they were married in July, he 20,

she 14, pregnant and illiterate, signing her name with a cross. The union, Danby wrote, "resulted in a precarious and unhappy life." In fact, Danby's own improvidence with money was a major source of his troubles. He had seven children by the illiterate Hannah and often left her alone with them, penniless. She used to get a friend to write to his patrons, asking them to send any money owed to her "and not to Mr Danby." In due course she ran off with another Bristol artist, Paul Falconer Poole, and Danby, in revenge eloped with a girl paid to look after the children. Thus "orphaned," the children were handed over to an aunt, who likewise deserted them. It was Danby's moral conduct and, perhaps even more, his refusal to apologize for it, which persuaded the Royal Academy not to elect him.[178]

Whatever the Royal Academy, led by its stiffer element, such as Farington, might do, artistic life tended to slip over into bohemianism. Turner, the greatest of the Royal Academicians, whom everyone was afraid or wary of, never married. There was endless speculation behind his back about whether either or indeed both of his two housekeepers, one named Mrs. Sophia Caroline Booth and the second, another Mrs. Danby, were his mistresses. Mrs. Booth's son, Daniel John, was widely believed to be Turner's, and Mrs. Danby's niece Hannah also came to live with them. Turner's final codicil to his will appointed Hannah and Mrs. Booth joint custodians of his gallery-foundation. But there is no conclusive evidence, either way, about Turner's sex life, or whether he had any.[179] Portrait painters, especially successful ones who moved, to some extent, "in society," were circumspect, of course. Ingres, who had married a dress designer, a *modiste*—he had a passionate love of drapes, textiles, and clothes of all kinds—later fell in love with a married lady and exchanged letters with her, at that date a certain sign that love was reciprocated. But it is not clear whether they met *à deux* and he certainly did not engage in a liaison. Thomas Lawrence, like Turner, never married, and it was generally assumed that he had dealings with various women. Otherwise, people said, how could one account for the fact that, despite his immense earnings—he was charging 700 guineas for a portrait when he died in 1830 and was hugely prolific—he never had any cash and was often in danger of arrest for debt? Lawrence swore he never gambled "as much as a five-pound note," so the explanation must be women. If so he was discreet. Nothing but rumor linked him with specific women, such as the Princess of Wales, though he was briefly engaged to both Maria and Sally Siddons.[180]

Writers were deeply divided on the rules which should govern sex and marriage. They were also inconsistent in their own behavior and attitudes. Byron, in Venice, boasted of his conquests in letters home to his friends and his publisher John Murray, knowing they would be read aloud to select male gatherings. Writing to John Cam Hobhouse and Douglas Kinnaird in 1819, he listed his chief mistress by name, adding *"cum multis aliis"* (with many others). "Some of them," he wrote, "are countesses—and some are cobblers' wives—some noble—some middling—some low—& all whores. . . . I have had them all and thrice as many to boot since 1817." He held it wrong to spend his patrimonial inheritance on fornication, but money earned by poetry was another matter: "What I get by my brains I will spend on my bollocks, so long as I have a *tester* or a testicle remaining."[181] On the other hand, still in Venice, he objected strongly to mixed bathing, even when the parties were married, as "very indelicate." There was some truth in the Rev. Charles Kingsley's later observation that Byron "was an Evangelical gone wrong."[182]

Shelley, on the other hand, strongly disapproved of Byron's promiscuity. But his own rules on sex were made up as he went along, to suit his inclinations. His first marriage, to an ordinary middle-class girl of 17, was an elopement. Harriet Shelley put up with a good deal from her husband in the way of debts, duns, constant moves to escape creditors and strange women residing in the house. But she did not warm to his attempts to set up love colonies or engage in wife swapping. He, in turn, abandoned her the moment he fell in love with Mary Godwin and upbraided her fiercely for not accepting the fact humbly and joining them as the junior member in a *maison à trois*. Mary's father, William Godwin, who at one time had disapproved of marriage altogether, was beside himself with rage when Shelley ran off with his daughter without being in a position to marry her. He refused to receive them until Harriet's despairing suicide allowed Shelley to make Mary "an honest woman," whereupon he boasted to his friends that Mary was marrying "the heir to a baronetcy and a considerable fortune."[183] Shelley was soon renting a big house in Great Marlow, for an extended family consisting of himself; the pregnant Mary; her stepsister Claire Clairmont with the baby, Allegra, whom she had just had by Byron; as well as Leigh Hunt and his wife Marianne, also pregnant; and Marianne's sister Bess. They built an altar to Pan in the woods, and the atmosphere was heavy with sexual innuendo. Mary was correcting the proofs of *Frankenstein* and Shelley was writing *Laon and Cynthia*, whose theme was incest.[184]

Incest seems to have obsessed this group of poets, though it must be remembered that in the early 19th century and for long afterwards, a husband who committed adultery with his wife's sister was technically guilty of incest. Both Byron and Shelley repeatedly returned to incest as a motif in their poetry—Shelley notably in *The Revolt of Islam*—though as a rule their publishers or printers insisted that the references be disguised. Byron almost certainly committed incest, even as we would understand it, with his half sister Augusta Leigh, and their passionate liaison was a contributory factor in the breakup of his marriage. Shelley might be said to have committed technical incest twice over. He seems to have had an affair with Mary's elder half sister, Fanny Imlay—a daughter of Mary Wollstonecraft by an earlier liaison—an ill-considered fling that led to Fanny's suicide soon after Harriet Shelley's. But he also, a year or so after the Great Marlow gathering, resumed sexual relations with Mary's other half sister, Claire Clairmont, in Italy, the consequence being a baby girl, Elena, duly placed in a Naples orphanage, where she died.[185]

Shelley seems to have played a role in corrupting Leigh Hunt, who was likewise accused of incest because of his behavior to his wife's sister. Hunt had married Marianne Kent when she was fourteen. She was never very intelligent, and had little education. Repeated pregnancies, plus Hunt's improvidence, soon reduced her to a slut—"a disgusting person," as Henry Crabb Robinson called her. Her one talent was for writing begging letters, a skill put to frequent use in the Hunt household. Hunt, under Shelley's influence, came to prefer her sister Bess, a brighter, livelier girl, author of the first book on potted plants. Haydon, Keats, and Hazlitt, all of whom went down to Great Marlow, were united in condemning the behavior there. Haydon testified that he had heard Shelley "hold forth to Mrs Hunt & other women present . . . on the wickedness and absurdity of *chastity*." Hunt, in response, had enraged Haydon by saying "he would not mind any young man, if he were agreeable, sleeping with his wife!" He added: "Shelley courageously adopted and acted on his own principles—Hunt defended them, without having energy to practise them, & was content with a smuggering fondle." Haydon wrote this comment in the margin of his copy of Medwin's *Conversations of Lord Byron,* and in his diary he went further: "His poor wife has led the life of a slave, by his smuggering fondness of her sister, without the resolution or the desire to go to the full extent of a manly passion, however wicked. He likes and is satisfied to corrupt the girl's mind, without seducing her person, to dawdle over her bosom, to inhale her breath, to lean against her thigh and play with her petticoats . . . shuts his eyes to tickle the edge of her stockings that his feeling may be kept tingling by imagining the rest." Bess used to get upset, and swig opium (and Marianne eventually became an alcoholic). Haydon, coming one morning to Hunt's house for breakfast, did not arrive till 11 A.M., knowing Marianne's hopeless habits, but found no meal. A hungry and exasperated Keats told him there had been a row; Bess had tried to drown herself in the pond, but had stuck in the mud and been rescued by two cabbies. Both men were disgusted by Hunt's endless sex talk. Hazlitt agreed: "It's always coming out like a rash. Why doesn't he write a book about it and get rid of it?"[186]

One reason why English antinomians like Byron, Shelley and Hunt went to Italy was that it was believed to have a tolerant attitude to sexual license, more so even than France in those days. (The excellent exchange rate was another powerful factor.) Byron claimed he had slept with about 200 Venetian women, "perhaps more," in the space of two-and-a-half years, at a total cost of £2,500.[187] Despite everything successive popes could do, women in many Italian cities felt that once they were respectably married (for prudence), they were entitled to take a *cavaliere servente* (for love). Even in papal Rome, the atmosphere was relaxed. Some blamed Bonaparte's sisters. Ingres, who dominated painting in Rome as Canova dominated sculpture, and who was obsessed by the naked female form in all its erotic aspects, was encouraged by Caroline Murat, Bonaparte's promiscuous elder sister, wife of his cavalry general and king of Naples, to excel himself in these suggestive nudes. Among them was his erotic masterpiece, the *Baigneuse de Valpincon,* also known as the *Grande Baigneuse.* It is a hymn to the beauty of a woman's back (Caroline's back was her strongest point). Delighted with this painting, Caroline got Ingres to paint for her his *Grande Odalisque,* another back-nude, in which, to strengthen his design, he actually inserted three vertebrae too many, though the viewer does not notice the back is too long. A third magnificent nude, the *Dormeuse de Naples,* also sold to the Murats, was lost in the ruin of their kingdom.[188]

Caroline's pretty younger sister, Pauline, patronized the other great artist in Rome, Canova, whom she persuaded to immortalize her. She married as her second husband Camillo Borghese, head of one of Rome's oldest families, who sided with Bonaparte and was given the government of Piedmont. In 1808 she was determined to have a permanent memorial of her body while it was still comely, and commissioned Canova to sculpt her naked, as Venus Victoria, the archetypal sex goddess who conquers men by her beauty. The sculptor, a pious man who had first made his reputation with tomb-figures, especially popes, was horrified. He compromised by offering to present her as Diana, fairly naked but associated with chastity. In a masterful Napoleonic manner, she insisted on Venus, and Canova, an old-fashioned and obedient artist who served every major court in Europe, complied. The result was his masterpiece of portrait sculpture. He did not quite accede to the princess's unblushing request, in that her private parts are covered. But her back—like Caroline she was proud of it—is naked to the cleft of her buttocks, and the statue is unquestionably erotic. Moreover, though Canova placed her on a mattress sculpted of marble, like her body, he used as a plinth a real bed of painted wood, which conceals a mechanism for turning round the entire statue for closer inspection. It is true that the statue was not on public view, unlike today (it is still in the Palazzo Borghese). But it was the custom, after dinner, to take friends of the family and special guests to inspect the work by candle-light—that was how Canova preferred all his statues to be seen—and the treat was especially notable when the Princess was in charge of the party and could draw attention to her finer points. The pope might issue decrees against tight-fitting trousers, but he could do nothing to stop these private exhibitions, which went on under his nose and continued until the Princess's death ten years after Waterloo.

Nor was this all. Pauline was celebrated not just for her back but for small and finely formed feet. The Roman nobility and distinguished visitors—especially the English—were invited to the Palazzo Borghese to see *La toilette des pieds*. Printed cards were issued. Women guests were just as fascinated as were the men. According to a description that Lady Ruthven, who had attended one session, gave to Augustus Hare many years later, when the guests arrived, they found Pauline with her little feet—exquisitely white, according to Lady Ruthven—displayed on a velvet cushion. At her command, her maids entered, touched the feet with sponges, and dusted them with powder. The Duke of Hamilton, a regular at the ceremony, used to take up one foot and tuck it into his waistcoat, "like a little bird."[189]

The Italians were unique in having the institution of the *cavaliere servente*, which unofficially recognized that illicit sex was most conveniently regulated by admitting it within the structure of indissoluble marriage. Other societies followed suit, less blatantly, if only because few people knew how to practice birth control successfully. The one exception was the United States, where adultery, however discreetly managed, was never socially condoned. We shall see, in due course, how sexual irregularity could shake Washington to its foundations. Americans were also unusual in permitting publicity for birth-control methods. By the early 1800s, birth control was widely practiced in Europe, especially in France, where by the 1820s it was having a perceptible effect on the birthrate. But knowledge, such as it was, was passed from mother to daughter; it was rare for European censors to permit marriage manuals even to refer to it. In 1826, Richard Carlile, who wrote early sex guides with titles like *Every Woman's Book* and *What Is Love?*, advocated inserting a small sponge soaked in quinine and water into the vagina after intercourse. But he was always in and out of the courts on charges of blasphemy or obscenity, and his books, regarded as pornography, were not widely distributed.

In some American cities, by contrast, books discussing birth control were freely on sale as early as the 1820s. Robert Owen's *Moral Physiology* (1831) remained in print for 40 years, and Charles Knowlton's *Fruits of Philosophy* (1832) reached its 10th edition in the 1870s. Owen favored *coitus interruptus* but also described the vaginal sponge and the condom or *bandrache,* made of oiled silk or thin animal skins. Knowlton recommended douching—the vaginal cap, soon to be the preferred method, was not yet available in the 1820s. What was more surprising, Samuel K. Jennings's *Married Lady's Companion,* published as early as 1808 and freely available in some states, recommended various methods to induce abortion—hot baths, bleeding from the foot, calomel, and aloes—though it is true the word was not used: "obstructed menses" was the euphemism he employed. Lawful—or, at any rate, condoned— abortion, up to three months of pregnancy, has a long history in the United States. By the 1820s courts in the cities tended to acquit "quickening" doctors as they were known, and the authorities were reluctant to prosecute anyway. In the first three decades of the 19th century, there was one (estimated) abortion for every twenty-five to thirty live births, and the ratio was rising rapidly—it was one to every five or six by the 1850s.[190]

In Europe, abstention was common. It was widely known, for instance, that the famous Coke of Norfolk, later Earl of Leicester, no longer had sex with Lady Leicester, since the doctors had warned her she could not safely bear another child. But the couple remained "on civil terms." Some marriages were never consummated at all.[191] Others were notorious for their lack of sexual content, Brougham's being a prime example. Brougham did not know how to cope with women. According to Harriet Martineau, "He knew many cultivated and intellectual women, but this seemed to be of no effect. If not able to assume with them his ordinary manner towards silly women, he was awkward and at a loss. . . . His swearing became so incessant, and the occasional indecency of his talk so insufferable that I have seen even coquettes and adorers turn pale."[192] He regarded marriage as a business matter. He proposed to the rich Georgiana Pigou, who turned him down flat, then turned to the recently bereaved Mrs. Mary Ann Spaulding, who had

£1,500 a year and a London house. Sydney Smith described her as "a showy, long, well-dressed, red-and-white widow." She was a hypochondriac and a sofa-lady even before they were married but, to the general amazement, produced two daughters, one of whom died young. Thereafter the Broughams barely exchanged a word. She dressed like a little girl in white, her face thickly powdered and rouged, and wore corsages of roses. With Brougham in his invariable black, they made a gruesome couple. She never went out with him because he discouraged invitations inviting her, and when he entertained at Brougham Hall in the Lake District, she remained invisible; his mother acted as hostess. But we have one account, from Creevey, of a dinner party in their Gill Street house, "damnable in cookery, comfort and everything else." Brougham, wrote Creevey, "was jawing about nothing from beginning to end, without attending to anyone and only caring to hear himself talk." Mrs. Brougham "sat like an overgrown doll at the top of the table in a bandeau of roses, her face in a perpetual simper without utterance." She was eventually consigned to a madhouse, where many felt her husband should follow her.[193]

With so many marriages dead from the start or dying from inanition, adultery, even if indiscreet, did not usually lead to the breakup of a marriage. The head of the Harley family, the Earl of Oxford, allowed his wife, once she had produced an undoubted heir, to have by different lovers a variety of children, known as the Harleian Miscellany, after the first Earl's historic donation of books. When she had a child by Sir Francis Burdett, the Earl said he would not provide for it, and Burdett produced £5,000 pounds, though it was stolen by one of her brothers. The couple lived in the same house but in separate quarters.[194] Few husbands would exercise this degree of toleration. When the beautiful Mrs. Dunnage was caught by her husband's brother James *in flagrante delicto* with Sir Thomas Turton—the newspapers got all the details— Mr. Dunnage felt he had no alternative but to sue for *crim-con.*, as it was termed, and Turton had to pay £5,000 damages. A similarly bad case—I am taking the two almost at random—concerned Mrs Guard, wife of an army colonel, a lady of ravishing beauty but lascivious, who had an intrigue with the son of an apothecary in Ottery St. Mary. This affair outraged the colonel's sense of social propriety and he sued, getting £3,000 damages; the offender, having no property, ran off to join Wellington's army in Spain.[195] If the lady left her husband's roof and— to use the early 19th-century euphemism—"placed herself under the protection" of her lover, then a separation, even a divorce, became almost inevitable in England, though not on the Continent. Jane Austen, who does not mince matters, shows a divorce following promptly when Maria Bertram runs off, albeit briefly, with Henry Crawford.[196]

A measure of discretion made such procedures, expensive and damaging even for the innocent party, avoidable. Byron used to boast that he had never damaged a marriage, though his letters were frank about the early 19th-century rituals of upper-class adultery. Lady Caroline Lamb, whose husband (later Lord Melbourne), himself a practiced adulterer, was irritated but long suffering, sent Byron a clipping of her pubic hair. So, in 1819, did the Countess Guiccioli, who had it mounted in a brooch of brilliants.[197] In this case, a papally approved separation did follow, since the strawberry-blond countess eventually went to live with Byron entirely; but Byron justified himself by arguing that the marriage had broken down completely long before he appeared on the scene.

It was more common, however, for a love affair between married persons to remain clandestine. An interesting case, because it is well documented, was Palmerston's affair with Lady Cowper. Lady Cowper was born Emily Lamb and was Lady Caroline's sister-in-law. Her mother, Lady Melbourne, though a good wife and mother—she gave excellent advice to her young admirer Lord Byron—was herself a notororious adulteress. Emily's true father was the Earl of Egremont. It is striking how often in the early 19th century adultery, like illegitimacy and divorce, ran in families. Palmerston was not Lady Cowper's only lover—he was fiercely jealous of his rivals—but he was certainly the most persistent one. Both played by the rules of the game. They corresponded in cipher, and Palmerston recorded their encounters in his diary in Italian, in both cases to fox inquisitive servants who might sell the information to newspapers. Thus, a Palmerstonian diary entry would read: "Fine night, *per il giardino, dalle 2 fin alle 5.*" This comment meant that he went to Lady Cowper through the garden door of her house and stayed from two till five. Sometimes there was a misunderstanding: "Failed *La notte per spaglio reciprico* waited from 2 to 5 in morning." It was an exhausting life for him, since he had a full day's work in the War Office, followed by attendance at the Commons, and these nighttime arrangements went on for many years. Cowper was complaisant, but the proprieties had to be observed at all times. He also had to be indulged in his own intrigues. Lady Cowper wrote to her brother Fred Lamb, a diplomat in Vienna: "Dear Lord C in the most *sheepish* way asked me the other night if I had any objection to Ly Sarah [Bayly] coming to P[anshanger, the Melbourne country house]. So I answered in the most frank, amiable manner, to be sure not, I shall be delighted, oh pray ask her directly. . . . *J'ai voulu lui donner un bon exemple.*"[198] When Lord Cowper finally died in 1837, the couple could marry, though it took Lady Cowper two years before agreeing to do so.

How should society react to adulterous or irregular couples? In the United States the answer was simple: They were excluded. On the Continent, as a rule, the answer was equally simple: They were included if discretion was observed. In England the answer was not simple and was becoming more complicated. Unlawful marriages were common even in the gentry class. Palmerston himself, as war minister, often had to settle the claims of rival officers' widows to pensions. In April 1817, for instance, he had to disappoint the granddaughter of the 1st Earl of Arran, who finally admitted that her marriage to a paymaster had been "private."[199] Upper class marriages that were contracted on the Continent, sometimes bigamously, were often regarded as invalid—Trollope was later to make good use of them as plot devices. Should such couples be "received"? Were such wives *sortable?* The rules were changing, not for the better in the eyes of the stiffer ladies like Mrs. Arbuthnot. In March 1797 Sir George Beaumont, another stickler for moral rules, noted with satisfaction that at a big party at the Duchess of Gordon's, when Lady Jersey, regarded as a fallen woman, appeared, other ladies "made a lane for her and let her pass unspoken to."[200] Twenty years later, however, Lady Jersey was ruling the roost at Almack's, the society ballroom, and deciding who got in.

Beaumont's view was that the rot had set in with Charles James Fox, who had "done more harm than any other man." Fox had introduced his longtime mistress, Mrs. Armstead, after he had finally married her, into the "highest society" and insisted she be invited to "the best houses," though—quite apart from her sins—"she had been very common."[201] All Tory moralists agreed that Holland House, headquarters-den of the Foxes, had a lot to answer for. Lady Holland herself, though a great power in society in some ways, was a fallen woman: She had left her husband to go and live with Lord Holland and had later got a divorce in order to marry him. Outside London that made her inadmissible in many homes. In 1814, Brougham, dependent in many ways on Holland House patronage, was "consternated" when the Hollands, returning from Scotland, asked to be put up at Brougham Hall and his mother refused to let them in. The mother said that "she herself was too old to be hurt by Lady Holland, or anybody of that kind, but that she had an unmarried daughter, then living with her, and therefore no Lady Holland should set foot in her house." Brougham added: "My mother was immovable, and there was nothing to be done but that I should go out to the carriage [and] make any excuse I could invent."[202] In London it was a different matter: the moralists considered it a great victory when the Queen persuaded the Regent not to invite Lady Holland and other adulteresses to his big fête.[203] Even in London, Lady Holland, fearing snubs, did not invite wives to "dine and sleep" at Holland House. No doubt many would have been glad to poke their noses into its splendid and famous rooms. Her dinner parties, therefore, were all-male affairs, apart from herself, one reason why they were so successful, claimed some men.

Impropriety, indeed, was often the reason and sometimes the excuse for excluding wives. Thus Farington noted the case of Mr. Penton, who seduced his wife's pretty maid; deserted the family home; took the girl to Italy, where she learned to sing professionally and became a leading diva; then brought her back to England, "where she sits at the head of his table." Stuffy people like Sir John Truern and Lord Thomond dined with them, to hear her sing afterwards, but they did not take their wives. Equally, Peel made no scruples about enjoying the millionaire Lord Hertford's magnificent hospitality at Ragley, but in view of the Marquess's notoriety, he would not take his precious Julia there. Other guests did bring their wives, however. A peer who was grand and rich enough could usually get away with anything as long as he did not actually insist that respectable wives curtsey to his mistress.[204] With such uncertain, changing rules, it was not surprising that lesser folk became confused. In 1820 in Pisa, where the Hunt family was occupying the ground floor of Byron's Palazzo Lanfranchi, the preposterous Marianne Hunt made a fuss about "receiving" the Countess Guiccioli, a gesture which made Byron, who loathed her and her ill-behaved children—"gypsies" he called them—grind his teeth with rage.[205]

One reason why society was less censorious was that more and more marriages were breaking down. Among writers and artists, the number of broken or irregular homes was enormous by the 1820s. The shipwreck of Coleridge's marriage was particularly poignant. In a sense Coleridge was pushed into marriage by his officious and censorious brother-in-law, Southey. The poet laureate had married Edith, one of the five beautiful Fricker sisters who supported themselves and their widowed mother in Bath by exquisite needlework. Coleridge was in love with Mary Evans but thought she was unresponsive. He became friendly with Edith's sister Sara to the point where Southey insisted he "regularise matters" by getting engaged to her. He then got a letter from Mary saying she loved him, but it was no good—hence his sad little poem, "On a Discovery Made Too Late," and his later remarks, whenever Bath was mentioned, "And there I had the misfortune to meet my wife." Sara, aged 21, little, blue eyed, plump, and fresh, was very much in love with Coleridge, and he tried to persuade himself he loved her. Certainly, he made an initial effort to get the marriage to work in ways most men of his day would have scorned, involving himself even in the housework. They moved into a cottage at Clevedon on the Somerset Coast, and a list survives, in Coleridge's hand, of items they needed, which he sent to his generous publisher, Joseph Cottle, in Bristol: "A riddle-slice. A candle-box. Two ventilators, two glasses for the wash-hand stand. One tin dust-pan. One small tin teakettle. One pair of candlesticks. One carpet-brush. One flour-dredge. Three tin [candle] extinguishers. Two mats. A pair of slippers. A cheese-toaster. Two large tin spoons. A Bible. A keg of porter. Coffee, raisins, currants, catsup, nutmegs, all-spice, cinnamon, rice, ginger and mace." He also compiled, under the heading *Desiderata,* another list: "1 set of better China. Two tubs and a pail. 4 urine pots. Two beds. Four blankets. Five pair sheets of the finer order, 2 pair for servant. A set of curtains. Pewter and earthenware." He brought into the household his young friend George Burnett, and one of his notebooks, "the Gutch," as it is known, shows that the two men used to get up at 6 A.M., clean the kitchen, light the fires, put on the kettle, clean "the insides of the boiling-pot," polish the shoes—all before Sara got the breakfast at eight o'clock. They also put the meat on the spit for dinner, while she did the vegetables, and they helped her wash the dishes.[206]

The marriage, starting on so hopeful and modern a note, was effectively destroyed within five years by Coleridge's absences; inability to work regularly and support his family; and, above all, by his opium addiction and drinking. Divorce was out of the question. There were no grounds for it, as Coleridge, with all his faults and despite the fact that he was now in love with Wordsworth's sister-in-law Sarah Hutchinson, was no adulterer. A formal separation would have been disastrous for Sara, since she did not possess a marriage contract specifically providing for her property rights, and so would have been entirely dependent on Coleridge's good faith, something which, thanks to his addiction, did not exist. Hence, Sara fought desperately against one. Southey reached the conclusion that Coleridge was not worth managing: "[He] besots himself with opium or spirits till his eyes look like a Turk's who is half reduced to idiocy by the practice—he calls up the servants at all hours of the night to prepare food for him . . . his present scheme is to live with Wordsworth—it is from the idolatry of that family that this has begun—they have always humoured him in all his follies, listened to his complaints of his wife, and when he has complained of his itch, helped him to scratch instead of covering him with brimstone ointment, and shutting him up by himself." But Coleridge later quarrelled with the Wordsworths too, and in the end it was Southey who had to house the deserted wife and bring up the children—not unjustly, since he was responsible for the marriage in the first place.[207]

Byron's separation from his wife Annabella Milbanke, in April 1816, by which time Coleridge had given up any attempt to live with Sara, confirmed the view of many that literary marriages were inherently unstable. Byron's influence over the next ten years was immense, and his supposed influence even greater. His friend Moore made a diary note in January 1820 of a Parisian lady who solemnly asserted "she considers these *Piqueurs* (the Monsters in Paris that stab women) to be the natural consequences of the study of Lord Byron's works, and the principles inculcated by him!"[208] Byron's desertion of his wife and his engaging in widely publicized immorality abroad branded the Romantic movement as inherently wicked. It set the pattern for 19th-century and indeed 20th-century, attitudes toward the artist. In a sense it was the first modern scandal. The exact reasons why Lady Byron left him are now irrecoverable. His affair with his half sister Augusta, though important later in stiffening his wife's resistance to a reconciliation, was not the cause. One factor was Byron's sexual tastes, including his wish to sodomize women, a relic of his youthful homosexuality. That was what Hobhouse referred to when he told Moore "I know more of Byron than anyone else and much more than I should wish anybody else to know"; he feared that news of such proclivities would damage the radical cause. Another entry in Moore's diary records a discussion with the singer Mrs. Robert Arkwright: "an intimate friend of Lady Byron's had told her such horrors of Lord Byron's conduct to his wife as were inconceivable and on the authority, as she supposes, of Lady Byron herself, not only (as Mrs R.A. said) 'attempts to corrupt her morals but things not to be named which without having heard them one could not even have imagined.' This evidently refers to certain beastly proposals—It was not only, she said————." At this point the entry breaks off.[209]

Another, and more prosaic, reason for the disaster is often overlooked. Byron could be sensible, faithful, and even uxorious, as his final phase with the Countess Guiccioli shows. But he married too young. There is another entry in Moore's diary, from 1819, of a conversation at Lord Methen's: "I mentioned what (I think) Scrope Davis said Lord Byron had told *him*—that the first night of his marriage, he waked in the middle of the night & there being a blazing fire in the room & the bed-curtains being of a deep crimson, he thought, from the red glow around him, that he was 'dead and damned' but 'on recollecting myself,' said he, 'I found it was worse, that I was—married!' "[210] Byron's joke covered what he had come to regard as an error of judgment. Thanks to the follies of his trustees over many years and the unforgivable sloth of his lawyer, Hanson—compounded by his own youthful extravagance—his affairs were in a pitiful condition by the end of the war. His debts were large, and the postwar depression, provoking a financial crisis, made it increasingly difficult to service them, let alone borrow fresh money against his considerable assets. He believed that marriage to Arabella, who he thought he liked and who was an heiress, would solve his problems. As a more experienced friend might have told him, it merely compounded them in the short term, by increasing his unavoidable expenses without giving him access to her capital. Over the winter of 1815–16 the credit squeeze tightened, and the crisis reached its low point in April 1816, the month when Byron's marriage broke up. His drinking and his often frenzied behavior—his wife thought he was mad at times—reflect his hopeless financial straits as much as anything else. Plenty of other people were in desperate trouble, too. This was the point at which the bank owned by Jane Austen's favorite brother, Henry, collapsed and left him penniless.

The truth is, Byron could not afford to live like a lord in London, or even in England. Lady Byron's return to her parents seemed to give him an easy way out; on the Continent he could and did live in style. But, of course, it made a retrieval of the marriage impossible. Many marriages collapsed at this time, financial stress adding to other factors. The lack of money helped to destroy Byron's marriage as surely as it did Coleridge's. It was as frequent a collateral cause of marital breakdown in early 19th-century England as it is today.

No doubt Byron was more inclined to see his marriage go beyond repair as he was an artist and the scandal did not affect his earning capacity, as it did in most callings. The Royal Academy might try to impose virtue on would-be members, as in the case of Danby—though Danby's behavior was exceptionally bad—but the fact is that by the early decades of the 19th century, prominent painters were splitting from their wives and getting away with it. Even in Catholic France, a court painter like David took the opportunity of the revolution to get a divorce, though he later had a reconciliation for the sake of his family. In 1810 the up-and-coming genre painter William Mulready (1786–1863), another Irish immigrant, separated from his wife Elizabeth. Elizabeth was the sister of his teacher, John Varley, and like other members of that gifted family a fine painter herself, so competitiveness may have led to the breakdown. But it does not seem to have done Mulready any harm; five years later he was elected ARA (Associate of the Royal Academy). John Opie, RA, was involved in more serious scandal. His wife went off with an Irishman, Major Edwards, and for a time he was involved with Mrs. Wollstonecraft, no less—he claimed she had thrown herself off Chelsea Bridge for the love of him. He even got a parliamentary divorce, so he could get married again to an heiress, Miss Booth. None of this behavior affected his fashionable practice or his election as the Royal Academy's professor of painting.[211]

All the same, people were beginning to associate artistic creativity with loose sexual morals. To someone like Southey, a man of great integrity, if a little stuffy, and as poet laureate the official head of his profession, the function of writers and artists was to raise the moral tone of society by their works, not lower it by their behavior. Thus, he denounced what he called "the Satanic school," not only because its members were wicked, but as far as he could see because their offenses brought them nothing but unhappiness: their "audacious impiety" merely "betrays the wretched feeling of unhappiness wherewith it is allied."[212] What struck him most about the Godwin-Shelley nexus was the mess they all seemed to make of their lives. Of the children in Godwin's household, Fanny Imlay, Mary Wollstonecraft's daughter, was illegitimate, though her father was known; she committed suicide. Mary Godwin was his own daughter, and legitimate, but by absconding with Shelley, a married man, was partly responsible for Harriet Shelley's suicide—she certainly felt so later. Mrs. Wollstonecraft's adult life was unhappy in the extreme, punctuated by disastrous love affairs and repeated suicide bids, though her death in childbirth was no one's fault. Godwin's second wife called herself Mrs. Clairmont, but she was, in fact, Mary Vial, the illegitimate daughter of a "Mrs." Vial by a man called Devereux. When she married Godwin, she already had two illegitimate children, Charles and Mary Jane (Claire); we do not know the identity of their father or fathers. Claire in due course had two illegitimate children, by Byron and Shelley; both were put into orphanages and died as infants. Shelley had seven children that we know of; two had to be made wards of Chancery, two died in orphanages, only one grew to adulthood. It is true that many infants died in those days, however careful their parents. But a child in a one-parent family or an orphan had little chance. No wonder Mary Shelley, contemplating the sole survivor, Percy, hoped passionately that he would grow up "ordinary": she had seen enough of the miseries of genius, bohemianism, and rebellion.[213]

Marital disasters, however, ran in establishment families, too. Madame Vigée Le Brun was divorced for desertion and her daughter, Julie Nigris, also had a broken marriage—that might be attributed to "artistic temperament." But it is astonishing how many of her aristocratic sitters were divorced or separated, among them Princess Yussoupoff, Countess Golivin, and Anna Potocka. The last had four husbands, all from some of the oldest families in Europe. The first husband, Prince Sanguszko, grand master of Lithuania, died hunting. The second, Prince Casimir Sapieha, she divorced three years later. The third, Count Kajetan Potocki, divorced her for adultery. The fourth, Prince Charles-Eugene of Lorraine, contrived to make the union last. Anna was unique in getting both her divorces approved by Rome.[214] The Esterhazys of Hungary were another case. Prince Nicholas II Esterhazy collected women and young girls; his wife, Princess Marie of Lichtenstein, was also promiscuous, her lovers including Baron Salomon Meyer de Rothschild, who advised her husband on money. They were a scandal to Europe, and their children proved profligate, too. England provided many examples, notably the Bulwer-Lyttons. Lord Lytton's mother, an heiress, was the child of a broken marriage. Her father, Richard Warburton Lytton, was, after the famous Porson, the best classical scholar of his day. But all he ever did was to write a Hebrew play, which could not be performed because he said he could not find a cast who could pronounce the language properly. He married a girl who boasted she had never opened a book, and they separated immediately after Lytton's mother was born. In due course Lytton's mother married a General Bulwer, produced children, then left him, saying he was so vile tempered she would never again set foot in his house. She brought Lytton up herself, but broke with him and cut him off when he married a penniless beauty called Rosina Wheeler. Rosina was also the child of separated parents. Their marriage, in turn, broke down, leading to a judicial separation in 1836: Rosina wrote a novel attacking him and spent the rest of her life dragging him through the courts.[215]

An even more striking case was provided by Wellington's family, the Wellesleys, and the Pagets, the family of Lord Anglesey, his Waterloo cavalry commander. Wellington himself was separated from his wife, the sister of poor "Ned" Pakenham. He told Mrs Arbuthnot all about his marital disaster on 27 June 1822, walking up and down the lawn at Brompton Park "late in the evening." It was a classic husband's lament. The Duchess "did not understand him." Her mind was "trivial and contracted"; he "might as well talk to a child," and as for "discussing political or important subjects," it was "like talking *Hebrew* to her."[216] His elder brother, Lord Wellesley, also had a broken marriage. He and his wife had separate London houses, and down at Dorking he kept a mistress, "publicly known as such," named Mrs. Douglas; she was "a woman of a low order" and he was said to "spend on her."[217] Two younger brothers, Gerald and Henry, had married sisters, daughters of the Earl of Cadogan—himself a womanizer—called Lady Emily and Lady Charlotte. Lady Charlotte, "who had been marked for great levity of manner before she married," became the mistress of Lord Paget (later 1st Marquess of Anglesey). Lord Paget left his wife for a time, returned "for his children's sake but said "He would visit Lady Charlotte Wellesley whenever he pleased." In due course, however, there were two divorces and a remarriage, Lady Charlotte leaving four children behind with her ex-husband. To complete the misery, Paget seduced Lady Emily, and that marriage broke up, too. All this explains Mrs. Arbuthnot's sense of outrage, in May 1820, when told Lord Liverpool objected to giving a vacant place in the order of the Garter to the Duke of Dorset, on the grounds that "some years ago he had got into a scrape by an intrigue with a married woman." In that case, she asked indignantly, why had he made Anglesey (as he was by then) a knight of the Garter? He had "fled from his own wife to the wife of another man, married her and then seduced her *sister*, and to complete the tale made his own wife tell the story of her sister's frailty to her husband."[218] The truth, of course, was that there were no clear rules of conduct any more. Mrs. Arbuthnot was expressing the bewilderment of multitudes and voicing the commonest refrain of the modern age: What are things coming to?

Marital breakdowns, however, meant different things to different classes. Wealthy and influential families like the Pagets and Wellesleys could get parliamentary divorces—the only valid form in England until the Act of 1857. Divorces also took place among the poorest classes, where no property was involved, though they were unlawful. They replaced the bigamous marriages which the Hardwicke Act made more difficult. If a wife was beaten too often or was deserted too long, she "returned the ring," in front of witnesses. A husband sometimes received a written "release." A man who remarried while his first wife was living was said to be "on a lease." A husband who allowed his wife to leave him and remarry "leased her out." In effect, the ground for these Common Law divorces was consent or living apart for at least seven years. These divorces had a certain fragile validity in law, but if one party reneged and made trouble, a bigamy prosecution might follow. Even if it did—and the authorities usually did not want to be bothered—juries were lenient.[219]

A traditional form of working-class divorce was the "wife sale." This form increased rapidly during the population shifts produced by the early Industrial Revolution and seems to have reached a peak in the years after 1815, especially in the manufacturing districts. The theory behind it was that the husband released himself from a (notional) premarital contract by accepting a total sum from a rival suitor. The object was to rid the husband of the responsibility for the wife's upkeep. The husband led the wife to the place of sale with a halter around her neck and handed her over to the new "owner." The purchaser was already connected to her and usually living with her, so the "sale" was merely the publication of a *fait accompli*. That was why it had to take place in the market square, sometimes with the approval of the parish authorities and even with legal advice. The buying was always prearranged, though sometimes a mock auction was held, the crowd beating tin kettles. If the husband was unpopular, however, the crowd might stop the auction and burn him in effigy. But by the 1820s justices of the peace were becoming increasingly hostile to these antinomian displays and instructed constables to break them up and arrest the ringleaders.[220] They continued clandestinely, of course, but most poor people seeking divorce no longer bothered with ceremony. If a marriage broke up, the parties moved—no problem in an increasingly volatile and mobile society—and, if opportunity offered, remarried. The risk of prosecution was remote.

In the middle ranks of society, where a parliamentary divorce was out of the question and a bigamous remarriage was dangerous, the only course was separation, formal or informal. Such breakups were much commoner than historians like to admit. Farington recorded literally dozens of them among his own extensive acquaintance. The pressures of the modern world—economic, psychological, not the least cultural—were already beginning to undermine the stability of the family in the early 19th century. The moralizers and champions of the family were among the victims. By a tragic irony, Cobbett published his optimistic and highly successful guide to domestic happiness, *Advice to Young Men and (Incidentally) to Young Women in the Middle and Higher Ranks of Life* in 1827, the same year his own marriage began to break up. He had always publicly portrayed his wife as perfect, his family life as idyllic. But the reality was different, and after the brawl at the Burdett testimonial dinner and his wife's attempted suicide, he retired to his study and a back bedroom and held no communication with any member of his family for 75 days. The final quarrel came when he was elected member of Parliament (as a result of the Reform Bill) and he returned from a late sitting of the Commons. He expected to find "the bowl of warm milk with a little tea in it which I always wish for in such a case" but found "neither bowl nor fire, and nobody but a man to let me in, though there was a wife, three daughters, two sons and two maidservants in the house, all in good beds of my providing. Too happy should I have been, however, if this had been *all*. But when I got into that bed which I so much needed . . . that *tongue* which for more than 20 years has been my great curse, and which would have worried any other man to death, suffered me not to have one moment's sleep . . . and as I saw that this was a mere *beginning* of a month of it, she breakfasting in bed every day, and having the sofa to lounge on, and the park to take exercise in, to provide the strength of lungs and the power of sustaining wakefulness at night, I also saw that I must get out of the house." So there was a separation and no reunion of the family until the noisy herald of the modern world lay dying.[221]

For middle-class people who wanted to remarry and for whom a legal divorce was more or less essential, the only hope was Scotland. The Scots did not have the Anglican church tradition (itself inherited from Catholicism) that marriage was indissoluble, and provided court divorces on the basis of marital crime. But, even in Scotland, it was much easier to make a marriage than to end it. To prevent collusion, the plaintiff (almost always a woman) had to swear what was called the Calumny Oath; lying was perjury, and if the state could prove it, the penalty was seven years' transportation. The Scots authorities were particularly suspicious of couples from south of the Border, and with good reason. There were many other legal pitfalls. Take the case of John Black, editor of the *Morning Chronicle,* a leading liberal daily. John Stuart Mill considered him the most important newspaperman of the day, "the first journalist who carried criticism and the spirit of reform into the details of English institutions." (He won, for instance, the right for newspapers to report preliminary proceedings in police courts.)

Black was a poor boy from Berwickshire, who in 1810 walked to London for work and raised himself entirely through his own efforts, as so many able Scotsmen did at this time. In 1812 he became hopelessly infatuated with the mistress of one of his bohemian friends and married her. She got him into debt, deceived him, and deserted him. By 1814 his infatuation had finally worn off, he had met an old lady friend, and Mrs. Black agreed, for a consideration, to give him a "Scotch divorce." She was willing to take the Calumny Oath and to go to Scotland and be domiciled there long enough to sue him on her petition. He, too, had to prove domicile. Whether the court would have accepted her oath is doubtful, but in any case it judged the proofs of domicile inadequate and turned down the petition. Black then "married" the lady friend, the first Mrs. Black found out, and blackmailed him. "This pertinacious persecution," we are told, "went on for many years."[222]

Hazlitt, who wrote for the *Morning Chronicle,* no doubt had Black's disastrous experience in mind when he determined on a Scottish divorce in 1822. His case is of exceptional interest, not least because it tells us so much about him as a person. Hazlitt was a great writer, perhaps the first truly modern writer in English. But as a person he was dangerous. He was an obsessive. He was obsessive about politics; about the Revolution; about the "betrayal" of Wordsworth, Coleridge, and Southey; and, above all, about his hero Bonaparte. But he was also obsessive emotionally and sexually. He wrote with great bitterness: "There is but one instance in which appetite hangs about a man as a perpetual clog and dead-weight upon the reason, namely the sexual appetite." Hazlitt's sexuality took a peculiar form. Though he married two middle-class women for financial and social reasons, his preference was, as he put it, for "humble beauties, servant-maids and shepherd-girls with their red elbows, hard hands, black stockings and mob-caps."[223] He was fascinated by the life of the women servants, "below stairs," and their bawdy talk.

This taste got him into trouble again and again. As I have already briefly mentioned, there was a distressing incident in the Lake District in 1803 when Hazlitt was staying there, still on good terms with Wordsworth's circle. Hazlitt fell for the daughter of a local "statesman" and tried to seduce her. What exactly Hazlitt did is not clear. The story got out only years afterwards, when Wordsworth, exasperated by Hazlitt's savage attacks, delivered as always in a high moral tone, told Haydon, Crabb Robinson, Lamb, and no doubt others why he had washed his hands of Hazlitt—the offense that had provoked the critic's enmity in the first place. Haydon recorded: "Some girl called him a black-faced rascal when Hazlitt, enraged, pushed her down, 'and because, Sir,' said Wordsworth, 'she refused to gratify his abominable and devilish propensities,' he lifted up her petticoats and *smote* her on the *bottom*.' "[224] The girl complained to the male members of her family, who raised up a Keswick posse, "not less than 200" according to Coleridge, and set out on horseback to find Hazlitt. Wordsworth thought they intended to have him ducked or imprisoned; Coleridge believed he might have been transported or even hanged, which suggests the girl was actually raped. Hazlitt had to flee in the middle of the night, leaving his clothes and paintbox behind, having borrowed, according to Coleridge, "all the money I had in the world and the very Shoes off my feet."[225]

In 1808 Hazlitt married Sarah Stoddart, a woman with a little property. Sarah was the sister of the *Times* editor, John Stoddart, and a close friend of Mary Lamb, through whom Hazlitt met her. The marriage produced three sons, only one of whom, William, survived. Sarah was a lively, easy-going woman, but she objected strongly to Hazlitt's spoiling of the boy, who obsessed him. He gave William money in the morning and told him it must be spent by the evening, to instill "generous notions," as he put it. He also, she said, took the boy "to the fives Courts and such places" even "when he went picking up the girls on the town." She had got used to Hazlitt falling for servant girls and consorting with prostitutes—"his tastes went that way," she said resignedly—but she did not want the boy ruined, too. As it was, John Keats found him "a little Nero."[226] Sarah was also exasperated by Hazlitt's failure to earn, or at any rate keep, enough money to support his family. By 1820 they were living apart. That year Hazlitt took bachelor lodgings off Chancery Lane, in the house of a tailor, Michael Walker, and promptly fell in love with one of his daughters, Sarah, or Sally as he called her. "Love" is an inadequate expression: He was totally infatuated. His friends were mystified. One of them, Bryan Proctor, wrote: "Her face was round and small, and her eyes were motionless, glassy." Perhaps what obsessed Hazlitt were her peculiar movements. Proctor said, "I never observed her to make a step. She went onwards in a sort of wavy, sinuous manner, like the movements of a snake."[227] In 1823 Hazlitt tried to set down what he felt in a remarkably frank book, the *Liber Amoris,* but even that conceals many aspects of his obsession. She would not sleep with him, but permitted him "liberties," and he was frantic with jealousy that she also granted them to other lodgers, younger and more handsome than he. In a letter to another friend, P. G. Patmore, he described how he overheard Sarah, her sister Betsey, her brother Cajah (short for Micaiah) and their mother sitting in the kitchen and arguing about which of their lodgers had the largest penis. They talked about Griffiths, their Welsh lodger. Betsey: "Oh! if those trowsers were to come down, what a sight there would be!" (a general loud laugh). Mother: "Yes, he's a proper one. Mr Follet is nothing to him." Cajah: "Then I suppose he must be seven inches." Mother: "He's quite a monster. He nearly tumbled over Mr Hazlitt one night." Sarah: *Inaudible.* Cajah: "Sarah says. . . ." Sarah: "I say—Mr Follet wears straps." "Can there be a doubt," Hazlitt commented in anguish to Padmore, "when the mother dilates in this way on codpieces and the son replies in measured terms, that the girl runs mad for size?" When Hazlitt gave her his most precious possession, a little china statue of Napoleon, as a love token, she told him it reminded her of a former boyfriend. At one time he actually hired a young man, a "Mister F," to attempt Sarah's seduction, to see whether she was promiscuous or not; nothing came of it.[228]

Hazlitt decided his only way of securing Sarah Walker was to divorce his present Sarah and offer his new Sarah marriage. That meant Scotland. An English divorce, even if obtainable, involving a private bill, was beyond his means. A later Royal Commission reported that for an English divorce *a vinculo matrimonii,* which permitted remarriage in certain circumstances, the cost "under the most favourable circumstances can hardly be less than £700 or £800; and when the matter is much litigated it would probably reach some thousands. In Scotland the average cost of rescinding a marriage is said to be £30 and that when there is no opposition £20 will suffice."[229] Hazlitt calculated that he could just about afford the sums involved and asked his wife to agree to take up residence in Edinburgh and petition on the grounds of his adultery. She consented, provided he paid her expenses. In all the circumstances—she had no prospect of remarriage herself—it was an act of kindness, for divorced women, however innocent, were objects of pity and contempt. But Sarah Hazlitt was a good-natured woman. Just before she was due to leave for Edinburgh, to take up her forty days' minimum residence, she ran into Hazlitt in the street. Hazlitt: "Ah, you there—and how do you do?" "Oh, very well, William, and how are you?" He said he was "just looking about" for his dinner. "Well, mine is just ready, a nice boiled leg of pork, if you like, William, to have a slice."[230]

Sarah Hazlitt was a formidable walker, and perhaps she welcomed the opportunity to see the Lowlands. Mary Lamb said she "in vain endeavoured to make her look on her journey to Scotland in any other light than a jaunt." At all events Sarah kept a diary of the episode. Some years later, Seymour Kirkup recorded how, in Florence, Hazlitt had turned the whole story of his divorce into a boastful anecdote, which he related with relish to W. S. Landor and himself: "They took the steamboat to Leith, providing themselves each with good law advice, and continued on the most friendly terms in Edinburgh till everything was ready: when Hazlitt described himself calling in from the streets a not very respectable female confederate, and for form's sake putting her in his bed and lying down beside her. 'Well, Sir,' said Hazlitt, turning more particularly to Landor, who had by this time thrown out signs of the most lively interest, 'down I lay, and the folding doors opened, and in walked Mrs H accompanied by two gentlemen. She turned to them and said: 'Gentlemen, do you know who that person is in bed along with that woman?' 'Yes, madam,' they replied politely, ''tis Mr William Hazlitt.' On which, Sir, she made a curtsey, and they went out of the room, and left me and my companion *in statu quo.* She and her witnesses then accused me of adultery, Sir, and obtained a divorce against me, which, by gad, Sir, was a benefit to us both."[231]

But this was Hazlitt's bravado. The divorce was in fact much more complicated, very dangerous for Sarah, and infinitely more sordid. They traveled to Edinburgh separately. She got there on 21 April 1822, paid 14s a week for lodgings, plus 2s "firing," and engaged a barrister and solicitor. The latter, John Gray, told her the case would last two months and cost £50.[232] She had to have various documents, her statement properly stamped, and the Oath of Calumny, which was bought from the law stationers, signed and duly witnessed. Hazlitt had put up in a terrible den, which shocked even the hardened Gray. "He told me," Sarah wrote, "that he was never more astonished than on going into No 21 James Street, for that the people he found there was a set of the lowest abandoned blackguards he had ever met with: who told him they would not say a word till he had treated them with Mulled Port: but that when they were half intoxicated he got out of them sufficient for his purpose. That the appearance of the house, people and everything about it was more infamous than anything that he had before any idea existed in Edinburgh at the present day. I said, I was not at all surprised at it, as those were the kind of people he associated with in London."[233] There were holdups and much anxious trouble over her oath. She used the time to walk to Roslin Castle and back, 17 miles; to Glasgow through the Trossachs, going by boat from Newhaven to Stirling, then the rest of the way on foot—170 miles in a week; then went walking in the highlands, another hundred miles or so and, after taking a canal boat to Glasgow, crossed to Ireland for ten days; finally, she walked to Dalkeith to see the duke of Buccleuch's painting collection.

The divorce finally came through on 17 July, and Hazlitt instantly left for London to propose to the other Sarah. When his solicitor Adam Bell, who had arranged everything for Hazlitt in Edinburgh, complained to the ex-wife that Hazlitt had departed without giving him a word of thanks, she replied that giving thanks "was what I never knew him to do for any body."[234] Hazlitt was also inaccurate in saying the divorce was a "benefit" to him. The landlady's daughter turned down his proposal in contempt and shortly afterwards married a young man of her own age. In his fury, Hazlitt threw the statue of Bonaparte on the ground and smashed it to pieces with his foot. Then, a few minutes later, he picked them all up and desperately tried to glue them together. The episode ended in complete disaster for him. He published the *Liber Amoris* in an attempt to exorcise his obsession, carefully concealing everyone's identity. But the enemies his bitter pen had made were soon on his trail. The *Literary Register* revealed all the names, to enable the public to see "what materials go to the composition of these liberal and radical rapscallions who take upon them the airs of philosophers, poets and politicians, disseminators of truth, improvers of taste, reformers of abuses, and ameliorators of mankind, as they call themselves." Sarah Walker and Hazlitt were thus dragged into the open and, worse, a week later *John Bull* published in full a highly embarrassing letter he had written to her. It is fair to say that his reputation, in his lifetime, never recovered.[235]

But at least Hazlitt got his divorce, and later made a second marriage (which also failed). For purposes of comparison, it is worth looking at a man who stuck to the English legal and ecclesiastical system. In January 1823, four months before Hazlitt published his *Liber Amoris,* Elizabeth, wife of a Captain Johnstone, ran away from him for the third time. On this occasion she met Lord Brudenell, heir to the Earl of Cardigan, and went to live with him in a Bond Street hotel. In June 1824 Johnstone brought an action against Brudenell for *crim.con.* damages. Brudenell did not defend it; he instructed his counsel to say that he did not have sexual intercourse with the wife until after she had left her husband. His counsel continued that his client was "a nobleman of the strictest honor, who had insisted that not the slightest reflection was to be made either upon the lady or the plaintiff in this case . . . his client would willingly submit to such damages as the jury might think it proper to award." Counsel referred to Mrs. Johnstone's "great personal charms and distinguished beauty," to Brudenell's "violent and irresistible attachment," and to the fact that he "could not be accused of having recourse to the arts of the seducer." The captain was awarded £1,000. Brudenell then sent him a message offering "to give him satisfaction." The captain told the Second: "Tell Lord Brudenell that he has already given me satisfaction: the satisfaction of having removed the most damned bad-tempered and extravagant bitch in the kingdom." For Brudenell, the end of this action, which had taken a year, was only the first hurdle he had to cross. There followed an ecclesiastical divorce and an Act of Parliament, and the guilty pair were finally able to marry on 26 June 1826, 3½ years after Elizabeth Johnstone had left her husband. Her new marriage also ended in hopeless ruin, and Brudenell, by then Lord Cardigan, went on to lead the Charge of the Light Brigade.

The Johnstone-Brudenell divorce, which was unopposed, gives some idea of the difficulties which faced George IV, when he, too, on ascending the throne, made up his mind to divorce his wife. In his case, there was no desire to remarry, but he could not bear the thought of Caroline enjoying the title and privileges of queen. The couple had lived apart for a quarter of a century, having separated for good almost immediately after the birth of their only child, Princess Charlotte. At first Caroline lived at Blackheath, where her behavior raised eyebrows. She had been brought up by her barrack-room father, his mistress and his coarse wife and had learned the facts of life at a very early age. She loved to shock, to display her ample charms—the portrait painter John Hoppner, RA, thought them "very bad—short—very full-chested— jutting hips"—in flimsy gowns. She also liked to dress up as a man; she was observed dancing with Sir Sidney Smith, the verbose hero of Acre, "he wearing her chemise and bedgown, she dressed in his clothes." Years before, old Horace Walpole had noticed she did not wash often enough.[236] In 1801 there were rumors Caroline was pregnant, followed the next year by her adoption of a son, officially said to be William Austin, son of a docker, but whom she declared privately to be an illegitimate son of Prince Louis-Ferdinand of Prussia. In 1806 the Whig government, then devoted to the Prince of Wales, set up what was known as the "Delicate Investigation." Four cabinet ministers reported that the child was, indeed, adopted, not hers, but that all the same the evidence of reliable witness gave "occasion to very unfavourable inter- pretations." The Tories, strongly opposed to the Prince, dismissed the evidence against her as "unworthy of credit," and Lord Eldon publicly defended the Princess's chastity.[237] But the Tories returned to power, and Whig opinion shifted round completely when the Prince became regent with full powers and failed to put the Whigs in office. From that point they began a systematic assassination of George's character, and the Tory government found themselves defending him. There was a corresponding shift over the Queen. To the Whigs she became an injured woman, to the Tories an adulteress. Thus, George's matrimo- nial problems were compounded and envenomed by something none of his subjects had to contend with—a political dimension.

The legal aspects of George's quarrel with his wife are immensely complicated.[238] There had been no English royal divorce since the reign of Henry VIII, as George I's divorce had taken place under Hanoverian law. If the Princess of Wales committed adultery, she was guilty of high treason under the Act of 1351, as would be her lover or lovers. Brougham, who became her legal adviser from 1811, warned her of this. Wellington related she had once asked him cryptically, "Why are Englishmen so afraid of being hanged?" which he took to be a reference to potential lovers (Canning was often mentioned) fearing to sleep with her.[239] Brougham further warned her (30 July 1814) not to go abroad: "Depend upon it Madam that there are many persons who now begin to see a chance of divorcing Your Royal Highness from the Prince. . . . As long as you live in this country I will answer for it that no plot can succeed against you. But if you are living abroad and surrounded by base spies and tools who will always be planted about you, ready to invent and to swear as they may be directed, who can pretend to say what may happen?"[240] But

Caroline was mortally offended by her exclusion from the peace celebrations and left England in August 1814.

Two months later she had engaged as her courier a former army quartermaster, the handsome, 32-year-old Bartolomeo Bergami. She made him a baron; installed his sister, whom she created Countess Oldi, as her lady-in-waiting; allowed her "court" to be taken over by the Bergami family; and, thus surrounded, made a much-publicized visit to Jerusalem, where she established the Order of Saint Caroline of Jerusalem, with Bergami as its grand master.[241] Englishmen on the grand tour brought back tasty tales of her check bouncing—two checks for £5,000 each which she had tried to cash in Vienna and Naples had both been "returned" by Messrs. Coutts—and her dancing: "a short, very fat elderly woman," wrote a shocked Lady Bessborough, "with an extremely red face (owing I suppose to the heat) in a girl's white frock-looking dress, with shoulder, back and neck quite low (disgustingly so) down to the middle of her stomach); very black hair [it was a wig] and eyebrows, which gave her a fierce look, and a wreath of light pink roses on her head."[242] As for her relations with Bergami, Brougham's brother James, sent out by him to put Caroline's finances in order, reported: "They are to all appearances man and wife, never was anything so obvious. . . . The whole thing is apparent to everyone."[243]

The death of the royal couple's only child, Charlotte, in 1817 removed George's last reason for refraining from exposing his wife's frailties. As king of Hanover, he had already been collecting evidence against her for two years, through Baron Ompteda, envoy to the Vatican, who wormed his way into her confidence. Now the Liverpool government was persuaded to finance a more formal enquiry, known as the Milan Commission, which took evidence from various witnesses, mostly Italian (and mostly unsworn) about Caroline's conduct. All this evidence was put into what was known as "the Green Bag." But the government was not anxious to open it publicly. Ministers did not regard their evidence as conclusive, rightly as it turned out, nor were they and their law officers at all sure what form the litigation should take. A divorce bill, a bill of Attainder, a charge of high treason, a suit in Doctors Commons (the quasi-ecclesiastical court)? All posed what seemed insuperable difficulties. An ordinary parliamentary divorce was not open to George because that could be defended, and the moment Caroline started to present evidence of her husband's infidelities, his case would collapse. What the ministers proposed was to buy Caroline off; they thought £50,000 a year, plus payment of her debts, would do it. So thought Brougham and so, probably, would have thought Caroline herself, if the proposition had ever been put to her unambiguously.

But it never was. There was too much muddle and misunderstanding, too many parties to any negotiations—George; his advisers (often changed and not always agreeing with him); the government, divided among itself; the Whigs; Wilberforce—who stuck his moral oar in—Caroline; Brougham, whom she never trusted; and not least the Radicals, led by the mayor of London, Alderman Wood, who made themselves her champions.

In the end, George effectively ruled out a private financial settlement soon after the death of his father made him king and brought matters to a head. He had an extremely pertinacious conscience, when he could be bothered to consult it. On 30 January 1820, he locked himself up with a collection of Anglican prayer books and worked himself up into a pious rage at the thought that the prayers for the King *and* Queen which their formularies laid down meant that "the wicked woman" would now be prayed for each Sunday in every church in the kingdom. Four days later, Croker rubbed salt into the wound by telling him: "If she is fit to be introduced to the Almighty she is fit to be received by men, and if we are to *pray* for her in church we may surely bow to her at court. The prayer for her will throw a sanctity round her which the good and pious people of this country will never afterwards bear to have withdrawn."[244] Thus mischievously advised, George commanded the cabinet to have Caroline's name taken out of the liturgy, the unspoken threat being that, if they refused, he would turn them out of office.

How seriously the threat ought to be taken, no member of the cabinet could decide. During the early stages of the Queen Caroline Affair, Peterloo was only a few months in the past, and the Six Acts had only just become law; the Cato Street Conspiracy took place, with the trial and execution of the conspirators following in due course. The economy was improving rapidly, but the political atmosphere was still tense. The ministers were not sure that if they left government, the Whigs would be willing or able to come in. How could they, in view of their support for Caroline and their constant abuse of the King, do his bidding in getting his marriage dissolved? But greed for office had never to be underestimated. The Whigs had moved through one 180-degree turn over George and Caroline, why not another? What Liverpool feared was a weak Whig government, which would give way to the Radicals and the mob, and so set in motion that fatal chain of events he had himself witnessed in Paris in 1789. One of the Cato Street gang who turned king's evidence, Hall, said in his deposition that Thistlewood had been to see Hobhouse, Byron's friend and the Radical member of Parliament for Westminster, and asked him if, in the event that

their *putsch* succeeded, he would be willing to become the head of a
provisional government, and that Hobhouse had said yes. Wellington
confided this secret to Mrs. Arbuthnot, who noted in her diary: "The
Duke said he dared say that Thistlewood had made the most of the
story in telling it to his confederates, but he had no doubt of the
interview having taken place and that, whatever Mr Hobhouse had
said, he had no doubt of his inclination to place himself at the head of
a revolutionary government."[245]

On the whole, then, the cabinet thought it less risky to humor the
king up to a point, even at the risk of further unpopularity, because they
could thereby retain control of the forces of order. So, with four or five
of their number opposed, they voted on 12 February to take the Queen's
name out of the liturgy. This ended any realistic hope of a compromise
and made it inevitable that the Queen would return to England to fight
her husband. It also compelled the government in logic to go further
and justify the change in the liturgy by putting some kind of proposition
to Parliament. Two days later, the cabinet sent the King a minute
pointing out that, in an ordinary divorce, the law gave the accused party
what was called "the right of recrimination," so the Queen could
accuse him of adultery, too. "If Your Majesty and the Queen were in
the situation of private individuals," it concluded, "it may be assumed
that a divorce could not possibly be entertained."[246] All the government
could do was to put forward a bill in Parliament which accused the
Queen of conduct unbecoming her title and, while allowing her a
defense to such charges, prevent her from making counteraccusations.
Then Parliament, sitting as judge and jury in its own case, could pronounce sentence, which might include stripping her of her marital
status but would certainly deprive her of her title.

Events between February and June, when the queen actually returned to England, showed how right the government was in hesitating.
By 1820 a government had to cope not just with the law and the King
and Parliament, but with public opinion. Public opinion was the great
new fact of the dawning modern world. And public opinion was changing, not least on the question of sexual morality. In the 1770s Samuel
Johnson had been able to proclaim, amid general agreement—at any
rate among men—that adultery by a husband, though equally wrong in
morals, was socially trivial compared to adultery by a woman, which
represented a threat to the rightful succession of property and title.[247]
The King, by thinking he could proceed against his wife without raising
the issue of his own numerous and flagrant adulteries—he was openly
living with Lady Conyngham at this time—was echoing Johnson's
ruling. But that was now fifty years ago, and it was plainly outmoded.

The relationship between the royal couple had been discussed for two decades, and the public had had plenty of time to reach a settled conclusion—that George bore a heavy responsibility for Caroline's conduct. As old Lady Melbourne put it, marriage at best "must be a lottery"; but for a man it was "better to have a bad wife than no wife—besides it is always a man's fault if his wife is *very* bad." Before her death, George's daughter Charlotte had reached the same conclusion: "My mother was bad," she told Baron Christian Stockmar, the Swedish-German doctor in her husband Leopold's suite, "but she would not have become as bad as she was if my father had not been infinitely worse." Jane Austen had made her mind up in 1813: "Poor woman, I shall support her as long as I can, because she *is* a Woman, and because I hate her Husband . . . if I must give up the Princess, I am resolved at least to think that she would have been respectable, if the Prince had behaved only tolerably by her at first." This became and remained the prevailing view, among men as well as women.

However, what made the Caroline Crisis unique was not the coincidence of views, but the fact that, by the spring of 1820, when it got going in earnest, every man and woman in the country *had* a view. Even children joined in. "At this period," wrote the 14-year-old Elizabeth Barrett, "when the base & servile aristocracy of our beloved country overwhelm with insults our magnanimous and unfortunate Queen"— she was referring to the change in the liturgy—"I cannot restrain my indignation, I cannot control my enthusiasm—my dearest ambition would be to serve her, to serve the glorious Queen of my native isle."[248] For the first time in English history, an issue had arisen in which the entire country became emotionally involved and everyone felt they had a right to an opinion. In its own way it was an important landmark in the road to democracy and a tribute to the new power of the press which made such national participation possible. Letters and diaries of the period often ignore every other salient event, Waterloo and Peterloo included. But it is rare, indeed, to come across any series which has no mention of the Caroline Crisis. "It let loose for a time," Cobbett wrote, "every tongue and pen in England." "It was the only question I have ever known," Hazlitt agreed, "that excited a thorough popular feeling. It struck roots into the heart of the nation; it took possession of every house and cottage in the kingdom." "Since I have been in the world," was Greville's comment, "I never remember any question which so exclusively occupied everybody's attention, and so completely absorbed men's thoughts and engrossed conversation."[249] It was the only issue in decades by which the countryside was as obsessed as London, and parts of England which had remained completely tranquil throughout the distresses of 1815–16 and the agitation of 1819 were now in a ferment.

It is not surprising, that Radicals of every shade, and most of the Whigs, joined in the agitation; tried to take it over; and gave it, as they thought, a political momentum. For a time it looked as though this strategy would pay handsome dividends. The general election, which had to be held at the beginning of a new reign and which the government brought forward before pro-Queen sentiment could influence the results, left the balance in the Commons much the same, in theory, but much less dependable in practice—the country gentlemen in particular were becoming uneasy.[250] The moment of danger came shortly after the Queen returned to England on 6 June, when she was escorted by mobs wherever she went and citizens were forced to "illuminate" whether they liked it or not, not only in London, but in many small towns and even villages. People passing Alderman Wood's house, where the Queen was staying, were pelted if they refused to raise their hats in respect. That was not unusual; more disturbing was the report that noncommissioned officers in many regiments were drinking the Queen's health in their messes. London was full of troops that had been brought into the capital as a precautionary move during the trial and execution of Thistlewood and his gang. They had shown complete steadiness then. Unlike the naval and army mutinies of the 1790s, the armed forces never showed the slightest disposition to disobey orders when putting down political and economic disturbances. But the rallying cry of an injured Queen introduced a quite different factor, calculated to appeal to martial and loyal breasts, reinforced, of course, by pressure from their womenfolk.

Wellington's closest confidante, Mrs. Arbuthnot, noted in her diary on 15 June 1820: "A mutiny in a battalion of the 3rd regiment of Guards. The grounds of their complaint were being too much crowded in their barracks, not having pay enough and too much duty. They were marched off the next morning for Portsmouth [where they could be under cover from heavy naval guns] and at night the mob collected round the King's Mews [now Trafalgar Square] and would not disperse till the Riot Act was read and the Life Guards charged them." Two days later, the rest of the regiment went off to Portsmouth. Wellington "went at 4 o'clock in the morning to see the start. They were very obedient and in perfect order but he said they did not show so much pleasure at the sight of him as they had always done before." The next day, the anniversary of Waterloo, he persuaded the Duke of York to inspect his own regiment, the 1st Guards: "The mob was collected in immense numbers and received the Duke [of York] with the most tumultuous applause [and] expressed loudly their affection for a Prince who was not afraid of shewing himself among them." Ten days later, she recorded Liverpool as saying "that the aversion to the King was rising to the greatest possible height, that the Guards in London were all drinking the Queen's health and had the greatest possible contempt for the King from thinking him a coward." He thought that if needs be the King should "go over to Hanover for a time while the storm here blows over, and have a regency here. We should soon be tranquil here with the Duke of York for our governor."[251]

In fact, by the beginning of July, Wellington had got the army fully under discipline again, and the government decided to go ahead with a measure. Almost at the last minute it fixed on a Pains and Penalties Bill (including an optional divorce clause) which would hear evidence of the Queen's misconduct; allow her to mount a defense, but not to counter-charge the King; and, if passed, strip her of her titles. It was introduced in the Lords to give it a more dignified and safer send-off, Liverpool opening the First Reading himself on 5 July. Essentially, it was a trial of Caroline's adultery with Bergami.[252] The evidence began on 19 August, and for the rest of the summer and well into the autumn, the nation was transfixed by this fascinating event. The following Sunday Wilberforce bought no less than 19 metropolitan newspapers to pore over reports of the week's proceedings. Even ministerial papers printed in full antigovernment documents, such as the Queen's petition. A pro-Queen pamphlet, A Peek at the Peers, sold 100,000 copies at 2d each. According to Cobbett, the Queen's Answer to the King sold 2 million copies in Britain and another half million in the United States. The British Museum has over 500 cartoons on the case which were printed in 1820, plus hundreds of pamphlets and placards.[253]

The trial gave many people who were anxious for a row a respect-able excuse to take to the streets. The troops might be steady, but no one could ask them to fire on a pro-Queen mob. Once a week there was a mass parade that, strictly speaking, was unlawful under the Six Acts. Creevey noted: "Every Wednesday the scene which caused such alarm in Manchester is repeated under the very nose of parliament and all the constituted authorities, and in a tenfold degree more alarming."[254] Mobs gathered daily outside Parliament during the trial, to cheer or hoot the arrival of those cast as heroes or villains in the drama. Once the proceedings began, ministers rather than the King, who kept well hid in his palace, were seen as the Queen's antagonists. Wellington became indignant when Lady Conyngham told him that the King was saying that his ministers were the source of his unpopularity: "Pray explain why I am unpopular? I have been but two years in England, and have certainly done nothing to deserve to lose the popularity I had. I had nothing to do with the Milan Commission and yet I am hunted down to the House of Lords every day and back again, while the Duke of York is as much applauded. What do you suppose is the reason of this? It is because I am thought to be a *King's Man,* and the Duke of York is applauded because, as it's his interest that the divorce should not pass, he is thought to be a *Queen's Man*—and then this is what you call the *Ministers being unpopular.* It is the *King* that is unpopular and we share it with him."[255]

However, the duke could also laugh at his predicament. Asked by the mob to express his loyalty to their heroine, he raised his hat and said: "God save the Queen! and may all your wives be like her!" Earlier disturbances on purely politicoeconomic issues had been ugly, humorless affairs, but the Caroline Crisis soon became richly comic. The first government witness was the Queen's former servant, Teodoro Majocchi. His appearance in the Lords startled her, and she began to run toward him screaming: *"Teodoro!"* His evidence was devastating for her, but he was completely destroyed under cross-examination by Brougham, who got from him (to a question that might have involved him in perjury), the reply: *"No mi ricordo* [I don't remember]." Seizing on this answer, Brougham relentlessly angled his questions to get the same reply 87 times, and *No mi ricordo* became the catchphrase of the day, arousing mirth even among village bumpkins. It was set to music and sung in imitation of a comic Italian tenor.

The government's difficulty was that all its key witnesses were Italians, associated in Londoners' minds with organ-grinding and monkeys. As Eldon put it: "Here they have settled all matters because they say sweepingly Italians are not to be believed." People quoted Nelson's remarks about Italy, from Southey's best-selling life: "A country of fiddlers and poets, whores and scoundrels."[256] The whole of London's vast and ingenious entertainment industry devoted itself to extracting the last ounce of popular enjoyment out of the trial and its procession of monoglot witnesses. At 48 Belvedere Place, Borough Road, a grand exhibition was held of Caroline memorabilia, including an enormous (35′ × 12′) painting by Carloni showing her entering Jerusalem in triumph. Mrs. Arbuthnot, while strongly anti-Queen, could not resist going to look at it. Afterwards, she snorted: "She is sitting *man-fashion* on an ass!"

In some quarters the unpopularity of the Lords caused glee. Sydney Smith dated a letter to Lady Mary Bennet in London, "October 1820, near Manchester," adding "While here I shall study the field of Peterloo." Then he went on: "Will the greater part of the House of Lords be thrown into the Thames? Will short work be made of the bishops?

If you know, tell me—and if you know that the bishops are to be massacred, write by return of post!"[257] As the trial went into its eighth week, familiarity bred—jokes. Lord Eldon took to drawing caricatures and showing them to the other judges, "which made them laugh." The Queen would sneak out to her robing room to play backgammon. All the time the evidence against her was piling up. "All one can say is," Mrs. Arbuthnot noted, "that if the Whig lords do not consider the disgusting details they have heard *proof,* the Whig ladies may in future consider themselves very secure against divorces." Sydney Smith agreed: "I have no more doubt about the Queen's guilt," he wrote to Lady Mary Bennet, "than I have of your goodness and excellence. But do not on that account do me the injustice of supposing that I am deficient in factious feelings and prejudices. . . . I sincerely wish the Queen may be acquitted, and the Bill and its authors thrown out. Whether justice be done to the royal Plaintiff is of no consequence: indeed he has no right to ask for justice on such points." This illogical conclusion—that the Queen was guilty, but should be acquitted—spread across the nation. Mrs. Arbuthnot had to admit that "the whole of the respectable yeomen and gentry of the country" were now "all convinced of her guilt" but "always say, 'But then the King is worse, and if she is bad he made her so.' "[258] This feeling spread to the Lords, with many backwoods Tories siding with the Whigs, who were solid against the bill. It is a significant fact that the growing weight of public opinion was now reflected even in the unreformed Parliament, even in this upper house.

On the Second Reading, the government's majority in the Lords fell to 28. By now, both the King and the cabinet were sure their policy was mistaken, but each was anxious to put the blame on the other and to avoid the responsibility of capitulating. Castlereagh and other ministers in the Commons were particularly anxious to abandon the bill because they were now sure it would not pass there. Brougham was threatening to argue recrimination in the Commons debates—there was no way of stopping him—and had proof that George had married Mrs. Fitzherbert. This might lead to a challenge to his legal right to the throne, with the Whigs, radicals and mob putting the Duke of York at their head, as a kind of Orléanist king, a Philippe Égalité. The idea terrified George and sent shudders through the older ministers. On the Lords Third Reading the government majority dropped to nine, and the cabinet took this as an excuse to drop the bill. The king was said to be "delighted." But Mrs. Arbuthnot reported "a terrible scene" in the cabinet and much recrimination. "Lord Liverpool was in phrenzy. His rage got so high that for a time it stopped all deliberation. He abused the Chancellor. He complained of the ill-usage he had received from several in the room, without particularising them, and ended by crying."[259]

Liverpool was understandably upset because he had not wanted the trial, had been forced into it, and was now left carrying the (dead) baby. But, as people were discovering, once public opinion enters the political process, it often becomes a mysterious and unpredictable business. Ordinary people, without access to society gossip, had been unaware of the more outrageous aspects of the Queen's life until the proceedings opened. They thought her simply an injured woman. As the evidence against her mounted, their conviction that the trial was unfair did not diminish, but they no longer regarded her as a heroine. They wanted the case dropped and the Queen to retire into obscurity. Once both these things happened, public interest in the matter collapsed, almost overnight. The play, as it were, had been running to packed houses for six months, everyone had seen it, and now they wanted something fresh. It suddenly became difficult even in London to keep a mob together. Outside it, the issue was dead. Farington noted that in Hemel Hempstead, for instance, a place with 4,000 inhabitants, only eight houses "illuminated" at the news that the government had dropped the bill, despite the fact that the Whig Earl of Essex had "sent money" to buy candles.[260] Indeed, Radical and Whig efforts to make further political capital out of the queen ran into a wall of public indifference. As Mrs. Arbuthnot's husband, one of the governmental managers, put it, "She is *blasted,* & that is sufficient." Only 18 peers signed protests asserting that adultery had not been proved. Over Christmas Tory members were able to take soundings among their constituents and returned to Westminster early in 1821 in good spirits, convinced that by merely dropping the bill, ministers had set themselves right with public opinion. Thus, by an odd paradox, justice was done and felt to have been done.

Mrs. Arbuthnot noted that when George IV opened Parliament on 23 January, he was "better received than we expected. The crowd was immense, but they were perfectly orderly." Two weeks later, on 8 February, Wellington attended Covent Garden and "was most loudly cheered by the whole house . . . standing up and waving their hats and hankerchiefs for near a quarter of an hour."[261] The anti-Queen faction was now taking heart, led by Theodore Hook's audacious Sunday paper *John Bull,* which began a case-by-case assault on the characters of prominent Whig ladies, and by April 1821 was selling over 9,000 copies a week, "more than any Sunday paper that ever was known." Mrs. Arbuthnot deplored its assault on "the character of woman," but pronounced it "a most ably written paper" and rejoiced to see it going for her bête noire, Lady Jersey, publishing the fact "that she *paints*, which she can't bear to be suspected of." This was an additional reason for Whig ladies to beg their husbands to call off the hunt against George IV, an exercise now regarded as hopeless.

In any case all were preparing for the King's coronation, long delayed but now celebrated with extraordinary splendor in the summer. The coronation brought out record enthusiastic crowds, and when the Queen, who was not invited, tried to gain admittance, she merely made herself look foolish. A few weeks later, on 7 August, the Queen was dead, probably from cancer of the stomach, for which she had doctored herself with "laudanum and nervous medicines." The body had to be moved from Hammersmith to Harwich, to take ship to Germany, for she had asked to be buried in Brunswick, and the hard core of the radical mob insisted it be taken through the West End; there was a mêlée with the Life Guards at Cumberland Gate, Hyde Park, and two men were killed. But that was all. The taste for violent street theater had suddenly disappeared, and it would not reappear for a decade. Liverpool found that he had inadvertently made the right decisions, and his government was now secure for the remainder of his political life. The Radicals, by putting all their eggs in the Queen's basket, had made a fundamental strategic error. The basket had suddenly vanished, taking their eggs with it, and leaving them with nothing. The economy had been recovering throughout 1820, almost unnoticed. By summer 1821 it was booming—the opening of the first modern trade cycle. The nightmare conjured up by Peterloo thus dispersed, the country woke up prosperous, and the Radicals found themselves yesterday's men, rebels without a cause or a following.

The Queen Caroline affair, however, had numerous long-term consequences. For Britain it opened the age of public-opinion politics and, not just in Britain but in the United States and France, too, opened a decade in which newspapers were to become crucial for the first time. It had a profound effect on women as a sex by demonstrating that not even a king could treat a woman's rights as if they were of no consequence. It also served to bring women into the arena of political discussion. The great Whig ladies had, in some cases, talked politics for more than a generation, and even in certain Tory drawing rooms, at least in London, ladies had tête-à-tête discussions of political figures. But that was all. Before 1820s, politics were never raised at dinner parties until the ladies had left the table. Jane Austen, a strict recorder of such conventions, never has her women take part in political chat, and, since for the sake of accuracy she refrained from writing a scene in which a woman was not present, that is why her novels never deal with politics as such. When, in *Northanger Abbey*, Catherine Morland is talking with Henry Tilney and he suddenly switches to politics, "it was an easy step to silence."

That was now changed. Women joined in the Caroline Affair with their tongues and their pens, in the streets and in the libraries, around the dinner tables and in pubs and drawing-rooms. Farington recorded a dinner party in Cowes on 28 August 1820, when the trial was at its height, a gathering of ordinary provincial people at the house of his nephew, a naval captain. Six ladies were present: four pro-Queen. The two anti-Queen ladies kept quiet, not having much of a case to put or not daring to put it; the pro-Queen ladies held the floor, one of them proclaiming that "it would turn out Bergami is a woman." Lower down the social scale, popular agitation sometimes took the form of all-woman marches, demanding the Queen's "rights." This, it seems, was the only phenomenon of the whole business that actually got a laugh from the King, for whom 1820 was a dismal year. It is not surprising that exclusively female agitation proved counterproductive. But on the wider point—the right of women to join in political arguments—1820 was a watershed. The genie was never put back in the bottle.

The 1820s also marked the point at which, almost imperceptibly, women moved into areas of activity hitherto exclusively male. Byron did not like his wife being a mathematical expert. One presumes he would have been still more irritated to see his only legitimate daughter, Ada, not only follow her mother in this respect but grow up to become the valued assistant of Charles Babbage, inventor of the first computer. But if Byron and Coleridge were hostile to learned women, most scientists had no such prejudice. Sir Humphry Davy strongly favored women being encouraged to do anything of which they were capable. He wrote: "The standard of the consideration and importance of females in a society is I believe likewise the standard of civilisation."[262] Charles Lyell, whose geological revolution in the 1820s foreshadowed the still-more-important anthropological revolution of Charles Darwin in the next decade, encouraged women scientists and enthusiastically applauded their work when it was merited. It was a woman, Mary Anning, who discovered the ichthyosaurus in 1823, at what had been Jane Austen's favorite resort, Lyme. "What a leap we have here," Lyell wrote in excitement, "and how many links in the chain will geology have to supply!"[263]

Lyell was also a close friend and supporter of Mary Somerville (nee Fairfax), the first woman scientist of real consequence, at whose house the leading men of science gathered. She was another brilliant Scot, born in 1780, the daughter of Admiral Fairfax, who had been with Wolfe in Quebec and at the Battle of Camperdown. Her mother, from a family of solicitors, was a highly nervous woman, terrified of thunder. During storms, she would take out her hairpins and sit reading the Bible, while the Admiral offered her grog: "Take that, Peg, it will give you courage, for we are going to have a rat-tat-too!" They gave their daughter no encouragement. She got no schooling until the age of ten, and she was eleven before she could read, even badly. But, like Dorothy Wordsworth, she was a passionate and most minute observer of nature. She collected fossils and stones and somehow got hold of a celestial globe. She taught herself Latin, then Greek. She became a highly proficient pianist, playing Mozart, Beethoven, Clementi, and Steibelt, and, like George Sand's mother, she could tune her piano and mend broken strings. She discovered algebra and geometry for herself. When the Admiral heard she had mastered Euclid, he said: "Peg, we must put a stop to this or we shall have Mary in a strait-jacket one of these days. There was ——— who went raving mad about longitude."[264] She got, however, more support from her uncle, the Rev. Dr. Somerville, Minister of Jedburgh, and through him was sent to Alexander Naysmith's school for ladies in Edinburgh—"The cleverest young lady I ever taught was Miss Mary Fairfax," Naysmith recalled. There she became an accomplished painter and she was also a superb needlewoman, making all her own dresses, even ball gowns.

For her first husband, Mary was talked into marrying a friend of her father's, Samuel Greig, who had been seconded to Saint Petersburg to organize the Russian navy and now acted as Russian naval commissioner in London. Greig "possessed in full the prejudice against learned women which was common at the time," but he died when she was only 33, leaving her a well-off widow, with the means to build up a splendid mathematical library. She then married her cousin, William Somerville, an army doctor who had traveled in South Africa and elsewhere and was a good scholar himself. At the time Dr. Somerville's sister wrote to his bride saying she "hoped I would give up my foolish manner of life and studies, and make a respectable and useful wife to her brother." In fact, the doctor, being a scientist, gave her every encouragement. She led a busy life, studying Homer or botany before breakfast while nursing her baby; writing in odd moments; and then, exactly like Jane Austen, pushing her manuscript under the blotting paper when interrupted. She noted: "A man can always command his time under the plea of business, a woman is not allowed any such excuse."

In 1816, however, her husband was made a member of the Army

Medical Board, which meant that they came to London, and during the 1820s Mrs. Somerville made her house in Chelsea the center of the country's scientific-social life, and herself one of the best-known women in the capital. When she published her book, *Physical Geography,* she recorded, "I was preached against by name in York Cathedral"—some churchmen were hanging on grimly to the Old Testament chronology worked out by Bishop Usher—but she also met with powerful encouragement. Brougham might not know how to talk to clever women, but he could see they should no longer be denied entrance to the world of science, and, on behalf of the Society for the Diffusion of Useful Knowledge, he wrote to her husband asking that she write their books on astronomy and Newton's *Principia.* Sir John Herschel was also delighted with the manuscript of her *Mechanics of the Heavens* and became her foremost advocate. In the 1820s and for many decades after, a woman could not hold a professorship, but Mrs. Somerville, by sheer brainpower and personality, had now shown she could win acceptance from her scientific peers.[265]

There is another significant aspect of her achievement. Her ability to reach a high professional standard, not just in her scientific work but in her painting, was another characteristic of the age. In some ways its most notable—and fragile—feature was the unity of vision and purpose still shared by scientists and artists. That is what we must now examine.

SEVEN

Forces, Machines, Visions

On 25 May 1812, while Bonaparte was planning his disastrous Russian campaign, there was a gigantic fire-damp explosion at the Felling Pit near Sunderland. The accident produced a sensation throughout Britain. Fire-damp deaths, caused by the open oil lamps used by the miners igniting inflammable underground gases, were common enough. But this catastrophe cost the lives of 92 men and boys, burned to death, suffocated or crushed by fallen rocks. Coal production in Britain was already by far the largest mining industry in the world, producing the energy to power the first phase of the Industrial Revolution and a rapidly growing export trade which was fueling the spread of steam engines throughout the world. More pits were being opened almost every week, and main shafts were being driven deeper underground. The deeper the workings, the greater the risk of explosions, the smaller the chance of anyone surviving them. Was this one problem to put a fierce brake on the whole industrial age? There was also the piteous human tragedy; a striking sermon preached over the massed coffins of the dead men and boys had a vast congregation in tears and was reprinted all over the country.[1] Colliery owners offered premiums to anyone who could invent a safety lamp. On 1 October 1813, Byron's future father-in-law, Sir Ralph Milbanke, led a number of public-spirited gentlemen in founding a society to promote the invention. Later that year a Sunderland physician, Dr. Clany, produced the first safety lamp. It worked, but it was too heavy and unwieldy for the colliers to carry. The owners again appealed for help, specifically calling on the director of the Royal Institution in Albemarle Street, Humphry Davy, already regarded as Britain's leading scientist. Davy came north and stayed with John Buddle, head engineer of the Wall End Colliery, and the two men went down the pit on 24 August 1815. Davy also went down Morden West, owned by a former pupil, Jack Lambton (later "Radical Jack," Earl of Durham, and one of the architects of modern

Canada). Davy then hurried south to work in his laboratory, his parting words to Buddle: "Do not despair, I think we can do something for you in a very short time."[2]

Six weeks later, the head engineer of the Grand Allies pits, George Stephenson, the greatest engine designer and builder of the age, but almost illiterate, produced another working safety lamp, much smaller and lighter than Clany's. Stephenson had been puzzling over fire-damp for some time because the bigger and more effective the engines he built to pump out the pits, the greater the risk of fire. On 21 October he insisted on testing the lamp personally, taking it underground at Killingworth Colliery, and to the most dangerous part of the mine. John Moody, the under viewer, later testified: "When we came near the Blower it was making so much more gas than usual that I told Mr Stephenson and Mr Wood [the head viewer] that if the lamp should deceive him we should be severely burned, but Mr Stephenson would insist on the trial, which was very much against my desires. So Mr Wood and I went out of the way at a distance, and left Mr Stephenson to himself, but we soon heard that the lamp had answered his expectations with safety. Since then I have been many times with Mr Stephenson and Mr Wood trying out his different lamps."[3] Stephenson worked hard on making his lamp lighter, both down the pits and at his cottage. He discussed the problem with the cleverest tinsmith in Newcastle, over a beer; his son George kept the sketch he made, stained with beer, and showed it to his father's biographer Samuel Smiles. Stephenson knew he had to demonstrate his lamp personally in an area of maximum danger, otherwise the colliers would not use it. He put his final version into action on 30 November 1816.

Meanwhile Davy had been busy. The first version of his lamp was ready by January 1816, when Buddle announced: "We have subdued this monster." Davy also took his invention underground, but his was essentially a scientific rather than an engineering process. His young assistant Michael Faraday later testified: "I was witness in our laboratory to the gradual and beautiful development of the train of thought and the experiments which produced [the lamp]."[4] Davy refused to take out a patent, not wishing to charge a fee to protect men's lives, but he insisted on the maximum publicity, believing that the interests of humanity were best served by the rapid diffusion of an idea once perfected. On 9 November, three weeks before Stephenson's final version was tested, Davy gave a sensational lecture at the Royal Society, "On the Fire-damp of Coal-Mines and on Methods of Lighting the Mine," announcing he had solved the problem.[5]

The competing inventions led to some undignified partisanship.

Davy wrote a foolish letter to Stephenson's supporters, rejecting their claims of priority. They replied that Stephenson's idea had been passed by the colliery doctor, Dr. Burnet, to Buddle, who gave it to Davy. The likelihood is that both men discovered the principle independently. The lamps were the same, except that Stephenson used a perforated plate instead of Davy's wire gauze. Stephenson quickly adopted the Davy gauze as superior, but kept to his glass chimney, which Davy's lamp had scrapped. As a result, the Stephenson, or "Geordie Lamp," was safer. There is no record of one going wrong. On 18 January 1825, on the other hand, a Davy lamp caused an explosion which cost the lives of 24 men and boys. By then, however, Davy had been universally credited with ending the problem. The state awarded him 2,000 pounds. The Tyne & Wear colliery owners presented him with a massive set of plate at the Queen's Head, Newcastle, on 13 September 1817, "Jack" Lambton in the chair. The Royal Society awarded him the Rumford Medal. The Regent made him a baronet. Alexander I, anxious to get in on any "progressive" act, sent him a huge silver vase, with the god of fire weeping over his extinguished torch. All Stephenson got was a purse of 100 guineas. It was not a question of class. Stephenson's backer, the Grand Alliance, was run by many grandees, and they were so annoyed by the honors paid to Davy that, two weeks after the Queen's Head dinner, they gave Stephenson an even bigger one, at the Newcastle Assembly Rooms, presenting him with a silver tankard and £1,000 raised by public subscription. Stephenson himself modestly gave priority to Clany. But it was no use. Davy remained the inventor of the safety lamp in the public's mind. He had won the publicity battle, and that, increasingly, was what mattered in the world.[6]

In the years after Waterloo, scientific invention was of passionate interest to a rapidly expanding British and international public. That was the most important new factor. But it was still possible for a moderately well-educated man or even woman—a manual on chemistry was specifically written to appeal to ladies—to grasp the latest scientific developments. Indeed, an empiric engineer like Stephenson, who had no schooling, worked at the frontiers of technology alongside scientists like Davy. Physics and chemistry, science and engineering, literature and philosophy, art and industrial design, theory and practice—all constituted a continuum of knowledge and skill, within which men roamed freely. The notion of separate, compartmentalized "disciplines," later imposed by universities, did not yet exist. Indeed, except in Germany and Scotland, where the modern university was just beginning to emerge, universities did not engage in the promotion of discovery. Oxford and Cambridge played virtually no role in the Industrial Revolution. Degrees, certificates, qualifications, all the apparatus of academic trade unionism, were still of little consequence, except in medicine, where they formed barriers to progress. Elsewhere, men sprang from nowhere to take the lead. A privileged elite might rule in Westminster, but advanced knowledge was a democracy. The opportunities for clever young men were enormous, especially in Britain— one reason why the dynamic of change was so powerful there.

Humphry Davy was born in December 1778, four years after William Wordsworth, six years after Samuel Taylor Coleridge. They were very much of the same generation and world. His father was a Cornish craftsman, a woodcarver and gilder, who specialized in picture frames and fireplaces (the Victoria and Albert Museum has one of his). Davy spent some time at Truro Grammar School, but his notebooks show he was largely self-educated, and he left at 16 (when his father died) to be apprenticed to a Penzance surgeon. The Cornish world in which he grew up was a world of poetry: Davy loved the weird beauty of the Marazion Marshes and Mounts Bay, and wrote countless descriptive poems, four of which were later published in Robert Southey's 1799 anthology. It was also, being mining country, a world of the new engines: five of Watts's steam engines had been installed the year Davy was born, and Watts himself came down to supervise them. Watts's son Gregory, who suffered from tuberculosis, lodged in the Davy house. Gregory had studied chemistry and geology in Edinburgh. He and young Davy went on rock-gathering expeditions together, a practice later ridiculed by Charles Dickens, but the commonest way, in those days, in which clever young people came to science. Before his early death, Gregory Watts taught Davy all he knew.[7] Davy was also befriended by a local member of Parliament, the polymath Davies Giddy Gilbert, who did all the theoretical mathematical calculations and paperwork for the great Cornish empiric engineer Richard Trevethick, whose inventions rivaled the Stephensons.' Through his medical work, Davy had become a passionate chemist. Gilbert gave him the run of his library and got him access to a laboratory. He introduced him to Dr. Thomas Beddoes, down in Cornwall on a geological expedition, who had just set up the paramedical Pneumatic Institution in Clifton and who now asked Davy to join him as his assistant there.

This was the Clifton described by Jane Austen in *Emma,* where Mrs. Eldon had lived with her married sister at Maple Grove and drove about in a barouche-landau. Beddoes hoped to make it into a spa as famous as Brighton and set up his institute to explore the use of "factitious airs" or gases in medical treatment. There was much experimenting there with opium and its derivative, "laughing gas" and other protoanaesthetics; indeed, Beddoes was the pivotal figure in a circle of drug addiction, of which more later. For Davy it was a matchless opportunity—typical of the way in which outstanding young men were given their chances in those days—for Beddoes not only arranged for him to give public lectures on chemistry but allowed him to design and run the new treatment center. Davy wrote to his mother: "[He] has given up to me the whole of the business of the Pneumatic Hospital."[8] Beddoes's wife was the younger sister of Maria Edgeworth, whose bestseller *Castle Rackrent* was published two years after Davy wrote this letter. The Beddoes home was a center of learning, literature, and the arts, where Davy met scientists like Erasmus Darwin, grandfather of Charles—the man who, above all others, propagated the new notion of "progress"—and poets like Southey, Wordsworth and Coleridge.

The conjunction of minds was important. In the early 1790s, the three poets had looked to politics to produce progress and to France as the arena where the great experiment to transform humanity was taking place. Wordsworth had been disillusioned by the time he returned from France; Southey soon followed. Both had abandoned their utopianism by the early 1800s and with it their optimism about the redemption and improvement of society, though they continued to believe that education—especially the mass education of the poor—would accomplish something. But there are, as Coleridge saw, two kinds of utopia, the political and the scientific. By 1800 he recognized that the political utopia would not work—would produce horrors, indeed—but he was toying with the idea of science effecting, by its advances, a complete transformation of the material existence of humanity. Davy seized on this notion and it became his creed. Science was to become the great redemptive force! And, within science, chemistry was to become the chief instrument whereby human misery would be reduced and new marvels created. At Clifton he found striking examples of the powers of chemistry. There was his new friend Thomas Wedgwood, son of the great potter Josiah, who was experimenting with silver nitrate to reproduce visual images and contributed the first essay on photography to the *Journal* of the new Royal Institute. Still more impressive was his own experimentation with laughing gas to kill the pain which forced surgeons like Cooper to operate at lightning speed so their patients, like poor George Wyndham, MP, did not die from its aftereffects. Davy noted: "As nitrous oxide in its externive operation appears capable of destroying physical pain, it may probably be used with advantage during surgical operations in which no great effusion of blood takes place."[9]

Davy's aim was to gather together all these heterogeneous experiments in a unifying theory of chemical action like Newton's laws of motion and to use chemistry to turn medicine into an exact science, instead of an empirical one. He wrote in his first important essay: "Thus would chemistry in connection with the laws of life become the most sublime and important of all sciences."[10] Davy's aim was to be fully realized only after 1945, following Alexander Fleming's discovery of penicillin. But in the meantime he pushed chemistry to the forefront of public attention. In 1801, the panjandrums of the Royal Institute, Sir Joseph Banks, President of the Royal Society, the international inventor Count Rumford—who had invented the first modern fireplace and much else and Henry Cavendish, who had recently discovered how to measure the density of the Earth, invited Davy to come to London to run the Royal Institute laboratory.[11]

Davy's acceptance marks the beginning of the modern scientific era in England. He not only turned the laboratory into the first scientific research institute, but developed extraordinary presentational skills which made him the best lecturer in Europe. He was a chemist by preference, but he ranged over the whole of science and technology. He had immense respect for the skills of craftsmen and studied their methods whenever opportunity offered. In 1797 Wordsworth and Coleridge had created English romantic poetry in the Somerset village of Nether Stowey, where Coleridge was living under the patronage of the local tanner (and literary enthusiast) Tom Poole. Coleridge had brought Davy down there. Davy had gone over Poole's tannery and had been instantly able to deduce and explain the scientific basis for what Poole was doing with his inherited skills. Poole said Davy's mind worked so fast it appeared to be intuition, though it was, in fact, reasoning. When Davy went to London, his first course of lectures, in the early winter of 1801, was on the chemistry of tanning and similar crafts. Then, from January 1802, came his "Introductory Chemistry" course. Its success was sensational. More than 300 people attended, including many society ladies who sent Davy sonnets and love tokens; dukes became 50-guinea subscribers. Davy was a small man, but he had brilliant eyes which fascinated people—"the finest eyes I have ever seen," wrote J. G. Lockhart, the biographer—and his soft, West Country voice enhanced the mesmeric affect. Lecturing was just then coming into fashion as the outstanding "serious" metropolitan entertainment—Tom Paine always referred to God as "the Great Lecturer"—and Davy was its first undoubted star. Davy kept his preeminence by the range of his successive courses. He gave lectures on minerology, on geology, on the applications of chemistry to agriculture—this last brought him invitations to leading country houses and an introduction to the Antigua heiress Jane Kerr of Kelso, whom he married. His Bakerian Lecture of 1806, "On Some Chemical Agencies of Electricity," showing how to make use of the new pile, or battery, invented by Alessandro Volta (1745–1827) in 1800, brought him the acclaim of the international scientific community, and the next year, using his own new techniques, he was able to isolate and name potassium and sodium.

Davy illustrated his lectures with spectacularly colorful and, if possible, fiery experiments, as near as possible to fireworks—it was the poet in him—and his "soda experiment" was particularly successful: He recorded that "the globules flew with great velocity through the air in a state of vivid combustion, producing a beautiful effect of continued jets of fire."[12] It was Davy's ability to make scientific advance visible and exciting which was part of his enormous appeal, particularly to artists. Coleridge promised Davy he would take up chemistry—"attack it like a shark" was his phrase—and when Davy published his *Elements of Chemical Philosophy* (1812), one of its earliest and most enthusiastic readers was the young Percy Bysshe Shelley.

Even before he got his hands on Davy's calm and masterly introduction to the enormous potential of science, Shelley had been fascinated by what it could do for mankind, though his notions were mixed up with gnosticism and Gothic horror-romance. We have already noted his interest in air travel. Electricity was another passion of his. In 1808, while a schoolboy in Dr. Bethel's house at Eton, he had electrified the doctor, who put his hand on a doorknob Shelley had connected to a Voltaic pile. He also blew up a tree stump with gunpowder he had made, and the doctor claimed he found him sitting in an alarming blue circle of spirit-flame trying to conjure up the devil. At all events, the doctor banned his entire chemical library. It was the same at Oxford, where Shelley connected himself to an electrical battery charged by turning a handle rapidly and made his hair stand on end, and he told his friend Hogg he was building an "enormous" electrical kit, "or rather combination of kits, that would draw down from the sky an immense volume of electricity, the whole ammunition of a mighty thunderstorm, and this being directed to some point would there produce the most stupendous results."[13] It was Shelley's noisy, smelly and dangerous experiments in his rooms at University College, almost as much as his public avowal of atheism, which led to his expulsion. There was more trouble in the Lake District, where he stayed under Southey's aegis. He did not, like William Hazlitt, try to seduce the local maidens—he already had a small harem of his own—but his hydrogen experiments alarmed the neighbors. One complained: "The country talks very strangely of your proceedings. Odd things have been seen at night near your dwelling."[14] Shelley still believed in political utopianism, but he reinforced it with the scientific variety of Davy. He had been studying Sir William Herschel's work on astronomy—he was the first poet to appreciate its importance—as well as Davy's chemistry book, and shortly after he bought the latter he wrote *Queen Mab* (1813). This remarkable if crude early masterpiece became a cult text among radicals for its extreme political views, but it is also striking for its scientific passages on the evolution of stars and suns, the image of the chariot in a fiery firmament which reveals the concept of electricity as a force. He believed science would replace religion: The unalterable laws of Newton and Davy would be substituted for the whims of a tyrannical Deity. Like Coleridge, he had a strong grasp of scientific principles and could set them down skillfully in verse. In Acts III–IV of *Prometheus Unbound*, in which he presents the Promethean Fire of antiquity in its modern form of electricity, he describes electrons in the atomic structure of matter:

> *A sphere, which is as many thousand spheres,*
> *Solid as crystal, yet through all its mass*
> *Flow, as through empty space, music and light;*
> *Ten thousand orbs involving and involved,*
> *Purple and azure, white and green, and golden,*
> *Upon a thousand sightless axles spinning.*

Shelley seems to have been pursuing a similar line to Immanuel Kant: that matter is fundamentally immaterial, the forces of electricity, magnetism and light forming a dynamic system akin to thought, with matter being no more than force in a state of rest.[15] Once man had mastered the force system, he could turn it to use to transform the prospects of mankind for the better. Like Lenin a hundred years later, he put his faith in electricity, which would give man dominion over nature. Hence, near the end of *Prometheus Unbound* comes the song of the earth:

> *The lightning is his slave; heaven's utmost deep*
> *Gives up her stars, and like a flock of sheep*
> *They pass before his eyes, are numbered, and roll on!*
> *The tempest is his steed, he strides the air;*
> *And the abyss shouts from her depths laid bare,*
> *Heaven, hast thou secrets? Man unveils me; I have none.*

Shelley would frequently set his little communes of women to work sewing together squares of silk to make balloons, which he would inflate with fiery wicks generating hot air, attach to them messages announcing political rights and the wonders of scientific progress and launch them to teach mankind. Thus, he sent his balloons across the Bristol Channel into south Wales in 1812, and in August 1816 he sent another fire balloon across the Lake of Geneva to astound and edify the burghers of Calvin's city.[16] That same summer, by the shores of the lake, he persuaded the 18-year-old Mary Wollstonecraft to write her tragic romance *Frankenstein,* the tale of a creature reborn by electricity, in which gothic horror, utopian idealism and science fiction combine.

Shelley was not the only gifted young man to see an electrified future at this time. Michael Faraday (1791–1867), one year older than Shelley, brought it appreciably closer. He was born poor, the son of a Yorkshire blacksmith and a Sussex farmer's daughter, both members of the Sandemanian sect, which banned swearing and many other things but taught self-improvement. He had no education other than a few years at a school for the poor, but as a bookbinder's apprentice, he read the works he bound, and they included Mrs. Janet Mercer's *Conversations in Chemistry More Especially for the Female Sex*. This was a revelation to him, and he longed for the chance to repeat the experiments it described: "Time, Sir, is all I require," he wrote to a friend, "and for time I will cry out most heartily. Oh! that I could purchase at a cheap rate some of our modern gent's spare hours!" He wrote to Sir Joseph Banks for help in pursuing scientific studies, but got no reply. But his brother, who followed their father in the forge, paid a shilling a week out of his wages for Faraday to attend lectures in natural philosophy in Fleet Street, and Faraday was given tickets for Davy's last set of lectures at the Royal Institute in 1812. He had been taught drawing by a French refugee, and his superbly illustrated notes of this series are in the institute's library. He was one of many scientists of this epoch who might, like Alexander Naysmith, have become a professional artist, and his ability to visualize his concepts and set them down in diagram form was an important factor in his genius. He bound his lecture notes and sent them to Davy, begging for a chance. Davy had been working for the government, testing experimental high explosives for siege works, and had injured the cornea of his eye. While waiting for it to heal, he needed a secretary, and sent for Faraday (1813). So at 22, "Mike," as he was known, became assistant to the greatest scientist in Britain, another example of the tremendous opportunities that able and forceful young men could grab for themselves.

Just after taking Faraday on, Davy got permission from Bonaparte, despite the war, to travel through Europe for scientific purposes. He took with him his wife, her maid Jane and Faraday as assistant valet. "Mike's" passport described him as having "a round chin, a brown beard, a large mouth and a great nose"; he kept it, along with an elaborate diary which provides a detailed account of their two-year journey.[17] In Paris, Joseph-Louis Gay-Lussac (1778–1850), who was Davy's exact contemporary and called by him "the head of the living chemists of France," introduced them to all the leading scientists. André-Marie Ampère (1775–1836), the French authority on electricity—Faraday was overwhelmed to meet him—gave Davy for analysis a piece of violet-colored substance found by the saltpeter manufacturer Courtois. Davy analyzed it in the portable laboratory he set up in the Hotel des Princes in the Rue de Richelieu and called it iodine; it soon became, after opium, the most useful item in the medical pharmacopoeia.[18] Davy was elected a corresponding member of the Imperial Institute, then set off with his party across the Alps. He treated the Tyrolese patriot Speckbacker for rheumatism and in gratitude was given the gun with which he killed 30 Bavarians in a day—Davy passed it on to Sir Walter Scott, who was delighted and hung it at Abbotsford. Peace broke out on their journey. In Rome they saw Pius VII return in triumph, his ceremonial litter borne by all the artists of the city, led by Antonio Canova. They ascended Vesuvius, making measurements and experiments, and in Pavia they met Volta, whom Faraday pronounced "the greatest living scientist."

Once back in London, Faraday helped Davy design the safety lamp in winter 1815–16. The next spring he gave his first lecture-course at the City Philosophical Society and published his first paper, an analysis of caustic lime. Faraday had none of Davy's lightning-flash brilliance of thought, and he was handicapped by an inadequate knowledge of mathematics, which meant that he could not always follow series of equations worked out by other scientists. But in some ways he was a better scientist than Davy. He was a much harder worker. After 1820, when he succeeded Banks as President of the Royal Society, Davy became something of a scientific diplomat, leaving the drudgery to others. He negotiated to bring government and science closer together. He tried to persuade George IV to found a Royal Newton College of Science. His idea was to gather together the Royal Observatory, the British Museum for Natural History, and the Royal Society into the kind of institution foreshadowed in Bacon's great tract, the *New Atlantis*, the whole financed by governmental money. He persuaded the Athenaeum to admit scientists. He helped Stamford Raffles found the zoo. He spent much of his time traveling, in the wake of his rich wife, tinkering with problems, like the gentleman-scientists of the 18th century. He tried to unroll the papyri found at Herculaneum and analyzed the waters of the baths at Lucca. In Ravenna he met Lord Byron and his mistress, the Countess Guiccioli. When Byron explained to her that Davy was the most famous scientist in the world and could do anything, she said, "Oh, then, *caro mio,* do pray beg him to give me something to dye my eyebrows black."[19] Lady Davy did not help his reputation. Miss Martineau called him "a martyr to matrimony." Faraday complained on their tour that she chattered incessantly; he said he was relieved that a storm in the Gulf of Genoa was so serious that, for a time, "Lady Davy was too terrified to talk." Henry Edward Fox noted in December 1820: "Lady Davy was so anxious and fidgety that she could hardly sit still or find time to scold Sir Humphry."[20]

By contrast, Faraday was indifferent to social life and avoided science power-politics, though as a lecturer he was as big a showman as Davy. His powers of work were formidable. Between 1815 and 1820 he systematically mastered virtually the whole of the science of the day. Three volumes in the Wellcome Medical Historical Library, for instance, consist of W. T. Brande's *Manual of Chemistry,* torn apart and interleaved with blank quarto pages on which Faraday put down bibliographical references and other notes. Faraday seems to have read every single publication in French and English which dealt with chemistry. He insisted on repeating others' experiments, writing at the end of his life: "I was never able to make a fact my own without seeing it. . . . If Grove, or Wheatstone, or Gassiot, or any other told me a new fact and wanted my opinion, either of its value or the cause, or the evidence it could give in any subject, I never could say anything until I had seen the fact."[21]

Faraday's thoroughness was to make him the most effective pioneer in the emerging science of electrical physics. The background is worth exploring because it illustrates the interplay between philosophy, literature and science at the birth of the modern world. The 18th century had failed to solve the problem of how heat, light, magnetism and electrical power fitted into the laws of motion and attraction Isaac Newton had set out in his *Principia* (1687). But Immanuel Kant, in his *Critique of Pure Reason* (1781) and still more in his *Metaphysical Foundations of Natural Science* (1786), had produced an inspirational insight. He was concerned not so much with science as with God. Was there a duality, of spirit and matter? Newton had been concerned only with matter— and with the advance of science, this pointed to a materialistic world and led to atheism. Kant wanted to bridge the gulf between spirit and matter and harmonize the physical and moral laws. As he saw it, space

THE BIRTH OF THE MODERN

and time were purely mental intuitions which made our grasp of external reality possible. The substance of thing-in-itself, *Ding an sich,* was hidden from human reason—reality was perceived, rather than led an independent existence. We perceive reality only through the forces, of attraction and repulsion, which work in space. Hence Kant dismissed the dualism of spirit and matter, replacing it by forces. The universe consisted, then, not of matter but of forces. Electricity, magnetism or any other observable effects were governed by laws of attraction and repulsion within a unified theory of forces, all of which were convertible into one another.

It is doubtful if the physical scientists could have proceeded as fast as they did in the early 19th century without this essentially metaphysical intuition. As early as 1798, Johann Wilhelm Ritter, having absorbed Kant—no easy matter, then as now—produced a unified electrochemical theory. The same year, Coleridge was in Germany and brought Kant's transcendental idealism back to England for his friends like Davy to digest. He argued that it was possible to create a universal science in which both matter and God were explicable: "For since impenetrability is intelligible only as a mode of resistance, its admission places the essence of *matter* in an act or power, which it possesses in common with *spirit;* and body and spirit are no longer absolutely heterogeneous but *may* without any *absurdity* be supposed to be different modes, or degrees in perfection, of a common substratum."[22] Both in his writings, and still more in his tremendous conversational monologues, which transfixed almost everyone who listened to them, Coleridge explored the Kantian insight: "The universe was a cosmic web," as he put it, "woven by God and held together by the crossed strands of attractive and repulsive forces." All forms of energy must be convertible; they were also indestructible. "What," he wrote to Tom Poole, "what if the vital force which I sent from my arm into the stone as I flung it in the air and skimmed it upon the water—what if even that did not perish?" Coleridge had thus stumbled upon what was to become the Principle of the Conservation of Energy.[23]

It was one of the great merits of both Davy and Faraday that they were prepared to read and listen to the poets. Indeed, one of the younger scientists, Charles Babbage, thought Davy might have become a great poet, had he persevered. They were also flexible in their ideas. Davy was always skeptical about his theories and conclusions: "Consistency in opinion," he noted, "is the slow poison of intellectual life, the destroyer of its vividness and energy."[24] Faraday was a skeptical man, too, slow to reach any conclusion until the evidence had been carefully verified and was overwhelming, always ready to look for phenomena which contradicted a hypothesis of his, and to drop it without complaint when it was refuted, constantly aware of error in any general statement. But he also believed in the utility of error, repeatedly quoting Bacon: "Truth is more likely to arise from error than from confusion." In 1819 he warned, in a lecture to the Philosophical Society: "The man who is certain he is right is almost sure to be wrong; and he has the additional misfortune of inevitably remaining so. All theories are fixed upon uncertain data, and all of them want alteration and support." By the time Faraday spoke these words, he was a mature scientist, and in intellectual terms approaching a complete one, perhaps the first complete scientist the world had known. But the process whereby he turned electricity into a practical force at man's disposal was assisted by a collective, international effort.

Volta's discovery that the source of electric power was contact between two metals in a solution enabled him to build his pile in 1800. The Royal Society acquired one the same year. Batteries of considerable size were built. Their importance was that they allowed scientists like Davy to conduct experiments; he used the Royal Institute battery to isolate sodium, strontium, magnesium, barium, and potassium, for instance, and he discovered the principle of the arc lamp as early as 1802, though it was of little use until electricity became cheap. The next stage was to put to the practical test the quasi-metaphysical concept of Kant and Coleridge that the world was governed by forces which were fundamentally indivisible and indestructible, based upon the principle of attraction and repulsion, of which electricity and magnetism were expressions. The Danish scientist Hans-Christian Ørsted had been working on Kant's notions for 20 years, and by winter 1819–20, he was able to describe the workings of electromagnetism, or the magnetic field. In July 1820, while London was transfixed by the Caroline Affair, he sent out a four-page announcement in Latin to leading European scientists, which rightly caused a sensation. Using it, Ampère was able to write his *Memorandum on the Theory of Electrodynamic Phenomena Deduced Solely from Experiment, Setting Out the Laws of Electrical Action* (1820–21), the work that won him the label, "the Newton of Electricity." Davy, assisted by Faraday and William Hyde Wollaston, began examining the implications of Ørsted's work from 1 October 1820. In the months that followed, Faraday began to write an account of this new branch of science, electromagnetism; to do so, he repeated, in his dogged way, all the previous experiments, and so discovered anomalies in Ampère's explanation of Ørsted's discovery. Being no mathematician, he could not follow Ampère's equations, but he knew they were wrong because his own experiments conflicted with what

Ampère was arguing. Ampère insisted mathematics could not lie and that if experiments did not correspond with his equations, it was because they were badly done. Faraday insisted on the paramountcy of experimental verification—the principle so courageously upheld by Albert Einstein over his General Theory of Relativity in 1915–18—and he knew his experiments were thorough and valid. How to explain the anomalies then? To do so, he devised an experiment involving a magnet in a basin of mercury, a wire, and a galvanic circuit. By thus surrounding a magnetic force by a current-carrying wire, he developed rotatory power; in effect, he had created the first electric motor. Faraday was slow to reach a conclusion, but once he was certain of it, he had a motto: "Work, Finish, Publish." Unable to consult Wollaston, who was on vacation, he announced what he had found in the October 1821 issue of the *Quarterly Journal of Science*. Two years later he wrote: "I have regretted ever since that I did not delay the publication, that I might have shown it first to Dr Wollaston."[25] Wollaston, who was furious, accused Faraday of stealing his ideas. Davy, who was beginning to be jealous, backed Wollaston and tried to prevent Faraday's election to the Royal Society—ineffectually, since he was duly elected in 1824.

Faraday was shaken by this row, but he pressed conscientiously forward. His work at the Royal Institution, however, did not permit him to work exclusively on electromagnetism. To retain the institution's support, the public had to be kept amused. One way Faraday did so was to pursue the analogy between sound, light and electricity. In 1828, lecturing on resonance, he illustrated it "by some striking experiments" using "many curious instruments of music from Java, for the loan of which the Institution was indebted to Lady Raffles," and by "some very novel and curious musical performances on the Jew's harp by Mr Eulenstein."[26] The next year he delighted his audience by producing a Mr. Mannin, who could whistle two notes at the same time. But Faraday was determined to master the problems of electromagnetism, always devising new experiments and apparatus—his background at the forge was important in this respect—and following the work of others in a wide range of foreign publications. He noted that in Albany, New York, Joseph Henry had created a new range of powerful electromagnets and that Moll of Utrecht had discovered that if you rapidly interchange the leads to the electromagnet, you achieve a reverse of polarity. Finally, in August 1831 he devised an iron ring, coiled round with copper wire, which allowed him to master the principles of electromagnetic induction. He now had not only the first electric motor, but, in essence, the first dynamo: He could generate power.

Faraday was merely at the beginning of his dramatic series of experiments in electricity, which he conducted for the next 30 years. But what was remarkable about his work between 1820 and 1831 was that by showing exactly how mechanical could be transformed into electrical power, he made the jump between theoretical research and its practical application a comparatively narrow one. The electrical industry was the direct result of his work, and its first product, the electric telegraph, was soon in use. This idea of cause and effect was of great importance, for both industry and governments now began to appreciate the value of fundamental research and to finance it. But it was transcendental in itself. Man progresses by finding successive power substitutes for his own puny muscles. The late-medieval, early-modern period had been enriched by the rapid spread of mills worked by sails and river wheels. From 1750 the age of wind and waterpower began to yield to the age of steam power. By the 1820s it was demonstrating its colossal impact and still greater potential; but already Faraday's work was adumbrating the age of electrical power, and with it the 20th century. Here, then, we have one of the foundation stones of modernity, put in place as a direct result of systematic scientific research—the first clear demonstration of the central relevance of scientific research to material progress. The episode also demonstrated the emergence of an international scientific community, circulating its ideas rapidly and so making possible a collective effort—in this case by men of six different nations, Italy, Denmark, France, the United States, the Low Countries and England. It demonstrated the less-welcome concomitant, too: Competitive jealousies in the fierce quest for the fame of discovery. This competitiveness was also new.

The intuitive physics of Kant and Coleridge foreshadowed electromagnetic theory, but they did not explain the nature of matter, on which the forces played. Kant, indeed, by positing immaterialism, actually pointed in the wrong direction. Coleridge at least was moving in the right one, taking Davy with him. He rejected the prevailing notion of an imponderable fluid, often called phlogistron: It was "a vulgar idea like that of the peasant, everything done by a spring; so everything must be done by a fluid." A more likely explanation, in Coleridge's view, was that "all *power* & vital attributes" depended on "modes of arrangement." Davy, thus prompted, put it in more "scientific" terms: "forms of natural bodies may depend upon different arrangements of the same particles of matter."[27] This foreshadowing of atomic theory is a striking demonstration of the importance of imagination in forming scientific hypothesis: Coleridge and Shelley could see possibilities in nature with the intuition of poets and so open the eyes of the experimental scientists. The early 19th century was a great age of science precisely because it was also a great age of poetry.

Coleridge, indeed, thought himself a natural philosopher, as much as a poet; that is, he deduced general principles by looking imaginatively at the visible world. He thought Wordsworth, by early training and habitual study outdoors, greatly his superior in this respect, and Wordsworth's sister Dorothy even better. After their first meeting, he noted "her eye watchful in minutest observation of nature"; if Dorothy had been a man, she might have made an ever finer poet than her brother or, more likely, a great scientist.[28] Those who are born and live in the mountains look carefully at nature, especially the weather, which changes from minute to minute and influences all else, including their lives. Such ingrained habits, combined with huge, inborn intelligence, may lead to science or poetry.

An outstanding example was Wordsworth's near-contemporary and neighbor John Dalton (1766–1844), born near the poet's Cockermouth, in the village of Eaglesfield, and educated at its tiny school. His father was a local statesman or sheep farmer. No one watches the weather more closely than do mountain shepherds and their boys, and Dalton, who seems to have had exceptional eyesight, began observing cloud formations when he was small. From age 12, he ran his own school. He was almost entirely self-taught, winning bets in candles to carry on his night studies. Thus, he absorbed mathematics, physics and chemistry, stressing to his pupils that they could do the same—"Yan might do it!" The only real teaching he had himself was from a blind man in Kendal.[29] From 1793 he was mathematics tutor at the New College, Manchester, where he remained for 30 years, living in a bed-sitting room and taking pupils at half a crown an hour, or 1s6d if there were two. Dalton was a Quaker and wore the Quaker dress, though he did not "thee" and "thou"; he went twice to church on Sunday, never dining out that day. He fell in love with another Quaker, Nancy, who was engaged to someone else, and anyway died young. So he remained a bachelor, and his first task each day was to light his laboratory fire. Dalton began work on chemistry in 1796 but remained an all-rounder: In 1801 he published *Elements of English Grammar*, which occasionally showed the failings of the autodidact—he thought "phenomenal" was the feminine of "phenomena." But by 1803 his chemistry papers had made his name well known in Europe, and Davy invited him to lecture at the Royal Institution. They did not get on. Dalton smoked a huge pipe, not done in those days by those aspiring to gentleman status. He said of Davy: "His principal failing as a philosopher is that he does not smoke." Davy was put off by Dalton's odd voice, gruff manners, strong accent, water drinking, and poor lecture style and the fact that his experiments often did not work. Davy's son called him "repulsive," his "voice harsh and brawling," his manner "dry and almost crabbed."

The fact is, Dalton was an outdoor scientist. He hated books and rarely read them; he said they contained too many errors. He trusted his own observations and the experiments he devised for himself. He was a tall, bony man with a typical statesman's stride, able to climb mountains effortlessly all day. From the time he was a boy, he kept a meteorological diary, and much of his work was done at high altitude. Over long years he studied cloud formations for hours at a time, remarking at the end of his life that "there was no such thing as genius, and if he had accomplished anything which the world considered valuable, it had been done by persevering industry directed to a single practicable object." His major discovery, he said, was made "when still young, before he had undertaken the special study of chemistry."[30]

By looking hard at Lake District weather, Dalton perceived the unity of matter; cloud, mist, rain, stream and torrent, and lake and sea and river were all one, changing their forms and positions as a result of continuous but minute variations in atmospheric pressure. Meditation on this, on the constitution of homogenous and mixed elastic fluids, led him step by step to form in his mind a distinct picture of self-repellent particles and thus, to the atomic constitution of matter. The next stage was the notion of atomic weights and multiple proportion—Dalton had a passion for exact numerical determinations, and his theory, as it evolved, brought chemistry into the category of the exact sciences. His theory was more or less complete by the time he published his *New System of Chemical Philosophy* in May 1808. Of course, it was defective in detail, but the intuitive insight, derived from direct observation of mountain weather, was what mattered; it was a classic example of a fundamental scientific discovery springing from an imaginative hypothesis. His atomic theory was subsequently confirmed, over the next generation, by observations and experiments all over Europe.

Recognition in England was slow, but it came. In 1832, Oxford University, just dimly beginning to grasp the importance of science, made him an honorary doctor of laws. Two years later, Babbage and Henry Brougham had him presented at Court. As a Quaker he could not wear a sword, so he refused to put on court dress. Instead he wore his Oxford gown, being persuaded—he was now color blind—that its forbidden scarlet was mud color. William IV thought he was a provincial mayor come to be knighted. The bishops at the levée were shocked, not by the fact that Dalton was a scientist—that did not interest them—but because he was a Quaker.[31]

Being an outdoor scientist, Dalton was not content with theory. His October 1820 paper, "Memoir on Oil, and the Gases obtained from it by Heat," read at Manchester College, laid the foundations of the modern oil and petrochemical industries. He was always poking about the mountain tops till the end of his life, looking for problems to solve, always carrying a thermometer and theodolite, sometimes much more equipment slung across a donkey. He investigated old mines and quarries and frequently corrected the maps. In July 1812, on the top of Skiddaw, while making observations, he first met two other self-taught scientists, Wilson Sutton and Jonathan Otley, the latter also carrying a barometer. The two men went with him on a giant walk over the tops to Wastdale Head; Dalton, who always reached a summit first, strode ahead with his equipment, Sutton complaining: "John, I wonder what thy legs are made of."

Otley, who came from Langdale, was in some ways as remarkable as was Dalton, and his origins were even humbler. He had no education apart from village schooling and set up as a basket- and swill-maker. He developed an intuitive grasp of minute mechanical functions, and for 55 years mended all the watches and clocks of Keswick, roaming the hills in his spare time to make observations. Otley was primarily a geologist, but he was interested in all natural phenomena and made himself a superb draughtsman. In 1818 he published the first modern, accurate map of the Lake District, and five years later he produced the summation of a quarter century of intense observation and note taking, *A Concise Description of the English Lakes and Adjacent Mountains*, illustrated by his superb outline sketches of all the hills. This was a pioneering volume, for not only had Otley worked out in detail the complex geology of the Lake District, he had also deduced general conclusions on cleavage, stratification and rock formation. He was still at it in 1852, when he was spotted high up in Borrowdale, aged 86, rowing near Friar's Crag and making notes for a record of water levels he had been keeping for half a century.[32]

Otley's geological mapmaking was part of an intense process of work and discovery which was making geology rival chemistry as the queen of the sciences. The emphasis in geology was shifting from the mineral formations of rocks to fossils. In 1815, William Smith, another self-educated man—a land surveyor by profession—effected a chronological marriage between the rock formations he had charted and the Rev. Benjamin Richardson's giant fossil collection in Bath, to produce the first general geological map of England. One of his disciples was the Rev. William Buckland, who gave the first lectures on minerology at Oxford. These lectures were very exciting, for Buckland liked to "enforce an intricate point with a Samsonic wielding of a cave-bear jaw or a hyena thigh-bone," and among his fascinated listeners was an Exeter College undergraduate, Charles Lyell (1797–1875). Lyell was not self-made: he came from a Scots family which, to use Jane Austen's phrase in *Emma*, "had been rising to gentility" for two generations. But, like Davy and Faraday, he illustrates the opportunities open to clever young men at this birth of the modern world. He was elected a Fellow of the new Geological Society the moment he took his degree and was world-famous while still in his twenties. Like Dalton and Otley, he thought through his eyes, making intense observations for hours at a time and taking copious notes. He went everywhere on foot, tramping over the Yarmouth estuary, hurrying to places where workmen were digging into the earth, so he could draw cross-sections—the coming of the railways delighted him for this reason—and clambering over sea cliffs and in quarries. His eyes taught him to think in terms of land dynamics, as Dalton's did in weather dynamics, and he had a rare imaginative grasp of the meaning of landscape, as do the greatest landscape painters, seeming to be able to peer inside it, to grasp what had happened and was happening.

Lyell dismissed Oxford science, still enmeshed in Aristotelian categories, as worthless—"treatisies of barren and abstract science," he wrote, "a world of terms in themselves unmeaning, & the most fanciful and laborious analysations and divisions of immaterial things which exist but in the mind."[33] He despised the university method, which was to read books and never to go anywhere, observe anything or conduct empirical research. Most dons supported the views of Abraham Godlieb Werner, of the famous Frieburg School of Mines, who taught a catastrophe theory, in which the world revealed by the fossils and bones of ancient monsters had been obliterated by a giant ocean. Clergymen referred to this world as "the former world." By contrast, they argued, the "present world" had been created by God about 6,000 years ago, exactly as described in the Book of Genesis. In contrast, the radicals supported James Hutton's *Theory of the Earth* (1785), which posited a very old, nonbiblical Earth: "In the economy of the world I can find no trace of a beginning, no prospect of an end."[34]

The Geological Society, not wishing to offend the clergy, which constituted a large part of its membership, tried to keep out of the clash between the Wernerians and the Huttonians, neither of whom had much empirical evidence to back their conclusions. Instead, it concentrated on intensive fieldwork and expeditions, which produced a more accurate and detailed geological map of England in 1819 and the formidable *Outlines of the Geology of England and Wales,* by W. D. Conybeare and William Phillips, in 1822. Lyell followed this line, though he extended his researches, from the age of 20, to the Continent. In France and Switzerland in 1818, he often walked 35 to 40 miles a day (his guide said *"Oui, c'est assez pour un monsieur"*), taking notes. The next year he was all over the north of England, his coach being stopped by a mob of 3,000 escorting Hunt into Manchester on the eve of Peterloo; at the Borrowdale Inn, before going to inspect some of Otley's rock formations, he picked up a volume of Shakespeare in the parlor and found "in the first page a reprimand from Mr Wilberforce in his own handwriting, written when he was here last year [visiting Wordsworth] to the Landlady, 'for having such ungodly books in the house.' "[35]

In 1820 and 1823, Lyell was again in France, the second time crossing the channel by the new 240-ton steam packet, the *Earl of Liverpool,* whose 80-horsepower engines did the trip in a mere 11 hours. He found Paris still the scientific capital of the world. All the members of the Académie des Sciences were full-time scientific researchers, who set high standards for published work. He was deeply impressed by the Musée d'Histoire Naturelle; official expeditions and private travelers deposited their collections and notes at the musée, where they were systematically catalogued by expert staff. There he found Jean-Baptiste Lamarck working on his study of invertebrate zoology and the paleontologist Baron Georges Cuvier; at the latter's salon, he met the great German scholar Alexander von Humboldt, who showed him round the superb Paris Observatory. But Lyell was not overawed. In a survey of the state of geological science which he published three years later, he noted the enormous number of scientific societies which had come into existence in Britain in the past decade—not just in London, like the Astronomical Society (1821), but in Bristol, York, and many smaller towns, in contrast with France, where Paris absorbed all.[36] The year before he had read Lamarck's *Philosophie zoologique,* which first suggested evolution by the transmutation of species. Now, in his 1826 papers, he argued that successive races of distinct plants and animals had inherited the Earth: They were all "parts of one connected plan" which was "not a fixed but a progressive one." The next year he speculated that if Lamarck was right, it "would prove that man may have come from an Ourangoutang." That notion might sound fantastic, but recent geologically discoveries likewise suggested possibilities which had hitherto seemed unimaginable: "What changes species may really undergo! How impossible will it be to distinguish & lay down a line beyond which some of the so-called extinct species have never passed into recent ones. That the earth is quite as old as [Lamarck] supposes has long been my creed." Like Dalton, he saw nature as dynamic: "Nature is not repose, but war. It is not rest, but change. It is not preservation but successive production & annihilation."[37]

Lyell was, by nature, a conservative and was alarmed by the prospect opened up by his reading and researches: that all existing theories of the origin of the Earth and its flora and fauna, including those compatible with the Bible, were untenable. But he was also, by nature, a scientist, and he persisted in accumulating masses of material found in his constant travels, to be shaped into a giant work on the principles of geological change. In 1828–29 he was on the Continent again, visiting not only Vesuvius but Etna in Sicily. The trip was decisive; he discovered that Etna was built on strata containing only species of shells and zoophytes still living in the Mediterranean. Most of Sicily had been formed since the time when the Mediterranean fauna first appeared, and plants and animals in Sicily were almost certainly older than the land itself—had migrated from Africa and Europe. Geological changes destroyed old land areas and created new ones more rapidly than a change of species appeared. Species had to be prepared to migrate and adapt themselves to avoid extinction and were thus engaged in a continual battle to survive. Lyell's researches in Sicily completely changed his view of the history of the Earth. He now became aware of the immensity of geological time, and of the gradual nature of geological change, ruling out catastrophes which made the biblical account plausible.

Between November 1829 and early summer 1830, Lyell was feverishly rewriting his *Principles of Geology,* which was published by John Murray in July 1830, just as the Paris mob was overthrowing the Bourbon regime. Its impact was even more revolutionary; indeed, the book is one of the most influential ever written. Lyell's object was "to explain the former changes of the earth's surface by reference to causes now in operation," and he showed that the speed of observable changes today was the same as in the past: There had been no tremendous upheaval, merely the continual, slow evolution under the twin forces of aqueous agents (rivers, seas), laboring to level the Earth's inequalities, and igneous ones (volcanoes, earthquakes) endeavoring to restore the unevenness of the Earth's crust. His first four chapters traced the history of geological inquiry. The next five, the core of the book, laid down his theory of what had happened and why. Then came 17 chapters illustrating the theory by describing actual aqueous and igneous processes. The second part (1832) dealt with the animal and the plant world, the third (1833), surveyed the entire history of geological formations. But it was the five "ideas" chapters in Volume One which contained the intellectual dynamite.[38]

Lyell was an adroit tactician. He made skillful use of approved theological writings, such as Bishop Butler's *The Analogy of Religion*, when they could be made to reinforce his conclusions or suggest they were less startling than naive Christians might suppose. His method was to play down the notion of an actual, let alone an inherent, conflict between science and revealed religion—an approach gratefully followed by Charles Darwin later—and to reassure believers. His private papers show, in addition, that he cut and tailored his key passages to arouse the minimum resistance from churchmen: "If I have said more than some will like," he wrote to his fellow scientist G. P. J. Scrope, "yet I give you my word that full *half* of my history and comments was cut out, and even many facts; because . . . it was anticipating 20 or 30 years of the march of honest feeling to declare it undisguisedly."[39] Lockhart, editor of the *Quarterly*, Scrope, the reviewer and Lyell himself consulted extensively about how the book was to be noticed in what was by far the most influential conservative publication in Britain.

Whatever the ethics of all this, Lyell's stealthy approach succeeded: The *Principles* won wide approval and got itself accepted as scientific orthodoxy before the fundamentalists realized that it had wrecked their biblical chronology completely. Like Davy and Dalton in chemistry and Faraday in electromagnetics, Lyell laid the foundations of the modern science of geology, and the *Principles* became its first textbook. But in his case, there was a religious dimension to be navigated; his achievement was to gain acceptance for his book, which was the first to treat the origin and history of the Earth on the assumption that all its phenomena could be explained naturally and discussed scientifically.

What Lyell failed to do, in his Volume Two, was to answer the question: How do species originate? He did not know the answer, or perhaps he was afraid to search for it too hard. That was left to Charles Darwin. But Volume One made Darwin's task much easier, both scientifically and in terms of winning social acceptance for his evolutionary theory. Darwin was 21 when the *Principles* first appeared, and he found it indispensible during his cruise on HMS *Beagle* in working out South American geology. He became Lyell's closest friend, though the great geologist was not exactly a social asset. Darwin's fiancée Emma dismissed him as "a dead weight" and grumbled: "Mr Lyell is enough to flatten a party, as he never speaks above his breath so that everybody keeps lowering their tone to him."[40] As scientific associates, however, they were well suited and formed a productive partnership. Their work has to be seen together, demonstrating for the first time how the Earth and what is on it evolve.

Lyell was not the only difficult dinner guest. He himself recorded the mathematician Charles Babbage in action at Wilberforce's house in Hendon, insisting that "the truth of a man's stories" depended on "the algebraic equation of his character." When Lyell criticized the paint-work on the house, Babbage interjected: "No: painting a house outside is calculated by the index minus one. That is to say, I am assuming revenue to be a function." With Lyell whispering and Babbage talking in equations, there was a curious episode during a dinner given by Charles Darwin's brother, when Thomas Carlyle shut both up by discoursing throughout dinner on how much better mankind would be without speech. "After dinner," wrote Darwin, "Babbage, in his grim-mest manner, thanked Carlyle for his very interesting lecture on the advantages of silence."[41]

Charles Babbage (1792–1871) was indeed a grim man: He looked grim, sounded grim and his thoughts became grimmer as he aged. He was grim with a reason; he saw the way to bring the future into the present, for the universal benefit, and found himself frustrated at every stage by human and material failures. He came from Totnes in Devon, the son of a partner in a successful Fleet Street banking house. As a young man he had an income of £300 a year and eventually (1827) inherited £100,000; he spent at least £20,000 on his scientific work. His lifelong fascination with machines began when as a small boy he saw the silver figure of a lady in Weeke's Mechanical Exhibition in Cock-spur Street. The lady danced, and the bird she held in her hand opened its beak, wagged its tail and flapped its wings. (By an extraordinary chance, Babbage was able to acquire the figure at an auction 40 years later, and it held pride of place in his drawing room.[42]) If, thought the little Babbage, machinery could do that, what could it not do? Babbage seems to have decided at an early age that the key to advanced machin-ery, in the long run, lay not so much in skilled craftsmanship as in calculation. He went to Totnes Grammar School, then a private acad-emy in Enfield, rising at 3 A.M. and working till 5:30 P.M. on mathemat-ics, including algebra. An early favorite was Maria Agnesi's *Analytical Institutions,* and he always held that, *ceteris paribus,* women made better mathematicians than did men. By the time he went to Cambridge at age 19 (1810) he was reading Lacroix's great work on differential and integral calculus. But, to his fury, he found that only Newton was studied at the university, and his tutor could not answer his questions. He himself, with help from John Herschel, had to create the Analytical

Society and publish its *Transactions*. The two men translated Lacroix together, wrote textbooks and papers, and updated mathematical tables. In winter 1813–14, as Bonaparte's empire was at last disintegrating, Herschel watched Babbage copying out logograms. "Well, Babbage, what are you dreaming about?" "I am thinking that all these tables might be calculated by machinery."[43]

Thereafter, the desire to make a machine to eliminate the growing number of elaborate calculations demanded by an industrialized world, and which had to be done by hand and brain, became an obsession with Babbage. A primitive calculating machine had been devised by Blaise Pascal in the mid-17th century. Gottfried Leibniz had produced another for his mathematical tables, and there was a machine known as Napier's Rods. Babbage regarded the rods as virtually useless: He wanted a machine which would not only calculate but print accurately any series of numbers determined by any law for which it was programmed. He seems to have fixed on two types of "engine," as he called them, in his early twenties. The first was a Difference Engine, to calculate and print tables. It was immediately useful because it would work out Admiralty tables of tides, longitudes, and so forth, but embodied comparatively unsophisticated principles. The second was the Analytical Engine, a highly versatile calculator which could be programmed to perform an immense variety of tasks. Babbage continued to work on the principles behind this machine for over 40 years, and there was no essential difference between it and the mainframe computers developed in the 1930s and 1940s.[44] Babbage invented computer science single-handedly and was 100 years ahead of his time. In this respect, he was by far the most original scientist of his day. But that, in a way, was his problem: He was too far ahead of the age.

There was no doubt about the need for his engines. Calculating clerks constantly made arithmetical errors, which were compounded by compositors when their handwritten tables were set. Writing to Davy, president of the Royal Society, in 1822, Babbage not only urged the need to eliminate the "intolerable labour and fatiguing monotony" of calculating work, "one of the lowest occupations of the human intellect," but pointed out that the French Board of Longitude printed series on the sun and moon contained at least 500 typographical errors. His projected machines, by contrast, calculated and printed in one operation and had a built-in self-correcting capability. Not only the elimination of drudgery, but infallibility and, above all, speed were his aims. One of the largest-scale sets of calculations, Babbage noted, was the French series on sines, tangents, and logarithms of numbers. This series consisted of 17 enormous folio volumes, one table alone containing over 8 million figures. A total of 916 people, included 14 highly skilled mathematical experts, working under 2 professors of the Academy of Sciences, had been needed to produce the work. Using machines, the work force could be reduced to 12, possibly less, and errors could be eliminated.[45]

Babbage thought he could build his Difference Engine in three years at the outside and was prepared to spend £3,000–£5,000 of his own money. But that amount would not be enough, so in early 1823 he requested a financial subsidy from the Treasury. The British government, unlike the French, was not accustomed to subsidizing science. It referred the request to a Royal Society committee, which included Davy, Herschel, and Brunel the elder. All but one agreed that money should be provided and so reported to Parliament. Babbage had a meeting with the Chancellor of the Exchequer, Fred Robinson, in 1824, at which he understood substantial funds would be made available and that the government would buy the machine when completed. But Robinson, with characteristic incompetence, kept no minutes, and a row broke out later about what was agreed. In the end, Babbage got over £7,500 from the Treasury, an enormous sum in those days, and much more than any British government had hitherto spent backing an invention. But in a sense, he was fighting against the spirit of the times. The more "progressive" members of the government thought the state should engage in as few activities as possible. They thought that the government's job was simply to remove the restrictions on private enterprise by dismantling the relics of mercantilism and introducing free trade, and that industry would do the rest. If Babbage's idea was viable, why did not he set up a company and appeal to the public for funds through the market?

Significantly enough, Babbage's strongest supporter in the government was the supposed reactionary, the Duke of Wellington. The Duke could see the military point of calculating machines, especially for the artillery, naval gunnery and navigation. To him, subsidizing Babbage was part of the nation's defense effort. Moreover, he was, as always, fascinated by machines, and Babbage's engines had a peculiar attraction for him—vast numbers of functional parts controlled by a single will that could be varied according to the problems set it—like an enormous army under a commander in chief. By comparison, Sir Robert Peel, the "modern," enlightened statesman, was much less enthusiastic: "I should like a little previous consideration," he wrote drily to Croker, "before I move in a thin House of country gentlemen a large vote for a wooden man to calculate tables."[46]

Babbage's difficulty was threefold, and it explains why his machines took much longer to build and cost infinitely more than he had first supposed. It took him some time to appreciate that he was trying to push forward the frontiers of science, not just at one point—imagining the machines in theory—but at several. In the first place, he had to invent a new language. How could the programs and actions of the engines be described? "I soon felt that the form of ordinary language was far too diffuse to admit of any expectation of removing the difficulty, and being convinced by experience of the vast power which analysis derives from the great condensation of measuring in the language it employs, I was not long in deciding that the most favourable path to pursue was to have recourse to the language of signs." To describe the complex procedures of the engines he thus resorted to combinations of Arabic and roman letters, upper and lower case, italics, arrows and other typographical devices. That did not help him with the public, which could not make head or tail of the result. Again, in conveying what the engines did, he was forced to use the analogy of the human brain. This analogy was in itself misleading and caused some people to overestimate what they could do—others to fear them. When the machine was "set" (we would use the word "programmed"), Babbage would say "it now *knows!*" He defended the use thus: "The words 'the engine *knows* etc' means that one out of many possible results of its calculations has happened, and that certain changes in its arrangements have taken place, by which it is compelled to carry out the next computation in a certain appointed way."[47] This kind of "explanation" actually confused the public still further. Babbage thought clearly—no one better—but he could not write or speak clearly, and he lacked linguistic imagination. Significantly, just as poets like Coleridge and Shelley could grasp atomic theory intuitively, so it took the young American poet Edgar Allan Poe (1809–49) to put the Difference Engine onto paper in words that ordinary people could follow, as he did in his story *The Chess Player of Maelzel*—foreshadowing the science fiction that H. G. Wells was to use to popularize science in the last decade of the century.

Babbage often failed to communicate even with fellow scientists. That was why he was so grateful for the support and understanding of Byron's beautiful child—"Ada! sole daughter of my house and heart!"[48]—whose mathematical genius, inherited from her mother, "the Princess of Parallelograms," he encouraged when she was still a girl. She was pretty, small, slight and dark, with her father's lovely speaking voice, and she wrote Babbage many remarkable letters as well as acted as his assistant. The wife of the mathematician August de Morgan described the scene when Babbage displayed his Difference

Engine at his house: "While the rest of the party gazed at this beautiful instrument with the same sort of expression and feeling that some savages are said to have shown on first seeing a looking-glass or hearing a gun, Miss Byron . . . understood its working and saw the great beauty of the invention."[49] This was some compensation to Babbage for the incomprehension he felt everywhere, which increased his sense of isolation and so his bitterness.

Babbage's second difficulty was perhaps insuperable. He was trying to build a computer in the age of cast iron, brass and mahogany. He had no lightweight materials whatever. Moreover, in laying down the highest specifications of accuracy, he was obliging his workmen to operate, again, at the limits of the existing technology and beyond. Every single part had to be handmade. His great incomplete engine, now in the Kensington Science Museum, is a beautiful and awesome object. But it also looks very expensive—and it was. In all except mathematics, Babbage was a gentleman-amateur of the old school. He could pick any kind of lock, but he could not operate a lathe or make his own parts. He should have set up his own company and employed a general manager to run its finances. He should have employed a showman to explain his purpose to the public. But most of all, he needed a head engineer, closely identified with him in the success of the venture. Instead, he used Joseph Clement, not as a fellow entrepreneur with a stake in the engines, but as an employee, under a cost-plus contract. Clement was an excellent craftsman, but a perfectionist, very slow; he was greedy, too, and incapable of controlling costs. Babbage never came to grips with this side of the venture. He seems to have been devoid of business sense, but too proud to ask for help. As late as 1829, by which time he had had about £5,000 of the government's cash and spent a fortune of his own, he was still having to ask basic questions about who owned the tools, patterns and drawings, and who paid the insurance. As a result, the entire project languished for want of funds. The Difference Engine did, in fact, perform some work, but it was never completed or went into production. The prototype Analytical Engine was never built, though Babbage made designs and parts. As a result, successive governments completely lost confidence in Babbage, and the affair had harmful long-term effects: The loss of so much taxpayers' money in a chimera that came to nothing was thereafter cited as a reason for refusing public funds for any kind of scientific research project. The fact that many of the tools to build the machines had to be specifically created for the purpose by Clement, who in the process became the leading machine-tool maker in Europe, and that major by-products in toolmaking thus flowed from the project—all were ignored.[50]

Babbage's falling-out with the government was particularly tragic because he was, perhaps, the first man to grasp the true nature of industrial society and foresee the boundless opportunities it offered mankind. Where his younger contemporary Karl Marx saw only the evils of industrial capitalism and even a man like Peel, whose father and grandfather had been the most successful entrepreneurs of their day, felt industrialization was a regrettable accident that had to be lived with and civilized, Babbage thought it the best thing that had ever happened to mankind. His thinking engines, which would abolish the drudgery of thousands of clerks, were paradigms of the way in which machines, infinite in number and variety, would end all the worst forms of labor, physical and mental, and gradually bring about a future in which prosperity would be combined with ever-increasing leisure. Babbage traveled all over Britain looking at manufacturing machinery, staying at inns for commercial travelers—he was often taken for one—accompanied by one of his skilled workmen, Richard Wright, both of them taking copious notes. He visited works in France, Austria, Germany, and Italy. A key article of his in a 1829 encyclopedia, "General Principles which Regulate the Application of Machinery," was the first attempt to put factory-based manufacturing industry at the center of economic discussion.[51] By comparative studies of machinery and processes, he originated a new science, operational research. He analyzed the pin-making industry and printing. His study of the economics of the post office led him to recommend to Rowland Hill the adoption of the penny post. He published the first reliable life insurance tables and the earliest comprehensive treatise on actuarial theory. A lot of the imaginative devices he conceived, such as clocking-on/off machines, water meters, and the hydroplane, were based on a confident assumption that rapidly developing technology would make them possible. Thus, the hydroplane required the kind of small, lightweight, compact propulsion unit later provided by the internal combustion engine. From his wide knowledge of different industries, Babbage saw technical advances in one branch stimulating development in others, and he believed a second industrial revolution was on the way, with highly sophisticated machines, often centrally controlled, raising productivity at a phenomenal rate and eliminating muscle labor. He clearly foresaw many of the industrial advances of the late 20th century but mistakenly believed they were imminent.

One reason Babbage was proved wrong was because society failed to avoid industrial class warfare, which he regarded as nonsense. He expanded his encyclopedia article into a book, *The Economy of Machinery and Manufactures* (1832), and was especially anxious that working men should read it because "a most erroneous and unfortunate opinion prevails among workmen in many manufacturing countries that their own interest and that of their employers are at variance." The result was Luddism and trade union restrictive practices, on the one hand, and the failure of management to use the talents and insights of their workers on the other. Trade unions, let alone machine breaking, simply drove industry from one part of the country to another, and if the unions were organized nationally, they simply benefited competitors overseas. But he opposed owners' trade associations as strongly as he did unions, and his hatred of manufacturers' combinations in the London Book Trade (an early version of retail price maintenance) led him to publish his book himself, with, for once, considerable commercial success. He argued passionately that workmen had as much interest as capitalists in installing the latest machinery and raising productivity, but this fact could only be brought home to them by payment by results, profit sharing and bonuses for operational improvements suggested by the men.[52] In his view, masters and workmen, scientists and engineers alike suffered from a defective education. Britain's whole educational system ought to be reorganized to meet the needs of an industrial society, dependent on ever-advancing technology to retain its world leadership in manufacturing.

What Babbage said proved to be true in almost every particular. More notice might have been taken of him if his engines had been seen to work. But his Difference Engine was little more than a showpiece and his Analytical Engine existed only on paper. From the mid-1820s he was attacked as a humbug and it was claimed that his project was a waste of public money—the most vicious denunciations coming from the holders of "scientific" chairs and lectureships at Cambridge. Increasingly grim and embittered, Babbage developed an extraordinary capacity for making enemies and for waging vendettas against them and institutions. When Davy died, Babbage failed to get Herschel elected President of the Royal Society; the royal Duke of Sussex was chosen. This failure knocked the stuffing out of Babbage's scientific reform movement and provoked his tract, *Reflections on the Decline of Science in England and on Some of Its Causes* (1830), which rightly drew attention to the lack of science education in Britain but blunted its impact by dragging in his personal grievances.[53]

Apart from arousing the interest of Wellington, Babbage made little impression on the politicians. Brougham was one of the many people with whom he did not get on. In any case, Brougham held weird scientific views and did more harm than good; his attacks in the *Edinburgh Review* were responsible for damning the perfectly valid wave theory of light advanced by the brilliant polymath Thomas Young (1773–1829). The Whigs were not interested in science. Peel, who was, insisted on backing the academic establishment. He made a contemptuous enemy of Babbage's machines, the feeble George Biddell Airy, Astronomer Royal, and as master of Trinity he installed his friend the Rev. William Whewell, who insisted that undergraduates take an arts course before studying science—though even Peel objected when Whewell argued that a century should elapse before new discoveries were included in Cambridge science courses.[54]

Scientific reformers like Babbage and Herschel turned in despair from Whitehall and Oxbridge to the provinces, setting up in 1831 the British Association for the Advancement of Science, which appealed to the public over the heads of the government and academia. It was classless as well as nonacademic, and that was important: Most scientific or "philosophical" societies, as they called themselves, had hitherto excluded men who did not look like gentlemen. In 1815 a self-educated Londoner, Timothy Claxton, was refused membership to a philosophical society: "I am a mechanic," he protested, "and though that is the reason why I wish to be admitted . . . it is the very reason also why I am not." Two years later he set up the first Mechanics Institute.[55] George Birkbeck, an Edinburgh doctor who practiced in London, became the driving force of the movement, setting up branches in Glasgow and London. In 1825, by which time there were 14 such institutes, Brougham became involved and produced a pamphlet, *Practical Observations on Education of the People*. Brougham was someone it was wise to keep well away from scientific research, but as a populist he had no equal in the 1820s. His tract led directly to the creation of 30 new institutes, and by the end of the year there were about 100, 20 in Yorkshire alone. The institutes adopted the rule that two-thirds of their managing committee had to be workingmen, defined as those who made their living by the work of their hands. They were self-supporting financially and ran their own reference and circulating libraries. By 1863, there were over 700.[56]

The movement drew attention to the real strength of industrial Britain: skilled workingmen, mostly self-educated. Its weakness was that, like the educational system as a whole, it tended to drift toward literature and the arts, instead of sticking to technology and science. Granted the state of Britain's universities, and the indifference of Whitehall and Westminster to educational reform, it may well be asked: How did the Industrial Revolution occur in Britain in the first place? The Industrial Revolution was a product mainly of the 1770s, with lift-off achieved in the 1780s.[57] The universities, as opposed to the grammar schools and Dissenting Academies, had little to do with it, and the government, nothing at all. Lord North went to his grave without knowing he had presided over an Industrial Revolution. The first historian of technology, Samuel Smiles, noted that "the educated classes of the last century regarded with contempt mechanical men and mechanical subjects." He quoted Dean Swift speaking of "that fellow Newton over the way—glass-grinder and maker of spectacles"—and pointed out that the great John Smeaton, who rediscovered the old Roman invention of water-resistant cement and built the Eddystone Lighthouse, was taken to task by his colleagues of the Royal Society for making a road across the Trent Valley, which they deprecated as "navvy work." Smiles added: "One of the most remarkable things about engineering in England is that its principal achievements have been accomplished not by natural philosophers nor by mathematicians but by men of humble station, for the most part self-educated."[58] In fact, this pattern continued well into the 19th century.

Even more than the scientists—Dalton, Davy, and Faraday—the technocrats came from nowhere and had nothing given to them except what they earned with their hands. George Stephenson began as a cowherd; Telford, a shepherd's son, as a stonemason. Alexander Naysmith started as an apprentice coach painter. His son James, inventor of the steam hammer, made a brass cannon at the age of nine. By 12 he insisted on making his own tools and would not buy chemicals from shops for his experiments. He and his father deplored getting things ready made. He wrote: "The truth is that the eyes and the finger—*the bare fingers*—are the two principal inlets to sound practical instruction." That was why he was glad to leave school to go into apprenticeship at the Carron Ironworks: "I have no faith in young engineers," he wrote later, "who are addicted to wearing gloves. Gloves, especially kid gloves, are perfect non-conductors of technical knowledge."[59] Joseph Bramah, the machine-tool inventor, creator of the first patent lock, the hydraulic press, the beer pump, the modern fire engine, the fountain pen, and the first modern water closet, started as a carpenter's apprentice and got his essential learning and experience from the local blacksmith's forge. Henry Maudsley, perhaps the ablest of all the machine-tool inventors, who created the first industrial assembly line for Brunel's block-making factory in Portsmouth, began work at 12 as a powder-monkey in a cartridge works and graduated in the smithy.

Joseph Clement learned nothing at school except to read and write and began helping his father, a humble handloom weaver; he too was a forge graduate. So was the great engine designer and manufacturer Matthew Murray of Leeds, who shared with James Fox of Derby the honor of inventing the first planing machines (1814). Fox began as a kitchen boy and butler. The Welshman Richard Roberts, another brilliant inventor of machine tools and power looms, including the Self-Acting Mule—described by Smiles as "one of the most elaborate and beautiful pieces of machinery ever contrived"—was a shoemaker's son, had literally no education, and began work as quarry laborer.[60] William Fairbairn, who designed and built the second generation of machinery for the textile industry in the 1820s, was the son of a Kelso gardener, who left school at age 10 to work as a farm laborer. John Kennedy, Fairbain's partner in this second industrial revolution and the first great builder of iron ships, was another poor Scot, who received no schooling except in summer and, like Bramah, started as a carpenter's boy. It was the same story with clever immigrants. Frederick Koenig, who built the first steam presses in London, was the son of a Saxon peasant and began as a printer's devil. Charles Bianconi, who created the first successful passenger transport system, in the remote west of Ireland of all places, was a packman from Lake Como.[61]

Such clever and enterprising men came to the British Isles because of the opportunities provided by its great wealth and, still more, by its free economic climate. The English universities might be comatose and the government indifferent to industry, but the law left the entrepreneur and the self-advancing artisan free to pursue their genius. Moreover, it was the only country with an effective patent system. As Koenig put it: "Almost every invention seeks, as it were, refuge in England, and is there brought to perfection, though the government does not afford any other protection to inventors beyond what is derived from the wisdom of the laws. [All this] seems to indicate that the Continent has yet to learn from her the best manner of encouraging the mechanical arts . . . after having lost in Germany and Russia upwards of two years in fruitless application, I at last resorted to England."[62]

That was not the only advantage of the free climate. In early industrial Britain, qualifications, degrees, certificates, professional rules and trade conventions were swept aside by masters and men who were anxious to get on. Maudsley did not bother about apprenticeships if he came across a clever lad. He gave James Naysmith a job straight away, on full wages. What mattered was quality of workmanship combined with ingenuity of ideas. This was why able young men got their chances so quickly—much more quickly and surely than they would today.

When Naysmith, in turn, set up his works in Patricroft, Manchester, he promoted skillful men rapidly, with big wage differentials determined by merit and productivity. The best men moved up from unskilled labor to craftsman, then to foreman, then to superintendent, and finally to partnership, though the last stage, in practice, was usually in a different firm. Naysmith laid down: "I believe that *Free Trade in Ability* has a much closer relation to national prosperity than even Free Trade in Commodities." Like Babbage, he rejected class warfare in industry as disastrous for all, not least because it stopped able young men from advancing to positions of authority. "In all well-conducted concerns," he argued, "the law of 'selection of the fittest' sooner or later comes into happy action, when a loyal and attached set of men work together for their own advantage as well as that of their employer."[63]

This "free trade in ability," born of the Industrial Revolution, was possible partly because large-scale industry first thrust itself forward in areas outside the reach of the old medieval guild-style restrictive practices. Even in an England where class distinctions were so important in most fields, they scarcely touched industry at any point as yet. Professional barriers were likewise leapfrogged. When the Liverpool–Manchester Railway was first planned in the mid-1820s, George Stephenson was made operative engineer, with another empiric, J. U. Rastrick, as assistant. Since the project involved laying line over marshland, over viaducts, and through deep cuttings, the highly qualified George Rennie was hired as a consulting engineer. Rennie told the directors of the company: "He would not object to Mr Jessop, Mr Telford or any member of the Society of Engineers being consulted, but he would not be associated in any way with Rastrick or Stephenson."

This piece of shameless professional trade unionism was simply brushed aside.[64] But with every decade, the tyranny of professional qualifications and apprenticeships was becoming more entrenched: in pharmacology, medicine, engineering, mining, architecture and printing (in law it was already absolute). Naysmith hated the apprentice system: "The arrangement we greatly preferred was to employ intelligent, well-conducted young lads, the sons of labourers or mechanics, and advance them by degrees according to their merits." His desire to promote on ability was his main bone of contention with the already aggressive Engineer Mechanics Trades Union. Union officials objected that men at Naysmith's Patricroft foundry were not "legally entitled to the trade," that is, had not served seven years' apprenticeship. Naysmith complained that the union's "persistent aim" was "an indolent equality," which he called "one of the greatest hindrances to industrial progress"—and high wages, too. The union objected that mere laborers from Worsley were being raised to the rank of mechanics and called their members out on strike. Half the work force complied. Naysmith broke the strike by shipping 64 Scots and their families from Glasgow to Liverpool, then by special train on the new railway to Manchester.[65]

Strikes sometimes worked, however, and there is evidence that unions were already acting as effective barriers to the self-advancement of able poor men. Fairbairn recorded: "When I first entered London, a young man from the country had no chance whatever of success, in consequence of the trade guilds and unions. I had no difficulty in finding employment, but before I could begin work I had to run the gauntlet of the trade societies; and after dancing attendance for six weeks, with very little money in my pocket, and having to 'Box Harry' [go without food] all the time, I was ultimately declared illegitimate and sent to seek my fortune elsewhere." He said there were then three competing mill-wright unions, formed "to exclude all those who could not assert their claims to work in London and other corporate towns. Laws of a most arbitrary character were enforced, and they were governed by cliques of self-appointed officers, who never failed to take care of their own interests."[66] Fairbairn, in his early working life, found himself constantly up against restrictive union practices. In Dublin he got a job in Robinson's Phoenix Foundry, whose owners had invented machinery to make nails, and so avoid importing them. But the Dublin union would not let the Robinsons use it, and it was scrapped unused: the nail-making trade gradually left Ireland, never to return. Fairbairn added: "The Dublin iron-manufacture was ruined in the same way; not through any local disadvantages, but solely by the prohibitory regulations enforced by the workmen of the Trade Unions."[67] By the 1820s, Irish trade unionists were emigrating to Britain, especially to Glasgow and Liverpool, stiffening the nascent British union movement with a strong element of political radicalism.

But nothing, as yet, could halt the march of the machines, great and small. Machine making was not a British monopoly—far from it. The French were the first to mount an exhibition specifically devoted to machinery, at the Conservatoire des Arts et Métiers, as early as 1796, and two years later these exhibitions became a regular, government-sponsored event. Dublin was the first to hold one in the British Isles, in 1824; London followed only in 1828.[68] Until about 1815 the French were ahead in tunneling and bridge-building machinery. They were the first, too, to discover the principles of sterilization and hermetic sealing for preserving food. This was the work of the Paris confectioner François Appert, who supplied food to Bonaparte's armies. But he used glass. It was the English who invented tinplate for the purpose, patented by Peter Durand in 1810, and it was Bryan Donkin who built the first canning factory at Bermondsey in 1812, to supply soups and preserved meat for the Royal Navy in the war against America. The type of tin can now in use, with locked side seams and double seams at the ends, was being made in Wakefield as early as 1824.

The Americans were also prolific inventors. Jacob Perkins of Philadelphia invented one of the first nail-making machines, fire-fighting devices, machines for printing bank notes and an engraving process said to be proof against currency forgers. The cost of labor made Americans particularly keen on agricultural machinery. In 1829 Jacob Bigelow of the Harvard Medical School published a 507-page compendium of new technology, arguing that the use of machines to replace muscle power was of central importance to America's rapid development and peculiarly suited to "American inventive genius." Steam power, he argued, was like the power of kings, and America must identify itself with technological advance.[69] But Britain was still by far the biggest market for machinery in the years after Waterloo. It was in London that Perkins set up shop in 1815. Ten years later he was trying to sell his steel machine gun, which fired 100 rounds a minute, to the Duke of Wellington; the Duke of Sussex thought it "Damned wonderful!" but the army would not buy. Some of the technology was merely a gigantic extension of the old. Thus, in 1817 the organ makers Flight & Robson displayed in London a giant mechanical organ, which had taken them five years to build at a cost of £10,000. The organ had 45 stops and 1,900 pipes, the largest being 24 feet high (thus topping the previous biggest, 16 feet, in Saint Bavo's, Haarlem), and was programmed to play Mozart, Beethoven and Weber overtures. Claire Clairmont went to see it three times, on the last dragging Thomas Love Peacock with her.[70]

Other marvels were very much the new technology. They included the first passenger lift, invented by Thomas Hornor, which went on display in Regent's Park in 1826, and, two years later, the first really efficient microscope, which solved the problem of achromatic aberration, shown at the Microcosm in Regent Street.[71] Of more concern to most people was the development of the rubber industry. The French had brought rubber from South America in the mid-18th century and called it *caoutchouc*. It was the chemist Joseph Priestley who gave it the English name when he said it was useful as a rubber for wiping out pencil marks. But mass use came only in 1820, when Thomas Hancock discovered how to handle it and developed machinery to cut it into joinable strips. The process was adopted by Charles Macintosh, who brushed it onto cloth to form an impervious layer. Hancock, in partnership with Macintosh, treated long lengths at high speed. A factory for mass production was opened in Manchester in 1824, and within a year the men-about-town were wearing Macintoshes in the London rain.

There were, however, two outstanding developments which really signaled the machine age. The first was the world's prototype production line, set up by the elder Brunel in Portsmouth. Brunel's experience illustrates the strengths and weaknesses of the various national systems. Mark Isambard Brunel was born in Normandy in 1769 and had the best technical education available anywhere in the world at that time, at the Royal College in Rouen, under Vincent Dulague, Professor of Hydrography, and Gaspard Monge, the inventor of mechanical drawing. He was driven by French political instability to emigrate to the United States, where he became Chief Engineer of New York and set up a cannon foundry. But America could not yet provide him with enough scope for his genius. Dining with the former Secretary to the U.S. Treasury, Alexander Hamilton, in 1798, he got news of the bottleneck in British naval expansion. The Royal Navy, he was told, required at least 100,000 rigging blocks a year. Each 74-gun ship of the line needed 922 blocks for its rigging, not counting spares. But the blocks were made by hand in Fox & Taylor's antiquated Southampton factory, and demand had long since outstripped their output. It was then, Brunel wrote later, that "the idea for block machinery came to me."

Brunel hurried to England and put his plans to the government. His first designs for block-making machinery were filed on 10 February 1801. The notion of an entire series of mass-production machines appealed strongly to Sir Samuel Bentham, the government's chief adviser (he was the brother of Jeremy Bentham). Bentham recommended that Brunel be given a contract. Brunel was also lucky to fall in with Maudsley, who had left Braham to set up on his own as a tool designer in 1798 and was probably the best mechanical engineer in the world for the purpose. In all Brunel designed 45 machines for the production line, all of which were made by Maudsley. The first blocks came off the line in 1803, and within three years of Bentham's letter of approval the whole concept was in operation. An examination of the production cycle at Portsmouth reveals the astonishing originality and subtlety of Brunel's mechanical mind.[72] One of his ideas in this series went back to Leonardo da Vinci; another anticipated developments not seen till the last quarter of the 19th century. Brunel's fertility was such that, when he ran into a bottleneck with his files and plans, he simply designed a copying machine, the Polygraph. When an old lady complained her fingers were stiff with arthritis, he sat down immediately and designed her a machine to shuffle her cards and another to wind her wool.[73]

What made Brunel's Portsmouth production line unique, however, was not just the inventiveness of the individual machines—though nothing like his mortising machine, the cone-clutch clamps of his hole-boring machine, or the split-nut in the pin-polishing machine, had ever been seen before. The historic novelty was the coordinating of these machines, which had interchangeable parts, into a single production line. Men who had grown old in the trade could not believe their eyes. Samuel Taylor, of Fox & Taylor, the existing contractors, flatly refused to believe machinery could replace skilled handcraftmen. When offered a partnership by Brunel, on 25–26 March 1801, he insisted that the existing method was perfect: "I have no hope of anything better ever being discovered, and I am convinced there cannot be." Exactly four years later, his firm lost its contract. The Portsmouth line was operated by 10 unskilled hands, who could not even read or write, and they produced as many blocks as 110 expert craftsmen at Southampton.

The employment of Maudsley in making the machine tools ensured that the quality of the blocks was at least as high and that the line did not break down. The new works recouped its capital in three years, and the Brunel-Maudsley line was still turning out the blocks used in assault landing craft which took part in the D-Day invasion of 1944; one was still at work in 1967. Visitors were awed. Maria Edgeworth noted: "Machinery so perfect appears to act with the happy certainty of instinct and the foresight of reason combined." Sir Walter Scott, after a tour of the plant in 1816, said he had never witnessed "such wonderful sights." Other manufacturers were as impressed as the laity, and Maudsley's machine-tool firm became a depository of the new technology and dispersed it rapidly through the more open-minded sectors of industry.[74]

Brunel was a practical man in a way that Babbage was not. He brought his inventions off the drawing board and into action with astonishing speed. Flushed with the success of his Portsmouth enterprise, he created the circular saw for timber handling (he had got the idea from a marble-cutting machine he saw in the United States) and installed 10-foot saws at a mill he set up in Battersea. An even bigger sawing mill, attached to the naval yard at Chatham, made the first large-scale use of framesaws and machine handling. To get the huge 100-foot-plus Russian oaks into his giant sawing-hall, he built a 860-foot-long railway, a 400-foot tunnel and cranes worked by hydraulic power. A central power supply pumped the water, fed the traveling crane, winched the tramcars, and operated the railway, what Brunel triumphantly called "untried combinations being brought to act in unison and harmony." He reduced the price of sawing from 3 shillings to 6 pence per 100 feet, and his circular saw was rapidly adopted all over Britain. Even more impressive was the boot factory he set up near his Battersea sawmill. The machinery was operated by 24 disabled soldiers and produced high-quality products for low prices: "common shoes" for 9s6d a pair, waterproof boots for 10s6, half boots for 12s, "superior shoes" for 16s and Wellington boots for £1. These prices were a third or less of handmade articles. Castlereagh wore "Brunel Boots," pronounced them excellent, and pushed their use by the British army. Boots with machine-riveted soles were worn by Wellington's veterans in the Peninsular and by his British units at Waterloo—their success was one reason why he favored machinery. Bonaparte's troops also wore Brunel boots, when he could get them.[75] Brunel, in fact, combined an almost intuitive physical skill—he once maneuvered a ship into Deal harbor when a panicking captain lost the confidence of passengers and crew—with superb theoretical inventiveness. He was a thorough experimenter, as well as a visionary, and both he and his son Isambard Kingdom Brunel were as practical as the Stephensons, George and his son Robert.[76]

But the elder Brunel, like Babbage, had a debilitating weakness: an inadequate grasp of the financial side of business. Like Babbage he needed a properly organized company with a financial manager. Instead, he kept his own accounts. James Sanson, a banker friend called in to straighten out the accounts, reported that they were "a most extraordinary jumble"; it was, he wrote, "as if one of your saws had walked to town." Like many other businesses, the boot factory was hit by the peace, and Brunel found himself with a £5,000 stock of unsold boots. When his Battersea mill burnt down, it was found to be inadequately insured. The mill was rebuilt, and new inventions flowed: a knitting machine, tinfoil, the first accurate stereotype plates and the first engraved cylinder anticipating gravure printing. None was fully developed for lack of capital, and debts were mounting. In May 1821 Brunel's obliging bank collapsed, and he found himself arrested for debt and put in the King's Bench. Wellington, remembering the boots, persuaded the Chancellor of the Exchequer to provide £5,000 to get Brunel out of trouble and keep him in Britain, "there being strong publick grounds for the Government to avail themselves of Mr Brunel's extraordinary talents."[77]

Three years before, Brunel had been fascinated to learn of the habits of the shipworm or *Teredo navalis,* a creature nine inches long and half an inch in diameter, which had sunk more sturdy vessels than all the cannon in history. Inspecting a piece of infested timber, he noticed that the worm's head was protected by strong boring shells like shields and its body by tunnel lining of its own secretion. He decided to use the principle of the worm to develop a deep-level tunneling machine and entered a Patent for Forming Drifts and Tunnels Under Ground, on 20 January 1818. Men had been tunneling through solid rock since antiquity, but this machine was designed to produce something never seriously attempted before: a soft-bed tunnel. The target was the Thames at London, where the bridges were grotesquely inadequate for the frantically expanding city. Even the Waterloo footbridge took £12,000 a year in tolls. At Wapping there were 350 exorbitant watermen with wherries. By the early 1820s over 4,000 wagons crossed London Bridge every day, creating infuriating traffic jams. It cost more to carry skins across the Thames from Wapping than across the Atlantic from Hudson's Bay, or so it was claimed. The first sub-Thames tunnel plan had been put forward in 1798, and attempts were made to solve the soft-bore problem; all failed.

Out of debtor's prison, the elder Brunel—now joined by his son Isambard Kingdom Brunel, who had been sent by his father to the Lycée Henri Quatre in Caen for a proper mathematics education—put forward his proposal. In conjunction with the entrepreneur William Smith, MP, spokesman for the slave trade, which was seeking to diversify itself in anticipation of further reforms, the Brunels got a bill through Parliament on 24 June 1824, authorizing them to tunnel under the Thames at Blackwall. The tunnel was designed to carry two carriages or wagons abreast. Brunel's worm method, or Great Shield as he called it, had a circular head end, nearly 38 feet in diameter, divided into 12 frames or cells, each housing an expert miner. Its outer walls overlapped the masonry lining of the tunnel, which was installed as the work progressed. After the miners in the cells completed each phased evacuation of the face, the entire apparatus was pushed forward by a giant hydraulic ram. Spoil was removed by a bucket-chain elevator worked by a new inverted-"V" engine he had designed (he was frustrated in his desire to use a new gas engine, ancestor of the internal-combustion engine, which he had invented).[78]

The entire system was new, and it aroused enormous interest. Indeed, both Brunels complained bitterly of interruptions to the work caused by the constant flow of distinguished visitors Smith brought along. Being new, the machinery was employed at the limits of tolerance of its cast-iron components and, equally important, the project pushed at the frontiers of mining geology. Had Brunel consulted Lyell, with his uncanny ability to "see" into the ground, he would have tunneled deeper; as it was, his expert surveys and borings underestimated the difficulties, especially the damage to the projected roof caused by Thames dredgers extracting gravel over many years. Even today, large-scale tunneling remains dangerous and unpredictably expensive. As always with the Brunels' schemes, there was inadequate financing. A letter young Brunel wrote in March 1825 indicates the slender margins: "I am at this moment without a penny. We keep neither carriage nor horse nor footman, only two maidservants. I am looking forward with great anxiety to this Gaz Engine. . . . How much more likely it is that all this will turn out to nothing! . . . the Tunnel may fail, and I most likely in such circumstances will cut my throat or hang myself."[79] Father and son carried an enormous burden. The old man at one stage did nine consecutive days, each of 20 hours, in the tunnel; the son worked even harder. But they were up against the frontiers of safety, too, and there the margins were too small. Both wanted visitors banned. The son noted in his diary, on 13 May 1827: "Notwithstanding every prudence on our part, a disaster may still occur—*may it not be when the arch is full of visitors!*" Four days later there was a roof fall, which might have been catastrophic, and work stopped. This shook the confidence of investors, already undermined by the financial panic of 1825–26 and the subsequent recession. Work resumed on 30 September 1827, but there was a second fall and a rush of water three months later. On 8 August 1828 work was suspended, and the tunnel was walled up. The tunnel was not finished until 1843.[80]

By this time, in any case, the public passion had switched to the even more spectacular expression of the power of machines—railways. The dispute over who invented rail travel will probably never be resolved. It was the creation of dozens, perhaps scores, of inventive men, all of them of humble origins, many mere workmen. The great majority were Geordies from the northeast coalfield, though some, including Richard Trevethick, who provided the key development of the high-pressure engine (1804), came from the Cornish tin-mining industry. This inventive work was wholly practical, carried out by hard-headed men seeking cheaper and more effective ways of doing things. There was no theoretical science, few plans. The motive was to do the same job—usually hauling coal from the pithead to the ports—at less cost. Essentially, steam-driven engines running on rails were more economical than were horses and canals. In the final years of the Napoleonic Wars, the cost of horse fodder was so high that two Leeds inventors, John Blenkinsop, who built the rack rails, and Matthew Murray, who built the engines, laid down a rack line to carry coal from the mines on the estate of Charles Brandling, who put up the capital, to Leeds. The rack

engines were called *Prince Regent* and *Salamanca*—names usually give
away the date—and each could do the work of 16 horses pulling 94 tons
on the level at 3½ miles an hour. They were more reliable than were
horses, worked round the clock, and lasted much longer (these two
were at work for half a century). When the wars ended, the price of
fodder fell, and horse-drawn tramlines competed successfully with canals. George Overton, the leading tramway builder, calculated that his
feeder tramway to the Brecon & Abergavenny Canal took only a year
to build and yielded 7 percent; a similar canal would take a decade and
yield 1 percent: "Railways are now generally adopted," he insisted,
"and the cutting of canals nearly discontinued." That statement was
true, but what Overton did not grasp was that the great Shire horses
which hauled his wagons were at the end, as it were, of their line of
development, the steam engine just at the beginning. George Stephenson knew it.

The problem with the early engines, even when they incorporated
high-pressure boilers, was that they were too weak. Stephenson's
Blücher, which had its first run on 25 July 1814 (when the Prussian
Marshal was the toast of London), driven by his elder brother James,
sometimes required a good human shove to get going. When, hauling
12 wagons weighing 36 tons up the incline near James's home, it would
nearly come to a standstill, and he would call out to his wife: "Come
away, Jinnie, and put your shoulder to her." This she would do, and
would get "her" moving; Jinnie also got up at 4 A.M. to light the fire in
Blücher's boiler.[81] George Stephenson's great merit, however, was that
he rightly believed that an engine type, however weak, could have its
horsepower progressively raised by practical improvements in the
boiler, valves, traction system, wheels and rails. No two of the scores
of engines he and his son Robert built were quite alike, and each was
more powerful than the last. When a group of businessmen from the
Aukland-Darlington coalfield got together in 1818 to promote a line to
get its coal cheaply to the sea wharves at Stockton-on-Tees, their first
thought was to employ Overton to build a horsedrawn tramway. But
by the time their bill was through Parliament, in April 1821, George
Stephenson convinced them it would be madness not to build a double
line for steam engines and to convey people as well as coal. Fired with
this belief, Edward Pease, head of the business committee, prophetically
declared: "If the railway be established and successful, as it is to convey
not only goods but passengers, we shall have the whole of Yorkshire
and next the whole of the United Kingdom following the railways."[82]

To build the Stockton–Darlington railway, the first in the world,
Stephenson set up his own engine-building company (later the long-

lasting Robert Stephenson & Company) in Newcastle and recruited line layers, blasters and tunnelers from all over the Tyne coalfield. Many of these handy, adaptable men, none of whom had more than a few years' schooling, later became famous entrepreneurs, first in Britain, then all over the world. The line was completed by early September 1825, and meanwhile Stephenson had built two engines, *Locomotion* and *Hope* at a cost of £550 each, plus *Experiment,* the first passenger coach. By the time the railway was due to open on 27 September there was excitement all over the northeast. Over 40,000 people were waiting in Stockton to see the *Locomotion* arrive with the first train, the *Experiment* plus 21 coal wagons, weighing 90 tons in all, which it had pulled over 8½ miles at an average of 8 miles per hour. No one in that vast crowd could doubt that railways were the conveyance of the future, and the opening, coming as it did at the height of the mid-1820s boom, prompted ambitious schemes to build passenger and goods railways all over Britain.

Few schemes survived the 1825–26 economic crash, but one that did was the grandiose project to link Liverpool, Britain's fastest expanding port, to Manchester, the textile-trade boomtown. The route Stephenson laid down involved huge viaducts, deep cuttings and track laid over marshy Chat Moss, which some engineers thought impossible. In the postcrash climate, raising the capital needed proved difficult, and the company had to take advantage of the Exchequer Loan Bill and borrow £100,000 from the government. Obtaining the loan involved getting route approval from Telford, engineer to the Loan Commissioners, and he forced Stephenson to amend his plans in certain key respects. The Geordie grumbled, but Telford was doubtless right.

The project involved earth moving on a scale never before attempted—the only comparable scheme was Telford's own 38-mile Birmingham & Liverpool Junction Canal, begun at the same time, January 1827. Track gradients had to be met by added engine power, and that was rising sharply as the competition increased. One of the elder Stephenson's protégés, Timothy Hackworth, produced at the end of 1827 a superb engine, the *Royal George,* which incorporated improved wheels and traction, and a big boiler protected by the first spring-safety-valve (*Locomotion* blew up and killed its driver). It was the world's first truly powerful locomotive. Young Robert Stephenson surpassed it the next year with his *Lancashire Witch,* built for the new Rolton & Leigh Railway, and in 1829 he produced the *Rocket,* the most famous engine of all.

The directors of the Liverpool–Manchester Railway held competitive engine trials at Rainhill on 6 October 1829, five rival engines taking part in front of 10,000 spectators. The *Rocket* beat its main contender,

Hackworth's *Sans Pareil*, averaging 14 miles per hour over 60 miles, and it weighed less and consumed less coal than any of the others. By spring 1830 Robert had built six more *Rocket*-type locomotives, each with improvements, leading to the ultimate version of the type, the *Northumbrian*. He was already working on a radical improvement, the *Planet,* which he delivered to the company three weeks after the official opening of the railways in September 1830. This opening was marred, as we shall see, by a significant political tragedy. But with passengers drawn by the *Planet* between two of the world's fastest-growing cities at speeds of 20 miles per hour or more, there could be no doubt that the railway age had begun.[83]

In due course, a poet like Wordsworth, watching the intrusive railway engine invade the remotenesses of his beloved Lake country, would see the machine as a threat to art, and from that view would flow the Manichean dualism which pits aesthetics and industry as irreconcilable enemies, Beauty and the Beast, the argument becoming further envenomed by the supposed conflicting interests of social welfare and the profit motive of the capitalist system. But at the dawn of modernity, men did not think in these terms. They saw art and science, industry and nature as a continuum of creation and the quest for knowledge as a common activity, shared by chemists and poets, painters and engineers, inventors and philosophers alike. Davy and Coleridge were allies in a common struggle to understand the elements. When Byron, Shelley and his wife sat down by the shores of the Lake of Geneva, their theme was the beauty and poetry of electricity. Men spoke of "the art of machine making," and those who designed the great new engines and structures were often artists, also, in the sense we understand the word today.

That superlative engineer-inventor James Naysmith was not the son of a great artist for nothing. His father taught him draughtsmanship from infancy (his brother Patrick and his sister both became professional artists) and he always regarded his graphic skills as essential. He wrote: "Mechanical drawing is the alphabet of the engineer. Without this, the workman is merely a 'hand.' With it, he indicates the possession of a 'head.' " Or again: "Drawing is the Educator of the Eye. It is more interesting than words. It is graphic language." The "principles" he drew up for young engineers could almost equally well be addressed to art scholars. "The fewest possible parts." "Guard carefully against the intrusion of more traditional arrangements." "Simplicity and directness of action." "Plain common sense in design." "Severe utility." "Gracefulness and form consistent with nature and purpose."[84] Among the engineers and machine-tool makers, drawing was regarded as an essential skill. When the young Westmorland lad Joseph Clements went to Glasgow to better himself, he had the shrewdness to take drawing lessons from Peter Nicholson, the writer on industrial carpentry, who designed power looms; when he showed Nicholson his copy of a loom, he was told: "Young man, *you'll do!*" In London with £100 saved, he went to Alexander Galloway's machine-tool show shop in Holborn at the end of 1813 and offered himself. "What can you do?" "I can work at the forge." "What else?" "I can turn." "What else?" "I can draw." "What, can you draw? Then I will engage you."[85] Nearly all these early inventors were superb draughtsmen. Some were more. Isambard Kingdom Brunel, whose father always said, "Drawing is the alphabet of the engineer," produced beautiful color-wash drawings of all his multifarious projects, only some of which, alas, survive.[86]

Moreover, their visual clarity, foundation of the sense of beauty, expressed itself in their creations. The few great engines which survive from the years 1815–30 often have an arresting grandeur of form. The immense waterwheels Fairbairn and Kennedy built for Kingman, Pinlay & Co.'s cotton mills in Ayrshire, in 1826–27, are regarded, even today, as among the most perfect hydraulic machines in Europe; they are also awesome in their beauty. You have only to look at the *Rocket* in the South Kensington Science Museum to realize that Robert Stephenson loved the creature he designed and built, that it lived, in his eyes. Nearby, on the floor above, the Difference Engine casts an aesthetic spell of its own. Inventors and engineers alike embellished their creations, whenever possible, in the artistic idiom of a gifted age. Brunel's great new sawing mill at Chatham had Regency wings, with a Moorish Great Sawing Hall. The motif of his tunnels and viaducts was Tuscan capitals and astragals. When Stephenson built the Stockton–Darlington line, the company engaged Ignatius Bonomi, son of the great Joseph Bonomi, as architect to design all its stonework, including the splendid Skerne Bridge. Telford was not the only engineer whose surviving works bear the stamp of a wonderfully consistent, if severe, love of the beautiful. The spirit of Leonardo da Vinci hovered over many of these hardheaded men, who were by no means as simple as they sometimes seemed. When John Rennie completed his new Waterloo Bridge in 1817—chosen by John Constable as the occasion for one of his most striking canvases—Antonio Canova said: "It was worth a journey from Rome to see." Like Brunel with his worm, the great American inventor Robert Fulton, who began life as a miniature painter, followed Da Vinci in basing his engines on nature, especially the movements of fishes.[87]

* * *

Art and invention went hand in hand, often in the same families. The Naysmiths were the outstanding example, but there were many others. From Ovingham, the next-door village to Wylam, where the Stevensons were born, came the Martins: John, the great apocalyptic landscapist and his brother Jonathan, who spent his life working on the problems of perpetual motion. Richard Parkes Bonington learned his art in French studios because his father went there to run a business exporting (secretly and unlawfully) English parts for textile machines.

The Bells of Edinburgh were a family of artists and medical men, brought up in the circle of Brougham and Jeffrey, Francis Horner, Scott and Cockburn. Both Charles and his brother John were superb draughtsmen (Charles had lessons from David Allan). John went on to become the leading operating surgeon of the day, Charles Bell to create anatomy as a modern science through the brilliance alike of his observation and his drawings. Was he a scientist or an artist? In fact he was both. His sumptuous quarto volume, *Essays on the Anatomy of Expression in Painting,* first published in 1806, then greatly enlarged and improved in later editions, was illustrated by his own drawings. David Wilkie, RA, did a few of the plates, and Sydney Smith helped Bell with the text, "to eliminate his Scotticisms." It was a landmark in the exploration of the human nervous system, and Charles Darwin, who used the third edition of 1844, found it invaluable in preparing his *Origin of Species.* But artists, amateur and professional alike, thought it a godsend. The delight of Queen Charlotte, a skillful watercolorist, was reported back to Bell, who ungraciously exclaimed: "Oh! happiness in the extreme that I should ever write anything fit to be dirtied by her snuffy fingers!" John Flaxman, RA, the Royal Academy's Professor of Sculpture, said the book "had done more for the Arts" than anyone else in the age.[88]

Bell was obsessed by the mind-body problem, to which he saw the nervous system as the key, and he thought art and science had precisely the same aim—"to lay a foundation for the study of the influence of the mind on the body." He not only gave special lectures to artists on anatomy (it was how he made his living when he first came to London), but he was fascinated by the way a painter, in depicting the human face, expressed the workings of the mind. Bell urged Wilkie to master this problem—how, for instance, to paint a scene showing a man or woman blushing, and why—and Wilkie's successful response made him the greatest genre painter of the age.[89]

It was Bell's great merit that he took a broad view of his science: "By anatomy . . . I mean not merely the study of the individual and dissected muscles of the face, body and limbs; I consider it as including all the peculiarities . . . which mark and distinguish the countenance, and the general appearance of the body . . . The anatomy of painting, taken according to this comprehensive description, forms not only a science of great interest but that from which alone the arts can derive the spirit of observation." He wanted artists to downgrade the study of antique casts and other forms of academic lifelessness and get out into the world, to observe and paint the real, to catch the moment of truth. Wilkie followed his advice, as his hundreds of studies show, and Bell's gospel was an important step on the road which, throughout the 19th century, was taking painters out of the studio and into town and country for the direct depiction of nature.[90]

Art, science and technology overlapped constantly in this exciting period of experiment. It was not just the engineers, like Clement and the Brunels, and the scientists, like Farraday and Otley, who saw the importance of graphic skills. Nor was it just the poets and philosophers who had an intuitive grasp of physics and chemistry. The great inventive genius of the musical scene in the late 1820s, Hector Berlioz, retained a lifelong interest in science, aroused when, as a medical student in Paris, he attended Gay-Lussac's lectures on electricity. His preoccupation with the technology of instruments and the theory of sound—his positive obsession with the emotional impact of huge orchestral *tutti*—were important parts of his creativity. Both he and Felix Mendelssohn were superb draughtsmen. Mendelssohn's watercolors of his travels, some of which survive, give important insights into his early compositions. The musical illustrations and notes which Berlioz compiled for his book on Beethoven, published in 1829, were as neat and clearly written "as a legal document." The great pianist Moscheles, who saw the original manuscript of the Romeo and Juliet Symphony on Berlioz's desk, described it as "exquisitely penned."[91]

Science touched the artist at a growing number of points. One of the most spectacular developments during the first three decades of the 19th century was the rapid growth in the publication of illustrated books (and prints) of all kinds, both luxury volumes produced by the Saxon immigrant-entrepreneur Rudolph Ackermann (1764–1834) in London, and new mass publications, ranging from textbooks and children's stories to illustrated newspapers and magazines. In addition to the professional engravers, hundreds of artists now derived their incomes mainly from such work, and even fashionable painters, like Wilkie, could double their earnings in the 1820s by reproductions. In the last prephotography age, artists had to keep up with the latest technology.

Some reproductive processes, of course, went back to the late-medieval period. Line engraving, done by the intaglio method—the picture cut into the surface of the plate, usually copper, filled with ink then printed under heavy pressure—went back to the mid-15th century. Etching, using copper coated with acid-resistant substance as a surface for the drawings, then repeated immersions in nitric acid baths, and drypoint, using a diamond-tipped steel needle to produce a burred line directly on copper, were developed by German, Dutch and Italian artists from c1500 onwards. But with these methods only the first few of the impression had any quality. An important variation was by Ludwig von Siegen of Utrecht in 1642, who produced a burr over the entire copper plate by using a serrated-edge rocker, then created a picture by scraping away the burr to get light tones and polishing the metal smooth for highlights. This method produced variations of tone and midtints and was called mezzotint. There were radical refinements in this method early in the 19th century and, as a result, Joseph M. W. Turner's great compendium of landscapes, the *Liber Studiorum* (1807–19), was done in *mezzo,* combined with etching, under the painter's direct supervision. All Constable's chief landscapes were mezzotinted by the great engraver David Lucas (1802–81). The method was used for popular prints of society portraits, too.[92]

The real technological breakthrough, however, came in 1768 when Jean-Baptiste le Prince bit the plate with acid through a porous ground of powdered resin fixed to the plate by heating: this process gave the effect of transparent tones of a wash drawing. This technique, aquatint, gradually spread through west and central Europe, especially when artists learned to combine it with etching: Goya became attached to it, between 1795 and 1825, using combinations of etching and aquatint. Paintings could be aquatinted in color by using separate plates for each hue, or the monochromes could be hand colored, and huge quantities of such work were sold in London and Paris from about 1800.[93]

In 1798, however, a Bavarian playwright, Aloys Senefelder, who was trying to find a means to duplicate his plays for rehearsals, stumbled on what he called "Chemical Printing." It was typical of an age that was becoming increasingly fascinated by chemistry and is based on the mutual repulsion of grease and water. The artist draws with greasy ink or crayon; the printer then chemically treats the surface to fix the grease; water is added, which avoids the greasy bits but is absorbed by the porous surface of the rest; the surface is now rolled with greasy ink, which sticks to the drawing and is repelled by the rest; a sheet of paper is now put on and the whole pulled through the press; an exact replica of the drawing is left on the paper. All kinds of surfaces, including metals and plastics, can now be used for this technique, but in the 1800s only porous stone was available, and the technique was thus known as lithography. Its outstanding characteristic is that it is neither cut in relief, like a woodcut, nor uses the *intaglio* method of incision, like line engravings, etchings, and the tints, but is a planographic or surface-method of printing. The artist treats the stone just as if it were paper: he can use pencil or crayon, brush and washes.

Lithography is a truly marvelous invention; its derivatives, such as offset and photo-litho, are infinite and are still being explored. But for artists, in the years 1810–30, when it came into widespread use, it seemed a miracle, for it allowed them to combine their subtlest effects with mass reproduction. Théodore Géricault used it for his brilliant watercolors of horses and men at work. Eugène Delacroix turned to it for his illustrations to Goethe's *Faust* of 1828, that masterpiece of romanticism. The same year, the young cartoonist Honoré Daumier fell on it voraciously as the perfect medium for his savage assaults on political and legal wickedness.[94] Lithography was used with equal success by many English town- and landscape watercolor artists. A typical (though also outstanding) example was Thomas Shotter Boys (1803–74). He learned lithography as a boy from the successful engraver George Cooke, who did Turner's *Picturesque Views on the Southern Coast of England* (1814–26). Boys worked on this great publication and on the *Cyclopaedia of Plants* produced by the creator of villa-suburbia, John Claudius Loudon.[95] In 1822, when he was 20 and already an expert lithographer, he went to Paris, where there was evidently a shortage of capable engravers. There he rapidly became a superb townscape watercolorist, in the circle of Bonington, Wyld and Louis Francia (who taught him). Boys developed a finer touch for watercolor lithography than any other painter since his day.

All these young and highly romantic artists were responding, spontaneously, to the staggering (and hitherto ignored) magnificence of French medieval towns. They all drew and painted out of doors, direct from nature. But Boys even carried lithographic materials in his pockets, so his drawings could be accurate and detailed, and the luminosity and atmosphere authentic. He thus made the highest-quality engravings of all his outdoor subjects because he wanted to inform the world, through mass reproduction, of the subtle beauty of what he had found.[96] Much of what he learned he passed onto his younger contemporary, William Callow (1812–1903), who was put to engraving in the artists' quarter of Marylebone at the age of 11 in 1823, working from 8 A.M. to 6 P.M. When he came to Paris in his teens, he and Boys scrambled all over the city together, painting watercolors and making lithographs. Together these two industrious and long-lived artists recorded a vast quantity of Western Europe, with extraordinary vividness and accuracy, for a mass public.[97] They were part of a wide movement whereby artists used new technologies for the visual education of the world.

It was characteristic of Boys, keen on any aid to accuracy, that he used the Graphic Telescope to record topographical details exactly. This useful instrument, which had the merit of fitting into a pocket, reduced a landscape to two dimensions on a flat surface and was invented by Cornelius, one of the Varley brothers.[98] Most artists did not disdain such aids and often invented gadgets to suit their particular work. They, too, were keen on chemistry to extend the range of colors and, equally important, to improve inadequate existing ones, such as the greens. Turner was so disgusted with the available greens and his inability to make a better one that he went to elaborate lengths not to use the color. Many artists mixed their own colors, and some held that doing so was the only way to get results. Thomas Girtin's first teacher, Edward Dayes, grumbled at the number of manufactured colors available in the first decade of the new century: "an evil so encouraged by the drawing-master and colour-man that it is not uncommon to give two or three dozen colours in a box, a thing quite unnecessary." But artistic experiments with color mixing, as the sad case of Sir Joshua Reynolds showed, could have disastrous results, and by the 1820s young artists who wanted to work almost entirely out of doors welcomed handy boxes—by 1827 Ackermann's shop was selling a compendium of 45 cakes of pigments, plus pencils, brushes, palette, slab chalk, and paper all for £3.13.6.[99]

These men did not see themselves as separate beings from scientists like Dalton and Faraday or engineers like Clements and Robert Stephenson, but rather, as fellow craftsmen. The great majority came from exactly the same world—the enterprising working class—and were keen to get on; to improve their skills; and, if possible, to revolutionize their trade. Turner, a characteristic example—he seems to have had no interests outside his profession—came from a family of Covent Garden shopkeepers, his father a barber and wig maker, son of a saddler, his maternal grandfather a butcher. David Roberts was the son of a shoemaker, William Mulready of a leather breeches maker. Turner's follower Augustus Wall Calcott came from a family of bricklayers, as did the architect Henry Holland. Antonio Canova's family were all stonemasons, and he made his name by creating a superb sculpted butter centerpiece for a Venetian feast. Bertel Thorvaldsen's father carved ships' figureheads, and Sir Francis Chantrey's made furniture.

John Singleton Copley's mother ran a tobacco shop; Gilbert Stuart's father, a snuff mill; Samuel Palmer's sold coal and books. William Callow's family were carpenters and builders; Sir Henry Raeburn's goldsmiths; Francisco Goya's gilders; John Varley's, instrument makers; and George Richmond's, innkeepers and horse dealers. A few, like Jean-Auguste-Dominique Ingres, had artist fathers (but his grandfather was a tailor, and he himself married a dressmaker) or came from a middle-class background: Thomas Cole's father founded a wallpaper business, John Constable's was a substantial miller. But the great majority of artists began humbly. "Limning or drawing is a bad trade," announced Varley Sr., and forbade his children to enter it. But all did, including his daughter Elizabeth. The topographical draughtsman John Preston Neale recorded: "Poor [John] Varley began the world with tattered clothes and shoes tied with string to keep them on. Yet nothing would damp the ardour of this determined, great man ... He rose early, drew till it was time to attend his situation [he was a silversmith's assistant], and set off with a large, ragged portfolio and a string over his shoulder, attached to it head first, at a full trot until he arrived at his master's'.[100] David Roberts, like many artists, began as an apprentice housepainter. His fellow apprentice, David Ramsay Hay, went on to transform housepainting, delighting his patrons with altarpieces, imitations of Pompeii and the like. Sir Walter Scott gave Hay the commission to transform his newly built Abbotsford, and this commission established D. R. Hay & Co. as the leading interior-decorating firm in Britain.[101] Other artists and architects, like Robert Smirke and Sir William Beechey, began as coach painters. Sir John Soane started as a footboy. Robert Clevely, the marine artist, was a simple caulker—and was laughed at for caulking in gloves.[102]

Artists saw themselves as craftsmen, who had to work hard at their trade in an increasingly competitive world. But the romantic element, which implied a subjective and personal vision, was growing. William Blake (1757–1827) hovered uneasily between the roles of artist-craftsman and poetic-visionary. He had an excellent training as an apprentice engraver and was extraordinarily innovative in everything he did—watercolors, illustration, color printing, work in tempera, prose and poetry. He had studied at the Academy Schools under Henri Fuseli, as his drawings indicated. Everyone in the world of arts and letters knew Fuseli. Coleridge called him Fuzzle or Fuzzly, a name the students adopted. They respected his teaching but disliked him. He forbade them to swear, but swore himself, his favorite rebuke being: "Sir, you are a damnation fool!" "You are a set of wild beasts," he would shout, "and I am your cursed keeper!" George Richmond later recorded a snatch of conversation. John Flaxman, RA, to Blake: "How do you get on with Fuseli? I can't stand his foul-mouthed swearing. Does he swear at you?' Blake: "He does." Flaxman: "And what do you do?" Blake: "What do I do? Why, I swear back, and he says, astonished: 'Vy, Blake, you are swearing!' But he leaves off himself." It was Fuseli who taught Blake that art was a highly emotional and intensely personal business. When painting, he said, "First, I sits myself down. Then I works myself up. Then I throws in my darks. Then I pulls out my lights."[103]

Blake, even more so than Goya, matured as an artist who saw no absolute line between the real world of nature, which he studied with minute intentness, like Dorothy Wordsworth, and the world of his imagination, which was both literary and religious. Nor did he draw much distinction between past and present, this world and the next. According to Richmond, "Before Blake began a picture, he used to fall on his knees and pray that his work might be successful." When Richmond complained to Blake and his wife of a lack of inspiration, Blake answered: "It is just so with us, is it not, for weeks together when the vision forsakes us. What do we do then, Kate?" "We kneel down and pray, Mr Blake."[104] Blake, despite relentless industry, did not meet with much professional success, but by 1815–20 he was becoming respected, even revered, as a painter's painter. Lawrence began to collect his drawings. A fellow artist, John Linnell, was responsible, in 1821, for commissioning Blake's greatest work, his watercolor illustrations for the Book of Job, completed in 1826, for which he received £150 for the copyright and 22 plates—the largest sum he ever earned.[105]

By the early 1820s, Blake was even, occasionally, seen in society. Lady Charlotte Bury was introduced to him at a party given by Lady Caroline Lamb. Her diary entry for 20 January 1820 reads: "A strange part of artists and literati and one or two fine folks, who were very ill-assorted with the rest of the company." She met an "eccentric little artist by name Blake; not a regular professional painter but . . . full of beautiful imaginations and genius . . . He looks careworn and subdued; but his countenance radiated as he spoke of his favourite pursuit and he appeared gratified by talking to a person who comprehended his feelings."[106] Richmond was only 16 when he first met Blake at a party given by Tatham the architect in St. John's Wood. He offered to escort Blake back to his house at Three Fountains Court, off the Strand. While Blake talked, Richmond said, "I felt as if I were walking on air and talking to the Prophet Isaiah." One remark of Blake's struck him with great force: "I can look at the knot in a piece of wood until it frightens me." Richmond, Linnell and their circle used to call Blake's rooms "the House of the Interpreter." One of them, John Giles, described Blake as "a man who had seen God, and talked to angels."[107] That, certainly, is what Blake himself believed. He told Crabb Robinson that "once, when he was carrying home a picture which he had done for a lady of rank, and was wanting to rest in an inn, the Angel Gabriel touched him on the shoulder and said 'Blake, wherefore art thou here? Go to, thou should not be tired.' He arose and went on unwearied."[108] Richmond said that when he entered Fountains Court, he used to plant a reverent kiss on the bell handle. But he admitted that Blake's room was squalid and untidy: "Once, Mrs Blake, in excuse for the general lack of soap and water, remarked to me: 'You see, Mr Blake's skin don't dirt.' "[109] As with Beethoven, visitors put up with the mess. Henry Crabb Robinson "found him in a small room which seems to be both a working-room and bed-room. Nothing could exceed the squalid air both of the apartment and his dress; but in spite of dirt—I might say filth—an air of natural gentility is diffused over him."[110]

In this room, Blake would describe his visions, which inspired a growing number of his drawings. While he did so, said Robinson, "it was in the ordinary unemphatic tone in which we speak of trivial matters . . . he said repeatedly, 'The spirit told me.' I took occasion to say, 'You use the same words as Socrates used. What resemblance do you suppose is there between your spirit and the spirit of Socrates?' 'The same as between our countenances.' He paused and added, 'I *was* Socrates,' and then as if correcting himself, 'a sort of brother. I must have had conversations with him, as I had with Jesus Christ. I have an obscure recollection of having been with both of them. . . .' He spoke with seeming complacency of himself, said he acted by command; the spirit said to him: 'Blake, be an artist and nothing else. . . .' [Blake added] 'I wish to do nothing for profit. I wish to live for art. I want nothing whatever. I am quite happy.' "[111] He told Robinson that the Voltaire-vision, in conversation, admitted he had blasphemed. "I asked in what language Voltaire spoke. He gave an ingenious answer. 'To my sensations it was English. It was like the touch of a musical key. He touched it probably French, but to my ear it became English.' " Sometimes Blake would draw his portrait heads of visions while visitors were present. " 'William Wallace,' he exclaimed, 'I see him now—there, there, how noble he looks—reach me my things!' Having drawn for some time, with the same care of hand and steadiness of eye, as if a living sitter had been before him, Blake stopped suddenly and said: 'I cannot finish him—King Edward I has stepped in between him and me.' 'That's lucky,' said his friend, 'for I want the portrait of Edward too.' Blake took another sheet of paper and sketched the features of Plantagenet; upon which His Majesty politely vanished, and the artist finished the head of Wallace.' " Most of these visionary heads have survived. They are often unexpected. There is a noble, very English-looking Mohammed, now in the Santa Barbara Museum. Canute looks saintly. Wat Tyler is young and handsome. King John and Edward I, meant to be villainous, look like decent fellows. The most sinister is Owen Glendower.[112] Visitors often discovered Blake holding imaginary sittings. One recorded: " 'Disturb me not,' he said in a whisper, 'I have one sitting to me.' 'Where is he and what is he—I see no one.' 'But I see him, Sir,' said Blake haughtily, 'there he is, his name is Lot—you may read of him in the Scriptures. He is sitting for his portrait.' "[113]

Among those who believed completely in Blake's visions was John Varley. Not that Varley was an unbusinesslike visionary himself; in many ways he was the most "scientific" artist and the central figure in the new British school which was making watercolor a major art form, and a popular one, too. This new art form combined the new cult of the British countryside, of which Wordsworth was the outstanding exponent, with important technical developments. Varley's friend W. H. Pyne pointed out in 1812 that "the love of exploring the beautiful scenery of our island" was "the greatest encouragement to landscape drawing" and that what the school was doing "may be almost considered as a new art." The Old Master style of using watercolor sketches of lightly tinted pen outlines, Pyne wrote, had nothing to do with the new British technique of pigments prepared with gum to achieve depths of tone for painted, finished works.[114] The pigment cakes made by William Reeves made possible astonishing brilliances, and the new woven "vellum paper" invented by the Kent manufacturer James Watman, which had "at once superseded all other fabrics," allowed artists to spread multiple washes on a surface unbroken by the old wiremarks of "laid" paper. In the 1780s Francis Towne and J. R. Cozens had been the first to use pure washes modeled by darker tints of the same color, in effect to model with color, rather than line.

Cozens had become insane and was looked after tenderly by Dr. Thomas Monro (1759–1833), the chief physician to the Bethlehem hospital. It was through Monro, a discerning and generous art collector, that the secrets of Cozens passed to his two young protégés, Thomas Girtin and Turner. The early, unsigned works of these two men are almost indistinguishable and are often known as "Monros." Girtin and Turner improved enormously on the earlier techniques, and so did Varley when he joined the Monro circle in the first decade of the 19th century. Varley would use new means to get depth and variety—scraping the paper, rubbing it with bread crumbs, sponging and cutting it; he would, said Pyne, "moisten and rub the paper clean away to get

brilliant highlights." "No artist," he added, "has ever studied his department with more abstract reasoning upon cause and effect." Pyne,
Varley and John Glover created the Watercolour Society (1804), which
within five years was attracting 23,000 people to its annual exhibition.[115]

These watercolor artists worked with heroic dedication. John
Glover would complete a major watercolor drawing in five hours exactly, and he was soon to carry his workmanlike methods to Sydney
and Tasmania, where he founded the Australian school of landscape
painting. Another fanatical worker was Anthony Van Dyke Copley
Fielding. Fielding and Varley married sisters. Varley would sit up all
night to work up his finished watercolors, known as "Varley's hot
rolls," because they were ready for breakfast. He averaged 44 major
watercolors a year. But he also taught. Indeed, he was probably the best
watercolor teacher who ever lived, for he insisted on outdoor work
from nature and he was particularly successful in encouraging gifted
pupils to develop their own manner, instead of imitating his. His pupils
included, besides Pyne and Fielding, Mulready (who married Varley's
sister Elizabeth), David Cox, Peter de Wint, John Linnell, William
Holman Hunt, and William Turner of Oxford. Many of them lived in
his house, at a fee of £100 (later £200) a year. Their ages varied from
13 to 18, and Varley, a keen boxing fan, would stage sparring matches
as well as painting competitions among them. He also gave lessons to
amateurs—the Earl of Tankerville, his sister Lady Mary Monck, the
Earl of Essex, the future Earl of Harewood—at a guinea an hour. After
much entreaty, he fitted in the future architect John Dobson "at five in
the morning, his time during the day being fully occupied." Elizabeth
Turner, daughter of a rich Yarmouth banker, said he was so enthusiastic about watercolor that "he would make everyone an artist, and as
good a one as himself . . . it is not Mr Varley's fault if we are not all
Michael Angelos."[116]

Varley was introduced to Blake by Linnell in 1818, and the two
established an instant rapport. It was not just that each admired the
other's work: They shared an interest in the paranormal. Varley, like
Fuseli, believed in the imminent Second Coming. He accepted the
claims of Joanna Southcott (c1750–1814), who persuaded over 20,000
followers that she would give birth to the Saviour at the age of 64 (but
died instead).[117] He was an ardent follower of astrology: "His pockets
were stuffed with almanacs" as a friend put it. "He entirely believes,"
wrote Elizabeth Turner, "in astrology, palmistry, raising of ghosts and
seeing of visions. . . . [He] was not happy until he had cast all our
nativities." He foresaw events and foretold that his house would burn

down (it is not surprising since it happened three times). On the back of Blake's drawing of Varley, now in the National Portrait Gallery, is written all the details of Varley's birth—"on 17 August 1778, 18 degrees 57 minutes, Sagittarius ascending."

Like Charles Bell, Varley accepted that physical expressions were closely linked to interior emotions, but he went further and accepted the pseudoscientific theories of Fuseli's fellow Swiss and friend Lavater, who believed that appearance was determined by innate moral and intellectual qualities. Fuseli helped to get Lavater's massive work on physiognomy translated into English, with 800 engravings, four of them by Blake. This five-volume tome became the basis for the phrenology theories of Franz-Joseph Gall and Johann Gaspar Spirzheim, whose own work appeared in London in the year of Waterloo.[118] Varley's own theory was that features do, indeed, reflect morals and the cast of mind, but that they are determined at birth by the stars. No wonder, then, that he was delighted by Blake's visionary heads, some of which he copied with the aid of his brother's Graphic Telescope, and used them for his own phrenological treatise, which Linnell illustrated.[119] According to Linnell, "Varley believed in the reality of Blake's visions more even than Blake himself." In fact, many of the heads were drawn at Varley's house in Great Titchfield Street, where they held evening sessions in the early 1820s; it was there that Blake produced his "head of the ghost of a flea" and other oddities.[120]

Men like Varley and Blake walked the borderline that divided the burgeoning new science and the old world of neoplatonism, necromancy and superstition, not without a strong itch for religion, usually of a Nonconformist variety. They all read the Bible regularly, but they followed Davy's lectures as well. In many ways, they looked forward to the pre-Raphaelites and even to the attitudes of William Morris and his following. The younger men, like Linnell and Richmond, clustered round a follower of Blake's, Samuel Palmer (1805–81), who lived in Shoreham, where his father, a Baptist, had had a "call," preached furiously, and was known to the village as "The Man of God." Palmer himself remained a religious fanatic all his life and put his views to his friends in immensely long letters—one to Richmond is 5,460 words. He thought of himself as "scientific," studied botany and geology, made elaborate drawings from nature, and used to quote with approval Mulready's dictum: "We cannot proceed a step without anatomy; and in landscape what is analogous to it."[121] He was fascinated by the work of Lyell, with his poetic understanding of "the underground," the muscles and bones of the land. But his own landscapes became, increas-

ingly, romantic imaginings. The younger art students, Linnell, Richmond, Edward Calvert and John Giles, used to go down from London
to Shoreham to see him, hitching a lift on a lumbering goods
wagon, or trudging the 20 miles on foot. They called themselves "The
Ancients." Once, Blake came with them and gave a demonstration of
Second Sight. Palmer would greet them with apples and green tea,
which he kept permanently on the boil. He was austere. One of his
sayings was: "A person living as an Epic Poet should be able to exist
on 5s2d a week." He was already, in his twenties, going bald, and wore
a long, flowing beard, a great rarity in those days. Even indoors he
sported a cloak. He would lead the Ancients in singsongs and readings
of Mrs. Radcliffe and Shakespeare.[122] These coteries, an increasing
feature of artistic life in the 19th century, often intermarried—Linnell,
for instance, wed Palmer's sister. The Ancients were strongly idealistic.
Richmond's diary for 7 April 1827, shortly after his 18th birthday,
records him doing portrait sketches, including one of Palmer, "in my
garret" (he lived on Half-Moon Street, then very much artists' territory), and continues: "Almighty God, grant that, in all my endeavours
in the year at hand to become useful to man, more perfect as an artist,
and above all better acceptable as a Christian, I may be instructed and
supported by Thy Holy Spirit."[123]

Their livelihoods were precarious. Even once-popular artists like
Richard Wilson, George Moreland and James Barry died destitute. The
number of people who were trying to live by art was growing fast.
Between 1800 and 1824, the number of artists exhibiting at the Paris
Salon nearly trebled, from 282 to 786. Seven years later there were
1,212. It was much the same in London. Indigenous art had flourished
during the long French wars, just as English Perpendicular architecture,
the first native style, emerged during the Hundred Years War. But with
the peace, the art-buying public tended to take vacations abroad and
often patronized French and Italian artists. Prices fell in London. Varley
had eight children and an improvident wife and, despite a superhuman
work load, he was declared bankrupt in April 1820, owing £4,140.2.4.,
and jailed. He underwent another seizure for debt in 1830. The diary
of Farington, who regarded himself as the Royal Academy's unofficial
almoner and made strenuous efforts to raise cash for indigent artists or
their widows, who were often left penniless, told many similar tales.
Richard Westall, RA, was another bankrupt, forced to sell all he had.
The historical painter Thomas Lane told Farington that to pay his
models, he was no longer able to afford meat "and lives on bread and
butter unless invited to the house of a friend."[124] Haydon, another
historical painter, entered in his diary on the eve of the New Year, 1826:

"After being deprived of my bread by the abuse of the press, an historical commission started up, gave me an opportunity again to burst forth, and saved me from ruin! On it depends my future subsistence and my power to bring up my boys like Gentlemen." He thanked God that he had, at present, enough money to live, adding: "And O grant health still to pursue my enchanting Art, & conclude what I have to do, to the honour of Thy gifts, and the satisfaction of my employers."[125] Alas, Haydon too met bankruptcy, and his life ended in suicide.

Who were artists' "employers" after 1815? The entire economic basis of art was changing. As with music, princely patronage was yielding to the market. Sir Thomas Lawrence and Canova—and David, until he fell from grace—who worked for the crowned heads of Europe, benefited from an old habit of courtly commissions which had not essentially changed since Rubens's day two centuries before. But they were two survivors from a rapidly dwindling band. In England, despite the vast increase in national wealth, there were scarcely half a dozen old-style patrons by 1820. True, three of them were exceptionally open-handed, making artists their friends and guests and encouraging them to use their picture galleries. Sir John Leicester, later Lord de Tabley, gave generous commissions to landscape painters, especially to record the famous tower and lake at Tabley in Cheshire, where artists were constantly housed.[126] William Bewick described how he, the Landseers (the engraver and his brilliant prodigy-son), Leigh Hunt, Keats and Haydon went to see Leicester's picture gallery in his London house: "He and Lady Leicester and their friends came in to see those remarkable men, and we were all introduced (a very unusual thing on such occasions)."[127] Even more friendly to artists was the immensely rich Earl of Egremont, whose Sussex palace at Petworth was a summer home for many painters, above all Turner, whose work there, in finished oils and color sketches, constitutes a permanent testimony to this great patron. Turner had for his special use the Old Library, over the Chapel, which he turned into a painting room, locking himself in. Even Egremont could get access to it only by giving two special knocks (Chantrey, by imitating them, once got in, too).[128] Egremont lived "magnificently," and 10, 20 or 30 people sat down to dinner at Petworth daily, many of them artists. He not only gave them hospitality and brought their works, but ran a discreet welfare service for those who were down on their luck. The miniaturist Ozias Humphrey, who went blind, received an annuity.[129] Haydon, threatened with bankruptcy, was sent £200. He left in his diary, on 15 November 1826, a grateful portrait of his Petworth host: "Such is Lord Egremont, literally like the sun. The very flies at Petworth seem to know there is room for their existence, that the windows are theirs. The dogs, the horses, the cows, deer and pigs, the Peasantry and the Servants, the guests and the family, the children and the parents, all share alike his bounty and opulence and luxuries. At Breakfast, after all the guests have breakfasted, in walks Lord E. First comes a grandchild, whom he sends away happy. Outside the window moan a dozen black spaniels, who are let in, and to them he distributes cakes & comfits, giving all equal shares. After chatting with one guest, and proposing some scheme of pleasure to others, his leather gaiters are buttoned on and away he walks, leaving everybody to take care of themselves, with all that opulence and generosity can place at their disposal, entirely within their reach. At dinner he meets everybody and then are recounted the feats of the day! All principal dishes he helps, never mind the trouble of carving. He eats heartily & helps liberally. There is plenty but no absurd profusion— good wines but not extravagant waste. Everything is solid, liberal, rich and English . . . The meanest insect at Petworth feels a ray of his Lordship's fire in the justice of its distribution."[130]

Egremont was particularly generous in letting artists study his art collection, an important aspect of patronage before the days of public galleries. So was Sir George Beaumont (1753–1827), who had acquired, from relatively modest means (he had £8,000 a year), a striking collection of Old Masters, which he made available to artists at his house in Grosvenor Square and at Coleorton in Leicestershire, a house he had rebuilt by George Dance in the Gothic style. A childless couple, the Beaumonts were both hypochondriacs, consuming a vast number of pills. They patronized Coleridge and Wordsworth, as well as painters; indeed, Lady Beaumont was so active in promoting Wordsworth's fame, it was, said Sir George, "as if she were paid to do it." In the gardens at Coleorton, they built a shrine to Milton, at the end of an avenue of trees, and another to Reynolds. Sir George was a passionate amateur painter and loved to encourage and befriend professionals. He supported Cozens when he went mad and educated the orphaned children of Julius Caesar Ibbotson. He discovered the struggling David Wilkie, and when the painter was ill and refused Beaumont's offer of £100, sent him three dozen of a famous port: "It is not in the power of man to colour well," ran the accompanying note, "or indeed paint with effect, if his port wine is not good; I have therefore taken the liberty of sending you a few bottles of such as you cannot get at the retailers." Wilkie painted the famous *Blind Fiddler* for him, and when Beaumont saw *The Village Politicians,* he was so overcome with delight he impulsely gave Wilkie one of his most treasured possessions, Hogarth's mahlstick.[131]

Over the years, Beaumont acquired various paintings by Wilson and Reynolds, two Rembrandts, a Poussin, three Claudes, Canaletto's *Stonemason's Yard* and—his own favorite—Rubens's superb landscape of his country house, *The Chateau de Steen,* which Lady Beaumont bought with a £1,500 legacy. When painters came to stay, they sketched and studied all day (never on Sunday), read Shakespeare and Wordsworth after dinner, and looked at the Old Masters by candlelight, a trick Beaumont got from Gainsborough. Haydon wrote: "We dined with the Claude and Rembrandt before us, breakfasted with the Rubens landscape, and did nothing, morning, noon or night but think of painting, talk of painting, dream of painting, and wake to paint again." When Constable came to stay in 1823, he was "bowled over" by the 30 superb Girtins, whose work he had never seen before, and mesmerized by the big oil landscapes. "Only think," he told his wife, "I am now writing in a room full of Claudes, Wilson and Poussins . . . the Claudes, the Claudes, are all I can think of here." Owners were more easygoing about their treasures in those days. Constable said he "dragged" various paintings into his bedroom and "slept with one of the Claudes every night" (they were usually kept in the Breakfast Room). Indeed, Beaumont lent him his small Claude, *Hagar and the Angel,* to copy. Beaumont's generosity was all the more notable in that he did not really admire Constable's work; like most of the older generation, he thought it "unfinished." In turn, Constable laughed at Beaumont's 18th-century preference for somber colors, especially browns. When Constable was painting *The Cenotaph,* his impression of the Reynolds shrine, Beaumont asked: "Will it not be difficult to decide the placing of the brown tree?" "Not in the least, for I never put such a thing into a picture."[132]

But these men were the last of their kind. Beaumont died in 1827, Egremont, aged 86, a decade later, his hearse preceded "by a group of artists, Turner at their head." No one replaced them. Artists were no longer prepared to accept the gentlemanly but firm authority that patrons like Beaumont expected to exert. Matters came to a head in 1815 over the British Institution. The British Institution had been founded in 1804 for the encouragement of British art, and its exhibitions were, after the Royal Academy itself, the chief shop window in which living artists could display their wares. The lists Farington gives in his diary show how well attended it was by the nobility. But the well-born connoisseurs wanted loan exhibitions of Old Masters, too, and when the first was held, in the year of Waterloo, there was an explosion of anger from the artistic profession. On the artists' behalf Robert Smirke produced an anonymous pamphlet, the *Catalogue Raisonné,* which

Beaumont and other patrons resented as an unmannerly personal attack. The dispute was envenomed by some vigorous articles by Hazlitt, who hated the Royal Academy painters and savaged the pamphlet unmercifully.[133]

Hazlitt, who has strong claims to be considered the first British art critic of significance, had a low opinion of British art and thought that the best way it could be improved was to raise the public's taste by exhibitions of Old Masters, especially the Italians. He thought patronage was finished. Artists must paint what they saw, in the way they saw it, and discerning private collectors—the market, in short—would sort out the good from the bad.[134] This was certainly the pattern of the future and is was already happening in the decade 1815–25. The grandees were being replaced by collectors like Dr. Munro, Turner's Yorkshire supporter, Walter Fawkes or Constable's Archdeacon Fisher. Not only were artists becoming more numerous, the range of people who appreciated art was being extended into the huge middle class. A sign of the times was Lawrence's funeral in January 1830, when, despite a snowstorm and thaw, thousands turned out to see the coffin taken from the home of the Royal Academy at Somerset House, where it had lain in state, to Saint Paul's, to be buried alongside Reynolds. Some 42 official coaches and 80 private carriages drove before bareheaded crowds along Fleet Street and up Ludgate Hill, all the shops shut and draped in mourning banners. "It is something to feel," Turner wrote, "that gifted talent can now be acknowledged by the many who yesterday waded up to their knees in snow and muck to see the funeral pomp."[135]

Another sign of the time was the opening of London's National Gallery to the public in May 1824. The notion of public galleries was by no means new; the Oxford Ashmolean goes back to 1683, the Vatican had begun displaying its collections and admitting the public in 1773, and soon afterwards Charleston set up the first public gallery in the Western hemisphere. But the democratization of art began in earnest in 1793, when the Revolutionary regime admitted the public to the royal collections in the Louvre. Thereafter it became French policy to concentrate in this palace-museum a comprehensive collection of paintings and sculpture which the Republican armies looted from churches, convents and palaces all over Europe. This procedure, which certainly made it easier for artists and connoisseurs to study the Old Masters, was strongly approved by Hazlitt when he first visited the Louvre during the Peace of Amiens in 1802—it was one of the reasons he admired Bonaparte. Public museums were also opened in the conquered territories. In 1807 Bonaparte created the Accademia in Venice; in 1808 his brother Louis, puppet-king of Holland, opened the Rijksmuseum in Amsterdam; and in 1809 the French brought together a huge collection of north Italian loot in the Brera, Milan. The De Medici collections were likewise displayed in the Uffizi in Florence. At the peace settlement, 1814–15, thanks to Castlereagh and Canova, many of the Louvre's stolen possessions were restored to their rightful owners (though the two greatest treasures of the Borghese Palace, the Winged Victory and the Venus de Milo, remained). The principle of publicizing art was retained, however. In 1817 Pius VII began a huge program to enlarge the Vatican Museum. In 1818–19 Ferdinand VII established and opened the Prado in Madrid. In 1823 Frederick William III set up the Berlin Museum (though the public was not generally admitted till 1830).

In January 1823, John-Julius Angerstein, the Lloyds financier, died, leaving his collection, among the best in Europe—it included Raphael's *Pope Julius II* and Rembrandt's *Woman Taken in Adultery*—on the market. Beaumont had long agitated for a National Gallery. As he put it in a letter to Wordsworth, in Rome it was "delightful to see people of all descriptions from the highest to the lowest" enjoying great art in the Vatican, whereas in London "our people" were forced to "devour the Panorama or Mrs Salmon's Waxwork." He now said to the government: *"Buy* Angerstein's collection and I will give you mine."[136] Happily trade was good, and the Chancellor of the Exchequer, currently known as "Prosperity" Robinson for that reason, produced £57,000 for Angerstein's 38 best pictures. The new National Gallery, temporarily set up in the financier's house, 100 Pall Mall, was visited by 24,000 people in its first six months.[137] Peel was one of the early trustees, and in due course many of the pictures from his superb collection, which included Rubens's *Chapeau de Paille*—he housed it in the 66-foot gallery of the house he built in Whitehall overlooking the Thames— went to the National Gallery, too.[138]

Painters welcomed public access to great collections because they thought it educated public taste and widened the market for their work. Just as the pianoforte and the birth of the "musical genius" like Beethoven was creating a huge middle-class public for concerts and music publishing, so the picture gallery, the print and the watercolor were persuading the middle class to buy art. The 19th century was to be the golden age of the professional painter: Never before or since has so high a proportion of the population, in Western countries, bought original works of art by contemporaries.

The days of high-Victorian academic splendor, when Lord Leighton held court at his Moorish palace in Kensington, Franz von Lenbach built the opulent Lenbachaus in Munich, and Frederick Edwin Church lorded it in Olana above the Hudson, were not yet.[139] But artists who knew how to run their business were already prospering in the expanding market, not alas without jealous criticism from their brethren. John Opie, who left £12,000, was said to be "a miser," sewing up caches of guineas (one contained 198) in his clothes. Alan Ramsay, who died even richer, "only twice painted not for money" and was accused of having "a cold and narrow mind." George Romney was "chained down by a spirit of avarice," so it surprised none that he left over £50,000. Sir Francis Chantrey, an exceptionally canny sculptor-businessman, saved up £150,000 and so was able to endow his famous bequest. His wife seems to have entered into the spirit of his trade, and when he died went to his studio "with a hammer and knocked off the noses of many completed busts so that they might not be too common."[140] Chantrey began life doing a milk round with a donkey and ended it shooting woodcock on the Earl of Leicester's estate at Holkham; he was so proud of killing a brace with one shot that he carved them in marble. Even watercolorists did well if hard-headed enough. Peter De Wint's wife Harriet related him naming the price of some drawings in guineas. Gentleman: "There are no guineas now, Mr Wint, so we'll call it pounds." "No you won't! My price, sir, is guineas." "Really, you don't mean to quarrel for the shillings?" "Don't I? The shilling are my wife's and I will quarrel with you for two straws, so take them or leave them."[141] (It was a hard age, but a charitable one: in 1821 De Wint gave £10 toward the cost of sending Keats to Italy in search of life-giving sun.)

The Royal Academy's annual show in May, which opened the London Season, was the best showplace by far. This explains why artists were so desperate to get elected to membership because then they could display works as of right. But there were many disadvantages. Somerset House was unsuited to the bigger canvases because the curving staircase—brilliantly portrayed in a famous Rowlandson drawing—was so narrow that they had to be hauled up with ropes. The wall space was grotesquely overcrowded, and everything depended on where your work was hung and what was near it. There were tremendous rows in consequence, not all of them recorded in Farington's diary. When Constable finally showed his *Opening of Waterloo Bridge,* done in 1817, he heightened it on varnishing day with vermilion and lake. The painting was hung next to Turner's *Helvoetsluys,* described by C. R. Leslie as "beautiful" but "a grey picture." Turner came several times into the room, looking from Constable's picture to his own, "and at last brought his palette . . . and putting a round daub of red lead, somewhat bigger than a shilling, on his grey sea, went away without saying a word. The intensity of the red lead, made more vivid by the coolness of his picture, caused even the vermilion and lake of Constable to look weak." Hence Constable's bitter comment: "[Turner] has been here, and fired a gun."[142]

Constable was constantly unlucky with varnishing days. In 1826 when he showed *The Cornfield*, Chantrey, who prided himself on being a rough diamond, said "Why, Constable, all your sheep have got the rot—give me the palette, I must cure them." He dabbled at the canvas, then threw the palette at Constable and ran off. In 1829, Chantrey again interfered with Constable's exhibit, *Hadleigh Castle*, and put a glaze of asphaltum over the foreground. "There goes my dew," said Constable, and took it off.[143] John Martin was another victim: In 1814 his sensational *Clytie* was ruined before the show opened when another artist spilled varnish right down the middle. He hated the Royal Academy thereafter and they, in return, never elected him.[144]

To escape the academy's limitations, artists sometimes followed the example of John Singleton Copley and Thomas Gainsborough and held their own shows. Even Blake had a show in 1809. From 1804 Turner used his house in Harley Street to display his wares, and after 1822 he designed and fitted his own permanent gallery, hung with red, a background chosen by Peel as well for his private gallery. Wilkie, a newcomer to success in 1812, attempted a show at 87 Pall Mall, but it flopped because, in deference to collective sentiment by the Royal Academy, which hated "puffing," he did not advertise it enough. In the post-1815 years, newspaper reports and reviews became of critical importance in getting the public to go to art exhibitions, another sign of the rising power of the press. It was newspaper publicity that turned the painting Wilkie did for Wellington, *Chelsea Pensioners Hearing the News of Waterloo*, into such a cynosure at the 1822 Royal Academy exhibition that, for the first time, railings had to be put up to keep the crowds back.[145]

One-man shows, especially of giant pictures, lured the press, but it was difficult to draw the line between art and showmanship, especially if the pictures were displayed on commercial premises, like the Egyptian Hall in Piccadilly. When Haydon finally completed his enormous *Christ's Entry into Jerusalem*, for which he used Hazlitt, Lamb, and other friends as models, Beaumont kindly allowed a preview at his Grosvenor Square house and invited a vast social throng. The occasion was dominated by Mrs. Siddons, celebrated for delivering platitudes in a wonderfully theatrical manner. According to Haydon's account, no one had dared to pronounce on the painting until "in walked, with all the dignity of her majestic presence, Mrs Siddons, like a Ceres or a Juno. The whole room remained dead silent, and allowed her to think. After a few minutes, Sir George Beaumont, who was extremely anxious, said in a very delicate manner, 'How do you like the *Christ?*' Everyone listened for her reply. After a moment, in a deep, loud, tragic tone, she said: 'It—is—completely—successful.' " From Grosvenor Square the monster was trundled to the Egyptian Hall to draw in the paying public. It failed to do so, and Haydon afterwards complained: "Is it not a disgrace to this country that the leading historical painters should be obliged to exhibit their works like wild beasts and advertise them like quack doctors?"[146]

The reason why Haydon's picture flopped was that it met stiff competition from renderings of one of the most horrific events of the time. On 2 July 1816 the French frigate *La Méduse,* flagship of a convoy taking soldiers and settlers to the new colony of Senegal, struck bottom off the coast of Mauritania, with 400 aboard. Its six lifeboats would hold only 250. For the rest a raft, 65 feet by 28, was built. Leaving lower ranks to the raft, the Captain took over the flotilla of boats, which were supposed to tow the raft ashore. But the towropes parted, and the raft was left to fend for itself. There were nightmare scenes aboard it. From the fourth day on, all those aboard practiced cannibalism—a subject which, like incest, seems to have exercised a dreadful fascination at the time—drank seawater and urine, and there was madness and murder. When a rescue ship found the raft, only 15 were still alive, of whom 5 died quickly. So 140 were lost in the horrors. The details, which the government tried to suppress, were leaked to the press. It emerged that the Captain, who was largely to blame, had been appointed by favoritism, so the affair turned political. In many ways, it was a dress rehearsal for the Dreyfus case of the 1890s. The ship's surgeon, who survived and wanted to tell the truth, was dismissed. He wrote a book, helped by another survivor (also dismissed), who opened a political pamphlet shop in the Palais Royale arcade, under the sign *Au Naufrage de la Méduse.* The scandal rolled on and on, the theme attracting a multitude of poets and, still more, painters.[147]

By 1819–20 the British public had become almost as keen on the tale as had the French. A melodrama, *The Shipwreck of the Medusa,* was a hit at the Coburg Theatre. A week after it opened, in mid-June 1820, the Egyptian Hall put on display, in a room adjacent to Haydon's *Christ,* Géricault's masterly *Le Radeau de la Méduse,* which had been the sensation of the 1819 Paris Salon and remains, in many ways, the greatest painting of the age. It attracted 50,000 people and killed any remaining interest in Haydon's exhibit.[148] An even bigger popular success was *Marshall's Marine Peristrephic Panorama of the Wreck of the Medusa French Frigate and the Fatal Raft,* a sequence of events, rather than a single canvas, and 10,000 square feet to Géricault's 432. Hundreds of thousands saw it in London and on tour. Touring was now important. Following the death of Benjamin West, his sons built a gallery in the garden of his house in Newman Street in 1821 and displayed 94 of his paintings. Over 95,000 people paid to see it in the first year, but attendance then tailed off, and the show was too cumbersome to take to the provinces.[149] On the other hand, *Napoleon on Board the Bellerophon,* worked up from sketches done in Plymouth harbor in 1815 by a then-unknown artist, Charles Eastlake, was bought by a syndicate of five Plymouth businessmen who made a fortune taking it all over Britain. Eastlake's profit on the deal came to £1,000, on which he went to Italy, ending up as president of the Royal Academy and head of the National Gallery.[150]

We have already examined the leading exponent of art showmanship, poor John Martin. But it is worth pointing out that no man illustrated better the overlap of art and technology at this time. When he first came to London, as he later recalled, he "supported myself and my family by pursuing almost every branch of my profession, teaching [he was drawing master to Princess Charlotte], painting small oil pictures, glass enamel painting, watercolor drawings"; he became a master of mezzotint, etching and drypoint, aquatint and lithography. At the same time, he had imaginative schemes for iron ships, maritime propulsion, coastal warning lights, new building materials, colliery safety and urban transport systems.

Like many people in a stinking world, he was particularly interested in designing a modern sewage system. His obsessions, indeed, help to explain his popularity, for they were widely shared. As the German painter G. F. Waagan put it, the reason Martin's paintings were so popular was that they united "the three qualities which the English require above all in art—effect, a fanciful invention inclining to melancholy, and topographical historical truth."[151] Exhibited in London, then in halls in all the major towns of the British Isles, Martin's monsters attracted larger crowds than any other paintings in the 1820s.[152] His mezzotints sold by the thousands, and his excellent line engravings, being cheaper, by the hundred thousand. He reinforced his popularity by allowing his work to be reproduced in magazines and annuals: *The Gem,* the *Keepsake, Amulet, Forget-Me-Not, Friendship's Offering,* the *Literary Souvenir.* Much of the hostility he met from fellow painters was humbug, for during the years 1815–30 the more successful of them were turning increasingly to the mass market of prints. Turner achieved immense sales with his topographical line engravings and with the mezzotints of his *Liber Studiorum*. By the end of the 1820s, genre painters like Wilkie and the new animal-sporting genius, Edwin Landseer, were earning more from prints than from the sale of their paintings. It was the same for Délacroix and Ingres in France.

Painters were as interested in mechanical reproduction as was anyone, for they had a strong financial interest in its improvement. They had not yet grasped the threat to their livelihood which would develop if the imaginative foundation their work supplied was eliminated by the machine. From Gainsborough on, they were intrigued by the technology of the effects of light and made increasing use of the refined *camera oscura* and its derivatives. (They were not the only ones; in the 1820s a version of this machine was used to detect pickpockets at horse races.) Brougham characteristically boasted in his old age that the paper on optics he wrote at age 16, portions of which were read to the Royal Society in 1796, anticipated the invention of photography, and it was only the scientific establishment's willful omission of this key passage which "witheld from humanity" the invention for decades.[153] In fact, the theoretical basis of photography was widely understood by about 1800. Experiments were conducted on producing and fixing optical images by Wedgwood, Davy, Coleridge and other members of the Clifton scientist-poet circle. Just as computing was held up by the absence of lightweight materials, so protophotography lacked suitable paper and fixatives. Thanks to the theoretical work of Samuel Klingenstierna of Uppsala and the practical experiments of Herschel, who produced many suitable lenses as well as the first giant observatory telescope, the optical problems had been solved by 1815. A workable shutter was developed in the 1820s.

The most persistent investigator was the theater designer and panorama painter Louis-Jacques Daguerre, a showman who oscillated between London and Paris with visual displays employing a variety of advanced technologies. Constable went to the private view in 1823 of Daguerre's new cinematic transparencies. He found it "very pleasing" and admitted it produced a "great illusion," but pronounced it "without the pale of art because its object is deception." He added: "The style of the pictures is French, which is decidedly against them. The place was filled with foreigners—& I seemed to be in a cage of magpies."[154] One of Daguerre's associates, the physicist Joseph Nicéphore Niepce, had meanwhile been using, as a light-sensitive medium, silver chloride, as opposed to the silver nitrate used by Wedgwood. In 1826 he contrived to produce and fix *View through a Window at Grasse*, often regarded as the first true photograph. But it was Daguerre's plates, made in the next decade, which aroused the awe and fear of a radically new way of presenting the world in two dimensions. As Charles Dauthendey, one of the earliest photographers, put it: "At first we did not dare look long at the images he produced. We were frightened by the clarity of the men, imagining that these small, indeed tiny, faces fixed on a plate could in turn look back at us!"[155]

Daguerre's cross-Channel commuting, the display of Géricault's *Radeau* to London crowds (it was not the only example; Le Thiers's *Brutus* was at the Egyptian Hall in 1816 and 18 of Le Jeune's Napoleonic battle-scenes in 1828), and the growing tendency of art dealers to operate from both London and Paris—all reflected a new phenomenon: the internationalization of the art world. Of course, great painters, from Hans Holbein on, had often moved from one court to another. Now, however, artistic ideas, like scientific ones, were crossing frontiers automatically and quickly. Artists moved around constantly, in search not of patrons but of new visions and techniques. As with music, the rise of a mass, middle-class market, which was buying prints and, increasingly, original works, was beginning to dissolve local peculiarities and to develop a European taste that, with the spread of collecting to the United States, Canada, Australia, Buenos Aires, Rio de Janeiro, and Mexico City, would soon be global. It was between Britain and France that artistic exchanges were most significant. Indeed, in the years 1815–30 it is almost correct to speak of an Anglo-French school of painting, which also constitutes the distant prehistory of the modern movement. More notable still, this was the first and only time that English painters exercised a powerful influence on French art, rather than vice-versa.

It was part of a wider phenomenon of English prestige, which sprang from the nation's triumphant emergence from the long wars; its enormous and growing empire; unchallenged maritime supremacy; industrial and commercial paramountcy; the world's strongest currency; and, not least, its concomitant—the aura of wealth and superiority that English travelers carried with them everywhere. Americans were to enjoy the same réclame in the years after 1945. The feeling that England was the paradigm of a successful nation, based on a superior constitution, was particularly strong in Restoration France, which with its Charter, limited monarchy and narrow-suffrage parliament, was almost an English creation. Not until the 1830s did Paris recover its position as the literary and artistic capital of Europe. In the meantime,

Scott and Byron had more readers in France than did any native authors. It was even the fashion, followed by Lamartine, De Vigny, Berlioz and many others, to marry English women. Lady Morgan, returning to France in 1829, had her Irish hackles raised by this Anglomania and protested: "Not a sanded floor, not a sullied parquet are now visible. Nothing but English carpets and English cleanliness. The *garçon* cries 'Coming up!' and the tea and muffins are worthy of the Talbot at Shrewsbury." In Paris she claimed it was hard to buy French confectionary, being offered instead "de crecker, de bun, de plomcake, de spice gingerbread, de mutton and mince-pie, de crompet and de apple-domplin." No French soap, only "de lavender-vatre" or "de Vinsor sopa." She boasted she was even offered a bottle of "genuine poteen." It disgusted her to see Parisian ladies in "shawls of tartan-plaid" straight out of "Valtre-Scott," feminists in English-style men's clothes and "Byron followers" with "open, short collar and a wild and melancholy look."[156]

However, there were intrinsic as well as general reasons why English painters influenced French art at this time. It was primarily the work of two men, Richard Parkes Bonington and John Constable. Like Keats and Weber, Bonington was a genius who was destroyed by tuberculosis as a young man (he died in 1828 at age 26). If he had lived, he might well have come to dominate European painting because he combined extraordinary originality, the highest technical skills, and immense industry. He was also an arresting personality, a romantic hero, to whom others evidently looked for leadership; this quality comes through in some magical depictions of him by his French follower Alexander Colin.[157] Whether he is truly a French or an English artist is a matter of opinion. He was born near Nottingham in 1802 and came to Calais in 1817 when his impoverished father, a former prison governor, tried to set up a lace-making business there, using smuggled machinery. In Calais he met a local painter, François-Louis-Thomas Francia. Francia had been a royalist refugee in London in the 1790s, working as an assistant in Barrow's Drawing School in Great Queen Street and Lincoln's Inn Fields and, more important, joining the circle of watercolorists, including Girtin and Turner, who met at Monro's house in the Adelphi. He seems to have absorbed all Girtin's more daring wash techniques, which even Turner envied, and from 1817 he transmitted them to Bonington.[158] This influence was the most important element in Bonington's formation as an artist, but he also benefited from a rigorous French training at the École des Beaux Arts. It incorporated the studio of

France's best teacher, Baron Antoine-Jean Gros, who had been taught by David. Bonington was one of the few artists, then or since, who have worked with equal virtuosity in both oils and watercolor. What was entirely his own, however, was a new and daring use of bright color. This was what most struck Gros, and he told his other students: "You do not pay enough attention to colour, gentlemen. Colour . . . is poetry, charm, life and nothing can be a work of art without life." He told Bonington: "You have found your path—follow it."[159]

Among the students, and even more impressed, was Delacroix. The two young men had met copying in the Louvre, became good friends, for a time shared a studio and went on painting expeditions together on both sides of the Channel. Delacroix was amazed by Bonington's light and color effects and especially by his watercolor highlights, essentially achieved by exploiting the white of the paper—Bonington made them, said Delacroix, "glitter like jewels."

Bonington turned his back completely on Claude and Poussin, a daring thing to do in the early 1820s, heightened his palette, and painted with a new realism, producing watercolors and even oils entirely out of doors. He painted, when he chose, at great speed, using such new devices as the "broken wash," oils as well as watercolor, often without any preliminary line, employing instead very fine brushes which he wielded like pencils. His townscapes and landscapes in both media thus give the impression of great freshness and audacity. In fact, Bonington was a highly cerebral and deliberative painter, who chose the spot from which he painted—in Paris, on the Normandy coast, in Venice and elsewhere in Italy—with great care, so that his pictures are superbly designed even though he painted exactly what he saw. The angle of his vision, his height from the ground, how little or how much to show—these things were carefully calculated, so that he "frequently coins views which have since become standard picture-postcard images."[160]

Bonington was also frenziedly energetic in traveling and producing. His output, despite his short painting life, is impressive, and since he was also businesslike and extremely shrewd in picking the bookshops which sold his work, he disposed of a good many. All these qualities help explain why he dominated an important section of the Parisian art world. This art world had a strong Anglo-French flavor. Its leading hostess was the daughter of Thomas Banks, RA, who was the wife, later the widow, of the British Embassy chaplain, the Rev. Edward Forster—their daughter married the great French sculptor Baron Henri de Triqueti. Mrs. Forster gave weekly parties that were attended by Delacroix and Ingres, Chopin and Berlioz, and scores of French and English artists. The English contingent included Boys, Callow and members of the great Fielding clan of engraver-painters—Copley, Theo, Thales and Newton.[161]

Boys and Bonington liked the Parisian girls. Fragments of notes, half in French, half in English, survive. Thus, from May 1826: "Dear Boys, Try and come this evening. Rivet and a few friends will be here [his *atelier* in the rue des Martyrs], avec the french model & tout cela pour rejouir le chrétien . . . votre ami Bonington."[162] Delacroix, on the other hand, followed the fashion of Parisian intellectuals and was in love with the English girl Elizabeth Salter, writing her letters in what he called "that develish English tongue." "I conceive," he wrote to her, "you are wearied to see me in stairs to the face of the whole house. . . . Oh my lips are arid since had been cooled so deliciously. . . . You are a cruel person which play afflicting the anothers. Nevertheless not be angry at it. I am a pitiful Frenchman and I bet I have told in this write a multitude of impertinence. . . . Why whisker not sting more."[163]

A few surviving sketchbooks of the young Camille Corot (he was six years older than Bonington), with views of Paris and the Normandy coast, testify to the vogue for open-air work which Bonington promoted and exemplified so brilliantly. Both Delacroix and Géricault shared his passion, at this time, for watercolor and lithography. Bonington, like his follower Boys, loved lithography. He was used extensively by the publisher Ostervald for his huge *Voyages pittoresques et romantiques dans l'ancienne France,* which began to appear in the 1820s.[164] When Bonington went to Venice in 1826, what he brought back and displayed at the Salon of 1827 was so stunning that it revived artists' interest in the drowsy city. There must then have been a score or more professional artists in Paris who looked on him as their leader: John Scarlett Davis, E. W. Cooke and James Holland, as well as Boys, Callow and the Fieldings among the English, and among the French Paul Huet and Jules Collignon, as well as Colin.

The critics referred to *le Boningtonisme,* by which they meant brilliant color, extreme freedom combined with exact dexterity in handling paint, low horizons and big skies, and dewy freshness. But by then Bonington was dying. He made heroic attempts to continue working right to the end. Indeed, he was still experimenting, trying out a new walnut-juice medium invented by the engraver W. J. Cooke, which enabled color to be washed over a brown ink. One of Cooke's apprentices, John Saddler, recorded: "Bonington after dinner, while reclining on two or three chairs, made sundry sketches with pen and brush, with the juice, and expressed his intention when he was better he would try the material further. . . . They were brought into the study to be thrown into the paper basket, but I took care of them . . . as the very last things

Bonington produced—he died after that visit." The last completed
watercolor, *The Undercliff*, worked up from a sketch of Normandy is
one of his most striking and original color compositions. On the back
his mother wrote: "August 6th & 7th 1828. The last drawing made by
our dear son about prior to his fatal dissolution. Never to be parted
with."[165]

Still more important, in the long run—and on both sides of the
Channel—was the work of Constable. Constable was born in 1776, two
years after Wordsworth. There were significant links between the two
men. Like all the greatest Romantics, they were self-obsessed. Curiously enough, what Constable disliked most in Wordsworth, whom he
knew well through the Beaumonts, was what he called his "egoism"—
precisely the term most people would have applied to Constable. Both
men were obsessed by their childhood and its physical surroundings in
nature. In 1829 Constable copied out Wordsworth's key lines: "My
heart leaps up when I behold / A rainbow in the sky; / So was it when
my life began / So is it now I am a man / So be it when I shall grow
old / Or let me die! / The child is father to the man." What the two men
shared amounted almost to a theory of art, which would have been
recognized by Chateaubriand (and later by Marcel Proust): that the
child has perceptions which are intuitive; when the man matures, he
pulls them out of his memories, examines and rationalizes them, and
finds that what they chiefly concern is the harmony of nature and man
(himself). In a sense, Wordsworth's entire *oeuvre* was a reexamination
in maturity of his childhood perceptions. Constable's egoism was similar. His biographer Leslie records that when asked if he painted a
picture for "any particular person," he replied: "Yes, Sir, it is painted
for a *very particular* person, the person for whom I have all my life
painted."[166]

It is important to grasp that Constable came comparatively late to
professional painting. For family reasons, his father was most anxious
that he should carry on the milling business and reluctant to let him
have time off for instruction. He eventually got some good teaching
from John Thomas "Antiquity" Smith (and at the Royal Academy), but
his painter's vision was formed long before he had any training and was
thus right outside the academic tradition. The browns and yellows and
hesitant blues of Claude and Poussin meant nothing to him. What he
painted all his life was essentially what he had seen, through his eyes
alone, as a child on the Stour and its banks. "I paint," he wrote, "my
own places best—Painting is but another word for feeling. I associate
'my careless boyhood' with all that lies on the banks of the Stour. They

made me a painter (& I am grateful), that is I had often thought of pictures of them before I had ever touched a pencil."[167] His drawing master Smith reinforced his own inclination to look at everything with the most minute attention and to note color as carefully as form, especially the greens: "The shades or degrees of this colour as it is distributed in nature are innumerable."[168]

Constable's paintings, even his slightest sketches, have one out-standing characteristic: accuracy. He was punctilious in showing agri-cultural processes and implements. As his younger brother Abraham put it: "When I look at a mill painted by John I see that it will *go round*."[169] But it was in rendering nature itself that he strove most earnestly for truth. Unlike Wordsworth (and Turner), he was not moved by the sublime. He dutifully went to paint in the Lake District, like all other English landscape artists, and to please his patron Fisher he often painted Salisbury Cathedral, but it was the Suffolk of the Stour which roused his deepest emotions. As he put it, in a letter to Fisher, "The sound of water escaping from mill-dams etc, willows, old rotten planks, slimy posts, and brickwork, I love such things. . . . As long as I do paint, I shall never cease to paint such places."[170] He liked the little canals, their barges and horses, as well as the river, sedges, reeds and flowers that grew on the banks; small figures doing agricultural tasks; trees bending over water; and skies above promising more water to come. Rendering these images truthfully was to Constable (as to Wordsworth) a moral action. "Every tree," he wrote, "seems full of blossom of some kind & the surface of the ground seems quite living— every step I take & on whatever object I turn my eye that sublime expression of the Scripture, 'I am the resurrection and the life' seems verified for me."[171]

Constable's progress was slow because he was teaching himself an entirely new way of painting nature. Comparing the 1802 version of *Dedham Vale* with the 1828 view done from the same spot, it is possible to see how much he had learned in that quarter century, making nature not only true but living, getting light and moisture down on his can-vas.[172] The vast majority of his work was done within a radius of three miles, and there, as he put it "my limited and restricted art may be found under every hedge." He produced thousands of sketches, but saw them as working tools, not as masterpieces. When John Linnell intro-duced him to Blake, and the latter, leafing through his sketchbook, exclaimed: "Why, this is not drawing, but *inspiration*," Constable— who really did not like other artists—snubbed him: "I never knew it before: I meant it for *drawing*." Sketches to him were units that he used to build up into a painting which transcended the subject and told everything about it. "A sketch of a picture is only like seeing it in one view," he wrote. "A sketch (of a picture) will not serve more than one state of mind—that which you were in at the time."[173] He was as industrious as Bonington and much more laborious, for he lacked virtuosity. There was no sudden change in his work, just a slow but progressive and cumulative movement toward his mature style and mastery of big spaces.

By early 1819 Constable was ready to tackle the large-scale canvas and began work on *The White Horse,* the first of his "six footers." He told John Fisher that this painting was "one of the strongest instances" of his realizing a "picture" he had thought of as a child. At the same time he moved to Albion cottage, Hampstead, and began to take an increasing interest in skies, often making them (like Bonington), the protagonist of the picture. This focus raised a problem, however: "Their difficulty in painting both as to composition and execution is very great, because with all their brilliancy and consequence, they ought not to come forward or be as hardly thought about in a picture any more than extreme distances are." Yet "that landscape painter who does not make his skies a very material part of his composition elects not to avail himself of one of his greatest aids. . . . [Skies] must and always shall with me make an effectual part of the composition. [There is no landscape] in which the sky is not the *key note, the standard of scale* and the chief *Organ of Sentiment. . . .* The sky is the *source of light* in nature and governs every thing."[174]

One result of Constable's trip to the Lake District was an increased interest in cloud formations, and there is little doubt that he followed the scientific work of Dalton and Otley. Scientific interest in weather grew rapidly after 1815. In 1818–19 Luke Howard published his notable work *The Climate of London,* and it was after reading it that Constable began his systematic sketches of clouds. Although he refused to accept that the panoramas or other illusionist tricks were genuine art, he thought it essential that painters should keep up with scientific and technical progress. He shared Cornelius Varley's interest in optics and physics. The times, he thought, were "scientific," and "in such an age as this, painting should be understood, not looked on with blind wonder, not considered only as poetic aspiration, but as a pursuit, legitimate, scientific and mechanical."[175]

By the early 1820s Constable was painting superbly and on a large scale. He might have gone further and faster and thus contracted the quarter century or so which separated his work from early Impressionism, but to some extent he had to bow to prevailing opinion, putting in and smoothing over a vast amount of detail which now looks almost fussy. Even so, he ran into great hostility. Fisher bought his first great work, *The White Horse,* for 100 guineas, "an act of generous patronage that the artist never forgot." He also bought *Stratford Mill.* Nobody else seems to have wanted either. It is arguable that, without Fisher, Constable might have abandoned painting as a profession. He told the archdeacon that "I should almost faint by the way when I am standing before my large canvases" were he not "cheered and encouraged by your friendship and approbation." He would "never be a popular artist—a Gentleman and Ladies painter—but . . . your hand stretched out teaches me to value my own natural dignity of mind."[176] The English art world of his day never valued Constable. Beaumont and Farington encouraged him but neither really liked his work. He had great difficulty in getting elected to the Royal Academy and, even afterwards, his work was unregarded by his colleagues: The same word recurs monotonously: "unfinished." W. P. Frith described an awkward scene at the hanging committee when Constable's *Willow by a Stream* was accidentally put with the pictures submitted by nonmembers of the academy and brought in to be judged. "The first judge said, 'That's a poor thing'; the next muttered 'It's very green'. . . . Constable rose, took a couple of steps in front, turned round and faced the Council. 'That picture,' said he, 'was painted by me. I had a notion that some of you didn't like my work, and this is pretty convincing proof.' "[177]

It was a different matter in France. When *The Haywain* appeared in the 1821 Royal Academy exhibition, Géricault, who was in England, saw it, marveled, and took the news back to Paris. The painting went on display again at the British Institute, priced at 150 guineas. The Paris dealer John Arrowsmith offered £70 but was turned down. But, early in 1824, he bought the picture, plus *A View on the Stour* and a small oil of Yarmouth for £250. He was back again in May with Van Bree, Director of the Antwerp Academy, and another Paris dealer, Claude Schroth, each of whom bought a painting. A third painting was sold to the Vicomte de Thulluson, who "says that I am a great man in Paris," Constable reported. Arrowsmith put the two big canvases on display in his Paris gallery, writing: "I can now, Sir, assure you that no objects of art were ever more praised." The *Haywain* and *Stour,* plus a view of Hampstead Heath, were all in the 1824 Paris Salon. After a few weeks, in response to demand, they were shifted to the Salle d'Honneur. The painter William Brockendon reported to Constable from Paris that he had heard a Frenchman say, "Look at these pictures by an Englishman—the very dew is on the ground."[178] In all, Arrowsmith bought 20 Constables and took them to France. The impact on French art was immediate and lasting. On studying Constable's colors, Delacroix went back to his studio and repainted the background of his masterpiece, *The Massacre at Chios*. The Barbizon School and the work of Theodore Rousseau were further consequences of "the Constable effect."[179] Bonington and two of the Fielding brothers were also in the 1824 Salon, and in 1827 the English contingent was even larger: Bonington and Newton Fielding; the great recorder of India William Daniell; a mezzotint of Wilkie's *The Rent Day;* two portraits by Lawrence, including his famous *Master Lambton;* but, above all, Constable's *The Cornfield*. Some critics said the jury had gone too far in admitting so many English works. In fact, French generosity, contrasting with the insularity of the Royal Academy, was shrewd: It was part of the process whereby French art was enriched from abroad and, even more important, whereby Paris became the art center of the world—above all of its advance guard, the place where artists came to learn and develop and show. Constable might have enjoyed more success in his life if he had joined Bonington there. But he hated the French; had no wish to set foot in France; and, in any event, was tied to his native subject matter. Had he been born a generation later, he might have made the move. As it was, his work became a milestone along the road toward the modern international school as much as an episode in English art.

The notion of an Anglo-French school was strengthened by the many visits French artists paid to England, made possible after 1815 by the growing ease and cheapness of travel. The *Annals of the Fine Arts* reported (1820): "Horace Vernet, son of the famous French animal painter, and a party of French artists, were hunting in Normandy, and on a freak they started for England and gave a call in the different artists here."[180] Both Géricault and Delacroix profited enormously, and in a variety of ways, from their English experiences. They were romantic archetypes, Delacroix of the robust-brigand, Géricault of the tragic-sufferer version. Delacroix, as an illegitimate offspring of Talleyrand, had romantic credentials by birth, and he gave an impression, with his black mane and massive black eyebrows, dark eyes and sallow complexion, of suppressed fury. Baudelaire was later to describe him as "a volcano artistically concealed beneath bouquets of flowers"; he made you think of "those ancient monarchs of Mexico . . . whose hand, skilled in human sacrifice, could immolate 3,000 human beings on the pyramidal altar of the Sun."[181] He seems to have fancied himself a Byronic hero and was certainly as assiduous a womanizer.

Géricault, on the other hand, was very likely a homosexual. He was born in 1791, into a rich middle-class family of Rouen property owners and lawyers, the same background as Flaubert. He came to Paris to run a tobacco firm, but a timely annuity from his mother made him independent. He developed, very early, a passion for horses, bought and owned many, and studied under the equestrian painter Carle Vernet. He drew and painted horses from life, in the English manner of Stubbs and Marshall, which he got indirectly through Vernet, though the passion with which he depicted them was unique. Horses fired his imagination in the same way that naked women made Ingres want to paint. One reason he liked England was because he found the men there more interested in horses than in women. He studied horses with the same devotion that Constable brought to clouds. His drawings and oil sketches show he knew exactly how their legs moved at speed, as finally proved 50 years later by the camera, though in his big paintings, to suit public taste, he followed the convention of the "flying gallop."[182] As a young man, he had an affair with his aunt by marriage and made her pregnant, a criminal offense. His parents looked after the child. Thereafter he never touched women. He was hypochondriacal, neurotic, a depressive and suicide prone, interested in death, executions and madness. As a hobby, he painted portraits of the insane, particularly monomaniacs, assisted by Dr. Etienne-Jean Georget, head of the Salpetrière women's asylum in Paris. Five portraits survive: a man suffering from delusions of military grandeur, a woman cursed with obsessive envy, a woman gambling addict, a kleptomaniac, and a compulsive kidnapper. These studies are much more "scientific" than are Goya's madmen, done 20 years earlier, which reflect conventional beliefs in how lunatics behave, and there is no doubt that Géricault knew a good deal about the subject. Two close relatives died insane, and he believed artists (and poets) like himself were particularly susceptible to mental illness. He seems to have been self-destructive—overspending, gambling and riding recklessly. He probably knew his life would be short, for his hypochondria was linked to acute back and chest pains which were real enough, caused in all probability by tuberculosis of the spine, from which he died.

One aspect of Géricault's studies of horses was interest in ichyphalic stallions and the covering of mares (horses copulating), the subject of two of his greatest watercolors.[183] He seems to have associated male blacks with stallions. From 1818 he formed a passionate friendship with Louis Bro, a black soldier in the Haiti troubles, and this friendship influenced his handling (and perhaps the selection) of the *Medusa* theme. There had been only one black on the raft. Géricault portrays three, one with a dominant position in the picture, using Bro as a model.[184] (He got Delacroix to pose for one of the white sailors, at the apex of the pyramid design.) The picture was an exercise in radical realism. He interviewed the survivors and even used some of them as models. But his exaggeration of the role played by blacks springs from his concern about their underdog role in society and his hatred of the slave trade, a topic which obsessed him. He was critical of this great painting, dismissing it as "a mere easel picture" (it is, in fact, 24 by 18 feet), but when he was invited to exhibit it in London, he went there in winter 1820 to make arrangements.

Géricault stayed in England 18 months, and the experience was critical to him in several ways. He developed the habit of constant outdoor sketching, transforming the poverty, squalor, drudgery and teeming creation of wealth of the world's greatest city into a new form of the sublime. He drew brilliant scenes of everyday life, from racing at Ascot to unloading cargo in the docks to the "bagging" of three felons just before hanging (Thistlewood, Tidd, and Ings), scenes in which the real heroes were usually the horses—chargers; hunters; racers; and, above all, the vast shire-horse drays, whose majestic beauty came as a revelation to him. He learned to use watercolor with great skill and to make superb lithographs from his drawings. He discovered English art. After watching Wilkie in his studio and returning again and again to the 1821 Royal Academy exhibition, where he found Constable and much else, he wrote to Vernet that it was now necessary "to be steeped in the English school. . . . The Exhibition just opened has confirmed me in the belief that colour and effect are understood and felt only here. You cannot imagine the beauty of this year's portraits, and of many of the landscapes and engravings, and of the animals painted by Ward and Landseer, aged eighteen—Old Masters themselves have not done better in this line. . . . I formed a wish at the Exhibition that a number of paintings then before me might be placed in our museum. I wanted them to be a practical demonstration, more useful than prolonged reflection."[185]

Back in France, early in 1822, Géricault began to harvest his English gleanings and to work on a great picture which would surpass his *Radeau*. In England he had met many antislavers and seen George Moreland's *The Slave Trade,* hitherto known to him only through a print. French feeling against slavery was growing, too, and Géricault intended to stimulate it by a tremendous propaganda picture, the power of which is indicated by surviving drawings.[186] But his disease was closing in, aggravated by riding accidents incurred in frenzied gallops on the thoroughbreds he loved. By February 1823 he was bedridden and scarcely left his room until his death 11 months later, another item in the sad catalog of artistic waste compiled by tuberculosis in the 1820s.

Géricault's *Radeau* was an important landmark in European art and illustrated two points which ensured the continuing strength of

French painting: the willingness of their artists to tackle contemporary public themes on the grandest scale and the magnanimity of the French state in supporting such efforts. By seizing on the *Meduse* scandal for the picture which would make or break his reputation, Géricault turned his back on the celebration of national military glory which had preoccupied most French artists for two decades and chose something which was implicitly an attack on the regime. It was the first indication of a shift of artists away from compliance and toward a radical criticism of society, a change of allegiance which would destroy the notion of a unified public culture, except in archaic or totalitarian states. Nevertheless, the Bourbon establishment took the painting to its conservative bosom. When it was first shown in 1819, it was awarded the Salon's gold medal. In 1824 it was bought by the Louvre. By the end of the 1820s it was already treated as a classic. Where Géricault pioneered, Delacroix followed. If Delacroix got his coloring from the English, he seized upon Géricault's dynamism, his exoticism and his political passion for resounding issues. Where Géricault painted blacks, Delacroix turned to Levantines (later Arabs). Instead of horses, he painted tigers, lions and leopards; the establishment and expansion of public zoos, such a feature of the years 1815–30, made this possible. He loved attending feeding time of the big cats at the Jardin des Plantes, when he was, as he put it, *"pénétré de bonheur."* Most of all, he developed a sharp nose for controversy.

In 1822 Delacroix exhibited his first big picture, *Dante and Virgil in Hell,* at the salon. The subject was anodyne, but the work was spotted by the journalist Adolphe Thiers, who was to play so significant a part in overthrowing the regime. Romantic writers were just turning against the Restoration under the slogan (coined in Belgium) of *le romantisme est le libéralisme en littérature,* and the case of Géricault showed that young painters could be recruited, too. Thiers hailed the work: "No picture reveals so clearly the future of a great painter."[187] Thus encouraged, Delacroix turned to the subject which, in the early 1820s, increasingly attracted the European intelligentsia: the liberation of Greece. With one or two exceptions, English artists (unlike the poets) avoided the Greek war, which is curious in view of their obsession with the Elgin Marbles. French painters rightly judged it a splendid theme to tackle. Taking up a Turkish atrocity that aroused peculiar abhorrence in Europe, Delacroix exhibited his *Massacre at Chios* at the 1824 Salon. This, like the *Radeau,* was a provocative, highly contemporary painting on the grand scale, and it incorporated the new sense of color that Delacroix was learning from the English. It made his reputation. Almost overnight he became, as it were, a public painter, a national asset, however dangerous. Hence, though intervention in Greek-Turkish affairs was against the policy of the Holy Alliance, the Bourbon government bought the work. As a result, Delacroix was able to visit England, May–August 1825. Bonington and the Fieldings took him to the galleries and introduced him to painters like Wilkie and Lawrence. He saw various Shakespeare plays. For the rest of the 1820s, Scott, Shakespeare and Byron became his literary mentors.

The "English factor" guided Delacroix's work at several levels. His *Portrait of Baron Schwiter* (1826) is done in the manner of Lawrence. His *Execution of the Doge Marino Faliero* is Byronic in subject matter, but the painterly influence is Bonington. He was also under Byron's spell when he painted *The Death of Sardanapalus* (1827), an impressive but monstrous creation, which hovers uneasily between the sublime and the ridiculous. It is supposed to show the dying Assyrian despot having his harem slaughtered so that no one who survived him should enjoy their favors. The theme is horrific enough in itself, especially when presented on such a scale and with Rubenesque opulence. What made it so difficult for Delacroix's admirers to defend, then and now, was that Sardanapalus (a self-portrait) does not look as if he is dying but as if he is enjoying the occasion. It has been compared to a sex-horror movie.[188] At the time, it aroused shock and fury and made Delacroix unpopular with sensitive as well as powerful people.

But Delacroix was a hard-working man who could always retrieve an error of judgment by new surprises (he was so prolific that, in the year before his death, there was an exhibition of just under 200 of his paintings, most of them enormous, and he produced 6,000 drawings and engravings). He had already returned to the independence theme with his *Greece on the Ruins of Missolonghi* (1826) and, now identified with the radicals, he worked the subject for all it was worth until the end of the decade. The Greek woman who dominates *Missolonghi* opens her arms in an appeal for help. It is a dress rehearsal for the great populist masterpiece with which Delacroix greeted the revolution of 1830, *Liberty on the Barricades,* in which Madame France looks behind to see if the mob is following her. That appealing if meretricious work made Delacroix the official artist, as it were, of the July Monarchy. Although the new government, which bought it, considered it too inflammatory to be shown often, Thiers, the impresario of the regime, loaded the painter with official commissions. It marked the end of the Anglo-French epoch in painting and confirmed the bifurcation which was taking France toward artistic radicalism, leaving the English happily engrossed with dogs and horses, lakes and mountains, legends, knights, maidens and melancholy.

*   *   *

There was, however, one exception: the most important figure of all. Turner's impact on the way in which artists paint the world, and on how those who love pictures see it, was as deep and lasting as Beethoven's impact on music and took place over a much longer span. Turner was born in 1775 when Chardin was still treasurer of the French Académie. He sold his first drawings when he was only 10 and was making his living as a teenage artist while Jean-Honoré Fragonard was still patronized by the court of Louis XVI. By the time Coleridge and Wordsworth were creating English romantic poetry in 1797, he was already a master making a distinctive contribution to the transformation of English painting. Yet he was still sketching and painting (albeit with failing power) in the late 1840s, when Camille Pissarro and Edouard Manet were just beginning to paint seriously. He was particularly fortunate in his father who, though a shopkeeper with little education, recognized Turner's brilliance when he was only eight or nine; saw that he got expert instruction in architectural and topographical drawing from the earliest possible age; stoutly defended his "genius," as he called it, when the boy was still an adolescent—"What!" he exclaimed indignantly, "*him* making drawings for Dr Monro at half-a-crown!"— became his first commercial agent; and, to the end (he died in 1829 at age 84), looked after his household, servants and money, stretched and prepared his canvases and varnished the finished pictures.[189]

Turner inherited his father's commercial acumen and businesslike habits. He always got up early, before sunrise; worked hard—he left a greater *oeuvre,* in finished paintings and watercolors, etchings and other prints, sketches and notebooks, than any painter who has ever lived—lived frugally, spent little, saved and invested. His money went for his art. While in his teens, he was able to finance sketching trips in Britain, and from 1802 to 1845 he was able to afford 19 extensive working visits to the Continent. Long before he was 21, he began to "lay up something in the Funds" and his professional life was a continuing success story. He exhibited his first big oil in 1796, when he was 21. By this time, he told Farington, he already had more commissions than he could handle. At 24, the earliest possible age, he was elected ARA, and three years later, to the Royal Academy. By 1803 he was already being widely imitated by young painters, and the next year he opened, in his Harley Street house, the first gallery entirely devoted to his work. This gallery was purpose built, probably in consultation with Sir John Soane, the leading gallery designer, and top-lit throughout, then a new device. His second gallery, begun in 1819, was even more elaborate. Turner was also instrumental in transforming the lighting at the Royal Academy and the British Institute.[190] Sales from his gallery, from the Royal Academy and the Royal Institution, and from his work for publishers brought him a handsome income.

By the end of the war, he had over £9,000 in the funds, plus land and two houses. He left about £150,000.[191] Never in his working life did he feel under financial pressure to make concessions to public taste. To be sure, he had a strong commercial sense. Under no circumstances would he reduce his prices, though he was willing to allow keen clients to pay in installments. He was as sharp about money as was Beethoven but much more sensible (and honest) in handling it. Anxious as he was to sell his work, his determination to follow his artistic judgment was at least as firm as Beethoven's and always prevailed. He never married, had no acknowledged children, never caused difficulties for himself by sexual entanglements and, unlike Beethoven, wasted no emotional energy on family disputes.

It is hard, then, to think of any great artist who won for himself, throughout his life, such complete freedom to develop his art in his own way. Happily this freedom was balanced by a sober and practical approach to painting. Turner never dramatized himself in the way Beethoven, Byron, Shelley, Chateaubriand and Berlioz did. Nobody could have been further from the new Romantic image of the suffering artist-genius-hero. He never complained of criticism, though there were times, especially in the decade 1805–15, when attacks by Beaumont and others did him damage.[192] He was a stoic and usually a silent man, who felt his work would speak for itself. David Roberts, the best of the younger landscape painters, contrasted Turner's modesty with Constable's egoism, "ever talking of himself and his works, and unceasing in his abuse of others."[193] Turner's entire life was devoted to the unostentatious acquisition of complete mastery over his craft in all its aspects. Descriptions of him at work remind one of Henry Maudsley using his tools or George Stephenson at work on an engine. He had the strong propensity of the age to take every possible advantage of scientific advance. Hence his concern with optics and studio lighting. He followed paint technology closely and made use of three newly developed colors—chrome yellow, cobalt blue and emerald green—as soon as they became available. His paint box, in the possession of the Tate Gallery, contains 10 yellows, four of them developed in his lifetime. The Turner watercolor box in the Royal Academy's collection has four reds, four browns, two blues, two greens and six yellows. Yellow, the color that was most susceptible to development through modern chemistry, was the basis of his coloring. Like many artists, now as then, he regarded the greens that were available as unsatisfactory and the portrayal of green as one of the insoluble problems of painting. In fact, he hated green. He told J. B. Pyne he wished he could "do without trees." His habit of painting palm trees yellow earned him a rebuke from William Westall: "I have travelled a great deal in the East, Mr Turner, and . . . I can assure you that a palm-tree is never of that colour: it is always green." Turner: "Umph! I can't afford it—can't afford it!"[194]

His severe practicality came out again in his attitude toward sketching. He always drew out of doors—drawing from the imagination was useless. When he was 67, to make preliminary sketches for *Snow Storm: Steam Boat off a Harbour's Mouth* (1842), he had himself lashed to the mast of the *Ariel* in a gale. He colored out of doors, too, when he could, notably in the superb series of large-scale watercolors of Welsh and Lakeland hills he did in the late 1790s. But like many artists on outdoor location, Turner resented the time taken from drawing by coloring (you can draw in the rain, but you cannot paint, especially in watercolor). For his first trip to Venice (1819), he only had five days, and on the first day he took a gondola ride from the entrance to the Canale di Cannaregio, upstream to where the Station now is, then slowly down the Grand Canal to the Salute and beyond, with pauses to sketch. In this way he produced 80 pencil sketches in one day (possibly two). He did a much smaller number of color sketches separately.[195] The same year Soane's son recorded him saying, "It would take up too much time to colour in the open air—he could make 15 or 16 pencil sketches to one coloured." But R. J. Graves, who watched him when he reached Naples, testified: "Turner would content himself with making one careful outline of the scene and . . . would remain apparently doing nothing, till at some particular moment, perhaps on the third day, he would exclaim 'There it is!' and, seizing his colours, work rapidly until he had noted down the peculiar effect he wished to fix in his memory."[196]

Eyewitness accounts of his 1813 painting tour of the West Country show the superb craftsman at work: quick, economical, industrious, all-observant. At Rame Head he went out in a small boat in heavy weather. The rest were seasick, but Turner "sat in the stern sheets intently watching the sea and not at all affected . . . like Atlas, unmoved." When he sketched, he "seemed writing rather than drawing." Then followed a 20-mile walk, with Turner "a good pedestrian, capable of roughing it in any mode the occasion might demand". Watching the ships in the Tamar one evening with De Maria, the Covent Garden scene painter, the two resolved a technical argument while viewing the setting sun. "You were right, Mr Turner, the ports cannot be seen. The ship is one dark mass." "I told you so, now you can see it—all is one mass of shade." "Yes, I can see that is the truth, and yet the ports are there." "We can take only what we see, no matter what is there. There are people in the ship—we don't see them through the planks." "True."

The young Eastlake, who watched Turner on this trip, said he often made his sketches "by stealth." Like the craftsmen and inventors he so much resembled, Turner sometimes seemed to be guarding the secrets of his trade. He had a spy hole in his gallery, so he could pounce on painters who made sketch-notes of the works displayed. His own sketches were sacred. Ambrose Johns, the Devon landscape artist who acted as his assistant on the 1813 trip, hoped Turner would give him a sketch as a reward but was disappointed. Instead he received, in due course, a small, finished oil. The sketches were the tools of Turner's trade, and he kept them for reference and use, sometimes a quarter century after they were made.[197] Over the years he built up a comprehensive visual archive of much of Britain and Europe.

But Turner would nonetheless ignore his own record in pursuit of an imaginative effect he had conceived (possibly on another occasion in a different place). His *Regulus,* painted in Rome in 1828, had its lighting scheme completely transformed by Turner on the walls of the British Institute in London, watched by an astonished Sir John Gilbert: "He was absorbed in his work, did not look about him but kept on scumbling a lot of white into his picture—nearly all over it—The picture was a mass of red and yellow in all varieties. Every object was in this fiery state. He had a large palette, nothing on it but a huge lump of flake-white: he had two or three biggish hog-tools to work with, and with these he was driving the white into all the hollows and every part of the surface.... The picture gradually became wonderfully effective, just the effect of brilliant sunshine absorbing everything, and throwing a misty haze over every object. Standing sideway at the canvas, I saw that the sun was a lump of white, standing out like the boss of a shield."[198]

We have considered Turner's technical approach at length because he had more effect on other painters, in the long run, than any master since Rembrandt and should be seen as the ultimate progenitor of the modern movement in art. His craftsmanship has to be emphasized, but it should also be grasped that the dynamic of his art was strongly intellectual and emotional. Like Beethoven he was little educated outside his craft, but he read widely all his life, seized on ideas, thought about them, transformed them, and applied them in his art. Modern research has revealed that the literary and intellectual content of his work is much greater than hitherto supposed.[199]

It was characteristic of Turner that, like Delacroix but unlike most English artists, he constantly returned to public themes—Greek independence, the slave trade, industrialization—even though his references are sometimes upstaged by his artistic exuberance. He remained faithful always to his belief that painting is a form of language, that it is essentially descriptive, and that its object is to tell the truth about nature, seen objectively. He believed that paintings have a moral purpose, too, to instruct and improve—hence the literary content—but that they do so by showing the effect of light on objects. In no sense was he an abstract or "uncommitted" painter. To understand light, he studied optics and the current theory of color. He knew classical theory, as explained by Aristotle and Pliny, and Newton's seven-color system; he was familiar with what Kant and Goethe had to say about color; and followed the work of Thomas Young, which Brougham tried so hard to discredit. He certainly read *Chromatics,* published in 1817 by George Field, who spent much of his life improving pigments available to artists. He also read the manuscript essay, *Letter on Landscape Colouring,* by his friend Sawrey Gilpin, who did the animals in some of Turner's early landscapes.[200] But in the end Turner had to work out his own way not merely of distinguishing colors, but of actually getting them onto the canvas—a very different matter—when suffused by varying lights. It was here that his original genius manifested itself.

Almost from the start Turner was adventurous in using color and depicting light. By 1810 he was credited with founding the "white school," which waged war against the browns and sepias of the classicists and moved decisively into the upper range of colors. Oddly enough, most contemporaries, their minds conditioned to the lower color key of Claude, Poussin and their infinite followers, had lost the capacity to look directly at the colors of nature and saw Turner's high chromatic vision as "invention." The supposedly radical *Examiner* referred to his "intemperance of bright colour." The *Literary Gazette* accused him of replacing "the magic of nature" by the "magic of skill," when, in fact, he was trying to do the opposite and use truth to destroy artificial conventions.[201]

The term *white painters* was a hostile expression which scared Turner's followers and might have deflected a lesser man from his purpose. As his paintings became larger and lighter, the public was, for a time, deterred. One of his greatest, *Frosty Morning* (1813), now damaged by cleaning, remained unsold, as did *Apulia* (1814), which Turner hoped would win the prize at the British Institution. His decision to close down his first gallery that year may have been prompted by these reverses.[202] But in the year of Waterloo, both his *Dido Building Carthage* and *Crossing the Brook* won instant and almost universal acclaim, except from Beaumont and his friends, and their power to hurt was undermined by the *Catalogue Raisonné* row that summer. Turner followed this success by painting the superb *Decline of the Carthaginian Empire* (1817), with its blaze of setting sun—now darkened by destructive cleaning—and he was soon building his new gallery. The next year his *View of Dort* raised the chromatic pitch still higher. Henry Thomson, RA, who got an early view, described it to Farington as "a very splendid picture" with colors so brilliant "it almost puts your eyes out." Happily this magnificent canvas, which was bought by Walter Fawkes and remained in his family, is still in perfect condition. There was no precedent for this blaze of color. Even Constable, not a man given to praise his contemporaries, called it "the most complete work of genius" he had ever seen.[203]

But it was on his first visit to Venice in September 1819 that Turner finally released himself from the restraints of Old World painting, though no one could have known it at the time. In his four months in Italy, he filled 19 sketchbooks with hundreds of tiny drawings and notes (100 in Venice alone), plus many watercolor studies of Rome and Naples on a ground of gray wash. Twice on Lake Como and four times in Venice, immediately after his arrival, he did on-the-spot watercolor studies while the impact of the north Italian light, which he had never experienced before, was still fresh. Dazed by the interaction of sky, still water and buildings in misty dawn, in full sunlight, and at sunset, he used pure and translucent color for naturalistic purposes, something no one—not even he—had done before.[204] None of these studies was seen for many years, or even developed by Turner into finished oil paintings at the time. But they all marked the point at which he discovered, through the experience of his own eyes, the truth of Goethe's observation that we perceive the visible world through light, shade and color, rather than by our actual knowledge of solid forms.[205] Henceforth Turner was concerned not so much to draw objects and color them as to paint the effects of light itself—its translucence and opacity; its manifestations in cloud, water, fog, mist, snow and steam; and its capacity to transform, dazzle, ennoble, terrify, explain and inspire wonder. Turner now began to set himself problems, in rendering light on a two-dimensional flat surface with inadequate chemical colors, problems which he could not solve and are, by their nature, insoluble. As he grew older, he grew more and more interested in photography, spending hours questioning the American photographer J. J. E. Mayall about its physical basis: "He came again and again, always with some new notions about light."[206] It was as though he wanted to know what science could do in areas where art was inadequate. But if no painter could surmount the problems, Turner's heroic efforts to grapple with them, in the 1820s and after, produced astonishing work, only half-understood at the time, which the young John Ruskin was to devote much of his life to explaining and which would excite a multitude of painters not yet born.[207]

There was another sense in which Turner stood at the threshold of the modern age. He was probably the last great painter who believed that he and his scientific contemporaries were involved in the same task: to explain the Earth, by laws and equations and experiments, on the one hand, by visual presentation on the other, to those who lived on it. He and the scientist and technologist still spoke roughly the same language and belonged to recognizably the same culture. In the late 1820s he discovered an affinity with Shelley. The poet was then dead, but Turner found he had tried to put down air and atmosphere and infinite spaces in words, as Turner was himself seeking to do in paint. So, too, he felt an affinity with Faraday; they were both experimentalists, working skillfully with their hands as much as with their eyes and their brains, to explore the physical secrets of the world.

But as the 1820s progressed, it became harder to maintain that all men of genius could speak to one another. There was a sad moment at Lowther Castle in 1827, when Sir Humphry Davy and William Wordsworth met for the last time. Wordsworth later complained to a correspondent that it had no longer been a meeting of kindred spirits: "His scientific pursuits had hurried his mind into a course where I could not follow him, and had diverted it in proportion from objects with which I was best acquainted."[208] The parting of the ways between art and science, the bifurcation into two—indeed into many—cultures was only one aspect of modernity. Turner's pursuit of light in his paintings of the 1820s suggested not only the clarity but the confusion, the chaos even, of nature. The new world coming into existence inspired awe edging into fear, as well as admiration. The great forces now unleashed, the machines on the march, the visions unveiled, signaled destruction and phantasmagoria almost as much as progress. To these aspects we now turn.

EIGHT

Masques of Anarchy

In June 1819, while the English radicals were organizing their summer mass marches, a more formidable exploit took place which might have made the subject of a sensational Turner canvas: Simón Bolívar, Generalissimo of the newly proclaimed republic of Venezuela, crossed the high Andes with his army of liberation. The achievement was more remarkable than the crossing of the Alps by Bonaparte or even Hannibal, two events which certainly excited Turner's imagination. By 1819 the Alps were being penetrated even in their highest reaches. The summit of Mont Blanc had fallen as far back as 1786, the Meyers had climbed the Jungfrau in 1811 and Maynard the Breithorn in 1813. While Bolívar struggled on the *alteplano*, J. N. Vincent was conquering one of the summits of Monte Rosa. The high Andes, by contrast, were almost totally unexplored; the first major peak, Cotopaxi (19,350 feet) was not climbed till 1872.[1] Bolívar had no proper maps, only Indian guides. His raggle-taggle army, the most reliable unit of which was the so-called British Legion of Peninsular veterans, now mercenaries, had only light clothing. Among the camp followers were wives, mistresses and children. The ascent was all the more remarkable because the approach-march during the rainy season was itself horrific, and it was succeeded by the trackless swamps and moors of the high plateau. There were almost daily crossings of unbridged ravines and mountain torrents, in which much equipment, including saddles, was abandoned or fell into the abyss. At one campsite above the snowline, one of the women gave birth.[2]

Once on the other side of the *alteplano*, Bolívar struck at the heart of Spanish-held Colombia. The week before Peterloo, he entered the capital, Bogotá, and took what remained of the garrison prisoner. Then he rode on, the Venezuelan civil authorities, led by the Vice President, Francisco Santander, taking over the city. On 10 October, Santander decided to execute the 38 captured officers from the royalist garrison and had them brought out of their cells and lined up in the Cathedral Square, in what was rapidly becoming a Latin American set-piece tradition. Why he wanted to kill them never emerged, then or since. A passerby who objected to the procedure on the grounds that Bolívar had reprieved the prisoners was shot on the spot. After the firing squad had done its work, Santander harangued the silent crowd and rode off, preceded by musicians; he was heard to be singing a song specially composed to mark the slaughter. Later he commented: "I find a special pleasure in having all Goths [Spaniards] killed."[3]

What was the explanation for this medley of heroism and savagery? Who was Bolívar, and what was he trying to do? The "liberation" of Spanish America (except for Cuba) was one of the central events of the early 19th century, bringing into existence an entire continent of independent states, the greatest nativity of nations in world history until the mass decolonization of the 1960s. It was the direct consequence of Bonaparte's assaults upon the old European order, and especially of his destruction of the Spanish monarchy in 1808. Events in Latin America thereafter, which have had abiding consequences to this day, reflected the instability and moral degeneration which accompanied the Bonapartist armies wherever they went. The first modern European dictator spawned a teeming progeny across the Atlantic, and the characteristics of Revolutionary France, where libertarian rhetoric and democratic constitutions went hand in hand with mass killings and unbridled tyranny, were rapidly transplanted there. What happened south of the Rio Grande in the years 1815–30 epitomized all the hopes and fears, but, above all, the ambiguities, of the modern world which was being born.

The Spanish empire, on the eve of its dissolution, lacked dynamism and enterprise, but was, in many respects, rich and civilized, distinguished by its noble baroque cities. Madrid itself, an immense place with over 200,000 inhabitants, was famous for its Calle de Alcala, the widest street in Europe, which could take 10 carriages abreast, and for its magnificent Botanic Gardens near the Prado Palace. It was one of the cleanest cities on Earth and well policed. Some of the New World towns, like Santiago de Chile and Lima in Peru, were even richer. Alexander von Humboldt (1769–1859), the Prussian naturalist and traveler, who was in Mexico City in 1804, just before the empire was engulfed by the Napoleonic Wars, wrote that "[it] recalls Berlin but it is more beautiful." He praised its chemical laboratory, its botanical gardens, its famous School of Mines, its well-stocked Academy of Painting and Sculpture.[4] The month before Britain and Spain were at war, the Morning Post called Mexico City "the richest and most splendid city in the world, the center of all that is carried on between America and Europe on the one hand, and between America and the East Indies on the other."⁵ Its huge, well-lit squares ranged from Spanish Renaissance and baroque to late Palladian. The grandiose baroque cathedral had recently been refaced in neoclassical marble, and the brilliant Manuel Tolsa was still working on the dome and lantern. The regular plan of the city, a fusion of Aztec features and the new town-planning criteria of the *conquistadores,* had been praised by visitors since the late 16th century, and the black-and-red volcanic stone of the 17th- and 18th-century public buildings was now acquiring the dignified patina of age. Fine parks, like the Alameda, had been added and adorned with statuary and fountains.⁶ There were, said Humboldt, innumerable libraries, public and private. Equally striking was the beauty and the purity of the currency, both gold and silver. In the 1840s many looked back to the last decade of the empire as a golden age.⁷

The chain of events set in motion first by the American Revolutionary War, then by the French Revolution, brought disaster to this opulent but fragile colonial system, which had experienced no large-scale violence for 300 years. Local "patriots" studied the American constitution; they read the "Declaration of the Rights of Man." The first "liberation juntas" began to appear in 1794. After the taking of Trinidad in 1797, Britain began to finance revolts against the mother country. Early "liberators" like Francisco Miranda were on William Pitt's payroll. Some American politicians, like Aaron Burr, planned to detach provinces from Spain long before General Jackson actually did so. And from about 1800 American mercenaries were likewise available.

But there were multitudes of crosscurrents. Some of the richer creoles, that is, Latin Americans of pure white stock, known as "Spaniards," resented the authority wielded by officials straight from Spain, known as "Europeans." Others were terrified of the upheaval that independence would bring. Humboldt reported that the rich "see in revolutions nothing but the loss of their slaves, the spoilation of the clergy and the introduction of a religious tolerance they deem incompatible with the purity of the prevailing worship. . . . They prefer not to exercise some rights than sharing them with everybody." They were, he added, particularly worried by the possible loss of their titles and decorations. The clergy were likewise divided: The bishops tended to side with the Spanish government, the lesser clergy and the religious orders (like the Catholic clergy in Quebec) to wish to seal off Latin America from European secularism. They had never forgiven the Spanish court for suppressing the Jesuits and feared that their immense properties would be confiscated.⁸ All these fears were heightened when

Spain fell under the influence of Bonapartist France, regarded by many
creoles and clergy alike as antichrist. The slaves were proindependence,
thinking it might bring their liberation with it, as in Haiti, though they
knew that the slaves had not been emancipated in the United States. On
the other hand, the poor, the free blacks, the Indians, and many low-
caste mixed-race groups, looked to the crown for protection against
worse injustices than they already suffered. There was also the peculiar-
ity of constitutional attitudes. Spain itself was a collection of crowns
and kingdoms—León, Castile, Catalonia, Navarre—and the empire
consisted not so much of colonies as of viceroyalties. A kingdom, or
viceroyalty, might break away but remain, in a sense, Spanish. It is
significant that the earliest rejections of the authority of Madrid were
the work of "Europeans," not creoles. What happened was not so much
a war of liberation as a civil war, and that is one reason it was so
prolonged and savage.

The first detonator was the war between Britain and Bonaparte-
dominated Spain, which broke out on 12 December 1804. To finance
the war, the Madrid government adopted a scheme of peculiar ineptitude. Virtually all Latin American landowners, large and small, were in
debt, as indeed they were in the southern United States. The usual thing
in Mexico and elsewhere was for owners to mortgage their land to set
up chantries in return for perpetual annual payments, usually 5 percent.
Madrid decided to impose a forced loan by the compulsory redemption
of these mortgages. The sum demanded was 40 million pesos. Since
many could not raise the funds to pay, there were bitterly resented
forced sales of land at public auctions. The rich and powerful had
enough pull to bribe or argue for exemption. The rest experienced, or
feared, ruin. The scheme realized only 12 million pesos all of which, the
Mexicans believed, went straight to atheist Paris, thus adding religious
to economic resentment. The loan might have been designed to alienate
the entire indigenous ruling class.[9]

Then in 1808 came the Spanish revolt against the Bonapartists. This
was the second detonator. The real breakdown of order within the
empire began, indeed, in European Spain. At one time four different
juntas—those controlled by Joseph Bonaparte and Ferdinand VII and
the juntas of Seville and the Asturias (later the Junta Central) were
issuing peremptory orders to the Indies. The Indies responded by setting up their own juntas, consisting of senior officials, archbishops and
other dignitaries. But the Spanish juntas did not recognize the overseas
juntas; instead they insisted that delegates be sent to their Junta Central
and, from 1811, that deputies be elected for a cortes, or parliament.

This ruling immediately raised the problem of proportional representation. There were 17 million people in the Indies: 3 million whites, 4 million blacks and 10 million Indians. The allocation of 24 deputies to the Indies was fair if only whites were counted. But like the southern states at the 1787 Federal Convention, the creoles wanted the other races counted in, and their quota raised accordingly, even though they, as whites, proposed to exercise all the power. In any event, it proved impossible to reach a similar compromise to the one worked out in the United States, whereby a slave counted as three-fifths of a white. The struggle, then, had a constitutional origin as well as a financial one. If the Spanish Central Junta had proved more effective in organizing resistance to France, the Indies might have followed it. But it was feeble and cowardly. News of the hopeless situation in Spain reached Caracas in spring 1810, and there was a confused coup on 19 April. The nominal viceroy was dethroned. The crowd outside government house shouted "Death to the French! Long live the Fatherland, religion, Ferdinand VII!" But the new self-appointed junta immediately behaved like an independent government. Other cities took similar action. In Mexico, a priest from a wealthy family, Miguel Hidalgoy Costillo, staged a coup on 10 September and proclaimed an independence crusade under the protection of the patroness of New Spain, the Black Virgin of Guadalupe.

The Latin American revolution was thus, in origin, a conservative move in a civil war. But it was soon envenomed by two factors: the political theory of Rousseau, as disseminated by the French Revolution, and warlordism. In a way they were the same, for the first was employed to legitimate the second by means of the totalitarian notion of the General Will. Almost from the start, there was no attempt to achieve consensus, in communities divided by class, wealth, race and allegiance. All the principal actors endeavored to impose their personal authority by force in the name of "the people." The first cycle of violence began in Mexico. Father Hidalgo, already aged 57 in 1810, collected an army of 25,000 ruffians behind his black Virgin, stormed Guanajuato, massacred its garrison, and stole silver bars and coins worth 3 million pesos. Thus funded, he assembled 80,000 men, but drew back from an assault on Mexico City itself. Instead he took over the press in Guadalajara, one of only four in Mexico, and published a newspaper, *El Despertador Americano*, which proclaimed a radical program: for the Indians, the abolition of the poll tax and the initiation of land reform; for the blacks, the abolition of slavery; and for the creole poor, the end of the liquor taxes and the tobacco monopoly. The army, theoretically loyalist, retook rebel-held towns and retaliated for the massacre by slaughtering every follower of Hidalgo it could lay its hands on. In July 1811 Hidalgo, his brother and their three lieutenants were taken while trying to slip into the United States and were garroted after a trial of sorts. Their heads were put in iron cages at the Granary in Guanajuato, where they rotted for some time.[10]

In Venezuela the rhetoric of the French Revolution and the constitutionalism of the American concealed an increasingly vicious struggle for power. A Congress, formed on 1 July 1811, passed a "Declaration of the Rights of the People" imposing popular sovereignty as "imprescriptable, inalienable, indivisible; liberty, security, property, equality before the law, temporariness of public office and last but not least happiness as the aim of society." Four days later the Republican faction, led by Francisco de Miranda, a quasi-professional revolutionary who had been paid £1,000 a year by the British government to cause trouble, (though he wore the uniform of a French general, circa 1795) pushed through an American-style Declaration of Independence. This declaration made Venezuela a sovereign state while promising to "uphold in its pure and intact state the Holy, Catholic and Apostolic Roman Religion, one and exclusive in these lands, and to defend the mystery of the Immaculate Conception."[11]

As in Mexico, the atrocities began early. Despite its overall tranquility, there had always been a certain spirit of lawlessness in the Spanish-American empire, a feeling that European niceties need not always be observed. The 16th-century expression, "No peace beyond the line" (that is, beyond mid-Atlantic), remained valid, especially in the Caribbean area. Great Spanish officials often acted beyond their authority. If they were successful, they were honored and rewarded; if unsuccessful, they were disgraced or executed. The 18th century had seen a progressive improvement in enforcing respect for the law and reducing violence. All this progress was now rapidly reversed. No sooner had independence been declared and liberties guaranteed than Miranda had a dozen supporters of King Ferdinand beheaded and put their heads in cages hung at the entrance to Caracas. Thereafter the war became cruel on both sides.

Into this arena of violence now stepped a man who was well able to exploit it. Simón Bolívar had the courage and enterprise to take an army over the Andes. But he allowed no human consideration to stand in his way either. He was born in 1783, a generation younger than the one that produced Bonaparte, Wellington and Jackson; he belonged, rather, to the age group of Peel and Van Buren, Schubert and Byron, Faraday, Shelley, Géricault and Lammenais. His mother ran the family

slave-estate with an iron hand; his father was an indiscriminate womanizer (and rapist). His sole effective parent was the slave Hipolita. Both
his parents died when he was a child. In 1799 he went to Europe with
a tutor, Simon Carreno, who encouraged him to read not only Voltaire,
Rousseau and Holbach, but Helvetius, Hume, Spinoza and Hobbes.
Bolívar was particularly struck by Hobbes's stress on man's dynamic
need for perpetual movement, which corresponded with his own restlessness. At age 18 he married an older woman, but she died fewer than
two years later, leaving him a widower at age 20. Thereafter he became,
like his father, an indiscriminate womanizer. Père de Lacroix, one of his
early biographers, had from Bolìvar himself an unsavory story of being
thrown out of a London brothel by angry women. When drunk, his talk
tended to become obscene. He pursued woman as archetypes, not as
persons. He never sought to remarry. He counseled friends to remain
single. He seems to have had no desire to beget an heir (though he
probably left a natural son in France, like Wordsworth). There ran
through his life an unbroken thread of loneliness and pathos. He was
a romantic hero manqué. It would have been fascinating to see what
Byron, who repeatedly expressed the wish, in the years 1816 to 1819, to
go to Latin America and help the cause of independence, would have
made of him.[12]

Bolívar's early moves in the war of liberation were confused and
contradictory. He had both Negro and Indian blood, though not much
of either, and in practical matters identified with the landowners. He
could quote Voltaire (so could many people), and he spoke the language
of political idealism. When in London, he met reformers like William
Wilberforce and the educationalist Thomas Lancaster. He learned how
to use the press and manipulate public opinion, especially in London
and Washington. He always knew how to sound the note of progress.
But his idealism did not run deep. He pursued power for its own sake,
or rather he wanted responsibility only on his own terms, which were
authoritarian, and when it was not forthcoming, he retired like Coriolanus. He always lied when convenient. He had no respect for law.
When his brother died at sea, he took his brother's fortune, which
doubled his own, quite unlawfully. When he could, he bullied the
courts for his own financial benefit, seeking wealth not for itself but as
the means to acquire power. He wanted arms, men and a frigate waiting in the bay if things went wrong and he needed to leave in a hurry.

Bolívar invented many of the operatic clichés in the rise and fall of
Latin American dictators. But some he learned from Miranda, later
known as "the Precursor." Miranda had been repeatedly in revolt, then
in exile, and his 1811 Republic, in which Bolívar was his military

assistant, failed, too. The truth is, that it had no real popular support. It was always possible to assemble a crowd to shout *"Viva la Revolución!"* in front of Government House, but the crowd ran for cover at the first whiff of hostile grapeshot. On 26 March 1812 a major earthquake destroyed much of Caracas, killing 10,000 people. It was seen as God's vengeance for the sin of rebelling against the sacred person of Ferdinand. There is a vignette of Bolívar, scrambling over the smoking ruins in his shirtsleeves and shouting, above the screams, "If nature opposes us, we will fight against her and force her to obey us!" Did he really strike this Promethean attitude? If so, it was a touch of Shelley, rather than of Byron, who would have laughed at him.

In any event, Bolívar's next steps were far from heroic. The royalist commander, Admiral Monteverdi, proved more resolute than Miranda expected. If the insurgents began the atrocities, the royalists certainly compounded them. Cities were sacked. The execution squads got to work. There was looting and plunder, in which Bolívar joined enthusiastically. Slaves were emancipated; others staged revolts. What Miranda could not do was to find enough volunteers to carry on the struggle; recruits were so reluctant they had to be manacled. On the other hand, private armies began to emerge, and warlords to command them. There were bands of armed blacks; bands of mulattoes. Monteverde, a Canarian with his disciplined Islanders (as they were called) and his marines, commanded the most effective force. In July 1812 Miranda capitulated to him, then made off. He no doubt intended to go into temporary exile again. But Bolívar decided to change sides, delivered Miranda under arrest to the royalists in return for a passport, and planned to go to Spain to fight under Wellington. He changed sides again when he learned that Monteverde had confiscated his estates. But by then it was too late to save his old commander. Miranda was taken to Spain and died in a Cádiz prison four years later. He used to lift the heavy chain which riveted him to two pillars and say bitterly, "To think that the first link in this chain was forged by my countrymen."[13]

There followed many years of warlordism, in which Bolívar gradually emerged as the most intelligently ruthless. His great biographer, Salvador de Madariaga, wrote that he had "the soul of a *mestizo,* in which conquered and conquerors cohabited." But however questionable his idealism, there was no doubt about his hatred, especially of Spanish rule. He wrote of "a continent separated from Spain by immense seas, more populous and richer, submitted during three centuries to a degrading and tyrannical dependence." It was "the harshest tyranny every inflicted on mankind." Sometimes he spoke as if he were an indigenous Indian: "The ferocious Spaniard vomited on the coast of

Colombia to convert the world's most beautiful region into a vast and odious empire of cruelty and loot." "[He] signalled his arrival in the New World with death and desolation; he wiped out from its earth the original race; and when his fury found no more beings to destroy, he turned against his own progeny settled in the soil he had usurped."[14] This was to sound a new note of anti-European propaganda, adumbrating much of the rhetoric against colonialism which was to be so notable a feature of the 20th century.

From November 1812 Bolívar set up as a liberator on his own account, at first on a small scale, with 500 men and 15 armed river craft—no more than a guerrilla leader, in fact. But this too was a portent. His first manifesto stressed "practical means" rather than "ideas." It complained: "We had philosophers instead of leaders, philanthropy instead of legislation, dialectics instead of tactics and sophists instead of soldiers." It denounced "popular elections" and "the tolerant system" as "criminal clemency." What this meant was dictatorship (his), achieved through ruthlessness. Here once more was the modern revolutionary pattern.

The civic virtues of the Spanish New World were never entirely to recover from the devastation of the civil wars which swept over it in waves from 1812 to the early 1820s. There were dozens of insurgent commanders, often representing racial interests—white, mestizo, black, or various combinations—but always anxious to steal each other's troops, who were constantly deserting. Hence warlords condoned looting, though they usually denied it took place. There were regional loyalties, too. Both sides used a strong position in one province to invade and loot its neighbor. On the Spanish side there were regional loyalties as well. Castilians, Catalans, Basques, Galicians, Islanders— each tended to stick together and persecute others. In due course, royalist cruelty and blindness made independence inevitable, but both sides practiced atrocities. One of Monteverde's commanders, a former penal-colony officer named Cerveriz, paid a *peso fuerte* for every ear of an insurgent brought to him. An eyewitness testified that his men "brought out many persons who were hidden on the estates and mutilated and killed them." His Catalan troops used to wear the ears on their hats.

The insurgents also rewarded slaughter. From 1814 to 1815 on, many of their officers were Bonapartist veterans with experience in repressive warfare. An insurgent "War to the Death" plan had 15 articles, 6 on how to extort money. Article Two states that "the first and chief aim [is] to destroy in Venezuela the accursed race of European Spaniards, including the Islanders. . . . Not a single one must remain alive." Article Nine states that "the presentation of heads of European Spaniards, including Islanders, is sufficient to deserve reward and a commission in the army: any private presenting 20 such heads shall be promoted ensign; if 30, lieutenant; if 50, captain, and so forth." Both sides used the word *extermination* constantly. Basques were to be exterminated, or creoles, or whites, or blacks, or French—this last was an echo of the Spanish war of liberation. But in Latin America "French" usually meant French-speaking blacks from Haiti, who fought on both sides.[15]

Bolívar adopted these articles in part. He avoided terror if he thought it counterproductive. But he showed no qualms about using it when it suited his purpose. He did not punish his commander Antonio Briceno when Briceno offered freedom to any slave who murdered his Spanish-European master. When Briceno decapitated two Spaniards of over 80 and sent their heads to Bolívar with a letter written in their blood, all the Liberator did was to warn him that he must first obtain authority for such proceedings. His own proclamation of June 1813 sentenced to death all Europeans who did not "actively and effectively" help the "patriots." All "Americans" were to get a general pardon for atrocities, and Europeans would be classified as "Americans" if they changed sides: "Spaniards and Canarians, be sure of death even if neutral unless you act effectively for American liberty! Americans, be sure of life even if guilty!"

Bolívar "liberated" Caracas in August 1813, with an army of only 1,700 men, by cowing the Europeans with terror and forcing the creoles to back him. He then executed as many as he killed in battle. He wrote to the Congress of New Grenada that he had advanced through nine cities and *pueblos,* "where all Europeans and Canarians, almost without exception, were shot." An eyewitness recorded that one of Bolívar's commanders, Ribas, gave a banquet where one officer proposed a toast: that they "solemnised the act by every one of the guests drinking the death of a prisoner of his choice. The idea was greeted with acclamation. The list was completed and, within half-an-hour, 36 persons perished on the Cathedral Square."[16] As the armies grew in size, the killings mounted. Bolívar's own "Manifesto to the Nations of the World on the War to the Death," 24 February 1814, justified the execution of 1,000 prisoners. Rafael Diego Merida, whom Bolívar made minister of justice, and the man he appointed governor of Caracas, Juan Bautista Arizmendi, were traders in death. Juan Vicente Gonzales recorded: "Morning and afternoon, shootings went on in the main square [of Caracas] and in the slaughterhouse ... To save ammunition, sometimes the victims were murdered with machetes and knives." In La

Guaria, "the victims came out in pairs, joined by shackles each carrying the wood which was to burn his body." Often huge stones were used to smash heads. "Over such scenes could be seen running with delight, dressed in white and adorned with yellow and blue ribbons, deadly nymphs who, on the bloody and muddy remains, danced the obscene dance known as the *Palito*."

As the war in Europe ended, leaving much of Latin America still in ferocious combat, Bolívar himself sounded a note of despair (he had just inspected the ruins of one of his own estates): "The war is becoming more cruel and the hopes of a prompt victory I had aroused in you have vanished. . . . We are living terrible days. Blood flows in streams. Three centuries of culture, of enlightenment and of industry have vanished." This statement contradicted his earlier analysis of Spanish colonialism. No matter: Bolívar was rarely interested in the truth of what he said, merely its effect. Statements, manifestos, were like bullets, tools of power. He told his friend Francisco Iturbe, who took alarm at some democratic message: "Have no fears about the coloured people. I flatter them because I need them. Democracy on my lips and"—he put his hand on his heart—"aristocracy here."[17]

Bolívar was never able, like Washington, to create a volunteer citizen army. He always had to rely on mercenaries or "patriots," who were in it for the loot. With the Bonapartists chased out of Spain, Madrid was able to concentrate on the New World, and the odds against Bolívar lengthened. In June 1814 he had to abandon Caracas, carrying off jewels and 27,912 ounces of silver, looted from churches, his future war chest. But the royalist commander, José-Tomas Boves, did not give the people, least of all the opinion-forming classes, the peace they plainly wanted. Though white himself, he was an antiwhite racist. His troops were mestizos, blacks, *llaneros* (horsemen), or *zambos* (Negro-Indian). He killed all the whites he could lay his hands on, his object being to clear the main Venezuelan plain of whites and replace them with mestizos. He had the white males speared to death "like bulls in the ring" and forced their wives to dance the *pirquirico* and other rustic measures, encouraging them with his whip.

Boves behaved like a savage. And some of the insurgent leaders were savages, too. Antonio Paez, an illiterate peasant, had lived in the wilds from the age of 17, when he committed murder and fled from justice. He lived by lassoing wild cattle, in huts furnished with horses skulls and heads of alligators. He dressed in skins, his only food saltless meat, his weapons homemade spears. When war came, he formed a cavalry band, attracting many followers who admired his exploits—he could ride his horse across a river in a flood, carrying his spear in his teeth—

and his refusal to place any restraints on loot and rape. He was, in fact, a bandit, and there were many such. Creatures like Boves and Paez created a moral climate into which even the few decent men involved were relentlessly sucked, like a swamp. A particularly sad case was Pablo Morillo, appointed royal commander in 1815, a man of humble origins who had risen under Wellington and absorbed disciplined notions of how an army should behave. He was unfortunate in that his arrival coincided with a brief truce and amnesty, in which men like Arizmendi were released. This monster, of mixed creole and Indian blood, was described by a British sailor as having "a peculiar ferocity of expression, which his smile only increases. His laugh never fails to create a momentary shudder, and the dreadful distortion of the muscles of the face which it produces can only be compared with that of the hyena when under similar excitement."[18] Once at large, Arizmendi and others raised the cruelty stakes, and Morillo gradually abandoned his humanity under the ferocity of the struggle. In the last six months of 1816, for instance, he executed 102 men.

In official letters home, Morillo also drew attention to the growing tendency of the clergy, especially the orders (the Augustinians, in particular, though not the Capuchins) to side with the insurgents and provide moral justifications for their enormities. As far back as the early 16th century, the Franciscans had tried to prevent cruelties to the Indians in New Spain, and the Jesuit had protected the Indians in Paraguay. But in the circumstances of 1812–22, it was the royalists who were upholding the rights of the downtrodden, especially the Indians and the blacks, and the activist clergy were motived not by compassion but by ideology. "Where the priest has been of the right kind," wrote Morillo, "the people have imitated him. [But] many or most of the priests have been the instigators of the new ideas." The phenomenon of a politicized clergy, preaching abstract "justice" and revolutionary change, was new and yet another portent.[19]

Since opinion in New Spain was so divided, and there was so little genuine enthusiasm for independence or willingness to fight for it—apart from those seeking power and plunder—why was the restored Spanish government unable to impose its will? After all, from 1814 to 1815, legitimacy had been restored all over Europe and the Holy Alliance existed precisely to uphold its authority, if needs be by force. In Spain itself people of all shades of opinion, from absolute monarchists to ultraliberals, opposed independence for the colonies. There was no equivalent in Spain to the Whig opposition in England which had sided with the American colonists in the 1770s. The insurgents had no Burke to put their case in Madrid. The Spanish, conservatives and liberals alike, could not believe that the Americanos could be so shamefully unjust and ungrateful as to break the links with a mother country which had provided the human and financial resources to bring the New World all the benefits of European civilization. It is true that the factions in Spain disagreed on many points. The liberals believed that once constitutional rule was properly established in Spain, the colonists would see the error of their ways. The monarchists thought that the revolt was entirely due to the growth of liberalism at home and that once liberalism was effectively suppressed, insurgency would gradually peter out. Hence, during the two constitutionalist periods, 1810–14 and 1820–23, and during the absolute rule by Ferdinand VII, 1814–20 and 1823 onwards, governments in Madrid flatly refused to concede independence. All used force to suppress it.

The military effort was by no means insignificant. In the years 1811–20, 30 military expeditions were dispatched: three to Havana, seven to Veracruz, five to Lima, one to La Guaira, two to Costa Firme, five to Montevideo, one to Maracaibo, three to Portobelo, two to Santa Marta and one to Puerto Rico—thus covering the entire continent. These armadas involved a total of 47 warships with 1,004 cannon, and 177 transports with a combined tonnage of 47,086, carrying 2,390 officers and 44,689 men. The manpower was not far short of the entire regular Spanish army of the early 1820s.[20] Troops and ships were backed up by unanimous propaganda from all quarters of Spanish opinion which persisted long after the New World was irretrievably lost. The liberal proclamation of 1814 set the keynote: "Do not be ungrateful to your parents. Such ingratitude is a scandalous monstrosity." Miranda was always referred to as "the traitor." Miguel Hidalgo was "the most bloodthirsty man America has ever known." Father José María Morelos, another Mexican clerical insurgent, "says mass to his soldiers wearing a general's hat, two blunderbusses, and a sword stuck in a belt round his vestments."[21] Toward the end of the 1820s, the Spanish historian Mariano Torrente published a multivolume account of the revolt denouncing the insurgents as "terrorists, monsters of barbarity, corrupt and bloodthirsty" and relating innumerable episodes of cruelty and gruesome massacre. Its theme was that an evil minority had imposed its will on the majority, who were loyal subjects, by terror.[22] The liberals always defended Spain's colonial record. As late as 1843, Francisco Martinez de la Rose, who had been liberal prime minister in 1822, told a congress of historians: "Few nations have treated their colonists with such wisdom and kindness; few have ruled them with laws so favourable to the indigenous population."[23]

But if everyone in Spain opposed decolonization, the actual colonial lobby was narrowly based. Because of the monopoly system, it amounted, in practice, to the town of Cádiz. The wars of liberation ruined Cádiz, but it had to watch impotently while they continued, not being strong enough on its own to mobilize the nation.[24] Everyone else made the right political noises; nobody was prepared to do anything. The indifference of the public was a distant foretaste of the supine mood with which most British, French, Belgians and Portuguese greeted decolonization, voluntary or enforced, in the 1950s and 1960s. In particular, Spaniards were prepared neither to pay nor to fight. All kinds of medieval devices were employed to finance the armadas, plus some modern ones, such as the sale of copper and mercury stocks. But efforts to get the public to contribute were rejected or evaded. A levy on bullfight tickets failed. Theater owners likewise declined to collect a surcharge on tickets. Ferdinand contributed a total of 15,483,980 pesos from his privy purse, including money set aside to support his aged parents. No one followed his example. There was a lot of speechifying, but no action; as the old Spanish proverb said, "Day of much, eve of nothing." A few officers were keen to make a military name in America, but most officers, and all the men, did not want to go at all. The government failed to keep its promises of pay and promotion for those who were fighting overseas or of crediting them with extra years' service. Many contracts were not paid either, and it became increasingly difficult to get supplies for loading. Some units could not be got aboard without being disarmed. Americano agents and (it was said) freemasons were active at the quaysides, sowing disaffection, especially before the Plate expedition of 1818–19. In the end, the expedition had to be abandoned.[25]

The war effort was further frustrated by the extraordinary way in which Spain was governed, especially under Ferdinand. In the years 1808–26, there were 51 ministers of war, 46 prime ministers, and 40 ministers of finance. The average tenure of a prime minister was 4.6 months and of a war minister, 4.2 months. The Ministry for the Indies was repeatedly abolished and re-created.[26] There was grotesque inefficiency in prosecuting the war under both types of regime. The liberals handed over decision making to parliament: "Every proposal had to be examined and reported on by diverse and often overlapping committees"; the committees showed no sense of urgency and by the time they reported, the situation had changed, usually for the worse.[27] Ferdinand, on the other hand, ruled through a series of consultative bodies and was continually creating new ones. All these bodies produced was what the Navy Minister, José Vasquez Figueroa, called "a morass of conflicting papers" (December 1816). The entire administrative system was double- and triple banked, containing at each level a multiplicity of layers. The Council of the Indies, the Council of State, the Council of War, the Council of the Treasury, and the Council of the Admiralty all had a say in decisions. They were joined, as the revolt spread, by ad hoc bodies, such as the Junta de Generales (1814) and the Junta de Pacificatión (1815). Everyone involved seems to have thought it imperative to produce a huge document on the cause of the revolt. When control over the war was placed in single hands, an experiment tried in 1816–17, all the rest ganged up against him. There was no cabinet system. In theory Ferdinand was an autocrat, but all this meant in practice was that he had his own *camarilla* of weird drinking cronies. They included his former bodyguard whom he made Duque de Alagon and to whom he gave vast estates in Florida just before Jackson took it, and an ex-dancing master, Antonio de Urgarte, whom he put in charge of the Plate expedition. The expedition collapsed in a welter of fraud, mutiny and sabotage.[28]

Ferdinand's mismanagement meant that he threw away two of his strongest cards: control of the sea and support from his fellow autocrats. In 1817 Ferdinand secretly arranged with Alexander I to buy warships from Russia. The warships included five 74-gun battleships and three 44-gun frigates, for which the Tsar charged 13.6 million rubles or 18 million reales. To raise the money, Ferdinand used the £400,000 Britain paid him for abolishing the slave trade. The deal was handled by his *camarilla*. The Navy Minister, Vasquez Figueroa, knew nothing of it until the fleet actually sailed into Cádiz harbor. According to the court, the ships were "fully armed and ready for immediate long-distance service." According to the Captain-General of Cádiz, his surveys showed that, except for one battleship and one frigate, the ships were "totally useless." In fact, little use was made of them, and repatriating their Russian crews cost almost as much as the purchase price.[29]

In the meantime the crown was losing control of the Pacific, hitherto maintained from Callao, the port of Lima, as a result of actions by British, Irish and American mercenaries. In 1817 the Irishman Raymond Morris, a member of the Irish Legion (it was commanded by one Devereux who claimed descent from the Elizabethan Earl of Essex), seized the brig *Aguila,* 22 tons. The *Aguila* was joined by the East India ship *Windham,* bought and renamed *Lautaro,* after one of the Masonic lodges, and commanded by George O'Brien and J. A. Turner, with marines under Captain William Miller. On 27 April 1818 they won a victory over two Spanish warships blockading Valparaiso, as usual flying the British flag until they were close. In due course they were

joined by the American brig *Columbus,* renamed *Araucana,* under the
Yankee skipper C. W. Wooster, and the *San Martin,* a former Royal
Navy battleship, commanded by William Wilkinson. In November
1818 this little squadron was put under the command of Lord Cochrane, flying his flag in the battleship *O'Higgins* as Admiral of the
Chilean navy. In 1819–20, with characteristic efficiency, he completed
the destruction of Spanish naval power in the eastern Pacific.[30]

The Anglo-Saxon military contribution was also substantial. Officially, Castlereagh declared neutrality. The Regent issued a proclamation, 27 November 1817, forbidding any of his subjects to take part in the
war. But George Hippersley, one of the mercenaries who left an account,
related that when he recruited the first British Legion, which sailed that
month, "no interference . . . from the British government obtruded itself;
and all concerned felt convinced that the Ministry . . . tacitly consented to
the exertions that we were making in the cause of Spanish South-
American independence."[31] This first contingent, of five regiments in five
ships, numbered only 800, but it was well equipped. One ship was lost in
a storm, but by the early summer of 1818 about 150 had already reached
the fighting zone. Most of these men had enlisted for drink and duly got
drunk. But they fought well. When Hippersley presented his first accounts in June 1818, Bolívar raised many questions. "Having then twirled
up his mustachios, and looking fierce, he repeated these questions. I
turned up and twisted my mustachios (which were as large as his own,
though not so black) and . . . expressed my astonishment at his refusal to
settle my account." The affair ended amicably with Bolívar buying
Hippersley's fine-feathered cocked hat, which he fancied. A second,
much larger British contingent, of 2,000 Peninsular veterans, arrived in
spring 1819, many to take part in the Andes crossing.[32] The arms of these
mercenary forces were supplied, as a speculation, by a committee of
London merchants, who were breaking into the trading monopolies as
Spanish power receded. Indeed, any "liberation" cause in the years
1815–30 could usually succeed in raising money in London by one means
or another. On the other hand, the big banking houses, like the Rothschilds and Barings, who were usually happy to float enormous loans for
the autocracies, would not do so for Ferdinand, whom they regarded as
too risky.

By this time the royal cause was virtually lost. In the south, the
former Spanish army officer José de San Martín (1778–1850), had organized a formidable military machine in Argentina, based in Mendoza,
where he made his own weapons, including cannon, and ran cloth mills
to clothe his troops. He declared the United Provinces (as they were first

called) independent on 9 July 1816, and the following January he crossed into Chile, taking Santiago on 14 February 1817. He set up the Chilean Bernardo O'Higgins as Supreme Director of the new state and went on to win the decisive battle of Maipú on April 2, 1818. Bolívar's great march across the high Andes brought him, too, to the shores of the Pacific and close to the remaining centers of Spanish power on the west coast of the continent.

Much fighting remained to be done because at no stage was the liberation popular. Nowhere was Bolívar's army greeted with genuine enthusiasm. At a late stage in the struggle, one of the first British envoys on the scene, Colonel Hamilton, passed the main jail in Bogotá and noticed it was full of young men. He supposed, he said, there were many robberies. No: "These prisoners were only young *volunteers,* from the Province of Neyva, going to join a newly-raised regiment at Bogota." They were "confined for the night, to prevent their running away." The Colonel added: "On the road we met some more volunteers with their hands tied together."[33] Campaigns were decided essentially by desertions, changes of side by senior commanders, bribes and terror. Bolívar admitted, in one of his letters to Santander, that he had to touch "violent springs" to set in motion success—martial law, freeing the slaves, theft; "We have asked and taken all public and private funds within our reach."

What Bolívar did not admit were the many forgeries he had made of letters between royal commanders and Madrid. The special object of these forgeries was to turn international opinion, above all in Britain and the United States, against Spain. Thus, he had Morillo writing to Ferdinand on his entry to Santa Fe de Bogotá: "Every person of either sex who was capable of reading or writing was put to death. By thus cutting off all who were in any way educated, I hope effectually to arrest the spirit of revolution."[34] Bolívar also forged, for home consumption, "secret treaties" and copies of Royalist newspapers giving alarming accounts of the collapse of order in Spain. In the event, these last inventions proved unnecessary, since on 1 January 1820, as a result of a revolt by middle-ranking army officers, who arrested their generals, there was a liberal coup in Spain and in March the King was forced to resurrect the 1812 constitution and call a cortes. Morillo was instructed to arrange an immediate armistice, and did so. He had been badly wounded and lost much of his vitality; he wanted to go home. He and Bolívar met, on 27 November 1820. There was a great deal of high-sounding talk about justice, honor, liberty, and idealism. Both men got drunk, were carried to bed, and slept in the same room.[35] Then Morillo went back to Spain, and in due course the liberal government there resumed the war.

By this time, however, opinion was focusing on the future shape an independent Latin America would take and the likelihood of recognition by the Anglo-Saxon powers. Both Bolívar and San Martín appreciated that it was necessary to play the constitutionalist, even the democratic, card, to win over opinion at home and abroad. San Martín was a less ambitious man, and in 1822 withdrew his claim to rule a continental empire by handing over Lima to Bolívar. For his part, Bolívar retained his Coriolanus streak and made periodic and dramatic renunciations of authority. He also made genuflections toward both the United States and the British constitutions and incorporated bits of them in various schemes he drew up. But in power, with an army at his back, all his instincts were autocratic. His low stature (five feet six inches or less) and his love of uniforms made him fear that people would compare him to Bonaparte. But how could they avoid doing so? Bonaparte was to set the pattern of dictatorship for a century, above all in Latin countries. Without his suborning, then overthrow, of the Spanish monarchy, the revolt in New Spain could not have occurred as it did. In a sense, the independence of Latin America, and the violent and unstable form that independence took, were his most enduring legacies.

Moreover, it is obvious that Bolívar often thought in Bonapartist terms. That meant, in effect, that his duty was to re-create the Spanish empire as a unity, with himself as king in all but name. He saw the Spanish Americans as a single race, telling the Angostura Congress, 18 February 1819: "We are not Europeans, we are not Indians, but an intermediate species between the Aborigines and the Spaniards, American by birth, European by right." In his heart he knew this statement to be untrue. In a letter to Vice President Antonio Narino on 21 April 1821, he speaks of "the astounding chaos of patriots, Goths, egoists, Whites, coloureds, Venezuelans, Cundinamericans [Indian slang for whites], republicans, aristocrats, good and bad people, and all the gang of categories in which the several classes subdivide." How could, he asked, such a collection of violently conflicting interests rule themselves through the civil institutions of congresses and parliaments? Only military rule could hope to provide the disciplined framework within which the General Will of the people could operate.

However, Bolívar's difficulty was that he could not persuade himself that the popular will was sound. By the early 1820s he had seen too many horrors enacted, many of his own making. Behind his own will to power was despondency and self-doubt, a fundamental pessimism which Bonaparte never knew. "I put no trust in the moral sense of my countrymen," he wrote, "and without republican morality there can be no free government." "Neither liberty nor laws nor the most thorough education will make of us moral men," he told Santander, "let alone republicans and true patriots. Friend, it is not blood that runs in our veins but vice mixed up with fear and error."[36] He could not run Colombia, or the new state named after him, Bolivia, as civil states, and Venezuela was already in the hands of the half-savage José Antonio Paez. The truth is, Bolívar did not really like, respect or honor his fellow Americanos, and at times he felt they were not worth ruling. Colonel Henderson noted: "He observed to me that all his labours in the last 18 years appeared to be bringing no other result than the opening of Colombia to the commerce of the European nations."[37]

Commerce was certainly one consequence, though "opening" is not the right word. Since the late 1790s, under wartime conditions and with the British navy ruling both the Atlantic and the Pacific, British goods had been entering Spanish American ports. The real question was whether the United States, Britain and possibly France would go further and actually seize chunks of the disintegrating Spanish empire. That was what Jackson did in Florida. At one time Aaron Burr had a plan to detach the whole of Mexico from Spain. The British had made two attempts to set up a colony in the Buenos Aires region. In 1820 the British Governor of Trinidad, Sir Ralph Woodford, reported that the United States government was negotiating with Bolívar to get part of the Venezuelan coast and he urged that Britain, for security reasons, take the mainland near Trinidad. That area had been "nearly abandoned" by both insurgents and royalists and "two companies from the garrison would be the extent of military force required" to make "this desirable acquisition." But Bathurst, at the Colonial Office, turned down the proposal as "altogether at variance with those principles of strict neutrality" that the Crown had "uniformly maintained."[38] In practice, as we have seen, Britain was not entirely neutral. It became much less so after the liberal regime in Spain ran into difficulties in 1821–22 and the risk of an intervention by Bourbon France grew. France had already reestablished itself in the West Indies, to some extent, and another French puppet government in Madrid might well enable Paris to acquire chunks of the empire for itself. Britain and the United States had a common interest in preventing such an outcome.

The first official move to treat the independence of the former colonies as a *fait accompli* came on 8 March 1822, when President James Monroe sent a message to the U.S. Congress proposing to recognize the new republics. Three months later Castlereagh, though unwilling to go so far, accepted that, for sea-trading purposes, the new countries' flags were valid. The question became more acute after the Congress of Verona authorized the Holy Alliance to intervene in Spain to restore the autocracy, and preparations proceeded in France to carry out the mandate. On 11 February 1823, Canning, now British Foreign Secretary, made a speech at Harwich hinting strongly that war must follow if France either invaded Portugal or took a military and naval role in Latin America. The French army duly entered Spain on 6 April and took Madrid on 24 May and Cádiz on 30 September. Even before the French army got to Cádiz, the springboard for the New World, Canning had written a letter (20 August 1823) to Richard Rush, the U.S. Minister in London, proposing a joint declaration that neither Britain nor America would annex any part of the collapsing Spanish empire and both would oppose such action by any other power (that is, France). President Monroe consulted his two predecessors, Thomas Jefferson and James Madison, about how he should respond. All three wanted to accept Canning's offer, though Jefferson qualified it by urging the seizure of Cuba; he thought the crisis "more important than anything that has happened since our union."

At cabinet meetings on 7 and 26 November John Quincy Adams, as Secretary of State, argued successfully that it would be more dignified if the United States acted alone: America should "avow our principles explicitly to Russia and France [rather] than come in as a cock-boat in the wake of the British man o'war." Adams had nothing but contempt for the new republics, regarding their constitutional pretensions as worthless: "As to an American system, we have it; we constitute the whole of it; there is no community of interests or of principles between North and South America."[39] He thought them likely prey if legitimist Europe came back into the hemisphere. Once the Holy Alliance was granted access, Adams told the cabinet, "the ultimate result of their undertaking would be to recolonise them, partitioning them out among themselves. Russia might take California, Peru and Chile, France Mexico . . . as well as Buenos Aires." France, he added, was said to be intriguing to get a Bourbon prince on the Mexican throne and to reopen the Louisiana deal: "The danger therefore was brought to our own doors, and I thought we could not too soon take our stand to repel it."[40]

The Monroe Doctrine followed five days later (2 December 1823). It asserted that "the American continents, by the free and independent condition which they have assumed and maintained, are henceforth not to be considered as subjects for future colonisation by any European power." The United States did not intervene in Europe or its wars: "We have never taken part, nor does it comport with our policy to do so."

"With the movements in this hemisphere," however, "we are of necessity more immediately concerned . . . We owe it therefore to candour and to the amicable relations existing between the United States and those powers to declare that we should consider any attempt on their part to extend their system to any portion of this hemisphere as dangerous to our peace and safety." With existing colonies, "we have not interfered and shall not interfere." But from now on European intervention in "the affairs of independent countries" [the new republics] would be "the manifestation of an unfriendly disposition towards the United States."[41]

The Monroe Doctrine was the first major entrance of the United States on the stage of geopolitics. It was made, however, within the framework of the new "special relationship," for it was Washington's adoption of a British suggestion, and whatever Adams said, the high tone adopted was made possible and submission to it effective, only by the power of the Royal Navy. In effect, Holy Alliance Europe had lined up behind the Spanish crown, and the Anglo-Saxons behind the insurgents. Already, in addition to British naval and military volunteers, the London banks, hitherto hesitant, had decided to back the republics. In 1822 Gran Colombia, Bolívar's principal foundation, had at last succeeded in negotiating a loan as a government, and this loan was rapidly followed by the sale in London of bonds from the new governments of Argentina, Chile, Mexico, Peru and the emerging Central American Federation (as well as Brazil).[42] The number of British mercenaries was growing rapidly. Lord Holland now put through Parliament a private bill making such service lawful.[43] The same week the Monroe cabinet first met to discuss his doctrine, Canning named British consuls to Montevideo, Buenos Aires, Chile and Peru, with instructions to negotiate commercial treaties. Vast quantities of armaments, bought on credit, were shipped from Liverpool, Bristol, and London to the insurgent armies. French bayonets put Ferdinand back on his throne, but Holy Alliance Europe had no alternative but to accept the Monroe Doctrine or, rather, the inhibition by the British navy that underwrote it.

In South America itself there was a grand-opera climax in 1824, culminating on 9 December 1824, when Bolívar's leading general, Antonio Sucre, won what was termed the "decisive" Battle of Ayacucho in the Peruvian highlands. This battle was stage-managed, since most of the royalist generals had agreed to capitulate before it started. After it, the Viceroy, 15 generals, 16 colonels, 552 other officers and 2,000 men surrendered on generous terms; most went straight into the republican armies. At the end of the month, Canning recognized Colombia, thus setting in motion an irreversible process of acceptance. Two years later he was claiming credit for the whole thing, telling the City of London Fathers (12 December 1826): "I called the New World into existence, to redress the balance of the Old."

How was this New World to be governed? The omens from Mexico were not good. On 24 February 1821, the royalist commander, Colonel Agustín de Iturbide, changed sides, and announced: "At the head of a brave and independent army, I proclaim the independence of North America" (an interesting piece of terminology). He entered Mexico City in September as "the liberator." Eight months later he staged a military coup, the first in the independent history of Latin America, and made himself emperor. But this act involved recognizing a rival war-lord, the guerrilla leader Vicente Guerrero, as "marshal of Southern Mexico," in effect co-ruler. Joel R. Poinsett, President Monroe's special envoy, who was busy organizing a network of lodges, known as York Rite Masons, as an instrument of Washington's influence—the conservative, anti-Washington party in Congress were Scottish Rite Masons—inspected the contents of the Mexican Treasury (none) and predicted that Iturbide would last only as long as his private war chest. This prediction proved accurate. In September 1822 Guerrero and the commander at Veracruz, Antonio López de Santa Ana, staged another coup. Iturbide abdicated and, when he tried to make a comeback in 1824, was shot by a firing squad.[44] Hence in the first 18 months of Mexico's independence, the constituted government was twice overthrown by military power. Two more coups, one civil in 1828, one military the next year, followed, and the decade ended with the execution of Guerrero in January 1831.[45] The political instability was accompanied by the debauching of the currency, the seizure of church property and the repudiation of debts.

Farther south, the huge territories carved out of the empire by Bolívar and Sucre were themselves unstable entities, both in their frontiers and in the way they were governed. Almost everywhere, power rested in the hands of the white landowners who actually lived in the cities, where they shared some authority with the rising mercantile oligarchies. Other races and classes counted for nothing. The uniforms were gorgeous. There was a good deal of ceremony. Bolívar would enter each capital as a conqueror, on horseback, and would be greeted by "nymphs" (as they were always called) dressed in white, who would present him with garlands. The nymphs were usually recruited from a local brothel. One of the nymphs who serenaded him in Quito in June 1822 was a woman of 25, Manuela Saenz, battle hardened in the war of the sexes, who promptly became his most powerful, and last, mistress. Bolívar's next step would be to go to whatever congress or legislature was gathered and (as he put it in Lima in September 1823), "prostrate myself at the foot of the civil power, to recognise the sovereignty of the nation and manifest my submission to it." He would hand over his sword, the deputies would hand it back to him, and he would carry on as before. Other generals also went through these pantomimes. At the old university town of Chuquisaca, Bolivia, Antonio José de Sucre was obliged to climb into a red-and-white Roman chariot drawn by 12 young men, then to be taken through the streets hidden behind immense pyramids and obelisks made of cardboard to an "Ionic Temple," where six nymphs in white recited poetry.[46] Sucre, however, did not allow his head to be turned by these attentions and remained loyal to Bolívar. Indeed, as long as Sucre lived, the Liberator was secure.

Bolívar's insecurity was, rather, inward. He never put on weight with success. Like Andrew Jackson, though a much shorter man, he remained gaunt, thin, almost fragile. At 45, he had crisp, graying hair, huge mustachios, a big brow, a triangular face and a long chin. Many eyewitnesses recorded him looking morose, or worried, sometimes despondent. He wore a black handkerchief around his neck, a blue greatcoat, blue trousers, long boots and spurs. He carried with him an atmosphere of extraordinary sadness, punctuated by manic episodes. He must have been one of the most restless men who ever lived. Apart from his constant traveling the huge distances that separated the great cities, through jungles and swamps, across the mountain barriers and barren uplands, he remained in motion even when he arrived at his destination. He walked fast; he rode fast; when torrential rain made movement impossible, he swung and rocked himself violently in a hammock. He wriggled his body while he talked. He fidgeted at meals. His passion was dancing. The arrival of the waltz was a godsend to him, it was so fast and furious. On campaign, in the evenings, he would eat hurriedly, summon the womenfolk—his various mistresses always traveled with him—and dance, then disappear to dictate orders, returning to dance again. At his famous meeting with San Martín at Guayaquil, there was a night of tremendous dancing, in which Bolívar participated with enthusiasm, while San Martín sat, rigid as a statue, radiating ferocious disapproval. There was another notable meeting, early in 1827, between Bolívar and the de facto dictator of Venezuela, Paez. Each would cheerfully have hanged the other, but there was much embracing, backslapping, mutual expressions of love and undying esteem, lies, bombast, a great feast, nymphs in white, and not least an all-night dance, in which both men joined.

There is an eyewitness account of another characteristic evening, this time at Bolívar's villa in Bogotá. At the banquet, Bolívar sat alone at the head of the table, with 30 dignitaries down the sides. Behind him hung his portrait, with the simple message, "Bolívar is the God of Colombia." After many toasts, he stepped onto his chair, to orate, then onto the table, "and with long paces walked from one end to the other, breaking plates and glasses and upsetting bottles. The tumultuous crowd seized him at the other end and carried him in triumph to the reception hall."[47]

At times Bolívar wielded enormous personal authority. He possessed, wrote O'Leary, one of the mercenaries, "a power more absolute over a considerable part of South America . . . than the most exalted monarch of Europe over his dominions."[48] He certainly considered turning himself into an emperor, like Bonaparte, or into a sort of reconstituted Inca. But the fall and exile of San Martín, the constitutional duels between military and civilians in Mexico, the first of the assassinations (General Monteagudo in 1825) left him in little doubt of the transience of his own authority.

In 1825 Bolívar seriously considered a condominium with Britain. "Our American federation cannot last," he wrote to one of his lieutenants, "if it is not taken under British protection. If we tie ourselves up with England we shall exist, and if not we shall be infallibly lost." Although later on, Americanos would resent "England's superiority," that problem could be faced when it arose. These ideas were put to Canning, through diplomatic channels, but the reply came back: All Britain wanted was respect for maritime law, an end to undue United States influence, the signature of a peace treaty with Spain, and the suspension of efforts to free the last remaining Spanish colonies, Cuba and Puerto Rico. Bolívar's international diplomacy did not prosper. He hankered after some kind of federal union of the Spanish-speaking states. To this end he summoned, from Lima, the first Pan-American Congress, which met at Panama on 22 June 1826. He had not wished to invite the United States, or Haiti and Brazil for that matter. In any event, the U.S. delegation did not arrive in time. But Chile was now in anarchy and its representative could not attend. Buenos Aires, whose President Bernadino Rivadavia was barely hanging on to office (he was ousted the following year) declined. The Congress broke up on 15 July, having achieved little.

Bolívar continued to brood over British links. He was, with all his faults, an imaginative man, who thought big, a true child of the modern in some ways. He had picked Panama, then a mere town in the Guatemalan Republic, which included all Central America, because he wanted to build a canal there. The British envoy Henderson reported home on 14 July 1827: "General Bolivar [took] the opportunity to request if an occasion offered I would assure the British capitalists of his desire to give the greatest facility for opening a communication at the Isthmus between the two oceans . . . he would even make the territory neutral."[49] But the following year, the first war between the newly independent states broke out, between Colombia and Peru. There were intermittent conspiracies and *pronunciamentos,* a few battles, in one of which Sucre beat the Peruvians at Tarqui, at least 1,500 being killed—a higher casualty figure than in any of the set pieces in the long wars of independence.

Bolívar continued both to use the rhetoric of constitutionalism and to impose a personal rule which was as absolute as he could make it. But his despondency and sense of hopelessness increased, and he saw a dark age ahead. "A host of tyrants," he wrote to Sucre, "will rise from my grave and every one of them will be a Sulla or a Marius to drown in blood their civil wars."[50] The final blow was the assassination of Sucre in June 1830. In the last years of the 1820s, almost all governments were unpopular as the effects of the 1825–26 smash and depression made themselves felt. Latin American states no longer found it easy to raise money in Europe. The war made Colombia bankrupt, and Bolívar was held accountable for it. He was blamed, too, for the greed and extravagance of Manuela Saenz. The Liberator was now sick, probably from malaria, and was losing the will to govern. Just before he fell from power, 27 August 1830, he pronounced: "America is ungovernable. He who sows a revolution ploughs the sea." When Bolívar left his palace, the crowds were letting off fireworks and burning him and Manuela in effigy. Four months later he was dead (17 December 1830), his last words curiously summoning up all his restlessness: "Let us go, the people do not want us in this land . . . my baggage, take it on board the frigate."[51]

The independence that Latin America obtained in the 1820s thus turned to disillusionment and bitterness, and the savagery of its birth was written into the title deeds of its component parts. The notion that colonial empires could be disbanded and turned into nurseries of constitutional utopias was thus exploded 140 years before the 20th century reenacted the experiment on an even larger and more tragic scale. Bolívar thought the only answer was personal absolutism—his—but the arena in which he tried to establish it was too large. Another autocrat proved it was workable, after a fashion in a smaller theater, well protected by nature. Paraguay was a natural entity whose only access from the mouth of the Plate was by a single river. The Jesuits had tried and failed to create a Christian utopia there by protecting the Indians from European exploitation. They had not been able to keep the creoles out entirely, but they planted notions in thoughtful heads. One such thoughtful man was José Gaspar Rodriguez Francia, a member of the junta which proclaimed the independence of the province of Paraguay in 1811. Two years later, Francia was designated one of two consuls charged with ruling the new country. In 1814 the Congress in Asunción, Paraguay's little river-capital, voted him absolute power for three years, and in 1816 he was made dictator for life, with the title El Supremo, a post he held until his death in 1840. In due course Thomas Carlyle made him the hero of a characteristically perverse and perceptive essay, which greatly annoyed liberals like John Stuart Mill.[52] A few Latin American scholars, such as the great Argentine jurist Juan Alberdi, agreed with Carlyle: "America does not know the story of [Paraguay] save as related by its rivals. The silence of isolation has left calumny victorious. . . . Dr Francia proclaimed the independence of Paraguay from Spain and preserved it against her neighbours by isolation and despotism—two terrible means that necessity imposed on him in the service of a good end."[53]

Even today, comparatively little is known about Francia and his rule. He seems to have been born between 1757 and 1766. At various times he claimed his family was French or Portuguese from São Paolo. His father managed a tobacco plantation. His doctorate—everyone always called him "Dr. Francia"—was in theology, but he had a master's degree from Cordoba University in either philosophy or law. Certainly, he practiced as a lawyer until called to power and achieved a high reputation for service to the community, incorruptibility, austerity and (among the Indians) magic.[54] His strategy of government was based on negatives: keeping out Europeans, Brazilians, and Argentines; limiting contacts with all foreign countries to the barest civilities; denying the church the right to do anything except administer the sacraments and run charitable works and (under strict supervision) schools; and excluding from power all creoles. His isolationism began because, initially, Argentina laid down that he could not trade without its permission. He decided not to trade at all and refused to accept Argentina's envoys. He did receive Brazil's, but declined to join with Brazil in 1827 when it fought Argentina, calculating correctly that it would lose. The various presidents and dictators of Argentina viewed him with detestation. But just as they could stop him trading down the river so he could stop them coming up it. They thought about forcing their way up the river, but decided it would be difficult, perhaps impossible, and anyway not worth it. Francia's persecution of "old Spaniards" and upper-class creoles dated from the earliest days of independence and was strengthened both by what he observed of events elsewhere in Latin America and by an abortive conspiracy they mounted against him in 1820–21. He had all the conspirators arrested and executed them in public, at the rate of eight a day, to the delight of the citizens, especially the Guaraní Indians. Hence, unlike the other new republics, where the white creoles and *Peninsulares* took all power, treating the poor, the mestizos and the Indians as mere cannon fodder, in Paraguay the revolution was accompanied by profound social changes in which the indigenous inhabitants became the dominant economic force.[55]

Francia ran the country on the receipts of a governmental monopoly in tobacco and *yerba maté,* the local drink. He prevented the growth of a trading and commercial middle class, as well as a landowning aristocracy. Brazilian and all other foreign merchants were pushed out to Hapua, following the policy which, as we shall see, was pursued by the Chinese government when it concentrated foreign trade in Canton. The regime was described by one historian as a "secular replacement" for the former "Jesuit communist empire."[56] In fact, property was not held in common. The government was essentially paternalistic, but with a degree of attention to detail which would have been impossible on a larger scale. Francia personally decided which crops should be planted and supervised any commercial deal of consequence. A visitor recorded: "He knew exactly the cost of a hoe or axe, and he used to count and measure the needles and thread necessary for a uniform."[57] He insisted on a high standard of manners: Every male had to wear a hat to be doffed, and all women were expected to curtsy. The atmosphere was that of the 18th century before the fall of the Bastille. The deputies wore 18th-century three-corner hats and red or brown wigs.

A Scottish merchant, John Parish Robertson, who was in Asunción for some time, painted a curiously arcadian picture of Francia's Paraguay. The junta came and went on prancing horses, wearing knee breeches and heavy sabers, saluting elaborately with their cocked hats, attended by gorgeously dressed but barefoot servants. These superbly trained horses performed an elaborate dance before Dr. Francia, before backing out. Much of the state ceremonies were carried out in the open air, beside a lake. The banquets tended to be picnics. Robertson saw mounted friars carrying umbrellas, their horses also trained to dance. Then the friars dismounted and did their own stately saraband. Indeed, there was a great deal of dancing all around—Bolívar would have enjoyed it—under the benign but watchful eye of the doctor. Robertson described Francia's study as being equipped with a celestial globe and a theolodite, with a large telescope standing on the veranda outside. The shelves held 300 books in French and Latin, as well as in Spanish, mainly on law and science. The doctor had read Voltaire, Constantin de Volney and Rousseau: He believed strongly in the General Will, as exercised by himself. His face was "dark, and his black eyes very penetrating. His jet-black hair combed back from a bold forehead and hanging in natural ringlets over his shoulders gave him a dignified and striking air. He wore on his shoes large golden buckles, and at the knee of his breeches the same." All his clothes were black, worn with "a large scarlet *capote*"; he held "a maté-cup in one hand, a cigar in the other, a little urchin of a negro in attendance by his side."[58]

Francia's army was small, but he had a multitude of informers, who gave him his reputation for omniscience. His rule was based on a combination of awe, fear and respect—the fact that he lived modestly and drew only a third of his salary was in striking contrast to the dictatorial plundering going on elsewhere. As the traveler Richard Burton put it, Francia was able to "show to the world in the reclusive kingdom of the Jesuits the sole exception to republican anarchy."[59] The weakness of his system, however, was that it made no provision for continuity, and after his death his successors ended Paraguay's isolation, embarked on war and so destroyed the Garden of Eden. What Francia's lifework showed was that, in the right geographic circumstances, the new world of the modern could be kept at bay, but only for a time.

The favorite dance in Asunción, Robertson noted, was a Sarandigs, which involved a great deal of noisy heel tapping. The fact that friars performed it was by no means unusual in Latin America at this time. At Bahia, in nearby Brazil, the nuns danced enthusiastically, both in their convents and in public churches, especially on certain feast days. There, in Rio de Janiero and elsewhere, there was no Dr. Francia to impose decorum. At Pernambuco, travelers found not only frenzied dancing but lovemaking going on in the churches, especially in the Imperial Chapel, where the congregation consumed ices and sherbets in between the noisy sambas, *congadas* and *resiados*. At the church door traders sold phallic rosaries made of pastry, and within, sterile women rubbed themselves, half naked, against the legs of the statues of Christ, in the hope of conceiving. In 1817 the canons of the church of São Goncalo of Olinda tried to ban such practices on the ground that they scandalized European visitors.[60] Brazil was a slave country whose contacts, over two centuries, had been closer with Africa than with Europe, and, unlike Spanish America, it raised few social barriers to racial intermarriage. Much of the slavery was informal, so free and servile met, made love and begat children. The cultures of Europe, Africa and the Indies blended. Brazil was the nearest approach to a multiracial society in the world, and in some ways the freest, or most anarchic— though, unlike most of its Spanish American neighbors, generally non-violent. Long before the United States, Brazil was the world's first melting-pot society. It was also, unlike Paraguay, a largely open one.

Here again, Bonaparte had changed the course of history, for following his invasion of Portugal and the transfer, by the Royal Navy, of the ruling family to Rio, Brazil's ports were opened to international trade. In 1808, 90 foreign ships called at Rio. Two years later the total was 122, rising to 217 by 1815. In 1820 there were 354, most of them British. Even in 1808, over 100 British merchants were operating from Rio, most of them in the import-export trade, and by the treaties of 1810, Britain got Most Favored Nation status and extraterritoriality for its citizens. In effect, during the Napoleonic Wars, Brazil became a British economic colony, though the situation was unlikely to last. Emigrants poured in from all over western and southern Europe, the British virtual monopoly of world trade came to a natural end, and the age of steam arrived. In 1815 Bahia got its first steam-driven sugar mill, installed by Scots and Lancashire engineers. By 1834 it had 64 of them. The first steamboat arrived in 1819; 10 years later, there were scores of them paddling upstream in the vast rivers.[61]

Happily escaping wars of liberation, Brazil was, in fact, experiencing one of the first economic and demographic explosions of the modern world, which was taking place against a political background of cheerful confusion. From 1808 to 1815, the country was officially a viceroyalty. In 1815 it became part of what was called the United Kingdom of Portugal, Brazil, and the Algarve. Following the liberal revolution in Spain, King João returned to Lisbon in 1821, leaving Prince Pedro as Regent. When Prince Pedro received an ultimatum from the liberal-dominated cortes in Lisbon on 7 September 1822, he drew his sword, shouted "Independence or death!"—that was the only ceremony—and had himself crowned "Constitutional Emperor" three months later. No one was required to die.[62]

In Brazil, as in the United States beyond the Appalachians, there was land and opportunity for anyone who chose to work for it. In 1808 Rio, already growing fast, had 60,000 people. By 1820, the population had doubled to 120,000. A British observer made a revealing, if estimated, breakdown of the city's population: 1,000 court (including servants), 1,000 government employees, 1,000 capitalist and rentier planters, 500 lawyers, 200 doctors, 2,040 merchants plus 4,000 clerks,

1,250 mechanics, 100 street vendors, 200 fishermen, 1,000 soldiers, 1,000 sailors, 1,000 free blacks, 12,000 slaves and 4,000 housewives.[63] There was already a magnificent national library of 60,000 volumes (1814), a medical school (1816), and an imposing French Cultural Mission (1818). Indeed, if the English ran the economy, the French were busy insinuating their culture, especially in architecture. It was Grandjean de Montigny who designed the magnificent new Customs House at Rio (1826). Brazil's first school of architecture was based on the Paris École des Beaux Arts.

As cities with grandiose public buildings arose almost overnight and men hacked their way into the interior, the speed at which Brazil grew amazed the world. Not everyone liked it. The Emperor Pedro's mother, Dona Carlota Joaquina, hated the country and used to say *"Nao e terra de gente"* (Not a country for gentlefolk).[64] But for poor Europeans, Germans, Welsh and Scots, as well as Latins, Brazil held more attractions in the years 1815–30 than did any other territory except the United States. It was already called "the country of the future," a name it still bears today, alas.

Outside Rio and a few other big towns, the writ of the government did not always run. Men settled their own disputes in the interior, carved out little empires, killed Indians, and hanged bandits, if they could catch them. There were periodic slave revolts, mostly on a small scale, but a big one at the diamond mines of Minas Gerais in 1821, which seized control of the provincial capital, Vila Rica. Mercenaries hired by the diamond junta, assisted by the Bishop of Mariana and armed friars, put down the revolt, and 1,000 blacks were slaughtered.[65] But the lot of the slaves was improving rapidly, partly because the whole thrust of British policy was to end the slave trade and encourage manumission. The slave-trade interest reacted with fury, but most Brazilians, after 1815, would not support a rigidly divided society on the lines of the southern United States.[66] There were still 1,930,000 slaves, nearly all black, in 1818, but the number of freed blacks had risen to 585,000 and was to double in the next dozen years. Miscegenation was almost universal, beginning in slavery with white masters keeping harems of black women, then continuing, often with intermarriage, in the increasingly multiracial free world. At the time of the Minas Gerais revolt, there were in the province more mulattoes (171,572) than whites (131,047) and almost as many as blacks (211,559). In Bahia visitors rarely found faces with purely European features.[67] Free black and mixed-race girls, complained the moralists, were responsible for Brazil's easygoing sexual ways; its endless dancing, carnivals and feasting; and its tendency to turn religion into a lighthearted celebration of carnality. Around 1820 two European travelers recorded a rhyme in Bahia: "A pretty mulatto girl / Need not practise devotion / She offers her dainty self / Towards her soul's salvation"; and on the Matto Grosso they noted: "A dark girl is hot spice / A white girl is cold soup / A dark one forever / And a white one never."[68]

The Emperor Pedro, under pressure from his Portuguese-born court, produced an official definition of "black" and ordered the militia and army to exclude from its ranks, as a security measure, anyone whose great-grandparents were black. In an effort to reverse the spread of Afro-American cuisine, even in the best circles, he brought over 17 French chefs and 10 French bakers and pastry chefs. But he himself, like most arrivals, found the relaxed atmosphere of Brazil congenial. He lived openly with his mistress, Domitila de Castro, by whom he had five acknowledged children—others were born to mulatto women—while his wife Dona Leopoldina, a plain Austrian archduchess, pursued her botanical and geological studies, often going up-country on prolonged specimen-gathering expeditions.[69] He did not himself operate a formal color bar, receiving at court men and women of all races, and granting full diplomatic honors to the ambassadors of African potentates, such as the King of Benin, who sent envoys to Rio in July 1824. Mulattoes and even blacks held high governmental posts. As the French Ambassador reported (1834), "in Brazil today . . . no situation is inaccessible to men of colour."[70] Pedro was highly civilized, gifted even. He wrote music—one of his symphonies was performed in Paris—and cultivated the friendship of Gioacchino Rossini. It was in his day that Brazilian towns acquired the taste for building enormous opera houses. His broad-mindedness ensured his survival. In 1831, without any fuss, he handed over the throne to his son, and his 1824 constitution lasted 65 years, a record for Latin America. His reign illustrated the undoubted fact, which became plainer as the 1820s proceeded, that a society which rejected Paraguayan-style isolation and which wanted to benefit from world trade, steam and industrialization had, in practice, to liberalize itself politically.

This principle was beginning to make itself felt in Europe as well as the Americas. The 1814–15 Vienna settlement had left legitimacy in power everywhere, and the Holy Alliance was designed to keep it there. As Castlereagh and Wellington foresaw, the system would not work. The world was marching on more relentlessly than ever now that its substance was no longer being squandered on senseless wars. As the speed of travel doubled and trebled in a decade, ideas and people moved faster, too: Great bridges were built; roads were straightened; harbors were transformed; machines began to power the workshops; steam began to drive the presses; universities were expanded; and doctors, scientists, engineers, merchants, manufacturers, teachers and writers daily increased in number and strengthened their position in society. The stability imposed by Vienna had already been undermined, even before the Congress met, by the gradual collapse of Spanish rule in the Americas. If the emperors had really wanted to stop the rot, that is where they should have started, by underwriting Spain's overseas armadas or at least by helping Spain pay for them. But they did nothing until the effects were felt in Madrid.

Bearing in mind Ferdinand VII's chronic lack of ready money and his bewildering methods of conducting the government—Pedro Cevallos, the Foreign Minister, did not discover that Spain had joined the Holy Alliance until four months after the King had made the deal—the survival of his regime even until 1820 was remarkable. There were, in fact, numerous revolts, usually with a regional basis and led by disgruntled army officers—Mina in Pamplona (1814), Porlier in Corunna and Santiago (1815), the Triangulo Conspiracy to murder Ferdinand (1816), and Lacy in Catalonia and Vidal in Valencia in 1817. In many ways the revolt which toppled Ferdinand was the weakest. It started in Cádiz in 1819 and gathered strength because the Army of the South was concentrated there in the hope of sending them to Buenos Aires. Agitators found it easy to stir up the men as they waited in the cantonments. The mutiny was led by middle-ranking officers, but it succeeded because the sergeants and corporals did not want to go to America.[71]

That let in the liberals, mostly exiles or "jailbirds," as Ferdinand called them (he had locked them up when he returned in 1814), and their easy success gave a false idea of their real strength. The liberals found themselves in power for reasons which had nothing to do with their program. In fact, their main support came from the educated middle class and a small "enlightened" section of the aristocracy. They had no appeal for the lower orders, about whom they knew nothing. It is likely that Ferdinand, who used his secret police chiefly to keep him in touch with tavern and peasant opinion, was better informed about popular wishes than was any newspaper editor in Madrid.

The liberals themselves were divided, like Gaul, into three parts. The moderates, who were mostly practicing Catholics, formed the government. They excluded from it the former Bonapartists, who had backed the French in 1808–14 and were therefore "traitors." Thus rebuffed, this section turned into the new regime's most vehement enemies, made common cause with the royalists, and actually sided with the French army when it intervened in 1823. Then there were the liberal extremists, the *exaltados* of the clubs, violent anticlericals and levelers whose slogan was: "The poor cannot pay taxes, therefore the rich must." They could when they chose bring out the Madrid mob (or, rather, their mob; the royalists had a mob, too) against liberal ministers, and they had links with the Army of the South, which remained undependable once the government resumed its attempt to subdue the Americas.

In theory, the governing liberals ought to have done well. The international economy was in full boom. Living standards were rising rapidly in Britain and France, Holland, Scandinavia, parts of Germany and even in Lombardy. The liberals, with their middle-class base, ought to have been able to take full advantage of the trade-and-credit expansion. But they could not persuade parliament, sunk in a bog of committees and paper, to authorize clear orders, and when orders did finally emerge, they were not obeyed. The rich paid their taxes no more than did the poor; nobody did. Thus, Europe's first indigenous liberal government—that is, one not imposed from without and upheld by foreign bayonets—danced a masque of anarchy and began to collapse by the end of 1822.

At this point the archetypal Romantic, François-René Chateaubriand, entered the scene. Unlike the younger romantics, such as Victor Hugo, he was not losing his passion for Catholicism, the spirit of medieval chivalry, honor and legitimacy. On the contrary, it burned ever brighter in his breast, and it was fanned by the belief that events in Spain offered France the opportunity to reenter the western hemisphere. America had obsessed him since he visited it in his youth, as the great work of French literature on which he was now engaged, his *Mémoires d'Outre-tombe,* was to make clear. What Adams and Canning feared, he wished to promote. From the Congress of Verona, where he was representing France, he sent back to Villèle, the Prime Minister, an exaggerated account of the enthusiasm the other powers felt for a French expedition to Spain, to restore the fallen Ferdinand.[72] Before the end of the year, he found himself Foreign Minister, charged with an interventionist policy, and in the spring he sent the Duc d'Angoulème across the Pyrenees with 90,000 men. At a secret session of the Chambre des Députés on 8 February 1823, he painted a glowing picture of France as the divinely ordained protectress of Spain, of Cuba as a French Jamaica and of South America restored to legitimacy but its people enfranchised and holding out grateful arms to France. He claimed to have received assurances from Russia, Prussia and Austria that they would help France if Britain openly backed the insurgents in the Americas.

It was on this basis that the French army bombarded its way into
Cádiz in July 1823. But that action, in turn, as we have seen, brought
to the fore the new Anglo-Saxon "special relationship" and in due
course the Monroe Doctrine and explicit warnings to France from
Canning.[73] The French were told that although they might be allowed
to convey Spanish troops to Havana in French ships, the British navy
would not permit them to transport a French army across the Atlantic.
By the end of the year, Paris was climbing down hastily and counting
the cost of what was proving to be an expensive undertaking in Spain.
Bonaparte's troops had always lived off the lands they occupied, but
this Bourbon expedition, to avoid antagonizing Spanish opinion, was
paying its way. By spring 1824 the shoe was pinching, and in July
Chateaubriand was sacked.

Long before this point, the Holy Alliance's one great exercise in
foreign intervention had served to reveal the complexities of Spanish
politics. If the liberals were divided into three, equally there was not one
form of legitimacy in Spain, but two. Ferdinand VII, far from being the
"Crowned Tiger" as portrayed by liberal propagandists like Carlo Le
Brun, was a man of some moderation, rather like his cousin Louis
XVIII. But, like Louis, he had a more unbending younger brother, Don
Carlos. In July 1822 Ferdinand had refused to sanction the overthrow
of the liberal government by a march of the guards on Madrid. The true
legitimists, as they saw themselves, then turned to Don Carlos as their
leader, and before the end of the year civil war had begun.

The civil war quickly became three cornered. Spanish rural troops
and militia hunted down royalist or Carlist bands when they could.
Royalist juntas formed and held out in Galicia, Navarre, and Aragon.
Many villages were divided down the middle, with the local militant
atheist and the militant parish priest urging on the parties. So both
royalists and liberals began to develop strong local followings, which
were to perpetuate and transmute themselves, through many open
commotions and deceptively tranquil intervals, until they exploded in
the merciless civil war of 1936–39. In the circumstances of 1822–23, the
royalists were not strong enough to overcome the regular army, whose
senior officers were mostly liberals: hence the French military intervention. But this intervention, as the French discovered, solved nothing.
Ferdinand, back on the throne, was now seen as a cryptoliberal by the
Carlist reactionaries, and his French protectors as a bodyguard of
atheists. From 1823 to 1830, all the plots and risings were monarchist.

But if the legitimists were divided, prefiguring the Carlist wars to
come, when Ferdinand tried to strike his brother from the succession,
the abyss which already separated Catholics from anticlericalists wid-

ened, too. The purging of religious orders had begun in 1822, when monasteries and convents were accused of sheltering royalist conspirators. In 1823 the liberals massacred the monks of Mora del Ebro for "counter-revolutionary activities" a term which had just come into use. With the throne restored, their bodies were exhumed and pronounced "uncorrupted and of a sweet odour," and the canonization of the martyrs duly followed.[74] So did a purge of liberal army officers, some of whom (it was said) starved to death in consequence. The liberal clubs and the masonic lodges preached hatred of priests, monks and nuns. The militant clergy worked on the pious bourgeoisie and nobility and further enflamed any suitable mob which formed. There were many unpunished murders. On both sides, what were in effect private armies began to form. The royalist partisans, 100,000 strong, if ragged, had their own inspector general, who acknowledged no official military superior.[75] The masonic lodges, which included many ex-officers, organized in more clandestine fashion. Spain's real difficulty, as it began to enter the modern world, was that the rival forces were too evenly balanced to allow one to prevail easily: hence the duration and ferocity of its civil commotions. The horrors of Latin America had feedback, too, for many on both sides had fought across the Atlantic and been corrupted by the cruelties.

Faced with the tendency of the nation to crumble into warring factions, the strategy of Ferdinand's restored government, in so far as it had one, was to accelerate the modernizing process, in the hope of making itself appear progressive. The new Prado museum was opened to the public. Some roads were built. A stock exchange was opened. The King was seen at the theater, shaking hands with dramatists like Leandro Moratin. Poets and artists were put on the royal payroll. So were journalists. The 1820s were the first decade of real press power, in Spain as in most other civilized countries. Every effort was made to attract industry and promote trade, culminating in the Industrial Exhibition in 1828, one of the first. But the attempt to present Ferdinand as a resurrected enlightened despot failed. How could it succeed? Everyone knew he was not enlightened but a travel-stained opportunist whose one aim was survival. Nor did he possess the power to be a despot. The events of 1820 brought the first crack in legitimist Europe, and as the decade progressed, experience showed it could not be mended.

The threat to what Friedrich von Gentz, *éminence grise* of the Vienna settlement, called "the public order" came increasingly from aninomian elements of all kinds dressing themselves in fashionable ideological clothes. The French Revolution had opened an era of intense politicization. Perhaps the most significant characteristic of the dawning modern world, and in this respect it was a true child of Rousseau, was the tendency to relate everything to politics. In Latin America, every would-be plunderer or ambitious bandit now called himself a "liberator"; murderers killed for freedom, thieves stole for the people. In Spain, during the 1820s, believers and nonbelievers, those who liked kings and those who hated them, began to regard their faith, or lack of it, as a justification for forming private armies which defied the lawful authorities. Organized crime now took a party label and put forward a program and thereby became better organized and a more formidable threat to society.

Thus violence acquired moral standing and the public was terrorized for its own good. Many years before, Samuel Johnson, in upholding the rights of authority, had qualified his defense by pointing to a corresponding and inherent human right to resist oppression: "Why all this childish jealousy of the power of the Crown? . . . In no government can power be abused long. Mankind will not bear it. If a sovereign oppresses his people to a great degree, they will rise and cut off his head."[76] The French Revolution had lowered the threshold of abuse at which men rose. It proved that cutting off royal heads was easier than had previously been thought and did not bring down the heavens. That undoubted fact was now a permanent temptation to every enemy of society who wished to acquire moral respectability for his crimes. It operated, in particular, throughout the Mediterranean area, where every government oppressed its subjects to some degree and there were usually no lawful forms of redress. In the past, men with a grievance had suffered in silence or taken to the hills and robbed. Now the hitherto resigned joined secret societies, and the bandits called themselves politicians.

Nowhere had this process gone further than in Italy, a notable theater of the Napoleonic Wars, both in their military and ideological aspects. Bonaparte politicized Italy, taught people to rise and overthrow ancient masters, and enabled those of inordinate ambition and appetites to pin Liberty to their caps. The British, controlling the seas, sought to organize and finance resistance to the Emperor's New Order, as they were to do a century and a half later against Nazi-occupied Europe. Bonaparte did not examine the moral character of the men who served his ideological purposes and his puppet regimes. Nor did the British inquire too closely into the good faith of those they paid and armed to bring the Francophile governments down. As in Latin America, they put victory before law and justice. Thus both antagonists helped to spread corruption in a country where it had always found a ready soil.

Central and southern Italy (including Sicily), prime theaters of misrule, had always bred outlaws, from the time of Rome's servile wars, and ferocious bandit-hunters. It was the custom to decapitate these malefactors and deck the town walls with their heads. The Papal States and the Kingdom of Naples were notorious for banditry. When Sixtus V became Pope in 1585, he demanded brigands' heads from his officials, and he was served in such quantities that the heads lay under the walls of Rome "as thick as melons in the market," while his Castel San'Angelo was decked out with quartered corpses; when complaints were made about the insufferable stench of the dead, Sixtus replied that "the smell of living iniquity was far worse." This endemic curse (and the response of the authorities to it) was envenomed, aggravated and politicized by the French incursion in Italy and the "patriotic" resistance. The number of murders in the Papal States was already enormous in the late 1790s. John Flaxman, in Rome to study antique sculpture, reported it was running at 1,500 annually and totaled "30,000 during the reign of the present pope."[77] Professional murderers were easily renamed God's warriors when they turned against French atheists and their collaborators. In Naples, the "crusade" launched by General-Cardinal Fabrizio Ruffo against the French forces enfranchised thousands of bandits in the cause of Christian monarchy and encouraged thousands of others to join them in lucrative and honorable service.

This was the problem faced by Marshal Joachim Murat, Bonaparte's brother-in-law, when the Emperor made him King of Naples in 1808. Murat was a brilliant cavalry commander who knew nothing of police operations against bandit-guerrillas. He summoned the help of a young expert, General Manhes, who had made a name for himself putting down papal insurgents in the Abruzzi. Manhes was only 32 at the time and of startling beauty. His first, chilling proclamations in Calabria were treated as a joke. In effect, he held local officials responsible for crimes committed in their districts and hanged them without mercy. To save their lives and avoid torture, the locals, from mayors to peasants, were forced to betray the outlaws, often members of their own families. One chief thus arrested, the famous Benincasa, was brought to Cosenza. Manhes ordered both his hands to be lopped off and tied round his neck; then he was to be taken to his home in San Giovanni in Fiore and hanged in front of it. He refused the last rites, ate whatever was put in his mouth "with real pleasure," slept soundly the night before his execution, "and died admired for his brutal intrepidity." This eyewitness account was by Pietra Coletta, the local Intendant, who said of some of the horrors perpetrated by Manhes that he lacked "the courage to relate them." In due course all the main roads were lined with decapitated bandits and every town wall in the province was decked with their heads.[78]

The fact that Murat had given General Manhes carte blanche for these atrocities eventually cost Murat his life. Murat had backed Bonaparte during the Hundred Days; lost his own kingdom at the Battle of Tolentina, five weeks before Waterloo, and fled to Corsica. Metternich then offered him asylum, and a British frigate was waiting to take him to Trieste. Instead he mustered 250 followers and seven *felucce* and landed at Pizzo on 7 October 1815 to win back his throne by the kind of guerrilla movement he had suppressed when he occupied it. He did not, however, dress as a guerrilla should. Always known as the Dandy King, he flaunted a gorgeous uniform crowned by a feathered hat with diamond clasps. He was recognized; the reception was chilly at first and rapidly became hostile as the mob was joined by innumerable relatives of Manhes's victims, who now at last saw the chance for revenge. Murat narrowly escaped being torn to pieces—one woman, whose four sons had been executed by Manhes, tore off part of his moustache—and was frog-marched to the Bourbon authorities, who had him court-martialed and shot. His last words were: "Aim at the heart but spare my face." King Ferdinand of Naples was said, probably falsely, to keep his skull as a souvenir.[79]

The end of the Napoleonic Wars did not end the violence of the Italian countryside or diminish the number of murders in the towns and cities. But the restoration of legitimacy changed the party labels of politicized crime. In Austrian-ruled territory, antinomian elements could still play the patriotic card. Everywhere they used the liberal one. What remained to be seen was the value of these cards in ordinary Italian eyes. The Congress of Vienna, as we have seen, left Austria supreme in Italy. Metternich had sought an Italian confederacy, under an Austrian president, as he obtained in Germany, but Savoy-Sardinia, which had pan-Italian ambitions, and the Pope, who valued his independence, refused to agree. All the same, Metternich got a great deal. Lombardy, Venice, the Trentino, and the Valtellina were knocked into the Kingdom of Lombardy-Venezia and handed to Austria outright. The Emperor Francis's brother got Tuscany; his sister, Parma; and a cousin, Modena, and Austrian forces were given the right to garrison three citadels in the Papal States. Ferdinand of Naples was required to sign a perpetual defensive alliance with Austria, which, in effect, conceded to the Habsburgs the right of military intervention.

It would be absurd to pretend the settlement was popular with

Italians. The Italians disliked the Austrians almost as much as they had come to detest the French. The first Governor of Lombardy, Bellegarde, warned Metternich in 1816: "I shall never tire of repeating that it is absolutely necessary to abandon the idea of a future, albeit slow, assimilation of these provinces within the German body of the Empire . . . [let alone] complete fusion." Four years later his successor, Strassoldo, likewise wrote to Metternich: "The Lombards have been and always will be unable to get used to the Germanic forms imprinted on the government of their country. They loathe them and they detest the system of uniformity by which they have been put on a par with Germans, Bohemians and Gicians."[80] That statement was doubtless true, and the Lombards also detested conscription into the Austrian army, which meant eight years' service outside Italy unless they could afford to buy themselves out. They resented as well the new tariff barriers, which made British and French goods dear and Austrian cheap.

On the other hand, the Austrian administration kept all the best ideas of the Napoleonic period and most of the civil servants who had implemented them. Justice was impartially administered. It was the most efficient and least corrupt of any Italian government. Tuscany and Parma were also comparatively well run and much more liberal in trade. The Papal States were highly taxed, corrupt, lawless, priest ridden and very Italian. Naples was also very Italian, as well as corrupt, lawless and priest ridden, but it had low taxes, especially on the poor. Sardinia was the most authoritarian, indeed reactionary—it was much influenced by the supreme ideologist of legitimacy, Joseph De Maistre—but the most noisy and consistent in beating the Italian national drum.

The dilemma, then, for Italians who were seeking to overthrow the Vienna settlement was that the areas of maximum grievances did not coincide with the areas under foreign occupation. Quite the contrary, if anything. And political crime, which could be put to use in the cause of "liberation" was likewise most prevalent where the misrule was unarguably of Italian origin. This dilemma might have been resolved by political education if the secret societies, which constituted the only organized opposition, had been capable of it. But in the north, where they were liberal, anticlerical, and progressive, they appealed only to the educated middle classes and "enlightened" aristocrats. In the south they had a more popular base, through their links with rustic outlaws and urban undergrounds, but tended to become criminalized in consequence. In any case, the menace of the societies or sects was much less formidable than the police forces of legitimacy liked to claim. Like the

Comintern in the 1930s, they were a European phenomenon and, to some extent, coordinated and centrally directed. But unlike the Comintern, they did not have an ultimate national base, where they could be trained and from which money and arms could flow.

The most important figure, or so it was supposed, was Filipo Michele Buonarroti (1761–1837), a Pisan by birth, and proud of his descent from Michelangelo. Becoming a naturalized French citizen, he took part in the French Revolution and was imprisoned and deported for his part in the conspiracy organized by François-Emile Babeuf, the proto-communist who tried to overthrow the Directory. He came out of prison in 1809 and immediately resumed underground work in northern Italy with Republican elements in the French occupation and local malcontents and "patriots." He founded a network called the Adelphi, which migrated to Geneva when the Austrians took over Lombardy and changed its name to the Sublime Perfect Masters.

The Sublime Perfect Masters combined illuminism, freemasonry and radical politics with a good deal of pretentious symbolism. Its structure was hierarchical, only the most senior levels knowing its inner secrets, and Buonarroti came close to the isolated cell system of modern terrorist groups, which makes them so difficult to destroy, even if penetrated. The various police forces never discovered much about his apparatus, which is the reason we know so little about it. In theory it was formidable, since it had links with a Directive Committee in Paris which coordinated Orléanist, Jacobin, Bonapartist, and Republican subversion, with various German groups, such as the Tugendbund and the Unbedingten; with Spanish Masons and *comuneros;* and even with a Russian group called the Union of Salvation, the whole supposedly existing under a mysterious body, also in Geneva, called the Grand Firmament. In Italy, the Sublime Perfect Masters had links with the Carbonari, which operated in the center and the south. Contact was maintained by special handshakes, secret codes, invisible ink and other devices that are dear to the heart of a healthy schoolboy. But it is a notable fact that Buonarrotti, in particular, and the networks, in general, never once succeeded in organizing a successful conspiracy or one which can fairly be said to have got off the ground. Moreover when uprisings did take place and governments were overthrown, as in Spain in 1820, Buonarroti—like Marx, and indeed Lenin, later—was taken completely by surprise.

In northern Italy, subversion was close to surface respectability. In fact, for a time it produced a newspaper, *Il Conciliatore* (1818–19), which propagated romantic literature (just being classified as "progressive"), Bell-Lancaster schools, the theories of Jeremy Bentham, hydraulics and steam engines. These topics, on the whole, were what middle-class Lombard intellectuals discussed, rather than slitting Austrian throats. The Carbonari, uninterested in Science, were more blood-thirsty and more formidable. Their origin may have been in the char-bonniers, or charcoal cutters, of the Franche-Comté, a secretive, lawless trade, "modernized" by Freemasons and brought to Italy by the former Jacobin Briot, who was Intendant of Chieta and Cosenza under the French occupation. They were subsidized by the British and spread rapidly after the 1812 Russian disaster fatally undermined French au-thority. In the postwar period they had sympathizers in many towns, big and small, even in the administration, and links with all the big groups of brigands. But such a network, like the proto-Mafia in Sicily and Freemasons almost everywhere, was inherently corrupt, devoting its energies to trade-offs and governmental "jobs," protection rackets, smuggling, and contract assassinations as much as to politics. Where money was to be made, the Carbonari were often effective. Where the object was political, its branches—like the sectarians in the north—proved themselves uncertain, irresolute, divided, and ineffectual. The political underground as a whole, as Metternich pointed out privately in 1817, was also in a continual state of osmosis: "In design and principle divided among themselves these sects change every day and tomorrow may be ready to fight each other."[81] What they offered, to a few educated, sometimes well-born, Italians, was an escape from the boredom of autocracy.

This was the world to which Byron, fleeing his wife, came in 1816. His letters give a day-by-day account of his self-imposed exile. "Miss Milbanke appears in all respects to have been formed for my destruc-tion," he wrote. "She—or rather the Separation—has broken my heart—I feel as if an elephant had trodden on it."[82] But soon Italy was exerting its manifold charms. In Milan's Ambrosian Library he exam-ined a lock of Lucretia Borgia's hair ("the prettiest and finest imagin-able"), saw bandits on the Lombardy Plain ("they come upon you in bodies of thirty"), inspected the tomb of the Capulets in Verona and reached Venice in November ("the greenest island of my imagination"). There he settled to enjoy a life of unqualified hedonism. He took rooms with "a Merchant of Venice," promptly fell in love with the merchant's wife Marianna ("like an antelope"), seduced her "according to the incontinent Continental system," and soon declared: "We are one of the happiest unlawful couples on this side of the Alps." By the New Year he had additional mistresses: "Never a 24 hours without giving or receiving from one of three (and occasionally an extra or so) pretty unequivocal proofs of mutual contentment."[83] He liked the theaters, which did not open till 9 P.M. ("all this is to my taste"), found he could get a box for the season at the Fenice ("it beats *our* theatre hollow in beauty and scenery") for a mere £14, as opposed to £400 at Covent Garden or Drury Lane) and rented the Moncenigo Palace on the Grand Canal for a modest £200 a year. He had his own gondola and 13 servants, plus a nurse for his child, Allegra, by Claire Clairmont. The household were nearly all male, "my ragmuffins—a damned bad set as ever I sailed with."

Harassed by duns in London, Byron found he could live in Italy like a lord or a prince; in 2½ years he spent £5,000 but "more than half was laid out on the Sex—to be sure I have had plenty for the money—that's certain—I think at least 200 of one sort or another—perhaps more."[84] He studied Armenian at a local monastery, made forays to Florence, Rome, and other towns, saw bandits guillotined, attended "the circumcision of a suckling Shylock" ("I have seen three men's heads and a child's foreskin cut off in Italy"), provoked two rival mistresses into a fistfight, cursed the English tourists ("a parcel of staring boobies who go about gaping"), got himself "clapt" by a lady ("to be sure it was *gratis*—the first gonorrhea I have not paid for") and won a race swimming from the Lido back to his palace, beating the Chevalier Angelo Mengalda, who had swum the Danube and Beresina under fire.[85] He returned repeatedly to his favorite painting, Giorgione's *Tempesta*, then in the Mandrini Palace, acquired another beauty, Margarita ("the figure of a Juno—tall and energetic as a Pythoness, with eyes flashing and dark hair streaming in the moonlight"), rode and walked with Shelley along the empty, desolate Lido sands, thus inspiring *Julian and Maddalo*, fell into the Grand Canal, found indigestible "a kind of Adriatic fish called Scampi," and wrote home for supplies of "toothbrushes; tooth powder; magnesia; Macassar oil and corn-rubbers," all unobtainable in Italy.[86]

During this period Byron had not been idle. He wrote a great deal of poetry, including further cantos of *Childe Harold* and much of *Don Juan;* plays; and lyrics. He sorted out his financial affairs, and began to save money for some grand, preferably military, adventure. He had had a radical upbringing from his mother, reflected in his few speeches in the House of Lords, and his politics were always populist, though in no way democratic. He thought Shelley's views extreme and unworkable, almost ridiculous. He pictured himself as a parliamentary grandee at the opening of the English Civil War and when there was talk of a rising in Britain in 1819, he said he would return, "get a 'Charge of Horse' in the ensuing struggle" and "Shoot Castlereagh"—"if nobody else will . . . I will take that service on myself."[87] But in all his Venetian letters there is no mention of local politics, and this omission is significant, for Venice, whose trade the Austrians had penalized to build up Trieste, ought to have been seething with discontent. In fact, Venice was apathetic, like so much of Italy.

Then on 6 April 1819, Byron announced he had "fallen in love with a Romagnalo Countess from Ravenna." Teresa Guiccioli was "as fair as Sunrise—and as warm as Noon—a sort of Italian Caroline Lamb, except that she is much prettier and not so savage—but she has the same red-hot head." He followed her from Venice to Ravenna, where her husband the Count, a rich but elderly and miserly man, had a town palace, and conducted a characteristically Mozartian-Italian intrigue with her, involving a priest, a chambermaid, a female friend called Fanny and a Negro page boy.[88] They became lovers, Byron renounced all his other ladies ("I am living in strictest adultery"), moved into the upper floor of the Guiccioli Palace, and was discovered "quasi in the fact" by the angry Count. Teresa's father, Count Gamba, who had always detested her husband, appealed on her behalf to the Pope for a judicial separation, which was granted. Teresa, Byron, Gamba and his son Pietro became firm allies. Byron's own friends found it hard to believe in her permanency at first. Indeed, Thomas Moore reported him as saying in October 1819, "I say, Tom, you might have been my salvation for if you had come [to Italy] a little sooner, I'll be damned if I would have run away with a red-haired woman of quality."[89] Shelley described Teresa as "a very pretty, sentimental, innocent Italian, who has sacrificed an immense fortune for the sake of Lord Byron and who, if I know anything of my friend, her and human nature, will hereafter have plenty of leisure and opportunity to repent her rashness."[90] In fact, the Countess proved to be Byron's last and longest love—many years later, her second, French, husband used to introduce her in the Paris salons with the whispered addition "la dernière maitresse de milord Byron." Her effect on the poet was entirely beneficial. She not only kept him faithful to her, but got to him to lead a sensible, less selfish life. Shelley, visiting him at Ravenna, found he had "completely recovered his health and leads a life totally the reverse of that which he had at Venice."

To be sure, some of Byron's propensities remained, including his habit of surrounding himself with exotic beasts. Byron's establishment, Shelley noted, "consists, besides servants, of ten horses, eight enormous dogs, three monkeys, five cats, an eagle, a crow and a falcon; and all these, except the horses, walk about the house which every now and then resounds with their unarbitrated quarrels." He added a footnote:

"I have just met on the grand staircase five peacocks, two guinea hens and an Egyptian crane."[91] Through Teresa, however, Byron at last gained a serious purpose in life besides his poetry, which he did not believe a sufficient occupation for a gentleman. For the Gambas were a political family. The Count and his son were both members of a branch of the Carbonari, and in August 1820 they inducted Byron into the sect. Suddenly, he conceived a vocation for irredentist politics and felt himself filled with the spirit of Italian independence. Through Teresa, he was part of the struggle. He wrote to Moore at the end of the month: "What do Englishmen know of Italians beyond their museums and saloons? Now I have lived in the heart of their houses, in parts of Italy freshest and least influenced by strangers—have seen and become a portion of their hopes and fears and passions and am almost innoculated into a family. This is to see men and things as they are."[92]

What Byron meant was that hitherto he had been a mere rebel against convention and established morality. Now he was committed to a cause. Among Italian nationalists, the desire to strike a blow—what kind was never clear—had been rising throughout 1819. There was much plotting and whispering, but rather less leadership. Every *capo di carbonari,* every Sublime Perfect Master, appeared to be waiting for a sign, preferably from abroad. In autumn 1819 reports of Peterloo, grotesquely exaggerated, reached Italy. In Italy, the "provocation" of the Manchester yeomanry seemed a stroke of fortune. Moore, in Florence, was told that Nocolini, the leading nationalist writer in Tuscany and "a violent anti-government man," had said that "the massacre of Manchester was a lucky event for English liberty and exclaimed: "Would to God that the Archduke would this night order 400 Tuscans to be sabred!' "[93] But no such spark was struck. The Austrians plodded on, sober, honest and tiresomely bureaucratic, but never violent unless attacked. Then came the Spanish liberal coup of 1 January 1820. When news reached Italy, the nationalists felt ashamed. The quasi-clandestine *Romagna Collector* asked on 30 March 1820: "Is Italy to be the *last* nation of Europe?" The only response came from Naples. There the Carbonari, besides its links with discontented peasants and the bandits, had a wide middle-class following: junior army officers, merchants, shopkeepers and even some priests. On the night of 1 July a revolt of army officers and Carbonari broke out. It was led by a priest, Luigi Minichin. Part of the army under General Gugliemo Pepe deserted to it. King Ferdinand capitulated and granted a Spanish-type constitution under his son Francis as Regent. Carbonari pressure got the salt tax halved and some power devolved to local governments, that is, to the sects and their outlaw allies. But the government set up by the Regent was ultramoderate and could not make up its mind how to deal with the Austrians who, in accordance with a decision taken by the powers at the Conference of Troppau, were sending an army south to restore "public order." To make matters worse, there was a copycat rising in Palermo two weeks later, which declared Sicily independent of Naples; the Neopolitan Carbonari did not control the Sicilian Mafia, and the liberal government was so furious that it sent out an army to put the revolt down. In the rest of Italy, every local group of conspirators was waiting for the next to move. The Lombards did nothing. Nothing was heard from France or from the center of the supposed web of conspiracy in Geneva.

Byron's letters from Ravenna show him waiting in a fever of impatience. Being a foreigner, he felt he could not take the lead himself. The most he could do was to buy arms and store them in his house, concealed in the quarters of his menagerie. There were countless rumors and one or two actual skirmishes. On 9 December 1820, Byron reported that a commandant (major) had been shot near his door and carried up to his apartment for succor. That was the nearest he got to any violence. Three months later the planned Carbonari rising was aborted when its plans were betrayed and some leaders were arrested (24 February 1821). The first Byron knew of it was when frightened Italian friends asked if they could hide their guns at his house. He complied with these requests without much enthusiasm; if his house was searched, he might be expelled, or worse. Within 10 days the Austrian army beat General Pepe's Neapolitans at Rieti, and the revolt in the south collapsed. Up north, in Piedmont, a revolt finally came, two days later (9 March 1821) and six months too late. There was a small skirmish, in which 10 people were killed. Then the cities that had risen were quickly subdued by Austrian and Savoyard troops. By April it was all over and the police could start picking up suspects at their leisure. On 22 June they arrested Byron's ferociously bearded but kind-hearted Venetian servant Tita. On 10 July Pietro Gamba was taken into custody and banished. As a rich English nobleman with European fame, Byron was immune, but he felt it safer to transfer himself in the autumn to Tuscany, now the least-oppressive state in Italy, and rent a palace in Pisa. The Italian uprising, if the word is not too strong for it, had been a total fiasco: ill-planned; ill-led; and, above all, ill-followed. For whatever reason— lack of courage and, equally important, lack of real grievances—Italy did not want independent nationhood enough to fight for it. The Congress of Vienna frontiers were to endure till 1859 and even then they were overthrown mainly through French military intervention. Disgusted and disillusioned, Byron began to think of wider fields of action.

In Pisa Byron renewed his friendship with Shelley and the two poets found a new interest: the sea. Byron, whose affairs now prospered and who was accumulating what he called a war chest, had a Genoese shipyard build him a schooner, which he called, significantly, the *Bolivar*—he was still thinking of joining the cause there. Shelley, with more slender means, commissioned the *Don Juan,* a small craft only 24 feet long but built for speed, with twin mainmasts and schooner rigging. He and a new friend, Lieutenant Edward Williams of the East India Company, devised additional rigging, which made the boat still faster and extremely dangerous. Shelley's personal life was reaching another crisis, for he was falling out of love with his second wife, Mary, and in love with Williams's beautiful, guitar-strumming wife Jane. On 8 July 1822 Shelley and Williams were taking the *Don Juan* back from Livorno, where its extra rigging had been fitted, to Lerici, where the Shelleys and Williamses were sharing a summer villa. A storm was brewing and the pair were warned not to embark. They did so, under full sail, and the last person to see them, as the storm broke, reported that one (supposedly Shelley, who had a mania for speed) was seen to stop the other lowering the sails, seizing him by the arm "as if in anger." The boat went down 10 miles from shore, still under full sail, and both men drowned.[94] Thus another intense poetic flame was extinguished—Keats had died of tuberculosis in Rome the year before. Byron, in accordance with Shelley's wishes, arranged for his body to have a Viking's funeral on the seashore.

This gruesome episode brought Byron into close contact with an adventurer, Edward James Trelawny. Trelawny had connections with the Greek nationalists who had risen against Turkish rule in 1821. He planted in Byron's head the idea of returning to Greece, scene of his exciting youthful travels, as a liberator. The moment was well chosen. Greece was now ousting Latin America, in the minds of Europe's liberal intellectuals, as the cause of the moment. The insurgents had enjoyed some initial success, but three months before Shelley's drowning, in April 1822, the Turks had perpetrated a fearful atrocity. Greek ships had appeared off the island of Chios, in the hopes of raising a revolt there. The local Turkish Governor carried out a massacre to forestall it. There had been other brutal, large-scale killings, by both sides, but this one captured the European imagination. As we have seen, Delacroix made it the subject of his greatest painting. Rossini planned an opera, which eventually became *The Siege of Corinth.* Greece began to obsess European radicals in the way that Spain was to do in the 1930s or Vietnam in the 1960s, with Chios as a kind of Guernica or My Lai. On 3 March 1823, John Cam Hobhouse, Sir John Bowring and Thomas

Gordon, with 22 other "friends of Greece," set up a London Greek Committee, to raise money, buy arms, and dispatch volunteers to aid the Greeks. The committee also established links with similar committees in Paris, Munich, Stuttgart, Berne, Madrid, Marseilles and Zurich. Eight bands of volunteers were soon on their way. A month after the London Greek Committee was formed, one of its supporters, a former Irish sea captain, Edward Blaquiere, called on Byron in Genoa, where the poet was now living, and begged him to be their chief on Greek soil. By early June, Byron had decided; he sold the *Bolivar;* charted a three-masted clipper, the *Hercules;* and wrote to Trelawny asking him to join the expedition: "I am at last determined to go to Greece—it is the only place I was ever contented in."[95]

Byron was already sufficiently familiar with the structure of Greek society and the way the Turks ruled it to realize that the cause of Greek independence was not quite what it seemed. But his personal knowledge was out of date, and the situation had become far more complex and squalid since 1811. The Greek revolt was part of the process whereby the Ottoman-Turkish Empire, all-powerful in the 16th century, still formidable in the 17th century, manifestly in decay in the 18th century, was being dismembered. Two great powers had been competing for the spoils. Russia had been pushing down from the north, defeating Turkey in two acquisitive wars, 1768–74 and 1787–92. Its aim was to control the Black Sea, recover Constantinople for Christianity, assert a Russian overlordship over the Christian peoples of the Balkans, acquire access to the Mediterranean and strengthen its position in Western Asia. France aimed, long before the Revolution, to found on Turkey's ruins a French empire in the eastern Mediterranean to compensate for its losses to Britain in India and Canada.[96] France had designs on Cyprus, Crete and Egypt, and it sought, by modernization and military-assistance programs, a position of paramountcy at the Ottoman court.

Within Turkey, a fierce and often bloody debate raged between the modernizers and the fundamentalist Moslems. Western-oriented Turks pointed out that Turkey had fallen behind powers like Russia and France in military technology and that to escape dismemberment, it had no alternative but to introduce modern ideas on how to fight wars. The fundamentalist position was put by the historiographer Vasif, writing in about 1800: "The imperial state should not demean itself and condescend to learn unfamiliar martial sciences from those [the French] who belong to the same kind [are fellow Christians] as its enemies [Russia]. Success or failure depends on the conduct of Almighty God. The beliefs

of the Christian nations are contrary to this, as they follow the doctrine
of a school of philosophers according to which the Creator has no role
in particular matters (Heaven forfend!). As war is one of such particular
matters, they believe that the side superior in material means of warfare
becomes victorious. [But] how is it possible to attribute victory merely
to the perfection of the means of warfare and defeat to lack of those
means? [Hence] to accept aid from the French . . . is bound to bring
immediate and ultimate disaster and fatal consequences, besides the
fact that their purpose is not entirely friendly, and trusting the Christians is not permitted."[97]

This tortuous view is set out at length because it represented majority opinion in Turkey until the end of the 1820s, not merely among the
clergy but in sections of the fighting classes. In 1785 the reformist
Sadrazam [Prime Minister] Halil Hamid, who had accepted French
military advisers, was dismissed and murdered along with other pro-
Westerners; the placard attached to his body before it was thrown into
the Bosphorus read: "The Enemy of the [Islamic law] and the State."
Selim III, who came to the throne in 1789, began a more cautious
reform, based upon what Turkish advisers in Paris considered the
characteristics of a modern state: (1) a disciplined army; (2) orderly
finances; (3) honest, educated and patriotic civil servants; and (4) economic prosperity encouraged by a reliable framework of law and order.
Selim sent young men to be educated in the West and appointed a
Council of Ten, all members of the younger, more secularized generation, to advise him. Embassies were set up in Paris, London, Vienna,
Berlin and Madrid. French military experts were admitted, and military
schools were set up. In May 1807 an alliance of ulemas (priests), janissaries (palace guards), derebeys (feudal chieftains and provincial nobles) and ayans (other notables) seized power, murdered all the young
westerners—whom they accused of conspiring to dress all Turks like
Franks—and set up a janissary dictatorship. A compromise was
reached between the fundamentalists and the surviving reformers under
which a new sultan, Mahmud II (reigned 1808–39) was put on the
throne, with a form of constitution known as the *Ittifak,* the first
attempt to put down on paper the respective functions of the various
Turkish governing bodies and to distinguish between ruler and ruled.[98]
In practice, however, conservative methods prevailed, and it was not
until 1826, as we shall see, that the fundamentalists received their first
real setback. The new factor, from about 1800, was a growing British
presence in the eastern Mediterranean, anxious to frustrate both Russian and French designs and inclined, if anything, to keep the Ottoman
Empire together as the best means of securing this aim.[99]

MASQUES OF ANARCHY 675

Meanwhile the authorities in Constantinople continued to rule the empire by traditional methods. The West found it hard to understand them. Westerners, whether legitimists or constitutionalists, believed in sets of rules delineating power precisely, enforced in courts. In Turkey, as in most independent oriental states, including China and Japan, the ruler's power was theoretically absolute, but in practice it devolved on subordinates by a series of personal deals. There were never any rules about how these deals were made or unmade, and all in the end depended on the strength of character, cunning and physical resources of ruler and satrap. In North Africa, as we have seen, most but not all power was devolved on the beys of Algiers, Tunis and Tripoli. In Egypt, from 1805 onwards, the local ruler was Muhammad Ali (1769–1848), whom we will examine in detail shortly. In Greece, power had gradually been acquired by an Albanian Moslem, Ali Pasha (1741–1822), known as the Lion of Janina, whose barbarous court culture was observed by the young Byron in 1809–10 and brilliantly described in *Childe Harold.*

This erosion of the Ottoman Empire was proceeding simultaneously with the disintegration of Spanish power in the Americas, and in both situations, enlightened European opinion favored the insurgents. But the differences were important. Spain and its empire shared a common language, culture and religion. In the Balkans, Ottoman rule was more a military occupation by a racial and religious enemy whose culture was alien and repellent. The Greeks had defended Europe from invasion by Asiatic hordes since the days of the Persian Empire. In the 1820s, Greeks and Turks were in the forefront of an intercontinental clash which continues to this day. That, at any rate, was how Greek leaders presented it in their independence rhetoric, especially when directed at French, British and German audiences. The reality was very different. Greek and Turks had lived together in the Balkans for many centuries, as occupied and occupier, and had reached many compromises. At no point did this spirit of compromise flourish more mightily than during the long reign of Ali Pasha. Ali Pasha had gained power through murder and brigandage and had taken full advantage of the violence and instability provoked by the long Napoleonic Wars. As in Latin America, these wars had favored insurgents challenging the power of established authority, who might be helped by the French or the British or both in succession. Ali Pasha changed sides frequently and so prospered. He also benefited, in a rough and ready fashion, from the growing availability, which the wars accelerated, of modern weapons, mass-produced, sold, stolen and circulated. He acquired arms from both sides and equipped his men not only with modern muskets and rifles but with cannon.

Thus established as the leading Moslem power in Greece, the Lion of Janina ruled by the time-honored Ottoman method of favoring the growth of certain elites which could be managed. These elites were, in the first instance, the ecclesiastical leaders and the *Phanariots,* senior civil servants associated with the imperial administration (the word comes from the Constantinople lighthouse district where it was situated). To them Ali added three provincial groups: in the Peloponnese, the so-called *primates,* big landowners and tax farmers; in the islands, the shipowners and merchants; and, most important, especially in Rumelia, the chiefs of the authorized paramilitary bands, known as *armatoles.*[100] Why were the *armatoles* so important? Here again it was necessary for Westerners to make a radical adjustment. They saw society in terms of clear distinctions between the law-abiding and the criminal classes. That distinction had become blurred, as we have seen, in Latin America, where the war of independence turned liberators into brigands, and vice-versa. It was becoming blurred in Spain, where private armies flourished, and in Italy, especially in the south, where liberal secret societies merged imperceptibly into organized crime and robber bands. But whereas in Italy bandits were still recognizably such and sported gangster nicknames like Brother Devil, Mammon, Big Saber and Black Belly, in Greece the bandits were called Agamemnon and Socrates, Achilles and Nestor and could attain the highest respectability.[101]

As Ottoman power declined, anarchy in Greece spread, especially in the coastal areas, where lawlessness, including piracy, was reinforced by the long Napoleonic wars. Peasants fled inland or abandoned the lowlands for the mountains; plow land was given up to pasture, and the wealth of the community was increasingly vested in huge flocks of sheep and goats, which produced meat, milk and wool—and economic and political power. Enormous flocks of sheep, often 10,000 or even more, accompanied by 2,000 shepherd-horsemen, operating under chiefs, made their seasonal migrations from winter to summer pasture and back. Alliances were formed between the owners of the pasture and the owners of the flocks. Whereas in the highlands of northern and western Europe—Scotland being a prime example—ancient pastoral societies were disintegrating, in Greece they were growing stronger. Ali Pasha was the outstanding figure in this galaxy of patriarchal overlords, underwriting his political power by seizing peasant holdings and consolidating them into huge estates, called *chifliks,* for winter pasture;

maintaining vast flocks; and using mounted men as both shepherds and warriors.[102]

In this insecure society, no one from the Pasha down was immune to threat, and force, not law, was the only guarantee that you kept what you possessed. No one looked to the theoretical central authority for protection. Loyalties were local. The extended patriarchal family, whose ties were blood, foster brotherhood and godparentage, was the chief political institution. The patriarch protected, and in return he ruled, settling rows, punishing crimes, laying down standards of behavior. The external threat might come from anywhere, but locally it came from the bandits or *klephts,* bands of debtors, jailbirds, fugitives, misfits, victims, and adventurers, who could not flourish in society but took to the hills to live by violence. The klephts robbed unguarded travelers, sometimes carried out mass attacks on villages, and straddled the passes through which flocks, caravans and officials had to pass. The tendency of 19th-century intellectuals to portray them as Romantic heroes in verse, opera and novels, and of 20th-century academics to categorize them as primitive social revolutionaries, runs against all the reliable contemporary evidence. Depositions show they were young men, often with a shepherd background, who took to the hills at the age of 16 or 17, as a result of a false arrest, being done out of an inheritance, or a similar grievance. Most acquired legal patrons and did not like to embarrass them by sensational robberies or demands for ransom or by killing soldiers, in which case the hunt for them became intense. If confronted by army units, they usually ran away, not so much out of cowardice as from a desire not to cause trouble to their patrons. They levied contributions from the peasants and protection money from landowners, which were their main sources of income, not robberies. They also made deals with owners of migratory sheep, which, moving as flocks of 3,000 or 4,000, often destroyed crops as they came down from the mountains to winter pasture, and so needed protection. The brigands supplied it.

On the whole, the *klephts* respected the shepherds, from whom they usually sprang, but despised the peasants, who were there simply to be exploited. As one western observer put it, the *klephts* "habitually plundered Christians and accidentally murdered Mussulmans . . . it is an egregious error to suppose they had not a great share in perpetuating the barbarism that gave them birth." They tended to attack those they feared least, the poor.[103] However, most were poor themselves, and their self-image was of a have-not whose crimes were justified by a cruel world. The possessions found on captured bandits included expensive weapons (the bandit ideal was to have guns inlaid with silver); a heavy silver chain; a telescope; expensive rings; watches; and collections of British, French, Dutch, Austrian and Russian coins.[104] Their clothes were poor, not exotic, and filthy. They ate from tin-coated copper dishes stolen from peasant homes. Each carried a large bag or *tova*, with flour and salt for their bread, and cheese. Their society was strictly male, for their "laws" specifically excluded women from the bands, and most bandits were unmarried. Homosexuality may have been common, for responsible Greek leaders tried hard to discourage young boys from joining the gangs.

With no women, bandits made their own coarse pita bread, mended their shoes from sole leather they carried with them, and had needles and thread to patch their clothes—tights, a cotton or wool kilt to the knee, a cotton shirt, a woolen waistcoat, cloth tied around the waist and a leather belt, a brimless cap and a woolen cloak that served as bedroll. Pita and cheese were their staples, but they loved goat or mutton roasted on a spit when available (not on days of abstinence). Chickens they despised as fit only for townsmen. Beef did not exist in their world. The roasted animal was cut into portions, allocated by lot. The chief then "read" the shoulder bone. Sometimes they got wine and *raki* from monasteries. Usually they had no wine and drank only water, unless they distilled a coarse spirit for themselves. Their bands were 10 to 20, linked by blood or foster relationships. Bigger bands were difficult to feed and clothe without straining relations with the local peasants. As a result they always avoided battles with authority, if possible, and seldom used the firearms they carried—their main weapon was a long dagger, the *giatagan*. They were always on the move, carrying heavy loads, and unless they invested shrewdly in sheep, they seldom, if ever, became rich. In short, their lives were frugal, grim and brutal. If caught, they were tortured to confess or disgorge, and they tortured in turn, pouring scalding oil or butter on chests, cutting off the nose or one or both ears, breaking knees with axes or stones.[105] The peasants feared them at least as much as they feared any other kind of authority.

Ali Pasha greatly extended the practice of granting amnesty to leaders of such bands of klephts and enlisting them to supress mountain crime. These *armatores*, or paramilitaries, authorized to carry arms, were each under a *kapitanos*, who was put in charge of an area called an *armatolik*, where brigands were active. It is important to grasp that a klepht chief became a kapitanos precisely because he had been a successful bandit and had built up a band that was strong in reputation, men and sheep. It was the ambition of every such leader to attract the attention of authority by his prowess and thus be allowed to pass the frontier from illegality to legality. When selected, a klepht-turned-kapitanos was formally licensed by the Turkish authorities in the presence of the Christian notables and hence was empowered to collect taxes in return for providing security. In effect, it was a legal protection racket. The increase in armatores under Ali Pasha meant that by the 1820s they had become the power elite in Rumelia, Thessaly, Epirus and southern Macedonia. Local folk songs often told the tale of how a bandit became a famous and rich kapitanos. The most widely praised kapitanos was Georgios Karaiskakis, who became a bandit at 15, fought his way up to captain status, boasted of his bastardy, was foul mouthed and quick tempered but generous to his men if they showed bravery, and decked himself out in glittering clothes adorned with expensive jewels, the spoils of war.[106] Another, about whom opinion was divided, was Odysseus Androutsos, who married his 13-year-old daughter to Trelawny. He had made himself celebrated by winning a wager with Ali Pasha, who had bet the most beautiful women in his harem, against Odysseus's head, that he could not outrace the Pasha's fastest horse. He was said to be brave, strict on discipline, knew all his men, was respected and feared by them, paid them well, had vast family connections, was impetuous but not imprudent, was violent only for a set purpose, cruel only when necessary and combined nobility with generosity. Others said he was deceitful, bloodthirsty, greedy and without scruples, caring for nothing except to become ruler of an independent province.[107]

The existence of so many paramilitary forces, controlled by Greeks, prepared the way for a Greek independence movement on the ground. In 1820 Ali Pasha brought it a step nearer by rebelling against the sultan. The Porte had Ali assassinated in 1822, but before that happened there had been a good deal of fighting between rival Moslem forces, while the Greek captains watched and steadily increased their power. In the meantime the liberal risings in Spain and Naples proved infectious, and in spring 1821 the *Philiki Etairia*, or Society of Friends, proclaimed Greek independence. This movement was led essentially by educated, westernized Greeks of the diaspora, like Alexandros Mavrokordatos (1791–1865) and John Capodistria (1776–1831), who had all kinds of schemes for introducing parliamentary government, the rule of law, and modern education. Capodistria, indeed, had been one of Alexander I's chief ministers and an architect of the settlement at the Congress of Vienna. But they had no armies and few followers in mainland Greece.

The initial success of the revolution was mainly the work of the captains, who had quite other ideas. Most of them simply seized what towns they could and set up fiefdoms of their own. Odysseus made himself master of Athens. Dimitrios Makris took absolute power in Aetolia and ran it like a family estate. Adritsos Siafakas became ruler of Kravari. These, and other captains, paid little attention to Mavrokordatos, who as President of the new Greek assembly was supposed to be in charge of the revolutionary war. They refused to join together to take the chief fortresses, which the Turks still held and which, provided the Moslems could establish command of the sea, were springboards for the reconquest of the country. Instead, the captains often behaved like independent warlords—as their equivalents did in Latin America—and had territorial disputes among themselves. They made deals with the Turks when it suited them, and local bishops, representing the provisional government, complained they often treated the peasants more cruelly than either Ali Pasha or the Sultan had.[108]

It may be that Byron, with his international prestige and his curious blend of romanticism and cynicism, which gave him so clear an understanding of the brigand mentality, was the right man to unite the Greeks and would eventually have become their first sovereign. But he moved slowly. The *Hercules* set sail from Italy on 16 July 1823, his party including Trelawny, Pietro Gamba, Byron's faithful valet Fletcher, and the bearded Tita. Byron's first stop was the Ionian Islands, then run as a British protectorate. But he was moved on by the authorities, who were anxious that Corfu should not become a transit camp for European volunteers, thus compromising British neutrality. He reached Greek soil, at Metaxata on one of the islands, early in September, and debated what he should do. His war chest was full, but it was enough only to buy influence, not to pay an army. The Greek government's entire income was only £80,000 a year, and all its hopes rested on raising a loan in London. Everyone in Greece thought Byron was a multimillionaire whose treasure would win the war. Byron received invitations from warlords and governors from all over Greece to join them in what they represented as the key point in the struggle. The Souliotes or Christian Albanians wanted him to take them on his payroll. It took him some time to sort out these conflicting pleas and to decide what to do.

On 22 November 1823, Byron was joined in Metaxata by Colonel Leicester Stanhope (1784–1862), heir to the Earl of Harington, who had proposed himself to the London committee as Byron's assistant. Stanhope had had a good deal of military experience, in the Buenos Aires expedition and the Mahratta War in India, but his main interest was in the media and the uses to which it could be put in assisting independence movements.[109] Once in Greece, he set about establishing an arsenal; collecting equipment; and laying plans for hospitals, a scientific laboratory, schools and a postal service back to Britain. He lectured the Greeks on strategy, stressing how important it was to take the fortresses of Lepanto, Patras, Rio and Antiro. He calculated that these fortresses could be taken with 1,000 irregulars, six 12- or 18-pounders, 50 German artillerymen, two bomb boats and a special shipload of Congreve rockets which had been bought by the London committee and was on its way, under an expert from the Woolwich arsenal, William Parry. Byron formed a low opinion of Stanhope and his "high-flown notions [from] the Sixth Form at Harrow or Eton." He wanted to see action, and he accused Stanhope of doing too much talking. He was particularly contemptuous of the Colonel's printing press and his *Telegrafo Greco,* a propaganda sheet distributed in various languages. "It is odd," he complained, "that Stanhope, the soldier, is all for writing down the Turks, and I, the writer, am all for shooting them down."[110]

Byron finally crossed to Missolonghi, on the mainland, on 6 January 1824. He believed that the Greek efforts to raise money in London would bear fruit. Since the loan would be made to the Greek government, on the security of the future country, the cash would have to be put into the hands of Mavrocordatos, as head of it, and the mere possession of the money would bring the various factions to heel under his leadership. By going to Missolonghi, Byron signaled his backing of this plan. But the loan took time. Two Greek deputies, with plenary powers to negotiate it, arrived in London only at the end of January. The London committee gave a banquet for them at the Guildhall, attended by Canning, the Foreign Secretary—an important point—and a contract was signed with London banking houses on 27 February, the loan being floated two days later. The loan was nominally worth £800,000, floated at 59 percent, and raised £472,000; £310,000 was actually transferred to Greece. The rate of interest was 5½ percent, so the Greek government had to pay back £40,000 annually. On the other hand, the investors had absolutely no guarantee they would ever receive a penny, in interest or in capital. The London committee thought Byron would be the ideal man to ensure that the cash was prudently spent.

Meanwhile, Byron was restless. He collected a force of 2,000 insurgents, including 500 souliots, whom he paid himself. His aim was to take the fortress of Lepanto, but his plan was delayed by the arrival of a Turkish naval squadron. Parry and his rocket team docked on 7 February but the Welshman's response to reaching the front was to go on a drinking bout. His men, civilian artificers, were terrified by the souliots, who tried to raid their stores for explosives, and demanded to be sent back to England. Irritated by the inaction and anxious to get out of Missolonghi, which was notoriously fever ridden, Stanhope left it for Athens on 21 February, in an attempt to make peace between the factions and to form a united front for the offensive. He arranged a meeting at Salona for the last week in April and invited Byron to join them there: "I implore you to quit Missolonghi and not to sacrifice your health, and perhaps your life, in that bog." The letter was entrusted to Trelawny to deliver, but on his way, Trelawny met soldiers who told him that Byron was dead. Byron had caught fever. His initial and sensible response was not to let the doctors, of whom there were several in the camp, come near him. The doctors' sovereign remedy was bleeding, and that was the one thing Byron always feared. But as the fever rose, his friends and followers, to whom he was everything in the world, became anxious and begged him to do as the doctors wished. In his weakness, he eventually gave way and the doctors, competing in their zeal, set to work. He was, in effect, bled to death, succumbing on 19 April. So the bearer of the European *Zeitgeist* left the stage. Stanhope, who had received peremptory orders to rejoin his regiment, took the poet's body back to England, and the leadership of the British contingent passed into other hands.

Byron might have served as a symbol of unity, though his last letters were not optimistic. His removal left all to Mavrokordatos, a civilized, learned man—he spoke seven languages and had taught Greek to Mary Shelley at Pisa in 1819—but no war leader. In Nauplion, where the government had now gathered, all awaited the arrival of the "English money." Greece's struggle for liberty had brought out all the rogues. There was Andres Londos, Primate of Vostitza, who claimed to have drunk with Byron in 1809 and had been seldom sober ever since. There was Sisinis, Primate of Gastouni, whom Stanhope said "lived like a Turk," surrounded by whores, soldiers, dirt and misery, drinking the fine Glarenza wine of his province—from which he got the title he bestowed on himself, "Duke of Clarence." In autumn 1824 the first slice of the loan arrived, £80,000, quickly followed by a further £50,000. The barrels of money were received with cries of *"Zito i Anglia!"* George Finlay, the most dependable of the British eyewitnesses, recorded: "Remeliot captains and soldiers received large bribes to attack their countrymen. No inconsiderable amount was divided among members of the Legislative Assembly, and among a large group of useless partisans, who were characterised as public officials. Every man of consideration in his own estimation wanted to place himself at the head of armed men, and hundreds of civilians paraded the streets of Nauplion with trains of kilted followers, like Scottish chieftains. Panariots and doctors of medicine who [before the money came] were clad in ragged coats and lived on scanty rations . . . emerged in all the splendour of brigand life, fluttering about in rich Albanian habilments, refulgent with brilliant and unused arms, and followed by diminutive pipe-bearers and tall henchmen . . . Nauplion certainly offered a spectacle to anyone who could forget it was the capital of an impoverished nation struggling through starvation to establish its liberty."[111]

Meanwhile, disaster struck the revolution from an unexpected quarter. While Turkey itself had failed so far to overcome the weakening force of fundamentalism, the story in Egypt had been very different, thanks to the enterprise, greed and resolution of one man, Muhammad Ali (1769–1849). Ali was of the same generation as Bonaparte, Wellington and Jackson, and like them a politician-soldier and in some ways the most consistently successful of them all. He was also a portent: the first of the reformer-tyrants to emerge from what we would now call the Third World. The earlier designs of Louis XVI's government on the Middle East were first carried into action in summer 1798, when Bonaparte landed an army in Egypt on 1 July and entered Cairo, after a devastating battle, three weeks later. The aim of an eastern Mediterranean French empire proved abortive, for Nelson destroyed Bonaparte's fleet on 1 August, the Corsican returned to France a year later, and in August 1801 the remaining French capitulated to the British land forces. The British withdrew in March 1803, under the terms of the Treaty of Amiens, but Egypt, unlike Turkey, had now experienced not just one but two occupations by Western powers, and the effect was a secular awakening.

Bonaparte had contrived not only to impose a new political structure of quasi-representative "Divans," but to provoke a popular uprising in Cairo. This last strategy was a new weapon in Moslem politics. It caught the imagination of Muhammad Ali when he arrived as second in command of the Ottoman forces that took over when the British withdrew. Like Ali Pasha, Muhammad Ali came from Albania, as did his troops, and he was equally ambitious. Within two years he had formed a populist alliance with the artisans of the bazaars and the Cairo poor, organized for him by a demagogue named Umar Makram, and the students of the al-Azhar university, organized by their rector. In 1805, at a word from Ali, all the shops shut; the Cairo poor rose, forming themselves into a street-militia led by a greengrocer; the ulemas of the al-Azhar set up religious war chants; and Ottoman rule collapsed ignominiously. This kind of Middle Eastern *putsch*, installing in power a group of young officers, was to become commonplace in the 20th century, but in 1805 it was a shattering novelty.[112] The Porte felt it had no alternative but to appoint Ali viceroy, and the man he replaced, Khurshid Pasha, said with disgust as he left, "I have been ousted by the *fellahin*" (the common people).

In reality no one was a victor, least of all the Cairo poor, except Ali himself. Umar Makram was soon in exile. His mob was harshly taught who was master. The university ulemas were turned into frightened puppets. The old Mamluk warlords, who had ruled Egypt, after a fashion, for centuries, were inveigled into the Cairo citadel for a celebration in March 1811 and butchered. After this bloodletting, Ali settled down to absorbing all the Mamluk tax farms and other possessions into his personal economic empire. By 1815 he was not only absolute dictator of the country, but the owner of a large percentage of its land and property. Western envoys and Middle Eastern experts (the latter a new species introduced by Bonaparte's Nile expedition) applauded the end of Mamluk power, while delicately averting their gaze at the manner. But they were mistaken in supposing that Ali would now travel the Western way by introducing constitutional reforms, a free press, mass education, and a postal service—all the Benthamite nostrums that Colonel Stanhope was to press on the Greeks. Ali was, indeed, willing to receive Western assistance in modernizing his army, creating a fleet, and manufacturing his own arms. But reforms which did not increase his revenues; consolidate his hold on the country; and, above all, expand his military power—as a prelude to building an empire of his own—were not to his taste. In the years after 1815, he recruited many former Bonapartist army and naval officers to train his troops and to found schools of cavalry, artillery, military medicine and engineering, and a naval academy. He also used them to help form elite corps of regulars from a specially selected slave population. He was perhaps the biggest dealer in slaves in the world during the second and third decades of the 19th century, drawing them from the entire Sudanese-Nile basin as well as East Africa. With the help of the French consul-general, he set up a system of conscription which forced large numbers of peasants into his army; that was the victory of the fellahin![113]

Ali's internal rule, far from being constitutionalist, was a continuation of Ottoman tyranny, made more oppressive in many ways by the fact that it was much more efficient and closely supervised by Ali himself. We have, for almost the first time, an accurate, detailed account of life in an oriental despotism, thanks to the industry and perception of Edward William Lane, a brilliant mathematician and engraver who spent much of the 1820s in Egypt for reasons of health, and returned with a vast collection of notes and drawings. The book he then published opened a new window into the East.[114] Lane said that

Ali's chief victims were the peasants, who were taxed arbitrarily according to their ability to pay, rather than by any other criterion; the system, he said, was essentially the same as that run by the Pharaohs. Ali had dispossessed virtually all private proprietors, allotting the former owners proportionate pensions, theoretically for life: "The farmer therefore has nothing to leave to his children except his hut, and perhaps a few cattle and some small savings." Ali had also robbed the religious and charitable foundations. As sole landowner, he increased his revenues by putting pressure from above, transferred downwards, through governors of provinces and districts, to the sheikhs of each village. The instrument of collection was the bastinado: "When the population of a village does not yield the sum required, their sheikh is often beaten for their default. . . . All the *fellahin* are proud of the stripes they receive for withholding their contributions and are often heard to boast of the number of blows which were inflicted on them before they would yield up their money." Lane added: "Ammianus Marcellinus gives precisely the same character to the Egyptians of his time." The fellahin said, echoing Ammianus: "The more readily the peasant pays, the more he is made to pay."[115]

Cairo, as described by Lane, was run by the secret police, themselves answering to Ali's Albanian military. The secret police had no distinguishing uniform, and their first task was to visit coffee shops and listen; their second was to enforce the tax system. The Wali, or head policeman, ran the "public women," all of whom paid taxes to Ali, though these taxes were sometimes farmed—leased to private taxgatherers. If the Wali heard of a woman committing adultery, the woman was promptly classified as a prostitute and taxed. The police went around with the military on their night rounds. The curfew was imposed an hour and a half after sunset, at which point anyone outside his house (other than the blind) had to carry a lantern. Anyone else was challenged: "Who is that?" "A citizen." "Attest the unity of God." "There is no God but God." On night patrol, the Wadi was always accompanied by a torchbearer, carrying a *shealeh* (rather like a western dark lantern) which flared up when waved violently, and an executioner. Curfew breaking was punished by a beating on the spot, and "the Chief of Police [had] an arbitrary power to put any criminal or offender to death without trial"; inferior officers also had this power, but it was now rarely used.

By day, the markets were toured on horseback by an officer called the *Mohtesib*, preceded by a man carrying a pair of scales and followed by an executioner and guards. Checks for evasion of economic laws or taxes were made on the spot, and floggings carried out the same way.

"Once," wrote Lane, "I saw a man tormented in a different way, for
selling bread deficient in weight. A hole was bored through his nose,
and a cake of bread about a span wide, and a finger's breadth in
thickness, was suspended to it by a piece of string. He was stripped
naked, with the exception of having a piece of linen about his loins, and
tied, with his arms bound behind him, to the bars of the windows of
a mosque called the Ashrafeeyeh, in the main street of the metropolis,
his feet resting on the sill. He remained there about three hours." In
1825, Lane said, the *Mohtesib* frequently clipped the ears of offenders,
cutting off the lobe, and "a butcher, who had sold some meat wanting
two ounces of its due weight, was punished by cutting off two ounces
[of flesh] from his back." A seller of vermicelli paste was forced to sit
on his copper stove "and kept so till he was dreadfully burned!" Butchers were usually punished "by putting a hook through their nose and
hanging a piece of meat from it." Lane once saw the market guards, for
no apparent reason, punish a seller of earthenware water bottles by
smashing them all against his head.[116]

Such justice was administered without resort to the courts, which
were in some respects even more arbitrary, according to Lane's account, since a large element of bribery entered, as well as physical
torture. "When a person denies the offence of which he is charged, and
there is not sufficient evidence to convict him, for some ground of
suspicion, he is generally bastinadoed, in order to induce him to confess. . . . A thief, after this discipline, generally confesses: 'The Devil
seduced me, and I took it.'" The punishment was forced labor or army
service for petty offenses. The chief judge, or *kadi,* bought his place
from the government; his deputy, or *naib,* actually presided in court,
and the real work was done through the Bahi Turguman or chief
interpreter, who understood the demotic speech. Bribery operated at
every level, from first arrest to court of appeal, though some of the sums
were tiny, a piastre (two pennies) or two. In cases involving property,
the kadi got 2 percent of its value, and 4 percent in disputes over
legacies. In nonproperty cases, the naib fixed the fees, with all the court
officials, down to the writers, getting a slice. "The rank of a plaintiff or
defendent, or a bribe from either," wrote Lane, "often influences the
decision of a judging. On some occasions, particularly in long litiga-
tions, bribes are given by each party, and the decision is awarded in
favour of him who pays highest." Lane was afraid his readers would
not believe this account, so he gave details of a shocking case related to
him by the secretary and Iman of the Sheikh El-Mahdi, then the Supreme Mufti (religious judge) of Cairo.[117]

Since all legal offices were purchased, the higher ones directly from

Ali, he got a cut of all judicial incomes. But he or his household judged all cases involving his own property, a great part of the total wealth of the country, and anyone found stealing it was invariably executed. Egypt was essentially governed by a series of councils, which Lane listed, all appointed by Ali himself, so there was no devolved authority. Nor, though Ali was careful to remit tribute to the Sultan, and respected the fundamental laws of the Koran, as he saw them, was there any rule of law. His dominion was unlimited: "He may cause any one of his subjects to be put to death without the formality of a trial or without assigning any cause: a simply horizontal motion of his hand is sufficient to imply the sentence of decapitation."[118] But Lane insisted that Ali was severe or draconian rather than positively cruel, and he included among his merits the fact that he had stopped the Egyptians from insulting foreigners and infidels.

This last was an important point as far as Western governments were concerned, since the Suez land route to the East was used by a rapidly growing number of people. As his army grew and his authority expanded, Ali made himself responsible for the safe conduct and decent treatment of Western Christians visiting the holy places. For London, Paris and Berlin, it was convenient to have a man in charge in Cairo who was strong, predictable and (so far) respectful of Western interests. In 1813–14 he had a cadastral (land) survey made; that survey was "progress," though his object was to raise his land revenues. He started a salaried civil service; that was progress, too, though Westerners did not inquire if the salaries were paid. He set up a printing press and published the *Official Gazette*, another sure sign of progress, though it merely printed the news the government wished known. He sent 200 students abroad, to learn administration and other imperial skills: unquestionable progress, though his object was to extend his power into Arabia and up the Nile. But Britain found his acquisitiveness convenient, for the severe defeats he inflicted on the Saudi Wahhabis in 1814 and 1818—as we have seen—suited Britain's Persian Gulf policy well and made it easier for it to put down piracy.[119] If his motive in forcing his way up the Nile—he went beyond the cataracts and up to the junction of the Blue and White Niles—was really to get gold and slaves, it began the penetration of major African rivers by steam-powered vessels which was becoming British policy.

The up-country fundamentalist revolts that Ali's forward thrust, with its secularizing overtones, provoked, often led by *Mahdis* or revivalist saviors, themselves adumbrated the fundamentalist backlash the British and Egyptians would face together from the 1880s onwards, culminating in the Battle of Omdurman in 1899. In short, Muhammad

Ali, though a monster in some ways, appeared to be a man with whom the powers could do business, to their mutual advantage. The way he treated his people, shocking though it might be, was his own affair.

Moreover, the success of Ali's reforms, limited though they might be to increasing revenue and military power, was evident in the authority he exercised right up the Nile Valley and in much of Arabia and Palestine-Syria. It was noted in Constantinople.[120] It encouraged Mahmud II to make some cautious moves in the same direction. Indeed, in some ways Mahmud became more of a modernizer than Ali in the 1820s. When Ali introduced the Bell-Lancaster system of pupil-teachers, he limited it to his military academies, whereas in 1824 Mahmud tried to make primary education compulsory for the entire Turkish population. His decree reads: "Whereas according to our Moslem faith, learning the elements of religion comes before everything else, taking precedence over all worldly considerations, most people avoid sending their children to school in these days and prefer to teach them a trade as artisans or apprentices when they reach the age of five or six, because of their desire to earn money quickly. This leads to widespread illiteracy and ignorance of religion, and hence has been the cause of our misfortunes. [For all these reasons] no man hence shall prevent his children from attending school until they have reached adult age."[121] Mahmud also did important work in introducing Turkey to the concept of impersonal law, especially the term *adalet*, which in 19th-century Turkish usage came to signify equity or just treatment for all, irrespective of creed or social standing and according to enacted laws. Unlike the Islamic law or *Seriat*, or the *Kanus*, decrees peculiar to individual rulers, *adalet* was justice as such. It was a secularist notion because it implied that there was a source of justice apart from God (the Koran) and his appointed ruler or vicar. To push this concept forward, Mahmud made use of minority communities, especially Greeks, Armenians and Jews, and his aim was to abolish the system of *millets*, that is, totally separate (but not equal) racial and religious communities.

Ironically enough, this policy ran into strong opposition from the Western envoys, personified by the increasingly powerful British diplomat Stratford Canning (1786–1880), who wanted extraterritorial rights of protection over Catholic, Orthodox and Protestant millets—in effect, all Europeans who did business in Ottoman lands. This opposition acted as a brake on secularism. There was an internal obstacle, too, since the janissaries continued to murder any reformers who raised their hackles until 1826, when Mahmud plucked up courage to oust them for good.[122] Thereafter he set up a Western-style government,

with a prime minister, departmental heads, and carefully defined ministries, including the key Board of Useful Affairs, which included education, commerce, agriculture and industry.

Until then Mahmud had to be content with sartorial and sumptuary
reforms. He hated beards, especially long ones—they were almost unknown in Europe in the 1820s—and he went around with scissors
snipping them off. He also cut off what he saw as surplus ribbons (on
men, of course; he did not dare to touch women's dress). He hated
Turkish saddles and the oriental style of riding. He liked to go around
the country haranguing people on these topics. He told his ministers to
sit in his presence. He went on steamer trips. He tried to learn French.
He dismissed his ancient Turkish band and imported a German one. He
dressed in breeches, stockings, and a Western coat, even in trousers,
and ordered his court to follow suit. He objected particularly to the
enormous curly toed shoes and baggy pants that most Turkish men
wore and to the decorative paraphernalia of traditional sartorial grading.

Until the 1820s, every Turk carried his curriculum vitae in his dress,
distinguished minutely in origins, social and religious status, occupation, and career by fine touches of badge, jewelry, color, shape and
fitting. Mahmud now set about introducing uniformity. Many Westerners, as well as the entire Turkish religious community, objected. Marshal Marmount, who seems to have been everywhere in these years,
inspecting and commenting, was highly critical of this attempt to "abolish the gradations of rank." But the American James E. DeKay, whose
Sketches of Turkey is the most perceptive account of the country during
the 1820s, pointed out that Mahmud was legitimating what was beginning to happen anyway. DeKay noticed that Turkish troops had
dropped their "loose, slipshod slippers" in favor of "stout, serviceable
shoes securely fastened by leather strings"; had replaced their "huge
balloon *chaksheers*" which "impeded [the soldier's] every movement"
by "woollen trowsers"; and had dropped the "glittering and flowing
jubbee [gown] and *bayneesh* [robe] in favour of a right-bodied blue
jacket." DeKay was particularly glad to see that "the turban, infinitely
varied in shape and colour, often ragged and frequently dirty, suggesting the idea of walking toadstools" was now yielding to a "tidy red cap
with a blue tassel gracefully descending from its crown." In short,
Turkish soldiers were now "scarcely distinguishable from the regulars
of any European nation." Turbans, indicating grades, not least among
the religious, were particularly sensitive items of dress, and Mahmud
failed to replace the army's with the tall caps equipped with visors (to
shelter the eyes from the sun) now favored by European headquarters.

The ulemas insisted that Islamic law makes it necessary for all believers to touch the ground with their forehead while praying, and so the visor had to go, the Turks ending up, like the Egyptians, with the fez, an undistinguished piece of headgear that was actually of European origin.[123]

The Greek revolt of 1821 undoubtedly accelerated the Turkish move toward Western models, especially in military matters. Indeed, it did more than that. Ali, while consolidating and extending his rule, had always acknowledged the Sultan as his ultimate superior and declared himself willing to oblige the Sultan, within reason and at a price. In 1822 Mahmud asked Egypt's help in putting down the Greeks. Ali, who had a substantial navy, trained and to some extent officered by Frenchmen, sent it across to Crete with an expeditionary force, and in two years reduced the island to submission. The commander of the force was Ali's son, Ibrahim Pasha, a formidable general and great perpetrator of atrocities. He was credited with a plan to land on the mainland; occupy the Morea; slaughter or drive out the Moriots; and repeople it with Egyptian fellahin, of which there were, then as now, a large surplus. With Byron dead, Stanhope gone and the London committee useless—its latest cargo had been a consignment of 90 watercolors to encourage Greece to join the mainstream of Western culture—the squabbling Greeks had no notion of how to meet this impending catastrophe, for the Egyptians had command of the sea.

In Athens, Odysseus was bitterly discontented because he had got none of the English loan. In late autumn 1824, his son-in-law Trelawny advised him to return to his headquarters-cave on Parnassus, lie low, and wait until the Egyptians landed and did so much damage that the other Greeks would turn to him as a savior. But the cunning Odysseus for once overreached himself, ignored the advice, and instead negotiated a truce with the Turks. As a result he found himself besieged in Athens by another kapitanos, Tannis Gouras, and obliged to surrender in March 1825. Odysseus was held captive in the Frankish Tower of the Acropolis. His dead body was found at the bottom of it on 17 June. Gouras said he was trying to escape and his rope had broken; more likely he was hurled down. Trelawny had taken his own advice and hidden in the cave, where he was shot twice, in the back and neck, by a spy, "Captain" H. G. Whitcombe, but survived and eventually returned to England (without his wife, however). This sordid affair, one of many internal battles on the Greek side, helps to explain the steady deterioration of their fortunes. Ibrahim Pasha duly landed 4,500 troops at Methoni on the mainland on 24 February 1825, and he quickly got ashore a second division, plus artillery. Former Bonapartist officers were prominent in these operations. Missolonghi fell to him in April 1826, the town of Athens in August, and the Acropolis the following June. The Greek response to these calamities was further civil war.

The London money was now spent, and it had achieved nothing. What was the West to do? The Russians were waiting for an opportunity to intervene in the name of Orthodox solidarity and to take their empire to the Bosphorus. The French had military advisers on both sides and stood to enhance their position in the eastern Mediterranean whatever happened. In London, Canning was not, as the Greek liberals supposed, an out-and-out philhellene. His primary concern was to keep the Russians out of Greece. He also had, like Palmerston then and later, a profound fear of the French. An opportunist and an inspired improviser, he played Greece, as he had played events in Latin America, by ear. While the romantic and adventurous Chateaubriand was in charge of French foreign policy, Canning was ultrasuspicious. He declined to discuss the Greek question with the French, telling the cabinet that he knew what they were up to in Greece anyway, since all their letters from there had to pass through the British-controlled Ionian Islands and were stealthily opened and read. He wrote to Lord Granville on 15 November 1824: "[In Greece] too I have traced Chateaubriand's agents, perplexing the unhappy Greeks with I know not what absurd fantasies of elective monarchies and crusades against the infidels with new Knighthoods of Malta at three and sixpence a head."[124] After Chateaubriand was booted out of office, Canning was less worried by what the French might do—the British had a large naval superiority in the Mediterranean—but in the meantime, the success of the Egyptian forces increased the risk of Russian military intervention. Canning now began to move toward the notion of a joint intervention of the "civilised powers" to effect a settlement or at least avert a wider war.

This idea was a historic development, one of the great milestones toward modernity, for it envisaged three of the powers using their joint forces in a peacekeeping role. Both Canning and his predecessor Castlereagh had strongly opposed interventionism on ideological grounds, as practiced by the Holy Alliance, because its object was to impose or sustain a particular type of government, which ran directly counter to the Zeitgeist. It was therefore unlikely to work, apart from its intrinsic immorality. The possibility now emerging was for three of the powers to get together on an ad hoc basis for the purely empirical reason that it was the best way to stop hostilities and prevent them from spreading. That proposal was entirely to the British taste and, Canning thought, a workable one. And so it proved—though not in quite the way he envisioned.

Canning began his work by tackling Russia in late autumn 1825, taking advantage of the death of Alexander I to send Wellington to Saint Petersberg to represent Britain at the ceremonies and work on the new Tsar, Nicholas I. The ploy succeeded, and an Anglo-Russian protocol was signed, 4 April 1826, under which Greece was to become autonomous, but remain a tributary Ottoman state; all Turks were to leave its territory; and the Sultan was to join with the powers and the Greeks in designating a ruler (who would be, in Canning's view, a surplus member of the British royal family). That done, Canning next turned to the French. The Bourbon government stood to gain whichever side won, and the new King, Charles X, disapproved of rebellion as such, even against a Moslem ruler; on the other hand, French opinion was overwhelmingly philhellene. Canning went to Paris in September–October 1826 to bring France into the arrangement. The following April, after Liverpool's stroke, he became Prime Minister and put the whole thrust of his new government behind his Greek policy. The result was the Treaty of London, 6 July 1827, a landmark agreement which, for the first time, created a great power concert for peace, backed by a force-in-being. Its terms followed the protocol, but its preamble stated that the three great powers were intervening with their naval power to put down piracy and safeguard commerce. This was the truth, though not the whole truth, since the war had led to a terrifying increase of piracy in Greek waters and beyond, and both sides were commandeering or sinking peaceful vessels. A week after the treaty was signed, orders went out to the British, Russian and French fleets in the area: If both sides accepted the terms, well and good; if the Greeks accepted and the Turks refused, the fleets were to prevent military or naval reinforcements from either Turkey or Egypt from reaching Greek waters. In short, the combined peacekeeping force was to quarantine the area. Much subsequent experience, notably in the 20th century, has shown how unlikely it was that such vague and optimistic orders, given on behalf of the international community, would in practice be carried out to the satisfaction of those who issued them.

It is important to add that others in the West were working on what might be called a technological solution to the Greek problem. The Moslems had been doing well by deploying their naval superiority, but they had not yet embraced naval steam power. Admiral Cochrane was now tired of naval service in South America, where his job was done, and was available for further adventures in a radical cause. A further slice of London money, some £155,000, became available in 1825, and the idea was to equip Cochrane with a purpose-built steam fleet of six vessels. If the proposal were adopted, the philhellene Edward Ellice told the Greek deputies, "Within a few weeks Lord Cochrane will be at Constantinople and will burn the Turkish vessels in the port." Cochrane was to be paid £37,000 on account and a further £20,000 when Greece was free.

The plan, however, ran into the crosscurrents of the rapidly burgeoning international arms industry. Ellice signed a contract with Brent & Co. to build a corvette, the *Perseverance,* and with Alexander Galloway of Smithfield to fit engines. But Galloway was already doing business with Muhammad Ali in Egypt—his son was at work there and hoping to get the job of resident engineer at Alexandria—so the firm went slowly in building the engines. The London committee also tried to place contracts with American yards for two "big" sailing frigates of 1,500 tons, at a cost of $247,000 each. But American yards were busy supplying the new naval needs of Colombia, Peru and Mexico, as well as their own government's; prices were rising fast; and, in the end, the Greeks had to sell one frigate to pay for the other. Of the six steam warships, only four were built and only the *Perseverance,* renamed the *Karteria,* which reached Nauplion on 14 September 1826, saw effective service. Her two 42-horsepower engines were not powerful enough for her 400-ton deadweight and let her down at critical moments. The paddles were too heavy and high in the water, and her speed under steam was barely seven knots. To get enough steam, her furnaces had to be stoked to the point where her boilers risked bursting. On the other hand, her English master, Captain Hastings, found her highly maneuverable: Using her paddles, she moved forward or backwards at will and rotated rapidly, thus bringing all her massive 64-pounder guns to bear on any target. Hastings, a gunnery expert, devised means of heating shot in the furnaces and slinging it up to the gun breeches. The *Kanteria* never had the good fortune to face a sailing squadron in open water or, better still, come across one in a calm. She wreaked devastating destruction on Turkish shore batteries, firing 18,000 hot shells in her first year of service, and became a legend in those waters. But the technological armageddon never took place.[125]

Instead Greece was finally freed by an international muddle. The man at the middle of it was Admiral Sir Edward Codrington. We last came across him gazing sadly at the mess poor 'Ned" Pakenham made of the New Orleans assault. He was now a senior naval figure, appointed to command the Mediterranean fleet, and sailing there in February 1827, with his flag in the 84-gun battleship *Asia,* and all his family on board. He had put his wife ashore at Livorno (or Leghorn as the English called it) and took up station in Greek waters. His letters to Lady Codrington (and others) give us a blow-by-blow account of the first armed international peacekeeping mission, as he saw it, supplemented by his *Narrative of His Proceedings in the Mediterranean,* which he had printed for private circulation in 1828.[126]

Codrington's mission was bedeviled not merely by its intrinsic difficulty, but by political instability in London. The same month he sailed for the Mediterranean, the long years of Liverpool's rule were brought to an end by a stroke. Canning did not succeed in forming his government until April, and during its short existence he was coping with a host of political problems and growing ill-health—he died in August. But at least he got the treaty through and sent out Codrington's orders in accordance with it. And his policy was clear, at any rate in his own mind: Greece was to be a genuinely autonomous state, but the Ottoman Empire was to be preserved. Canning's death, however, led to the premiership of Fred Robinson, now Viscount Goderich, one of the weakest in British history—so weak, indeed, that it could not meet Parliament and collapsed ignominiously early in 1828. That collapse, in turn, brought in Wellington, who thought that the principal object of British policy was the maintenance of Turkey as a barrier both to Russian and French acquisitiveness. So Codrington's orders were drafted by Canning; his actions took place under Goderich, who was harassed by his tiresome wife and had no firm views on Greece; and were judged by Wellington, who was a pro-Turk.

The orders themselves certainly warranted Codrington acting as he did, but they would also have allowed him to act differently.[127] Once Canning was dead, he got no further directions of any consequence from the top, though he had several letters from the Duke of Clarence (later William IV) who held the post of Lord High Admiral. It was later said that one of the letters contained the phrase, "Go in, my dear Ned, and smash those Turks!" but all those that survive enjoin caution and begin, "My Dear sir." Codrington's complaint was that he heard all too little from London. He was shocked to read the full text of the Treaty of London in *The Times,* two weeks before his own copy, supposedly rushed out to him by the government, reached him, and long before Stratford Canning got it. "Only think!" he wrote to his wife, telling her of the leak, it was supposed to be "a profound secret!"[128] Codrington was the first commander in chief in history who had to rely, for news of what was going on, on the press, in his case *The Times* and *Galignani's Messenger,* published in Paris.

*   *   *

Like many, perhaps most, naval officers, Codrington was a mild Whig. He was also, to use Jane Austen's phrase, a "reading man," well versed in the classics, who took Xenophon's *Anabasis* and Mitford's *Greece* to read on station. But there is no evidence he was a philhellene or was much influenced by any pro-Greek sympathies. He had too many other things to bother about. As senior commander of the peace force, he had to deal with six nations: Greece, Egypt and Turkey, all at war; Austria, theoretically neutral but whose warships, he discovered, were in secret communication with the Ottoman fleet; and France and Russia, his associates but deeply suspicious of each other: the horrors and atrocities of the 1812 campaign still rankled on both sides. In Codrington's first function, to put down piracy, he was hampered by an archaic law and frustrated by the Greek authorities, whom he rightly held responsible for its increase. In various letters addressed to "the persons exercising the functions of government in Greece," he complained of attacks on British and Ionian commerce by ships flying Greek naval colors or pirates who he knew were being protected by the Greek authorities. He enclosed schedules of "insults and injuries" and demands for compensation, especially for hostilities by Greek naval vessels against the British-run Ionian coastguards.[129]

When the admiral got to Nauplion, where the Greek government sat, he was disgusted by the feuding between the Greek bands and by the dirt of the place: "The filthiest town with the worst streets and most wretched houses I ever saw." The government's headquarters did not impress: "The wooden stairs by which we ascended seemed hardly able to bear our weight and the floor of the room itself was little better. There was no ceiling to the room and the swallows were flying about it amongst the rafters." He found himself receiving clamorous deputations: "I have been thrown into odd situations at different times when on service but I did not expect to be called upon to *make harangues to Greek citizens.*" He found a few Greeks noble, but most "mendacious, greedy and scoundrelly." "Piracy in all its different shapes daily increases," he complained to his son. "The Greek authorities, knowing that most of the principal people among them are owners of pirate vessels, are afraid or ashamed to do what is requisite for its suppression. . . . The Greek and Turks are more attached to their vices than to their country and therefore I feel no attachment to either." The Greeks were "cruel, treacherous people," just as Mitford described them. He related to Lady Codrington the endless discussions and late nights spent arguing with people he knew to be liars and of "listening to a detail of low-bred dishonesty, accompanied by cruelty in the execution and producing disastrous consequences with the thermometer at 91 degrees and the light sand thickening the air and

irritating the eyelids." The temperature in his cabin was 95 degrees "and
in De Rigny's [the French Admiral's] more." The Russian Admiral Count
Heiden, he said, was "a plain sailing officer" and did exactly what he
requested; De Rigny was pro-Egyptian and hated Greeks, and his behavior was influenced by the fact that many French naval officers were
serving as mercenaries on the Egyptian fleet. "I trust," Codrington wrote
to his wife, "I shall have health and nerves to stand up to all the
responsibilities attached to [my mission]. . . . But in truth I should make
a better chief if I had you at my elbow, let the regulators of naval affairs
say what they may!"[130]

But if Codrington disliked the Greeks, he was appalled by Turkish
atrocities. Riding at anchor off Scio, he recorded: "Out of 120,000
souls, 30,000 were murdered in cold blood and the houses reduced to
ruins. . . . I have never contemplated a scene more sickening in the mind
than this view of Scio." He referred to "the avenging wrath of the
de-capitating Sultan." His detestation of the continuing slaughter undoubtedly pushed him in favor of settling what he saw as an endlessly
messy problem by action. As always in eastern affairs, then and since,
the temptation was to enforce order by the use of the technological
superiority of the civilized West: "One strong act of coercion would
place the Porte at our mercy and we would then settle the whole matter
as we chose."[131]

In the event, however, the matter was taken out of Codrington's
hands by Muslim intransigence. Once he heard of the Treaty of London, Ibrahim Pasha decided that the three great powers were not
bluffing. But he could not peruade the Sultan to climb down. Like
George III over the United States and Spain over Spanish America,
Mahmud was unwilling to admit that nationalism was the wave of the
future (if indeed it was). The combined Egyptian-Turkish fleet sailed
from Alexandria before Codrington received his instructions, so he was
unable to bottle it up there, which would have avoided conflict.

Once he got his orders on 7 September he proceeded immediately to
cut the Muslim fleet off from the Greek coast. Instead it anchored in
Navarino. Codrington took up station outside and was joined by De
Rigny. Ibrahim Pasha signed a truce on 25 September, to await further
orders from the Sultan, but he tried to break it on 2–4 October by
sailing out to attack Greek ships of Patras. Codrington in the *Asia,* with
two frigates and a brig, forced him back. His blockading fleet was then
reinforced by the Russian squadron under Heiden. Despite the truce,
Ibrahim was continuing to murder and burn on land, and Codrington's
outraged protest was futile, since he could find no Turkish official who
was willing to receive it. At the same time, the season was advancing

and the weather was getting worse. Codrington faced the growing risk of a storm dispersing his combined fleet and allowing Ibrahim's fleet to get out and terrorize the coast. At this point he consulted the other two admirals, and all agreed they must proceed into Navarino bay and anchor in such a formation as to protect their own ships and prevent Ibrahim's from escaping. De Rigny sent a peremptory message to Letellier, Bompard and other French naval officers on the Muslim ships to leave them forthwith, *"si vous restes français."* But they declined to do so. Indeed, it was Letellier who arranged the Muslim ships in a horseshoe formation, which would force the Allies into the middle if they entered, and in such a way as to get the maximum assistance from shore batteries.

By entering the harbor, Codrington was accepting a high risk. The numerical odds were not much in his favor. He had three battleships, four frigates, four brigs, and a cutter; the French, three battleships, two frigates, and two cutters; the Russians, four battleships and four frigates. The Muslim fleet had only three battleships, but it had 17 frigates, four of them of the "big" variety; 30 corvettes, 28 brigs, and five schooners, plus dozens of transports. There were also five fireships, as well as the shore batteries. The gun count was 2,240 guns for the Muslims and 1,324 for the Allies, but many of the latter were of heavy caliber. Codrington's dispositions, when he took his ships in at 2 P.M. on 20 October, reflected his many anxieties, political as well as naval. He stationed the French squadron on the right, knowing that was where the French mercenaries were, so that only Frenchmen would have to fire on fellow countrymen. He put himself in the middle, so there was no contact between Russian and French ships, fearing they might be tempted to fire on each other. His orders included: "No gun is to be fired from the combined fleet without a signal being made for that purpose, unless shot be fired from any of the Turkish ships; in which case the ships so firing are to be destroyed immediately."[132] He stationed Captain Fellows in the *Dartmouth* near the entrance to watch for Muslim fireships. If the Muslim admirals were determined on a fight, they would have done well to wait till darkness and used their fireships then. As it was, Fellows saw the fireships preparing for action and sent first a pinnace, then a cutter, to order them to desist. The Moslems fired on the cutter and this began the action, which soon became general.

The Battle of Navarino lasted four hours and was won by superior Allied gunnery. The Muslims concentrated their fire on the *Asia,* and the horrors of a close-quarter naval action have never been better described than in a brilliant letter which Codrington's son Henry, who was serving as a midshipman on her, sent to his brother William.[133] Much of the action was fought in dense smoke and darkness, the air thick with an infinity of savage wood splinters sent flying by the impact of cannon shot on the bulwarks. An inch-thick projectile went through Henry's calf, another embedded itself in his thigh, a third smashed his collarbone. The Admiral was exposed and on deck throughout, and the Muslims later admitted they had appointed a squad of sharpshooters to kill him. His hat was pierced by a bullet. Another went through the sleeve of his coat. A third broke the watch in his fob. The Ship's Master and the Captain of Marines were both killed standing near him. He just avoided being crushed by the fall of the mizen-mast. The *Asia* was badly mauled on deck, but her thick oak sides prevented any real damage to the hull and her own broadsides were devastating. Codrington said he had never seen such successful shooting. The Allies lost 178 men killed, but all their ships survived. All the Muslim ships were crippled, and by morning only 29 out of 89 were still afloat. The slaughter was appalling—over 8,000 Turks and Egyptians dead—and it was compounded the next day when the Moslems decided to blow up their stranded or wrecked vessels, often with Greek galley slaves still chained on board.[134]

Thus, the first military peacekeeping mission in history ended in an exceptionally bloody encounter, which was variously received by the interested parties. For the Muslims, it was the second time in just over a decade that the West had used its superior military technology to enforce its wishes in the Mediterranean, and it was later seen as part of a continuing pattern. For the Greeks, it made their independence certain, and they greeted the news with delight. The Russians, too, were happy at the outcome, as were the French, though with qualifications, since they had been forced to take sides and thus undermine their position in Egypt. The British public greeted with rapture what they saw as a heroic victory against a cruel enemy. The Duke of Clarence was beside himself with joy—"I believe the Turk never before felt the British eloquence of our guns"—and immediately persuaded his brother, George IV, to award Codrington the Grand Cross of the Bath. Indeed, it rained medals; "more orders were given for the battle of Navarino than for any other naval victory on record."[135] The Admiral also got the Grand Cross of Saint Louis from Charles X, the Order of Saint George (second class) from Nicholas I, and the Gold Cross of the Redeemer from Mavrocordatos.

But that was the end of Codrington's rewards. The Goderich cabinet, after much dithering, especially from Huskisson, had sent him additional orders in October telling him to bear in mind "that we are not at war—that we do not desire to be at war—but that what we aim at is to part the combatants." These orders were dispatched four days before the battle and, of course, reached Codrington weeks afterwards.[136] Hence the government received the news of the "victory" with consternation and only just decided against recalling Parliament. Palmerston, the War Secretary, sourly observed: "The mere circumstance of our having made a bonfire of the fleet of our good ally at Navarino is not deemed a reason for assembling Parliament because this was not a declaration of war but only a slight act of remonstrance stuck parenthetically into an unbroken friendship."[137] George IV was quickly persuaded he had done the wrong thing, though it was too late to recall the cross: "I sent him the ribbon but he deserves the rope," he joked. When he opened Parliament on 29 January 1828, George IV was made by the government to refer to the battle as "this untoward event." But that phrase was going too far and evoked an uproar, forcing ministers to change course again and state publicly that "they did not make the slightest charge nor cast the least imputation on the gallant officer who commanded at Navarino." But Codrington was removed from his command by Wellington not for impetuosity but for letting the Muslims get into Navarino in the first place, which was absurd. No reason was given to Codrington himself. Indeed, there was much cabinet skulduggery; a surviving letter from Huskisson to Wellington suggests that the date on a cabinet dispatch to the consul in Alexandria was falsified to make the government look better in the eyes of Parliament.[138]

This was one of those rare occasions when Wellington came out badly. When Codrington returned to London, the two had a chilly meeting on 28 January 1829. The Admiral wrote an account of it immediately afterwards. "After waiting a long time" in the Prime Minister's antechamber, he was admitted, and Wellington promptly assured him there was no hostility toward him among the ministers. Codrington: "Then will Your Grace let me ask you why I was so superceded?" Duke: "Because you seemed to understand your orders differently from myself and my colleagues, and I felt we could not go on." Codrington pointed out that everyone on the spot he was able to consult—colleagues, Stratford Canning and other diplomats—understood the orders in the sense he carried them out, adding: "But let me ask Your Grace which is the part in which we differ?" Duke, after a pause: "You must excuse me." Codrington then bowed and prepared to leave. Duke: "If at any time, while in town, you should wish to say anything further to me, I should be happy to see you." Codrington: "Pardon me, Your Grace, but if you feel you cannot answer that simple question, I have nothing further to say, and it will be quite unnecessary for me to trouble Your Grace again" (retires).[139]

Ministers were afraid the Admiral might complain publicly and tried to buy him off with a pension of £800 a year. But he replied that first his officers and men should receive their victory bounty, denied to them because Britain was not officially at war, or, at least, they should have their clothes and bedding replaced free—many had lost everything they had—instead of it being docked from their pay. He was especially incensed about the case of one of his best signalers on the *Asia,* George Carlow. Because of his duties, brilliantly performed, Carlow was particularly exposed to fire. He received six wounds in his right thigh, one very severe, and five slighter ones; a musket ball in his left groin; one wound in his forehead; one on his lower lip; and one in the head, leading to the loss of one eye and damage to the optic nerve in another. He lost all his clothes and bedding and was now invalidated out of the service. But the government refused to give him a penny because he was not "totally disabled." Codrington eventually got him a pension of 6d a day, but he had to wait until the Whigs came to power. He himself became member of Parliament for Devonport in the first Reform Parliament before he finally, after repeatedly raising the matter in the Commons, got financial redress for the rest of his seamen. This was in 1834, over seven years after the action. That night he told his family: *"Now* I can go to bed without that subject weighing on my mind as it has done hitherto. For years past it has been my last thought at night and my first in the morning."[140]

Thus, the first experiment in a new form of international control by the civilized powers ended in confusion, misunderstanding and bitterness. Nor, in the long run, did the Greeks themselves benefit from Navarino in the way they expected. The effect of the battle was to bring the war of independence to a fairly rapid close and thus to give the captains of the bands and other guerrilla leaders an undue reputation among ordinary Greeks for winning it. In fact, the bands by themselves could never had beaten the Turks. The shrewder Greek nationalist leaders realized this fact. From 1825 they made efforts to form a properly trained national army. Navarino made it unnecessary, and when they set up an army in 1828–30, few guerrillas could be persuaded to join it. The guerrillas had grown accustomed to looting the Turks, they had acquired flocks and possessions, and they had no intention of leaving their way of life. Moreover, now that Greece was free, they enjoyed patriotic approval for their possession of *pallikaria,* a term that meant manliness, courage and endurance and which was peculiarly associated with bandit mythology. Was it not pallikaria which had defeated the Turks and made the Greeks free men? This false assumption that the ethics of the band were more important than the more prosaic business of establishing effective parliamentary institutions and the rule of law remained deeply embedded in the Greek political spirit. It has retarded the modernization and democratization of the country to this day. The cult of pallikaria gave rise to a corresponding capacity for national self-deception, a tendency to blame the failings of Greece on outside forces conspiring against Hellas and its people, and this tendency has also endured.[141]

Hence, we have seen that in Greece, no less than in the Spanish-speaking countries on both sides of the Atlantic, the anarchic, brutal and often cruel manner in which independence was won had enduring and baleful consequences for the future health of all these countries. The matrix of modernity was corrupt and flawed. Nor did the intervention of the more advanced societies, like Britain, France, and the United States—well-meaning though it often was—curb these anarchic and destructive tendencies, alas. So the forces of progress spread rapidly in these years, sometimes like a manumission, sometimes like a plague.

Fresh Air and Drowsy Syrups

After his rapturous first meeting with Samuel Taylor Coleridge in Bridgwater, Thomas de Quincey recorded: "About ten o'clock at night I took leave of him; and feeling that I could not easily go to sleep after the excitements of the day, and fresh from the sad spectacle of powers so majestic already besieged by decay, I determined to return to Bristol through the coolness of the night. The roads, though in fact a section of the great highway between seaports so turbulent as Bristol and Plymouth, were as quiet as garden-walks. Once only I passed through the expiring fires of a village fair or wake: that interruption excepted, through the whole stretch of forty miles from Bridgwater to the Hot Wells, I saw no living creature but a surly dog, who followed me for a mile along a park wall, and a man who was moving about in the halfway town of Cross. The turnpike gates were all opened by a mechanical contrivance from a bedroom window; I seemed to myself in solitary possession of the whole sleeping country: the summer night was divinely calm; and no sound, except once or twice the cry of a child as I was passing the windows of cottages, ever broke upon the utter silence."[1]

Even great trunk roads, as the passage suggests, were unfrequented at night in the early 19th century (the year was 1807), for few traveled after sundown, unless there was a full moon. More striking still, however, is the way in which De Quincey took for granted a walk of over 40 miles. It was typical of the age. That the poor walked everywhere (unless they hitched a lift on a wagon) was taken for granted. But the amount of long-distance walking done by the literary middle classes, who have recorded it, is also impressive. In the first three decades of the 19th century, the cost of travel was falling, particularly after 1815, but it was still expensive, and it remained so until cheap rail travel became available in the 1830s.

Coleridge and Southey walked roughly the same route De Quincey described, but in reverse, going from Bath by Bridgwater to Nether Stowey; it cost them nothing except the price of a bed in Cheddar—a single one they shared, Coleridge tossing and turning so much that Southey labeled him "a vile bedfellow." When Coleridge returned along the same route by post chaise, he made a note of the charges: Stowey to Bridgwater, 11s3d; to Piper's Inn on the Polden Hills 13s1½d; to Old Down 8s9d; to Bath 16s6d. In addition, he had to pay the driver on each lap 2s6d, and every turnpike charged 6d.

So people walked, women as well as men. When Keats went on his tour of Scotland in 1818, he went by public coach as far as Lancashire and on foot thereafter. Wordsworth, his sister Dorothy, and Coleridge began a similar Scottish tour together on foot, Coleridge branching off by himself at Stirling and continuing for nearly 300 miles until there was nothing left of his shoes. Dorothy Wordsworth, with a friend or relative, regularly walked from Penrith across the Pennines and moors to visit the Hutchinsons near Halifax. Hazlitt would walk from London to his writing base at Winterslow in Wiltshire. His first wife Sarah, while waiting for her Scottish divorce in Edinburgh, walked a total of over 200 miles to visit places of interest. Painters were great walkers, too, like "the Ancients" who walked from London to see their friend Samuel Palmer at Shoreham, over twenty miles away, or Michael Angelo Rooker, who spent his summers "on pedestrian excursions, 18 miles a day."[2] So were musicians: The young Richard Wagner, despite his short legs, walked from Dresden to Leipzig and back. Saving money was one motive, seeing nature another, exercise a third. When the painter John Hoppner stayed with the nautical Duke of Clarence at Petersham, he was taken off every day after dinner for "a walk of 10 or 12 miles."[3]

Nor was walking confined to the country. Lamb's letters give innumerable glimpses of him walking 5, 10, or 15 miles within the London area, and sometimes 30 or more in its northern outskirts. The young Macaulay regularly walked from central London to Clapham or Greenwich. London was not yet a multistory city, but was spread out over great distances with scores of thousands of one or two-story houses, often with substantial gardens. Countless numbers walked five or more miles to work and back; every morning, between seven and eight, you could see 90,000 people tramping across London Bridge to get to the City. But if a walk of 20 miles was nothing, there were some exceptional performers. The Scots agricultural expert, Captain Berkeley Allardice (1779–1854), was noted for "pedestrian feats." In 1807 he did 87 miles on hilly roads in 14 hours. The next year he started at 5 A.M., walked 30 miles grouse shooting, dined at 5 P.M., and walked 60 miles to his house at Ury in 11 hours; after attending to business, he walked 16 miles to Laurence Kirk, danced at a ball, returned to Ury by 7 A.M., and spent the next day partridge shooting, having walked 130 miles and been without sleep for two nights and three days.[4] The next year, at Newmarket, he walked 1,000 miles in a specified time for a 2,000-guinea bet, reducing his weight in the process from 13 stone, 41 pounds to 11 stone: "He walked in a sort of lounging gait . . . scarcely raising his feet two inches above the ground."[5] Another top performer was Jack Spiller, who had fought in General Burgoyne's army as a boy and walked all over the United States, from New York to New Orleans and from Richmond to Boston. He was 50 when he performed some of his feats and had not a tooth in his head.[6]

"Captain Berkeley," as he was known, and Jack Spiller were examples of a new type of celebrity who was making his appearance in the early 19th century, the Sporting Hero. In no respect did the modern age proclaim its arrival more significantly than in the rise of competitive, organized, regulated and mass-directed sports. In the past, sports usually had been regarded as the resort of the idle, frivolous, dissolute and even the disaffected—"sporting meetings" were often a pretext for treasonable gatherings of the discontented gentry and their followers. Suddenly, at the beginning of the century, it became identified with healthy outdoor exercise and, equally important, with moral cleanliness: *mens sana in corpore sano*. On 5 December 1815, what might be described as the first modern football match took place at Carterhaugh, in the Ettrick Forest. Football was not yet played according to the strict rules we would recognize, but it was clearly and consciously organized by authority. Before a crowd of 2,000, Selkirk fought Yarrow, Sir Walter Scott, as keeper of Ettrick Forest, backing Selkirk and the Earl of Home responsible for Yarrow. Selkirk wore "slips of fir," Yarrow "sprigs of heath." Their supporters carried banners. The Duke of Buccleugh kicked off. The first game lasted 90 minutes and was won by Selkirk; the second lasted three hours and was drawn or, rather, "inconclusive." James Hogg wrote a ballad for the Yarrow team, and Scott provided one for his Selkirk men. Four lines from Scott's fine ballad are worth quoting, for they mark the beginning of the British moral theory of games, which was to be carried across the world in the course of the 19th and early 20th centuries:

> Then strip lads and to it, though sharp be the weather
> And if by mischance you should happen to fall,
> There are worse things in life than a tumble on heather
> And life is itself but a game of football.[7]

The idea that football and similar team sports might be a form of education, particularly a way of producing healthy Christian gentlemen, would have struck most people before the year 1800 as absurd. Football was an ancient pastime, but it was almost invariably associated with hooliganism among the lower orders. All over Europe, governments had repeatedly banned it by proclamation and statute as being calculated to produce riot and injuries, sometimes deaths. It was played most in Protestant Britain, however, especially at Shrovetide as an alternative to the Continental carnival, which had Catholic overtones. It took countless forms, which varied according to the district.[8] In some places the ball was carried, in others it was kicked, in yet others both were allowed. There were teams of 10 or 15 a side, but in other cases there was no limit on the number of players. At Derby, which staged one of the most notorious Shrovetide games, 500 to 1,000 a side was common in the years 1810–20. Many places distinguished between what was called "civil play" and "rough play," the latter degenerating into a fight. Joseph Strutt, who wrote one of the first accounts of football (1801), said that when the game "hots up" in some places, "the players kick each other's shins without the least ceremony."[9] In Norfolk, where it was played with a small ball, carried or thrown, it was called "camping," and there was "kicking camp," the sporting version, and "savage camp," the free-for-all fight.

Annual intervillage or intertown matches lasted all day and at Derby, well into the night, by which time all were drunk. Tradesmen shuttered and barricaded their shops, magistrates stood by ready to read the Riot Act, and the churches tried to get the event banned. The Evangelicals and Methodists were particularly keen to destroy football. The Primitive Methodists would time their "camp meetings" to coincide with annual "wakes weeks," when football matches took place, in order to wreck them. Thus in 1823 they organized a huge camp meeting on the Sunday reserved for the annual football match between Preston and Heden, a notoriously bloody affair. But people were attached to the game, not least because it created local heroes. One observer of the Derby matches said they were rather like an election, though "a coarse sport." "I have known," he added, "a football hero chaired through the streets like a successful Member, although his utmost elevation of character was no more than a butcher's apprentice."[10]

It was the Enclosure Movement which precipitated the birth of modern football because in many cases it removed the common land over which the traditional game roamed. There were no pitches, as such, the "play" ranged over the open countryside and the object was often to get the ball into your home village and keep it there. When the

Enclosure Acts took away the commons, villagers petitioned the local gentry to donate land. Thus, the pitch came into existence, and since the land usually remained the freehold of the donor, he could ensure that civilized rules were drawn up and observed. Scott's organizing of the Carterhaugh game was precisely such an attempt to eliminate "savage play" because, he admitted, "the old clannish spirit was to apt to break out."[11] Backing the gentry was the growing influence of schools and universities, which in the years after 1815 began to organize sports in earnest. In the old quasi-ecclesiastical foundations, like Winchester, Westminster, Christ's Hospital and Charterhouse, football was first played in the grassy square formed by the cloisters. But in 1810 Westminster bought a 10-acre plot in Tothill Fields and marked out what was perhaps the first proper pitch, the bill for which survives. By the 1820s many major schools were playing football regularly, though often according to peculiar rules. The Stonyhurst version, going back to the 1590s, was played against a huge stone wall. Eton also had a "wall game" version, which in 1827 led to a desperate fight and was stopped by its notorious flogging head, John Keate. The college then became the first to stabilize the numbers at 11 a side and to introduce a new and key figure, the referee.[12] Four years before, at Rugby, a boy named William Webb Ellis had taken up the ball and run with it, in a game hitherto of the kicking variety, and that was the origin of the version which had since spread all over the world as rugby football, though its rules were not formalized until 1846.

American football also dates from the 1820s. The Princeton students started playing an organized game called "ballown" in 1820. Seven years later, at Harvard, freshmen and sophomores inaugurated an annual football fixture on the first Monday of the college year. But the rules were still a matter of argument, and the event was known as "Bloody Monday"; at Yale, a similar scrimmage was called the annual "Rush."[13] Standard British football, which became known as soccer in the second half of the century, was not yet rule-governed in the 1820s, but it was already being exported, first to the Danes, then to Brazil. Italy, where the game went back to antiquity, still clung to an archaic medieval version.[14]

Cricket, a much more recent game than football, proved easier to organize and standardize because the gentry had played it from the start, at a village level. They became its first heroes, and particularly talented members of their estate staffs, its first professional players. Squires infused the game with their own notions of "gentlemanly" behavior and "fair play," which really derived from dueling. In 1787 Charles Lennox persuaded the professional bowler of the White Conduit Club, Thomas Lord, to open a private ground which became the Marylebone Cricket Club, or MCC. Lennox—later the celebrated Duke of Richmond, whose wife gave the ball on the eve of Waterloo—was a superb all-rounder. Two years after he dueled with the Duke of York on Wimbledon Common, the antagonists were reconciled while playing a match at Lord's ground, billed as "England v the Hambledon Club." There had to be strict rules, with an undercurrent of honor, since the game was a duel between bowler and batsman. Indeed, some of the games, right up to about 1830, were single combat. Lord's found its final resting place in 1814 when it settled in St. John's Wood, but it took some years to assert its authority over the game. In June 1817, for instance, Lord Frederick Beauclerk, who was a distinguished clergyman, got up an England team of 11 to play 22 men of Nottingham at Lord's. The local justices of the peace said that stumps must be drawn [the game must end] no later than 7 P.M. because Luddite rioters were active. But when the game was ended, the angry crowd descended on the pitch.[15] The next year Lord's held a single combat between the leading amateur, George Osbaldeston, and a professional bowler, George Brown, from Brighton. Brown hurled a ball so fast that it went through a coat held by the longstop and hurt a dog on the far side of the ground. Osbaldeston, always known as "Squire," was, with Richmond, one of the three great men in the formative years of the game. He was a star of the new Eton and Oxford elevens and then in 1816 made 112 and 68 for the Marylebone Cricket Club v. Middlesex at Lord's. Like Captain Berkeley, he was a sporting-hero-all-rounder, a master of Foxhounds for 35 years and a superb shot who once killed 98 partridges with 100 cartridges.[16]

The third and greatest of the trio was William Ward (1787–1849), a director of the Bank of England and a member of Parliament for the City of London from 1826. Between 1810 and 1825, he was the best amateur in England. On 24 July 1820 he scored 278 at Lord's, which stood as the record for over a century until it was beaten by the great Jack Hobbs in 1925. But Ward was also a statesman of the game. When the Lord's ground was almost sold off as a building site in 1825, he whipped out his checkbook and bought it for £5,000, making it over to the MCC in perpetuity. He played a leading role in getting the rules into shape, including the key decision to admit overarm bowling in 1822.[17] The great problem was betting. Even the Rev.-Lord Frederick admitted he made £600 a year at the game. Leading London bookies, including the great gambling master Crockford, used to sit in front of the pavilion at Lord's to take bets, and the Green Man and Still in Oxford Street, where all the chief professional players lodged, was a hotbed of "off-pitch" betting. Inevitably, players became corrupted and had to be "warned off" Lord's. Schoolmasters and dons would not allow the game to be played regularly at their colleges unless the betting element was eliminated. So the first Oxford and Cambridge and Eton and Harrow matches, which date from the 1820s—and the first Gentlemen v. Players, which was even earlier (1819)—coincide with the first real attempts to eliminate gambling.[18]

Betting bedeviled two other rough sports, boxing and racing, and here the gentlemanly takeover and reorganization ran into the insuperable obstacle, at least on this point, of the gambling instinct of the gentry and nobility themselves. Prizefighting itself was unlawful, and zealous magistrates sometimes took considerable trouble to prevent matches from being held and to arrest the organizers. Important prizefights might be widely advertised, but the venue was announced only at the last minute and the crowds were forced to race across the country, rather like acid house parties in the 1990s.[19] With bare fists and an unlimited number of rounds, a death in the ring was always possible, and then justices of the peace were sure to act. On 22 October 1816, the Welsh champion Ned Turner (active 1805–20), went 68 rounds (about 85 minutes of actual fighting) with a boxer called Curtis at Molsey Hurst. Curtis was insensible when the 68th round ended and died a few hours later. The coroner's court returned a verdict of manslaughter against Turner, and he was indicted on a charge of willful murder, the jury bringing in a manslaughter verdict. Turner got two months. Once he was out of jail, he fought, on 26 March 1817, a grudge fight at Hayes against Jack Scruggins. The fight aroused unprecedented interest and a huge volume of betting, but it was ruined by the crowd pressing into the ring, despite the presence of a posse of prizefighters with whips to keep the ring clear. After many changes of place to avoid the authorities, the battle was resumed on 10 June at Sawbridgeworth in Essex, when Turner won, Scroggins being carried out of the ring after 72 minutes of battering. Members of both Houses of Parliament were present on these occasions, though gentlemen tended to watch outdoor fights from the safety of their coaches.

Prizefighting became an aristocratic sport in the 1790s, largely because of the popularity of boxing at the big public schools. It reached its climax in the decade 1815–25. It was a disreputable sport because of its illegalities and the many fights that were "fixed," and it attracted the lowest blackguards in London. The Westminster Fives Courts, Hazlitt's favorite haunt, was a notorious place for indoor fights. Heroes of the sport, great men in their day, usually ended in the gutter. Scroggins, whose real name was John Palmer, a short man (five feet four inches) but broad, "like the stump of a large tree," took to drink, crashed downhill, became a pothouse buffoon, and died destitute in 1836 at age 48. The Tinman, one of the heroes of Hazlitt's famous essay, "The Fight," was a Bristol man, Bill Hooper, who made saucepans in the Tottenham Court Road. When he took to prizefighting, he was patronized by the nobility, spoilt for his trade, and died of drink and venereal disease in great poverty. Henry Pearce, known as the Game Chicken, was another drinker, though the cause of his death at 32 was tuberculosis. Then as now, champion boxers used their prize winnings to buy public houses, which usually proved their ruin. That is what happened to one of the greatest, Tom Cribb. Cribb was a champion so long, 1805–20, that aspiring fighters who sought publicity would attack him in his pub; he insisted on bringing them before the magistrates for assault, "otherwise I could not carry on my business . . . for these swaggering blackguards." But his business failed all the same, and he, too, died destitute in 1848. Many fighters were Jewish: Aby Belasco, prominent in the years 1817–24; Daniel Mendoza; and Samuel Elias, known as Dutch Sam—though he was born in Petticoat Lane—a small man weighing only nine stone, but a terrific hitter; he, too, died of drink in 1816 at age 41.

There were even more blacks in prizefighting: "Massa" Kendrick and Jack Sutton, both champions in their day, and Bill Richmond, who came from Staten Island, New York. Richmond's patron was one of the wild Pitts, Lord Camelford, who owned two seats at the pocket borough of Old Sarum and threatened, if he was interfered with by the government, to return Richmond for one of them. Richmond might have made an excellent member of Parliament, for he seems to have been highly intelligent and was much respected. But most black fighters, like their white colleagues, led foolish private lives. The best of them was Thomas Molinea from Virginia, a fighter of outstanding courage but illiterate, overgenerous, and too fond of flashy clothes and women, who died of drink and venereal disease in 1818.

Irish boxers tended to go the same way. Jack Randall, said to be the best of them all, was killed by drink in 1828, at the age of 34, and Tom Shelton became another alcoholic with a strong propensity to suicide. "Any man has a right to hang himself," he said and took prussic acid in 1830.[20]

Two great men helped to bring respectability to the sport. John Jackson, who kept a gymnasium a in Old Bond Street and taught Byron to box, was one of the best-known figures of the Regency era. His father was an enterprising builder who constructed the Great Sewer of Blackfriars. "Gentleman John" was an all-around athlete, a short-distance running and jumping champion and a superb weight lifter, as well as a fighter; he could write his name while an 84-pound weight was suspended from his little finger. Artists called him "the finest-formed man in Europe." Just under six feet, weighing 14 stone, he had "noble shoulders"; a narrow waist; beautiful calves; delicate ankles; and small, fine hands. He dressed in a scarlet coat decorated with gold; frills of fine lace; a cotton stock; a looped hat with a broad black band; buff knee breeches; striped white silk stockings; a pale blue satin waistcoat, sprigged with white; and pumps with paste buckles. He walked down the London streets at 5 ½ miles an hour—according to an eyewitness— "the envy of all men and the admiration of all women."[21] Jackson was successful in business and generous. He did benefit performances for the Portuguese war victims in 1811, British prisoners of war in France in 1812, and Lancashire weavers in 1826. On 15 June 1814, at the Pall Mall House of Wordsworth's friend Lord Lowther, MP, he starred in a boxing fete before Alexander I and Marshal Blücher. For George IV's elaborate coronation in 1821, he recruited and commanded a numerous plain clothes force of prizefighters, who, dressed as royal pages, "preserved order." He died in 1845, rich and honored.

An even more remarkable success story concerned John Gully, son of a Gloucestershire butcher, who went into his father's trade, became a bankrupt at 21, then fought his way to the top in the years 1805–08. Like other prizefighters he put his winnings into a pub, the Plough, on Carey Street; did well; invested in bloodstock; and bred many winners at Ware Park in Hertfordshire. He owned Hetton Colliery near Sunderland and bought a fine estate at Ackworth Park, Yorkshire. Gully illustrates a point which strikes the historian of the early 19th century again and again: Not only in the United States but in supposedly class-ridden Britain, it was comparatively easy for an able, determined man to rise quickly, both in wealth and social status. For a professional boxer to become a member of Parliament or a congressman would be astonishing even today; Gully achieved it in 1832, when he became the member for Pontyfract in the first reformed Parliament.[22]

Even with the help of men like Gully and Jackson, it was not easy to gentrify boxing and to bring it within a legal, honest and respectable framework. Boxing remained a rough, if popular, sport, on the margin of criminality, until past the middle of the century. Even in the schools and universities it was not yet recognized as a "respectable" sport, unlike rowing, for instance, which became accepted with the founding of the Oxford-Cambridge race in 1827.

Horseracing was as corrupt and rough as prizefighting and attracted the same kind of undesirable people, but the gentry controlled more cards because they owned most of the horses and tracks. To eliminate popular races, Parliament passed an Act in 1740 stipulating that no lawful race could be worth less than £50 to the winner. This amount came from subscriptions and from publicans who paid for the right to erect beer tents on what was private land.[23] Entrance was free until grandstands were built. In the years 1815–30 races were still essentially local, since competing horses had to be walked to the course. In 1820, for instance, from Goodwood to Epsom or Ascot a walked horse took four days; to Newmarket, a week, and to Doncaster, two weeks.[24] So for all except the most important races, events were still for half-bred horses, hunters, or even ponies; heats were used, and the winner was the first entrant to win two heats. The big exception was Newmarket, famous since Charles II's day, where the common people were forcibly discouraged, and the races were watched by an upper-class elite of about 500, from horseback or carriages, the latter used "for invalids and ladies." At Newmarket, gambling and bloodstock trading were the purposes, and meetings were held periodically throughout the year. Most other meetings were annual, linked to local holidays and held in conjunction with balls and dinners.

In 1823, 87 out of 95 racecourses in England held only one meeting a year, but the movement toward multirace professionalism was already marked. The trend was accelerated by the discovery that races between horses that were less than five years old could make exciting contests. There was a rapid increase in the 1820s of races for two- or three-year-olds, and once younger horses ran, shorter races and lighter jockeys followed, with a tendency toward more scientific breeding.[25] So owners gradually ceased to ride their own horses, and a new breed of lightweight professional jockey emerged. By 1830 one expert was asserting that it was likely that "the three principal jockeys of England will earn, or at any rate receive, more money in a year than the whole professional staff of a modern university."[26]

With more money needed, and to be made, proprietors were encouraged to put up grandstands to which they could charge admission. The Duke of Richmond, son of the wicket keeper, set up in 1828 a public grandstand subscription for Goodwood, which he owned. The next year at Epsom a Yorkshire businessman, Charles Bluck, formed the Grandstand Association, which transformed a muddle of sheds into a modern-style grandstand. He, in turn, was bought out by a syndicate which built what was then the largest grandstand in the world; it could hold 5,000 people with seats for 2,500 on the roof, and it cost £14,000.[27]

During the 1820s, the elements of the world's first national racing system began to fall into place. Newmarket, with seven meetings a year, was the national racing center, where 400 out of the 1,200 blood race-horses trained. Ascot was the royal meeting and Epsom, the great mass racing event of the year, with over 100,000 attending the Derby. Don-caster was the top provincial course for the north of England, as Good-wood was for the south.

Presiding over it all was the archetypal instrument of sporting gen-trification, the Jockey Club, so-called from the days when owners (or their sons) rode their own horses in races. The Jockey Club came into existence in the mid-18th century, soon after Parliament began to legis-late about racing, and issued a growing number of directions at New-market on such matters as the weighing in of jockeys. It was, and to some extent remains, secretive—no list of members was published officially until 1835—but it began to issue a journal, the *Racing Calen-dar,* in 1807. The crucial year was 1816 when the *Calendar,* which printed the club's rulings, invited followers of the sport from all over England to submit matters in dispute to the club's senior steward.[28] The club reinforced its prestige by buying Newmarket Heath and endowing new races, such as the Two Thousand Guineas (1809) and the Thou-sand Guineas (1814). But the ability to enforce its jurisdiction was the key to its authority. In 1819 Doncaster became the first of many courses to accept its verdict. Two years later its right to "warn off" an of-fender—in effect, to ruin his career or sever his connection with the turf—was upheld in the courts.[29]

The establishment of the Jockey Club as the accepted controlling institution of a sport which not only had a mass following but involved enormous sums of money—far more, in comparative terms, than, say, international football, tennis or golf today—was of great importance because it set a new pattern of social control. The expansion of mass sport as the primary means of healthy outdoor recreation, first in Britain, then in other advanced countries, was one of the key develop-ments of the 19th century, the prelude to its worldwide spread in the 20th. In the modern world, sport was to come to mean more in the lives of most people than anything else, after home, family, jobs, peace and war—more, even, than religion. Its probity and discipline, therefore, was to become of great importance. What the Jockey Club established was that even in a sport like horseracing, which was peculiarly suscepti-ble to corruption, the most effective mode of control was not legislation and police, but the arbitrary rulings of an unelected body whose ver-dicts went unchallenged because the social status and wealth of its members made them disinterested. Racing was the first sport to profes-sionalize itself and attract a mass following, and the notion that its professionals should be closely supervised by eminent amateurs became the model for the regulation of all sport, first national, then international. Moreover, the emergence of the Jockey Club's authority in the 1820s came just in time, for the arrival of the railways in the next decade had perhaps a bigger impact on racing than on any other form of entertainment. The railways allowed the rapid transport not just of race goers but, more important, of racehorses across the country and thus led to the huge expansion of the sport.

There was irony in the railways' expansion of racing because ultimately mechanical transport was to destroy the horse's prime function. In the years 1815–30, however, the demand for horses, in quantity and still more in quality, was still increasing rapidly all over the world. That was the key to the career of William Moorcroft (1765–1825), one of the age's most gallant explorers. Moorcroft came from Lancashire and was studying medicine under the famous Liverpool surgeon John Lyon, when the outbreak of a devastating cattle plague among Derbyshire farms in 1783 led the authorities to ask the Liverpool Infirmary to send a student to see what help, if any, medical science could bring. Scientific veterinary surgery was then virtually nonexistent, though the French army had some skilled empiric horse doctors. Moorcroft was sent and became interested in the then largely unknown field of animal medicine. He told Lyon, on his return: "If I were to devote myself to the improvement of a degraded profession, closely connected with the interests of agriculture, I might render myself much more useful to the country than by continuing in one already cultivated by men of the most splendid talents."[30] Lyon was deeply upset, for Moorcroft was his favorite pupil, and he asked the head of the surgical profession, John Hunter of Leicester Square, to dissuade the young man. But Hunter's response was uncompromising: "If he were not advanced in years, he himself would on the following day begin to study the profession in question." So Moorcroft went to France to get some practical training, and in 1792 opened the first modern veterinary surgery at 224 Oxford Street. There were then 150,000 horses in London alone (over a quarter million by the 1820s). Moorcroft made a fortune but lost it all in a scheme to market machine-made horseshoes. Hence in 1808 he was glad to get a well-paid appointment as Superintendent of the East India Company's stud in Bengal.

In India Moorcroft was immediately confronted with a dramatic problem: the impossibility of getting sufficient quantities of high-quality horses to supply the company's army. At one end of the spectrum, English breeders were now producing—as Théodore Géricault was delighted to observe a few years later—bloodstock and draft animals of superlative quality. But these horses were expensive and hard to get hold of, and the best Moorcroft could do was to recommend the importation of small numbers for breeding. At the other end, poor-quality semiwild mustangs and other breeds were multiplying by the millions on the plains of the Americas, and indeed were beginning to do the same in Australia. What the company needed, to keep its grip on India, was a reliable, cheap horse that was capable of carrying a 252-pound dragoon at speed over long distances in rough country. Throughout the Orient, that is from Morocco to China, the native powers were remodeling their armies on European lines, increasingly with European mercenary officers. The same thing was happening on the borders of British India, and it threatened to tilt the military balance against the company, which had always been at a hopeless disadvantage in sheer numbers. What the company needed was a first-class cavalry arm and horse artillery, which would give it devastating mobility and the power to shock by driving deep into enemy territory and dictating terms in one sharp campaign. Without horses of great strength and endurance, Western military technology was not decisive.[31]

Moorcroft proposed to solve the problem by tapping a source almost on India's doorstep, the central Asian horse market and its horse fairs, where he believed the highest quality breeding stock could be cheaply obtained. But no European, and certainly no Englishman, had ever analyzed this source of supply, and to get to them Moorcroft had to travel in Asian disguise and to follow unexplored routes over the world's greatest mountain barrier, the Himalayas. In his search for horses, Moorcroft fortuitously set in motion two key modernizing processes: high-altitude exploration and what became known as the Great Game of central Asia. In 1811 he made his first journey in the central Himalayas. From May to August 1812, he and the Anglo-Indian Hyder Hearsey went right through the Himalayas, up the Daudi River and Gorge, onto Gartok and Lake Manasarowar on the Tibetan Plateau. In the years 1819–25, Moorhouse traveled through Kashmir, Ladakh, Waziristan and Afghanistan and across the Hindu Kush and the Oxus to Bokhara, where he died of disease or poison.[32]

This pioneering record of perilous travel has never been equaled. What he saw and heard led Moorcroft, for both humanitarian and strategic reasons, to advocate and persuade the Indian government to adopt a forward policy in the Himalayas. Moorcroft got close to the people because he treated patients wherever he traveled, sometimes 300 in a single day. He was particularly successful in fighting that scourge of the East, trachoma, since "the performance of operations on the horse has given me a boldness in operating on man which, doubtless bordering on temerity, might startle the regular surgeon. . . . The liberties I take are followed by a success which creates surprise even in one who, during the last 12 years, has had no small experience of operating on cases which would be considered incurable by discreet practitioners." He performed some drastic operations, unthinkable in Europe, to remove giant growths—one male patient was relieved of a cancerous mass weighing 8 pounds, 13 ounces.[33]

Moorcroft was a man of passionate sympathies who could not bear to observe the miseries inflicted by the decaying Gurkha Empire. In the summer of 1814 he persuaded the new governor general, Lord Hastings, to tackle the Gurkhas, who had already provided a pretext by constant raiding of the plains. That autumn General Ochterlony fought his way up the passes and reached Kathmandu the next year. Under the Treaty of Sagauli (1816), the Gurkhas surrendered the lowlands, withdrew from Sikkim and agreed to receive a British resident. The British thus acquired Simla and other hill stations, creating the world Kipling was to immortalize two generations later. They also began to recruit Gurkhas into their army, thus transforming the practitioners of an archaic and unsuccessful imperialism into brilliant defenders of the progressive version which replaced it.[34]

It was Moorcroft's humanitarianism which led him to invent the Great Game. Moorcroft believed Russian imperialism to be insatiable, inexorable unless opposed, and a great social and moral evil. When he first went into the Himalayas, Alexander I was still working closely with Bonaparte to undermine British world interests, a fact which had been worrying the authorities in Calcutta since 1808.[35] Moorcroft discovered, from the evidence of Russian trade goods (and even of French products) that Russians had penetrated much farther into central Asia than anyone had hitherto supposed. Even after all danger from Bonaparte was ended, Moorcroft's further travels, from 1819, convinced him that the Russian threat to India was now greater than ever, that "a monstrous plan of aggrandisement" was being prepared and put into operation, and that the pack animals and caravans carrying Russian goods were the forerunners of mighty armies. He believed, in particular, that the Russian agent Agha Mehdi (known to Russian historians as Mekhti Tafailov), who had been exploring the whole mountain area since 1808 on behalf of the Ministry of Foreign Affairs in Saint Petersburg, had been working out feasible military routes across the Himalayas.

What worried Moorcroft most was that the strategic territory Russia needed to acquire for a spring into India was nominally Chinese.

But the rule of Peking was vulnerable because the Moslems of the hills hated it and would rise to welcome anyone, such as the Russians, who came to end it. He calculated that a mere 60,000 Russian troops could end Chinese rule over Turkestan, and he even envisaged a rapid Russian conquest of China as a whole. British policy toward China revolved essentially around tea, and we will come to it later in this chapter. What Moorcroft feared was that the Russians would deliberately destroy the existing tea trade, reroute it, and take it over, the cost to Britain being "£2 million annually to the Exchequer, the comforts of the whole population of Great Britain to whom tea is now become a necessity of life, the employment of an immense capital and the subsistence of thousands."[36]

The answer to all these threats, Moorcroft argued, was for Britain to establish protectorates over Afghanistan and Ladakh and, above all, to annex Kashmir. Kashmir was a natural fortress with mountains for its walls, and a fertile one which could supply an army of half a million. With Kashmir, he told Calcutta, Britain "might mock any possible movement against her Indian possessions . . . but it may be said with truth that from the moment it falls into the possession of any other European power . . . the safety of British India is endangered."[37] Moorcroft believed that British rule would be welcomed and that it would transform Kashmir into what nature intended, "the Venice or Palmyra of Upper Asia." His warnings were taken seriously, his sinister death being an added reason for heeding them, and much of what he proposed was eventually done or tried. More important, he set in motion that delicate form of paranoia, known as the Great-Game mentality, which was to be part of the British Raj until the very instant of Britain's withdrawal in 1947 and which, in the form it took on the other side of the hill, was to obsess Russian policymakers as late as 1979, incite them to invade Afghanistan, and so bring the mighty Soviet empire crashing down in the next decade. It was quite an accomplishment for a veterinarian who set out to buy horses.[38]

The increasing specialization of the horse trade, which Moorcroft's career illustrated, was only one instance of the way in which scientific breeding was beginning to affect large sections of the animal world. There was a significant incident when Moorcroft and his companion Hearsey first met officials of the Tibetan government and handed over their ceremonial presents. Two unmistakably European-bred dogs, a pug and a terrier, said Moorcroft, emerged from the crowd and "suddenly rushed towards me, fondled, caressed me, frisked, jumped, barked and appeared as much rejoiced at seeing me as if they had recognised in me an old and favoured acquaintance." Recognizing, no doubt, his European smell, "they appeared desirous of showing their accomplishments by sitting up on their haunches and pushing forward their forelegs . . . as is sometimes taught to those animals in imitation of presenting firearms." Who, he asked, had brought the dogs? He was told "Ooroos" (Russians), thus giving Moorhouse the first disturbing intimation that the hand of Saint Petersburg had reached as far as Tibet.[39]

The growing fondness of men and indeed women from the advanced countries for well-bred dogs, especially of certain breeds, is reflected in the large number of names of dogs which have come down to us from the early 19th century. Dog names often gave away the country of origin of the breed. Thus, Henri de Saint-Simon, the founder of French socialism, had a dog, probably a setter, with the popular English dog-name of Presto. Presto was also the name of the dog which belonged to Lamb's friend Thomas Manning, the sinologist who was the first Englishman to explore Tibet. George Sand's spaniel also must have been English, for it was called Dash, probably the most common name for English dogs at the time. The dog belonging to the poet Thomas Hood, described as "large," was called Dash, too. He was given to Lamb to mind, got him into all kinds of trouble, and so figures largely in his correspondence. One of Lamb's many landlords, Owen, had a dog called Pompey and that was a common name as well. Among Byron's many dogs was a Pompey.

Byron also had a dog called Bosun, another favorite name, and this dog was a Newfoundland. These imported gun dogs, used as retrievers, were highly prized in the early 19th century. The leading expert on shooting, Colonel Peter Hawker, author of *Instructions to Young Sportsmen* (1825), described his "favourite Newfoundland dog" as "of the real St John's breed, quite black, with a long head, very fine action, and something of the otter skin, and not the curly-headed brute that so often and so commonly disgraces the name of the Newfoundland dog." The cricketing Duke of Richmond had a Newfoundland called Blücher, which means that it was almost certainly born in 1814, and it was this dog, by becoming fond of the rabid pet fox, which caused the Duke's death from hydrophobia. Byron's big dog Mutz, as his name suggested, came from Switzerland and was almost certainly a Saint Bernard. The poet proudly boasted that he "shuts a door when he is told," but the dog also stole a leg of mutton and was thoroughly worsted by a wild pig. Until sportsmen learned to appreciate the skill required to hit driven pheasants, which they began to do in the mid-1820s when modern-style shoots were first organized, they shot over dogs, usually point-

ers. Southey, a lifelong dog lover, had in succession pointers called
Rover and Dapper, and his friend Farmer Jackson had one called
Cupid.

Classical names were much favored. Young Edwin Landseer portrayed his dog Brutus in one of his first paintings, and I have noted
others called Ajax, Juno, many Caesars, Nero and Tully. John Black,
editor of the *Morning Chronicle,* who got into such matrimonial difficulties, had two enormous Newfoundlands called Cato and Pluto, "as
well known as himself." Juno and Pluto were also the names of pointers
belonging to the famous sportsman Colonel Thornton, who had them
painted by J.-C. Agasse, the Swiss painter who settled in England and
specialized in horses and dogs. Agasse also painted Sir John Shelley's
pointer, Sancho, but what he really relished was painting greyhounds.
Because of a white spot on the muzzle, many greyhounds were called
Snowball. Edward Topham had a Snowball. So did Agasse's chief
patron, George Pitt, later the 2nd Lord Rivers, who lived at Stratfield
Saye before the Duke of Wellington got it. Pitt kept many dogs, called
by names beginning with "P," such as Portia, when he was Pitt, and
with "R," such as Rolla and Rascal, when he became Rivers. But
Snowball was his most-fancied dog-name and one of his dogs, Young
Snowball, was an ancestor of the Prince Consort's favorite greyhound,
Eos. Agasse must have painted more named dogs than any other practitioner of his day. He did not, alas, paint Bluff, the treasured dog
belonging to the pretty actress Fanny Kelly, who turned down Lamb's
offer of marriage, so we do not know what breed it was.[40]

The English fondness for dogs and horses was undoubtedly at the
root of the growing movement for the kinder treatment of animals
which became prominent in the years after Waterloo. The battle itself,
as we have seen, was the first time that public attention was focused on
the sufferings of animals in combat, thanks to the work of Astley
Cooper and Charles Bell. Another development which caused outrage
was the attempt to avoid payment at tollgates by harnessing dogs,
instead of donkeys or horses (which had to be paid for), to carts. Not
that the English (and Scots) were the only people to object to overbur-
dened animals. The man who pioneered the decent treatment of horses
in the transport industry, at a time when many English coach-service
owners simply worked them to death, was Charles Bianconi from Lake
Como, who created public transport in the Irish West; he knew every
one of his 1,300 horses by name and made sure that each was well-fed
and groomed and—a vital point—got at least one rest-day a week.[41]

The English, however, were the first nation to become collectively
emotional about animals. The popularity of the public zoo at Exeter

Change in the years after 1810 was a big factor. Today zoos are often associated with cruelty by animal lovers, but their coming in the early 19th century allowed masses of ordinary people to see wild animals for the first time in a context free from fear and allowed them to be anthropomorphized. This was an important stage in public education.

The popularity of the Indian elephant Chunee, who arrived in 1809, has probably never been surpassed. Byron noted (1813): "[He] took and gave me my money again—took off my hat—opened a door—*trunked* a whip—and behaved so well that I wish he was my butler."[42] But Chunee's musts began to get worse in the 1820s, and early in 1826 the mistake was made of trying to cure him with purgatives—6 ounces of calomel and 55 pounds of Epsom salts. On 26 February the 12-foot creature began to break out of his cage, and the decision was taken to kill him. Elephant guns did not then exist, and no one knew how to perform the deed. Six years earlier Byron had provided an exciting account of a musk-ridden elephant breaking out in Venice, eating up an entire fruitshop, smashing into a church, and being finally destroyed by field guns from the Arsenal.[43] The killing of Chunee was even more prolonged and horrific and provoked outrage across the country. A long and learned correspondence followed in *The Times,* as did prints, pamphlets, a Sadlers Wells play and the exhibition of his skeleton. His agony was still remembered when Dickens wrote about him in the *Morning Chronicle* in the next decade.[44]

Chunee's martyrdom dramatized the struggle to outlaw cruelty to animals which was already intense by the mid-1820s. Between 1800 and 1835 Parliament debated no less than 11 bills seeking to make the deliberate ill-treatment of animals unlawful; all failed, mostly by narrow margins. Bearbaiting and bull running were the prime targets of the lobby. These were mainly rustic sports, practiced at a village level by the common people, often at annual fairs or wakes. A notorious example was the annual bull running at Stamford.

The reform movement was dominated by religious groups, overwhelmingly Nonconformist and Evangelical, and it was closely associated with the Society for the Suppression of Vice (1802), detested by intellectuals because it paid people to inform against purveyors of dubious literature. Many campaigners believed that cruelty to animals and sexual vice went together. Critics of the Stamford sports claimed they were also notorious for profligacy: "Many young women too were among the number, whose conduct was anything but modest. Indeed all classes seemed as if they had on that day license to cast off all appearances of decency and order, and plunge into every excess of riot, without shame or restraint."[45]

In Parliament, spokesmen for the blood-sports lobby claimed that the anticruelty bills were, in effect, class legislation, aimed at the pleasures of the poor. Opposing the first of them in 1800, William Wyndham, MP, pointed out: "The common people may ask with justice, why abolish bull-baiting and protect hunting and shooting?" Or, as Sydney Smith put it: "A man of £10,000 a year may worry a fox as much as he pleases . . . and a poor labourer is carried before a magistrate for paying sixpence for seeing an exhibition of courage between a dog and a bear! Any cruelty may be practised to gorge the stomachs of the rich, none to enliven the holiday of the poor."[46] Nonetheless, from 1815 popular blood sports were in rapid decline. In 1816 the Royal Cockpit at Westminster was demolished.[47] In 1822 a humane slaughtering measure, "An Act to Prevent the Cruel Treatment of Cattle," got onto the statute book. Two years later the Society to Prevent Cruelty to Animals (SPCA) was formed and immediately began to use this act to have promoters of bull baiting prosecuted.

In the early 1820s public opinion began to swing heavily against all sports involving cruelty to large wild animals, such as bears. In Staffordshire, once notorious for its popular blood sports, General William Dyott (1761–1847), a leading landowner, noted in 1824: "Refinement in manners of various classes [has] reached the little as well as the great": he saw the end of bull baiting in his neighborhood as part of a general movement to improve the behavior of society.[48] Under pressure from the SPCA, magistrates used troops of yeomanry and regular cavalry to stamp out the Stamford bull running.[49] The first specific Cruelty to Animals Act, which made all baiting of animals unlawful, was not passed until 1835, but by then bull- and bearbaiting had gone, cock throwing, the more ferocious version of cockfighting, had been abandoned, and even cockfighting lingered on chiefly in the wilder districts of the Midlands and North.[50] By the end of the 1820s English tourists were already beginning to poke disapproving noses into the Continental mistreatment of animals in ways that were now forbidden at home.

It was in the 1820s, indeed, that the English developed what Arthur Hugh Clough (1819–61) called "an almost animal sensibility of conscience." This sensibility was brought to bear on almost every aspect of life and became the driving force behind countless efforts to improve society, first at home, then abroad. The treatment of children, no less than animals, was brought into the legislative drive from the first decade of the century. The Health and Morals of Apprentices Act (1802) limited, for the first time, the working hours of pauper children ("parish apprentices," as they were termed) hired by factory owners and provided for their education. The big change, however, came after the war when the 1819 Factory Act banned parents from hiring out their children under age nine and limited the time worked in cotton mills by children aged nine from 16 to 12 hours a day. The difficulty faced by reformers was that the employment of children was often the only way to ensure they survived at all. The elder Brunel, who loved children, made every effort to give them jobs in his workshops "because I do not want them to starve."[51]

Half the population were aged 16 or under. There had been, by the 1820s, a revolution in infant mortality of a kind never before experienced by any society. In 1730 three out of four children born in London failed to reach their fifth birthday. By 1830 the proportion had been reversed. But married couples were still as philoprogenitive as ever—more so, indeed, since fewer women died in childbirth. The painter William Daniells's friend Mr. Wilkins, Sr., had 30 children, all living. The great financier Sir Robert Wigram had 15 sons and 5 daughters. The Rt. Rev. Henry Bathurst, Bishop of Norwich, was one of 36 children his father had by different wives.[52] Maria Edgeworth was one of her father's 22 children by four wives, whom he married at four, nine and seven months after bereavement.[53] John Gulley, the prizefighter-turned-gentleman, had 24 children, 12 each by two different wives.[54] These are a few examples, picked almost at random. The 90-year period 1760–1850 was the time of greatest fertility, for instance, in the history of English aristocratic women. A study of 50 women shows that they tended to marry at age 21 and had an average of eight children, the last at age 39.[55] Working women were even more productive, since they were less likely to practice birth control or deny their husbands.

It is true that more lower-class children died young. In Liverpool, the life expectancy of "gentlefolk" averaged 35 years and of laborers, 15 years. Life expectancy varied enormously by place, too; in Bath gentlefolk lived on average to 55, and even laborers to 25. In rural Rutland, the life expectancy of laborers averaged 38, more than for gentlefolk in either Manchester or Liverpool.[56] The London slums (the word first came into use in the 1820s) had a very high infant mortality rate. Dickens, born in 1812, was taken by his nurse, Mary Weller, to many lyings-in, and as a child he learned a lot about babies, including dead ones. He recalled the results of a multiple birth, "four or five," laid out "side by side on a clean cloth in a chest of drawers," reminding him of "pigs'" feet as they are usually displayed in a neat tripe-shop."[57]

In the United States, where likewise half the population were aged 16 or under, the infant mortality figures were improving rapidly in the 1820s, but even among whites, one in six or seven children never reached their first birthday. In the eastern states, families were just beginning to show signs of decreasing by 1830: in Massachusetts and Connecticut, the average number of children per family was only five; farther west, seven, eight or nine children were the norm.[58]

Even wealthy parents had to get accustomed to the idea of losing children, often with startling suddenness. But the stoicism, even indifference, with which the death of a child had been greeted in the 18th century was yielding to a higher sensibility. Wordsworth was devastated by the deaths of two of his children; in a sense, he never recovered from them. Children, their tragedies and sufferings, recur again and again in his poetry. While he, Coleridge and Southey set their faces against many political reforms in the years after 1815, they identified themselves with what Coleridge called "the hopeless cause of our poor little White-Slaves, the children in our cotton Factories, against the unpitying cruel Spirit of Trade, and the shallow, heart-petrifying Self-conceit of our Political Economists."[59] It was, above all, the exploitation of children which drove Southey to hate industrialization so bitterly. Southey noted that some of the most strident radicals, such as Burdett and Whitbread, were millionaire capitalists whose fortunes had been built from sweat and suffering. When Southey died, the most passionate tribute to his memory came from the great Earl of Shaftesbury, friend of the boy sweeps and the factory children: Southey, he wrote in his diary, was "essentially the friend of the poor, the young and the defenceless—no one so true, so eloquent and so powerful."[60]

At Greta Hall near Keswick, with its unmatched views over Derwentwater and the fells, Southey, his wife and her sister, Mrs. Coleridge, lovingly brought up their children together to an astonishingly high standard of accomplishment, as we have seen. Sara, the nine-year-old prodigy, was rather shocked when she stayed with the Wordsworths at Dove Cottage and later at Allan Bank. The poet, his wife Mary, and his sister Dorothy, though devoted to their brood, were "rather rough and rustic in their management of children." Sara said: "We left our beds at 4 A.M. and roamed about the kitchen barefoot." She remembered being washed in the kitchen tub. Miss Crump, who owned Allan Bank, looked down her nose at what she called "these irregular Scotchy ways" and accused the children of scribbling on the walls; they were, said Sara, "chid and cuffed freely enough, yet far from kept in good order."[61]

Intellectuals and writers tended to oscillate between neglecting their children and spoiling them. Shelley ceased to write to or think of his two children by his first wife Harriet, once the Court of Chancery had taken them out of his hands. Hazlitt, by contrast, unquestionably spoiled his son William.

Perhaps the worst brought-up children of the age were Leigh Hunt's. Byron got Hunt out to Italy to edit his projected periodical, the *Liberal,* but he was consternated when Hunt arrived with his slatternly wife Marianne, later described by Blackwoods as "a pert Abigail in a fifth-rate farce," and all their six offspring. The whole lot expected to stay in his house, and when he shifted from Pisa to Genoa, they followed. The children had been brought up in the ultrapermissive modern manner, and when Byron rebuked them, they answered back. They also proved extremely destructive: "What they can't destroy with their filth," said Byron, grinding his teeth, "they will with their fingers." He called them "Yahoos," "Blackguards," and "Hottentots" and tied his bulldog across the staircase to keep them out of his own quarters. Unfortunately, the dog went for the nanny goat the Hunts insisted on keeping to provide fresh milk for the Yahoos. Marianne noted in her diary: "Mr Hunt was much annoyed by Lord Byron behaving so meanly about the Children disfiguring his house, which his nobleship chose to be very severe upon. . . . Can anything be more absurd than a peer of the realm, and a *poet,* making such a fuss about 3 or 4 children disfiguring the walls of a few rooms—the very children would blush for him, fye, Lord B, fye!"[62]

Hunt, however, was careful, when he had a house of his own in Chelsea, to ban his children from his own room. When Thomas Carlyle visited Hunt, he found it the only tidy, well-furnished chamber in the place. The rest he called "the poetical Tinkerdom." Mrs. Hunt "looked devilish and was drunken"; the children were "a set of young, bronze-coloured gypsey faces. . . . The Frau Hunt lay drowsing on cushions, 'sick, sick' with a thousand temporary ailments; the young imps all agog to see me jumped hither and thither. One strange goblin-looking fellow, about 16, ran ministering about tea-kettles for us; it was all a mingle lazaretto and tinker's camp, yet with a certain joy and nobleness at heart of it." Jane Carlyle could not see the nobleness, having, as a near neighbor, to put up not only with the children's invasions but Marianne's improvidence. "She is every other day reduced to borrow my tumblers, my teacups, even a cup full of porridge"; the servant was always round—"Missus has got company and happens to be out of the article"—"Missus," noted Jane, "is the most wretched of managers. She actually borrowed one of the brass fenders the other day and I had difficulty getting it out of her hands: irons, glasses, teacups, silver spoons are in constant requisition and when one sends for them the whole number can never be found."[63] It is not surprising, then, that the later history of the Hunt children was almostly uniformly sad. The Godwin children, by contrast, were brought up strictly: made to work hard, write books at an early age, and speak only when they were spoken to. When Humphry Davy and Coleridge dined with William Godwin, young Hartley Coleridge hit the philosopher accidentally but painfully on the shins with a ninepin, producing an extraordinary explosion and a lecture for his sister Sara. Davy, a child lover, thought the "silence" of Godwin's own children "very oppressive."[64] These children, too, led tragic lives later.

In examining the lives of children brought up in the years 1815–30, one finds it hard to discern any uniform pattern. The methods parents employed seem to have varied as much as they do today. The notion that strictness was the rule is certainly false. When Spencer Madan arrived in September 1814 to tutor the three younger boys of the Duke of Richmond (three were already serving with Wellington), his diary reveals that he received conflicting instructions. He arrived at glorious Richmond House overlooking the Thames at Westminster (now demolished, but its great stone terrace is immortalized in two of Canaletto's most successful canvases[65]), to find, in addition to the boys, the duchess, her six daughters, and a bad-tempered Swiss governess. "Her Grace took the opportunity . . . to tell me that the boys were the most *headstrong* untoward young pickles she ever knew, and that my only way was to begin with extraordinary strictness and severity."

The next day Madan was summoned to Downing Street by the boys' uncle, Earl Bathurst, who "told me that his object in sending for me was to caution me against the temper of the Duchess generally, and in particular against what she might say about the boys . . . they were high spirited but well-disposed and that anything like severity wd. be the worst possible way of managing them."[66]

The second night "a servant came in to say the young gentlemen were in the kitchen throwing everything about and making such a riot that no servant could live in the house." The boys were rude to the governess, threw butter, and the eldest said to the middle boy, "If you hold the girls, I'll *lick* Mademoiselle." They clambered over the terrace railings "and slid down the posts to which barges are fastened, onto a coal barge below." The youngest, little Lord Arthur, was following, "but in getting down the post his foot slipped and he fell up to his chin in mud and water between two barges, and had he not been seen by two bargemen would most likely have been drowned." Madan added: "Lady Bathurst gave them a pound: with which they contrived to purchase a brace of pistols and some gunpowder." He found them ill-supplied with books and with no toys at all, so that when they were forbidden to play on the terrace, as too dangerous, they had nothing to do.[67]

From another eyewitness, we hear that "some of the younger sisters were in the habit of running down to the river, and giving sixpence to a bargeman to get them a Thames flounder, with which to propitiate their very cross Swiss governess."[68] When the family moved to the Continent, the boys continued to give trouble. According to Madan, Lord Sussex was good but stupid, Lord Frederick clever but bad, and they quarreled. One one occasion, "Lord Frederick despairing, I suppose, of convincing his brother by means of words, took up a heavy brass candlestick perhaps with a view of throwing light on the subject and gave his brother a blow of which he will carry the mark to the grave." The boy's nose was broken, he "had some severe headaches, was bled with leeches repeatedly & kept at home upwards of three weeks." The boys, said Madan, took no notice of anyone except himself: "If I were away therefore the house would be turned out of windows every evening, & there would be no end to their riots, let alone their pilfering the store-room, thrashing the maids, and sending out for red herrings and gin."[69]

Other parents went to enormous lengths to teach their children. Joseph Farington met on the Hastings Coach a Mr. Cassmajor, who told him his wife had "produced 15 children, nursed them all herself, and taught all her ten daughters languages, history, geography, drawing and painting." Lady Oxford did the same, "from ten till one each day" and "examines all books they have access to, no novels allowed ever."[70] The degree of severity, even cruelty, in this home teaching varied enormously. When George Sand was taught to write, she was forced into a machine devised by her writing master, a whalebone corset from head to waist, with a wooden bar to keep her elbow high and a brass ring on boxwood rollers for the pen and index finger.[71] John Ruskin, born in 1819, had parents who devoted themselves totally to his welfare, molding their lives, including where they lived, to his supposed interests. But the only toys he ever had were a box of bricks and a bunch of keys; when his aunt brought him a scarlet-and-gold Punch and Judy set, he never saw it again. He was not allowed to mix with other children. On Sundays all books were removed, and only cold food was served. His mother was his sole instructor until he was 10; from the earliest age, she read the Bible aloud to him, going straight through from beginning to end, then began the next day at the beginning. The night before he was three he was able to repeat the whole of the 119th Psalm.[72] On the other hand, from the age of six he was taken by his parents all over the British Isles and to Paris, Brussels, Bruges, Ghent and other Continental centers, traveling in a private carriage. He was shown cathedrals, castles and churches and was taught to draw and paint them and to study their architecture, taking notes on everything all the time. His earliest unsupervized notes, done in 1826 when he was seven, are headed "Incipient Action of Brain Molecules." In summer 1830, spent touring the Lakes, he wrote a 2,000-line poem as a record; he was then 11. The Sunday after he finished the poem, he saw Wordsworth at Rydal church and recorded in his diary: "Rather disappointed in this gentleman's appearance. He appeared asleep the greater part of the time. This gentleman possesses a long face and a large nose."[73]

John Stuart Mill, born in 1806, likewise was the recipient of the most intensive education from his father. Despite a full-time job at India House and the demands of his magisterial *History of India,* the older Mill, wrote his son, devoted "a considerable part of every day" to "the instruction of his children"; he "exerted an amount of labour, care and perseverence rarely if ever employed for a similar purpose." Mill said he could not remember the time when he began Greek: "I have been told it was when I was three years old." At eight he began Latin, and to teach his sister, and so on with the younger children; by then he had read all Herodotus, Xenophon, and the *Memorials* of Socrates; the lives of the philosophers by Diogenes Laertius; part of Lucian and the first six dialogues of Plato (the last when he was seven). At the age of eight he began Greek verse and read Pope's Homer—"I must have read it from 20 to 30 times through." "My father in all his teachings," Mill wrote, "demanded of me not only the utmost that I could do but much that I could by no possibility have done." He did his Greek at the same table at which his father wrote his *History,* and since he had no lexicon, he had to interrupt his father to ask about every word he did not know. He also had to read a good deal of history—Robertson; Hume; Gibbon; Burnet; Watson's *Philip II* and, his own favorite, Hooke's *History of Rome.* Then followed all the *Annual Registers.*

The Mill family lived at Newington Green. Each day, Mill would go for a long walk with his father and answer questions about his reading of the day before; he had to make notes while reading on slips of paper and was allowed to use these as *aides mémoire.* At 10, Mill began science: "I never remember being so wrapped up in any book as I was in Joyce's *Scientific Dialogues";* and "I devoured treatises on chemistry." At 12 there was logic, "an intellectual exercise in which I was most perseveringly drilled by my father." At 13, Mill senior "took me through a complete course of political economy." By the age of 14, Mill was much better educated than the overwhelming majority of university graduates today. None of this was rote learning either: "Anything which could be found out by thinking I never was told until I had exhausted my efforts to find it out by myself"; "my father," Mill added, "was fond of putting into my hands books which exhibited men of energy and resource in unusual circumstances, struggling against difficulties and overcoming them."[74] There were no holidays in the young Mill's life; few children, books or toys; no games at all; much walking with his father but no boy companions.

The childhoods of these prodigies, with devoted but overdemanding parents, sound grim, though both Mill and Ruskin grew up to be great men with an astonishing output of high-quality work and a huge influence on the intellectual life of their times. Nor did this kind of parental cramming, so typical of the age, necessarily involve severity. The young Robert Browning, born four years after Mill in 1812, received an unusually loving education from his parents. His father had a comfortable job at the Bank of England and was able to build up a large library at their house in what was then the Georgian paradise of Herne Hill, South London.[75] His mother, the daughter of a shipowner of German descent, was a superb pianist, with a gift for attracting butterflies and animals to her. Both, said Browning, "had a childlike faith in goodness. His father introduced him to Homer when he was five and read the whole of John Dryden's *Essay on Satire* to him as they walked on Nunhead Hill.[76] By this time Browning was already writing verse, his sister Sariana describing him as "a very little boy, walking round and round the dining-room table, and spanning out the scansion of his verses on the smooth mahogany."[77]

Like Mill and Ruskin, Browning was taught by his father to have an independent mind, but in addition was positively encouraged to read anything he wanted in his father's library. When he asked for Shelley's work—then much disapproved of and hard to find—his mother got it for him. His parents' view, as he put it, was that "no thought which ever stirred/A human breast should be untold" ("Paracelsus"). Browning was upset when, browsing around among his father's books, he came across, at the age of 12, Wolf's *Prolegomena in Homerum*, "proving" that Troy never existed. He also found horror stories, including Nathaniel Wanley's *Wonders of the Little World or a General History of Man in Six Books* (1678), which specialized in monsters, abortions, sex changes, tortures and executions. He plowed steadily through the metaphysical poets, then little regarded, Vasari's *Lives of the Painters,* Gerald de Lairesse's *Art of Painting in All Its Branches* (ca. 1700), his favorite book, the 50 volumes of the *Biographie Universelle,* bought when it was first published in 1822, Kant's philosophy, medicine, zoology, musical theory and much biblical scholarship. As Chesterton put it, Browning acquired his learning "in the same casual manner in which a boy learns to walk or play cricket."[78] At 16 his parents sent him to the new London University (1828) to learn modern languages. He grew up in a house which was full of music and pets—two dogs, a cat, a pony, monkeys, owls, hedgehogs, snakes, a magpie and at one time an eagle: not quite Byron's menagerie, but near it. Carlyle, riding from Cheyne Row over Battersea Bridge, met the young Browning, aged 18, on Wimbledon Common, and described him as "a beautiful youth," with dark, long, flowing hair and fashionable green riding jacket, 'turf and scamphood written all over him.' In fact he was well on the way to becoming perhaps the most learned poet in the history of English literature.[79]

It is notable in the early 19th century how many boys, as well as girls, were educated in effect at home, and in isolation from other children. Victor Hugo owed all his early education to his mother. Edward William Lane, later to be the leading authority on Egypt, was given a superb classical and mathematical education at home, mainly by his mother Sophia Gardiner, a niece of Gainsborough; when he went up to Cambridge he found he could do all the maths Tripos, and so did not stay. Pushkin, by contrast, was hated and ignored by his mother, who called him "Monster," and was taught to write Russian and read its literature by his personal house serf, Nikita Kozlov, who remained his lifelong valet and lived to bury him.[80] W. E. Forster, born in 1818, the son of Quaker missionaries, "learned to discuss grave social and political questions with his father and mother before he had learned to play with children of his own age."[81] He later told with relish the tale of how he was sitting, aged three, in a coach with his nurse, and a Kind Old Gentleman asked: "Where is your Papa, my dear?" "Papa is preaching in America." KOG: "And where is your Mama?" "Mama is preaching in Ireland." KOG: "!!!!!" Forster, who later put through the famous 1870 Education Act, creating free, compulsory schooling in England, was an only child, educated by his mother and by local clergymen. At 12 he was regularly reading the *Edinburgh Review* and commenting on political events in his diary. Thus, on the fall of the Wellington government in 1830: "As it is to be hoped that the Whigs now in power will fulfil their three great promises, viz. the abolition of slavery, retrenchment and moderate reform, I must confess I am glad of the change."[82] He did not go to a regular school till he was 14, when his hours were 6:30 A.M. to 6 P.M.

Herbert Spencer, born two years later in 1820, was likewise brought up without contact with other children, though he came from a family of teachers. The amount of knowledge he acquired at home was impressive, and when he was only just 11, he attended Dr. Sprutzheim's lectures on phrenology and was taking part in experiments in physics and chemistry. At age 12, the future polymath and creator of sociology was sent to his uncle's school, where he objected fiercely to learning Euclid, absconded and walked home—48 miles the first day and 47 miles the second day, reaching his house on the third. This determined boy was said to have "a strong disregard for authority and a tendency to question every explanation."[83] Most boys, given the choice, preferred education at home. Edward Bulwer Lytton was taught English, mathematics, and Latin by his adoring mother and, two brief experiences at school proving objectionable, successfully petitioned to have a private tutor at home until he was ready for Cambridge.

One reason Lytton hated school was that, like Herbert Spencer, he could not keep his pets there. The number and variety of pets children kept in the 1820s was remarkable. At Alfred Tennyson's house, there was a Newfoundland so big that it pulled his mother's donkey carriage. Tennyson had a pet owl which he trained to sit on his mother's head, occasionally descending to attack their pet monkey.[84] Some schools allowed boys to bring pets. At the Wellington House Academy, attended by Charles Dickens, there were various rodents and birds: "One white mouse, living in the cover of a Latin dictionary, was trained to run up ladders, draw Roman chariots, shoulder muskets, turn wheels and even make a very creditable appearance on the stage as the dog of Montargis," but later "fell into a deep inkstand, was dyed black and drowned."[85]

Schools could usually be relied on to teach the classics and mathematics well. But conditions were often bad and the discipline was severe. The young William Makepeace Thackeray, born in 1811 and largely brought up by a black servant, Lawrence Barlow, hated his first school, Arthur's in Southampton: "cold, chilblains, bad dinners, not enough victuals and caning awful!" Charterhouse was worse. When he arrived, the headmaster, John Russell, questioned him, then told the porter: "Take that boy and his box and make my regards to Mr Smiler and tell him the boy knows nothing and will just do for the lowest form."[86] Thackeray later wrote of the cruel masters "whose lips, when they were not mouthing Greek or grammar, were yelling out the most brutal abuse of poor little cowering gentlemen standing before them . . . fancy the brutality of a man who began a Greek grammar with *tupto,* I thrash." The beatings were fearful, and the boys "had to wash in a leaden trough under a cistern with lumps of fat yellow soap floating about in the ice and water." Fagging was "a form of slavery," since the boys were unsupervised: "torture in a public school is as much licensed

as the knout in Russia." Nor did the masters take any responsibility for
the boys' moral welfare: "Charterhouse morality—fresh, innocent
voices singing bawdy songs without knowing their intent." Thackeray
said "one of the first orders he received at Charterhouse was 'come and
frig me.' "[87]

Tennyson appears to have wanted to go to Louth Grammar School,
perhaps to escape the gloomy atmosphere at home, where his clerical
father was increasingly depressed, alcoholic and epileptic. His father
would not let him go there until he could repeat from memory on four
successive mornings all the odes of Horace. But, once there, Tennyson
found the headmaster, the Rev. J. Weaite, a sadist: "He thrashed a boy
more unmercifully for a false quantity than a modern headmaster today
[1870] would thrash a boy for the worst offence of which a schoolboy
could be guilty." One boy was in bed for six weeks after a beating.

Eton was another school that was notorious for flogging in the
1820s. W. E. Gladstone, in his later years, told some horrifying stories
of E. C. Hawtrey, the future headmaster and provost, who flogged
Gladstone himself when, as praepositor of the Remove (school prefect),
he tried to protect three boys who were due to be flogged by omitting
their names from his list. An eyewitness account of Hawtrey in action:
Hawtrey (to the praepositor): "Write down Hamilton's name to be
flogged for breaking my window." Hamilton: "I never broke your
window, Sir." Hawtrey: "Write down Hamilton's name for breaking
my window and lying." Hamilton: "Upon my soul, Sir, I did not do it."
Hawtrey: "Write down Hamilton's name for breaking my window,
lying and swearing." Hamilton was flogged the next day.[88] On the other
hand, it must be added that during his last three years at Eton, Gladstone received, or gave himself, a magnificent education in traditional
subjects, as well as in political debating. In 1826 Canning, recently
appointed Prime Minister, passed by the school on the way to Windsor
and asked to see the boy; he had heard of his abilities.[89]

Abraham Lincoln, born the same year as Gladstone, 1809, walked
four miles every day to Knob Creek in Kentucky to what was called a
"blab school," the children singing everything out loud. His father
could sign his name, his mother "made her mark" and they and all their
neighbors were afraid they had "the wrong kind of papers" for their
land. That was why the Lincolns moved to Indiana, where "the right
kind of papers" could be had, and where Abe and his sister Sally hiked
18 miles a day, there and back, to the local school. When their mother
died, of the "milk sick," their father promptly went to a widow he
thought available, proposed to her without ceremony—"I got debts"—
paid them, bought a license, and they married. This wife was also

illiterate; she said "she liked a man that didn't drink an' cuss none."
Their existence depended on barter: venison hams, bacon slabs, barrels
of homemade whiskey. The storekeeper would ask: "What kind of
money have you today?" Lincoln's skills were a woodman's: the trap,
the axe, the cleaver—he knew how to butcher. Men and women went
barefoot except in the coldest weather. Lincoln's uncle said, "We lived
the same as the Indians, 'ception we took an interest in politics and
religion." Lincoln once walked 34 miles just for the pleasure "of hearing a lawyer make a speech."[90]

Willpower, industry and an internal drive in a particular direction:
these raised the great men of the 19th century above their circumstances. Gustave Flaubert, born in 1821, son of a surgeon at a 600-bed
hospital in Normandy—he and his sister used secretly to watch their
father amputating legs—was educated largely by his mother at home
and was writing plays almost as soon as he could write at all. He seems
to have learned the art of storytelling from a well-read servant, Julie,
whose bad leg had kept her for a year in bed, where she read a lot, and
his culture he acquired from a teenage friend, who came from a more
civilized home and who introduced him to Goethe, Spinoza and poetry.
By the age of 15 he was, in effect, an inveterate writer, and formal
schooling played no part in it.[91] On the other hand, Charles Baudelaire,
born the same year, went to two of the best schools in Europe, the
Collège de Lyon and St-Louis-le-Grand in Paris, earned first-rate marks,
then contrived to get himself expelled for refusing to hand over a secret
note from a classmate, tearing it up and eating it instead.[92]

Neither of the two greatest composers of the midcentury, Richard
Wagner and Giuseppe Verdi, both born in 1813, had much of an
education of any kind. Wagner took after his mother, a tiny but electric
woman, so small that when she visited her daughter-in-law at Dresden,
"the maid took her in her arms like a baby and ran upstairs with her."
She was hypersensitive to cold and wore "nine caps, one on top of the
other, to keep warm." Wagner, too, was tiny, with a large head, and
"eyes as blue as the Lake of Lucerne"; he also suffered dreadfully in
winter, wearing layers of silk underclothes and padded dressing gowns.
"Her education was very defective," he admitted of his mother; when
Goethe and Schiller were pointed out to her on the Promenade at
Lanchstädt, she asked who they were. Wagner's real father was almost
certainly the actor Ludwig Geyer, and his education, if anything, was
theatrical.[93] Geyer tried him out first as a painter, then as an actor, then
sent him to the Dresden Kreuzschule, where he learned a little Latin and
Greek and much mythology. He came to music late, only after he had
been overwhelmed by Weber's *Freischutz,* and claimed in 1842: "In my

whole life I have never learned to play the piano."[94]

Both Verdi's parents, who came from innkeeping families near Parma, were illiterate. Verdi received a few years' teaching at the village school and was taught the organ by the local choirmaster. A wholesale merchant who supplied his father with liquor was responsible for getting him into the nearest *ginnesio* (grammar school), where he learned a little "humanity and rhetoric." He seems to have earned his living as an organist from the age of 10, and "from my thirteenth to my eighteenth year . . . I wrote an assortment of pieces, marches for brass bands by the hundreds, perhaps as many *sinfonie* that were used in church, five or six concertos or sets of variations for pianoforte which I played myself at concerts, many serenades, cantatas, and various pieces of church music, of which I remember only a *Stabat Mater*."[95]

Also born in 1813 was the Danish philosopher Søren Kierkegaard, who complained repeatedly in his *Journals* that he had no childhood. His father's first wife had died childless; the father had then seduced her maid and been forced to marry her. The family treated her as a nonentity—in effect, she remained a servant—and the father became a chronic depressive. He was already 57 when Kierkegaard was born: "An old man who was himself enormously melancholy . . . had a son of his old age upon whom the whole of that melancholy fell in inheritance," Kierkegaard wrote.[96] "I never knew the joy of being a child." The father "filled my soul with dread." Though a successful merchant in the hosiery trade, the father felt his sin had made him accursed of God. His son heard him say to a friend: "I am good for nothing. I can do nothing. My only wish is to find a place in some asylum." The son, and to some extent his elder brothers, inherited in full measure this guilt or *tingsind* (heaviness of spirit). When Kierkegaard's brother Peter, who became Bishop of Aalborg, was shown the entries in the *Journals* on guilt, he exclaimed: "That is my father's history, *and ours too!*" It is not surprising that Kierkegaard became obsessed with the tale of Abraham and Isaac, for the father-son relationship was unsoftened by any mediation from the shadowy mother; she was not mentioned once in all the 20 volumes of Kierkegaard's *Collected Papers,* and is only twice referred to in the Bishop's letters.[97]

Sent to the Copenhagen Borgerdydskole (the School of Civic Virtues, for merchant's sons) at the age of nine, Kierkegaard, who had never been allowed to play with other boys, found himself treated as "the Strange One," "the Peculiar One"; he was *Fremmed,* weird, as his contemporary Frank Welding put it, "a stranger and object of pity," "Søren Sock," "the Choirboy." His father gave him no money, so he had to borrow it, or cheat. He was also made to wear a jacket and knickers cut from dark, coarse tweed and knee socks and shoes instead of boots; he hated his clothes—"as a child I was mistaken for an old man." "Tender, frail, weak," he wrote, "in almost every way denied the physical qualities required to make me a whole human being like the others; melancholy, soul-sick, in so many ways deeply and inwardly unfortunate, one thing was given me—a mental superiority." He spoke and learned to write superb Danish and developed a fearsome capacity to use his tongue with savagery, so he was beaten up by other boys, and occasionally thrashed by the entire class. "As a sick man longs to cast off his bandages," he wrote, "so does my sound mind long to cast off . . . that sweaty, sodden poultice which is the body and its weaknesses."[98]

What was also striking about Kierkegaard's childhood was the relentless masculinity of the household. His sisters, Nicoline and Petrea, were treated like their mother, as servants, made to wait on their brothers and given little education. This treatment was becoming unusual by the 1820s, at any rate in northwest Europe. Girls were not as a rule educated to the same standard as boys, but a growing proportion were receiving regular lessons or being sent to schools. It is a point made repeatedly by Jane Austen (for instance, a propos the Musgrove girls in *Persuasion*) that young people, especially girls, were now much better educated than their parents. The number of girls' schools was growing fast. Most were of the type run by Mrs. Goddard in *Emma,* unpretentious but efficient, not "a seminary, or an establishment, or anything which professed, in long sentences of refined nonsense, to combine liberal acquirements with elegant morality upon new principles and new systems—and where young ladies for enormous pay might be screwed out of health and into vanity—but a real, honest, old-fashioned Boarding-school, where a reasonable quantity of accomplishments were sold at a reasonable price, and where girls might be sent to be out of the way and to scramble themselves into a little education, without any danger of coming back prodigies."[99]

Such a school Elizabeth Gaskell, born in 1810, the same year as Frédéric Chopin, Robert Schumann, and Alfred de Musset, attended in Knutsford, run by the six Unitarian sisters, the Misses Byerley. The Byerleys taught their 16 boarders (plus day girls) English reading, spelling, grammar, composition, geography, the use of globes, and ancient and modern history, all for 30 guineas a year (excluding washing), and, for extra fees, French, music, drawing, dancing, and arithmetic. The sisters had traveled, spoke fluent French and Italian, played well on their Broadwood piano, and taught harp and guitar. Mrs. Gaskell, virtually an orphan though part of a huge, ramifying family, with dozens of cousins her own age, was content there—"such happy days as my schooldays were," as she put it.[100]

This school must be reckoned good value. Boarding schools which only took girls from age 13 on, to be "finished," usually charged at least £100. That was the fee set by "the Misses Hodges, nieces of Sir John Carr," who took "six young ladies" in Bristol. In Bath, the Misses Broadhurst took a maximum of 10 girls and charged £120 each. Both these schools were "seminaries." London was more expensive. In Great Cumberland Street, Mrs. Leach and Miss Carden took up to 20 teenage girls for £140 a year. Farington's friend Battersbee had to pay £400 to get his girl "finished" in London, but this was a special year in which she would be taken to theaters and balls and would be introduced and "presented." Not everyone approved of girls' schools. Farington's friends Mrs. Offley and Miss Glover, both of whom had been to boarding school, told him they would not do the same for their daughters because of "the course pursued by girls there which vitiated others." But a well-run school could make a fortune for a wise and careful proprietor; Mrs. Stephens was said to have saved £60,000 during the years she kept a school in Queen's Square, and when she retired the goodwill alone was worth £5,000.[101]

The girls' schools of the 1820s were given a bad reputation by Charlotte Brontë's *Jane Eyre,* one of the most powerful novels ever written, based on her experiences at the Clergy Daughters' School at Cowan Bridge in Lancashire, to which she was sent in 1824, aged eight. Her two sisters, Maria and Elizabeth, were already there, and Emily was to follow. The fees were low, clergymen having to pay only £14 a year per girl (plus extras), but the school consisted of a converted row of cottages and had only recently opened. The place was very cold, and the two-mile walk to church on Sunday meant that they had to stay there for dinner, taking cold meat and bread with them (attending both services on Sunday was normal). The children, said Charlotte Brontë, "set out cold . . . arrived at church colder," and "during the morning service became almost paralysed." During her time, six girls died of tuberculosis, and others died in the typhoid epidemic of 1825; the dead included her two elder sisters. Maria, suffering from tuberculosis and too weak to get up (a blister had been applied on her side to cure her lungs) was violently jerked out of bed by one of the teachers, Miss Andrews, thrown onto the dormitory floor, and abused for "dirty and untidy habits." This scene was witnessed by the young Charlotte, who never forgave the school, and after Maria's death, her husband claimed it was the sitting in church in sodden shoes for two services which had done the irreparable damage. Charlotte, however, was only at the school 10 months, during its worst period. When the school moved to the much healthier area of Casterton, things improved. The appearance of Charlotte's novel led many old girls to defend the place hotly, and when Charlotte died, there was a long newspaper controversy on its merits.[102]

The school at Cowan Bridge, with all its faults, was one of thousands of new establishments opened in the years 1815–30; in both England and France more resolute efforts were made to reduce mass illiteracy than in any other comparable period, before or since. A precursor was the Quaker Joseph Lancaster, who at age 18 opened a neighborhood poor school in the Borough Road in London (1801). Lancaster taught his pupils to become "monitors" and repeat their lessons to other pupils. It was a rough-and-ready system designed solely to cope with large numbers; the monitors or pupil-teachers performed all the school functions, under strict discipline.[103] By 1804 Lancaster had 500 pupils, and three years later there were 45 schools run on these lines. But Lancaster was hopeless at running his finances and was imprisoned for debt in 1807. The idea, however, was attractive, and to a limited extent successful. From 1815 various efforts were made to implement it all over the world, notably in Spanish-speaking countries, the Middle East and India. Brougham became involved, through an organization pushing Lancaster's methods called the British and Foreign Schools Society, founded in 1814. In May 1816 he successfully moved a motion in the Commons setting up a committee "to inquire into the education of the lower orders in the Metropolis." He brought in Wilberforce, Mackintosh, J. G. Lambton, Romilly, Lansdowne, Horner and James Mill, a clever selection of radicals, Whigs and Tories. Introducing its first report a month later, he claimed that half the children of England got no education at all; in London there were 120,000 "without the means of education," up to 4,000 of whom were rented out by their parents to professional beggars.[104]

The difficulty of getting money from the Treasury to implement a Lancaster-type system was that, like almost any educational experiment in the 19th century, it was rapidly bedeviled by religious controversy. Lancaster would not teach religious doctrine, except in the most general terms. A rival reformer, Dr. Andrew Bell, had worked out a somewhat similar system in Madras, and brought it back to England. Each accused the other of plagiarism. Bell was an Anglican, and provided education in his monitorial system on traditional Church of England lines. He thus got the enthusiastic support of most Tories and the literary right, especially Southey, Wordsworth and De Quincey, all of whom were passionate believers in popular education, provided it was done in a framework of religious orthodoxy. The radicals, and liberal Anglican clergy like Sydney Smith, backed Lancaster.[105] Bell antagonized them further by the strict limits he placed on the process: "It is not proposed that the children of the poor be educated in an expensive manner ... Utopian schemes ... for the diffusion of general knowledge would soon confuse that distinction of ranks and classes of society, upon which the general welfare hinges. ... There is a risk of elevating by an indiscriminate education the minds of those doomed to the drudgery of daily labour above their condition, and thereby rendering them discontented and unhappy with their lot." To which Brougham angrily retorted: "Is it contended that persons of a certain yearly income engross among them all the natural genius of the human race?"[106]

This last argument was, in practice, irrelevant, for though the Bell-Lancaster systems succeeded in quantity—about a quarter of a million children were processed by them in the years 1805–25—by their very nature the amount they could teach was meager, one reason why other methods supervened when funds to pay teachers became more plentiful. There is no evidence that children were deliberately taught less at Bell-type establishments than at Lancaster's. But both men proved embarrassments to their partisans. Lancaster devised an elaborate system of punishments for unruly pupils. As a Quaker he would not wield the rod, but he put bad boys in shackles or in cages which were slung up to the roof, and some he tied to a pillar in the manner of Saint Sebastian. His financial embarrassments, too, became endless, despite much help.[107] Bell, by contrast, became very rich through various preferments, such as his mastership of Sherborne Hospital. According to De Quincey, he was worth £125,000. But he was notoriously avaricious and mean and had a public separation from his wife Agnes, daughter of a Scottish doctor. Agnes wrote him many letters endorsed on the outside: "To that supreme of rogues, who looks like the hangdog he is, Doctor (such a doctor!) Bell," and "To the ape of ape, and the knave of knaves, who is recorded to have once paid a debt, but a small one you may be sure—it was that he selected for this wonderful experiment—in fact it was 4½d. Had it been on the other side of sixpence he must have died before he achieved so dreadful a sacrifice." When Bell was staying in Grasmere at the cottage of a former soldier, Robert Newton, Mrs. Bell sent his host a message warning him to "look sharp" about Bell's rent. Another read; "If you have any regard for your family, don't grant him an hour's credit." Then (written twice): *"Cash down!"*[108] However, it should be added that by the time Bell died in

1832, over 12,000 schools had come into existence to practice his system, in Britain alone.

Despite much contradictory evidence, the overall impression is that the position of children was improving steadily in the early decades of the 19th century. Wrongs and cruelties about which society had hitherto been silent were now voiced and sometimes righted. Adults were becoming much more conscious of children as human beings with needs and rights, more interested in them, and more anxious to help. The notion that a child should be seen but not heard was being undermined; children were beginning to take part in conversations. Farington noted approvingly of his friend Major Reynell: "He talked about the way he is educating his children—makes them his companions—requiring nothing but obedience." Some were thought to go too far in this direction. Erasmus Darwin "makes it a rule never to contradict his children but to leave them their own masters." It was said that the painter Joseph Wright of Derby took the same line. Edmund Burke was "besotted" by his son, "who contradicted him without opposition," but Burke, all agreed, did go too far: The son was much disliked.[109] Many parents were extraordinarily sharp at looking for "genius" in their children, and nurturing it, often in ways we might consider indulgent today. Thanks to their parents, Shelley, Elizabeth Barrett Browning, Leigh Hunt and Bulwer Lytton all had their verses and/or fiction printed and published while still in their teens—Elizabeth Barrett Browning was only 14 when *Marathon* appeared. When Shelley went up to Oxford, his father, who had already enabled him to print a novel and a book of verse, wrote to the leading bookseller-printer there: "My son here has a literary turn. He is already an author and do pray indulge him in his printing freaks."[110]

It was a good time to be an infant prodigy. There must have been more of them in the early 19th century than at any other epoch, before or since. They ranged from "Miss Randall, the Celebrated Musical Child," 3½ years old, the daughter of a blind Welsh harper, who earned £400 by her London performances, to Master William Henry Betty (1791–1874), often called the Young Roscius, who astonished audiences in the first decade of the century by his Shakespearean performances when only 14 or 15. Pitt adjourned the Commons early so the members could see his Hamlet. His father bought him a £40,000 estate in the Midlands from his earnings and saved a further £34,000, so Betty was able to retire at 20 and live the life of a country gentleman for the next 60 years.[111] It was, however, the mass production of the piano and the growth of the middle-class audience which brought about the apotheosis of the prodigy. In the early 1820s, in Paris alone, there were Leontine Fay, Anne de Belleville, Larsonneur and George Aspull (from Manchester), all of them infant pianists, and the 13-year-old singer, Euphémie Boye. There also were the astonishing public performances of Clara Schumann, from the age of nine. But the truly outstanding wunderkind was the Hungarian boy Franz Liszt (1811–86).

Liszt came from a very poor family. His grandfather had 25 children and died penniless; his father, Adam Liszt, worked on one of the Esterhazy sheep farms, learned bookkeeping and so became an efficient agent for exploiting the talent of his gifted son. Adam played the piano, and Franz's genius came out at the age of five when he sang Ries's concerto in C-sharp minor after hearing his father play it on the piano. Adam taught him to play from memory, to sight-read, and to improvise—Bach, Mozart, Hummel, Beethoven—and when the boy was seven, a local merchant gave him a piano. The only schooling Franz had was as one of a class of 67 in a village room, 20 feet by 14, and he later bitterly complained he had never been able to remedy his lack of history, geography, and science.[112] But he had one decisive stroke of luck. His father could not afford to send him to Hummel, who charged one louis d'or per lesson. But the brilliant Austrian pianist Carl Czerny (1791–1857), who had been taught by Beethoven himself, agreed to take Liszt, aged 10, at no charge. Czerny was probably the finest teacher of piano who has ever lived. For 14 months he subjected the boy to intensive training—endless endurance exercises, scales in all keys, correct fingering, rhythm and tone. He forced Liszt to learn music at great speed, thus perfecting his sight-reading. The test came when Liszt was eleven, and the Viennese music publishers, to trap him, gave him Hummel's new concerto in B-minor; but the boy played it at sight. Czerny, who called him Puzzi, described him as "a pale, sickly-looking child, who while playing swayed about on the stool as if drunk." Franz was thin, weak in many ways, a fragile creature, who remained subject to fevers and fainting fits all his life. In 1822 the publisher Anton Diabelli invited 51 leading musicians in the German-speaking world to write variations on a waltz he had composed. The 11-year-old Liszt was the youngest. Except for Beethoven, all accepted. Most were rubbish; Liszt's was Czerny-like and clever, Schubert's was beautiful. Then Beethoven upstaged them all by writing a masterpiece, his 33 *Diabelli Variations*. The episode revealed the standing the boy already had in German music. But that was the end of his training because his father was desperate for him to earn money on the concert circuit. Franz's first major appearance, at Vienna in December 1822, led the *Allgemeine*

Zeitung to announce that "a young virtuoso has fallen from the clouds."[113]

Then followed tours all over Europe. Adam proved himself a skilled publicist and cleverly invited comparisons by following the routes Mozart had taken 60 years before. He also made a pioneering arrangement with the leading piano manufacturer in Paris, Sebastian Érard, who had just produced his epoch-making seven-octave piano with its "double-escapement" action, which enabled a player to repeat a single note rapidly. This piano perfectly suited Liszt's growing virtuosity. He was presented with the fourth such piano ever made, and it was agreed he would always use an Érard piano, provided one was shipped in advance to wherever he was playing. Thus, Liszt became the "Érard Artist"; the new piano and the prodigy's magic were associated in the public mind; and art and commercialism advanced together. Liszt's debut in Paris in March 1824, when the Italian Opera Orchestra, then the best in Europe, jumped to its feet to give him a spontaneous round of applause, made him a European celebrity. Lithographs of the boy, still only 12, were in all the print shops. Franz Gall, founder of phrenology, took a cast of his head. In London he performed before the entire musical establishment, including such outstanding pianists as Ries, Kalkbrenner, Clementi, Cipriani, Potter and Carmer. At Windsor, at George IV's request, he improvised on the waltz from *Don Giovanni*. A letter to a music publisher, now in the British Library, survives from this visit: "Dear Sir!!! I would be greatly obliged to you if you would take the trouble of coming to see me today at a quarter past three having finished a few pieces and as I want to have them engraved I am appealing to you to ask you to kindly hear them so that you don't buy a pig in a poke. Franz Liszt."[114] In Manchester there was the one setback: he had to share the program with the Baby Harpist, the Infant Lyra "not yet four years old"; as she was so tiny she had to climb onto a chair to play her miniature harp, still twice her size; she upstaged him. By 1827, when he was 16, Liszt had already made three tours of Britain, and when his father died that year, he gave up the circuit in disgust—he hated being a wunderkind, comparing himself to the performing dog Munito—and set himself up in Montmartre. There he took up smoking, drinking, womanizing, becoming the archetypal Romantic hero, suffered a nervous breakdown, was infected with religious mania, indulged in fashionable melancholy and despair, and was described as "pale and haggard," with "unspeakably attractive features," reclining on a sofa smoking a long Turkish pipe, lost in meditation, his smile "like the glitter of a dagger in the sunlight."[115]

Two years earlier Liszt had met in Paris another prodigy, Felix

Mendelssohn (1809–47), who had, however, come up the easy way. His family were bankers and that year (1825) his father felt so prosperous he moved into a vast Berlin mansion on the Leipzigerstrasse. Mendelssohn was bruised throughout his life by the blows of anti-Semitism and, still more, by the bitter arguments within his family about whether or not to convert to Christianity and add Bartholdy to their name.[116] But he never faced any financial problems. From the earliest age he had all the best tutors. Ludwig Berger, Clementi's disciple, taught him piano; he learned the cello and the violin to concert standard; his voice was trained at the Singakademie, whose director, Karl-Friedrich Zelter, also taught him composition. He had private tuition in Greek, Latin and modern languages and had a better general education than any other composer up to that time. As a gifted, beautifully spoken boy, he was introduced to everyone—Spohr, Spontini, Paganini, Weber and Cherubini. Zelter, a coarse Prussian, made a double-edged presentation of Mendelssohn, aged 12, to Goethe, as a genius, adding (in an imitation Jewish accent), "It would be quite a thing if a Jew-boy became an artist!" Goethe who, to his credit, always took meeting the young seriously, promptly set the boy to play unfamiliar Bach fugues, to improvise on unknown tunes, and to sight-read from his collection of Mozart and Beethoven manuscripts, as well as his own compositions. He then awarded his seal of approval. Mendelssohn reciprocated: "The sound of [Goethe's] voice is tremendous, and he can shout like 10,000 warriors."[117]

By the time Mendelssohn met Liszt, who was two years his junior, in Paris, he had been everywhere, knew everyone, done everything—he was an ultrasophisticated young man of the world, already composing with subtlety and elegance, his conversation knowing and witty, and his taste fastidious. His father went to immense lengths to ensure that he enjoyed Paris and all its civilized delights, introducing him to Rossini, Auder, Meyerbeer and Hummel. Of his fellow 16 year olds, born the same year, Tennyson and Gladstone were being flogged at school; Lincoln could still barely read or write; Charles Darwin was disgustedly studying elementary anatomy in Edinburgh; Edgar Allan Poe was penniless, almost starving; and Pierre-Joseph Proudhon was a printer's devil. The young Mendelssohn declared he found Paris, by comparison with Germany, frivolous and ignorant. Cherubini was "a burnt-out volcano"; Rossini's face "a mixture of roguery, boredom and disgust"; and little Liszt had "many figures, few brains." He thought Auber's music ridiculous—"it might be capitally arranged for two flutes and a jews-harp *ad libitum*." As for Meyerbeer's horn sonata, "I laughed so much I almost fell out of my chair."[118] It says a lot for Mendelssohn's inner goodness that the spoiled teenager matured into an exceptionally generous and disinterested servant of his art.

I suspect that the more sensitive parents, when they could afford it, indulged and promoted their children because they were painfully aware of the risk of losing them. Fewer children were dying in infancy, but if they survived the years of maximum danger, ages one to three, it by no means guaranteed that they would survive to maturity. In the early 19th century tuberculosis was probably the biggest single killer, and its ravages were fiercest among those aged 15 to 25. In the United States, up to the Civil War, it was the commonest cause of death, especially among young people and the middle-aged. It was particularly hard on poor young women living in towns. But it harvested youth from all classes. It killed Bonaparte's son, the King of Rome, when he was 21. It killed one of George III's daughters. It killed Bourbons and Hohenzollerns, Habsburgs and Romanovs. It killed Jackson's adored adopted son, Lyncoya, when he was 16, coming with startling suddenness, the shock hastening his wife's death.[119] It was often a fast killer, indeed. Lady Aberdeen, still in her twenties, died of it almost without warning, leaving her husband with four small children. Sometimes it was slow. The marquess of Abercorn's heir, Lord Hamilton, had relays of London doctors sent to him in Ireland over several years and "tried relief by inhaling air through a tube," but died in the end.[120] It massacred whole families, as with the Brontës. The "White Plague," as they called it, wiped out the family of Ralph Waldo Emerson's first wife, Ellen Tucker, killing her father and brother, then herself, then her mother and sister.[121] It killed countless children, too, including the enchanting little Mlle. Rivière, who figures in Ingres's finest portrait, *Madame Rivière* (1805). Governesses, being female, mostly young and poor, were a particularly high-risk category, though the notion, derived from Victorian fiction, that they were a particularly oppressed class, is much exaggerated: Sydney Ownerson, for instance, had an enjoyable time as governess, and I have noted other cases in which governesses were happy, confident, well paid and treated, and much loved.[122]

Tuberculosis was particularly destructive in the arts, killing among others Keats, Géricault, and Bonington, three young men of genius, already of outstanding accomplishment but just approaching their artistic maturity. An equally distressing case was that of Karl Maria von Weber (1786–1826), particularly since tuberculosis killed him just when, after many misfortunes and struggles, he was becoming the most successful composer in Europe. His father, himself a composer of sorts, ran a small traveling theater company, but was dissolute, dishonest and always in debt, and his troubles often involved his son. In 1820 the Berlin Opera produced Weber's *Der Freischutz*, which was an overwhelming success there and later all over Europe. The opera was particularly well received by British audiences after it had its first performance on 2 July 1823, at the English Opera House (the Lyceum, on the Strand). Indeed, it produced a phenomenon called "Freischutz Mania," songs, rhymes, prints, endless repetitions on hand-organs, a verse edition with illustrations by George Cruikshank, theatrical imitations and a crop of witch jokes. When Weber's *Euryanthe* failed at Vienna in 1823, Weber sank into an acute state of depression, aggravated by the onset of tuberculosis. But he roused himself when Charles Kemble of Covent Garden offered him £500 to compose a new work—which became *Oberon*—plus further handsome payments to conduct 12 performances and 4 oratorial concerts.

The trip to England in February 1826 was the greatest triumph of Weber's life, vividly described in his letters. He was escorted like royalty through the Customs House at Dover, put into a fine carriage which "dashed along like lightning" through "a country beyond all description charming" to the splendid home of Sir George Smart, organist to the Chapel Royal, where "everything is taken care of." He marveled at English luxury: "Every possible comfort is provided—a bathroom in the home!" Broadwood supplied him with a free piano wherever he went. "English life and manners," he wrote, "are thoroughly sympathetic to me." But he was already visibly ill, and his hosts were concerned. "People are all so good to me with their anxious care. No King can be served with greater love and affection in all things than I am. I am as much cosseted and caressed as a baby in arms. . . . I cannot be sufficiently grateful to Heaven for the blessings which surround me."[123] Weber was described as "a pale little man," with a big nose and a rather distinguished face in the shape of an isosceles triangle. When he arrived to conduct the first oratorio at Covent Garden, the audience gave him a 15-minute standing ovation, the orchestra played the overture to *Freischutz*, and he was in tears. But people noticed he coughed a lot: parcels of medicated sweets, lozenges and jellies were constantly delivered to Smart's house. Writing to his wife, Weber told her: "The excellence of flesh and fowl is indescribable. I have had set before me chickens which without exaggeration are as large as middle-sized geese with us. And the meat is so tender and juicy—ah! and the oysters!"[124]

There were 12 rehearsals for *Oberon,* involving exhausting physical strain, for Weber was frantic, as always, and terrified lest the new work should be accorded the, to him, inexplicable hostility which greeted *Euryanthe*, his favorite. He had to rewrite whole sections of the score to accommodate the voice of John Braham (1774–1856), the leading English tenor. Weber was now spitting blood, was ashy-pale, his hands trembling, his feet swollen. He had to play at a huge crush at the Marquess of Hertford's with the whole of the musical establishment but also 600 high-society people present; "not a creature listened . . . I heard but little of what I played myself." The opening night of *Oberon* on 12 April was an unprecedented success with, for the first time in England, calls for the composer at the end ("an undesirable Continental custom," as one newspaper put it). Every ticket was sold for all 12 performances. But six days later, unexpectedly because it was already spring, an appalling "London Particular" descended on the city: "a thick, dark, dark, yellow fog," Weber wrote in despair. "It is almost impossible to see without candles. Today is enough to kill one."[125] Six weeks later he was dead.

Medical science in the early 19th century was powerless to fight tuberculosis. Quacks claimed to be able to cure it. To see one of them, St. John Long, Bonington hurried back to England in 1828, of course to no avail. It was chiefly to find methods of treating tuberculosis that Dr. Thomas Beddoes set up his Pneumatic Institution at Clifton and put the young Humphry Davy in charge of experiments with gases and drugs at its Pneumatic Hospital. But not all Davy's intuitive genius was of the slightest use. In the early 19th century, the usual recommendation was a warm climate—hence Keats's dispatch to Rome—just as later in the century it became high altitude and Swiss sanatoriums. The outstanding mercy of the period was the discovery by Dr. Edward Jenner (1749–1823), the Gloucestershire general practitioner, of a satisfactory method of vaccinating against smallpox, and still more his extraordinary generosity, which accelerated its rapid adoption, at least in advanced countries, in the first quarter of the 19th century.[126] As a result, smallpox ceased to be a major killer in Western Europe, North America and Australia. Almost as important was the success of two French chemists, Joseph Caventon and Pierre-Joseph Pelletier, in isolating the quinine alkaloid of chinchona in 1820. Quinine was popularized by Royal Navy surgeons, who did a lot of experiments on the West African station, and by 1830 quinine was cheap enough for general use among whites in the tropics. It successfully contained malaria, though the connection with the mosquito was not proved until 1898.[127]

In other respects, doctors were short of effective weapons. But some advances were being made in surgery. The long Napoleonic Wars, in general a brake on human progress, produced marked improvements in the speed and skill with which surgeons performed drastic operations, and the daring and self-confidence with which they undertook them, as the writings of Doménique Larrey, Bonaparte's head military surgeon, make clear.[128] There was no effective form of anesthesia until C. W. Long of Jefferson, Georgia, used nitrous oxide gas in 1842. Hence surgeons in the early decades of the century had to operate rapidly, and to acquire this skill they needed real bodies for practice. In Britain, two acts of Parliament (1726 and 1751) made the bodies of executed felons, hitherto hung in chains, available for medical dissection. But the supply dwindled as juries, judges and the system of royal pardons united to reduce the number of executions. In the 15-year period 1805–20 they averaged only 77 a year. Hence the rise of body snatching.[129] Great surgeons like Sir Astley Cooper needed fresh bodies for their own work and, still more, to train their students, and they willingly cooperated with the gangs of criminals who supplied them.[130] Bransby Cooper, in his life of his father, gives biographical sketches of these "resurrectionists": Ben Crouch, Bill and Jack Hartnett, Tom Light, Hollis, Daniel and Butler. The gangs were usually in league with the badly paid caretakers of the burial grounds that were raided.

In the library of the Royal College of Surgeons in London there is a manuscript diary of 16 pages, covering 28 November 1811 to 5 December 1812, kept by a body snatcher, one Joseph Naples. It is strikingly matter-of-fact. Thus: "Friday 29 November 1811. At night went out and got 3, Jack, Ben and me got 2, Bethnal Green—Bill and Daniel 1 Batholow [hospital]. Crib opened [post-mortem] . . . Tuesday 10 December 1811. Intoxicated all day. At night went out and got 5 Bunhill Row. Jack almost buried. . . . Wednesday 8 January 1812. At 2 A.M. got up, the Party went to Harps. got 4 adults, 1 small, took 4 to St. Thomas. Came home, went to Mr. Wilson & Brooks, Daniel got paid £8.8.0 from Mr Wilson, I received £9.9.0 from Mr Brooks. Came over to the Borough, sold small for £1.0.0. Received £4.4.0 for adult. At home all night."[131] If bodies were too "bad," that is, decomposed, the gang drew the canine teeth and sold them, again to such places as St. Thomas's. Among the names mentioned in the diary are those of Cooper, Sir Charles Bell and other well-known surgeons.

Many of the bodies were sold to the private anatomical schools, which in London clustered in Soho, especially in Soho Square, where Bell settled in 1811. He was connected with the nearby Great Windmill Street School of Anatomy, as well as with the more reputable Middlesex Hospital from 1814.[132] The growth of such private-enterprise academies, where physicians and surgeons could be quickly and cheaply trained, reflected not only the enormous increase in urban population but the disproportionate rise in the demand for medical skills, as wealth increased and people were no longer prepared to bear, for instance, the pain of kidney stones, which could now be safely removed. The growing number of operations was directly connected to the practice of body snatching.

Edinburgh, where more British doctors and surgeons were trained than anywhere else, was also a center for body snatching, and in the 1820s the demand seems to have exceeded the supply. In 1827 an Irish canal-navvy, William Burke (1792–1829), took a room at Log's lodging house in Tanner's Close, Edinburgh, an establishment kept by an Ulsterman, William Hare. In November, Donald, a friendless old pensioner died in the house, and Burke and Hare, instead of burying the body, sold it to a well-known surgeon, Dr. Robert Knox, who kept a school of anatomy in the city. They were paid £7.10s. Their greed thus aroused, the two men, assisted by their wives, murdered at least 15 persons during the next 10 months, by luring them into the house, making them drunk, suffocating them—so as to leave no marks on the body—and then selling the corpses to Dr. Knox. In November 1828 the police were alerted and found one of the bodies in Knox's cellar. Hare turned King's Evidence, and Burke was tried, convicted and hanged.[133] The full extent of the various rackets associated with body snatching was never established. A House of Commons committee reported (1828) that in one winter a gang of six sold 312 bodies at an average price of four guineas. But a corpse could fetch up to 40 pounds. So great was the fear of resurrectionists in the 1820s that various security devices were manufactured, such as Bridgeman's Patent Wrought Iron Coffin, advertised as "the only Safe Coffin."[134]

Behind this gruesome business lay the infighting of an emerging medical profession. The Royal College of Physicians, who in 1825 moved into a grand new classical headquarters, built for them on Pall Mall East by Robert Smirke, felt themselves scientifically and socially superior to the surgeons.[135] Britain was the only country in Europe where, already, doctors were generally treated as gentlemen; so when they traveled on the Continent they concealed their profession, since otherwise they might not be "received" at its courts.[136] But the surgeons were coming up in the world. In 1823 one of them, Thomas Wakley, a friend and disciple of Cobbett, founded the *Lancet,* which stuck up for them, attacked the medical establishment, denounced the leading London hospitals and their staffs as "human slaughterhouses and professional butchers" (1829), sold a lot of copies, made a profit and became a power in the land.[137]

Surgery was also greatly enhanced in the years 1815–30 by the scientific anatomical studies of Charles Bell and, still more, by the professional success of Astley Cooper (1768–1841), who in 1827 became president of the Royal College of Surgeons. Cooper said that a surgeon had to have "an eagle's eye, a lady's hand and a lion's heart"—he might have added a greyhound's speed. Cooper's great merit was that he knew exactly what he was looking for and what to do when he found it. As one of his disciples put it: "For operating with alacrity, and well at the same time, I have never known his equal."[138] Without anesthetics, the maximum "safe" time a patient could stand being operated upon was reckoned to be 15 minutes. When the politician William Wyndham died in 1810, Sir Anthony Carlisle (1768–1840) told Farington that his death arose because the surgeon, Lind, "though a good cutter," took too long, 20 minutes, to removed a lump caused by a fall from his horse (the operation was probably unnecessary anyway). Carlisle said he died from the shock of the pain. The same nearly happened to the duke of Portland during a stone-removal operation; the stone broke in the surgeon's hands and it was 78 minutes before all the pieces were extracted.[139] A surgeon like Cline, who had never been known to take more than 15 minutes for the most difficult stone operation, was therefore regarded as a public benefactor, and Cooper was the fastest of all. Despite "incessant" labors, he had many more demands than he could handle. Once established, he never earned less than £10,000 a year, and in two years his fees were computed at £21,000 and £22,000. One grateful client, an elderly Jamaican planter named Hyatt, whose stone Cooper had swiftly removed, invited him to his house—he was recuperating and wore his nightcap—and handed him a cheque for £1,000, the largest fee ever recorded to that date.[140]

Surgeons could, to some extent, be judged by results. With physicians, it all depended on your view of medical science. Some members of the profession were cynical. Professor Nicholas, the anatomist, said the only difference between a young and an old physician was that "the former will kill you, the latter will let you die." Until in his weakness at Missolonghi, he allowed them to bleed him, Byron had always kept clear of doctors, relying instead on his own reading of *Thomas's Domestic Medicine*.[141] He was not the only celebrity who bled to death. So, in all probability, was Tsar Alexander I. In November 1825, aged 47, he was suffering from a fever, probably a form of malaria. He was bled repeatedly, no less than 35 leeches being applied behind his ears and at the back of his neck, until he succumbed.[142] Bleeding was known as "lowering." The absurd thing was that physicians disgreed constantly on whether a patient should be "lowered" or "raised" (that is, given fortifying food and drink). Farington records a row between two doctors on this point over the Marquess of Thomond, who was married to Sir Joshua Reynolds's niece and heiress. Sir George Baker wanted to lower him by taking out blood; Sir Francis Milman insisted on raising him by forcing him to drink three large glasses of Madeira daily, saying, "If once we lower him we shall never be able to raise him again, and he will sink and die; but we can at any time *lower him* if circumstances require it."[143] With the therapeutic debate conducted at this level, it is surprising that anyone put their faith in doctors. Apart from taking out blood, or putting in meaty food and fortified wine, they had few remedies. When they used anything powerful in the chemical line, they were liable to make appalling errors. Wellington complained that after he attended the trials of a new howitzer, he was left with a singing noise one ear. He went to Dr. John Stevenson (1778–1846), Britain's leading ear specialist. Stevenson poured in a solution of nitrate of silver, known as "lunar caustic," which completely deafened the Duke in one ear, caused intense pain and left him with a recurrent headache.[144]

As it was, quacks and peddlers of patent medicines flourished. One Godbold, a former gingerbread maker, produced a fraudulent compound with which he cleared £3,000 a year and bought himself a £30,000 house and park in Godalming. Sawinson, proprietor of the antiscorbutic, "Velno's Vegetable Syrup," likewise made enough to become the owner of a Twickenham estate which boasted a botanical garden. But at least he knew Latin and Greek, Farington noted, whereas Godbold was illiterate "and vulgar in conversation."[145] Most people dosed themselves but called in doctors when they felt they could afford it. A London doctor in high repute would cost you a guinea a visit. Carlisle, if called to operate "out of town," charged a guinea a mile to travel, plus £10 a day, or £70 a week. Private medical treatment could be just as ruinously expensive in the early 19th century as it is today. The Marquess of Cholmondely, in the course of an illness lasting 16–18 months, had to fork out fees of £2,700. Coutts, the banker, being old and often ill, thought it would be worth it to offer the Brighton practitioner Dr. Hooper £2,000 a year for life, to "attend him exclusively." But Hooper would not agree. On the other hand, doctors did not always get paid what they asked. When Dr. Pemberton spent months in northern Ireland trying to save Lord Hamilton from tuberculosis, all he was offered was a £200 annuity, which he turned down, since he said he "might die tomorrow" and had "left his practice in London and probably lost connections he might not recover." In the end he had to be content with a postdated bond for £2,000.[146] The worst payers were George III and his family. In theory a doctor summoned to Windsor, as a very large number were, got £20 a day retainer. But all grumbled they were never paid at all, or years in arearrs, after being forced to wait at the castle four days in the week to the neglect of their London practices. Sometimes they were given arbitrary sums in full settlement of their accounts. Thus Dumerque, the leading London dentist, who had attended the entire family for 18 months, put in a bill for £3,000. He was paid £1,500, take-it-or-leave it.[147]

There is no question, however, that, by the 1820s, successful doctors were already among the wealthiest section of the community. Dr. Alderson, practicing in Hull, realized £3,000 a year. Dr. Lubbock, of Norwich, aged 38 and the son of a baker, made an average of £4,000 a year. Dr. Matthew Baillie, probably the ablest physician in London until his death in 1823, made £10,000 a year or more, and at times rivaled Cooper's earnings. But such men were slaves to their profession. Alderson scarcely had time to eat a proper meal and "lived off Bohea and bread and butter." At various times Baillie complained to Farington that he had to work a 15- or 16-hour day and was "tired of it." If he were not able to spend "two months each summer at his house in Gloucester," he would soon "be under ground." He said he was "on duty 6.30 till 11pm at night" and when he got back "from rounds of visits, in morning and evening, has a quantity of letters to answer."[148]

Men like Baillie, who was exceptionally conscientious and would attend sick people for no charge if their means were slender, were setting new standards of behavior in a profession which was growing in wealth, in authority, and, above all, in numbers. Edinburgh quadrupled its output of new doctors in the early decades of the century: In the 1770s it was producing an average of only 213 a year; in 1820, its output was 1,139. There was a similar fourfold increase in the United States, 1790–1840, the key decade being the 1820s.[149] However limited medical knowledge might be, however inadequate the training, the greater availability of professional advice did make some difference. But if smallpox was now under control in advanced countries, other great scourges revealed the impotence of medical men. In Philadelphia; New York, Baltimore and, above all, New Orleans, yellow fever raged virtually unchecked during the 1820s. And the coming of cholera from the East, hitting Europe from 1829 to 1831 and the United States in 1832, was like a thunderclap, causing panic and demoralization everywhere.

Doctors were equally powerless when faced with mental disturbance, though it did not stop some of them from treating it with a variety of drastic methods. The age was both fascinated by madness, as the superb studies of Goya and Géricault suggest, and terrified of it. The secret practice of Dr. Johnson, who kept a padlock and chain so that Mrs. Thrale, his sole confidante, could bind him if he showed symptoms of madness, was by no means unusual. Madness and guilt were closely linked. Severe depression, as the case of Kierkegaard and his father makes plain, was not understood, least of all by those who suffered from it. Forms of mental disturbance were concealed, by the victim and by his or her family. The painter John Jackson, who married one of the daughters of James Ward, RA, did not discover she was "mad" until their wedding day.[150] Those who suffered from epilepsy, particularly if they were male, were pathetically anxious to hide it, since many doctors attributed it to masturbation or excessive sexual excitement. Epilepsy was unusually painful in the case of Tennyson's father, since he was a clergyman, Rector of Somerby in Lincolnshire, and his fits were frequent, once a week on average. His children were petrified of him, scattering at his approach, and there were frequent separations from his wife. He took refuge first in alcohol, then in opium.[151]

But if there was great ignorance of mental disturbance, society was compassionate toward the insane in ways we would find strange today. The family tended to accept responsibility for those of its members who became mentally ill. Even hopeless cases were kept at home, rather than buried and forgotten in institutions. Those who were put in asylums were visited, taken out and brought home for long spells. Charles Lamb's sister Mary suffered from recurrent bouts of insanity. In 1796 she stabbed her mother, who died of the wound. Her plea of insanity was accepted, and she was confined to an asylum until spring 1797, six months after the crime. Then, since she seemed to have recovered, Lamb was able to take her home. He looked after her for the rest of his life. Although her insanity returned from time to time, sometimes for months at a stretch, and he had to confine her in a private madhouse, she was thus enabled to lead a near-normal life and, indeed, to make a contribution to literature in the *Tales from Shakespeare,* one of the most popular children's books of the 19th century, which the Lambs wrote together.[152]

Lamb's fraternal devotion entailed sacrifice amounting to heroism. He fell in love with the actress Fanny Kelly (1790–1882), who often played Ophelia to Kean's Hamlet. By a horrible coincidence, a deranged admirer of hers, George Barnett, shot at her while she was performing at Drury Lane in February 1816, and some of the shot fell into the lap of Mary Lamb, who was in the audience. Three years later Lamb plucked up the courage to propose to Fanny, but she turned him down in a kind but firm letter, confiding to her syster Lydia that she could not bear the thought of a union "which would bring me into that atmosphere of sad mental uncertainty which surrounds [Lamb's] domestic life."[153] Neither ever married.

Keeping an acknowledged lunatic at home was not uncommon. The educationalist Joseph Lancaster refused to allow his wife to be committed; when she became violent, he "subjected her to severe hot-and-cold treatment."[154] There were many private asylums, where disturbed members of the family could be detained for a time, but they were not very secure places. David Davies, the deranged officer who shot and wounded Palmerston in 1818, had been confined to one but broke out and came to London; no effort was made to trace him. After his assassination attempt, he was found guilty but insane and detained "at pleasure." But he was evidently soon out, since three years later he wrote to his would-be victim asking to be reinstated in the army on full pay. Palmerston endorsed his letter"!!!!!."[155] But attitudes to madness were beginning to change. The Criminal Lunatics Act of 1800 began the modern penal approach to criminal lunacy, making it mandatory for the accused to be kept in strict custody in cases of murder, treason, and felony; if it had been on the statute book when Mary Lamb killed her mother, her brother could not have been given custody of her. Equally, there were the first hints of a more subtle penetration of the recesses and infirmities of the mind. In 1827 Johann Paul Friedrich Richter wrote in *Selina* of "the monstrous realm of the unconscious, the real inner Africa [of the soul]."[156]

Attitudes toward madness varied from country to country, but in most of the advanced countries, like Britain, the United States and France, state asylums were among the more progressive institutions, frequently visited by travelers. There was much less of a tendency than today to brush insanity under the carpet. If the House of Commons is any guide, many people who today would be treated as mentally disturbed were then classified as eccentrics, and their odd behavior was tolerated. In the period 1790–1820, for instance, members of the Commons included Lord Glerawdy, who was "once in Willis's care" (Dr. Francis Willis [1717–1807] specialized in treating mental disorders, looked after George III for a time and ran two private asylums). Other very odd members were Montague Mathew, a huge Irishman, who used to shout other speakers down in the chamber; Charles Trelawny, said to be "pathologically mean"; Nathaniel Halhead and Henry Drummond, both religious extremists who belonged to "prophetic" sects; the Earl of Bective, described as "a chattering, capering spindleshanked gaby"; Patrick Duigenan, who hated papists; Robert Deverell, an eccentric author; Sir John Macpherson, who wrote endless letters to members of the royal family; and John Pytches, who was driven mad by the gigantic dictionary he planned. Sir William Manners, Richard Wilson, William Cornwallis and William Beckford suffered from paranoia or persecution mania. All these men were allowed to carry on with their parliamentary duties, but about 20 members had to be forcibly committed to asylums during these years.[157]

In addition, seven MPs were judged to have committed suicide while their mental balance was upset. The increasing pace, industrialization, pressure, and complexity of life in the early decades of the 19th century was often seen as the cause both of insanity and of the suicides it so constantly produced. In France this theory appeared to receive confirmation when Henri Saint-Simon, the philosopher most associated with the modern age, particularly with industry, tried to kill himself. In the early 1820s, to finance his new philosophical system, he toured the French provinces, gouging cash out of industrialists, asking for 1,000 francs at a time, never small sums. Most slammed the door in his face; others accepted the brochures with which his pockets were crammed and even handed over money. He saw those who subscribed as members of a elite society with metaphysical overtones. At his headquarters above the Passage Hulot at 34 rue de Richelieu in Paris, crowds of similar eccentrics gathered: Captain Montgée, who designed floating mines and submarines; phrenologists like Dr. Gall, Dr. Broussais and Dr. Etienne-Marin Bailly, who was also an astronomer; and various more considerable men of science and letters. One of them described the place: "His apartment was a perfect model of most complete disorder. Not an unencumbered seat or chair. . . . On his desk were piled up books, papers, crusts of bread, dirty linen, various bottles."[158] By 9 March 1823, funds were low, and having written a despairing letter to the textile industrialist Ternaux and other subscribers, Saint-Simon loaded a pistol with seven bullets and tried to blow his brains out. A tradition in the movement claimed that he took out his watch and spent his last seven minutes on Earth having final thoughts about the organization of society. He managed to fire all seven shots, but they only grazed his skull, though one pierced his eye, which he lost.[159] The suicide attempt, which was much talked about, had the effect of bringing in considerable funds.

In Britain, substance was lent to the "modern bustle" theory of an increased suicide rate by a sudden crop among prominent MPs, beginning with the great liberal millionaire Samuel Whitbread in 1815; continuing with Sir Samuel Romilly, an outstanding lawyer and one of the Whig leaders, in 1818; and Castlereagh himself in 1822. Sixteen other members also committed suicide in the years 1790–1820.[160] But if we look at individual cases, there is no clear evidence to support the "bustle" theory. Whitbread, according to his doctor Sir Henry Halford, was worried by his health and by the fact that people he had persuaded to invest money in the rebuilt Drury Lane were at a loss because it could not pay a dividend.[161] In Romilly's case the explanation was clear: He had been shattered by the illness and death of his wife, to whom he was devoted, and which occurred in the most distressing possible circumstances. He cut his throat with a razor four days later.[162]

There is a mystery about Castlereagh's suicide, since he had always seemed to his friends to be happy, equable and well balanced. Castlereagh had indeed a fierce will to live, attested by the fact that he twice saved himself from drowning.[163] Mrs. Arbuthnot, one of his closest friends, on whom he had called for a chat almost every other day from early in her marriage, wrote a long entry in her diary on 29 August 1822, immediately after he, like Romilly, cut his throat, surveying the events which led up to it. The strain of running the Commons was clearly one factor. Although parliamentary sessions were much shorter than today, the pressure they put on key ministers was much greater while they lasted. No one today would think of combining the duties of foreign secretary and leader of the House, which was what Castlreagh, who loved both, insisted on doing. Shortly before his suicide, he had told Mrs. Arburthnot that he had been "completely knocked up by the Session. It had fagged him so excessively that frequently he had not been able to get out of bed till 2 or 3 o'clock"; he had sometimes not called on her because he had only just got up in time to go to the Commons. He was "excessively disgusted" with the treatment of him by the country-gentlemen members and found himself "always languid and worn and out of spirit."

One of the nasty aspects of early 19th-century society was the habit of sending anonymous letters (and inserting them in newspapers). On 5 August, a week before the suicide, Castlereagh called on Mrs. Arbuthnot, took her hand and asked her "in the most earnest manner" that if she had ever heard anything against him, to tell him "with no false delicacy." She admitted: "I had often heard he was a great flirt & very fond of ladies." He then "told me that about three years ago he had had an anonymous letter threatening to reveal he had been seen to go into an improper house." At that point they were interrupted, but the next day he called again and admitted to her that three years ago "he did go with a woman to an improper house, from which he was watched by a man, who the next morning wrote to tell him so & ask for a place." He said he had taken no notice at the time, but now thought "the purport of the letters was to accuse him of a crime not to be named [homosexuality] and this notion could not be put out of his head."[164] From that point on, he developed clear signs of paranoia, accusing various people, such as the Duke of Wellington and his own wife, of being in a conspiracy against him. Wellington told Mrs. Arbuthnot: "what a shock it was to him to see a man with so strong and calm a mind in a state bordering on insanity." Efforts to prevent him from hurting himself were at last taken, but on 12 August he used a small, concealed knife to sever the carotid artery in his neck. Wellington investigated the blackmail business and found it baseless, and it is clear from the deterioration of Castlereagh's handwriting from June 1822 onwards that the origin of his distress was physiological, not external.[165]

Suicide statistics in Europe for the early 19th century are not satisfactory and provide no proof that it was on the increase as a proportion of all deaths. Many prominent people killed themselves, or attempted to do so, from Bonaparte (who made an attempt in 1814 though not, curiously enough, after Waterloo) to poor Auger, the perpetual secretary of the Academie Française, who killed himself in a fit of depression at the triumph of romantic over classical-style literature. There were innumerable suicide attempts by women, such as Mary Wollstonecraft and Mrs. Cobbett, as a result of broken love affairs or family rows. Shelley's first abandoned wife may have been pregnant when she threw herself into the Thames, and he seems to have had a hand in the distress that drove Fanny Imlay to kill herself (he also made at least one suicide attempt).[166] Young women who committed suicide in the years 1815–30 were usually pregnant or abandoned or both.

Men who committed suicide had a variety of motives. The unfortunate Sir Richard Croft, the gynecologist in charge when Princess Charlotte died, was driven to kill himself by widespread public criticism, which probably accounts also for the suicide of Dr. André, the surgeon at Petworth.[167] Melancholy (often an early 19th-century synonym for guilt), caused by excessive religious zeal, was a common cause. Thus, the wealthy Mr. Stovin of Yorkshire, said to be "Methodistical," shot himself because he was "married to a beautiful woman whose sentiments on religious subjects did not agree with his."[168] Still more common was despair provoked by gambling losses. Sir John Bland shot himself in France after losing £34,000 at a sitting to Lord Inchiquin. Lord Cornwallis's aide de camp, Captain Parish, threw himself overboard from the Leinster packet ship after a similar disastrous session. Boswell's friend, the Hon. Andrew Erskine, took the same course. So did Colonel Buckeridge, who shot himself in his dressing room, leaving a wife and four children.[169] There are, naturally, some cases when a suicide is described as "unaccountable." But by far the biggest single reason for suicides among men was debt and business failure. One failed merchant threw himself out of a window at Hampton Court Palace. Another went to Windsor Great Park and shot himself there. Others took overdoses of such drugs as laudanum. Pistols and razors were, for men, the usual means. There was a crop of business suicides during the financial crisis of 1816, and another in the wake of the crisis of 1825–26.[170]

Early 19th-century doctors did not know how to treat those with suicidal tendencies other than by removing possible weapons. Sometimes potential suicides were "lowered"; Castlereagh, for instance, was bled several times when paranoid symptoms appeared. But doctors, it is only too clear, were baffled by many forms of illness. Indeed, they were baffled and frustrated by the general state of health, much of it, as they were only too painfully aware, caused by poverty. Most doctors now associate dirt with disease and advocate frequent washing. But Philippe Loutherbourg was looked upon as unusual, not least among artists, because "he washes himself all over every morning."[171] Still more unusual was the Lancashire farmhouse in which the great poor-law reformer Edwin Chadwick was born in 1801, where every child was washed every day. The time had not come when the German nationalist historian Heinrich von Treitschke would tell his Berlin students, "The English think soap is civilization," but their attitudes to washing already cut them off from most Continental nations, and indeed the United States, where English travelers found conditions in all but the newest hotels, and the failure to provide soap in any of them, unacceptable. The stress placed on cleanliness and constant bathing by dandies like Beau Brummell and Lord Byron was an important factor.

Byron's example also encouraged swimming, and that was one general health-giving form of therapy the doctors could prescribe. The success of Brighton sea bathing, simply by encouraging people to take more outdoor exercise, was marked, led to a crop of imitations and had an appreciable effect in improving public health, at least of the middle- and upper classes who could afford to patronize the new resorts. The old spa-baths and mud-resorts, to be found by their hundreds all over Europe, probably increased the quantity of ailments on balance by huddling patients together in highly unsanitary conditions, where they paid by the limb to be put in hot mud or often filthy water (7½d per leg at Saint Armand in Belgium, or 15d for the whole body) or drank the waters out of glasses that were seldom washed. By 1820, for this and other reasons, famous spas like Bath were in manifest decline. The income of the master of ceremonies had fallen from £2,500 a year to £1,000, and it was no longer possible to see or meet fashionable people in the public rooms—they attended private parties or did not patronize the spa.[172]

In contrast, sea resorts were multiplying. There was, for instance, Cromer, strongly recommended by Mr. Perry, Mr. Woodhouse's medical adviser in *Emma:* "The best of all the sea-bathing places. A fine open sea, he says, and very pure air."[173] When Farington was there, he discovered it had 49 houses and lodgings to be let to sea bathers, varying in price from half a guinea a week to 5½. "The air with all its freshness circulates without interruption," he noted, and "it has all the privacy of a country village."[174] Near Lyme was Charmouth, another resort praised by Jane Austen (in *Persuasion*), where modest-size houses were being built or converted for the retirement of people of "independent means." "We did not recollect," enthused Farington, "to have before seen a village where neatness & comfort were so manifest"—the first example in history indeed of a gentrified village.[175] By 1815 Torquay was already in the process of creation by Sir Lawrence Palk, grandson of a butcher and son of an Indian nabob. Palk "found only a few cottages" there but, "at great expense," he "built rows of neat houses, a fine pier on the south side to form a harbour," and "made walks upon the hills which surround the place."[176] This one-man creation of a new seaside resort was by no means unique. At Bournemouth, a landowner-entrepreneur L. D. C. Tregonwell built the first house on what had been a virgin site in 1810. By August 1824 Mrs. Arbuthnot was reporting: "I rode one day to a place called Bournemouth which are a collection of hills lately planted by a gentleman of the name of Tregonwell, who had built four or five beautiful cottages which he lets to persons who go for the sea-bathing. . . . I half agreed to take one next summer."[177] It is typical of Jane Austen's sharp eye for trends that the protagonist of her last, unfinished novel, *Sanditon,* Mr. Parker, is just such a pioneer: "The success of Sanditon as a small, fashionable Bathing Place was the object, for which he seemed to live," transforming "a quiet village" into "a profitable Speculation."[178]

By 1815, then, many physicians, such as Mr. Perry, were prescribing sea bathing, often recommending one resort and condemning others (Mr. Perry had no time for Southend, where the air was "very bad"). But much, perhaps most, of their advice centered on food and drink. In the towns, water was not usually safe to drink in this period. It had to be treated in some way. In northern Europe and North America they drank beer and in southern Europe, wine. In London, beer was now brewed in industrial quantities. Meux's Brewery, one of the biggest, constructed a colossal receptacle, 65 feet in diameter and 27 feet deep, at a cost of £510,000, which would hold 20,000 barrels of porter.[179] An agricultural laborer's family would drink two quarts of beer a day, five in August; but most of this beer was brewed at home. Increasingly, however, women were turning to tea and persuading their husbands to do the same. Tea drinking was not approved of by many doctors. The great Dr. Baillie told Lady Beaumont that *wine* and *tea* were great causes of human destruction."[180] Cobbett, in his *Cottage Economy,* put it more strongly: Tea was "a destroyer of health, an enfeebler of the frame, an engenderer of effeminacy and laziness, a debaucher of youth and a maker of misery for old age . . . the gossip of the tea-table is no bad preparatory school for the brothel."[181] Tea was brewed very strongly, and at 3s, 4s, or even 5s a pound, was not cheap. Medical opinion relented when in the 1820s the practice began of making a much weaker brew. Tea consumption was also increasing in the United States, at the expense of spirits. But even more in demand was coffee: from 1800 to the 1840s, Americans increased their coffee consumption by an astonishing 500 percent.[182] Doctors did not like that trend either.

The doctors' attitude toward alcoholic drinks varied. Drs. Baillie and Carlisle did not prescribe wine at all; indeed Carlisle never touched it (though he was a great trencherman). Other doctors would "raise" patients by prescribing port, madeira, Cape wine and other cordials (the unfortunate Croft was attempting to "raise" Princess Charlotte with a mixture of wine and brandy when he found she was dead). By 1820 everyone in London agreed that drinking was very much on the decline, by the standards of the late 18th century. Dr. Addington, Prime Minister, then Home Secretary, drank "perhaps 20 glasses of wine at his dinner" to "invigorate himself" before going to the Commons (but these would have been small, triangular-shaped glasses). Louis XVIII drank four bottles of port at dinner. Pitt drank only a pint of wine at dinner, but would "eat a wing of fowl in the evening" and "drink two or three tumblers of strong port wine and water." Dr. George Fordyce of Essex Street, one of the most "knowledgeable" doctors in London, "drank a bottle at dinner, one after dinner and one at supper" (he lived to be 65). But all these men were really 18th-century figures.[183] And, indeed, Pitt's doctors were anxious to stop him drinking any wine at supper. Many doctors went further and thought supper should not be eaten at all. That was because dinner was getting later and later and supper was now really unnecessary and kept people up late. Mr. Wood-house "liked to see the cloth laid" because "it had been the custom of his youth," but he compromised by trying to stop people eating anything set upon it.[184]

Doctors tried to get healthy people to eat less. They disapproved of the "great turtle dinners" of the City and the Bar, where merchants and lawyers competed to see who could eat the most plates of turtle soup, which included great greasy gobbets of highly flavored turtle meat. "Sir James Sylvester, recorder of London, the great gourmet of the Bar, confessed he was beaten by Lord Ellenborough when it came to eating turtle." The millionaire Mr. Penrice of Yarmouth, who inherited all Lord Chedworth's vast estates in Gloucester, achieved an unrivaled reputation as a "great eater" and "killed himself by overeating." Over-eating rich food also did in the famous Dr. Parr, "the Whig Dr. Johnson" in 1825. Middle-aged clergymen, like Parr and the Rev. Sydney Smith, were probably the greediest men in London in the years after 1815. Worst of all was the Rev. Dr. Lawrence who, at a dinner at the Duke of Portland's, "ate a whole plate of orange chips, believed to be poisonous in such quantity"; he was ill for a month. The Rev. Dr. Paley, the great theologian, was another example; he "would eat from all the main dishes and the side-dishes too—he called it skirmishing." But the aesthetes were greedy as well. R. Payne Knight would "take five or six eggs at breakfast; his rival, Uvedale Price, always had his own breakfast at eight, then if staying in a house where formal breakfast was served, would eat another, bigger one, at eleven.[185] At dinner Price was "so intent on eating" that he resented "anyone putting a question to him." When traveling he brought his own bread from his estate at Foxley. People were particular about their bread in England, and visitors noticed how fine it often was. Talma, the great French tragedian, who spoke excellent English, took up a piece of bread while dining with the Kembles and said, "How well you in England may be contented while you have such bread as this to eat, while in Paris there is no bread but coarse black bread."[186]

This superfine bread, however, was criticized by the first modern dietitian. In the 1820s the Bostonian Sylvester Graham began to campaign against overwhite bread. He argued that it was made from superrefined flour, which eliminated the healthiest ingredients. His approach was well in advance of his times. He disapproved of "the superabundance of animal food," which characterized diets in wealthy, advanced societies, and their excess of sauces, spices and stimulants. In the 1830s he was to publish the first dietary magazine, the *Graham Journal of Health and Longevity*.[187] English ideas on diet varied as much as they do today. One expert whom Farington consulted recommended no wine, "roasted apples for supper," "white biscuits instead

of bread," no "webb-footed animals," venison and game instead
of beef and mutton, no pork whatever, but plenty of "salmon, mack-
erell . . . whitings, soles, haddocks, turbot, all good." "He asked me if
I had warm feet, I said, Yes. *That*, he replied, was a good sign."[188]
George III, on the other hand, recommended simplicity, as the record
of a conversation he had with Lord Galloway revealed. George III:
"You have grown very round in the belly." Galloway: "I take a great
deal of exercise which makes me hungry and causes me to eat heartily."
George III: "I also take a great deal of exercise but when I sit down at
table I fix my eye on some one dish and dine off that *alone*. Your horse,
my lord, takes a great deal of exercise but he feeds simply and does not
grow round-bellied."[189] Byron, when dieting, avoided all meat and lived
mainly on boiled potatoes in vinegar. Many men, when trying to slim
down, ate only fish and dessert. Some limited themselves to two ounces
of meat a day. Kemble gave up drink and ate nothing on a day he was
performing, having his first food only after the play. Dr. Jenner, another "expert" on diet, told Lysons, the keeper of the records in the
Tower, to eat only meat and bread, no vegetables; no wine or malt
liquor either, and above all "no study."[190] Dr. Jackson, dean of Christ
Church, lived off milk. Sir Joseph Banks, president of the Royal Society,
was a vegetarian and teetotaler, eating nothing but puddings and boiled
vegetables.

Even in advanced countries, early 19th-century society was composed of many who got too little to eat (and drink; in winter, alcohol
was essential to those living in cold, unheated and often damp dwellings), and some who habitually ate and drank too much. The way in
which food was served, among those who had plenty, encouraged
overeating. There were usually only two courses at dinner, spread all
over the table, the second including sweet dishes. The standard work
on general household management, Elizabeth Raffald's *The Experienced English Housekeeper*, first published in 1769 and in its 13th
edition by 1815, shows a table layout of 25 dishes for the first course
and 25 for the second. The first course consisted of various soups, then
heavy meat joints, entire large fishes, pies and vegetables. The second
course included venison, game, poultry, hams, savory dishes, and various puddings, such as fishpond, moonshine, floating (and rocky) islands, sponge cakes, ornamental jellies, flummeries and syllabubs.[191] A
diner who regularly went skirmishing among these 50 dishes, like Dr.
Paley, was bound to become obese. Farington, who gave the main
course layouts for all the dinners he held at his house in 1808, showed
that even in a modest middle-class entertainment, for close family and

friends, it was usual to serve soup, fish, roasts, game and pies, often with several varieties of each.[192]

In the 1820s a new method of serving dinner, à la russe, was just coming into vogue among the more fashionable people. This was the modern system of serving each dish consecutively. It was reckoned to be vastly more expensive, since it required more servants and involved more "made" dishes, which could be properly concocted only by professional cooks trained in French cuisine, as opposed to preparing joints; hence such dinners were often sent in from professional caterers, which made them very expensive indeed. Resistance to dinners à la russe was very strong in England. A traditionalist like Anthony Trollope, born in April 1815, just before Waterloo, was still fighting a rearguard action in favor of the traditional spread in the 1850s and 1860s and attacking the Russian method in his novels; but by then he was defending a lost cause.[193] The French, with their fondness for what the English called "made" dishes and their brilliance at preparing them, were much quicker to adopt the multicourse service. Even in the 1820s, the English already had a reputation for "dull" food, that is, simple joints. While Talleyrand, as Foreign Minister and as Ambassador in London, spent an hour every morning with his chef, the Duke of Wellington, the representative Englishman, could not keep his famous French chef Félix, who left in anger, saying: "I serve him a dinner which would make Udé or Francatelli burst with envy, and he says nothing. I serve him a dinner badly dressed by the cook-maid, and he says nothing. I cannot live with such a master, were he a hero a hundred times over."[194] On the other hand, cookery books were beginning to sell well in England: John Murray was happy to give 2,000 guineas for the copyright of Mrs. Rundell's New System of Domestic Cookery, first published in 1819. And in serving breakfast, at least, the British were already accorded a special place. The German traveler Puckler-Muskau was served at a Welsh inn in the 1820s "smoking coffee, fresh guinea-fowl's eggs, deep yellow mountain butter, thick cream, toasted muffins, two red-spotted trout just caught, all produced on a snow-white tablecloth of Irish damask."[195]

However dinner was served or cooked, by the 1820s the medical profession was exerting pressure on people to eat less and to drink less. If the consumption of alcohol was on the decline in Britain, as most people believed, it was due not so much to improved morals as to higher duties. Drinking could be a problem in the House of Commons.[196] In the 1820s, however, MPs became much more sober. It was a different story in the United States, where the Vice President, Daniel D. Tomkin, had to be persuaded to leave Washington in 1822 because he could no longer perform his duties as presiding officer of the Senate. Other victims of alcoholism were Van Buren's brilliant protégé Samuel Talcott, Attorney General of New York; Erastus Root, the New York Lieutenant Governor; and Silas Wright, Senator and Governor. An interesting bill has survived for the dinner that Andrew Jackson gave on 18 February 1825, to thank 22 supporters for their work during the recent election. Washington's Franklin House Hotel charged him $46 for the 23-place dinner; the liquor, which included bowls of "apple-toddy" and punch, champagne, wine, brandy, whisky and cider, came to $48.65. The guests seemed to have consumed 14 bottles of wine, as well as four pints of spirits.[197] Spirit drinking was much more a problem in the United States than in Europe; by the late 1820s, American men were drinking, per capita, a yearly average of four gallons of pure, 200-proof alcohol. This, in turn, produced a reaction. The American temperance movement dates back to 1810, but it was in 1826, with the foundation of the American Temperance Society, that the drive for prohibition first acquired national dynamism, a portent of the future. By 1840, the temperance movement had already reduced per capita consumption from 4 gallons to 1.5.[198]

The big change, on both sides of the Atlantic, was the "improvement" in female habits. Snuff taking, very common among women up to about 1810, had gone almost entirely by 1830. It was an expensive and mainly a rich woman's habit. Poorer women smoked pipes. Horace Greeley (1811–72), creator of the *New York Tribune,* said that during his New Hampshire boyhood, around 1820, "it was often my filial duty to fill and light my mother's pipe." General Jackson's wife smoked a pipe until her death in 1828. So did Sir Robert Peel's grandmother.[199] But by the 1820s pipe smoking among women was confined to the elderly. Girls saw it as a "dirty" male activity. Cigarettes, in their turn, would attract women back to smoking, but in the early 19th century cigarette smoking was almost entirely confined to Spanish-speaking countries, though it was creeping into French habits. The Anglo-Saxon world did not begin to adopt the cigarette until the 1850s. In the meantime, smoking had been virtually banned from middle- and upper-class houses, unless they were large enough to have an isolated room for the purpose. The new rail companies reinforced the prohibition when, right from the start, they refused to allow smoking in first-class carriages because it upset the ladies. By the late 1820s, smoking in England was rapidly becoming an all-male, largely outdoor activity, and in New England, at least, the Americans were following suit. One of the criticisms of Dr. Parr was that he "smoked in the vestry."

By the 1820s, then, smoking was beginning to attract disapproval.

With drug taking, opinion was divided, confused and ill-informed. Drug addiction, indeed, was not yet recognized as a social problem, though the evidence suggests it was serious and widespread. The difficulty was that opium, in various forms, was the one really powerful and effective instrument the medical profession possessed. Surveying the pharmacopoeia around 1815, the great surgeon Astley Cooper said: "Give me opium, tartarised antimony, sulphate of magnesia, calomel and bank, and I would ask for little else."[200] It is significant that he put opium at the head of the list; almost every other physician and surgeon would have done the same.

Opium had been known to man for about 6,000 years. It is essentially the dried juice of the poppy, *Papaver simniferum*, a white flower growing to between one and two feet. The unripe heads are cut, and the milky juice that comes out is collected and allowed to dry. This crude drug, the stuff available in the early 19th century, contains a large number of alkaloids, of which the most important is morphine, 10 percent of the total alkaloid content.[201] Its use to soothe pain, induce sleep and promote a sense of well-being in patients had been recognized by doctors for millennia. The 16th-century doctor Paracelsus prescribed it a great deal, and he first used the term laudanum. Tincture (the liquid form) of laudanum was pioneered as a treatment by Dr. Thomas Sydenham in the 1660s. "God," he wrote, "has granted to the human race, as a comfort in their afflictions, no medicine of the value of opium, either in regard to the number of diseases it can control, or its efficiency in extirpating them. . . . Medicine would be a cripple without it."[202] This was still the general opinion of doctors in the early 19th century. The pleasurable aspects of opium were also appreciated, and as far back as the early 18th century, Dr. John Jones, author of *The Mysteries of Opium Reveal'd* (1700), had discussed and treated addiction. In 1793, Dr. Samuel Crumpe, who said he frequently took opium himself, wrote an important treatise on the drug, describing the characteristics both of addiction and withdrawal, but at no point did he condemn its use, even without medical supervision.[203]

Crumpe's attitude was understandable. Many, perhaps most, people could not usually afford to seek medical advice even from lowly apothecaries. That was the main reason why opium, along with other drugs, such as they were, was freely on sale, until the 1868 Pharmacy Act in Britain, and much later in most countries. Opium came in innumerable guises. The commonest was laudanum, or tincture of opium, which was mixed with distilled water or various forms of alcohol. There was also a camphorated tincture, known as paregoric. And there were many proprietory brands, such as Dover's Powder, much used in hospitals, in which opium was mixed with licorice; saltpeter; tartar and ipecac; Battley's Sedative solution, a sleeping draught of opium; calcium hydrate; sherry; alcohol and water; and Godfrey's Cordial, a similar draught for children, based on laudanum. Dr. Collis Brown's Chlorodyne, which proved the most durable—it is still on sale now, though diluted—did not come into use until later in the century, and contained the new "miracle drug," chloroform.

In the period 1815–30 the procedure was for the raw opium to be imported by a wholesale drug house, which either made its own preparations or sold it to licensed apothecaries. The Apothecaries Company gradually accumulated a selection of 26 opium preparations. William Allen of Plough Court, London, had 20 on his list in 1811. These preparations were comparatively cheap at wholesale rates—a box of 100 poppy capsules for less than 2 shillings, a three-dozen case of bottled opium draughts for 10 shillings. Wholesale goods went out by parcel post or on carrier's carts to local shops. Many local proprietary preparations, like the famous Kendal Black Drop, four times the strength of laudanum, were also generally available. Most apothecaries stocked not only tincture or camphorated laudanum but pills, lozenges, powders, plasters, "wines" and "vinegars," enemas and liniments, all of which contained opium. Some apothecaries were responsible about selling these products; they would question would-be purchasers and refused to sell to children. But every corner shop in the country sold the most popular preparations to anyone who could pay for them, including children. Laudanum, at 20–25 drops a penny, or 3d an ounce, was sold everywhere, by London costermongers and street traders, in pubs, by midwives, and by all grocers.

Bottled laudanum and opium in pillboxes were kept in most houses. Families often had their own laudanum-based recipes, handed down from mother to daughter, and used them for a vast variety of complaints, internal and external. Opium was widely used for sick children—corner shops carried notices, "Children's Draughts, a Penny Each"—and fractious babies. Mistakes were inevitable. The number of children, especially babies, who died from accidental overdoses is unknown but was clearly large. Sir Henry Maine (1822–88) was nearly killed as an infant by his anxious mother and aunt who administered an overdose of opium. He was lucky, surviving to become a great legal historian. Most overdosed babies simply went into convulsions and died. At Wisbech, in the Fen country, the doping of babies was responsible for excessive infantile death rates, as high as 206 per 1,000 even in the 1860s.[204]

The Fen country was notorious for opium taking in the 19th century, being one of the few places in Western Europe where white poppies were commonly grown. They had long been cultivated in physic gardens attached to hospitals. In the 1790s Dr. John Ball tried to grow them commercially at Williton in Somerset, reporting to the Society of Arts in 1794: "I think amazing quantities are [now] consumed every year, and am of opinion there is 20 times more opium used now in England only, than there was 15 or 20 years since, as great quantities are now used in outward applications, and it is continually advancing in price." He found the growing of opium to be labor intensive and experimented with child labor. Women, especially unemployed lace makers, were used at a successful opium farm at Winslow, Buckinghamshire. Medical and horticultural societies offered prizes for agricultural innovators who succeeded in growing "safe" opium, for example, from lettuce. In 1813 Dr. Howison, a former inspector of opium in Bengal, won the Caledonian horticultural society's prize by growing a double-red garden poppy in Scotland. In 1820 John Young got the Royal Society of Arts medal for successfully cultivating lettuce-opium, getting 56 pounds of high-quality opium an acre, with a profit of £50–£80 an acre.[205] But in the Fens, where suffering from rheumatism was universal and opium was a sovereign remedy, most people grew it in their gardens and used the dried juice for homemade poppy-head tea. Ely was known as the "opium-eating city." The stuff grown locally was poor quality, so more was imported. South Lincolnshire, Cambridgeshire, Huntingdon and the Isle of Ely probably accounted for half England's opium imports. Women and children were the biggest consumers, but everyone seems to have taken it occasionally. In Wisbech, you went into a shop, put a penny on the counter, the shopkeeper asked "The best?" you nodded, and a package of opium was handed over. The propensity in these parts was well known—Charles Kingsley has a passage on Fenland opium eating in *Alton Locke* (1850).[206]

The Fenland was exceptional, but most people in early 19th-century Britain dosed themselves with opium at some point in their lives. Farington took it in 1800 when he was "much lowered" by the death of his wife: "While I have taken laudanum it has supported my spirits a little, but having left it off I am fallen back to a most depressed state."[207] With his intense concern for all medical matters, he noted many instances when people took opium, and wherever possible he listed the dosage in his diary. Thus, a friend, Mrs. Batty, took "70 drops of laudanum daily." Another friend, the Rev. Dr. Cookson, took a daily dose of 100 drops, "to suppress the pain in his prostate." George IV took "250 drops" to get to sleep at night. Charles James Fox also took opium to sleep, but during the day, after being kept up at night in the Commons (the quantity is not given). Another friend, Mrs. Spicer, "takes drops by the spoonful," 100 drops per spoon, and she takes six spoonfuls. The Irish painter Francis Wheatley (always in trouble of one kind or another) "has lately taken 300 drops of laudanum in 24 hours . . . in brandy, to counteract effects of a paralytic kind." But at least he took them "by Dr Pitcairn's advice." Other habitual opium users simply swigged away, according to Farington's record. The wicked old Earl of Lonsdale measured it out "by the finger." Samuel Johnson's former friend, Topham Beauclerk, "took it regularly in vast quantities"; no wonder Horace Walpole told Farington that Beauclerk was "the worst-tempered man he ever knew." The Duke of Cumberland also took it "in enormous quantities."

According to Farington's entries, the range of maladies for which opium, or rather laudanum, was self-administered was very wide. One friend took it for "a nervous tic," another, the architect Robert Smirke, for "his Old Disorder" (probably a stricture in the penis). The actor Charles Kemble took it "before going on stage" to "keep down his asthma." Lord Grey, the Whig leader, took laudanum (and ether) for his "stomach complaint." Farington recorded a case of a clergyman who tried to kill himself by swallowing a bottle of laudanum and of a judge who died after what was probably an accidental overdose. But the only instance he noted in which pleasure was supposed to be the motive was the case of Henri Fuseli, widely supposed to take opium in order to induce the hallucinatory images of his drawings. When he asked Fuseli, however, the painter replied he did indeed use the drug but just to "induce sleep."[208]

There is evidence that writers and artists at this time, and later, took opium in various forms. When Byron's wife, thinking him insane, searched his belongings, she found a bottle of Black Drop (as well as a copy of De Sade's *Justine*). Shelley took laudanum, so did Keats, in the years 1819–20, and thought of it for suicide. While Sir Walter Scott was writing *The Bride of Lammermoor* (1818–19), he was taking 200 drops of laudanum and six grains of opium daily.[209] Elizabeth Barrett Browning began to take opium at an early stage in her life. She wrote to Mary Russell Mitford: "It *is* a blessed thing! Opium—opium—night after night!' Her husband was disturbed, when they married, to discover "sleep only came to her in a red hood of poppies." But she dispensed with opium when she was pregnant. Jane Carlyle was also a regular user, as was Wilkie Collins: "Who was the man who invented laudanum?" he wrote, "I thank him from the bottom of my heart."[210] But in all these cases, opium was taken to mask pain, alleviate sickness or cure insomnia, rather than for artistic or frivolous reasons. There was sometimes an artistic side-effect. James Thomson's *City of Dreadful Night* (1874) certainly reflected opium taking, though it was taken by Thomson to induce sleep, and some of the power of *Edwin Drood* (1870) comes from Dickens's experience of laudanum, though there, again, insomnia was the reason for taking it.

The more we look over the records of the early 19th century, the more addicts we discover, though in virtually every case the drug was first taken for medicinal reasons. William Wilberforce was originally prescribed opium for colitis in 1788. He became an addict, and 30 years later, in 1818, he was still taking a four-grain pill three times a day. He apparently was repeatedly treated by doctors to break the habit, but without success. George IV was probably a mild addict, though his use of the drug was almost inextricably mixed up with the excessive consumption of alcohol, which became marked in the 1820s. Laudanum was a much-used hangover cure, and Wellington complained of the King: "He drinks spirits morning, noon and night, and he is obliged to take laudanum to calm the irritation which the use of the spirits occasions."[211] Forms of opium, often in large quantities, were taken to alleviate the many horrors of India, and Englishmen who went there frequently came back addicts, usually mild, sometimes serious, ones. That had been the tragedy of Robert Clive, who died in a fit after doubling his customary dose.

A typical early 19th-century case of addiction was Sir James Mackintosh (1765–1832), one of the ablest men of the time, whose career fizzled out. The brilliant son of a needy army officer, he studied medicine at Edinburgh, took to law, wrote a good deal, and went out to India with the plum job of Recorder of Bombay, worth £5,000 a year. He almost certainly took opium first as a student, but by the time he came back from India in 1812, with a pension of £1,200 a year, he was an incurable addict. He was Professor of Law at Haileybury College, the training center for Indian service, Rector of Glasgow University (a sinecure), and a member of Parliament, 1813–32, but despite many predictions about his political future, it never materialized. Thomas Creevey wrote of him as "an indolent, thoughtless, innocent sort of man who will be continually in scrapes, and who will not get forward with all his extraordinary talents unless somebody take him up and push him on." Bulwer, referring to his writing, as well as to his political career, wrote that "no man, doing so little, ever went through a long life continually creating the belief that he would ultimately do so much." Earl Grey wrote: "With all his extraordinary talents he was, practically, quite useless," and when he became Prime Minister in 1830, he said he found it "impossible" to give Mackintosh anything more than a seat on the Board of Control (which ran India under a president, the effective minister).[212] The phrases which crop up again and again with reference to Mackintosh are that he lacked "superior energy of character" and showed "habitual indolence," the second almost certainly a code phrase for drug addiction.

It is significant that early in the century Mackintosh was associated with the Bristol-Clifton circle of Dr. Thomas Beddoes, who had a lifelong interest in powerful drugs. He had been a disciple of Dr. John Brown and edited his *Elements of Medicine,* which deals at length with opiates and was widely read, not least among literary men.[213] Mackintosh was related by marriage to Tom Wedgwood, the early photographic experimenter, who took opium to ease the pain of "a diseased lower gut" and likewise became an addict. Both were friends of Robert Hall, the well-known Baptist preacher, who took 120 drops a day, and Charles Lloyd, another addict. All belonged to the Beddoes circle. Brown had argued, in his book, that opium helped to prolong the state of imaginative excitability he called "the vital process," that is, artistic creativity, and it may be that Beddoes's Pneumatic Institution in Clifton, though primarily founded to produce a cure for tuberculosis and other lung complaints, was also a center for experiments with drugs not just for therapy but for artistic stimulation. When Humphry Davy worked for Beddoes, both at the institution and its associated hospital, which he helped to create, he conducted many experiments with what they called "factitious airs" or "artificial airs," of which nitrous oxide or "laughing gas" was one. Davy recorded after taking the gas: "A thrilling, extending from the chest to the extremities, was almost immediately produced. I felt a sense of tangible extension highly pleasurable in every limb; my visual impressions were dazzling, and apparently magnified, I heard distinctly every sound in the room, and was perfectly aware of my situation. By degrees as the pleasurable sensation increased, I lost all connection with external things; trains of vivid visible images rapidly passed through my mind and were connected with words in such a manner as to produce perceptions perfectly novel. I existed in a world of newly connected and newly modified ideas. I theorised. I imagined I made discoveries."[214] This passage is particularly interesting because it anticipates by 150 years the illusions entertained by mid-20th-century literary men who experimented with hallucinatory drugs in the belief that they would expand their artistic perceptions.

*   *   *

It is at this point that Coleridge joins the story. Like Mackintosh and the other members of the Beddoes circle, he had read Brown and had been intrigued with his references to "the vital process." Like Davy, he was fascinated by dreams and visions and anxious to induce them. Davy tried the nitrous oxide on his patients who suffered from paralysis and noted their reactions. One said: "I felt like the sound of a harp." But he persisted in taking the oxide and other preparations himself. He sometimes "respired six quarts of newly-prepared nitrous oxide."[215] He was reckless, as scientists who experiment on themselves sometimes are—J. B. S. Haldane was an outstanding example in the 20th century—and he encouraged Coleridge, who often joined him at Clifton, to be reckless, too. Coleridge inhaled the gas deliberately after a heavy dinner, Davy after drinking a bottle of wine in fewer than eight minutes; they both used it to cure hangovers. They drew others into their experiments. Coleridge's brother-in-law Robert Southey wrote to Tom Southey: "Davy has actually invented a new pleasure. . . . Oh Tom, I am going for more this evening! It makes one strong and so happy!"[216]

The circle used other drugs besides laughing gas. Tom Wedgwood, for example, was anxious to sample Bang, then the term used for pot or Indian hemp. When he asked Davy to get him some, Davy referred him to Beddoes, who, he said, had just got a consignment from the East Indies. In 1803 Coleridge got a small packet of Bang from Sir Joseph Banks and wrote to Wedgwood (17 February 1803): "We will have a fair trial of *Bang*—do bring down some of the Hyoscyamine Pills—& I will give a fair trial of opium, hensbane, & Nepenthe. Bye the bye, I always considered Home's account of the *Nepenthe* as a *Banging* lie."[217] The exchanges of letters between Davy and Coleridge make it clear that although both were interested in the therapeutic qualities of drugs, both also took drugs for aesthetic and even self-indulgent reasons. Davy was then planning a huge epic poem about Moses; wrote tales with a morbid note; and, like Keats, induced in himself union-with-all-living-things trances in which, he wrote, "I should have felt pain in tearing a leaf from one of the trees." It seems likely that he and Coleridge experimented with opium together. While Davy was helping to prepared for the press the second edition of *Lyrical Ballads*, Coleridge wrote to him from the Lake District: "My dear fellow, I would that I could wrap up the view from my House in a pill of opium and send it to you! I should then be sure of seeing you in the fall of the year."[218] Coleridge's letters at this time were full of lighthearted references to drugs—"Red Sulfat" and "Compound Acid" are mentioned—particularly to certain people, those who shared the mystique of the drug culture.

Yet Davy matured to do great work in the field of science, and
Coleridge sank into addiction. Indeed, it is likely that he was already
addicted, though mildly, at the time of the Clifton experiments. While
still at school, Christ's Hospital, he suffered from rheumatic fever, for
which laudanum in substantial doses was then the standard treatment.
In the late 1790s he was again prescribed laudanum for rheumatic
pains, which the doctors described as nervous, "originating in mental
causes." He was given 25 drops every four hours. The pains may well
have been the result of opium, which the doctor presumably was unaware of, and Coleridge added to his prescribed doses by further supplies of his own. Most of the symptoms of which Coleridge complained
throughout his life—"internal rheumatism," "flying gout" and cramps
in his arms and legs—were due to his addiction, though he could not
bring himself to admit it.

Thomas de Quincey, 13 years younger than Coleridge, first bought
opium in 1804, when he was 19, from a druggist in Oxford Street:
"When I asked for the tincture of opium he gave it to me as any other
man might do; and furthermore, out of my shilling, returned to me
what seemed to be a real copper halfpence." De Quincey's motive was
to alleviate a stomach-ache and because he feared tuberculosis, but it
is almost certain that he, like Coleridge before him, was in search of
sensation. In due course he, too, became an addict, his daily dose rising
to 320, then 480 drops; on one occasion he took 8,000 drops.

These figures do not mean very much, since there was no standard
drop then and much of the opium sold was weak. Coleridge's addiction
became serious after 1800–1, when he first got hold of Kendal Black
Drop, which was invented by a Quaker family called Braithwaite, who
sold it in Kendal alongside ironmongery and marble chimneypieces. It
was expensive: 11 shillings for a four-ounce bottle. When Mrs. Braithwaite died in 1825, she left her daughter, who carried on the trade, over
£10,000. Two other Quaker families produced rival, cheaper versions,
and publicity was generated by carefully spread rumors about women
stirring it at dead of night wearing masks. In March 1821 the *Lonsdale
Magazine* gave what it said was the recipe: the "best Turkey opium
dried," mixed with saffron and cloves, strong acetic acid and rectified
spirit, the compound to be left to stand for a week.[219] The point about
the Black Drop, however, was its strength, and once Coleridge became
accustomed to take it, a complete cure for him was not possible. By the
time Coleridge and De Quincey met in 1807, both were addicts. Each
at various times accused the other of taking opium for pleasure, while
testifying to the purity of his own motives. Both lied. Lying and opium
were inseparable, one reason why it is so hard to elucidate the medical

history of such men. It is notable, however, that women were much less inclined to conceal or try to justify their addiction: Coleridge's daughter Sara, who also became addicted, was matter-of-fact about it.[220]

Coleridge and De Quincey, whatever they said and wrote about opium, remained ambivalent about it. Coleridge's notebooks, which he kept from 1794 until his death 40 years later, reflect the history of his addiction. They show that he had powerful fantasies and daydreams, even without opium, and that the drug first hindered, then killed, his poetic imagination. Occasionally, Coleridge professed his determination to warn others about the dangers of opium. Writing to one of his publishers in September 1816, he referred to "the anguish of my mind concerning . . . [addiction], my anxiety to warn others against the like error in the very commencement, and the total absence of all concealment, have been far more than the thing itself the causes of its being so much and so malignantly talked about. For instance, who has dared blacken Mr Wilberforce's good name on this account? Yet he has been for a long series of years under the same necessity. Talk with any eminent druggist or medical practitioner, especially at the West end of the town, concerning the frequency of this calamity among men and women of eminence."[221] Yet the same year, by allowing another publisher, John Murray, to publish in conjunction *Kubla Khan, Christobel* and *The Pains of Sleep,* Coleridge allowed the notion to circulate that his best poems were written as a result of opium taking. De Quincey was no better. His *Confessions of an Opium Eater,* published in the *London Magazine* in 1821 and as a book the following year, warned of the horrors of opium: "Farewell, a long farewell to happiness. . . . Farewell to smiles and laughter! Farewell to peace of mind, to tranquil dreams, and to the blessed consolation of sleep! . . . Here opens on me an Iliad of woes: for now I enter upon *the Pains of Opium.*"[222] Yet he also called the drug "O just, subtle and all-conquering opium! . . . Eloquent opium! . . . Thou hast the keys of paradise, O just, subtle and mighty opium!"[223] The book may have led as many to opium as it deterred; certainly, it was disastrous in the case of another fine poet, Francis Thompson.[224]

From Coleridge's and De Quincey's writings, however, it is possible to gather that the addiction and its consequences followed a similar course. First, De Quincey noted, "intellectual torpor . . . more oppressive and tormenting from the sense of incapacity and feebleness, from the direct embarrassments incident to the neglect and procrastination of each day's appropriate labours, and from . . . remorse." This description exactly paralleled Coleridge's problems from about 1800 onwards. Next came optical hallucinations and horrible nightmares, and what De

Quincey called "deep-seated anxiety and funereal melancholy" and "suicidal despondency" (many addicts in the 1810s and 1820s did, in fact, commit suicide). De Quincey said he became "awestruck" at the approach of sleep and feared "death through overwhelming terrors." Coleridge also referred to the "terror and cowardice . . . of sudden death." Family life degenerated and, still worse, wives and dearest friends were seen as enemies and conspirators. Coleridge's wife Sara was the first to grasp the nature and seriousness of his addiction, complicated by his heavy consumption of brandy, which he took to keep the opium on his stomach, and she fought against it. That led to their separation, and Coleridge's delusions about her, reflected in dozens of his brilliant letters, destroyed her character in the eyes of his admirers, then and for a long time afterwards.[225]

In the early 19th century doctors were rarely successful in treating drug addiction, since they did not understand and often failed to recognize its symptoms. In 1801, when Coleridge was in an appalling state after taking quantities of Black Drop, the local practitioner, Dr. John Edmondson, visited him almost daily and said he was quite baffled. In 1810 Coleridge was again treated, by the clever and imaginative Dr. Carlisle, but to no effect. Drs. Tuthill (1811), Gooch (1812), Parry (1813), Daniel (1814), Brabant (1815) and Adams (1816), all of them able, likewise could do no good. But Joseph Adams at least grasped the magnitude of the problem and in 1815 arranged for Coleridge to go into a supervised residence with the surgeon James Gillman, at his house in Highgate. There Coleridge remained until his death in 1834. At times he still secretly obtained from Dunn, the Highgate chemist, three-quarters of a pint of laudanum, a five-day supply. But gradually he accepted a regimen, in which he took only carefully supervised doses. This regimen not only prolonged his life (his death from heart disease reflected the rheumatic fever that had led him to take opium in the first place and had nothing to do with his addiction), but enabled him to develop a separate career, as a philosophical writer on politics and religion.[226]

The cases of Coleridge and De Quincey were important not only because of their intrinsic interest, but because they served to open up a topic hitherto concealed and obscure. Until De Quincey's *Confessions* appeared in 1821–22, addiction had never been debated. De Quincey's ambivalence was noted at the time, and in 1823 an anonymous *Advice to Opium Eaters* was published to reinforce what were thought to be the wholly inadequate warnings in his book. Coleridge's agonies, though known to a growing circle of friends, were never confessed in his lifetime, at least publicly. In 1837, however, his old Bristol publisher

Joseph Cottle, with the help of Robert Southey, put out memoirs that
included many of Coleridge's letters referring to his addiction, though
the texts were barbarously edited. The publication of the memoirs led
his old custodian, Dr. Gillman, to make public his own account of
Coleridge and his troubles, which came much closer to the truth.[227]
Thus, the facts about addiction began to emerge, though with what
may seem to us deplorable slowness. And Western societies were still
more reluctant to grasp the significance, and the immorality, of the
international trade in dangerous drugs.

Opium imported into Britain, which reached an annual total of
22,000 pounds by 1830, came almost entirely (80–90 percent) from
Turkey, where it was grown by the peasants east of Smyrna. Large-
scale production was impossible, and it was highly labor intensive,
every member of each peasant family joining in. There were three
sowings a year, in November, December and February–March, and
harvesting May through July. The poppies grew to between six and
eight feet, with blue-and-white seeds, and the growth was so concentrated that the Turks took systematic precautions to avoid inhalations
during the night. Speculators bought the crop in advance, at high
interest rates, and a crop might be sold four times over before it was
marketed. The raw opium was packed in gray calico bags, sealed, then
put into oblong wicker baskets and taken to Smyrna by mule. In
Smyrna the experts tested it, marking it in carats (24 carats was pure
opium).

Smyrna, or Turkey, opium was distinguished by its shape; it came
in two-pound flat slabs, waxy, browny-black, wrapped in leaves. Egyptian opium came in flat round cakes; Persian, in sticks; and Indian, in
balls, the size of a double fist, weighing 3½ pounds, and packed in
two-story chests of mangowood, having 20 compartments with a ball
in each. Smyrna opium, which included the Persian supplies, was
packed into airtight zinc-lined wooden cases, then taken across Europe
by ancient trade routes, through Italy, Germany, France, Malta, Gibraltar and Holland, though from 1815 onwards it also went by ship
directly to Liverpool and Dover but chiefly to London. When the Levant Company monopoly ended in 1825, there was free competition
among the Turkish merchants, who used the drug brokers of Mark
Lane and Mincing Lane to sell it, at regular auctions at Garraway's
Coffee House near the Royal Exchange.[228] The trade was carefully
supervised by the authorities, but they were concerned about purity and
adulteration, not about addiction.[229] Indeed, during the 1820s, the duty
on imported opium, along with most other duties, was reduced from 11

shillings to 9 shillings a pound. The retail prices of high-quality opium then fell to about 30 shillings a pound.

The international circulation of opium in the early 19th century was at the root of many of the modern difficulties between the West and the Far East, and that is one reason it is worth examining in detail. But the more we examine, the more we stumble on mysteries. And the first mystery is this: Why were some societies more susceptible to opium taking than were others? The drug was grown in the Levant and the Middle East, but did not generally cause problems. It was widely used in Turkey for hedonistic purposes. It was chewed, rather as the Americans chewed tobacco. In 1810 Farington cross-questioned a friend of his named Brown, who had traveled widely in the area, about the "habit of chewing opium which prevails among the Turks. He said this habit is acquired gradually and as by stealth. It is considered to be disgraceful and they secrete the opium in their handkerchiefs to avoid being observed."[230] Social disapproval, however, was sufficient to keep the practice under control: the Porte, which benefited financially from the Smyrna trade, did not find it necessary to act against the poppy growers. Likewise, opium had been grown in India for thousands of years. Indeed, some people referred to India as "the Mother of Opium." Since the 16th century, growers in west India had been organized into a regular trade, rather like at Smyrna, by the Portuguese of Goa, and the product was known as Malwa (as opposed to "Turkey"). In 1773 the British East India Company organized the opium growing in its dominions into a rival monopoly trade, advancing money to the *ryots* (farmers) to promote it; this opium was known as Patna, and was of a higher quality than was Malwi. Opium was cheap in India and always had been. Why did not the Indians, who had so many miseries to bear and were vulnerable to so many other scourges, physical and social, become addicted to opium? We do not know. The fact is that they did not.

This brings us to China, and the mystery of the Chinese addiction to opium. Opium appears to have reached China in the first century A.D., having been brought from India and Indochina by Buddhist priest-doctors, who used it as a medicine. The Chinese then began to cultivate it themselves in Yunnan province, as they still do.[231] It was known as *a-fu-yung*. In Sung, and still more in Ming times, it became the leading medical product, as elsewhere. Each Ming emperor received an annual tribute from Thailand of 200 pounds for himself and 100 pounds for his empress.[232] It first figured in the records of European trading companies that were operating in Asia in the early decades of the 17th century, when small quantities were exported from India to the Dutch settlers in Java.

China, at that time and indeed until the Opium Wars of the mid-19th century was, theoretically at least, a sealed country, the government having a monopoly on all transactions with the outside world. Chinese economic theory, which was highly irrational, even by the usual standards of economic theory, held that it was fatal to the well-being of the country to allow either silver or people to leave it. Nevertheless, Chinese people, for their own good reasons, wished to leave, as they still do—"Boat People" constitute an ancient phenomenon. From the 16th century, the Portuguese had run a trading post in Macao, which the Chinese government permitted because it formed a convenient conduit for their monopoly dealings with the outside world. Chinese who were anxious to leave tended to go through Macao. The Chinese government blamed the Portuguese for this exodus, just as they later blamed the British for their opium problem. But the Portuguese could not prevent runaway Chinese from crossing into their post. Far from encouraging these movements, they did everything in their power to persuade the runaways to return home. But the Chinese, who were in effect refugees, though whether of the political or economic variety it is hard to say, begged to be allowed to stay. The Portuguese way of dealing with the problem was to ship them out and, since the Chinese were hard and intelligent workers who made themselves useful, colonies of them began to form all over Southeast Asia, especially in areas of European settlement.

One such colony was in Java, where the Chinese formed an artisanal and shopkeeping middle class, between Dutch rulers and Indonesian peasants. In Asia, the Portuguese took snuff. The Dutch smoked tobacco. During the 17th century, the Dutch settlers in Java took to adding a pinch of opium (from India) to their tobacco, mixing in a little arsenic for good measure, and smoking the mixture. The Chinese in Java copied them. Over a period, however, the Chinese reduced the quantity of tobacco and increased the quantity of opium, until they were eventually smoking pure opium. They then passed this addictive habit back into mainland China. By 1729 opium smoking was so prevalent in China, and its social consequences regarded as so serious, that the authorities acted. Among other things, they asked the East India Company, which was shipping small quantities of Indian opium to China, not to do so; and the company, anxious to keep good relations with Peking, immediately complied.

Why did the Chinese, over less than a century, develop such an extraordinary and unpredictable taste for smoking opium in a pipe?

That is another mystery, for which no historian has been able to provide an explanation. Then again, why did the measures of 1729 fail to have an effect? That, too, is a mystery, though explanations can be ventured, and they are twofold. The first point is that British trade with China, conducted largely through India, expanded rapidly in the 18th century, but caused increasing concern to the East India Company because of its imbalance. The British, like other Europeans, had always imported Chinese silks in considerable quantities. The new factor was tea. Chinese tea, from Canton and Macao, first reached England in 1652, the same year as coffee and cocoa. The English took to all three, but tea, in particular, slowly but surely became a national obsession, which spread to the Scots, Welsh and Irish, too. Why? Another mystery. Tea was *cha* or *char* (a form still used in the British army). The British upper classes called it tay and spelled it thus until Victorian times. By 1820 the British were importing 30 million tons of tea annually, nearly all of it from China (some also came from Formosa, then Japanese). Tea cost £40 a ton in Canton, and the duties on it when it reached Britain formed the biggest single item in the Exchequer's revenues. The same year, David Scott, the Commissioner for Assam in India, sent specimens of a species of camellia to the Linnean Society in London for analysis. This species was a wild tea plant; the Indians, who did not drink tea, had never bothered to cultivate it. Ten years later, the Indian tea industry started, and eventually it was to oust Chinese tea decisively in the British taste.[233] But that was for the future.

The export trade in tea to Britain was important for the Chinese economy, though the government in Peking did not grasp its significance. In 1810 Farington's friend Mr. Barrow, an expert on the Orient, who had been a member of the embassy Lord Macartney took to China in the 1790s, told him that over 3 million Chinese were employed growing the tea the British consumed.[234] Apart from its size, the tea trade was helping to modernize China by spreading cash cropping through large areas of Fukien, central China and Kwantung, as more and more farmers switched to monoculture for the market.[235] The difficulty, as far as the East India Company was concerned, lay in selling China sufficient British or Indian products to pay for the tea (and silk).

Chinese consumers were not keen on British manufactured goods, such as cottons. Why? The rest of the world liked them. Here we have another mystery. The Chinese would take a certain amount of raw Indian cotton; a few luxuries; mechanical toys, known as "sing-sings"; and small quantities of precision instruments, such as telescopes. But even these imports were strictly illegal. The Chinese court would not recognize that trade had to be a two-way process. With the huge and continuing increase in British tea imports, the Chinese had an export surplus in the first decade of the 19th century of $26 million, an enormous imbalance for the times. The Chinese authorities were delighted as this surplus, mainly in the form of Spanish-American silver dollars, poured into their coffers. But it could not last; indeed, even by 1800 it was in the process of being transformed by the increase in Chinese opium imports.

Why the demand for opium in China leaped so dramatically in the late 18th- and early 19th centuries is another fact that is hard to explain. Certainly, the Chinese population was rising fast. Between the late 17th century and the White Lotus Risings of the late 18th century, China had enjoyed a century of internal peace, which seems to have made possible a population explosion, the total doubling from 150 million to over 300 million. From 1779 to 1850 there was a further 56 percent increase, bringing the total to 450 million.[236] Nothing like this increase had ever been seen before in world history. As the numbers rose, the percentage who used and became addicted to opium rose accordingly. Then again, there seems to have come a point, around 1800, when the opium habit in China became, as it were, "critical" and changed from a minority to a popular taste. This change may have coincided with the fall in the price of opium and the increase in its quality, produced by the competition between Malwa and Patna.

Another factor was the East India Company's loss of centralized control of the China trade on the British side. The company's monopoly of British trade with India ceased in 1813 and though in theory the company kept a monopoly of the China trade until 1833, many private trading houses in Calcutta ran what was called a "country" trade with China long before then. These private trading houses were the most active in supplying opium. The Portuguese were still very much in the trade, with their Malwa, and so from about 1805 were the Americans, who shipped Turkey opium from Smyrna: "With one or two exceptions," wrote a contemporary, all American houses in the Far East engaged in the China opium trade.[237] But it was the British who were the most successful in selling the Chinese opium, absorbing over 80 percent of the trade, probably because their Patna was the best. Patna was sold at auction in Calcutta, bought by private merchants, and then leaked into China through Macao. In the years 1800–18, the yearly average was 4,000 chests, each of 140 pounds. From 1817 to 1819, when the East India Company retired from the fray at the request of the Chinese government, the private houses took over completely and the quantities rose dramatically. By 1822–30 the British were exporting to China an average of 18,760 chests a year, and during the early 1830s, the exports topped the $18 million–mark, making opium the world's most valuable single-commodity trade.[238]

As a result, China began to lose silver on a huge scale. The trading surplus turned into a deficit which, in the years 1828–36 alone, cost China $38 million. The effect on the Chinese population was also drastic. By 1830 the Chinese authorities said that 1 percent of the population smoked opium and that the city of Süchow alone had 100,000 addicts. Westerners estimated about 12.5 million smokers, one-third of them heavy, and the figure, still estimated, was raised to 15 million later in the century.[239] The curse of addiction struck most heavily at elements of the ruling class: successful soldiers, wealthy landowners, senior clerks and governmental officials. One senior Chinese official reported: "Everywhere transactions are slow and the revenue does not come in. Money is expensive and bullion depreciated. That is because it is leaving the country in large quantities, being drained by the opium trade. This is the work of the English. This people, not having enough to live on at home [a common Chinese official belief about Europeans] tried to bring other countries into subjection by first weakening their inhabitants. . . . Now they have come to China and brought us a disease which will dry up our bones, a worm that gnaws at our hearts, a ruin to our families and our persons. Since the Empire first existed it has run no such danger. It is worse than a world deluge, than an invasion of wild beasts. I demand that the smuggling of opium be inscribed in the code among the crimes punished by death."[240] Unless the trade was stopped, another official warned, "Heads of families would no longer be able to admonish their wives, masters would no longer be able to restrain their servants, teachers to train their pupils . . . It would mean the end of the life of the people and the destruction of the soul of the nation."[241]

There is, however, no evidence that the British government wanted to force on China what Peking called "foreign mud." Quite the contrary. Both the government and the East India Company were prompt to comply with the wishes of the Chinese government to respect its ban on opium, which was reiterated and reinforced from 1817. In trading terms, however, the Chinese craving for opium was convenient to Britain, indeed to all the advanced countries which did business with China. A British official was later to admit: "We bring the Chinese nothing that is really popular among them. . . . Opium is the only 'open sesame' to their stony hearts."[242] But there was never any question of high-pressure salesmanship or of the need for salesmanship of any kind: The demand for opium in China was incessant and insatiable. "Opium is like gold," one merchant said, "I can sell it at any time."[243]

*   *   *

The truth is that Chinese addiction to opium was not a disease transmitted by the British but a symptom of deep-seated weaknesses in the Chinese government and society which growing contacts with the West were beginning to expose. China was an ancient human construct which had contrived to hold itself together, but had failed to modernize itself. It was as though the Byzantine Empire had somehow survived into the 19th century, without essentially modifying the ideas of the Emperor Justinian. Indeed, in some ways 19th-century China was more archaic than was 6th-century Byzantium. To begin with, it had no effective state currency. One of the reasons that opium was so popular in China was that it became a highly effective substitute currency. In theory China had a silver and copper coinage, with 1,000 copper pennies to a silver tael. But the silver was not in coin form but in bullion, as in ancient Egypt; it had no quality standard; and the coins fluctuated wildly in uniformity. The coins were also heavy to cart around. Hence, the moment the Chinese made contact with the West in the 16th century, they began to use its more dependable currencies, chiefly Spanish silver, what they called the *peng-yang* or standard dollar. These currencies were accepted for tax purposes and were the normal currency in Canton until 1853 and Shanghai until 1857. The Chinese government's attempts to create a paper currency had been abandoned and were not revived until the end of the 19th century. Periodic attempts by authority, for instance by the Tao-kuang Emperor in 1829, to stop the use of foreign dollars, were ineffective for the simple reason that Peking had failed in one of the fundamental purposes for which a government exists, to maintain a reliable currency of its own. Once opium began to arrive in high-quality, consistent units, it, too, was eagerly seized upon as a medium of exchange. It was the only commodity for which merchants or the general public were always ready to offer cash or barter at steady rates. In many ways it was better than Spanish silver because it was much lighter. Chinese who had to travel carried it like we do traveler's checks. It was safer, too: Silver betrayed itself by its weight, and its owner was liable to be murdered by boatmen or bearers.[244]

The absence of its own currency was merely one of China's structural weaknesses. These had been less important when the empire was a self-contained system that had little contact with the outside world and a relatively stable population. But in the 18th century, the population explosion set up all kinds of strains within the old structure—addiction to opium may have been one response to them—and these strains were sometimes exacerbated by attempts by Westerners to trade—attempts, it should be noted, which were welcome to the Chinese people, as opposed to its government. The government itself was built on pride made more dangerous by ignorance. Like many of the official credos of antiquity, Chinese state theory held that the Chinese were the only true "people"; that other races were inferior or malevolent, "devils"; that its civilization was the true repository of grace, art and knowledge; and that China had nothing useful to learn from outside and much to fear from the destructive propensities of foreigners. Several embassies had been sent from Europe at the end of the 18th and in the early 19th century. All had met with various degrees of hostility. The most recent was Lord Amherst's in August 1816: Amherst's secretary, Henry Ellis, left a vivid description of how he was denied an imperial audience; pushed and manhandled; exposed to gaping crowds; and, finally, after much effort, accorded the minor courtesy of a free breakfast.[245]

Throughout this period, all efforts by Western states to negotiate with the Chinese government, at any level, were rebuffed. Westerners, whatever their status, were merely the recipients of decisions. This treatment might have been more acceptable to them if they had been able to perceive any merit in the system which treated them with such contempt. But the system was little understood, and all its ostensible activities, which Westerners could observe in their daily contacts, ranged from the stupid to the outrageous. China was a theocracy, a society run for religious purposes. The Emperor was *Teen-tze,* Son of Heaven, the vicar on Earth of the celestial powers, like the Pope. His divine right rested on the study of the principles of government in the sacred books, and his most important function was to perform sacrifices, especially during the winter solstice. The Board of Rites in Peking was the most powerful body in the empire. Next came the Board of Censors, which checked all officials, including, in theory, the Emperor himself. Since only the Teen-tze could perform certain key ceremonies, national calamities like floods, pestilence and foreign intrusions were judged to be the consequence of his ritual errors, and he was obliged to publish a self-scourging decree, admitting himself unworthy and promising repentance. China was held together not so much by race, since the Chinese varied at least as much as European nationalities, or language, since Mandarin was like Latin in medieval Europe and was not spoken by the people who had their own different tongues, as by ethics. Ethics included the right of rebellion when the Emperor was deemed unworthy, and that was how dynasties changed, the consensus deeming the ruling family sinful.[246]

China liked to think of itself as eternal and immutable, but it was subject to the same dynamics as was any other society, and the rapid population growth which began in the 18th century was making it unstable. It was prone to outbursts of popular religion, which could take political forms. In 1796 there was a serious revolt of the White Lotus cult, a syncretistic blend of Buddhism, Taoism, Manicheism and other faiths, which went back to the 11th century and reappeared periodically, sometimes overthrowing dynasties. The cult was vegetarian, had married clergy, put out vernacular holy books, featured radical preachers, and practiced Messianism. In some ways, it resembled Methodism or the Camp Revivalism of the United States. In others it was like the secret societies and political banditry of southern Europe, both protecting and exploiting the peasants in their fortified villages. It resisted authority in many ways: by smuggling salt, which was an imperial monopoly; by counterfeiting coin; and by dealing in opium. The White Lotus leaders identified themselves with the late medieval Ming dynasty, which they wanted to restore in place of the "corrupt" Ch'ing. Their armies were not large, and it is likely that only about 10 percent of the rebels actually belonged to White Lotus, since provincial governors were less likely to be punished by Peking for disturbances in their districts if they classified rebels as members of "heterodox sects." So the White Lotus movement did not have the strength to seize and hold big cities. But it had fortified villages that successfully resisted Ch'ing armies and it was, for a time, an effective guerrilla movement.

Imperial policy was to launch search-and-destroy drives, which burned villages and sometimes massacred the peasants. The government left the walled towns alone. In areas where rebels were strong, the authorities set up strategic hamlets where they concentrated people and grain, to deny both to the rebels; this policy was known as *chien-pi ch'ing-yek,* "Strengthening the Walls and Clearing the Countryside." They also introduced a militia system and sometimes hired bandits as mercenaries. At times the Ch'ing regular forces, militias and mercenaries numbered up to 600,000 men, but many of the units were mutinous or pillaged on their own account. It took a decade to bring the rebellion under any kind of control, and even in 1805 it was only driven underground, to flare up again in 1813 and again in the 1820s, especially in the border areas.[247] It spawned other movements: the *Pa-kue chiao,* or Eight Diagrams Society; the *I-ho ch'yuan,* or Boxers; and the *Ho-wei pien,* or Tiger-Tail Whips. These joined existing secret societies or Triads, which by the early 19th century had spread all over Yangtse Province and beyond, going under such names as *San-ho hui* (Three Harmonies Society), *San-tien hui* (Three Dots Society), and *T'ien-ti hui* (Heaven on Earth Society, known collectively as the *hung* or Vast Gate men).[248] Like the secret societies of early 19th-century Europe, they were part-idealist, part-criminal, antinomian, destructive of order, exciting to the young, attractive to radicals and to grudge-mongers of all ages.

These secret societies flourished because the empire, while in theory a highly ethical concept, was in practice the negation of ethics, being corrupt from its highest to its lowest official. Indeed, at a time when Western societies—Britain and Austria were good examples—were making strenuous and increasingly successful efforts to purge corruption from their central governments and local administrations, China was becoming more corrupt.

China was that worst of all systems: a society run by its intelligentsia, a cathedocracy ruled from the scholar's chair. In Peking there were the boards. Outside it were 18 provinces administered by viceroys, who had direct access to the Emperor, were summoned to him periodically, were appointed and dismissed by him, and were chosen (theoretically) on merit because they had no hereditary fiefs. Below them were the *Taoutai,* the intendants of the circuit, who reported to the viceroys. Then came the prefects of each department, who reported to the intendants. At the bottom rung were the *Hsein,* or districts, each with a walled city ruled by a magistrate, who reported to the prefects. All these officials were bureaucrats, chosen by examination in Confucian studies and other archaic disciplines and for their ability to speak and write elegant Mandarin.

The system was obnoxious because it placed scholars at the top, followed in descending order by farmers, artisans and merchants. What it meant in practice was that the country was ruled by those who were good at passing highly formalized examinations. So early 19th-century China, with its rapidly increasing population, had many of the symptoms of underdeveloped Third World societies today, especially an overproduction of literate men (not technocrats or scientists) in relation to the capacity of the political and economic system to employ them usefully. The educational system trained Mandarins for official life in its narrowest sense, not for anything else, least of all commerce. The number of governmental jobs and the quotas for degrees were fixed for all time by statute.

As the intelligentsia grew in size, the ethics of the system were progressively destroyed. Degrees, studentships and places in the academies, as well as the statutory jobs themselves, were all in time put up for sale. Each official was provided with nonstatutory supernumeraries, endless *doppelgängers,* and there were huge increases in clerical staffs and secretariats. All these men had high notions of their worth and

healthy appetites for power and money. All that they had been taught
at the academies was how to write examination essays. All they learned
in their jobs was how to translate the miniscule slice of power each
exercised into money, in the form of bribes from those whose activities
they controlled.[249] The Emperor forced all those who he appointed,
from viceroys to board members, to pay him large sums for their jobs.
They extorted money from those below them to recoup and to enrich
themselves in turn. All officials had to pilfer to satisfy the swarming,
grasping entourages of bureaucratic insects which surrounded any job
of consequence. Ultimately, the money had to come from the taxes of
the peasants and the bribes squeezed out of the town merchants.

Hypertrophy of the bureaucracy and the consequent corruption not
only impoverished the country and led to the smoldering discontent
which the secret societies expressed, but progressively destroyed the
country's institutions. One reason it took a decade to put down the
White Lotus was that the army was as corrupt as everything else. Funds
were stolen by generals, including the Commander in Chief, who reported back phony battles and imaginary body counts. Three other
central institutions of the empire—the grain tribute, the salt monopoly,
and the Yellow River Conservancy—were also undermined in the first
quarter of the 19th century. The tribute was the collection of the rice
tax from eight provinces in south and central China, which was taken
to Peking by river and canal in boats, manned by hereditary official
boatmen, who lived in military colonies along the Grand Canal and
sailed in fleets of up to 100 grain junks. The grain should have been sent
by sea, which would have been quicker and cheaper and would have
avoided all the greedy middlemen along the route. But doing so would
have involved a radical change. As it was, the system was a bottomless
pit of idle bureaucrats and corruption. The hereditary boatmen did not
actually sail the junks, which were manned by deputies, up to 50,000 of
them, mainly vagrants known as *shui-shou*. But all had to paid. The
number of people involved in collecting and transporting the grain rose
steadily; the cost rose, too; the burden on the peasants grew; and the
final yield fell.

In 1824 there was a crisis, when the grain fleets got stuck in the silt
while trying to cross the Yellow River en route to Peking. This crisis
was an excellent opportunity to switch to the sea route, and some in
Peking wanted to take it, but vested interests prevailed. The only upshot was that many disgruntled boatmen organized themselves into
secret societies, with White Lotus programs, thus forming another
lawless element in the state. In the salt monopoly, a similar pattern of
bureaucratic proliferation and avarice led, in this case, to a huge in-

crease in salt smuggling. Smuggling was conducted by desperate men, and if effective steps were taken to block their smuggling routes, they switched to simple brigandage.[250]

The most striking evidence of breakdown was in the Yellow River Conservancy, whose great historic mission was to keep the Yellow River flowing properly and to ensure that the Grand Canal functioned. The key point was Huai-an, where the canal crossed the river, a miracle of archaic technology made possible by a system of feeder lakes which transferred water from river to canal. Bureaucratic corruption led to neglect and inefficiency and the silting up of the system. This silting threatened the state's two main sources of revenue, the grain tax and the salt monopoly, because the grain fleets could not get through Huai-an, as in 1824, and the floods which silting inevitably produced wrecked the main evaporating system and salt factories at Liang-huai. There were lurid tales of three-day banquets and lavish theatrical entertainments taking place among the mandarins who controlled the system, while the silting and wrecking went on unchecked.[251]

Westerners who had to deal with the Chinese could observe these ominous and visible signs that the empire was coming apart and it reinforced their exasperation at the contemptuous manner in which the Chinese authorities treated them. Moreover, like it or not, if they wanted to trade with China, they had to descend into the vast labyrinth of corruption themselves. All foreign trade had to be done through Canton (except in the north where there was a Russian trading post at Kiakhta), where Chinese merchants or hongists bought monopoly licenses from the Imperial government. The trading area of the port was effectively run by the Imperial Superintendent of Maritime Customs, known to Westerners as the hoppo. He bought his office for a three-year period, and he had not only to transmit the official customs dues to the government in Peking but to send 855 silver taels annually to the Emperor's privy purse. To get this amount and to become a millionaire in his three-year period, he put the squeeze on the hongists. To pay him and others, the hongists put 10 percent of their profits into a secret Consoo Fund, which exacted a 3 percent levy on foreign imports in addition to formal duties. Foreign traders thus found themselves part of a double or even multiple system of payments, some official, most unofficial, in fact, bribes. In addition, they all had to sweeten the officials they dealt with by giving them presents, the "sing-songs," or musical boxes and toys, that the mandarins loved.[252]

It is important to grasp that no Westerner who traded with China had the slightest respect for the system and its officials. All longed for its overthrow. They also saw that the hongists were being milked dry by the squeezing officialdom. In fact, most hongists were in debt to the East India Company, which had to give them advance payment for tea to keep them in business. The company would not touch opium, since it was banned, and made little money out of the tea trade because of the innumerable "bites." The private merchants saw the opium trade not only as the only way, granted the oppressive system, they could make a reasonable profit, but as one means of getting back at the officials who ran it. They did not believe for one second that the Chinese government was concerned about the moral welfare of its subjects and had declared the trade contraband for that reason. In this they may have been mistaken. A few Chinese officials were decent, honorable, and incorrupt and their worries about opium addiction were genuine. But the government as a whole disliked the opium trade mainly because it led to the flight of silver. That is why they banned it. And most officials disliked it simply because since it was banned, it was more difficult and often impossible to get their "bite" of its profits. Not that opium trading, being unlawful and involving smuggling, eliminated bribery. It merely shifted the opportunity to exact bribes from one set of Chinese officials to another. Indeed, it is possible that officialdom banned the trade in the first place thinking it would offer fresh opportunities for exacting percentages, then found that it was more difficult to control and milk than was lawful commerce.

Certainly, no British merchant who traded in opium on or off the China coast felt he was doing wrong, any more than the 26,000 owners of apothecary shops and the like in Britain thought they were wrong in selling laudanum to the public. In 1827 William Jardine, a partner in a traditional China trade merchant house, joined forces with James Matheson, to form what was to become the most powerful firm in the entire Far East. Matheson had been selling opium off the coast and had become aware of the colossal demand for the product in China; he thought, rightly, that the trade was only just beginning. Jardine had also traded in opium, working for a Parsi firm that sold Malwa. Once, in Canton, an iron bar had fallen on his head from a scaffold, and he had walked on. The Chinese called him Iron-Headed Rat—a compliment. Both Jardine and Matheson saw themselves, and were seen, as honest merchants, anxious to turn an honest penny. Their firm eventually became a byword for high standards of dealing and public service. But in 1827 they were buying fast clippers to get increasing quantities of opium into China under the noses of the Chinese authorities.[253]

The cynicism with which Western traders viewed the Chinese authorities was reinforced by the conditions in which they were obliged to live and work. A ship desiring to trade stopped at the outer anchor-

age of Canton until the hoppo came on board and, on receipt of official
dues, presents, and his customary bribe, gave a "chop" (pass) to proceed up-river to Whampoa Island. There you had to get another chop
to trade. At Canton itself the permanent Western trading community,
fewer than 200 British, 50 or so Americans ("flowery-flag devils"), a
score or so Portuguese, who operated mainly from Macao, plus a few
other Westerners and Parsis, occupied a strictly controlled area with an
800-foot seafront, divided into 13 houses, each extending inland about
130 yards. There was a fetid ditch on each side, and two streets, China
Street, on which the houses opened, and Hog Lane, full of spirits
shops—"nothing so narrow or so filthy," wrote one visitor, "exists in
a European town."[254] All the non-opium trade went through Canton.
So did much of the opium, but covertly under the *Cumsha* ("golden
sand" or bribe) system. This system was recorded in great detail by a
British merchant. The ship carrying opium anchored outside Canton.
The official, or mandarin, came aboard. If his interpreter demanded
"all same custom," that meant the usual bribe, $40 a chest, and all he
needed to be sure of were the number of chests being carried. When the
cash was handed over, the mandarin announced "Kaou-tsze" ("I am
departing"), which meant that the deal was concluded and junks could
be sent out to pick up the chests. But the purchase price for the opium
was handed over in the usual way in Canton itself.[255]

Despite this blatant evasion of Chinese law by the very officials who
were charged with its application, all of whom, as everyone knew, had
to remit percentages to Peking in one form or another, many regulations were strictly enforced on the Canton traders. The traders' movements were carefully controlled. One regulation read: "Foreigners are
not to row about the river at pleasure but to take the air only on the
8th, 18th and 28th day of the month; foreign barbarians may visit the
flower-garden but no more than ten at a time." No house could employ
more than eight Chinese servants, and the authorities were particularly
suspicious of the Chinese interpreters employed by the merchants. The
Westerners often became fond of these loyal and unoffending creatures,
who were liable to be savagely punished by the mandarins if their
employers broke the rules.[256]

There can be no doubt that, for the ruling Chinese intelligentsia,
Westerners were physically repellent and their culture was loathsome.
The mandarins were particularly critical of big Western noses: *Ta-pi-
tze,* "big nose," was their collective term. They also had a strong
aversion to Western clothes. Lin Tse-hsu, the Commissioner eventually
appointed to put down opium smuggling, who was an honest and in
some ways a great man, left a note, which has survived, of a visit to

Macao: "The bodies of the [Western] men are tightly encased from head to toe in short jackets and long, close-fitting trousers, so that they look like actors playing the part of foxes, hares and other such animals," he wrote, adding: "They really do look like devils." He also noted: "devil-slaves, called black devils, who come from the country of the moors. . . . They are blacker than lacquer and were this colour from birth." He was shocked by the fact that European women "part their hair in the middle" and "wear low-cut dresses, exposing their chests" and by Western marriage customs: "Marriages are arranged by the young people themselves, not by their families, and people with the same surname are free to marry one another, which is indeed a barbarous custom."[257]

Above all, Chinese ruling-class attitudes reflected the hatred of intellectuals for business. A fragment of a conversation between an emperor and one of his advisers has survived. Emperor: "It is plain that these barbarians always look on trade as their chief occupation and are wanting in any high purpose or striving for territorial acquisitions." Sage: "At bottom they belong to the class of brutes. It is impossible that they should have any high purpose."[258] Yet the mandarins were particularly hostile to Westerners who learned their language and studied their culture. Suspicious as they were of Chinese interpreters, whom they believed to have been corrupted by daily contact with the hated traders, they were deeply upset when Robert Morrison, who had been on the Amherst mission, spoke Chinese, and had translated the Bible into Mandarin, was appointed the official interpreter of the East India Company.[259] The Chinese government made its opinions of Westerners and their morals public by plastering Canton with large-character wall posters and by enforcing petty restrictions that, for instance, prevented Westerners from using rickshaws except when it was raining.

One regulation which caused Westerners wry amusement and led to a lot of trouble was Regulation Two: "Neither women, guns, spears nor weapons of any kind may be brought to the factories." The mandarins' objection to Western women was even more ferocious than their dislike of the traders. When, from time to time, the wife of a merchant insisted on coming to Canton and the authorities found out, they would put up insulting and obscene wall posters, accusing the West of corrupting Chinese morals. Not all Westerners objected to this rule, however. One who found it convenient was the brilliant London artist George Chinnery, who lived in Macao from 1825 till his death in 1852 and whose work provides a superb pictorial record of the Far East in the second quarter of the 19th century. Chinnery came to Macao to avoid paying the large debts he had accumulated in Calcutta and, still more, to escape from his wife Mary Anne, whom he called "the ugliest woman I ever saw in the whole course of my life." Whenever there were rumors that Mary Anne was pursuing him to Macao, he would go up-river to Canton, feeling he was safe there. But some women made their way up-river, too, especially American wives, who were the most persistent. In 1829 Abigail Low, wife of William Low, partner in the big American firm of Russell & Co., and her niece Harriet Low—Chinnery painted a pretty portrait of her—insisted on visiting Canton. The next year, Mrs. Baines, wife of a British marine trader, followed suit. But the mandarins objected so strongly on this occasion, not only putting up wall posters but cutting off food supplies and withdrawing all the Chinese servants, that the community had to give way.[260]

The flight of silver from China that began to accelerate in the 1820s increased corruption at every level of government; made the authorities far more tense in dealing with foreigners; and, for the first time, began to persuade the Western traders that a showdown with China was inevitable. Westerners were becoming aware, on altruistic as well as commercial grounds, of the enormous possibilities presented by the largest consumer market in world history and of the chance to bring enlightenment and possibly good government to the great mass of oppressed Chinese, whom they saw as highly intelligent, decent people crushed by a system which was both totalitarian and incorrigibly inefficient. They began to demand a more forceful approach to dealing with Peking. Almost every day Western merchants in Canton were made aware not just of the corruption but of the cruelty of the regime. They loathed seeing the Chinese forced to prostrate themselves before the retinues of chaired mandarins, surrounded by brutal soldiers and chain men, who shackled those who failed to kowtow.[261] They were outraged when their interpreters were humiliated, beaten, tortured, imprisoned and, in some cases, executed without trial.

Indeed, the conflict between Western and Chinese notions of justice was ultimately fatal to coexistence on Peking's terms. When a Chinese person was killed, even accidentally, as a result of the Western presence, the authorities demanded a victim to execute. They were not interested in his guilt; the punishment was a necessary public ritual, to save face and appease the celestial powers. As far back as 1784, a Chinese had been killed, quite by chance, during the firing of a ceremonial salute. The mandarins insisted that the unfortunate gunner be handed over to them for execution. The business was made still more objectionable by the method the mandarins used, ritual strangulation, beheading being ruled too honorable. Incidents were always possible in the conditions created by the authorities in the Canton settlement, for sailors who were sent on brief leave from the merchant ships in the anchorage were liable to get drunk in Hog Lane and embroiled in fights. In 1807 a Chinese was killed by a sailor in just such a brawl. This killing was solved by bribery. In 1820 another accidental killing was fortunately "atoned" for by the purely coincidental suicide of a sailor. But the following year, an Italian from an American ship accidentally killed a Chinese woman, during an argument, by throwing an olive jar at her. The Chinese demanded him for execution. The Americans at first refused, but when the mandarins imprisoned their interpreter and took other forceful measures, they weakly complied, and the wretched man was strangled. The British were revolted by this American surrender and swore that they would under no circumstances do the same.[262]

In other parts of the world, extraterritoriality and consular courts had solved the problem of conflicting ideas of justice. The Chinese authorities not only refused to entertain such a solution, but flatly declined even to discuss it, or any other problem, with the Western powers. Indeed, they went out of their way to be provocative. A typical incident involved a prisoner being brought for execution in front of the Canton factories. A cross was driven into the ground, the prisoner's neck and outstretched arms being attached to it. The merchants protested at the space being used for such a purpose, and the proceedings were violently broken up by a charge of British sailors from an Indiaman, who could not stomach such barbarity.[263]

Such cultural confrontations were inevitable as trade spread across the world and increasingly rapid and reliable forms of transport annihilated distance. Perhaps the most important single aspect of modernity was the way in which, almost imperceptibly, mankind was transforming itself into a single global community, in which different races and civilizations, now touching at all points, simply had to come to terms with each other. These frictions were usually solved by debate and agreement, with both sides recognizing the mutual advantage of peaceful conduct. Sometimes the unilateral threat or use of force smoothed the way for the West. But in China, the merchants, and behind them—it might be a long way behind them—their governments in Europe and North America were up against the largest nation on Earth, embodying the oldest continuous civilization on Earth, its present state pitiable perhaps, but bolstered by an arrogant self-confidence based upon profound ignorance. Thus, the stage was being prepared for a long, and still continuing, tragedy of East and West, of which the coming Opium Wars were the first episode. The Chinese mandarins, so confident in their superior knowledge, were unaware that they were facing the greatest naval power the world had ever seen, which was currently, in the 1820s, reinforcing its ability to penetrate the world's great rivers by developing steam warships. One of them was now to demonstrate its capacity to alter geopolitics by a striking exhibition not far from China's shores.

Enormous Shadows

Early in 1825, nearly 500 miles up the River Irrawaddy in Burma, a curious battle took place between the new and the old world, when the East India Company's steam warship *Diana* chased a Burmese imperial war prau up-river. These praus were perhaps the most fearful oar-driven craft ever devised. They carried a mass of fighting men and were driven at seven to eight miles an hour by 100 double-banked oars, wielded by highly trained oarsmen. In their river environment they were just as formidable as the vast triremes of antiquity, and they enabled the kings of Burma to pursue an aggressive policy of expansion over a large part of Southeast Asia and up along the Bay of Bengal. Captain Marryat, who watched their performance from the *Larne* sloop of war, which he commanded, pronounced them "Very splendid vessels."[1] But Marryat, who commanded the naval forces in the First Burma War, was also responsible for bringing the *Diana* into Burmese waters. He was the first to grasp the vital point that shallow draft steam-powered vessels, whether paddle or screw, were ideally suited to river warfare.

The *Diana* had been launched at Kiddapore in 1823. She had paddles driven by a 60-horsepower engine, which would burn either coal or wood. As a result, she was almost self-fueling for jungle-river work; she had merely to pull into the side while her crew cut timber. Moreover, her own engineers could service and, if necessary, repair her simple power unit and for eight years she never had to go into dock. Marryat insisted on taking the *Diana* as part of his force, for she could tow a train of troop-carrying vessels up-river whether or not there was any wind. What he did not foresee, until it happened, was that she would prove a decisive weapon against the giant war praus. She simply put on full power and chased the praus up river. After four or five hours of continuous rowing, the Burmese oarsmen collapsed (in some cases, died) from exhaustion, and once the prau was stationary, it was holed and sunk at leisure by the *Diana*'s deck guns. The *Diana*, in fact, was the first modern gunboat, and she introduced the era of gunboat diplomacy. As one observer, describing the steam-oar race to the death, put it: "The muscles and sinews of men could not hold out against the perseverance of the boiling kettle."[2]

The performance of the *Diana* was widely noted, and conclusions were drawn all over the world. In China, which in 1829 saw the first Western steamboat the *Forbes,* also built at Kiddapore, William Jarndyce recognized the capacity of the steamboat to push up and dominate China's great rivers in ways that no sailing warship dared risk. "A few gunboats alongside this city," he wrote from Canton, where the follies, corruption, and cruelty of the regime was becoming daily more apparent, would overrule any "caprice" of the local authorities by "the discharge of a few mortars."[3] In large parts of Asia and Africa, the arrival of military steam power was felt by many Westerners, for altruistic as well as commercial reasons, to be an almost divine deliverance, a means whereby the horrors and oppressions of native rulers could be brought to an end. In West Africa, Robert Macgregor, one of the men behind the first great Niger expedition (1832–34), noted: "By [Watt's] invention every great river is open up to us." He saw not just the Mississippi, but "the Amazon, the Niger and the Nile, the Indus and the Ganges" mastered "by hundreds of steam-vessels, carrying the glad tidings of 'peace and good-will to all men' into the dark places of the earth which are now filled with cruelty."[4] In many cases, those who were most anxious to use the new gunboats were the missionaries who wanted to end slavery, cannibalism, human sacrifice, and other unspeakable evils. They were inclined to see the hand of the Almighty in the emergency of naval steam technology.[5]

European imperialism, that is, the desire to acquire territory and administer it directly, was not a primary force at this stage, except in Tsarist Russia. The British, in particular, were interested in two things: promoting trade and suppressing slavery. But they were determined to defend their existing possessions. It is important to grasp that the European empires were not the only ones. China was an empire. So was Japan. Ethiopia was an enormous empire in East Africa. Some of these empires were archaic. Others, like the empires of the Persians and the Ottomans, were in manifest decline. But some, especially in western and southern Africa, were new and expanding. Others were exceedingly aggressive.

One of the most obnoxious to its frightened neighbors was the Burmese empire, with its court at Ava (near the future Mandalay). In the late 18th and early 19th centuries, it was moving into what is now Thailand and south down the Tenasserim coast. It was also pushing

west into the Bramaputra Valley and threatening the outworks of the
East India Company's position in Assam. The company sent missions
to Ava in 1803, 1809, 1811 and 1813, to remonstrate and to warn, all
to no purpose. What it accomplished instead was to reveal, to Western
eyes, the full horrors of the Burmese system of government. Michael
Symes, head of two of these embassies, described King Bodawpaya,
whose long and bloody reign ended in 1819, as "a child in his ideas, a
tyrant in his principles and a madman in his actions."[6] Early 19th-
century Western opinion saw him rather as we see Saddam Hussein of
Iraq or Muammar Qaddafi of Libya in the 1990s.

King Bodawpaya conducted ceremonial massacres of potential rivals, sometimes killing entire families, including their children and even
their servants. He was particuarly harsh toward his own family: In a
series of bloodbaths, he murdered every member of it who might conceivably claim his throne. Rebels who tried to overthrow him had their
entire native districts destroyed, every man, woman and child in the
area being killed; cattle slaughtered; and crops and even trees burned
or uprooted. After every massacre he built what he called an Atonement
Pagoda. In fact building pagodas was to him both the supreme pleasure
and an overriding religious duty. He built pagodas as the pharaohs built
pyramids, depopulating entire regions to recruit slave labor for these
projects, provoking famine and starvation. To raise taxes, he had compiled what the British called the Burmese Domesday Book, an astonishing record of social and economic conditions, unique in Southeast
Asian history, written on palm leaf and the thick local paper, *parabaik*.

The King was in some ways a religious fanatic. He persecuted those
he branded heretics and imposed the death penalty for drinking alcohol
or smoking opium. But the Buddhist priesthood regarded him as a
dangerous zealot, and when they tried to limit his theocratic mania, he
confiscated their property. If he oppressed the Burmese, he was still
more savage toward their neighbors, conducting plundering expeditions into Thailand, pushing forward his frontiers and launching
search-and-destroy missions into the wilder parts of his dominions
occupied by non-Burmese populations. Much of this activity was to
finance his masterpiece, a pagoda 500 feet high, the largest in history,
for which he recruited many thousands of slaves and deported tribesmen. It remained unfinished at his death.[7]

The British, like all the rest of the King's neighbors, regarded him
as a menace. His depredations produced a huge increase in desperate
refugees and a consequent rise in dacoitry (banditry). Some refugees
crossed into British territory and became a problem there. During the
Napoleonic Wars, French raiders, apparently with the King's consent,

used Burmese seaports as bases from which to attack British shipping in the Bay of Bengal.[8] Burmese oppression and imperialism produced a series of guerrilla revolts which tended to spill over into British-controlled territories. Nor did the problems end when Bodawpaya died. In fact, they increased. Bodawpaya's successor, King Bagyidaw, was a weak man under the thumb of an ambitious general, Maha Bandula. For most of the period 1815–19, the British in India were occupied with the Maratha wars, and the Burmese court conceived a mistaken idea of British power. The Burmese began to pursue guerrilla bands into British territory and, in the process, captured local people who were engaged in elephant roundups for the East India Company; they were taken off as slaves. In winter 1823–24 the Burmese army, which was 60,000 strong, began a full-scale invasion with the object of capturing the British post at Chittagong. The Burmese had already occupied British-owned islands in the Bay of Bengal, but the seizure of Chittagong was a threat to Calcutta itself. On 5 March 1824, the Governor General, Lord Amhurst, reluctantly declared war.

The First Burma War was not aimed at annexation but it was a foretaste of what could be expected when a Western superpower came into conflict with an archaic oriental state, however formidable. Not that the British war effort, which was grudging and feeble, hampered at every point by financial restrictions dictated from London and reinforced by the East India Company, was in any way impressive. On the contrary, it illustrated serious and continuing weaknesses in British imperial power. The 47th Bengal Native Infantry refused to embark on ships to go across the "black water" to Burma, citing religious-caste prohibitions; mutinied at Barrackpore; and had to be disciplined and disbanded—an ugly foreshadowing of the Indian Mutiny to come. The British sent two overland columns into Burma, up the Bramaputra into Assam and into Arakan from Chittagong, and an amphibious expedition to take Rangoon and proceed up the Irrawaddy to Ava. All three were ill-planned and ill-equipped and, in particular, lacked medical supplies and personnel to meet the hazards of warfare in a tropical rainforest. Here again, the muddle and waste of the Crimean War were adumbrated. There were 15,000 British casualties, the overwhelming majority of them dying from dysentery, malaria, scurvy, dropsy, ulcerated legs and cholera.

The main thrust came from the waterborne force up the Irrawaddy. It had a 50-gun ship, the *Liffey;* four 20-gun sloops; four East India Company cruisers; and masses of schooners, gun brigs, and transports carrying 9,000 white and native troops. In addition to the *Diana,* there were two other steamboats; the *Enterprise,* used as a troopship, and the

Pluto, for coastal bombardment. The Burmese abandoned Rangoon without a fight, confident that their river fastnesses would protect them. That illusion was dispelled by the *Diana*. But Marryat, who published his account of the war, complete with drawings, was impressed by Burmese resourcefulness: their ability to build formidable stockades at short notice, their fireships made up of rafts of 40 canoes tied together and stocked with jars of petroleum, and their general intelligence. "I never met with any Burman who could not read or write," he recorded. In addition to their courage, inventiveness and skill, he found them "the most even-tempered race I ever met with, always gay, always content under any privation. . . . The English seamen were particularly partial to them and declared them 'the best sort of chaps they had ever fallen in with.' " Marryat was often ill with fever, and he was bitterly critical of the authorities who could send men on this kind of expedition without any attempt to provide them with suitable tropical uniforms, mosquito netting, and antimalarial stores. There was no milk, fresh meat, fish, fruit, or vegetables, only salt pork and biscuits. By the end of 1824, of the 3,586 whites in the original force, 3,115 were dead. Marryat believed that it was only the superiority of British weapons that gave them victory.

But the *Diana* made all the difference, and her ability to get the force 500 miles up-river demoralized the Burmese command. Arakan, Pegu and Tenasserin fell. When the Burmese counterattacked with their large forces, they fell victims in huge numbers to British firepower. General Bandula was killed in such an attack on 1 April 1825, and thereafter a British victory was only a matter of time. Marryat handled the naval forces skillfully, and *Diana's* Congreve rockets and mortars proved devastating.[9] By early 1826 the British were only 45 miles from Ava, the capital, and the Burmese army surrendered at Yandaboo. The treaty signed there, 24 February 1826, forestalled a British occupation of the capital. Under the treaty, the Burmese agreed to withdraw from Assam, give up Arakan and Tenessarim, recognize the independence of Main-pur, admit a British resident at Ava and pay a £1 million indemnity—cheap, under the circumstances, for the war had cost Britain £14 million, 10 times an Indian campaign. Burma's neighbors were delighted with the British victory. King Bagyidaw sank into a melancholy and eventually went mad. But Burmese governments continued to take an unrealistic view, rather like the authorities in Peking, of what they could or could not do while existing in close proximity to a Western superpower, and their arrogance eventually led to annexation.[10]

* * *

The dynamic relationship between the British power in India and the Burmese empire, in which the first was, seemingly inexorably and against its will, drawn into absorbing the second, was only one example of the way the modern world was taking shape. As trade brought Westerners into contact with other civilizations all over the world, so their notions of how affairs should be conducted came into irreconcilable conflict with those of local rulers. The British in India, with few exceptions, did not want an empire. In the years after Waterloo, some of them thought that Indians no longer showed the same respect for British authority. Farington's friend Mrs. Peache, back from Calcutta, told him that "the natives would no longer get out of their palanquins and bow" when they passed Europeans and that there was "less salaaming."[11] But equally, many of the British in India did not desire this kind of subservience. The East India Company itself was old-fashioned; conservative, inactive, run by committees (rather like the old Spanish Empire in the Americas); and, above all, obsessed by financial economy. During the 1820s, parsimony became its leading principle of administration. In 1828 Lord Ellenborough, as president of the Board of Control (the Whitehall department which oversaw the East India Company), warned the company that unless it reduced its expenses, its charter would not be renewed. By far the easiest way to cut costs was to rule out military or naval expeditions.[12]

Money, then, was one factor which worked against Western expansion. On the other hand, there were ideas and feelings about justice. Britain was going through a progressive, peaceful revolution in which governmental corruption was being stamped out, criminal law reformed, trade made free, industry established, mass education introduced, towns paved and lit by gas, transport improved and almost every aspect of daily life altered for the better. The young men who were sent out to India, like the traders in Canton, came face to face, beyond the boundaries of direct British rule, with societies that were sunk in squalor and apathy, ruled by men who were indifferent to their subjects' welfare, lazy and avaricious at best, and actively cruel and aggressive at worst. Their itch to reform these iniquities was constant, and reforming them meant a forward policy—annexation or taking the native princes under British supervision.

An outstanding but also typical example of the British reformer was Mountstuart Elphinstone (1779–1859). Elphinstone had come out to India in 1795, aged 15, and had served first as the legal assistant to the Registrar at Benares, then transferred to the diplomatic side, which worked with native princes. He had been political assistant to Wellington in the First Maratha War; Resident in various places; envoy to

Kabul, and, finally, Resident in Poona. His journals reveal him to be exceptionally hard working, determined to improve himself and everyone and everything around him.[13] "We rise at four and read Sophocles, generally about 200 lines, till it is time to ride," he recorded. He would gallop hard for two hours, his horses never lasting more than a year. Then: "We sometimes read on our return which takes place about seven. After breakfast business generally prevents our beginning Xenophon, which is our forenoon's lesson, till eleven; we then read 20 or 30 pages, eat a sandwich and read separately—I Tacitus and the books on the French Revolution till two; and then we read Grotius until evening."[14] As with other able British administrators in India, there was a slight strain of melancholy about his existence. A younger son, without inheritance, he had come out, as they all did, to "make a competency," which he worked out at £1,500 a year. To save enough to produce this amount would take him to age 42, when he would retire, "too old to set up a wife and family, and likewise too old to mix in society."[15] But that did not mean he lacked dedication to his work; on the contrary, he was fiercely devoted to it.

Elphinstone was in at the kill of the old Maratha empire. British policy was to have protective treaties with friendly rulers. It had one with the Amir of Sind, with the Shah of Persia, with the Amir of Afghanistan, and with Ranjit Singh, ruler of the Punjab. Sometimes the British assisted these rulers to consolidate their power over their more unruly subjects. The object was to surround British India with friendly buffer states, self-governing but guaranteed to resist diplomatic or military penetration by powers like Russia or France, rather than actual frontier colonies. But, of course, if a ruler turned nasty or died and his successor proved aggressive, then Britain might, reluctantly, move in. Much of central India was nominally ruled by rajas, in reality by their ministers or *peshwas,* and by the fierce Pindaris or irregular military bands, composed of Marathas, Arabs, Jats, Afghans, criminal tribes, and other marauders. Elphinstone, as Resident at Poona, had to oversee these very unsatisfactory native personages and was continually frustrated by the wickedness and ruin they caused and his inability to stop it. The most important of the *de facto* rulers was the Peshwa Baji Rao. In 1802 he had provoked a revolt by a powerful noble, Jaswant Rao, by having his brother trampled to death by an elephant. The revolt was successful, the Peshwa fled to the British, and they reinstated him by force, in return for a treaty which gave them control over his foreign relations. But the Peshwa continued to be an unsuitable ruler, Elphinstone reporting in 1815 that "the greater part of [his] time that is not occupied by religion is devoted to vicious indulgences."[16] After trouble over his favorites, Elphinstone imposed a more severe treaty in 1817. That treaty provoked the Peshwa into a revolt of his own, making common cause with all the Maratha and Pindari bands who were willing to take on British power. In the course of 1817, the British mobilized an army of 120,000, under Sir John Malcolm, which defeated the huge but disorderly coalition forces. The result was a major reconstruction of central India. The Peshwa surrendered and was exiled. The Deccan was annexed to the Bombay Presidency. The Pinari bands were exterminated or broken up, the leader of the worst of them, Chitu, being driven into the jungle where he was eaten by a tiger. The old Maratha empire ceased to exist. In Poona, its most important city, with a population of 110,000, the local bankers and merchants asked for permanent protection against their old military rulers. Elphinstone was appointed "Sole Commissioner of the Territory Conquered from the Peshwa"; given a salary of 50,000 rupees a year (plus expenses); and, in effect, allowed to provide the uncorrupt and disinterested system of modern government he favored.

Thus a huge chunk of the old world, a medieval system based on feudalism, which had somehow contrived to prolong itself into the early 19th century, disappeared into the oubliette of history. Not only the absolute rulers, like Baji Rao himself, but their feudatories, who provided cavalry in proportion to their incomes and status, had to be dealt with by Elphinstone. General Malcolm, assigned to march Baji Rao to his place of exile in Bithur (where he was supervised by a British military commissioner), noted in a letter to Elphinstone: "[Baji and his court] have the *best water* whenever we halt, they have tents, camels, bullocks, coolies, cash whenever required, and every species of civility, attention and respect, but all ideas opposite to their situation [their powerlessness] are crushed the moment they appear."[17] The Peshwa died under surveillance. His brother Chimnaji Appa was also exiled under guard. Both got generous stipends. Some dangerous men, like Trimbakji Dengle, the Peshwa's favorite, who was violently anti-British, were imprisoned in forts until they died. The great feudatories, or *jagidars*—they held territorial *jagirs* in return for military service— were dealt with on their merits, with regard to the degree of freedom and the amount of cash they were allowed. But such grand figures as the Jagadir of Nipani, the Desai of Kittur, Madhav Rao Raste, Ganpart Rao of Tasgaon, Chintaman Rao of Sangli, and Gopal Rao of Jamknandi, their names reading like a litany of the ancient south Asian chivalry, would wage war or oppress their subjects no more.[18] When Indian power reemerged, it would be in the shape of *pandits* and lawyers, professional politicians of the big cities.

Thanks to the paradoxical attitudes of men like Elphinstone, the resurrection of Indian power was set in train at the very moment that Britain was destroying the old ruling class and putting in its own administrators. Long before Thomas Babington Macaulay set the course for India to be educated into independence, Elphinstone decided, at the moment he was taking over power in January 1819, that such was the only responsible direction for British policy. He wrote to Malcolm; "The acquisition of knowledge by their subjects may have lost the French Haiti and the Spaniards South America, but it preserved half the world to the Romans, gave them a hold on the manners and opinions of their subjects and left them a kind of moral empire long after their physical power was destroyed. Knowledge seems to overturn tyrannical and maintain moderate governments & it is therefore to be hoped that it may strengthen ours. But at any rate the danger from it is distant and uncertain & we have no more right to stifle the growing knowledge of our subjects than Herod had to massacre the Innocents because he believed that one of them was to dethrone him."[19]

The notion of a "moral empire" in India, that is, British rule justified by its success in improving the lot of ordinary Indians, began to establish a powerful grip on the imaginations of some British administrators in the 1820s. It became particularly marked when Lord William Bentinck came out as Governor General in 1828. Bentinck put it in these words: "English greatness is founded on Indian happiness."[20] The essence of liberal imperialism, of which he was the founder, was that the ruling power must respect the religion, customs and susceptibilities of the ruled, subject to two qualifications: They must not be allowed to obstruct changes needed to give Indians a better life and prepare them, in the long term, for participation in government, nor could they be tolerated if they ran counter to fundamental humanitarian instincts. In this respect, the model was the Roman empire, which likewise left many local ways unchanged but would never tolerate human sacrifice.

Bentinck set about abolishing the more horrifying religious practices, such as female infanticide and offering children to the Ganges. He also acted against suttee, the killing, voluntary or involuntary, of the widows of the nobility and royalty. Suttee was based upon a misunderstanding of Vedic texts and had become institutionalized under the rajputs during the Middle Ages. The Emperor Akbar had tried to abolish it, but with the Mongol empire's decay, the practice had actually increased. As many as 64 women were put on the pyre of one raja, and it was calculated that in Bengal alone 700 women were burned alive each year. Bentinck's Regulation in Council of 1829 lays down: "The practice of *suttee,* or burning or burying alive the widows of Hindus, is illegal and punishable by the Criminal Courts." Within a decade, suttee had been discontinued, and none of the disastrous consequences foretold by the priests occurred. (It has enjoyed a sporadic revival since Indian independence in 1947.)

Another institution banned was *Meriah*, the human sacrifice to fertility gods in Orissa, though this practice was not eliminated until the mid-1850s. Efforts were also begun to break up the criminal tribes and end the outrageous cult of *Thuggee*, whose initiates murdered travelers in enormous numbers. Some modern Indian historians have argued that there was no such cult and that the large number of murderous robberies on the road reflected the breakup of the Mongol empire and the anarchy caused by the Maratha bands and the Pindaris. For India's new rulers to present Thuggee as a religious practice was "a convenient way of disowning responsibility for its actual origin in the British period."[21] But this argument would imply that the confessions of innumerable Thugs, which describe the cult dedicated to the goddess Kali—one man confessed to over 900 murders, another to 500—were deliberately fabricated, and that Sir William Sleeman, the dedicated soldier-policeman who over six years brought over 1,500 Thugs to justice, was a liar and manufacturer of evidence on a colossal scale.[22] At all events, Thuggee was ended, and travel on the Indian roads (later the railways) became, by Indian standards, remarkably safe.

By the end of the 1820s, India was thus a benevolent paternalism, direct rule by Britain marching alongside a variety of arrangements in which Indian princes and British residents collaborated. But there was never any question of who was the senior partner. Under Lord Moira, Governor General from 1812 to 1823, the imperial title, still held by Akbar Shah II, was not exactly abolished. But Akbar was slighted by raising the Nawab of Oudh, Ghaziel-Din Haidar (reigned 1814–27) to the status of King, the change being formally gazetted at Windsor in 1819. But since the new King was dominated by his upstart butler Agha Mir, a sinister, "dark, harsh, hawk-nosed" creature, according to Bishop Reginald Heber of Calcutta, Moira insisted that the British Resident be given equal precedence.[23] In the Ashmolean Museum in Oxford, there is a remarkable ten-inch-high bronze, Mughal work from Lucknow, circa 1820, showing a cavalcade of the King of Oudh and the Resident. The bronze is strikingly symbolic of the way the British worked in princely India. King and Resident are each mounted on elephants, and there is a show of equality, but both are surrounded by British redcoats.[24]

*   *   *

The kind of liberal imperialism the British were adopting in India in the 1820s eventually spread into their other east Asian possessions, especially into the Malay archipelago which they began to develop from their new and flourishing base in Singapore. But other European nations were slow to bring liberal notions into their overseas possessions. In the Philippines, the policy of Spain, in occupation since 1565, was confused and tended to be backward looking. From 1762 to 1764, the forces of the British East India Company had occupied the capital, Manila, as part of the operations of the Seven Years War, and though they withdrew after peace was concluded, Spanish military and naval prestige in the area never recovered. Indeed, until the Spanish began to introduce steam gunboats in the 1830s, their control over many of the 7,100 islands was nominal. There were Muslim or animist raids against Christian towns, when thousands were massacred or taken into slavery—the Philippines was a prime source for slaves throughout the Southeast Asian market. Nor was this the only challenge to Spanish authority. There was a revolt of white liberals in 1815, provoked by Ferdinand VII's suppression of the liberal constitution in faraway Madrid, and in 1823 mutinous native troops nearly succeeded in storming Manila. The Spanish tried to bolster their increasingly precarious rule by savage counterattacks on their many enemies and by a general policy of xenophobia. They feared the French and Dutch; still more the British; and, increasingly, the Americans, who were eventually to get the colony in 1898. In 1800 a royal edict had forbidden any non-Spanish whites to live in the Philippines. In 1820, during a serious outbreak of cholera, the Spanish government deliberately whipped up mob fury against "disease-carrying foreigners," and eight years later, there were renewed edicts against Europeans engaging in trade or visiting the outlying islands.[25]

The Dutch in Indonesia, which the British had also restored to them (in 1814–15), were likewise anxious to keep out other Europeans. The first Governor General after the British withdrew, Baron Van der Capellen, deliberately set about reversing all the liberal measures introduced while Stamford Raffles was in charge, especially in the policy toward the natives. Like the Spanish in the Philippines, he wanted to turn Java into a hermit state, sealed off from the outside world and its ideas. He ignored regulations laid down by the far-from-progressive Dutch government if they seemed to him too "advanced." His policy was to make the colony profitable by an alliance between his government and the more powerful native chiefs to bring masses of native laborers into the plantation economy. In theory the slave trade was forbidden and headmen were not allowed to hire out their villagers (who were serfs). In practice, Dutch officials encouraged and paid the native authorities to supply forced labor for the expanding coffee plantations and the teak forests. It was the prelude to imposing the so-called Culture System, which abolished the freedom of peasants.

The Culture System was the work of another antiliberal governor, Johannes Van den Bosch, a self-made man who had been a prisoner of war of the British during the Napoleonic Wars and who loathed all they stood for, especially their notions of personal liberty and free trade. His two hate-figures were Adam Smith and Raffles. Bosch argued that the natives were too ignorant and lazy to be left alone. Each peasant farmer was given a quota and forced to produce it. A percentage had to be for export, and was sold to the Dutch, taken to the Netherlands in Dutch ships and marketed there. The system began with indigo and sugar, then was expanded to include tea, coffee, tobacco, cotton, cochineal, pepper and cinnamon. The outgoing ships brought Dutch products for sale in a market closed to all other Europeans.

The system was originally hedged with some safeguards for the natives, but these were gradually dropped, and Java became a serf country in which the peasants had to work 200 days a year, unpaid, for the government.[26] It was enormously profitable to the Dutch government, paying off part of its huge national debt and, from the 1830s, financing its railway system. It also gave Java a road network, and in some ways the colony flourished, the population rising from 6 million in 1815 to 9.5 million 20 years later. But it brought a rebellion, 1825–30, led by Dipo Negora, the native prince of Jogjakart, who was outraged when the Dutch drove a road over a sacred tomb. The Prince called himself "the chosen of Allah to drive out the Kaffirs," as he called the Dutch, and his guerrilla bands massacred Dutch officials, plantation overseers and their Chinese allies, who acted as estate middlemen, like the Jews in Eastern Europe. Hitting back, the Dutch followed the example of Peking in fighting the White Lotus revolt by building fortified strong points, linked by their new strategic roads, from which search-and-destroy missions were launched. Thus, alongside liberal imperialism in Asia, the Dutch were establishing another tradition of exploitative commercial imperialism, which was to be widely followed in Africa, especially by the Belgians. In Indonesia itself, where they were already absorbing other islands in addition to Java during the 1820s, the Dutch were setting the pattern of white-native hatred which was to mold this vast and populous country during the crucial decade of the 1940s and beyond.

In Indochina, where the French had been active since the 1760s, they steered a course halfway between the liberal imperialism of the British and the commercial imperialism of the Dutch and Spanish. The situation in the 18th and early 19th centuries was complex because, in addition to the predatory Burmese, there were two other local imperialisms. When not fending off Burma, the Siamese empire periodically thrust into Cambodia from the west, while the aggressive and militaristic Vietnamese attacked it from the east. French policy, through its great missionary bishop Pierre-Joseph-Georges Pigneau, was to build up and Christianize the Vietnamese empire, taking members of the Nguyen royal family to Paris to be educated. With French help, the Emperor Nguyen Anh succeeded in uniting all the Vietnamese lands in 1802, for the first time in history, and took the title Emperor Gia Long. But French efforts to ensure that his successor was a francophile failed. Minh-Mang, who came to the throne in 1820, was anti-Western, anti-Christian and pro-Chinese. He rejected repeated French missions, refused to receive a consul, broke off relations with France, made Confucianism the state creed and finally ordered a general persecution of Christians.[27] The French eventually followed the pattern set by the British in Burma in 1824–26 and intervened with amphibious forces, thus ending Vietnam's attempt to remain a hermit state.

The one wholly successful hermit state in the region, which succeeded in absorbing only what it wished from the outside world and rejecting the rest, was Japan. But in doing so, it prepared an ominous future for itself in the 20th century. In the 1820s Japan conducted itself in many ways like China. At Nagasaki it permitted a small Dutch commercial settlement of a dozen traders, who were allowed neither to travel inland nor to bring their wives. The trade was grudgingly conceded, one ship a year, and the Japanese maintained they really had no need for Dutch manufactured imports, though these goods were much prized among the ruling class and the merchant-tycoons. Equally, they were reluctant to part with their main export, copper, smelted at the imperial town of Sakai. Like the Chinese, the Japanese thought that sending their metals abroad was a weakening process, living on capital, and under no circumstances would they allow silver or gold to leave. Japanese were forbidden to travel on pain of death if caught, and no junk over 50 tons could be built, except for the imperial navy. So there were no Japanese boat people, though the country was already beginning to develop signs of overpopulation.

With virtually no natural resources (even the copper was beginning to run out by the 1820s), limited land, and a hostile climate—cold spells, drought at times, floods, typhoons, severe spring frosts and plagues of insects—the incessant fear in Japan was famine. The possi-

bility of imminent mass starvation was becoming a driving force in
Japanese life and remained so until, from the 1950s, the development
of a vast export economy removed it. In the 1820s this fear was reinforced by terror of foreign predation. The Dutch, who attached little
importance to their Nagasaki station, sometimes used American ships
instead of their own. The Japanese did not like this practice; they were
vaguely aware of America as a huge entity far to the east but growing
toward them. They feared the British, too; British ships, nosing about
Japanese waters, were always warned off, and when Captain Pellew,
the future victor of Algiers, made an unauthorized call at Nagasaki in
the frigate *Phaeton* in 1808 and the local authorities did not succeed in
detaining him and his ship, the affair was seen as a national disgrace,
and many ritual suicides had to take place.[28]

The Japanese also feared the Russians, driving across the northern
Pacific in pursuit of high-quality furs, especially the skins of sables,
seals, otters, and arctic foxes, and actually competing with Japan for
territory. The Russians were setting up posts in the area. From 1795
they had one at Urup, which was much resented by the Japanese, who
responded by fortifying Yezo in Saghalin and the South Kuriles. The
Japanese dispatched their leading cartographer and mathematician, Ino
Chukei, to map Yezu and its surroundings and had all the nearby
waters sounded and charted for future naval operations. Special naval
vessels were built to show and plant their sun flag. When Governor
Rezanov of the Tsarist Far East Company took an embassy to Nagasaki
in 1804, the Japanese not only refused to receive it but detained him by
force for six months. Released, he fitted out two warships, which
conducted a series of revenge attacks in 1806–07, burning Japanese
junks and their settlements at Kushunkotan, Iterup, and Hakodate.
These attacks led to further Japanese military and naval measures, and
in 1825, following a British landing on the coast, in which cattle were
stolen and peasants were killed, the famous Expulsion Decree, *Uchi-
harai-Rei*, was issued. The decree listed all the outrages committed by
the Russians and other white races and went on: "The continuation of
such insolent proceedings, as also the intention of introducing the
Christian religion, which has come to our knowledge, will no longer be
received with indifference. . . . If foreign vessels should come near any
port whatsover, the local inhabitants should unite to drive them away
. . . [and] if any foreigners land they must be arrested or killed and their
ships destroyed."[29]

Japan's growing xenophobia took different forms. One was the
persecution of Japanese who had foreign contacts. In 1823 a brilliant
Bavarian scientist, Philip Franz van Siebold (1797–1866), came to

Nagasaki as physician to the trading post and began to study Japanese fauna, flora and language. He had a villa nearby at Narutaki, and many Japanese scholars came there to consult him, especially about astronomy and cartography. In 1828 there was a sinister and significant incident when the authorities discovered that one of Siebold's scholar-friends had given him a map of Japan, a capital offense under Japanese law. Siebold was arrested, questioned on his knees, held under duress for nine months, and finally expelled in October 1829.[30] Many of his friends were tortured and died in prison, including the court astronomer Takahashi, whose body was preserved in salt until it could be formally tried and condemned. The principal university at Edo, the capital (now Tokyo), issued a solemn decree condemning Western learning as wicked and useless.

Hatred of foreigners also took the form of a reassertion of aristocratic privileges against the pretensions of merchants and manufacturers. Japan was not a cathedocracy like China, run by a caste of intellectual-officials. It was a militaristic feudal empire, where ultimate power rested in the hands of fierce landowners and their knights, known as "the Two-Sworded Men." But in many ways, it was a money as well as a feudal economy, rather like Europe in the late Middle Ages, with a growing degree of intermediate technology and a thrusting middle class of manufacturers and traders threatening the dominance of the old military and landed elites. Of the other three imperial towns (in addition to Nagasaki), Edo (Tokyo) was a parasitic court city; Kyoto, the ancient capital, was the main manufacturing and industrial center; and Osaka (of which Sakai and its smelters formed little more than a suburb) was the distribution center, where food and goods were stored. Osaka had more than 100 medieval-type guilds or *kumis,* entry to which was carefully guarded and had to be bought. The kumis covered all occupations: the wholesale rice kumi had 1,351 members and the bathhouse kumi, 2,004, there were 52 moneychangers, 613 pawnbrokers and 50 booksellers. The most important kumi were the Ten Kumi, which dealt in paper, oil, drugs, dry goods, cotton, lacquer ware, ironware, earthenware, wine and matting. Kumi elsewhere in Japan were merely branches of the Osaka ones, and these, in turn, were beginning to be organized, in the 1820s, into giant trusts or cartels. The Japanese had never heard of monopoly capitalism, but they were finding their way to it.

Those who ran the cartels were becoming immensely and ostentatiously rich. Their huge feasts and their outbidding each other in paying vast sums for the first bonito of the season or the first fruit of the eggplant enraged the old nobles and their Two-Sworded Men, and from

the 1820s onwards there were brutal attempts to enforce ancient sumptuary laws. The luxurious villas of rich but low-born people in Edo
were demolished. Ichikawa Danjuro, Japan's most famous actor, who
had become flamboyantly wealthy, was banished to the countryside.
Farmers were forbidden to appear in Edo at all. Storytelling halls,
teahouses, and archery booths—all centers of middle-class pleasures—
were closed. Novels and decorative signboards were prohibited. All the
professional women hairdressers lost their licenses, and women were
told to dress their own hair. Women were forbidden to take lessons in
many exotic skills, such as flower arranging, miniature gardening and
interior decoration. Merchants and their families were confined to
dressing in cotton, hemp and simple silk. Imported silk from China was
forbidden, as were crepe, satin and *habutaye*. The regulations, culminating in a decree of 1841, were extremely detailed, regulating hairpins, combs and even tea cakes. A woman who was found dressing
above the norm was stripped naked and paraded through the streets.
Corruption of the police soon mitigated the severity of the regulations,
but they reminded all the money men that those who wielded the sword
had the ultimate power.

There was a third, and ultimately most important, manifestation of
xenophobia, whose roots went back into the 18th century: a fundamentalist revival of Shinto, the ancient national religion. Japan like China
was a theocracy, and it had never even changed its dynasty, since when
heirs failed there were co-options into the divine family. But for 200
years the *tenku* or mikado had reigned but not ruled. Instead, Japan
was a shogunate, the Shogun being the Emperor's generalissimo, pre-
server in peace, leader in war. The Emperor performed certain religious
ceremonies, which only he could do, but the Shogun was the government. The shogunate was hereditary, too, resting in the Tokugawa
family, and the 11th Tokugawa Shogun, Iyenari, who was born in 1773,
was one of the most enduring, ruling from 1793 to his abdication in
1837 (he died in 1841). During Iyenari's long shogunate, the elements
of the crisis which was to end the system in 1868, restore the Emperor
to power and begin the modern history of Japan, were already beginning to appear. Iyenari was the greatest of the feudatories, his lands,
scattered all over Japan, formed the largest domain of all, including 3
to 4 million urban dwellers. But he was not all-powerful. The three next
largest feudatories, the Kaga, Satsuma, and Sendai lords, known as the
Great Kokushu, reported directly to the Emperor, and all 16 of the
biggest lords were treated with elaborate respect and ceremonial when
they came to see the Shogun in Edo.

Moreover, the Shogun had to observe elaborate protocol when

dealing with the Emperor, who was by no means powerless. The procedure was as follows: The Shogun communicated his will to the Rojo,
or Great Council. The Rojo transmitted it to a court official called the
Shoshidai in Kyoto, the imperial city where the Mikado lived. The
Shoshidai sent it to another official called the Tenso, who brought it to
a third, the Kwampaku, who finally laid it before the Mikado himself,
a divine personage by the name of Ninko during the years 1817–46.
Ninko's reply was then transmitted, with some variations, by reversing
the process. Every stage involved elaborate ceremonies and huge expenses. Moreover, the early 19th century was a time when many archaic
procedures were being revived. Ninko's coronation in 1817 was celebrated with prodigious splendor and the revival of the ancient practice
that when a Mikado or Shogun abdicated (retired), a new palace was
built for him. Each palace required several hundred officials to administer it. New titles were constantly being awarded. Ninko made Iyenari
first Minister of the Right, then Minister of the Left, finally Chancellor
of the empire, each occasion being an excuse for expensive junketings.
Every anniversary was celebrated, too. An extra tier of government was
added by the custom of each Shogun having an official favorite, in
Iyenari's case, during the 1820s, Mizuno Tadashige, who was behind
the draconian sumptuary purge.

Much of the time of the myriads of courtiers and officials was spent
paying elaborate visits to each other, courtiers going to Edo, officials to
Kyoto. Institutions duplicated each other. A Junior Council was added
to the Great Council. There were three Great Magistrates, representing
different archaeological layers of bureaucratic duplication. As in China,
every official had his hangers-on. As in China, all had to be bribed to
get any action. Officials and courtiers constantly gave each other costly
presents. Most of the ceremonies were paid for by the Shogun. In
addition, the Shogun had to keep up the palace district of Edo Castle,
a city within a city, with duplicate palaces—the Main Palace and the
Nishi Maru.

The Shogun's own scale of living was profligate. He had 350 court
ladies and 250 female attendants. The most powerful mistresses and
concubines were known as the Ladies of the Great Interiors. All were
divided into factions, often on religious grounds. Iyenari's family usually belonged to the Jodo Buddhist sect, but he was persuaded by one
of his concubines to convert to the Nicheren sect. This conversion was
a serious financial matter for rival bands of monks and produced a
constant maelstrom of intrigue in the world hermetically sealed from
real Japan by the palace walls.

The Japanese were by no means wholly silent about the failings of their rulers. Ceremonial expenditures got some of them deeply into debt to the Osaka money men. The Shoshidai Saki, known to owe millions, was lampooned as a bankrupt in Kyoto wall posters. The Shogun Iyenari himself was criticized. It was said he did little work, merely summoning the Great Magistrates to chat with him in his private gardens, and that, in particular, he neglected to look at the letters put in the "Complaint Boxes." His constant need for money to finance the ceremonial afflatus, reflected in a steep rise in the tax- and bribery levels, was a further grievance.[31]

A more profound force at work, reflecting a general dissatisfaction with the shogunate system and a desire that Japan should return to its pristine religious origins, began to gather force about this time. Like the White Lotus movement in China, it was a form of religious fundamentalism, but more articulate and intellectualized. Above all, it was xenophobic, being directed against the Chinese in the first instance but embracing all foreigners and all alien ideas and customs. It preached a return to Japan's primeval form of religion, Shinto, from which the institution of the Mikado sprang.

The greatest of the Shinto revivalists, Mabuchi (1667–1769), wanted to strip Japanese culture of all its Chinese accretions, especially Confucianism. "In ancient times," he wrote, "when men's characters were straightforward, it was not necessary to have a complicated system of manners and morals such as Confucius taught." Nor did the Japanese, being essentially good people, need one now. The Chinese did, because they had a disposition to evil, and that was why their country was so disorderly. They had likewise tried to corrupt the brave and honest Japanese with their Confucian ideas, and the results had been bad for Japan, as all could see. "The Japanese, as honest men, could do without such teaching."[32]

Mabuchi's doctrine became the basis for the far more important literary work of Moto-ori, a physician of prodigious energy, who in his spare time from medical practice wrote 55 books in 180 volumes. In some ways, he is the Japanese Rousseau. His *Kojiki-den,* his central work, was written in the years 1764–96, but the printing of it was not complete until 1822. Thereafter it circulated widely in educated circles. It is astonishing that the Shoguns did not censor Moto-ori's book. Their short-sighted reason may have been that it modernized and enormously improved written Japanese, stripping it of its accretions of Chinese imported words and bringing out the pristine strength of the native tongue. Moreover, the *Kojiki-den* was a patriotic compendium of Japanese lore, containing history and cosmology, as well as philosophy and religion, like a medieval *Summa*. But there can be no doubt that it was subversive of the shogunate and ultimately fatal to it. Moto-ori was a religious fundamentalist of the more obscurantist kind, who believed in primitive shinto with its 8 million deities, reproduced fables and myths as fact, and rejected the kind of abstract philosophy which China had brought to Japan. But he also showed the hard practicality and the concrete imagery which the Japanese character relishes, and this imagery—plus his glorious language—explains his influence.

Japan under Shinto, Moto-ori argued, was a Garden of Eden, simple, rustic, true, and pure. The Mikado was a great monarch and exercised his enormous power wisely. Then came Confucianism from China, deceiving the innocent Japanese with its pseudo-religious sophistries and bringing with it the tendency toward civil war, which was endemic in China. (The contrast between disorderly, divided China and disciplined unitary Japan is a constant refrain of Moto-ori.) In due course came the emasculation of the Mikado, Japan's man-god: "Since the introduction of Chinese manners, the sovereign, while occupying a highly dignified place, has been degraded to the intellectual level of a woman. Real power fell into the hands of servants, and though they never actually assumed the title, they were sovereigns in fact, while the Mikado became an utter nullity." One reason Moto-ori rejected Chinese religious ideas was that they portrayed China as the center of the universe and all humanity as its natural subjects or tributaries. The truth, he wrote, was different. The sun was God, and the sun goddess had been born in Japan. It was Japan which was the center of the universe, and all human beings were subject to it, actually or potentially. As descendants of the sun goddess, the Mikados were divinely appointed to rule not only Japan but the the entire world.[33]

Moto-ori produced a fundamental shift in Japanese thinking. He became the center of a Japanese cultural revival. The Shogun made him an honored official, despite the fact that his works identified the Shoguns with Chinese cultural imperialism and were to be, over the half century from 1822, the basis for the exultant and finally successful slogan "*Sonno Jo-i*—Honor the Emperor and Expel the Barbarians!" Men and women from all over the country came to listen to him. Events appeared to bear him out. The fact that China was in increasing trouble with foreign intrusions, as the Japanese knew, proved his analysis. The Japanese had always been told that the Chinese were "the Elect Nation." Now Moto-ori taught them to see their neighbors as the wretched, crushed, humiliated inhabitants of what he called "a dirty country." It was, rather, the Japanese who were the elect nation. This assertion, so deeply attractive to Japanese xenophobia and racialism, was reinforced by the multitudinous works of Moto-ori's leading disciple, Hirata, born the same year as the U.S. Declaration of Independence. Hirata's cosmology and creation story confirmed Japanese preeminence. It begins: "Why Japan is the Country of the Gods." All the thousands of Shinto gods, he argued, had been born in Japan, none abroad. Hence every Japanese is descended from a god and is born with a perfect disposition, of pure heart and spirit, corrupted only by foreign influences. "Between the Japanese people," he wrote, "and the Chinese, Hindus, Russians, Dutch, Siamese, Cambodians and the other nations of the world there is a difference of kind rather than of degree." Hence, the Japanese must take steps to keep the corrupting foreigners out. His works developed into a kind of defense manual against Russian, Dutch and Anglo-Saxon penetration.

It was indeed inevitable that Shinto fundamentalism would eventually produce a militaristic spirit, as well as the overthrow of the shogunate, and it is remarkable that a subversive like Hirata should have been allowed to publish and teach openly in Edo throughout the 1820s and beyond (not until 1836 was a book of his censored and not till 1840 was he banished to his home town). Equally important, however, was the impact of a revived and modernized Shinto on Japanese society. Shinto merely taught about deities. It had no ethical or moral code; to make it a workable religion for modern Japan, it had to be given one. But this ethical code was produced according to the needs of the new, highly militarized state which emerged in Japan in the second half of the 19th century, thus giving a religious underpinning to a form of totalitarianism which was both primitive and highly sophisticated. And, as its "elect nation" philosophy slowly switched from a purely defensive posture, as the hermit state left its cell and became acquisitive and imperialistic, fundamentalist Japan eventually became the terrifying aggressor state of the 1930s and early 1940s.

It is a curious fact that in the 1820s similar tendencies were operating on the other side of the globe in Europe, despite the absence of any cultural contact. The 19th century was the great age of racism, prompted probably by the huge and visible increases of population, the beginnings of a demographic revolution which would sweep the entire world and is still raging in parts of it today. But whereas in the Far East, the "elect nation" racist ideologies of China and, now, Japan, were clothed in the priestly robes of religious cosmogony, in Europe they tended to wear rationalist and philosophical garments. Underneath, however, were the same flesh and bones of gullible men, easily persuaded by their rulers and intellectual guides that they were, in essence, and could be in reality, supermen, ruling the world.

In Germany, as we have seen, Bonapartist oppression had roused the sleeping giant of German nationalism. The restoration of imperial and princely power, with its police and censorship, could not put the monster to sleep or keep it aroused only for brief periods. The 1819 murder by K. S. Sand, of the antiliberal dramatist August Kotzebue, who had ridiculed the German student movement, followed by Sand's execution and the Karlsbad Decrees, merely divorced nationalism from old-fashioned authority. The decrees dissolved the student movement, set up commissions to investigate subversive activities, and reinforced the power of the police to arrest political activists and close down newspapers. They were drawn up at the instigation of Metternich and the Austrian throne and rubber-stamped by the federal Diet. They were provocative, rather than effective—some of the south German states would not enforce them—and in the long term made revolution more, not less, likely. Moreover, they set some German intellectuals thinking along the lines of France's development in the 1790s, of a marriage between nationalism and the overthrow of all existing order. In a perceptive comment, the Rhineland journalist Joseph Gorres, whose paper, the *Rheinischer Merkur,* was banned under the decrees for criticizing the Prussian government, warned that a German revolution, when it came, would be just as much a menace to the peace of Europe as the French Revolution had been. It would "inevitably end with the expulsion of all ruling dynasties, the destruction of all ecclesiastical forms, the extermination of the aristocracy and the introduction of a republican constitution. Then, when it has found its more fortunate Wallenstein, it will step beyond its frontiers and destroy Europe's whole rotten political system as far as the frontiers of Asia, because every revolutionised nation becomes a conquering one."[34]

Moreover, there was a growing chance that any German revolution of destruction would be conceived in terms of an "elect nation" asserting its rights with brutal force. There was, in the early 19th century, an important bifurcation between the French and the German approach to the world. The French, when in a revolutionary mood, were nationalist, but they were also internationalist; they thought in terms of "civilization," of which to be sure they were the leading exponents but which they shared with many other races. The Germans were beginning to think in terms of "culture"—theirs. Nicholas de Condorcet's *Historical Tableau of the Progress of the Human Spirit* (1793–94), one of the most powerful influences on French academic thinking in the period 1813–30, saw man as a long way on his voyage through time—middle-aged, fortyish and *désabusé*, as well as hopeful, rather like France herself, a well-worn entity, a little battle scarred by experience.[35] The Germans, on the other hand, who were not yet a united nation, saw man as young, fresh, and one step above the brute in some ways, but vigorous, capable of changing the Earth: a young Siegfried, stepping out of the primeval forest, but with the power of a god in his sword arm. The forest was German; so was the representative man. This was not the primitive view of a Moto-ori, a pagan believer in 8,100 gods, but of highly sophisticated academics in the world's best network of universities, of which there were now 19 in Germany.[36]

Johann Gottlieb Fichte (1762–1814), who held the chair of philosophy at the newly constituted University of Berlin, the most formidable of these institutions, wrote a series of works in the last phase of the Napoleonic Wars stressing both the intellectual and moral primacy of Germany and the way it could become, as he saw it, a boon to the whole of mankind through the agency of the modern state. Why, he asked, was there not in the German language a specific word for "character"? It was because to be German was to be automatically endowed with character. The Germans, he stated, were an *Urvolk*, the Chosen People of Nature. There was no need for them to learn to be civilized. On the contrary, they had an obligation to teach others their own natural civilization. To realize their world mission, however, they must first fulfill their mission as a nation, become the great nation their natural endowments made possible. The nation was inseparable from the state, which gave it form, discipline, purpose and, by its coercive power, kept the evil within man in check.

Fichte was much impressed by Niccolò Machiavelli and saw life as a continuing struggle for supremacy among the nations. The nation-state most likely to survive and profit from this struggle was the one which extended its influence over the lives of its people most widely. And such a nation-state—Germany was the obvious example—would naturally be expansive: "Every nation wants to disseminate as widely as possible the good points which are peculiar to it. And, as far as it can, it wants to assimilate the entire human race to itself in accordance with an urge planted in men by God, an urge on which the community of nations, the friction between them, and their development towards perfection rest."[37]

This was a momentous statement because it gave the authority of Germany's leading academic philosopher to the proposition that the power impulse of the state was both natural and healthy, and it placed the impulse in the context of a moral world view. Fichte's state was totalitarian and expansive, but it was not revolutionary. Its "prince" ruled by hereditary divine right. But "the prince belongs to his nation just as wholly and completely as it belongs to him. Its destiny under divine providence is laid in his hands, and he is responsible for it." So the prince's public acts must be moral, in accordance with law and justice, and his private life must be above reproach. In relations between states, however, "there is neither law nor justice, only the law of strength. This relationship places the divine, sovereign rights of fate and of world rule in the prince's hands, and it raises him above the commandments of personal morals and into a higher moral order whose essence is contained in the words, *Salus et decus populi suprema lex esto.*" This was an extreme and menacing statement that justified any degree of ruthlessness by the new, developing nation-state in its pursuit of self-determination and self-preservation. The notion of a "higher moral order," to be determined by the state's convenience, was to find expression, in the 20th century, in what Lenin called "the Revolutionary Conscience" and Hitler "the Higher Law of the Party." Moreover, there was no doubt what kind of state Fichte had in mind. It was not only totalitarian but German. In his *Addresses to the German Nation* (1807), he laid down as axiomatic that the state of the future can only be the national state, in particular the German national state, the German Reich.[38]

Fichte's campaign on behalf of the future Reich was continued and developed by the great philsopher who eventually occupied his chair in Berlin, Georg Wilhelm Friedrich Hegel (1770–1831). It is worth looking at Hegel in some detail. Not only was he the most important philosopher of the 19th century, whose notion of a dialectical progression from the lowest to the highest forms was to influence every academic discipline as well as his own, from theology to history, he was also a striking example of how, in the dawning modern world, the penmen were forming a devastating alliance with the swordsmen. This alliance was taking place in a primitive version in Japan—but a Japan soon to take a huge leap from intermediate to advanced technology. In Germany the process was more sophisticated, but not in essence very different. The common assumption is that intellectuals and soldiers are natural enemies. Not so. Intellectuals tend to be fascinated by power, not least military power, and are only too anxious to harness the soldiers to the chariots of their ideas. Equally, the soldiers and the politicians who both direct and are carried along by them have no objection to attaching intellectual horsepower to their gun carriages.

Hegel illustrated this tendency better than anyone. No intellectual has ever been a more dedicated servant of state power. In appearance, temperament, habits, virtues and vices, he was the archetypal academic.

He loved accuracy and precision. Both the well-born Nuremberg lady he married, Marie von Tucher, and his earlier girlfriend, Nanette Endel, accused him of habitual pedantry. In his dealings with women, indeed, he was "insufferably condescending."[39] The only things that mattered to him in life were a dutiful, respectable wife and a secure academic job. Announcing triumphantly that he had been appointed philosophy teacher at a gymnasium (high school), he wrote to his friend Isaac von Sinclair: "I . . . have what personally counts most for me: a fixed career and . . . an official occupation linked to my studies."[40] Thereafter he struggled and intrigued to get a university post at Tübingen and, finally, the apex of his ambition, the chair at Berlin. Already at Tübingen he was known to students and colleagues as *Der Alte,* the Old Man. His letters are quintessentially donnish, full of dull high-table gossip about jobs, fellowships, chairs, salaries, perks, free lunches and creature comforts. He noted that the defeat of the French had brought a blessing: "We have been liberated from ersatz coffee, and from our supplementary income as councillors we can now procure real Java coffee."[41]

Hegel was determined to put philosophy in a proper academic straitjacket: "Philosophy must assume a regular structure as teachable as geometry," he wrote to Von Sinclair. "My task is to invent that scientific form."[42] "Philosophy instruction in the universities," he insisted, "can accomplish what it ought—*an acquisition of definite knowledge*—only if it adopts a *definite methodical procedure,* encompassing and *ordering detail!* In this form alone can it be *learned* like any other science." He deplored the mere pursuit of *"thinking for oneself."*[43] In trying to Euclidize philosophy, he succeeded only too well, his methods and his dialectic providing what became a system of intellectual engineering, irresistibly attractive to the clever students who attended his lectures in Berlin and formed the Young Hegelians: Bruno Bauer, Ludwig Feuerback, David Friedrich Strauss, Arnold Runge— and, not least, that outstanding product of young Hegelianism, Karl Marx, who transformed Hegel's intellectual engineering into a system of social engineering, with incalculable consequences for the 20th century.[44]

Hegel was archetypally academic, but like many such men, he enjoyed proximity to power. Much of his intriguing for jobs revolved around his desire to be at the center of things, to live, as it were, in the pocket of the colossus. Getting to Berlin was the greatest thing in his life: "I have come here to be at the heart of events instead of in a province," he wrote. And, "the satisfaction one thinks one will find in private life is after all deceptive and insufficient." "Everyone must maintain a connection with the state and work on its behalf." "Being at the centre of things [in Berlin] . . . has the advantage of giving more accurate knowledge of what is happening, so that one can be more assured of one's interests and job." He quoted with complacency the "Biblical saying": "Strive first for food and clothing and the Kingdom of God will fall to you all by itself."[45]

Not only did Hegel like to be near power, he almost worshipped its physical, personal manifestation. When Jena was occupied by the French in 1806, he wrote exultantly: "I saw the Emperor—this world-soul—riding out of the city on reconnaissance. It is indeed a wonderful sensation to see such an individual, concentrated here at a single point, astride a horse, reach out over the world and master it." He saw Bonaparte the lawgiver as a kind of apotheosized don; as he put it, "The great professor of constitutional law sits in Paris." Again: "It is only from heaven, ie from the will of the French Emperor, that matters can be set in motion."[46] When Bonaparte fell, Hegel wrote (29 April 1814): "It is a frightful spectacle to see a great genius destroy himself. There is nothing more tragic [in Greek literature]. The entire mass of mediocrity, with its irresistible leaden weight . . . has succeeded in bringing down the highest to the same level as itself."[47]

By this point Hegel no longer believed in a personal god, except for the purposes of securing or retaining academic appointments. His metaphysic revolved around what he called the "world-spirit," an irresistible dynamic force which embodied the march of progress from lower to higher forms. Bonaparte had embodied this world-spirit on behalf of France, but with his fall, France fell out of the picture, and the spirit settled elsewhere, in Germany: "The purely abstract formal freedom of the French Republic passes out of its own self-destructive actuality over into *another land*—I had in mind here a specific *land*—of self-conscious spirit in which in this actual form it passes for truth itself. . . . The new form of *moral* spirit is at hand."[48] This was merely an academic philosopher's way of saying that world intellectual and spiritual leadership was now passing from France to Germany. Hegel, it is important to note, was not an "elect nation" or "master-race" theorist, like Motoori or Fichte. That was a static historical concept, and his historicism was dynamic. What he taught was much more plausible: In every big epoch, there is a "nation of world-historical consequence" which bears the universal spirit at that particular stage of development. Such a nation, *for that time,* is entitled to absolute privileges over all the others. It should behave as the spirit willed it and will be dominant in the world. And that nation was now Germany.[49]

It was characteristic of Hegel that he tended to see his world-spirit in terms of military metaphors or gigantism, exerting ruthless power.

This, of course, was one reason why Marx found Hegel's ideas and writings so attractive. Writing in July 1816, Hegel dismissed the statesmen of the Congress of Vienna, contrasted with the all-powerful Bonaparte they had replaced, as "ant, flea and bug personalities." "I adhere to the view," he added, "that the world-spirit has given the age marching orders. These orders are being obeyed. The world-spirit, this essential power, proceeds irresistibly like a closely-drawn armoured phalanx." Nothing can stop it. "They can perhaps reach the shoelaces of this colossus, and smear a bit of boot-polish or mud, but they cannot untie the laces, much less remove the shoes of gods once the colossus puts them on. Surely the safest thing to do, internally and externally, is to keep one's gaze fixed on the advancing giant." Those who oppose it are "powerless vermin."[50]

The colossus was the visible embodiment of the state, which to Hegel, as well as to Fichte, was the highest form of human institution. When a particular state, in its turn, embodied the world-spirit, it was entitled to do what it pleased and, in particular—Hegel was careful to state this—to use war to achieve its desires. He turned his back decisively on Immanuel Kant's notion of perpetual peace. No authority had the right to arbitrate between states, he argued. The "national force" is the intellectual legacy of the past plus the nation's present and future demands. Representing this national force, the state has absolute autonomy and the right to pursue its interests, if necessary, by war. This was the first time that a leading German philosopher, and one who had made a point of attempting a general rationalization of how the world behaves and progresses, had thrown the whole weight of his academic reputation behind the proposal that war had the unqualified and definite sanction of history and a place in the world-view.[51]

This philosophy was what intelligent young Germans were to be taught, throughout the 19th century and beyond. A new force had entered the world: the force of history. Whether you called it a world-spirit or described it as a colossus giving not just people but entire epochs "marching orders," ordinary men and women, however many of them there were, could not stop history pursuing its predetermined course, and the great men of the time, however powerful they seemed, were merely puppets stuck in the swaying howdah on the vast back of the advancing elephant. The idea of history as something more than a collection of facts, as a positive force with an irresistible momentum of its own, was attractive to an age which was discovering its past and developing new scholarly skills.

Archaeology was one of the most exciting of the budding sciences in the early 19th century. In Italy, Herculaneum had been unearthed in 1738 and Pompei in 1748, but accurate plans of the sites began to appear only in 1812, when François Mazois, under the patronage of Caroline Murat, began to produce his huge folio presentation of the ruins, a project completed in 1828.[52] This followed closely on Vivant Denant's elaborate record of the three-year work accomplished by the 175 savants who followed in the wake of Bonaparte's expedition to Egypt. Such volumes opened the eyes of the educated world to the astonishing splendors of remote antiquity.[53] Britain was almost equally fascinated by the quest into the distant past, for it had obtained the bulk of the Egyptian antiquities found by the French teams, including the Rosetta Stone, as well as the Elgin Marbles, the first large-scale abstractions from the growing number of sites in Greece and Turkey.

Happily, the deciphering of the hieroglyphics, the most ancient of the Egyptian languages, was a combination of British and French scholarship. For centuries these inscriptions had baffled or rather deluded scholars because it was believed they were allegorical rather than linguistic. The discovery of the Rosetta Stone in 1799, and its eventual installation in the British Museum, gave scholars the chance for a fresh start. This ceremonial artifact, inscribed by Egyptian priests in 196 B.C. in honor of the young king, Ptolemy Epiphanes, had identical texts in hieroglyphics, the demotic and Greek. A Swedish scholar-diplomat, Åkerblad, had the first shot at using the Greek to illuminate the demotic and indeed identified various proper names in it, but unfortunately labored under the illusion that the demotic was exclusively alphabetic. In 1814, the great English polymath Thomas Young, chief physician at Saint George's Hospital, London—we have already come across him as a victim of Brougham's arrogance—got hold of a copy of the stone and Åkerblad's findings. He immediately spotted Åkerblad's mistake and realized there was a close connection between the demotic and the hieroglyphs (characters). He set about it scientifically, dividing up all three sections into component words, and he soon had Greek/demotic values for 86 groups, most of them correct. Two years later, having examined additional material—passages from the famous *Book of the Dead,* written in hieroglyphics and hieratics on papyrus, and also in the British Museum—he established the equivalence of the pictorial and cursive forms of the signs and became certain that the language was essentially phonetic. He proved that the cartouches, or royal rings, contained names of kings and queens and was able to identify some. He found the characters "f" and "t," which were alphabetic, in the hieroglyphs and discovered the key principle of homophony—different characters possessing the same powers.[54]

However, it was the young Frenchman Jean-François Champollion (1790–1832) who made the real breakthrough. Unlike Young, Champollion was not a polymath scientist but a philologist who, when not yet 12, knew some Arabic and Hebrew, was studying Coptic, and formed the ambition to solve the problem of the Rosetta Stone. He had political problems, being an ardent Republican, but he stuck doggedly to unraveling Egyptian secrets and studying the country's history—he published *L'Égypte sous les pharaons* in 1814—which gave him a solid background of knowledge the other code crackers lacked. He identified the relationship between hieroglyphic, hieratic and demotic and then proceded to transliterate and identify systematically royal cartouches, using not only the Rosetta Stone but other inscriptions and papyri, including an important inscripted base and obelisk that the traveler W. J. Bankes brought back from the Nile island of Philae to his park at Kingston Lacey. Bankes forwarded to Champollion a lithograph of these hieroglyphs, together with Young's work (though Champollion never acknowledged it). The more material Champollion had to work on, the more identifications he made, and on 29 September 1822, he was able to read to the Royal Academy of Inscriptions his famous *Lettre à M. Dacier* [perpetual secretary of the academy] *relative à l'alphabet des hyeroglyphes phonétiques*, generally considered the beginning of modern Egyptian studies. In this work, he gave transcriptions of the hieroglyphs of over 70 rulers. Two years later he produced his *Précis du système hieroglyphique*, in which, for the first time, whole phrases and sentences of ancient Egyptian were translated and the underlying linguistic system was illuminated.[55]

The unraveling of the linguistic mysteries of Ancient Egypt served as an inspiration to generations of scholars who would not rest until all the outstanding problems of antiquity were solved. For the first time we begin to hear of "scientific history," especially in German universities, and archives of every kind began to be sorted out and systematically preserved and key documents published. The passion for history was not just a scholarly enthusiasm but a popular one, spurred by the enormous, worldwide success of Sir Walter Scott's novels.

Scott was one of the first historical novelists to take the trouble to get the details of dress, armor, architecture, and speech right when portraying an earlier age, and his example was followed not only by other writers, French and English, but by painters. In the 1820s historical paintings suddenly became immensely popular. On both sides of the Channel, certain key figures inspired painters as diverse as Richard Parkes Bonington and Paul Delaroche—Henri IV, Queen Elizabeth, Mary Queen of Scots, Cardinal Richelieu, Cardinal Mazarin, Oliver

Cromwell, and Charles I. The influence of William Shakespeare, seen primarily as a historical dramatist, was immense, especially among the operatic composers, who increasingly turned to historical themes.

The rich began to redorate their houses in "period" styles, not just a mish-mash of "classical," "Gothic," or "Tudor," but with the beginning of attention to consistent period details. They still made mistakes. When the interiors of Apsley House were redone in 1829, in what was termed Louis Quatorze, what the Duke of Wellington actually got was *Régence:* Not that he cared—he was much more worried about the enormous bill.[56] For the first time, however, the principles of historical research began to be systematically applied to architecture, furniture, china, silver, and not least painting and sculpture.

Equally important, especially at the level of the growing middle-class readership, was the publication of historical texts. In April 1818, after much persuasion, the publishers Bray & Upcott were allowed by the Evelyn family to bring out the diaries of John Evelyn. These diaries were a critical and a popular success, and as a result Magdalene College, Cambridge, decided to have the shorthand diaries of Samuel Pepys, bequeathed to it as part of his magnificent library, transcribed and published, too. The work was farmed out to an impoverished sizar of Saint John's, John Smith, who completed it in April 1822, and it was then incompetently edited by the master of Magdalene's brother, Lord Braybrooke. Nonetheless, the diary, published by Henry Colburn in a set of two quartos at the hefty price of six guineas, was a triumph. Francis Jeffrey in the *Edinburgh Review,* Scott in the *Quarterly, The Times,* and others all received it enthusiastically. Only Sydney Smith ("Nonsense") and Thomas Creevey ("trash") were the odd men out.[57] Not to be outdone, the French in 1829 began publication of the court diaries of the duc de Saint-Simon, with their incomparable account of the last years of Louis XIV and the regency which followed.

The Germans were beginning to rediscover their lost musical heritage. Between 1750 and 1800, no complete work by Bach was printed; Bach was regarded as an out-of-date musical pedant. Even by 1820 little of Bach's music was in print. Mendelssohn learned about the *St. Matthew Passion* from his great-aunt Sara Levy and the musical director Karl Friedrich Zelter, who had a complete manuscript of the work. But Zelter thought the work was unperformable, and it was only after Mendelssohn arranged a private family performance in his house in winter 1827, that serious plans to revive the work were made. The 20-year-old Mendelssohn worked on the arrangement and the cutting of the immense score with the actor Edouard Devrient and observed wryly: "To think that a comedian and a 'Jew-boy' must revive the greatest Christian music in the world!" By the time of the performance, 11 March 1829, Mendelssohn, who conducted, knew it by heart. Word had got around that a great musical event was to take place, and the concert hall in Berlin was sold out. There was a grand party of the intellectual elite at Zelter's house afterwards. Frau Devrient whispered to Mendelssohn: "Do tell me, who is the stupid fellow sitting next to me?" Mendelssohn (behind his napkin): "The stupid fellow next to you is the philosopher Hegel."[58]

Hegel was an appropriate guest on this occasion because no one has ever done more to instill historical consciousness, to make men and women aware that time is dynamic and that the story of humanity is a progression: we must use the past to reconsider the present and forecast the future. But Hegel was not the only historicist writing in the 1820s. In some ways Henri de Saint-Simon was even more strongly attached to the notion of historical dynamism. Everyone had grasped that 1789 had started a momentous epoch in world history, that the Earth could never be the same place afterwards. But Saint-Simon was the first philosopher to link the Revolution with the entirely new process of capitalist industrialization. He realized that what was happening, especially in Britain, was going to have a far more fundamental effect on the lives of ordinary people, in the long run, than a mere change of regime. What was vital was to link the inevitable political changes with an understanding of the economic changes so that the benefits of industry could, for the first time in history, raise the living standards of ordinary people to an acceptable level.

Saint-Simon did not, like Thomas Malthus, think the population explosion would have catastrophic consequences. On the contrary, he identified it as a symptom of progress (as it was) and as something the world, through industrialization and mass production, could accommodate (as it has).[59] Though a determinist like Hegel, he did not see a role for a master race, such as the Germans. Rather, he envisaged the advanced European races as a whole using their new knowledge and technology and a new spirit of unity to raise the entire world to their own rising levels. These races would coalesce, under an elected parliament on the British model; form a government general; undertake vast public works; and then, as a substitute for Europe's wars, conduct a global crusade to civilize the world: "To people the globe with the European race, which is superior to all other races, to open the whole world to travel and render it as habitable as Europe, that is the enterprise through which the European parliament could continue to engage the activity of Europe and always keep up the momentum."[60]

Saint-Simon developed a philosophy of history, less metaphysical and more optimistic than Hegel's. With Augustin Thierry, he wrote a pamphlet for the Congress of Vienna, *De la réorganisation de la société européenne,* in which he declared robustly: "The Iron Age of humanity lies behind us. The Golden Age of the human species is not behind us, it is before us. It lies in the perfection of the social order."[61] How would the "social order" be "perfected"? First, by throwing out religion and substituting "terrestrial and positive morality" for "celestial." Then by getting rid of kings, nobles and priests and replacing them by a meritocracy: especially industrialists and scientists.[62] Saint-Simon invented the terms *industrialization* and *industrialist.* The men who could create and run huge factories, mines, smelters, and ports and build roads and canals were clearly those who should constitute the new ruling class. Saint-Simon is often classified as the first socialist, and in a sense he is. Following from Jeremy Bentham (whom he often quoted), he believed that, given the right system, the vast majority of mankind could be made prosperous and happy. He had a particular urge to raise up "the poorest and most numerous class." He believed in welfare transfers to the poor, coining the phrase—soon to be a commonplace of the Left—"*A Chacun selon sa capacité, à chaque capacité selon ses oeuvres.*"[63] However, this was a doctrine of work, rather than communism, and Saint-Simon's ideas point in a liberal-democratic-market direction, rather than in that of a totalitarian command economy.

Nevertheless, there are three respects in which Saint-Simon's influence on Marx, who was seven at the time of his death, was decisive. Though Marxism would have been impossible without Hegel's dialectic, it could not have come into existence without Saint-Simon. First, Saint-Simon saw the coming historical changes in terms not of individuals but of classes, and of classes whose international common interests were replacing their national ones. He called the class of the future, which would take history into its own hands and change it—because it was the most numerous—*les industriels.* Later socialists, especially Marx, preferred the ancient Roman term *proletariat,* but the concept was the same. Indeed, the essence of Saint-Simon's political teaching is a class theory based upon a philosophy of history leading to a materialist millennium—exactly the same as Marx's.

Second, as with Marx, Saint-Simon thought that the decisive, inevitable moment would come at a time of crisis in the existing system. He did not relish the prospect, as Marx was to do, but such a "boiling over" was bound to come, and then the new ruling class would firmly, calmly and, he hoped, peacefully take charge and begin the ordering of human society by reason.[64] This transformation would enable the energy that hitherto had been wasted by being directed by man against man in the interminable struggle for domination, to be directed by man to subdue nature: "The only useful action that man can perform is the action of man on things. The action of man on man is always in itself harmful to the species because of the twofold waste of energy it entails."[65] With this transformation—and here we come to the third key point Marx took from Saint-Simon—most of the functions of the state would disappear. He did not actually use the term "wither away," but he wrote that the need for governmental action would be "reduced to nothing or almost nothing." Only managerial action would be required. By eliminating poverty, idleness, ignorance, and other sources of public disorder, the industrial society would make it possible to drop all the coercive powers of the state. Thus utopia, or something very like it, would be complete.[66]

The trouble with these determinist philosophers was that they were constantly changing their minds about what history was certain to do. Each had a map of the future, but the contours of these maps were always unstable. Hegel switched from Bonaparte to the Hohenzollerns and from a French Republican future to a German monarchical one. Saint-Simon abandoned his prediction that religion would disappear because it was out of date (in the early 1820s he saw it as an 18th-century notion). It is a significant comment on the growing power of religion in the second decade of the 19th century that Saint-Simon was forced to admit: "The present generation has caused to vanish from our books and conversation that tone of frivolity . . . in matters of religious belief which the past generation flaunted . . . even in the salons of our idlers it is reputed to be in bad taste. It has been replaced by a general feeling of respect for religious ideas which is based on a conviction of their present need."[67] Not that he became religious himself; his last secretary, Leon Halévy, said he spent much of his final years reading trashy novels by Madame de Genlis and Paul de Kock, commenting grandly: "The history of the human heart, well or ill-narrated, can only be there."[68] But he found antireligious attitudes bad for subscriptions. So at the end of his life, he invented a novel concept, outlined in his final work, *Nouveau Christianisme* (1825) a confused and insincere tome which became—such is literature and life—the best known and most often translated of his books.

It is notable that during the 1820s other philosophers were hedging their bets about religion. Hegel ceased to hold, or at least to print, views hostile to orthodox faith, though he did so partly to keep his chair in Berlin; and during the last decade of his life, a quasi-religious tone crept into his writing, which helped to make it more influential then and later. Utopians who could not bring themselves to adapt to the more religious spirit of the age by embracing traditional brands, invented new ones. Saint-Simon was moving that way, clearly, and, as we have already seen, some of his followers, like Enfantin, actually set up churches soon after his death, combining religiosity with feminine liberation and free love. It was a great age for new creeds: In 1830 Joseph Smith (1805–44) had the first of his revelations, in Manchester, New York, about the Book of Mormon, the foundation document for his Church of Jesus Christ of Latter-Day Saints.

Another of Saint-Simon's disciples, Auguste Comte, almost moved from utopianism to pseudo-religion. He had the sense to spot an important fallacy in his patron's approach (later shared by Marx), that the aggressive pursuit of power is an ineradicable characteristic of man, which will not disappear when one system is transformed into another, but will be enthusiastically exercised by those in charge of the new one. He learned this by experiencing how Saint-Simon actually behaved toward his secretaries, above all, himself. He did not like Saint-Simon's new industriels either: "Today," he wrote to a friend, "those people think they are coming into the sole possession of power and they are growing impertinent like nobles. . . . If they were given free play they would make mere engineers of scientists, who would be put on bread and water if they failed to invent a new gadget a week."[69] However, when Comte was in a position to employ secretaries, he behaved no better than his old master, and as soon as he elevated himself to the position of *Grand-Prêtre de l'Humanité*, he became as imperious as any ruling industriel.

Comte was a brilliant graduate of the École Polytechnique and retained many of the characteristics of that remarkable school. He was an enthusiastic taxonomist, ordering the world into categories and types, good and bad. He believed in numbers. He has some claims to be considered the worst writer who ever lived, and his works read just as badly, if not more so, in French as in translation. In 1824, in reply to criticism, he insisted that style was of no importance. He said he wrote "scientifically." Later, however, he laid down rules of style: no sentence longer than five lines of print; each paragraph to have no more than seven sentences; all books to have seven chapters; each chapter to have three parts and each part seven sections; each section must have a lead paragraph of seven sentences, followed by three paragraphs of five sentences each.[70]

We have seen how Comte completely reversed his ideas on women. But his views on many aspects of politics, economics, science, and society were equally volatile, and he changed his Positive Philosophy, which is essentially a taxonomy of the sciences and a history of social evolution, into a religion (with humanity as the god), on what can only be considered a whim. The taxonometrical approach then continued, with secular gods, goddesses and holy people being classified. Yet among intellectuals, Comte was to become by far the most revered figure of the 1840s. John Stuart Mill, George Eliot and Professor Huxley thought the world of him. Comte's positivism was as attractive to the radical intelligentsia in the mid-19th century as Marxism was in the mid-20th century. Nor is this surprising: Positivism and Marxism have a good deal in common.

The early 19th century was rich in imaginative intellectuals who believed they had discovered the keys to utopia but whose ideas had totalitarian overtones that were to find concrete expression in the horrific state systems of the 20th century. Some of their ideas were so ridiculous, and were expressed in such preposterous language, as to make the more extravagant beliefs of medieval Christianity seem plausible by comparison. Yet highly educated men (and sometimes women, though much more rarely) who found the beliefs of Christianity or Judaism incredible, accepted and propagated their fantasies. The core of Saint-Simon's disciples, for instance, were emancipated young Jews—Benjamin Olinde Rodrigues, his cousins Émile and Isaac Pereire, Gustave d'Eichthal and Leon Halévy—all of them clever and extremely well read, who turned down the Talmud but found the absurd Nouveau Christianisme of Saint-Simon to be the true Gospel.[71]

Saint-Simon's younger contemporary Charles Fourier (1772–1837), a businessman from Lyons, put forward some even more extravagant notions. Like Comte he had a passion for numbers and categories. He predicted the ideal world he was creating would last 80,000 years, 8,000 of them an era of Perfect Harmony, during which the North Pole would be milder than the shores of the Mediterranean, the sea, no longer salt, would turn into lemonade, and the world would contain 37 million poets equal to Homer, 37 million mathematicians equal to Newton, and 37 million dramatists equal to Molière, though he modestly added, "These are approximate estimates." Every woman would have four lovers or husbands simultaneously. Fourier's utopia was elaborated under neologistic chapter headings such as Pre-lude, Cis-lude, Citerpause, Trans-appendice, Ulter-logue, and so forth, which appealed to the intelligentsia of the day.[72] Despite their oddness, Fourier's ideas not only drew to him intelligent men and women but even persuaded them to join with him in pilot ventures. He recruited a "liberated order" of like-minded people forming a phalange or phalanx of 1,620 souls living in a *phalanstère*, a combination of garden city and agricultural commune. Some of these phalanstères were set up for a time in the 1830s, and Fourier himself was acknowledged later as one of the founding fathers of International Socialism, his ideas contributing, in due course, to Hitler's notions of town-and-country planning; fascist organizations in Spain, Rumania and elsewhere; and Stalin's grim agricultural communes.

A similar, though less fantastical, socialist utopia was set up by Robert Owen (1771–1858), first at New Lanark in Scotland, later at New Harmony in Indiana, and elsewhere. New Lanark was much visited in the second decade of the century, for Owen had married the daughter and heiress of David Dale, who built the New Lanark cotton mills, and he therefore had both people and resources to experiment with, until the business began to fail in consequence. But shrewd observers were not taken in by his proclaimed socialist benevolence. They detected a hard note of authority underneath. Robert Southey was there on 28 September 1819, after his Highland tour with Thomas Telford, and was shown around by Owen himself. The buildings, he recorded, had "a regular appearance, such as belongs to a conventual or eleemosynary establishment" and seemed very clean with no smell—an amazing omission for urban Scotland in the early 19th century. A large building, with ball-, concert- and lecture rooms had just been completed, for "the formation of character." Owen explained it all, using a model and a picture stick. Southey watched boy fifers play while 200 children did gymnastics: "They turned to the right or left, faced about, fell forward and backwards, and stamped at command, performing manoeuvres, the object of which was not very clear, with perfect regularity." After going over it all, Southey concluded that "Owen in reality deceives himself." His factory-colony differed "more in accidents than in essence from a [slave] plantation." His workers "happen to be white" and are free "to quit his service," but "while they remain in it they are as much under his absolute management as so many negro slaves." Owen actually called them "human machines . . . and too literally believes them to be." Moreover, added Southey indignantly, "he jumps to the monstrous conclusion that because he can do this with 2,210 persons who are totally dependent on him, all mankind might be governed with the same facility." What Owen would not admit, even to himself, was that his "system, instead of aiming at absolute freedom, can only be kept in play by absolute power."[3]

All Owen's colonies not only failed financially but disintegrated because, in free societies like Britain and the United States, his colonists or workpeople were at liberty to escape from his rules. The danger, in the Anglo-Saxon world, was that utopian philosophers, with their totalitarian leanings, might be allowed to experiment on the nonfree. Jeremy Bentham (1748–1832) was not a marginal figure in British society. Some of his ideas passed, via the Whigs and the Radicals, into the mainstream of social welfare policy. His "utilitarianism," assiduously propagated by Evangelicals like James Mill, evoked nods of approval from grave statesmen, even skeptical ones like Sir Robert Peel and cynics like Lord Palmerston. But Bentham suffered from the totalitarian itch, too, and he was always anxious to get his hands on the poor or the criminal, to improve or reform them. He produced elaborate plans both for what he called "pauper management" and for his "panopticon," or model prison. The prison was to be a single unit, so constructed and secure as to be managed by a single person. The paupers were to be placed in "industry-houses," originally 250 of them, housing 500,000 people, rising, at the end of 21 years, to 500 houses holding a million people, the entire poverty class of South Britain (England). In both cases ownership and management would be in the hands of private enterprise. These managements would be vested with wide coercive powers, not only over the men, women, and children already in the houses, but over people outside who ought to be there.

Bentham had a wide definition of *the poor:* it included "all persons, able-bodied or otherwise, having neither visible nor assignable property, nor honest or sufficient means of livelihood"; "non-adults of divers descriptions, being without prospect of honest education"; "insolvent fathers of chargeable bastards"; "also mothers of ditto." The managements would have "powers of *apprehending*" all such people "and detaining and employing them." Bentham also wanted to treat as criminals and *apprehend* people who were likely, because of their social and economic status, to fall into crime, whether or not they had committed one. Thus, the industry houses would be kept stocked up with people, and to make the job of rounding up potential inmates easier, Bentham proposed "a *universal* register of names, abodes and occupations." Once inside, people were to be reformed. They could, in theory, get out again, but only on what he called "the self-liberating principle." This principle was as follows: "No relief but on the terms of coming into the house . . . and working out the expense." This, interestingly enough, was the same principle proclaimed, though not followed, at Auschwitz, where the ironwork entrance gates contained the slogan: "Work Makes Free." Indeed, there were many respects in which Bentham's industry houses adumbrated the work camps set up in Hitler's Germany and Lenin's Russia over a hundred years later.[74]

Bentham's industry-house scheme was part of the largest proposal for social engineering ever put forward in Britain, on which he worked until his death in 1832. Some of it was embodied in the Whig 1834 Poor Law Amendment Act, which replaced all outdoor poor relief and forced paupers into 600 workhouses—run, however, not by private enterprise but by local authorities. The totalitarian social engineering behind Bentham's plan, however, was never put into practice, and even the workhouses were eventually replaced by state insurance, an idea, by a strange paradox, imported from Bismarck's Germany. Bentham feared that Britain would never find the hardheaded resolve to implement his scheme, since the British preferred "the most inveterate mischiefs to the most simple and efficient, if unaccustomed, remedies."[75] This was a slander. The British had a long tradition of respect for personal liberty, imperfectly followed at times but always deep, and it was reinforced by an interpretation of Christianity which saw all human beings as essentially individuals, to be treated as such, and not as raw material for schemes, however well meaning, which handled them as though they were sand or earth or stones, to be shifted about by governmental machines.

Edmund Burke had articulated these national objections to totalitarian utopianism with great force before the turn of the century, but it was Samuel Taylor Coleridge who, after 1815, was their most subtle and original champion. A myth was propagated, in his own day and after, by friends-turned-opponents like William Hazlitt, that Coleridge was a revolutionary-turned-reactionary. In fact, Coleridge repudiated few of the views he had held as a young man, except support for violence and personal attacks on statesmen like the younger William Pitt.[76] His mature political views developed naturally from the philosophy he had imbibed (chiefly from Immanuel Kant) or worked out for himself in his twenties and thirties. The problem, as he saw it, centered on one question: How do you reconcile the claims of men and women as individuals to their duties to society? Until about 1815, as we have seen, Coleridge was a pitiful victim of opium, which poisoned his relationships with his wife and many of his friends and ruined him as a poet. But after 1815 he reduced his dependence and then began to organize his thoughts on public issues. However, throughout his life he always balanced duties against rights, individualism against society.

Unlike William Godwin, Coleridge did not believe man to be naturally good. He always accepted the reality of evil, as distinct from mere error, and this acceptance rightly tempered any optimism he might feel about the future of mankind. He never fell into the crucial error, made so significantly by Shelley, by his mentor Godwin and by so many Continental idealists and utopians and their countless followers, of loving mankind in general but treating human beings in particular with heartless contempt or cruelty. Coleridge saw personal affections as the key to any true humanitarianism. They expand "like the circles of a Lake—the Love of our Friends, parents and neighbours leads us to the love of Country to the love of all Mankind. The intensity of private attachment encourages, not prevents, universal philanthropy."[77] The individual, the object of love, had to be at the heart of any scheme for general improvement. From Kant, he derived the vital notion that a person should never be treated as a thing. That was the true objection to slavery: "A Slave is a person perverted into a Thing. Slavery, therefore, is not so properly a deviation from Justice as an absolute subversion of all morality."[78] But people in factories might be treated as things, too, and it was important to use the right language in referring to them. He detested such terms as *the labouring poor* and, still more, *hands*. Workers were to be treated "not as hands or as machines but as men capable of being educated." He was especially concerned with "the hopeless cause of our poor little White Slaves, the children of our cotton factories, against the unpitying cruel spirit of trade, and the shallow, heart-petrifying self-conceit of our political economists."[79]

Coleridge, however, while perceiving persons as individuals, also saw them as living, functional parts of an organism. Here, again, the economists were wrong. There is a record of a fierce exchange between him and the most formidable economist of the age. Coleridge: You appear to consider that society is an aggregate of individuals." Harriet Martineau: "I certainly do!"[80] For him, society was always more than the sum of its parts, and he used an arresting image: "A male and female Tyger is neither more nor less whether you suppose them only existing in their appropriate wilderness, or whether you suppose a thousand Pairs. But Man is truly altered by the coexistence of other men; his faculties cannot be developed in himself alone, and only by himself."[81]

Man owed duties to the social organism, as well as drew rights from it. Both had to be seen in a religious and a secular context. Coleridge was always a believing Christian (albeit he sometimes called himself a Unitarian as a young man) who in maturity identified himself with the Anglican Church. Jesus Christ, he believed, was a radical. Christianity was "a religion for democrats." It taught the rights of man "in the most explicit terms." It "commands its disciples to go everywhere and teach those rights." The Bible is "the Statesman's Manual."[82] As he grew older, however, he made a distinction between religious and social morality. Religious truths must be communicated to all, whatever the consequences, because the Church is "the only pure democracy," seeing all individuals as equal in the sight of God. The state, by contrast, has to deal with unequal classes and interests. Not that Coleridge had a class view of society, like Saint-Simon. Quite the reverse: "The phrases—higher, middle and lower classes . . . are delusive; no such divisions as classes actually exist in society. There is an indissoluble blending and interfusion of persons from top to bottom."[83] Nonetheless, religion dealt with inner motives, the law with external actions. The law could not dictate to conscience without "a busy and inquisitorial tyranny.' Hence, "not the practice of *virtue* but the peace of Society and the Legality of the Individual's actions are the objects of the Law; these secure, we may safely trust to Religion, Education and Civilisation for the rest."[84]

Coleridge distrusted most forms of political agitation, such as secret societies, clubs, and "movements," especially if they had a working-class composition, since he distrusted the uneducated masses. But he rejected both government by fear (as in Hobbes's *Leviathan*) and by reason (as in Rousseau's *Social Contract*). What he really believed in was government by consensus. Government, he thought, had to be expedient and rule by a form of consent. A wise statesman judged the rightness of political actions by their likely consequences. In practice, the constitution had to be a balance between "the forces of permanence" (the landed interest) and "the forces of progression" (the commercial interest), both informed and restrained by "a continuing and progressive civilisation." This balance was created by a third factor, the national church, or what he called "the clerisy," which promoted the education of the nation.[85] The clerisy was an endowed national class, distributed partly in universities, but mainly throughout the country, in every community, so as to leave no locality "without a resident guide, guardian and instructor." The object of the whole was "to preserve the stores, to guard the treasures, of past civilisation, and thus to bind the present with the past; to perfect and add to the same, and thus to connect the present with the future; but especially to diffuse through the whole community, and to every native entitled to its laws and rights, that quantity and quality of knowledge which was indispensible both for the understanding of those rights, and for the performance of the duties correspondent." He thought such a system, if pursued thoroughly, would secure an equality at least, perhaps a superiority, in civilization over its neighbors—more important in the long run than "fleets, armies and revenue" in producing "defensive and offensive power."[86]

Coleridge's vision was a noble one, and it had some impact on events after his death, since he had many disciples, like Thomas Arnold, the great headmaster of Rugby School. Thanks, in part, to Coleridge, religion was both a reforming and conciliatory voice in Victorian Britain. But it was also a divided voice. The clerisy could not work as the effective civilizing force Coleridge envisioned as long as religion was a battlefield between High, Low and Broad Church Anglicans, Nonconformists of countless sects and increasingly aggressive Roman Catholics, with Parliament constantly intervening in their arguments. And in no area of policy were they more bitterly split than over the control of education. Nevertheless, the teachings of Coleridge and those he influenced, following in the tradition of Burke, were one reason why Britain did not take the totalitarian path at any time in the future.

Coleridge's work was curiously paralleled by another admirer of Burke, Joseph de Maistre (1753–1821), though from the perspective of a Catholic, rather than an Anglican. De Maistre came from a family which had worked its way into the ruling class of Savoy. All his life he served its royal family. He must have been one of the most learned men of his age, certainly the best read among its statesmen. He read Aquinas and other theologians, Locke, Hobbes, Bacon, Newton and Hume; Voltaire, Rousseau and other "enemies"; and vast amounts of science and travel writing. He inherited a large library from his grandfather, added to it until, in 1792, when he fled from the advancing French revolutionaries, it contained 2,621 volumes and constituted the most impressive private library in Savoy. Moreover, he knew what his books contained, for he filled 5,000 pages of *registres des lectures*, notes from 760 works in eight languages. He also wrote as fine a French as Chateaubriand, though he barely set foot in the country and only visited Paris at the end of his life. His French was too good—too witty, at least. It made his superiors at the stuffy Court of Savoy regard him as dangerously frivolous, a lightweight, though no man of his time took life, and especially politics, more seriously. And, though immensely energetic and healthy in other respects—a man who worked and read hard all his days—he suffered from narcolepsy, so that he was liable to drop off in the middle of an important interview—a handicap in a court and diplomatic career.[87]

De Maistre spent the first 20 years of his career as a magistrate; then, from 1792, he spent a decade in exile, in Switzerland, Venice and Sardinia. Next in 1803, he went to Saint Petersburg, where he spent 14 years as envoy to the Tsar; finally, he was Minister of Justice in Turin, the Savoyard capital. His writings are voluminous; they include his great book *Considérations sur la France* (1796), in which, like Burke, he drew the lessons of the Revolution, and *Du Pape* (1819), in which he made the case for a reinvigorated papacy as a balancing force in international morality and great-power politics. But he summed up his thoughts, using the dialogue form he loved—it was so useful in putting both sides of the case—in his *Les Soirées de Saint-Petersbourg*, published in 1821 just after his death.

As with Coleridge, there is a myth about De Maistre, which presents him as an ultrareactionary. He was much more complicated than that, however. The kind of governing system he admired was the British because it had no written constitution but had evolved organically over hundreds of years, with different estates, each playing an appropriate part, and many checks and balances. He thought the British fortunate because they had, over the years, modified their constitution quietly and almost imperceptibly. The French constitution, on the contrary, had been destroyed by Louis XIV, who had turned France into an absolute monarchy, undermining the rule of law, emasculating and trivializing the nobility, and so preparing its violent overthrow in the long run. Other nations had gone the same way. As he put it, "the governments of Europe had aged and their decrepitude was only too well known to those who wanted to profit from the situation to execute their deadly projects." In France, above all, there was no more unity, no more energy, no more public spirit, a revolution was inevitable."[88]

But revolution was not the way. "We are habituated to one kind of government. Let us perfect it as much as possible. Let us denounce the abuses of government with respect and moderation. But let us hold onto it." Governments should not be overthrown, or "remade according to idealistic theories," but should be brought "back to their eternal and hidden principles." He thought it "impossible that an entire nation wisely asks for a reform without it being granted."[89] What had to be avoided was the pride of individual philosophers, like Voltaire or Rousseau, who thought they could reshape the universe by their own unaided intellects. This arrogance invited divine retribution. "In all the acts of the French Revolution, one can hear the voice of divinity saying, 'I want to show you what you can do without me.' "

De Maistre, in fact, constructed from the events of the 1790s a theodicy of revolutions: For the arrogance of the intelligentsia and their liberal supporters in power, the entire people is made to suffer, for "in moments of Revolution, the sovereign power brusquely comes nearer to man and clasps him tightly." But from the sufferings of the innocent, lessons can be learned and future mistakes can be avoided. The greatest lesson was the realization that mankind belongs to a social organism of which God is part: "We are all attached to the throne of the Supreme Being by a subtle chain that restrains us without enslaving us."[90] Man is less likely to want to shake off the chain and so commit monstrous atrocities if religion is strong. Alas, in the past, monarchies, especially the French, had undermined the church by the erosion of Gallicanism. De Maistre, even in the dark days when Bonaparte was trampling over a prostrate Europe, was certain the traditional order would be restored, but he believed it would be far stronger, because more humane and civilized, if the papacy was able to act as a restraining force within kingdoms and among them. The trouble was that De Maistre had a high opinion of Pius VII (reigned 1799–1823). After meeting him, he wrote enthusiastically to his daughter, "I believed I had seen St Peter instead of his successor." He was not willing to face the fact that the Papal States were among the worst administered territories in Europe, and his failure to answer this point weakened his case for many readers.

One reason De Maistre admired Pius VII was that the Pope had restored the Jesuits. Like Coleridge, De Maistre believed in education as a cure for many sicknesses in society. Like Coleridge he wanted a clerisy. In his judgment the Society of Jesus, suitably reformed, improved, and backed by enlightened governments, provided one. Once at the court of the Tsars, he saw his opportunity. De Maistre had much more influence there than at the court of Savoy. The Russians, a superbly literary people, liked his wit and brilliancy. One of their leading writers, Alexander Stourdza, called him "the outstanding personality" at Alexander I's court. De Maistre's fear was that Romanoff Russia would go the same way as Bourbon France—as in the end it did—by making too many concessions to French rationalism and liberalism. Especially after the Treaty of Tilsit (1807), he tried to resist French influence at Alexander's court. He dissuaded the Tsar from creating a written constitution, and he encouraged him to allow the Jesuits to play a notable part in improving Russia's educational system. In particular, he was successful in getting the great Jesuit college at Plotsky raised to the status of an independent university.[91] He also had the effect of pushing the general drift of Russian education away from rationalism: Of the five men who were ministers of public instruction in the years 1810–48, four of them, Count Razumovsky, Prince Alexander Golitsin, Admiral A. S. Shishkov, and Count S. S. Uvarov, were all members of De Maistre's intellectual circle in Saint Petersburg.[92] But his plan to use the Jesuits as a clerisy to reform Russia on traditionalist lines ran headlong into the wave of nationalism which swept over the country in 1812 and after. The Jesuits were seen as a threat to the orthodox Church and the spirit of Holy Mother Russia. Hence, they were expelled from Saint Petersburg and Moscow in 1815, and from the rest of the country five years later.[93]

*   *   *

Whether the Jesuits, even backed by the authority of the state, could have done what De Maistre wanted them to do—create an educational climate in which the Russian regime developed the organic capacity to reform itself from within—is doubtful. In the post-Napoleonic period, Russia, with its backwardness, brutality, and obscurantism, was an insoluble problem. In some ways, it was like Japan—arrogantly sure of its own ways, proud of its race and culture, and drawing on deep wells of intolerance and xenophobia. Toward the end of the 17th century, Russia's rulers perceived that the West was acquiring superior military power because it had developed, through scientific knowledge and technology, greater wealth-generating power. Japan was to make the same discovery 200 years later, in the 1860s. The response of the elite in both countries was the same: to take from the West what was industrially, that is militarily, useful, but to keep the gates closed to the free flow of ideas. As Peter the Great put it: "We need Europe for a few decades, but then we must turn our back on it."[4] This idea did not, however, prove possible, any more than in the end selective isolation proved possible for Japan. In the 18th century, Russia was drawn increasingly into Europe's politics and settlements until finally, in the age of Bonaparte, she had to fight for her existence. But the same wave of nationalism that the War of 1812 provoked, and which drove out the Jesuits, also generated a furious Russian military response which carried her armies into the heart of Europe and to Paris itself in 1813–15. This was a crucial event in Russian history: it marked the point at which Russia's fate became inseparably linked with Europe's. For to take the army into Europe was to Europeanize it. And the army was not just an instrument of Russia: It *was* Russia.

Muscovy, later Russia, was perpetually fighting. Warfare was its organizing principle. As we have seen, because of Russia's geography, climate, and primitive agriculture, she constantly required more land. The perpetual need to expand, the ever-growing frontiers and the endless territories requiring garrisons meant that by Peter the Great's time, two-thirds of the labor of the entire country went directly to manning, supporting and feeding the army. So did most of the taxes, the revenues from the crown lands and the profits of trade and industry, almost all of which were state monopolies. In 1705 military expenditures were 80–85 percent of the state's revenues. At this point Tsar Peter introduced the tax on "souls," or Capitation Tax, which tripled national revenues, and at the same time introduced fixed recruitment quotas. Male Russia was thus divided into the souls who went into the army and the souls who paid for it. It became the first country to run a systematic system of military conscription on a perpetual basis, whether the nation was at peace or at war. The landlords were the instruments whereby taxes were collected from peasant fathers and recruits drawn from peasant sons. Their sons, in turn, supplied the officers, and since officers needed education, quasi-military schools were organized to provide it, so in effect the compulsory military service of five years was extended back into childhood.

To integrate society still further with the army, Tsar Peter replaced the old aristocratic gradations with a "scientific," military "table of ranks" in 1722. Thereafter, right to the end of the 19th century, rank or *chin,* to use the Russian word, was the key to social status. A man who had not served as an officer and therefore had no *chin* was a nobody. Lower middle-class families strove desperately to get their sons a lieutenancy in the army or the rank of a commissar in the civil service. These were the 14th or lowest ranks, but both provided *chin* and therefore some kind of access to the privileges of the ruling caste, a snout in the trough. The army itself took rank over the bureacracy, or, rather, no bureaucrat would progress far without military *chin.*[95]

Hence when the army went into Western Europe at the end of the great wars, it was as though the heart and mind of Russia had been briefly transferred there. The officers, especially the younger ones, were astonished at what they found: not merely the wealth and sophistication, but the sense of freedom. They were struck by the easy manners of the Germans and French, as opposed to the frightened, sullen, suspicious demeanor of Russians, terrified of authority in countless forms. It was their first experience of the effects of the rule of law, which enabled the individual to look the powers-that-be in the face. One of them, V. Raevskii, visiting a veterinary school, was particularly intrigued to discover that even animals were regarded as creatures with some right to be treated well.[96] The young officers also, for the first time, became aware of the potentiality of the press and education. Some of them had been connected, in the years 1812–15, with a printing press attached to the Russian armies advancing into Europe, which put out propaganda material urging the European peoples to join with them in the liberation struggle against Bonaparte. They learned how to write for a mass public. In France they found open political discussion, debates and parties. They came across the Lancaster system, which was spreading from England into the Continent, and when they returned to Russia they set up the first army schools, run on Lancastrian methods.[97]

Post-Napoleonic Russia offered some, if not many, opportunities for the returning officers to spread the ideas they had found in the West. Traditionally, the press in Russia was an instrument of the state: Tsar Peter had set up the first newspaper in 1703, and Catherine the Great had sponsored the satirical magazines which appeared during her reign. Under Alexander I, however, publications had multiplied, and not all, directly or indirectly, were controlled by the government. By 1815 it was possible for a writer to live by his efforts. More books were being written and published. The number of bookshops in Moscow, for instance, had risen from 2 to 20.[98] Alexander had created the Ministry of Education in 1802, and while the Minister was usually a conservative and the ministry's prime function was to serve the state's interests, the ministry did promote literacy and found institutions. By the early 1820s there were six universities: Moscow, Dorpat, Saint Petersburg, Kharkov, Kazan and Vilna, with another serving Finland. University students were numbered in hundreds, but there were 5,500 secondary school students, a lot by previous Russian standards.[99]

Yet such educational progress was merely to scratch the surface of an immense, cruel, despairing, and corrupt tyranny. In the 1760s, Catherine the Great had ended the government monopoly ownership of land. Henceforth the country was administered by 100,000 private landlords and 50,000 senior bureaucrats. The landlords were concentrated in the Russian heartlands, the bureaucrats at the periphery. Beneath the crown, they were the exploiting classes. They were left alone to squeeze the peasants provided they handed over to the crown their quotas of recruits and taxes, and provided they kept out of politics. Russia was, in effect, farmed. The farming by the landlords was obvious, but bureaucratic farming was just as intensive. Until Peter the Great's day, officials were paid no salaries. They were to "feed themselves from official business," *kormiatsia ot del*. Later, salaries were paid, but under Alexander I they were still so tiny—only about 10*d* to 2*s* a month in English money—that "feeding," *kormlenie*, was the way they made their living. As in China and Japan, bribery and peculation were ubiquitous, inevitable and incorrigible. As late as 1883, the conservative Russian historian Nicholas Karamzin, asked to describe Russian governmental life, put it as follows: "What goes on in Russia? Thieving."[100]

There was no way in which the oppressed subject could get redress against officials. Until the 1860s, the government never initiated legal proceedings unless it was itself the injured party. In theory a subject had access to the courts. But there was no concept of legal sovereignty, no rule of law. Indeed, there was no distinction between laws, decrees or administrative ordinances. Many were not published and only the official charged with enforcing them knew about them. All Russian governmental activities were conducted on a "need to know" basis. Very senior officials were wholly unaware of policies or actions outside their

purview. Only the Tsar, like a medieval monarch, knew all. But his
entourage, and others, might keep dangerous or distressful or embarrassing knowledge from him. So in the end, no one was fully informed.
For even a senior minister or bureaucrat to inquire was dangerous.
Strictly speaking, every act of government was a state secret.

In 1802 Alexander I had decided to "modernize" his government.
He issued a manifesto, and it was characteristic of Russia that it was
not rebels, or conspirators, or a parliament or a party which issued a
manifesto, but the Tsar. This manifesto set up ministries, as opposed
to the medieval royal council, including the Ministry of the Interior, or
MVD, which survives to this day. In the guise of reform, the MVD was
actually a piece of audacious social engineering. It was essentially a
police ministry, but with a mandate to exercise extraordinary power
over Russian life. National happiness, said the manifesto, "could only
be realised when the government has salutory means, not only to
correct all overt manifestations of evil, but especially to eradicate the
very roots of such evil, and to deter all causes which might give rise to
the destruction of the general or private tranquillity, to reveal and
anticipate the needs of the people, to prudently, zealously and actively
assist the observance and affirmation of order necessary for all, and to
increase the national wealth and productivity that serve as foundation
for the power and might of the empire."[101]

This was a manifesto for a totalitarian state, or rather an order
transforming an archaic totalitarian society into a modern one. Police
in Russia had all kinds of functions apart from suppressing crime:
billeting, tax collection, passport work, running lunatic asylums, controlling rabies and heresy, enforcing sanitation laws, directing public
works and improving agriculture. They "confiscated" the children of
beggars, supervised servants' liveries, built and regulated inns for foreigners, and listened for and punished any swearing in public. Subject
to the interests of the state, themselves often confused, they did anything their superiors told them to do. The creation of the MVD gave
them further and more positive functions.[102] The MVD was a state
within the state. Chateubriand had shrewdly noticed this tendency, in
relation to France, in 1816: "The Minister of Police is the more formidable because his powers touch the business of all the other ministers
or rather, he is the sole Minister. Is not a man who has the *gendarmerie*
of France at his disposal, for which he does not account to the legislature, in fact a king?"[103]

However, in France the threat was mitigated after 1815 by the fact
that trials were open and reported by a largely free press. In Russia

most trials were conducted in secret, especially if they involved the state, and in any case there was no press to report them outside Saint Peterburg and one or two other towns. There was also a category of offences, *slovo i delo* (word or deed crimes) against the sovereign power. The police operated a secret system of private denunciations (often rewarded with payments) which allowed these crimes to be discovered. They were then investigated in "secret chanceries" which had their own prisons and whose very existence was unknown outside higher government. Men died in these prisons by torture or starvation; they were often just forgotten. Such oubliettes were supposedly abolished by Catherine, with a lot of public fanfare, but substitutes were immediately and privately created.[104]

An exercise in this deception, so characteristic of the Russian state, occurred simultaneously with Alexander's "reform" manifesto of 1802 which set up the MVD. Catherine had privately created an internal security organ, called the Secret Expedition (of the senate), which made secret arrests and used torture. Alexander abolished it and told the world he was doing so: "From now the power of law alone shall protect our proper dignity and the integrity of the empire." In fact, its functions were immediately and secretly transferred to the Military Government of Saint Petersburg. When the first head of the MVD, V. P. Kochubey, asked the Governor General whether he had a secret police apparatus in the capital, he was sent a list of its agents and a summary of their duties: "The secret police office concerns itself with all objects, actions and speeches that tend towards the dissolution of the autocratic power and the security of the government . . . all that relates to the Tsar personally or to his administration."[105] Alexander, while professing liberalism, was constantly tinkering with this network, adding to it and changing its name (rather as, in Soviet Russia, the Cheka became the GBU, then the OGPU, then the NKVD, finally the KGB). In September 1805 he set up a special section to deal with foreigners, plus in 1807 the wartime Committee for the Dispatch of Crimes Threatening the Public Safety. The same year he extended the network to cover Moscow inns, salons, and clubs. Three years later he abolished the committee and replaced it with the Ministry of Police, or PolMin, created by A. D. Balashov, the son of a French emigré police expert. In 1817 Alexander, impressed by the Austrian police arrangements during the Congress of Vienna, set up the Gendarmes of Internal Security. Two years later the MVD Minister, Kochubey, wrote a memo to Alexander complaining of the multiplicity of overlapping police bodies in Saint Petersburg: "The city boils over with spies of all kinds, foreigners and Russian, salaried and volunteers." He claimed they all used disguises, including the

Minister of Police, who seems to have been a sinister and disreputable fellow, employing his men as agents-provocateurs to enhance his work load and protect his job. Kochubey urged that the PolMin be absorbed into the MVD. Alexander agreed to the change, though he certainly did not object to the different services competing with and reporting on each other. Quite the reverse: Since he alone received all the reports, he believed such duplication enhanced his personal security. So in 1821, he created yet another network, an army secret police, and there were further police "reforms" in 1822.[106]

The grip of the police, both open and secret, on all sections of the Russian people was reinforced by the growing practice of the MVD, under both Alexander and his successor, Nicholas I, to issue decrees and circulars, both to officials and to the general public, which had the force of law. Alexander had given it discretionary power to do so, and we must assume that he and Nicholas were consulted before one came out, though this assumption is not demonstrable. What is certain is that these *diktats* became the biggest single source of the extension of state power in the 19th century and the system was taken over and exercised from the moment Lenin seized power in 1917. The first two diktats came in 1810. By 1820 they averaged 10 a year; by 1825, 16 a year; and thereafter rose quickly to 180 a year.[107] They became the "legal" basis on which the government could do anything it pleased, though their legality did not mean that an official could be brought to book for exceeding the limits they laid down. This precise point was raised, à propos of censorship, with Count Benckendorff, who ran the main organ of the secret police in the later 1820s. He took the view, also held by some academic legal experts in Russia, that the function of law was not to promote and enforce justice, but simply to maintain order. Justice was something that lay in the hand of God. Law was something that enabled the state to perform its function. Hence, as he put it, "Laws are written for subjects, not for the authorities."[108]

How could the spirit of reform, even of the benevolent kind which De Maistre favored, operating organically from within, set about transforming such a system? The only lawful reform could come from above, the only licensed reformer was the Tsar. Alexander I found, like Catherine before him, that once he set about changing the system, it showed signs of breakdown; therefore, he found himself not only reimposing but increasing the central authority to prevent anarchy. He ended up with a far more autocratic state than he had inherited. What other forces were there to do the job? There was a small but growing intellectual class, including doctors, teachers, engineers, and other professional men, even a few writers.

* * *

Russian secular literature had scarcely existed in the 18th century, but once it began to find its voice, its lungs expanded with dramatic speed to produce, in the second half of the 19th century, one of the world's greatest literatures. In the years 1815–25 it was just beginning. It revolved around the Arzamas Society, called after a small town in central Russia, which began to meet in Saint Petersburg from 1815 onwards. Many of its members were young, well-born army officers, like Prince M. F. Orlov and Nicholas Turgenev. These young men had recently served in the West or had been fascinated by accounts of those who had. Indeed, the army provided the bulk of the intelligentsia at this time. The society's star was Alexander Pushkin, born in 1799 and just beginning to write. Pushkin had published his first poem at 1814 when he was only 15—even in Russia it was a fortunate time for the teenage literary genius—while attending the Tsarkoe-Selo Lyceum, built by Alexander in the park of his summer residence to train brilliant young men for state service. Two years after he graduated, he had published, while still only 21, his *Russlan and Ludmilla,* which made him famous—almost a national hero. He then went en poste in the public service, at Odessa, but in 1824 was dismissed for holding political views and ordered to live with his family near Pskov.

In internal exile Pushkin began his greatest work, *Eugene Onegin,* and wrote most of his best poems. But as a rule the poems had to circulate in *samizdat.* For the censorship was strict. The few newspapers or magazines which did not belong to the state were allowed to publish only news which had already appeared in official organs, and all creative work was supposed to be read and approved before publication. The responsibility for censorship rested with the Ministry of Education, and was conducted chiefly through a Saint Petersburg committee, by men who were themselves professors or writers. In June 1815 one of De Maistre's friends, Admiral Shishkov, proposed the formation of a Corps of Censors who were to be "mature, of good morals, learned, connoisseurs of the language and of literature" and whose duty was not merely to suppress evil but improve the quality of what was good. Tsarist Russia saw nothing incongruous in a system designed not merely to censor books but to produce them. Nor did it regard as odd a double-banking device whereby the PolMin also had a censorship department which pounced on anything the official censors had let through and which it did not like. Alexander, who was always tinkering with the censorship as he was with his police forces, appointed a third body in 1820 to draw up new rules. Four years later he put Admiral Shishkov in charge of education. The old salt declared: "It seems that

all our places of learning have been transformed into schools of vice."
He said he was determined to purge Russian youth of "pseudo-intellectual cerebrations, vapourous dreaming, swollen pride and sinful self-
conceit."[109] He finally got his chance to create his corps in 1826 when
Nicholas I asked him to create a new censorship system. The statute the
Admiral drafted reflects his personal and literary tastes. It banned
absolutely "mere thoughtlessness," any use of the word "constitution,"
"personal insults of any kind" and "any reference to a quarrel which
is *useless* to the readers." All "morbid subjects" were "best left unmen-
tioned." Forbidden topics included mesmerism, magic, phrenology,
astrology, and all superstitions, as well as secret societies and political
parties. The Admiral was particularly hard on grammatical errors and
citations from medical texts. Finally, his code threatened to close down
any publication which did not display "a beneficent mode of
thought."[110]

Against this background of totalitarian oppression, albeit administered with characteristic Russian carelessness and inefficiency, there
was no real possibility of a civilian reform movement developing.
Change could only come through the army, in particular, the younger
officers who had seen a different world in the West. The Decembrist
Movement of 1825 is of great importance because it was the first time
a group of middle-ranking officers conspired to overthrow a regime
they judged incapable of reforming itself. It set the pattern for countless
such coups from that day to this, in Europe and the Middle East, in
Africa and Asia, and throughout the Spanish-speaking world. The
Decembrists took inspiration from the 1820 conspiracy in Cádiz. But
that was essentially a mutiny of troops who did not want to serve
abroad. Theirs was in every way an altruistic scheme, resting on the
highest principles, to improve their country, above all morally. It dates
from 1816, when units from the West began to return home, and their
officers asked: What, then, must we do to save Russia? The founding
group were all aristocrats and guards officers: Prince Sergei Troubet-
skoi; I. D. Yakushkin; the two Moravyov brothers, Alexander and
Nikita, and the brothers Matthew and Segei Muravyov-Apostol. The
Secular Catechism produced by the last of these six strikes their characteristic tone, which was both righteous and fundamentalist. "For what
purpose did God create man? So that he would believe in Him, be free
and happy." "What does the Holy Writ command the Russian people
and army to do? To repent of their long servility and, rising against
tyranny and lawlessness, to swear: let there be one Tsar for all—Jesus
Christ in heaven and on earth." "Consequently, God does not like

Tsars? No: they have been cursed by Him as oppressors of the people. But God loves Man."[111] The first group recruited a general, Count Michel Orlov, whose brother was afterwards to run the Secret Police, and four more generals later became involved. But the conspirators were mostly captains, majors and, above all, colonels (30) in their twenties and thirties. All were of gentry stock or above. At least 25 were writers and poets. Literature, the diffusion of knowledge, improvements in technology and trade, scientific research—these were their interests. The most forceful of them was Colonel Pavel Pestel, son of the Governor General of Siberia. Pestel had fought and been wounded at Borodino, at age 19, later commanded a regiment with great gallantry and (as we have seen) got into trouble in the Caucasus. He was also the most learned of them.[112]

Characteristically, the conspirators first modeled their organization on Pushkin's Arzamas Society, but they added Masonic overtones and they changed its name several times, altered its rules and objects, and finally split it into two halves, north and south. This restlessness paralleled the constant osmosis of its enemies, the secret police and the censorship. Into the thinking of the Decembrists went a cocktail of foreign influences: the Spanish liberals; the notions of the Carbonari and the German student bund; the Scottish Enlightenment, especially Adam Smith; English ideas of the rule of law; and American constitution making. In general, they looked to the West. In 1820 Nikita Muravyov, on behalf of the northern section, wrote a political program, stating: "The source of the supreme power is the people." It abolished serfdom and guaranteed peasants the ownership of their houses and plots, but also said that the landlords could keep their estates. It abolished guilds, titles and ranks; ended military colonies; established trial by jury and freedom of speech and religious worship; and provided for the police to be elected. All citizens were entitled to vote, but property qualifications were required for those elected to office. In all essentials it was the U.S. Constitution: an elected "Supreme Official of the Russian Government" (but called an emperor not a president), who held a veto over legislation but could be overruled by a two-thirds vote of the bicameral legislature—the latter divided into a Duma or Senate and a Chamber of National Representatives. The country was to be rearranged into 13 semisovereign states.[113]

For the southern section, however, Pestel produced sets of proposals which were both more radical and more nationalistic. He wanted a republic run by a single chamber. He declared that an aristocracy of wealth (as in America) was even worse than one of rank and proposed that all land (and all factories) should become the property of the state.

Peasants and paupers would all be members of a *volost:* "Every Russian
will be completely assured of the necessities of life, and will be certain
that in his *volost* he can always find a piece of land which will assure
his nourishment." But the rest of the land would be the state's, rented
out to "enterprising persons" or retained as state farms for scientific
agriculture. His scheme was much closer to the utopian models being
bandied about by Owen, Saint-Simon and others and, indeed, much
closer to the Soviet regime which actually came into existence a hundred years later. It had other disquieting aspects. He envisaged a
"higher" or political police, as a check on the ordinary criminal one, the
administration, and the generals. It was to be "ennobled" by the "deep
moral quality" of its chief and was to use secret agents (known only to
the chief) and a special gendarmerie. "Secret investigations," he wrote,
"[are] . . . not only permitted and legal but are even most desirable and
the only means by which the higher police can achieve the purposes
assigned to it."[114]

Pestel's state was also highly centralized, not a federation of states,
and it retained universal military service as the means to pursue an
expansionist policy. "The races which because of their weakness," he
wrote, "are subject to a larger state and cannot enjoy their own political
independence, must necessarily submit to the power or protection of a
large neighbouring state and may not invoke the right to nationhood,
in their case fictious and non-existent." These "weak" peoples included
"Finland, Estonia, Livland, Courland, White Russia, the Ukraine, New
Russia, Bessarabia, the Crimea, Georgia, the entire Caucasus, the lands
of the Khirgiz, all the Siberian peoples"; all were to "merge their
nationality completely with that of the dominant people." And, to
provide security for all, further annexations would be necessary in
Moldavia, the Transcaucasus, nomad lands and Mongolia, "so that the
entire course of the Amur river, from the Dalai Lake on, belongs to
Russia." Pestel spared the Poles inclusion in the new unitary republic,
but only on condition that they adopted a political system similar to
Russia's. Pestel's Greater Russia might be described as enlightened
imperialism of the Jacksonian kind, offering absorption as Jackson
offered it to the Indians, but equally it might be seen as an adumbration
of Stalinist imperialism with even a "free" neighbor like Poland treated
as a satellite.[115] There was a further difference between the northern
and southern proposals. The northerners would simply have offered
their plan to a constituent assembly. Pestel's plan would have been
imposed. Indeed, despite his constant use of the word "free," it is hard
to believe he was constitutionalist or a democrat in any sense.

Pestel and the northerners quarreled over means, as well as ends. It

was clear they would have to use violence at some stage. But how much
and when? It is at this point that outside events impinged on their
thinking. Odessa, then as now, was Russia's great Mediterranean-style
seaport, crowded with exotic minorities. It housed thousands of Greeks
and was the main base for Greek plotting against the Ottomans. In 1814
the Greek minority there formed the *Philike Hetaireia,* the Society of
Friends, to liberate Greece. One of its members was a Greek officer
serving in the Russian army, Alexander Ypsilanti. Ypsilanti knew various members of the later Decembrist conspiracy though he did not
actually belong to their group. Like them, however, he watched the
revolts in Spain and in Naples closely. On March 4, 1821, he led a small
army of Greeks and Rumanians across the Moldavian frontier, as a first
move to liberate all the Balkans from Turkish rule. His action was
timed to coincide with the Peloponnesian revolt in Greece, which began
the following month. Ypsilanti believed he had, or would get, the Tsar's
backing. But Alexander, as a member of the Holy Alliance, was unwilling to identify himself with revolutionary forces anywhere. If revolution occurred, he was happy to profit from it, especially in areas like the
Balkans where he had territorial ambitions. But he would not directly
overthrow legitimate authority. The insurgents reached Bucharest,
when deep divisions between Greeks and Rumanians became apparent.
The Turks then moved in large forces, and Ypsilanti, lacking Russian
help, was crushed.[116]

This episode enormously embittered the Decembrists, especially the
southerners, against the Tsar. As early as 1822, they began actively to
discuss a military coup. Pestel favored the extermination of the royal
family and held two conferences with various Polish nationalists to
prepare for it. The Poles were to murder the Viceroy in Warsaw,
Alexander's brother the Grand Duke Constantine; Pestel's men were to
kill the Tsar. Suicide squads of young officers were to be formed for this
purpose. In return, the Poles would get their (limited) independence.
But when Pestel took his plan to Saint Petersburg for a conference with
the northerners in March 1824, they turned it down. In the end, no
common approach to assassination was agreed. Indeed, nothing was
agreed. Northerners, southerners and Poles never drew up a coordinated timetable. There was, in fact, no timetable, and the Decembrist
conspiracy was detonated by events.[117]

On 19 November 1825 Tsar Alexander, aged 48, died suddenly in
Taganrog. There were rumors of murder and even suicide, but the
likelihood is that he had a high fever and was, in effect, bled to death
by his doctors. Throughout the country, army officers swore allegiance
to the elder of his two brothers, Grand Duke Constantine. What no-

body knew was that, five years before, Constantine, having married a Polish wife and liking his life in Warsaw, had renounced his rights to the succession. Alexander had then, in 1822, drawn up a will-manifesto, appointing Grand Duke Nicholas his successor, But in true Russian fashion, not only did it remain secret but even the two Grand Dukes did not know its precise contents. When Alexander died and the will was opened, Nicholas tried to persuade Constantine to change his mind, but without success. On 14 December (old style), Nicholas reluctantly assumed the throne, and all officers in Saint Petersburg were summoned to swear allegiance, a second time, to him.

At that point the northerners decided to stage their coup. The incompetence on both sides of the political equation, even by Russian standards, was striking. The various police networks had no knowledge of the conspiracy, despite the carelessness of those involved. By chance, Pestel had shown his hand in the south and was actually arrested the day before the swearing, December 13; but the authorities in Saint Petersburg and the northerners were unaware of his arrest. Fortunately for the house of Romanoff, the northerners, on the fateful day, displayed an extraordinariy combination of irresolution, stupidity, cowardice and treachery. Of the troops in and around Saint Petersburg, they were able to muster only a small percentage and marched no more than 3,000 to Senate Square. That was their only act. The troops stood in the square for several hours, under the command of a mere lieutenant, who had no orders. Huge crowds of civilians gathered in and around the square. Some historians believe they would have favored a coup, had any appeal been made for their support. None was. As subsequent interrogations showed, only one of the conspirators had any real contacts with the people. The rest were essentially intellectuals in uniform. While the troops stood idle in their ranks, their leaders argued. Prince Sergei Trubetskoi, who was to have been appointed temporary dictator had the conspirators taken over, deserted them. His two assistants, who appeared in the square, behaved like idiots (one of them later committed suicide).

Nicholas, who had more resolution than his enemies, had meanwhile been gathering troops and surrounding the square. He then made his appearance on the scene and even at that stage could have been assassinated. But nothing was done. At last the new Tsar had cannon brought up and opened fire with canister. Between 60 and 70 of the rebel troops were killed and the rest fled.[118] When they got the news, the southerners rose, too, more from despair than from any other motive. Without Pestel, they did nothing effective, and the 1,000 men they collected were soon dispersed. The Poles, having been kept in the dark throughout, never rose at all.

Nicholas was shaken and dismayed at the carnage in the square. Surveying it, he muttered bitterly: "What a way to begin a reign!" His next actions were to determine the course of Russian history for many decades. He was not a divided soul like his brother Alexander, but a straightforward one. He believed in order. He was by training an army engineer. Nicholas had "icy blue eyes" set in "the head of a bald Medusa."[119] He was a generation younger than Alexander and had no feelings about the French Revolution. He was interested in the physical manifestations of the modern age, not its ideas. He had made a grand tour of Europe in 1816. He liked looking at bridges, docks and canals. Unlike Southey, he was most impressed by the discipline and uniformity at Owen's New Lanark. But what pleased him most of all was the Prussian army: "Here, there is order, there is a strict, unconditional legality, no impertinent claims to know all the answers, no contradiction, all things flow logically from one to the other. No one commands before he has first learned to obey. No one steps in front of anyone else without lawful reason. Everything is ordained to one definite goal; everything has its purpose. That is why I feel so well among these people and why I shall always hold in honour my calling as a soldier. I consider the whole of human life to be merely service, everyone serves."[120]

As Tsar, Nicholas immediately reorganized the government. Everyone got new uniforms. Smoking was forbidden in the streets of Saint Petersburg. The wearing of "old gray hats" was also banned (it reminded him of Jews).[121] Much of the confidential work was entrusted to Balts of German origin. In particular General-Count Alexander Benckendorff (1783–1844) created yet another secret police apparatus, whose full title was Section Three of the Private Imperial Chancellery. A fellow German, M. I. Von Vock, was appointed its first director. By a queer, but characteristically Russian, paradox, the new apparatus embraced the proposals for a "higher police" set out in Pestel's program, which had fallen into the hands of the authorities.[122]

Nicholas's regime was even more secretive than his brother's. It was run by furtive committees; often, a minister had to give evidence to one although he was not supposed to know of its existence. The Third Section was typical of this atmosphere. Everyone knew it operated from a house near the Chain Bridge. In fact, distinguished visitors to Saint Petersburg were supposed to pay a formal call on Benckendorff there—Pushkin was once severely rebuked for not doing so. But all its activities were a state secret. The section itself always called, searched and made arrests at night, and brought prisoners to the Chain Bridge house in closed coaches driven through the deserted and darkened streets. Alexander Herzen, whose wife gave premature birth after one such visit, said there was no reason for such methods except "the histrionic passion of policemen, especially secret ones." Most of those they arrested were allegedly involved in secret societies, but the section made little distinction between conspiratorial gatherings and regular, innocent meetings with friends. Often those who were pulled in did not even know the charge against them until they were already in Siberian exile.[123]

For the first decade of Nicholas's reign, Benckendorff was closer to him than was anyone else, and the Tsar took a detailed interest in all the Third Section's doings, including helping to pick its bizarre personnel. Vock, a doctor's son, had been in detective policing all his adult life and loved interrogation. He invented many of the "they say" techniques used until 1989–90 throughout Eastern Europe. He had "an immense growth of hair" above his right eye, which winked incessantly and made him look frightening. He also invented the principle that anyone, whatever his class, who refused to inform on others was himself guilty of treason, a working assumption of the Soviet KGB until recently.[124] He was devoted to his work to the exclusion of anything else, and in 1830 his annual report welcomed the coming of cholera, which was new to Russia, on the grounds that "it has deflected minds from political matters." The next year he died of it.[125] Other Third Section people included a devious Kentish engineer John Sherwood; the courtesan Madame Sobanskaya; the Botanist Boshniak, the poet Viskovatov, the converted Jew Platanov; and an exceptionally unscrupulous journalist, Thaddeus Bulganin, who had served on both sides in the Napoleonic Wars and was the son of a murderer. Like many other section members and agents, Bulganin had done time in prison, and he used his position to terrorize other journalists, overawe the censors and build up a personal publishing empire. Pushkin caricatured him as Figliarin, the juggler.[126] Nicholas, despite his stuffiness and love of order, seemed to have taken a keen interest in this disorderly crew. We have a comic glimpse of the Tsar and Benckendorff poring over Bulganin's review of the Seventh Canto of Pushkin's *Eugene Onegin*, ending with Nicholas angrily pronouncing it "unjust and vulgar." Tsar: "Count, I order you to call in Bulganin and order him to print no more literary criticism whatever from now on. And, if possible, close down his paper!"[127]

*   *   *

Tsar Nicholas's relationship with Pushkin, indeed, casts a revealing light on the strange intimacies of his dismal regime. The Tsar's literary tastes ran to Sir Walter Scott and Paul de Kock, but he realized that Pushkin, his contemporary, was a national asset who ought to be cultivated. He puzzled over the poems, circulating in *zamisdat*, especially an obscene one on the Immaculate Conception, the *Gabrieliad*. Whether he was in country exile or in the city, Pushkin was a cynosure: People stood up in their boxes when he went to the theater. Countless reports about him poured into the Third Section. His country neighbor, a retired general, reported that he dressed in a peasant blouse with a red sash and straw hat, visited fairs, and had got off his horse to let it run free, saying "Even a horse needs freedom!" Boshniak the botanist was sent down to see if he was really inciting a peasant revolt, but concluded he was a fine fellow. The Tsar, who wanted a cat-and-mouse relationship with the poet, curiously adumbrating Joseph Stalin's with the composer Dmitri Shostakovich, badgered Benckendorff to let Pushkin come to Saint Petersburg. The count general, who sometimes suffered complete lapses of memory in which he could not even recall his own name, readily agreed; he had forgotten who Pushkin was or why he was in exile. Pushkin was taken straight from two years' exile in a remote province to the Tsar's private apartments: odd bits of dialogue from their long talk (8 September 1826) have survived. Tsar: "What would you have done if you had been in Saint Petersburg on 14 December?" Pushkin: "I would have been in the ranks of the rebels." Tsar: "I expect to see many verses from your pen." Pushkin: "The censorship is very strict." Tsar: "I will be your censor." Pushkin: "I am deeply moved."[128] This statement was confirmed in a letter to the poet from Benckendorff: "The sovereign himself will be the first critic of your works, and your censor." Thereafter the Third Section received and transmitted regular reports on the progress of Pushkin's work. "He is writing a historical play." "It is said there is nothing 'liberal' in *Boris Godunov*." "All he needs is guidance." "We can expect the most beautiful works from his genius." The atrocious Bulganin became jealous of all this attention and took to sending anonymous letters denouncing Pushkin to the Third Section, even though he worked there. The Tsar ran into Pushkin at a court ball and asked him to recite a wicked, unpublishable epigram which, he had heard, the poet had written about Bulganin. Pushkin did so. Tsar: "Clever!"

With all his power and single-mindedness, the Tsar nonetheless mishandled the Decembrist conspiracy. There was no difficulty about unraveling the plot itself. It may be that the Saint Petersburg mob would have joined the conspirators if they themselves had been more resolute. But among their own social circles, everyone turned against them. Ten days after the failed coup, Nicholas reported to his brother Constantine: "Here everyone has helped me in this terrible work. Fathers led their sons to me. All want to be an example, and the main thing: they want to see their families cleansed of such personalities and even suspicions." If Nicholas had executed all those involved, it is likely he would have met with the approval of most of the Russian ruling class. But he did no such thing. No fewer than 579 people were brought to trial. Of that number, 290 were acquitted, 134 were found guilty of minor offenses and degraded, four were expelled from Russia, 20 died during or before trial, the fate of 9 is unknown and 121 were judged primary conspirators. Of the 121, only 5 were hanged. Siberian exile with hard labor was given to 31; 85 got shorter terms in prison. The sentences were totally inconsistent. Michel Orlov, one of the founders of the whole movement, was released under police surveillance. Pestel was hanged, though he had played no part in any insurrection, being under arrest. Michael Lunin, who was in Warsaw and totally inactive, got a long sentence and died in the Akatui Mines 20 years later. Peter Falenburg, whose connection with the group was slight, also got a long Siberian term.

If Nicholas had hanged all, their cause would have died with them. Among the masses, among even their own house servants, they were not popular. Agents reported the servants saying: "They have begun to hang the masters and send them into exile. A pity they don't hang them all!" As it was, the cruelties inflicted on the exiles made them legends while they were still alive; some even survived to write their memoirs. A few were kept in chains for many years. Others were put in a prison with no windows. Some, including teenagers, vanished into fortresses for decades. But there were also acts of clemency. In 14 cases women were allowed to join their husbands or sons. They, too, helped to create and perpetuate the legend and the mythology of the Decembrists. The conspiracy was still a living melodrama at the end of the 19th century when it was appropriated by Lenin. In the short term, the Decembrists must be ranked among the most unsuccessful plotters in history. In the long term, they played a decisive part in delegitimizing and destroying the regime they hated.[129]

One reason they were able to do so was that, being intellectuals but, unlike most intellectuals, sacrificing themselves for their ideas, they set up a fatal split between the educated class and the ruling class. This split tends to occur in any modern society. But in Russia the split became an unbridgeable gulf; as Alexander Herzen put it, "them—and us." It became the most important single fact in Russian politics. The split was opened by Tsar Nicholas's handling of the conspiracy and widened by his subsequent actions. Nothing appeals to intellectuals more than the feeling that they represent "the people." Nothing, as a rule, is further from the truth. But in Russia, from 1825 onwards, the regime, by acts of deliberate policy, pushed intellectuals and the masses closer. An autocratic regime, especially a monarchical one, never finds it difficult to pursue a populist policy. Tsar Nicholas went in the opposite direction. The writers and journalists who were used by the regime deliberately emphasized its antipopulism. Michael Pogodin, the governmental historian, wrote in 1826: "The Russian people are marvellous, but only in potential. In actuality, they are low, horrid and beastly." They "will not become human beings until they are forced into it." The governmental journalist Nicholas Grech emphasized: "There are many devils among them. Therefore police, and a severe police, is a necessity both for the state and for all private individuals." Alexander had been too "meek," too "full of kindness and compassion. This is too good for the vile human species. Now there I love our Nicholas! . . . When he hits, whether they like it or not, they sing *God save the Tsar!* . . . Why be crafty, when one can issue orders and use the whip?" Thaddeus Bulganin joined the chorus: "It is better to un-chain a hungry tiger or hyena than to take off the people the bridle of obedience to authorities and laws. There is no beast fiercer than a raging mob!"[130]

Such attitudes, reflected in laws and actions, allowed intellectuals to pose as the champions of a sovereign people and encouraged them, in so doing, to relish the fantastic utopian schemes now being elaborated by other intellectuals farther west. Educated idealists in Russia tended increasingly to turn away from Anglo-Saxon precedents and constitu-tionalism and toward men like Fourier and Saint-Simon. They read Hegel, too, and other protototalitarian ideologues. When Marx's writ-ings reached Russia in the 1880s, the ground was thus well prepared; it might almost be said that a section of educated Russia was already Marxist.

The Decembrist conspiracy and its aftermath were thus one of the great turning points in history, a sinister signpost toward the horrors of the 20th century. Almost everything about this event had a gruesome symbolism, not excepting the executions of the five officers the Tsar did choose to hang, on 13 July 1826. The gallows had been hastily and badly erected during the previous night, on the glasis of the Peter-Paul Fortress. The morning was dark and misty, so fires were lit near the square into which all the prisoners had been herded to witness the deaths. At 3 A.M. the condemned men were led out. Their epaulettes and uniforms were stripped off and cast on the flames. Much vodka had been drunk. There was laughter and buffoonery, one man, Iakubovich, wearing a plumed officer's hat, high boots, and a short dressing gown down to his knees. The five condemned men had notices saying "Criminals—Regicides!" hanging round their chests. They were blessed by the Archpriest Myslovskii, even Pestel (a Lutheran) receiving his viaticum. The ropes were then put on, hoods slipped over their faces, and the supports pulled away. Three of the men fell off, unharmed. One of the generals in charge ran up shouting, fatuously: "Faster, faster!" Muravev, rolling on the ground where he had fallen, shouted: "My God! In this hopeless country they cannot even hang people properly."[131] It was the authentic voice of Russia, despairing but also ironic. Moments later all five men were dead.

The Decembrist affair became a watershed in Russia, but outside it no one took much notice. The Duke of Wellington, in Saint Petersburg for the funeral of Alexander, was busy negotiating with the new government terms under which the Allies would hold the ring in Greece. The thing which struck him most about Russian affairs was the long delay in holding the funeral and the disgusting state of the corpse, which was becoming unfrozen and was manifestly decayed. In any case, the rest of Europe was preoccupied with its own difficulties. For in the same month the Decembrist coup failed, the advanced world was hit by a new and frightening phenomenon: the first modern financial crisis.

ELEVEN

Crash!

On 14 December 1825, the day the radical colonels tried to overthrow the Tsarist monarchy, intense pressure threatened to destroy a supposedly even more secure institution: the Bank of England. Founded in 1694 by William III to finance his French wars, the bank had become, by the mid-1820s, easily the most powerful and august financial organ in the world. For more than 20 years, its physical appearance, on its four-acre site off Threadneedle Street, had been progressively transformed by Britain's most original architect, Sir John Soane. Soane had created five immense halls, composed of subtle curves, arches and vaults, lit by dim light from lunette windows above, and across whose marble floors daily shuffled an immense concourse of people, marshaled by tall men in long-tailed pink coats and scarlet waistcoats.[1] On that day, however, the usual cloistered calm beneath the marble, in the bank's vast strong rooms, had yielded to a frenzied search for gold, as its officials ransacked the reserve boxes for their last remaining stocks of sovereigns. As the public demanded specie for their paper and country banks recalled their deposits to save themselves from ruin, the bank found itself, for the first time in its history, in serious danger of running out of cash.

Early on 17 December, John Charles Herries (1778–1855), financial secretary to the Treasury, called on Mrs. Arbuthnot and told her that "such has been the extraordinary demand for gold to supply the country bankers and to meet the general run upon them that the Bank of England was completely drained of its specie and was reduced to 100,000 sovereigns, with which it would have to open today and meet demands of probably four times that amount."[2] Quite by accident, however, bank officials that day stumbled upon a huge, unmarked chest, thought to contain bonds, which proved on opening to be crammed with sovereigns—£1.5 million in solid sterling. They were hastily made available for over-the-counter transactions. Three days later, the bank was again down to 60,000 sovereigns, but by this stage the private banker Nathan Rothschild, used by the bank to keep up its gold stocks, had got his hands on 200,000 more, and had 25 couriers ranging all over Europe buying sovereigns wherever they were to be found. Thus, the bank avoided a suspension of payments and saved its credit.[3]

To discover why and how the bank had got itself into this mess, we must retrace our steps some years. The Napoleonic Wars, like all great wars, were largely financed on credit, producing a huge increase in governmental indebtedness and fundamental changes in the international banking system. Just as William III's wars against Louis XIV led to the creation of the Bank of England itself, so the efforts to subdue Bonaparte brought into power and prominence a new type of private banking house to raise loans for governments and provide them with cash. Britain, the world's richest country and the most consistent of Bonaparte's opponents, required specie not only to finance its colossal navy and its Peninsular army, but to subsidize its Continental allies. To do so, it needed to sell at least £20 million of loan stock every year of the hostilities. The London market could not absorb this amount directly, so tranches of it were sold to contractors who found customers.

In 1803 one of these contractors was Nathan Rothschild (1777–1836) then a young man who had recently transferred his activities to London after a successful spell in the Lancashire cotton trade.[4] He had one stroke of extraordinary fortune in acquiring working capital. After the calamitous Battle of Jena in 1806, the elector of Hesse-Cassel transferred his personal reserves to London and invited Nathan to invest it in British securities. The banker was thus able to build up his own resources while serving the elector's interests. He also practiced the traditional Jewish skill of transferring bullion and specie securely under difficult conditions. In the years 1811–15, he and J. C. Herries, then also a young man and British Commissary in Chief, contrived to transport £42.5 million in gold safely to Wellington's army in Spain, half of it handled directly by Nathan or by his younger brother James, operating from France.[5] By the end of the wars, Nathan was a major financial figure in London, as James was in Paris, while their eldest brother, Amschel, was in charge of the family's original headquarters in Frankfurt. In 1816 a fourth brother, Salomon, set up a Vienna branch of the business, while in 1821 a fifth brother, Karl, completed the Rothschild European network with a bank in Naples.

From 1815 the Rothschilds led a new movement in international banking. Governments had always financed war on credit. Now the Rothschilds made it possible for them to raise comparable or even greater sums to accelerate peaceful progress. It was, in its own way, perhaps the key factor in the birth of the modern world because it made so many other developments possible. In the decade 1815–25 more securities were floated than in the whole of the preceding century. Most of this credit was raised in London, with the House of Rothschild in the van. Nathan did not normally deal with volatile Latin American regimes— we will come to them shortly—but with solid European autocracies: Austria, Russia and Prussia. He became banker to the Holy Alliance, and in the years 1818–32 he handled 7 of the 26 foreign government loans raised in London (plus one jointly), conjuring up a total of £21 million, 39 percent of the whole.[6]

No country was more avid to take advantage of the growing sophistication of the banking system and the new financial markets than was the United States, for none was more in need of credit for development. In the years 1816–21 alone, six new states were created; in size and potential power, it was like adding six new European countries. European financial techniques were quickly copied and embellished; the surge of credit, in terms of existing capital, was doubled, trebled and multiplied manyfold. The United States was already creating for itself a reputation for massive borrowing against its limitless future. That, and its sheer size, meant, in turn, a need for a large number of banks, and the United States was also already notorious for the proliferation of its banking system. America's rapid development would have been impossible without it, but the individual banks lacked effective supervision and control.

A central bank, the Bank of the United States, had been created in 1791. It was modeled on the Bank of England. But it had many enemies in a country where states saw themselves as sovereign. When its 20-year charter ran out in 1811, Congress refused to recharter it. States, on the other hand, were happy to charter banks, and the number of state banks rose from 88 in 1811 to 208 two years later. Each state bank was empowered by the state legislature to issue bills up to three times its capital. In practice, however, there was little check upon the ratio, and most banks issued well beyond the legal limit.[7] Hence, in good times at least, securing a state charter for a bank was an easy way to make money. A new kind of economic-financial power was coming into being, which ran directly counter to the original concept of the United States as a majestic rural society based upon landed property.

The first to perceive the implications of this phenomenon was John Taylor of Carolina, as he was known (1753–1824), a Virginia farmer who served in the Senate and in 1814 published a vast, 700-page work,

An Inquiry into the Principles and Policy of the Government of the United States. He distinguished between "natural" property, such as land, and "artificial" property created by legal privilege, of which banking wealth was the outstanding example. Paper-money banking, he argued, benefited an artificially created financial aristocracy at the expense of the hard-working farmer: "the property-transferring policy invariably impoverishes all labouring and productive classes." He saw the right to issue money as a form of indirect taxation, adding, "Taxation, direct or indirect, produced by a paper system in any form, will rob a nation of property without giving it liberty; and by creating and enriching a separate interest, will rob it of liberty without giving it property." Taylor compared the new financial power to the old aristocratic and ecclesiastical power, with the bankers using "force, faith and credit, as the two others did religion and feudality."[8] What particularly angered Taylor was the diabolical skill with which financiers had invested "fictitious" property, such as bank paper and stock, with all the prestige and virtues of "honest" property.[9]

Taylor's arguments, suitably vulgarized, were to become common coin as the darker side of the credit boom and the proliferation of banks manifested itself. During the War of 1812, the United States was awash with $2 and $5 dollar bills issued by mushroom banks. Such gold as there was flowed into New England, especially Boston, whose state banks were the most secure. By 1813 Boston notes were at a 9–10 percent premium in Philadelphia. The New England banks refused to take notes from banks in the West and South at all. In 1814, the final year of the war, the first banking crisis broke: Every bank outside New England was forced to suspend payments, and many honest investors were ruined.

The response of Congress was to reverse its earlier decision and set up (10 April 1816) the Second Bank of the United States (SBUS). But the remedy proved worse than the disease. The congressmen who legislated the SBUS into existence were so suspicious of a strong central government that they gave the bank a great deal of independence. In 1824 its President, Nicholas Biddle, was to write to President Monroe saying that suggestions by the Secretary of the Treasury "will be most respectfully considered by the Board of Directors, and cheerfully agreed to, if not inconsistent with their duties to the institution."[10] That statement would have been acceptable coming from the Bank of England, which was a nongovernmental body. But the federal government owned 20 percent of the SBUS's stock and appointed 5 out of 25 directors. It was geared into the fiscal operations of the nation. Thus, importers paid their customs duties in private bank notes; these notes went to the

SBUS, which gradually came to hold large quantities of the paper of all banks, and it was through these holdings that it regulated them. That, at any rate, was the theory.[11]

In fact, during the immediate postwar period, when the wartime boom continued, the push west and south proceeded rapidly, and vast number of emigrants entered the United States, the SBUS, as the lender of last instance, was ultimately responsible for pumping a prodigious amount of inflationary paper into the system. Its first President, William Jones (1760–1831), a former congressman and Madison's Navy Secretary, knew little of banking and had some dubious business friends—he fitted nicely into Taylor's demonology. He responded too enthusiastically to Henry Clay's demand that America should develop the West by borrowing against its future. In the years 1815–19, the boom was fueled chiefly by the sale of and speculation in land. The manufacturing sector in New England was not doing well, primarily because of dumping by British firms.

But industry was then only a tiny fragment of the U.S. economy, which was still essentially agricultural, and which expanded on an unprecedented scale, thanks to cotton. All over the world people wanted cheap cotton goods from Lancashire, and the Liverpool importers could not get enough cotton to keep the ever-growing number of looms busy. From 1815 the price of American cotton rose rapidly, reaching 31½ cents a pound at one point in 1818. That in turn fed the land boom. In these years new public land was sold primarily to raise revenue, rather than to benefit the settlers. Settlers had to pay $2 an acre for land in minimum blocks of 160 acres. However, they had to put only 25 percent down. The rest they borrowed from the banks, on the security of the property. The $2 was a minimum; in the South potential cotton land was sold as high as $100 an acre in the boom years. The SBUS effectively financed this land boom by its easy credit policy.[12]

In a curious adumbration of the 1920s Wall Street boom, when speculators were allowed to buy stock on credit, the SBUS allowed land investors to pay the second installment on their purchase by credit, again raised on the security of the property, in effect a second mortgage. Jones's principal aim was to pay high dividends to the SBUS's stockholders. The more he lent, especially through the SBUS's score of branches, the more profits the bank made and the greater the dividend. Amazing though it may seem, the SBUS—America's central financial institution—dealt in bits of paper known as racers, short for race horse bills. A racer was a bill of exchange paid for by other bills of exchange, which thus rushed around rapidly from one debtor to another, ac-

cumulating charges and yielding less and less face value in the process.
It was a typical bit of 19th-century ruin-finance, beloved of novelists
like Thackeray and Trollope, who used such devices to get their gullible
heroes into trouble. This kind of paper explains why needy people got
so little for what they undertook to repay. But then, of course, they
often could not repay it anyway, which was why the credit system was
so inherently unstable.[13]

Jones's easy credit policy was aggravated by the unsupervised activities of the bank's branch offices, some of which were in the hands of
amateurs or crooks. In Baltimore, the SBUS branch was run by two land
speculators, James A. Buchanan and James W. McCulloch. These men
financed their vast speculative purchases by taking out unsecured loans
from their own branch, in effect putting their hands in the till. Buchanan borrowed $429,049 this way, McCulloch $244,212, and the first
teller a further $50,000.[14] The credit expansion was used to buy all
kinds of property, including town houses—it was the first urban house-
price boom in U.S. history—but most of it went for land. Thanks to
Jones, the debt on public land alone rose from $3,042,613 in 1815 to
more than five times the amount, $16,794,795, three years later. To
some extent, the increase in paper money and credit was inevitable. In
the postwar period, as a result of the closure of many Latin American
mines by the independence struggle, gold was in short supply all over
the world. But Jones went too far, especially in financing land deals in
the South and West, and everyone else in the banking fraternity followed suit.

There were some warning voices. On 14 March 1818, John Jacob
Astor (1763–1848), the German immigrant who had set up the American Fur Company 10 years before and was now the dominant figure in
the trade—as well as a big property owner in Manhattan—accused the
SBUS directors of discounting too freely. They had made money so
cheap, he complained in a letter to Albert Gallatin, "that everything else
has become Dear, & the Result is that our merchants, instead of
shipping produce, ship Specie, so much so that I tell you in confidence
that it is not without difficulty that Specie payments are maintained.
The different States are going on making more banks & I shall not be
surprised if by & by there be a general Blow Up among them."[15]

By the time Astor wrote, the blowup was on its way, for Liverpool
cotton importers, alarmed by the high price of U.S. cotton, had
switched orders to East India. The number of bales of Indian cotton
which were imported by Britain rose from 117,955 in 1817 to 227,300
in 1818. As more Indian cotton came in, the Liverpool price of U.S.

cotton wavered and began to fall toward the end of 1818. When the news reached America in December, the price of cotton dropped in one day from 32 to 26 cents, then slipped further to a New Orleans average of only 14.3 cents. The drop in U.S. cotton prices, in turn, savaged land prices, which fell from 50 to 75 percent, and there was a further knock-on for the banks, which found themselves with collateral in land now worth only a fraction of their loans, which were irrecoverable. Many of these state-chartered banks were bucket shops anyway. According to Hezekiah Niles (1777–1839), the enterprising publisher of *Niles's Weekly Register,* one of our best sources of general information for the period, all you needed in these years to start a bank which issued notes were plates, presses and paper. Notes were easily forged, too: Niles claimed that counterfeit notes from at least 100 banks were circulating by 1819. To get a state legislature to charter your bank was the easiest thing in the world: all you needed was to talk to a few state senators, who were often rewarded by an easy seat on your board. Premises were often provided by a converted church, forge or inn. By 1819 there were at least 392 chartered banks and many more uncharted ones, and in the meantime the debt on public lands had jumped another $6 million in 12 months to stand at $22 million.

Once the cotton and land prices began to fall, Jones compounded his earlier errors by abruptly reversing his easy credit policy. He ordered branches of the SBUS to accept only its own notes, demanded immediate cash payments on notes issued by state banks, and refused to renew loans. That order immediately began to smash the state-chartered banks and ruin their investors.[16] The land deeds that state banks held as collateral passed into the vaults of the SBUS. Many congressmen, seeing the future of their electors thus put in the power of a central bank they had never wanted anyway, turned with fury on Jones. Jones was easily dealt with. A congressional committee soon discovered the Baltimore business, and in January 1819 Jones and his entire board were forced to resign. President Monroe appointed as his successor the austere and experienced figure, Langdon Cheves, who took over in March, finding the SBUS "a ship without a rudder or sails or masts . . . on a stormy sea and far from land."[17] The only way Cheves could save the SBUS was by intensifying the deflationary policy belatedly adopted by Jones. He did so and managed to keep the SBUS solvent and open. But everyone else had to pay for it. As a contemporary expert, William Gouge, put it: "The Bank was saved and the people were ruined."[18] The congressional anti-central-bank lobby, outraged by the manner in which the SBUS had assassinated the banks in their states, tried to get Congress to revoke its charter immediately. Failing at that, they urged state legislatures to tax it out of existence.[19]

At this point there stepped into the argument one of the most influential figures in American history. If one man can be said to have wedded the United States indissolubly to the capitalist system, it was John Marshall (1755–1835), appointed Chief Justice of the Supreme Court in 1801, a post he held for 34 years. This proved to be one of the most critical appointments in American history, for Marshall believed in a strong central authority and he used his office to assert this interpretation of the Constitution at a time when most of the presidents— Jefferson, Madison, Monroe and Jackson—tended to favor states' rights. He also upheld the rights of property, including what Taylor called "artificial" property, at a time when it was coming under attack. Above all, he asserted, fully and systematically and for the first time, the right of the court to play its full part in the Constitution, by, in effect, making law through the process of interpretation. As he put it in one of his judgments: "We must never forget that it is a constitution we are expounding . . . something organic, capable of growth, susceptible to change." He was a man of strong character, great charm, and subtly persuasive power, who phrased his arguments, written or spoken, in elegant and sinewy English. During the six to eight weeks the Court sat each term, he and his fellow justices lived in the same Washington boardinghouse, so that, as his biographer put it, Marshall was "head of a family as much as he was chief of a court."[20] Though less learned than some of his colleagues, he was absolutely dominant among them. In 34 years, he found himself in a dissenting minority only eight times out of over 1,100 judgments, 519 of which he wrote himself.[21]

Like his great contemporary, Lord Chancellor Eldon, Marshall was a self-made man, born in a Virginia cabin. Like Eldon, he was an elitist, in every fiber of his being. He did not exactly look the part: He was tall, thin, gangly, ill-dressed, not always too clean, very gossipy and gregarious, not at all aloof. But he had read Edmund Burke's *Reflections on the French Revolution* when it was first published, and to the end of his days he had a profound distrust of the people, especially the mob. In his view, popular power was essentially vested in state legislatures, which were the first to enfranchise unpropertied people. Hence, he was a centralist and, other things being equal, would find for the federal government. He had read Adam Smith's *Wealth of Nations,* too, and he believed with measured passion that capitalism was the means whereby Americans would take possession and fructify the great spaces to the west. He had none of Taylor's qualms in asserting the rights of capitalism and the power of property. Quite the reverse. He believed that the correct interpretation of the Constitution by the Court was the quickest and most efficient means of enabling capitalism to do its job of developing the vast territories which Almighty God, in His wisdom, had given the American people, just as He had once given the promised land to the Israelites.

Marshall was not the only outspoken defender of property in these years. Daniel Webster (1782–1852), the leading New England orator, made a dramatic plea for the property base in politics at the Massachusetts Constitutional Convention of 1820: "Power *naturally* and *necessarily* follows property," as he put it.[22] The banker Nicholas Biddle referred to "men with no property to assess and no character to lose," as though possessions and virtue went hand in hand.[23] Jeremiah Mason, another lawyer turned central banker, argued: "As the wealth of the commercial and manufacturing classes increases, in the same degree ought their political power to increase . . . in a country where wealth greatly abounds, I doubt whether any other foundation for a stable, free government can be found."[24] Such men, however, were unable to stem the tide of one-man–one-vote democracy in the legislatures. By contrast, Marshall, with his subservient colleagues, was able to turn the Supreme Court into an elitist fortress, using all the resources of the U.S. Constitution and the English Common Law to assert the gravitational value of property and commercial law and so to prevent the United States from falling victim to the anticapitalist demagoguery which repeatedly swept across the states of Latin America and hindered its wealth-producing process. In doing so, he became one of the principal architects of the modern world.[25]

Marshall set the parameters for his work as early as 1803, when in *Marbury v. Madison* he asserted the constitutional power of the Supreme Court to engage in judicial review of both state and federal legislation and, if needs be, to rule it unconstitutional. Viewing, as he did, the Constitution as an instrument of national unity and safety, he claimed that it not only set forth specific powers but created its own sanctions by its implied powers. These sanctions were particularly necessary when, with the spread of the suffrage, politicians made populist assaults on property to appease the mob. To Marshall, it made little difference whether an actual rabble stormed the Bastille by force or a legislative rabble tried to take it by an unconstitutional statute. His first great blow for property came in 1810 in *Fletcher v. Peck,* when he overturned the popular verdict by ruling that a contract was valid whatever ordinary men might think of its ethics.[26] Fourteen years later, in the key case of *Gibbons v. Ogden,* he struck a lasting blow for entrepreneurial freedom by ruling that a state legislature had no right to create a steamboat monopoly. This interpretation of the commerce clause of the Constitution, in effect, insisted that the U.S. Congress was supreme in all aspects of interstate commerce and could not be limited by state statute in that area. "The subject," he wrote, "is as completely taken from the state legislatures as if they had been expressly forbidden to act on it."[27]

But 1819 was Marshall's *annus mirabilis* in defense of property. Early in February his Court ruled, in *Sturges v. Crowninshield,* that a populist New York State bankruptcy law in favor of debtors violated the Constitution on contracts. Later the same month, in *Dartmouth College v. Woodward,* the Court laid down that a corporation charter was a private contract which was immune from interference by a state legislature. But the most important decision came in March, over the banking crisis. The attempt by the states to suppress the SBUS came to a head in Maryland, which tried to destroy the bank's Baltimore branch by taxation. As we have seen, there was everything wrong with the branch, but taxation was not the right way to remedy it. The errant McCulloch, on behalf of the branch, refused to pay the taxes demanded. In the resultant case, *McCulloch v. Maryland,* the Court had to rule not only on the right of a state to tax a federal institution but on the right of Congress to set up the bank in the first place. The judgment came down magisterially in favor of the central power and the status of the SBUS, which thus survived and flourished.[28]

But what of the country? By the time the Marshall Court delivered its verdict, the nation was in the midst of its worst economic and financial crisis since its foundation. As we have seen, frantic efforts were made to halt the flow of immigrants pouring into New York and Boston. On 27 May 1819 John Quincy Adams, then Secretary of State, was writing in his diary: "The banking bubbles are breaking." Agricultural prices were collapsing, "the merchants are crumbling in ruin; the manufactures perishing, agriculture stagnating, and distress universal in every part of the country." Six week later he reported: "[Treasury Secretary] Crawford told me . . . the banks are breaking all over the country, some in a sneaking and some in an impudent manner, some with sophisticated evasions and others with the front of highwaymen."[29] The public raged against the collapsed banks, which had swallowed people's money and, often, the deeds of their farms, but, above all, it cursed *the* bank, which remained intact and was now systematically foreclosing businesses and holdings. By mid-1819 the SBUS owned half Cincinnati, America's flagship boom-city, and enormous tracts of prime land throughout the West and much of the new South. By foreclosing, it got flourishing businesses very cheaply and land at less than half its average real value. When the panic subsided and property values rose again, the bank's assets rose rapidly, and it was able to sell off its foreclosed properties at a hugh profit. It had been exceptionally foolish and, because of its privileged position, its folly had been rewarded.

The true case against the bank was that an institution made possible by the credit of the nation had, during the scare, put its own survival before the national interest. No doubt Cheves would have answered that if the SBUS had fallen, the national financial position would have been even worse. But that was not how the critics saw it. With some justice, they held the SBUS responsible for the credit boom in the first place, from which it alone had emerged enriched. To them, the SBUS's behavior had not been foolish but calculated and evil. Three years before, Mary Shelley had created her Frankenstein's Monster, and now a real, institutionalized monster had risen in America's heartland to wreak havoc. That was exactly the term ruined Westerners used to describe the triumphant force of finance of which the bank was the symbol. Senator Thomas Benton of Missouri (1782–1858) roared in anguish: "All the flourishing cities of the West are mortgaged to this money power. They may be devoured by it at any moment. They are in the Jaws of the Monster. A lump of butter in the mouth of a dog—one gulp, one swallow and all is gone!" And now the Court had ruled that the states might not even tax the Monster to get some of their money back! It was a constitutional scandal.

Moreover, as the disclosures about the Baltimore branch indicated, there was corruption in the air, too. There was, indeed—more than the public realized. As always happens when firms go bankrupt, ugly deals and practices came to light, involving leading members of the administration, including William Crawford, John Calhoun (1782–1850) the War Secretary, and even President Monroe himself. These men were not personally corrupt, but each tolerated indefensible activities by underlings and political cronies, rather as President Harding was to do in the 1920s. The now-bankrupt Johnson Brothers Company of Kentucky was advanced $250,000 of federal money to provide four steamboats for the Yellowstone Expedition of 1818. The boats turned out to be useless. Monroe, as well as Calhoun, was involved in this transaction. It led to Crawford and the U.S. Treasury investigating various aspects of Calhoun's departmental activities. In reply, Calhoun's friend Thomas L. McKenney, former head of the Office of Indian Trade, set up a new paper, the *Washingtonian Republican and Congressional Examiner,* specifically to attack Crawford and *his* doings. That action led to a mutually damaging newspaper war with the pro-Crawford papers, and to a congressional investigation, by Crawford's allies, of McKenney's Indian administration. Crawford's men also got onto the circumstances surrounding the building of an army base called Fortress Monroe, in which it turned out that the brother-in-law of Calhoun's chief clerk had mysteriously been awarded a $300,000 contract. Calhoun hit back, in turn, and was able to show that Crawford had allowed the U.S. Treasury and the SBUS to transfer money from the bank to certain troubled state banks in violation of the law, while allowing government contracts to be paid in low-quality state-bank paper money.[30]

All these accusations and rumors seemed to lead, in the view of the more imaginative public, back to the Monster, standing at the center of a secret network of corrupt power, whose lifeblood was the hated paper money. The worries within the Monroe administration about growing popular hostility to "the system" were discussed by Calhoun and Adams during a ride in May 1820. The panic, said Calhoun, had aroused "a general mass of disaffection to the government, not concentrated in any particular direction, but ready to seize upon any event and looking out anywhere for a leader. . . . It was a vague but wide discontent caused by the disordered circumstances of individuals but resulting in a general impression that there was something radically wrong in the administration of the government." On which Adams commented in despair: "Government can do nothing . . . but transfer discontents, and propitiate one class of people by disgusting another."[31] The truth is, the great crash of 1819 ended the age of innocence in America, the epoch when government was generally trusted to do the right thing. It introduced a pause, in which the rapidly growing electorate looked around, as Calhoun rightly prophesied, for a leader to voice their discontents, especially against the money power. Soon they were to find him, in the tall, angular shape of the fierce General Andrew Jackson.

In the meantime, the difficulties the Americans had experienced with too much paper money had been duly noted in Westminster, where the Committee of Secrecy of the House of Commons presented its Second Report, 6 May 1819, "on the expediency of the Bank resuming cash payments."[32] The Bank of England (and Britain) had been forced by wartime conditions to go off the gold standard in 1797; that is, the bank then ceased to be obliged by law to pay out gold for its own paper. When peace came, the world gold shortage made it impossible for the bank to resume payments in gold coin (sovereigns or guineas) because it simply did not possess enough of them to redeem all its notes.

But in 1816 the brilliant businessman and economist David Ricardo (1772–1823) pointed out convincingly that there was a halfway house.

Ricardo, like Chief Justice Marshall, was a student of Adam Smith. Moreover, he was the first economist since Smith to have a profound effect on the way governments actually behaved. Ricardo was another of those child prodigies in which the age specialized. His father was a Sephardic broker from Amsterdam who came to London and was chosen for one of the dozen brokerships reserved for Jews in the City. Six of his sons followed him there, including David, who at the age of 14 was judged so clever that he became his father's principal confidant.[33] But David broke with his family by falling in love with a beautiful Quaker girl, Abigail Delvalle, and marrying her outside his faith, becoming a Unitarian; his father "went into mourning for him as though he were dead" and left him a mere £100 in his will, "as token of forgiveness."

By then, however, Ricardo was well launched on his own account. He speculated cunningly in East India Company stock and, like Nathan Rothschild, contracted successfully for many of the governmental loans between 1811 and 1815. He reinvested his profits with immense success in country properties, which he bought and sold, and by the end of the war he could retire from City business with the huge income of £28,000 a year.[34] He had already started to write about financial matters. In February 1819, when the American banking crisis was just beginning, he bowed to the entreaties of friends, including James Mill, and went into Parliament, by the simple expedient of buying the borough of Portarlington from Lord Portarlington for the sum of £4,000, as part of a loan of £25,000 to the impecunious peer. He had already, however, established his name as the leading authority on currency problems. He fretted that an unbacked paper currency was certain to lead to inflation, and in September 1809 he had written a series of articles for the *Morning Chronicle* showing how this could happen.[35] When peace came, he renewed this crusade for a metallic backing. He accepted that the Bank of England could not yet get enough gold coin for its paper to be fully convertible, but he argued, in *Proposals for an Economical and Secure Currency* (1816), for his intermediate solution: The bank should turn its gold stocks into standard ingots, which could be used by merchants who needed bullion to make gold payments abroad.[36] Once in the House of Commons, he was able to press his plan with vigor. Despite his "shrill voice" and "broken" speech, his remarks in the House were to the point and well received, and he proved the most influential of all the witnesses examined by the Committee of Secrecy. At all events, the committee accepted his plan.[37] It was duly adopted by the bank, and the first gold ingots issued on 1 February 1820, were known as "Ricardos."

The gold ingots proved an immense success and led to the adoption of full convertibility much sooner than anyone, even Ricardo, expected. The world rise in the price of gold had meanwhile promoted intensive surveying and mining, which by 1820 was bringing supply into line with demand. By spring 1821, the bank's agents had been able to buy enough gold to risk a sovereign backing for its paper, and an act of Parliament was promptly passed enabling it to return to the gold currency standard on 1 May. The effect of this move was to increase immensely worldwide confidence in the British economy and the expansion of international trade. It intensified a manufacturing and commercial boom which had begun in the second half of 1819 and was now well under way. In the process, and almost incidentally, the new wave of confidence enabled the battered American economy to recover rapidly. So the U.S. paper crisis of 1819 was erased by the British gold boom of 1821.

The rapid expansion of the world economy in the early 1820s marked the upswing of the first modern trade cycle. It had innumerable consequences. One was to make the new species of expert, the economist, appear—at least for a time—to be the guide and philosopher of mankind. Ricardo, whose great work, *The Principles of Political Economy and Taxation,* had first appeared in 1817, was not the only practitioner to catch the ear of the powerful, indeed the reading public as a whole. Thomas Carlyle had not yet denounced economics as "the dismal science."[38] On the contrary, it was held in almost reverential respect. When Harriet Martineau was learning economics in the 1820s and applying her lessons instantly to best-selling moral tales—*The Rioters, The Turn-Out* and so forth—there were not yet rival schools of economists, but a single stream of doctrine running from Adam Smith (attended by various heretics), through Thomas Malthus and Ricardo. When Smith wrote, British merchants were not yet ready for free trade, hence the hostile term he used to describe its opponents, *mercantilism.* By the 1820s all that had changed. British industry and commerce had established such a commanding lead over the rest of the world that the entire mercantile community in such cities as London, Glasgow, Liverpool, Manchester and Birmingham were free traders to a man and were petitioning Parliament to be allowed free trade.

Economics was not so much a subject to be studied as a theory which its advocates believed was unarguable. The only problem, in their view, was how to teach it to the working classes, to stop them from burning hayricks and smashing machines when times were hard.

Its "iron laws" were as true and immutable as Isaac Newton's. As the *Quarterly Review,* by no means extreme in such matters, put it in October 1825: "It would be a real blessing if the working classes could be made acquainted with some of the fundamental principles of Political Economy, such as the laws of population . . . the circumstances which regulate the market of corn, or the market of labour. They would then perceive that inequality does not originate in the encroachments of the rich or the enactments of the powerful, but has been necessarily coeval with society itself in all its stages; they would learn that the recompense of labour is governed by definite principles—and we are grateful for any measures which may tend to diffuse such knowledge."[39] Hence the gratitude society felt for Miss Martineau, whose brilliant, up-to-the-minute tales—as Leslie Stephen later put it, she had the true journalistic talent of "turning hasty acquisitions to account"[40]—had precisely the common-man appeal.

But much weightier tomes also circulated in large numbers. Publishers paid Malthus and James Ramsay McCulloch, author of *A Discourse on . . . Political Economy* (1825), impressive sums, running into thousands of pounds, for their works. The universities were suddenly discovering economics. McCulloch got the first chair in the science set up at the new University of London. Nassau Senior was appointed to the new one endowed at Oxford. Articles on economics occupied an enormous amount of space in the reviews. Judges, too, were discovering its iron laws and gave tendentious lectures about them from the bench, to scowling machine breakers and arsonists.[41]

Indeed, the only people who were opposed to economics, apart from the diehard agricultural interest, were the more militant working men, especially those who belonged to trade unions. And the more enlightened leaders of opinion hoped to reconcile even them, by a systematic policy of conciliation and reform. By 1820, when the postwar recession had visibly yielded to good times, the Liverpool government turned from repression to liberalism. The year was marked by numerous City and manufacturers' petitions in favor of free trade and, what was more surprising, by the favor with which they were received in the Commons and indeed the government.[42] The move toward free trade, and so lower import duties and prices, was slowed down by the immense fuss over Queen Caroline and the endless troubles created by George IV, but it was later accelerated by two important ministerial changes: the return to the government of Sir Robert Peel as Home Secretary in 1822 and the shift of William Huskisson (1770–1830) to the Board of Trade the next year.

Huskisson was an odd and difficult man, a former Pittite and now a Canningite, much given to self-pity and, at times of crisis, indecisiveness, but widely acclaimed as brilliant and original. His father had been no more than a gentleman farmer (the estate when sold brought in £13,500), but Huskisson had been largely educated in Paris, where he had mixed in intellectual circles. Indeed, he was the nearest to an intellectual who had yet held high government office in Britain, and a doctrinaire to boot. His own financial activities on the stock exchange had been sometimes reckless, if not actually dishonest, and certainly far from successful.[43] But in economics he was a passionate student of Ricardo (as well as Smith) and thought he knew all the answers. As the boom progressed and the government surplus rose, he persuaded an already half-convinced cabinet to accept large reductions in duties, which had an immediate effect on prices and stimulated the economy still further.[44] Indeed, this was the first instance in history in which a "natural" economic upswing was turned into a raging boom by the deliberate use of the levers of policy by a politician in office.

Sir Robert Peel was in every way a more formidable statesman than Huskisson, with a much wider, though nondoctrinaire, philosophy of government. He was the son of the most successful early cotton millionaire, but his father, the first baronet, had never intended him to go into the family business: He was to be Prime Minister. Peel had a superb career at Harrow, where he easily outshone Byron ("I was always in scrapes," wrote Byron, "and he never; in school he always knew his lessons, and I rarely"). At Christ Church, then academically the best Oxford College, he took a double first. Indeed, for his final examination, conducted then, as usual, orally and in public, his fame was such that the schools were packed, one eyewitness reporting: "What is very rare, the Examining Masters separately thanked him for the pleasure they had received . . . the whole assembly was actuated with one sentiment of applause."[45] Within a year he was in Parliament. His ministerial ascent was as rapid as he cared to make it. Peel was a rich man, who formed one of the best private art collections in Europe; married the great beauty of the day, Julia Floyd (much admired by the Tsar and by London's wealthiest bachelor Hughes Ball, known as Golden Ball[46]); and had a life and career which, externally, seemed of unalloyed bliss and success. Whether he felt guilty about his own good fortune—there is no evidence of it in his letters—he certainly had an unusual sympathy for the poor and a determination to do everything in his power, subject, of course, to the "iron laws," to improve their lot.

Once in the Home Office, he made, for instance, the first serious effort actually to enforce such factory legislation as was already on the statute book. In this regard, he followed in his father's footsteps. In 1802 the elder Sir Robert Peel had carried through Parliament the Health and Morals of Apprentices Act, which limited the hours worked by boys and girls under age 16 to 12 a day, forbade night shifts and made provision for the children to receive adequate clothing. From 1816, acting as parliamentary spokesman for Robert Owen, he pushed through the parliamentary committee which eventually produced the far more comprehensive 1819 Act, which applied to all children working in cotton mills. Sir Robert, Senior, was motivated by compassion, but his legislation was not entirely disinterested: Well-capitalized firms like his own could afford to be humanitarian, and he was anxious to eliminate unfair competition by forcing bad employers to match his own standards—this was a point neither Engels nor Marx was ever able to understand.[47] But the weakness of the 1802 and 1819 acts is that they did not provide for a factory inspectorate, and it was hard to get people to pluck up enough courage to lay information before the magistrates. The younger Peel changed all this. He made a particular point of exhorting clergymen justices of the peace to take action, for instance, in Macclesfield in March 1823, and he encouraged Byron's friend, John Cam Hobhouse, to bring in the Cotton Mills Regulation Bill of 1825. At Wigan, a bad area where the justices were negligent, he threatened them with an Act of Parliament, which would have removed jurisdiction from their hands and put it under the county magistrates, unless they took action against bad employers themselves.[48]

It was characteristic of Peel that he made his move against Wigan at the instigation of John Doherty, Secretary of the Cotton-Spinners' Union. Peel was, in fact, the first British minister, perhaps the first in any country, to have friendly and constructive dealings with a trade union leader. He believed that unions ought to be brought into the country's legal system, as a necessary check on the power of employers, and he made this goal a part of the comprehensive reform of the English criminal and civil law and its enforcement. Let us look, first, at the law reform program as a whole. The task occupied him throughout the 1820s and culminated in his creation of the first modern law-enforcement agency, the Metropolitan Police, in 1829.

Peel had to carry this program through against the worst possible background: a crime wave. Though political agitation declined sharply after 1819, ordinary criminality seems to have increased dramatically, not only because London and other towns and cities were growing fast, but because all classes were becoming wealthier, yet policing was inadequate or in some places nonexistent. In the period 1809–16, 47,522 crimes were committed in England and Wales, leading to 29,361 convictions. These convictions produced 4,126 death sentences, of which 536 were actually carried out. During the somewhat longer period 1817–27, crimes committed rose to 93,718, with 63,418 convictions and 7,770 death sentences, of which 579 were carried out.[49] The significant features of the 1820s figures, both due to Peel, are the percentage rise in convictions and the decrease in hangings. Peel regarded the operations of the law in England with horror. He thought there were far too many laws and statutory crimes; and, above all, too many carrying capital punishment. While not an opponent of hanging as such, he was appalled by the frequency with which the rope was employed. He was determined to reduce the number of statutory capital crimes.

But Peel put first things first. If the public was to accept a reduction in hanging, it had to be persuaded that adequate, secure and salubrious prisons existed to house the felons thus spared. So Peel began with the first national reform of Britain's prisons, passing two acts in 1823 and one in 1824. These acts consolidated all the prison legislation going back to Edward III's time in the 14th century; built modern, uniform jails (though still paid for by local rates), and provided for standard discipline, visits by justices of the peace and a national inspectorate, and for the health care and education of prisoners.[50] Peel had had personal experience of prisons, since his younger brother William, his fellow MP for Tamworth, the family borough, had spent a month in the King's Bench Prison in 1820 following a dueling row. Indeed, it is a curious fact that many more members of the upper-middle or upper classes went to prison in the early nineteenth century than nowadays: Jane Austen's highly respectable aunt, Mrs. Leigh-Perrot, for instance, nearly received 14 years' transportation when falsely accused of shoplifting and spent seven months in Ilchester jail.[51] A famous letter Peel wrote to Sydney Smith, another prison reformer, shows how deeply he felt about the whole problem of criminality, despairing, as he put it, at the "vast harvest of transportable crime that is reaped at every assize. . . . The real truth is, the number of convictions is too overwhelming for the means of proper and effectual punishment. I despair of any remedy but that which I wish I could hope for—a great reduction in the amount of crime."[52] Peel believed that the long-term remedy was a progressive rise in the national standard of living, and in the early 1820s it began to look increasingly possible, for the first time in history. But in the meantime, as he told Lord Liverpool in a letter of 12 October 1822, he was determined to meet the law reformers at least halfway and codify outmoded laws.[53]

In 1823 Peel carried two acts which repealed capital punishment for many forms of larceny and for a variety of crimes, such as breaking river banks and impersonating Chelsea pensioners. He did this quickly and smoothly by the extraordinary tact with which he transformed the judges, including Lord Tenterden, the Lord Chief Justice, from potential enemies of reform into active friends.[54] He paid deferential visits to Bentham, accompanying him on what the sage called his "anteprandial circumgyrations" of his garden in Queen's Square, Westminster, where John Milton had lived when he was Oliver Cromwell's Latin secretary; but he got precious little practical help from that quarter and wisely ignored most of Bentham's views about prisons. His most useful mentor was W. O. Russell's *Treatise on Crime* (1819).

In March 1825 his Juries Regulation Bill consolidated 85 statutes, and in 1826 and 1827 he put through no less than five acts which consolidated hundreds of criminal statutes and amounted virtually to a new criminal code. He followed these acts in May 1828 with two further acts, one abolishing what was known as petty treason (murder of husbands by wives, masters by servants and bishops by inferior clergy), the other simplifying the law of rape and other sex offenses, and a bill dealing with the law of evidence. Finally, in 1830, he consolidated 120 forgery statutes into one. This program reduced 398 criminal statutes into 9 and involved reforms in over 90 percent of the cases which came before the courts. It was the most ambitious program of law reform since the work of Henry II in the 12th century, and in its own quiet, unfussy way was as comprehensive a reform of the law as the Napoleonic Code in France. One immediate and striking consequence was a drop in hangings. In the 1780s hangings had averaged 56 a year. In the years 1816–22 they fell to an average of 27 a year. On 1 April 1830, Peel was able to tell the Commons, with satisfaction, that the average had dropped to 17.[55]

A vital part of this criminal-law-reform program was the first attempt to integrate the trade unions into society by legalizing at least some of their activities. Peel was pressed to do so not only by union leaders like Doherty, but by his own colleague Huskisson and by such economists as McCulloch. Trade unions had existed *de facto* if not *de jure* since the time of Charles II in the 1660s; but active unionists who urged workmen to strike against their employer had always faced charges of conspiracy under the Common Law which carried a minimum penalty of seven years' transportation. Combination in restraint of trade had likewise always been a Common Law offense. In 1799–1800 Parliament had passed the Combination Acts, which made most forms of trade unionism unlawful by statute. These acts reduced the penalty for most offenses to three months, but conspiracy charges under

Common Law remained, and employers could invoke the 1799 Treason and Sedition Act, which dealt with secret oaths.[56]

However, as everyone knew, trade unions continued to exist, disguised as public houses and benefit societies and used Masonic methods of control and concealment. Indeed, they were often active, and ruling-class opinion was by no means always antiunion, even when the unions organized strikes. During the Newcastle strike of keelmen (the boatmen who took coal to deepwater ships) in October 1822, for instance, the Duke of Northumberland wrote repeatedly to Peel, as Home Secretary, emphasizing the peaceful behavior of the men. The Home Office, for its part, was always anxious to keep out of trade-union disputes, leaving masters and men to settle them by direct bargaining. Above all it was most reluctant to send troops. Peel's policy was to leave such matters, if they got out of hand, to the local justices of the peace. He wrote letters to them applauding the impartial enforcement of the law: magistrates sometimes prosecuted and convicted employers who paid their men with "truck" (in kind), which might be unlawful.[57] The prevailing view among enlightened London opinion, though not among employers, was that trade unions were fundamentally benign bodies that could safely be freed from some legal restraints at least. This case was powerfully put by McCulloch himself in an article in the Edinburgh Review in January 1824, and it was followed almost immediately by Peel's decision to end the Combination Laws.[58]

Peel's first 1824 Act (5 George IV cap. 46) consolidated all arbitration statutes and substituted a single method; the second (5 George IV cap. 95) made it lawful for workmen to combine to determine wages, hours and conditions of work, and to persuade fellow workmen to break an existing contract and refuse to accept a new one. The second act set an important precedent, the foundation of all subsequent trade union permissive legislation, for it awarded the unions a privilege—the right to break contracts—denied to any one else, whether individuals or institutions. The two bills went through Parliament almost without debate, the general assumption being that they would help to produce industrial peace.[59]

Never was an illusion more ill-founded. The consequence of lifting legal penalties produced the first real wave of organized strikes in British history—indeed, in world history—followed by what can only be described as a "Winter of Discontent." Workmen leaders appeared as if from out of the ground all over the industrial areas and now did openly and on a bigger and more effective scale what they had hitherto done secretly. There were strikes among the spinners and weavers of west Scotland, among the textile workers of Lancashire and among the colliers in both the Lancashire and the Midlands coalfields. Most alarming, among the shipwrights and seamen of both the northeast coal ports and of the Port of London, there was a highly effective and menacing strike which for a time halted London seagoing traffic— something which had never happened before in the port's existence, which went back to Roman times.[60] Many of these disputes went on throughout the winter and well into 1825.

Moreover, some of the most destructive and frightening aspects of modern trade unionism at its worst made their instant appearance. It was as if a huge and fearsome monster, long chained in its lair, had suddenly been unleashed. There were widespread demands for the introduction of the closed or union shop; for restrictions on entry, especially for apprentices, and on the introduction of new machinery; for the dismissal of unpopular (efficient) foremen; and for limitations of every kind on the recruitment of new labor. In short, most unions immediately produced long shopping lists of requirements, each of which tended to lower productivity, raise manufacturers' costs or restrict the employer's right to run his business. All were backed by threats of strikes. What was particularly alarming were the harsh and often brutal effort by union leaders and militants to compel their fellow workmen, whether they liked it or not, to back these demands. New union rules, now lawful, not only enforced a wide range of restrictive practices but introduced entry fees, forced levies of wages, and inter-union action, or what are now called secondary strikes, whereby groups of workmen not in dispute go on strike to back up those who are. The new activity of "picketing," often violent, began outside workplaces where a strike had been declared, to prevent nonstriking workmen from entering it. The so-called English Disease of the years 1945–79, thus went back to the 1820s.

There was a good deal of terrorism, too. The word *blackleg* made its appearance. In the Lancashire cotton districts, a union passed a sentence of death on four men thus accused, one of whom was actually murdered. Many nonstriking seamen were assaulted. A Lancashire miner was almost beaten to death. A Glasgow weaver was shot in the back. In Ireland, where violence was never far beneath the surface, no fewer than 10 nonstrikers in Dublin were murdered and 70 were injured.[61] Joseph Hume, MP, and the London reform-organizer Francis Place, who had played a major part in getting the legislation passed and who both had strong trade-union connections, made desperate efforts to persuade the militants to exercise moderation, but without success— another modern touch.

Among manufacturers there was something like panic, and great pressure was brought on Peel to restore order. In 1825 he set up a Committee of Inquiry into the working of the legislation, and when it reported promptly introduced an amending bill (6 George IV cap. 129). This bill not only reaffirmed the unlawfulness of violence, threats and intimidation in the pursuit of union aims but created the new offenses of "molestation" and "obstruction." Each was punishable by three months' imprisonment, though the accused had the right to be tried before at least two justices of the peace (not one) and on payment of £10 bail could go to Quarter Sessions and be tried before a jury. In effect, the amendments forbade the use of collective power to promote violence. As Peel put it, "Men who . . . have no property except their manual skill and strength ought to be allowed to confer together if they think fit, for the purpose of determining at what rate they will sell their property. But the possession of such a privilege justifies . . . severe punishment of any attempt to control the free will of others." The amendments, however, reaffirmed the right to combine "for the sole purpose of consulting upon and determining the rate of wages and prices"—thus retaining the element of privilege which is the basis of all modern trade union law—and Peel retained his view that such privilege was justified: "I think the law with regard to combination as it now stands is founded upon just principles and I believe it will ultimately be as effectual as law can be."[62] For the moment the agitation died down, though more for economic than for legal reasons; but Britain, then the world's greatest manufacturing country, was now pointed along the road which led ultimately to an all-powerful form of trade unionism, and industrial unrest would shortly return, as we shall see.

If the unions, however, were flexing their muscles, the political wing of the working-class movement was in sharp decline, as rising wages, high employment and better living standards pushed the distress of 1816–19 into the back of men's memories. The 1820s introduced all kinds of changes, not least to the dens in Soho, North London and the East End (especially Finsbury and Bethnal Green), where the violent men and women of 1819 met. The lowering of duties on imported coffee made the beverage relatively inexpensive compared to porter, the pub staple, and, in turn, produced a shift from licensed premises to coffee-houses as meeting places of those planning radical political change. There was an accompanying growth of respectability as the agitators turned from violence, arms and drilling to education, propaganda, and doctrine; as with Saint-Simon in France, there was a shift to "theory," preparing the way for Chartism in the 1830s and Marxism in the 1880s. Some of those who were most active in the Peterloo year moved from politics toward other, more promising, though not less unlawful, ways of earning a living, especially prostitution and pornography. There had always been a certain amount of pimping on the Far Left. As long ago as 1819, one of Arthur Thistlewood's group had been running a brothel from the same premises he used to sell seditious publications. But in the 1820s many more radicals, despairing of revolution, went into the vice trade, especially in Soho. In 1828 one of the most prominent of them, William Edgar, was revealed running a business pimping for his own wife. Two years later, Robert Wedderburn got a two-year sentence for operating a bawdy house, in which again his wife took a prominent part. The tiny Waddington, or "Little Waddy," who had once made a lifesize paste dummy of Castlereagh, which he could operate from inside, and flourished a Bible whenever the spirit moved him, was charged in 1822 with being drunk and assaulting a watchman in Windmill Street. He was convicted again the next year of attempted sexual assault on an 11-year-old girl who was delivering laundry to his cell. Fellow prisoners, then as now, aggressive toward those guilty of corrupting children, tossed him in a blanket and badly injured his back.[63]

Other agitators turned from radical pamphlets and newspapers to publishing obscenity. The bridge here was the Queen Caroline crisis, during which radical material attacking George IV and the government had become increasingly bawdy, Lady Conyngham, in particular, featuring in indecorous poses. After that cause disappeared, the men who wrote, drew and printed the material turned to pornography as such, often using premises in Soho, which, to this day, deal in girlie magazines and peepshows. The big change came in August 1822 with the exposure of the Rt. Rev. Percy Jocelyn, Bishop of Clogher (1764–1843). Jocelyn was a notorious pluralist and a member of the Society for the Suppression of Vice. As far back as 1811, he had been accused of homosexuality by a man named James Byrne, but had succeeded in getting his accuser transported.[64] However, in 1822, he was actually discovered *in flagrante delicto* with a guardsman in the back room of a London tavern, eight witnesses being prepared to swear they had witnessed an act of buggery. The affair aroused an immense sensation, for Jocelyn was the son of one earl and his mother the daughter of another, and he had high political connections. He avoided trial by slipping off to Scotland under an assumed name. Radicals suggested that the escape of "the Arsebishop" had been made possible by the complicity of Lord Sidmouth, until recently Home Secretary, and who was also accused of protecting Thomas Warburton's private madhouse where female lunatics were exploited.[65] This gave a slight political edge to the affair, but essentially it was handled by the former radicals as an opportunity to descant on a forbidden and highly obscene topic.

One of the radicals, William Benbow, having milked the Bishop's sins for all they were worth, went on to other exposés of clerics in his *The Crimes of the Clergy or the Pillars of Priest Craft Shaken* (1823). He then began to ransack Irish history for more cases of clerical scandal and, having exhausted that vein, turned to France. That led him directly into French pornography, which he began to print in translation. He had been prosecuted by the Society for the Suppression of Vice for obscene publications before, whereupon he changed his premises to a shop in Leicester Square, which he called "The Byron's Head." The shop was described by Shelley, shortly before his death, as "one of those preparatory schools for the brothel and gallows: where obscenity, sedition and blasphemy are retailed in drams for the vulgar."[66]

Just down the square was a similar shop run by another former radical, George Cannon, who had once been a dissenting minister under the name Erasmus Perkins. In 1815 he had been close to Percy and Mary Shelley, then both violently anticlerical, and had supplied them with documents. Shelley, in return, had given him copies of *A Refutation of Deism* and *Queen Mab,* extracts from both of which appeared in the first issue of the *Theological Inquirer,* which Cannon published in March 1815. By the mid-1820s, however, the bankruptcy of radical politics had tempted Cannon into pornography, and he was putting out such works as *The Philosophy of Birch Discipline, Voluptuous Night, Festivals of Passion* and De Sade's *Juliette* (in French). The law caught up with the Rev. Erasmus, or whatever his real name was, in October 1830, when he was arrested for publishing obscene libel and subsequently sentenced to 12 months' imprisonment. Other publishers who had been extreme radicals in 1815–20 but who turned to pornography in the 1820s were John Benjamin Brookes, who specialized in sadomasochism in the Opera Arcade; John Duncombe, once the owner of the *Republican,* who was repeatedly convicted for publishing obscene books, including *Fanny Hill,* from 1821 on; and John and William Dugdale, associates of the ferocious Watsons, who ran porn shops from various addresses in Drury Lane, Holywell Street and elsewhere, using a variety of pseudonyms.[67]

The 1820s is thus the first decade in history in which it is possible to point to a connection between general prosperity, which produced a rise in living standards among all classes, and the process of depoliticization. This was to become a familiar phenomenon in the history of the advanced countries, with political activity subsiding during the upswing in the trading cycles and resuming during the downswing. But prosperity had a ratchet effect: From the early 19th century onwards, the level attained at the end of each complete cycle was always higher than at the beginning, so the politics of desperation began to be succeeded by the politics of aspiration; hunger passed out of the equation.

In the United States, the effects of the 1819 bank crisis were soon pushed aside by the huge tide of wealth which swept over the land during the 1820s, though its memory remained burned in many hearts. Improvements affected everyone. The Argand, the Astral, and other patent oil lamps replaced candles in countless homes. Efficient cooking stoves replaced the slow and labor-intensive business of cooking over open fires. Mass-produced chairs, selling at 30 to 75 cents each, doubled the number of chairs per household from 1800 to 1830, and from 1820 many households began to acquire sofas. By 1830 inventories for probate showed that nearly a quarter of American households now had carpets. Cheap Lancashire cottons, which transformed the appearance of working-class women in the years 1815–30, were joined by cheap, mass-produced shoes—by 1835 American manufacturers were turning out 15 million pairs a year; during the 1820s, indeed, most children and all adults acquired shoes.

The biggest visual change in standards was in housing. Successive editions of Asher Benjamin's *American Builder's Companion*, first published in Boston in 1806, which reached its 6th reprint by 1827, reflect higher spending. There was a change from wood to brick, from long houses with a roof axis to gable houses, from one- to two-stories. Instead of every room having beds, there were now distinct bedrooms, and the sharing of beds, universal until the second decade of the 19th century, became increasingly rare, except among married couples and children. Travelers, notably lawyers and salesmen, were no longer prepared to share beds, or even bedrooms, with strangers in hotels which advertised themselves as first class. Indeed, the new Tremont House Hotel in Boston, which opened its doors in 1829, not only provided separate one- and two-bed rooms but no less than eight bathrooms and eight water closets.[68]

During the 1820s, for the first time, the United States began to compete with Britain in providing the latest technological luxury. In many respects, rapidly expanding America was still a rural and primitive country. But on its East Coast and in one or two other areas, it was already in the forefront of progress. An outstanding example was refrigeration. The rich had long since learned how to cut ice in winter and store it for summer use. Stone icehouses, half buried in the ground, were a feature of the parks which surrounded the English and French

country houses of the 18th century. George Washington had one at
Mount Vernon, Thomas Jefferson at Monticello, and James Monroe at
Ash Lawn.[69] From 1815 onwards, supplying ice to the urban upper- and
middle classes became a major business. The Cornish mining engineer
Richard Trevithick, who had some ideas for making an ice-producing
machine, discovered that in 1828, "as much as £100,000 a year was paid
in [London] for the use of ice."[70]

There was a lot of money to be made out of ice in America, too, as
Frederick Tudor of Boston discovered when he began to tackle the
problem systematically. Tudor was the son of Washington's judge-
advocate-general, but turned from law to business and invention. He
designed a syphon pump for bilges and new ships' hulls and was the
first man to bring an English steam locomotive to New England. But his
main work was as an iceman. He first began to ponder the problem of
ice efficiency in 1805 when, at 21, he shipped 130 tons of Massachusetts
winter ice to Martinique. It took him 15 years to master the various
aspects of supply and demand. The ice came from New England ponds,
though in the exceptionally warm winter of 1818, suppliers had to hack
it off Labrador icebergs with picks. Using as his main source the Fresh
Pond near Cambridge, Tudor designed a new ice cutter with iron
runners and saw teeth, which cut the ice into regular, uniform blocks
which were easily packed into carts and ships, thus greatly reducing
melting. Then he had to design an efficient icehouse by timing the
melting process of different materials and thus discovering exactly the
right insulator. The successive ice-storage buildings he put up in
Havana, Charleston, and the West Indies gradually reduced the seasonal loss to at little as 8 percent or even less. At the same time, he
worked hard to create a steadily expanding demand by pushing the
consumption of iced drinks and ice cream and by proving to the manufacturers and sellers of both that refrigeration was cheap.

Nathaniel Jarvis Wyeth, who owned the Fresh Pond and became the
manager of Tudor's ice factory in 1824–25, worked out some of the
detailed technology which, from the 1830s, produced the first ice-mak-
ing machines. But it was in the 1820s that Wyeth discovered that
sawdust could prevent blocks from melting in transit, thus hugely
increasing the distances that ice could be profitably transported and, at
the same time, finding a profitable use for a waste product of the Maine
lumber industry. By the mid-1820s Tudor was getting 1,000 tons of ice,
gathered in a day, from every acre of pond, and shipping it all over the
world, including countries like Persia. By 1833 he was taking ice to
Calcutta.[71] The real improvement, however, was in getting the ice from
the ponds into the specially designed iceboxes which, during the 1820s,

were to be found in a growing number of middle-class homes in Boston, Baltimore, New York, and other cities, becoming, as the *New York Mirror* put it, no less an "article of necessity" than a carpet in the drawing room.

It is in the 1820s, indeed, that the historian first becomes conscious of the growing speed with which technology could bring improvements in ordinary ways of life and the luxuries of the rich could pass down the social scale. From his experiences in Long Island, William Cobbett was able to include a design for an ice-house in his *Cottage Economy*, arguing that ordinary yeoman families ought no longer to be denied a convenience for keeping meat, milk, butter and eggs fresh in all seasons.[72] Much of the new technology again, was first exploited thoroughly by public institutions, rapidly growing in size and numbers in the years 1815–30, rather than by the rich. Tudor expanded ice production, an early example of a high-tech, capital-intensive industry, by persuading hospitals to take regular deliveries. As the leading historian of the English country house has put it, "On the whole, hospitals, prisons and lunatic asylums were centrally-heated and lit by gas long before country houses."[73] (This was a point made by the young Disraeli through the voice of Lord Marney, in his novel *Sybil*.) The elite, at any rate in Britain, did not always welcome new technology with open arms. At Newstead Abbey, as long as he still lived there, Byron continued to use the old monastic water supply, including the lead cistern in the cloister *lavatorium*. Charles Sylvester, a commercial advocate of domestic "improvements," who expected the wealthy to set an example, complained bitterly in 1819: "Nothing can be more preposterous and inappropriate than the prevailing construction and management of a gentleman's kitchen. As for the boasted comfort of an Englishman's fireplace, we see it accompanied with evils which loudly call for remedy."[74]

All the same, in the years 1815–30 there was a huge effort to improve the comfort and efficiency of life in the houses of the aristocracy. Wellington, who loved gadgets of every kind, put in hot-water pipes to heat Strathfield Saye when he took it over. By 1819 the mill owner William Strutt had installed a hot-air heating system, adapted from garden hothouses, in his house in Derby (and in the Derby County Infirmary). According to the Germany tourist Puckler-Muskau, there was certainly hot-air heating at the duke of Bedford's Woburn in the 1820s, as there was at Bowood, the great Wiltshire palace of Thomas Moore's friend, the Marquess of Lansdowne. Ducted hot-air systems were installed at Coleshill, Berkshire, in 1814 and at Abercairn, Perthshire in 1829.[75] As in America, patented oil lamps were rapidly replacing candles in the 1820s. By 1830 the Duke of Rutland's vast Belvoir Castle was completely lit by oil lamps and had a special lamp room where the lamps were housed and maintained; during the Duke's annual 16–17 weeks of residence, 600 gallons of oil were consumed.[76] Modern fireplaces, based on the pioneering design of the Anglo-American Count Rumford, were replacing the old open fireplaces, and efficient stoves were appearing to heat hallways, corridors and staircases. Lord Dundonald had introduced gas lighting into his Scottish castle as early as 1787, though only in its hall. But the early gas systems were hot, smelly and expensive, and did not produce much light. From 1815, however, they improved rapidly, and in 1818 the Regent took the risk of fitting gas chandeliers in his Brighton Pavilion. That set the trend. In 1823, during the boom years, Sir Walter Scott decided to go the whole hog at his new Abbotsford and put in both steam heating and gas lighting, making it one of the most modern houses in Scotland, despite its Gothic fantasy.[77]

Other improvements became common after 1815, notably bathrooms and water closets. The Earl of Moira, at Donington Park in Leicestershire, installed two bathrooms and six water closets. His wife had one of the latter, plus a bathroom, opening off her dressing room. He himself had a bathroom and water closet opening off his study (which he also used as his powdering room) on the floor below. How did his guests bathe? By the traditional method: A footman brought a hip bath into the bedroom, and maids filled it from big hot-water jugs. But guests could now summon these menials by pulling bells, connected to an elaborate signal station in the kitchen and servants' hall.

The fussier guests, however, expected bathrooms of their own, and from the early 19th century onward there was a growing stress on comfort, as opposed to grandeur, in the houses of the rich. John Nash introduced huge picture windows, which brought lawns and borders almost into the house itself. Turnpike roads, fast coaches, and then the first railways made country-house visits far more frequent (and shorter), and the age of the house party began. A new term, *lounging*, made its appearance. The old state bedrooms on the ground floor were pushed upstairs—indeed, by the 1820s all bedrooms were upstairs in most houses—and more rooms became available for diversions. The age of Samuel Johnson, when everyone sat in a circle and conversation was general, was over. Fanny Burney's *Diary* relates the smart heiress Miss Monckton saying, "My whole care is to prevent a circle," what Maria Edgeworth termed "all the ladies sitting in a formal circle, petrified into perfect statues." Instead guests chatted in groups or pairs or pursued their own individual pleasures, often in the library, which was now fitted with comfortable chairs and little tables. "No more the cedar parlour's formal gloom," wrote Humphrey Repton, but "tis now the living room" where guests "their different plans pursue."[78] The accent, increasingly, was on having fun, as the wars were forgotten and the times of famine receded into the past. With more ground-floor space, ballrooms were installed. And it was not always necessary, as in *Mansfield Park,* for ordinary rooms to be converted for private theatricals. With the country-house theater all the rage, stages, drop curtains and elaborate machinery were installed in many of the bigger houses, at Wynnstay, Blenheim and Wargrave, for example; the private theater at Chatsworth, built in 1833, still survives.[79] Much more use was made of the gardens for entertaining. "Company" breakfasts moved outdoors, were held later, and became "garden parties," with archery and other sports in which ladies could join.

The outstanding example of modern technology put to domestic use was the Regent's Royal Pavilion at Brighton. Not only was the Regent among the first to install gas, he also helped to design a vast "steam kitchen," which became part of the tour when he escorted guests round the palace. The structure was completed by 1816, elaborate culinary equipment was installed in 1817-18, and various improvements were carried out well into the 1820s. The Great Kitchen itself was 45 by 36 feet, with magnificent day lighting supplied by a high ceiling lantern of 12 sash windows. There were further big sash windows at the east and west ends to supply cross-ventilation. At night, light was provided by giant copper wall lamps with tin reflectors and four big Argand hexagonal lanterns. (Gas lighting was thought too risky.) The floor was in the new covering known as oil cloth, easy to clean, and the roof was supported by four cast-iron columns, ornamented with copper leaves, to give the illusion of palm trees decorated with bamboo stems. In the center, flanked by four large L-shaped "preparation tables," made of beech, was a 13-foot-long steam table, fitted with a cast-iron top and bound in brass. This steam table had a multitude of water pipes to heat it, so that a large number of prepared dishes could be kept warm. A local observer, Charles Wright, in his book *The Brighton Ambulator* (1818), described this device as "an admirable specimen of mechanical invention" and the whole kitchen as an exercise in which "every modern improvement to facilitate the process of the culinary art has been introduced in all its boasted perfection."[80]

The steam came from a large copper boiler, which also heated a whole series of hot closets, and the main north wall had a 23-foot range of stewing stoves, with, on the south wall opposite, a giant open fireplace for roasting, flanked by cast-iron stewing and broiling stoves.

The strong upward draft from the main fire turned a metal fan set in the chimney; the power thus generated, by a system of chains, gears, and pulley, turned the spits below. There were five spits, operating simultaneously but at different speeds, enabling the chef to serve multiple roast dishes on a single menu—when the great French maître-chef Marie-Antoine Carême (1784–1833) worked briefly for the Regent, he could thus serve a dinner which included no fewer than 36 entrées, though he declined generous offers to leave France and enter George's regular service. Each heating apparatus was equipped with copper awnings, which drew away heat, smells and steam, and had gutters to deal with the condensation of water, so the Great Kitchen was itself a clean and healthy place to work in—perhaps the first in history. The Great Kitchen was surrounded by five minor kitchens, also equipped with stewing stoves, ovens and hot closets, where pastries and puddings were made, and next to the Confectioner's Room, which produced the sorbets and ice creams, was an ice room, where ice from the icehouse in the garden was stored in lead bins. The water which operated the whole system came from a water tower, into which well water was steam pumped and then distributed through iron mains and hundreds of yards of lead pipes. The kitchen, in short, was the ultimate in advanced steam technology before gas and electricity were adapted for cooking.[81]

If only the rich could afford the latest household appliances, ordinary consumers benefited from better, cheaper clothes, shoes, furniture and transport, and from the reduction in prices of many goods brought about as the government moved toward free trade. The economic boom, felt everywhere but most intensively in Britain, sent governmental revenues soaring, and in the years 1823–25, the new Chancellor of the Exchequer earned himself the name "Prosperity" Robinson by across-the-board reductions in taxes and duties. Indeed, many taxes and duties were abolished. In 1823 Robinson scrapped all the assessed taxes in Ireland and many in England: out went taxes on windows, male servants, wheeled vehicles, ponies, mules, horses and mules engaged in agriculture and trades, many categories of house and garden servants, clerks and shopmen of traders, and scores of similar categories. The tariff on foreign wool and all restrictions on the export of British wool were ended. Duties on Newcastle coal imported to London by sea were cut. The prohibitive duties on imported foreign silk, which led to so much smuggling, were cut to 30 percent *ad valorem*. So were duties on rum and other spirits. Many inland duties went altogether, so that Britain, and to a great extent Ireland, became the largest free-trade area in the world. All kinds of ancient regulations, quotas, bounties and taxes, which interfered with the free flow of goods and services, were dumped, leaving the market to determine price and quantity.[82]

By February 1825 Robinson was boasting that the current prosperity had "nothing hollow in its foundation, artificial in its superstructure, or flimsy in its good result." It is odd, indeed—but then history is full of such paradoxes—that this nervous, indecisive, sometimes ridiculous and in many ways profoundly silly man was the first statesman in history to outline the notion of a consumer society. Having cut taxes on imported wines; Scotch, Irish and English spirits; cider, iron and hemp, carts, carriages, houses and lodgings, he philosophized on what was happening to the world. "There is a principle," he told the Commons, "in the constitution of social man which leads nations to open their arms to each other, and to establish new and closer connections, by ministering to mutual convenience—a principle which creates new wants, stimulates new desires, seeks for new enjoyments and, by the beneficence of Providence, contributes to the general happiness of mankind. . . . it is always alive, always in motion and has a perpetual tendency to go forward—and when we reflect upon the facility which is given to its operation by the recent discoveries of modern science, and by the magical energies of the steam engine, who can doubt that its expansion is progressive, and its effect permanent?"[83] Robinson had stumbled on an important truth: modern science and industry could turn the luxuries of one generation into the necessities of the next. His notion of a universal, steadily increasing prosperity, powered by technology and free trade, was a heady one. Charles Lamb, who often spoke for the *homme moyen sensuel*, put it more prosaically. Praising Robinson in a letter to Bernard Barton, he called the government "the best ministry we ever stumbled upon. Gin reduced four shillings in the gallon, wine two shillings in the quart. This comes home to men's minds and bosoms."[84]

Britain was not alone in Europe in enjoying the prosperity of the 1820s. France had followed her into the postwar slump and, about a year later, followed her out of it. The 1820s were the first decade in French history in which something approaching general prosperity made its appearance. Compared to Britain, France was an industrially backward country. Most of its steam power was imported from Britain, and often the men to operate the engines: Up to 1,400 British "experts" were working in French mining and industry by 1824. The number of steam engines, which the French still called "force pumps," rose only from 200 in 1818 to 572 in 1830. Even at the end of the decade, only 29 blast furnaces used the modern coking process, the remaining 379, supplying 86 percent of national production, still used charcoal.[85] During these years, efforts were made, often by Bonaparte's former marshals, Marmont and Soult, to merge small pits and forges into four major mining-and-metal firms. But probably the most efficient industry in France was the traditional silk manufactures of Lyons, where the number of looms jumped from 7,000 in 1817 to 42,000 in 1832.[86]

Though well behind Britain, France was still richer than any other European country, and Paris, which grew from 622,000 in 1811 to 800,000 at the end of the 1820s, was becoming a major financial center: During the twenties boom, France lent over 525 million francs abroad. Small savers, as well as big ones, were important. French factory conditions were as bad as the worst in Britain, and the wages were lower. But these wages were, on average, higher than any hitherto enjoyed in French history—strikes were rare in the 1820s—and men saved from them. The peasants saved, too, at a time when the density of France's rural population was the highest the country had ever known. Some thought, indeed, that money had become France's only god. A collective complaint from the Gironde to the Villèle ministry in 1827 read: "The basis of all our laws is wealth: the condition of all distinction is gold: the reward pursued by everyone is riches."[87]

This statement was not, in fact, true. One of the most striking things about Restoration prosperity in France, particularly in the years 1820–25, was the growth of the printing industry and the increase in reading. Printing was one area in which France made a decisive contribution to new technology. Many French inventions were first conceived during the Napoleonic period but only commercialized after the wars were over. Around 1800, Louis-Étienne Herhan had invented the cliché, a stereotype plate made from special wax molds imprinted by a sheet of type. The cliché came into massive use after Bonaparte (and his censors) departed, changing the book trade from a craft into an industry. Hitherto, editions had rarely exceeded 500 copies, charged at 7.50 francs a volume, so that a three-volume title sold at 22.50, more than the weekly wage of a skilled laborer. Printer-publisher-booksellers could not get credit from banks and had to borrow at 15 percent from small moneylenders. With the cliché, the same plate could be used for a 10,000-copy impression, without resetting or wearing out the printers' type, which was expensive. Another invention, Nicholas-Louis Robert's papermaking machine, also came into commercial use around 1814–15, when it was put into production by the mills of the Firmin-Didot family on the Somme; by 1827 at least four machines were producing giant continuous rolls of paper. Then again, a system for mass-producing printers' ink, devised by Pierre Lorilleux in 1808, was commercialized immediately after peace came, and 11 Paris firms were using it by 1827.

The biggest factor in longer runs and lower costs were the presses themselves. The fastest handpress could not produce more than 250 sheets an hour. As far back as 1790, William Nicholson had invented the rubber roller, which made mechanical presswork possible. But large-scale mechanical printing even in London had to wait until the last years of the wars, and France did not get its first Nicholson press until 1823, though four years later there were 11 in Paris alone. And France produced her own printing technologist in Ferdinand Koenig. The slowest mechanical press put out 1,000 sheets an hour. The Nicholson did much better, but it was still clumsy and, at 36,000 francs each, expensive. Koenin developed a faster press at one-third the cost. Much of the Parisian printing trade remained small scale: even in 1833, 34 of the printers there (from a total of 80), owned 819 handpresses and only 54 mechanical ones. But the combination of new processes and machinery had a dramatic effect on the cost of books and the number of books in circulation. From 1815 onwards book prices dropped by 50 percent. During the early 1820s it was easy to find a new title at only 3 francs. At the same time, press runs of 2,500 became common.

Whole new categories of readers came into the market. The book trade had probably the highest growth rate of any industry in France, with cheap editions of classics like the collected works of Molière, Racine, and Voltaire running into 10,000 sets. The number of booksellers in Paris jumped from 373 in 1815 to 945 in 1845, a rate of advance that was 50 percent over the expansion of the city's population. These shops were often much bigger than their predecessors, and, with increasing competition, their owners for the first time permitted browsing, hitherto confined to shops stocking secondhand books. The arcades of the Palais Royale, with their great stocks of new books, became a huge attraction for book lovers from all over France and Europe, though it must be said they were also the center of the vice trade (there were 163 licensed brothels in Paris in 1824, and 2,653 registered prostitutes, with about 15,000 unregistered). What was perhaps most remarkable was the huge number of new books published. Titles recorded by the *Bibliographie de France* rose from 3,357 in 1815 to 8,272 in 1827—the latter to remain the highest level until the second half of the century. For the first time, too, Parisian publishers employed commercial travelers to sell the new titles to provincial bookshops.[88]

As a result, the Restoration, at any rate up to 1827, when the economic crisis really took a grip on the trade, was a glorious, productive, and remunerative epoch for authors. Many writers who were in exile under Bonaparte flocked back to Paris to publish banned works for the first time or republish books that had been printed abroad. The historian Edgar Quinet (1803–75), then an ambitious young man, called the decade 1815–25 "a sort of intoxication of reawakened thought, an appeased thirst of the soul after years in the desert of the Empire."[89] The poets benefited most: In 1827, 537 new volumes of poetry were published in Paris, as against 295 new novels, though thereafter the novelists slowly took the lead. The rapid growth of primary schools under the restored monarchy, especially in Paris and its surroundings, produced metropolitan literacy rates, around 1820, of 84 percent for men and 60 percent for women. In 1814 there were virtually no commercial libraries in Paris; by 1820 there were 32, and 10 years later 150. Most commercial libraries had only about 5,000 titles, but Madame Cardinal's, in the Rue des Canettes, had 20,000, the majority new. Natives and visitors alike noted the growth of working-class literacy and reading habits. Writing of Louis XV, Lady Morgan trilled: "There is scarcely a porter, a water-carrier or a commissionaire, running the streets of Paris, who is not more learned and enlightened than this royal patron of letters of the Augustan age."[90] Literacy and reading habits were all improving. As one young visitor to Paris in 1824 put it, "The love of study is the true spirit of the century, this is the dominant passion which has won all walks of life, all classes, all conditions. One could mistake the streets and boulevards for the doors to the Académie."[91]

There was a marked increase in the number of professional writers, that is, those who could make a living from books and articles; the list of those paying income tax rose even faster, which indicates that the living was a good one. The great trash writer of the age, Paul de Kock (1794–1871), a mere 200 francs-a-month bank clerk under Bonaparte, hit the jackpot with the saucy *Georgette* in 1820—not only Saint-Simon but Macaulay and the young Elizabeth Barrett enjoyed it—and by 1826 was getting 20,000 francs a novel. He systematized his work, pouring out 200 plays and 400 volumes of novels, which earned him a luxurious Paris apartment and two country houses. "I'm greedy and I admit it," he smirked in his *Memoires*. He anticipated what Charles-Augustin Saint-Beuve later called *littérature industrielle*, including Alexandre Dumas's "fiction factory," in which he and 73 assistants composed adventure stories.[92] Many others did well as the 1820s progressed, Victor Hugo getting 15,000 francs a book and 10,000 for reprinting his earlier works. In 1830 Alphonse-Marie-Louis Lamartine sold his *Harmonies poétiques* for the impressive sum of 27,000 francs, and Ladvocat, the archetype of the new entrepreneur-publishers, who had Goethe, Byron and Schiller on his list, as well as Hugo and Saint-

Beuve—"the god whose golden figure became the symbol of successful publishing," as Augustin Thierry described him—offered Chateaubriand 55,000 francs for his memoirs."³ These figures were exceptional, of course. It was calculated that a successful play made 15,000 francs; a top-selling novel, 5,000; a volume of history, 1,000; and a book of poetry, 500. But Augustin-Eugène Scribe (1791–1861) got it right when the writer in his play *Marriage d'argent* (1828) asserted: "Thank heavens we no longer live in times when talent worked only for rich patrons. Artists today in quest of fame and fortune have no need to resort to such means. Real artists remain true to themselves, work hard—and the public judges and rewards them." Scribe himself was a tycoon of the new *littérature industrielle,* with a record of over 300 plays (some written with collaborators).

Alongside the growth of a large professional class of writers—whose collective weight and influence grew steadily as the 1820s went on—was a huge printing industry, which employed more skilled (and well-paid) workers than any other in the capital. By the end of the decade, in Paris alone, 61,000 copies of newspapers were being sold every day. The number of periodicals in Paris increased tenfold from 1815 to 1830, and the printer Paul Deport calculated that sheets printed for nonperiodicals tripled in the 12 years from 1814. The economist and statistician Baron Dupin, who covered Belgium as well as France, thought the printing trade's 9.25 percent annual growth rate was the highest of any sector. He wrote: "However extensive, however rapid, have been the development of our physical activities and the rise in our material wealth, the development in our intellectual activity and the increase in our literary wealth have been even more extensive and rapid."⁹⁴ The Paris pressworkers alone, 4,500 strong, constituted a formidable force, highly literate, well read and organized, and with strong views, and were to play—as we shall see—a decisive role when times became hard again and discontent rose.

That was the difficulty about prosperity: It was fragile and, as economists had not yet learned, there was no chance that the rapid expansion of the years 1819–25 would be maintained at the same rate. No sector of the new world economy was more volatile and fragile than were the newly independent republics of Latin America. Until they got their independence, the republics had all been part of a closed Spanish imperial economy. This economy had been increasingly penetrated by British exporters during the long Napoleonic Wars, especially during the years when Spain had been Britain's enemy and the Royal Navy had no scruples about enabling British merchant ships to break Spain's colonial embargoes on foreign trade. Once the new states got de facto independence, which they did increasingly after 1817–18, they threw the ports they controlled open to trade, most of it British.

Simón Bolívar in Colombia, Augustín de Iturbide in Mexico, Bernadino Rivadavia in Argentina and Bernardo O'Higgins in Chile all officially adopted free trade. It made sense to them because they used import-export taxes as their main sources of revenue, to pay their armies and officials. In Mexico, for instance, customs supplied the government with 50 percent of its income and in Argentina the figure was as high as 80 percent. The British mercantile community, in turn, responded with enthusiasm. Within a year or two there were 60 British commercial houses in Rio de Janeiro, 20 in Bahia, 16 in Penambuco, 40 in Buenos Aires, 10 in Montevideo, 20 in Lima and 14 in Mexico City and Veracruz. The British commercial penetration of Argentina was particularly thorough. Indeed, the country was for many decades a British economic colony.[95] British exporting firms in London, Bristol and Liverpool sent anything they could lay their hands on: enormous quantities of cheap textiles, of course, but quantities of inappropriate heavy woolen goods, too. Brazil, for instance, got woolen blankets, skates and warming pans; the blankets were used as screeners in the gold washings, the skates for knives and door latches and the pans for boiling sugar.[96] Local governments also imported huge quantities of military equipment of all kinds, as long as fighting against Spain continued. Firms like Anthony Gibb & Son arranged all these deliveries and sometimes raised money and provided other services to the governments. Gibb & Co. was a worldwide venture, with 86 clients in Spain and 26 elsewhere in Europe; by 1826 it had 31 clients in the new Americas.[97]

The slogan of the new countries, governments and people alike, was Spend, Spend, Spend. To pay for the imports, gold and silver specie, all of it of fine quality, was gathered from the colonial treasuries and private hoards—replaced by new government paper—and production in existing mines was stepped up. One reason Britain was able to return to the gold-bullion standard in 1819 and the Bank of England to resume payments in specie two years later, was that so much specie was flowing in from Latin America. From Peru alone, the British consul in Lima, Charles Ricketts, calculated that Royal Navy ships in the years 1819-25 had carried back to Britain 27 million pesos of fine gold and silver.[98] As the rage for imports intensified, local Latin American governments overspent their revenues, and the whole continent was drained of specie. Overspending introduced a new phase in the economic cycle—state loans and the formation of companies to open new gold and silver mines.

Up to 1822 the London capital market had dealt mainly with Continental countries associated with the Holy Alliance. But in that year Bolívar's Colombia signed a foreign loan contract with a group of London bankers. This move was rapidly followed by other newly independent governments. "England is the first to be interested in [a loan to Peru]," Bolívar wrote, "because she desires to form a league with all the free nations of America and Europe against the Holy Alliance, in order to put herself at the head of all these peoples and rule the world."[99] Of the foreign-government loans raised in London from 1822 to 1826, Latin American countries, chiefly Argentina, Brazil, Chile, Colombia, Mexico, Peru and the Central American Federation, took £20 million out of a total of £25 million. These loans were accompanied by commercial treaties, negotiated through the British consulates which Canning established in Buenos Aires, Montevideo, Santiago, Lima and elsewhere from October 1823 onwards. Bolívar's Colombia (which then included Venezuela and Ecuador) alone got over £9 million in British money.[100]

High interest rates, twice those charged to Continental governments, were paid on the loans, and bonds from Latin American countries were bought and sold at fancy prices on the London Stock Exchange right up to the coming crash. There were various unsound aspects of these issues. Theoretically, a country like Colombia ought to have had much larger revenues than the viceroyalty it succeeded, since it imposed its own customs dues and property taxes. In practice, however, it paid its troops in paper, soon devalued, and the troops, in turn, looted local customs offices and branches of the state tobacco monopoly for cash. Everyone who had power or arms followed suit. This was Bolívar's own fault. At various times he expressly commanded his men to steal to live and authorized the looting of gold and silver vessels from churches and convents. There was also a huge amount of contraband, which bypassed the customs, often run by governmental officials and generals. Everyone who could, had his hand in the state till. So the Finance Ministry disposed of only a fraction of its nominal income. Bolívar himself complained, a little late in the day in July 1825, that "most agents of the government are robbing it of its life blood [customs revenues] and this should be proclaimed in all the public papers and elsewhere."[101] As a result, there were not enough funds in cash to pay for government arms purchases. Lopez Mendez, Bolívar's arms-purchasing agent in London, found himself thrown into the Marshalsea for nonpayment of arms bills: By 1820 he owed £500,000 to about 200

British firms. The governmental loans were designed to pay such debts and embark on other purchases.

In some cases the loans helped to finance economic growth. In Argentina, which saw less fighting than the other states and was better administered, the government had a surplus by 1824, and its loan raised in London was used to launch, with considerable success, its own central bank, the Banco de Buenos Aires. Indeed, Argentina was prospering mightily until it involved itself in an idiotic war with Brazil from 1826 to 1828. Mexico also used loan money constructively, to expand its silver-mining industry. But other loans were frittered away, chiefly on arms. Only a portion of the nominal value of the loans was actually received by the governments. Intermediaries and agents on loan issues, both Latin American and British—highly respectable firms like Barings went into this kind of work—made outrageous profits, sometimes 20 percent of the net figure. Commissions were huge. Richardson & Co., in conjunction with Herring, Powles & Graham and Barclay, Herring, made £500,000 from two Colombian loans. In addition to their cut, bankers also played the market on loans, selling the Latin American securities when the price rose, buying when it fell and using the proceeds of loans to finance exports of British goods and getting a further commission on that.

From 1823 onwards the Latin American mining boom began, money being raised in London to finance new gold and silver mines and expand old ones. Mining got a further impulse in February 1825, when the first news of the decisive victory over Spain at Ayacucho (9 December 1824) reached London. These mining companies were privately owned but they often involved public officials, both in Latin America and in Britain. Thus, the head of the Argentine government, Rivadavia, held shares in various mining companies. Lucas Aleman, the Mexican Foreign Minister, became Chairman of the United Mexican Mining Association. The London-based New Brazilian Mining Company had a 12-man board of directors, eight of whom were British members of Parliament. By 1825 members of Parliament were on the boards of no fewer than 19 Latin American mining companies. The young Benjamin Disraeli wrote a 135-page propaganda pamphlet to boost investment in these mining ventures, of which there were 26 registered in London by the middle of 1825.[102] Some, probably most, of these projects were sound, especially if viewed in the long term. British, French and German mining engineers were hired to do the surveying. One of them was Robert Stevenson, who drew up plans in 1825 for a railway from Caracas across the ferocious mountains to the coast; he was working for Herring, Powells & Graham, who were also interested in the project to build a canal across the Isthmus of Panama. But most of the London promoters were simply interested in making quick capital gains as the boom mounted. There were also plenty of crooks involved, both in mining ventures and the loans business. Borja Mignoni, in conjunction with B. A. Goldschmidt & Co., cheated the Mexican government of vast sums over its 1825 loan. They gave Mexico only 50 percent of the nominal value of the bonds, but sold them in London for 80 percent. Thus, Mexico had to pay, in effect, twice the already large interest rates. A Scotsman, Gregor MacGregor, who had commanded a division of Bolívar's army and later married Bolívar's niece, came to London in 1822 as the official representative of an imaginary country he called Poyais and marketed £200,000 of its bonds; he also sold fictitious land there.[103]

Latin American transactions were the principal element in the last phase of the upswing, the London bull market which ran from summer 1824 to autumn 1825. But all kinds of paper were being sold in London at high prices, and shrewd operators made handsome gains while the frenzy lasted. For the first time, from 1823 to 1825, shares of prospective passenger railroads came onto the market. Mrs. Arbuthnot noted on 16 March 1825: "There is a railway going to be made between Liverpool and Manchester which promises to answer immensely. We have 10 shares in it for which we gave £3 apiece and which are now worth £58 each, and they are expected soon to be worth above £100. I am very fond of these speculations and should *gamble* greatly in them if I could, but Mr Arbuthnot does not like them and will not allow me to have any of the American ones as their value depends upon political events and he thinks in his official position it would be improper."[104]

Arbuthnot was right to be chary. Most of the railway projects were sound and were eventually built and made money, though never as much as the optimists expected. But the bull market, while stimulating investment in an expanding cotton industry and in gas and steamship and iron and coal companies—all of them valid—produced dozens of risky ventures and some outright dishonest ones. One dishonest scheme was the Equitable Loan Company, "to carry on the business of pawnbroking on a large scale." Another was an enterprise to cultivate mulberry trees and silkworms in England and Ireland. The object of these schemes was to make quick capital gains for the men who devised them, rather than to conduct a genuine business. The Bank of England, followed by other banks, adopted policies which made credit available and pumped extra circulating money into an economy which, by the summer of 1824, was beginning to show signs of overheating. Robinson, the most important financial minister in the world, did not think he needed to have a financial and credit policy as such, as long as he balanced his budget. It did not occur to him to tell the central bank what or what not to do. Peel wrote to Henry Goulburn, who had much more cautious and sensible views about financial management, in 1823: "Robinson tells me that the Bank of England has undertaken the lending of Money on mortgage entirely of their own free will, and without any expression of a wish on the part of the government."[105] This was a highly inflationary scheme which encouraged landowners to borrow money against their estates and so put an extra £1.5 million in circulation, much of which was invested in unsound ventures.

Up to the last months of 1824, opinion in London was with the government, both in its tax-cutting program and in the rapid reduction of import duties which Robinson and, still more, Huskisson, had brought about. The manufacturing interest also, as was natural, favored the expansionist, free-trade policy. But in November 1824 the exchanges moved against Britain, when the huge exports of capital for foreign-government and private loans and the growing imports of consumer goods led to a reversal of the inflow of gold and silver, which now began to leave the country in growing quantities. At this point City opinion turned sour, and there was increasing criticism of Huskisson, now seen by the practical men of business as a dangerous ideologue. On 30 April 1825 Mrs. Arbuthnot recorded an alarming conversation with Herries, the Financial Secretary to the Treasury, who knew more about the foreign exchanges and the movement of gold than did any other member of the government. Herries complained that Huskisson was both wrongheaded and arrogant. He had cut tariffs and "done it all without saying one word to any human being. . . . His tone in addressing the House [of Commons] was that of the Prime Minister, and he never appeared to consider the Chancellor of the Exchequer *as any thing*. Rothschild had been with Mr Herries and had told him that the consequence of admitting foreign goods (which had not been met with corresponding liberality on the other side of the water) was, that all the gold was going out of the country. He had himself sent two millions within the last few weeks; the funds fall rapidly and *no advantage* is gained by any human being."[106]

The stock exchange bull market increased the feeling of unease in some minds. Wellington, in particular, was anxious. "He thinks," Mrs. Arbuthnot noted, "the greatest national calamities will be the consequences of this speculation mania, that all the companies are bubbles invented for stockjobbing purposes, and that there will be a *general crash!*[107] This prediction was in March 1825, and the Duke was right. Indeed, within weeks, the buying of stocks began to slow down and some stocks declined in value. Gold became increasingly scarce and the Bank of England began to ration its discounts. That meant credit automatically began to restrict itself, and business activity slowed. The anxiety spread when in June the House of Commons found itself debating the issue of whether an individual was justified in refusing Bank of England notes and demanding gold. The fact is that gold was becoming hard to get and businessmen could not always find the cash to meet their payrolls. The inability to meet payrolls, in turn, restricted consumer spending. From early October the price of commodities, especially cotton, sugar, coffee, tea, iron and tin, began to fall, and these falling prices affected all the other markets. Latin American mining shares had been drifting a little since January, but at the end of October they fell dramatically and the panic began to gather momentum. In early November cotton-trading firms started to fail. The Bank of England tightened credit still further, and other London banks began to call in bills, chiefly from the country, to strengthen their reserves. The calling in of country bills hit the country banks and at the end of November the leading bank in Plymouth ran out of cash and shut its doors.

That introduced the black month of December 1825, the beginning of the first world financial crisis. On 9 December the *Times* announced the failure of the big financial house of Wentworth, Chalmer & Co., a key London firm with links to many Yorkshire banks. Four days later came the collapse of Peter Pole, Thornton and Co., "among the most considerable in London" and linked to no fewer than 47 country banks. This closing set off the real panic the same day. No one had any gold. A contemporary account read: "An extraordinary number of country bankers from all parts of England were in town yesterday [13 December] either for the purpose of procuring specie and bank notes as a protection against a run on them, or to ascertain by their own observations the state of affairs among their London friends. Several of them were to be seen in each of the leading banking houses, anxiously awaiting their turn for an interview with the principals. . . . The gloom within doors, and the events which provoked it, were sensibly felt on the Stock Exchange."[108] "The bullion office of the Bank," the *Times* reported, "was beset by a multitude of persons waiting to convert bank notes into sovereigns."[109] Thanks to the discovery recorded at the beginning of this chapter, the flow of gold coins over the counter continued, and huge quantities in strongboxes were moved in fast post chaises to the country banks, to save those of them which had kept their doors open. Special scales were used to weigh the gold coins, so that they did not have to be counted individually.

The critical day was 16 December, when Liverpool summoned a meeting of the whole cabinet but pointedly excluded Huskisson, by now so hated and distrusted in the City that it was thought that his presence would simply intensify its fears. Huskisson, it should be added, was in no way abashed by his role in provoking the crisis. Quite the contrary: He privately expressed the hope that the Bank of England would fail and close its doors, thus enabling Parliament to revoke the bank's charter and reissue it on more liberal lines. Indeed, he tried to persuade Liverpool that he should *order* the bank to suspend payments, and at one point the Prime Minister was inclined to follow this advice until told by a furious Herries that if he did so, his office would be unable to pay either the army or the navy, which might well mutiny. Huskisson compounded his irresponsibility by manufacturing or passing on rumors that Rothschilds was failing and getting Canning to inquire, through the Foreign Office, into the solvency of its Paris branch. In fact, as already noted, Rothschild was doing his best to scour Europe for gold to keep the bank's doors open, and the cabinet, after sitting well into the night, decided this was the right policy. The same afternoon, 700 leading City figures had met at the Mansion House to proclaim their confidence in the system, and this meeting effectively ended the acute panic, since enough sovereigns were now circulating, at any rate among the London and country banks, to persuade most traders that all high-quality bank paper was dependable. Most of the banks thus survived, but only by recalling loans and "screwing almost to destruction every farmer, manufacturer and other customer in the country from whom they could get their money."[110]

One political victim of the crisis was Robinson. The day after the long cabinet meeting, Mrs. Arbuthnot recorded: "Mr Herries said that the City merchants appeared to have the utmost contempt for Mr Robinson, who was wholly without plans or expedients and who did not appear to have the least idea what to do." Three days later she noted that banks were still "breaking in every direction, and as the circulation is entirely in local notes, there is now in fact no circulation for gold cannot be supplied and everything is at a stand. In the manufacturing districts they do not know how to pay the wages and serious riots are expected. . . . The state of the country at this moment is extraordinary. There is no circulating medium, no means of getting money or of paying for any thing. Sir Charles Knightley, a gentleman of large property near Daventry, came to London two days ago and was obliged to ride part of the way and to borrow a few sovereigns, which his little girl had hoarded, to be able to pay for his journey, and told us that at this moment he has not the means of getting a shilling. The bank he deals with has suspended its payments."[111]

The first modern financial crisis produced, in turn, an economic depression whose effects were worldwide, deep, lasting and of great historic importance. One of the biggest London houses to go under was B. A. Goldschmidt, with £400,000 of unpayable bills in a total debit sheet of £1.2 million. Goldschmidt dragged down with it the house of Herzs in Frankfurt, the German money capital, and that closing, in turn, destroyed Benecke in Berlin and Reichenbach in Leipzig. In Vienna, Fries, one of the top four banks, broke, and its senior partner, David Parish, drowned himself in the Danube.[112] There were failures of key financial houses and banks in Amsterdam, Saint Petersburg, Rome, Madrid and Paris. Most of the French and Belgian banks survived, but the shortage or recall of credit produced an acute depression in heavy industries and the textile trades. Indeed, throughout Europe, the spread of the Industrial Revolution from Britain was set back the best part of a decade. In Britain itself the credit squeeze produced widespread recession and unemployment, followed by unrest. The first trouble came in January 1826 when the Norwich weavers rioted and the militia was called in. In April the Lancashire weavers followed suit, with violence in Rochdale, Manchester, Blackburn, and Preston. In May there was rioting in Bradford among the wool workers, and "great distress" was reported from Dublin.

Britain's difficulties were compounded by a sharp downturn in trade with Latin America. Dozens of British firms that had been set up in the years 1820–25 specifically to trade with the new republics went into liquidation. With imports from Britain (and elsewhere) dwindling, state revenues from the customs fell abruptly, and the new governments were unable to service their borrowings. Their difficulties were increased by the collapse of London houses which had floated the loans. Barclays, which had been guilty of wild speculation, closed its doors in August 1826, losing the Mexican government 300,000 pounds. The collapse of Goldschmidts made almost inevitable the failure of the government of Peru to pay interest on its bonds. Other governments followed suit. As a result, investors started to sell their Latin American bonds for whatever the bonds would fetch—very little, in most cases. By the middle of 1827, all but one of the new countries had defaulted and, in most cases, payments were not resumed for two decades. Negotiations about how to solve the debt crisis dragged on into and beyond the midcentury, and in the case of Mexico was an important factor in the foreign military intervention of the 1860s. With the exception of Brazil, which seems to have escaped the worst of the financial backlash, no Latin American country was able to raise state loans in the European money markets until the 1850s. This failure in itself held up economic development. Worse still was the knock-on effect that the defaults of governments had on private venture capital, especially in mining. The projects surveyed and started during the boom were generally sound. But in 1826 the flow of working capital dried up, and most of the schemes were abandoned, not to be resumed (if at all) for many years. Shares held in London became virtually worthless, and this discouraged other projects.[113]

Thus all the high hopes raised by the independence movement were dashed. The new states, caught up in an international turmoil they did not understand, turned on each other in fury and began to quarrel about frontiers. The Argentine-Brazil war of 1826–28, which closed the River Plate to commercial traffic and so made a bad economic situation worse, was a harbinger of many small but destructive wars. The Royal Navy frequently had to be used to protect British shore interests or back up commercial negotiations or simply to keep ports open.[114] These events left lasting scars and help to explain both the edgy relationship between Latin American countries and the northern world and the spasmodic development of these countries. Curiously enough, however, the losses sustained by European investors in Latin America in 1826–27 had no long-term deterrent effect: Each generation, including our own, has had to learn anew the risks of lending money to Latin American governments.

The economic disaster, so powerful in its consequences for states and governments, affected countless individuals, institutions and groups in different ways. The Bank of England, recently so triumphalist with its gold standard, had to draw in its almighty horns. Its staff, over 800 at the peak of the boom, was reduced to 650. Salaries were frozen or cut, and many clerks had to supplement their income by becoming (among other guises) coal merchants, booksellers or tea dealers or running a butcher's shop or an eating house. Their easy hours, 9 A.M. to 3:30 P.M., were extended, and the long, 90-minute dinner hour (if they worked till 5 P.M.) was reduced. Their old medieval holidays, which included the feasts of Saint Matthias, the Conversion of Saint Paul, and Saint Philip and Saint James, were largely abolished. In addition, discipline generally was tightened up; the clerks were forbidden to bring "strong liquors" into the office, smoke cigars while on duty, grow moustaches or wear top boots. What all this had to do with the crisis is not clear, but it was yet another sign of the coming of modernity. The economists were also knocked off the elevated pedestal they occupied while the boom was on. The great McCulloch not only lost much of his savings, but his plan to produce a vast tome explaining economics to the common man had to be abandoned as uneconomic. Instead he decided to publish the section on wages himself as a shilling pamphlet. The pamphlet failed, and he sold only half an edition of 2,000. "I lost my pains and £40 by this effort to improve their Sovereign Majesties," he commented sourly. "When I commit another *faux pas* of the same sort my friends had better get me to shut up."[115]

One economist for whom the crisis brought personal disaster was Harriet Martineau. The family textile business run by her father, Thomas Martineau, was badly caught by the collapse in demand, being left with a heavy inventory which lost half its value. Thomas's hair turned white; he had to rewrite his will, reducing his daughters' portions; and he died before 1826 was out. The firm staggered on till 1829, then finally subsided, and his daughters had to live by their needles or, in Harriet's case, her pen. Harriet was very bitter about the behavior of the trade unions during the crisis year. "The unemployed weavers," she wrote, "who would not take work at the wages the manufacturers could afford, kept a watch at the city gates [of Norwich] for goods brought in from the country. They destroyed one cartload in the street, and threw the cart into the river; broke the manufacturers' windows; cooped in a public-house three men from the country who had silk canes about them; and kept the magistracy busy and alarmed for some weeks. About 12,000 weavers in Norwich were then unemployed and the whole city in a state of depression, the more harassing from its contrast with the activity and high hope of the preceding year."[116]

Charles Lamb was exceptionally lucky in that he had been allowed to retire, after working at East India House for 33 years, in March 1825, at the crest of the boom. The Honourable Company gave him, *ex gratia*, a generous pension of two-thirds of his final salary—he would never have got anything like that a year later, when all was economy and retrenchment; indeed, it is most improbable that he would have been allowed to retire at all (he was only 51).[117] The need to economize helps to explain the East India Company's savagely ungrateful treatment of Stamford Raffles, who was refused compensation for his losses at sea and presented with a bill for £20,000. Raffles's distress was increased by the collapse of the City firm run by his friend Thomas McQuoid, carrying down with it £16,000 of Raffles's savings, and he died only three months after receiving the Company's shocking letter, dispatched in January 1826 at the nadir of the financial slump.[118]

The arts were badly affected. For a time, at least, building schemes in London and elsewhere came to a complete stop. Many architects were unemployed. Lord Holland and J. W. Ladbroke, who were busy developing their estates north of Hyde Park, in what was then known as "Kensington Gravel Pits," in the years 1820–25, ran out of cash and halted work on the housing later known as Holland Park and Ladbroke Grove—work was not resumed until 1839. This was a great area of artistic settlement in the early 19th century—among the painters who lived there were Augustus Wall Calcott, William Mulready, David Wilkie, John Linnell and Wilkie Collins—and their hopes of getting handsome new "villas" with spacious gardens were disappointed.[119] Many artists were hit personally by the crash and loss of commissions. Joseph Turner's patron, the Yorkshireman Walter Falkes, died just before the storm broke, and the Fawkes family lost heavily by the collapse of the main bank in Wakefield in December 1825. Turner, who was often secretly generous, tided them over with a timely loan. He noted in a letter the following May the severe effect of the crisis on the illustrated book trade, one of his main sources of income: "The crash among the publishers has changed things to a standstill and in some cases to loss." He added laconically; "I have not escaped."[120] Some painters were almost ruined. John Martin, as might have been expected, lost most of his savings in one of the collapsed banks, where there was an element of fraud, too. Benjamin Robert Haydon, as might also have been expected, set up a caterwauling in his diary. "These commercial distresses have reached me," he noted on 27 February 1826. "My employer could not pay me, I could not pay others, and these last five weeks I have been suffering the tortures of the inferno." The next day he added: "To see one's Friends all about one, harassed to Death, men of the greatest Genius and rank, is really painfully afflicting." He gave a gruesome account of Fred Robinson, now totally discredited as a financial wizard, making a vacuous speech on 6 May 1826, at a dinner of the Artists' Benevolent Fund, of which he was chairman. The artists gave him a none-too-warm reception, believing him partly at least responsible for their financial troubles, in some cases serious. One man who was badly hit was Thomas Lawrence, present at the dinner in his capacity as President of the Royal Academy. Haydon, always jealous of Lawrence, recorded with grim relish: "As a specimen of Lawrence, on that very morning a man told him if he did not pay his bill due, he would arrest him, before going to the dinner. . . . I was never arrested [for debt] and saw a lawyer, but Lawrence had been before me."[121]

Some of the cleverest men in the kingdom were ruined. One to go down was the brilliant engineer Sir William Congreve, inventor of the long-distance rocket. Congreve had recently devised a new kind of canal lock, worked by hydropneumatic machinery, and the first gas meter. But he had invested heavily in the Arigna Mines Company, which went bust scandalously in 1826, and thereafter he was forced to live penuriously in Toulouse, where two years later he died.[122] Many writers, some of them outstanding, were hit. The crash, which was particularly severe throughout the publishing industry, affected newspapers, magazines and, above all, books. It more or less finished William Hazlitt, whose career was in the doldrums anyway; after 1826 he recedes into the shadows.[123] Such men could just keep going by column-inch journalism, but, for the time being, big advances on speculative books were out of the question. Henry Crabb Robinson noted in his diary, 9 June 1826: "The booksellers are in a deplorable condition. [Alaric] Watts [a young editor and publisher] says that with the possible exception of Colburn and Longman, he doubts whether any of them are solvent."[124]

Indeed, there was one spectacular publishing crash, which changed the life of the man who was then the world's most widely read writer, Sir Walter Scott. In 1825 Scott was the world's richest author and had already spent £76,000 on his Gothic palace of Abbotsford, where the world came to admire and enjoy his splendid hospitality. He was also buying land, which was reasonable: His income was easily £10,000 a year. However, there was a hidden weakness in his financial position. Scott's original publisher had been John Ballantyne, an enterprising soul but a poor man of business. Ballantyne got into difficulties as early as 1813, and Scott came to his rescue. Scott induced a far more formidable Edinburgh publisher, Alexander Constable, to take over from Ballantyne the publication of Scott's entire output. From an author's point of view, the new arrangement worked spectacularly well, for Constable quadrupled Scott's sales. However, by bailing out Ballantyne, who was technically bankrupt, Constable had been obliged to take over all his debts, at ruinous rates of interest. Scott had also signed papers to keep Ballantyne out of jail. Sir J. Gibson Craig, who knew all the facts, held Scott responsible for a dangerous arrangement, which Scott made still more risky in 1822. From 1816 to 1822, James Ballantyne had been simply Scott's paid literary manager. After 1822 Scott took him into partnership, defining the terms in a "missive letter" and becoming responsible for Ballantyne's liabilities up to 46,000 pounds. So both Constable and Scott were now heavily involved in the Ballantyne family's fortunes, rather as Shelley plunged into the black hole of William Godwin's finances.

Their involvement might not have mattered so much if Constable, who was in many ways the best publisher of the day, had not become involved in another disaster area, the London financial house of Hurst, Robinson & Co. Operating extensively from London, as well as from Edinburgh, Constable used Hurst, Robinson as his London agents, and his and their finances were somewhat intermingled. Unknown to Constable, Robinson, a swaggering Yorkshireman, had been speculating with the firm's money on his own account. In particular, he had been doing vast deals in Kentish hops. On the strength of these ventures, he moved the firm to palatial new offices at the corner of Pall Mall and Waterloo Place. The firm was thought to be worth £350,000. In fact, once the commodities market turned down decisively in summer 1825, it was in increasing trouble.[125]

In October the banks began putting pressure on firms like Hurst, Robinson to reduce their liabilities. Robinson, in turn, went to Constable. The latter was already worried about the Ballantyne debts, as well as his own. When things looked serious, he took all his Ballantyne bills to Scott, offering to exchange them for those Ballantyne had granted to Scott. Scott felt unable to do this, and Constable had to have the bills discounted. Scott thus became liable for both sets, amounting to a further £40,000. In November 1825 Scott heard a fearsome rumor that Constable's banker was threatening to foreclose on his account. On 22 November he wrote in his journal: "The general distress in the City has affected Hurst, Robinson, Constable's great agents. Should they go, it is not likely that Constable can stand. . . . Thank God I have enough at worst to pay forty shillings in the pound." That may have been true then, but Constable threw all his resources into trying to save his agents, not knowing how hopeless the business was, and urged all his associates, including Scott, to do the same. So Scott became more deeply involved; indeed early in December he was persuaded to borrow 10,000 pounds on the security of Abbotsford and throw it into the kitty. By 18 December, however, he knew the awful truth, writing in his journal: "My extremity is come. . . . I suppose it will involve my all." He thought it all most unfair, for he had shown no financial arrogance himself, was "not taken in my pitch of pride." Simply because "London chooses to be in an uproar . . . in the tumult of bulls and bears, a poor inoffensive lion like myself is pushed to the wall."[126] All three firms broke in January 1826, Ballantyne with liabilities of £117,000; Hurst, Robinson, with over £300,000; and Constable, with £256,000. All went bankrupt, Constable eventually paying 2s6d to the pound (Robinson paid 1s3d).

Scott's personal debts were less than £33,000 but the various bonds and discounted bills of Constable, Ballantyne and Robinson came to a

further £86,000, making his total liabilities £104,081. He was bitter and
cursed the whole race of publishers, noting in his journal: "Whitaker,
the rascally bookseller, whose slip for £200,000 or thereabouts has
brought ruin nearly on the trade, kept seven hunters and be damned to
him!" He added, on 17 January 1826: "He that sleeps too long in the
morning, let him borrow the pillow of a debtor." The previous day he
had refused breakfast, but at dinner his staunch servants had forced him
to eat "some fine mutton chops." Scott got, it must be added, precious
little sympathy from some of his literary peers. The Wordsworths were
profoundly shocked, or said they were, to discover that a man of
letters—"and a baronet too," as Dorothy Wordsworth piously observed—should have involved himself in sordid business partnerships.
Leigh Hunt, up to his ears in permanent debt himself, laughed at the
news, though he was careful to weep crocodile tears for public consumption. Other writers on the Left, jealous of Scott's success and
hating his Toryism, jeered.

In fact, Scott extricated himself from the appalling mess, which
would have buried alive any other writer, with a grim sense of duty
which amounted almost to nobility. He was determined not to go
bankrupt and thus to deprive his creditors of most of their money. He
held discussions with the banks and other firms involved and came to
a compromise with them. They would not press him for immediate
payment or foreclose, and he, in turn, would remain solvent. They
would allow him to retain his salary as sheriff and clerk of court and
to live at Abbotsford rent free. In return, he would devote all his
working hours to paying off the debt. There was no discharge clause in
the agreement, since Scott intended to pay in full. He was profoundly
grateful to the bankers, and in spring 1826, when a jittery government
threatened legislation that would make banknotes of less than £5 unlawful—thus hitting at the £1 notes beloved of the Scots—he wrote a
pamphlet defending Scottish bank issues, as a result of which the bill
was recast to exclude Scotland.[127]

Scott had no illusions about what the agreement meant for him. He
had always worked hard and was now 55. He had been looking forward to retirement amid the joys of Abbotsford. Now, he wrote in his
journal of 24 January 1826: "I will be their vassal for life and dig in the
mine of my imagination to find diamonds." In the harsh publishing
conditions of 1826, he nonetheless managed to sell his *Napoleon* for the
huge sum of £18,000. By Christmas 1827, having produced £40,000 in
two years of frantic exertions, he was able to pay a first dividend of six
shillings in the pound. He continued to work at full pressure, and on
15 February 1830, he had a stroke. But he struggled on. He produced

another three shillings in the pound in December that year. At his death in 1832, £54,000 was still outstanding, but his life insurance policy accounted for £22,000 of it. The publisher Cadell, Constable's former partner, then paid off the rest on the security of Scott's copyrights, and these had discharged the debt in full by 1847. So honor was saved and Scott's estate passed safely to his heirs. Much of Scott's later *oeuvre* was hackwork and reads like it, but we must not imagine that his last years were without comforts. When he sold his Edinburgh house as part of the settlement, its wine cellar was loaded into carts and taken to Abbotsford; 350 dozen bottles of port and claret and 35 dozen of spirits went to join a much larger depository, of over 1,000 dozen bottles, at the country mansion.[128]

Another victim of the crash, who nearly went under—and almost went to jail—but survived to climb the heights was the young Benjamin Disraeli. He celebrated his 21st birthday, in dead trouble, on 21 December 1825, when the panic was raging. For such a youngster, he had already seen much of life. Four years before at age 17, he had been articled to a firm of solicitors in Frederick's Place, Old Jewry, and from this base he had begun to nose his way all over the City with a view to making a fortune, fast—a handsome, palefaced youth, with long, jet-black curls and a devastating taste in canary and ruby waistcoats, lavender trousers, prussian-blue jackets and masses of cheap jewelry. He and a fellow clerk, T. M. Evans, cooked up various investment schemes, buying on margin, which was then lawful. Disraeli's father Isaac, a bookish man and author of anecdotal volumes of history, was a gentleman of leisure, but much too sensible to give any money to his imaginative son. So any shares young Disraeli bought were on credit.

In November 1824 Disraeli and Evans began to buy into the Latin American mining market, and it was at this time that Disraeli met two more substantial figures with an interest in it. Once was Robert Messer, son of a rich stockbroker. The other was John Diston Powles, head of a major financial house that was heavily involved in the Latin American boom. Powles had made personal loans worth £120,000 to one of the new republics and had helped to float mining companies there. He was outraged when, early in 1825, old Lord Chancellor Eldon, who shared Wellington's skepticism about the boom, denounced the new floatations as another South Sea Bubble. Disraeli offered his already-prolific pen and wrote the pamphlet already mentioned, at Powles's instruction, and had it put out by Byron's publisher, John Murray, whom he had met through old Isaac. The work was a piece of astonishing cheek, for though much of it was a scurrilous attack on Eldon, it was dedicated (without permission) to his cabinet colleague Canning, the Foreign

Secretary. It was the first of three pamphlets on City matters which Disraeli scribbled in 1825. All were full of wild exaggerations and occasional downright lies. In the first, for instance, urging readers to buy Latin American shares, he described himself as "one whose opinions are unbiased by self-interest." In the third, he portrayed Don Lucas Aleman, the Mexican Foreign Minister, who had been heavily bribed by the mining companies, as "a pure and practical patriot!"[129]

Disraeli not only persuaded Murray, normally a canny Scot, to publish these works on credit, but contrived even to sell him some mining shares. Growing bolder, he put to Murray a much more ambitious scheme, in July 1825. There was much dissatisfaction, especially among Tories and City men, with the *Times,* whose editor, Thomas Barnes, had taken (they thought) a pusillanimous line at the time of Peterloo, deploring the loss of life and blaming it on the authorities. It was also critical of financial speculators. The attempt to start the rival *New Times* having failed, Disraeli now proposed a further shot at breaking the near-monopoly grip of the Thunderer by a new daily to be called—he proposed—the *Representative*. He brought Powles and Murray together and outlined the project. He was to be the manager; Scott's son-in-law Lockhart, the editor; and Murray, the publisher: Murray would hold 50 percent of the stock and Disraeli and Powles, 25 percent each. An agreement was signed on 3 August 1825, and Disraeli was given until December to subscribe his capital. Disraeli had all the wiles of a born con man and so mesmerized even his father, who knew him of old, that Isaac referred to the proposed paper as "the new intellectual Steam Engine." Murray later admitted ruefully that he had "yielded" to Disraeli's "unrelenting excitement and importunity."[130]

At all events, Disraeli went up to Scotland twice, each time staying with both Lockhart and Scott. He went to Scott with the warmest recommendation from Murray, who termed him "my most particular and confidential young friend." But Scott was not taken in. He thought at first that Murray was sending him old Isaac and was astounded to greet the young and heavily scented apparition at Abbotsford gates. Looking closer, he found that the young man did resemble his father, whom he did not like. As he put it crudely to a correspondent, describing the visit, "for sayeth Mungo's *Garland,* Crapaud piccanin, Crapaud himself," adding "the young coxcomb is like the old who [be]got him."[131] Lockhart, on the other hand, was quite won over, apparently swallowing Disraeli's promise that as part of the deal he would be found a seat in Parliament and that he would be coming to London "not to be an Editor of a Newspaper but the Director-General of an Immense Organ, and at the head of a band of high-bred gentlemen and important interests.''[132] Disraeli reported exuberantly to Murray in London, his letters referring to Scott, whom he termed enthusiastic, as "the Chevalier," and urging: "When M [code name for Lockhart] comes it will be most important that it should be distinctly proved to him that he *will* be supported by the great interests I have mentioned to him. . . . He must see that, through Powles, all America and the Commercial Interest are at our beck."

Disraeli seems to have lied glibly to all concerned. He claimed that Wilmot Horton, the Under-Secretary for War and Colonies, and Sir John Barrow, the Secretary to the Admiralty—two exceptionally hard-headed men who were most unlikely to be moved by the arm-waving eloquence of a 20-year-old dandy—"are *distinctly in our power.*" Back in London he began hiring staff and organizing an office. He told one correspondent that "the most celebrated men in Europe" had promised to write for his paper: "I have received six letters from different correspondents in the Levant and Morea." He informed Lockhart that he had already signed up correspondents throughout South America, Mexico and the United States and in every important city in Europe, as well as in Liverpool, Glasgow, Manchester, Birmingham, and other home cities. He said he had persuaded Dr. Copleston, the provost of Oriel, to become university correspondent, a barefaced lie.[133]

Then, abruptly at the beginning of December, Disraeli disappeared from the gestation of the *Representative*. He had been due to take up his shares, but had no money, and by this point credit was unobtainable. Indeed, he was deeply in debt. The margin speculations in mining into which he had ventured with Evans had been disastrous from the start. Buying in during November 1824, he had lost £400 even before the end of the year, £1,000 by the end of January 1825, and a massive £7,000 by July. The *Representative* scheme had followed immediately as a bold stroke to redeem his losses, but when the market finally collapsed, he had no alternative but to pull out, leaving the paper to go on to disaster without him. The *Representative* was launched on 25 January 1825, at the worst possible time, with advertising scarce and subscriptions thin. Murray kept it going for six months and lost £26,000; it ceased publication on 26 July. By that time Disraeli had written and published (22 April) his first novel, *Vivian Grey,* in which the hapless Murray was ridiculed, thus adding personal insult to financial injury. Evans vanished into a sponging house, Messer went bankrupt and Powles's firm collapsed (though he eventually paid 20 shillings in the pound, plus interest). Disraeli survived and, amazingly, escaped the Marshalsea or the King's Bench, though his losses and debts became the source of all his subsequent financial troubles, until they were resolved by his marriage to a rich woman and the generosity of the Cavendish-Bentincks, Dukes of Portland.[134]

Noblemen and politicians were bowled over like ninepins by the crash. One who just survived and, like Disraeli, went on to Elyseum, was Palmerston. His finances were always problematical, for although he owned vast estates in Sligo, Hampshire and Yorkshire, plus town properties in London and Dublin, he also invested heavily in them and had large liabilities. His net landed income was £10,150, from which he had to find £3,100 in annuities to dowagers and so forth, plus £2,596 in mortgages and interest on loans. He also paid out irregular sums in blackmail to ex-mistresses and other people who had a hold over him.[135] This was one reason why he was so keen on having an official salary, holding governmental office for a total of 50 years, a record. In 1824, his job as War Secretary brought him £2,480 a year, and he was eager to supplement it. Hence, at the end of December 1824, he decided, as most people had already done, to plunge into the stock market. He was a month later than Disraeli and no more successful. He bought into Pesco-Peruvian, Pearl Fisher, Welsh Mines and the Norfolk Railway. In March 1825 he was invited to join the board of Pesco-Peruvian. Ministers were not then automatically debarred from holding company directorships, and Palmerston was tempted by the handsome salary. He consulted Canning, who after hemming and hawing replied, "I should incline to—no." He did, however, join the boards of the Welsh Iron & Coal Company, the Cornwall & Devon Mining Company and the Welsh Slate, Copper & Lead Mining Company.

Palmerston went in at the top of the market, and most of his shares were sliding within a month. In the companies in which he was not a director, he may have lost as little as £1,600, but his total losses were at least £5,000. The only company in which he made any money was Welsh Slate, of which he eventually became a controlling shareholder. It did not pay a dividend till 1833, but by the 1860s it was earning him £9,500 a year.[136] At the time, however, the 1825–26 crash brought Palmerston near financial disaster, forcing him to such economies as selling new leases, cutting allowances and putting his servants into cheaper liveries. There is a hint that he may have come close to political disaster, too. When Liverpool retired after a stroke in February 1827, and Canning was eventually asked to form a government, he first offered the Chancellorship of the Exchequer to Palmerston. But twice in April and May 1827, Palmerston was obliged to reply, in the House of Commons, to unpleasant allegations about his directorship of the Cornwall & Devon Mining Company. Palmerston had always been aware that the company's secretary, John Wilkes, known appropriately as "Bubble," was a fraud. "Bubble" was connected with all the companies with which Palmerston was involved, and Palmerston had written of him in September 1825 that he was "a bit of a rogue if Nature writes a legible hand; at the same time he is a clever fellow & as long as his interest goes hand in hand with ours will probably do well by us."[137] By the time the attacks were made on Palmerston in the Commons, "Bubble" had gone to ground, and the chairman of Devon & Cornwall Mining, Peter Moore, was actually in jail. To modern eyes, Palmerston was lucky to escape political ruin. As it was, Canning hastily withdrew his offer of the Treasury—indeed, it is amazing that he made it in the first place—and appointed Herries instead. Canning's withdrawal of the appointment had important political consequences, for it meant that Palmerston was more loosely attached to the government than hitherto; he left it soon after Wellington became premier and refused to rejoin it, moving toward the Whigs. His detachment was an important milestone in the demise of the Tory ascendancy, which we will soon be examining.

The economic depression also had an important psychological effect on Peel, who, together with Palmerston, was to dominate British politics for the next two decades. Peel had begun public life as a hard-line traditionalist whose unwillingness to bend to popular agitation or violence had been stiffened by long service as secretary of state in Ireland, where he was known as "Orange" Peel. But he was a sensitive, thoughtful, and compassionate man who could not, like his friend John Wilson Croker, turn his face from the spectacle of popular suffering. The crash left his own immense fortune largely untouched, but he knew from his Manchester connections the depth of the distress in the manufacturing districts, and as Home Secretary he was called in 1826 to take emergency steps to maintain order in many parts of Britain. He used troops again and again, though not as often as his critics wished. Nor was he content merely to enforce the law. He organized and largely contributed to a private relief fund which raised £60,000.

Peel was not prepared to support direct governmental intervention, as some radicals urged, in the form of subsidies to hard-hit industries—indeed, he denounced such proposals, to Goulburn, as "quackery." But he favored suspending the Corn Law under discretionary (but unused) powers the government possessed to admit cheap foreign corn, thus bringing prices into line with the lower wages now being paid. Indeed, when the harvest of 1826 turned out poor, that is exactly what he did, arranging for the ports to be opened by Order in Council on 1 September 1826. This action dramatically foreshadowed his great surrender of the entire protectionist cause 20 years later, but in a sense it did more than that. When told by diehard agricultural-interest MPs in the Commons that he was bowing to the mob, he flashed back: "Sir, there are two sorts of courage which may be displayed in respect to them. There is the courage to refuse to accede to such demands at all. And there is another kind of courage—the courage to do that which in our conscience we may believe to be just and right, disregarding all the clamour with which these demands may be accompanied."[138] Noble words, from a man emerging as one of the great statesmen of the age, and marking a fundamental change in the way the more intelligent traditionalists were reacting to the challenge of the modern economy and the rise of popular urban power. The idea that constitutional conservatives might concede reforms not because of, indeed despite, the screams of the multitude, but simply because they were morally justified was a new one. It forms a fitting prelude to our last section: the first coming of democracy.

TWELVE

The Coming of the *Demos*

Toward the end of the 1820s, the world moved a decisive stage nearer the democratic age. This advance came about not through one dramatic incident, such as the storming of the Bastille, whose results were bound to be ephemeral, but by a combination of many factors and forces—the growth of literacy, the huge increase in the number and circulation of newspapers, the rise in population and incomes, the spread of technology and industry, the diffusion of competing ideas—and, not least, by the actions of great men. Governing elites began to realize that the right of the few to monopolize political power was no longer graven in stone. With various degrees of reluctance, they faced the likelihood that the magic circle would have to be expanded and more people admitted. So the process began whereby first some, then most, and finally all found themselves participating in the political process. It was not inevitable, as we shall see; accident, coincidence, miscalculation, individual willpower and collective violence all played a part. Nor was it necessarily progress: Organized human societies have existed for 8,000 years, and democracy has been a form of government, in some places and there only fitfully, for a mere two centuries; it is early days to judge. But, welcome or alarming, the entry of the *demos* onto the great stage of history in the late 1820s was a grand and unmistakable fact, the culminating event in the way the matrix of modernity was forged.

The prime theater of experiment was, perhaps naturally, the new world of the Americas where, between the 1770s and the 1820s the first great wave of decolonization had swept away the old monarchical order of Europe. In the south and center, paper constitutions, often radical, written and approved in the first flush of independence, proved largely worthless in the face of naked power conveyed by land, money and, above all, guns and sabers. In the north, and above all in the United States, where the roots of constitutionalism and the rule of law were deep and tenacious, it was a different matter.

Not that the great republic was designed to be a democracy: quite the reverse. The grave and substantial men who shaped its constitution deplored the "tumults, heats and ferments" of popular rule. They thought in terms of a high-minded oligarchy, based on landed property. They particularly disliked the spirit of party, though they had inherited the concept from England. They thought that great matters should be settled by consensus and that the principal pillars of the republic—presidents, governors, and senators—should be elected not directly by voters but by experienced legislators. George Washington himself was chosen informally and, on both occasions, elected unanimously, without contest. In his Farewell Address, he warned the nation against government "of a popular character" and the "horrid enormities" of party. The 85 constitutional essays published in *The Federalist* (1788), written mainly by Alexander Hamilton and James Madison and termed by Thomas Jefferson "the best commentary on the principles of government which has ever been written," likewise denounced repeatedly "the pestilential influence of party."[1] Nonetheless, Jefferson founded the Democratic-Republican party in 1795 and, when Washington refused to stand again, thus beginning the tradition of two-term presidents, the 1796 election was fought on a party basis. The election was won by the Federalist, John Adams. But after 1800, when Jefferson and Madison put forward the first true party platform, known as the Kentucky and Virginia Resolves, the Democratic-Republican party became so strong that it was able to nominate and elect, through the electoral college provided for in Article II, Section I (2) of the Constitution, three two-term presidents in a row: Jefferson, who served from 1801 to 1809, Madison (1809–17), and James Monroe (1817–25).[2] In each case, the retiring President was succeeded by his Secretary of State, thus ensuring a smooth transfer of power, and it was widely assumed that Monroe would also hand over the presidency to his Secretary of State, John Quincy Adams, in March 1825. So indeed he did, but in circumstances of great bitterness, even scandal. That was the spark which ignited the powder keg of American democracy.

Discontent with the political establishment, which amounted, in effect, to a rejection of oligarchy and the system of indirect election, had been growing for some years. Monroe had been 60 when he became President in 1817 and still wore breeches and top boots; he stood for the Old World. He had fought in the War of Independence; had been hailed, as Minister to France, by the National Convention as "Citoyen Monroe" and taken a seat on its benches; had sheltered Tom Paine; and, as Secretary both of War and State, had cleaned up the mess left by the burning of the city of Washington. In the 1816 election he got the votes of all the states except Massachusetts, Connecticut and Delaware, being elected, as one newspaper put it, "with less bustle and *national* confusion than belongs to a Westminster election for a Member of Parliament in England."[3] He was called "the last of the Revolutionary farmers," and shortly after taking over in Washington, he went on a three-month tour of 13 states to reunify the country after the stress of the war years and to boost its morale. "He wore a plain blue coat, a buff under-dress, and a hat and cockade of the revolutionary fashion. . . . The demon of party for a time departed and gave place to a general burst of National Feeling."[4] His visit to Boston was especially signifi-cant, for Massachusetts was a stronghold of federalism and, as we have seen, had been hostile to the war from the start. But there, too, he was well received and the *Colombian Centinel (sic)* called the visit "an event which has a more direct tendency than any other . . . to remove prejudices and harmonise feelings, annihilate dissensions and make us *one people.*" It added: "During the late Presidential Jubilee many per-sons have met at festive boards, in pleasant converse, whom party politics had long severed. We recur with pleasure to all the circum-stances which attended the demonstration of good feelings."[5]

The phrase caught on. The times were often called, then and later, the Era of Good Feelings. But if any such spirit of harmony ever prevailed, it did not last, and it certainly did not survive the bank crisis of 1819. The period was already marked by a growing feeling, espe-cially beyond the eastern littoral, that something was fundamentally wrong with the way the system operated and that dark and sinister forces were at work, especially in Washington itself. A case can be made for describing the Monroe presidency, and the rule of John Quincy Adams who formed its appendage, as the first great era of corruption in American history. Indeed, the word itself was used with increasing frequency. Many Americans came sincerely to believe that their govern-ment, both administration and Congress, was corrupt, and this at a time when, in Britain, the traditional corruption of the 18th-century Walpoleian system was being slowly but surely extruded from public life. Of course, by corruption Americans of the 1820s did not mean simply the use of bribes and stealing from the public purse. They also meant the undermining of the constitutional system by secret deals, the use of public office to acquire power or higher office, and the giving of private interests priority over public welfare. But they thought there was plenty of simple thieving, too. Nor was criticism confined to the administration's open opponents. As was already noted, William Crawford, at the Treasury, and John Calhoun, at the War Department, each accused the other of tolerating, if not actually profiting from, skulduggery.

These internecine feuds became envenomed and inveterate as the Monroe regime progressed. There was particular bitterness over patronage and appointments, always a source of favoritism and sometimes worse. There is a striking entry in Adams's diary, recording a furious quarrel, during the last months of the presidency, between Crawford and Monroe. The two men had met to discuss nominations for federal customs officers, which were posts of supreme importance because of the growing volume of cash handled. Monroe was difficult, and finally Crawford rose to go, saying: "Well, if you will not appoint the persons well qualified for the places, tell me who you will appoint, that I may get rid of their importunities." Monroe replied "with great warmth, saying he considered Crawford's language as extremely improper and unsuitable to the relations between them; when Crawford, turning to him, raised his cane, as if in the attitude to strike, and said: 'You damned infernal old scoundrel!' Mr Monroe seized the tongs at the fireplace in self-defence, applied a retaliatory epithet to Crawford and told him he would immediately ring for servants himself and turn him out of the house. . . . They never met afterwards."[6]

One reason good feeling had turned to ill-feeling was that both Crawford and Calhoun, as well as Adams, wanted to succeed Monroe and were campaigning actively. Both Crawford and Calhoun used agents in their departments, whose duty it was to dispense money, as political campaigners; they were given gold and silver but allowed to discharge payments in paper as a reward. Since each knew what the other was doing and circulated rumors to that effect, such activities became public knowledge. Then again, Crawford authorized one of his supporters in the Senate to inspect federal land offices, at public expense, during which the Senator lobbied and made speeches in favor of the Treasury Secretary's candidacy. Many members of the administration, it was claimed, had been given "loans" by businessmen seeking favors—loans which were never paid. But Congress, it was said, was corrupt, too. Senator Thomas Hart Benton of Missouri served as "legal representative" to the great operator of the fur trade and real estate tycoon John Jacob Astor and managed to push through the abolition of the War Department's "factory" system, which provided Indians with clothing and tools and so competed with Astor's own posts. The fact that the War Department's system was corrupt, as Benton easily demonstrated in 1819, was not the point: What was a senator doing working for a millionaire? Benton was not the only one. The great Massachusetts orator, Daniel Webster (1782–1852), received a fee for "services" to the hated Second Bank of the United States (SBUS). One modern historian described Webster as "a man who regularly took handouts from any source available and paid the expected price."[7] Astor seems to have had financial dealings with various other men high in public life, as well as Benton. Indeed, he even loaned $5,000 to Monroe himself in 1812; this sum was repaid, though not for 15 years. He lent the huge sum of $20,000 to Henry Clay during the panic year 1819, when commercial credit was almost impossible to come by. Clay was then Speaker of the House. He combined his job as Speaker with work for the SBUS—indeed, he continued to serve the bank until he became Secretary of State in 1825.[8] From 1821 to 1822, America's growing number of newspapers began, for the first time, to campaign against Washington's lack of standards. "Enormous defalcation" was practiced by paymasters in the navy, announced the *Baltimore Federal Republican,* and this was only "one of innumerable instances of corruption in Washington." The *New York Statesman* referred to "scandalous defalcations in our public pecuniary agents, gross misapplications of public money, and an unprecedented laxity in official responsibilities."[9]

It was in 1822, when these goings-on in the capital became the subject of angry public debate, that General Andrew Jackson first seriously contemplated running for president. It was clear that he wanted office. But he would not seek it. He thus contrived a pose which was to become a postural cliché for countless candidates to come. Seeing himself as a national hero, summoned by public opinion to rule, he said: "I give the same answer—that I have never been a candidate for any office. I never will. But the people have a right to choose whom they will to perform their constitutional duties, and when the People call, the Citizen is bound to render the service required."[10] However, Jackson had many passionate supporters, chiefly from his army days, and two in particular saw to it that the people did call. They were both former majors, who had married sisters: William Berkeley Lewis, Jackson's quartermaster in the southern wars, and John Henry Eaton, who had written his campaign biography. They served as his campaign managers—the first in presidential history—and as part of their jobs, they had the Tennessee legislature elect him to the U.S. Senate, where he served from March 1823. Jackson went the 900 miles to Washington partly by stage and by steamboat, when available, but mainly on horseback. People turned out to gape and question him when they heard he was passing through, the first stirrings of a mighty engine of populism.

In town Jackson lodged at William O'Neale's boardinghouse, on I

Street, just east of 21st Street, then a salubrious neighborhood. The place had been recommended to him by Eaton, who had been its star boarder since he became a senator in 1818, and it was enlivened by the presence of the owner's daughter, Margaret (Peggy) O'Neale Timberlake, who was to play an important, if unwitting, part in Jackson's life and the evolution of the U.S. presidency. Peggy had married, at age 16, a U.S. Navy purser, John B. Timberlake, and had a son and two daughters by him. But his duties took him abroad a good deal, and in his absence men assumed that Peggy, who was pretty, pert, self-centered, talkative and flirtatious, was available. Not so: She was very likely chaste; indeed shortly after Jackson's arrival, she complained to him that one of his cronies, Richard Keith Call, had "grossly insulted" her (made a pass). Jackson, who liked bold women who stood up to him in conversation, found her "an admirable woman," and Eaton, now a widower, something more.[11]

Washington was then a slow, idle, Southern city. Its chief boast was its 91,665 feet of brick pavement, though it also had, at the corner of Pennsylvania Avenue and 13th Street, the Rotondo, with its "Transparent Panoramic View of West Point and the Adjacent Scenery." Banquets for the legislators, which were frequent, began at 5:30 P.M. and proceeded relentlessly through soup, fish, turkey, beef, mutton, ham, pheasant, ice cream, jelly and fruit, taken with sherry, a great many table wines, madeira and champagne. There was, besides, much drinking of sherry cobblers and gin cocktails, slings made with various spirits, juleps, snakeroot bitters, timber doodly and eggnogs. For Jackson, the best aspect of Washington was the variety of churches. He was inclined to the mystic views of Emanuel Swedenborg, the Upsala pantheist and theosopher, whose notions of the Deity, as the general put it, were "the most soo-blime that tapped the drum ecclesiastic."[12] But Jackson liked to shop around, and he went to different denominational services every Sunday. He disliked official Washington, and the more he saw of its ways, the more he protested that fundamental change was needed.

Jackson no longer thought it possible to return to the Jeffersonian notion of a pastoral America run by enlightened farmers. "Experience has taught me," he wrote in 1816, "that manufactures are now as necessary to our independence as to our comfort."[13] But the bank crisis of 1819, and the overwhelming corruption (as he saw it) to which it was the prelude, made him sure that "a general cleansing" of Washington was imperative if the Union was to survive. He was the first candidate to grasp with both hands what was to become the most popular theme in American campaigning history: "clean the rascals out."

Jackson saw himself as an outsider against the insiders, and since most Americans felt themselves to be outsiders, too, he could if he chose play the democratic card. And he did choose. When Governor of the Florida Territory, he had ruled that mere residence was sufficient to give an adult male the vote. He reiterated this view in 1822. Every free man in the nation or state should have the vote, since all were subject to the laws and punishments, both federal and state, and so they "of right, ought to be entitled to a voice in making them." He added, however, that each state legislature had the duty to adopt such voting qualifications as it thought proper for "the happiness, security and prosperity of the state."[14] The more people who had the presidential vote, the better, since if, as he believed, Washington was rotten, it gave them the means of remedy: "The great constitutional corrective in the hands of the people against usurpation of power, or corruption by their agents, is the right of suffrage; and this when used with calmness and deliberation will prove strong enough—it will perpetuate their liberties and rights."[15] Jackson, then, was instinctively a democrat, and it is no accident that he created the great Democratic party, which is still with us. He thought the people were instinctively right and moral, and Big Government, of the kind he could see growing up in Washington, instinctively immoral. His task was to liberate and represent that huge, moral popular force by appealing to it over the oligarchic heads of the ruling elite. Here was a winning strategy, provided the suffrage was wide enough.

How far the strategy and its articulation were Jackson's own is hard to assess. He had read little. His grammar and spelling were shaky. The "Memorandoms" he addressed to himself are an extraordinary mixture of naïveté, shrewdness, ignorance, insight and prejudice. His tone of voice, in speech and writing, might be termed subbiblical. His formal oratory adumbrated the speeches with which Charles Dickens adorned the Eatanswill election in The Pickwick Papers 12 years later. "I weep for my country," he asserted, often. Banks, Washington, the War Department and enemies in general were "The Great Whore of Babylon." Hostile newspapers poured on him what he called "their viols of wrath." He himself would "cleanse the orgean stables." By contrast, Eaton was a skilled, even sophisticated writer, and it was he who worked the "clean up Washington" theme into an integrated national campaign, the first modern election campaign, in fact. In early summer 1823, Eaton wrote a series of 11 articles, signed "Wyoming," for the Philadelphia paper, the Columbian Observer. These articles attracted wide attention, were reprinted in pamphlet form as The Letters of Wyoming, and were reproduced in newspapers across the country.[16]

The theme, worked out in impressive detail and couched in powerful rhetoric, was that the American government had fallen into the hands of Mammon, and the voters must now ensure that it returned to the pure principles of the Revolution. It was by far the most impressive electioneering tract laid before the voters anywhere.

Whether it had much effect was doubtful. The bank scandal was not forgotten, but America, like Western Europe, was enjoying a boom. In his last message to Congress, Monroe felt able to state: "There is no object which as a people we can desire which we do not possess or which is not within our reach."[17] Reporting the message, the London *Times* said it described "an amount of national prosperity . . . superior to all that has been recorded of any community on earth."[18] All the same, political bitterness mounted steadily. Congress was a shambles of recrimination and mudslinging. Monroe complained to his old chief, Madison: "I have never known such a state of things . . . nor have I personally ever experienced so much embarrassment and mortification."[19] For the first time during an American election, personalities were savagely attacked by both speakers and press. Even the thick-skinned Henry Clay was moved to protest: "The bitterness and violence of presidential electioneering increase. . . . It seems as if every liar and calumniator in the country was at work day and night to destroy my character."[20]

Once Eaton's *Letters of Wyoming* appeared, Jackson himself came under fire, in a forthright pamphlet, *An Address on the Presidential Question*, written by Jesse Benton and published in Nashville, which accused Jackson of dueling, gambling, racing and cockfighting. A more damaging, because more temperately phrased, attack came from the former Treasury Secretary, Albert Gallatin, who asserted that whenever Jackson had been entrusted with power he had abused it. Had he not said he would like to hang the leaders of the Hartford Convention? Latin America provided plenty of examples of generals seizing power and destroying freedom, and "General Jackson has expressed a greater and bolder disregard for the first principles of liberty than I have ever known to be entertained by any American."[21] Lengthy passages from this warning appeared in many newspapers. It found echoes. Thomas Richie, of the *Richmond Enquirer,* claimed he "scarcely ever went to bed . . . without apprehension that he would wake up to hear of some *coup d'état* by the General."[22]

Yet Jackson was an outstanding candidate. Tall, slender, handsome and fierce, he looked tremendous, but his consumptive cough, white face, hair going from gray to white and the fact that he often seemed ill and frail, helped; it made people feel protective. He had a reputation for wildness, rages and severity, but when men actually met him, they found him courteous as well as awesome. "He wrought," wrote Josiah Quincy, "a mysterious charm upon old and young." He appealed particularly to women. "He appears to possess," testified Mrs. Sarah Seaton, wife of the editor of the *National Intelligencer,* "quite as much *suaviter in modo* as *fortiter in re* . . . a polished and perfect courtier in female society and polite to all" (December 1823). Two months later, Daniel Webster testified: "General Jackson's manners are more presidential than those of any of the candidates. . . . My wife is for him decidedly."[23] Of course, wives did not have votes, but they had husbands, and American women were much less diffident than were British or French ones in speaking their political minds.

In short, Jackson had that most valuable of all qualities for a presidental candidate, charisma. He was also known throughout the nation, and that, too, was important in a crowded field. Originally, there were five candidates: Jackson, Clay, Calhoun, Crawford and Adams. But a stroke in 1823 made Crawford a weak runner, and Calhoun withdrew to become vice presidential candidate on both the Adams and Jackson tickets. Clay was powerful in the new West but nowhere else, so in practice it was a race between Adams and Jackson.[24]

The election of 1824 was an important landmark in American constitutional history for more than one reason. The electoral college system was still a reality, but this was the first election in which popular voting loomed large. In Georgia, New York, Vermont, Louisiana, Delaware and South Carolina, the electors of the President were chosen by the state legislatures; elsewhere there were already statewide tickets, though voting by districts still took place in Illinois, Maine, Tennessee, Kentucky and Maryland. The number of voters was larger than ever before, but, with the country prosperous, no wrathful rising of the people took place. In Massachusetts, where Adams was a favorite son, only 37,000 votes were cast, against 66,000 for governor the year before. In Ohio, where 76,000 had turned out for the governorship race earlier in the autumn, only 59,000 voted for the presidency. Virginia had a white population of 625,000; only 15,000 votes were cast, and in Pennsylvania, where the population was already over a million, only 47,000 voted.[25] Low turnouts were already a feature of the American approach to politics. All the same, with a total of 356,038 votes cast, Jackson, with 153,544, emerged the clear leader, and Adams, the runner-up, was over 40,000 votes behind with 108,740.[26] Jackson was also well ahead in electoral college votes, having 99, against 84 for Adams, 41 for Crawford and 37 for Clay. He carried 11 states, against 7 for Adams and 3 each for the other two. By any reckoning, then, Jackson was the winner. However, under the Twelfth Amendment, if no presidential candidate secured a majority of the electoral votes, the issue had to be taken to the House of Representatives, which picked the winner from among the top three, voting simply by states. That, in practice, made Clay the broker. As the fourth runner, he was excluded from the play-off. But as Speaker of the House, he determined who would win it.

The House was due to meet on 9 February 1825. Jackson got to Washington on 7 December after a 28 days' journey, putting up at Gadsby's Tavern (also owned by O'Neale). He claimed, in a letter to his old army crony, John Coffee, that he was taking no part in politics until the outcome was decided: "There are various rumours . . . but whether any of them is founded on fact I do not know, as I do not . . . join in any conversation on the subject of the presidential election. . . . Mrs Jackson and myself go to no parties [but remain] at home smoking our pipes. (This was a formidable operation: His wife had clay pipes, but Jackson smoked "a great Powhaten Bowl Pipe with a long stem," puffing out until the room was "so obfuscated that one could hardly breathe.")[27] According to rumors, Clay's people put out feelers to Jackson, asking what offices would be given to them if Jackson was elected. Andrew Wylie, President of Washington College, later asked the General to confirm this rumor: "Is that a *fact?*" Jackson: "Yes, Sir, such a proposition *was* made. I said to the bearer, 'Go tell Mr Clay, tell Mr Adams, that if I go to that chair, I go with clean hands.' "[28]

Adams and Clay were less squeamish, though both had disliked each other since the Ghent negotiations. Clay called on Adams twice, on 9 January 1825, at 6 P.M., spending the whole evening there, and again on 29 January. The first meeting was probably the decisive one, though Adams's diary, while recording it, is uncharacteristically reticent about what took place. The key sentence in Adams's account is this: "He wished me, as fast [surely "far"] as I might think proper, to satisfy him with regard to some principle of great public importance, but without any personal considerations for himself." The passage concludes: "In the question to come before the house between General Jackson, Mr Crawford and myself, he had no hesitation in saying that his preference would be for me."[29] In view of Adams's character, there are two possible explanations for what took place. One is that there was no explicit bargain, but an understanding that if Adams could bringing himself to think Clay suitable, he would give Clay a great office; the other was that a bargain was struck, and the normally high-minded Adams could not bring himself to write about it. In all events, the story of a Clay-Adams bargain was already circulating by mid-January, John Campbell of Virginia writing to his brother David: "Letters from Washington inform us that Adams is certain to be the president. Clay & him have compromised . . . Bargains & sales are going on . . . as infamous as you can imagine. This office and that are held out provided you vote this way and that, etc, etc. What is this but bribery and corruption?"[30]

Nonetheless on 9 February Clay got Adams the White House. Congress was jampacked and tense. In those days the House was a semicircle of pillars of Potomac marble. Each representative's desk carried a snuff box, and there was a personal spittoon at the side. Between the pillars were sofas on which privileged guests lounged. Others crammed the galleries behind. Clay was working against time, believing that if he could not get the vote for Adams on the first round, the affair would drag on and Jackson was bound to win. Indeed, the Pennsylvania militia had threatened to march on Washington if the General "did not get his rights." Clay needed 13 states to bring Adams home and he had lined up only 12 when the House met. The case of Kentucky was particularly scandalous, since Clay cast it for Adams although Adams had not received a single Kentucky vote in the electoral college.

The swing state was New York, whose casting vote was held by old, rich, dotty, and indecisive General Stephen Van Rensselaer, the "Patroon," who had come such a cropper in the Canada Campaign. Van Rensselaer was notoriously henpecked. Asked if he had read Von Humbolt's latest work, he turned to his wife: "Have I read Humbolt's work, my dear?" "*Certainly* you have read it!"[31] Clay pressed the old man to vote for Adams, but according to the autobiography written by his New York colleague, Martin Van Buren, Van Rensselaer "took his seat fully resolved to vote for Mr Crawford. But before the box reached him, he dropped his head upon the edge of his desk and made a brief appeal to his Maker for his guidance in the matter—a practice he frequently observed in great emergencies—and when he removed his hand from his eyes he saw on the floor directly below him a ticket bearing the name of John Quincy Adams. This occurrence, at a moment of great excitement and anxiety, he was led to regard as an answer to his appeal, and taking up the ticket he put it in the box."[32] Whether Clay or God decided the matter, Adams got his 13th state and was president on the first ballot. Webster and John Randolph of Roanoke were the tellers. Clay read out the results. There was clapping and hissing in the galleries, whereupon a South Carolina Jacksonite ordered the galleries to be cleared, and this was done by the sergeant at arms. As the congressmen shuffled out, Randolph said: "It was impossible to win the game, gentlemen. The cards were stacked." Representative Cobb of Georgia went further, bellowing "Treachery, treachery! Damnable false-hood!"[33]

When the committee of the House waited on Adams at his house on F Street to tell him the result, "sweat rolled down his face. He shook from head to foot and was so agitated he could hardly speak."[34] Jackson's first reception of the news was cool. Adams's diary records that Adams met the General at a party which Monroe gave at the White House that evening and found him "altogether placid and courteous." The General had a lady on his right arm, and another eyewitness described the meeting. Jackson: "How do you do, Mr Adams? I give you my left hand for the right, as you see, is devoted to the fair. I hope you are very well, Sir." Adams: "Very well, Sir. I hope General Jackson is well." The eyewitness was struck by Jackson's affability and Adams's coldness.[35]

But the General's behavior was a mask. His adopted son and aide, Andrew Donelson, had already, that evening, coined the phrase "a corrupt bargain has been struck." Indeed, six days before, a Jackson supporter, Senator George Kremer, had published an article, "Another Card," in the *Intelligencer,* accusing Clay openly of having corruptly sold his support to Adams. The assumption was that Clay would become Secretary of State, the office which, for the last four presidencies, had been the prelude to the White House itself. Jackson said he refused to believe so shocking a fact. But the day Clay's appointment became known, 14 February, his wrath overflowed. "So you see," he wrote to Major Lewis that evening, "the *Judas* of the West has closed the contract and will receive the thirty pieces of silver. His end will be the same. Was there ever witnessed such bare-faced corruption?"[36] The cry, "corrupt bargain," was taken up all over the country. The way in which Jackson, having got most suffrages, most electoral votes, and most states, was robbed of the presidency by a furtive deal seemed, to many people, to confirm exactly what Jackson had said in his campaign was wrong with Washington and what he had been elected to change. It was the voters, as well as Jackson, who had been swindled.

Foreigners saw it differently. For the first but not for the last time, Europeans were struck by the mysterious workings of American public morality. Bargaining for office in return for votes was an absolute commonplace of British politics and occurred in every other country where parliamentary constitutions had been tried. Yes, replied the Jacksonites, and that is precisely what is wrong with the Old World and unacceptable in the New. It was not only the Jacksonites who were upset. Adams himself was always uneasy about the Clay appointment; it went a long way to wrecking his presidency. Clay was repudiated by

many of his supporters in his own state, Kentucky, who deserted him
to form a Jackson party. He tried to defend himself, but made matters
worse by giving different versions. First, he said that "as a friend of
liberty," he could not allow the White House to go to "a military
chieftain." But in a circular to his constituents, he said his reason was
that Jackson "lacked statesmanship." He eventually produced two
further defenses of himself, equally contradictory. Jackson was delighted by Clay's lack of nerve, rightly perceiving it was a mistake to
reply. "How little common sense this man displays," he wrote to
Coffee. "Oh, that mine enemy would write a book! . . . Silence would
have been to him wisdom."[37]

Jackson and his supporters were determined to reverse the result as
soon as they lawfully could. So the 1828 election campaign effectively
began in spring 1825. The Tennessee legislature immediately renomi-
nated Jackson for President. In a 15-minute discourse, "perhaps the
longest political speech in his career," Jackson accepted, giving the
"corrupt bargain" as his chief reason for doing so. Indeed, the bargain
gave the General his route into the politics of the masses, under the
banner of Popular Sovereignty, since the essence of the charge he leveled
against Adams and Clay was that the will of the voters had been defied
by corrupt politicians. These politicians thought the fuss would die
down. But it never did. Jackson and his men ensured it was kept alive.

From its very inception, Jackson declared war on the Adams administration. As he put it in a letter to Henry Lee, he had originally trusted
Adams's integrity, but after the Clay appointment, "I do not think the
human mind can resist the conviction that . . . Mr Adams by the
redemption of a pledge stood before the American people as a participant in the disgraceful traffic of Congressional votes for executive
office. From that moment I withdrew all intercourse with him."[38] A
huge, unbridgeable fissure opened between the administration and the
Jacksonites. From this point opposition in Congress became systematic.
The modern American two-party system began to emerge. All over
what was already an enormous country, and one which was expanding
rapidly, branches of a Jacksonite popular party were formed in 1825–
26, and scores of newspapers lined up behind the new organization,
including important new creations like Duff Green's *United States Telegraph*. As the political system polarized, more and more established
politicians swung in behind the General: Van Buren came, bringing his
New York machine. So did the remains of the old Crawford faction,
Randolph of Roanoke, McDuffie of South Carolina, Livingstone of
Louisiana, Sam Houston of the West, Calhoun and Benton. Thus as-

sembled what was to become one of the great and enduring popular instruments of the modern age, the Democratic party.[39]

It was not, however, the first fully organized and financed democratic mass movement. The credit for the first must go to Ireland and to Daniel O'Connell, and we must break off for a space from Jackson's progress to the White House to see how the Liberator, as he was known, did it. Ireland was a chronically discontented country which, from time to time, became actively ungovernable. Castlereagh's plan to solve the Irish problem by the Act of Union failed when George III refused to accompany it with Catholic Emancipation—that is, removing the disabilities which banned Roman Catholics from political office, Parliament and most official jobs. The Irish birthrate was probably the highest in the world at this time. Some relief was provided by emigration to Britain.

The Irish started arriving in Britain in the 1790s as seasonal laborers, but from 1815 they came as permanent settlers. Everywhere they formed the lowest level of what were now termed "slum dwellers." Entire Irish families lived in cellars. Indeed, towns which did not, on the whole, have houses with cellars, like Nottingham, Birmingham and Leicester, did not have an Irish problem. But in Glasgow, Manchester, Liverpool and London, the Irish settled by the hundred thousand.[40] They were hated in the towns and still more in rural areas where they depressed wages. When they appeared in Lincolnshire, "the native labourers assembled in great numbers and drove them away." As we have seen, the Irish were emigrating to North America in great numbers, too. Even so, the home population was over 7 million by 1820 and heading quickly for 8 million, in a country which in times of poor harvests could barely feed 5 million.[41] Three-quarters of these masses, including all the poorest, were Catholics. That was the main reason why Ireland could not be absorbed into the British system, as Scotland and Wales had been. Irish poverty was envenomed by the feeling that it was caused by what was seen as alien rule. The fact that the seat of royal government was still called Dublin Castle—it was, and is, not so much an actual castle as a rambling collection of dingy buildings—was symbolic of the defensive and indeed military nature of sovereignty.

The young Robert Peel was Chief Secretary to the Lord Lieutenant, or Viceroy, from 1812 to 1818, and his letters and speeches provide a fascinating and often rueful insight into the insuperable difficulties of governing Ireland with dignity and justice. Much of ordinary Irish life, then as now, was lighthearted, warm, free and easy and fun, lit by flashes of brilliant wit and creative passion. But the business of governing was a morass of corruption, lies, hatred and fear. The Protestant Irish enjoyed the privileges of what was called the Ascendancy and howled for patronage day and night. But they did little in return. It was difficult to get Irish members of Parliament, even if they were members of the government, to attend twice a year at Westminster. Peel's baptism of fire was to manage the 1812 Irish elections, a disgusting business involving the careful use of what seem to us minute sums of governmental money to corrupt electors and borough owners without falling foul of the antibribery clauses of Curwen's Act.[42] He also had to deal with incipient rebellion at the time of the Hundred Days, when 5,000 troops had to be rushed out of Ireland to Flanders, leaving the garrison dangerously weak. Even after Waterloo, Lord Whitworth, the Viceroy, had to lock up what he called "blackguards running about the streets in the night denying the victory and asserting that Buonaparte was the conqueror."[43] The *Dublin Evening Post* gave joyful prominence to any French success. Like the other popular papers, it was vociferously anti-British and nationalist. All the popular papers were unscrupulous, full of libel and falsehood, and flatly refused to report the actions of the government truthfully.

As a result, Peel was obliged to support an exiguous "loyalist" press with subsidies from the Secret Service fund and what was called the Proclamation Fund. Thus, the *Dublin Journal* got £1,500 a year (its revenue was £2,490 and its expenditures, £2,430). The *Patriot* got the same, and further sums went to the *Correspondent*. Their circulations were tiny—the *Patriot's* as little as 750. Peel wanted to get rid of the whole rotten system. But, as he told the Commons on 26 April 1816, the so-called free press was the chief cause of violence in Ireland. "What could be said," he asked, "in favour of a press which never sought to enlighten the public mind, which never aimed at the dissemination of truth, which never endeavoured to correct the morals or improve the happiness of the people? On the contrary—the most studious efforts were made to keep alive and foment discord and the malignant influence of the worst passions."[44]

All this was doubtless true. But the government itself was unscrupulous. In the predominantly Presbyterian north, it furtively encouraged the growth of Orange Lodges, which dated from the 1790s, while preventing them from emerging as an alternative power structure. Peel admitted, in a letter to the Viceroy in July 1814, that his object was to keep the lower classes in the north and, indeed, in the whole of Ireland disunited, since if they came together, the Protestants would be bound to adopt Catholic nationalism "and therefore a cordial concurrence in hating the British connection." He hoped they would always be divided: "The great art is to keep them so, and yet at Peace or rather not at War with one another."[45]

Dublin Castle was rather like what Talleyrand said of Tsarist Russia: never as strong as it looked, never as weak as it looked. In the last resort, it could invoke the Irish Convention Act of 1793, which made unlawful the election and assembly of any unauthorized bodies purporting to represent the people. But it was not a despotism. Indeed, it was very much subject to the rule of law, and so vulnerable to partisan juries and a nationalist movement led by brilliant and far-from-scrupulous barristers.

The most gifted of these barristers was Daniel O'Connell (1775–1847), Peel's particular bête noire. Peel came from a strongly Protestant family, but he was far from being an Orangeman; indeed, when he first arrived in Dublin, he changed all the family facings on his servants' livery, which fortuitously had been orange. So it was a bitter point that O'Connell promptly dubbed him "Orange" Peel, a name that stuck. O'Connell was the exact contemporary of Charles Lamb, J. M. W. Turner and Jane Austen. He was born a favored member of a swarming clan which inhabited a remote penisula in County Kerry, traditionally the poorest part of Ireland (and its people rated by other Irishmen as the stupidest). Here, in the wild southwest, it was possible for a family like the O'Connells, who traced their gentry status back to Edward III's time but had remained Catholic, to survive the fiercest phase of the Ascendancy simply because their land was so poor and undeveloped. They were graziers, merchants and smugglers. Most were poor. A few were rich, much richer than they seemed. The richest was O'Connell's uncle, known as Hunting Cap. He was hereditary chief, having as the symbol of authority the crooked-handled knife or *sgian na coise cuime*. The peasants obeyed him. He was childless and, the young Daniel quickly earning a reputation as a clever and spirited lad, Hunting Cap made him unofficial heir and undertook his education.[46]

In short, O'Connell belonged to the indigenous and, to some extent, unconquered Irish aristocracy. His status was important to him and was ignored by his Ascendancy and English opponents who saw him as a counter-jumping attorney. For most of his life, he was a substantial landowner, his lands bringing him in nominally about £4,000 a year, though not much in cash. His adoption by Hunting Cap was a mixed blessing. The old patriarch was overbearing and exacting, and the response of his dependent was a mixture of servility and deception, as his letters painfully reveal. This uneasy relationship, akin to that between Ireland and the dominant English, bred in O'Connell a habit of intrigue and concealment which became a hallmark of his political character. Initially, his upbringing was Celtic, in that he was fostered out to the wife of a herdsman, lived in a mud cabin and spoke Gaelic. All his life he moved and conversed at ease among the peasants, indeed, among men and women of all classes in the countryside; this facility was one of the sources of his strength both as a barrister and as a politician. But at a time when nationalists all over Europe, from Finland to Hungary, were turning to the native vernacular as a source of unity, he rejected Gaelic. He used it only when there was no other means of making himself understood. He thought English would be the first world language and for the Irish to opt against it would be to reject their entrance ticket to the modern world: "The superior utility of the English tongue, as the medium of all modern communication," he said, "is so great that I can witness without a sigh the gradual disuse of Irish."[47]

His emotional loyalty was, rather, to a larger concept: Ireland as part of European Catholic civilization. His national idea was not what Eamon de Valera actually implanted in the young Irish state of the 1920s and 1930s, of a Celtic isle cut off from the materialist chaos beyond, but the proselytizing Ireland of the Dark Ages, sending out Latin-speaking scholars and saints to the world. In the 17th and 18th centuries, the Irish Catholic gentry had to seek their fortunes on the Continent, chiefly as soldiers. His Uncle Daniel was a count of France and a general in the Bourbon army. His own outlook was cosmopolitan, internationalist, turning instinctively to Paris, Vienna and even New York as much as to London. His boyhood dream was to be his country's Washington. Later he saw Bonaparte as Ireland's friend. Later still, he identified with Simón Bolívar, another "Liberator," and proudly dispatched his son Morgan, aged 14, to join the Irish Legion fighting for freedom against Spain.[48]

O'Connell's Europeanism was reinforced by his schooling in the Jesuit colleges run for the sons of British Catholic gentry in Flanders. Hunting Cap's decision to send him to Saint Omer and the University of Louvain had an unforeseen effect, for it made the youth an eyewitness to the turmoils and terror created by the French Revolution. Just as Lord Liverpool never forgot the horror of the fall of the Bastille, O'Connell formed from these events a lifelong conviction that violence was evil and ultimately futile. His constitutionalism was reinforced by luck, often a decisive factor in politics. During the disastrous Irish rebellion of 1798, O'Connell was bedridden with rheumatic fever. This illness not merely prevented him from taking part, but allowed him to view the rising with detachment and learn the lesson—the folly of armed conspiracy and the salient truth that the Irish masses could not be trusted except under firm leadership. By instinct and conviction, he supported hierarchical order. He not only joined but enjoyed the militia, and he developed a profound respect for monarchy, which led to accusations of flunkeyism during George IV's highly successful state visit to Dublin in 1821. But he was justified by events in his belief that nonviolent mass agitation was the right way for Catholic Ireland to progress toward equality.

However, from his earliest entry into public life, he rejected the path taken by the Welsh and the Scots toward integration. His chief reason was religion. As a young man he went through a phase of radical skepticism. Marriage ended that. His wife Mary was another (but penniless) O'Connell. He wed her in secret and without Hunting Cap's permission, and as a result lost half his inheritance. But Mary restored his faith and thereafter he was a strict Catholic, observing all the holy days, fasts and abstinences.[49] His Catholicism made possible his emotional identification with the Irish peasants and the priests who ministered to them. But his Catholicism was not ultramontane. As we have seen, Chateaubriand's great work, *Le Génie du Christianisme,* laid the foundations of Catholic populism and thus eventually of a revived, independent papacy. But in the years 1815–30, the Pope was still heavily dependent on one or another of the Great Powers. During the Congress of Vienna, anxious to secure the return of the Papal States in full, Pope Pius VII was quite prepared to make a deal with London over Catholic Emancipation and allow the British Crown a veto on appointments of Irish Catholic bishops. O'Connell saw such a veto not merely as an infringement of religious liberty but as a denial of Irish nationalism. "I am sincerely a Catholic but I am not a Papist," he asserted. Clergy selected by a cynical alliance between the British government and Rome were unacceptable: "The *Crown Priests* will be despised and deserted by the people, who will be amply supplied with enthusiastic anti-Anglican friars from the Continent."[50] The struggle over the veto split the Irish Catholic leadership, but, in the long run, it operated decisively to O'Connell's advantage, enabling him to drive off the political stage the old upper-class, conformist Irish spokesmen and replace them with his own followers and policies.

O'Connell rose to power through the Bar, to which he was called in 1798. He became one of the most hard-working and successful advocates in Irish history. He was wonderfully at home in court, a magisterial examiner in chief, a deadly cross-examiner, more learned in the law than the great majority of judges and never afraid to stand up to them. His greatest merit was that he became totally absorbed in his client's case, as though it were his own, and could concentrate his whole energies on getting a favorable verdict. Even his bitter opponent Peel admitted that if great issues were at stake, O'Connell was the man he would brief.[51] Within a decade he was making the then-enormous sum for a junior of £5,000 a year. By 1827, he was making £7,000. But as a Catholic he was not only banned from Parliament and thus from high legal office, not only excluded from a judgeship, but he could not even take Silk (become a King's Counsel), which disabled him from accepting briefs in the most important cases. As a Silk he could have earned £20,000–£30,000 a year in Westminster. It was this kind of discrimination which made the ablest Catholics so bitter.[52] Hence, the real rewards of the bar were denied O'Connell, and the large income he continued to make as a junior was achieved only at the cost of relentless drudgery, which became increasingly hard to sustain as he grew older.

Nonetheless, his political rise was rapid. As early as 1808, he was the leading spokesman for Catholic Ireland. A political leader, especially a nationalist, can to some extent master events, but equally he is a victim of them, too, and O'Connell is a case in point. When Bonaparte bestrode Europe like a colossus and England's cause faltered, the chances of rapid Emancipation looked good. O'Connell consolidated his reputation with a tremendous forensic triumph during the Magee libel trial of 1813, when he crushed the Protestant Attorney General with a vituperative display of rhetoric such as had never before been heard in Dublin.[53] This trial made him a national figure. An eyewitness recorded his morning walk in Dublin: "When breakfast was over, his burly form excited attention as he moved towards the Four Courts, at a pace which compelled panting attorneys to toil after him in vain. His umbrella shouldered like a pike was his invariable companion. The military step which he has acquired in the Yeomanry, strangely blended with the trot characteristic of an active sportsman in the mountains of Kerry, gave him the appearance of a highland Chieftain—a similarity increased when his celebrity as an agitator began to ensure him a tail of admiring followers whenever he appeared in public."[54]

However, in the decade that followed the Magee case, O'Connell's political career and the cause of Emancipation both marked time, as England was everywhere triumphant. On both sides of the Channel, the bulk of the middle classes, whatever their religion, joined the ruling class in resisting reform. The repressive laws and police power were one factor, but it was primarily the spirit of the times which favored the existing order. In Ireland an additional element was the skill with which Peel, despite all his grumblings, operated the Dublin Castle machine. As long as Peel was in charge, there was little chance of O'Connell getting the better of it.

In the bitter contest between the two men, there appears to have been real dislike on O'Connell's side, matched by contempt on Peel's. It is a curious comment on the twisted values produced by English rule that Wellington, whose family was established in Ireland and who was born and raised there, denied he was Irish. He even looked down his nose at Peel, whose grandfather came from nowhere: "Peel has no manners," as he put it. Peel, in turn, despised O'Connell, whose family had held their lands since the 14th century, as a vulgar comic, little better than a stage Irishman.

Unfortunately, there was a tiny element of truth in this view. O'Connell was a tall, handsome man, with flashing blue eyes and jet-black hair, and at times he carried himself like a prince. But he had weaknesses, characteristic of his time, place and race. For one thing, as was already noted, there was his propensity to get himself involved in duels, often with friends, colleagues and relatives as much as with enemies—a habit which harmed his reputation as much as it did Jackson's. Then again, O'Connell was always in constant trouble over money. However hard he worked, however much he earned and got from Hunting Cap and other members of his family, he was always in debt. A recent analysis of his unpublished correspondence with his wife and others reveals a pitiful tale of extravagance, concealment, "cheques in the post," guarantees, endorsed bills, post-obit bonds and all the other apparatus of 19th-century improvidence with which William Godwin, Percy Shelley, Leigh Hunt and others were so familiar.[55] He was always a generous man, foolishly ready to guarantee other men's debts. In 1815 a friend for whom he had gone security went bankrupt, dragging O'Connell with him and leaving him liable for £8,000. There were many other instances of his financial imprudence. But, equally, he borrowed from others. In 1817 his exasperated brother James, who tried to sort out his financial affairs, thrust into his hands a list of his debts totaling £19,000 and including an infinity of small sums owed to relatives, friends and clients, few of whom could ever expect to be repaid.[56] His financial problems and his efforts, both serious and comic, to solve them were well known to Dublin Castle, through its spies, and so to Westminster, and this helps to explain the derision he often evoked in English ruling circles.

Yet in a way it was O'Connell's very Irishness, with its weaknesses, as well as its strengths, which enabled him to speak for his country as no one had ever spoken before and to become the first modern populist politician. He was an Irishman in the way Jackson was an American: Both expressed, in a heightened and exaggerated manner, some charac-

teristic traits, prejudices, attitudes, likes and dislikes of their countrymen. Both were quintessentially of their time and place. But O'Connell,
while lacking Jackson's huge will and fierceness, had a political brain
of great originality and showed organizational skills of no mean order.
It was these qualities which enabled him to create the first modern
machine of mass politics.

O'Connell's machine rested on three forces. The first was a rabid
and coordinated press. In 1823, sensing that the spirit of the age had
moved again and that a more liberal spirit was in the air, O'Connell
founded the Catholic Association to work for emancipation from legal
disabilities. The 1820s, in the United States, Britain, France and Germany, was the first great age of newspaper power. Ireland was no
exception. Once Peel left Dublin Castle, the system of subsidized governmental newspapers began to collapse. By the early 1820s it was
nonexistent. From 1823 four out of the six large-circulation newspapers
were 100 percent behind the association. Three of them, the *Dublin
Evening Post,* run by F. W. Conway, and the *Morning Register* and the
Weekly Register, edited by Michael Staunton, were completely in
O'Connell's pocket. These were highly political papers, which reported
the speeches of O'Connell and his satraps in immense detail and were
read out loud in gatherings and public houses all over Catholic Ireland.
O'Connell's domination of the Catholic media ensured that his association's propaganda reached into every chink and cranny of the south.[57]

The second leg of the tripod was finance. O'Connell repudiated
violence; instead, he introduced peaceful mass agitation, and his newspapers told the Irish peasants how they should set about it. As far back
as 1784, a proposal had been made of levying a "Rent" of £1 a year over
every Catholic family to provide funds for the emancipation movement.
On 4 February 1824, O'Connell launched a new and simple form of this
idea through his newspapers. Each Catholic household should put in a
penny a month, something which even the poorest could afford. Together these contributions brought in £50,000 a year. This sum was to
be spent on legal aid for the Catholic poor, especially those appearing
before "Orange" magistrates; on subsidizing and expanding the Catholic press; on educating the poor; on church and school buildings; and
on parliamentary business, particularly the presentation of mass petitions drawing attention to Irish grievances.[58] What O'Connell had not
initially perceived, but which he soon grasped as the Rent was
launched, was that the very act of collecting and contributing not only
raised funds but bound militants and the people together into a mass
organization, operating from a nationwide network of committee
rooms, and forming the third leg of the tripod. Giving their pennies

transformed the sentimental support of the peasants into genuine commitment. Collecting turned thousands of middle- and lower-middle-class Catholics into active campaigners. The priests were drawn in, for collections had to be taken at church doors to get the pennies of those without their own homes, such as house servants. Within two years of first organizing the Rent, O'Connell found himself the master of an octopuslike machine, whose tentacles stretched into every village of Catholic Ireland and which could easily be transferred from financial to electoral purposes.[59]

The effects of the financial crash of 1825, and the depression which followed the next year, gave O'Connell his political opportunity. During the boom years, Protestant liberals like Maria Edgeworth were confident that rising prosperity would enable Ireland to solve its difficulties without any fundamental erosion of British rule. In the peak boom year 1825, Edgeworth received Scott and his son-in-law Lockhart at Edgeworthtown, which impressed them both. "Here we had the opportunity," wrote Scott, "of seeing in what universal respect and comfort a [Protestant] gentleman's family may live [in Ireland] and in far from its most favoured district, provided only they live there habitually, and do their duty as the friends and guardians of those among whom Providence has appointed their proper place. Here we found neither mud hovels nor naked poverty but snug cottages and smiling faces all around."[60] Miss Edgeworth herself was touchingly optimistic about the future, writing to an American friend in May 1825: "English capital, now overflowing, will flow over here, set industry in motion all over this country and induce habits of punctuality, order and economy. . . . Vast companies of men of science and commercial enterprise have been formed in England for working our mines, establishing manufactures—making canals—working slate quarries, mills etc, in Ireland. One of the companies begins its prospectus with these words: 'Our Capital is Two Millions.'"[61]

Alas, by the end of the year, all this was gone with the wind. The £2 million never materialized, nor did any other of the proposed English investments. Ireland, even more than Britain, sank into deep distress, as landlords ceased to spend freely and even raised rents and commerce went into sharp decline. The optimism disappeared. At the 1826 general election, O'Connell's new organization swept all before it at a trial run in Waterford. The peasant 40-shilling freehold voters, overwhelmingly Catholic, deserted governmental candidates in droves, not only in Waterford, but all over the country. Once the Irish Catholic tenantry stood united, shoulder to shoulder, landlordism as the electoral framework of the Ascendancy ceased to work. It was O'Connell's association and its Rent which brought this unity into existence. No movement of this kind, and certainly not on this scale, had ever before been launched in the British Isles or even in France. In the United States, it was still in embryonic form in 1826. It was at this point that O'Connell's repudiation of violence paid handsome dividends. Dublin Castle had no real answer to the man who played the constitutional game. O'Connell did not break the law, but he challenged it by exposing its basic inequity. His candidate at Waterford was necessarily a Protestant sympathizer, for a Catholic, being unable to take the oaths, could not occupy his seat in Parliament. But if a Catholic could not sit in Parliament, he could put up for it.

During 1827, as his movement grew, O'Connell determined to make the gesture himself. An opportune by-election vacancy in Clare the next year provided the opportunity. For the first time, O'Connell, as candidate, was able to put himself publicly and lawfully at the head of a mass movement. He began to address huge gatherings, which came not only from all over Clare but from all over Catholic Ireland. Later, in the early 1840s, one of them was to total over a million men, women and children—the largest political gathering, so far, in world history.[62] Those days were not yet, but the gatherings in Ireland during the Clare election were already vast. Much of the mobilizing was done by parish priests, who tore off their vestments at the end of mass and led their parishioners in demonstrating. For the final gathering for the vote, in June–July 1828, which took place in the county town, Ennis, each group of tenant farmers, sometimes 100 or 200 strong, marched from their landlords' estates in column, and when they reached the county town, solemnly and publicly repudiated their masters' instructions to vote for the Ascendancy candidate, Vesey Fitzgerald. Their solidarity was their strength. A landlord might kick out one tenant for disobedience, but he could not expel them all.

Moreover, all the 3,000 men who had the vote were accompanied by perhaps 10 times as many wives and children, friends and supporters. O'Connell had 150 priests in the town, plus his own lay militants, who saw to the housing and feeding of the throng and to their discipline, for it was vital that the law be kept and violence avoided. When the one pro-Ascendancy priest, Father John Coffey, was about to lead a group of tenants to vote for Fitzgerald, they were snatched away from him with the words, shouted out by an O'Connell priest, Father Murphy of Corofin: "Men, are ye going to betray your God and your country?" And at the entrance to the election booth itself, Fitzgerald's own tenants were marched into the O'Connell camp by a ferocious declaration from another nationalist priest, Father Tom McGuire: "Ye have heard the tones of the tempter and charmer, whose confederates have through all the ages joined the descendants of the Dane, the Norman and the Saxon in burning your churches, in levelling your altars, in slaughtering your clergy, in stamping out your religion. Let every renegade to his God and his country follow Vesey Fitzgerald, and let every true Catholic Irishman follow me."[63] When the polls closed, O'Connell led by 2,057 to 982, having secured 67 percent of the votes cast—by the standards of the early 19th century an overwhelming victory. As Fitzgerald put it, "I have polled all the gentry . . . to a man [but otherwise] the desertion has been universal." He was writing to Peel, who saw the event, quite rightly, as a watershed in history: "We were watching," he informed Sir Walter Scott, "the movements of tens of thousands of disciplined fanatics, abstaining from every excess and every indulgence, and concentrating every passion and feeling on one single object."[64] Here, indeed, was the demos taking the center stage of history, or as Shelley would no doubt have seen it, the Demogorgon emerging from its lair.

What was the British government to do, faced with this unmistakable breakdown in its system for ruling Ireland? In theory it was a strong government, particularly in terms of Irish policy. On 17 February 1827, Lord Liverpool, after 15 continuous years as Prime Minister, had suffered a debilitating stroke and had to retire. Some six weeks later, on 10 April, George Canning had formed a ministry of liberal Tories and moderate Whigs. His difficulties were enormous in view of the continuing economic recession and the gathering diplomatic crisis over Greece and Turkey, but it was the collapse of his health which wrecked his ministry. On 8 August he died, and after some maneuvering, George IV invited the discredited Fred Robinson, now Viscount Goderich, to form a ministry. He did so, but from the start, his government never worked. From early December various ministers, such as the Chancellor of the Exchequer, John Charles Herries, and William Huskisson, Secretary of State for the Colonies, were threatening to resign—Huskisson, put in, withdrew, and reproffered his resignation six times. By early January, the Treasury was without funds; no King's Speech had been prepared for the meeting of Parliament, due in 10 days' time, and Goderich was advised he stood in danger of impeachment unless he got things moving. On 8 January he went to the King and resigned, bursting into tears as he did so (George IV: "Here, take this handkerchief!"), though an equerry, to whom Goderich gave a lift in his coach back from Windsor to London, says he laughed as well as cried, and fell fast asleep when they reached Hounslow.[65] Thus "Prosperity"

Robinson achieved his tiny niche in history by becoming the first and so far the only Prime Minister never to have met Parliament—"a transient and embarrassed phantom," as Disraeli later called him.[66]

Disgusted with the liberal, or "wet" Tories, George IV turned (25 January) to the unbending or "dry" ones in the shape of Wellington and Peel. Wellington became Prime Minister, with Peel as his right-hand man in the Commons. This promised to be the strongest government since the Younger Pitt in his heyday. Disraeli recorded in *Sybil:* "The conviction that the Duke's government would only cease with the termination of his public career was so general that, the moment he was installed in office, the Whigs smiled on him; political conciliation became the slang of the day, and the fusion of parties the babble of clubs and the tattle of boudoirs."[67]

O'Connell, like Peel, realized a watershed had been passed. As he put it, immediately after the Clare by-election on 10 July 1828: "What is to be done with Ireland? What is to be done with the Catholics? One of two things. They must either crush us, or conciliate us. There is no going on as we are."[68] His somber belief was that with Wellington in power, the choice would be: crush. When Liverpool had his stroke, O'Connell had written to a colleague in alarm: "We are here in great affright at the idea of the Duke of Wellington being made Prime Minister. If so, all the horrors of actual massacre threaten us. That villain has neither heart nor head."[69] In fact, Wellington had both heart and head, and nothing was more likely to persuade him of the necessity for a timely concession than the lawful and emphatic expression of public opinion in Ireland—not the rabble, as he saw, but sober and industrious tenant farmers—which the Clare election constituted. The Duke, indeed, soon convinced himself that change must come; his problem was to convince his colleagues, especially Peel, and his sovereign. He worked on Peel through the summer and autumn and by November, Peel agreed to surrender a lifelong conviction. In his case, there was a personal sacrifice. He was member for Oxford University, next to the City of London and the County of York the most highly prized seat in the country. He felt he had no honorable alternative, having now decided to support Catholic Emancipation, but to resign it and seek reelection, in February 1829. Many Oxford dons, then as now, were attached to lost causes. Now it is Marxism; then it was exclusive Protestant privilege. They threw Peel out, and he was forced to take temporary refuge in a government borough.

In moving the Emancipation Bill through the Commons, Peel was adamant that he was doing the right thing, taking the occasion to state a philosophical doctrine which was to become of ever-growing importance as the 19th century ushered in the modern age. However attached a conservative statesman might be to a particular position, he argued, the need to maintain national order, impossible without a general consensus, was paramount. He would not admit, therefore, that his previous opposition to Emancipation was "unnatural or unreasonable." But nor was his decision to end such opposition. "I resign it, in consequence of the conviction it can no longer be advantageously maintained; from believing that there are not adequate materials or sufficient instruments for its effectual and permanent continuance. I yield, therefore, to a moral necessity which I cannot control, unwilling to push resistance to a point where it might endanger the Establishments which I wish to defend."[70] The King proved more difficult, partly because he kept changing his mind and retracting any agreement to submit to the Duke's earnest persuasions. But finally he yielded, remarking bitterly: "Arthur [the Duke of Wellington] is King of England, O'Connell is King of Ireland and I suppose I am Dean of Windsor."[71]

So the demos triumphed, and the Catholics got their rights. Britain was a liberal parliamentary regime under the rule of law and, once Clare had spoken, Emancipation was inevitable. The event was critical to Ireland, for it not only put O'Connell, with his matchless eloquence, into the Commons, but led, in time, to the creation of the Irish Parliamentary Party, to the Repeal and Home Rule movements, and finally to the creation of the Irish Free State in 1922. But it was central to Britain, too, for it set a key precedent, of government bowing to the clearly expressed will of a national majority, whether it had the vote or not, and so to parliamentary reform.

By the time O'Connell won the Clare election, General Jackson too was well on the way to harnessing the demos to his presidential chariot and sweeping triumphantly into Washington. As with O'Connell, the principal engine driving him to power was the expanding popular press. As far back as 31 July 1824, before he was even elected President, John Quincy Adams had complained in his diary: "There are eight or ten newspapers of extensive circulation published in various parts of the Union acting in close concert with each other and pouring forth continual streams of slander upon my character and reputation, public and private."[72] He soon had far more cause for complaint. Shortly after the "corrupt bargain" row began, Jackson, who advanced $3,000; Eaton, James K. Polk and other supporters amassed money to enable one of the General's favorite journalists, Duff Green, to buy out the old *Washington Gazette,* rename it the *United States Telegraph,* and turn it into the principal Jacksonian newspaper.[73] This paper became the model for all the Democrat papers, of which were there soon 50 throughout the country. The level of argument was no higher than that advanced by Fathers Murphy and McGuire at the Clare hustings. It was envenomed by a degree of personal abuse and malice which make present-day American elections seem tame. There was a particular concentration on what went on in the White House. This focus also was not entirely new. Monroe had made various efforts to make the presidential mansion more like the palace of a European head of state. He had the East Room, where Mrs. Adams, wife of the second president, had once hung out her washing to dry, furnished for the occasion of the marriage of his younger daughter. This action was resented, and when, in April 1824, it was revealed that the late Colonel Lane, Commissioner of Public Buildings, had embezzled several thousand dollars, Congress held an inquiry, and its chairman, Congressman John Cocke of Tennessee (a supporter of Jackson) summoned the President to answer questions. Monroe, Adams recorded in his diary, "desired the person who brought him the message to tell Cocke that he was a scoundrel, and that was the only answer he would give him."[74]

With Adams President, thanks to his "bargain," still more attention was focused on the mansion. A White House inventory revealed that it now contained a billiard table and a chess set. Both had been paid for, as it happened, out of Adams's own pocket. Nonetheless, Representative Samuel Carson of North Carolina, a Jacksonian, demanded to know by what right "the public money should be applied to the purchase of Gambling tables and Gambling furniture?"—a question quickly parroted in the *Telegraph* and its satellite journals.[75] For good measure, these journals added that Adams, who was now portrayed as a raffish fellow, instead of the grim stick he actually was, had pandered to the Tsar while ambassador in Saint Petersburg, by supplying him with a young American girl. Adams was referred to as "the pimp of the coalition."[76]

Jackson's opponents hit back just as hard. The *National Journal* asserted: "General Jackson's mother was a *Common Prostitute*, brought to this country by British soldiers! She afterwards married a *Mulatto Man,* with whom she had several children, of which number *General Jackson is one!*" When Jackson read this statement, he is said to have burst into tears, but he was still more upset by attacks on his wife and the validity of their marriage. These attacks could have led to murder. Criticism of Mrs. Jackson's chastity had started during the 1824 election. As early as 6 January 1825, the General had written to a friend, "with a pen that fairly stabbed the paper," that he was prepared to challenge her accusers to a duel: "I know how to defend her!"[77] Clay was thought to be behind these rumors, and Jackson's supporters swore revenge. One of Clay's Kentucky supporters warned him: "For God's sake be on your guard! A thousand desperadoes . . . would think it a most honourable service . . . to shoot you."[78] In fact Clay felt it necessary to fight over the "corrupt bargain" accusation when Senator Randolph accused Adams and himself of forming "the coalition of Blifil and Black George . . . the Puritan and the Black-leg." Randolph and Clay fought a duel on the banks of the Potomac, just where the Washington National Airport now lies. Neither was hurt, but Clay's bullet went through Randolph's coat (he bought the Senator a new one).

It is remarkable that Clay did not have to fight Jackson, too. In late 1826 Jackson's camp heard that an Englishman called Day, a former debt collector, now a private detective, had been in Nashville and Natchez gathering information about Mrs. Jackson's former and present marriages. His findings went to Charles Hammond, editor of the pro-Clay *Cincinatti Gazette*. "Do they dare to invoke *her sacred name?*" demanded the General. He wrote a passionate letter to his friend Sam Houston, who had recently, after practicing shooting under the General's approving eye at the Hermitage, killed a campaign opponent in a duel. "I have lately," he told Houston, "got an intimation of some of [Clay's] secret movements, which if I can reach with positive and responsible proof I will wield to his political and perhaps his actual destruction!"[79] The rumor about Mrs. Jackson finally got into print in an election handbill, whereupon Hammond felt justified in reprinting it, and it was printed again in Adams's paper, the *National Journal*. Jackson got a committee of 10 prominent men in the Nashville area to draw up a statement of the facts, accurate as far as can now be ascertained, and it filled 10 columns in the *Telegraph* and Jackson's nationwide press. Hammond replied with a pamphlet, *A View of General Jackson's Domestic Relations,* in which he asked: "Ought a convicted adulteress and her paramour husband to be placed in the highest offices of this land?" At this point, Jackson wrote a long, deliberately insulting letter to Clay which, if sent, would have resulted in a duel. But having got his feelings off his chest, he was persuaded by his friends, who knew that yet another duel would have been fatal to the General's electoral chances, to lock it in his desk. Instead, the *Telegraph* printed a report asserting that Mr. and Mrs. Adams had lived in sin together before they were married, adding for good measure that the President was an alcoholic and a sabbath breaker.[80]

*   *   *

The presidential campaign of 1828 was perhaps the most scurrilous in American history, certainly the most vicious up to that time. The "leak" made its first appearance. Adams complained: "I write few private letters. . . . I can never be sure of writing a line that will not some day be published by friend or foe. Nor can I write a sentence susceptible of an odious misconstruction but it will be seized upon and bandied about like a watchword for hatred and derision."[81] But in some ways the Adams camp was more unscrupulous than Jackson's. It was asserted, for instance, by Samuel Southard, a former senator from New Jersey and now Secretary of the Navy, that the victory at New Orleans was entirely due to Monroe, who had prevented Jackson from going absent without leave and ordered him to face the foe. Jackson wrote a letter delivered personally to Southard and told Houston: "I wish to put down that vile slander and expose the slanderer . . . and if such an order as alluded to is on file, the *villian* who has placed it there shall be unrobed while I am living and the nation advised of the Treachery and hypocrisy of their public functionaries."[82] Pamphlets attacking Jackson included one dealing with his purchases of slaves, calculated to go down well in antislavery New England, entitled *General Jackson's Negro Speculations, and his Traffic in Human Flesh, Examined and Established by Positive Proof*. A document which became still more notorious was the widely circulated and displayed Coffin Handbill, under the headline "Some Account of Some of the Bloody Deeds of General Jackson." It summoned up all the available ghosts to haunt Jackson's Macbeth, including his dueling victims, Arbuthnot, Ambrister, the six Tenessee militiamen executed in Alabama, and young John Woods. It was illustrated with coffins, 18 in all.[83] Harriet Martineau related that in New England, where the anti-Jackson propaganda was universally put about and generally believed, a schoolboy, asked by his teacher who killed Abel, replied, "General Jackson, ma'am."[84]

Gradually, however, the Jackson machine developed the capacity to respond quickly, calmly, and factually to attacks on the General and to get their answers printed in the press all over the Union. Indeed, having won the midterm elections and so deprived the administration of its majorities in both houses of Congress, the Jacksonian Democrats had clearly got the upper hand by the time the campaign began in earnest in 1828. They had, to put it bluntly, the more salable candidate. Such items as campaign badges and fancy party waistcoats had first made their appearance in 1824, but it was in 1828 that the real razzmatazz began. The Jackson campaign slogan was cleaning up Washington and stopping high government spending, but the real thrust was a combination of the General's reputation as a military hero and the slogan's mass presentation by a strong media force.

This media contingent was increasingly led by an exceptionally cunning journalist, Amos Kendall (1789–1869), editor of the *Argus of Western America,* who in 1827 had deserted Clay and joined the Democrats.[85] Jackson had long been known by his soldiers as Old Hickory, after what was generally thought to be the hardest wood in creation.[86] This nickname was now used, by Jackson's journalistic advisers, under Kendall's inspiration, as a kind of campaign symbol. "Hickory Clubs" were created all over the country. Hickory canes and hickory sticks were sold to Jackson's supporters and flourished at meetings. Hickory trees were planted in pro-Jackson districts of towns and cities, and hickory poles were erected in the villages—some were still standing in 1845. There were parades, barbecues, and street rallies. The beginning of election gimmickry included the first campaign song, *The Hunters of Kentucky,* which proved enormously successful. It told of the great victory of January 1815 and of "Packenham [sic]" and "his brags"—of how he and his men would rape the girls of New Orleans—the beautiful girls "of every hue" from "snowy white to sooty"—and of how Old Kentucky had frustrated his dastardly plans and killed him.[87]

The General himself made few campaign speeches. The aim of his minders was to keep him in the background, fearful that he might say something violent and indiscreet. In fact, the General was happy with these tactics. He argued that it was hard to "bear things with calmness and equanimity of temper," but that he could and did do so: "My political enemies have not judged of me rightly. They cannot provoke me to an act of rashness—should the uncircumcised philistines send forth their Goliath to destroy the liberty of the people & compel them to worship Mammon, they may find a David who trusts in the god of Abraham, Isaac and of Jacob, for when I fight, it is the battles of my country. I am calm & composed, trusting to the lord of hosts, I believe him just & therefore look forward to a time when retributive Justice will take place, & when Just atonement can be *required and enforced!*"[88] There is a good deal of evidence that Jackson could always keep his temper when required and that his rages were simulated to achieve his ends.[89]

Not only was the General an ideal candidate. He also had the ideal second in command in the shape of the small, fiercely energetic, dandified figure of Martin Van Buren (1782–1862), with his reddish-blonde hair, snuff-colored coat, white trousers, lace-tipped orange cravat, broad-brimmed beaver-fur hat, yellow gloves, and morocco shoes.[90] If Van Buren dressed as self-indulgently as the young Disraeli, he had something the latter never possessed: a modern-style political machine. With Van Buren, the age of American machine politics opens. By 1828 Van Buren was the most powerful man in New York State at a time when ambitious politicians hestitated between running for governor there and running for president in Washington. Van Buren came from the pure Dutch backwater of Kinderhook in Albany County, which Washington Irving used as the setting for his Rip Van Winkle stories. There were 17, including slaves, in the family (New York State did not complete Abolition till 1818) and little money, but Van Buren, while still a teenager, got a toehold in local politics as an articled clerk in a New York City law office.

Even in the early 19th century, New York politics were immensely complex and baffling to outsiders, but they were the very air Van Buren breathed. He grew up in them, during the long struggle between the great political adventurer Aaron Burr (1756–1836) and De Witt Clinton (1769–1828), the state's governor who built the Erie Canal. Both these men were innovators. Burr had turned an old Jeffersonian patriotic club, the Society of Saint Tammany, whose members met to drink, smoke and sing in an old shed, into the nucleus of a big-city political organization. Clinton invented the "spoils system," whereby an incoming governor turned out officeholders and rewarded his supporters with their jobs. Van Buren's contribution was to amalgamate the two, and he did so by switching his support from the declining Burr to the rising Clinton, then turning against Clinton and taking over as soon as he felt strong enough.[91]

Van Buren was the first political bureaucrat. He was a quiet-spoken man with no rhetorical gifts, but he had a subtle lawyer's mind and an immense capacity for hard work. He demonstrated, in his long struggle with Clinton, that the man who got the details right and controlled the best organization would win in the end. His Tammany men were called Bucktails by their enemies, a sneer at their rustic origins, but he taught them to be proud of the name and to wear the symbol in their hats, just as the Democrats later flaunted their symbolic donkey. Branching out from Tammany, he constructed an entire statewide system of the party. His main party newspapers in Albany, the state capital, and New York City, propagated the party line and supplied printed handbills and ballots for statewide distribution. The line was then repeated in the country newspapers, of which Van Buren controlled 50 by 1827. The line was set by the party elite, who consisted of lawyers and placemen. Even by the 1820s the United States, and especially New York, was a lawyers' paradise. Frequent sessions in New York's complex court system kept the lawyers moving. Van Buren used them as a communications artery to townships and villages even in remote parts of the state. Similarly, officeholders who were appointed by the governor's council were the basis for party pressure groups everywhere. Van Buren's own political views sprang from the nature of his organization. The party identity must be clear. Loyalty to majority vote in political councils must be absolute. All measures must be fully discussed and agreed on, and personal interests must be subordinated to those of the party. As his biographer put it: "Van Buren's ideas were innovative in that he identified all of the parts and integrated them into a unified political structure which, once it came into being, supplied its own momentumm and its own ideology, an organic mass responding to change yet usually under control."[92]

Was this new kind of political machine, then, totally amoral? Not exactly. Van Buren was always torn between high-mindedness and the political ruthlessness needed to make his machine effective. In 1816 he masterminded the crooked seating of a Republican from Ontario County long enough for him to take part in a critical vote. But he then wrote: "The case was in truth one of those abuses of power to which parties are subject, but which I am sure I could never again be induced to countenance."[93] When his Bucktails took over the state early in 1821, Van Buren conducted a massacre of officeholders at the council's first meeting. He had the Bucktails vote out of office 11 county sheriffs, the chief officers of the militia, the secretary of state, the attorney general, the comptroller and treasurer, the superintendent of common schools, and the mayors of New York and Albany. In subsequent weeks he combed through 6,000 minor posts, removing Federalists, Clintonians and even unreliable Bucktails. This proscription was unprecedented. It brought from Clinton, who had invented the system, howls of rage. He wrote to the Old Patroon, Stephen Van Rensselaer: "The whole state is alive for office and next week will exhibit a scene of office-hunting heretofore unknown in the annals of the community."[94] On the other hand, though Van Buren now had the power to smash it, he supported Clinton's great project of the Erie Canal because he thought it was in the interests of New York and the United States, despite the fact that the canal, triumphantly completed on 2 November 1825, enabled Clinton to regain the governorship.

The Erie Canal was important politically, as well as economically. To open it, the newly elected Governor Clinton went to Buffalo and embarked for eastern New York on the *Seneca Chief*, a special state steamboat decorated for the gala, followed by another, the *Young Lion of the West*. Both steamed majestically 400 miles downriver to Albany, taking several days, with cannon salutes at every lock and landing, the banks lined with farmers and townsmen. Then the nautical cortege moved into the Hudson River and journeyed on to New York City, where Clinton poured a symbolic keg of Lake Erie water into the Atlantic Ocean.[95] The canal, as Van Buren saw it, involved tens of thousands of jobs and countless contracts, all controlled by New York State and therefore at the disposal of its governing party machine. And that is the principal reason he threw his resources behind Jackson. Adams made it clear during his presidency that he was a big-government, big-federal-budget man, who believed that Washington should be the prime engine behind public works projects—roads, canals, ports, welfare services, education and culture: the infrastructure and the superstructure which would turn the increasingly wealthy United States into the greatest nation on Earth. Jackson hated such ideas because he associated big government with George III and colonial rule, and he believed that Adams and his elitist, East Coast allies would turn America into a tyranny run in the interests of landowners and bankers. Van Buren joined forces with Jackson not because he opposed such projects, but because he wanted them planned and carried through by the individual states and by the party machines which controlled them. As Senator for New York and campaigning for his seat again, he said in his 1827 acceptance speech: "It shall be my constant and zealous endeavour to protect the remaining rights reserved to the states by the Federal constitution and to restore those of which they have been divested by construction."[96]

Most of 1827 Van Buren spent building up the new Jackson Democratic party nationally, exercising prodigies of tact to win support from difficult men like Benton of Missouri, a great power in the West, and the great but bibulous orator John Randolph, who was often "exhilarated with toastwater." He traveled along poor roads in jolting carriages through Virginia; down to Georgia to conciliate old, sick Crawford; through North and South Carolina; and then back to Washington, commuting between there and Albany. Thus, for the first time, the Democratic "solid South" was brought into being. In February 1828 Clinton died of a heart attack, clearing the way for Van Buren to become Governor of New York State. Van Buren campaigned vigorously to keep the job. Indeed, he spent seven weeks in July and August electioneering in the sticky heat of grim new villages in upstate New York, carrying basic provisions with him in his carriage, for none were to be had, complaining of insects, humidity, and sudden storms which turned the tracks into marshes. He brought with him entire cartloads of posters, Jackson badges, bucktails to wear in hats, and hickory sticks. He was the first American politician to assemble a team of professional writers, not just for speeches but to be lent to newspapers to write election propaganda. Artists and writers who supported the Jackson campaign included Nathaniel Hawthorne; James Fenimore Cooper; the sculptor Horatio Greenough; the historian George Bancroft; William Cullen Bryant, then the leading American poet; and another well-known poet, William Leggett. Apart from Ralph Waldo Emerson, most of America's writers seem to have backed Jackson at this time. As Harriet Martineau put it, Jackson had the support of the underprivileged, the humanitarians, the careerists and "the men of genius."

In many other respects—and always excluding New England—the Jacksonians outgunned Adams, especially in New York. Adams wrote bitterly in his diary: "Van Buren is now the great electioneering manager for General Jackson [and] has improved as much in the art of electioneering upon Burr as the state of New York has grown in relative strength and importance in the Union."[97]

Thus America swung into its first modern election. Adams made a lackluster candidate and the times were against him. The crash of 1825–26 in Europe had hurt even America, isolated though it increasingly was from the storms and stresses of Europe by its own huge expansion inland. Cotton had been badly hit. The 1820s saw the first major strikes in the United States, culminating in a carpenters' strike in Philadelphia which led to the formation of the Mechanics Union of Trade Associations, the earliest American workers' federation covering an entire city.[98] Workingmen were as opposed to bankers as was Jackson himself. They hated being paid in bank notes. A particular grievance of theirs was that if an employer went bankrupt, they had no lien on him for wages, sometimes paid monthly or even semiannually. And the number of employers who went bankrupt was enormous. The *National Gazette* reported on 15 November 1827, that in New York alone there were 1,972 men in prison for debt, some for less than $3. These debtors were given neither food nor bedding, just a quart of soup every 24 hours. In the second half of the 1820s, it was estimated that the number of people who were imprisoned annually for debt in the United States reached 75,000.[99] Moreover, in the four years since the 1824 election, vast numbers of voters, many with little or no property, had been added to the electoral rolls. Most of these people, without quite knowing why, leaned toward Jackson, whom they saw as their champion. There were no real issues in 1828, but Jackson successfully identified Adams with the established order, with property, privilege and oligarchy. His victory was part of a much wider movement, a spirit of the age, which at the end of the 1820s, in Europe as well as America, was displacing those in possession.

This was the first popular presidential election. In Delaware and South Carolina the state legislatures chose the electors of the college, but in the other 22 states, they were selected by all the voters, who were roughly equivalent (except in Virginia, Louisiana, and Rhode Island) to the adult white male population. Thus, the demos came to America. A total of 1,155,340 white males voted, over 800,000 more than in 1824, and in all the circumstances Adams did well to get 508,064 suffrages, carrying the New England states, New Jersey and Delaware and getting a single college vote in Illinois and a majority in Maryland. Even in New York he got 16 out of 36 college votes, for Van Buren was only able to carry the state for Jackson, despite all his efforts, by a plurality of 5,000. That gave Adams a total of 83 electoral college votes. But Jackson took all the rest, 178, and his popular vote was 647,276.[100] There was also evidence that America was moving toward a national two-party system. In 1824 no one voted for Jackson in Massachussets, Connecticut, New Hampshire or Rhode Island, and no one voted for Adams in North Carolina or Kentucky. In 1828 there were substantial minorities in all the states. The vote, however, was decisive enough to send Jackson to the White House with a clear popular mandate and to end the old indirect, oligarchical system forever.

In those days voting for President started in September and ended in November, but the new incumbent did not take office until March. Jackson arrived in Washington on 11 February, a sad and bitter man. Early in December his wife had gone to Nashville to buy clothes suitable to her new position. While waiting, she picked up a campaign pamphlet defending her against charges of adultery and bigamy. Hitherto the General had concealed from her the true nature of the smear campaign waged against her honor, and the shock of grasping its enormities was too much. She took to her bed and died on 22 December. After her funeral, Jackson said grimly: "I pray God I may not be allowed to have enemies to punish. I can forgive all who have wronged me, but will have fervently to pray that I may have grace to enable me to forget or forgive any enemy who has ever maligned that blessed one who is now safe from all suffering and sorrow, whom they tried to put to shame for my sake!"[101]

Hence, Jackson came to Washington, putting up at Gadsby's, a widower. But he was not alone; from all over the 24 states, his followers congregated on the capital—a huge army, more than 10,000 strong, of the poor, the outlandish, the needy, the hopeful. Washington in the 1820s was by no means an elegant city. It was built on a swamp.

Two-foot snakes were liable to invade drawing rooms. Pennsylvania Avenue was not yet paved. In the dry season it was a dustbowl, in the wet season, "the mud is frightful and one sinks down above the ankles"; smart carriages deposited dressed-up ladies into quagmires.[102] But the city was stuffy in its own way, especially after four years of the saturnine presence of Adams. Now the Apostolic Succession of elite presidents had been ended and a man of the people had been chosen. Washington society was appalled as his followers crowded in, many in dirty leather clothes, "the inundation of the northern barbarians into Rome," as someone put it. Jacksonians drank the city dry of whiskey within days. The hotels tripled their prices, to $20 a week, and the invaders slept five to a bed, then on the floors, then spilled over into Georgetown and Alexandria, finally sleeping in the fields. "I never saw such a crowd here before," wrote Daniel Webster. "Persons have come 500 miles to see General Jackson and *they really seem to think the country has been rescued from some dreadful disaster.*"

But many had also come to demand jobs and besieged the General in Gadsby's; Jackson protested that he represented the people, not the party, as he put it. Clay, the retiring Secretary of State, joked sardonically about the moment "when the lank, lean, famished forms, from fen and forest and the four quarters of the Union, gathered together in the halls of patronage; or stealing by evening's twilight into the apartments of the President's mansion, cried out, with ghastly faces and in sepulchral tones, 'give us bread, give us Treasury pap, give us our reward!' "[103]

There was much ill-feeling. Jackson refused to call on Adams, blaming him for the slanders on his wife. As a result, Adams left the White House at 9 P.M. on 3 March and boycotted the inaugural the next day. Washington's population had doubled in size, and the inaugural itself was a demotic saturnalia, reminiscent of scenes from the early days of the French Revolution but enacted against a background of the strictest constitutional legality—Demogorgon tamed, as you might say, but not yet taught good manners. It was sunny and warm. The inauguration took place on the East Portico of the Capitol, and by 10 A.M., a vast crowd had assembled there, held back by a ship's cable. At 11 A.M., Jackson emerged from his hotel and, escorted by soldiers, walked to the Capitol in a shambling procession of New Orleans veterans and politicians, flanked by "hacks, gigs, sulkies, woodcarts and a Dutch waggon full of females." By the time he had walked up Pennsylvania Avenue, the Capitol was surrounded by 30,000 people. At noon, the marine band played *The President's March;* there was a 24-gun salute; and Jackson, according to one critical observer, Mrs. Margaret Bayard

Smith, "bowed low to the people in all their majesty." The new President had two pairs of spectacles, one on the top of his head and the other before his eyes, and read from a paper, but nobody could hear a word of the swearing in. Then he bowed to the mob again and mounted a white horse to ride to the presidential mansion. "Such a cortege as followed him," gasped Mrs. Smith, "country men, farmers, gentlemen mounted and dismounted, boys, women and children, black and white, carriages, waggons and carts all pursuing him."[104]

Suddenly, to the dismay of all the gentry watching from the balconies of their houses, it became obvious that this vast crowd was all going to enter the White House. To some, it seemed like the mob taking over the Tuileries; "raving democracy" would enter—without a formal invitation card—"the President's palace." One watching Supreme Court Justice said that those who poured into the building ranged from "the highest and most polished" to "the most vulgar and gross in the nation—the reign of *King Mob* seemed triumphant."[105] Soon the entire ground floor of the White House was crammed. Society ladies fainted, others grabbed what they could get. "It would have done Mr Wilberforce's heart good," wrote one present to Van Buren (who was still in New York), "to see a stout black wench eating a jelly with a gold spoon in the President's house."[106] Clothes were torn in the melee; barrels of orange punch were knocked over; men with muddy boots jumped on "damask satin-covered chairs," worth $150 each, to see better; and china and glassware "worth several thousand dollars" were smashed. To get rid of the mob, the White House servants took huge stocks of liquor onto the lawn, and the hoi polloi followed, "black, yellow and grey," wrote Van Buren's correspondent, "many of them fit subjects for a penitentiary." Jackson, sick of it all, climbed out by a rear window, went back to Gadsby's and ate a steak, already a prime symbol of American prosperity. He declined, being in mourning, to join 1,200 people at the ball that evening in Signor Carusi's Assembly Rooms—a more sedate affair since invitation was by ticket only. The scenes at the White House were the subject of much pious moralizing in Washington's many places of worship that Sunday. At the posh Unitarian church, the pastor preached indignantly from Luke 19:41: "Jesus beheld the city and wept over it."[107]

There was more weeping and gnashing of teeth over Washington jobs as Jackson men ousted the old guard. Mass firings and new appointments had long been the custom in Pennsylvania and other states, as well as in New York, but it was Jackson who first applied it to the federal government. One of Van Buren's sidekicks, Senator William L.

Marcy, told the Senate that such "removals" were part of the political process, adding "To the victors belong the spoils of the enemy." The term stuck, and Jackson will forever be associated with the spoils system at a national level. Mrs. Smith reported that with many leading officials about to be expelled, Washington was "gloomy—so many changes in society—so many families broken up—and those of the first distinction—drawing rooms now empty, dark, dismantled." Adams was outraged, recording in his diary on 27 April 1829: "The removals from office are continuing with great perseverance. The customs houses in Boston, Philadelphia and New York have been swept clear, also at Portsmouth, New Hampshire and New Orleans. The appointments are exclusively of violent partisans ánd every editor of a scurrilous and slanderous newspaper is provided for."[108] It is true that Jackson was the first president to appoint journalists to senior jobs—Amos Kendall, for instance, got a Treasury auditorship. But Jackson's defenders pointed out that the total number of men removed was not as great as his enemies claimed. Of 10,093 governmental appointees, 919 were removed in the first 18 months, but over the whole eight years of Jackson's presidency, only 10 percent of all officeholders were replaced and in most areas the majority of jobholders remained.[109] Many of those who were sacked were clearly unsuitable: 87 had jail records.

The Treasury, in particular, was deplorably ill-staffed. David Campbell, brother of the new Treasurer, reported: "a considerable number of the officers . . . are old men and drunkards. Harrison, the First Auditor, I have not yet seen sober."[110] Other old Treasury men were crooks. One of them fled and was caught, convicted and sentenced. Nine others were found to have embezzled, including Adams's friend Tobias Watkins, who stole $7,000. Within 18 months, Kendall and other nosy appointees discovered that $500,000 had been taken from the Treasury, apart from thefts involving army, navy and Indian contracts. The Register of the Treasury, Nourse, who had defaulted for $10,000, had been there since the Revolution and pleaded to be allowed to stay, on account of his age. Jackson: "Sir, I would turn out my own father under the same circumstances!" But in one case, he relented. At a White House reception, a sacked postmaster at Albany, who had fought under Washington, accosted Jackson and told him: "The politicians want to take my office from me and I have nothing else to live on." He began to take off his coat to show his wounds to the President, who said angrily, "Put on your coat at once, Sir!" But the next day he took the man's name off the sackings list: "Do you know that he carries a pound of British lead in his body?"[111]

Oddly enough, Van Buren, the spoils-system expert, had nothing to do with the early mass dismissals and appointments because he was not in Washington. Not until 14 February 1829 did Jackson send him a letter, asking him to become Secretary of State and urging him to get to Washington quickly for talks on matters "purtaining [*sic*] to the general interest of the country."[112] The letter took five days to reach Van Buren in New York, and it was some time before Van Buren could resign the governorship, settle his affairs there—handing over to his machine, known as "the Albany Regency"—and join Jackson. Once in Washington, he found that many disastrous decisions and appointments had already been taken. Van Buren had acquired an encyclopedic knowledge of political personalities, their virtues and defects, throughout the United States—rather like that possessed by Richard Nixon in our own time—and he could have saved the new President from many grievous errors. He was particularly upset that no cabinet post had been given to the powerful Virginians; indeed, one Jackson man, Thomas Richie, editor of the *Richmond Enquirer,* complained bitterly that federal jobs had gone to a score of partisan editors all over the country and that it was an attempt to subvert the press.

Van Buren was able to square Richie, but he failed to reverse the most disastrous appointment of all. This was the selection of Samuel Swartwout as collector of customs in the Port of New York, a post which involved handling more cash than any other on Earth—$15 million in 1829. Swartwout was an old crony of Aaron Burr; an enemy of Van Buren; and an adventurer well known for his improvidence, fast women, horses and stock market gambling. His sole claim to office was that he had backed Jackson in New York before Van Buren had. When the latter protested, the President said he could not now withdraw the offer. Van Buren's aide, Churchill C. Cambreleng, snorted: "If our collector is not a defaulter in four years I'll swallow the Treasury." So it proved. In due course, Swartwout fled to Europe, taking with him $1,222,705.09, the biggest official theft in U.S. history and worse than all the Adams administration's peculations put together.[113]

Equally serious, in the long run, was Jackson's failure to consult the shrewd Van Buren about cabinet appointments. As a result, the President put together a cabinet which, apart from Van Buren himself, was weak and inappropriate. Almost all its members had to be sacked within two years.[114] The worst move was Jackson's decision to make his old comrade and crony Major Eaton the new War Secretary. Van Buren had a low opinion of the Major; he thought him indiscreet and negligent, not a man to confide in: "Through his habitual carelessness about his letters one runs the risk of having one's highly confidential correspondence finding its way into one of the committee rooms [of

Congress] folded up in a petition on behalf of some good fellow who has no friend except the Major."[115] But a far more serious objection was the moral status of Peggy Timberlake, now Mrs. Eaton. Various old friends came to Jackson and begged him not to appoint Eaton for this reason alone. His response was to settle the matter by leaking the appointment to Duff Green, his pocket editor, who promptly published it in the *Telegraph*. The reason for Jackson's obduracy was that he held himself responsible for the marriage. Since Timberlake's death, which rumor held was suspicious, Eaton had been managing the widow's affairs, and rumor also held that they were cohabiting. Eaton had come to Jackson in 1828 and asked his advice. Jackson said: Marry her. So Eaton had proposed, and they planned to marry in spring 1829. Then suddenly, in November 1828, Jackson told them to marry straight away, and they did, on 1 January 1829.[116]

This imprudent appointment set in motion a chain of bizarre events which were to change permanently the way in which America governed itself. Amos Kendall, who dismissed the worst rumors against Mrs. Eaton as baseless, summed it all up when he said: "She is too forward in her manners." She was pert, egotistical, selfish, pushy and only 29. The other cabinet matrons, older and plainer, loathed her from the start. Disliking her, they were inclined to listen to rumors about her chastity and to cite her sexual behavior as their reason for cutting her. There was an ugly foretaste of things to come at the inaugural ball when some important ladies pointedly refused to sit with her. Once the administration moved into office, the rumor machine got busy with a vengeance. This situation was to be expected, since Jackson's own men had operated the first successful smear campaign in American history. This nasty event had occurred in 1827 when the *Telegraph* had published unpleasant innuendos against the Adamsite Speaker of the House, John W. Taylor (1784–1854). The worst Taylor appeared to have done was to make objectionable conversation to two ladies in the Washington–Baltimore stage, rather like Laurel and Hardy in *Way Out West*. But he was nonetheless ousted.[117] Mrs. Eaton, however, was accused of sleeping with 20 men, as well as Eaton, before their marriage. What made matters worse was that the most damaging rumors were circulated not by the administration's enemies, but by the wives of its senior members, who gave them substance by their behavior. If old Rachel Jackson had lived, she might have had the authority to push the wives into line or, more likely, the skill to dissuade Jackson from making the appointment in the first place. But her place as mistress of the White House was taken by the 20-year-old Emily Donelson, wife of Jackson's adopted son. Emily was used to running a big plantation establishment and had no difficulty bossing the White House with its 18 servants. But she loathed Peggy Eaton from the start and pronounced her as "held in too much abhorrence ever to be noticed."[118] So on this issue, Jackson was not even master in his own household.

The row was social and moral but it had growing political undertones. Van Buren quickly spotted that Jackson would never yield, and so he moved smartly into the pro-Eaton camp. He and the President took to taking long rides together, during which they mulled over everything, including the refusal of cabinet wives to be in the same room with Mrs. Eaton, let alone invite her to their houses. Mrs. Calhoun, wife of the Vice President, felt so strongly on the point that she refused for a time even to come to Washington. Van Buren was in no social difficulty because he was a widower and was happy to invite the Eatons to dinner. The British Minister, Sir Charles Vaughan, and the Russian Minister, Baron Krudener, were equally free to entertain the lady, being both bachelors. But various members of the cabinet were at the mercy of their wives, or said they were.

The Peggy Eaton row was the first good thing to happen to Adams since he lost the presidency, and he recorded gleefully in his diary that Samuel D. Ingham, the Treasury Secretary; John M. Berrien, the Attorney General; John Branch, the Navy Secretary; and Colonel Nathan Towson, the Paymaster General, had "given large evening parties, to which Mrs Eaton is not invited. On the other hand the President makes her doubly conspicuous by an overdisplay of notice. At the last drawing-room, the night before last, she had a crowd gathered round her, and was made the public gaze. But Mrs Donelson . . . held no conversation with her. The Administration party is slipped into a blue and green faction upon this point of morals. . . . Calhoun heads the moral party, Van Buren that of the frail sisterhood." He went on to relate that Van Buren spent three-quarters of an hour trying to persuade Mrs. Donelson to call on Mrs. Eaton, which she terminated with the words: "Mr Van Buren, I have always been taught that 'honesty is the best policy.' Upon which he immediately started up, took his hat, and departed."[119]

For once, Van Buren was at a loss how to cure what he called "the Eaton Malaria." No one had ever been a stronger believer in the conspiracy theory than had Jackson, and at first he concluded that the entire anti-Eaton camp was being orchestrated by Clay. But Emily Donelson told him she had never set eyes on Clay. She said she would, if forced, receive Mrs. Eaton, but on no account would call on her. She said she hated her "bad temper" and "meddlesome disposition"; her "society [was] too disagreeable to be endured." The cabinet wives, who also disclaimed knowledge of Clay, agreed. "The ladies here," wrote

Mrs. Donelson to Mary Coffee, daughter of Jackson's old comrade, "with one voice have determined not to visit her."[120] They called Mrs. Eaton "La Bellona," a term said to have disgusting implications in Italy. Mrs. Ingham was leader of the opposition. Jackson's first big formal cabinet dinner was a catastrophe, since the wives, led by Mrs. Ingham, refused to address a word to La Bellona. When Van Buren gave a similar dinner, Mesdames Ingham, Berrien, Branch and Barry (wife of the Postmaster General) refused to come, so a tearful Mrs. Eaton declined, too. The *Washington Journal,* noting that both Van Buren and Vaughan had broken the boycott, accused them of trying to force "an unworthy person" on pure Washington society. Madame Huygens, wife of the Dutch Minister, planned a dinner party without inviting Mrs. Eaton, or so it was alleged. The President promptly accused her of "conspiring" and threatened a big American-Dutch row. Mrs. Huygens denied it all. At this point Jackson read the riot act to three cabinet ministers: They *must* ask Mrs. Eaton to their wives' dinner parties.

By this time Jackson was beginning to switch the blame from Clay to a vague category he referred to in his letters as "villians." He also blamed "females with clergymen at their head" who thought they could settle "who shall & shall not come into society—and who shall be sacrificed by their secret slanders."[121] The clergymen concerned were the Rev. J. M. Campbell, Pastor of the Presbyterian church which Jackson often attended in Washington, and an old acquaintance, the Rev. Ezra Stile Ely of Philadelphia. Both believed the gossip—that Mrs. Eaton had been dissolute as a girl; that she had a miscarriage when her purser-husband had been at sea for a year; and that she and Eaton, long before they married, had traveled together. Jackson exchanged some remarkable letters with Ely on the subject. He had Campbell over to the White House several times to try to argue him out of his accusations. He spent immense amounts of his time engaging in amateur detective work, rummaging up "facts" to prove Mrs. Eaton's innocence, sending investigators to examine hotel registers and interviewing witnesses. At 7 P.M. on 10 September 1829, he summoned what must have been the oddest cabinet meeting in American history to consider what he termed Eaton's "alleged criminal intercourse with Mrs Timberlake." It was thought that Eaton himself should not attend, but Campbell and Ely were there. The meeting began with a furious exchange between the President and Campbell about the date of the supposed miscarriage— was it 1821 or 1826? There then followed a dispute about whether the Eatons had been seen in bed in a New York hotel or merely sitting on a bed. The cabinet sat in speechless embarrassment as the clergymen droned on, often interrupted by the General's exclamations—"By the

Eternal!" "She is as chaste as a virgin!" and so forth. Campbell refused to withdraw his accusation and finally rushed out of the room, swearing he would prove it in a court of law. The cabinet meeting then broke up.[122] Mrs. Eaton does not seem to have been particularly grateful to the President for his heroic, indeed preposterous, efforts on her behalf: She took them all for granted. She was not, indeed, an agreeable woman. Her black servant boy, Francis Hillery, later described her as "the most compleat Peaice of deception that ever god made, and as a mistres: it would be Cruelty to put a dum brute under her Command."[123]

Not all the President's men, however, nor the President himself, succeeded in clearing Mrs. Eaton's name, and she never established herself in Washington society. Her ultimate fate, in fact, was pitiful. When Eaton died in 1856, leaving her a wealthy widow—like most of Jackson's friends, including Van Buren, he had speculated successfully in land—she found herself an Italian dancing master, Antonio Buchignani, and married him. Buchignani not only defrauded her of her property, but ran off with her granddaughter. All the same, she left her mark on the way America is governed.

One of the most fascinating aspects of history is the way power shifts from formal institutions to informal ones, where it is really exercised. This happened in England, in the 17th and 18th centuries, when the decision-making process gradually moved from the Royal Council to the cabinet, originally a furtive and rather disreputable body. When the Americans set up their own government, they adopted the cabinet from Britain, though in strict constitutional terms they gave the institution little status. Nonetheless, it survived for the early generations after Independence, as part of the governing system, and it was still functioning effectively under John Quincy Adams. Jackson, however, was the first president to be elected by an overwhelming popular vote and this fact, in a sense, gave him an unprecedented mandate to exercise the truly awesome powers which the U.S. Constitution confers on its chief executive. From the outset of his tenure, an informal group of cronies had begun to confer with him in the White House. They included Donelson; Major Lewis; Isaac Hill, the former editor of the New Hampshire *Patriot;* and Amos Kendall, now working in the Treasury. This "kitchen cabinet," as its enemies called it, also included two members of the formal cabinet, Eaton and Van Buren.

Until the Mrs. Eaton affair proved insoluble, Jackson made some effort to have policy decided in the official cabinet. But he became increasingly convinced that the "conspiracy" against Mrs. Eaton and himself was a political, rather than a moral, one, and that the real "villians" were not two pettifogging clergymen but his own Vice President, John Calhoun, and his wife Floride. It is true that Floride was perhaps the most adamant of Mrs. Eaton's critics, but it is likely that the suspicions of plotting by Calhoun were first lodged in the President's mind by Van Buren, who not for nothing was known as "the little magician." Behind his spells was the deep, often hidden but steadily growing antagonism between North and South. Van Buren stood for the commercial supremacy of the North, Calhoun for an extreme version of states' rights, and it was not difficult for the Secretary of State to persuade his President that the notion of sovereignty being peddled by Calhoun was a mortal threat to the Union itself. What was more natural, then, than for Calhoun, leader of a much wider "conspiracy," to subvert Jackson's cabinet, using Mrs. Eaton as a pretext? This conclusion gradually formed in the President's mind. In April 1831, following a plan of Van Buren's, he acted: Van Buren resigned, to avoid any suspicion of partisanship, and almost all the other cabinet ministers were sacked, leaving Calhoun isolated for the rest of his term. Van Buren's reward was to be made heir apparent, getting the reversion first of the vice presidency (during Jackson's second term), then the presidency itself.[124]

In the meantime, power shifted steadily from the old cabinet to the new one. The new cabinet held no meetings. It had no agenda. Its membership varied. People thought its most important member was Kendall. Certainly, Kendall wrote Jackson's speeches. The General would lie on his bed, smoking and uttering thoughts. The ex-editor would then dress them up in presidential prose. The Jacksonian congressman Henry A. Wise termed him "the President's *thinking* machine, and his *writing* machine—aye, and his *lying* machine." Harriet Martineau, reporting Washington gossip, wrote: "He is supposed to be the moving spirit of the whole Administration; the thinker, planner and doer, but it is all in the dark . . . work is done, of goblin extent and with goblin speed, which makes men look about with a superstitious wonder; and the invisible Amos Kendall has the credit of it all."[125]

It is unlikely, however, that Kendall had the most influence on the President. Jackson listened more to Donelson (except about Mrs. Eaton), to Lewis and to Van Buren. But Kendall symbolized to observers what was happening to government. The old cabinet had been designed to represent interests from all over the Union. Its members were a cross section of America's ruling class, in so far as it had one—they were gentlemen. The kitchen cabinet, by contrast, brought into the exercise of power hitherto excluded classes, such as journalists.

Kendall despised the old society of Washington, trying to ape, as he saw it, London or Paris manners. He thought late dinner was "a ridiculous English custom." He disapproved of low-cut dresses for women. Drinking champagne, especially in the evening, was an abomination to him. The idea that men such as Kendall were now helping to rule the country horrified Adams and all who thought like him. But what could they do? It was the march of the masses. Jackson, by wooing them successfully, by conjuring them from out of the ground, not only set up a new political dynasty which was to last, with one or two intervals, almost up to the Civil War, but changed the power structure of America permanently. The kitchen cabinet, which proliferated in time into the present enormous White House bureaucracy and its associated agencies, was the product of the new accretion of presidential power made possible by the personal contract drawn up every four years between the President and the mass electorate. That a man like Kendall came to symbolize these new arrangements was appropriate, for if Jackson was the first man to sign the new contract of democracy, the press was instrumental in drawing it up.

The press, indeed, was the new dynamic force in the 1820s, setting the pace of political change in all the advanced societies. It was associated with the latest technology, a process begun in 1813 when John Walter of the London *Times* bought the first two double presses worked by steam. Not all proprietors favored steam. James Perry, the Aberdonian who owned the *Morning Chronicle,* when he learned what the machines cost, refused even to look at them, "alleging that he did not consider a newspaper worth as many years purchase as would equal the cost of the machine."[126] The print workers were also vehemently hostile. Though the manual labor involved in working the old newspaper handpress was so exhausting "that the stoutest constitutions fell a sacrifice to it in a few years," they would not have steam printing at any price, believing it would mean fewer jobs. To avoid their hostility, the workmen making the steam machines had to sign an agreement to forfeit £100 if they leaked the news. To avoid a strike and possible violence, Walter devised a strategy for introducing steam printing which in some ways anticipated Rupert Murdoch's when he introduced new computer technology in the 1980s and won "the Battle of Wapping." Walter made his plans in secret, smuggling the parts of the machines into Printing House Square and assembling them furtively. It was nearly two years before he could go ahead. Then, suddenly at 6 A.M. on 29 November 1814, Walter appeared among the print workers and announced: "The *Times* is already printed by steam!" He warned them that a force was standing by to suppress violence, but said he would pay their wages until they found alternative employment.[127] Thus, the steam era of newspapers opened, and all followed where the *Times* led, Perry included. Perry eventually made over 100,000 pounds from the *Chronicle,* one of the earliest media fortunes, of which there were soon many in the 1820s.

Even with steam printing, at 1,100 sheets an hour, sales were not enormous. A newspaper could survive on a circulation of 3,000–5,000 a day, which might rise to 10,000 for special events. Most newspapers were written for educated people. Even in the 1820s the *Times* continued to print the details of atrocious murders or sex crimes in Latin. But a popular press was emerging toward the end of the decade, when the publishing entrepreneur William Clowes opened a huge print works south of the Thames at Blackfriars, equipped with 20 large Applegart & Cowper steam presses. On these presses, he proceeded to print the *Penny Cyclopaedia,* which sold 75,000 copies of each issue, and the *Penny Magazine,* with a strongly scientific content, which sold 200,000. He was soon employing 500 men at his works, and one of his errand boys, John Parker, went on to create the Cambridge University Press.[128] Slowly, the modern newspaper was taking shape. In the early 1820s, Theodore Hook introduced the first true gossip column, "Sayings and Doings," in *John Bull.* With steam printing and regular deliveries, people found newspapers increasingly habit forming. "It is extraordinary," the painter Haydon noted in his diary (17 September 1827) "to what a pitch I long for the news of the day, knowing as I do the lies & the folly & the humbug of the daily surmises of the Editors, but so it is, and as I get older I find it increases. . . . I make more noise and disturbance if the *Times* is not on time, than if my Butcher had not sent my children's dinner!"[129]

What was also noticeable was the tendency of journalists to lean toward radicalism and against the established order, whatever it might be. As far back as 1809, Charles Long, MP, the Paymaster General, told Joseph Farington: "All the reporters of the debates in the House of Commons have a byass in favour of *opposition* even though they are employed by papers which profess to support government."[130] But there was nothing the politicians could do about it. Attempts to defy the press usually failed. Long liked to quote a saying of Edmund Burke's, that at the rate things were going, the press would soon be as important as Parliament. At one time a reporter who was seen taking notes in the Commons Gallery would have been ejected, said Long. Now, he told Farington, "the Reporters are admitted to a small room & are let into the gallery to take their places, where in making their notes they omit,

approve and disapprove as their disposition to party inclines them."
George Canning told Sir Thomas Lawrence that when William Windham, MP, attacked the parliamentary reporters, they abruptly stopped
publishing his speeches. As a result, said Canning, he was "very anxious
to appease them," and this had "caused much laughter" among other
Members.[131]

It was not long before Macaulay, referring to the parliamentary
gallery, coined the phrase "the Fourth Estate." The press was becoming
respectable as well as growing increasingly powerful. All kinds of people wrote for it, often secretly. Canning's journalistic activities were
well known, but Palmerston and even Peel contributed anonymously to
the progovernment newspaper, the *Courier*. John Wilson Croker, MP,
the Navy Secretary and another *Courier* contributor, told the Treasury
Secretary, Joe Planta, in 1829: "I have heretofore conveyed to the public
articles written by Prime and Cabinet Ministers, and sometimes have
composed such articles under their eye—they supplied the *fact,* and I
supplied the *tact.*" He advised Planta to do the same and added that he
"should throw in, here and there, such a slight mixture of error or
apparent ignorance, as should obviate suspicion of its coming from so
high a source."[132] These government leaks were, of course, balanced by
others. One of the clerks in the War Office, all of whom hated Palmerston, regularly transmitted embarrassing documents and facts to
Perry's *Morning Chronicle,* an opposition paper.[133]

If politicians increasingly wrote for the press and used it, so did
clergymen and even women. The Rev. Henry Bate Dudley, the Curate
of Hendon, edited the *Morning Post* and then started the *Morning
Herald,* which became the Regent's paper. In gratitude George made
Dudley a baronet and prebendary of Ely. Dudley also seems to have
been on close terms with Lady Hertford, once the Regent's Mistress,
and used her as a writer. In 1824 George IV told Wellington that "she
was the cleverest woman he ever knew in his life, and that all the *jeux
d'ésprit* in the the newspapers against the Opposition were her writing,
and that he had seen her write them and send them to . . . Dudley, who
was the person employed to insert them in the papers."[134]

Journalism, indeed, was often now well paid. Robert Southey made
a good living from occasional articles in the *Quarterly,* which paid him
£100 a time, a prodigious sum for the age (for purposes of comparison,
Peel's new police constables were paid £50 a year, a skilled artisan got
about £75 a year, and a sergeant major in the guards got £200 a year).
Even the young Thomas Babington Macaulay got £90 for a review, but
then he was worth it—he saved the *Edinburgh Review* in 1825 by his
vigorous polemics.[135] Journalism was, in fact, big business: In the 1820s

the *Times* paid £48,000 a year in stamp duty and £16,000 in advertisement tax. Yet the British were still ambivalent about the press (as they are to this day), reading it, needing it, but believing there was something disreputable about it. When the *Lancet* reported Sir Astley Cooper's lectures in 1823, the great surgeon complained he felt "disgraced and degraded" by his name appearing in the papers.[136] The hostility was social, and hypocritical. As Robert Stephen Rintoul, who founded the *Spectator* in 1828, put it: "Men who cannot breakfast without one, in the evening pretend to be hardly cognisant of such things. Men who in private life look to them almost for their sole stock of opinions are found in public sneering at their contents, thus despising that with which they are crammed to the very mouth."[137] His point was certainly sustained by the circulation figures and by the growing volume of advertising; by 1830 London alone supported nine dailies.

Yet it was also true, as the young William Makepeace Thackeray and Edward Bulwer Lytton complained, that in France journalists had a much higher social status than in Britain—probably higher than in America until Jackson arrived in the White House.[138] Indeed, in the Restoration, 1815–30, despite all the efforts to curb them, journalists probably exercised more power than in any other country. It was writers—journalists and historians, but, above all, journalist-historians—who destroyed the Bourbons in the 1820s. During these years, it has been said, "only a hyphen separates the journalist and the historian." August Thierry (1795–1856), historian of the Norman Conquest; François Guizot (1787–1874), who wrote at enormous length on French and European civilization and representative government; and François-Auguste Mignet (1796–1884), who is still read today, were all prolific and highly successful journalists, too. But it was Adolphe Thiers (1797–1877) who was the most significant example of the type. He was a tiny (five feet two inches) Provençal from Marseilles, born, as were so many in France, out of wedlock. His father then married his mother, but promptly disappeared for 25 years, returning in the end only for dollops of cash. So Thiers, like Victor Hugo, was brought up in a one-parent family by an adoring mother and grandmother. And, like William Wordsworth, he developed an extraordinary knack, all his life, of surrounding himself with women who worshipped him. He acquired as a mistress, and also as a third mother, Sophie Dosne, wife of a self-made property millionaire. She had two daughters, Elise and her pretty younger sister Felicité, who adored him. As soon as Elise was of age, he married her for her *dot*, acquiring Felicité for her looks as part of the bargain. He spent the rest of his life with the three of them, who formed, as one of his biographers put it, "*L'Administration, la Poupée, L'Admiration*—all he really wanted from women was an audience, a secretariat and a commissariat."[139]

Thiers's domestic arrangements are significant because they illustrate his mother's verdict that he was one of the cunningest men who ever lived. As she put it, "Anyone foolish enough to let him mount behind their carriage will soon find him sitting inside."[140] He was a fast, incessant talker and a fanatical worker. After attending one of Bonaparte's military *lycées*, he qualified as a lawyer and made his name, like Rousseau, by winning an essay prize. He was then taken on by the Duc de la Rochefoucauld as his secretary; and with contacts made in the Duke's circle, he hoisted himself aboard the *Constitutionel*, the liberal daily. *The Constitutionel* was the best-written and, together with the *Journal des Débats*, the widest-selling newspaper in France, with over 20,000 subscribers, one-fifth of the total sales of newspapers in Paris in 1826. Thiers showed himself a journalist of extraordinary versatility. He quickly became the most highly regarded political commentator in the country. He also wrote on the arts. At the salon of 1822, he spotted and promoted Eugène Delacroix, then 22 and 2 years his junior; made him famous; and helped convert him to liberalism. He always wrote favorably of Delacroix's major works, like the *Massacre of Chios,* and when he became minister of commerce and public works in 1830, he commissioned Delacroix to paint the murals in the Salon du Roi at the Palais Bourbon.

Thiers wrote brilliantly on the Spanish problem in the early 1820s, his articles later appearing in book form.[141] But he also wrote on financial matters, and in consequence got to know leading money men like Lafitte, Ternaux, Baron Louis and Delessert. These men arranged for him to have shares in the paper, and he joined its board, no mean step upwards. In the 1827 debate on the press laws, Casimir Perier stated that the receipts of the *Constitutionel* were currently 1,373,976 francs, out of which 450,000 francs went for the stamp tax, 102,000 francs for delivery costs, 394,000 francs for editorial and printing, leaving profits of 375,000 francs for its 10 shareholders and directors.[142] Through his financial articles Thiers also met Alexis-André Dosne: not only did Dosne's wife become Thiers's mistress but Dosne also lent him 100,000 francs (never repaid) to buy a big house on the Rue St. Georges and qualify as an elector. In the meantime, Thiers had established himself as a leading author by signing a lucrative contract with the *Constitutionel's* associated publishing house to produce a history of the French Revolution, something no one (Madame de Staël excepted) had yet dared to tackle. His *Histoire de la Revolution française,* which appeared in 10 volumes from 1823 to 1827, proved highly readable, made him famous and earned him a fortune.[143]

Thiers belonged to a group known as the *Idéologues,* who saw themselves as the natural successors to the Encyclopedists of the 18th century. They were middle class and proud of it, detested the ancien régime but deplored the excesses of the Revolution, repudiated Bonpartism, accepted the Charter but were suspicious of the Bourbons, and were supporters of parliamentary government without being democrats. Their model was Britain, which they saw as economically and militarily successful because it had the right system—a constitutional monarchy with the parliamentary right to change it if the monarch misbehaved. That was what the English had done in 1688, and the slogan "1688" was often used in France in the 1820s, especially by Thiers. As he put it, "It was not a popular rising which drove out the Stuarts, it was the aristocracy which deserted them." His message to the Bourbons was that they must observe the principle: *"Le Roi regne et ne gouverne pas."*

Representative government was a new idea in France. Chateaubriand was teaching it to the former émigrés and the country gentry, Benjamin Constant to the Imperialists, and Thiers aimed at the businessmen and the intellectuals of the younger generation.[144] Thiers thought that France would soon go the same way as Britain. The process had already started. Like so many of the philosophical-historical writers of the 1820s—Hegel being the outstanding example—he was a determinist. But he did not believe in inevitability. Rather, as he said in his history of the Revolution, "all is achieved by *entraînement"*—and that impulse was provided by writers like himself.[145]

When they returned, the Bourbons were well aware of the fragility of their regime and the need to win the battle of ideas. They started with the huge initial advantage that their government, in cultural matters, was extremely liberal by comparison with Bonaparte's. Whereas Bonaparte's censors had even cut lines from Corneille and Racine, the Bourbon press-and-publication policy, though it veered around considerably and in the end tried repression, was usually good to writers. Indeed, the years 1815–25 were a marvelous time to be a young writer in Paris, as the rapid launching of the careers of Hugo and Thiers testifies. Not only the writers but the workmen who printed their books stood shoulder to shoulder in favor of the Charter.

The Bourbons were given an early warning about the dangers of censorship in September 1816. In his memoirs, Guizot described what happened. Chateaubriand's *Of Monarchy According to the Charter* appeared that month. Its printer forgot or refused to deposit the statutory five copies at the Bureau for the Regulation of the Book Trade. On 18 September the police arrived at the printers to seize all the bound copies and unbound sheets and put seals on the formes of type. While they were so occupied, Chateaubriand arrived, in a foaming rage, and led a rush of "infuriated workmen." They broke the seals and recovered the formes, and (according to the police report) "they cried loudly and with a threatening air, 'Long live the liberty of the press!' 'Long live the King!' "[146] The warning was heeded. Louis XVIII, who did not mind being compared to Charles II, the English restorer of kingship, and, like that Merry Monarch, had no intention of "going on my travels again," was happy to woo writers rather than war with them.

In one way or another, the Restoration government spent enormous sums of money trying to create a cultural climate favorable to the regime. Newspapers were bought through intermediaries and subsidized. Important ministries usually owned or controlled a paper which presented the minister's views. Comte Jean-Baptiste Villèle, Prime Minister from 1822 to 1828, had three newspapers at his disposal: one for the Quai d'Orsay, another for the Interior Ministry and the third for the Finance Ministry. Their combined sales, however, were small, a mere 14,000 in Paris, while papers critical of the government sold 49,000.[147] At least three ministries, plus the Privy Purse, controlled by the King himself, offered pensions to writers. By 1823, Hugo, as an up-and-coming force—Louis XVIII read, encouraged and criticized his early works—was getting state pensions totaling 3,200 francs. Chateaubriand was sweetened by being made a Peer of France, Ambassador to London (1822) and Minister for Foreign Affairs (1823–24).

Even larger sums were spent on the positive promotion of the regime by the staging of fêtes, or public spectacles, and the lavish subsidy of the Comédie Française and the Opéra. The Opéra, the most important and expensive of the theaters, was closely identified with the prestige of the monarchy. Until 1824 it was under the direct supervision of the minister of the Royal Household, the Duc de Doubeauville, and was financed from the Civil List and from a special Fund for the Theaters. When the Duc withdrew, it passed to his son, Viscount Sosthènes de la Rochefoucauld, who was the biggest landowner in France and supplemented its huge expenditures from his own pocket. For its big productions, a great many state figures were involved. The *Architecte des menu plaisirs et dessinateur du cabinet de sa Majésté* was in overall control. Costumes and scenery came under the aegis of the state painter, Ciceri, who was given vast sums to achieve spectacular effects.[148] Men in high places paid great attention to details. Wellington was quite right in asserting that the underclothes of the Opéra's ballet dancers were a matter of concern to French governments. Rochefoucauld, or perhaps his Viscountess, thought them too scanty, and strove (though in vain) to get them reinforced. The Parisian authorities were not alone in this preoccupation. At La Scala in Milan, according to Captain Gronow, the Austrian Governor insisted that the dancers wear knee-length pantaloons of sky-blue color, "so tight that the outline of the figure was more apparent, and the effect produced more indelicate, than if the usual gauze inexpressibles had been worn."[149]

The Opéra was supposedly expected to pay its way, but, in practice, it served to make the regime seem splendid and conciliate its natural supporters. *Billets de faveur* were issued by the thousand, and there were *entrées de tolérance*. The doors were guarded by royal halberdiers, who kept unsuitable-looking people out, whether or not they had paid, and let grand people in, often for nothing. Gentlemen of the Chambers, *fonctionaires* of the Civil List, senior members of the Garde Nationale and the Tuileries police could always get in free, wearing their smart uniforms. For the first three performances of a new production, the house was completely "papered." If you belonged to the *beau monde* and dressed well you never needed to pay for your seat at the Opéra.[150] The object was to put on a show in which the audience was as important as the performance, to make the regime seem established, eternal, secure. The operas themselves were spectacles, rather than great art, with stories based mainly on classical mythology, and music by Niccolò Piccinni, Christoph Gluck and A.M.G. Sacchini.

On 16 September 1824, the huge, immobile form of Louis XVIII breathed its last, and his younger brother, now 66, became King as Charles X. Charles was universally suspected of holding reactionary views, but in many ways he seemed better equipped than his brother to run a monarchy that depended for its survival on putting on a good appearance. He was good-looking, slim, and did not stuff himself with rich food and wine (four bottles a dinner) like Louis. Whereas Louis had to be, literally, carried into his capital, like an ikon, Charles rode into it on horseback. His friends put it about that he had not had a mistress since 1804. His manners were excellent. Wellington, who knew both men well, thought him more intelligent than his brother. The new King certainly did his best to impress the nation with traditional splendor. Louis had never been formally crowned. In fact, there had been no coronation in France since 1775. On 6 October 1793, the National Convention had deliberately destroyed the vial containing the special coronation chrism, the Holy Oil of Rheims, which had been delivered to Saint Remi by a dove from heaven in the time of King Clovis

(466–511). So how could the divine right be conferred? Charles, however, had been impressed by George IV's stage management of his elaborate coronation in 1821 and was determined to do even better. The Archbishop of Rheims duly announced that some of the precious oil had been miraculously saved in 1793, secretly kept, and would now be used. He was supported by Chateaubriand, who wrote a pamphlet, *Le Roi est meurt, vive le Roi!,* insisting that a coronation was essential to sanctify the regime.[151]

The event was made into a festival of the arts, as well as politics and religion. Gioacchino Rossini was hired to write an elaborate new opera, *Il Viaggio de Rheims,* which celebrated Charles's solemn progress toward his coronation city and was a satirical interpretation of Madame de Staël's famous romantic novel, *Corinne.* The best singers in Europe, Pasta, Levasseur, Donzelli and Pellegrini, were hired to perform it at a special royal gala, which was a huge success.[152] In preparation for the ceremony itself, honors were showered on writers. Lamartine and Hugo were made chevaliers of the Légion d'Honneur and were invited to attend. Hugo decided to go; bought himself knee breeches, silk stockings, a sword and buckled shoes; and drove to Rheims in a cabriolet hired for 10 francs a day. The day before the actual ceremony, which was on 29 May 1825, Hugo, who had been inspired with a passion for Gothic architecture by Chateaubriand, went all over the great cathedral, and that evening, in his hotel, he read *King John,* his first discovery of Shakespeare and an important event in his literary life.

Charles X had been determined that everything should be done in medieval fashion, so he had preceded the event by a ritual three weeks' hunting in the forests, then was nearly killed in a carriage accident when a gun salute frightened the horses. The service itself, however, passed without untoward incident. The regalia, created specially by the first craftsmen of Europe, was embellished with 68,812 precious stones, at a cost of 21 million francs. When the King entered Rheims, he was presented with the city's traditional gifts: champagne and Rousselet pears. He then ordered the release of 50 prisoners. The doors of the cathedral opened at 6 A.M., and the ceremony began an hour later. Bonapartist marshals like Soult and Jourdan had roles to play, incongruously some thought. For the anointing with the Holy Oil of Rheims, Charles lay flat on the ground in a white satin garment, in which were seven openings so that the oil could be inserted in all the orifices of his body. The service ended soon after noon, and the next day the Chief Royal Physician lined up 121 victims of scrofula. Charles, now the Lord's anointed, "touched" each of them, saying the ancient words: "The King touches you, God cure you." Hugo rather enjoyed all this spectacle, but he then ran into Chateaubriand and was treated to a furious denunciation of the vulgarity and elaboration of the event: "I should have interpreted the coronation very differently," thundered the sage. "I would have had the church undraped and bare; the King on horseback; two books displayed open—the Charter and the Gospels— religion linked with liberty!"[153]

Chateaubriand's disapproval was characteristic of the ill-success which met Charles X's cultural policy. The truth is, the tide was changing. The medievalism which was fashionable in the decade 1815–25 was yielding to a wilder form of romanticism. One sign of the times was the changed French attitude toward Shakespeare. When a British troupe had presented a season of Shakespeare in Paris in 1822, the season had been a disaster. It was denounced as an "aide de camp de Wellington" and "an invasion." There were riots. Performances were hissed. Actresses, when curtsying, were injured by viciously thrown coins. When Desdemona lay on her couch, a voice shouted, "Where's the chamberpot?" Then, in 1825, opinion began to shift. Hugo's enthusiastic discovery of Shakespeare was a sign of the times—he always had a sharp nose for the latest cultural trend. Another enthusiastic promoter of Shakespeare was a clever young medical student from Boulogne, Charles-Augustin Sainte-Beuve (1804–69), who was in Paris by 1825 writing for the new and radical *Globe*. Even more important was Stendhal (or Henri Beyle, to give his real name 1783–1842), from Grenoble, who was so outraged by the hostility to the English troupe that he published *Racine et Shakespeare* (1823), a furious defense of romanticism, which he defined as "the art of presenting to people the works that, in the actual state of their beliefs, give them the greatest pleasure." This was to endow romanticism with something it had not possessed before, a political ideology which fitted in well with the new liberalism of the mid-1820s. When the English actors returned with Shakespeare in 1827—*Hamlet* and *Romeo and Juliet*—but also Sheridan's *The Rivals,* all done in English, they got an enthusiastic reception. Kemble's performance as Hamlet, the quintessential brooding romantic hero, as the French saw him, was hailed a triumph, but the real star of the play was the Ophelia of the beautiful Harriet Smithson, aged 27, tall, blue-eyed and with a thrilling voice. Her Irish accent was a handicap with London audiences, but the French were unaware of it. Her mad scene was a sensational success: Audiences wept and howled with emotion. Delacroix, Hugo, Alfred-Victor de Vigny, Alexandre Dumas and Sainte-Beuve all raved about the girl. This new world of Shakespeare, wrote Dumas, "has the freshness of Adam's first sight of Eden."

One who was overwhelmed by *Hamlet* was the young Hector Berlioz (1803–69). Like Stendhal, Berlioz came from Grenoble and had fled to Paris to escape the dull household of his doctor father and his mother's puritanical belief that all musicians were automatically sent to Hell.[154] After seeing the play, he recorded: "I had to acknowledge the only dramatic truth . . . the pitiable narrowness of our own poetics, decreed by pedagogues and obscurantist monks. I saw, understood and felt that I was alive, and that I must 'arise and walk.' "[155] Equally important, he fell in love with Harriet Smithson, and eventually—after many romantic turmoils—married her.

Berlioz personified the reasons that Charles X's cultural policy would not work. He was typical of the new, middle-class, highly intellectual professional musicians, not content to just to play and compose, but needing to understand and create, destroy and rebuild. He was a brilliant instrumentalist, especially on the guitar (like Karl Maria von Weber and Niccolò Paganini), but also on the flute and clarinet. When he got to Paris, he became a musical journalist and musicologist, as well as a performer-composer. He studied the scores of the classics in the Royal Conservatoire Library, and when he attended a performance in which unauthorized changes in instrumentation were made, he would rise from the pit like an avenging angel and shout: "Where are the trombones?" or "It's a piccolo, scoundrel!" He badgered Rochefoucauld to give him facilities to perform the grandiose works he was already composing and imagining, including a mass which he finally put on in the church of Saint Roch, famous as the place outside which Bonaparte gave the mob its "whiff of grapeshot." It went down well. Berlioz records that afterwards he met "August" (after the Emperor Augustus), who was the boss of one of the main theater claques, known as "the Romans" (because they decided the fate of gladiators). Auguste: "Why didn't you tell us you made your début at St Roch's the other day? We'd have gone in a body." Berlioz: "I didn't know you were so fond of religious music." Auguste: "We don't like it at all. But we would have warmed up your audience." Berlioz: "How? You can't applaud in a church." Auguste: "No—but you can cough, blow your nose, move your chair, scrape your feet, hum, lift your eyes up to Heaven—all the tricks. We could have given you a real success, just like a fashionable preacher."[156]

These claques spread over Paris like the plague in the 1820s. Some were mercenary. Others were ideological. But both types were increasingly hostile to the old, the conservative, the royalist. One object of their hatred, and Berlioz's, was Salvatore Cherubini (1760–1842), now in his late sixties, an archconservative who had been boss of the Conservatoire as long as anyone could remember, serving all regimes. Cherubini had a face like a gallows and was reputed to be the rudest man in Europe, the list of those he insulted ranging from Berlioz himself to Franz Liszt and César Franck. When the father of Adolphe Adam presented him as a baby, Cherubini's only response was, "What an ugly child!" When a famous violinist died, he said: "Small tone, small tone!" He loathed Beethoven and pronounced Bach's harmonies "barbarous." It was typical of the muddles of the state's cultural policy that Berlioz, a most persistent and importunate young man—as Harriet Smithson discovered—was able to get his way by setting Rochefoucauld against Cherubini.

In 1828, much to Cherubini's disgust, a ministerial decree established the Société des Concerts du Conservatoire, to give regular concerts of serious music, with a specific mandate to perform the works or new or neglected composers. This move was an excellent example of the way in which Charles X's cultural gestures proved counterproductive. The first season, under Francis Haberneck (1781–1849), one of the last of the violin-conductors and a passionate Beethovian, opened with well-rehearsed and brilliantly played performances of Beethoven's Third, Fifth and Seventh Symphonies. The old monster had died the year before, hallowed in Vienna and London, but still little known in Paris. The series had a sensational success with Parisian audiences, akin to the Shakespeare revival of 1827, reinforcing it and adding yet more dynamism to the the process which was politicizing romanticism. Were not Beethoven's symphonies revolutionary music, just as Shakespeare's drama was revolutionary poetry?[157]

This combination of forces began to have an increasing effect on official culture, pushing it toward novelty, radicalism and what contemporaries saw as realism. There was a growing demand for artists to get away from classic myths and to take on topical subjects, which were "significant" and often had a political "message." Just as Géricault's *Le Radeau de la Méduse* and Delacroix's *Massacre de Chios* dealt with the events of the day, so theater turned to issues. The movement began in the commercial boulevard theaters, proved popular, spread to the Comédie Française, and finally lapped at the foundations of the Opéra itself, the very citadel of Bourbon culture.[158]

The first sign that the Opéra was "going modern," albeit initially in a purely nonpolitical way, appeared in 1822 with Ciceri's big illusionist production of *Aladdin* (by Nicole and Benincori), using gas lighting, diorama and other scientific techniques supplied by his partner Louis-Jacques Daguerre. This production was followed in 1824 by a production of Weber's *Der Freischutz*, which was a huge success, though the score and text were much messed up. The watershed year was 1825, when documents in the Opéra's archives reveal the result of "modernist" pressure on staging, singing, music, artists, acting styles and costumes, as well as on the subject matter.[159] Then, in October 1826, with deliberate relevance to the struggle in Greece to throw off Turkish rule, came a production of Rossini's version of *Le Siège de Corinth,* about the Greek-Turkish war of 1459. Its success encouraged further and more daring innovation.

It has to be understood that a censorship of sorts operated throughout these years, but it was not difficult to fox it. A version of the first popular revolt in Naples had been done in 1825 on the boulevards and in 1826 at the *Opéra Comique,* in a libretto by Lafontelle and Moreau with music by Carafa. Performance of the second version had been allowed only after six series of changes following the censor's objections, but it was a smash hit, and many of its songs became popular airs. As a result, the playwright Augustin-Eugène Scribe (1791–1861) and the composer Daniel-François Auber (1782–1871) conceived the idea of yet another version, this time a sophisticated, "serious" one, for the Opéra. Scribe cleverly cooked the plot to get round the censors. The device of the dumb girl; the fact that the revolutionary leader was not only killed but seen to be killed by a wicked, undisciplined mob; the presence of an angry Vesuvius as symbol of divine retribution on the mob—these concealed both from the Opéra's own examining body of writers and musicians and the censors the real radical thrust of *La Muette de Portici.* No text was ever gone over more carefully, but all that the censors asked to be removed were a few phrases: *il faut armer le peuple, le people est maître, votre reine est à vos genoux,* and so forth.[160] Once the text was cleared, the immense resources of the Opéra were devoted to a spectacular production. The censors thought Auber's music was too highbrow to be popular, but they did not foresee Ciceri's brilliantly realistic sets, which permitted immense and dramatic crowd scenes, or the costumes, which drew sharp class distinctions and gave the production a flavor of class warfare. To top it all, the production team was sent to La Scala to study its famous volcano machinery, and the Vesuvius explosion alone would have sold out the house.

The first night, 29 February 1828 (it was a leap year) proved a popular success of a kind the Opéra had never known. By an odd coincidence, no prince from the reigning family was present, but Louis-Philippe, the Duc d'Orléans and his entourage were there in strength. Sensing something was afoot, an immense crowd had gathered outside the theater, which gave added relish to the scenes enacted within. The rumor spread that the regime had forced upon Scribe the ending—the triumph of reaction, rather than of the mob. The applause was thus not a response to the tragedy, but solidarity with the mob on stage. It was, in short, a highly subversive opera, duly denounced in the progovernment *Moniteur Universel* of 2 March. But by that time its success was so marked that ministers had no alternative but to let it run for 100 performances. They then set up a new committee of surveillance at the Opéra, but it was too late. The public had learned how to "read" musical drama politically, and the barcarolle-choruses of *La Muette* were already being sung everywhere. When a gala performance was given for the visiting King of Naples on 3 May 1830—an odd choice of piece, you might think—the Duc d'Orléans remarked: "It is we who are dancing on a volcano."[161]

Hence the demos, which was sweeping the United States in 1828, came to Paris the same year via grand opera. Worse was to come for the Bourbons. Their white knight, Victor Hugo, not only deserted them, but placed himself at the head of their enemies. Having discovered Shakespeare, he wrote in his new, wilder mood a poetic and revolutionary drama, *Cromwell*. He gave a full reading of it on 12 March 1827, in front of a select few, including his new young friend Sainte-Beuve. The next day Sainte-Beuve, who was to become perhaps the greatest literary critic of the 19th century, wrote him an immensely long and constructively critical letter. As a result, Hugo published the play with a preface, in which he effectively assumed the leadership of French romanticism. The preface had a terrific impact on young people, belaboring them with Manichean dualism, reflected in Hugo's own brilliant black-and-white wash drawings.[162]

A few weeks later, there was a scandal at the Austrian embassy in Paris. Some Bonapartist guests gave their names under the titles the *Empéreur* had awarded them: the Duc de Tarante, the Duc de Dalmatie, the Duc de Trévise and the Duc de Reggio. The majordomo, under instruction, perhaps from Metternich, perhaps from the Quai d'Orsay, shouted them out as Marshal Macdonald, Marshal Soult, Marshal Mortier and Marshal Oudinot. Such an episode would have aroused laughter in London, where a dual aristocracy was unknown, and plain incomprehension in Washington. But in Paris it was dynamite. In its own way it was the French equivalent of the Mrs. Eaton scandal. The marshals immediately called for their carriages and left, swords clinking, boots stamping angrily down the embassy stairs. Hugo, outraged, rushed for pen and paper and produced his famous *Ode de la colonne*. This ode, plus the preface to *Cromwell*, made him the idol of Young

France. The Ode was reviewed with enthusiasm by Sainte-Beuve, and that sealed their friendship.

The young critic moved to 19 rue Notre-Dame-des-Champs. It was almost next door to Number 11, where Hugo lived in a quiet and beautiful house, with a large, romantic garden and lake, spanned by a rustic bridge, with open country and windmills beyond. There, he and his wife Adèle gathered about them all the clever young men, who by 1829 were already calling Hugo *Maître* (he was 27). Adèle was always pregnant or recovering from childbirth, otherwise neglected, and it did not take Sainte-Beuve long to fall in love with her. The once-censorious Hugo was now discovering sex, as well as radical politics—the two were connected in his mind—and commenced a long career of promiscuity which lasted into his eighties. He was now rich, immensely fit—he had "sharks' teeth which could crunch a peach-stone"—and roaring for action. Sainte-Beuve, though two years younger, was his political mentor. Alfred de Vigny noted sadly in his journal, on 23 May 1829, that Hugo "was with Sainte-Beuve, a small, rather ugly man with a commonplace appearance and a back that is more than bent, who when he talks pulls obsequious and flattering grimaces like an old woman. . . . Victor Hugo is dominated politically by this clever young man who has succeeded . . . in making him completely and quite suddenly change all his opinions. . . . He has just told me that on thinking things over he has decided to leave the Right. . . . The Victor whom I loved is no more. *That* Victor was a bit of a fanatic for religion and royalism, as chaste as a young girl . . . it suited him and we liked him as he was. Now he has taken a fancy to bawdy talk and has become a liberal. . . . He began life as a mature man, and is only now entering on adolescence."[163]

Just over six weeks later, on 10 July 1829, Hugo read to a group at his house the text of his new drama, *Marion de Lorme,* set in the reign of Louis XIII. Those listening included De Vigny and his enemy Sainte-Beuve; Dumas; Alfred De Musset; the 30-year-old Honoré Balzac, who had just written *Les Chouans,* his first success; Prosper Merimée; the poet Emile Deschamps and the critic François Villemain. There were many interjections and ecstatic outbursts, and when Hugo finished, Dumas "waved his arms in a frenzy of enthusiasm . . . he seized the poet and, lifting him off his feet with a Herculean effort, shouted 'We will carry you to glory!' " The eyewitness added: "I can still see the immense Dumas stuffing himself with cakes and roaring out, with his mouth full, *'Superbe! Superbe!.'* "[164] However, when the play was read by the censors, they turned it down flat. The issue was taken before the Prime Minister, now the Vicomte de Martignac, a more liberal man than

Villèle. But even he thought the portrait of Louis XIII was "a threat to the monarchy." An angry Hugo appealed to Charles himself, and it says a lot for the value attached to the approval of intellectuals that the King gave the poet an immediate audience. Having read the script, he upheld the censorship but offered Hugo yet another pension as a *douceur*. Hugo turned it down with indignation, went home and immediately began work on a new drama, which was to become *Hernani,* the most notorious play of the 19th century. *Hernani* was begun on 29 August and finished fewer than four weeks later on 25 September. The Comédie Française accepted it for immediate production on 5 October, giving it priority over De Vigny's *Le More de Venise* to punish him for his arrogant behavior at the rehearsals. But Hugo would not hear of it: He knew he was approaching the biggest test of his life and he did not want any more enemies than were necessary. Besides, he needed to prepare his forces for the opening night, finally set for 25 February 1830.

Hernani was the first modern play, a fighting text symbolizing a cultural conflict which is still being fiercely waged today: between youth and age, freedom and convention, breaking the rules and upholding them, between innovative extremism and artistic tradition, the avant-garde and the canonical. Its preposterous plot, ending in the joint suicide by poison of Hernani and his heroine, Dona Sol, does involve wicked behavior by a king, but the impact of the play was not directly political. The play outraged conservatives because it assaulted their notions of cultural rectitude. It used ordinary language. It exhibited crude passions. People were killed, and died, on stage. To us it seems unbelievable melodrama. To the young in 1830, it brought to the stage a new and thrilling note of realism: This was life as it actually was, shorn of stupifying theatrical conventions going back to the Renaissance.[165]

Having chosen his battlefield, Hugo had no intention of fighting fair. Where his artistic aims were at stake, he was totally unscrupulous, thus setting a pattern for the future: that art is more important than fusty notions of right and wrong. During rehearsals, he deprived the hitherto all-powerful Mademoiselle Mars of the part of Dona Sol because he thought she lacked commitment to the new movement. More important, he did not hesitate to engage in cultural terrorism to ensure the play an enthusiastic reception, employing all the ruffianism of the claque system on an unprecedented scale. The premiere was dominated by his own army. Its commander was the 22-year-old poet Gérard de Nerval, another doctor's son, a wild and dangerous youth who was to become insane and hang himself 11 years later. De Nerval assembled a strong-arm claque of students from the Beaux Arts, the Polytechnique and other colleges. What better, said Hugo, than to "set waving locks against the bald-pates, the future against the past?" Adèle Hugo, who had her own bodyguard of bearded young men, studied plans of the auditorium and the door exits, to get the tactical details right. On 25 February Sainte-Beuve and Hugo were at the theater eight hours before the curtain went up, to watch their men filing in and taking up stations. They had special red tickets marked *Hiero*—from the war cry of the fanatical Muslim Almogavares, *Hiero despierta te*—"Steel flash forth." Hugo called them his Ironsides. When the usual bourgeois and upper-class patrons filed into the stalls and boxes, they were horrified by the long and spiky haircuts of the students and by the grotesque garments of some of Hugo's friends—Théophile Gautier was sporting a rose-red doublet, sea-green trousers and a blue dress coat with black velvet facings. From the gods came the menacing cry of the young, "Off with the heads of the baldies!" Uncommitted theatergoers found that anything other than applause or noises of approval was not tolerated, and if they hissed or merely sat on their hands, they were liable to get their faces slapped—a serious business in 1820s Paris, where it was grounds for a duel. There was, too, a faint whiff of money about it all. During the interval, on the pavement outside, a leading publisher, Mame, offered Hugo 5,000 francs for the first book rights and actually produced some 1,000-franc notes, which the poet pocketed.

Afterwards, the Hugoans met at the offices of their paper, the *Globe,* and decided to publish not so much a laudatory notice as "a victory bulletin." Later performances were organized in the same way. In a letter written at the end of the first week of March, Sainte-Beuve reported; "The first three performances, supported by friends and the *romantic* section of the audience, went off very well. The fourth was stormy, though victory went to our tough lads. . . . The receipts are excellent and with a little more help from our friends the Cape of Good Hope is almost rounded." The *National,* the new liberal paper founded by Thiers a month earlier, objected, however, not so much to the play as to Hugo's thugs—"neither restraint nor common decency." One of the actors complained in his journal: "Unashamed log-rolling . . . high-born women taking part . . . Theatre always full and always the same row, which does no good to anyone except the box-office." The commercial success was enormous, but some literary men, such as Turquety, were contemptuous of Hugo's self-publicizing: "He flies into a rage whenever anything critical appears in print and . . . has threatened to thrash the theatre-critic [of the *Quotidienne*] without mercy. . . . He now looks upon himself as a man in a great official position."[166]

By the time *Hernani* had triumphed at the box office, Charles X's regime was clearly heading into a crisis. There was violence in the air. Two weeks before the first-night performance, the long saga of the Greek revolution had finally ended when, at a conference in London, the new state was declared sovereign and independent under the protection of Britain, France and Russia. Greek independence effectively marked the end of the Holy Alliance. In the continuing conflict between Christians and Moslems in the Mediterranean, however, a new showdown was at hand. The chastisement of the Barbary pirates by British and Dutch naval forces had brought no lasting repentance from the Bey of Algiers. Depredations on Western commerce had been resumed. Christian slaves were still held in the infamous city, and Charles X and his ministers were increasingly convinced that naval bombardment was not enough. France had recovered its military confidence since the Waterloo disaster. Expeditions to Spain (1823) and Greece (1828) had been militarily successful, and plans were now well advanced to exorcise once and for all the specter of Moslem terrorism, hostage taking, and piracy by an occupation of Algiers by the Bourbon army.

This bellicose mood was reflected in a general stiffening of the regime toward all its opponents, at home as well as abroad. Thiers's new *National,* harping constantly on his comparison between the Bourbons and the Stuarts, insisted that Charles X was treading the same road as had James II and would meet the same end—expulsion and exile. Certainly, Charles's behavior, once his coronation was over, had exhibited signs of James II's fatal combination of ideological rectitude and political folly. In 1825 his government had passed the Sacrilege Law, punishing insults to Roman Catholic beliefs, services and privileges in a way almost calculated to resurrect the huge but latent forces of anticlericalism and win them a multitude of new recruits from the younger, highly educated generation.[167] It was followed the same year by the Compensation Act, which went much further than any of Louis XVIII's measures to restore property to former *émigrés* and victims of the Revolution. By a curious irony, the biggest single beneficiary of the law was the Duc d'Orléans (and his sister), who was soon to reciprocate Charles's generosity by replacing him.[168]

The third highly offensive measure was the Primogeniture Act of 1826, part of a series of moves by Charles and his ministers to switch political power away from the monied and toward the landed classes. Politically this act made no sense. The haute bourgeoisie were no threat to Charles until he alienated them. But once they grasped the full measure of his contempt, their money flowed into the coffers of the opposition, particularly into its newspapers, refinancing the old, founding the new. In addition to the *National,* the *Temps* was started in

October 1829 to defend the principles of the Charter; the *Globe* of Hugo and his friends was transformed from a weekly into a daily; and two more liberal papers, the *Journal de Paris* and the *Tribune des Départements,* were revived. Contrary to rumor, the cash for the *National* was not provided by Talleyrand. As Chateaubriand caustically remarked: "Monsieur le Prince de Talleyrand"—he had a special nasal tone of voice for pronouncing this title of infamy, conferred by Bonaparte—"did not contribute a *sou.* He simply sullied the tone of the paper by pouring into the common fund his stock of corruption and treachery." The money was, in fact, supplied by the financier Laffitte.[169]

There was no threat to the regime as long as the twenties prosperity continued, as it did for somewhat longer than in Britain. But by mid-1827, France was in a full depression. The years 1815–26 had been the Indian summer of France's preindustrial economy, but by the end of 1827, France's traditional textile trade, particularly silk, was being hit by the international downturn in trade, and the new cotton mills suffered, too.[170] The infant coal-mining industry was down as well, and by 1828 the Haute Banque was doing only 50 percent of the business of the year before. The 1827 harvest was bad, 1828's was no better and 1829's was worse. In France, unlike Britain, famine was still a real threat, and in some ways the conditions in the late-1820s were worse than those in the 1780s that had helped to precipitate the Revolution.[171] During the previous famine in 1816–17, France had allowed the free import of grain, but since then it had operated restrictions not unlike Britain's Corn Laws, and there was no one in the government like Peel who was prepared to act empirically to lift them.

What was so serious about France's troubles were the coincidental disasters in so many industries. The industrial crisis was heightened by the attempts of British textile firms to export their overproduction. There were riots in the French trade as men and women were laid off. There was a crisis in the wine trade—one of the biggest employers of labor in France—in response to a glut and high foreign tariffs. By 1829–30, many people in France were hungry. Bands of beggars, mainly women and children—one-parent families—roamed the countryside, particularly in the north. During the winter, crowds of angry women stormed the warehouses of food merchants in the towns, in desperate attempts to bring down prices.[172]

In Paris, young men like Berlioz and De Nerval were well fed, but they seem to have felt the same burning sense of oppression and exclusion as did the destitute. Berlioz wanted to make a big noise, literally as well as metaphorically, and he was using De Nerval's translation of

Goethe's *Faust* (1828) to work on a vast opera which was eventually to become *The Damnation of Faust*. Some of the opera was already written, and these *Eight Scenes from Faust* were published to form his Opus 1, what Ernest Newman was to call "the most astounding Opus 1 in musical history." Berlioz was the first to appreciate the possibilities opening up by the creation of large, highly professional orchestras and the systematic study of orchestration. If Beethoven had essentially created the form of the new music, Berlioz produced its sound. Not all the younger composers liked what he was doing. Felix Mendelssohn, an ingenious and graceful orchestrator himself, thought Berlioz "a very pleasant man," but thought that in his compositions "all the instruments have a hangover and vomit music." He said he would like "to bite [Berlioz] to death."[173] But, then, Mendelssohn had played the score only on the piano; he had not experienced the sound itself. By 1830 little of Berlioz's music had been performed. How could he get his hands on the orchestras and auditoriums he needed, as long as horrible old men like Cherubini barred the way, vetoing this, objecting to that?

There was a huge age frustration in France: cultural, political, economic and social. The Belgian sociologist Baron Dupin calculated that in 1827 only one-ninth of Frenchmen were over age 57, but they constituted half the "political nation," with votes, money and power.[174] This one-ninth had been adults under the ancien régime and looked back on it with nostalgia. Nobody else knew what they were talking about. The average life expectancy was only 36. Nearly 70 percent of the population was under age 40. Yet 40, even under the Charter, was the minimum age for a *député*. A fiercely ambitious and immensely successful man like Thiers could not sit in parliament. In 1828 a Genevan called James Fazy published a ferocious pamphlet called *De la Gerontocratie*, in which he denounced everyone over 40 as an old man. "They have reduced France," he fumed, "to 7–8,000 asthmatic, gouty, paralytic, eligible candidates with enfeebled faculties." The Empire might have killed young men—but at least it promoted them first. By 1830 the young felt blocked. France, said Fazy, was full of angry young men, briefless barristers, doctors without patients, college graduates tapping their feet in ministers' waiting rooms.[175] It was a feature of the Restoration that as the ministers got older, writers and artists were younger when they achieved fame.[176] In 1830 Gautier was 19; Chopin and De Musset, 20; the future Napoleon III, 22; Dumas, 26; Berlioz and George Sand, 27; Hugo, 28; Balzac, 31; Delacroix, 32; and Thiers and De Vigny, 33. Only Guizot was over 40. Balzac saw France, especially Paris, as "a ceaseless struggle between young and old for power, wealth

and success," a battle between "a wan and colourless youth [and] a
senility bedizened in the attempt to look young."[177]

All the same, a revolution of young against old in 1830 was not
inevitable; nothing in history ever is. The fall of the Bourbons was
brought about by stupidity and incompetence, compounded by sloth.
Having, as it were, willed a confrontation by their legislative measures,
Charles and his advisers moved toward it in a dreamlike trance. Under
Villèle, the cabinet system had been virtually abandoned. King and
minister simply did business together. But in the worsening economic
climate of 1827, the liberals and the ultraroyalists ganged up against
Villèle, and he lost the elections, retiring finally in January 1828, a bitter
man. No successor was appointed. The work was done by Vicomte de
Martignac, a lawyer from Bordeaux, who held only the title of Interior
Minister. De Martignac was chiefly interested in composing songs,
writing vaudeville shows, having *soupers* with pretty actresses, and
sleeping with them afterwards. There was a drift, rather than a drive,
toward liberalism. The press laws were loosened. Censorship was
relaxed. Right-wing prefects were removed.

The King did not like the way things were going. He tried to bring
in Jules de Polignac as premier in January 1829, and finally succeeded
in August. The new man was the son of Marie-Antoinette's favorite, a
Catholic ultra whose princedom came from the Pope. He had spent a
lot of his life in prison or under arrest and had the curious disassocia-
tion from life of the long incarcerated. Like many prominent Frenchmen of his time, he was an Anglophile and married to an English-
woman, but he understood nothing of English constitutionalism. In
November the cabinet was revived, but no one knew how to work it.
At its meetings, "the King would cut up paper into strange shapes and
carefully carried away his finished work at the end of the session.
. . . M. de Polignac and De Montel covered the notebooks in front of
them with pen sketches. M. de Chabrol spent his time stabbing sticks
of sealing-wax with a stiletto. . . . If someone fell asleep, the King would
laugh. If he wanted him woken up, he would offer him his snuff box."[178]
The supposedly strong men were Count Louis Bourmont at the War
Ministry and Count François de la Bourdonnaye, the Minister of the
Interior. The latter frightened the radicals because he symbolized the
White Terror of 1815. He was reported to have said: "One can govern
easily enough with gallows and prostitutes." But when the crisis came,
both men proved useless.

If Charles X had serious intentions of getting a firmer grip on the
country, he should have acted the moment the Polignac government

was in place. But nothing was done for six months, while the effects of the disastrous 1829 harvest were felt and the economy slumped further. Parliament was prorogued until 2 March 1830, when it promptly passed a vote declining to invest the new government with constitutional authority. Charles should have dissolved the parliament immediately, but again there was an unexplained delay. No doubt the government was obsessed with the coming Algerian conflict. The operation, as it happened, was a complete and rapid success. Troops began landing on 14 June, the buildup was complete four days later and Algiers itself fell on 5 July. The force commander, General Bournmont, issued a communiqué claiming that in 20 days France had "destroyed a state whose existence had wearied Europe for three centuries." This claim was echoed by Monsignor Quelen, the Archbishop of Paris: "Three weeks were enough to humiliate and reduce the proud Moslems to the weakness of a child." The Archbishop then added meaningfully: "Thus may the enemies of our lord and king be treated always and everywhere; thus may be confounded all those who dare to rise up against him."[179]

Some of the opposition then changed their tune. Thiers's shift of front is reflected in the 16 contradictory articles he wrote before, during and after the Algiers invasion: first outright condemnation, then a neutral analysis of the historical background, then a cautious approval of the military, followed by warm congratulations and an attack on the government for taking credit due only to the soldiers. Thiers also adumbrated the new, offensive French imperialism which was to take shape later in the century, calling for the occupation of Tunis and Tripoli and the penetration of the interior.[180] The conquest of Algiers was an impressive demonstration of western firepower and organization and marked the point at which other European powers began to emulate the rapid expansion of Britain's overseas empire which had taken place over the past generation. Casualties were slight, and the operation was crowned with an unexpected bonus. Bournmont found in the Bey's secret coffers enough cash to pay for the entire war.

The victory should have brought Charles a massive political bonus, but once again he got the timing all wrong. He did not dissolve parliament until 16 May. Other incomprehensible delays meant that the voting took place on 23 June and 3 July, just at the point when all the hazards of the Algiers expedition were most obvious, but before it ended in complete triumph. Hence, the result was a humiliating defeat for the regime. Only 143 governmental supporters were elected, and the ranks of the liberal opposition swelled from 221 to 274. The King now took the steps he had funked the previous August. For months Talleyrand had been predicting that 1830 would be decisive, *une année aux orages*—a storm year. Thiers had been predicting a royal coup for weeks, and now he openly challenged Charles in a headline: "Break the Laws or Get Out!" But the King did not need to act unconstitutionally. He merely invoked Article 14 of the Charter, which gave the sovereign emergency powers in time of crisis. On Sunday 25 July, a week after the challenge from the *National*, Charles dissolved the new parliament, ordered fresh elections, changed the electoral qualifications and suspended freedom of the press.

These four ordinances were a combination of force and folly. The third reduced the number of deputies to 258 and decreed their election by colleges, instead of directly by the voters. It thus went in exactly the opposite direction of the trend in the United States and it was particularly inapposite in France for two reasons. First, it completed the process whereby power shifted back from the commercial and monied classes to the landowners. Second, it overlooked the opportunity of taking, in the light of the Algiers triumph, a populist line by lowering the franchise, appealing to the masses and dishing the liberal intelligentsia. This was what Napoleon Bonaparte had done in 1799 and Louis Napoleon was to do in 1851. Charles thus narrowed the basis of his support to the nobility and gentry.

And where were the nobility and the gentry in July 1830? Sitting in their country chateaux, naturally. They certainly were not available to turn out in the streets of Paris. Many army officers from the Paris garrison were in the country, too, where they had been voting, as ordered. Charles himself was absent from his post. The day after he issued the ordinances, a Monday, instead of observing reactions, he and son were out all day hunting in Rambouillet, and did not get back till 11 P.M. Worst of all, the King, having willed the end—a semi-authoritarian royalist state—neglected to provide the means. Paris was now a city of 800,000 inhabitants, a large number of whom were unemployed, and many of whom were hungry. To hold down this inflammable mob, Marshal Marmont had only 12,000 troops, short of officers, and 1,300 lifeguards. It might have been different if the King had been on the spot to encourage his men. But Charles stayed outside the capital, in his palace. As De Vigny put it in his diary, "[Charles] thinks he can play Bonaparte. But Bonaparte was there, standing behind the cannon at St Roch. Charles X is at Compiègne."[181]

The July Days, as they came to be known, were the first time the media overthrew a government. Editors supplied the leadership, the printworkers the rank-and-file. As a wag put it, the revolt was "an alliance of the *blouson* and the frock-coat."[182] One American eyewitness, Calbe Cushing, claimed that it was a bourgeois youth revolution:

"[Students] came forth as a body, particularly the young men of the Polytechnic School . . . instantly gaining the confidence of the people."[183] Delacroix's famous summation of the affair, *Liberty Leading the People at the Barricades,* indeed shows *Polytechniciens* following the half-naked Marianne. But police reports and other evidence indicate that most of the young men at the barricades were artisans, especially printers. Compositors and pressmen, many employed in and around the Palais Royale, formed the only occupational group who appear regularly in police reports.[184] The truth is, the second ordinance, which effectively shut down the Parisian press, persuaded the printers that they either had to come out onto the streets to fight for their jobs, or starve. The editors, led by Thiers, who were striving to keep the presses rolling, offered them leadership, and the printers responded. On 25 July Thiers wrote a collective protest signed by 44 journalists from 11 papers. On 26 July a huge crowd appeared in front of the Foreign Ministry building. It was led by 5,000 printers and their lads. That evening Thiers had his protest distributed in 6,000–7,000 handbills, and despite the ordinance, he got 2,321 copies of the *National* printed that night. The *Globe* ran off 359 copies and the *Temps,* 5,151. The protest urged a tax strike and called on shops and businesses to close. The actual fighting began when the printers at the *National* refused to admit the police, and the doors were broken down. The government eventually issued warrants for the arrest of various journalists, but by then it was too late: the journalists were carefully hidden in the suburbs.[185]

Meanwhile the mob was out and barricades had gone up. The police complained that the printers, in groups of 30 or more, roamed around killing them and luring them into narrow alleys, where they could be attacked from all sides. When the army became involved, they were not much more effective. Marmont first dispersed his men in small units to attack the insurgents everywhere. When this strategy proved ineffectual, he concentrated them around the Place de la Concorde. The 5th and the 53rd regiments, drawn up in the Place Vendôme, but almost without officers, deserted. When Marmont replaced them with the Royal and Swiss Guards from the palace, the Louvre was invaded by the mob, and he was forced to withdraw his concentration to the Champs-Elysées.

Paris was a very dangerous place to be out. On the night of the 27 July, Adèle Hugo gave birth yet again, with bullets whistling over the garden and her husband sitting with an Argand lamp writing his *Ode to Young France.* The English painter William Callow and his studio-partner Newton Fielding came out of their den in the Rue St. Georges the next day to buy food. They were forced to put on *tricoleur* cockades and were nearly killed in consequence: "We were about to cross a street to get to the River Seine," wrote Callow, "when we were suddenly stopped by a bystander, which act doubtless saved our lives for the next moment a volley was fired down the street by a detachment of soldiers and the road was strewn with killed and wounded."[186] About 1,800 of the insurgents were killed and 4,500 were wounded. The casualties might have been higher. De Vigny reported the case of an officer in the Sixth Regiment of the Guards who refused to order his men to fire because the Rue de Rivoli was full of women and children. When his colonel threatened to put him under close arrest, he blew his own brains out.

By the end of 28 July Marmont had contrived to lose 200 men killed, 800 wounded and 1,500 missing—mostly deserters. He had had enough, and the next day he pulled out of the city completely, to reconcentrate outside. Observing the withdrawal up the Champs-Elysées from his window on the corner of the Rue St. Florentin, Talleyrand commented sardonically: "At five minutes after noon, the elder branch of the Bourbons ceased to reign." His enemy Chateaubriand put it a little differently: "Yet another government flinging itself from the towers of Nôtre Dame." Saint-Beuve, who had been caught by the crisis in Honfleur, hurried back and went straight to the offices of the *Globe* in the Rue de Richelieu, which he reached that evening, to find all was over. He wrote enthusiastically: "Here was the last act of the drama that had begun in 1789: arbitrary rule ended, a just age beginning—endless possibilities."[187]

Endless possibilities—but for whom? In fact, the coming of the demos to France produced a result not unlike that in the United States two years before: a division of the spoils. The first to get a post was the Duc d'Orléans, who became King. This choice was Thiers's idea, again following English precedent in 1688, to invite the member of the royal family who was most likely to behave respectably to occupy the throne. Thiers and his friend Mignet, backed by Laffitte, drafted an Orléanist proclamation and stuck it up all over Paris on 30 July. It was no more than a piece of imaginative journalism: "Charles X can never again enter Paris—he caused the blood of the people to be shed. The Republic would expose us to fearful divisions. It would embroil us with Europe. The Duc d'Orléans is a prince devoted to the cause of the Revolution. . . . The Duc d'Orléans is a citizen king. The Duc d'Orléans has carried the *tricoleur* under the enemy's fire. The Duc d'Orléans has declared himself. He accepts the Charter as we have always wanted it. It is from the French people that he will hold his crown."[188] In fact the Duc d'Orléans at this stage had not even been consulted. However, that same day Thiers went to the Duc's chateau at Neuilly. The Duc was not there, but his sister, Madame Adelaide, was, and the little historian persuaded her that if Orléans did not accept quickly, the crown would be offered either to Charles X's grandson or to Bonaparte's son, the Duc de Reichstadt in Vienna. The lady saw the force of this argument and promised to deliver her brother. Thiers said grandly (this is his account): "Today you place the crown in your house." He hurried back to Paris to report to the deputies who were meeting at the Palais Bourbon, and by midnight the Duc was there, too, with the title Lieutenant General of the Kingdom.[189] Charles X abdicated two days later, and on 7 August Orléans was proclaimed King of the French.

Then the provision of jobs for the boys began in earnest. The workers were not ignored completely. Though the general depression continued for the next two years, and many starved, the Paris print workers were rewarded: Even the unemployed ones got work. One of the undeclared objects of the revolution was to get cheap governmental loans to keep businesses going, especially in the badly hit publishing trade. The Law of October 1830 provided short-term, no-interest loans, and 57 publishers immediately applied; 2 million francs were distributed among them.[190] Other workers, however, felt they had been cheated. One young man who had played a modest role in the journalistic offensive against Charles X was the 22-year-old print-artist Honoré Daumier (1808–79). The son of a frame maker, Daumier, like Thiers, came from Marseilles, but did not have the same love of lucre. Quite the contrary: If ever there were a life-long radical, it was this brilliant and savage artist. Three days before the fatal ordinances were announced, Daumier had published his first successful lithograph, which proved tragically prophetic. It showed a soldier loading his musket and saying: *"Pas ton chemin, cochon."*[191] There followed, in quick succession, 19 other superb political cartoons, reflecting the fall of one regime and the birth of another. Daumier shared to the full the feeling of many workingmen that they had been cheated; they had fought for a revolution, the fruits of which had gone to others. On 20 November 1831, the young artist participated in a fracas at Lyons, the first purely working-class rising of modern times. This rising succeeded in driving the National Guard out of town, but was then brutally put down by Marshal Soult on behalf of the new regime. Daumier got six months in prison.[192] He emerged, to portray the spoils system and its pear-shaped monarch with wonderful fidelity and bitterness.

There was certainly no lack of material. The July Revolution was a triumph for the middle class or, at any rate, its upper reaches. The qualifying age for a deputy was lowered from 40 to 30, for an elector, to 25. Lower tax- and property qualifications increased the electorate from 90,000 to 166,000 (roughly one-third of the new electorate, 618,000, created by the Great Reform Bill in Britain two years later). One of the first to get his share of the spoils was Thiers. His mistress's husband, Dosne, completed the conveyance of his house in the Rue St. Georges, and three days afterward he became thus qualified, Thiers was elected deputy for Aix. Dosne, in return, was made Receiver General of Taxes for Brest. Laffitte became Minister of Finance, and the little deputy for Aix became his Undersecretary and a Councillor of State. Thiers went on to hold offices in six governments.[193]

A large number of journalists got jobs, even more than in Jackson's administration. Both François-Auguste Mignet and François Guizot became Councillors of State, Guizot a Minister in addition. The *National*'s manager, Robert Gauja, became a Departmental Prefect. Victor Cousin became a Life Peer and Minister of Public Instruction, in charge of the university system. Pierre Dubois, editor of the *Globe,* became Deputy for the Loire-Inferieur. On hearing about this appointment, Sainte-Beuve, one of the few to get nothing, addressed Dubois as "Monsieur le Deputé de la Goire-Inferieur." This taunt led to some characteristic French face slapping and a challenge. Ludicrous though it may be to imagine Sainte-Beuve dueling, especially with a mousy, ink-stained man like Dubois, the encounter did take place, in the Romaineville woods. Immediately before the duel, Sainte-Beuve conscientiously finished his current article, on Denis Diderot, slyly inserting a quotation hinting at his love for Adèle Hugo. It poured with rain, and Sainte-Beuve insisted on keeping up his umbrella throughout. Happily, both men were myopic. At 20 paces they fired, each missing. They loaded, fired again and missed again. At that point, the weary seconds called it a day. Dubois went on to become Headmaster of the École Normale Supérieur. Among other *Globe* journalists, Charles de Remusat, Duvergier de Hauranne, and Comte Duchatel became deputies, the last also Minister of the Interior. The paper's art critic, Louis Vitet, became an Inspector of Ancient Monuments; so did Prosper Merimée. The assistant editor of the *National* got the job of Secretary to the Speaker. Even Henri Beyle (Stendhal), who had demanded a prefectship, got the consulate in Trieste. Never before or since have so many journalists and academics got their snouts in the trough at the same time. As the empty-handed Sainte-Beuve put it, "the corrupt men of ten regimes joined forces with yesterday's roués, with feverish counter-jumpers and sweaty intruders, to form a veritable scum on the surface of the land." De Tocqueville made the same point more judicially: "The middle classes entrenched themselves in all posts, increased the numbers of those posts hugely, and became used to living almost as much by public funds as by their own labours."[194]

The new French revolution was well received by the Anglo-Saxon powers, since it produced stability under a responsible-seeming, middle-class constitutional sovereign. President Jackson expressed his warm approval. Monroe, on his last public appearance (26 November 1830), took the chair at a mass meeting in Tammany Hall to celebrate Charles X's downfall. The British government was officially surprised by the July Days, since only two days before the crisis broke, the new King, William IV, had been made to say by his ministers in the King's Speech at the opening of Parliament: "It is with the utmost satisfaction that I find myself enabled to congratulate you on the general tranquility of Europe."[195] Whitehall was a little alarmed at the violence in Paris, but pleased when the new regime paid elaborate court to Sir Charles Stuart, the British Ambassador. Talleyrand was quickly dispatched to London as envoy and persuaded Wellington that he ought to accept King Louis-Philippe, as he was now called, *"faute de mieux, crainte de pis"* (for want of a better and for fear of a worse). Indeed, once they realized the new regime was only interested in commerce and cash, the British were mightily relieved, believing strongly in Samuel Johnson's maxim: "Sir, a man is seldom so innocently employed as when he is getting [i.e., making] money."[196]

The words put into William IV's mouth, however, were peculiarly inept in view of the fact that most people had been expecting trouble, not just in France but elsewhere. Not only had the 1829 harvest been a disaster, but the winter of 1829–30 was ferocious and the spring wet and cold. Britain was recovering from the depression, Scandinavia was doing well—the Danish *riksfaler* rose in value from 1828—Spain and Portugal were prosperous, and Poland had had a good harvest in 1829. But all central Europe was in great distress. Indeed, trouble had already broken out before July, in Switzerland of all places. And, as in France, it started with radical press criticism and attempts to suppress it. Switzerland, as we have noted, moved in a strongly conservative direction after the end of Bonaparte's tyranny. But it appeared content because it was becoming increasingly affluent in the 1820s. One third of the active population owned their own land. The country was starting to industrialize, making silk in the north, watches in the Jura, and cotton in the Aargau-Appenzell-Glarus triangle. It already had strong banks and was making increasing use of waterpower. It was exporting dairy products from an efficient agricultural sector. During the decade, it enjoyed its first tourist boom, mainly from England.

But prosperity, as in Britain and the United States, tended to encourage middle-class agitation for a greater share in government. There was a particularly strong objection to the new press laws of 1823, imposed under pressure from Austria and France, which resented the ease with which political exiles made hostile propaganda from the safety of Switzerland. Despite the censorship, Switzerland—like every other advanced country—was acquiring powerful newspapers in the 1820s: the *Neue Zürcher Zeitung* (1821), the *Nouveliste Vaudois* of Lausanne (1824), the *Journal de Genève* (1826), the *Appenzeller Zeitung* of Basel (1828) and the *Osservatore del Ceresio* of Lugano (1829). The last spoke for the radicals of the Ticino, the poorest part of the country and the one most under Austrian influence. The regime of Giani-Battista Quadri, backed by Vienna, was increasingly unpopular in the later 1820s; the winter of 1829–30 was punctuated by peasant riots and violence in the towns, egged on by pamphlet warfare, and when Quadri closed down the *Osservatore* and prosecuted its editor in March 1830, the opposition boiled over. Being Swiss, it took a moderate form: radical constitutional changes were pushed through the cantonal diet on 23 June and confirmed by a plebiscite. The significant development was that when Quadri appealed for Austrian military intervention, he failed to get it. Thus began what the Swiss called the Regeneration, which over the next three years liberalized the constitutions of all the cantons.[197]

These Swiss events were accelerated by the July Days, but the country where the French revolution had most immediate and permanent effect was the Netherlands. Castlereagh's allocation of Belgium to the Dutch crown as part of his overall strategic scheme to contain French expansionism was the one aspect of it which did not work. Once again, it was the regime's press and cultural policy which precipitated disaster. William I, the last *Stadtholder* of Holland, who assumed the title of Sovereign Prince of the Netherlands in 1813 and acquired Belgium and Luxembourg two years later, was an exceptionally able, hardworking and narrow-minded man. From 1816 he made vigorous efforts to promote industry behind a high tariff wall. He went into partnership with John Cokerill to build the biggest works on the continent at Seraigne, near Liège. He set up the Société Générale des Pays Bas pour Favouriser l'Industrie Nationale (1822). He invested heavily in the new state company, the Nerderlandsche Handelsmaatschappij (1824), which revived the East Indies trade.[198] His high tariff policy, if anything, helped the Belgians rather than the Dutch. But in politics William behaved like a virtual dictator, running a highly restrictive constitution. He himself appointed the members of the upper house, and the lower house was chosen by indirect vote of the provincial assemblies, themselves based on a strict property franchise. Hence, a comparatively trivial economic affront—in 1830 it was a new tax on milling—could cause disproportionate resentment, especially in Belgium, where William was regarded as an alien ruler.

William had no notion of the principle of divide and rule. The Belgians had been at loggerheads for centuries (they still are) over language. But instead of seeking to conciliate the Flemings, thus separating them from the French-speaking Walloons (or vice versa), William drove them together in common hatred by insisting that all governmental business be conducted in pure Dutch. He might, again, have divided the Roman Catholics from the atheistic liberals. Instead he united them by closing Catholic seminaries, on the one hand, and shutting down or censoring newspapers, on the other hand. Belgium, like France, was full of clever, frustrated young men, wanting jobs and, failing to find them, looking for trouble. The violence in Paris, followed by the rapid change of regime there, created an explosive force in Brussels, another fast-growing city where unemployment, thanks to the continuing depression, was heavy. The spark was supplied by a sensational premiere, at the Opera House, of *La Muette de Portici,* which the authorities, despite the experience in Paris, had inexplicably allowed to be staged. It was the superb singing of a young French tenor, Albert Nourrit, of Massaniello's key aria, "The Sacred Love of the Fatherland," which not only brought down the house but virtually sent the audience out into the streets. Rioting swept through the city on 25–26 August and led to the formation of the Committee of Public Safety, which became the eventual Belgian government. When William sent his Dutch troops into Brussels in September, and armed Dutch began to fire on unarmed Belgians, the province was lost: The "Four Days" led to an ignominious Dutch defeat and withdrawal, and by October the Dutch had lost control everywhere except Maastricht, Antwerp and Luxembourg.[199]

The de facto secession of Belgium was in clear breach of the Vienna settlement, but the Holy Alliance was now dead and the great powers could not agree what to do. Prussia was for doing nothing. There was already trouble enough in Germany, where the demos was on the march. On 31 August a Protestant mob rioted against the Roman Catholic monarchy in Saxony, followed quickly by violence in Hesse, where the Elector's mistress was unpopular and bread prices had been put up, and in Brunswick, where the ruling Duke was hated. Prussia, in fact, was the first (after Britain) to recognize the new French regime, as soon as it received assurances that France had no claims on its Rhineland (31 August). Austria followed five days later, Metternich having agreed with Count Karl Nesselrode, the Russian Foreign Minister, that Louis-Philippe represented no threat to either of them as long as his new France agreed to remain within its existing frontiers. The breakup of the "big" Netherlands, with the possibility that Belgium might join France, raised some anxiety, which was quickly dispelled when France vigorously rejected any such desire. What Metternich really feared was the spirit of revolt spreading to Italy: He wanted to make friends with the new French regime to prevent it intervening south of the Alps. Hence, when the Dutch King asked for Austria's help, he (like the conservatives in Switzerland) was turned down. The chief aim of the British was to get a guarantee of Belgian independence. The British had been so angered by William I's high tariff policy that they were glad to see his kingdom split up. In conjunction with the French, they arranged for a conference on Belgium to be held in London, and this conference arranged an armistice on 21 November. The following month Britain, France, Prussia, Austria and Russia agreed on Belgium's separation from Holland. This diplomatic process, with some minor military alarms and excursions, led to the creation of a Belgian monarchy, for which Britain nominated a suitable German princeling, and the guarantee of the new state's sovereignty, independence and neutrality by the Treaty of London in 1839—the famous "scrap of paper," which brought Britain into the First World War.[200]

The only European ruler who favored strong measures against the wave of bourgeois democracy was Nicholas I of Russia, who did not agree with his Foreign Minister. Nicholas was seriously thinking of some sort of intervention when, in November 1830, the unrest spread to Poland. This was not surprising. Poland had not been much affected by the depression in most of Europe, but the 1830 harvest, unlike its bumper predecessor, was a failure, followed by sharp rises in the price of grain, beer and vodka. The Poland created by the Congress of Vienna, a constitutional state under the Russian autocrat, was in many ways a wretched place. It was satisfactory to the Russians because it gave them a militarily defensible western frontier. Until 1830 Russia ensured the cooperation of the "Political Nation" in Poland by greatly favoring the landed classes. The constitution Alexander I gave the Poles in 1815, while stipulating, in its first article, that Poland was indissolubly linked to Russia, gave all local political power and rights of justice to about 5,373 landlords. These landlords formed the top tier of a Polish gentry which numbered, in 1827, some 301,971 (including 62,593 heads of families), out of a total population of 4,137,634.[201] The gentry ranged from the two great, rival princely families, the Potockis, "the

Uncrowned Kings of Ruthenia," the traditionalist patriots, and the Czartoryskis, "the Upstart Family," who stood for constitutional reform, down to poor but nonetheless proud squireens. They believed they had a divine right to monopolize political power, and they were fierce fighters—they supplied some of the best regiments in both Bonaparte's and the Tsar's armies—but they did not trouble themselves with anything else, especially commerce and industry. Maritime trade was entirely in the hands of the German towns: Riga, Danzig, Elbing, Königsberg, and Memel. Internal commerce and much else was run by the huge Jewish minority.

At the bottom of the heap were the peasants. They were serfs, who performed labor services and required a passport, obtainable with difficulty only at the local noble's court, even to leave their villages. In short, they were *glebae adscripti,* tied to the earth, a form of servitude going back to the late Roman Empire. The Polish Diet, entirely controlled by their masters, denied the truth of this. It repeatedly ruled that since there were no serfs in Poland, no labor services, and no restriction of movement, there was no need to introduce reforms.[202] The peasants were of various grades, Full Peasants, Half Peasants, Quarter Peasants and even lower levels, depending on the amount of land they cultivated. But all were downtrodden, cringing and servile. One visitor wrote: "The Polish peasant is in every part of the country extremely poor, and of all the living creatures I have met with in this world, or seen described in books of natural history, he is the most wretched. He is in a worse condition than the Russian serf, who is at least maintained by his master."[203] It was forced peasant labor which made Polish wheat so competitive in Western markets and led Britain and other countries to introduce Corn Laws. When the corn-export market collapsed in the 1820s, and tax revenues fell, Poland could barely support its 40,000-strong army (commanded by the Viceroy, Grand Duke Constantine), which absorbed half the national revenue. Peasants and landlords hated each other. Many estates, indeed, were in the hands of stewards, and there was a saying, "the steward may hang the peasant for all the lord knows." There was another saying, "To work on the desmesne," that is, not at all—the peasants did as little as they possibly could. The gentry's policy was to keep the peasants drunk on cheap vodka. There were vast numbers of legal rural distilleries (as well as illicit ones), and often a condition of the peasant's tenure was that he could buy only the lord's vodka. Many of the distilleries, and the inns that served it, were leased to Jews. As an extreme form of "truck" (payment in kind), hired laborers were given vodka tickets instead of wages, rather as Chinese laborers were paid in opium. The peasants drank vodka in vast quantities and gave it to their fractious children, as the British used laudanum. Vodka kept the peasants tame, but in any case the legal system was stacked against them. From 1824 lawyers who represented peasants were made responsible for verifying their complaints and could easily land themselves in jail.[204]

It is important to grasp the plight of the peasants because it is one reason the Polish revolution of 1830 failed: It meant nothing to four-fifths of the population because it would have done nothing for them. In some ways, however, Poland was like other European countries in 1830. Gentry and middle class alike were tasting the delights of the new press. The Russian-backed regime was doing everything it could to keep cultural life under its control. Censorship was imposed in 1819, first on periodicals, then on all printing. In February 1825 Tsar Alexander ordered that only the opening and closing sessions of the diet be opened to the public, and the reporting of speeches was restricted. Gentry liberals, like Count Radonski, who took part in the Neapolitan rising of 1820, and the brothers Wincenty and Bonawentura Niemojowski, were put in jail or under house arrest. Students were forbidden to go to foreign universities. Secret societies were banned—but continued to exist. There were uniformed police all over Poland. Cossacks patrolled the frontiers. Grand Duke Constantine had his own secret police (but only two detectives). So did the Tsar's personal commissioner, Senator Novosiltsev. The Russians also set up a gendarmerie and a municipal police force. There was even a body which coordinated these various rival police forces, the Central Office for Police for Warsaw and the Kingdom. But only £12,500 a year was available for all secret police activities and the 200 agents, who included criminals, counts, Germans, Jews and foreign merchants, were often corrupt. The incompetence of the authorities was exceeded only by the inefficiency of the endless conspirators who tried to overthrow them. Every plot against the regime in the 1820s contained a high-born traitor, like Count Karski in 1821 or Prince Jablonowski in 1825–26, who revealed it to the police. The Quisling figure is a recurrent type in Polish history. In the second half of the 1820s, conspiracies tended to drift into the hands of younger officers, who resented the old-fashioned way Constantine ran the army, and who joined forces with students in the Warsaw and Cracow cafés.

The romantic movement was sweeping Poland, as everywhere else. Indeed, it is probably true to say that the influence of the romantic mind on Poland was stronger than anywhere else. No other artist, not even Berlioz, embodied the romantic spirit more completely than did Frédéric Chopin (1810–49), the son of a Frenchwoman and a Polish exile from the Vosges. Chopin's father returned to Warsaw to work as a tutor in private families and as a teacher at the Warsaw high school.[205] Chopin was largely self-taught in piano because his only music tutor was a violinist, but he produced his first published piece in 1817, when he was seven (he was a year younger than Mendelssohn), and it was, typically, a polonaise, a form which he used (together with the mazurkas, the nocturne and the waltz) to blend in his music the romantic spirit sweeping Europe and the new Polish nationalism. He must have had the subtlest ear ever possessed by a pianist. As Mendelssohn said, Chopin "does things on the piano as original as Paganini on the violin, and brings about miracles one would not have believed possible."[206] He listened intensely and always heard the piano as a series of voices, speaking a special music language. He loved singing, and his piano playing and teaching were based on vocal training. He made the piano not only sing, both tenor and soprano, but even have breathing pauses. He heard bad pianos as objectionable animals—a loud one, he said, was "like a dog barking." He gave to the piano what Berlioz gave to the orchestra, a new "modern" tone, a new range of sound-emotions. When he played, Berlioz said, "you have to go near him and listen closely"; often "the hammers merely brush the strings." "I have never heard," said Liszt, "such delicacy and refinement of playing."[207] Chopin published his Opus 1, a rondo, as early as 1825, but it was three years later, with his Rondo à la Mazur, that he first began to make an impact on the musical scene. He was one of thousands of very young, often gifted men in Warsaw at the end of the 1820s, exploring Polish history, poetry and folklore and its traditional music and mythology to throw off their huge frustrations at living in an almost-bankrupt country governed by an alien regime. Many attended the new University of Warsaw. Few had a job, or any prospect of one. Unemployment among young intellectuals was a feature of most European capitals in 1830, with high birthrates and a general recession, but there were proportionately more in Warsaw than anywhere else.

As it happened, however, the actual leader of the rising, in its early stages, was little educated, a cadet-instructor named Piotr Wysocki, who seems to have been in charge of the conspiracy from the end of 1828. Wysocki missed two opportunities to launch his coup with the murder of Nicholas I, who was in Warsaw in 1829 for his coronation as Polish king and again in May–June 1830 when he opened the diet. The July Days in France brought Poland's conspiratorial classes to fever pitch, for the country always looked to France for cultural and constitutional leadership. Even so, it was only when Grand Duke Constantine learned something of the potential plot and drew up a list of suspects for arrest that Wysocki decided to make his move. He fixed the date as 29 November, since on that day public buildings in Warsaw had a guard mounted by the Fourth Infantry, some of whose officers were in the conspiracy. But no proper plans were drawn up, and prominent people who were in a position to help were not informed. It might well have turned out to be a fiasco like the Decembrist coup in Saint Petersburg had not the date chosen, by pure accident, coincided with price increases. The signal for the rising, the burning of the brewery, was bungled. The attack on the Belvedere Palace failed, and Constantine escaped. Many popular senior officers refused to join the rising and were slaughtered. Solid citizens stayed indoors. But as soon as the city workers heard firing and realized their betters were up to mischief, they poured into the streets and started breaking into shops and drink stores. When the soldiers saw the mobs getting at the vodka, they joined in.[208] The result was an orgy of destruction and anarchy, and the authorities lost control of the city. This was the only time the popular mob itself made its appearance in Poland, and the gentry revolutionaries got the backing of the people. But, for a time, it was decisive. Constantine refused to intervene from outside the city, since his only dependable troops were Russians and he feared to antagonize the Poles, as Dutch William had in Brussels by using Dutchmen against Belgians. The senior Polish member of the regime, Prince Adam Czartoryski, tried to appease the mob by putting liberals on the governing council, meanwhile drafting Polish troops into the city. But the troops refused to fire on fellow Poles, and there was a growing fear that they would attack the Russian army, waiting outside. There were furious arguments, day after day, among the Polish gentry as to what to do next, culminating in the selection of a conservative soldier, General Josef Chlopicki, as dictator.

The general had no notion of attacking the Russians and merely wanted to negotiate his way peacefully out of a mess. Constantine wrote to his brother Nicholas that he hoped the General would become *"le second Monck de l'histoire."* (Monck was the army commander responsible for restoring Charles II in 1660.) But, in characteristic Polish fashion, the General was a dictator without dictatorial powers. As in France, the United States and elsewhere, Polish journalists and writers were trying to put themselves at the head of the movement for change. Their chief spokesman was the literary critic and poet Maurycy Mochnaki, who declared the events of 29 November to be "the start of a new Renaissance," a "rising of the nation." Another of the romantic writers, J. B. Ostrowski, said Poland should invite the intervention of "the liberal powers," Britain and France. Writing in the journal *New Poland,* he asserted: "The French Revolution of 1830 is the final act, the closing of the great scene of the Middle Ages, and the birth, the first light of dawn of a new Europe."[209] Cholopicki asserted: "I have decided to declare myself dictator because otherwise, what with these Moch-nackis and clubs, there will be no discipline, order or firmness any-where." When Ostrowski and others began to talk in irredentist terms, of incorporating Prussian and Austrian Poland and bringing, as Os-trowski put it, "onto the stage of history a new nation, 20 million strong, a nation which may have a decisive influence upon Slavdom and Europe in its resurrection," the General saw it as national suicide: "You, gentlemen, see in war the birth of the Polish nation, I only its grave." But the Supreme National Council, a self-appointed body of leading landowners, army officers and writers, would not give him authority to arrest troublemakers, and he resigned. The diet and its galleries became an engine of nationalist emotion, powered by hot air. Tsar Nicholas was deposed by acclamation. A national government was elected. The army was ordered to defend the new country.

Even the romantics of the Mochnacki camp, however, were careful to insist that their revolution was "national not social." They had no desire or intention of changing the archaic class structure of Poland or of giving even the merchant and artisanal classes in the towns, let alone the peasants in the countryside, any share in government. The Polish revolt was thus a rising of the upper crust, the *gratin,* and it was not enough. Some of them were brave officers, but they lacked manpower. By the time he got the news of his deposition, Nicholas had amassed an army of 80,000 men, and he immediately ordered it to cross the Polish frontier. It was twice the size of the Polish army and put it to flight at Ostrolenke on 26 May 1831. On 8 September, after a two-day battle, the Russians entered Warsaw, and it was all over. So Nicholas won the war, but he lost any hope of Polish cooperation. Thereafter the Poles always regarded Russia, as they still do, as their national enemy. The major powers which opposed Russia always raised Poland as a debat-ing and bargaining point. This in turn led the Poles to be overoptimistic about the level of foreign support they could command. So the modern Russian-Polish problem, still with us, came into existence.[210]

Meanwhile, what of Britain? Could the center hold again? The depression that began in 1826 caused some disturbances, as we have seen, but no revival of violent political radicalism. By 1828–29 trade and manufacturing were picking up again. In October 1829, writing in the *Lion,* the old radical publisher, atheist and jailbird Richard Carlile disgustedly described going to a meeting of the London Radical Reform Association to hear "Orator" Hunt, who was still at it: "You now look in vain for the energy and daring of the Radical Reformers of 1816 to 1820. There was then a general expectation that the cry of Radical Reform was to be followed by insurrection. . . . but now it is tame, it is hopeless, it is flat, stale and unprofitable. I am more than ever a reformer, but I could not act with and join in the doings, the littleness, of these men."[211] There was no obvious extraparliamentary leader. Right-thinking people talked apprehensively of "socialists"—the word was just coming into use at the end of the 1820s. But there was confusion about what socialists stood for, as illustrated by this exchange at one of the early Parliamentary committees of inquiry into social problems. Committee member: "You tell us that the railway navvies are mostly infidels. Would you say they are also socialists?" Clergyman witness: "In practice, yes; because, though most of them appear to have wives, few of them are really married."[212]

Nonetheless, there was much distress, especially in agriculture, and 1830 opened on a note of gloom. In Staffordshire, General Dyott wrote in his diary on 1 January: "I believe a year never opened with less cheering prospects to a country than the present for Old England; distress attending all classes of the community, agriculturals particularly from the low prices. Wheat 8s, barley 4s8d, oats 3s3d, beef 4½d to 5d, mutton the same. Meetings held in various parts of the Kingdom to represent the distress of the country."[213] This pessimism proved justified: Distress in rural areas continued, and unrest and violence, a phenomenon that came to be known as the Swing Riots, began in June, a good month before major trouble occured on the Continent. Indeed, there is little evidence that events in France and Belgium had much impact on the English poorer classes.[214]

The biggest factor was the introduction of labor-saving agricultural machinery. Firms like Ransome of Ipswich, Garrets of Leiston, Wood of Stowmarket, Burrell of Thetford, Hensman of Woburn, Holmes of Norwich, and Tasker of Andover were producing and marketing sophisticated agricultural machinery, such as threshers, which appealed strongly to the more commercially minded farmers because they saved time, which was important at harvest time in hitting the market before prices went soft. On smaller farms, machines made a cost differential of only about 10 percent, but the differential rose to 30 percent or more on the 17,000 farms of over 300 acres.[215] The first firing of ricks began at Orpington in Kent on 1 June. The first destruction of machinery followed toward the end of the harvest and also occurred in Kent, at Lower Hardres near Canterbury, on the night of 28 August. Kent, of course, was the nearest to the Continent, and it may be that the drift to violence was aggravated by reports and rumors crossing the Channel. August also saw trouble in Surrey, and in October the trouble spread to Sussex and then to 17 other counties, though in some it was brief.[216] By the third week of October about 100 machines were reported destroyed. The peak of the violence occurred in the last two weeks of November and the first week of December. In some areas special constables were sworn in, and the gentry and farmers armed themselves. There were threats against the clergy, to get them to reduce tithes (and these threats were sometimes supported by the farmers). In Uffington in Lincolnshire, Lady Charlotte Bertie recorded in her diary that a band of 450 men was roaming only 10 miles away, burning ricks and breaking machines. Her step-father, the Rev. Peter Pegus, armed himself with two swords, a double-barreled shotgun and a brace of pistols.[217] Some agitators were arrested. On 16 December a well-dressed middle-class merchant from Luton, John Saville, was found at Stradisfal in Suffolk, with £580 in notes and masses of inflammatory posters signed "Swing" in his possession: he had been traveling all over the Eastern counties in a green gig. He got 12 months.[218]

The general response of the authorities, and indeed the farmers themselves, was appeasement. Some landlords had recommended that their tenant farmers should not introduce more machinery even before the trouble started. After August many farmers discarded or even destroyed their machines to save their houses and ricks from being burned. When the first case of machine breaking came up at East Kent Quarter Sessions on 22 October, the chairman, Sir Edward Knatchbull, discharged seven men, who pleaded guilty, with a 2¾-day sentence and a caution, in the hope that, as the *Times* reported, "the kindness and moderation evinced this day by the magistrates would be met by a corresponding feeling among the people."[219] In Berkshire the justices issued a printed notice in November: "To the labouring classes. The Gentlemen, Yeomanry, Farmers and others, having made known to you their intentions of increasing your Wages to a satisfactory extent; and it being resolved that threshing machines shall not again be used; it is referred to your good sense that it will be most beneficial to your own permanent Interests . . . to withdraw yourselves from Practices which tend to destroy the Property from whence the very means of your additional Wages are to be supplied." A notice issued the same month by a group of Norfolk justices of the peace said it "begged to recommend" that "owners and occupiers of land" should "discontinue the use of threshing machines."[220] This trend had sinister implications for Britain's future, for it meant a deceleration in the application of modern mechanical technology to agriculture, in which, up to this time, Britain had led the world. It was to have disastrous consequences in the 1870s,

when steam-driven ships brought to free-trade Britain the first transatlantic grain produced on vast, low-cost midwestern U.S. farms. It combined with a similar spirit of appeasement which was evident in industry, where some manufacturers were already making deals with unions
which led to the introduction of restrictive practices and the loss of
productivity. In the late 1820s, at a time when Britain seemed supreme
in producing both food and goods with maximum efficiency, there were
portents of her long-term relative decline. But for the moment, appeasement brought peace.

That was as well, for after a decade of political somnolence, the
demand for fundamental reform was growing again. One reliable index
of political intensity is the number of political prints produced, which
can be gauged from the vast stocks held in the British Library. Artists
and print sellers mirrored middle-class opinion, which veered according
to events. The publication of new prints tended to bunch in the late
spring and late autumn, when Parliament was in session. They averaged
only one a week in the 1760s; rose to about five a week in 1810–20; and
then, after lithography began to replace the expensive single copper
prints in about 1820, they doubled to an average of 10 a week in 1830.
The principal artists—James Gillray, George Cruikshank, Thomas
Rowlandson, James Sayers and their many followers—switched from
social to political satire, and back again, in accordance with public
interest. The peak cycles for political prints reflected the crisis years
1813–16, 1819–20, and 1830–32. There was a dramatic peak in 1820
over the Queen Caroline divorce trial. Early in 1830 a new peak began
to build up, and continued until the crisis was resolved with the passing
of the Great Reform Bill in 1832. The number sold likewise rose, from
50,000 to 200,000.[221] The number of newspapers was growing, too, and
equally important the number of copies printed. By 1830 the total
number of newspapers bought by English readers had risen from 16
million in 1801 to over 30 million. Newspaper sales rose rapidly in 1830,
another index of a quickening political pulse.

Behind this process was a growing belief that constitutional reform
was now inevitable and imminent. The impetus was provided by Daniel
O'Connell's great victory in the Clare election, and the Wellington-Peel
surrender over Catholic emancipation in early 1829, which demonstrated that reform was possible under the existing system. But the shift
of the logjam really went back to 1828. The more liberal members of
the government, Huskisson and Palmerston especially, were against
reform in general, but favored it in particular. They reasoned as follows. Population, wealth and economic power were shifting from the

traditional English heartlands of the southeast to the Midlands and north. This was a long-term process. From statistics we now possess, we can see that, over the period 1693–1843, the following counties fell at least 10 places in the wealth table: Bedfordshire, Berkshire, Buckinghamshire, Dorset, Essex, Hampshire, Huntingdon, Northamptonshire, Suffolk and Wiltshire. Meanwhile the following rose at least 10 places: Cheshire, Derbyshire, Durham, Gloucestershire, Lancashire, Nottingham, Staffordshire and Yorkshire.[222] Huskisson and Palmerston did not possess such precise information, but they were well aware of the trend and they thought Parliament should do something about it, if only to appease middle-class public opinion. From time to time, a traditional borough, with a small electorate, was exposed as grossly corrupt. Then, they argued, it should be stripped of its representation, and the seat or seats given instead to one of the new manufacturing towns that were not represented at all. As Palmerston put it, he wanted the franchise "extended to a great town not because [I] am a friend to reform in principle, but because [I] am its decided enemy. To extend the franchise to large towns . . . was the only mode by which the House could avoid the adoption, at some time or other, of a general plan of reform . . . When people saw such populous places as Leeds and Manchester unrepresented, whilst a green mound of earth returned two Members, it naturally gave rise to complaint."[223]

Palmerston was speaking about the cases of two corrupt boroughs, Penryn and East Retford. He wanted them disenfranchised and their seats to go to Leeds and Manchester. Peel proposed a compromise, under which Retford was enlarged, and the Penryn seats went to Manchester. Unfortunately, on 28 May 1828, there was a muddle over the motion, and both Huskisson and Palmerston ended by voting against the government of which they were both members. Huskisson, a great ditherer, first resigned, then withdrew his resignation, then wavered. Wellington, who did not understand what the muddle was about—he was a member of the Other House—but was sick of Huskisson's half-hearted support, insisted the resignation had been put in, and accepted it. This precipitated a general withdrawal of the old Canningites, a matter which was, characteristically, settled as follows. The Foreign Secretary, John Ward, Lord Dudley (1781–1833) was even more indecisive than was Huskisson. He "stroked his chin, counted the squares of the carpet three times up and three times down, and then went off in an agony of doubt and hesitation." Palmerston and William Lamb (1779–1848), the Irish Secretary, caught him up, and the three ministers walked slowly down the Westminster street, their cabriolets following. Dudley: "Well, now we are by ourselves in the street, and nobody but the sentry to hear us, let me know, right and left, what is meant to be done—'in' or 'out'?" Palmerston: "Out!" Lamb: "Out!—though very regretfully, since he had voted with the government." Palmerston went home and wrote his letter of resignation the same night, and so did Dudley, but "he had to be taken by the arms, with Lamb on his right and Palmerston on his left, and marched down the Foreign Office steps."[224] Lord Ellenborough recorded in his diary that Wellington told him he had no alternative but to let Huskisson and his friends go. He "knew the men he had to deal with. The Canningites all entertained an erroneous and exaggerated view of their own consequence, which existed in the minds of none but themselves. They were always endeavoring to lord it. In this case, if he had solicited Huskisson to remain, he would have been [Prime] Minister instead of himself."[225]

This was the beginning of a great parting of the ways, the prolegomenon to a true two-party system, though men did not realize it at the time. Wellington was pleased to have got rid of some difficult colleagues and made his administration more homogeneous. But running a government was not the same as running an army. The Duke had despised old Liverpool. But Liverpool understood something the Duke did not: that the awkward squad are often the people most worth having in your ministry—that is how he had remained Prime Minister continuously for 15 years, an achievement never since equaled. These departures left Wellington with Peel as his only heavyweight colleague, the only senior minister capable of defending the government successfully in the Commons. The rest were subalterns, and Palmerston noted with relish that "the Duke begins to find that it is not quite so pleasant a thing as he thought it, in the long run, to do everything himself; and that the subservience of his colleagues does not quite compensate for the helplessness which arises from that want of energy and information by which alone that subservience & absence of individual opinion can be created."[226] Moreover, Palmerston, having left the government and sacrificed his ministerial salary—an important consideration with him—was not prepared to allow it an easy passage. He wanted to be back in office on his own terms, possibly with Earl Grey's Whigs, who had formed the hard core of the Opposition for two decades. On 1 June 1829, he set out the new parameters of British politics and related them to what was happening across the Channel. "There are," he told the Commons, "two great parties in Europe; one which attempts to bear sway by the force of public opinion, and another which endeavours to bear sway by the force of physical control, and the judgement, almost unanimous, of Europe assigns the latter as the present connection of England. The principle on which the system of this party is founded is, in my view, fundamentally erroneous. There is in nature no moving power but mind [and] in human affairs this power is opinion; in political affairs it is public opinion; and he who can grasp this power, with it will subdue the fleshly arm of physical strength . . . those statesmen who know how to avail themselves of the passion and the interest and the opinions of mankind are able . . . to exercise a sway over human affairs far out of all proportion greater than belong to the power and resources of the state over which they preside."[227]

This was the first of a series of major speeches which suddenly brought Palmerston to the very forefront of Commons debate in 1829–30 and caused Peel increasing concern. By spring 1830 Peel had other worries. Though he and the Duke had carried Catholic Emancipation easily with the help of Opposition votes, they had not been forgiven by a powerful group of Tory ultras who from now on voted regularly against the government. They made getting the government's business through the Commons increasingly difficult, for—another disquieting phenomenon—many of the country gentlemen were becoming reluctant to vote regularly. Peel pressed Wellington to enlarge the basis of the ministry's support by taking back Palmerston. This the Duke was willing to do, but Palmerston insisted that others come back with him, and the Duke refused. Then, on 26 June 1830, George IV died and was succeeded by his nautical brother as William IV. The succession entailed by law the dissolution of Parliament and a general election, held in July–August. The event offered Wellington an excellent opportunity to do a handsome thing which was also in the national interest: to resign as Prime Minister and to advise the new King to call on Peel to form a fundamentally reconstructed government. There is reason to believe the Duke thought about it and even began a letter to Peel on the subject. But the letter was never sent, and his change of mind was almost certainly due to the influence of Mrs. Arbuthnot.[228]

The Duke's greatest weakness was that he tended to listen to pretty women, who flattered him, rather than to serious, somewhat solemn colleagues like Peel. In this way, he was very like General Jackson. Indeed, it could be said that he had his own kitchen cabinet. The Lord Chancellor, Lord Lyndhurst (1772–1863), told the diarist Charles Greville that the "Duke's little cabinet (the women and the toad-eaters)" hated Peel and destroyed any good feeling that might have existed between the Prime Minister and his chief colleague.[229] Why Mrs. Arbuthnot, who was not a stupid woman and held sensible views on most subjects, disliked and underrated a great statesman like Peel is not clear. It was, I suspect, a case of personal antipathy. Peel had red hair, a feature which many women disliked in the second quarter of the 19th century.[230] Quite unintentionally, his manner was chilly and sometimes even repulsive. Indeed, the awe in which men held him was to cost him his life: An acquaintance who saw him in Hyde Park in 1850 riding a hired horse known to be a bolter was too afraid of Peel to speak to him; the horse threw Peel a few moments afterwards, and he died in agony three days later. In Mrs. Arbuthnot's case, however, Peel's chief failing was his unwillingness to call on her and have cozy chats about politics as Castlereagh had always done, and the Duke did. But Peel was completely devoted to his own beautiful and spirited wife Julia and was simply not interested in other women. In any case, he regarded calling as a waste of time, and he probably thought, as did others, that Mrs. Arbuthnot was the Duke's mistress. He was rather puritanical about such things, being middle class. At all events, the offer was not made, and the Duke remained in control with an increasingly discontented second in command.

The 1830 election brought mixed blessings for the government, and one absolute disaster. Peel's two parliamentary brothers lost their seats. John Wilson Croker, his most effective front-bench colleague, was defeated at Dublin University, and had to come in later at Aldeburgh, a pocket borough. In mid-August, Joe Planta, now Chief Whip, sent Peel a list which seemed to show an overall gain for the government of 17 seats, giving it a total of 368 against 234 for the Opposition, a majority of 134. But these figures did not mean much. To have a working majority, a government needed a theoretical majority of at least 100, since many members of Parliament simply did not turn up when requested. This tendency became more marked toward the end of the 1820s because the continual process of "economic reform" (the removal of corruption and synecures), which had been going on since the 1780s, was now having a real impact on governmental patronage. Wellington often complained that he had nothing to give away. Just when the spoils system was getting a grip on the United States federal government, it was vanishing in Britain. This had an increasing effect on the reliability of governmental support. Simultaneously, and no doubt reflecting the rising political temperature, the Opposition was becoming more cohesive and disciplined. It could now regularly pull out almost its full numbers—200 members or more—and that was perhaps the biggest threat of all.[231]

The absolute disaster for the government was the sudden reemergence, bigger, noisier, more popular, and more dangerous than ever before, of Henry Brougham. Just before the old Parliament had been dissolved, he had made a tremendous speech on slavery, threatening the government that he was now going to campaign for absolute abolition and that he intended to smash them to atoms if they resisted. This harangue made a huge impact in the north, and the editor of the *Leeds Mercury*, Edward Bains, had Brougham nominated for the greatest electoral prize in the kingdom, one of the four Yorkshire county seats. It was so vast and expensive that it had been contested only four times in the past 100 years, each time coinciding with a major national crisis: the hated Excise Tax in 1734, war and the fall of Walpole in 1741, the slave trade in 1807, and now slavery and reform. The previous contest had forced Lords Harewood and Fitzwilliam to fork out £100,000 each for their sons, and in 1826 John Marshall had had to pay £30,000 even without a contest.[232] There were over 20,000 electors, covering a wide social range, so victory in a contest was a real indication of public opinion, especially if the campaign was fought on issues, rather than simply being a power-and-prestige contest between two grand local families. The notable fact about Brougham's candidacy was that he was the first non-Yorkshireman to stand since the mid-17th century; he could not even plead the slender local connection he flaunted in Westmoreland in 1818. The campaign took place against the fiery background of the fall of the regime in Paris, impending events elsewhere in Europe, and the rising rural agitation in England. It also took place during the York Assizes: Brougham battled in court for his clients in the morning, then rushed by fast post chaise to all the towns within a range of 30 miles from the county town. He was addressing 70,000 people a day, among the largest meetings ever held in Britain, rivaling even Daniel O'Connell's monster assemblies.[233]

On 7 August Brougham was declared elected. That evening he had to observe the old custom of riding round the castle yard at York on a charger, with spurs, cocked hat, and sword. He called it "the proudest moment of my life. My return to parliament by the greatest and most wealthy constituency in England was the highest compliment ever paid to a public man." Lord Althorpe, leader of the Commons Whigs, echoed him: "the greatest reward that ever was bestowed on a public man, and the greatest that can be." The *Edinburgh Review* called it "the most extraordinary event in the history of party politics."[234] It was felt that he could now speak not only for Yorkshire, but for all its great, unrepresented industrial cities. The Whig member for Newcastle, William Orde, called him "the Member for Yorkshire, or rather one should say the Member for Leeds, Huddersfield and Sheffield."[235] Newspapers and magazines all over the country echoed this theme. So, in Yorkshire at least, the demos had moved, too, and Brougham—even more famous as a journalist than as a lawyer—was leading it in triumph to Westminster. At the end of August 1830, Brougham seemed set to become, as

Jackson had become in the United States, Britain's first true populist leader. The moment he got to London he announced he was to lead an out-and-out campaign for parliamentary reform.

Governments in long-term decline often find that their luck runs out. So it happened now. The end of the decade saw the first dramatic climax in the transport revolution that was sweeping the world. In the late 1820s, both Paris and London got their first well-organized systems of public transport. In Paris, the new Compagnie des Omnibus had 100 horse-drawn buses, charging 5 sous a ride and taking 30,000 passengers a day. Its smaller competitors took another 30,000.[236] Early in 1829, an English coach builder, George Shillibeer (1797–1866), who had been working in Paris and had built the latest buses, decided to sell his business, come to London and set up a similar network. To cope with London's increasing traffic jams, he designed a small and more maneuverable bus, drawn by only two horses, with 12 passengers inside and two on top. The service started in June 1829 and proved an instant success. By summer 1830 he had a fleet of 20 buses, and others were imitating him. Leigh Hunt was ecstatic: "By the invention of the omnibus, all the world keeps its own coach, and with what cheapness! No plague with servants, no expense for liveries, no coachmakers' and horsedoctors' bills, no keeping one's fellow creatures waiting for us in the cold nighttime and rain, while the dance is going down the room or another hour is spent bidding goodbye and lingering over the comfortable fire. We have no occasion to think of it at all until we want it, and then it either comes to your own door, or you sally forth, and in a few minutes see it hulling up the street."[237] The big transport event of 1830, however—indeed, one of the key moments in world transport history—was the opening of the first long-distance passenger railway, the Liverpool and Manchester line, on 15 September. As we have seen, this great project of the Stephensons involved not only enormous expenditures, but the mastering of unprecedented difficulties in laying the track through difficult country. The completion of the railway, at the very frontiers of 1820s technology, was a matter of intense satisfaction for all concerned, not least its most enthusiastic political supporter, William Huskisson, who held Canning's old seat in Liverpool. For the opening he arranged for both Wellington and Peel, as well as scores of other celebrities, to come north and travel on the first service.

It was at this point that politics made a fatal entry. The rural riots; the explosions on the Continent; the election and the triumph of Brougham; and above all, the growing pressure for parliamentary reform had brought the Duke round to Peel's view that an effort should be made to enlarge the government's support by bringing back the liberals and former Canningites. In this process Huskisson was a key figure because if he laid down impossible conditions, the reshuffle was not practicable. On the other hand, if he proved friendly, the Duke could go ahead, and the sooner the better. The trip north, it was thought, would be an excellent chance for an informal chat with Huskisson outside the hothouse atmosphere of Westminster. Indeed, without this inducement, the Duke might not have gone at all because he did not like railways ("Depend upon it, Sir, nothing will come of them!").

The arrangements for the opening were as follows. There were eight trains leaving Manchester. One carried the Duke, Peel, Huskisson and 80 of the grandest guests. This train was pulled by the Northumbrian, driven by George Stephenson himself, taking the south track. The other seven trains, taking the rest of the guests, followed on the north track at close intervals. At Parkside, 17 miles from Liverpool, all the engines stopped to water, the idea being that the Duke's train should then remain standing, while the other seven passed in procession, by way of salute. Then all would proceed into Liverpool for elaborate dining and wining. Parkside was reached in 56 minutes, and the duke's train stopped as planned. Huskisson and some others then got out onto the track to stretch their legs. This was standard practice while coaching long distance, and no one had yet appreciated how dangerous it might be on the new railways. When the Duke, sitting in his big state carriage, saw Huskisson, he waved in greeting, and so Huskisson hurried forward. This was the obvious moment for the chat. The Duke opened his door and held out his hand. At that moment someone saw the Rocket, with the third train, approaching on the north track, and shouted "Get in! Get in!" Two men flattened themselves against the Duke's carriage. Prince Esterhazy, Liszt's first patron, was hauled into another compartment. But Huskisson, who was suffering from acute rheumatism after attending George IV's long, chilly funeral, characteristically dithered, then lurched forward, stumbled while trying to get round the open door of the Duke's carriage, lost his balance and fell onto the north track just as the Rocket thundered down. The wheels passed over Huskisson's thigh and crushed it. He said: "I have met my death." Stephenson acted with admirable presence of mind. He had Huskisson lifted into the first coach, uncoupled the rest, then thundered to Eccles at the reckless speed of 36 miles an hour. There, the poor man was taken to the vicarage, and medical assistance was brought, but it was too late. Had Astley Cooper been one of the guests, it might have been a different matter.[238]

This first fatal railway accident proved a nail in the government's coffin, too. With Huskisson dead, the plan to enlarge the government lost much of its point. Negotiations continued into November, but the Duke was not prepared to concede much and Peel, seeing his mood, lost interest. With one three-year interval, Peel had been in office 20 years. He was increasingly reluctant to go on with a master who appeared neither to trust nor to confide in him. The Duke, often reasonable, could also be intransigent and peremptory. The fall of the Bourbons had not frightened him at all. He made a point of entertaining poor Marshal Marmont, when he arrived in London, a refugee. On a visit to Woolwich Arsenal, he arranged for the Marshal to meet the English soldier who had shot off his arm at Salamanca and had then lost one of his own at Waterloo. "Ah, *mon ami*," said Marmont, embracing him, "every man gets his turn!"[239] As the autumn progressed, the Duke became increasingly tetchy. He had been shocked by the unexpected death earlier in the year of Sir Thomas Lawrence, who had painted him many times and whom he enjoyed bullying. "Lawrence is a man of no mind," he would say. "Set the thing before him, he can do it. But he has no invention." He liked to recount an exchange after he had sat for Lawrence for three hours. "Pshaw, Sir Thomas, that is not like my sword." "Please, your Grace, I'll do it again next time." "No. Do it now." "I must go to the Princess Augusta's, your Grace." "No, now, you *must* put my sword right, it is really bad." "Ha!" the Duke would conclude, "it was done."[240] Now the President of the Royal Academy was gone, bringing to an end a great epoch in English painting. Was another great epoch ending in politics?

When Parliament met, Brougham was at once active and threatened to bring in a motion for radical reform on 16 November. On 2 November the House of Lords debated the King's Speech, which promised both firmness at home and abroad and conciliation. Earl Grey spoke for the Opposition. The Duke replied for his government. He was now barely on speaking terms with Peel, who seemed tired, listless and fatalistic, and he certainly had not discussed what he would say with his deputy. It is not clear how carefully he had considered it himself. Grey had said he favored reform but was not committed to any particular proposal. Wellington answered him: Not only was he, as Prime Minister, opposed to all particular proposals so far brought forward, he was opposed to reform in principle. The present system was as near perfection as possible, he asserted. It was better than anything else in any other country. If he was asked to draw up a constitution for a new country, he could produce no more admirable model than Britain's exactly as it stood. Its great virtue was that it was heavily weighted in favor of landed proprietors. Hence, not only was he not prepared to bring in any reforms, but he would resist with all his power reforms proposed by anyone else.[241] When he sat down, there was a stunned silence. He turned to his colleague Lord Aberdeen, who had succeeded Dudley as Foreign Secretary: "I have not said too much, have I?" The Scots Earl replied drily, "Ye'll hear of it." When he was leaving the Lords, someone asked Aberdeen what the Duke had said and he answered: "He said that we were going out."[242]

The same evening, Croker had a little chat with Palmerston. They had first become close governmental colleagues more than 20 years before. "Well, I will bring the matter to a point," said Croker. "Are you resolved, or are you not, to vote for Parliamentary Reform?" "I am." "Well then, there is no use in talking to you any more on this subject. You and I, I am grieved to see, shall never again sit on the same bench together."[243] On 15 November, the day before Brougham's motion on reform was due, the government was beaten, 233–204, on a Civil List vote. The truth is, once Wellington had slammed the door on any kind of reform, Peel had given up in despair. He told Wellington that 17 of their usual supporters had voted against or paired, all the former Canningites and Huskisson supporters had voted against, plus all the Tory ultras, and of the 66 English county members present, 49 had voted against, too. That was the measure of the way in which opinion was now moving in favor of reform, and of the cost of the Duke's intransigence. The Duke said nothing but, talking to Mrs. Arbuthnot later, he blamed Peel, in effect, for ratting. "There was no man in our cabinet," he added, "who cared one pin about parliamentary reform or anything else, excepting a quiet life."[244] It was the first time a government had been turned out on a Commons vote since 1804. More seriously, it was the end of the great, sustained governing alliance which had been created by Pitt the Younger in the early 1780s and which, with one or two minor intervals, had steered Britain through the Industrial Revolution, the greatest war in its history, and a difficult and dangerous aftermath. It was an immense watershed in the nation's development, opening the way directly to a Whig government, a two-party system, and a fundamental reform in the suffrage and composition of the House of Commons.

But there was to be no surrender to radicalism, no putting the demos on the throne. Earl Grey, summoned (16 November) by William IV to form a government, had no intention of allowing real power to slip from the hands of the great landed families to which he belonged by birth and connection. There was to be no equivalent in England of the storming of Washington by the hungry place seekers or the lavish reward of journalists and writers in Paris. The first problem Grey had to deal with was Brougham. Brougham's Yorkshire victory had seemed to place the political world at his feet. But in his impatience and vanity, he simply kicked an own-goal. He had told his Yorkshire constituents: "Nothing on earth shall ever tempt me to accept place." Had he waited, he might well have led, in a year or two, an irresistible populist movement on the scale of Jackson's, which would have made him the first man in the kingdom, or possibly even the first president of an ex-kingdom. Grey's initial offer to him was the Attorney Generalship, which Brougham felt was an insult. By 19 November Grey was convinced that he could not form an effective government unless Brougham was in some way muzzled, since Brougham would speak in the House of Commons as the people's voice against the Whig ministers. So he then, with great cunning, offered Brougham the Lord Chancellorship, which meant a transfer to the House of Lords. Brougham again refused. But he was then cornered by Althorp (Grey's lieutenant), the Earl of Sefton; the Whig Chief Whip, Duncannon; and his own brother James. Althorp told him that unless he agreed to accept the Woolsack, Grey would decline to form a government. "You take upon yourself the responsibility," he warned, "of keeping our party for another 25 years out of power, and the loss of all the great questions which will follow, instead of their being carried." Brougham's brother James spoke to the same effect. At this point, according to Brougham's own account, he gave in.[245] In truth, however, there was another factor. To a lawyer from nowhere, especially a Scotsman, the Lord Chancellorship of England was a glittering, a truly dazzling prize. To get it in one bound, never having held office before, and to get it with the assurance of everyone that he was sacrificing ambition to high-minded duty, was a temptation that proved irresistible. Brougham was indeed dazzled. Thus blinded to his long-term interest, he fell into the trap.

Once the trap was sprung, and Brougham was irretrievably promoted to the Lords, never to dominate the Commons again, the Whigs, and indeed others, could afford to laugh. As Wellington said, "Nobody cares a damn for the House of Lords, the House of Commons is everything in England, and the House of Lords nothing."[246] The Secretary to the Privy Council, Greville, recorded the general astonishment and delight among the ruling class at "a charm having been found potent enough to lay the unquiet spirit a bait rich enough to tempt his restless ambition . . . all men feel that he is emasculated and drops on the Woolsack as on his political deathbed. Once in the House of Lords, there is an end to him, and he may rant, storm and thunder without hurting anybody."[247] The taming of Brougham was regarded as such a coup that William IV promptly claimed all the credit for it. "You are all under a great obligation to me," he boasted to Lord Holland. "I have *settled* Brougham. He will not be dangerous any more."[248]

With the Brougham problem disposed of, Grey could set about his own division of the spoils. There were plenty of jobs for the boys—and for the girls, too, in the shape of the top court appointments, such as Mistress of the Robes—but it was the great Whig families who got them all. Some unconsidered trifles were thrown to the journalistic dogs. Macaulay, who came into the Commons as member for Calne, got a commissionership at the Board of Control, which governed India, and was eventually to make his fortune there, winning himself the leisure to write his best-selling *History of England*. Sydney Smith got a canonry at Saint Paul's (though not the bishopric he craved). Mackintosh, another *Edinburgh Review* man, also got a commissionership, and Jeffrey, its editor, was made Lord Advocate. But all this was small beer. The key posts went to what Disraeli called "the Venetian oligarchy." Lamb, for instance, now Lord Melbourne, became Home Secretary, and Palmerston, Foreign Secretary. With two exceptions, every member of Grey's cabinet was a peer or the heir to a peerage. Its members owned more land than any of its Tory predecessors. The Tories had been rather adventurous in bringing forward men from the new classes: Sidmouth, the son of a doctor; Canning, the son of an actress; and Peel, the son of a self-made mill owner, just as later they were the first to give the leadership to a man of Jewish origin and to a woman. But the Whigs believed in "the simple, old-fashioned snobbery of the pound sterling and strawberry leaves."[249] They kept the real power in the hands of a small group of interrelated families, all very rich, all deriving their fortunes from broad acres. In due course, their Reform Bill gave a measure of power to the middle classes, enfranchising one in six adult males. But for the present, land, as always in the past, remained the basis for the direct exercise of power. Indeed, the first thing the new Whig ministers did was to launch a ferocious series of prosecutions of the Swing rioters. Over 2,000 rioters were brought to trial in 30 counties, the vast majority of them simple country laborers. A quarter of them were transported.[250] Thus, the modern age began in Britain, too, with a series of ambiguities, contradictions, and ironies.

All over the advanced world, men knew that life was changing, irrevocably and at increasing speed. Writers and artists were particularly aware of it. But they were sharply divided in their response. Some, like Macaulay and Berlioz, rejoiced noisily in the opportunities it offered. Others hated it. Rossini almost stopped composing forever, so detestable did he find the new world being born. Southey, Coleridge and Wordsworth all feared and opposed the notion of a Reform Bill. Southey recorded that Lord Lowther seemed to have aged 20 years in a few months and that Wordsworth was switching his savings to the American funds—an imprudent decision, as it turned out.[251] Wordsworth, hearing about the Liverpool–Manchester Railway, could see it, in his mind's eye, creeping up through Lancashire and then turning left into his beloved Westmorland, a more terrifying threat even than Brougham. He had always seen himself as a distant observer of the changing world, perched on a hilltop, looking down through the clouds and mist, his mind torn between wonder at its beauty and fears about its future. The image found expression in one of his early poems, *A Night-Piece,* composed in 1798 though not published until 1815.

Three years later, this notion was visualized in a remarkable painting by Caspar David Friedrich (1774–1840), *Wanderer Above a Sea of Fog* (1818), now in the Kunsthall, Hamburg. Friedrich was four years Wordsworth's junior and shared with him a passionate love of nature, which like Wordsworth he reconstructed to suit his own artistic purposes. Like Wordsworth, he made use of the device of the halted traveler, the *Ruckenfigur,* who stops to gaze down into the landscape below. Friedrich thought the new, modern world horrific. The Industrial Revolution, to his mind, was a disaster for civilization. He particularly blamed the English for carrying it through. Examining a print done by the new technique of steel engraving, which filled him with revulsion, he said it had been done "either by an Englishman or a machine." "I am not so weak," he wrote, "as to submit to the demands of the age when they go against my convictions. I shall leave it to time to show what will come of it—either a brilliant butterfly, or a maggot."[252] His wanderer, dressed in a frock coat, looking down from a rock into a sea of mist from which mountains and pinnacles emerge, is a symbol of humanity contemplating the new world taking shape. You cannot see what the man thinks of what he observes: He turns an enigmatic back to the viewer.[253]

If writers and artists were divided about welcoming modernity, they were confused, too, about whether it had all arrived or was just beginning. Writing about his great love-hate figure Coleridge, in *The Spirit of the Age* (1825), Hazlitt thought "the world is growing old. We are so far advanced in the arts and sciences, that we live in retrospect, and dote on past achievements. The accumulation of knowledge has been so great, that we are lost in wonder at the height it has reached, instead of attempting to climb or add to it. . . . What *niche* remains unoccupied? What path untried?" But few agreed with him. His friend Lamb, who had much less taste for progress than did Hazlitt, felt that mankind was just at the beginning of its modern adventure and viewed the future with considerable anxiety, especially during the climactic year 1830. On 18 September, three days after Huskisson became the first railway accident victim, Lamb held in his arms the dying Hazlitt, worn out, disappointed, disillusioned. Hazlitt heard about events in France and Belgium with satisfaction, but his spirits were low: "Ah, I am afraid Charles," he said, "that things will go back again."[254] They were his last words.

Three months later, right at the end of the year, Lamb wrote a remarkable letter to his old friend George Dyer, on the wonders and evils of modern inventions. In particular he dwelt on that simple but vital new product, the Lucifer Match, which had first come on the market three years before, in 1827. It was an enormous boon to the housewife and countless other people who had to get up early to light fires and lamps. It was also a blessing, he noted, to the followers of Captain Swing. Lamb was now living in a cottage at Enfield, north of London, where the uttermost suburbs ended and the fields and farms began.

"Poor Enfield, that has been so peaceable hitherto," he told Dyer, "has caught the inflammatory fever, the tokens are upon her! A great fire was blazing last night in the barns and haystacks of a farmer, about half a mile from us. Where will these things end? There is no doubt of its being the work of some ill-disposed rustic; but how is he to be discovered? They go to work in the dark with strange chemical preparations unknown to our forefathers. There is not even a dark lantern to have a chance of detecting these Guy Fauxes. We are past the iron age and have got into the fiery age, undream'd of by Ovid. . . . It was never good times in England since the poor began to speculate on their condition. Formerly they jogged on with as little reflection as horses; the whistling ploughman went cheek-by-jowl with his brother that neighed. Now the biped carries a box of phosphorus in his leather-breeches; and in the dead of night the half-illuminated beast steals his magic potion into a cleft in a barn, and half a county is grinning with new fires. . . . What a power to intoxicate his crude brains, just muddlingly awake, to perceive that something is wrong in the social system—what a hellish faculty above gunpowder. . . . What temptation above Lucifer's! Why, here was a spectacle last night for a whole county—a bonfire visible in London, alarming her guilty towers and shaking the Monument with an aguefit—all done by a little vial of phosphor in a clown's fob! How he must grin, and shake his empty noddle in clouds, the Vulcanian Epicure! Can we ring the bells back-wards? Can we unlearn the arts that pretend to civilise, and then burn the world? There is a March of Science. But who shall beat the drums for its retreat?"[255]

Answer came there none, nor ever can.

NOTES

ONE
A Special Relationship

1 Malcolm J. Rohrbough, *The Trans-Appalachian Frontier: People, Societies and* Institutions, *1775–1850* (Oxford, 1978), 359.

2 *Dictionary of National Biography,* compact ed., vol. 2, 1574–75; Colonel John Gurwood, *Wellington's Dispatches 1799–1815,* 13 vols. (London, 1834–39), vol. 6, 434.

3 For the battle, see C. B. Brooks, *The Siege of New Orleans* (New York, 1961); and Robin Reilly: *The British at the Gates* (New York, 1974). An earlier account is Alexander Walker, *Jackson and New Orleans* (New York, 1856). From the British viewpoint, there is H. F. Rankin, ed., *The Battle of New Orleans, a British View: The Journal of Major C. R. Forrest* (London, 1961). I have mainly followed the account in Robert V. Remini, *Andrew Jackson and the Course of American Empire, 1776–1821* (New York, 1977), 260–87.

4 Lady Bourchier, *Memoire . . . of Sir Edward Codrington,* 2 vols. (London, 1873), vol. 1: *The American Campaign,* 309ff; letter of 9 January 1815, 335–36.

5 J. S. Bassett, ed., *Correspondence of Andrew Jackson,* 6 vols. (Washington, 1926–33), vol. 1,1. For basic biographical data, I follow Remini.

6 James Parton, *Life of Andrew Jack-son,* 3 vols. (Boston, 1866), vol. 3, 699; quoted in Remini.

7 A. C. Buell, *History of Andrew Jackson,* 2 vols. (New York, 1904), vol. 2, 410–11; quoted in Remini.

8 Remini, 11.

9 Letter to Amos Kendall, 9 January 1844, Jackson Papers in the Library of Congress, quoted in Remini, 23.

10 Remini, 120–23.

11 Ibid., 184–85.

12 For these various ailments, see Remini, *Andrew Jackson and the Course of American Freedom, 1822–32* (New York, 1981), 1–3.

13 Parton, vol. 3, 63–65.

14 See E. F. Heckscher, *The Continental System* (London, 1922); F. E. Melvin, *Napoleon's Navigation System,* 4 vols. (London, 1922).

15 Text of the order is in *Hansard* x, 126ff., and is given in Heckscher, Appendix 1.

16 See A. L. Burt, *The United States, Great Britain and British North America from the Revolution to the Establishment of Peace After the War of 1812* (London, 1940).

17 A good modern discussion of the Orders in Council is given in Chester New, *The Life of Henry Brougham to 1830* (Oxford, 1961), chap. 6: "Repealing the Orders in Council," 58ff.

18 For the "Chesapeake Incident," see

W. P. Cresson, *James Monroe* (Chapel Hill, 1946), 230–35.

19 C. F. Adams, ed., *The Memoirs of John Quincy Adams,* 12 vols. (New York, 1874–77), vol. 6, 196.

20 J. B. McMaster, *A History of the People of the United States from the Revolution to the Civil War,* 6 vols. (New York, 1895), vol. 4, 199ff.

21 Quoted in J. W. Pratt, *The Expansionists of 1812* (New York, 1925), 112.

22 Samuel F. Bemis et al., eds., *The American Secretaries of State and Their Diplomacy,* 17 vols. (New York, 1927–67), vol. 3, 223.

23 Edgar McInnis, *Canada: A Social and Political History,* rev. ed. (New York, 1958), 194.

24 For examples, see William Atherton, *Narrative of the Sufferings and Defeat of the North-Western Army under General Winchester* (New York, n.d.), 25–31, 56–67; Elias Barnall, *Account of the Hardships etc. . . . . of those Heroic Kentucky Volunteers and Regulars . . . in the Year 1812–13* (New York, n.d.), 36–38, 49–54.

25 McMaster, vol. 4, 7.

26 *Niles's Weekly Register,* vol. 3, 283, p. 4.

27 *Lansingberg Gazette,* September 1813; *True American,* 7 October 1813. Details in McMaster.

28 McMaster, vol. 4, 40.

29 Portrait reproduced in H. W. Dickinson, *Robert Fulton, Engineer and Artist* (London, 1913).

30 Ibid., 17–21.

31 Ibid., 73–93, 125.

32 Kathryn Cave, ed., *The Diary of Joseph Farington,* 16 vols. (New Haven, Conn., 1978–84), vol. 6, entry for 29 May 1803, 2040–41. See also entry for 26 May 1803, 2038 (hereafter called *Farington's Diary*).

33 Quoted in Dickinson, 182–87, 194–99.

34 *Edinburgh Evening Courant,* 31 August 1815.

35 C. W. Pasley: *An Essay on the Military Policy and Institutions of the British Empire* (London, 1810), 448. For details of his life and career, see *Dictionary of National Biography,* compact ed., vol. 2, 1604.

36 For Shrapnel, see *Dictionary of National Biography,* compact ed., vol. 2, 1919.

37 For biographical details, see ibid., vol. 1, 422; and R. G. Thorne, ed., *History of Parliament: The House of Commons, 1790–1820,* 5 vols. (London, 1986), vol. 3, 493–94.

38 For the technology of the rockets, see Kenneth Mason, *Gunfire in Barbary* (London, 1982), Appendix, "The Rocket Brigade," 185ff.

39 *Quarterly Review,* May 1811.

40 R. W. Chapman, ed., *Letters of Jane Austen,* 2nd ed. (Oxford, 1979), 304.

41 Southey to Scott, 13 January 1813, quoted in Geoffrey Carnall, *Robert Southey and His Age: The Development of a Conservative Mind* (Oxford, 1960), 124.

42 Wordsworth to Pasley in W. Knight, ed., *Prose Works of William Wordsworth* (London, 1896) vol. 1, 315–16.

43 C. C. Southey, ed., *Life and Correspondence of Robert Southey* (London 1849–50), vol. 3, 307, quoted in Carnall, 128ff.

44 The Earl of Dundonald, *Autobiography of a Seaman,* 2 vols. (London, 1860), vol. 2, 227–45.; D. Thomas, *Cochrane* (London, 1978), 192–98.

45 *Farington's Diary,* vol. 12, 4547, 7 July 1814.

46 *Dictionary of National Biography,* compact ed., vol. 1, 751.

47 Chrisopher Lloyd, *Captain Marryat and the Old Navy* (London, 1939), 113.

48 Ibid., 94.

49 But reinstated the following year.

50 McMaster, vol. 4, 116.

51 Lloyd, 147–48.

52 See the description of American frigates in *Farington's Diary,* vol. 15, 5251.

53 Lady Bourchier, 310.

54 *Farington's Diary,* vol. 12, 4407, 20 July 1813.

55 Lloyd, 165ff.

56 Quoted in ibid., 148.

57 The anecdote was told by James Bos-

well, son of the great biographer; *Far-ington's Diary*, vol. 13, 4492, 18 April 1814.

58 S. M. Hamilton, ed., *The Writings of James Monroe*, 8 vols. (New York 1898–1903), vol. 5, 245ff.

59 McMaster, vol. 4, 138ff.

60 Anne H. Wharton, *Social Life in the Early Republic* (Philadelphia, 1902), 172.

61 L. B. Cutts, ed., *Memoirs and Letters of Dolly Madison* (New York, 1886), 110ff.

62 Letter of 28 August 1814, in Lady Bourchier, 315ff.

63 Wharton, 172.

64 McMaster, vol. 4, 155.

65 Lady Bourchier, 317.

66 Quoted in Lloyd, 168–69.

67 Quoted in W. P. Cresson, *James Monroe* (Chapel Hill, 1946), 274.

68 Dale Van Every, *The Disinherited: The Lost Birthright of the American Indian* (New York, 1976).

69 Remini (1977), 301.

70 Reginald Horsman: "British Indian Policy in the North-West, 1807–12," *Mississippi Valley Historical Review*, April 1958.

71 J. F. H. Claiborne: *Mississippi as Province, Territory and State* (Jackson, 1880), 31, quoted in Remini (1977).

72 A. J. Pickett, *History of Alabama* (Charleston, 1851), vol. 2, 275; see also, H. S. Halbert and T. H. Hall, *The Creek War of 1813–14* (University of Alabama, 1969), 151–60.

73 Jackson to Rachel Jackson, 4 November 1813, Jackson Papers in the Library of Congress, quoted in Remini (1977); Davy Crockett: *Life of Davy Crockett* (New York, 1854), 75.

74 This was Lieutenant Richard Keith Call. See J. Doherty Jr., *Richard Keith Call, Southern Unionist* (Gainsville, 1961), 6; quoted in Remini (1977).

75 Jackson to Rachel Jackson, 29 December 1813, Jackson Papers in the Library of Congress, quoted in Remini (1977), 194.

76 For this episode, see Remini (1977), 198–99; J. Reid and J. H. Eaton, *Life of Andrew Jackson* (University of Alabama, reprint 1974), 63–70; Amos Kendall, *Life of General Andrew Jackson* (New York, 1844), 216–17.

77 Jackson to Rachel Jackson, 29 December 1813, Jackson Papers in the Library of Congress, quoted in Remini (1977), 201.

78 Reid and Eaton, 142–43; quoted in Remini (1977), 212.

79 Jackson to William Blount, 31 March 1814 and to General Thomas Pinckney 28 March 1814, in John Spencer Bassett, ed., *The Correspondence of Andrew Jackson*, 6 vols. (Washington, 1926–33), vol. 1, 488–89, 490; quoted in Remini (1977), 214.

80 Bassett, vol. 1 491–92.

81 The speech as given in Reid and Eaton, 164–65; another, similar, version is in Anne Royall, *Letters from Alabama* (Tuscaloosa, 1969), 91–92, this one having been written within three years of the event.

82 Angie Debo, *The Road to Disappearance* (Oklahoma, 1967), 82; Remini, 219.

83 Text of treaty in Charles Kappler, *Indian Affairs: Laws and Treaties* (Washington, 1903), vol. 2, 107–9; letter quoted in Remini (1977), 232.

84 Jackson to Secretary for War John Armstrong, 10 August 1814: *American State Papers, Military Affairs* (Washington, 1832–61), vol. 3, 792.

85 Quoted in Remini (1977), 240.

86 Jackson to W. Allen, 23 December 1814, Jackson Papers in the Library of Congress, quoted in Remini (1977), 154.

87 Norman Gash, *Pillars of Government . . . 1770–1850* (London, 1986), 31.

88 For the treaty making, see F. L. Engelman, *The Peace of Christmas Eve* (New York, 1962); F. A. Updyke, *Diplomacy of the War of 1812* (New York, 1915); Bradford Perkins, *Castlereagh and Adams: England and the United States 1812–23* (New York, 1964).

89 The full Adams diary is in C. F. Adams, ed.; I have used here the handier selection, Allan Nevins, ed.,

Diary of John Quincy Adams 1794–1845 (New York, 1951). The enemies list is given in the entry for 23 November 1835.

90 Entries for 8 and 23 September 1814, in Nevins.

91 Nevins, entry for 4 October 1814, 139.

92 Ibid., entry for 27 November 1814, 145.

93 Ibid., entry for 11 December 1814, 148.

94 Ibid., entry for 25 September 1814, 136–37.

95 Ibid., entry for 13 August 1814, 125.

96 For Goulburn, see *History of Parliament, 1790–1820,* vol. 4, 44–46.

97 Nevins, entry for 1 September 1814, 131.

98 Ibid.

99 Ibid., entry for 8 September 1814, 133.

100 *Annals of Congress, 1814–15,* 100. For Gcre, see *Biographical Dictionary of The U.S. Congress 1774–1989* (Washington, D.C., 1989), 1078.

101 McMaster, vol. 4, 234ff.

102 Nevins, 144.

103 Ibid., 154.

104 McMaster, vol. 4, 274–75.

105 C. J. Bartlett: *Castlereagh* (London, 1966), 236–37; Perkins, *Castlereagh and Adams,* 122–33.

106 Nevins, 151.

107 See J. L. Wright, *Britain and the American Frontier 1783–1815* (Athens, Ga., 1975), 172ff; F. L. Owsley, "Role of the South in the British Grand Strategy in the War of 1812," *Tennessee Historical Quarterly,* Spring 1972; the consequences of the Battle of New Orleans are well analyzed in Remini (1977), 298ff.

108 Text in Fred Israel, ed., *Major Peace Treaties of Modern History 1648–1967* (New York, 1967) vol. 1, 704.

109 Quoted by Daniel J. Boorstin, *The Americans: The National Experience* (London, 1966), 271.

110 Nevins, 214.

111 Text in V. Harlow and F. Madden, *British Colonial Development 1774–1834: Select Documents* (Oxford, 1953), 483ff.

112 Jackson to Monroe, 2 June 1818; Monroe Papers in the New York Public Library, quoted in Remini (1977), 364.

113 Ibid., 357–58.

114 Castlereagh to Sir Charles Bagot, British Minister in Washington, 2 January 1819, printed in P. C. Brooks, *Diplomacy and the Borderland: The Adams-Onis Treaty of 1819* (University of California Press, 1939), 117.

115 Adams to Erving, 28 November 1818, printed in W. C. Ford, ed., *John Quincy Adams, Selected Writings,* 7 vols. (Boston, 1913–17), vol. 6, 474ff.

116 George Dangerfield, *The Era of Good Feelings* (London, 1953), 152.

117 Nevins, 240.

118 Ibid., 252.

119 See A. P. Newton, "International Colonial Rivalry in the New World," in J. Holland Rose, A. P. Newton, and E. A. Benion, eds., *Cambridge History of the British Empire* (Cambridge, 1941), 525ff; texts of treaties are in *United States Treaties and Conventions,* 931–93; and *British and Foreign State Papers,* vol. 12, 38–43.

120 H. W. V. Temperley, *Cambridge History of British Foreign Policy* (Cambridge, 1938), vol. 2, 73.

121 Nevins, entry for 14 February 1827, 370.

122 *Farington's Diary,* vol. 7, 2492, 6 June 1805.

123 A. D. Godley, ed., *Poetical Works of Thomas Moore* (London, 1910), 117.

124 F. Bamford and the Duke of Wellington, eds., *Journal of Mrs Arbuthnot, 1820–32,* 2 vols. (London, 1950), vol. 1, 421.

125 *Dictionary of National Biography,* compact ed., vol. 2, 2226.

126 J. J. Coss, ed., *Autobiography of John Stuart Mill* (New York, 1944), 5–6.

127 See Michael Foot, *The Politics of Paradise: A Vindication of Byron* (London, 1988), 90ff.

128 Leslie A. Marchand, ed., *Byron's Letters and Journals*, 11 vols. (London, 1973–82), vol. 3, 236; vol. 9, 171; vol. 8, 240; vol. 3, 218; vol. 9, 49.

129 Anne P. and John M. Robson, eds., *Works of John Stuart Mill: Volume 22 Newspaper Writings, December 1822–July 1831* (Toronto, 1986), 235–37; the article appeared 9 January 1831, and was commenting on Jackson's 1830 Message to Congress.

130 Review of travel books about America, *Edinburgh Review,* 1818. Reprinted in *Collected Works of the Rev. Sydney Smith,* 3 vols. (London, 1854), vol. 2, 15ff.

131 Ibid., 16.

132 Ibid., 115.

133 Ibid., 367ff; 373.

134 Hulme's account is published as an appendix in J. E. Molpurgo, *Journal of a Year's Residence in the United States of America, 1819, by William Cobbett* (London, 1983); passages quoted on pp. 254, 259, 256–57.

135 Ibid., 192–93.

136 Ibid., 227, 195.

137 Ibid., 216–17.

138 R. W. Chapman, ed., *The Oxford Illustrated Jane Austen,* 6 vols. (Oxford, 1982), vol. 4, 25.

139 Frederick Marryat, *A Diary in America* (London, 1839),

140 Una Pope-Hennessy, ed., *Margaret Hall: The Aristocratic Journey: Letters of Mrs. Basil Hall* (London, 1930); Patrick Shirreff: *A Tour Through North America* (Edinburgh, 1835).

141 Quoted in Jack Larkin, *The Reshaping of Everyday Life, 1790–1840* (New York, 1988), 167–68.

142 Johanna Johnston, *Life, Manners and Travels of Fanny Trollope* (London, 1979), 149ff.

143 Noah Webster, *Rudiments of English Grammar* (Hartford, Conn., 1790), 80.

144 William Thornton, *Cadmus, or a Treatise on the Elements of a Written Language* (Philadelphia, 1793), quoted in David Simpson, *The Politics of American English 1776–1850* (Oxford, 1986).

145 Simpson, p. 25, for example.

146 *Leviathan,* Part 1, chap. 4.

147 Ibid., Part 1, chap. 5.

148 Quoted in Larkin.

149 See the list in J. A. Gere and J. Sparrow, eds., *Geoffrey Madan's Notebooks* (Oxford, 1981), 26.

150 R. G. Thwaites: *Original Journals of the Lewis and Clark Expedition,* 8 vols. (New York 1904–05); for American neologisms and borrowings, see Boorstin, 282–84.

151 *Collected Works of the Rev. Sydney Smith,* vol. 2, 122–23.

152 See Martin Green, "The God That Neglected to Come: American Literature 1780–1820," in Marcus Cunliffe, ed., *American Literature to 1900* (London, 1986), 53ff.

153 Ibid., 55.

154 Walter A. Reichart, *Washington Irving and Germany* (University of Michigan, 1957), 22–23, 42.

155 H. A. Pochmann: "Irving's German Sources in the *Sketch Book,*" *Studies in Philology,* 1930, 477–507.

156 Pierre M. Irving, ed., *Life and Letters of Washington Irving,* 3 vols. (London, 1962), vol. 2, 8–9.

157 Ibid., vol. 1, 128.

158 Cunliffe, 78.

159 Irving, vol. 2, 56.

160 Ibid., vol. 2, 24.

161 Jackson's remark quoted in Samuel Eliot Morrison, *History of the American People,* 3 vols. (Oxford, 1972), vol. 2, 161.

162 Otto von Pivka, *Armies of the Napoleonic Era* (Newton Abbot, 1979), 253ff.

163 Erik W. Austin: *Political Facts of the*

United States Since 1788 (New York, 1986), Table 5.1.

164 C. R. Fay, "The Movement Towards Free Trade, 1820–53," in *Cambridge History of the British Empire* (Cambridge, England, 1941), 388ff.

165 Mason, 42–43.

166 Austin, *Political Facts,* Table 7.1.

167 Alexander Kucherov, "Alexander Herzen's Parallel Between the United States and Russia," in J. S. Curliss, ed., *Essays in Russian and Soviet History* (Leiden, 1963), 3. Herzen was writing in 1857.

TWO
The Congress Dances

1 Thomas Barnes, *Parliamentary Portraits* (London, 1819), 18–19, quoted in J. E. Cookson, *Lord Liverpool's Administration: The Crucial Years, 1815–22* (Edinburgh, 1975), 37.

2 Philip Henry, Earl Stanhope, *Notes on Conversations with the Duke of Wellington* (Oxford, 1938), 28–29.

3 Elizabeth Longford, *Wellington: The Years of the Sword* (London, 1969) 383–84.

4 M. Brialmont and G. R. Gleig, *Life of Arthur, Duke of Wellington,* 4 vols. (London 1858–60), vol. 1, 6.

5 Longford, 98–99.

6 Ibid., 402, 184, 321–22, 299–300, 185, 218. Many similar remarks are recorded.

7 Stanhope, 30.

8 William Hazlitt, *Political Essays, with Sketches of Public Characters* (London, 1820), preface.

9 Hazlitt, *Life of Napoleon* 4 vols. (London, 1828).

10 Quoted in Jean Clay, *Romanticism* (trans. London, 1981).

11 See Peter Campbell: *French Electoral Systems since 1789* (London, 1965), 50ff.

12 Ingvar Andersson: *A History of Sweden* (trans., London, 1956), 316, 330.

13 Stewart Oakley: *The Story of Denmark* (London, 1972), 7–14.

14 For the significance of Goya's subject matter, see the sections on his paintings in Hugh Honour, *Romanticism* (London, 1977); Clay; Kenneth Clark: *The Romantic Rebellion* (London, 1973).

15 Honour, 217–18 and fn 3, p. 355.

16 E. H. Gombrich, "Imagery and Art in the Romantic Period," *Meditations on a Hobby-Horse,* 2nd ed. (London, 1971), 120–25.

17 George Sand, *Histoire de Ma Vie* (Paris, 1853–54).

18 Quoted by Isaiah Berlin, *Four Essays on Liberty* (Oxford, 1969), ix.

19 Frank Eyck, ed. and trans., *Frederick Hertz: The German Public Mind in the 19th Century* (London, 1975), 15–16.

20 Honour, 221.

21 Alan Palmer, *Metternich* (London, 1972), 75.

22 The event is well described in Harold Nicolson, *The Congress of Vienna* (London, 1946), 4ff.

23 August Fournier, *Napoleon I* (Leipzig, 1889), vol. 3, 108.

24 For this trip, see Armand-Augustin-Louis, Marquis de Caulaincourt and Duc de Vicence, *Memoires,* 3 vols. (Paris, 1933).

25 Quoted in Palmer, 91.

26 Quoted in ibid., 99; Nicolson, 42.

27 Quoted by Nicolson, 93.

28 Ibid., 95.

29 Louis to Talleyrand 21 October 1814, quoted in ibid., 225.

30 Quoted in ibid., 107.

31 Ibid., 108.

32 Stanhope, 126.

33 Leslie A. Marchand, ed., *Byron's Letters and Journals,* 11 vols. (London, 1937–82), vol. 4, 277–78.

34 See the "Chronology of Jane Austen's Life," in Deirdre le Faye, ed., *Jane Austen: A Family Record* (London, 1989), xvff.

35 Stanhope, 25–26.

36 Metternich gave this account in a letter to Croker, reproduced in L. J. Jennings, ed., *Letters and Papers of John Wilson Croker*, 3 vols. 2nd ed. (London, 1885), vol. 3, 233ff.

37 Nicolson, 227–28.

38 Longford, 393–94.

39 *Journal of Mrs. Arbuthnot*, 28 July 1821, 112–13.

40 John Gore, ed., *Creevey* (London, 1949), 136.

41 Antony Brett-James, *The Hundred Days: Napoleon's Last Campaign from Eye-witness Accounts* (London, 1964), 39.

42 Beatrice Madan, ed., *Spencer and Waterloo: The Letters of Spencer Madan, 1814–16* (London, 1970), 166–67.

43 Figures from Longford, 456–57.

44 Marquess of Anglesey, *One Leg: Life and Letters of Henry William Paget* (London, 1963), 149–50.

45 Longford, 472. Kathryn Cave, ed., *The Diary of Joseph Farington*, 16 vols. (New Haven, Conn., 1978–84), vol. 14, 5091 (hereafter called *Farington's Diary*).

46 Wellington, *Dispatches*, 12 vols. (London, 1834–38), vol. 12, 529.

47 Gore, 141–42.

48 Stanhope, 173.

49 Lady Bourchier, *Memoire . . . of Sir Edward Codrington*, 2 vols. (London, 1873), 345; *Reminiscences of Captain Gronow*, 2 vols. (London, reprint, 1984), vol. 2, 204–05.

50 J. H. Dible, *Napoleon's Surgeon* (London, 1970), 238ff; for Larrey's contribution to military medicine, see R. G. Richardson: "Larrey: What Manner of Man?" *Proceedings of the Royal Society of Medicine* (London) vol. 60 (July 1977).

51 Gronow, vol. 2, 273–74.

52 Vincent Cronin, *Napoleon* (London, 1971), 405–07.

53 Jennings, *Croker Letters*, vol. 1 (London, 1984), 73.

54 W. Robertson Nicol, ed., *Southey's Journal of a Tour of the Netherlands*

55 R. D. Altick: *The Shows of London* (Cambridge, Mass., 1978), 239–41; *Farington's Diary*, vol. 14, 4891, 24 August 1816.

56 Gordon N. Ray, *Thackeray: The Uses of Adversity 1811–1846* (Oxford, 1955), 66.

57 Sketch of the face in the Victoria and Albert Museum; drawing of funeral in the British Museum Print Room; Christopher Lloyd, *Marryat* (London, 1973), 193ff.

58 Nicolson, 234–35.

59 Duff Cooper, *Talleyrand* (London, 1939), 308.

60 Nicolson, 68.

61 Ibid., 63ff.

62 For Castlereagh's background and early career, see *House of Commons, 1790–1820* (London, 1986), vol. 5, 278ff; C. J. Bartlett, *Castlereagh* (London, 1966), 4–39; Ione Leigh, *Castlereagh* (London, 1951), 15–40.

63 W. S. Dowden, ed., *The Journal of Thomas Moore*, 2 vols. (Newark, N.J., 1983), vol. 1, 343.

64 Mary Campbell, *Lady Morgan: The Life and Time of Sidney Owenson* (London, 1988), 1.

65 *Mrs. Arbuthnot's Journal*, vol. 1, 176–85.

66 Peter Dixon, *Canning, Politican and Statesman* (London, 1976), 136–37.

67 Palmer, 112–13.

68 Nicolson, 127.

69 Palmer, 90.

70 Prince Clement de Metternich, *Memoires*, 2 vols. (Paris, 1880), vol. 1, chap. 1.

71 Nicolson, 88–89.

72 Cooper, *Talleyrand*, 12ff.

73 *Geoffrey Madan's Notebooks* (Oxford, 1984), 12.

74 See Saint-Beuve's five *causéries* on Talleyrand in *Nouveaux lundis*, 13 vols. (Paris, 1863–70).

75 Letter to Count Philip Stadio, Austrian Foreign Minister, September 1808, quoted in Palmer, 58.

76 Walpole to Castlereagh, 9 August 1814, quoted in Nicolson, 119.

77 Quoted in Henri Troyat, *Alexander of Russia* (trans., London, 1984), 296–98.

78 *Farington's Diary*, vol. 14, 4761, entry for 11 January 1816.

79 Quoted in C. Osborne, *Schubert and His Vienna* (London, 1985), 22.

80 D. T. Orlovsky, *The Limits of Reform: The Ministry of Internal Affairs in Imperial Russia 1802–1881* (Cambridge, Mass., 1981), 5–6.

81 Grenville to Buckingham, 8 May 1814, quoted in Elie Halévy: *England in 1815*, 2nd ed. (trans., London, 1949), 8, fn.

82 Hibbert, *George IV* (London, 1973), 31–32; Nicolson, 109–11.

83 *Ingram's Memorials* (London, 1837).

84 Nicolson, 115.

85 Gore, 117.

86 *Farington's Diary*, vol. 13, 4534, 9 June 1814.

87 *Farington's Diary*, vol. 7, 2364.

88 Nicolson, 160–63; Palmer, 131.

89 Nicolson, 141ff.

90 Palmer, 135.

91 Ibid., 137–38.

92 Nicolson, 197.

93 For Stein's proposals, see Constantin de Grunwald, *Baron Stein: Enemy of Napoleon* (trans. London, 1940), 271–79.

94 Quoted in Golo Mann, *History of Germany since 1789* (trans. London, 1968), 45.

95 *Byron: Poetical Works* (Oxford, 1970), 146–50.

96 Osborne, 15.

97 Michael Hamburger, ed., *Beethoven: Letters, Journals and Conversations* (London, 1984), 102–03.

98 Osborne, 25.

99 August Fournier, *Die Geheimpolizei auf dem Wiener Kongress* (Berlin, 1913), 289; Martin Cooper, *Beethoven: The Last Decade 1817–1827* (Oxford, 1970), 16.

100 For the workings of the police, see Donald Emerson, *Metternich and the Political Police: Security and Subversion in the Habsburg Monarchy* (The Hague, 1968).

101 Carl Bertuch: *Tagebuch den Wiener Kongress* (Berlin, 1916): Commandant Weil, *Les Dessous du Congress de Vienne,* 2 vols. (Paris, 1917); Nicolson, 204–05.

102 Nicolson gives the terms of the "secret treaty," 177–78, and terms of the agreement on Poland-Saxony, 179–80.

103 Quoted in Palmer, 142.

104 Nicolson, 241.

105 Ibid., 252ff.

106 See R. Darnton, *Mesmerism and the End of the Enlightenment in France* (Cambridge, Mass., 1968); August Viatte: *Les Sources occultes du romantisme: illuminisme-philosophie 1770–1820.* 2 vols. (Paris, 1928).

107 Henri Troyat, *Alexander of Russia* (trans. London, 1984), esp. chap. 13, 240–60.

108 Nicholas Mikhailovich, *L'Empereur Alexandre I,* 2 vols. (Saint Petersburg, 1910), vol. 2, 215ff.

109 Quoted in Alan Palmer, *Alexander I: Tsar of War and Peace* (London, 1974), 333. See also E. J. Knapton, *The Lady of the Holy Alliance: The Life of Julie de Krudener* (New York, 1939).

110 Raymond Carr, *Spain, 1808–1939* (Oxford, 1966), 120ff.

111 *Journal of Mrs. Arbuthnot,* 2 January 1821, 62.

112 Hamburger, 92ff.

113 This was Beethoven's version, given by Bettina von Arnhem in a letter to Prince Hermann von Pückler-Musskau; Hamburger, 117–18.

114 See Carl Dahlhaus, *Nineteenth-Century Music* (trans. Berkeley, Calif., 1989).

115 Immanuel Kant, *Kritik der Urteilskraft,* trans. J. F. Bernard (London, 1951).

116 Peter le Hurey and James Day, *Music and Aesthetics in the 18th and Early 19th Centuries* (Cambridge, England, 1981), 343–44.

117 Honour, *Romanticism,* 119ff.

118 Ibid., 120–21; the question is from André Coueroq: *Musique et Littérature* (Paris, 1923) 11–48.

119 Cooper, *Beethoven: The Last Dec-*

ade, 60: Berlioz in *Le Correspondent*, 11 April 1829, quoted in Jacques Barzun: *Berlioz and the Romantic Century*, 3rd ed., 2 vols. (New York, 1969), vol. 1, 99.

120 Hamburger, 86–96.

121 Dahlhouse, chap. 1.

122 For Beethoven's health, see Cooper, *Beethoven*, Appendix A: "Beethoven's Medical History" by Edward Larkin, 439ff.

123 Quoted in Cooper, *Beethoven*, 78.

124 Hamburger, 165.

125 Ibid., 174–75.

126 Ibid., 182.

127 Cooper, *Beethoven*, 455ff; see also, A. W. Thayer, *Life of Ludwig van Beethoven*, reissue, 3 vols. (London, 1960) vol. 3, 42ff.

128 For a slightly different version of this episode, see Thayer, vol. 3, 83–84.

129 Ibid., vol. 2, 269.

130 Quoted in Cooper, *Beethoven*, 37; Hamburger, 219.

131 Hamburger, 207–09.

132 A. Azevedo, *Gioacchino Rossini: Sa vie et ses oeuvres* (Paris, 1824), 21.

133 Richard Osborne, *Rossini* (London, 1986), 15.

134 John Rosselli: *The Opera Industry in Italy, from Cimarosa to Verdi* (London, 1984), 72–73; W. S. Rose, *Letters from the North of Italy*, 2 vols. (London, 1819) vol. 1, 123.

135 Byron, *Letters and Journals*, vol. 6, 132.

136 Osborne, 48.

137 G. W. F. Hegel: *Briefe von und an Hegel* (Leipzig, 1887), 154, quoted in Osborne, 57.

138 Rosselli, 40.

139 Byron, *Letters and Journals*, vol. 6, 18.

140 Osborne, 63ff.

141 Adam Carse, *The Orchestra from Beethoven to Berlioz* (Cambridge, 1948).

142 C. Humphries and W. Smith: *Music Publishing in the British Isles*, 2nd ed. (Oxford, 1970), 28–37.

143 D. S. Grover, *The Piano* (London, 1976), 85–92.

144 *Farington's Diary*, vol. 13, 4525, 27 May 1814.

145 Jane Austen, *Emma*, chap. 8.

146 Barzun, vol. 1, 35 and fn. 3.

147 See Marcel Brion, *Daily Life in the Vienna of Mozart and Schubert* (trans., New York, 1962).

148 *New Oxford History of Music* (Oxford, 1982), vol. 8, 17.

149 Osborne, 84ff.

150 Quoted in ibid., 96–97.

151 Quoted in ibid., 38.

152 Quoted in Honour, 245ff; see also Rudolph and Margaret Wittkower, *Born Under Saturn* (London, 1963).

153 Willard Bissel Pope, ed., *Diary of Benjamin Robert Haydon* (Cambridge, Mass., 1963), vol. 3, 7, 8, 62–63; entries for 16 and 18 February 1825 and 2 December 1825.

154 Ibid., 39, 119, 115; entries for 13 August 1825 and 10 and 7 July 1826.

155 William Dunlap, *Address to the Students of the National Academy of Design* (New York, 1831), quoted in Honour.

156 F. R. Rontiex, *L'Histoire du romanticisme en France* (Paris, 1829).

157 *Farington's Diary*, vol. 12, 4384, 2 July 1813; Cronin, 284ff; for De Staël's biographical details, see J. C. Herold, *Mistress to an Age: A Life of Madame de Staël* (London, 1958).

158 See the comparison between De Staël and George Sand in Donna Dickenson, *George Sand* (Oxford, 1988), 24–25.

159 Herold, 418–23.

160 For Byron on De Staël, see esp. *Letters and Journals*, vol. 3, 131, 207, 227, 247ff. and further refs. in vol. 12, Index, 154.

161 Norman Gash, *Lord Liverpool* (London, 1984), 45–46.

162 Byron, *Letters and Journals*, vol. 3, 273; *Journal of Mrs. Arbuthnot*, 135.

163 Guillaume de Bertigny de Sauvigny, *The Bourbon Restoration* (trans., Philadelphia, 1966) 27–37.

164 Daniel Reznick, *The White Terror and the Political Reaction after*

Waterloo (New Haven, Conn., 1966); Sauvigny, 134.

165 Campbell, *French Electoral Systems Since 1789* (London, 1989), 57–61.

166 Sauvigny, 127.

167 Quoted in ibid., 269.

168 Ibid., 270–71. The quotation is from Le Comte Mole, *Sa Vie, ses memoires,* 6 vols. (Paris, 1922–30).

169 For Restoration texts and so forth, see J. Vidalenc, *La Restauration* (Paris, 1968); and A. Jardin and A. Tudesq, *La France des Notables* (Paris, 1973).

170 Quoted in Sauvigny, 261; see Lammartine's autobiography, *Les Confidences* (Paris, 1849).

171 H. J. C. Grierson, *Letters of Sir Walter Scott 1808–11* (London, 1932), 495.

172 F. Ewen, *The Prestige of Schiller in England, 1788–1859* (New York, 1932).

173 Quoted in Mann, 58.

174 Full text of the translation is given in R. E. Chapman, ed., *The Novels of Jane Austen* (Oxford, 1980), vol. 3, 475–539.

175 A. O.Lovejoy: *Essays in the History of Ideas* (London, 1940).

176 Germaine de Staël, *De l'allemagne.*

177 Print (1827) in the Bibliothèque Nationale; reproduced in Clay, 6 (Fig. 5).

178 The Gérard is reproduced in Clay, Fig. 359; the Ingres is in the Musée Ingres, Montauban.

179 Francois Mazoi, *Les Ruines de Pompeii* (Paris, 1812–38).

180 Vivant Denon, *Voyage dans la Basse et dans la Haute Egypte* (Paris, 1802).

181 It is now displayed in Apsley House, Wellington's old London home, which is part of the Victoria and Albert Museum. See Charles Truman, *The Sèvres Egyptian Service 1810–12* (London, 1982); and Judith Nowinski, *Baron Dominique Vivant Denon* (London, 1970).

182 It is now in the Musee de l'Armée, Paris.

183 Warren Roberts, *Jacques-Louis David: Revolutionary Artist* (Chapel Hill, N.C., 1989), 95ff.

184 Ibid., 168, 172.

185 Ibid., 191.

186 Italo Faldi, *La Galeria Borghese: Catalogo della Sculture della xvi al xix secolo* (Rome, 1954), 45.

187 Guiseppe Pavanella and Mario Praz, *L'Opera Completa del Canova* (Milan, 1976).

188 At present, the property of the Duke of Bedford, at Woburn Abbey.

189 Fred Licht, *Canova* (New York, 1983).

190 The statue was destroyed by fire in 1850, but there are three preparatory *bozzetti,* or models, in the Gipsoteka, the museum devoted to Canova's sculpture in Passongo, near Treviso.

191 This amazing colossus, 141¼ inches high, was once at the head of the main staircase in the Museo Nationale, Naples, but has now been pushed into a dingy doorway.

192 For a contemporary account, see J. M. Thiele, *Life of Thorwaldsen* (trans., London, 1865).

193 See his *Discours prononce par Louis-Simon Auger, séance publique des Académies, 24 Avril 1824* (Paris, 1824).

194 Quoted by J. S. Allen, *Popular French Romanticism: Authors, Readers and Books in the 19th Century* (Syracuse, N.Y. 1981), 80.

195 Quoted in André Maurois, *Victor Hugo* (trans. London, 1956), 76.

196 Ibid., 92–93.

197 Ibid., 94.

198 Adèle Foucher, *Victor Hugo raconté par un temoin de sa vie,* 2 vols. (Brussels, 1863).

199 Letters of 3 February 1822, and 4 March 1822, printed in the volume *Lettres à la Fiancée,* in Victor Hugo, *Oeuvres complètes,* 45 vols. (Paris, 1904–52).

200 Henri Guillemin, *Victor Hugo par lui-même* (Paris, 1951), 50.

201 Foucher, vol. 2, 7, 12.

202 Virginie Ancelor, *Les Salons de Paris* (Paris, 1866), vol. 1, 25–26.

203 Chateaubriand, *Essai sur la Littérature Anglaise*, in *Oeuvres de Chateaubriand* 18 vols. (Paris, 1853), xv.

204 E. V. Lucas, ed., *Letters of Charles and Mary Lamb*, 3 vols. (London, 1935), vol. 2, 328, 333; vol. 3, 106.

205 Jan Reynolds, *William Callow RWS* (London, 1980), 10.

206 George Rudé, *The Growth of Cities and Popular Revolt 1750–1850*, deals particularly with the size of Paris; for population figures, see J. F. Bosher, *French Government and Society 1500–1850* (London, 1973), 166–190.

207 Sauvigny, 243.

208 Ralph G. Allen, "The Eidophusikon," *Theatre Design and Technology* (London, December 1966).

209 The quotation is from an account by Gainsborough's contemporary, William Henry Pyne; see Jonathan Mayne, "Thomas Gainsborough's Exhibition Box," *Victoria & Albert Museum Bulletin*, July 1965.

210 Quoted in Altick, 120–21.

211 Ibid., 217–18.

212 For Childe, see *Dictionary of National Biography*, compact ed., vol. 1, 365.

213 For Gurney, see ibid., vol. 1, 858.

214 Jane Austen, *Persuasion*, chap. 17.

215 For the precursors of Panorama, see Ralph Hyde, *Panoramania: The Art and Entertainment of the All-embracing View* (London, 1988), chap. 1, 45–56.

216 For Barker's and Girtin's views of London, see ibid., 62–63, 68–69.

217 Altick, 163–67; Helmut and Alison Gernsheim, *L. M. J. Daguerre: The History of the Diorama and the Daguerrotype* (London, 1956).

218 For an illustration of the graphic telescope, see Leslie Parris, *Landscape in Britain 1750–1850* (London, 1973), 125.

219 Hyde, 79–80.

220 Altick, 141ff.

221 For a contemporary account, see the chapter on the Colosseum in J. Britton and C. A. Pugin: *Illustrations of the Public Buildings of London* (London, 1838), which also includes one on the Diorama. There is a cross-section of the Colosseum machinery reproduced from the *Literary Gazette*, 31 January 1829, in Hyde, 81.

222 *Blackwoods*, No. 15 (1824), 472–73, quoted in Altick, 181.

223 Lord John Russell, ed., *Memoirs, Journal and Correspondence of Thomas Moore*, 8 vols. (London, 1853–56), vol. 5, 178.

224 *The Prelude*, vol. 7, 244–64.

225 For these definitions and others, see Andrew Wilton, Introduction, *Turner and the Sublime* (London, 1980). The quotation from Knight is in his *Analytical Inquiry into the Principles of Taste* (London, 1805) and from Ruskin in his *Modern Painters* (London, 1843), vol. 1, Part 2, chap. 3.

226 For Loutherbourg, see William T. Whitley, *Artists and Their Friends in England 1750–99*, 2 vols. (London, 1928), vol. 1, 353–55.

227 Joseph Cowell, *Thirty Years Passed Among the Players* (New York, 1845), 38.

228 See Pieter van der Merwe, "Roberts and the Theatre," in Helen Guiterman and Briony Llewellyn, eds., *David Roberts* (London, 1986), 27–44.

229 See James Ballantyne, *Life of David Roberts RA* (London, 1866); there is a photocopy of *Robert's Record Book* (1829) in the Guildhall Library, BR643: Merwe, 31–32.

230 Allan Nevins, ed., *Diary of John Quincy Adams 1794–1845* (New York: 1951), 169.

231 Quoted in G. M. Young, ed., *Early Victorian England 1830–65*, 2 vols. (Oxford, 1934), vol. 1, 418, fn. 3.

232 T. S. R. Boase, *English Art, 1800–70*

(Oxford, 1959), 21; Gerald Reitlinger: *The Economics of Taste* (London, 1961), 71; Altick, 186–88.

233 Quoted in Kenneth Clark, *Romanticism in Art* (London, 1973).

234 The first is now in the City of Bristol Art Gallery, the second is in the Victoria and Albert Museum; see Francis Greenacre, *Francis Danby* (London, 1988),

235 See his interview with the *Illustrated London News*, 17 March 1849.

236 William Feaver, *John Martin* (London, 1975).

237 Allston's unfinished *Belshazzar's Feast* is now in the Museum of Fine Arts, Boston.

238 Letter to Bernard Barton, 11 June 1827; E. V. Lucas, *Letters of Charles and Mary Lamb*, vol. 3, 97–98.

239 William Bissel Pope, ed., *The Diary of Benjamin Robert Haydon* (Cambridge, Mass., 1963), vol. 3, 1825–32, 10–11, entry for 8 March 1825.

240 For details, see Thomas Balston, *John Martin, His Life and Works* (London, 1947); and Christopher Johnstone, *John Martin* (London, 1974).

241 Washington Irving, *The Sketchbook of Geoffrey Crayon, Gent* (New York, 1820).

242 William Dunlap, *History of the Rise and Progress of the Arts of Design in the United States* (New York, 1834), 357.

243 Oswaldo Rodriguez Roque, "The Exaltation of American Landscape Painting," in *American Paradise: The World of the Hudson River School* (New York, 1988), 21–48.

THREE
The End of the Wilderness

1 Kathryn Cave, ed., *The Diary of Joseph Farington*, 16 vols. (New Haven, Conn., 1978–84), vol. 12, 5 September 1812, 4209 (hereafter called *Farington's Diary*).

2 See entry for Gurney, *Dictionary of National Biography*, compact ed., vol. 1, 858.

3 For Manning, see C. A. Prance, *Companion to Charles Lamb: A Guide to People and Places* (London, 1983), 218–21.

4 De Sauvigny, 211.

5 Jane Austen, *Mansfield Park*, chap. 2.

6 *Letters of Charles and Mary Lamb*, vol. 1 (London, 1938), 206.

7 Ibid., vol. 1, 94.

8 Jane Austen, *Emma* (London, 1815), chap. 34.

9 John Adolphus, *The Political State of the British Empire, Containing a General View of the Domestic and Foreign Possessions of the Crown*, 4 vols. (London, 1818), vol. 2, 36 and fn. 1; *A Return of the Number of Persons Employed* [in government] (London, 1828).

10 *Farington's Diary*, vol. 12, 3 September 1813, 4419.

11 Ibid., vol. 15, 11 August 1801, 93.

12 Ibid., vol. 16, 8 December 1821, 5676.

13 John Niven, *Martin Van Buren: The Romantic Age in American Politics* (Oxford, 1983); Marcus Lee Hanson, *The Atlantic Migration, 1607–1850* (Cambridge, Mass., 1940), 153.

14 Allan Nevins, ed., *The Diary of John Quincy Adams 1797–1845* (New York, 1951), 180.

15 Bernard Pool, ed., *Croker Papers* (London, 1967), 32; Norman Gash, *Mr. Secretary Peel* (London, 1985), 118.

16 R. S. Surtees, *Plain or Ringlets?* (London, 1860), 184ff.

17 Turner to Charles Eastlake, 22 January 1829, quoted in Andrew Wilton, *Turner Abroad* (London, 1982), 80. The watercolor is reproduced as Plate 1.

18 *Farington's Diary,* vol. 4, 1436; vol. 9, 3462–63; 21 May 1809.

19 G. R. de Beer, ed., *A Journey to Florence in 1817 by Harriet Charlotte Beaujolais Campbell* (London, 1951), 87.

20 *Journal of Mrs. Arbuthnot,* 49.

21 Roger Price, *The Modernisation of Rural France: Communications Networks and Agricultural Market Structures in 19th Century France* (London, 1983), 43.

22 Anthony Wagner and Antony Dale, *The Wagners of Brighton* (Chicester, 1983), 22.

23 *Farington's Diary,* vol. 8, 4 October 1806, 2876; vol. 11, April 16, 1811, 3912; vol. 12, 11 September 1813, 4423; vol. 13, 25 September 1815, 4710–11.

24 Alastair Penfold, ed., *Thomas Telford: Engineer* (London, 1980), 47.

25 Jack Larkin, *The Reshaping of Everyday Life, 1790–1840* (New York, 1988), 224–25.

26 See Addington's letters and diaries in B. W. Perkins, ed., *Youthful America* (Berkeley, California, 1960).

27 Larkin, 229.

28 W. J. Reader, *Macadam: The McAdam Family and the Turnpike Roads, 1798–1861* (London, 1980), 17.

29 N. W. Webster, *The Great North Road* (London, 1974), 20–21.

30 W. D. Jones, *"Prosperity" Robinson: The Life of Viscount Goderich, 1782–1859* (London, 1967), 123.

31 *Farington's Diary,* vol. 14, 4 September 1817, 5079.

32 De Sauvigny, 202–27.

33 Jane Austen, *Persuasion* (London, 1817), chap. 2. Details of services from *Cary's New Itinerary* (London, 1828).

34 A. J. Mill, ed., *John Stuart Mill's Boyhood Visit to France* (Toronto, 1961), 10.

35 Larkin, 216.

36 Reader, 15–16.

37 The *Treatise on Carriages,* first published in 1801 in London, was a price guide, illustrated by 60 copper plates; Felton was a coachmaker in business at 36 Leather Lane, Holborn. For a modern survey, see R. W. Chapman's Appendix, "On Carriages and Travel," in the *Oxford Illustrated Jane Austen,* vol. 3, 561ff.

38 See the list in Harold Nicolson, *Helen's Tower* (London, 1937).

39 Mary Campbell, *Lady Morgan: The Life and Times of Sidney Owenson* (London, 1988), 209–10.

40 Reader, 16.

41 Seymour Dunbar: *A History of Travel in America,* 4 vols. (Indianapolis, 1915); Charles Goodrich, *Universal Traveller* (Philadelphia, various dates), gives contemporary routes and details.

42 Quoted in Larkin, 223; see also, E. W. Bovil, *English Country Life 1780–1830* (London, 1962), 153; T. Cross, *Autobiography of a Stage Coachman,* 2 vols. (London, 1861).

43 *Farington's Diary,* vol. 1, 14, 76, 242.

44 Bovil, 136.

45 Sir Herbert Maxwell, ed., *The Creevey Papers,* 2 vols. (London, 1903), vol. 2, 129.

46 *Farington's Diary,* vol. 2, 20 July 1796, 613; vol. 16, 6 November 1821, 5746; vol. 9, 13 November 1808, 3375.

47 Penfold, 19; C. H. Herford, ed., Robert Southey, *Journal of a Tour in Scotland in 1819* (London, 1929), xxiiff.

48 Osborne, *Rossini,* 32–39.

49 T. K. Derry and T. I. Williams, *A Short History of Technology* (Oxford, 1979), 429–30.

50 J. L. McAdam, *Report from the Committee on Highways and Turnpike Roads, 1810–11,* reprinted in McAdam, *Observation on the Present System of Roadmaking* (London, 1823), 29.

51 Reader, 33.

52 J. L. McAdam, *The Management of*

Trusts (London, 1825); see also, McAdam, *Minutes of Evidence to Select Committee on Highways* (London, 1819).

53 Edwin Pratt, *History of Inland Transport and Communications* (London, 1912), 318.

54 Reader, 14.

55 For his early life and chronological details of his career, see Brian Bracegirdle and Patricia H. Miles, eds., *Thomas Telford* (Newton Abbot, 1973).

56 Nikolaus Pevsner, *The Buildings of England: Shropshire* (Harmondsworth, 1974), 80.

57 For Telford as a bridge innovator, see A. W. Skemton, "Telford and the Design for the New London Bridge," in Penfold, chap. 4, 62ff.

58 Bracegirdle and Miles, 28.

59 Ibid., 34–36.

60 See Barrie Trinder, "The Holyhead Road," in Penfold, 41–61.

61 J. Rickman, ed., *The Life of Thomas Telford* (London, 1838), 213.

62 Bracegirdle and Miles, 71.

63 R. A. Paxton: "The Menai Bridge 1818–26, the Evolution of the Design," in Penfold, 84ff.

64 The master plan is adumbrated in Thomas Telford, *A Survey and Report of the Coast and Central Highlands of Scotland* (London, 1803).

65 C. H. Herford, ed., *Robert Southey: A Journal of a Tour of Scotland in 1819* (London, 1929).

66 Ibid., 13, 26, 31–32.

67 Ibid., 40–41, 55ff.

68 J. R. Hume, "Telford's Highland Bridges," in Penfold, 151ff.

69 *Southey Journal*, 98ff.

70 Ibid., 62, 76, 82, 85–86, 89.

71 Ibid., 157, 167ff, 182ff, 202–24.

72 *Farington's Diary*, vol. 4, 1 December 1799;, 1313, vol. 9, 8 May 1808, 3273; 21 June 1809, 3493.

73 For details of the times, see G. M. Young, *Early Victorian England*, vol. 1; *Farington's Diary*, vol. 10, August 28, 1810, 3729.

74 Cf. figures produced for the *Parliamentary Select Committee on Steam-Carriages*, (1831); Penfold, 118–19.

75 Edmund Burke, *A Philosophical Inquiry into the Origin of Our Ideas on the Sublime and Beautiful* (London, 1757).

76 This masterly work was demolished in 1901; see John Summerson, *Life and Works of John Nash, Architect* (London, 1980), 73–74; a print of it is Plate viii in Summerson's earlier book, *John Nash* (London, 1949); cf. Nicholas Taylor, "The Awful Sublimity of the Victorian City," in H. J. Dios and Michael Wolff, eds., *The Victorian City: Images and Realities*, 2 vols. (London, 1973), vol. 2, 431–47, and Plate 306.

77 Penfold, 128.

78 Derry and Williams, 601ff.

79 For more details, see L. T. C. Rolt, *George & Robert Stephenson: The Railway Revolution* (Harmondsworth, 1978), 7–23.

80 Ibid., 53.

81 Quoted in ibid., 35.

82 See A. E. Pease, ed., *The Diaries of Edward Pease* (London, 1907).

83 Penfold, 128.

84 For details of Gurney's efforts, see *Dictionary of National Biography*, compact ed., vol. 1, 858.

85 Quoted in Rolt, 190–92.

86 *Parliamentary Select Committee on Steam-Carriages* (1831).

87 *Letters of Spencer Madan*, 39.

88 See Ann Blainey's life of Leigh Hunt, *Immortal Boy* (London, 1985), 124.

89 Maurice Collis, *Raffles* (London, 1966), 134.

90 *Farington's Diary*, vol. 1, 6 September 1794, 235.

91 Ibid., vol. 12, 2 September 1812, 4208.

92 Richard Holmes, *Shelley: The Pursuit* (London, 1974), 715–29; Joan Rees, *Shelley's Jane Williams* (London, 1985), chap. 6, 96ff; F. L. Jones, ed., *Maria Gisborne and Edward Williams, Their Letters* (Oklahoma, 1951), 149.

93 Figures in Derry and Williams, 370; H. I. Chapelle, *The Baltimore Clipper* (New York, 1981).

94 Ibid., 366; Peter Kemp, ed., *Oxford Companion to Ships and the Sea* (Oxford, 1976), 915–16.

95 E. C. Smith, *A Short History of Naval and Marine Engineering* (Cambridge, 1938).

96 H. W. Dickinson, *Robert Fulton: Engineer and Artist* (London, 1913), 218.

97 Ibid., 234–38.

98 Ray Allen Billington, *Westward Expansion: A History of the American Frontier* (New York, 1949), 332; Larkin, 226.

99 W. M. Lowrey, "The Engineers and the Mississippi," *Louisiana History*, 5 (1963), 233ff.; W. E. Lass, *History of Steamboating on the Upper Missouri* (New York, 1962).

100 Samuel Smiles, ed., *Naysmith's Autobiography* (London, 1883), 39.

101 For a drawing of it, see Peter Jackson, ed., *George Scharf's London: Sketches and Watercolours of a Changing City 1820–50* (London, 1987).

102 Reproduced in Derry and Williams, Figure, 194.

103 The 1804 essay is printed in J. Laurence Pritchard, *Sir George Cayley: Inventor of the Aeroplane* (London, 1961), Appendix 1, 219–21; his "Air Navigation" paper was published in *Nicholson's Journal*, September 1809.

104 See J. E. Hodgson: *The Papers of Sir George Cayley, 1799–1826* (Newcomen Society, London, 1933); for the tractor concept, see Pritchard, 146ff; for the mechanical hand, 161–73; for rail safety, 174–87.

105 Pritchard, 227.

106 Ibid., 48ff, 21.

107 For the Adelaide Gallery, see Altick, *The Shows of London*, 376ff; the anecdote about Wellington is related in W. P. Frith, *Autobiography*, 2 vols. (London, 1887), vol. 1, 27.

108 For these various episodes, see Holmes, *Shelley*, 24, 149–50, 344.

109 For Shelley's interest in science as a weapon of social reform, see Carl Grabo, *The Magic Plant: The Growth of Shelley's Thought* (Chapel Hill, N.C., 1936), 5–7, 21ff.

110 Shelley, *The Witch of Atlas*, esp. lines 290–448.

111 Derry and Williams, 369.

112 See Hanson, 172–77.

113 Southworth Allen Howland, *Steamboat Disasters and Railroad Accidents in the United States* (New York, 1840), describes this and other calamities; see also, Daniel J. Boorstin, *The Americans: The National Experience* (London, 1966), 105ff.

114 Pool, 62.

115 R. G. Albion, *Square-riggers on Schedule* (Princeton, N.J., 1938), chap. 1, 2, 4, 6.

116 Hansen, 178ff.

117 D. F. MacDonald, "The Great Migration," in C. J. Bartlett, ed., *Britain Pre-Eminent* (London, 1969), 54–75.

118 See Colin Clark, *Population Growth and Land Use* (London, 1967), 106–07, Table III.14.

119 E. E. Lampard: "The Urbanising World," in Dios and Wolff, vol. 1, 3–58, and Table 1.1.5. It is not always easy to get comparable figures on population and urban growth rates, and I have seen statistics that somewhat conflict with the ones I have given here. For dates of census or estimates, cf. A. F. Weber, *The Growth of Cities in the 19th Century* (New York, 1899), Table 112.

120 Lampard, 4.

121 British Museum, reproduced in Dios and Wolff, vol. 2, Plate 338.

122 Figures from S. C. Johnson, *A History of Emigration from the United Kingdom to North America, 1763–1812* (London, 1913), Appendix 1, statistical tables.

123 Hansen, 79–80.

124 Ibid., 90. For early records of immi-

gration and their treatment, see A. H. Spear, "Marcus Lee Hansen and the Historiography of Immigration," *Wisconsin Magazine of History*, 44 (1961), 258ff.

125 James Flint, *Letters from America* (Edinburgh, 1822).

126 Hansen, 103.

127 C. F. Adams, ed., *Memoirs of John Quincy Adams*, 167.

128 Emanuel Howitt, *Selections from Letters Written . . . [in] 1819* (Nottingham, 1820), 217. Robert Browning, "The Lost Leader."

130 *Niles Weekly Register*, 18 (1820), 157–58; a complete run of *Niles* was printed in facsimile in 1947.

131 Hansen, 114–15.

132 Ibid., 110–12.

133 *Select Committee on Emigration from the United Kingdom, Fourth and Fifth Reports, Parliamentary Papers* (London, 1826), 1826–27.

134 Colin McEvedy and Richard Jones, *Penguin Atlas of World Population History* (Harmondsworth, 1978), 285–87, 313–14, 327; H. R. Jones: *A Population Geography* (New York, 1981), 254; A. W. Crosby: *Ecological Imperialism: The Biological Expansion of Europe 900–1900* (Cambridge, England, 1986), 3–5.

135 Sydney Smith, *Works* (London, 1854) vol. 2, 119–20; this originally appeared in the *Edinburgh Review* (Spring 1820).

136 *Hansard*, vol. 33, 126ff; Chester New, *Life of Henry Brougham to 1830* (Oxford, 1961), 166–69.

137 Hansen, 153, 159–61.

138 Richard Pipes, *Russia Under the Old Regime* (London, 1974), 14–16; see also, W. H. Parker: *A Historical Geography of Russia* (London, 1968) and M. Raeef, *Siberia and the Reform of 1822* (Seattle, 1956).

139 J. C. Brown, *A Socio-economic History of Argentina, 1776–1860* (Cambridge, England, 1979), 149–50; David Rock, *Argentina, 1516–1982* (London, 1986), 99.

140 C. M. H. Clark, *History of Australia,* 2 vols. (Cambridge, England 1962–68), vol. 2, 69.

141 G. M. Theal, *History of South Africa, 1798–1828* (London, 1903), 202ff.

142 Ray Allen Billington, *Westward Expansion: A History of the American Frontier* (New York, 1949), 265–66, 290ff, 310ff.

143 Donald J. Carmony in the *Indiana Magazine of History*, 61 (1965); quoted in Malcolm J. Rohrbough, *The Trans-Appalachian Frontier: People, Societies and Institutions 1775–1850* (Oxford, 1978), 168–69.

144 Ibid., 171–72.

145 For details, see P. J. Treat, *The National Land System 1785–1820* (New York, 1910); and B. H. Hibberd, *A History of the Public Land Policies* (New York, 1924).

146 Quoted in Boorstin, 75.

147 See Paul D. Evans, *The Holland Land Company* (Buffalo, 1924).

148 Freeman Cleaves, *Old Tippecanoe: William Henry Harrison and His Times* (New York, 1939).

149 Remini, 331–32.

150 Niven, 185.

151 See Wakefield's *Letter from Sydney* (London, 1829) and *England and America* (London, 1833).

152 *Hansard*, 3rd series, 33, 852.

153 H. Hale Bellot, *American History and American Historians* (London, 1952), chap. 4, "The Settlement of the Mississippi Valley," 108ff.

154 F. S. Philbrock, *The Rise of the West, 1754–1830* (New York, 1965), 314–15.

155 See Elijah Iles's own account, *Sketches of Early Life and Times in Kentucky, Missouri and Illinois* (Springfield, Ill., 1863); Rohrbough, 178ff.

156 Rohrbough, 361–62; R. C. Buley, *The Old North-West: Pioneer Period 1815–40* 2 vols. (Indianapolis, 1950).

157 Quoted in Rohrbough, 211.

158 *Emma* (London, 1816), chap. 3; ad-

vertisement quoted in Rohrbough, 216.

159 *Historical Statistics of the United States, Colonial Times to 1957* (Washington, D.C., 1960); Rohrbough, Table 2, 163; Table 3, 204.

160 Quoted in Rohrbough, 235–36.

161 J. C. Buchanan, *Travels in the Western Hebrides* (London, 1793), vol. 6, see T. C. Smout, *A History of the Scottish People, 1560–1830* (London, 1972), 328ff; see also, Eric Richards, *A History of the Highland Clearances* 2 vols. (London, 1982–85).

162 *Select Committee on Emigration, Third Report, Parliamentary Papers 1827*, 59; see Smout, 329–30.

163 Southey, *Journal of a Tour in Scotland*, 137.

164 Figures in Marjorie Harper, *Emigration from North-East Scotland*, 2 vols. (Aberdeen, 1988), vol. 1, 35–37, Tables 1 and 2a.

165 Quoted in Richard Ormond, *Sir Edwin Landseer* (Philadelphia, 1982), 6.

166 C. Dickens, *Life of Charles J. Matthews*, 2 vols. (London, 1879), vol. 2, 49–51.

167 *A Guide to the Wilderness* (Dublin, 1810), quoted in Kay S. House, *James Fenimore Cooper: Cultural Prophet and Literary Pathfinder* (New York, 1988), 97.

168 Quoted in Edwin C. Rozwenc, ed., *Ideology and Power in the Age of Jackson* (New York, 1964).

169 Hansen, 146–47.

170 See Clarence Golides, "The Reception of Some 19th-Century American Authors in Europe," in Margaret Denny and W. H. Gilman, eds., *The American Writer and the European Tradition* (Minneapolis, 1950), 113–14; Preston A. Barba, *Cooper in Germany* (Bloomington, Ind., 1914), 73–78.

171 Halvden Koht, *The American Spirit in Europe* (Philadelphia, 1949), 111; H. W. Hewett-Thayer, *American Literature as Viewed in Germany*,

1818–61 (Chapel Hill, 1958), 24. See also, Ray Allen Billington, *Land of Savagery, Lady of Pioneers: European Images of the American Frontier in the 19th Century* (New York, 1981).

172 Jackson to Calhoun, August 24, 1819; R. L. Meriwether and W. E. Hemphill, eds., *Calhoun Papers*, 5 vols. (New York, 1957–91), vol. 4 271–72.

173 C. C. Royce: *Indian Land Sessions in the United States* (Washington, D.C., 1900), 682–83; Grace Woodward, *The Cherokees* (Norman, Okla., 1963), 135; Arrell M. Gibson, *The Chickasaws* (Norman, Okla., 1971). See also Remini, vol. 1, 327ff.

174 For the "removal" policy, see Bernard Sheehan, *Seeds of Extinction* (Chapel Hill, N.C., 1973), 243ff; Reginal Horseman: "American Indian Policy and the Origin of Manifest Destiny," in F. P. Prucha, ed., *The Indians in American History* (New York, 1971).

175 Mary E. Young, *Redskins, Ruffleshirts and Rednecks* (Norman, Okla., 1961), 40; Remini, 338.

176 C. J. Kapler, ed., *Indian Affairs: Laws and Treaties*, 2 vols. (Washington, D.C., 1904), vol. 2, 135–37, 174–77.

177 F. P. Prucha, "Andrew Jackson's Indian Policy: A Reassessment," *Journal of American History*, December 1969.

178 J. S. Basse II and J. F. Jameson, eds., *Jackson Correspondence*, 6 vols. (New York, 1926–35), vol. 2, 376.

179 Remini, 362.

180 Billington, *Westward Expansion*, 301.

181 For Cass, see F. B. Woodford: *Lewis Cass, the Last Jeffersonian* (New York, 1950).

182 *North American Review*, Spring 1827, 365–442, and January 1830, 64–109.

183 Quoted in Rohrbough, 273.

184 Ibid., 277.

185 Nevins, 313.

186 Ibid., 318–19.

187 For the republic, see Henry Thompson Malone, *Cherokees of the Old South: A People in Transition* (Athens, Ga., 1956), 74–90.

188 Billington, *Westward Expansion* 315–16.

189 A. De Tocqueville, *Democracy in America*, 2 vols. (New York, 1945), vol. 1, 352ff.

190 Malone, 178–79.

191 See A. W. Crosby, "Ecological Imperialism," in Donald Worster, ed., *Ends of the Earth: Perspectives in Modern Environmental History* (Cambridge, England, 1988), 108 and refs., note 9; Alexander Gillespie, *Gleanings . . . at Buenos Aires* (Leeds, 1818) 136ff.

192 A. J. Tapson, "Indian Warfare on the Pampas During the Colonial Period," *Hispanic American Historical Review*, 12 (February 1962); J. P. and W. P. Robertson, *Letters from South America*, 3 vols. (London, 1843), vol. 2, 274–75; J. A. Beaumont, *Travels in Buenos Aires and . . . the Rio de la Plata* (London, 1828), 55.

193 David Rock, *Argentina, 1516–1982* (London, 1986), 104–05; for Rosas, see John Dynch, *Argentine Dictator: Juan Manuel de Rosas 1829–52* (Oxford, 1981).

194 J. C. Brown, *A Socio-Economic History of Argentina, 1776–1860* (Cambridge, England, 1979), 114ff; Rock, 99.

195 Darwin quotations from *The Cruise of the Beagle* (London, 1840) and *The Descent of Man* (London, 1871).

196 Edgar McInnis, *Canada: A Social and Political History*, rev. ed. (New York, 1958), 202ff.

197 William Kingsford, *History of Canada*, 10 vols. (London, 1887–98), vol. 9, 241ff.

198 For Papineau's views, see Fernand Puellet, *Lower Canada 1791–1840: Social Change and Nationalism* (trans., Toronto, 1980), 50, 109, 150–01, 190ff.

199 Kingsford, vol. 9, 179–82.

200 Gourley's *Sketches of Upper Canada* are published as an introduction to his *Statistical View*, 2 vols. (London, 1822); Kingsford, vol. 9, 208ff, esp. 236 fn.

201 Kingsford, vol. 9, 108–55, gives a hostile account of Selkirk; see also, J. M. Grey: *Lord Selkirk of Red River* (London, 1963), and E. E. Rich, *The History of the Hudson's Bay Company 1670–1870*, 2 vols. (London, 1958–59).

202 McInnis, 190ff.

203 Quoted in C. R. Boxer, *Four Centuries of Portuguese Exploration, 1415–1825* (Johannesburg, 1965), 27.

204 A. W. Crosby, *Ecological Imperialism: The Biological Expansion of Europe, 900–1900* (Cambridge, England, 1986), 140; see P. D. Curtin, "Epidemiology and the Slave Trade," *Political Science Quarterly*, June 1968.

205 Quoted in G. S. Graham, *Great Britain in the Indian Ocean 1810–50* (Oxford, 1967), 41–42.

206 For a general account, see W. M. Macmillan, *Bantu, Boer and Britain; the Making of the South African Native Problem* rev. ed. (Oxford, 1963); J. D. Omer-Cooper, "The Nguni Outburst," in J. E. Flint, ed., *The Cambridge History of Africa c1790–c1870*, vol. 5 (Cambridge, England, 1976), 319–351.

207 See M. D. Malcolm, ed., *The Diary of Henry Francis Flynn* (Pietermaritzberg, South Africa, 1950), 16.

208 H. Kuper, *An African Aristocracy* (London, 1947); Omer-Cooper, 328–32.

209 Richard Elphick and Hermann Giliomee, eds., *The Shaping of South Africa Society, 1652–1820* (London, 1979), Table 10.1, 360.

210 Charles Darwin, *The Origin of Species* (London, 1839), chap. 3; Her-

bert Spencer, *Principles of Biology* (London 1964–67), chap. 12.

211 Elphick and Giliomee, vol. 3, 223.

212 Ibid., 338–57; T. R. H. Davenport, *South Africa: A Modern History* (London, 1977), 34.

213 Hermann Giliomee, "The Slachternek Rebellion of 1815," in Elphick and Giliomee, 348ff.

214 Anna Steenkamp's diary quoted in Davenport, 40.

215 *Memoirs of Charles Matthews*, 4 vols. (London, 1839), vol. 4, 136–37.

216 Robin Hallett, "Changing European Attitudes to Africa," in Flint, esp. 458–96, 481.

217 J. C. Pritchard, *Researches into the Natural History of Mankind*, 2 vols., 3rd ed. (London, 1939), vol. 1, 97.

218 Church Missionary Society, *Missionary Papers* (London, 1816), vol. 1, quoted in Hallett, 476; G. R. Mellor, *British Imperial Trusteeship 1783–1850* (London, 1951), 257.

219 W. F. Freund, "Rulers and Ruled in Cape Colony," in Flint, 225–26.

220 See Macmillan, 6, 9ff; *Dictionary of National Biography*, compact ed., vol. 2, 1654.

221 Macmillan, 17–18.

222 For the coloreds, see W. M. Macmillan, *The Cape Colour Question* (London, 1927).

223 Macmillan, *Bantu, Boer and Britain*, 10.

224 Ibid., chap. 5: "A Moving Frontier in the East—A Neutral Belt," 71–84.

225 Ibid., 20.

226 V. V. Obolensky-Ossinky, "Emigration from and Immigration into Russia," in I. Ferenczi and W. F. Willcox, eds., *International Migrations, II* (New York, 1969), 521–80.

227 Quoted in H. Tinker, *A New System of Slavery: The Export of Indian Labour Overseas, 1830–1920* (Oxford, 1974), 44–45.

228 R. Willock, *Bulwark of Empire: Bermuda's Fortified Naval Base* (Princetown, 1962), 44ff.

229 For a general survey, see N. and P. R.

Shergold, "Transportation as Global Migration," in Ferenczi and Willcox, 28ff.

230 *Sussex Weekly Advertiser*, 2 October 1786; *United Services Journal*, December 1846; quoted in Bill Beatty: *Early Australia: With Shame Remembered* (London, 1962).

231 Beatty, 4, 17–18.

232 Robert Hughes, *The Fatal Shore* (London, 1987), 175.

233 For this controversy, see Manning Clark, "The Origins of the Convicts Transported to Australia 1787–1852," *Historical Studies: Australia and New Zealand*, 7 (Sydney 1956); L. L. Robson, *The Convict Settlers of Australasia* (Melbourne, 1965); A. G. L. Shaw, *Convicts and the Colonies* (London, 1966): J. Hirst: *Convict Society and Its Enemies* (Sydney, 1983). These studies, plus Hughes, stress the "criminal class" interpretation. A recent study, Stephen Nicholas, ed., *Convict Workers: Reinterpreting Australia's Past* (Cambridge, 1988), seeks to disprove it.

234 Nicholas, 3–8.

235 Deborah Oxley, "Female Convicts," in ibid., 85ff.

236 "Proceedings of the Bench of Magistrates *re* Prostitution on the Ship *Janus*," in F. Watson, ed., *Australian Historical Records*, 35 vols. (Sydney, 1914–25), vol. 10,

237 Beatty, 21.

238 Ibid., 28–29.

239 C. M. H. Clark, *History of Australia*, 2 vols. (Cambridge, England, 1962), vol. 1, 282.

240 See Oxley, Table 6.2, 92.

241 Clark, vol. 1, 290.

242 A. Atkinson and M. Aveling: *Australians 1837* (Sydney, 1987), 287.

243 Father Bernard Ullathorne, *The Horrors of Transportation Briefly Unfolded* (Dublin, 1836).

244 See J. V. Barry, *Alexander Maconachie of Norfolk Island* (Sydney, 1925).

245 Stephen Nicholas, "Care and Feeding of Convicts," in Nicholas, 180ff.
246 Clark, vol. 1, 304.
247 Beatty, 13.
248 Nicholas, 19.
249 Crosby, *Ecological Imperialism*, 283; Nicholas, 8.
250 Nicholas, 8ff, 93–94, 98ff, 145–46.
251 Clark, vol. 1, 279.
252 Ibid., 269–70, 303.
253 Macquarie to Bathurst, 17 October 1814, *Australian Historical Records*, vol. 8, 316.
254 Clark, vol. 1, 308–10.
255 Ibid., 314.
256 *Report of the Commision on Inquiry into the State of the Colony of New South Wales,* House of Commons, 19 June 1822.
257 Sydney Smith's first essay on Botany Bay appeared in the *Edinburgh Review* in April 1819; his review of Bigge's report was in the issue of January 1823; S. Smith, *Articles in the Edinburgh Review,* 3 vols. (London, 1854), vol 2, 55ff, 302ff.
258 For Macquarie, see M. H. Ellis, *Lachlan Macquarie: His Life, Adventures and Times,* 3rd ed. (Sydney, 1958).
259 See the anthology of press and contemporary documents, A. Birch and D. S. Macmillan, eds., *The Sydney Scene, 1788–1960* (Melbourne, 1962).
260 For Bennet, see *History of Parliament: House of Commons 1790–1820,* vol. 3, 178ff.
261 Beatty, 136–37.
262 See Anon., *History of Samuel Terry* (London, 1838).
263 For Wentworth, see A. C. V. Melbourne, *William Charles Wentworth* (Brisbane, 1934).
264 G. C. Bolton, *A Thousand Miles Away: A History of North Queensland to 1920* (Sydney, 1970).
265 Macquarie to Bathurst, 30 June 1815, *Australian Historical Records,* vol. 8, 467.
266 Macquarie to Bathurst, 24 March 1815, *Australian Historical Records,* vol. 8, 369–70.
267 Quoted in Clark, 315–16.
268 *Sydney Gazette,* 7 November 1818, quoted in Clark, vol. 1, 317.
269 Mansfield to General Commissioner, 23 November 1821, quoted in Clark, vol. 2, 3.
270 Leading article, *Sydney Monitor,* 19 November 1838.
271 J. W. Beattie, *Glimpses of the Lives and Times of the Early Tasmanian Governors* (Hobart, 1905), 36ff.
272 F. Debenham, ed., *Voyage of Captain Bellinghausen to the Antarctic Seas, 1819–21* (Hakluyt Society, London, 1945), vol. 2, 355ff.
273 Clark, vol. 2, 118ff.
274 C. Turnbull, *Black War: The Extermination of the Tasmanian Aborigines* (Melbourne, 1948), 72–76.
275 N. J. B. Plomley, ed., *Friendly Mission: The Tasmanian Journals and Papers of George Augustus Robinson 1829–34* (Hobart, 1866).
276 Beatty, 184.
277 *Parliamentary Papers* (1840), vol. 7, 582, Q1047.
278 J. R. Elder, ed., *Letters and Journals of Samuel Marsden, 1765–1838* (Dunedin, 1932), 60ff.
279 For white-Maori hostility, see K. Sinclair: *The Origins of the Maori Wars* (Wellington, 1957).
280 R. A. Cruise, *Journal of Ten Months Residence in New Zealand* (Christchurch, 1974), 20; Crosby, *Ecological Imperialism,* 236–37.
281 V. O. Kliuchevski: *Kurs russkoi istorii,* 5 vols. (Moscow, 1937), vol. 1, 21; quoted in A. S. Donnelly, *The Russian Conquest of Bashkiria, 1552–1740: A Case Study in Imperialism* (New Haven, Conn., 1968).
282 See A. P. Okladnikov, "The Ancient Population of Siberia and Its Culture," in M. G. Levin and L. P. Potapov, eds., *The Peoples of Siberia* (Chicago, 1956).

283 For the penetration of Siberia, see R. J. Kerner, *The Urge to the Sea: The Course of Russian History, the Role of Rivers, Portages, Ostrogs, Monasteries and Furs* (New York, 1942).

284 D. W. Treadgold, *The Great Siberian Migration* (Princeton, N.J., 1957), 32–34.

285 Walter Kolarz, *Russia and Her Colonies* (New York, 1955), 255.

286 Donnelly, 101–38, esp. table of punishments, 138.

287 Richard Pipes, *Russia Under the Old Regime* (London, 1974), which has an excellent account of the problems posed by the climate, 4ff.

288 Ibid., 5.

289 W. H. Parker, *A Historical Geography of Russia* (London, 1968), 158.

290 Lieutenant-General William Monteith, *Kars and Ezeroum: With the Campaign of Prince Paskiewitch in 1828–9* (London, 1856), 155.

291 Quoted in J. F. Baddeley, *The Russian Conquest of the Caucasus* (London, 1908), 96–97.

292 Ibid., 130–32.

293 Charles Darwin, *The Cruise of the Beagle* (London, 1962 ed.), 433.

294 Crosby, "Ecological Imperialism," 108, 109, 113–15.

295 Ibid., 109; A. H. Clark, *The Invasion of New York by People, Plants and Animals* (New Brunswick, N.J., 1949).

296 A. Marriott and C. K. Rachlin, *American Indian Mythology* (New York, 1968), 174ff.

297 For many more examples, see Crosby, *Ecological Imperialism*, 32ff, 205–06; E. M. Curr, *The Australian Race*, 2 vols. (Melbourne, 1886), vol. 1, 213–14.

298 Anna Brownell Jameson, *Winter Studies and Summer Rambles in Canada* (London, 1838).

299 *Two Years Before the Mast* (Boston, 1840).

300 For Douglas, see *Dictionary of National Biography,* compact ed., vol. 1, 559; W. Wilks, ed., *Douglas's Journal* (London, 1914); and Anon., *David Douglas: Botanist at Hawaii* (Honolulu, 1919).

301 Billington, *Westward Expansion,* 513–14, 554ff.

302 Ronald T. Takaki, *Iron Cages: Race and Culture in 19th Century America* (London, 1980), 154ff.

303 Andrew Jackson, *Third Annual Message to Congress,* 1830.

304 Geoffrey Blainey, *The Tyranny of Distance* (Melbourne, 1967).

305 *Journal of Mrs. Arbuthnot,* 319.

306 G. F. Berkeley, *My Life and Recollections,* 2 vols. (London, 1865), vol. 1, 297.

307 Quoted in E. W. Bovill, *English Country Life, 1780–1830* (Oxford, 1962), 122.

308 *Haydon Diary,* vol. 3, 51.

309 C. C. Southey, ed., *Life and Correspondence of Robert Southey,* 3 vols. (London, 1849–50), vol. 3, 326–27.

310 Quoted in Clay, *Romanticism,* 18.

311 Osborne, *Rossini,* 79ff.

312 Andrew Lees, *Cities Perceived: Urban Society in European and American Thought, 1820–1940* (Manchester, 1985), 7–9.

313 John Byng, *The Torrington Diaries,* 4 vols. (London, 1934–38), vol. 2, 222.

314 *Journal of Thomas Moore,* vol. 1, 33.

315 *Reminiscences and Recollections of Captain Gronow, 1810–1860,* 2 vols. (Surtees Society, 1984), vol. 314; *Journal of Mrs. Arbuthnot,* 63.

316 Bovill, 116. See M. Hadfield, *Gardening in Britain* (London, 1860), chap. 6.

317 For an interesting analysis of Loudon's influence, see L. Davidoff and C. Hall, *Family Fortunes: Men and Women of the English Middle Class, 1780–1850* (London, 1987).

318 J. M. MacKenzie, *The Empire of Nature: Hunting, Conservation and*

British Imperialism (Manchester, 1988), 89.

319 Figures in MacKenzie; see S. D. Neumark, *Economic Influences on the South African Frontier* (Stanford, 1957); T. Pringle, *Narration of a Residence in South Africa* (London, 1838), 38ff.

320 MacKenzie, 203ff.

321 Ibid., Appendix 1, 312ff.

FOUR
World Policeman

1 Douglas Johnson: "The Maghreb," in J. E. Flint, ed., *The Cambridge History of Africa, Volume V, 1790–1870* (Cambridge, England, 1976), 99–124.

2 Kenneth Mason, *Gunfire in Barbary* (London, 1982), 29.

3 Ibid., 35–37.

4 Sir Henry Bunbury, *Narrative of Some Passages in the Great War with France* (London, 1810), 232.

5 See C. N. Parkinson, *Edward Pellew, Viscount Exmouth: Admiral of the Red* (London, 1936).

6 For a detailed account of preparations for the engagement and the bombardment itself, see Mason, 85ff, 116ff.

7 For an eyewitness account by one of Exmouth's secretaries, see Abraham Salame, *Narrative of the Expedition to Algiers, 1816* (London, 1819).

8 *Dictionary of National Biography*, compact ed., vol. 2, 1627.

9 Michael Jenkins, *Arakcheev: Grand Vizier of the Russian Empire* (London, 1969).

10 Ibid., 90–91.

11 Robert Porter, *Travelling Sketches in Russia and Sweden* (London, 1809), Letter xxciii, September 1806.

12 Quoted in Jenkins, 86.

13 Quoted in Richard Pipes, "The Russian Military Colonies, 1810–1831," *Journal of Modern History*, September 1950.

14 Jenkins, 147.

15 Quoted in ibid., 185.

16 Ibid., 221.

17 *Voyage de Monsieur le Maréchal Marmont, Duc de Raguse*, 2 vols. (Brussels, 1841), vol. 1, 1.

18 Quoted in Jenkins, 190.

19 Jack Larkin, *The Reshaping of Every-day Life, 1790–1840* (New York, 1988), 184.

20 Jenkins, 197.

21 Hugh Seton-Watson, *The Russian Empire 1801–1917* (Oxford, 1967), 162–63.

22 Jenkins, 252.

23 Ibid., 246ff.

24 Quoted in Pipes, *Russia Under the Old Regime* (London, 1974), 105.

25 For the legislative and legal background, see U. B. Phillips, *American Negro Slavery* (New York, 1918) and K. M. Stamp, *The Peculiar Institution* (New York, 1956).

26 Paul L. Ford, ed., *Thomas Jefferson: Writings*, 10 vols. (New York, 1892–99), vol. 9, 416.

27 William Peden, ed., *Thomas Jefferson: Notes on the State of Virginia* (New York, 1955), 155; Ronald T. Takaki, *Iron Cages: Race and Culture in 19th Century America* (London, 1980), 43–46.

28 For Jefferson's dilemmas over slavery, see Fawn M. Brodie, *Thomas Jefferson: An Intimate History* (New York, 1974); and John Chester Miller, *The Wolf by the Ears: Thomas Jefferson and Slavery* (New York, 1977).

29 Irving Brant, *The Fourth President: A Life of James Madison* (London, 1970), 249.

30 Ibid., 610–11.

31 Harriet Martineau, *A Retrospect of Western Travel*, 3 vols. (London, 1838).

32 Brant, 639–40.

33 Allan Nevins, ed., *Diary of John Quincy Adams 1794–1845* (New York, 1951), 3 March 1820, 231.

34 J. P. Mayer and Max Lerner, eds., *De*

Tocqueville: Democracy in America, 2 vols. (New York, 1966), vol. 1, 373–74.

35 Nevins, 96.

36 For these and other examples, see Leon Litwack, *North of Slavery: The Negro in the Free States, 1790–1860* (Chicago, 1961), 167; Takaki, 113–14.

37 Nevins, 228, 246–47.

38 Peter Kolchin, *Unfree Labor: American Slavery and Russian Serfdom* (Cambridge, Mass., 1987), 366, Table 11.

39 Ibid., 364; see P. D. McClelland and R. J. Zeckhausen, *Democratic Dimensions of the New Republic: American Interregional Migration, Vital Statistics and Manumissions, 1800–60* (Cambridge, England, 1982).

40 Henry Hobhouse, *Seeds of Change: Five Plants That Transformed the World* (New York, 1986), 144ff.

41 Derry and Williams, 287ff; Samuel Smiles, *Industrial Biography: Ironworkers and Tool-makers* (London, 1863), 322ff; Hobhouse, 142.

42 Hobhouse, 141.

43 Constance M. Green, *Eli Whitney and the Birth of American Technology* (New York, 1950).

44 Quoted in Hobhouse, 181 note 20.

45 J. G. de R. Hamilton, ed., *The Papers of Thomas Ruffin,* 4 vols. (Raleigh, N.C., 1918–20) vol. 1, 198, Graham to Ruffin, 9 November 1817.

46 Jan Lewis, *The Pursuit of Happiness: Family and Values in Jefferson's Virginia* (Cambridge, England, 1983); Hobhouse, 153.

47 Billington, *Westward Expansion,* 198–99.

48 Hobhouse, 158.

49 Ibid., 183 fn., 34.

50 Nevins, 226.

51 Helen T. Catterall, ed., *Judicial Cases Concerning American Slavery and the Negro,* 2 vols. (New York, 1924), vol. 1, 311.

52 Ibid., vol. 2, 59.

53 Ibid., vol. 2, 57, 334. See George Dangerfield, *The Era of Good Feelings*

(London, 1953), 211ff for these and other cases.

54 Quoted in Dangerfield, 211ff.

55 Kolchin, 372.

56 *Annals of Congress,* 15th Cong., 2nd Sess., vol. 1, 1204.

57 Monroe, *Writings* vol. 6, 116; *Cresson,* 348.

58 Text of Missouri Compromise in *Annals of Congress,* 16th Cong., 2nd Sess., 1128; Dangerfield, 217–42, text on 241–42.

59 James E. Cutler, *Lynch-Law: An Investigation into the History of Lynching in the United States* (New York, 1905), 24–31.

60 W. D. Jordan, *White over Black: American Attitudes Toward the Negro, 1550–1812* (Chapel Hill, N.C., 1968), 115–20.

61 Herbert Aptheker, *American Negro Slave Revolts* (New York, 1943), 270ff; J. C. Carroll, *Slave Insurrections in the United States, 1800–65* (New York, 1938), 94–100.

62 For Nat Turner, see Herbert Aptheker, *Nat Turner's Slave Rebellion* (New York, 1966).

63 Hobhouse, 74.

64 J. H. Rodrigues, *Brazil and Africa* (Berkeley, Calif., 1965), argues this case.

65 Ibid., 42–49.

66 Salvador de Madariaga, *Bolivar* (trans., London, 1952), 25–26.

67 Hobhouse, 74–75; see N. Deerr, *The History of Sugar* (Oxford, 1971).

68 See David Nicholls, "Haiti: Race, Slavery and Independence, 1804–25," in Leonie J. Archer, ed., *Slavery and Other Forms of Unfree Labour* (London, 1988), 224–37.

69 Baron de Vastey, *An Essay on . . . Hayti* (Exeter, 1823), 245.

70 Quoted in Nicholls, 234.

71 Quoted in ibid., 236.

72 Baron de Vastey, *Political Remarks . . . Concerning Hayti* (London, 1818), 26, 74.

73 See J. Holland Rose, A. P. Newton, and E. A. Denion, eds., *Cambridge*

History of the British Empire (Cambridge, 1941), chap. 5, "Abolition of the Slave Trade," 188ff; Hobhouse, 70ff.

74 Kathryn Cave, ed., *The Diary of Joseph Farington*, 16 vols. (New Haven, Conn., 1978–84), vol. 3, 901; other references to Beckford's income in the same source. are vol. 2, 613, vol. 4, 1173–75.

75 For the debate over numbers, see P. D. Curtin, *The Atlantic Slave Trade: A Census* (Madison, Wisc.: 1969); Paul Lovejoy, "The Volume of the Atlantic Slave Trade," *Journal of African History*, 1982; J. D. Fage, "African Societies and the Atlantic Slave Trade," *Past and Present*, November 1989.

76 Thomas Clarkson, *History of the Abolition of the Slave Trade*, 2 vols. (London, 1808).

77 James Boswell, *Life of Dr. Johnson* (London, 1904) vol. 2, 153–56.

78 T. B. Howell, *State Trials*, 33 vols. (London, 1816–26), vol. 22, 1–82.

79 Clarkson, vol. 1, 117–26, 230, vol. 2, 188–92, 346–55; *Parliamentary History*, 27.

80 For the Clapham Sect, see E. Howse, *Saints in Politics* (London, 1952): S. Meacham, *Henry Thornton of Clapham 1760–1815* (Cambridge, Mass., 1964); David Spring, "The Clapham Sect: Some Social and Political Aspects," *Victorian Studies*, 5 (1961–62).

81 R. I. and S. Wilberforce, *Life of Wilberforce*, 5 vols. (London, 1838), vol. 4, 239, 241.

82 W. L. Mathieson, *British Slavery and Its Abolition* (London, 1926), 118; L. J. Ragatz, *Fall of the Planter Class in the British Caribbean* (London, 1928), 52.

83 *Black Dwarf*, 26 October 1819.

84 William Nais, *Reason for Using East India Sugar* (London, 1828).

85 T. W. Reid, *Life of the Rt Hon W. E. Forster* (Bath, 1970 reissue), 21.

86 J. S. Colquhoun, *Life of Wilberforce*, 2nd ed. (London, 1867); New, *Brougham*, 122.

87 *The Slavery of the British West Indies Delineated*, 2 vols. (London, 1824–30).

88 *Edinburgh Review*, April 1838.

89 R. Coupland, *Wilberforce* (London, 1923), 341.

90 *The Times*, 30 November 1813.

91 *Parliamentary Papers*, 1824, vol. 24, 427.

92 *Hansard*, 1826, vol. 14, 1160; *Hansard*, New Series, vol. 11, 961ff, 1294ff.

93 C. W. Vane, ed., *Memoirs and Correspondence of Viscount Castlereagh . . . edited by His Brother*, 12 vols. (1848–53), vol. 10, 73, 1 August 1814.

94 Sir Charles Webster, *The Foreign Policy of Castlereagh, 1812–15* (London, 1831), 413–24; *The Foreign Policy of Castlereagh, 1815–22* (London, 1925), 454–66.

95 Sir Charles Webster, *Britain and the Independence of Latin-America, 1812–30* (Oxford, 1938) vol. 1, 171; Rodrigues, 117–19.

96 H. G. Soulsby, *The Right of Search in Anglo-American Relations, 1814–62* (London, 1933); New, *Brougham*, 139–41.

97 For these and further details, see H. S. Klein: *African Slavery in Latin America and the Caribbean* (Oxford, 1986), 249–32.

98 Helen Taft Manning, *British Colonial Government After the American Revolution 1782–1820* (New Haven, Conn., 1933), 479; D. M. Young, *The Colonial Office in the Early 19th Century* (London, 1961), 36ff.

99 Nicolson, *Congress of Vienna*, 211–16.

100 C. W. Newbury, ed., *British Policy Towards West Africa: Select Documents, 1786–1874* (Oxford, 1965), 140–42.

101 G. S. Graham, *Great Britain in the Indian Ocean 1810–50* (Oxford, 1967), 138–39.

102 John Peterson, *Province of Freedom: A History of Sierra Leone, 1787–1870* (London, 1969); Leslie Bethell, "Mixed Commissions for the Suppression of the Atlantic Slave Trade," *Journal of African History*, 7 (1966), 1.

103 E. L. Fox, *The American Colonisation Society* (Baltimore, 1919), 33.

104 See Chrisopher Fyfe, "Free Slave Colonies in West Africa," in *Cambridge History of Africa*, 170–99.

105 J. F. Ade Ajaye and B. O. Cloruntimehin, "West Africa in the Anti-Slave Trade Era," in ibid., 200–21.

106 *Select Documents*, 62ff.

107 F. K. Macohney, "African Leadership in Bathurst in the 19th Century," *Tarikh*, 2 (1962), 11, cited in Fyfe.

108 *Select Documents*, 142.

109 Ibid., 144ff.

110 Brantz Mayer, ed., *Captain Canot: Or Twenty Years of an African Slaver* (New York, 1854), 262–63, quoted in C. W. Newbury: *The Western Slave Coast and Its Rulers* (Oxford, 1961), 37–38.

111 Richard Lander, *Records of Captain Clapperton's Last Expedition to Africa*, 2 vols. (London, 1830), vol. 1, 238–39, quoted Newbury, 38.

112 Graham, 63.

113 Quoted in ibid., 147.

114 Ibid., 14.

115 Ibid., 134, 141–43.

116 Ibid., 145, fn. 1.

117 Ibid., 65 and fn 1.

118 W. C. Devereux: *A Cruise in the "Gorgon"* (London, 1869), quoted in ibid., 11.

119 Richard Burton, *Zanzibar, City, Island and Coast*, 2 vols. (London, 1872), vol. 1, 304.

120 Graham, 173.

121 Various authorities give different figures for naval strength. See William James, *The Naval History of Great Britain . . . 1793–1820*, 6 vols. (London 1822–24 and later eds.), vol. 3, 357; vol. 6, 505; for a general account, see Elie Halévy, *England in 1815*, 2nd ed. (trans., London, 1949), 45–46, and fn. 5.

122 Lloyd, *Captain Marryat and the Old Navy*, 172–33.

123 Halévy, 59–60.

124 For further details, see G. M. Young, *Early Victorian England*, 2 vols. (Oxford, 1934), vol. 1.

125 Graham, *Great Britain in the Indian Ocean*, 1–2; John Gleason, *Genesis of Russophobia in Great Britain* (Cambridge, Mass., 1950).

126 Charles Dupin, *The Commercial Power of Great Britain*, English ed., 2 vols. (Paris, 1825), vol. 1, Introduction.

127 C. E. Fayle, *A Short History of the World's Shipping Industry* (London, 1933), 217.

128 See Graham, 8–9 and fn. 4.

129 *History of Parliament: The House of Commons 1790–1820*, vol. 3, 159–60; *Dictionary of National Biography*, compact ed., vol. 1, 111.

130 *Journal of Mrs. Arbuthnot*, vol. 1, 158–59.

131 *Autobiography of [Sir] Henry Taylor*, 2 vols. (London, 1885), vol. 1, 138ff.

132 D. M. Young, *The Colonial Office in the Early 19th Century* (London, 1961), Appendix 8, 282–84.

133 R. J. W. Horton, *Exposition and Defence of Earl Bathurst's Administration of . . . Canada* (London, 1838), quoted in Young, 53.

134 Ibid., 34ff.

135 Taylor, *Autobiography*, vol. 1, 67–68; Young, 180.

136 L. Strachey and R. Fulford, eds., *Greville Memoirs*, 8 vols. (London, 1938), vol. 3, 65–66.

137 Young, 136.

138 Quoted in ibid., 183.

139 For Barrow, see his *Autobiographical Memoir* (London, 1847) and Christopher Lloyd, *Mr. Barrow of the Admiralty: A Life of Sir John Barrow* (London, 1970).

140 For Castlereagh's arguments on the

East Indies issue, see his letter to Liverpool, 19 April 1814, printed in V. Harlow and F. Madden, eds., *British Colonial Developments, 1774–1834: Select Documents* (Oxford, 1953), 67.

141 Maurice Collis, *Raffles* (London, 1966), 34ff.

142 *Select Colonial Documents,* 64ff; Lady Raffles, *Memoir of Sir T. S. Raffles* (London, 1830), 69–71.

143 See the paper he wrote for Canning, 23 October 1817, printed in *Select Colonial Documents,* 68ff.

144 Quoted in Collis, 140.

145 Raffles to Colonel Addenbrooke, 10 June 1819, printed in *Select Colonial Documents* 73.

146 Collis, 156–57.

147 Letter to Addenbrooke, cited above. The colonel was a former equerry to Princess Charlotte and Raffles's main contact with royal circles.

148 For Raffles's family life, see Emily Hahn, *Raffles of Singapore,* rev. ed. (Kuala Lumpur, 1966).

149 Collis, 163–70.

150 William Marsden, *History of Sumatra* (London, 1811).

151 Quoted in Mildred Archer, "India and Natural History: The Role of the East India Company 1785–1858," *History Today,* November 1959.

152 For details and further examples, see ibid.

153 Graham, 132.

154 *Select Colonial Documents,* 76.

155 Graham, 245.

156 H. Dodwell, *The Founder of Modern Egypt* (Cambridge, 1931), 45–46; L. G. Johnson, *General T. Perronet Thompson, 1783–1869* (London, 1957), 100ff; Graham, 249ff.

157 G. W. Earl: *The Eastern Seas, or Voyages and Adventurers in the Indian Archipelago* (London, 1837), 384. See also Captain Henry Keppel, *A Visit to the Indian Archipelago,* 2 vols. (London, 1853), vol. 1, 281. Graham devotes a chapter to a thorough discussion of the problem in "Piracy in Malay Waters," 362ff.

158 Cf. the minutes on Siam policy by Governor-General Lord Amhurst, 23 July 1827, quoted in Graham, 374.

159 See Owen's letter to J. W. Croker at the Admiralty, 20 July 1830, quoted in ibid., 364.

FIVE

Can the Center Hold?

1 Wordsworth to Lonsdale, 13 and 20 December 1817, printed in Mary Moorman and Alan G. Hill, eds., *Letters of William and Dorothy Wordsworth: The Middle Years, Part II 1812–20* (Oxford, 1970), 404–05, 406.

2 Wordsworth's Bond of Office, listing his duties as collector of stamps, a post he held until 1842, is at the National Trust property, Dove Cottage, Grasmere; see Mary Moorman, *William Wordsworth: A Biography. The Later Years, 1803–1850* (Oxford, 1965), 242–53, for all the circumstances surrounding the job. For all dates involving Wordsworth, I have followed F. B. Pinion, *A Wordsworth Chronology* (London, 1988).

3 *The Prelude,* Book 6, 108.

4 Leigh Hunt, *The Feast of the Poets* (London, 1815), 99; P. P. Howe, ed., *William Hazlitt, Collected Works,* 21 vols. (London, 1930–34), vol. 7, 143.

5 Haydon, *Autobiography,* vol. 1, 269ff. Keats's account is in M. B. Forman, ed., *Letters of John Keats,* 3rd ed. (Oxford, 1948), 73–78, letter to George and Thomas Keats, January 5, 1818.

6 Haydon, *Autobiography,* vol. 1, 272.

7 See Forman, 75, fn. 1; Keats's later and misleading version was recorded by C. W. Dilke in his annotated copy of Lord

Houghton's *Life and Letters of Keats* (London, 1848).

8 See Catherine Macdonald Maclean, *Born Under Saturn: A Biography of William Hazlitt* (London, 1943), 381ff.

9 Forman, letters, dated 25–27 June 1818, 154–60, and 17–21 July 1818, 184–90. See Robert Gittings, *John Keats* (Harmondsworth, 1978), 327ff.

10 Allan Nevins, ed., *Diary of John Quincy Adams 1794–1845* (New York, 1951), 177.

11 L. E. A. Eitner, *Géricault: His Life and Work* (London, 1983), 225.

12 See Kathryn Cave, ed., *The Diary of Joseph Farington*, 16 vols. (New Haven, Conn., 1978–84), vol. 2, 17 December 1795, 446 (hereafter called *Farington's Diary*).

13 See J. Stevenson, *Popular Disturbances in England, 1700–1870* (London, 1979); for a different view of the barrack-building program, see E. P. Thompson, *The Making of the English Working Class* (Harmondsworth, 1976), 663. "England in 1792 had been government by consent and deference, supplemented by the gallows and the church-and-king mob. In 1816 the English people were held down by force." I have found no convincing evidence to support this extreme interpretation.

14 A. P. Thornton: *The Habit of Authority* (London, 1966), 79.

15 Roger Wells, *Wretched Faces: Famine in Wartime England, 1793–1801* (Gloucester, 1988), esp. the final chapter, "Paradoxes, Ironies and Contradictions," 315–39. Wells sees the possessing classes as essentially divided between the compassionate and the hard-hearted.

16 J. R. Weston, "The Volunteer Movement as an Anti-Revolutionary Force, 1793–1801," *English Historical Review*, 21 (1956); Wells, 260–73.

17 *An Essay on the Principles of Population*, 2 vols. (London, Everyman ed., 1914), vol. 2, 187, 211–12.

18 J. Tann, "Cooperative Milling: Self-help during the Grain Crises of the Napoleonic War," *Agricultural History Review*, 28 (1980).

19 Quoted in Wells, 334.

20 For lists of disturbances during these years, see A. P. and J. M. Robson, eds., *Works of John Stuart Mill*, vol. 22, *Newspaper Writings*, December 1822–July 1831 (Toronto, 1986), xx–xxl.

21 Quoted in F. G. Darvall, *Popular Disturbances and Public Order in Regency England; Being an Account of the Luddite and Other Disorders in England during . . . 1811–17, and of the Attitude and Activity of the Authorities* (London, 1934), 310.

22 Quoted in G. D. H. Cole, *Life of Cobbett*, 3rd ed. (London, 1947), 180; for Maitland, see *History of Parliament: Commons 1790–1820*, vol. 4, 528–29; *Dictionary of National Biography*, compact ed., vol. 1, 1301.

23 *Emma*, vol. 3, chap. 3.

24 See Thompson, 667 and fn. 1; for Cartwright's career, see F. D. Cartwright, *Life and Correspondence of Major Cartwright*, 2 vols. (London, 1826).

25 Daniel Green, *Great Cobbett: The Noblest Agitator* (London, 1983), 438ff.

26 Louis Simond, *Journal of a Tour and Residence in Great Britain* (London, 1815).

27 Green, 350–58.

28 For Hunt's background and early life, see Ann Blainey, *Immortal Boy* (London, 1985), 3ff; Dickens's admission about Skimpole is in a letter to Mrs. Richard Watson, written in September 1853, quoted in ibid., 189.

29 *Dictionary of National Biography*, compact ed., vol. 1, 1034; Blainey, 62–71.

30 For these and other details, see E. W. Bovill, *English Country Life 1780–1830* (Oxford, 1962), 32ff.

31 He was still doing it in 1822; see *Jour-*

nal of Mrs. Arbuthnot, 137, entry for 23 January 1822.

32 F. L. Carsten: *A History of the Prussian Junkers* (London, 1989), 89.

33 See speech by William Huskisson in the Commons, 16 May 1814, *Parliamentary Debates,* vol. 27, 920.

34 *Farington's Diary,* vol. 2, 546, 562–83.

35 *Examiner,* 10 May 1812; *Political Register,* 30 May 1812; see Geoffrey Carnall, *Robert Southey and His Age: The Development of a Conservative Mind* (Oxford, 1960), 140ff.

36 Kenneth Bourne, *Palmerston: The Early Years, 1784–1841* (London, 1982), 156; for Flood, see *Parliamentary History: House of Commons 1790–1820,* vol. 3, 778ff.

37 Details are in Bourne.

38 William Hone, *The Report at Large of the Coroner's Inquest on Jane Watson* (London, 1815); *Edinburgh Annual Register 1815,* 79–85; W. D. Jones, *Prosperity Robinson: The Life of Viscount Goderich, 1782–1859* (London, 1967), 60–4.

39 Gronow, *Reminiscences,* vol. 1, 220–21.

40 L. J. Jennings, *The Croker Papers,* 3 vols. (London, 1884), vol. 1, 59; Croker to Canning, March 13, 1815.

41 Thompson, 293ff; W. M. Gurney: *Trial of James Watson* (London, 1817); *Independent Whig,* 27 July, 3 August, 12 October 1817; *Farington's Diary,* 16 June 1817, vol. 14, 5038.

42 William Cobbett, *Rural Rides,* 2 vols. (London, 1830), 30 October 1821, 11 October 1822. For rural disturbances, see *Annual Register* (1816), 93; *Annual Register* (1817), 9, 61–65, 76, 191; *Report of the Secret Committee of the House of Lords appointed to Inquire into certain Meetings and Combinations Endangering the Public Tranquility* (London, 1817).

43 See W. H. R. Curtler, *A Short History of English Agriculture* (Oxford, 1909); Bovil, 29–32.

44 Cobbett, *Rural Rides* 25 October 1825.

45 Quoted in A. N. W. Stirling, *Coke of Norfolk and His Friends,* 2 vols. (London, 1908).

46 Quoted in E. J. Hobsbawm and George Rudé, *Captain Swing* (London, 1969), 43.

47 *Political Register,* 20 October 1825.

48 Hobsbawm and Rudé, 24 and fn.; these figures date from the early 1880s.

49 George Eliot, *Impressions of Theophrastus Such* (London, 1879), 45.

50 *Pig-Killers and Paupers: The Diaries of the Rev. William Holland* (Newton Abbott, 1974).

51 The story is recounted by Smith himself in *Letters to Archdeacon Singleton* (London, 1837); see Saba, Lady Holland, *A Memoir of the Rev. Sydney Smith, by His Daughter,* 4th ed. (London, 1855), 6.

52 S. L. Ollard and Gordon Crosse, *Dictionary of English Church History* (London, 1912), 28. The remark about the king is in *The Times,* 12 February 1848.

53 Ollard and Crosse, *Dictionary of National Biography,* compact ed., vol. 1, 1022.

54 Morgan Cove, *An Essay on the Revenues of the Church of England,* 3rd enlarged ed. (London, 1816); Scott is quoted in W. R. Ward. *Religion and Society in England, 1790–1850,* 1972), 106–07.

55 *First Letter to Archdeacon Singleton;* see Alan Bell, *Sydney Smith: a Biography* (Oxford, 1980), 178–79.

56 Ward, 9–10.

57 Bell, 149.

58 *The Times,* 27 September 1819, quoted in Thompson, 752.

59 For Hay, see Ward, 125.

60 For the building program and so forth, see Ward, 108 and fn. 4, p. 310; 109ff; J. H. Overton, *The English Church in the 19th Century, 1800–33* (London, 1894), 145ff; for criticism, see *Manchester Guardian,* 30 June, 11 August, 1 September 1821, 6 July 1822.

61 William Roberts, *Memoir of Hannah More*, 4 vols. 3rd ed. (London, 1838), vol. 3, 423–24.

62 Ibid., vol. 3, 327.

63 For Hannah More, *Dictionary of National Biography*, compact ed., vol. 1, 1415; G. W. E. Lewes in *Dictionary of English Church History*, 374–75; Rev. Henry Thompson, *Life of Hannah More* (London, 1838); Mary Gwladys Jones, *Hannah More* (London, 1952).

64 T. S. Grimshawe, *Life of Legh Richmond* (London, 1828), 319.

65 See Hazlitt's description of the occasion in his famous essay, "On My First Acquaintance with Poets."

66 For Evans and Wedderburn, see Iain McCalman, *Radical Underworld: Prophets, Revolutionaries and Pornographers in London, 1795–1840* (London, 1989), 101ff, 133ff.

67 *Farington's Diary*, vol. 10, 3689; 12 July 1810.

68 Ibid., vol. 4, 1266, 1274.

69 Ibid., vol. 6, 2085ff.

70 Ibid., vol. 16, 5520.

71 Ibid., vol. 10, 3652–53.

72 Ibid., vol. 13, 4553.

73 *History of Parliament: House of Commons 1790–1820*, vol. 2, Constituencies, 175ff; ibid., vol. 16, 4925.

74 Charles Dickens, *Pickwick Papers* (London 1836–37), chap. 13; the story is set in the mid-1820s.

75 *Geoffrey Madan's Notebooks* (Oxford, 1981), 5.

76 *Journal of Mrs. Arbuthnot*, vol. 1, 36, 39, 61.

77 The notice, still preserved at Strathfield Saye, was hung in the porch.

78 *Farington's Diary*, vol. 3, 874.

79 Ibid., vol. 13, 4725.

80 Ibid., vol. 3, 884.

81 Cresson, *Monroe*, 359; Nevins, 260, 188.

82 Nevins, entry for 19 August 1822, 287.

83 Ibid., 297, 348–49.

84 Ibid., 368, 378, 382.

85 John Niven, *Martin Van Buren: The Romantic Age of American Politics* (Oxford, 1983), 232–34.

86 Frances Trollope, *Domestic Manners of the Americans* (New York, 1949), 125; Remini, *Jackson* (1981) 157–58; Marquis James, Andrew Jackson, *Portrait of a President* (New York, 1937), 257ff.

87 Haydon, *Diary*, vol. 3, 491–92.

88 Kenneth Bourne, *Palmerston: The Early Years, 1784–1841* (London, 1982), 112–18.

89 Ibid., 123.

90 Norman Gash, *Mr. Secretary Peel* (London, 1985) 297ff.

91 Jane Austen, *Persuasion* (1817), chap. 8.

92 Elie Halévy, *England in 1815*, 2nd ed. (trans.; London, 1949), 38–39.

93 See the list, and so forth in A. Aspinal and E. A. Smith, eds., *English Historical Documents 1783–1832* (London, 1959), 86–87.

94 Ibid., 87.

95 Lord Colchester, ed., *Lord Ellenborough's Political Diary 1828–30*, 2 vols. (London, 1881), vol. 1, 104.

96 Ibid., vol. 1, 155–56; Bathurst manuscript, quoted in Aspinal and Smith, 93, fn. 1.

97 *Ellenborough's Diary*, vol. 1, 76.

98 For Lady Salisbury's Diary, 1 September 1836, recording Wellington's recollections, see Carola Oman, *The Gascoyne Heiress: The Life and Diaries of Frances Mary Gascoyne-Cecil 1802–39* (London, 1968), 210.

99 This is Arbuthnot's account, recorded in Lady Salisbury's Diary, 9 September 1837; see Oman, 212.

100 George IV to Wellington, 17 July 1823, Wellington manuscript, printed in Aspinal and Smith, 181f. For the sumner row, see ibid., 180f.

101 For its origins, see D. L. Keir, "Economical Reform, 1779–1787," *Law Quarterly Review*, July 1934; for details, see A. S. Foord, "The Waning of the Influence of the Crown," *English Historical Review*, vol. 11, 1947; for Burke's speech, see *The*

Works of Edmund Burke 8 vols. (1894–1900), vol. 3, 229ff.

102 *Observations Respecting the Public Expenditure and the Influence of the Crown* (London, 1810).

103 Halévy, *England in 1815*, 10, fn. 2; 15, fn. 3.

104 Bourne, *Palmerston*, 88–89.

105 See *passim*, W. S. Dowden, ed., *The Journal of Thomas Moore*, 2 vols. (Newark, N.J., 1983); for details of the fraud, see Lord John Russell, ed., *Memoires, Journal and Correspondence of Thomas Moore*, 8 vols. (London, 1853–56).

106 The key entries are *Farington's Diary*, vol. 13, 4747, 4750–51, and ibid., vol. 14, 4842ff.

107 For details of the physical arrangements at the Commons, see R. G. Thorne, ed., *History of Parliament: House of Commons 1790–1820*, vol. 1, Survey, 333ff.

108 *Farington's Diary*, vol. 9, 3463, 21 May 1809.

109 Ibid., vol. 12, 4157.

110 T. H. S. Escott, *Club Makers and Club Members* (London, 1914), 64.

111 Chester W. New, *Life of Lord Brougham to 1830* (Oxford, 1961), 390ff.

112 *Letters of Sir Charles Bell* (London, 1870), 295–96.

113 Sir Herbert Maxwell, ed., *The Creevey Papers*, 2 vols. (London, 1903), vol. 1, 249–50; Sir Samuel Romilly, *Memoirs*, 3 vols. (London, 1840), vol. 1, 412–13.

114 Samuel Bamford, *Passages in the Life of a Radical* (London, 1844), 27.

115 George Pellew, *Life of Sidmouth*, 2 vols. (London, 1847), vol. 1, 153–54.

116 Harriet Raikes, ed., *Thomas Raikes's Journal*, 4 vols. (London, 1856–57), vol. 3, 207–08.

117 *House of Commons, 1790–1820*, vol. 3, 288–89.

118 These and the following figures are compiled from ibid., vol. 1, Survey.

119 Ibid., 280.

120 Ibid., 291.

121 Ibid., 330–32.

122 Ibid, 295.

123 For many examples, see ibid., 288–91.

124 Ibid., 291, for a full list.

125 *House of Commons 1790–1820*, vol. 3, 278–81; vol. 5, 31–33.

126 Published in Jennings, *The Croker Papers*, vol. 1, 367–72.

127 *House of Commons 1790–1820*, vol. 1, Survey, 4, 42.

128 *Farington's Diary*, vol. 7, 2694.

129 For Middlesex, Yorkshire, and Westminster, see *House of Commons 1790–1820*, vol. 2, Constituencies, 258ff, 436ff, 266ff.

130 *Farington's Diary*, vol. 7, 2694; vol. 8, 2867, 2870–71.

131 Ibid., vol. 14, 5031; *House of Commons 1790–1820*, vol. 2, 96–99.

132 *Farington's Diary*, vol. 2, 483; vol. 8, 2899.

133 Ibid., vol. 13, 3050, 3058.

134 *House of Commons 1790–1820*, vol. 2, 104–05, vol. 4, 456–57.

135 *Farington's Diary*, vol. 6, 2017.

136 *House of Commons 1790–1820*, vol. 2, 13–14; ibid., vol. 4, 1161.

137 Bourne, *Palmerston*, 247–48.

138 For the background, see Hugh Owen, *The Lowther Family* (London, 1990).

139 R. S. Fergusson, *A History of Westmorland* (London, 1894), 153ff; and R. S. Fergusson, *Cumberland and Westmorland MPs from the Restoration to the Reform Bill of 1867* (London, 1871),

140 W. W. Douglas, "Westmorland in Politics: The Westmorland Election of 1818," *Modern Language Notes*, 43 (London, 1948), 437ff.

141 M. K. Danzinger and F. Brady, *Boswell: The Great Biographer, 1789–1795* (London, 1989), esp. 5–6, 21ff, 49–86.

142 Alexander Carlisle, *Autobiography* (London, 1861), 418–19.

143 *Farington's Diary*, vol. 9, 3281, 3357, 3363, 3367.

144 W. A. Knight, *Life of Wordsworth*, 3 vols. (London 1889), vol. 1, 98.

145 Moorman, 60–63.

146 Wordsworth's side of the correspon-

dence is printed in Moorman and Hill; and ibid.

147 Shelley to Peacock, 20 April 1818, printed in Roger Ingpen, ed., *Letters of Percy Bysshe Shelley*, 2 vols. (London, 1914), vol. 2, 597.

148 For an extensive discussion of Wordsworth's political views, see Moorman, 330–63.

149 Wordsworth to James Losh, 4 December 1821, Moorman, vol. 1, 96–99.

150 Wordsworth to Catherine Clarkson, 4 June 1812, Moorman and Hill, 451.

151 Wordsworth to Daniel Stuart, 7 April 1817, ibid., 783–84.

152 Ibid., 804.

153 For Brougham's family background and early life, see New, 2–32.

154 Dorothy Wordsworth to Thomas Monkhouse, 5 January 1818, Moorman and Hill, 409–10.

155 Ibid., 410ff.

156 For Brougham's maneuvering for seats, see, *House of Commons 1790–1820*, vol. 3, 266ff.

157 Brougham to Lord Holland, 28–29 June 1818, quoted in ibid., vol. 3, 274.

158 Wordsworth's reports to Lonsdale are in Moorman and Hill, esp. 418–19, 423, 426–29, 431, 434, 441, 468.

159 Printed as *Two Addresses to the Freeholders of Westmorland* (Kendal, 1818); see J. E. Wells, "Wordsworth and De Quincey in Westmorland Politics 1818," *Publication of the Modern Language Association of America*, 5 (1940), 1080–1128.

160 All this description is from Dorothy's letters to Sara Hutchinson, 24 March, and to Mrs. Clarkson, 30 March, Moorman and Hill, 443ff, 448–49, 453ff.

161 Ibid., 438–39, 462.

162 For De Quincey's relations with the Wordsworths, see R. Gittings and J. Manton, *Dorothy Wordsworth* (Oxford, 1985), 165–67, 174–80, 191–92, 203–04.

163 Wordsworth to Lonsdale, 3 August 1818, Moorman and Hill, 478; the

exchange of letters with De Quincey is in J. E. Jordan, ed., *De Quincey to Wordsworth: A Biography of a Relationship* (Berkeley, Calif., 1962), 318ff.

164 For De Quincey as editor, see the unpublished doctoral thesis by F. S. Janzow, *De Quincey Enters Journalism: His Contributions to the Westminster Gazette 1818–19* (Chicago, University Library Archives).

165 Moorman and Hill, 479.

166 *House of Commons 1790–1820*, vol. 4, 460.

167 See ibid., vol. 1, Survey, 255ff, 272ff; for details, see *The Late Elections. An Impartial Statement of All Proceedings etc.* (London, 1818).

168 Thomas Reid, *Collected Works* (Edinburgh, 1863), vol. 2, 538.

169 James Boswell, *Journal for 1778*, quoted in Alistair Smart, *The Life and Work of Alan Ramsay* (London, 1952), 164.

170 For the lives of both Alexander Naysmith and his son, see Samuel Smiles, ed., *James Naysmith: An Autobiography* (London, 1883).

171 For Naysmith's landscape painting, see Duncan Macmillan, *Painting in Scotland: The Golden Age* (Oxford, 1986), 14ff.

172 T. A. Marcus, ed., *Order and Space in Society* (Edinburgh, 1982), 138.

173 John Knox, who was probably a pupil of Naysmith, did the same for Glasgow in 1825–26.

174 *The Life and Times of Lord Brougham Written by Himself*, 3 vols. (London, 1871), vol., 1.

175 *Farington's Diary*, vol. 15, 5 August 1819, 5394–95.

176 J. Clive, *Scotch Reviewers: The Edinburgh Review, 1802–15* (London, 1957), 419, list Brougham's contributions; for Smith's role, see *Memoirs of Sydney Smith* vol. 1, 31.

177 Henry Thomas, Lord Cockburn, *Life of Lord Jeffrey*, 2 vols. (Edinburgh, 1842), vol. 1, 118; New, 19; A. Aspinall, *Lord Brougham and the Whig Party* (London, 1927), 5.

178 For the *Quarterly*, see H. Shine and

H. Chadwick, *The Quarterly Review Under Gifford* (Chapel Hill, N.C., 1949), which identifies contributors and the like.

179 For Byron's varied reactions to the attack at the time, see *Byron's Letters and Journals, In My Hot Youth*, 157ff.

180 *Farington's Diary*, vol. 13, 4626, 21 May 1815.

181 George Spater, "Cobbett, Hazlitt and the Edinburgh Review," in J. H. Weiner, ed., *Innovators and Preachers: The Role of the Editor in Victorian England* (Westport, Conn., 1985), 293ff.

182 J. W. Warter, ed., *Selections from the Letters of Robert Southey* (London, 1856), vol. 2, 222–23 (17 May 1811) and vol. 3, 46 (18 October 1816).

183 Carnall, *Southey*, 148–49.

184 See my essay on Croker, "A Very Bad Man?" *Statesmen and Nations* (London, 1971), 200ff.

185 Mary Campbell, *Lady Morgan: The Life and Times of Sidney Owenson* (London, 1988), 177–96.

186 "Letter to William Smith" (1817), reprinted in *Essays* (London, 1832), vol. 2, 23.

187 *Farington's Diary*, vol. 9, 3351–52.

188 Jane Austen, *Letters*, no. 31; quoted in Deirdre Le Faye, ed., *Jane Austen: A Family Record* (London, 1989), 55.

189 For historical consciousness in the early 19th century, see Honour, *Romanticism*, 190–93.

190 For sales figures and sums earned, see *Dictionary of National Biography*, compact ed., vol. 2, 1875; see also, *Farington's Diary*, vol. 15, 5396.

191 Scott's review, *Quarterly Review*, March 1816, is reprinted in B. C. Southam, *Jane Austen: The Critical Heritage* (London, 1968), vol. 1, 1811–70, 58–69. Jane Austen's reactions to the review are in *Letters*, no. 127.

192 *Farington's Diary*, vol. 5, 1955, vol. 14, 5129, vol. 15, 5329.

193 *Farington's Diary*, vol. 6, 2078.

194 See C. A. Prance, ed., *Companion to Charles Lamb* (London, 1983), entry on "John Lamb," 185–87.

195 Le Faye, 158.

196 For Godwin's influence on Shelley see William St. Clair, *The Godwins and the Shelleys* (London, 1989), 313ff; for Godwin and Wordsworth, see P. H. Marshall, *William Godwin* (New Haven, Conn., 1984), 128ff.

197 Edith Morley, ed., *Henry Crabb Robinson on Books and Their Writers*, 2 vols. (London, 1938), vol. 1, 183–84; St. Clair, 394; Marshall, 321.

198 Southey to Governor Bedford, 10 September 1816, quoted in Carnall, *Southey*, 152–53.

199 *Southey's Life and Correspondence*, vol. 6, 13.

200 P. P. Howe, ed., *Hazlitt's Works* (London, 1930–34), vol. 7, 193–94.

201 *Byron's Letters and Journals*, vol. 7, 83.

202 Jack Simmons, *Southey* (London, 1945), 166–67.

203 For the League of Incest row, see *Byron's Letters and Journals*, vol. 1, 10; vol. 6, 76; 82–83, 126; vol. 7, 102.

204 For an interesting analysis of the political implications of these and other works of the period, see Marilyn Butler, *Romantics, Rebels and Reactionaries* (Oxford, 1981), esp. "War of the Intellectuals," 138ff.

205 Benett failed in 1818, but won the seat the following year at a by-election; see *House of Commons 1790–1820*, vol. 3, 172–73; for Crabbe, see René Huchon: *George Crabbe and His Times, 1754–1832* (trans., London, 1968), 454–55.

206 See J. M. McQuiston's illuminating analysis of the Lowther manuscript, "The Lonsdale Connection and its Defender, William, Viscount Lowther, 1818–30," *Northern History*, vol. 4, 1975–76.

207 The invitation was first disclosed in Cuthbert Southey's *Life and Correspondence*; it is questioned by the official *History of the Times*, but confirmed by Crab Robinson's

Diary. See Simmons, *Southey,* 156–57.

208 Letter to William Smith, 1817, reprinted in *Essays* (London, 1832), vol. 2, 23.

209 Letter of January 4, 1817, quoted in Carnall, *Southey,* 167.

210 *Life and Correspondence,* vol. 3, 334.

211 To Governor Bedford, 5 November 1819, quoted in Carnall, *Southey,* 168.

212 Milton, *Paradise Lost,* Book 2, line 965; Demogorgon is also mentioned in Spenser's *Faerie Queene,* iv, ii, 47.

213 *Black Dwarf,* 27 October 1819.

214 C. D. Yonge, *Life and Administration of . . . Liverpool,* 3 vols. (London, 1868), vol. 2, 408–09.

215 *House of Commons 1790–1820,* vol. 1, 355.

216 McCalman, *Radical Underworld,* 135.

217 Philip Ziegler: *Addington* (London, 1965), 370.

218 Samuel Bamford, *Passages in the Life of a Radical* (first pub. 1844; reissued Oxford, 1984), 19.

219 George Pellew, *Life and Correspondence of . . . Sidmouth,* 3 vols. (London, 1847), vol. 3, 2.

220 This act remained on the Statute Book until 1967.

221 *Hansard,* first series, vol. 41, 38.

222 Norris to Sidmouth, 5 August 1819; Sidmouth to Exmouth, 15 August 1819; printed in Bamford, 136, and Ziegler, 370.

223 This description accords well with the superb full-length watercolor of Sidmouth by George Richmond in the National Portrait Gallery.

224 Bamford, 65–66, 75–81, 83–84, 85–88, 111–12.

225 Ibid., 131–33, 136.

226 For two recent books on the subject, see Donald Read, *The Massacre and the Background* (Manchester, 1985); and John Belchem, *Orator Hunt* (Oxford, 1985).

227 See esp. the *Times,* 19 August 1819.

228 Bamford, 146.

229 For Mutrie's account, see Philip Lawson, "Reassessing Peterloo," *History Today,* March 1988.

230 Thompson, *Making of the Working Class,* 749ff, presents this case, implausibly in my view.

231 Bamford, 158.

232 For an illuminating analysis of governmental activity in the aftermath of Peterloo, see J. E. Cookson, *Lord Liverpool's Administration, 1815–22* (Edinburgh, 1975), 178–99.

233 Ziegler, 373ff; Canning to Liverpool, 14 October 1819, Canning manuscript, quoted Cookson, 181–82.

234 *House of Commons 1790–1820,* vol. 1, 300.

235 For the timetable, see ibid., 387.

236 For an analysis of the Six Acts, see New, 196–97.

237 For details of the many plots, see E. Aylmer, ed., *Memoirs of George Edwards* (London, 1820); *Dictionary of National Biography,* compact ed., vol. 2, 2068.

238 Now in the Rouen Musée des Beaux-Arts.

SIX
Honorable Gentlemen and Weaker Vessels

1 Allan Nevins, ed., *Diary of John Quincy Adams 1794–1845* (New York, 1951), 179.

2 Kathryn Cave, ed., *The Diary of Joseph Farington,* 16 vols. (New Haven, Conn., 1978–84), vol. 6, 2359 (hereafter called *Farington's Diary*); Christopher Hibbert, *George IV: Regent and King* (London, 1973), 147ff.

3 *Journal of Mrs Arbuthnot,* 24 February 1821, 75.

4 Ibid., 24 March 1821, 154.

5 Nevins, entry for 14 May 1817, 182.

6 *Farington's Diary,* vol. 8, 3147.

7 Ibid., vol. 2, 621.

8 A. Wagner and A. Dale, *The Wagners of Brighton* (Chichester, 1983), 36–37.

9 Jane Austen, *Pride and Prejudice* (London, 1813–14), chap. 16.

10 *Farington's Diary*, vol. 16, 5516.

11 Jennings, *The Croker Papers*, vol. 1 205.

12 *Farington's Diary*, January 18, 1794, vol. 2, 293.

13 Henry, Lord Holland, *Memoirs of the Whig Party during My Time*, 3 vols. (London, 1852–54), vol. 3, 143–44.

14 *Journal of Mrs Arbuthnot*, 81.

15 *Farington's Diary*, 24 June 1796, vol. 2, 589.

16 Ibid., vol. 1, 71.

17 *Journal of Mrs Arbuthnot*, 7 February 1822, 142.

18 Ibid., 11 January 1826, 306. Manners-Sutton was the Speaker; for his wife, see L. Strachey and R. Fulford, eds., *The Greville Memoirs*, 8 vols. (London, 1938), vol. 2, 178.

19 Quoted in Hibbert, 103.

20 H. C. R. Landon, ed., *Collected Correspondence and London Notebooks of Joseph Haydn* (London, 1959), 122–24; Bernard Pool, ed., *The Croker Papers* (London, 1967), diary entry for 12 January 1822, 69; Haydon, *Diary*, entry for 29 January 1826, 79.

21 *Journal of Mrs Arbuthnot*, 29 October 1823, 271.

22 Hibbert, 107.

23 Christopher Hibbert, *George IV* (Harmondsworth, 1973), 345.

24 P. Fitzgerald, *Life of George IV*, 2 vols. (London, 1881), vol. 2, 289.

25 Hibbert, 117–19.

26 *Farington's Diary*, vol. 4, 1330; vol. 10 3669.

27 For leading architects c1815, see John Summerson, *Georgian London* new ed. (London, 1988), 190ff.

28 *Journal of Mrs Arbuthnot*, 334.

29 For Scharf's work, see Peter Jackson, ed., *George Scharf's London: Sketches and Watercolours of a Changing City 1820–50* (London, 1987).

30 John Harris, *The Public Buildings of Westminster Described* (London, 1831).

31 Altick, *The Shows of London*, 227.

32 See Henry Mayhew, *The Shops and Companies of London* (London, 1865), esp. "Elegant Male Assistants."

33 Jane Austen, *Persuasion* (London, 1817), chap. 5.

34 Humphrey Ward, *History of the Athenaeum* (London, 1926); Summerson, 241.

35 Clive Wainwright, "Walter Scott and the Furnishing of Abbotsford," *Connoisseur*, January 1977.

36 Charlotte Gere, *Nineteenth-Century Decoration: The Art of the Interior* (London, 1989), 47, 106.

37 Ibid., 98–99.

38 Ibid., 106.

39 See L. E. A. Eitner, *Géricault: His Life and Work* (London, 1983), where this point is argued.

40 Aileen Ribeiro, *Dress and Morality* (London, 1986), 120–21.

41 Ibid., 122; the Place ref. is BM Addit. Mss., 27827, 50–52, 27828, 118.

42 J. P. Malcolm, *Anecdotes of the Manners and Customs of London* (London, 1818), 449; Ribeiro, 120.

43 Jane Austen, *Persuasion*, chap. 4.

44 Lady Bourchier, *Memoire . . . of Sir Edward Codrington*, 2 vols. (London, 1873), vol. 1, 343.

45 *Farington's Diary*, vol. 9, 3300–01; vol. 10, 3713.

46 Ibid., vol. 1, 13 July 1793.

47 Thomas de Quincey, *Recollections of the Lakes and the Lake Poets*, first published in *Tait's Edinburgh Magazine*, November 1838–August 1840. My quotation is taken from the Penguin edition, 135.

48 John Niven, *Martin Van Buren*, 207.

49 *Farington's Diary*, vol. 2, 404.

50 Ibid., vol. 14, 4853.

51 Harriet Martineau, *Autobiography*, 3 vols. (London, 1877), vol. 1, 310–12.

52 W. Jesse, *The Life of George Brummel Esq* (London, 1844).

53 Kenneth Clark, *The Romantic Rebellion* (London, 1973).

54 James Boswell, *Life of Johnson*, 2 vols. (Everyman ed.), vol. 1, 430–31, 463, and fn.; vol. 2, 463–64. See also

Boswell, *Tour of the Hebrides*, entry for 19 September 1773.

55 *Gentleman's Magazine*, 1789, vol. 2, 463, 565.

56 For a general historical survey during these years, see V. G. Kiernan, *The Duel in European History* (Oxford, 1988), esp. 187ff.

57 Gronow, *Reminiscences* vol. 1, 104–15.

58 Remini, *Jackson*, vol. 1, 120–23, 184–85.

59 Mrs. F. E. Ellet, *The Court Circle of the Republic* (Hartford, 1869), 104.

60 J. E. D. Shipp, *Giant Days, or the Life and Times of William H. Crawford* (New York, 1909).

61 John J. Crittenden to Clay, 15 February 1825, Crittenden Papers, quoted in Marquis James, *Portrait of a President* (New York, 1937), 120.

62 Remini, vol. 2, 320.

63 *Farington's Diary*, vol. 8, 2981.

64 E. J. Morley, ed., *Henry Crabb Robinson in Germany, 1800–15* (London, 1929), 104–38.

65 J. C. Herold, *Mistress to the Age: The Life of Madame de Staël* (London, 1958), 428.

66 M. F. Zirin, trans and ed., *The Cavalry Maiden: Journals of a Russian Officer in the Napoleonic Wars, by Nadezhda Durova* (Bloomington, Ind., 1988), 197.

67 David Margashak, *Pushkin: A Biography* (London, 1967), 298–301; Sidney Monas, *The Third Section: Police and Society Under Nicholas I* (Harvard, 1961), 197–228.

68 *Byron's Letters and Journals*, vol. 5, 143, 19 December 1816.

69 R. Baldick, *The Duel* (London, 1965), 144.

70 It is put forcibly by Kiernan, chap. 9, "The Psychology of Honour," 152–64.

71 *Memorials of His Time* (Edinburgh, 1856).

72 *Farington's Diary*, vol. 6, 2262.

73 *Parliamentary History: House of Commons 1790–1820*, vol. 4, 562ff.

74 Kiernan, 209.

75 Oliver MacDonagh, *Daniel O'Con-*

nell: *The Hereditary Bondsman, 1775–1829* (London, 1988), 135–36.

76 Stendhal, *On Love* (Harmondsworth, 1974), 149–50.

77 Norman Gash, *Mr. Secretary Peel* (London, 1985), 164–67; MacDonagh, 138–42.

78 W. F. Moneypenny and G. E. Buckle, *Life of Benjamin Disraeli*, 6 vols. (London, 1910–20), vol. 1, 287–95; R. E. Foster, "Peel, Disraeli and the 1835 Taunton By-election," *Somerset Archaeology and Natural History* (Taunton), 1982.

79 William Makepeace Thackeray, *Collected Works*, vol. 4, 317ff; Gordon N. Ray, *Thackeray: The Uses of Adversity, 1811–46* (Oxford, 1955), 85.

80 Lord Morley, *Life of Gladstone*, 3 vols. (London, 1902), vol. 1, 27; Lord Malmesbury, *Memoirs of an Ex-Minister* (London, 1885), vol. 1, 21.

81 *Croker's Correspondence and Diaries*, vol. 2, 407–08.

82 *Journal of Thomas Moore*, vol. 1, 312–13, mid-April 1820.

83 Ibid., vol. 1, 93–94, 29 November 1818.

84 Ibid., vol. 2, 545; Leslie Marchand, *Life of Byron*, vol. 3, 967–68.

85 *Byron's Letters and Journals*, vol. 11, 145, 30 March 1824.

86 Haydon, *Diary*, 24 May 1826.

87 M. Alic, *Hypatia's Heritage* (London, 1986), 104–05.

88 Kiernan, 203.

89 *Farington's Diary*, vol. 6, 2219–20; vol. 7, 2722; vol. 10, 3645.

90 Ibid., vol. 15, 5210.

91 Ibid., vol. 6, 2414.

92 Sir William Blackstone, *Commentaries on the Laws of England, Continued to the Present Time by John Williams*, 4 vols., 11th ed. (London, 1791), vol. 1, 430.

93 R. H. Graveson, *Status in Common Law* (London, 1953), 135.

94 E. Stanton, S. Anthony and M. Gage, *History of Women's Suffrage*, 6 vols. (Rochester, N.Y.: 1881–1922), vol. 3, 289.

95 Patricia Licie, "Marriage and Law Reform in 19th Century America," in

E. M. Craik, ed., *Marriage and Property* (Aberdeen, 1984), 141–45.

96 Jennifer Birkett, "A Mere Matter of Business: Marriage, Divorce and the French Revolution," in Craik, 119–37; J. F. Traer, *Marriage and the Family in 18th Century France* (Ithaca, N.Y., 1980), 131.

97 M. Poster, *The Utopian Thought of Restif de la Bretonne* (New York, 1971). The quotations are from *Les Françaises,* 4 vols. (Neufchatel, 1786), vol. 3, 63. 69.

98 *Moore's Journal,* 31 January 1819.

99 This point is argued forcefully in Gert Schiff and Werner Hofmann, *Fuseli* (London, 1975), 13–19. *The Henpecked Husband* is now in the Kunsthaus, Zurich; *Symplegma* is in the Victoria and Albert Museum, London.

100 *Mill's Collected Works, Vol. xxii: Newspaper Writings 1822–31,* 43ff.

101 For Thompson, see Philip Mallett, "Women and Marriage in Victorian Society," in Craik, 159–89.

102 Domenique Desanti, *A Woman in Revolt: A Biography of Flora Tristan* (trans., New York, 1976).

103 Pamela Pilbeam, "The Economic Crisis of 1827–32 and the 1930 Revolution in France," *Historical Journal,* 32, no. 2 (1989).

104 Claire G. Moses, "Saint-Simeon Men, Saint-Simeon Women: The Transformation of Feminist Thought in 1830 France," *Journal of Modern History,* June 1980, 240–67.

105 For Comte's letters to Mill, see P. E. de Berredo and P. Arnaud, eds., *Comte: Correspondance Generale* (Paris, 1973), vol. 2, 288ff.; see also, Wolf Lepenies, *Between Literature and Science: The Rise of Sociology* (Cambridge, England, 1988).

106 Madame Vigée Le Brun, *Memoirs* (trans., London, 1904), 49; Joseph Ballio, *Elizabeth-Louise Vigée Le Brun* (Fort Worth, 1982).

107 *History of Parliament: House of Commons, 1780–1820,* vol. 2, 458.

108 *Moore's Journal,* vol. 2, 423.

109 W. D. Jones, *Prosperity Robinson* (London 1967), 125ff; Violet Dickinson, ed., *Miss Eden's Letters* (London, 1919), 124; Charles Greville, *Diary,* 23 February 1830.

110 See the diary of Lady Salisbury, 17–20 November 1833, in Oman, 95; and Elizabeth Longford, *Wellington: Pillar of State* (London, 1972), 302.

111 Bournem 224ff.

112 André Maurois, *Victor Hugo* (trans., London, 1956), 16–17, 30–42.

113 *Farington's Diary,* vol. 1, 52.

114 J. S. Allen, *Popular French Romanticism* (Syracuse, N.Y., 1981), 153.

115 Quoted in Bovill, *English Country Life, 1780–1830,* 16.

116 *Emma,* vol. 1, chap. 4.

117 *Farington's Diary,* vol. 5, 1633.

118 Ibid., vol. 5, 1871.

119 E. V. Lucas, *Life of Charles Lamb,* 2 vols. (London, 1905), vol. 2, 13; William Hazlitt, *Dramatic Essays* (London, 1895), 69.

120 See Brian Fothergill, *Mrs. Jordan: Portrait of an Actress* (London, 1965), for details.

121 Osborne, *Rossini,* 68, fn. 1.

122 For Mrs. Serres's misfortunes, see *Farington's Diary,* vol. 6, 2355–56.

123 Joan Chissell, *Clara Schumann: A Dedicated Spirit* (London, 1983), 4–9.

124 For short biographies of all these women writers, see *Companion to Charles Lamb.*

125 Claire to Mrs. Jefferson Hogg, 1 February 1833, printed in Lady Jane Shelley, ed., *Jane and Mary* (London, 1882), vol. 4, 1175.

126 E. L. Griggs, ed., *Collected Letters of S. T. Coleridge,* 6 vols. (Oxford, 1956–71), vol. 2, 375.

127 B. K. Mudge, *Sara Coleridge: A Victorian Daughter, Her Life and Letters* (New Haven, Conn., 1989), 267ff.

128 The autobiographical fragments are printed as Appendix 3, in Phillip Kelley and Ronald Hudson, eds., *The*

Browning Correspondence, 2 vols. (Winfield, 1984), vol. 1, 1809–26, 347–62.

129 Frederick Locker-Lampson, quoted in J. A. Gere and John Sparrow, eds., *The Notebooks of Geoffrey Madan* (Oxford, 1981), 11

130 Kelley and Hudson, vol. 2, 1–5. 6–20, 47ff.

131 Michael Hurst, *Maria Edgeworth and the Public Scene* (London, 1969), 23–34; Mrs. R. L. Edgeworth, *A Memorial of Maria Edgeworth,* 4 vols. (London, 1867), vol. 3, 19–22.

132 Quoted in Campbell, *Lady Morgan,* 188.

133 Ibid., 212–13.

134 *Farington's Diary,* vol 6, 2378.

135 Revel Guest and Angela V. John, *Lady Charlotte* (London, 1989), 31.

136 Ibid., 166ff, 178–83.

137 Salvador de Madariaga, *Simon Bolivar* (trans. London, 1952), 629.

138 *Farington's Diary,* vol. 3, 1048.

139 The documents are reproduced as Appendix A in Zirin, 227ff.

140 Donna Dickenson, *George Sand* (Oxford, 1988), 129.

141 Curtis Cate, *George Sand* (London, 1975), 56–68, 73.

142 Ibid., 87ff.

143 George Sand, *Histoire de ma vie,* 4 vols. (Paris, 1854–55), vol. 1, 203.

144 They are given in Dickenson, 82.

145 Thomas Carlyle, *Latter-Day Pamphlets,* collected ed. (London, 1972), 68–70.

146 George Sand, *Journal Intime,* 25 June 1837.

147 Cate, 222–23; Dickinson, 94–95.

148 Cate, 92–93.

149 Cecil Woodham-Smith, "They Stayed in Bed," *The Listener,* 16 February 1956.

150 Lant Carpenter, *Principles of Education* (London, 1820), 41–42.

151 Harriet Martineau, *Autobiography,* 2 vols. (London, 1877), vol. 2, 166.

152 R. K. Webb, *Harriet Martineau: A Radical Victorian* (London, 1960), 102ff.

153 Martineau, *Autobiography,* vol. 1, 152; the articles on female writers of divinity and on women's education appeared in the Unitarian *Monthly Repository,* October 1822, February 1823.

154 Quoted in Guest and John, 30.

155 For a different view of Jane Austen's social doctrine, see Butler, 105–07.

156 R. C. Newman, *A Hampshire Parish* (Petersfield, 1976), 97–98. See also, J. R. Gillis, *For Better or Worse: British Marriages 1600 to the Present* (Oxford, 1985), 110ff.

157 H. and P. Coombs, eds., *Diary of a Somerset Rector, 1803–34* (Bath, 1971), 63–64.

158 *House of Commons 1790–1820,* vol. 1, 280; *Farington's Diary,* vol. 8, 3015; vol. 9, 3903; vol. 12, 4431.

159 *Farington's Diary,* vol. 14, 4997.

160 See Ziegler, *William IV,* Appendix B, 296.

161 *Farington's Diary,* vol. 5, 2053; vol. 15, 5329.

162 Alan Bell, *Sidney Smith: A Biography* (Oxford, 1980), 141.

163 Roger Price, *A Social History of 19th Century France* (London, 1987), 73–81.

164 *Farington's Diary,* vol. 10, 3735.

165 Gillis, 219.

166 Beaty, *Early Australia,* 181; *Farington's Diary,* vol. 2, 647; vol. 14, 4913.

167 *Farington's Diary,* vol. 4, 1341.

168 Ibid., vol. 5, 1691.

169 Maurois, 130.

170 Osborne, 15.

171 Chissell, 16ff.

172 R. B. Beckett, ed., *John Constable's Correspondence,* 6 vols. (Suffolk Records Society, 1962–68), vol. 2, 18 February 1816; J. L. Fraser, *John Constable, 1776–1835* (London, 1976), 80–97.

173 For the background to this marriage, see Oliver McDonagh, *The Hereditary Bondsman: Daniel O'Connell, 1775–1829* (London, 1989), chap. I.

174 *Farington's Diary*, vol. 15, 5134; vol. 4, 1269.
175 *Journal of Mrs Arbuthnot*, vol. 1, 137; ibid., vol. 4, 1268; vol. 6, 2140; vol. 15, 5201; vol. 16, 5578.
176 *Letters of Spencer Madan*, vol. 11; Kingsford, vol. 9, 161ff.
177 *Farington's Diary*, vol. 13, 4739; vol. 15, 5173, 5409ff; vol. 16, 5455.
178 Francis Greenacre, *Francis Danby* (London, 1988), 11, 30.
179 A. J. Finberg, *Life of J. M. W. Turner RA*, 2nd ed. (Oxford, 1961), 155, 415.
180 Kenneth Garlick, *Sir Thomas Lawrence* (London, 1954), 9, 18–19.
181 *Byron's Letters and Diaries*, vol. 6, 91–92.
182 Quoted in G. M. Young, *Early Victorian England*, 2 vols. (Oxford, 1934), vol. 1, 417.
183 F. L. Jones, ed., *Letters of Percy Bysshe Shelley*, 2 vols. (Oxford, 1964), vol. 1, 389–91, 391–92, 394, 396; letters of 14 July, 27 August, and 15 and 16 September 1814.
184 Blainey, 100ff.
185 For Fanny Imlay, see Richard Holmes, *Shelley: The Pursuit* (London, 1974), 347ff; for the baby Elena, about whose parentage there is continuing dispute, see Doris Langley Moore, *Lord Byron: Accounts Rendered* (London, 1974), 302; *Byron's Letters and Journals*, vol. 5, 160–62, vol. 7, 174, 191; Ursula Orange, in "Elise, Nursemaid to the Shelleys,' *Keats-Shelley Memorial Bulletin*, 1955, argues that Claire Clairmont was not the mother of Elena.
186 Haydon's marginal notes are in the Roe-Byron Collection at Newstead Abbey; quoted in Moore, *Accounts Rendered*, 301–02; Blainey, 97–99.
187 *Byron's Letters and Journals*, vol. 6, 65.
188 See the chapter on Ingres, in Clarke.
189 Italo Faldi, *La Galleria Borghese: Catalogo delle scultore dal xvi al xix seculo* (Rome, 1954), 45; see Fred

Licht, *Canova* (New York, 1983), Introduction; Augustus Hare, *The Years With Mother* (London, 1952), 184.
190 J. D'Emilio and E. B. Freedman, *Intimate Matters: A History of Sexuality in America* (New York, 1988), 59ff, 65–66, 76.
191 *Farington's Diary*, vol. 4, 1173; vol. 8, 3089.
192 Martineau, *Autobiography*, vol. 1, 310–12.
193 *Creevey Papers*, vol. 2, 89; Robert Stewart, *Henry Brougham: His Public Career, 1778–1860)* (London, 1985), 133–35; New, *Brougham to 1830*, 176; *Sydney Smith Letters*, vol. 1, 309.
194 *Farington's Diary*, vol. 11, 3967, 3973.
195 Ibid., vol. 3, 854–55; vol. 10, 3555.
196 *Mansfield Park* (London, 1812), vol. 3, chap. 17.
197 *Byron Letters and Journals*, vol. 6, 231.
198 Bourne, 186, 224.
199 Ibid., 151.
200 *Farington's Diary*, vol. 3, 793.
201 Ibid., vol. 11, 4230.
202 Quoted in New, 50.
203 *Farington's Diary*, vol. 11, 3956.
204 Ibid., vol. 8, 2873; Gash, *Mr Secretary Peel*, 268.
205 Blainey, 124ff.
206 Berta Lawrence, *Coleridge and Wordsworth in Somerset* (Newton Abbot, England, 1970), 58ff, 73–74.
207 For the separation of the Coleridges, see Molly Lefebure, *The Bondage of Love: A Life of Mrs. Samuel Taylor Coleridge* (London, 1986), 170–205.
208 *Journal of Thomas Moore*, vol. 1, 303, 25 January 1820.
209 Ibid., vol. 2, 558, 29 May 1822, and entry for 16 October 1827.
210 Marcia Poynton, *Mulready* (London, 1986), 64–65.
211 *Farington's Diary*, vol. 2, 441–42, vol. 3, 704–06.

212 Southey, *Poetical Works,* vol. 10, 206.

213 For details of Godwin's household, see William St. Clair, *The Godwins and the Shelleys* (London, 1989), esp. chap. 18, 238ff.

214 Details in Ballio. For her sitters, see Elizabeth-Louise Vigée Le Brun, *Souvenir de Madame Vigée Le Brun,* 3 vols. (Paris, 1835–37).

215 See *Life, Letters and Literary Remains of Edward Bulwer, Lord Lytton, by His Son* (London, 1883); *Life of Edward Bulwer, First Lord Lytton, by His Grandson* (London, 1913); Earl of Lytton, *Bulwer Lytton* (London, 1948).

216 *Journal of Mrs Arbuthnot,* vol. 1, 167–69.

217 *Farington's Diary,* vol. 11, 3950, vol. 12, 4171, 4479.

218 Ibid., vol. 9, 3470; *Journal of Mrs Arbuthnot,* vol. 1, 16, 8 May 1820.

219 Gillis, 209ff.

220 *Notes & Queries,* Third Series, vol. 4, 5 December 1863; S. P. Menefee, *Wives for Sale: An Ethnographic Study of British Popular Divorce* (New York, 1981); Gillis, 211–18.

221 George Spater, *William Cobbett: The Poor Man's Friend,* 2 vols. (Cambridge, England, 1982), vol. 2, chap. 24, describes the family quarrels.

222 For Black, see *Dictionary of National Biography,* compact ed., vol. 1, 163; *Works of John Stuart Mill,* vol. 22, Introduction.

223 *Collected Works of Hazlitt,* vol. 1, 46; vol. 8, 236.

224 Haydon *Diaries,* vol. 2, 470.

225 *Coleridge Letters,* vol. 4, 692–93, 669–70, 735. Hazlitt's biographers tend to gloss over this incident or deny it; see, for example, Stanley Jones, *Hazlitt: A Life* (Oxford, 1989), 10, where the girl is described, on no evidence at all, as "a local hoyden" and Hazlitt is called "a trusting victim."

226 R. W. Wardle: *Hazlitt* (Lincoln, Nebr., 1971), 249ff.

227 B. W. Proctor, *An Autobiographical Fragment,* ed., Coventry Patmore (London, 1877), 181–82.

228 Quoted in Wardle, 305., 337, 358–61.

229 *First Report of the Royal Commission on Divorce* (London, 1853), 21. For the legal differences between English and Scottish marriage and divorce law, which were complex, see O. R. McGreggor, *Divorce in England* (London, 1957) 11–15.

230 Wardle, 304.

231 Quoted in Malcolm Elwin, *Landor: A Replevin* (London, 1958), 223.

232 Her detailed account of the divorce is in W. H. Bonner, ed., *Journals of Sarah and William Hazlitt, 1822–31* (Buffalo, N.Y., University of Buffalo Studies, 1959), vol. 24.

233 Wardle, 344–45.

234 Jones, 337ff.

235 Quoted in Cecil Woodham-Smith, *The Reason Why* (London, 1953), 12–14.

236 *Farington's Diary,* vol. 4, 1324; vol. 8, 3078; vol. 2, 559.

237 *Proceedings and Correspondence Upon the Subject of the Inquiry into the Conduct of the Princess of Wales* (London, 1807); *Brougham Memoirs,* vol. 2, 425; *Letters of George IV,* vol. 2, 282, 359.

238 The best account of the legal-political strategy, as seen by the Liverpool government, is in Cookson, *Lord Liverpool's Administration,* 200–14, 228–300; Brougham's strategy is summarized in New, 79–100, 101–18, 228–62.

239 Stanhope, *Conversations with Wellington.*

240 *Brougham Memoirs,* vol. 2, 253ff.

241 Hibbert, *George IV: Regent and King,* 134–35.

242 *Farington's Diary,* vol. 15, 5178; *Leveson Gower Correspondence,* vol. 2, 534–35.

243 *Letters of George IV*, vol. 2, 280ff.

244 *The Croker Papers*, vol. 1, 159.

245 *Journal of Mrs Arbuthnot*, vol. 1, 17.

246 New, 231. The original draft of the minute was even stronger.

247 James Boswell, *Life of Dr. Samuel Johnson*, vol. 1, 347–48.

248 Lady Melbourne to Fred Lamb, 12 February 1820, quoted Bourne, 186; Hibbert, *George IV*, 484; Jane Austen to Martha Lloyd, 16 February 1813, in R. W. Chapman, ed., *Selected Jane Austen Letters 1796–1817* (Oxford, 1956), 137; *Browning Correspondence*, vol. 1, 353.

249 Quoted in Thea Holme, *Cobbett* (London, 1979); *Collected Works of Hazlitt*, vol. 20, 136; *Greville Diary*.

250 Cookson, 215–16.

251 *Journal of Mrs Arbuthnot*, vol. 1, 23–26.

252 For the lawyers involved and procedures, see New, 248.

253 Dorothy George, *Catalogue of Personal and Political Satires . . . in the British Museum* (London, 1952), vol. 10. For an interesting account of the propaganda in-fighting, see T. W. Lacquer, "The Queen Caroline Affair: Politics as Art in the Reign of George IV," *Journal of Modern History*, September 1982, 417–66.

254 *Creevey Papers*, 332.

255 *Journal of Mrs Arbuthnot*, vol. 1, 39, 81. She reported Wellington's conversation with Lady Conyngham on 28 February 1821, but it had taken place in September 1820.

256 For the trial, see J. Nightingale, ed., *Memoir of the Public and Private Life of . . . Caroline, Queen of Great Britain* (London, 1920); Horace Twiss, *Life of Lord Chancellor Eldon*, 3 vols. (London, 1844), vol. 2, 386; Mark Stovey, ed., *Letters of John Clare* (Oxford, 1985).

257 Altick, *Shows of London*, 409; *Journal of Mrs Arbuthnot*, vol. 1, 33; N. C. Nowell, ed., *Selected Letters of Sydney Smith* (London, 1956), 144.

258 *Journal of Mrs Arbuthnot*, vol. 1, 44.

259 Ibid.

260 *Farington's Diary*, vol. 16, 5596.

261 A. Aspinal, ed., *Correspondence of Charles Arbuthnot* (Camden Society, London, 1941), 30; *Journal of Mrs Arbuthnot*, vol. 1, 64, 69–70.

262 Davy quoted in Anne Treneer, *The Mercurial Chemist: A Life of Sir Humphry Davy* (London, 1963), 119–20.

263 L. G. Wilson, *Charles Lyell: The Years to 1841* (New Haven, Conn., 1972), 124–25.

264 Martha Somerville, *Personal Recollections from Early Life to Old Age of Mary Somerville* (London, 1873), 2–6, 17, 37ff, 54.

265 Ibid., 129, 161ff.

SEVEN
Forces, Machines, Visions

1 The sermon is reprinted in J. A. Paris, *Life of Sir Humphry Davy*, 2 vols. (London, 1931).

2 For the early history of mine safety, see *Report of the Select Committee on Safety in Mines* (Parliamentary Papers, London, 4 September 1835).

3 Moody's testimony on 23 December 1816, is reprinted in L. T. C. Rolt, *George and Robert Stephenson* (Harmondsworth, 1978), 27.

4 Anne Treneer: *The Mercurial Chemist: A Life of Sir Humphry Davy* (London, 1963), 171–74.

5 The published version, "On the Safety Lamp; with Some Researches on the Frame," is in John Davy, ed., *Collected Works of Sir Humphry Davy*, 9 vols. (London, 1939), vi.

6 For the arguments about priority and documents, see Rolt, 30–33; and Trenner, 174.

7 Watt's early death inspired Davy's belief in personal immortality, set out in

his essay "The Proteus" in *Consolations of Travel* (London, 1829). For Davy's poems, see Robert Southey, ed., *Annual Anthology*, vol. 1 (Bristol, 1799).

8 Letter to Mrs. Davy, 11 October 1798; Treneer, 31.

9 Wedgwood's essay is "An Account of a Method of Copying Paintings upon Glass and of Making Profiles by the Agency of Light upon the Nitrate of Silver," *Journal of the Royal Institution*, vol. 1; for Davy and nitrous oxide, see F. F. Cartwright, *The English Pioneers of Anaesthesia* (London, 1952); Treneer, 42–45. For "progress," see David Spadafora, *The Idea of Progress in 18th Century Britain* (New Haven, Conn., 1990).

10 Humphry Davy, *Researches, Chemical and Philosophical* (Bristol, 1800).

11 R. B. Jones, *The Royal Institution: Its Founder and Its First Professors* (London, 1871).

12 Quoted in Treneer, 95.

13 Richard Holmes, *Shelley: The Pursuit* (London, 1976), 24, 44–45.

14 Quoted in Carl Grabo, *The Magic Plant: The Growth of Shelley's Thought* (Chapel Hill, N.C., 1936), 59.

15 Ibid., 122–27.

16 Holmes, 344.

17 It is published in T. Martin, ed., *Faraday's Diary*, 7 vols. (London, 1932–36).

18 Treneer, 146–47.

19 Leslie A. Marchand, ed., *Byron's Letters and Journals*, 11 vols. (London, 1937–82), vol. 7, 98.

20 Treneer, 197–98; L. Pearce Williams, *Michael Faraday* (London, 1965), 40.

21 Letter to Dr. Becker, 20 October 1860, quoted in Williams, 27.

22 J. Shawcross, ed., *Coleridge: Biographia Literaria*, 2 vols. (Oxford, 1958), vol. 1, 88.

23 T. E. Sgedd, ed., *Coleridge: Works*, 7 vols. (London, 1884), vol. 1, 150, *Biographia Literaria*, vol. 2, 49; E. H. Coleridge, ed., *Letters of Samuel Taylor Coleridge*, 2 vols. London, 1894), vol. 1, 283.

24 Quoted in Treneer, 39.

25 "Historical Statement Respecting Electro-Magnetic Rotation," *Quarterly Journal of Science*, 15 (1823).

26 *Quarterly Journal of Science*, 25 (1828), quoted Williams, 177.

27 Humphry Davy, *Elements of Chemical Philosophy* (1812), in Davy, *Collected Works*, vol. 4; Williams, 68–71.

28 Ernest de Selincourt, *Dorothy Wordsworth: A Biography* (Oxford, 1933), 75.

29 W. H. Henry, *Memoirs of John Dalton* (London, 1854), 9–11, 49–50, 217.

30 Ibid., 220, 218.

31 Anthony Hyman, *Charles Babbage, Pioneer of the Computer* (Oxford, 1982), 178–80; ibid., 185–89; H. D. Rawnsley, *Literary Associations of the English Lakes*, 2 vols., 2nd ed. (Glasgow, 1901), vol. 1, 210ff.

32 Rawnsley, vol. 1, 126ff; Charles Leitch, *Jonathan Otley* (London, 1880); most of Otley's papers are in the *Kirkby Lonsdale Magazine* and the *Transactions of the Cumberland Association*.

33 Quoted in L. G. Wilson, *Charles Lyell: The Years to 1841: The Revolution in Geology* (New Haven, Conn., 1972), 56.

34 James Hutton, *A Theory of the Earth* (London, 1785 and subsequent eds.), 304.

35 Quoted in Wilson, 86.

36 Charles Lyell, "On Scientific Institutions," *Quarterly Review*, June 1826; "Transactions of the Geological Society," *Quarterly*, September 1826.

37 Wilson, 180.

38 Analysis of the work is in ibid., 278–80.

39 Ibid., 277.

40 Ibid., 446–47, 456–59, 506.

41 Charles Lyell, *Letters and Journals*, 2 vols. (London, 1881), vol. 1, January 13, 1831; Nora Barlow, ed., *Autobiography of Charles Darwin 1809–82* (London, 1908), 112.

42 Charles Babbage, *Passages in the Life of a Philosopher* (London, 1864), 425–27.

43 Quoted in Maboth Moseley, *Irascible Genius: A Life of Charles Babbage, Inventor* (London, 1964), 49.

44 Hyman, 48; for early calculators, see Brian Randell, *The Origins of Digital Computers* (Springfield 1973).

45 Moseley, 67, 70–72.

46 Ibid., 98–101, 17.

47 Ibid., 19–20. See Charles Babbage, "On a Method of Expressing by Signs the Acts of Machinery," *Royal Society Paper*, 16 March 1826.

48 *Childe Harold*, Canto iii.

49 Quoted in Mosley, 157.

50 Hyman, 124–25 and 170 (fn.); 76–77.

51 *Enclyclopaedia Metropolitana* (London, 1829).

52 Charles Babbage, *Economy of Machinery and Manufactures* (London, 1832), 250–51, 229.

53 See Anthony Hyman, ed., *Science and Reform: Selected Works of Charles Babbage* (Cambridge, 1989).

54 Hyman, *Babbage*, 149 (fn.).

55 See his *Hints to Mechanics* (London, 1839).

56 New, *Brougham*, 332–39; Thomas Kelly, *George Birkbeck* (London, 1957).

57 Roudo Cameron, "The Industrial Revolution, a Misnomer," in Jurgen Schneider, *Wirtschaftskräfte und Wirtschaftswege*, 5 vols. (Stuttgart, 1981), vol. 5, 367–76, plays down the part played by Britain in the Industrial Revolution and emphasizes the Continental contribution.

58 Samuel Smiles, *Lives of the Engineers* 3 vols. (London, 1861–62), vol. 1, xvi, 9.

59 Samuel Smiles, ed., *Naysmith's Autobiography* (London, 1883), 94–97.

60 Samuel Smiles, *Industrial Biography: Iron-Workers and Tool-Makers* (London, 1863), 183ff, 200, 236–37, 259, 262–63, 266–67.

61 Samuel Smiles, *Men of Invention and Industry* (London, 1884), 157–59, 226.

62 Frederick Koenig, Letter to *The Times*, 8 December 1814.

63 Smiles, *Naysmith Autobiography*, 217–28, 220–23.

64 Rolt, 114.

65 Smiles, *Naysmith Autobiography*, 222ff.

66 William Fairbairn, *Useful Information for Engineers*, 2nd series (London, 1860), 211.

67 Smiles, *Industrial Biography*, 313.

68 See K. W. Luckhurst, *The Story of Exhibitions* (London, 1951).

69 Jacob Bigelow, *Elements of Technology . . . on the Application of the Sciences to the Useful Arts* (Boston, 1829).

70 Altick, *Shows of London*, 359.

71 S. Bradbury, *The Microscope, Past and Present* (Oxford, 1968).

72 See K. R. Gilbert, *Brunel's Block-Making Machinery at Portsmouth* (London, 1978).

73 Paul Clements, *Mark Isambard Brunel* (London, 1970), 29.

74 Ibid., 34–36.

75 Derry and Williams, *Short History of Technology*, 288–89.

76 Alfred Pugsley, ed., *The Works of Isambard Kingdom Brunel: An Engineering Appreciation* (London, 1976).

77 Brunel's splendid letter of thanks to Wellington (10 August 1821) is published in Clements, 73.

78 For Brunel's tunneling system, see Clements, 87, 96–100, 116–17.

79 Ibid., 107.

80 Rolt, 63.

81 Ibid., 50–53.

82 Ibid., 68.

83 Ibid., 135ff, 188ff.

84 Smiles, *Naysmith's Autobiography*, vii, 125, 439.

85 Smiles, *Industrial Biography*, 240–41.

86 Clements, 118.

87 Dickinson, *Fulton*, 73ff.

88 Sir Gordon Gordon-Taylor, *Sir Charles Bell: His Life and His Times* (Edinburgh, 1958), 7–9, 20–22.

89 J. W. Mollet, *Sir David Wilkie* (London, 1881), 8.

90 Duncan Macmillan, *Painting in Scotland: The Golden Age* (Oxford, 1986), 156ff.

91 Jacques Barzun, *Berlioz and the Romantic Century*, 2 vols, 3rd ed. (New York, 1969), vol. 2, 101, fn. 45.

92 A. M. Hind, *A History of Engraving and Etching*, new ed. (London, 1923); J. Buckland-Wright, *Etching and Engraving* (London, 1953).

93 S. T. Prideaux, *Aquatint Engraving* (London, 1909).

94 Philippe Grunchec, *Géricault's Horses* (Lausanne and London, 1982–85), 62, 70, 94ff.; Lorenz Eitner, ed., *Delacroix* (London, 1964), 67–70; Roger Passeron, *Daumier* (Fribourg, 1979–81), 35ff; Loys Delteil, *Honoré Daumier: Le Peintre-graveur illustré*, 11 vols. (Paris 1926–30), reproduces 4,000 of his lithographs; see also, T. E. Griffiths, *Rudiments of Lithography* (London, 1956).

95 See the entry for Boys in *Ottley's Biographical and Critical Dictionary of Recent and Living Painters and Engravers* (London, 1866).

96 James Roundell, *Thomas Shotter Boys 1803–74* (London, 1974), 29–30.

97 Jan Reynolds, *William Callow RWS* (London, 1980), 8–10.

98 See Martin Butlin, "Blake, the Varleys and the Patent Graphic Telescope," in M. D. Paley and M. Phillips, eds., *William Blake: Essays in Honour of Sir Geoffrey Keynes* (London, 1973); there is a photo of the telescope in Leslie Parris, *Landscape in Britain, c1750–1850* (London, 1973), 125, fig. 305.

99 Marcia Poynton, *Bonington, Francis and Wyld* (London, 1985), 46ff.

100 C. M. Kauffmann, *John Varley 1778–1842* (London, 1984), 12.

101 Ian Gow, "The First Intellectual House-Painter," *World of Interiors*, May 1984.

102 Kathryn Cave, ed., *The Diary of Joseph Farington*, 16 vols. (New Haven, Conn., 1978–84), vol. 2, 308 (hereafter called *Farington's Diary*).

103 A. M. W. Stirling, *The Richmond Papers* (London, 1926), 9.

104 Ibid., 25–26.

105 Martin Butlin, *Paintings and Drawings of William Blake*, 2 vols. (New Haven, Conn., 1981), vol. 1, 409ff; vol. 2, 319–20. He had earlier (1805) done a set of 21 Job watercolors. The Linnell set is catalogued in vol. 1, 551, and plates in vol. 2, 733–53.

106 G. E. Bentley, ed., *Blake Records* (Oxford, 1969), 249–50.

107 *Richmond Papers*, 24–25.

108 Mona Wilson, *Life of William Blake* (Oxford, 1971), 327.

109 *Richmond Papers*, 25.

110 Derek Hudson, ed., *The Diary of Henry Crabb Robinson: An Abridgement* (Oxford, 1967), 87 (entry for 17 December 1825).

111 Ibid., 83–87.

112 The visionary heads are in Butlin, *Paintings and Drawings of Blake*, vol. 1, text, 495–531, and vol. 2, plates 909–59ff.

113 This and the Wallace anecdote are in Bentley, 496–99.

114 W. H. Pyne's (anonymous) "Observations on the Rise and Progress of Painting in Watercolours," was published in *Ackermann's Repository of the Arts* (London, 1812–13). Pyne supplied more information in a further essay published in the *Somerset House Gazette* for 1823–24.

115 Ibid.

116 Kauffmann, 33–39.

117 J. F. C. Harrison, *The Second Coming: Popular Millenarianism, 1750–1850* (London, 1979).

118 J. K. Lavater, *Essays in Physiognomy Designed to Promote the Knowledge and Love of Mankind*, 5 vols. (London, 1789–98); Drs. Gall and Sputzheim, *The Physiognomical System* (London, 1815).

119 John Varley, *Treatise on Zodaical Physiognomy, Part One* (London,

1828). The second part never appeared.

120 Kauffmann, 42ff.

121 R. Lister, ed., *Letters of Samuel Palmer* (Oxford, 1974).

122 *Richmond Papers*, 20ff.

123 Ibid., 30.

124 *Farington's Diary*, vol. 12, 4157.

125 Haydon, *Diary*, vol. 3, 73–74.

126 See Peter Cannon-Brookes, *Paintings from Tabley* (London, 1989).

127 Thomas Landseer, ed., *Life and Letters of William Bewick* (London, 1871), 170.

128 A. J. Finberg, *Life of J. M. W. Turner RA* (Oxford, 1961), 325.

129 *Farington's Diary*, vol. 10, 3142.

130 Haydon, *Diary*, 166–68.

131 Margaret Greaves, *Regency Patron: Sir George Beaumont* (London, 1966), 75–78. See also, Felicity Owen and D. B. Brown, *Collector of Genius: The Life of Sir George Beaumont* (New Haven, Conn., 1988).

132 For Constable's visit, see R. B. Bennett, ed., *John Constable's Correspondence*, 6 vols. (Suffolk Records Society, 1962–68), vol. 2, 27 October 1823; Greaves, 56ff; J. L. Fraser, *John Constable, 1776–1837: The Man and His Mistress* (London, 1976), 133–34.

133 See Jones, *Hazlitt*, 254ff.

134 For Hazlitt's art criticism, see John Barrell, *The Political Theory of Painting from Reynolds to Hazlitt* (New Haven, Conn., 1986), 314ff.

135 Letter to George Jones, quoted in Finberg, 320.

136 Beaumont to Wordsworth, 27 December 1821, Dove Cottage Trust; Beaumont to George Agar Ellis, 27 January 1824, quoted in *The Builder*, 4 May 1867. The events leading to the establishment of the National Gallery are recounted in *"Noble and Patriotic": The Beaumont Gift 1828* (National Gallery, London, 1988).

137 Felicity Owen, "Sir George Beaumont and the National Gallery," in ibid., 10–16.

138 Gash, *Mr. Secretary Peel*, 272–79.

139 *Leighton House* (Department of the Environment, London, 1980); *Franz von Lenbach 1836–1904* (Stadtische Galerie im Lenbachhaus, Munich, 1987); Clive Aslet, *The American Country House* (London, 1990), 35–47.

140 *Farington's Diary*, vol. 2, 353, 11, 432; vol. 8, 3016; and S. Baring Gould, *Cornish Characters* (London, 1890), 288.

141 Walter Armstrong, *Memoir of Peter de Wint* (London, 1888); see also, David Scrase, *Drawings and Watercolours of P. de Wint* (Cambridge, 1979).

142 C. R. Leslie, *Autobiographical Recollections*, 2 vols. (London, 1860), vol. 1, 202.

143 Fraser, 160, 173.

144 William Feaver, *John Martin* (London, 1975).

145 For the history of this painting, see A. Cunningham, *Life of Sir D. Wilkie*, 3 vols. (London, 1843), vol. 2, 72; Haydon, *Autobiography* (London, 1853), vol. 1, 351–52.

146 Haydon   *Tabletalk*   (undated), quoted in Altick, 404.

147 For the background, see L. Eitner, *Géricault's Raft of the Meduse* (London, 1972).

148 L. Johnson, "The Raft of the Medusa in Great Britain," *Burlington Magazine*, 96 (August 1954); S. Lodge, "Géricault in England", *Burlington Magazine*, 108 (December 1965).

149 See H. Von Erffa and Allen Staley, *The Paintings of Benjamin West* (New Haven, Conn., 1986), 161; figures in Altick.

150 Altick, 409 (fn.).

151 Quoted in Feaver, 10.

152 For the Martin revival, see the catalog of the 1975 loan exhibition, *John Martin 1789–1854,* (London,

153 *Transactions of the Royal Society,* vol. 36 (1796), 227–77; New, *Brougham,* 14–16.

154 Letters to Archdeacon Fisher, 29 September 1823, quoted in Altick, 166.

155 Quoted in Clay, *Romanticism,* 19; see H. and A. Gernsheim, *L. J. M. Daguerre: The History of the Diorama and the Daguerrotype* (London, 1956).

156 See her *France in 1829–30,* 2 vols. (London, 1830), esp. vol 1.

157 There is a portrait of Bonington by Colin in the Ashmolean and two drawings, one asleep, one sketching from a boat, by the same artist, in the Musée Carnavalet, Paris.

158 For the relationship between the various painters of the circle, see Pointon, 25ff, 33ff; and Carlos Peacock, *Richard Parkes Bonington* (London, 1979), 24ff.

159 Pointon, 43.

160 Ibid., 46.

161 For details, see Reynolds, 6–18.

162 Quoted in Roundell, 21.

163 Quoted in Eitner, *Delacroix,* 15.

164 A. Curtis, *L'Oeuvre gravé et lithographique de R. P. Bonington* (Paris, 1939).

165 Poynton, 60; *The Undercliff,* with inscription, is in Peacock, color plate xx.

166 C. R. Leslie, *Life of Constable* (London, 1845), 239.

167 Bennett, vol. 6, 23 October 1821.

168 J. T. Smith: *Remarks on Rural Scenery* (London, 1797).

169 Fraser, *Constable,* 22.

170 Quoted in Leslie, *Constable,* 74.

171 Quoted in Hugh Honor, *Romanticism* (London, 1979), 86–94; see Karl Kropber, "Constable and Wordsworth: The Ecological Moment in Romantic Art," *Journal of the Courtauld & Warburg Institutes,* vol. 34 (1971), and his study *Romantic Landscape Visions: Constable and Wordsworth* (Madison, Wisc., 1975).

172 Kenneth Clark, *The Romantic Rebellion* (London, 1973), 263ff.

173 Bennett, vol. 4, 293, 142.

174 Letter to Fisher, 23 October 1821, ibid., vol. 6.

175 Note found by C. R. Leslie attached to Lecture IV of *John Constable's Discourses;* for the weather studies, see Kurt Badt, *John Constable's Clouds* (London, 1950).

176 Undated; Bennett, vol. 6, 63.

177 W. P. Frith, *My Autobiography,* 2 vols. (London, 1887), vol. 1, 237–38.

178 Bennett, vol. 4, entry for 19 June 1824; vol. 6, entry for 17 December 1824.

179 See the argument in Clark, 265–83.

180 Quoted in Lorenz Eitner, *Géricault: His Life and Work* (London, 1983), 214.

181 Quoted in Eitner, *Delacroix,* 5.

182 Eitner, *Géricault,* 235; see also Philippe Grunchec: *Géricault's Horses: Drawings and Watercolours* (London, 1985).

183 *Stallion Led by Two Arabs to Cover a Mare,* Musée Bonat, Bayonne; *Scene of Covering,* private collection, Paris, respectively plates 89, 91 in Grunchec, *Géricault's Horses.*

184 F. H. Lem, "Le Thême du negre dans l'oeuvre de Géricault," *L'Arte,* vol. 27, 1962.

185 Eitner, *Géricault,* 215ff.

186 Now in the possession of the École des Beaux Arts, Paris. Géricault was also planning a painting of the Inquisition.

187 Eitner, *Delacroix,* 6.

188 See Clark's treatment of the picture in *The Romantic Rebellion.*

189 Finberg, *Turner,* 318.

190 For galleries, see John Gage: *Colour in Turner* (London, 1969), chap. 9, 148–64; J. Bolton' ed., *Sir John Soane, Lectures on Architecture* (London, 1829), 126; D. Stroud, *The*

Architecture of Sir John Soane (London, 1961), fig. 37. For Turner's foreign trips, see A. Wilton, *Turner Abroad* (London, 1982).

191 Finberg, 232–34, 443.

192 Ibid., 195.

193 Walter Thornbury, *Life of J. M. W. Turner RA*, 2 vols. (London, 1862), vol. 2, 45.

194 A. T. Story, *James Holmes and John Varley* (London, 1894), 121; John Burnett; *Turner and His Works* (London, 1852), 70; Gage, 19.

195 Lindsay Stainton, *Turner's Venice* (London, 1985), 13–14.

196 Quotations from Gage, 35.

197 Quotations from Finberg, 198–202. For the spyhole, see Gage, 166.

198 Quoted Finberg, 169.

199 Much of this appears in *Turner Studies* (London, Tate Gallery, 1982 ff).

200 Gage, 56–57.

201 Finberg, 289.

202 Ibid., 197, 208–09.

203 Bennett, letter to C. R. Leslie, 14 January 1832.

204 Stainton, *Turner's Venice*, 16; this volume reproduced one of the Como sketches and all four of the Venetian, plates 1–5.

205 Johann von Goethe, *Theory of Colours* (trans., London, 1840), xxxviii–xxxix.

206 Quoted in Andrew Wilton, *Turner and the Sublime* (London, 1980), 104.

207 Gage, 145–47.

208 Wordsworth to Sir John Stoddart, 1831, quoted in Treneer, *Davy*, 214.

EIGHT

Masques of Anarchy

1 For a chronological list of the first Alpine ascents, see Francis Keenlyside, *Peaks and Pioneers* (London, 1975), Appendix 1, 232–33.

2 A description of the crossing is in Daniel F. O'Leary, *Memoirs* (London, n.d.).

3 Salvador de Madariaga, *Bolivar* (trans., London, 1952), 359–61.

4 Alexander von Humboldt, *Travels in America* (trans., London, 1880).

5 *Morning Post*, 15 October 1804.

6 For the ground plans and growth of Mexico City, see Leonardo Benevolo, *The Architecture of the Renaissance*, 2 vols. (trans., London, 1973), vol. 1, 450ff; vol. 2, 999ff.

7 For the empire in its last phase, see S. de Madariaga: *The Fall of the Spanish American Empire* (trans., London, 1947), chapter 1.

8 M. P. Costelloe, *Church Wealth of Mexico* (Cambridge, England, 1967).

9 Jan Bazanet, *Concise History of Mexico, 1805–1944* (Cambridge, England, 1977), 6–7.

10 Ibid., 19.

11 For texts, see Madariaga, *Bolivar*, 156.

12 Byron to Hobhouse, 3 October 1819, in Leslie A. Marchand, ed., *Byron's Letters and Journals*, 11 vols. (London, 1937–82), vol. 6, 226.

13 For Miranda, see Enrique Piniero, ed., *Jose Francisco Heredia: Memorias sobre la Revoluciones de Venezuela* (Paris, 1895).

14 Madariaga, *Bolivar*, 76–77.

15 Ibid., 189–99.

16 José Domingo Diaz, quoted in ibid., 210–11.

17 Ibid., 209, 224–26.

18 Quoted in ibid., 277.

19 General Morillo to Ferdinand VII, 31 May 1816, quoted in ibid., 291.

20 Figures in M. P. Costeloe, *Response to Revolution: Imperial Spain and the Spanish-American Revolution 1810–40* (Cambridge, England, 1986), 101–02.

21 Quotations in ibid., 21–26.

22 *Historia de la revolucion Hispano-America*, 3 vols. (Madrid, 1829–30).

23 Quoted in Costeloe, 22.

24 J. Fontana, ed., *Le Economias espanola al final del Antiguo Regimen*, vol. III *Comercio y Colonias* (Madrid, 1982).

25 M. J. Quin, ed., *Memoirs of Ferdinand VII* (trans., London, 1824), 229–30.

26 T. E. Anna, "Institutional and Political Impediments to Spain's Settlement of the American Revolution," *The Americas*, 38 (April 1982).

27 Costeloe, 9.

28 Ibid., 14, fn. 21; for various charges against Ferdinand, see C. Le Brun, *Vida de Fernando Septimo, Rey de Espana* (Philadelphia, 1826), 68–70.

29 R. H. Bartley, *Imperial Russia and the Struggle for Latin American Independence 1808–1828* (Austin, 1978), 121ff. The secret treaties between Ferdinand and the Tsar of August 1817 and 27 September 1819, were published by the *Morning Chronicle*, December 1823.

30 See the detailed account in Thomas Cochrane, Earl of Dundonald, *Autobiography of a Seaman*, 2 vols. (London, 1860).

31 G. Hippersley, *A Narrative of the Expedition [which] Joined the Patriotic Forces in Venezuela, etc.* (London, 1819).

32 It is described in George Chesterton, *Peace, War and Adventure*, 2 vols. (London, 1853).

33 Madariaga, *Bolivar, 555*, fn.

34 Printed in *Recollections of the War of Extermination . . . in the Republics of Venezuela and Colombia* (London, 1828); see ibid., xii.

35 Ibid., 382–83.

36 Bolivar to William White, 26 May 1820; Bolivar to Francisco Santander, 7 April 1820.

37 Quoted in Madariaga, *Bolivar, 576*.

38 The episode is described in ibid., 352–53.

39 John Quincy Adams, *Memoirs*, vol. 5, 126.

40 Allan Nevins, ed., *Diary of John Quincy Adams 1794–1845* (New York, 1951), 311.

41 For the background to the Monroe Doctrine, see Cresson, *Monroe*.

42 J. F. Rippy, *British Investments in Latin America 1822–1949* (Minneapolis, 1959), 23ff.

43 Eric Lambert, "Los Legionarios Britanicos," in J. Alberich et al., eds., *Bello y Londres* (Caracas, 1980), vol. 1, 355–76.

44 For Poinsett's account of the first two coups, see his *Notes on Mexico* (London, 1823). For Iturbide, see W. S. Robertson, *Iturbide of Mexico* (Chapel Hill, N.C., 1952).

45 M. P. Costeloe, *La Primera republica federal de Mexico, 1824–35* (Mexico City, 1975).

46 For these ceremonies, see Madariaga, *Bolivar*, 434–35, 510–11ff.

47 Ibid., 70, 440, 541ff, 551.

48 Daniel F. O'Leary: *Memoirs* (London, n.d.).

49 Quoted in Madariaga, *Bolivar*, 585.

50 Ibid., 523.

51 Ibid., 647.

52 *Foreign and Quarterly Review*, 3 (July 1843).

53 Quoted in George Pendle, *Paraguay*, 3rd ed., (Oxford, 1967), 31.

54 Gilbert Phelps, *The Tragedy of Paraguay* (London, 1975), 19ff.

55 See Horton Box, *The Origins of the Paraguayan War*, 2 vols. (University of Illinois, 1927).

56 Ibid.

57 Richard Burton, *Letters from the Battlefields of Paraguay* (London, 1870).

58 J. P. and W. P. Robertson, *Letters from Paraguay*, 3 vols., 2nd ed. (London, 1839), vol. 1, 330–36.

59 Burton, *Letters*.

60 Gilberto Freyre, *The Masters and the Slaves: A Study of the Development of Brazilian Civilisation*, 2nd ed. (trans. New York, 1956), 256–57.

61 E. B. Burns, *A History of Brazil* (New York, 1970), 101–02.

62 Ibid., 109.

63 John Luccock, *Notes on Rio . . . and*

the Southern Part of Brazil (London, 1820), 41.

64 Quoted in Joao Paudia Calogeres, A History of Brazil (trans., Chapel Hill, N.C., 1939).

65 J. H. Rodrigues, Brazil and Africa (Berkeley, Calif., 1965), 66.

66 Charles Webster, Britain and the Independence of Latin America 1812–30 (Oxford, 1938), vol. 1, 171.

67 Rodrigues, 53.

68 Quoted in ibid., 64–65.

69 Freyre, 73; Sergio Correa da Costa, Every Inch a King: A Biography of Dom Pedro I, First Emperor of Brazil (New York, 1953).

70 Rodrigues, 71.

71 Raymond Carr, Spain 1808–1939 (Oxford, 1966).

72 Chateaubriand, Le Congres de Verone, 2 vols. (Paris, 1832), vol. 1, 173; Maurice de Palaeologue, The Romantic Diplomatist (trans., London, 1939).

73 For British information on French intentions and reactions, see the dispatches from Paris of Sir Charles Stuart to Canning, 10 February, 5 May, 12 June and 7 July 1823; W. F. Reddaway, "Anglo-French Colonial Rivalry, 1815–48," in Cambridge History of the British Empire, 241ff; Adams, Memoirs, vol. 4, 26 November 1823.

74 Carr, 143 and fn. 1.

75 Ibid., 149, fn. 2.

76 James Boswell, Life of Dr. Johnson (Everyman Edition), vol. 2, 170.

77 Kathryn Cave, ed., The Diary of Joseph Farington, 16 vols. (New Haven, Conn., 1978–84), vol. 2, 443 (hereafter called Farington's Diary).

78 Norman Douglas, Old Calabria (London, 1956) 222ff. Manhes denied the Benincasa story when it was published in Paris in 1835.

79 Harold Acton, The Bourbons of Naples (London, 1956), 565.

80 Quoted in Stuart Woolf, A History of Italy, 1700–1860 (London, 1979), 239.

81 Quoted in Denis Mack-Smith, The Making of Italy, 1796–1870 (London, 1968), 31; ibid., 250–51.

82 Letter to Augusta Leigh, 8 September 1816; to John Murray, 15 October 1816; texts in Marchand, vol. 5.

83 Letter to Thomas Moore, 17 November 1816; Douglas Kinnaird, 27 November; Augusta Leigh, 18 December; John Murray, 2 January 1817.

84 Letter to Wedderburn Webster, 8 September 1818, Marchand, vol. 6.

85 Marchand, vol. 5, 255; to Moore, 28 January 1817; Marchand, vol. 6, 54–55; to J. C. Hobhouse, 25 June 1818.

86 Marchand, vol. 5, 213; vol. 6, 68; letter to Hobhouse, 1 February 1819.

87 Ibid., vol. 6, 143.

88 Letter to Hobhouse, 6 April 1819; to J. Hoppner, 2 June 1819.

89 Moore's Journal, vol. 1, 224.

90 Letters of Shelley, vol. 2, 936.

91 Ibid., to Mary Shelley, 7 August 1821; to Thomas Love Peacock, 10 August 1821; vol. 2, 889ff.

92 Marchand, vol. 7, 170–71; letter to Thomas Moore, 31 August 1820.

93 Moore's Journal, vol. 1, 234–35.

94 For Shelley's boat and his drowning, see F. L. Jones, ed., Maria Gisborne and Edward E. Williams: Their Journals and Letters (London, 1946), 149; Richard Holmes, Shelley: The Pursuit (London, 1974), 729; Edward Dowden: Life of P. B. Shelley, 2 vols. (London, 1886), vol. 2, 534ff.

95 For Byron and the philhellenes, see Douglas Dakin, The Struggle for Greek Independence, 1821–33 (London, 1973), 107ff; Terence Spencer, Fair Greece, Sad Relic (London, 1954).

96 For the roots of French policy, see L. Pingaud, Choiseul-Gouffier: La France en Orient sous Louis XVI (Paris, 1887), 95ff.

97 Quoted in Niyazi Berkes, The Development of Secularism in Turkey (Montreal, 1964), 66.

98 Ibid., 90–91.

99 For the origins of British Near East policy, see Harold Temperley, En-

gland and the Near East (London, 1936), 16–20.

100 J. A. Petropoulos, *Politics and State-craft in the Kingdom of Greece, 1833–43* (Princeton, N.J., 1968), 24ff.

101 For names of Italian bandits, see Woolf, 250ff; for a general discussion of Greek bandits, see J. S. Koliopoulos, *Brigands with a Cause: Brigandage and Irridentism in Modern Greece* (Oxford, 1987)

102 For a contemporary account of the pastoral system, see W. M. Leake, *Travels in Northern Greece*, 4 vols. (London, 1835), esp. vol 4.

103 "Brigandage in Greece," *Saturday Review*, 6 May 1871; George Finlay, *History of the Greek Revolution*, 3 vols. (Edinburgh, 1861).

104 Koliopoulos, 241–42.

105 Ibid., 255, 266–67.

106 Julius Millingen, *Memoirs of the Affairs of Greece* (London, 1831), 37.

107 Leicester Stanhope, *Greece in 1823 and 1824*, 2nd ed. (London, 1825), 103ff; L. E. Richards, ed., *Letters and Journals of Samuel Gridley Howe*, 2 vols. (Boston, 1906), vol. 1, 75–77.

108 Koliopoulos, 44–49.

109 For Stanhope, see *Dictionary of National Biography*, compact ed., vol. 2 (1981).

110 Dakin, *Struggle for Greek Independence*, 116.

111 Finlay, *History of the Greek Revolution*.

112 For Muhammad Ali's rise to power, see H. H. Dodwell, *The Founder of Modern Egypt: A Study of Mohammed Ali* (Cambridge, 1931), chaps. 1 and 2.

113 For the military reorganization, see P. M. Holt, "Egypt and the Nile Valley," in J. E. Flint, ed., *Cambridge History of Africa, volume 5, c1790–1870* (Cambridge, 1976), 13–50.

114 E. W. Lane, *An Account of the Manners and Customs of the Modern Egyptians, Written in Egypt During the Years 1833–5*, new ed. (London, 1890; original published 1836).

115 Ibid., 115–17.

116 Ibid., 108, 110–11.

117 Ibid., 103–06.

118 Ibid., 99.

120 Dodwell, 45ff.

121 Quoted in Berkes, 100–01. For education in Ali's Egypt, see J. Heyworth-Dunne, *Introduction to the History of Education in Modern Egypt* (London, 1939), 113 fn.

122 For the destruction of the janissaries, see A. P. Caussin, ed. and trans., *Mehmed Esad: Precis historique de la destruction du corps des Jannisaires par le Sultan Mahmoud en 1826* (Paris, 1833), presented in English in Temperley, 16–20.

123 James E. DeKay, *Sketches of Turkey in 1831 and 1832* (New York, 1833), 226; Berkes, 124–25.

124 Quoted in Dakin, *Struggle for Greek Independence*, 174.

125 Ibid., 168ff and 172, fn.

126 It is reprinted, with all the admiral's letters, in Lady Bourchier, *Life of Admiral Sir Edward Codrington*, 2 vols. (London, 1873), vol. 1, 585ff.

127 For this point, see *Dictionary of National Biography*, compact ed., vol. 1, 400.

128 Letter to Lady Codrington, 7 August 1827, Bourchier, vol. 1, 401.

129 See, for example, Codrington's letters of 5 July and 8 August 1827 in Bourchier, vol. 1, 377–78, 406.

130 Letters of 7, 9, and 25 August in ibid., vol. 1, 401ff, 408ff, 428.

131 Ibid., vol. 1, 395ff.

132 Orders printed in Bourchier, vol. 2, 69.

133 Printed in ibid., vol. 2, 86ff.

134 Dakin, 227–28; Bourchier, vol. 2, 81ff.

135 Clarence to 4th Earl of Mayo, 12 November 1827, Royal Archives, Add. 4, quoted in Zeigler, *William IV*, 137; *Continuation of Jane's Naval History* (London, 1860), vol. 6, 372.

136 For the orders, see Jones, *Prosperity Robinson*, 179, which also has a full

discussion of how the government reacted to the news of the battle.

137 Palmerston to William Lamb, 15 November 1827, printed in L. C. Sanders, ed., *Lord Melbourne's Papers* (London, 1889), 108.

138 Letter printed in Bourchier, vol. 2,

175. It was printed by the government after Huskisson's death.

139 Bourchier, vol. 2, 441.

140 *Ibid.*, vol. 2, 500–10, 496–97.

141 This important point, with which I agree, is conclusively argued in Koliopoulos, 73, 325.

NINE

Fresh Air and Drowsy Syrups

1 Thomas de Quincey, *Recollections of the Lakes and the Lake Poets* (first published in book form 1854; my text from the Penguin ed., Harmondsworth, 1970), 56.

2 Kathryn Cave, ed., *The Diary of Joseph Farington,* 16 vols. (New Haven, Conn., 1978–84), vol. 3, 674 (hereafter called *Farington's Diary*).

3 Ibid., vol. 1, 151.

4 *Dictionary of National Biography,* compact ed., vol. 1, 25.

5 H. D. Miles, *Pugilistica, The History of British Boxing* (Edinburgh, 1906), 438.

6 *Farington's Diary,* vol. 2, 421.

7 J. W. Lockart, *Life of Sir Walter Scott,* 7 vols. (Edinburgh, 1837), vol. 3, 395–99.

8 For examples, see Robert W. Malcolmson, *Popular Recreations in English Society, 1700–1850* (Cambridge, England, 1973), 34ff.

9 Joseph Strutt, *Glig-Gamena Angel-Deod, or the Sports and Pastimes of the People of England* (London, 1801), 79.

10 William Hutton, *History of Derby* (London, 1791), 218.

11 Quoted in Percy M. Young, *A History of British Football* (London, 1968), 61.

12 Ibid., 61, 65, 67.

13 A. M. Weyland, *American Football: Its History and Development* (New York, 1926).

14 A. H. Fabian and G. Green, eds., *Association Football,* 4 vols. (London, 1960); see also, G. Green, *History of Association Football* (London, 1960).

15 H. S. Altham, *History of Cricket,* 2

vols., new ed. (London, 1962), vol. 1, 54–55.

16 See E. D. Cumming, ed., *Squire Osbaldeston* (London, 1926).

17 *Gentleman's Magazine,* (1849), 206; *Dictionary of National Biography,* compact ed., vol. 2, 2198.

18 Altham, 58ff and chap. 7 66ff; G. M. Young, *Early Victorian England,* vol. 1, 268–69.

19 Miles, 381–82.

20 Ibid., 412, 109, 181, 263–73, 288, 360, 327.

21 Quoted in ibid., 98.

22 Michael Stenton, ed., *Who's Who of British Members of Parliament* (London, 1976), vol. 1, 1832–85, 172; *Dictionary of National Biography,* compact ed., vol. 1, 856.

23 See *Select Committee on Gaming* (Westminster, 1844), vol. 6, 1031.

24 Wray Vamplew, *The Turf: A Social and Economic History of Racing* (London, 1976), 27.

25 See the figures in H. Rous, *On the Laws and Practice of Horse-Racing* (London, 1850), x.

26 Quoted in J. C. Whyte, *History of the British Turf* (London, 1840), xviii.

27 E. E. Dorling, *Epsom and the Dorlings* (London, 1939), 54ff.

28 For the rise of the Jockey Club, see Vamplew, chap. 6, 77ff.

29 R. Black, *The Jockey Club and Its Founders* (London, 1891), 257; see also, Roger Mortimer, *The Jockey Club* (London, 1958).

30 Quoted in Garry Adler, *Beyond Bokhara: The Life of William Moorcroft* (London, 1985), 13.

31 Ibid., 49–50.

32 H. H. Wilson, ed., *Moorcroft and Trebeck's Travels* (London, 1841), for details.

33 Adler, 295–96.

34 See J. Pemble, *The Invasion of Nepal: John Company at War, 1814–16* (Oxford, 1971).

35 See G. Adler, "Britain and the Defence of India: The Origins of the Problem, 1798–1815," *Journal of Asian History*, 6 (1972).

36 *Report to the Authorities in Calcutta, Christmas 1822*, quoted in Alder, *Moorcroft*, 267.

37 Quoted in ibid., 295.

38 G. Adler, "Standing Alone: William Moorcroft Plays the Great Game, 1808–25," *International History Review*, 2 (1980); G. Morgan, *Anglo-Russian Rivalry in Central Asia 1810–1895* (London, 1981).

39 Adler, *Moorcroft*, 147.

40 F. E. Manuel, *The New World of Henri de Saint-Simon* (Cambridge, Mass., 1956), 328; *Companion to Charles Lamb*, 89–90, 176–78, 218–21; *Letters of Charles and Mary Lamb*, vol. 2, 292; *Byron's Letters and Journals*, vol. 5, 103–04, 127, 144, 217; vol. 6, 108, 235, and fn.; Bovill, *English Country Life 1780–1830*, 164, fn. 1; *Literary Associations of the English Lakes*, vol. 1, 47; *J-L Agasse, Sporting Paintings*, passim.

41 Smiles, *Men of Invention and Industry*, 235–36, 245.

42 Letter of 14 November 1813, quoted in Altick, *Shows of London*, 309.

43 Byron to Hobhouse, *Byron's Letters and Journals*, vol. 6, 108.

44 Altick, 312–13; Dickens's article was cut when *Sketches by Boz* appeared.

45 J. F. Winks, *The Bull Running at Stamford* (London, n.d.); text of a Baptist sermon delivered 15 November 1829, quoted in Malcolmson.

46 *Parliamentary History*, 35 (18 April 1800), 207, quoted in Malcolmson, 153; *Edinburgh Review*, January 1809.

47 For this institution, see Fiona St. Aubyn, ed., *Ackermann's Illustrated London* reissue (London, 1985), 178–79.

48 R. W. Jeffrey, ed., *Dyott's Diary 1781–1845*, 2 vols. (London, 1907).

49 Malcolmson, 127ff; see also Appendix, "The Reform Movement Against Cruelty to Animals," 172–73.

50 Muriel Jaeger, *Before Victoria: Changing Standards of Behaviour, 1787–1837* (London, 1967).

51 Paul Clements, *Mark Isambard Brunel* (London, 1970), 42–43.

52 *Farington's Diary*, vol. 8, 3275; vol. 9, 3424; vol. 12, 4216.

53 Michael Hurst, *Maria Edgeworth and the Public Scene* (London, 1969), 11–12.

54 *Dictionary of National Biography*, compact ed., vol. 1, 856.

55 See R. Guest and A. V. John, *Lady Charlotte*, 33.

56 See table in Young, *Early Victorian England* vol. 1, 433.

57 Quoted in Fred Kaplan, *Dickens: A Biography* (London, 1988), 45.

58 Larkin, *Reshaping of Everyday Life*, 69, 75.

59 *Coleridge Letters*, vol. 4, 922.

60 Edwin Hodder, *Life of the Earl of Shaftesbury*, 3 vols. (London, 1886), vol. 1, 262.

61 Autobiographical fragment written by Sara Coleridge for her daughter Edith, dated 8 September 1851, printed in B. K. Mudge, *Sara Coleridge: A Victorian Daughter. Her Life and Essays* (New Haven, Conn., 1989), Appendix, 249–66.

62 Blainey, 130–31.

63 Ibid., 160–61.

64 Treneer, 57.

65 At Goodwood House, Sussex.

66 Beatrice Madan, ed., *Spencer and Waterloo: The Letters of Spencer Madan, 1814–15* (London, 1970), 12–13.

67 Ibid., 19, 25–26.

68 Hon. Mrs. Swinton, *Life of Georgiana, Lady de Ros* (London, 1893).

69 *Madan*, 166–67.

70 *Farington's Diary,* vol. 13, 4447; vol. 8, 2885.

71 George Sand, *My Life* (trans, London, 1979), 6ff.

72 E. T. Cook, *Life of Ruskin,* 2 vols. (London, 1911), vol. 1, 7–8, 13.

73 Ibid., 25, fn. 1.

74 J. J. Coss, ed., *Autobiography of John Stuart Mill* (New York, 1944), 3–22.

75 Ruskin, who also lived there as a child, described it in his *Praeterita* (first pub. 1886–89, Oxford ed., 1949), 25ff.

76 See Browning's poem "Development" in his last collection, *Asolando* (London, 1889).

77 Quoted in Edmund Gosse, *Father and Son* (London, 1907), 20.

78 G. K. Chesterton, *Robert Browning* (London, 1903), 48.

79 Donald Thomas, *Robert Browning: A Life Within Life* (London, 1982), 11–17.

80 See David Magarshak, *Pushkin, a Biography* (London, 1967), 13, 19.

81 Quoted in T. Wemyss Reid, *Life of the Rt. Hon. W. E. Forster* (Bath, reprint 1970), 38.

82 Ibid., 37, 45.

83 David Duncan, *Life and Letters of Herbert Spencer* (London, 1908), 9–13.

84 Robert Bernard Martin, *Tennyson: The Unquiet Heart* (Oxford, 1980), 18.

85 From "Our School" in *The Uncommercial Traveller;* see Fred Kaplan, *Dickens, a Biography* (London, 1988), 45ff.

86 *Thackeray Works,* 17 vols. (Oxford, 1908), vol. 17, 495.

87 Ibid., vol. 2, 706, "Slaughter House"; vol. 11, 52; G. N. Ray; *Thackeray: The Uses of Adversity, 1811–46* (Oxford, 1955), 86 and 452 n. 39.

88 F. Lawley in the *Daily Telegraph,* 20 May 1898; John Morley, *Life of Gladstone,* 3 vols. (London, 1903), vol. 1, 32ff.

89 Morley, vol. 1, 34; Canning had known Gladstone's father when he was a member of Parliament for Liverpool.

90 Carl Sandburg, *Abraham Lincoln: The Prairie Years* (New York, 1926), vol. 1, 19ff, 28, 48.

91 Benjamin F. Bart, *Flaubert* (Syracuse, N.Y., 1967), 6–19.

92 Claude Pichois, *Baudelaire* (trans., London, 1989), 49–50.

93 John Chancellor, *Wagner* (London, 1978), 5.

94 Ernest Newman, *Life of Richard Wagner,* 3 vols. (London, 1933), vol. 1, 17–24, 37, 52–53, 57.

95 Statement by Verdi in 1853, quoted in Frank Walker, *The Man Verdi* (London, 1962), 7.

96 Quoted in Josiah Thompson, *Kierkegaard* (London, 1974), 34.

97 Ibid., 13–15.

98 Ibid., 7.

99 Jane Austen, *Emma* (1816), vol. 1, chap. 3.

100 Winifred Gérin, *Elizabeth Gaskell* (Oxford, 1976), 24–30.

101 *Farington's Diary,* vol. 11, 3864; vol. 9, 3342; vol. 6, 2124; vol. 10, 3502; vol. 6, 2696; vol. 14, 4914.

102 See the *Halifax Guardian,* June–August 1857; C. K. Shorter, *The Brontes: Life and Letters,* 2 vols. (London, 1908) vol. 2, Appendix 8; Winifred Gérin: *Charlotte Bronte: The Evolution of Genius* (Oxford, 1967), 1–15.

103 Joseph Lancaster, *Improvements in Education* (London, 1803); and *The British System of Education* (London, 1809).

104 Chester New, *Brougham to 1830* (Oxford, 1960), 210ff.

105 Carnall, *Southey,* 135; Sydney Smith, *Edinburgh Review,* November 1810.

106 See Brougham's articles in the *Edinburgh Review,* April 1810 and November 1811, and Southey's in the *Quarterly Review,* October 1811.

107 For Lancaster see *Dictionary of National Biography,* compact ed., vol. 1, 1162.

108 De Quincey: *Recollections of the Lakes and the Lake Poets;* the section on Bell was added in 1854; for Bell,

see *Dictionary of National Biography,* compact ed., vol. 1, 128. For the controversy, see David Salmon, ed., *The Practical Parts of Lancaster's "Improvements" and Bell's "Experiment"* (Cambridge, 1932).

109 *Farington's Diary,* vol. 3, 776, 697, 771.

110 Holmes, *Shelley: The Pursuit,* 36, 48.

111 *Dictionary of National Biography,* compact ed., vol. 1, 152–53; *Farington's Diary,* vol. 8, 4257.

112 Alan Walker, *Franz Liszt: The Virtuoso Years 1811–47* (London, 1983), 57.

113 Ibid., 76–78.

114 British Library, Ad. Mss., 33965, fol. 237–42, printed in Walker, 105.

115 Wilhelm von Lenz, quoted in Walker, 135–36.

116 Eric Werner, *Mendelssohn: A New Image of the Composer and His Age* (trans, London, 1963), 32ff.

117 Werner, 21.

118 Quoted in ibid., 24–25.

119 Remini, *Jackson* (1981), 4ff.

120 *Farington's Diary,* vol. 11, 4089; vol. 13, 4526.

121 Larkin, *Reshaping of Everyday Life,* 80.

122 Campbell, *Lady Morgan,* 46; *Farington's Diary,* vol. 14, 5050–51, 5053, 5058, 5116–17, 5127, 5347ff.

123 Weber's letters are printed in the biography by his son: Max Marie von Weber, *Karl Maria von Weber,* 2 vols. (trans., London, 1865), vol. 2, 427ff.

124 Ibid., vol. 2, 441.

125 Ibid., vol. 2, 455–56, 460.

126 For Jenner's generosity, see *Farington's Diary,* vol. 3, 659ff; vol. 8, 2820. He never charged artist, poets, or writers for treating them.

127 Philip Curtin, *The Image of Africa: British Ideas and Action, 1780–1850* (Madison, Wic.: 1964) 82, 192–93; see also Curtin's "The White Man's Grave": Image and Reality, 1780–1850," *Journal of British Studies,* 1961.

128 See J. H. Dible, *Napoleon's Surgeon* (London, 1970), esp. 119ff, 244ff; see also R. G. Richardson: "Larrey—What Manner of Man?" in *Journal of the Royal Society of Medicine,* July 1977.

129 See Logan Clendening, ed., *Source Book of Medical History* (New York, 1960), 355ff.

130 Gordon Gordon-Taylor, *Sir Charles Bell: His Life and Times* (Edinburgh, 1958), 29–30.

131 Bransby Blake Cooper, *Life of Sir Astley Cooper, Bart.* 2 vols. (London, 1843); J. B. Bailey, ed., *Diary of a Resurrectionist* (London, 1896).

132 See Gordon-Taylor, 181–82.

133 See Anon., *Trial of William Burke* (Edinburgh, 1829); *Dictionary of National Biography,* compact ed., vol. 1, 261.

134 *Wooler's British Gazette,* 13 October 1822.

135 George Clark, *History of the Royal College of Physicians of London* (Oxford, 1966), vol. 2, 1675–1858, 652ff.

136 Dr. W. C. Wells, *Two Essays* (London, 1818), 361–62.

137 Clark, 666–67.

138 John Flint South, *South's Memorials* (Sussex repro. 1970), 32, 56.

139 *Farington's Diary,* vol. 10, 3673; vol. 7, 2777.

140 Ibid., vol. 16, 5581, 5883; vol. 14, 4902; *Dictionary of National Biography,* compact ed., vol. 1, 433.

141 See E. J. Trelawny, *Records of Shelley, Byron and the Author* (first pub. 1858; Penguin ed., 1973), 203–04.

142 Henri Troyat, *Alexander of Russia* (trans., London, 1984), 293ff.

143 *Farington's Diary,* vol. 8, 3107.

144 *Journal of Mrs Arbuthnot,* vol. 1, 192.

145 *Farington's Diary,* vol. 3, 1094.

146 Ibid., vol. 8, 2889; vol. 12, 4209; vol. 14, 5116; vol. 10, 3516.

147 Ibid., vol. 10, 3828; vol. 2, 356; vol. 11, 3982, 4054; vol. 1, 270–71.

148 Ibid., vol. 6, 2401; vol. 7, 2629; vol. 10, 3705–7; vol. 14, 4769.

149 Andrew Lees, *Cities Perceived: Urban Society in European and American Thought, 1820–1940*

(Manchester, 1985), 17–18; Larkin, *Reshaping of Everyday Life*, 87.

150 *Farington's Diary*, vol. 15, 5291.

151 Martin, *Tennyson*, 27–8.

152 For Mary Lamb's other writings, see *Companion to Charles Lamb*, 187ff.

153 For the theater incident, Lamb's proposal, Fanny's reply, and the letter to her sister, see *Letters of Charles and Mary Lamb*, vol. 2, 193, 254–56; *Companion to Charles Lamb*, 176–78.

154 *Farington's Diary*, vol. 12, 4404.

155 Bourne, *Palmerston's Early Years*, 160.

156 L. J. Rather, "Disraeli, Freud and Jewish Conspiracy Theories," *Journal of the History of Ideas*, January–March 1986.

157 For details and further examples, see *House of Commons 1790–1820*, vol. 1, 330ff.

158 Quoted in Manuel, 328.

159 "Notice historique" in *Saint-Simon: Oeuvres*, vol. 1, 104–06.

160 For details, see *House of Commons, 1790–1820*, vol. 1 332.

161 *Farington's Diary*, vol. 13, 4663.

162 Ibid., vol. 15, 5278–80.

163 Ibid., vol. 9, 3524.

164 *Journal of Mrs Arbuthnot*, vol. 1, 176–85.

165 Bartlett, *Castlereagh*, 262–63; Ione Leigh, *Castlereagh* (London, 1951), 353–63; H. M. Hyde, *The Strange Death of Lord Castlereagh* (London, 1959), 182–90.

166 For these two women, see Louis Schutz Boas, *Harriet Shelley: Five Long Years* (Oxford, 1962), 183ff; Holmes, *Shelley: The Pursuit*, 347ff.

167 *Farington's Diary*, vol. 15, 5156–57ff.; vol. 8, 3171.

168 Ibid., vol. 9, 3325.

169 Ibid., vol. 2, 307; vol. 4, 1479; vol. 2, 336; vol. 13, 4592–93.

170 For typical business suicides, for example, see ibid., vol. 1, 90; vol. 4, 1300; vol. 4, 1479; vol. 8, 2862–63, 2987–88, and 3095; vol. 9, 3543; vol. 10, 3808; vol. 14, 4905.

171 Ibid., vol. 6, 2224.

172 See *Farington's Diary*, vol. 16, entry for 16 September 1820.

173 *Emma* (1815), vol. 1, chap. 12.

174 *Farington's Diary* vol. 12, 4184–85.

175 Ibid., vol. 10, 3546.

176 Ibid., vol. 10, 3562.

177 *Journal of Mrs Arbuthnot*, vol. 1, 333.

178 Jane Austen, *Sanditon* (unfinished, 1817), chap. 2; printed in *Oxford Illustrated Works of Jane Austen*, vol. 6, *Minor Works*, 370ff.

179 *Farington's Diary*, vol. 2, 350.

180 Ibid., vol. 7, 2709.

181 Quoted Young, *Early Victorian England*, vol. 1, 21.

182 Larkin, 174–75.

183 *Farington's Diary*, vol. 6, 2033; vol. 8, 4502, 2937–38; vol. 10, 3537.

184 *Emma*, vol. 1, chap. 3.

185 *Field's Memoirs of Dr. Samuel Parr*, 2 vols. (London, 1828); *Farington's Diary*, vol. 12, 4281; vol. 14, 4999; vol. 8, 3107; vol. 15, 5206; vol. 14, 4969.

186 *Farington's Diary*, vol. 14, 5040.

187 Larkin, 178–79.

188 *Farington's Diary*, vol. 3, 815–16.

189 Ibid., vol. 4, 1319.

190 Ibid., vol. 13, 4513.

191 For Mrs. Raffald, see Jane Grigson, "Entrepreneur Among the Entrees," *Country Life*, 14 December 1989.

192 *Farington's Diary*, vol. 9, 3329ff.

193 Richard Mullen, *Anthony Trollope* (London, 1990), 438ff.

194 Quoted in Young, 135.

195 E. M. Butler, ed., *A Regency Visitor, the English Tour of Prince Puckler-Muskau* (London, 1957).

196 *House of Commons 1790–1820*, vol. 1, 342.

197 Marquis James, *Jackson: Portrait of a President*, gives the bill in its entirety.

198 Larkin, 285–86, 295–97.

199 Quoted in Larkin, 168; Gash, *Peel*, 35.

200 Cooper, vol. 2, 474–76.

201 For methods of collecting opium in

the years 1800–30, see V. Berridge and G. Edwards, *Opium and the People; Opiate Use in 19th Century England* (London, 1981), xviiiff.

202 See J. D. Comrie, ed., *Selected Works of Thomas Sydenham* (London, 1922).

203 S. Crumpe, *Enquiry into the Nature and Properties of Opium* (London, 1793).

204 Berridge and Edwards, 21–25; for Maine, see *Dictionary of National Biography*, compact ed., vol. 1, 1298.

205 Berridge and Edwards, 13–15; G. E. Trease, *Pharmacy in History* (London, 1964) 156.

206 See "Opium Eating in the Fens" and the map, p. 41, in Berridge and Edwards.

207 *Farington's Diary*, vol. 4, 1427.

208 Ibid., vol. 3, 925; vol. 6, 5487; vol. 11, 4034; vol. 8, 2818; vol. 13, 4611; vol. 3, 964; vol. 9, 3363; vol. 1 221; vol. 10, 3669; vol. 3, 984; vol. 6, 2134; vol. 14, 4917; vol. 15, 4996; vol. 9, 3379; vol. 15, 5052; vol. 3, 660; vol. 4, 1300.

209 A. Hayter, *Opium and the Romantic Imagination* (London, 1968), 293; Holmes: *Shelley: The Pursuit*, 111–15, 392–93.

210 Elizabeth Barrett Browning and Wilkie Collins, quoted in Berridge and Edwards, 57.

211 Ibid., 58–59.

212 Lytton Bulwer, *Historical Characters* (London, 1868), vol. 2, 93; Grey to Lord Holland, 2 November 1835; *House of Commons 1790–1820*, vol. 4, 498–502.

213 It was originally published as *Elementa Medicinae* (1780) in Latin. Beddoes translated it.

214 "Fourth Research," in *Researches, Chemical and Philosophical* (London, 1800).

215 Trenner, *Humphry Davy*, 42ff.

216 Quoted in ibid., 44–45; Davy testified differently in his book, but it was heavily censored for publication.

217 Quoted in Molly Lefebure, *Samuel Taylor Coleridge: A Bondage of Opium* (London, 1977), 62–63.

218 Ibid.

219 Ibid., Appendix 1, 493–95; *The Braithwaite Will Cause and the History of the Black Drop* (Kendal, England, 1872).

220 B. K. Mudge, *Sara Coleridge: A Victorian Daughter: Her Life and Essays* (New Haven, Conn., 1989), 147–48.

221 Kathleen Coburn, ed., *Notebooks of Samuel Taylor Coleridge* (Oxford, 1957).

222 Earl Leslie Griggs, ed., *Collected Letters of Samuel Taylor Coleridge*, 6 vols. (Oxford, 1956–71), 1028.

223 David Masson, ed., *De Quincey: Collected Writings*, 14 vols. (Edinburgh, 1889–90), vol. 3.

224 Brigid M. Boardman, *Between Heaven and Charing Cross: The Life of Francis Thompson* (New Haven, Conn., 1988) 45ff.

225 Molly Lefebure has largely restored the balance in *The Bondage of Love: A Life of Mrs Samuel Taylor Coleridge* (London, 1986); see esp. pp. 133ff.

226 L. E. Watson, *Coleridge at Highgate* (London, 1925).

227 Joseph Cottle, *Early Recollections: Chiefly Relating to the late Samuel Taylor Coleridge during his Long Residence in Bristol*, 2 vols. (London, 1837); James Gillman, *Life of Samuel Taylor Coleridge* (London, 1838), of which only the first volume was published.

228 J. H. Heap, "The Commerce of Drugs," *Pharmaceutical Journal*, 16 (1903); Berridge and Edwards, 4–9.

229 *Parliamentary Papers; First Report of the Select Committee on the Adulteration of Food, Drink and Drugs*, (Westminster 1854–5).

230 *Farington's Diary*, vol. 10, 3605.

231 For an account of the Chinese use of opium see Austin Coates, *Macao and the British, 1637–1842: Prelude to Hong Kong* (Hong Kong, 1988), 63ff.

232 Wolfram Eberhard, *A History of China*, 4th ed. (London, 1977), 298.
233 For an account of the Sino-British tea trade up to 1830, see Henry Hobhouse, *Seeds of Change: Five Plants that Transformed the World* (New York, 1986), 95–124.
234 *Farington's Diary*, vol. 10, 3612.
235 John K. Fairbank, ed., *Cambridge History of China, Volume X, Late Ch'ing, 1800–1911* (Cambridge, England, 1986), Part 1, 171ff.
236 Ping-ti Ho: *Studies on the Population of China, 1368–1953* (Hong Kong, 1960).
237 See H. H. Lindsay, *Is the War with China a Just One?* (London, 1840), 14; J. M. Downs, "American Merchants and the China Opium Trade, 1800–40," *Business History Review*, Winter 1968.
238 Fairbank, vol. 10, i, 172.
239 Jonathan Spence, "Opium Smoking in Ch'ing China," in F. Wakeman and C. Grant, eds., *Conflict and Control in Late Imperial China* (Berkeley, Calif., 1975), 143–73.
240 Quoted in Roger Pélissier, *The Awakening of China, 1793–1949* (trans., London, 1967), 54–55.
241 Pina-chia Kuo, *A Critical Study of the First Anglo-Chinese War, with Documents* (Shanghai, 1935), 213.
242 W. H. Mitchell, Hong Kong official, to Sir George Bonham at the Foreign Office, 15 March 1852, FO 405/2, 410, quoted in Yen-p'ing Hao: *The Commercial Revolution in 19th-century China: The Rise of Sino-Western Mercantile Capitalism* (Berkeley, Calif., 1986), 55, fn. 97.

243 Quoted in Michael Greenberg, *British Trade and the Opening of China 1800–42* (London, 1951), 118.
244 Yen-p'ing Hao, 34–55.
245 Henry Ellis, *Journal of the Proceedings of the Late Embassy to China, etc.* (London, 1817), 183–86.
246 Costin, 13ff.
247 Fairbank, vol. 10, i, 138–42.
248 Ibid., 134ff.
249 Ibid., 110ff.
250 Ibid., 119–26.
251 Ibid., 127.
252 H. B. Morse, *The Chronicles of the East India Company Trading to China, 1635–1834*, 3 vols. (Oxford, 1926–29), vol. 3, 155.
253 Coates, 143–44.
254 For the Canton settlement, see J. F. Davis, *The Chinese: A General Description of the Chinese Empire and Its Inhabitants*, 2 vols. (London, 1836) vol. 2, 24–26. Davis was the chief superintendent of the British East India Company.
255 This account, "By an Old Resident," is in W. C. Hunter, *The Fan Kwae at Canton Before Treaty Days, 1825–44* (London, 1882), 65–69.
256 For the detailed regulations, see Hunter, 28–30.
257 Quoted in Arthur Waley, *The Opium War Seen Through Chinese Eyes* (London, 1958), 68–69.
258 Quoted in Costin, 11.
259 For Morrison, see Coates, 114ff.
260 Costin, 9; Coates, 148.
261 Pelissier, 48.
262 Costin, 5–7; Coates, 133–34.
263 Hunter, 73–77.

TEN
Giant Shadows

1 Lloyd, *Captain Marryat and the Old Navy*, 217; Marryat's own account of Burma is in *Diary on the Continent of Asia* (London, 1840).
2 *United Service Journal*, 2 (London, 1841), 215.
3 Quoted by K. M. Pannikar, *Asia and Western Dominance* (New York, 1969), 97.
4 Quoted in K. O. Dike, *Trade and Politics in the Niger Delta 1830–85* (Oxford, 1956), 238.
5 D. R. Headrick, "The Tools of Imperialism: Technology and the Expansion

of Empire in the 19th Century," *Journal of Modern History*, June 1979; F. J. C. Hearnshaw, *Sea-Power and Empire* (London, 1940), 190–91.

6 Quoted in D. G. E. Hall, *A History of South-East Asia*, 3rd ed. (London, 1968), 584.

7 D. G. E. Hall, ed., *Michael Symes: Journal of His Second Embassy to the Court of Ava in 1802* (London, 1955) describes Bodawpaya and his rule.

8 Henri Cordier, *Historique abrégé des relations de la Grande Bretagne avec la Burmanie* (Paris, 1894), 8ff.

9 W. F. B. Lawrie, *Our Burmese Wars* (London, 1880), 46, 71–72.

10 For the postwar situation in Ava, see John Crawfurd, *Journal of an Embassy . . . to the Court of Ava in the Year 1827* (London, 1829); and G. E. Harvey, *British Rule in Burma 1824–1942* (London, 1946), chaps. 1 and 2.

11 Kathryn Cave, ed., *The Diary of Joseph Farington,* 16 vols. (New Haven, Conn.: 1978–84), vol. 11, 3995, vol. 14, 4786 (hereafter called *Farington's Diary*).

12 Graham, *Great Britain in the Indian Ocean,* 373ff.

13 His personal diaries are used in T. E. Colebrooke, *Life of . . . Mountstuart Elphinstone,* 2 vols. (London, 1884); for the Bombay secretariat records, see G. W. Forrest, ed., *Selections from the Minutes and Other Official Writings of . . . Mountstuart Elphinstone* (London, 1884).

14 Quoted in Kenneth Ballhatchet, *Social Policy and Social Change in Western India, 1817–30* (Oxford, 1957), 2–3.

15 Letter to Edward Strachey, Registrar in Benares, quoted in ibid., 3.

16 Letter to the governor general, quoted in Colebrooke, vol. 1, 289.

17 Malcolm to Elphinstone, 9 August 1818, quoted in Ballhatchet, 45.

18 See Ballhatchet, chap. 4: "The Fate of the Old Rulers," 43–76.

19 Elphinstone to Malcolm, 27 January 1819, quoted in ibid., 249.

20 For Bentinck, see John Rosselli, *Lord William Bentinck: The Making of a Liberal Imperialist, 1774–1839* (London, 1974).

21 See Hiralal Gupta in the *Journal of Indian History,* August 1959.

22 See Francis Tuker, *The Yellow Scarf: The Story of the Life of Thuggee Sleeman, or Major-General Sir William Henry Sleeman, 1788–1856, of the Bengal Army and the Indian Political Service* (London, 1961).

23 Bishop Reginald Heber, *Narrative of a Journey through India from Calcutta to Bombay,* 2 vols. (London, 1828), vol. 2, 53.

24 Stuart Carey Welch, *India: Art and Culture 1300–1900* (New York, 1988), describes and reproduces the bronze.

25 Hall, *History of South-East Asia,* 709ff.

26 For the workings of the system see ibid., 546–47.

27 Ibid., 426–35, 644ff.

28 James Murdoch, *A History of Japan,* rev. ed. by J. H. Longford (London, 1926), vol. 3, *The Tokugawa Epoch 1652–1868,* 497ff, 517ff.

29 Ibid., 528.

30 See the entry in Siebold's diary, 16 December 1828, quoted in ibid., 556–57.

31 Ibid., 438ff.

32 Quoted in Sir Ernest Satow, *The Revival of Pure Shinto* (London, 1920).

33 Murdoch, 482–83.

34 Quoted in Golo Mann, *A History of Germany since 1789* (trans., London, 1968), 61.

35 Marie-Jean-Antoine-Nicolas de Condorcet, *Tableau historique des progrès de l'ésprit humaine* (Paris, 1795).

36 For a map of Germany's university system in 1818, see Christa Jungnickel and Russel McCommach, *Intellectual Mastery of Nature: Theoretical Physics from Ohm to Einstein,* 2 vols. (Chicago, 1986), vol. 1, *The Torch of Mathematics 1800–70,* xxiv–v.

37 See Johann Gottlieb Fichte, *Ueber Machiavelli* (Koenigsberg, 1807); Friedrich Meinecke, *Cosmopolitanism and the National State* (trans., Princeton, N.J., 1970), 78–79.

38 Meinecke, 81. See *Reden an die Deutsche Nation*, (1807) printed in Johann Gottlieb Fichte, *Werke*, (Berlin, 1860ff) vol. 7.
39 Cf., for instance, his letter to his wife, No. 476 in Clark Butler, trans and ed., *Hegel: The Letters* (Bloomington, Ind., 1984), 610.
40 Butler, letter No. 167, 288.
41 Ibid., 307–08.
42 Ibid., 288.
43 Ibid., 340.
44 For Hegel's dialectic, see Michael Rosen, *Hegel's Dialectic and Its Criticism* (Cambridge, England, 1982); Hans-Georg Gadamaer, *Hegel's Dialectic* (trans. New Haven, Conn., 1982); J. E. Toews, *Hegelianism: The Path Towards Dialectical Humanism, 1805–41* (Cambridge, England, 1980).
45 Butler, 129–30, 142–44.
46 *Ibid.*, 114, 141, 159–60.
47 *Ibid.*, 306–07.
48 *Ibid.*, 307–08.
49 *Hegel Werke*, vol. 8, 433; see Meinecke, 201.
50 Butler, 325.
51 Meinecke, 199.
52 Francois Mazoi, *Les ruines de Pompei* (Paris, 1812–28).
53 Vivant Denon, *Description de l'Égypt*, 24 vols. (Paris, 1809–13).
54 For a summary of Young's work, see Alan Gardiner, *Egyptian Grammar*, 3rd ed. (Oxford, 1976), 9–10.
55 For Champollion, see ibid., 10–13; C. W. Ceram, *Gods, Graves and Scholars* (Harmondsworth, 1974), 124ff.
56 Elizabeth Longford, *Wellington: Pillar of State* (London, 1972), 262.
57 For the prepublication history of the *Diaries*, their transcription, editing, and reception, see R. C. Latham and W. Matthews, eds., *The Diaries of Samuel Pepys*, 11 vols. (London, 1983), vol. 1, xxvff.
58 E. Werner, *Mendelssohn* (London, 1963), 100.
59 F. E. Manuel, *The New World of Henri Saint-Simon*, (Harvard, 1956) 227–28.
60 *Oeuvres choisis* (Paris, 1830), vol. 2, 289.
61 Ibid., vol. 2, 328.
62 These ideas are set out in his partwork, *L'Industrie* (Paris, monthly 1816–18) and in *L'Organisateur*, November 1819.
63 *Doctrine de Saint-Simon: Exposition, première année 1829*, 2nd ed. (Paris, 1830), 70. This was from the lecture-course on Saint-Simonism given by Auguste Comte after Saint-Simon's death.
64 Saint-Simon's class theory is set out in *Le Système industriel* (Paris, 1821) and *Le Catéchisme des industriels* (Paris, 1823–24), esp. chap. 2, 130.
65 *Oeuvres complètes* (Paris, 1830), vol. 20, 126–27, 192.
66 Ibid, vol. 20, 199–202; see Manuel, 311.
67 *Oeuvres complètes*, vol. 19, 41.
68 Manuel, 344–47.
69 Auguste Comte, *Lettres à divers*, vol. 2, 34–35, 93; for Comte's break with Saint-Simon see Manuel, chap. 29, "The Master Denied," 332–43.
70 Lepenies, *Between Literature and Science: The Rise of Sociology*, 20.
71 For Saint-Simon's Jewish followers, see Manuel, 346–47.
72 Fourier's ideas are presented in *La Théorie des quatres mouvements* (Paris, 1808), *Traité de l'association domestique et agricole* (Paris, 1822) and *Le Nouveau monde industiel* (Paris 1829–30).
73 Robert Southey, *Journal of a Tour in Scotland*, 261–5.
74 For a description of Bentham's proposals, see Gertrude Himmelfarb, "Bentham's Utopia," in Himmelfarb, ed., *Marriage and Morals Among the Victorians* (London, 1986), 111–43; see also, John Bowring, ed., *Works of Jeremy Bentham* 11 vols. (London, 1838–43), vol. 8.
75 Quoted in Himmelfarb, 121 fn.
76 *Coleridge Letters*, vol. 4, 719; John Colmer, "Coleridge in Politics" in R. L. Brett, ed., *S. T. Coleridge* (London, 1971), 249.
77 *Lectures on Revealed Religion* (Bristol, 1795).

78 Unpublished sermon from 1799; see Colmer, 268–69.
79 *Coleridge Letters*, vol. 4, 922.
80 Quoted in Colmer, 264.
81 *Coleridge Letters*, vol. 2, 1197.
82 Ibid., vol. 1, 282; Colmer, 245–46.
83 Sara Coleridge, ed., *Coleridge: Essays on His Own Times*, 3 vols. (London, 1818), vol. 1, 91; *Table Talk*, 20 March 1831.
84 Marginal note, quoted in Colmer, 252.
85 These themes are developed in *Lay Sermons* (London, 1816–17) and *On the Constitution of Church and State* (London, 1830).
86 *Church and State*, (London, 1830), chap. 5, 49–50.
87 Richard A. Lebrun, *Joseph de Maistre: An Intellectual Militant* (Montreal, 1988), 4, 37ff, 45ff, 233.
88 *Lettres d'un Royaliste savoisien*, in *Oeuvres complètes*, 14 vols. (Lyons, 1884–86), vol. 7, 84ff.
89 Ibid., 148, 152.
90 This is the opening sentence in *Considerations sur la France*, ed., R. Johannet and F. Veremale (Paris, 1936), 23.
91 De Maistre's *Essai sur le principe générateur des constitutions politiques* (1810) was written with Alexander in mind; his *Mémoire sur la liberté de l'enseignment publique* (1812) has reference to the Jesuits.
92 Lebrun, 209.
93 See J. T. Flynn, "The Role of the Jesuits in the Politics of Russian Education," *Catholic Historical Review*, 66 (1970).
94 Quoted in Richard Pipes, *Russia under the Old Regime* (London, 1974), 113.
95 For the importance of *chin*, see Nicholas Turgenyev, *La Russie et les Russes*, 2 vols. (Paris, 1847), vol. 2, 47; Pipes, 125.
96 Mark Raeff, *The Decembrist Movement* (Princeton, N.J., 1966), 20, fn. 22.
97 Ibid., 19, fn 19; 21, fn. 23.
98 Sidney Monas: *The Third Section: Police and Society under Nicholas I* (Cambridge, Mass., 1961), 124ff.
99 N. V. Riasanovsky, *A Parting of Ways: Government and Educated Public in Russia 1801–55* (Oxford, 1976), 65.
100 Quoted in Pipes.
101 Quoted in D. T. Orlovsky, *The Limits of Reform: The Ministry of Internal Affairs in Imperial Russia, 1802–81* (Cambridge, Mass., 1981), 5.
102 Monas, 34.
103 Chateaubriand, *De la Monarchie selon la charte* (Paris, 1816), 28.
104 Monas, 34.
105 Ibid., 37.
106 Ibid., 42ff.
107 See the table in Orlovsky, *Limits of Reform*, 36.
108 Quoted in Pipes, 290.
109 Quoted in Hugh Seton-Watson, *The Russian Empire, 1801–1917* (Oxford, 1967), 170.
110 Monas, 139–40.
111 Quoted in Raeff, 120ff.
112 Monas, 56.
113 For details of various plans proposed, see Seton-Waton, 86ff; Riasanovsky, 92ff; Raeff, 40ff.
114 Seton-Watson, 180; Monas, 56; Riasanovsky, 91; Raeff, 150–51.
115 Raeff, 134–36.
116 Seton-Watson, 179–81; for further details, see R. W. Seton-Watson, *A History of the Rumanians* (Cambridge, England, 1934).
117 Seton-Watson, *Russian Empire*, 190ff.
118 For the events in Senate Square see the documents cited in Raeff; see also, Raeff, *Imperial Russia, 1682–1825: The Coming of Age of Modern Russia* (New York, 1971).
119 Monas, 10.
120 Quoted in Riasanovsky, 106; see Monas, 12.
121 C. de Grunwald, *Tsar Nicholas I* (New York, 1955), 203.
122 Monas, 61–5.
123 Ibid., 122–24.
124 Ibid., 100–03.
125 Ibid., 89.

126 Ibid., 118ff.
127 Ibid., 203–04.
128 A. Mazour, *The First Russian Revolution, 1825* (Berkeley, Calif., 1937), 212–13.
129 See the judgment of Raeff in *The Decembrist Movement*, 27; for inconsistencies in sentencing, see Monas, 75–83.
130 Quoted in Riasanovsky, 116–17.
131 Quoted Raeff, *Decembrists*, 177.

ELEVEN
Crash!

1 For the architecture of the Bank of England, see Summerson, *Georgian London*, 141–43; St. Aubin, *Ackermann's Illustrated London*, 104–5; *Architectural Monographs: John Soane* (London, 1983), 61–75.

2 *Journal of Mrs Arbuthnot*, vol. 1, 426.

3 The story about the chest was told by Alexander Baring, Baron Ashburton (1774–1848). See *Journal of Mrs Arbuthnot*, vol. 1, 427; Sir John Clapham, *The Bank of England* (New York, 1945), 100.

4 S. D. Chapman, *The Foundation of the English Rothschilds, 1793–1811* (London, 1977), 20ff.

5 Bertrand Gille, *Histoire de la Maison Rothschild*, 2 vols. (Geneva, 1965–67), vol. 1, 45ff; F. Crouzet, *L'Économie Britannique et le blocus continental 1806–13* (Paris, 1958), 842.

6 Harold Pollins, *Economic History of the Jews in England* (East Brunswick, 1982), 95ff; see also, K. Helleiner, *The Imperial Loans* (Oxford, 1965).

7 For the growth of U.S. banks, see M. G. Myers, *A Financial History of the United States* (New York, 1970).

8 John Taylor, *An Inquiry into . . . the Government of the United States* (Philadelphia, 1814), 275; Arthur M. Schlesinger, *The Age of Jackson* (London, 1946), 24.

9 For Taylor, see R. E. Shalhope, *John Taylor of Caroline* (Columbia, S.C., 1980).

10 W. P. Cresson, *James Monroe* (Chapel Hill, N.C., 1946), 333; Raymond Walters, Jr, "Origins of the Second Bank of the United States," *Journal of Political Economy*, 53 (1945).

11 Quoted in George Dangerfield, *The Era of Good Feelings* (London, 1953), 168–69; see W. B. Smith, *Economic Aspects of the Second Bank of the United States* (New York, 1953).

12 Leon Schur, "The Second Bank of the United States and Inflation after the War of 1812," *Journal of Political Economy*, 68 (1960).

13 Dangerfield, 181; see R. C. H. Catterall, *The Second Bank of the United States* (New York, 1903), 28–32, 160 n.

14 Catterall, 45–50.

15 Quoted in Dangerfield, 179–80.

16 See Murray N. Rothbard, *The Panic of 1819* (New York, 1962).

17 Quoted in Catterall, 68.

18 William M. Gouge, *Paper Money and Banking*, 2 vols. (Philadelphia, 1833), vol. 2, 109.

19 E. L. Bogart, "Taxation of Second Bank," *American Historical Review*, 17 (1912).

20 Albert J. Beveridge, *Life of John Marshall*, 4 vols. (New York, 1916–19), vol. 4, 87.

21 See Max Lerner, "John Marshall and the Campaign of History," *Columbia Law Review*, 39, no. 3.

22 See the *Journal of . . . the Convention of Delegates Chosen to Revise the Constitution of Massachusetts* (Boston, 1820).

23 Quoted in Schlesinger, 14.

24 Mason to George Ticknor, 3 April 1836, quoted in ibid.

25 For a range of views on Marshall's significance, see the symposium by

Carl B. Swisher et al., *Justice John Marshall: A Reappraisal* (New York, 1955) and E. S. Corwin, *John Marshall and the Constitution* (New York, 1919).

26 Beveridge, vol. 3, 586ff.

27 Dangerfield, 165; see Felix Frankfurter, *The Commerce Clause under Marshall, Tainey and Waite* (Cambridge, Mass., 1937).

28 See H. J. Plous and G. Baker, "McCulloch v. Maryland; Right Principle, Wrong Case," *Stanford Law Review*, 9 (1957).

29 Allan Nevins, ed., *Diary of John Quincy Adams 1794–1845* (New York, 1951), 216–17, entries for 27 May and 10 June 1819.

30 For these and other examples of corruption in the Monroe government, see Remini, *Jackson*, vol. 2, 18–23.

31 Quoted in Schlesinger, 35ff.

32 See Hansard's *Parliamentary Debates*, vol. 11, 152–78, for the full text.

33 See the biographical entry in P. Sraffa and Maurice Dobb, eds., *Works and Correspondence of David Ricardo*, 10 vols. (Cambridge, England, 1951–55), vol. 10, 1–105.

34 For further details about Ricardo's finances, see *House of Commons 1790–1820*, vol. 5, 11–13.

35 Published as a pamphlet, *The High Price of Bullion* (London, 1810).

36 David Ricardo, *Proposals for an Economical and Secure Currency with Observations on the Profits of the Bank of England* (London, 1816).

37 The passages in its report are reprinted in A. Aspinall and E. A. Smith, eds., *English Historical Documents 1783–1832* (London, 1959), 594–95.

38 Thomas Carlyle, *On the Nigger Question* (London, 1849).

39 *Quarterly Review*, vol. 32 (October 1825), 420–21.

40 *Dictionary of National Biography*, compact ed., vol. 1, 1332 (this entry is by the dictionary's first editor, Sir Leslie Stephen).

41 For instance, Mr. Justice Alderson at Dorchester, reported in *The Times*, 12 January 1831. For the popularity of economics in the 1820s, see R. K. Webb, *Harriet Martineau, A Radical Victorian* (London, 1960), 102ff.

42 Cookson, *Lord Liverpool's Administration*, 228.

43 For his financial dealings see *House of Commons 1790–1820*, vol. 4, 270ff, esp. 271.

44 See Anna Lingelbach, "William Huskisson as President of the Board of Trade," *American Historical Review*, 43 (1937–38) 759–74; the best survey of Huskisson's economic views is in C. R. Fay, *Huskisson and His Age* (London, 1951).

45 Quoted in Norman Gash, *Mr. Secretary Peel* (London, 1985) 57–58.

46 Gronow, *Reminiscences*, vol. 2, 90.

47 See Maurice Walton Thomas, *The Early Factory Legislation* (Leigh-on-Sea, England, 1948).

48 Gash, 353–54; A. A. W. Ramsay, *Sir Robert Peel* (London, 1928), 72–74.

49 Leon Radzinowicz, *A History of English Criminal Law and Its Administration since 1750*, 4 vols. (London, 1948–68), vol. 1, 588–89.

50 Sidney and Beatrice Webb, *English Prisons* (London, 1922), 73ff.

51 William Austen-Leigh et al., *Jane Austen: A Family Record*, (London, 1989) 106–07.

52 Quoted in Gash, *Peel*, 318.

53 Letter in C. D. Yonge, *Liverpool*, 3 vols. (London, 1868), vol. 3, 215.

54 Radzinowicz, vol. 1 589, n. 84.

55 *Speeches of Sir Robert Peel*, 4 vols. (London, 1853), vol. 2, 131.

56 For attitudes toward unions, 1815–24, see the Home Office papers printed in A. Aspinall, *The Early Trade Unions* (London, 1949).

57 For details of disputes, 1822–24, see ibid., 352–79.

58 "Combination Laws—Restraints on Emigration," *Edinburgh Review*, 39 (January 1824), 315ff.

59 Élie Halévy, *The Liberal Awakening* (trans., London, 1949), 206–09.

60 For details of the London port strikes, see speech of Thomas Wallace, 25 June 1825, in *Parliamentary Debates,* New Series, vol. 13, 1400.

61 These figures are from Halévy; Gash, *Peel,* 349, gives the number killed in Dublin as two.

62 Letter to Leonard Horner, 29 November 1825, printed in C. S. Parker, *Peel,* 3 vols. (London, 1891–99), vol. 1, 379–80.

63 McCalman, *Radical Underworld,* 187–88, 192–93.

64 Ibid., 206ff.

65 There is a brief entry for Jocelyn in the *Dictionary of National Biography,* compact ed., vol. 1, 1081; see also, Henry Cotton, *Fasti ecclesiae Hibernicae: The succession of the Prelates and Members of the Cathedral Bodies of Ireland,* 4 vols. (Dublin, 1845–78). He is known to have died in Edinburgh.

66 Quoted in McCalman, 205.

67 Ibid., 80–81, 204–05.

69 Larkin, *Reshaping of Everyday Life,* 139, 125, 165.

70 Derry and Williams, *History of Technology,* 698.

71 Boorstin, *The Americans,* 10–16.

72 William Cobbett, *Cottage Economy* (Oxford, 1979; original work published 1822), 183–91.

73 Mark Girouard, *Life in the English Country House* (New Haven, Conn., 1978), 263.

74 Charles Sylvester, *Philosophy of Domestic Economy* (London, 1819), quoted in ibid., 262.

75 See C. J. Richardson, *A Popular Treatise on the Heating and Ventilation of Buildings* (London, 1837); Herman Ludwig Heinrich von Puckler-Muskau, *Tour in England. . . . ,* 4 vols. (London, 1832), vol. 3, 209.

76 J. Eller, *Belvoir Castle* (London, 1841), 334; Girouard, 265.

77 J. G. Lockhart, *Life of Sir W. Scott* (London, 1896) 500–01.

78 L. Gibbs, ed., *Diary of Fanny Burney* (London, 1940), 79–85; Maria Edgeworth, *Ormonde* (1817); H. Repton, *Fragments on the Theory of Landscape Gardening* (London, 1816).

79 Girouard, 236.

80 For a detailed modern description of the kitchen, see Jessica Rutherford, "Steam Cuisine," *Country Life,* 14 December 1989.

81 There are numerous acquatints by A. C. Pugin of the kitchen quarters of the Royal Pavilion in John Nash, *View of the Royal Pavilion* (London, 1826).

82 For details, see *Hansard,* Second Series, vol. 10, 655, 1226–27, vol. 11, 595–96.

83 *Hansard,* Second Series, vol. 12, 722.

84 To Bernard Barton 20 March 1826, *Letters of Charles and Mary Lamb,* vol. 3, 37.

85 Bertier de Sauvigny, *The Bourbon Restoration,* 224.

86 Quoted in ibid., 245.

87 J. S. Allen, *Popular French Romanticism: Authors, Readers and Books in the 19th Century* (Syracuse, N.Y., 1981), 104ff, 112–13.

88 De Sauvigny, 243; ibid., 116–17.

89 Edgar Quinet, *Histoire de mes idées* (Paris, 1855).

90 Lady Morgan, *France in 1829–30,* 2 vols. (London, 1830), vol. 1, 383.

91 Hypolyte Mazier de Heaume, *Voyage d'un jeune Grec a Paris,* 2 vols. (Paris, 1824), vol. 1, 143–4, quoted Allen, 195.

92 Charles-Paul de Kock, *Memoires . . . écrits par lui-même* (Paris, 1873), 160; Allen, 92–96.

93 Allen, 121; Thierry quote from *Le Moniteur,* 12 September 1854; Marie Jeanne Durry, *La Vieillesse de Chateaubriand, 1830–45,* 2 vols. (Paris, 1933), vol. 1, 363.

94 Quoted in Allen, 127.

95 See H. Ferns, *Britain and Argentina in the 19th Century* (Oxford, 1960), chaps. 3–5; Vera Reber, *British Merchant Houses in Buenos Aires 1810–80* (Cambridge, Mass., 1979).

96 D. C. M. Platt, *Latin America and British Trade, 1806–1914* (London, 1972), 23.

97 D. C. M. Platt, ed., *Business Imperialism: An Inquiry Based on British Experience in Latin America* (Oxford, 1977) vol. 1, 62.

98 A. Gayer, W. Rostow, and A. Schwartz, *Growth and Fluctuation of the British Economy, 1790–1850*, 2 vols. (Oxford, 1953), vol. 1, 171–210, gives overall statistics for the 1820–25 boom.

99 Quoted in Leland Jenks, *Migration of British Capital to 1875* (New York, 1927), chap. 2.

100 For foreign loans issued in London, see *Parliamentary Papers*, 1822, vol. 20, no. 145, "Loans Contracted on Account of Great Britain for Each Year since 1793."

101 Quoted in Manuel Perez Vila, ed., *Simon Bolivar: Doctrina del Liberador* (Caracas, 1979), 204.

102 Benjamin Disraeli, *An Enquiry into the Plans, Progress and Policy of the American Mining Companies* (London, 1825).

103 Victor Allan, "The Prince of Poyais," *History Today*, January 1952.

104 *Journal of Mrs Arbuthnot*, vol. 1, 382.

105 12 November 1823, quoted in W. D. Jones, *Prosperity Robinson*, 114.

106 *Journal of Mrs Arbuthnot*, vol. 1, 391.

107 Ibid., vol. 1, 382.

108 T. Tooke and W. Newmarch, *A History of Prices and the State of Circulation, from 1793 to the Present Time*, 6 vols. (London, 1838–57), vol. 4, 336.

109 The *Times*, 15 December 1825.

110 The *Times*, 16 December 1825; *Annual Register*, 1826, 12.

111 *Journal of Mrs Arbuthnot*, vol. 1, 428.

112 Gille, vol. 1, 159–61; Stuart Bruchey, *Robert Oliver, Merchant of Baltimore* (Baltimore, 1956), chap. 6.

113 See Claudio Veliz, "Egana, Lambert and the Chilean Mining Association of 1825," *Hispanic-American Historical Review*, 55 (1975).

114 D. C. M. Platt, *Finance, Trade and Politics: British Foreign Policy 1815–1914* (Oxford, 1968), chap. 6.

115 Quoted in Webb, 106.

116 Harriet Martineau, *Autobiography*, (London, 3 vols. 1877), vol. 1 97–99.

117 See Lamb's famous essay on retirement, "A Superannuated Man." For Lamb's relationship with the East India Company, see Prance, *Companion to Charles Lamb*, 100–101.

118 For details, see Lady Raffles, *Memoir of the Life and Public Services of Sir S. Raffles. . . .*

119 There is a full description of early 19th-century Kensington in Marcia Poynton, *Mulready* (London, 1986), Introduction.

120 Finberg, *Turner*, 294–97; Thornbury, *Turner*, vol. 2, 130.

121 *Diary of B. R. Haydon*, vol. 3, 85–86, 96–97.

122 For Congreve, see *House of Commons 1790–1820*, vol. 3, 493–94.

123 See Stanley Jones, *Hazlitt: A Life* (Oxford, 1989), chap. 17: "The Final Years," 376ff.

124 Derek Hudson, ed., *Diary of Henry Crabb Robinson: An Abridgement* (Oxford, 1967), 91.

125 The clearest account of Scott's financial disaster is not in any of the biographies, but in the entry in the *Dictionary of National Biography*, compact ed., vol. 2, 1875ff.

126 A day-by-day record of this hectic period in Scott's life is in Edgar Johnson, *Sir Walter Scott: The Great Unknown, Volume 2, 1821–32* (London, 1970), 952–56.

127 See Croker's letter to Wellington dealing with this issue, 20 March 1826, printed in *Croker's Correspondence and Diaries*, vol. 1, 313ff. Croker wrote a reply to the pamphlet.

128 Johnson, *Scott*, 977.

129 W. F. Moneypenny, *Life of Benjamin Disraeli,* 6 vols. (London, 1910), vol. 1, 57ff; Robert Blake, *Disraeli* (London, 1966), 26.

130 Samuel Smiles, *Memoir of John Murray,* 2 vols. (London, 1891), vol. 2, 217.

131 Scott, *Letters,* vol. 9, 245; Johnson, *Scott,* 944.

132 Moneypenny, vol. 1, 64–65.

133 Ibid., 70–78.

134 Blake, 26. For a portrait of Disraeli at this time, see B. R. Jerman, *The Young Disraeli* (Princeton, N.J., 1960).

135 Bourne, *Palmerston; the Early Years,* 253–55.

136 Ibid., 260–64.

137 Ibid., 264.

138 Quoted in Gash, *Mr. Secretary Peel,* 364.

TWELVE

The Coming of the *Demos*

1 Seventy-seven of the papers were originally published in New York newspapers in 1787–88 under the signature "Publius"; eight were added later, and all appeared in book form as *The Federalist,* 2 vols. (Philadelphia, 1788).

2 See Morton Borden, *Parties and Politics in the Early Republic, 1789–1815* (New Haven, Conn., 1967); and Richard Hofstadter, *The Idea of a Party System, 1780–1840* (New York, 1969).

3 *Niles Register,* 5 March 1817.

4 Samuel P. Waldo, *A Narrative of a Tour of Observation, . . .* (Hartford, 1820), describes the presidential progress.

5 *Colombian Centinel,* 12 July 1817; see G. Dangerfield, *The Era of Good Feelings* (London, 1953), 96.

6 Allan Nevins, ed., *Diary of John Quincy Adams 1794–1845* (New York, 1951), entry for 14 December 1825, 353ff.

7 R. V. Remini, *Andrew Jackson,* vol. 2, 397, n. 14, lists various villainies of Webster.

8 Ibid., 398, n. 23.

9 *Baltimore Federal Republican,* 4 September 1822; *New York Statesman,* 6 August 1822, quoted in ibid., 13–14.

10 Letter from Jackson to Dr. James C. Bronaugh, 18 July 1822, quoted in ibid., 37.

11 Opinions varied greatly, then and since, about Peggy O'Neale's character; for the Eatons, see A. Johns and D. Malone, eds., *Dictionary of American Biography* (Oxford, 1930), vol. 5, 609ff; vol. 14, 41ff. *The Autobiography of Peggy Eaton* was dictated in 1873 and published (New York) in 1932; it followed the publication of Queena Pollock, *Peggy Eaton, Democracy's Mistress* (New York, 1931), apparently based on authentic sources but not documented.

12 Henry A. Wise, *Seven Decades of the Union* (Philadelphia, 1881) 100–03.

13 Letter to Benjamin Austin, 9 January 1816, quoted in Schlesinger, *Age of Jackson,* 18.

14 H. J. Doherty, Jr., "Andrew Jackson on Manhood Suffrage: 1822," *Tennessee Historical Quarterly,* 15 (1956), 60.

15 Letter to James Buchanan, 25 June 1825, quoted in Remini (1981), vol. 2, 30–31.

16 See R. P. Hay, "The Case for Andrew Jackson in 1824: Eaton's Wyoming Letters," *Tennessee Historical Quarterly,* 29 (1970); G. L. Lowe, "John H. Eaton, Jackson's Campaign Manager," *Tennessee Historical Quarterly,* 11 (1952); Remini (1981), 76.

17 J. D. Richardson, ed., *Messages and Papers of the Presidents, 1789–1902* (Washington, D.C., 1907), vol. 2, 16.

18 Quoted in Cresson, *Monroe,* 467.

19 S. M. Hamilton, ed., *Writings of James Monroe,* 7 vols. (New York, 1893–1903), vol. 6, 286.

20 Quoted in Carl Schurz, *Life of Henry*

Clay, 2 vols. (Boston, 1887), vol. 1, 231.

21 Quoted in Remini, vol. 2, 79–80.

22 Van Buren, *Political Parties,* 322.

23 Letter to Ezekiel Webster, 22 February 1824; *Daniel Webster, Private Correspondence* (New York 1902) vol. 1 346.

24 See J. F. Hopkins, "Election of 1824," in Arthur Schlesinger, Jr., and F. L. Israels, eds., *History of American Presidential Elections, 1789–1968,* (New York, 1971), vol. 1.

25 See Marquess James, *Andrew Jackson: Portrait of a President* (New York, 1937), 99ff.

26 These figures are from E. W. Austin, ed., *Political Facts of the United States since 1789* (Columbia 1986), Table 3.1, 92ff. Remini (1981), gives Jackson 152,901 and Adams 114,023.

27 Letter to Coffee, 27 December 1824, *Jackson Correspondence,* vol. 3, 270; Wise, 110–11.

28 Quoted in James, 135.

29 Nevins, 335; there is a full discussion on the negotiations in ibid., chap. 5, 100–34.

30 Quoted in James, 116.

31 Ibid., 125.

32 Quoted in Nevins, 342 fn. Van Buren's account, in his *Autobiography* (edited for the American Historical Association *Report,* 2 (1918), by J. C. Fitzpatrick, has been disputed; see James, 521 fn. 106.

33 See Gaillard Hunt, ed., *The First Forty Years of Washington Society, by Mrs. Margaret Bayard Smith* (New York, 1906), 181.

34 Ibid., 186.

35 S. G. Doorich, *Recollections of a Lifetime,* 2 vols. (New York, 1857), vol. 1 403–04.

36 *Jackson Correspondence,* vol. 3, 276.

37 See Clay's letter to Francis Brook, 28 January 1825, in Calvin Coulton, ed., *Works of Henry Clay* (Memphis, Tenn., 1855), vol. 4, 111.

38 7 October 1825, *Jackson Correspondence,* vol. 3, 291.

39 James, 144–45; see also, R. V. Remini, *Martin Van Buren and the Making of*

the Democratic Party (New York, 1959).

40 See Charles Dickens's description of Seven Dials ("an Irish labourer and his family in the back kitchen"), in *Sketches by Boz* (London, 1836).

41 Young, *Early Victorian England,* vol. 1, 15–16.

42 Gash, *Mr. Secretary Peel,* 105–06.

43 Ibid., 134.

44 Ibid., 126–29; *Peel Speeches,* 4 vols. (London, 1853), vol. 1, 62.

45 This revealing admission is in the Peel Papers, BM Additional Mss 40287 f34, quoted in Gash, 147.

46 For O'Connell's background and early life, see Oliver MacDonagh, *Daniel O'Connell: The Hereditary Bondsman, 1775–1829* (London, 1988), 7–29 (hereafter referred to as *O'Connell,* vol. 1).

47 This was in 1833; see W. J. O'N. Daunt, *Personal Recollections of the Late Daniel O'Connell,* 2 vols. (London, 1848), vol. 1, 14–15.

48 MacDonagh, *O'Connell,* vol. 1. 169–71.

49 For Mary O'Connell, see ibid., 71–74, 150, 158, 313–14.

50 John O'Connell, *Select Speeches of Daniel O'Connell,* 2 vols. (Dublin, 1854–55), vol. 1, 447–48; M. R. O'Connell, ed., *Correspondence of Daniel O'Connell,* 5 vols. (Shannon, 1972ff), vol. 2, 35.

51 MacDonagh, *O'Connell,* vol. 1, 187–88.

52 See *Dublin University Magazine,* July 1839, quoted in ibid., 149–50.

53 O'Connell, *Select Speeches,* vol. 1 244–304.

54 A Munster Farmer, *Reminiscences of Daniel O'Connell . . .* (London, 1847), 18, quoted in MacDonagh, *O'Connell,* vol. 1, 117. (The farmer was William Forbes Taylor.)

55 See ibid., 83–84, 152–57, 184–86, 191–98, 202–04ff; see also, the second volume of Oliver MacDonagh, *Daniel O'Connell: The Emancipist 1830–47* (London, 1989), 14–16, 75–76, 124–25, 214–18ff. (hereafter referred to as *O'Connell,* vol. 2).

56 MacDonagh, *O'Connell*, vol. 1, 156–57.

57 Ibid., 207–08.

58 The workings of the association and its finances are described in Sir Thomas Wyse, *Historical Sketch of the Late Catholic Associations of Ireland*, 2 vols. (London, 1829), which contains documents of its proceedings. For the Rent, see MacDonagh, vol. 1, 210.

59 For the growth of O'Connell's political strategy, see James Aloysius Reynolds, *The Catholic Emancipation Crisis in Ireland, 1823–29* (Yale, 1954).

60 Quoted in Michael Hurst, *Maria Edgeworth and the Public Scene* (London, 1969), 46–47.

61 Quoted in ibid., 42–43.

62 This was the figure given by a hostile source, the *Times*, for the attendance at the hill of Tara, 15 August 1843; see MacDonagh, *O'Connell*, vol. 2, 229–30.

63 Michael MacDonagh, *Daniel O'Connell and the Story of Catholic Emancipation* (London, 1929), 161–62.

64 Peel to Sir Walter Scott, 3 April 1829, quoted in Parker, *Peel*, vol. 2, 99–100.

65 For the disintegration of the Goderich ministry, and its undignified end, see Jones, *Prosperity Robinson*, chap. 7, "How a Government Fell," 169–204.

66 Benjamin Disraeli, *Endymion*, 3 vols. (London, 1880), vol. 1, 25.

67 *Sybil*, Book 1, chap. 3.

68 Quoted in MacDonagh, *O'Connell*, vol. 1, 255.

69 27 February 1827, printed in O'Connell, *Correspondence*, vol. 3, 291.

70 Quoted in Gash, 570.

71 George IV was fond of this epigram and repeated it in various versions; see Eliabeth Longford, *Wellington: Pillar of State* (London, 1972), 171, 181, and 192.

72 Nevins, 327.

73 For details, see Remini, *Jackson*, vol. 2, 125–26.

74 Nevins, 319–20, entry for 10 April 1824.

75 Remini, *Jackson*, vol. 2, 130; James, *Jackson*, 145.

76 Remini, *Jackson*, vol. 2, 133. The accusation about pimping was made in a campaign biography of Jackson written by Isaac Hill of New Hampshire.

77 Letter to C. P. Tutt, 6 January 1825, quoted in James, *Jackson*, 120.

78 John J. Crittenden to Clay, 15 February 1825.

79 Jackson to Houston, 15 December 1826, *Jackson Correspondence*, vol. 3, 325.

80 *United States Telegraph*, 16 June 1827.

81 Nevins, 372, entry for 18 March 1827.

82 Quoted in Remini, *Jackson*, vol. 2, 121.

83 An original of the Coffin handbill is in the North Carolina State Historical Commission in Raleigh and is reproduced in James, *Jackson*, 158–59.

84 Harriet Martineau, *Society in America*, 3 vols. (London, 1837), vol. 3, 166.

85 For Kendall, see William Stickney, ed., *The Autobiography of Amos Kendall* (New York, 1872).

86 For its origins, see Remini, *Jackson*, vol. 1, 180.

87 The two best verses are quoted by Remini, *Jackson*, vol. 2, 134.

88 Quoted in ibid., vol. 2, 127.

89 Schlesinger, *Age of Jackson*, 40–41.

90 This description of Van Buren is quoted in James, *Jackson*, 188–89; see also, John Niven, *Martin Van Buren: The Romantic Age in American Politics* (Oxford, 1983), 5ff, 207.

91 For the background, see Alvin Kass, *New York Politics 1800–30* (New York, 1965).

92 Niven, 64–65. For further details, see De Alva S. Alexander, *A Political History of the State of New York, 1774–1882*, 3 vols. (New York, 1906–09).

93 Letter of 5 February 1816, quoted in Niven, 54.

94 Clinton to Stephen Van Rensselaer, January 1821, quoted in ibid., 90.

95 For a full description, see Jabez D. Hammon, *History of Political Parties*

in the State of New York, 2 vols. (New York, 1846).

96 Quoted in Niven, 180.

97 *Adams Memoirs,* vol. 7, 272; Martineau, *Society in America,* vol. 1, 13–14; Schlesinger, *Age of Jackson,* 369.

98 J. R. Commons et al., *History of Labor in the United States,* 4 vols. (New York, 1915–35), vol. 1, 176ff, 190.

99 Schlesinger, *Age of Jackson,* 134–36.

100 For the voting system in 1828 and an analysis of the votes, see R. V. Remini, "The Election of 1828," in Schlesinger and Israels, *History of American Presidential Elections,* vol. 1 and in Schlesinger, *Age of Jackson,* vol. 2, 145ff; see also, Austin, *Political Facts of the United States since 1789,* tables 3.1, 3.2 and 3.3, 92ff.

101 Quoted in Wise, 115.

102 For a description of the place in 1819, see F. D. Scott, trans. and ed., *Baron Klinkowstrom: America 1819–20* (New York, 1952).

103 To Mrs. Webster, 19 February 1829, *Webster: Private Correspondence* (Boston, 1875), vol. 1, 470; the Clay quotation is from a Senate speech, 1832.

104 Gaillard Hunt, ed., *Margaret B. Smith: The First Forty Years of Washington Society* (New York, 1906), 484–91.

105 *Life and Letters of Joseph Storey* (Boston, 1851), vol. 1, 563.

106 James Hamilton to Martin Van Buren, 5 March 1829, quoted in James, 187.

107 Quoted in Samuel Eliot Morrison, *History of the American People* (Oxford, 1972), vol. 2, 16.

108 Hunt, 257; Nevins, 396.

109 E. M. Eriksson, "The Federal Civil Service under President Jackson," *Mississippi Valley Historical Review,* July 1827; S. H. Aronson, *Status and Kinship in the Higher Civil Service* (Cambridge, Mass., 1964), says the men Jackson appointed did not differ much from those chosen by Jefferson or Adams; for a review

of the controversy, see F. W. Muggleston, "Andrew Jackson and the Spoils System: A Historiographical Survey," *Mid America,* 1977, vol. 59; Remini, *Jackson,* vol. 2, 183ff, gives a spirited defense of Jackson's removals and appointments.

110 Campbell to his wife, 3 June 1829, quoted in James, *Jackson,* 192.

111 Remini, *Jackson,* vol. 2, 187–88; J. W. Forney, *Anecdotes of Public Men* (New York, 1873), 2.

112 Niven, 228.

113 Ibid., 240–45; Van Buren, *Autobiography,* 268–69; Remini, *Jackson,* vol. 2, 198–99.

114 For details see Remini, *Jackson,* vol. 2, 160ff.

115 Quoted in Niven, 228.

116 Remini, *Jackson,* vol. 2, 161–63.

117 Dangerfield, *Era of Good Feeling,* 194.

118 Quoted in James, *Jackson,* 202.

119 Nevins, 400, entry for 6 February 1830.

120 Quoted in Pauline Wilcox Burke, *Emily Donelson of Tennessee* (Richmond, Va., 1941), vol. 1, 178.

121 Jackson to John McLemore, 29 December 1829, quoted in Remini, *Jackson,* vol. 2, 213.

122 Jackson's dealings with the clergymen and the cabinet meeting are described in James Parton, *Life of Andrew Jackson,* 3 vols. (Boston, 1866), vol. 3, 186–205; see also, Remini, *Jackson,* vol. 2, chap. 11, "The Eaton Imbroglio," 203–16.

123 Quoted in Remini, *Jackson,* vol. 2, 207.

124 For various views of the cabinet crisis, see Schlesinger, *Age of Jackson,* 66ff, Remini, *Jackson,* vol. 2, chap. 18, "The Purge," 300–14; Niven, *Van Buren,* 255ff.

125 Stickney; Wise, 117; Martineau, *Society in America,* vol. 1, 257–58; Wise's remarks were in a speech in the House, 21 December 1838; there is an amusing portrait of Kendall in Schlesinger, *Age of Jackson,* 67–72.

126 Smiles, *Men of Invention and Industry,* 167 fn.

127 A. F. Johnson, *Catalogue of Specimens of Printing Types* . . . (London, 1962), Introduction; Smiles, 168–70.

128 Smiles, 216–17.

129 Haydon, *Diary*, vol. 3, 220–21.

130 Kathryn Cave, ed., *The Diary of Joseph Farington*, 16 vols. (New Haven, Conn., 1978–84), vol. 9, 3217ff, entry for 6 February 1808.

131 Ibid., vol. 10, 3497, 3619, entries for 26 June 1809 and 23 March 1810.

132 *Croker Correspondence and Diaries*, vol. 2, 21ff; letter to J. Planta, 21 August 1829.

133 Bourne, *Palmerston: The Early Years*, 123.

134 *Journal of Mrs. Arbuthnot*, vol. 1, 299, entry for 11 April 1824.

135 Young, *Early Victorian England*, vol. 2, 5ff; see the discussion on what policemen, footmen, and so on needed to be paid in *Croker Correspondence*, vol. 2, 16–21.

136 Samuel Squire Sprigge, *Life and Times of Thomas Wakley, Founder . . . of the Lancet* (London, 1897), 85.

137 *Spectator*, 17 September 1831.

138 Edward Bulwer-Lytton, *England and the English*, 2 vols. (London, 1833), vol. 1, 264–68.

139 C. Pomeret, *Monsieur Thiers et son siècle* (Paris, 1948), 92–100.

140 Quoted in J. P. T. Bury and R. P. Tombs, *Thiers. 1797–1877, a Political Life* (London, 1986), 2.

141 *Les Pyrénées et le Midi de la France* (Paris, 1823).

142 Bertier de Sauvigny, *Bourbon Restoration*, 294.

143 Bury and Tombs, 12–14.

144 See S. Hilmes, *Benjamin Constant and the Making of Modern Liberalism* (New Haven, Conn., 1984), chap. 5.

145 *Histoire de la Révolution française*, 10 vols. (Paris, 1823–27), vol. 1, 294.

146 François Guizot, *Memoirs to Illustrate the History of My Time*, 2 vols. (trans., London, 1858), vol. 1, Appendix, 417–30.

147 Bertier de Sauvigny, *Bourbon Restoration*, 294.

148 Françoise Waquet, *Les Fêtes royales sous la Restauration ou l'ancien régime retrouvé* (Paris, 1981), 2–18.

149 Gronow, *Reminiscences*, vol. 1, 241.

150 Alphonse Royer, *Histoire de l'Opéra* (Paris, 1875), 24; see Jane F. Fulcher, *The Nation's Image: French Grand Opera as Politics and Politicised Art* (Cambridge, England, 1987), 11–15.

151 For details of the political motivation of the coronation, and the event itself, see V. W. Beach, *Charles X of France: His Life and Times* (Boulder, Colo., 1971), 197–205.

152 Richard Osborne, *Rossini* (London, 1986), 70–71.

153 *Victor Hugo Racontée*, vol. 2, 99.

154 For a description of Berlioz's parental background, see David Cairns, *Berlioz, Volume One: The Making of an Artist* (London, 1989), 22–37.

155 *Mémoires de Hector Berlioz*, 2 vols. (Paris, 1870), vol. 1, 98; there is an English translation of this work by David Cairns, *The Memoirs of Hector Berlioz* (London, 1977). For the Berlioz attitude to the 1827 Shakespeare season, see Jacques Barzun, *Berlioz and the Romantic Century*, 2 vols., 3rd ed. (New York, 1969), vol. 1, 80ff.

156 Hector Berlioz, *Evenings with the Orchestra* (trans. New York, 1956), 75–76.

157 Cairns, *Berlioz*, 246ff; Berlioz *Memoirs*, vol. 1, 45–6.

158 See James Billington, *Fire in the Minds of Men: Origins of the Revolutionary Faith* (New York, 1980).

159 Fulcher, 19; her whole chapter "La Muette de Portici and the New Politics of Opera," 11–46, is worth study; see also, Nicole Wild, *Un Demi-siècle de décor de l'Opéra de Paris: Salle Le Pelétier 1822–73* (Paris, 1976), 17ff.

160 Fulcher quotes extensively from the censors' reports, which survive, 29–32.

161 *Nouvelle Biographie générale* (Paris, 1968), vols. 37–38, 950, quoted in Fulcher, 46.

162 André Maurois, *Victor Hugo* (trans., London, 1956), 123.

163 Alfred de Vigny, *Journal d'un poète* (Pleiade ed., Paris, 1973), 892–93.

164 Eduard Turquéty, quoted in Maurois, *Hugo*, 142.

165 Ibid., 146–157.

166 The events that preceded and followed the production of *Hernani* are described in Adèle Hugo's *Victor Hugo raconté par un temoin de sa view* (Paris, 1863), and by Theophile Gautier in his unfinished *Histoire du romantisme* (Paris, 1874).

167 M. Hartman, "The Sacrilege Law of 1825 in France: A Study in Anti-Clericalism and Mythmaking," *Journal of Modern History* (1972).

168 See Pamela Pilbeam, "The 'Liberal' Revolution of 1830 in France," *Bulletin of the Institute of Historical Research*, June 1990; James Roberts: *The Counter-Revolution in France* (London, 1990), chap. 6, "Charles X," 94ff.

169 Bury and Tombs, *Thiers*, 20–24.

170 De Sauvigny, *Bourbon Restoration*, 355–58.

171 J.-P. Gonnet, "Esquisse de la crise économique en France de 1827–32," *Revue d'histoire économique et sociale*, 33 (1955), 290ff.

172 Pamela Pilbeam, "The Economic Crisis of 1827–32 and the 1830 Revolution in France," *Historical Journal*, 32 (1989), 319ff.

173 Eric Werner, *Mendelssohn*, 170.

174 Charles Dupin, *Situation progressive des forces de la France depuis 1814* (Brussels, 1827), 11ff.

175 Quoted in De Sauvigny, *Bourbon Restoration*, 239.

176 For figures, see Allen, *Popular French Romanticism*, 191.

177 Honoré de Balzac, *La Fille aux yeux d'or*.

178 Baron d'Hausse, *Mémoires*, 2 vols. (Paris, 1896–97), quoted in De Sauvigny, *Bourbon Restoration*, 271.

179 Quoted in De Sauvigny, *Bourbon Restoration*, 439.

180 Thiers's "imperial" articles were published in the *National* on 14, 20, and 22 July 1830; see Bury and Tombs, *Thiers*, 25.

181 Louis Ratisbonne, ed., *Alfred de Vigny: Journal d'un poète* (Paris, 1882), 45ff.

182 E. Newman, "The Blouse and the Frock-Coat," *Journal of Modern History*, March 1974.

183 Calbe Cushing, *Review, Historical and Political, of the Late Revolution in France*, 2 vols. (Boston, 1833), vol. 1, 159–60.

184 See David Pinkney, "The Crowd in the French Revolution of 1830," *American Historical Review*, October 1964; and Pinkney, *The French Revolution of 1830* (Princeton, N.J., 1972), 159–60.

185 See D. L. Rader, *The Journalists and the July Revolution in France* (The Hague, 1973),

186 Jan Reynolds, *William Callow RWS* (London, 1980), 8.

187 Quoted in A. G. Lehman, *Sainte-Beuve: A Portrait of the Critic 1804–42* (Oxford, 1960), 111. For a blow-by-blow account of the "July Days" by an eyewitness, see the diary kept by a Swiss admirer of Sainte-Beuve: Juste Olivier, *Paris en 1830* (Paris, 1951).

188 Quoted in Bury and Tombs, *Thiers*, 30.

189 Ibid., 35.

190 Allen, 193.

191 Roger Passeron, *Daumier* (trans., London, 1981), 49.

192 Ibid., 61–62.

193 Bury and Tombs, *Thiers*, 42.

194 De Tocqueville, *Mémoires* (Paris, 1890), 6; Sainte-Beuve: *Oeuvres complètes* (Pleiade ed.) vol. 1, 476; both quoted in Lehmann, 115.

195 Clive H. Church, *Europe in 1830: Revolution and Political Change* (London, 1983), 27.

196 W. F. Reddaway, "Anglo-French Colonial Rivalry 1815–48," in *Cambridge History of the British Empire* (Cambridge, 1941), 241ff.

197 Church, chap. 5, 57–69.

198 For details, see Yves Schmitz, *Guillaume Ire et la Belgique* (Paris, 1954).

199 Church, 83ff.

200 For the background see Eugène de

Guichen, *La Révolution de 1830 et l'Europe* (Paris 1916); and Réné Dollot, *Les Origins de la neutralité de la Belgique et le système de la barrière, 1609–1830* (Paris, 1902).

201 This last figure is from 1830; for Poland's demographics, see R. F. Leslie, *Polish Politics and the Revolution of 1830* (London, 1956), 46–47.
202 Ibid., 73.
203 P. Harro-Harring, *Poland under the Dominion of Russia* (London, 1831), 255–56, quoted in Leslie, 50.
204 Leslie, 62–63.
205 For the family background, see Adam Zamoyski, *Chopin: A Biography* (London, 1979), 11–15.
206 Mendelssohn to his mother, 23 May 1834, quoted in Jean-Jacques Eigeldinger, *Chopin: Pianist and Teacher as Seen by His Pupils* (Cambridge, England, 1986), 267.
207 Quoted in ibid., 272, 273–74.
208 For the origins of the rising, see Leslie, 122–23.
209 *New Poland*, 24 January 1831, quoted in ibid., 149.
210 See the conclusions of Leslie's book, 279–80; see also, Marian Kukiel, *Czartoryski and European Unity, 1770–1861* (Princeton, N.J., 1955).
211 The *Lion*, vol. 4, 451, 9 October 1829, quoted in Carnall, *Robert Southey and His Age*, 182.
212 Young, *Early Victorian England*, vol. 1, 443.
213 R. W. Jeffery, ed., *Dyott's Diary, 1781–1845*, 2 vols. (London, 1907), vol. 2, entry for 1 January 1830.
214 See Norman Gash, "English Reform and the French Revolution," in R. Pares and A. J. P. Taylor, eds., *Essays Presented to Sir L. Namier* (London, 1956); see also, M. I. Thomis, *Threats of Revolution in Britain* (London, 1977).
215 See E. J. Hobsbawm and George Rudé, *Captain Swing* (London, 1969), Appendix 4, "The Problem of the Threshing Machines," 359–65.
216 Hobsbawm and Rudé provide a table showing the spread and duration of the riots, 170; on 196 they print a chronological graph of the incidents.
217 Revel Guest and Angela V. John, *Lady Charlotte* (London 1989), 6–7.
218 Hobsbawm and Rudé, 161–62; report in *East Anglian*, 11 January 1831.
219 The *Times*, 25 October 1830, quoted in Hobsbawm and Rudé.
220 Quoted in ibid., 156.
221 For this quantitative survey of prints, see H. T. Dickenson, ed., *The English Satirical Print 1650–1832: Caricatures and the Constitution, 1760–1832* (Cambridge, England, 1986), Introduction, 13–14, 19–20.
222 Figures in C. H. Lee, *The British Economy Since 1700: A Macro-Economic Perspective* (Cambridge, England, 1986), 129.
223 27 June 1828, *Hansard*, Second Series, vol. 19, 1538.
224 Bourne, *Palmerston: The Early Years*, 286.
225 Lord Colchester, ed., *A Political Diary, 1828–30, by Edward Law, Lord Ellenborough*, 2 vols. (London, 1881), vol. 1, 115.
226 Kenneth Bourne, ed., *The Letters of the 3rd Viscount Palmerston to L & E. Suliven, 1804–63*, Camden Society, fourth series, 23, 1979, 213.
227 *Hansard*, Second Series, vol. 21, 1643–70.
228 Gash, *Mr. Secretary Peel*, 634–35.
229 *Greville Diary*, vol. 5, 15 December 1830.
230 See, for instance, such characters as Uriah Heep in *David Copperfield* by Charles Dickens and the Rev. Obadiah Slope in *Barchester Towers* and various other novels by Anthony Trollope, such as *Orley Farm;* red-haired men are seen as particularly villainous in the novels of Mrs. Gaskell; see, for example, *Wives and Daughters*.

231 For an illuminating discussion of Peel's growing difficulties, see Gash, *Peel*, chap. 17, "The Last of the Old Regime," 599ff.

232 For the characteristics of the Yorkshire county seats, see *House of Commons, 1790–1820*, vol. 2, Constituencies, 435–40.

233 Lord Denman to his wife, in Joseph Arnoud, ed., *Memoir of Thomas, 1st Lord Denman*, 2 vols. (London, 1873), vol. 1, 312; for the Yorkshire election, see New, *Brougham*, 417–10.

234 *Brougham's Life and Times*, vol. 3, 42–43; *Edinburgh Review*, Autumn 1830, 582.

235 Letter to R. Kennedy, 23 September 1830, in H. Cockburn, ed., *Letters Chiefly Concerned with the Affairs of Scotland, 1818–52* (London, 1874), 236–37, quoted in New.

236 De Sauvigny, *Bourbon Restoration*, 208.

237 Quoted by Carson Ritchie in "Move Along Please: A Study of George Shillibeer," *Country Life*, 11 (October 1990).

238 For a memorable description of the accident, see L. T. C. Rolt, *George and Robert Stephenson* (Harmondsworth, 1978), 196–200.

239 *Greville Diary*, 28 August 1830.

240 A version of this story is given in *Haydon's Diary*, vol. 3, 70–71, entry for 13 December 1825.

241 For this occasion, see Elizabeth Longford, *Wellington: Pillar of State*, 226–28.

242 Sir A. Gordon, *Aberdeen* (London, 1893), 104.

243 *Croker Correspondence and Diaries*, 11, 74.

244 *Journal of Mrs Arbuthnot*, vol. 2, 26 December 1830.

245 *Brougham's Life and Times* vol. 3, 79.

246 Sir H. Maxwell, ed., *The Creevey Papers*, 2 vols. (London, 1903), vol. 1, 287.

247 *Greville Memoirs*, vol. 2, 64–65, entry for 20 November 1830.

248 Le Marchant Diary, 30 November 1830, printed in A. Aspinal, ed., *Three Early 19th Century Diaries* (London, 1952). For the way in which Brougham became Lord Chancellor, see Robert Stewart, *Henry Brougham: His Public Career, 1778–1868* (London, 1985), 248–51; and J. B. Atlay, *The Victorian Chancellors*, 2 vols. (London, 1906), vol. 1, 293.

249 Evelyn Waugh, *Brideshead Revisited* (London, 1945).

250 See Hobsbawm and Rudé, 242, for figures and references.

251 Carnall, *Southey*, 183–84.

252 Quoted in William Vaughan et al., eds., *Caspar David Friedrich, 1774–1840: Romantic Landscape Painting in Dresden* (London, 1972), 40, 44.

253 For a discussion of this painting and its links with Wordsworth, see J. L. Koerner, *Caspar David Friedrich and the Subject of Landscape* (London, 1990), 182ff; the painting is reproduced as Plate 77.

254 For his death, see Stanley Jones, *Hazlitt*, 380–81.

255 *Letters of Charles and Mary Lamb*, vol. 3, 298–99; to George Dyer, 20 December 1830.

Index

1073